Your Office

Microsoft Office® 2010

VOLUME 1
Second Edition

Amy Kinser

HAMMERLE | HOGAN | LENDING

O'KEEFE | STOUT | STOVER

PEARSON

Boston   Columbus   Indianapolis   New York   San Francisco   Upper Saddle River
Amsterdam   Cape Town   Dubai   London   Madrid   Milan   Munich   Paris   Montréal   Toronto
Delhi   Mexico City   São Paulo   Sydney   Hong Kong   Seoul   Singapore   Taipei   Tokyo

Editor in Chief: Michael Payne
Acquisitions Editor: Samantha McAfee
Product Development Manager: Laura Burgess
Editorial Project Manager: Anne Garcia
Development Editor: Nancy Lamm
Editorial Assistant: Laura Karahalis
Digital Media Editor: Eric Hakanson
Director, Media Development: Cathi Profitko
Production Media Project Manager: John Cassar
Director of Marketing: Maggie Moylan
Marketing Manager: Nate Anderson
Marketing Coordinator: Susan Osterlitz
Marketing Assistant: Darshika Vyas
Managing Editor: Camille Trentacoste
Senior Production Project Manager: Rhonda Aversa
Procurement Lead: Natacha Moore
Senior Art Director: Jonathan Boylan
Manager of Rights & Permissions: Jenn Kennett
Manager, Cover Visual Research & Permissions: Karen Sanatar
Cover Design: Anthony Gemmellaro
Composition: GEX Publishing Services
Full-Service Project Management: GEX Publishing Services

Credits and acknowledgments borrowed from other sources and reproduced, with permission, in this textbook appear on appropriate page within text.

Microsoft, Windows, Word, PowerPoint, Outlook, FrontPage, Visual Basic, MSN, The Microsoft Network, and/or other Microsoft products referenced herein are either registered trademarks or registered trademarks of the Microsoft Corporation in the U.S.A. and other countries. Screen shots and icons reprinted with permission from the Microsoft Corporation. This book is not sponsored or endorsed by or affiliated with the Microsoft Corporation.

Pearson Education Ltd., London
Pearson Education Singapore, Pte. Ltd.
Pearson Education, Canada, Inc.
Pearson Education–Japan
Pearson Education Australia PTY, Limited

Pearson Education North Asia Ltd., Hong Kong
Pearson Educación de Mexico, S.A. de C.V.
Pearson Education Malaysia, Pte. Ltd.
Pearson Education, Upper Saddle River, New Jersey

Library of Congress Cataloging-in-Publication Data

Microsoft Office 2010 / Amy Kinser ... [et al.]. — 2nd ed.
          p. cm. — (Your Office ; v. 1)
     Includes index.
     ISBN-13: 978-0-13-305158-2
     ISBN-10: 0-13-305158-7
     1. Microsoft Office. 2. Microsoft Word. 3. Microsoft Excel (Computer file)
     4. Microsoft PowerPoint (Computer file) 5. Microsoft Outlook. I. Kinser, Amy.
     HF5548.4.M525M52498 2013
     005.5 — dc23

2012033349
10 9 8 7 6 5 4 3 2 1
ISBN-13: 978-0-13-305158-2
ISBN-10: 0-13-305158-7

Dedications

I dedicate this series to my Kinser Boyz for their unwavering love, support, and patience; to my parents and sister for their love; to my students for inspiring me; to Sam for believing in me; and to the instructors I hope this series will inspire!

Amy Kinser

I dedicate this book to my husband, John, and my two boys, Matthew and Adam. They provide me with all the support, love, and patience I could ever ask for—thank you, boys!

Patti Hammerle

I dedicate this work to my parents, whose constant encouragement and unwavering support have led me to believe that anything is possible.

Lynn Hogan

I dedicate this book to my mother, Dagmar, for inspiring my love of books. And to Art, for keeping life going while I work too much and for making life so much fun when I'm not working.

Diane Lending

This book is a product of the unselfish support and patience of my wife and daughters, Bonnie, Kelsie, and Maggie, and of the values instilled by my parents, Paul and Carol. They are the authors—I am just a writer.

Timothy O'Keefe

I dedicate this work to my beautiful wife, Jackie. She is the spark to my plug, the sugar on my crème brûlée, the lime in my Corona. She is the universe in which I exist.

Nathan Stout

This book is dedicated to the memory of Linda Condry. I miss her every day.

Barbara Stover

My work is dedicated to those who taught me all I ever wanted to know and answered all the questions I was never afraid to ask.

Hilda Federico

I dedicate this to my husband, Jim. He is my support and my rock.

Joyce Thompson

I dedicate this book to my amazing wife, April. Without her support and understanding this would not have been possible.

Brant Moriarity

I dedicate this book to my girlfriend Anny, for generously sacrificing her time to provide feedback and support me through the writing process; to my network of friends; to my Vice President at Passaic County Community College, Dr. Jackie Kineavy, who supported me in pursuing my dream of writing; and to my students, who make this all worthwhile.

Eric Cameron

About the Authors

Amy S. Kinser, Esq., Series Editor

Amy holds a B.A. degree in Chemistry with a Business minor from Indiana University, and a J.D. from the Maurer School of Law, also at Indiana University. After working as an environmental chemist, starting her own technology consulting company, and practicing intellectual property law, she has spent the past 12 years teaching technology at the Kelley School of Business in Bloomington, Indiana. Currently, she serves as the Director of Computer Skills and Senior Lecturer at the Kelley School of Business at Indiana University. She also loves spending time with her two sons, Aidan and J. Matthew, and her husband J. Eric.

Patti Hammerle, Access and Integrated Projects Author

Patti holds a B.A. in Finance and an M.B.A. from Indiana University Kelley School of Business. She is an adjunct professor at the Kelley School of Business in Indianapolis where she teaches "The Computer in Business." In addition to teaching, she owns U-Can Computer Manuals, a company that writes and publishes computer manuals primarily for libraries to teach from. She has also written and edited other computer application textbooks. When not teaching or writing, she enjoys spending time with family, reading, and running.

Dr. Lynn Hogan, Word Author

Lynn has taught in the field of Computer Information Systems for the past 30 years. She is the author of *Practical Computing* and has contributed chapters for several computer applications textbooks. Specializing in microcomputer applications, she currently teaches at the University of North Alabama. She earned an M.B.A. from the University of North Alabama and a Ph.D. from the University of Alabama. Lynn resides in Alabama with her husband and two daughters, Jenn and Alli.

Dr. Diane Lending, Access Author

Diane Lending is a Professor at James Madison University where she teaches Computer Information Systems. She received a Ph.D. in Management Information Systems from the University of Minnesota and a B.A. degree in Mathematics from the University of Virginia. Her research interests are in adoption of information technology and information systems education. She enjoys traveling; playing card and board games; and living in the country with her husband, daughter, and numerous pets.

Dr. Timothy P. O'Keefe, Excel Author

Tim is Professor of Information Systems and Entrepreneurship, Chairman of the Department of Information Systems and Business Education, and M.B.A. Director at the University of North Dakota. He is an Information Technology consultant, cofounder of a successful Internet services company, and has taught in higher education for 29 years. Tim is married to his high school sweetheart, Bonnie; they have two beautiful daughters, Kelsie and Maggie. In his spare time he enjoys family, cherished friends and colleagues, his dogs, traveling, and archery.

Dr. Nathan Stout, Excel Author

Nathan received an M.B.A in Organizational Behavior and Human Resources and a Ph.D. in Management Information Systems from Indiana University. He has been teaching Information Systems courses for more than 15 years, primarily teaching large introductory courses. He enjoys developing materials in a variety of media to enhance students' learning. He has received teaching excellence awards as well as recognition for innovative teaching. When not teaching, he enjoys hiking, canoeing, and landscaping during the day and relaxing with his wife in the evenings.

Barbara S. Stover, PowerPoint Author

Barbara received her B.S. degree from Ohio University and her M.A. degree from The George Washington University. Her teaching career has spanned 35 years, with 25 years as a professor in the Information Technologies department at Marion Technical College in Marion, Ohio. She authored *Your Office: Getting Started with Outlook*.

Hilda Wirth Federico, Windows 7 Author

Hilda has taught computer literacy and applications courses at Jacksonville University in Florida for more than 20 years. When not teaching or writing, she enjoys traveling around the world and learning about different cultures. The uniquely configured keyboards in different countries have been very challenging. Her current goal is to see the sites recently declared the New Seven Wonders of the World. So far, she has visited six of the seven destinations.

Joyce Thompson, Common Features Author

Joyce Thompson is an Associate Professor at Lehigh Carbon Community College where she has facilitated learning in Computer Literacy and Computer Applications, Cisco, and Geographic Information Systems since 2002. She has been teaching computer applications for over 20 years. She received her M.Ed. in Instructional Design and Technology. Joyce resides in Pennsylvania with her husband and two cats.

Brant Moriarity, Cloud Collaboration Cases Author

Brant Moriarity earned his B.A. in Religious Studies/Philosophy from the Indiana University College of Arts and Sciences and his M.S. in Information Systems from the Indiana University Kelley School of Business. He has worked as a database programmer, data analyst, web developer, and consultant. He is currently a Lecturer at the Indiana University Kelley School of Business and in charge of several web systems for students, faculty, and staff. His research interests include mobile app development for student engagement and course administration. In his spare time he enjoys live music, good food, and spending time with his wife and son.

Eric Cameron, Windows 8 Appendix Author

Eric holds a M.S. in Computer Science and a B.S. degree in Computer Science with minors in Mathematics and Physics, both from Montclair State University. He is an Assistant Professor at Passaic County Community College, where he has taught in the Computer and Information Sciences department since 2001. He maintains a professional blog at profcameron.blogspot.com. He is also occasionally an adjunct professor at Bergen Community College. He wrote *Your Office: Getting Started with Web 2.0*.

Brief Contents

Contents

ACCESS MODULE 1

INTEGRATED PROJECTS

Acknowledgments

The *Your Office* team would like to thank the following reviewers who have invested time and energy to help shape this series from the very beginning, providing us with invaluable feedback through their comments, suggestions, and constructive criticism.

We'd like to thank our Editorial Board:

Marni Ferner
University of North Carolina, Wilmington

Jan Hime
University of Nebraska, Lincoln

Linda Kavanaugh
Robert Morris University

Mike Kelly
Community College of Rhode Island

Suhong Li
Bryant University

Sebena Masline
Florida State College of Jacksonville

Candace Ryder
Colorado State University

Cindi Smatt
Texas A&M University

Jill Weiss
Florida International University

We'd like to thank our class testers:

Melody Alexander
Ball State University

Karen Allen
Community College of Rhode Island

Charmayne Cullom
University of Northern Colorado

Christy Culver
Marion Technical College

Marni Ferner
University of North Carolina, Wilmington

Linda Fried
University of Colorado Denver

Linda Fried
Pace University

Jan Hime
University of Nebraska, Lincoln

Emily Holliday
Campbell University

Carla Jones
Middle Tennessee State Unversity

Mike Kelly
Community College of Rhode Island

David Largent
Ball State University

Freda Leonard
Delgado Community College

Suhong Li
Bryant Unversity

Sabina Masline
Florida State College of Jacksonville

Sandra McCormack
Monroe Community College

Sue McCrory
Missouri State Unversity

Patsy Parker
Southwest Oklahoma State Unversity

Alicia Pearlman
Baker College, Allen Park

Vickie Pickett
Midland College

Rose Pollard
Southeast Community College

Leonard Presby
William Paterson University

Amy Rutledge
Oakland University

Cindi Smatt
Texas A&M Unversity

Jill Weiss
Florida International University

We'd like to thank our reviewers and focus group attendees:

Sven Aelterman
Troy University

Angel Alexander
Piedmont Technical College

Melody Alexander
Ball State University

Karen Allen
Community College of Rhode Island

Maureen Allen
Elon University

Wilma Andrews
Virginia Commonwealth University

Mazhar Anik
Owens Community College

David Antol
Harford Community College

Kirk Atkinson
Western Kentucky University

Barbara Baker
Indiana Wesleyan University

Kristi Berg
Minot State University

Kavuri Bharath
Old Dominion University

Ann Blackman
Parkland College

Jeanann Boyce
Montgomery College

Cheryl Brown
Delgado Community College West
Bank Campus

Bonnie Buchanan
Central Ohio Technical College

Peggy Burrus
Red Rocks Community College

Richard Cacace
Pensacola State College

Margo Chaney
Carroll Community College

Shanan Chappell
College of the Albemarle, North Carolina

Kuan-Chou Chen
Purdue University, Calumet

David Childress
Ashland Community and Technical College

Keh-Wen Chuang
Purdue University North Central

Amy Clubb
Portland Community College

Bruce Collins
Davenport University

Charmayne Cullom
University of Northern Colorado

Juliana Cypert
Tarrant County College

Harold Davis
Southeastern Louisiana University

Jeff Davis
Jamestown Community College

Jennifer Day
Sinclair Community College

Anna Degtyareva
Mt. San Antonio College

Beth Deinert
Southeast Commuunity College

Kathleen DeNisco
Erie Community College

Donald Dershem
Mountain View College

Bambi Edwards
Craven Community College

Elaine Emanuel
Mt. San Antonio College

Diane Endres
Ancilla College

Nancy Evans
Indiana University-Purdue University, Indianapolis

Linda Fried
University of Colorado, Denver

Diana Friedman
Riverside Community College

Susan Fry
Boise State University

Virginia Fullwood
Texas A&M University, Commerce

Janos Fustos
Metropolitan State College of Denver

Saiid Ganjalizadeh
The Catholic University of America

Randolph Garvin
Tyler Junior College

Diane Glowacki
Tarrant County College

Jerome Gonnella
Northern Kentucky University

Connie Grimes
Morehead State University

Babita Gupta
California State University, Monterey Bay

Lewis Hall
Riverside City College

Jane Hammer
Valley City State University

Marie Hartlein
Montgomery County Community College

Darren Hayes
Pace Unversity

Paul Hayes
Eastern New Mexico Universtiy

Mary Hedberg
Johnson County Community College

Lynda Henrie
LDS Business College

Deedee Herrera
Dodge City Community College

Cheryl Hinds
Norfolk State University

Mary Kay Hinkson
Fox Valley Technical College

Margaret Hohly
Cerritos College

Brian Holbert
Spring Hill College

Susan Holland
Southeast Community College

Anita Hollander
University of Tennessee, Knoxville

Emily Holliday
Campbell University

Stacy Hollins
St. Louis Community College Florissant Valley

Mike Horn
State University of New York, Geneseo

Christie Hovey
Lincoln Land Community College

Margaret Hvatum
St. Louis Community College Meramec

Jean Insinga
Middlesex Community College

Jon (Sean) Jasperson
Texas A&M University

Glen Jenewein
Kaplan University

Gina Jerry
Santa Monica College

Dana Johnson
North Dakota State University

Mary Johnson
Mt. San Antonio College

Linda Johnsonius
Murray State University

Carla Jones
Middle Tennessee State Unversity

Susan Jones
Utah State University

Nenad Jukic
Loyola University, Chicago

Sali Kaceli
Philadelphia Biblical University

Sue Kanda
Baker College of Auburn Hills

Robert Kansa
Macomb Community College

Susumu Kasai
Salt Lake Community College

Debby Keen
University of Kentucky

Melody Kiang
California State Universtiy, Long Beach

Lori Kielty
College of Central Florida

Richard Kirk
Pensacola State College

Dawn Konicek
Blackhawk Tech

John Kucharczuk
Centennial College

David Largent
Ball State University

Frank Lee
Fairmont State University

Luis Leon
The University of Tennessee at Chattanooga

Freda Leonard
Delgado Community College

Julie Lewis
Baker College, Allen Park

Renee Lightner
Florida State College

John Lombardi
South University

Rhonda Lucas
Spring Hill College

Adriana Lumpkin
Midland College

Lynne Lyon
Durham College

Nicole Lytle
California State University,
San Bernardino

Donna Madsen
Kirkwood Community College

Paul Martin
Harrisburg Area Community College

Cheryl Martucci
Diablo Valley College

Sherry Massoni
Harford Community College

Lee McClain
Western Washington University

Sandra McCormack
Monroe Community College

Sue McCrory
Missouri State University

Barbara Miller
University of Notre Dame

Michael O. Moorman
Saint Leo University

Alysse Morton
Westminster College

Elobaid Muna
University of Maryland Eastern Shore

Jackie Myers
Sinclair Community College

Bernie Negrete
Cerritos College

Melissa Nemeth
Indiana University–Purdue University,
Indianapolis

Jennifer Nightingale
Duquesne University

Kathie O'Brien
North Idaho College

Patsy Parker
Southwestern Oklahoma State University

Laurie Patterson
University of North Carolina, Wilmington

Alicia Pearlman
Baker College

Diane Perreault
Sierra College and California State University,
Sacramento

Vickie Pickett
Midland College

Marcia Polanis
Forsyth Technical Community College

Rose Pollard
Southeast Community College

Stephen Pomeroy
Norwich University

Leonard Presby
William Paterson University

Donna Reavis
Delta Career Education

Eris Reddoch
Pensacola State College

James Reddoch
Pensacola State College

Michael Redmond
La Salle University

Terri Rentfro
John A. Logan College

Vicki Robertson
Southwest Tennessee Community College

Dianne Ross
University of Louisiana at Lafayette

Ann Rowlette
Liberty University

Amy Rutledge
Oakland University

Joann Segovia
Winona State University

Eileen Shifflett
James Madison University

Sandeep Shiva
Old Dominion University

Robert Sindt
Johnson County Community College

Edward Souza
Hawaii Pacific University

Nora Spencer
Fullerton College

Alicia Stonesifer
La Salle University

Cheryl Sypniewski
Macomb Community College

Arta Szathmary
Bucks County Community College

Nasser Tadayon
Southern Utah Unversity

Asela Thomason
California State University Long Beach

Joyce Thompson
Lehigh Carbon Community College

Terri Tiedeman
Southeast Community College,
Nebraska

Lewis Todd
Belhaven University

Barb Tollinger
Sinclair Community College

Allen Truell
Ball State University

Erhan Uskup
Houston Community College

Michelle Vlaich-Lee
Greenville Technical College

Barry Walker
Monroe Community College

Rosalyn Warren
Enterprise State Community College

Eric Weinstein
Suffolk County Community College

Lorna Wells
Salt Lake Community College

Rosalie Westerberg
Clover Park Technical College

Clemetee Whaley
Southwest Tennessee Community
College

MaryLou Wilson
Piedmont Technical College

John Windsor
University of North Texas

Kathy Winters
University of Tennessee, Chattanooga

Nancy Woolridge
Fullerton College

Jensen Zhao
Ball State University

Martha Zimmer
University of Evansville

Molly Zimmer
University of Evansville

Matthew Zullo
Wake Technical Community College

Additionally, we'd like to thank our myitlab team for their tireless work:

Jerri Williams
myitlab content author

Ralph Moore
myitlab content author

LeeAnn Bates
myitlab content author

Jennifer Hurley
myitlab content author

Jessica Brandi
Associate Media Project Manager

Jaimie Howard
Media Producer

Cathi Profitko
Director, Media Development

Preface

The *Your Office* series is built upon the discovery that both instructors and students need a modern approach to teaching and learning Microsoft Office applications, an approach that weaves in a business context and focuses on using Office as a decision-making tool.

In this second edition, the focus was on making this an even stronger tool for students:

- Increasing the font size
- Adding in collaboration and Web 2.0 cases
- Identifying the areas of business explored in each case or example
- Calling out which exercises are paired with videos and with my**it**lab

The process of developing this unique series for you, the modern student or instructor, required innovative ideas regarding the pedagogy and organization of the text. You learn best when doing—so you will be active from page 1. Your learning goes to the next level when you are challenged to do more with less—your hand will be held at first, but progressively the cases require more from you. Because you care about how things work in the real world—in your classes, your future jobs, your personal life—these innovative features will help you progress from a basic understanding of Office to mastering each application, empowering you to perform with confidence in Windows 7, Word, Excel, Access, PowerPoint, and Outlook.

No matter what career you may choose to pursue in life, this series will give you the foundation to succeed. *Your Office* uses cases that will enable you to be immersed in a realistic business as you learn Office in the context of a running business scenario—the Painted Paradise Resort and Spa. You will immediately delve into the many interesting, smaller businesses in this resort (golf course, spa, restaurants, hotel, etc.) to learn how a business or organization uses Office. You will learn how to make Office work for you now as a student and in your future career.

Today, the experience of working with Office is not isolated to working in a job in a cubicle. Your physical office is wherever you are with a laptop or a mobile device. Office has changed. It's modern. It's mobile. It's personal. And when you learn these valuable skills and master Office, you are able to make Office your own. The title of this series is a promise to you, the student: Our goal is to make Microsoft Office *Your Office*.

Key Features

- **Starting and Ending Files:** Before every case, the Starting and Ending Files are identified for students. Starting Files identify exactly which Student Data Files are needed to complete each case. Ending Files are provided to show students the naming conventions they should use when saving their files.
- **Workshop Objectives List:** The learning objectives to be achieved as students work through the workshop. Page numbers are included for easy reference.
- **Active Text:** Appears throughout the workshop and is easily distinguishable from explanatory text by the shaded background. Active Text helps students quickly identify what steps they need to follow to complete the workshop Prepare Case.
- **Quick Reference Box:** A boxed feature that appears throughout the workshop summarizing generic or alternative instructions on how to accomplish a task. This feature enables students to quickly find important skills.
- **Real World Advice Box:** A boxed feature that appears throughout the workshop offering advice and best practices for general use of important Office skills. The goal is to instruct students as a manager might in a future job.
- **Side Note:** A brief tip or piece of information that is aligned with a step in the workshop quickly advising students completing that particular step.
- **Consider This:** In-text questions or topics for discussion which allow students to step back from the project and think about the skills and the applications of what they are learning and how they might be used in the future.
- **Troubleshooting:** A note related to the active text that helps students work around common pitfalls or errors that might occur.
- **Concept Check:** A section at the end of each workshop made up of approximately five concept-related questions that are short answer or open ended for students to review.
- **Visual Summary:** A visual representation of the important skills learned in the workshop. Call-outs and brief explanations illustrate important buttons or skills demonstrated in a screenshot of the final solution for the Workshop Prepare Case. Intended as a visual review of the objectives learned in the workshop; it is mapped to the objectives using page numbers so students can easily find the section of text to refer to for a refresher.
- **NEW! Business Application Icons:** Clearly identify which application of business is being used in cases and examples; for example, Finance, Marketing, Operations, etc.
- **NEW! myitlab Icons:** Identify which cases from the book match those in my**it**lab.
- **NEW! Video Icons:** Cue students to watch the associated video at specific parts in the text. These include **Workshop Videos** that follow the steps of the Prepare Case and **Real World Interview Videos** that feature a real business person discussing how he or she uses Office on a day-to-day basis.

Instructor Resources

The Instructor's Resource Center, available at **www.pearsonhighered.com**, includes the following:

- AACSB mapping that identifies which cases and exercises in the text speak to AACSB certification.
- Annotated Solution Files with Scorecards assist with grading the Prepare, Practice, Problem Solve, and Perform Cases.
- Data and Solution Files

- Rubrics for Perform Cases enable instructors to easily grade open-ended assignments with no definite solution.
- PowerPoint Presentations with notes for each chapter are included for out-of-class study or review.
- Lesson Plans that provide a detailed blueprint to achieve workshop learning objectives and outcomes and best use the unique structure of the modules.
- Complete Test Bank, also available in TestGen format
- Syllabus templates for 8-week, 12-week, and 16-week courses
- Additional Perform Cases for more exercises where you have to start "from scratch."
- Additional Cloud Collaboration cases
- Workshop-level Problem Solve Cases for more assessment on the objectives on an individual workshop level.
- Scripted Lectures provide instructors with a lecture outline that mirrors the Workshop Prepare Case.
- Flexible, robust, and customizable content is available for all major online course platforms that include everything instructors need in one place. Please contact your sales representative for information on accessing course cartridges for WebCT or Blackboard.

Student Resources

- Student Data Files
- Workshop videos walk students through a case similar to the Prepare Case, which follows the click path and individual skills students learn in the workshop. There is one video per workshop.
- Real World Interview videos introduce students to real professionals talking about how they use Microsoft Office on a daily basis in their work. These videos provide the relevance students seek while learning this material. There is one video per workshop.

Pearson's Companion Website

www.pearsonhighered.com/youroffice offers expanded IT resources and downloadable supplements. Students can find the following self-study tools for each workshop:

- Online Study Guide
- Workshop Objectives
- Additional Workshop Cases
- Additional Capstone Perform Cases
- Glossary
- Workshop Objectives Review
- Web Resources
- Student Data Files

myitlab for Office 2010 is a solution designed by professors for professors that allows easy delivery of Office courses with defensible assessment and outcomes-based training. The new **Your Office 2010** system will seamlessly integrate online assessment, training, and projects with myitlab for Microsoft Office 2010!

myitlab for Office 2010 Features...

- **Assessment and training built to match *Your Office 2010*** instructional content so that myitlab works with Your Office to help students make Office their own.
- **Both project-based and skill-based assessment and training** allow instructors to test and train students on complete exercises or individual Office application skills.
- **Full course management functionality**, that includes all instructor and student resources, a complete Gradebook, and the ability to run a variety of reports including detailed student clickstream data.
- **The most open, realistic, high-fidelity simulation** of Office 2010 makes students feel like they are learning Office, not just a simulation.
- **Grader, a live-in-the-application project-grading tool,** enables instructors to assign projects taken from the end-of-chapter material and additional projects included in the instructor resources. These are graded automatically, with detailed feedback provided to both instructors and students.

Visual Walk-Through

Common Features workshop efficiently covers skills most common among all applications, reducing repetition and allowing instructors to move faster over such topics as save, print, and bold.

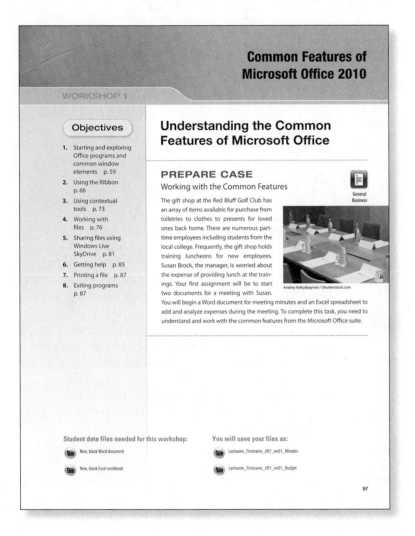

Business Area Icons

Customer Service

Finance & Accounting

General Business

Human Resources

Information Technology

Production & Operations

Sales & Marketing

Research & Development

Video Icons

Student Videos

Real World Interview Videos

Unique Structure Providing for Customizability for Each Course: Instructors can choose to teach with modules in order for students to achieve a higher level understanding of the skills, or go more basic and traditional with the workshops alone.

Workshops: Similar to a chapter, introduces concepts through explanatory text and integrates Active Text so students actively work through the Prepare Case the entire time.

Modules: An organizational structure that provides for the synthesis of skills and concepts introduced over two grouped workshops. Requires students to successfully retain and use skills they have learned over multiple workshops in new contexts.

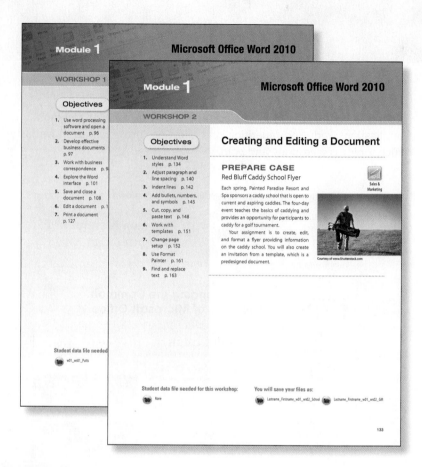

Module Capstone: An assessment section that appears at the end of each module. The Module Capstone is composed of Practice, Problem Solve, and Perform Cases that require students to use the skills learned over the two workshops to complete projects.

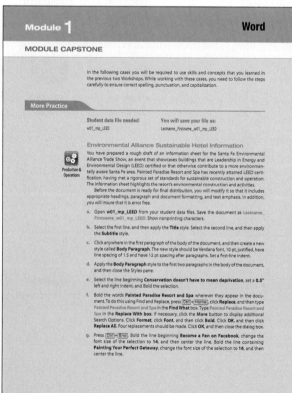

Clear Objectives with page numbers identify the learning objectives to be achieved as students work through the workshop. Students see these first at the workshop opener, and again at the Visual Summary.

The **Visual Summary** is a quick visual review of the objectives learned in the workshop, and is mapped to the Workshop using page numbers so students can easily refer back for a refresher.

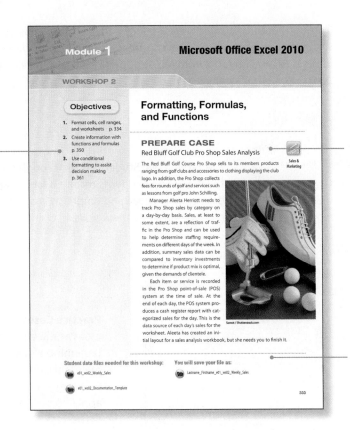

The Running Business Scenario is the basis of the Prepare Cases. This illustrates for students how businesses use Microsoft Office in the real world.

Starting and Ending Data Files clearly list the names of starting data files and naming conventions for the ending solution files prior to each case.

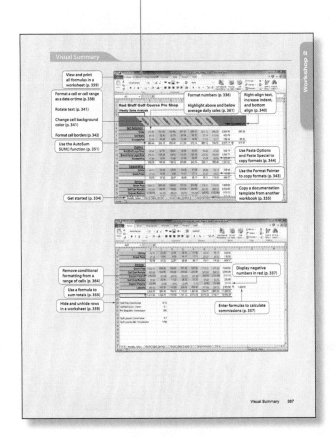

Throughout the modules there are four different cases characterized by the level of instruction or hand-holding that students receive. The goal of the progression of these cases is to take students from an introductory level all the way to mastery, so students can learn to make Office their own.

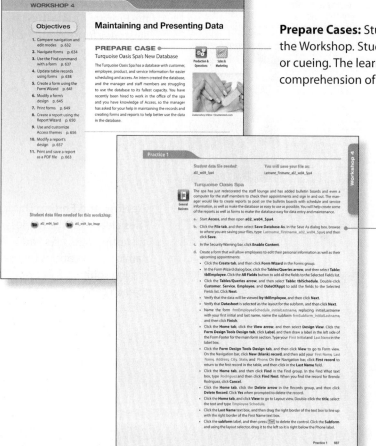

Prepare Cases: Students walk through these cases in the Workshop. Students receive a lot of hand-holding or cueing. The learning emphasis is on knowledge and comprehension of new skills.

Practice Cases: Students work on these cases at the end of the workshop and at the beginning of a Module Capstone. They often maintain the same or similar scenario as the Prepare Case. The learning emphasis is on applying previously learned skills.

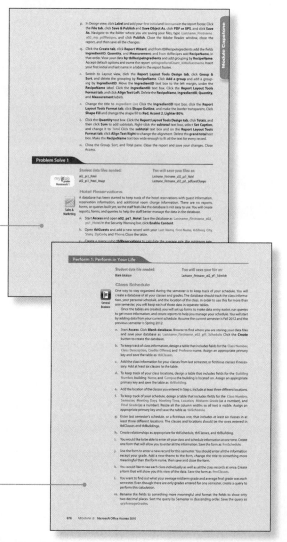

Problem Solve Cases: Students work on these cases at the end of the Workshop and in the Module Capstone. The learning emphasis is on analyzing and synthesizing previously learned skills.

Perform Cases: Students work on these at the end of the Module Capstone. Most of these cases require students to work completely from scratch to solve business problems in a variety of scenarios: typical student lives, future careers, and evaluating how others have performed. The learning emphasis is on synthesizing, creating with, and evaluating projects using previously learned skills.

Troubleshooting a note in the Active Text that helps students work around common pitfalls or errors that might occur.

Active Text boxes appear throughout the Workshop and are easily distinguishable from explanatory text by the shaded background. Active Text helps students quickly identify what steps they need to follow to complete the Prepare Case and gets them hands-on from start to finish.

Side Note identifies a brief tip or piece of information for a step in the Workshop.

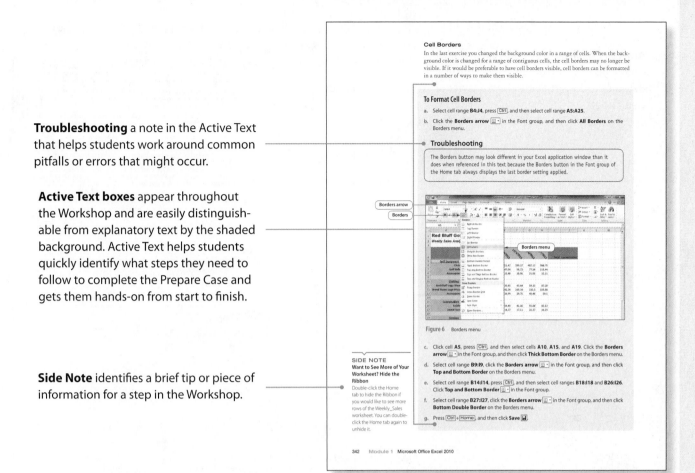

Real World Advice boxes appear throughout the workshop, offering advice and best practices for general use of important Office skills. The goal is to instruct students as a manager might in a future career.

Consider This is an in-text question or topic for discussion that allows students to step back from the project and think about the applications of what they are learning and how that might be used in the future.

Quick Reference boxes appear throughout the Workshop, summarizing generic or alternative instructions on how to accomplish a task. This feature enables students to quickly find important skills.

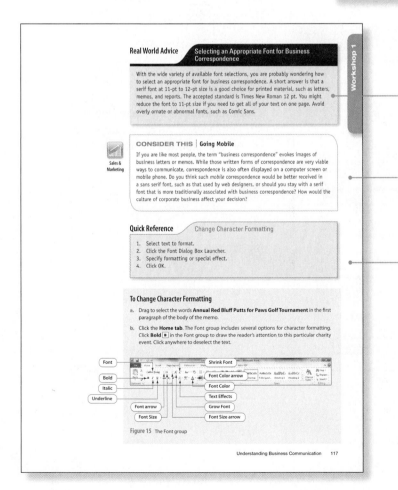

Concept Check at the end of each workshop is made up of approximately five concept-related questions that are short answer or open ended.

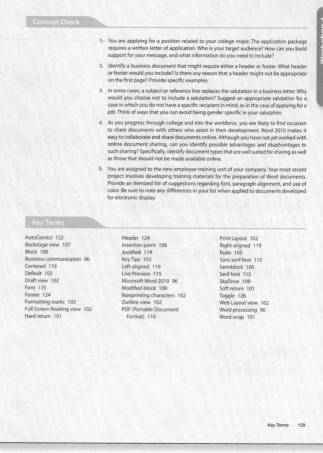

Concept Check

1. You are applying for a position related to your college major. The application package requires a written letter of application. Who is your target audience? How can you build support for your message, and what information do you need to include?

2. Identify a business document that might require either a header or footer. What header or footer would you include? Is there any reason that a header might not be appropriate on the first page? Provide specific examples.

3. In some cases, a subject or reference line replaces the salutation in a business letter. Why would you choose not to include a salutation? Suggest an appropriate salutation for a case in which you do not have a specific recipient in mind, as in the case of applying for a job. Think of ways that you can avoid being gender specific in your salutation.

4. As you progress through college and into the workforce, you are likely to find occasion to share documents with others who assist in their development. Word 2010 makes it easy to collaborate and share documents online. Although you have not yet worked with online document sharing, can you identify possible advantages and disadvantages to such sharing? Specifically, identify document types that are well suited for sharing as well as those that should not be made available online.

5. You are assigned to the new employee training unit of your company. Your most recent project involves developing training materials for the preparation of Word documents. Provide an itemized list of suggestions regarding font, paragraph alignment, and use of color. Be sure to note any differences in your list when applied to documents developed for electronic display.

Key Terms

AutoCorrect 122	Header 124	Print Layout 102
Backstage view 107	Insertion point 106	Right-aligned 119
Block 100	Justified 119	Ruler 105
Business communication 96	Key Tips 102	Sans serif font 115
Centered 119	Left-aligned 119	Semiblock 100
Default 102	Live Preview 115	Serif font 115
Draft view 102	Microsoft Word 2010 96	SkyDrive 109
Font 115	Modified block 100	Soft return 101
Footer 124	Nonprinting characters 102	Toggle 126
Formatting marks 102	Outline view 102	Web Layout view 102
Full Screen Reading view 102	PDF (Portable Document	Word processing 96
Hard return 101	Format) 110	Word wrap 101

Key Terms 129

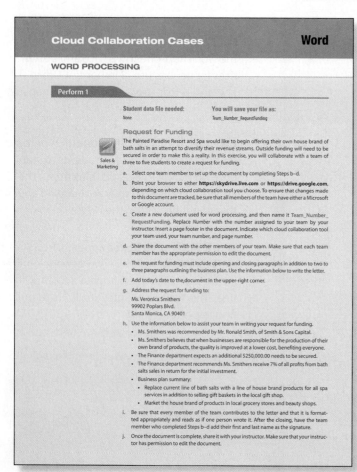

Cloud Collaboration Cases

Word

WORD PROCESSING

Perform 1

Student data file needed:
None

You will save your file as:
Team_Number_RequestFunding

Request for Funding

The Painted Paradise Resort and Spa would like to begin offering their own house brand of bath salts in an attempt to diversify their revenue streams. Outside funding will need to be secured in order to make this a reality. In this exercise, you will collaborate with a team of three to five students to create a request for funding.

Sales & Marketing

a. Select one team member to set up the document by completing Steps b–d.

b. Point your browser to either **https://skydrive.live.com** or **https://drive.google.com**, depending on which cloud collaboration tool you choose. To ensure that changes made to this document are tracked, be sure that all members of the team have either a Microsoft or Google account.

c. Create a new document used for word processing, and then name it Team_Number_RequestFunding. Replace *Number* with the number assigned to your team by your instructor. Insert a page footer in the document. Indicate which cloud collaboration tool your team used, your team number, and page number.

d. Share the document with the other members of your team. Make sure that each team member has the appropriate permission to edit the document.

e. The request for funding must include opening and closing paragraphs in addition to two to three paragraphs outlining the business plan. Use the information below to write the letter.

f. Add today's date to the document in the upper-right corner.

g. Address the request for funding to:
Ms. Veronica Smithers
99902 Poplars Blvd.
Santa Monica, CA 90401

h. Use the information below to assist your team in writing your request for funding.
- Ms. Smithers was recommended by Mr. Ronald Smith, of Smith & Sons Capital.
- Ms. Smithers believes that when businesses are responsible for the production of their own brand of products, the quality is improved at a lower cost, benefiting everyone.
- The Finance department expects an additional $250,000.00 needs to be secured.
- The Finance department recommends Ms. Smithers receive 7% of all profits from bath salts sales in return for the initial investment.
- Business plan summary:
  - Replace current line of bath salts with a line of house brand products for all spa services in addition to selling gift baskets in the local gift shop.
  - Market the house brand of products in local grocery stores and beauty shops.

i. Be sure that every member of the team contributes to the letter and that it is formatted appropriately and reads as if one person wrote it. After the closing, have the team member who completed Steps b–d add their first and last name as the signature.

j. Once the document is complete, share it with your instructor. Make sure that your instructor has permission to edit the document.

Cloud Collaboration Cases introduce students to web 2.0 technology and encourage teamwork and collaboration.

Dear Students,

If you want an edge over the competition, make it personal. Whether you love sports, travel, the stock market, or ballet, your passion is personal to you. Capitalizing on your passion leads to success. You live in a global marketplace, and your competition is global. The honors students in China exceed the total number of students in North America. Skills can help set you apart, but passion will make you stand above. *Your Office* is the tool to harness your passion's true potential.

In prior generations, personalization in a professional setting was discouraged. You had a "work" life and a "home" life. As the Series Editor, I write to you about the vision for *Your Office* from my laptop, on my couch, in the middle of the night when inspiration struck me. My classroom and living room are my office. Life has changed from generations before us.

So, let's get personal. My degrees are not in technology, but chemistry and law. I helped put myself through school by working full time in various jobs, including a successful technology consulting business that continues today. My generation did not grow up with computers, but I did. My father was a network administrator for the military. So, I was learning to program in Basic before anyone had played Nintendo's Duck Hunt or Tetris. Technology has always been one of my passions from a young age. In fact, I now tell my husband: don't buy me jewelry for my birthday, buy me the latest gadget on the market!

In my first law position, I was known as the Office guru to the extent that no one gave me a law assignment for the first two months. Once I submitted the assignment, my supervisor remarked, "Wow, you don't just know how to leverage technology, but you really know the law too." I can tell you novel-sized stories from countless prior students in countless industries who gained an edge from using Office as a tool. Bringing technology to your passion makes you well rounded and a cut above the rest, no matter the industry or position.

I am most passionate about teaching, in particular teaching technology. I come from many generations of teachers, including my mother who is a kindergarten teacher. For over 12 years, I have found my dream job passing on my passion for teaching, technology, law, science, music, and life in general at the Kelley School of Business at Indiana University. I have tried to pass on the key to engaging passion to my students. I have helped them see what differentiates them from all the other bright students vying for the same jobs.

Microsoft Office is a tool. All of your competition will have learned Microsoft Office to some degree or another. Some will have learned it to an advanced level. Knowing Microsoft Office is important, but it is also fundamental. Without it, you will not be considered for a position.

Today, you step into your first of many future roles bringing Microsoft Office to your dream job working for Painted Paradise Resort and Spa. You will delve into the business side of the resort and learn how to use *Your Office* to maximum benefit.

Don't let the context of a business fool you. If you don't think of yourself as a business person, you have no need to worry. Whether you realize it or not, everything is business. If you want to be a nurse, you are entering the health care industry. If you want to be a football player in the NFL, you are entering the business of sports as entertainment. In fact, if you want to be a stay-at-home parent, you are entering the business of a family household where *Your Office* still gives you an advantage. For example, you will be able to prepare a budget in Excel and analyze what you need to do to afford a trip to Disney World!

At Painted Paradise Resort and Spa, you will learn how to make Office yours through four learning levels designed to maximize your understanding. You will Prepare, Practice, and Problem Solve your tasks. Then, you will astound when you Perform your new talents. You will be challenged through Consider This questions and gain insight through Real World Advice.

There is something more. You want success in what you are passionate about in your life. It is personal for you. In this position at Painted Paradise Resort and Spa, you will gain your personal competitive advantage that will stay with you for the rest of your life—*Your Office*.

Sincerely,

Amy Kinser

Series Editor

Welcome to the Painted Paradise Resort and Spa Team!

Welcome to your new office at Painted Paradise Resort and Spa, where we specialize in painting perfect getaways. As the Chief Technology Officer, I am excited to have staff dedicated to the Microsoft Office integration between all the areas of the resort. Our team is passionate about our paradise, and I hope you find this to be your dream position here!

Painted Paradise is a resort and spa in New Mexico catering to business people, romantics, families, and anyone who just needs to get away. Inside our resort are many distinct areas. Many of these areas operate as businesses in their own right but must integrate with the other areas of the resort. The main areas of the resort are as follows.

- The **Hotel** is overseen by our Chief Executive Officer, William Mattingly, and is at the core of our business. The hotel offers a variety of accommodations, ranging from individual rooms to a grand villa suite. Further, the hotel offers packages including spa, golf, and special events.

   Room rates vary according to size, season, demand, and discount. The hotel has discounts for typical groups, such as AARP. The hotel also has a loyalty program where guests can earn free nights based on frequency of visits. Guests may charge anything from the resort to the room.

- **Red Bluff Golf Course** is a private world-class golf course and pro shop. The golf course has services such as golf lessons from the famous golf pro John Schilling and playing packages. Also, the golf course attracts local residents. This requires variety in pricing schemes to accommodate both local and hotel guests. The pro shop sells many retail items online.

   The golf course can also be reserved for special events and tournaments. These special events can be in conjunction with a wedding, conference, meetings, or other event covered by the event planning and catering area of the resort.

- **Turquoise Oasis Spa** is a full-service spa. Spa services include haircuts, pedicures, messages, facials, body wraps, waxing, and various other spa services—typical to exotic. Further, the spa offers private consultation, weight training (in the fitness center), a water bar, meditation areas, and steam rooms. Spa services are offered both in the spa and in the resort guest's room.

   Turquoise Oasis Spa uses top-of-the-line products and some house-brand products. The retail side offers products ranging from candles to age-defying home treatments. These products can also be purchased online. Many of the hotel guests who fall in love with the house-brand soaps, lotions, candles, and other items appreciate being able to buy more at any time.

   The spa offers a multitude of packages including special hotel room packages that include spa treatments. Local residents also use the spa. So, the spa guests are not limited to hotel guests. Thus, the packages also include pricing attractive to the local community.

- **Painted Treasures Gift Shop** has an array of items available for purchase, from toiletries to clothes to presents for loved ones back home including a healthy section of kids' toys for traveling business people. The gift shop sells a small sampling from the spa, golf course pro shop, and local New Mexico culture. The gift shop also has a small section of snacks and drinks. The gift shop has numerous part-time employees including students from the local college.

- The **Event Planning & Catering** area is central to attracting customers to the resort. From weddings to conferences, the resort is a popular destination. The resort has a substantial number of staff dedicated to planning, coordinating, setting up, catering, and maintaining these events. The resort has several facilities that can accommodate large groups. Packages and prices vary by size, room, and other services such as catering. Further, the Event Planning & Catering team works closely with local vendors for floral decorations, photography, and other event or wedding typical needs. However, all catering must go through the resort (no outside catering permitted). Lastly, the resort stocks several choices of decorations, table arrangements, and centerpieces. These range from professional, simple, themed, and luxurious.

- **Indigo 5** and the **Silver Moon Lounge**, a world-class restaurant and lounge that is overseen by the well-known Chef Robin Sanchez. The cuisine is balanced and modern. From steaks to pasta to local southwestern meals, Indigo 5 attracts local patrons in addition to resort guests. While the catering function is separate from the restaurant—though menu items may be shared—the restaurant does support all room service for the resort. The resort also has smaller food venues onsite such as the Terra Cotta Brew coffee shop in the lobby.

Currently, these areas are using Office to various degrees. In some areas, paper and pencil are still used for most business functions. Others have been lucky enough to have some technology savvy team members start Microsoft Office Solutions.

Using your skills, I am confident that you can help us integrate and use Microsoft Office on a whole new level! I hope you are excited to call Painted Paradise Resort and Spa *Your Office*.

Looking forward to working with you more closely!

Aidan Matthews

Aidan Matthews
Chief Technology Officer

Microsoft Windows 7

Understanding the Windows 7 Desktop and Managing Windows

PREPARE CASE

Painted Paradise Golf Resort and Spa Employees Explore Microsoft Windows 7

Information Technology

Aidan Matthews, Chief Technology Officer of the Painted Paradise Golf Resort and Spa, has just replaced all computers on the resort property. The new computers came with Microsoft Windows 7 installed. Due to a poor economy, Aidan decided not to upgrade to Microsoft Windows Vista when it was released several years ago. His staff has been using computers that were still running Microsoft Windows XP.

Monkey Business Images / Shutterstock.com

There is a considerable difference between Windows XP and Windows 7, and Painted Paradise employees have asked for help in making the transition. They are anxious to take advantage of the many new features in Windows 7 as soon as possible. You have been asked to plan a workshop to train personnel in all departments to use their new computers efficiently. Aidan has asked that you start by using Windows 7 default settings. He wants you to focus on fundamental skills but would also like you to introduce new features that will enhance productivity. Staff members will be encouraged to personalize their own computers once they become familiar with the basic features of Windows 7.

Student data file needed for this workshop:

  Student Data Files folder

You will save your files as:

  Lastname_Firstname_w701_ws01_Folders

  Lastname_Firstname_w701_ws01_Compressed

  Lastname_Firstname_w701_ws01_Search

  Lastname_Firstname_w701_ws01_Golf

Understanding Windows 7

SIDE NOTE
Windows 8

Microsoft released Windows 8 at the end of 2012. It includes an all-new touch interface as well as other new features. See the Windows 8 Appendix for more information about this release.

Microsoft Windows 7 is the latest version of the Windows **operating system**. The operating system is **system software** that controls and coordinates the computer hardware to make other programs run efficiently. The operating system acts as an intermediary between **application software**—programs that help the user perform specific tasks, such as word processing—and the computer hardware and helps the user perform essential tasks such as displaying information on the computer screen, saving data on a storage device, and sending documents to a printer. You can have multiple programs open at the same time and switch between programs easily using several different methods.

Microsoft releases a new version of Windows every few years to take advantage of improvements made to hardware and to add new features. Windows 7 replaces Windows Vista, which was released in 2007. Windows 7 uses a **graphical user interface (GUI)**, an interface that uses **icons**, which are small pictures that represent commands, programs, and documents. This type of interface helps the user interact with the hardware and software more easily.

Several versions of Windows 7 are available including the Home Premium, Professional, Ultimate, and Enterprise editions. Painted Paradise Resort is using the Home Premium edition, which is most likely what you are using on your home computer. Large universities or businesses may use one of the other versions. All four of these versions include the **Windows Aero** experience that incorporates subtle animations and translucent glass windows on your desktop.

Starting Windows 7

Windows 7 starts automatically when your computer is turned on. Several different things might occur, depending on where you are using your computer. If you are using your computer at home and you are the only user, most likely you will go directly to the Windows **desktop**—the working area of the Windows 7 screen. If several people in your family share the same computer, a welcome screen will show an icon for each user. You must **click**—press the left mouse button one time—your user icon, and then you may be asked to enter a password. This prevents other users from accessing your documents or other personal data. Your school or business may have a different logon procedure because many people may be sharing a network.

To Start Windows

a. Turn on your computer, and then wait a few moments. If necessary, follow any logon instructions required for the computer you are using. The Windows desktop is displayed.

Recycle Bin

Desktop

Mouse pointer

Taskbar

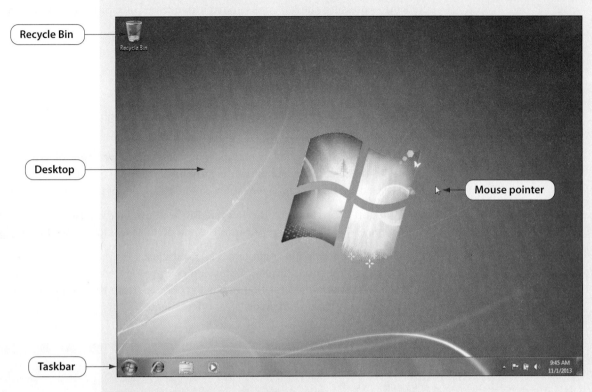

Figure 1 Windows 7 default desktop

Exploring the Windows 7 Desktop

The Windows 7 default desktop shows a blue background with the Windows logo in the center of the screen. The **Recycle Bin**—a storage area for files that have been deleted—is in the top-left corner and may be the only icon visible on the desktop. You will also see a **mouse pointer**—an arrow that shows the position of the mouse—somewhere on the screen. A mouse or other pointing device is used to interact with objects on the screen, to open programs, or select commands. Pointing to an object often brings up a **ScreenTip**, which provides a name or other information about the object to which you are pointing. **Right-clicking**—pressing the right mouse button—opens a **shortcut menu**—a group or list of commands—containing **context-sensitive** commands related to the right-clicked item.

At the bottom of the screen is the **taskbar**, which displays the Start button, pinned taskbar buttons, the notification area, and the Show desktop button. The taskbar is now taller than in previous Windows versions. Several program buttons are already pinned to the taskbar, and buttons for programs that you open will be placed on the taskbar temporarily.

Windows 7 allows you to personalize and customize your desktop. Therefore your background may be different, and there may be many more icons on your desktop. Your taskbar may even be in a different location. In this section, you will learn to identify desktop elements and understand the taskbar and Start menu.

Identifying Desktop Elements

You will begin your workshop by asking Painted Paradise Resort employees to explore the Windows 7 desktop. They will examine various elements on the desktop and learn correct terminology.

Pointing to a desktop icon highlights it and may bring up a ScreenTip. **Double-clicking**—pressing the left mouse button two times in rapid succession—an icon opens the program that the icon represents.

To Explore the Windows 7 Desktop

a. Using your mouse, point to the **Recycle Bin**. The icon is highlighted.

b. Double-click the **Recycle Bin**.

The Recycle Bin window opens, showing all files that have been deleted. Your window may fill the screen or some of the **desktop background**—the picture or pattern that is displayed on the desktop—may show around the edges of the Recycle Bin window.

c. In the top-right corner of the **Recycle Bin** window, you will see the Minimize , Maximize, and Close buttons common to all windows. Click **Close**.

d. Point to the **Recycle Bin** again, and then **right-click**.

A shortcut menu is displayed, showing context-sensitive commands or commands that can be performed relating to the Recycle Bin. Note that you can also open the Recycle Bin by clicking Open on the shortcut menu.

Shortcut menu

Figure 2 Context-sensitive shortcut menu

e. Point to a blank area on the desktop, and then **right-click**. A different shortcut menu appears, listing options that can be performed relating to the desktop.

f. Click a blank area of the desktop to close the shortcut menu without making a selection.

Real World Advice Using the Recycle Bin

Files sent to the Recycle Bin remain on the computer's **hard drive**—a disk drive inside your computer, also called the local drive—until the Recycle Bin is emptied. As long as a file is still in the Recycle Bin, it can be restored to its original location. This is similar to putting a piece of paper in a trash can. As long as the trash has not been emptied, you can still retrieve the piece of paper. However, once the Recycle Bin has been emptied, the file is gone.

If you are certain that you will not need a file again, you can bypass the Recycle Bin by holding down Shift when you press Delete. Note that only files deleted from your hard drive are placed in the Recycle Bin. Files deleted from a **USB flash drive**—a small storage device that plugs into your computer's USB port—or other auxiliary storage devices are not sent to the local Recycle Bin and can only be restored if the auxiliary storage device maintains a separate Recycle Bin.

Understanding the Taskbar

The taskbar is the long horizontal bar at the bottom of your screen and is twice as tall as in previous versions. The taskbar is visible most of the time and consists of several sections:

- The **Start button**, located on the far left of the taskbar, opens the Start menu.
- The Pinned taskbar buttons let you start programs with one click.
- The middle section displays temporary buttons for programs and documents that are open.
- The **notification area**, which displays information about the status of programs running in the background, also includes a clock.
- The Show desktop button is on the far right.

Clicking the Start button opens the **Start menu**, which is the major link to your computer's programs, management tools, and file storage structure.

To the right of the Start button are three pinned taskbar buttons representing Internet Explorer, Windows Explorer, and Windows Media Player. Microsoft assumes that these are programs that will be used frequently, so they are pinned permanently to the taskbar when Windows is first installed. You can pin more program buttons to this area, arrange them in any order you prefer, and unpin them when they are no longer needed. When you open a program or file, a corresponding temporary button appears in the area to the right of the Pinned taskbar buttons. When the program or file is closed, the button is no longer displayed on the taskbar.

The notification area, on the right side of the taskbar, contains icons representing programs running in the background and displays information about the status of those programs. The Show hidden icons arrow on the left of the notification area opens a window with additional icons. The time/date control shows the current time and date or the time and date to which your computer is set. Clicking on the time/date control opens a window showing a calendar and clock and allows you to make adjustments to the date and time. The **Show desktop button** is on the far-right end of the taskbar. When one or more program windows are open, this button lets you **peek**—turn open windows transparent to reveal the desktop—at the desktop for a moment, or return to the desktop with just one click.

To Explore the Taskbar

a. On the left side of the taskbar, point to **Start** 🔵. After a few seconds a ScreenTip appears, identifying the button.

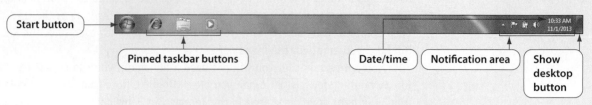

Figure 3 Taskbar

b. In the Pinned taskbar buttons area, point to the **Internet Explorer** button 🔵, and then read the ScreenTip. Repeat this step for the other buttons in the Pinned taskbar buttons area. Your pinned buttons may differ.

c. Point to several icons in the notification area, and then read the ScreenTips. These will vary on different computers. To the left side of the notification area, point to and then click **Show hidden icons** ▪. A small window with additional icons opens. Click a blank area of the desktop to close this window.

d. Point to **date/time.** A ScreenTip with the day and date is shown. Click **date/time**.
   A window opens with a calendar of the current month and a clock with the current time. You can adjust the date and time in this window. Click a blank area of the desktop to close this window.

e. On the far right of the taskbar, point to **Show desktop** ▪. Read the ScreenTip.
   Because you are already at the desktop, pointing to or clicking this button will have no effect. You will use this button later in the workshop when several windows are open.

Using the Start Menu

Clicking the Start button opens the Start menu, which allows access to everything on your computer—programs, management tools, and the file storage structure. You can open the Start menu by clicking the Start button on the left side of the taskbar or by pressing the Windows logo key. Desktop keyboards usually have two Windows logo keys, located near the left and right of the [Spacebar]. Notebook computers, except Macs, usually have only one Windows logo key, located to the left of the [Spacebar]. Your keyboard may or may not have one depending on your computer.

On the Start menu, some options include an arrow leading to a **Jump List**—a list displaying commands or files related to the option. Jump Lists are new in Windows 7 and can take you directly to documents, pictures, songs, and other items on the computer. When you point to a program, the Jump List displays a list of files recently opened with that program, and you can click any file on the list to open it. Other Jump Lists may offer a choice of commands. You can also open a Jump List by right-clicking any program icon on the taskbar.

To Open the Start Menu

a. On the left side of the taskbar, point to **Start** ⊙. Click the left mouse button. The Start menu opens. Programs listed on your Start menu may differ.

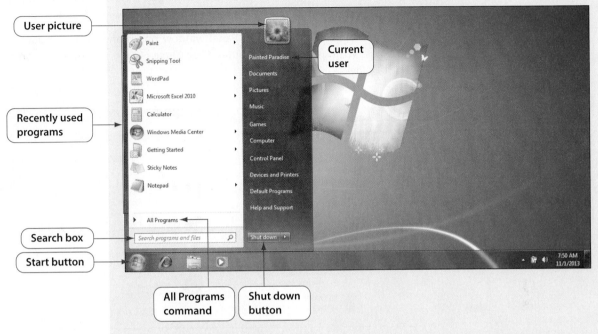

Figure 4   Start menu

b. Click **Start** ⊙ again to close the Start menu. You can also close the Start menu by clicking on a blank area of the desktop.

Understanding the Start Menu

The Start menu opens with two vertical side-by-side panes. The large left pane provides access to programs and other utilities installed on your computer. The right pane provides access to user documents, pictures, and music, as well as management tools and settings. This is also where you go to log off from Windows or to turn off your computer.

You will explore both panes of the Start menu with Painted Paradise Resort staff.

Exploring the Right Pane of the Start Menu

The right pane of the Start menu is divided into three sections. The top section provides quick access to various storage locations. It displays your user account picture and user name and links to the Documents, Pictures, and Music libraries. As you point to an item, it is highlighted, a ScreenTip is displayed, and the picture at the top of the pane changes to correspond to the item to which you are pointing.

The middle section allows access to games installed with Windows 7—and games installed by the computer manufacturer—as well as to the Computer window in Windows Explorer.

The bottom section provides access to computer management tools including links to the Control Panel, Devices and Printers, Default Programs, and Help and Support. At the bottom of the right pane is the Shut down button, which allows you to switch users, log off, lock the computer, restart the computer, put the computer in sleep or hibernate mode, and shut down the computer.

To Explore the Right Pane

a. On the taskbar, click **Start** ⊕. The Start menu opens, displaying two vertical panes.

b. Notice the picture at the top of the right pane. This represents your User Account. Point to each item on the right side of the Start menu. Read the ScreenTip and notice how the picture at the top of the pane changes to correspond to whatever you are pointing to.

c. Click **Control Panel**. The Control Panel window opens and displays options that let you adjust settings on your computer. Click **Close** ⊠ in the top-right corner of the Control Panel.

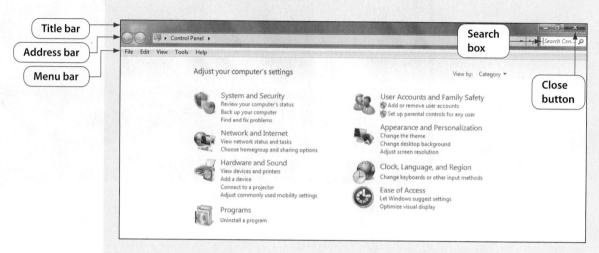

Figure 5 Control Panel

d. Click **Start** ⊕. On the right pane of the Start menu, click **Help and Support**. The Windows Help and Support window opens. A list of options appears that will help you learn more about Windows and using your computer. Click a topic to explore and read the information.

e. Click **Close** ⊠ in the top-right corner of the Windows Help and Support window.

f. Click **Start** ⊕. In the bottom-right corner of the right pane, point to, but do not click, **Shut down** ⬛. This button has two parts, the Shut down button, sometimes called the Power button, and an arrow.

g. Point to the **arrow** ▷. A menu is displayed with a list of options that lets you switch users, log off, lock the computer, restart the computer, or put the computer in sleep or hibernate mode.

Shut down options

Figure 6 Shut down button options

h. Click a blank area of the desktop to close the Start menu.

Exploring the Left Pane of the Start Menu

The left pane of the Start menu contains the Recently Opened programs list, which displays links to the last 10 programs that were opened. This list changes as you use different programs. The number of programs that are shown can be changed and programs can be removed. Your list of recently opened programs will differ.

Programs that you want to have available at all times can be added to the **pinned programs area** at the top-left side of the Start menu. This list will not be visible until the first time an item is pinned to this area. Your Start menu may already show programs in the pinned programs area.

Some programs on the left side of the Start menu display Option arrows. Pointing to a program with an Option arrow displays a Jump List—a list of tasks or recently opened files associated with that program.

To Open a Jump List

a. On the taskbar, click **Start** ⊛. The Start menu opens.

b. On the left side of the Start menu, point to the **Getting Started arrow** ▸. A Jump List opens listing various options.

Jump list

Getting Started selected

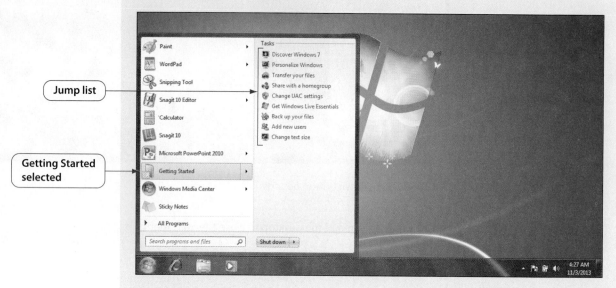

Figure 7   Getting Started Jump List

Troubleshooting

> If you do not see Getting Started, point to any other program that shows an arrow ▸.

c. Point to several other programs that show an arrow ▸ to display the Jump List associated with each program. When you point to a program, the Jump List displays a list of files recently opened with that program. You can "jump" to a specific file by clicking on it in the Jump List, and the file will open in the associated program.

d. Click a blank area of the desktop to close the Start menu.

Understanding the All Programs Menu

The **All Programs** command at the bottom of the left pane of the Start menu provides access to the programs and utilities installed on your computer. You open this menu by pointing to All Programs and waiting a moment or two. It is not necessary to click All Programs.

Some programs are available directly; others are stored in folders. The list is arranged alphabetically with programs at the top followed by folders. You need to use the **scroll bar**—a bar that appears when all items are not visible—on the right of the All Programs menu to see all available options. **Drag**—hold the left mouse button while moving to a different location—the **scroll box**—the box in the scroll bar used to reposition the items on the list—up and down until you locate the program you want.

When the All Programs menu opens, the All Programs command changes to Back. If you do not want to start a program, close the All Programs menu by pointing to Back and you will return to the standard Start menu.

To Display the All Programs Menu

a. Click **Start** 🔵 to display the Start menu.

b. Near the bottom of the left side of the Start menu, point to **All Programs**. After a few moments, the All Programs menu opens. Note that All Programs is replaced with Back.

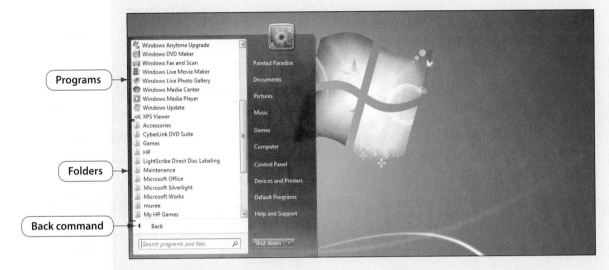

Figure 8 All Programs menu

c. Drag the scroll box up and down to examine the items in the All Programs menu. Programs are arranged alphabetically at the top of the list, followed by a list of folders.

d. Point to **Back**. After a few moments, the menu returns to the original Start menu. You can also click Back to return to the Start menu.

e. Click **Start** 🔵 or click a blank area of the desktop to close the Start menu.

Understanding the Start Menu Search Box

In the bottom-left corner of the Start menu, you will see the Start menu **Search box**—a box in which you type a word or phrase to search—with the insertion point flashing. The Search box helps you quickly find anything stored on your computer. Type any character in the Search box, and Windows will display programs, Control Panel items, documents, and other items containing that letter. As you add more characters, Windows will refine the search results. You can open any item that appears in the search results by clicking it, or you can open the folder containing that item by right-clicking the item and then clicking Open File Location.

To Use the Start Menu Search Box

a. Click **Start** 🔘. An insertion point flashes in the Search box at the bottom of the left pane of the Start menu.

b. Type the letter **c** in the Search box. After a few moments the search results display a list of Programs, Control Panel items, Documents, Music, and Pictures containing the letter "c."

Troubleshooting

If you do not see Calculator under Programs at the top of the list, continue typing the word "calculator" until Calculator appears under Programs near the top of the list.

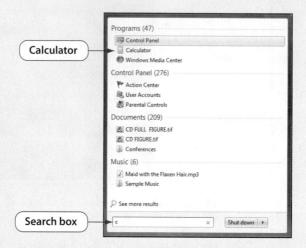

Figure 9   Search results

SIDE NOTE
Calculator Window
The Calculator window cannot be resized. Notice that the Maximize button—the middle button—in the top-right corner is dimmed. This indicates that this option is not available.

c. Click **Calculator** to open the Calculator program. A calculator window is displayed.

d. Click **Close** in the top-right corner to close the Calculator window.

Working with Windows

As the word "windows" implies, almost everything you view on your computer screen is displayed in a **window**—a rectangular frame that displays a program, folder, or file. Windows contain common elements such as a **title bar**, **address bar**, **menu bar**, **command bar**, and **status bar**. Figure 10 describes these elements in more detail. Windows can be moved, resized, **minimized** to a taskbar button, and **maximized** to fill the entire screen. Several windows can be open at the same time and can be manipulated in the same way. In this section, you will learn to move, size, and manage both single and multiple windows.

Screen Element	Description
Title bar	Bar at the top of a window that displays the Minimize, Maximize/Restore Down, and Close buttons on the right side. It may also display a program icon, the name of the active program, and the name of the open document or file.
Address bar	A toolbar that contains the navigation path to the current folder, file, or window. It is located under the title bar.
Menu bar	A toolbar from which you can access menus of commands.
Command bar	A toolbar that displays commands related to the open window.
Status bar	Located at the bottom of windows, this provides information about the selected window or object.

Figure 10   Common screen elements

Opening and Managing Windows

There are several ways to open windows. You have already opened windows using the right pane of the Start menu and the Search box in the left pane. More often you will use All Programs in the left pane of the Start menu because it provides access to everything on your computer. When a window is open, a temporary program button is added to the pinned buttons area on the taskbar.

All windows have similar components. The bar at the top of a window is the title bar. On the right side of the title bar are three control buttons that let you minimize, maximize (or restore down), and close a window. If a window is maximized, the center button changes to the Restore Down button. Clicking this button when the window is maximized **restores** the window to its previous size and location. Most windows display these three control buttons. If a window cannot be resized, the center button is usually dimmed. **Dialog boxes**—boxes that present information or require a response from the user—may display only a Close button.

The title bar can be used to move a window that is not maximized to another location on the desktop. Double-clicking the title bar maximizes a window or restores a window. Many windows also display icons on the left side of the title bar that represent the program that is open. Clicking the icon opens a menu of commonly used commands. To the right of this icon, many Microsoft programs display a Quick Access Toolbar with Save, Undo, and Redo buttons. Additional buttons can be added to the Quick Access Toolbar. Program windows also display the name of the document or file that is open and the name of the program you are using.

To Understand the Elements of a Window

a. Click **Start** 🔵 to open the Start menu. On the right pane of the Start menu, click **Control Panel**. The Control Panel window opens.

b. If the Control Panel window does not fill the screen, click **Maximize** 🔲 near the far right of the title bar. The Maximize button is in the center of the three control buttons if the window is not maximized. When the window is maximized this button becomes the Restore Down button 🔲.

c. Locate the address bar under the title bar. This shows the path to wherever you are currently located. The address bar indicates that you are at the Control Panel. Locate the Search box on the far right side of the address bar.

d. The menu bar displays below the address bar (press Alt to display the menu bar if it is not visible). Click **View** and notice the drop-down menu. Point to the other commands on the menu bar and observe the commands.

SIDE NOTE
Menu Bar Commands
When you click a menu bar command, some items on the drop-down menu may be grayed out. This means that those options are not available at that time. Only commands that are shown in black can be selected.

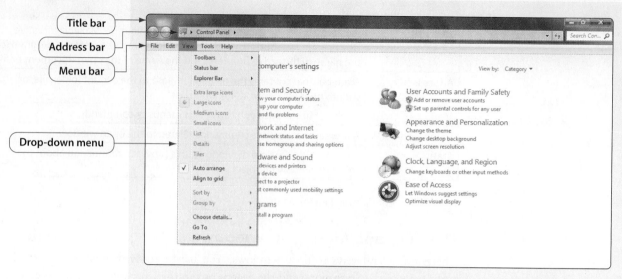

Figure 11   Control Panel with View menu

e. Click **Close** [×] to close the Control Panel window.

Moving and Sizing a Window

You can move a window that is not maximized by clicking its title bar, holding down the left mouse button, and then dragging the window to a new location.

The borders of a window contain options that let you resize the window. Point to any corner until you see a diagonal resize pointer [⬉] or [⬈], and then drag the corner in or out to resize the window both vertically and horizontally. Pointing to the top or bottom border displays a vertical resize pointer [↕]; pointing to the left or right border displays a horizontal resize pointer [↔]. Use these pointers to resize the window as you like.

You will use the WordPad program in the following exercise to practice moving and resizing a window. Notice that the WordPad title bar is slightly different than the Control Panel title bar. It displays an icon representing the program on the far left. Click this icon to display a menu of options. To the right of this icon, the Quick Access Toolbar contains three buttons that are displayed by default: Save, Undo, and Redo. Clicking the arrow to the right of these buttons displays the Customize Quick Access Toolbar menu that lets you add other buttons to the Quick Access Toolbar. The title bar also displays Document, the current file name, and WordPad, the name of the open program. The word "Document" will be replaced with the name of the file once it is created and saved. WordPad also displays a Ribbon, which is common to many Microsoft applications, including programs in the Microsoft Office suite that you will use for other workshops in this textbook.

To Move and Size a Window

a. Click **Start** 🌐 to open the Start menu. Point to **All Programs**, and then wait until the All Programs menu opens. If necessary, use the scroll bar so you can see the Accessories folder. Click **Accessories**, and then click **WordPad**. The WordPad window is displayed, and a WordPad button is added to the taskbar.

b. If your WordPad window is maximized and fills the screen, click **Restore Down** 🗖 , the middle button on the right side of the title bar.

c. Point to and click the **WordPad** title bar. Hold down the mouse button, and then drag the WordPad window so the top border is about 1" below the top of your screen. Dragging the title bar moves the window to a different location.

d. Point to the **bottom border** of the WordPad window until you see the Vertical Resize pointer 🔼. Drag the border so it is about 1" above the taskbar at the bottom of the screen. Dragging a border resizes the window.

e. Repeat this process with the left and right borders of the WordPad window so each is approximately 1" from either side of the screen.

WordPad window resized

Figure 12 WordPad window

Troubleshooting

If one of your borders is off the screen so you cannot see the resize pointer, use the title bar to drag the window so the border is visible.

f. Point to the bottom-right corner of the WordPad window until you see the Diagonal Resize pointer 🔲. Drag the corner of the window up and to the left until the window is about three-fourths the original size.

Minimizing and Restoring a Window

Minimizing and closing a window appear to do the same thing. However, it is important to understand that the two procedures are quite different. When you minimize a program, the window is removed from the screen, but the program is still running on the computer. The program button on the taskbar shows that it is still available but not active. When you close a program, the window is removed from the screen, and the program closes and is removed from computer memory. When a program is closed, the program button is removed from the taskbar.

To Minimize and Restore a Window

a. On the right side of the WordPad title bar, click **Minimize** 🔲. The window is removed from the screen, but notice that the WordPad button is still displayed on the taskbar.

b. Point to **WordPad** 🔳 on the taskbar. A preview window is displayed, giving you a chance to see what the window looks like. Click **WordPad** 🔳. The WordPad window is the same size and in the same location where it was before it was minimized.

Maximizing and Closing a Window

You can maximize a window by using the Maximize button on the right side of the title bar. You can also double-click the title bar of a window to maximize it or to restore it. If a window fills the screen, double-clicking the title bar restores the window to its former size and location. If the window does not fill the screen, double-clicking the title bar maximizes the window. Dragging the title bar so the pointer touches the top of the screen also maximizes the window, if your computer has Aero capabilities.

To Maximize and Close a Window

a. On the right side of the WordPad title bar, click **Maximize** 🔲. The WordPad window fills the entire screen.

b. Double-click the **WordPad** title bar. The window is restored down to its previous size.

c. Point to the **WordPad** title bar, and then drag it to the top of the screen until the mouse pointer 🔳 touches the top of the screen. You will see a translucent image that fills the screen. Release the mouse button and the WordPad window is maximized.

d. Click **Close** 🔳 on the right side of the WordPad title bar. If a dialog box appears asking if you want to save changes to the document, click **Don't Save**. The window closes. The WordPad button no longer is displayed on the taskbar, and the program is removed from memory.

Working with Multiple Windows

Often you will want to work with several programs at the same time to move data between them. Or, you may want to have several windows open in the same program so you can compare different documents. Learning to manage multiple windows makes it easy to get to a window that you want quickly. You can also arrange open windows in ways that help you work more productively. Windows 7 makes it very easy to work with several programs and windows at the same time.

To Open Multiple Windows

a. Click **Start** 🔵. If WordPad is on the recently opened programs list, click **WordPad**. If not, click **All Programs**, click **Accessories**, and then click **WordPad**. The WordPad window opens, and a WordPad program button is displayed on the taskbar. If necessary, maximize the WordPad window.

b. Click **Start** 🔵. If Paint is on the recently opened programs list, click **Paint**. If not, click **All Programs**, click **Accessories**, and then click **Paint**. The Paint window opens, and a Paint program button is displayed on the taskbar. If necessary, maximize the Paint window. It covers the WordPad window on the screen.

c. Click **Start** 🔵. In the right pane of the Start menu, click **Control Panel**. If necessary, Maximize 🔲 the Control Panel window. The Control Panel window opens, and a Control Panel button is displayed on the taskbar. The Control Panel button is highlighted to indicate that it is the active program.

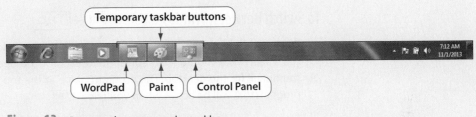

Figure 13   Program buttons on the taskbar

Switching Between Windows

Even though multiple programs are open, you can only work in the **active window**—the window in which you can move the mouse pointer, type text, or perform other tasks. This is the window that is on top or in front of any other windows. Only one window can be active at a time. Figure 14 shows several methods for switching between windows.

Switch Option	Method
Taskbar buttons	On the taskbar, click the button for the program that you want to work on to switch to that program. The program appears in front of the other windows and becomes the active window.
Alt+Tab	Press and hold [Alt] and then press [Tab] repeatedly to cycle through all open windows. When the program you want is highlighted, release [Alt].
Aero Flip 3D	Hold down the [🔲] and press [Tab] repeatedly. Release the [🔲] when the window you want is at the front of the stack. Or, click any part of a window in the stack to display that window.

Figure 14   Switching between programs

You will demonstrate these features and encourage Painted Paradise Resort staff to try them all. After experimenting with all of the methods, most people settle on the one or two methods they prefer.

To Switch Between Windows Using Taskbar Buttons

a. Point to **WordPad** on the taskbar. A preview window appears showing a thumbnail of a blank document in the WordPad window.

b. Point to **Paint** on the taskbar. The preview window displays a thumbnail of the Paint window. Click the **Paint** button on the taskbar. The Paint window opens and becomes the active window.

c. Click **Control Panel** on the taskbar. The Control Panel window opens and becomes the active window.

You can also switch between windows by using the Alt + Tab key combination.

To Switch Between Windows Using Alt + Tab

a. Press and hold down Alt and then press Tab. A window appears in the center of the screen with thumbnails representing each of the open programs. There is also a thumbnail for the desktop. The program name at the top of the window indicates the program that will be active when you release Alt.

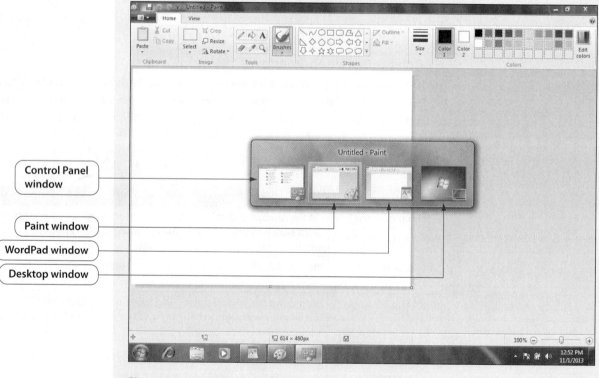

Control Panel window

Paint window

WordPad window

Desktop window

Figure 15 Alt + Tab window showing Paint highlighted

b. Hold down Alt and then press the Tab key repeatedly, until the Paint thumbnail is highlighted and Untitled - Paint appears at the top of the window. Release Alt. The Paint window fills the screen and becomes the active window.

If available, using Aero Flip 3D provides another method for switching windows.

To Switch Between Windows Using Aero Flip 3D

a. Hold down ⊞ and then press Tab. All open windows and a window representing the desktop are arranged in a cascading display. Press Tab to cycle through the windows. Each time you press Tab, a different window moves to the forefront. When you see the window you want, release Tab.

Desktop window

WordPad window

Paint window

Control Panel window

Figure 16 Aero Flip 3D with three programs and the desktop

b. Hold down ⊞ and then press Tab repeatedly, until the Control Panel window is at the front of the stack. Release ⊞. The Control Panel window fills the screen.

Peek lets you look past all open windows straight to the Windows 7 desktop.

To Use Peek to Look at the Desktop

a. On the right side of the taskbar, point to **Show desktop** ▌. The desktop is displayed temporarily.

b. Move the pointer away from Show desktop. Your screen displays the Control Panel window.

c. Click **Show desktop** ▌. The screen displays the desktop.

d. Click **Show desktop** ▌ to return to the previous window.

When multiple windows are open you can minimize all but the active window by using **Shake**—shaking the title bar to minimize all other windows. Shake is another feature in the Aero experience.

SIDE NOTE
Windows Logo Key
Look on your keyboard for the ⊞. If your keyboard does not have a ⊞, you will not be able to take advantage of this feature.

To Use Shake to Minimize Windows

a. On the right side of the Control Panel title bar, click **Restore Down** 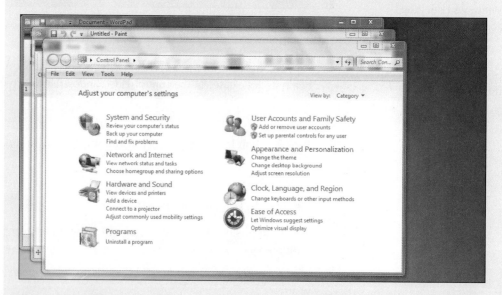.
b. Point to the **Control Panel** title bar. Click and hold the mouse button and then shake the title bar back and forth. All other program windows are minimized to the taskbar, and the Control Panel window is the only window visible on the screen.

Arranging Windows

You can control how windows are arranged and displayed on your screen. Cascading windows places open windows on top of each other with just the title bar and a small portion of the border visible. The active window is on top. To make a different window active, click on any portion of the window that is visible.

You can also stack windows to arrange them vertically on the screen or arrange them side by side to display them across the screen. Using Snap is an easy way to arrange two windows side by side so each takes up half of the screen.

SIDE NOTE
Undo Cascade Command
The Undo Cascade command (from Windows XP) is no longer available in Windows 7.

To Cascade Windows

a. Make sure that the **Control Panel, WordPad**, and **Paint** windows are open and that corresponding buttons are displayed on the taskbar. (If necessary, click the WordPad and Paint buttons on the taskbar so they are no longer minimized.)

b. Point to a blank area on the taskbar and right-click. A shortcut menu appears. Click **Cascade windows**. All open windows are cascaded one on top of the other with the title bar and a small portion of the left border visible. The window on top is the active window.

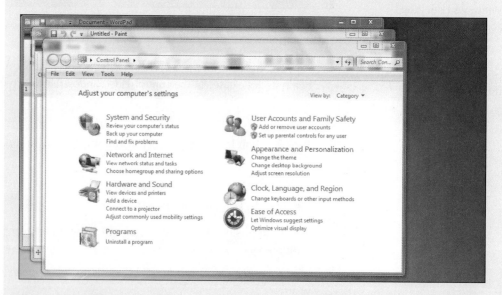

Figure 17   Cascaded windows

c. Click anywhere on the edge of a window that is not active to bring it to the front and to make it the active window.

Open windows can be stacked vertically on the screen. This works best when only two or three windows are open.

To Show Windows Stacked

a. Make sure that the **WordPad**, **Paint**, and **Control Panel** windows are open.

b. Point to a blank area on the taskbar and right-click. A shortcut menu appears. Click **Show windows stacked**. All open windows are stacked vertically on the screen.

c. Click in the **WordPad** window to make it active. Notice that the Close 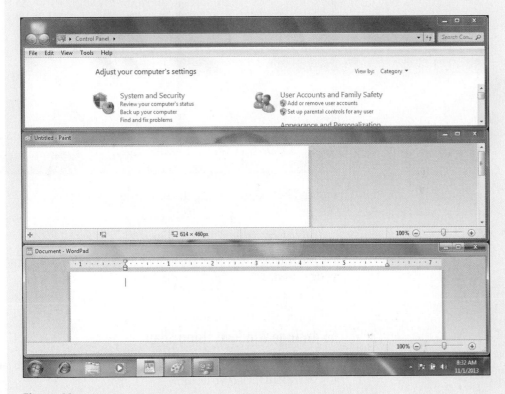 button in the active window turns red.

Figure 18   Windows stacked (Close button of active window shows red)

Open windows can also be displayed side by side.

To Show Windows Side by Side

a. Make sure that the **Control Panel**, **WordPad**, and **Paint** windows are open.

b. Point to a blank area on the taskbar and right-click. A shortcut menu appears. Click **Show windows side by side**. All open windows are displayed side by side.

c. Click in the **Paint** window to make it active. Notice that the Close button in the active window turns red.

Figure 19 Windows displayed side by side

Snap is a quick way to arrange open windows by dragging them to the edges of your screen.

To Arrange Windows Using Snap

a. **Close** ⊠ the Control Panel window so only WordPad and Paint are open. Make **WordPad** the active window.

b. Point to the **title bar** of the WordPad window and drag to the left until the mouse pointer ⍿ touches the left edge of the screen. When you see a translucent image filling the left half of the screen, release the mouse button. The WordPad window is arranged on the left half of your screen.

c. Point to the **title bar** of the Paint window and drag to the right until the mouse pointer ⍿ touches the right side of the screen. When you see a translucent image filling the right half of the screen, release the mouse button. The Paint window is arranged on the right side of your screen.

d. **Close** ⊠ all windows.

Personalizing the Desktop

Windows 7 offers many ways to personalize and customize the desktop. Some personalization leads to higher efficiency and more productivity. Other customization is just for fun and might become distracting if overdone.

Because the Painted Paradise Resort personnel are now familiar with Windows 7 basics, in this section you will show them a few ways to personalize their computers.

Adding Shortcuts to the Start Menu, Desktop, and Taskbar

To work efficiently, you want to access programs that you use regularly as quickly as possible. Shortcuts can be added to the Start menu, the desktop, and the taskbar. The method you choose will depend on the way you like to work. People concerned with working productively try to use as few keystrokes or mouse clicks as possible. You suggest that Painted Paradise Resort employees create several types of shortcuts and then choose the method that works best for them.

Adding Shortcuts to the Start Menu

When a computer is new, there are no shortcuts in the pinned programs area on the top of the left side of the Start menu. Programs can be opened from the Recently Used Programs list, but the programs on this list keep changing as you work with new programs. To make sure a program is always available on the Start menu, you can pin it permanently to the top of the list. To do this, you must first locate the program and then right-click it and click Pin to Start Menu. When you pin a program to the Start menu, it is always available in the area above the recently open programs list until you decide to remove it.

To Add a WordPad Shortcut to the Start Menu

a.   Click **Start** 🌐. Point to **All Programs**, click **Accessories**, and then right-click **WordPad**. A shortcut menu is displayed.
   If the program you want to pin to the Start menu is in the Recently Used Programs list, just right-click it to display the shortcut menu.

b.   Click **Pin to Start Menu**. The shortcut menu closes, but the All Programs menu is still open. Point to **Back** to return to the Start menu. The WordPad shortcut is added to the pinned programs area at the top of the left side of the Start menu.

c.   To test the shortcut, click **WordPad** in the pinned programs area. The WordPad program opens and is displayed in its previous location and size. **Close** ✖ the WordPad program.

Adding Shortcuts to the Desktop

Shortcuts can also be added to the desktop. When a program icon is visible on the desktop, the program can be opened by double-clicking the icon or right-clicking the icon and then selecting Open from the shortcut menu. Shortcuts display an upward pointing arrow in the bottom-left corner of the icon. Deleting a shortcut removes the shortcut from the desktop but does not affect the program with which it is associated.

To add a program shortcut to the desktop, you must first locate the program. Right-click the item, click Send to, and then click Desktop (create shortcut). The shortcut icon appears on your desktop.

Real World Advice   Desktop Shortcuts and Icons

Most of the icons you add to your desktop will be shortcuts to programs. If you delete a shortcut, the shortcut is removed from your desktop, but the file, program, or location that the shortcut links to is not deleted. You can also save files or folders to the desktop. If you delete files or folders from your desktop, they are moved to the Recycle Bin, where you can permanently delete them or restore them if necessary.

To Add a Calculator Shortcut to the Desktop

a. If necessary, make sure the desktop is visible. Click **Start** ◉. Point to **All Programs**, click **Accessories**, and then right-click **Calculator**. A shortcut menu is displayed.

b. Point to **Send to**, and then click **Desktop (create shortcut)**. **Close** the Start menu. A Calculator shortcut is placed on the desktop. Notice the arrow in the bottom-left corner of the shortcut.

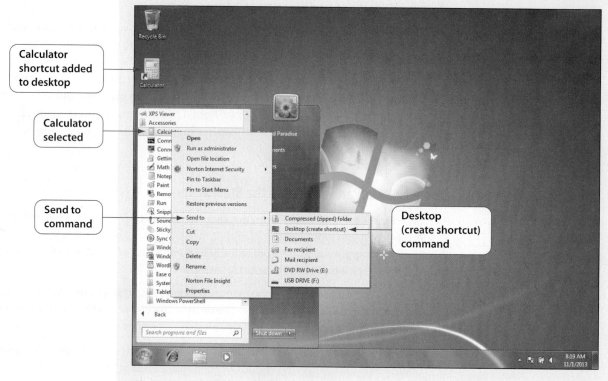

Figure 20 Calculator shortcut

Arranging Icons on the Desktop

Adding shortcuts to the desktop often places them in strange places. You can organize the icons so your desktop will always be neat. Just as you would want to keep the top of your desk organized, it is also good practice to keep your computer desktop organized.

To Arrange Icons on the Desktop

a. Point to a blank area on the desktop and right-click to display a shortcut menu. Point to **View**. This menu gives options for displaying icons on the desktop. Make sure there is a check in front of **Align icons to grid** and **Show desktop icons**. If necessary, select **Medium icons**.

b. With the menu still open, point to **Sort by**. A menu opens that allows you to sort icons by Name, Size, Item type, or Date modified.

c. Click **Name**. The Calculator icon is aligned neatly with other icons on your desktop and is placed in alphabetical order.

Adding Shortcuts to the Taskbar

By default, Windows 7 comes with three programs pinned to the taskbar: Internet Explorer, Windows Explorer, and Windows Media Player. Other programs can be added to the pinned buttons area of the taskbar. You might want to add a shortcut for Word or Excel or other programs you use daily. Locate the program you want to add to the taskbar, right-click the program, and then click Pin to Taskbar. Programs added to the taskbar are the fastest to open, as only one click is required.

You will show resort staff how to add a Snipping Tool button to the taskbar. The **Snipping Tool** is a feature in Windows 7 that allows you to capture screen shots, or **snips**, of any object on your screen. You can capture the entire screen, just a window, or a dialog box. You can also drag the cursor around a rectangular area of your screen or draw a free-form shape around an object. The Snipping Tool creates files that can be printed or submitted electronically. Later in this workshop you will create and save snips that can be submitted to your instructor.

To Add a Snipping Tool Shortcut to the Taskbar

a. Click **Start** . Point to **All Programs**, click **Accessories**, and then right-click **Snipping Tool**. A shortcut menu is displayed.

Icons sorted by name

Pin to Taskbar command

Snipping tool selected

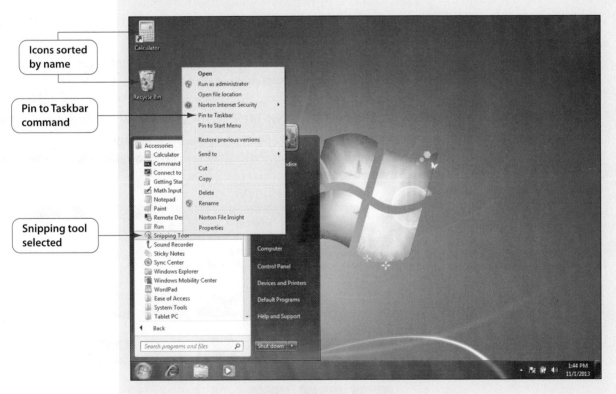

Figure 21   Shortcut menu after right-clicking Snipping Tool

b. Click **Pin to Taskbar**. The shortcut menu closes and a Snipping Tool icon is added to the right of other shortcuts already on the taskbar. **Close** the Start menu.

Changing the Appearance of the Desktop

Resort employees have been anxious to personalize their new computers. You will show them several ways to do this. Windows 7 comes with a number of different desktop backgrounds that can be used instead of the default background with the Windows logo. Other desktop backgrounds can be downloaded from the Internet. Some people may even choose to use their own personal photos as the desktop background.

Screen savers are another way of changing the appearance of your desktop. A **screen saver** is a moving graphic that starts when a computer sits idle for a specified amount of time, such as 10 minutes. It prevents others from seeing work on your screen if you walk away from your computer.

A selection of **gadgets**—mini programs that can be added to your desktop—is installed with Windows 7. Some are very useful, such as a clock or headlines that are constantly updated. Note that you must have an Internet connection for gadgets to be updated regularly. Other gadgets may be just for fun such as puzzles and games. If you would like to add more gadgets, there is a link in the Gadgets gallery to the Windows website where you can download more gadgets.

Changing the Desktop Background

The **desktop background** is the first thing you see when you open Windows 7. Most people want to change the background from the default background that is installed with Windows to something more pleasing to them. The background is definitely a personal choice, but it should not make it more difficult to perform tasks. Further, in a business setting the background should be professional and inoffensive. You will choose a background where desktop icons will still be easy to see.

To Change the Desktop Background

a. Point to a blank area on the desktop and right-click to display a shortcut menu. Click **Personalize**. The Personalization window opens.

b. On the bottom left of the window, the Desktop Background thumbnail shows the current background picture. (Make a note of this background so you will be able to return to it later.)

c. Click **Desktop Background**. If necessary, Maximize ▣ the gallery of backgrounds opens, arranged by categories. If necessary, select Windows Desktop Backgrounds from the Picture location list.

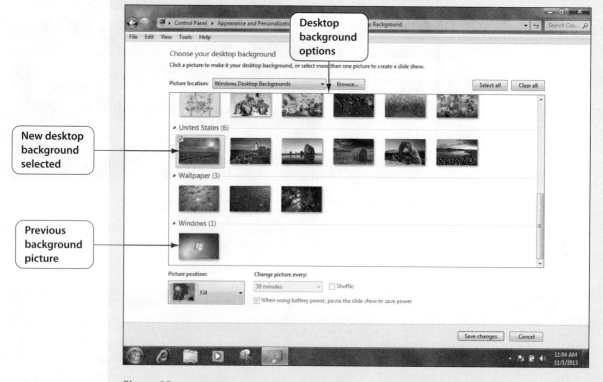

Figure 22 Desktop Background gallery

d. Scroll to locate the **United States** category, and then click the first thumbnail showing a sunset. A check appears in the top-left corner and a highlighted frame is displayed around the picture.

e. On the bottom-right of the screen, click the **Save changes** button. You return to the Personalization window, and the sunset picture is displayed as the Desktop Background thumbnail. Click **Close** ⬛ to return to the desktop. The picture you chose is now the desktop background.

New desktop background

Figure 23 New desktop background

Selecting a Screen Saver

A screen saver begins after your computer is idle for a predefined period, making the desktop not visible. Several screen savers are installed with Windows 7. The **Wait time**— the time before the screen saver starts—default is 10 minutes, but this can be adjusted. You will ask staff members to shorten the wait time to just 1 minute so they can observe the effect of setting a screen saver without having to wait a long time.

To Set a Screen Saver

a. Point to a blank area on the desktop and right-click to display a shortcut menu. Click **Personalize**. The Personalization window opens.

b. On the bottom right of the window, click **Screen Saver**. The Screen Saver Settings dialog box is displayed.

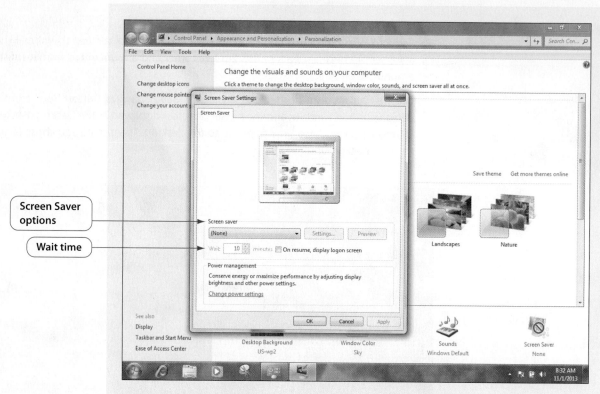

Screen Saver options

Wait time

Figure 24 Screen Saver Settings dialog box

c. Under Screen saver, click the **Screen saver arrow**, click **3D Text**, and then observe the preview in the screen at the top of the dialog box. If the default text has not been replaced with another message, you will see **Windows 7** revolving in the center of the Preview window.

d. Under Screen saver, click the **Screen saver arrow**, click **Mystify**, and then observe the **preview**.

e. Make note of the current Wait time. Click the **arrow** until the Wait time box displays **1 minutes**. Click **OK**, and then **Close** the Personalization window. You return to the desktop.

f. Wait approximately 1 minute without touching the mouse or keyboard. The Mystify screen saver will start. Move the mouse or press any key to return to the screen that was active before the screen saver started.

g. Repeat Steps a and b. Set the Wait time to **10 minutes** or to the time that was set before. Click **OK** and then **Close** the Personalization window.

SIDE NOTE
Setting Screen Saver Wait Time

Using a wait time of 1 minute is for demonstration purposes only. It would be very annoying to have the screen saver start so quickly. A much more reasonable wait interval would be the 10 minute default.

Adding Gadgets to the Desktop

Gadgets are small programs that can be placed anywhere on your desktop. You can easily add one or more gadgets and then remove them when they are no longer needed. If your gadgets are covered by open windows, you can use the Show desktop button to take a quick look at your gadgets without having to minimize any windows. There is also an option to always keep a gadget on top of any open windows.

When you point to a gadget, control buttons appear to the upper right. Each gadget has two, three, or four control buttons. A Close button removes the gadget from the desktop, and a Drag gadget button lets you move the gadget anywhere on the screen. Some gadgets can be customized with a Size button to make the gadget larger or smaller. Other gadgets, such as the Clock gadget, have an Options button that offers a variety of choices, such as different styles of clocks.

To Add Gadgets

a. If necessary, close any gadgets displayed on your desktop by pointing to the gadget and then clicking **Close** ![Close] at the top of the gadget control displayed to the right of the gadget. Repeat to remove all gadgets.

b. Point to an open area of the desktop, and then right-click to display a shortcut menu. Click **Gadgets**. The Gadgets gallery window displays. You may have more than one page of gadgets.

Gadgets available on your computer

Online link to other gadgets

Figure 25   Gadgets window

c. In the Gadgets window, point to the **Clock** gadget, and then double-click. The Clock gadget is displayed in the top-right corner of the desktop and shows the time set on your computer.

d. In the Gadgets window, double-click the **Calendar** gadget. The Calendar gadget appears below the Clock gadget and displays today's date.

e. Click **Close** ![Close] to close the Gadgets gallery.

f. Point to the **Calendar** gadget. Three control buttons are displayed to the right of the Calendar gadget. Point to each button and read the ScreenTips. Click **Larger size** ![Larger size]. A calendar for the current month is displayed above the date.

g. Point to the **Clock** gadget. Point to each Gadget control button and read the ScreenTips. Notice that the middle button is the Options 🔍 control button. The Clock gadget cannot be resized. Click the **Options** 🔍 button. The Clock dialog box opens, enabling you to customize your clock.

h. Use the arrows to select Clock **6 of 8**. Click **Show the second hand**, and then click **OK**. Clock #6 replaces the original clock and displays a second hand.

i. Point to the **Clock** gadget, and then click the **Drag gadget** button ▦ and drag the Clock gadget to the left about 2".

j. Point to the **Calendar** gadget, and then point to the **Drag gadget** button ▦. Drag the Calendar gadget up so it is placed in the top right of your screen.

Figure 26 Clock and Calendar gadgets on desktop

During your training at Painted Paradise, you will want to return everything to its original state after your demonstration. Then, employees can add their own personalization and practice the skills you demonstrated. The following steps will remove all shortcuts and gadgets and return to the former desktop background.

To Return to the Original Desktop

a. Point to any buttons that were added to the taskbar. Right-click, and then click **Unpin this program from taskbar**.

b. Right-click any shortcuts added to the desktop. Click `Delete`, and then click **Yes**.

c. Open the **Start** menu. Right-click any shortcuts added to the pinned programs area. Click **Unpin from Start menu**. **Close** the Start menu.

d. Point to each gadget, and then click **Close** ❌.

e. Right-click the desktop, click **Personalize**, and then click **Desktop Background**. Click the original background, and then click **Save changes**. You will return to the Personalization window.

f. Click **Screen Saver**. In the Screen Saver Settings dialog box, click the **arrow**, and then select the original screen saver. Check to make sure the Wait time was adjusted to the former time. Click **OK**. **Close** ❌ the Personalization window.

Shutting Down Windows 7

Some people like to leave their computer on all the time. In a lab you may be asked to leave the computers on and just log off as the user. At home, you might want to switch users or put your computer to sleep to conserve power. All of these tasks can be performed by using the Shut down button on the Start menu.

There are two parts to the Shut down button. When you click Shut down—also called the power button—your computer closes all open programs, along with Windows itself, and then completely turns off, along with the display. If updates are waiting to be installed, Windows does this first and then shuts down your computer. Sometimes, the installation of updates can take some time. Be patient, as Windows updates are important. Do not try to hurry the process by turning off the computer with the power button.

If you point to the Open arrow ▷ on the right side of the Shut down button, a menu appears with several choices. You can switch users or log off. You can also lock or restart the computer or put it in sleep or hibernate mode. Figure 27 shows the result of each of these options.

Shut down menu option	Result
Switch user	If you have more than one user account on your computer, this is an easy way for another person to log on to the computer without logging you off or closing your programs and files.
Log off	When you log off from Windows, all of the programs you were using are closed, but the computer is not turned off.
Lock	Lock prevents other people from accessing your computer or viewing your work if you need to step away from your desk for an extended period of time.
Restart	Restart is often used when updates or new programs are installed and the computer must be restarted.
Sleep	Sleep is a power-saving state. Sleep saves all open documents and programs, and allows the computer to quickly resume full-power operation when you want to start working again.
Hibernate (laptops only)	Hibernation is a power-saving state. Hibernation saves your open documents and programs to your hard disk and then turns off your computer.

Figure 27 Shut down menu options

SIDE NOTE
Logging Off
In a classroom, your instructor might ask you to log off but leave the computer on for the next student. Students in the last class of the day might be asked to shut down the computers.

To Shut Down Windows 7

a. First decide if you want to switch users, log off, restart your computer, or shut down completely. Click **Start**.

b. If you want to turn off the computer, point to and then click **Shut down** on the bottom of the right pane of the Start menu.

c. If you do not want to turn off the computer, point to the **Open arrow** ▷ on the right of the Shut down button. Choose the option you want from the menu.

Using Windows Explorer

Windows Explorer—a program used to create and manage folders and files—uses a hierarchical storage system similar to what you would use in an office. You can see a representation of this storage structure by displaying the contents of available drives in Windows Explorer. It displays icons that represent the contents of your computer including drives, folders, and files. It is easy to move from one location to another in the file hierarchy by using various elements in the Windows Explorer window.

At the top of window, the title bar contains the typical control buttons that let you minimize, maximize (or restore down), and close the window. Below the title bar is the address bar, which is very useful for navigating between various folders and files. It displays the path to wherever you are currently located. The classic menu bar is hidden by default, but it is still available. If you choose to turn on the menu bar, it appears below the address bar. The command bar is below the address bar or menu bar. The commands on this bar change to match whatever task you are doing. On the right of the command bar are buttons that let you change the view of your window or get Help information.

The Windows Explorer window can be divided into five panes. On the left is the **Navigation pane**, which displays the contents of your computer grouped under the headings: Favorites, Libraries, Homegroup, Computer, and Network. On the right is the **Preview pane**, which displays the contents of a selected file. The Preview pane is off by default so it will not be visible until you open the pane. At the top is the **Library pane**, which displays only when a library is selected. At the bottom, the **Details pane** displays the properties of the selected file or folder. The area in the center of the window is the **Content pane**, which displays the content of whatever is selected in the Navigation pane. When a folder is selected, the contents of the folder are shown in the **file list**. All of the panes can be turned off with the exception of the Content pane. It is, however, not practical to turn off the Navigation pane, since that would make navigating between folders and files very difficult. The Preview pane can be easily turned on and off as needed by using the Preview pane button on the right side of the command bar. In this section, you will learn to open and navigate Windows Explorer and become familiar with files, folders, and libraries.

Opening and Navigating Windows Explorer

You can view all the drives, folders, and files that are part of your computer's storage system using Windows Explorer. Windows Explorer opens with the Libraries folder selected in the Navigation pane. By default, the Windows 7 installation includes four standard libraries: Documents, Music, Pictures, and Videos. Each contains two folders, a personal folder and a public folder that can be shared with others.

SIDE NOTE
Displaying Menu Bar
Display the menu bar temporarily by pressing the ALT key. Press ALT again to hide the menu bar.
To display the menu bar permanently, follow these steps:
1. Click Start and type "folder option" and press ENTER. The Folder Options window will display.
2. Click the View tab and under Advanced Settings, select Always show menus. Click OK.

To Open Windows Explorer

a. On the taskbar, click the **Windows Explorer** button 🗔. The Windows Explorer window opens. If necessary, maximize the window.

Troubleshooting

If the Windows Explorer button is not available on the taskbar, click the Start button, point to All Programs, click Accessories, and then click Windows Explorer.

b. On the **command** bar, click **Organize**, and point to **Layout**. Make sure that the **Menu bar**, **Details pane**, **Navigation pane**, and **Library pane** are selected. If necessary, click **Preview pane** to clear the check.

c. On the menu bar, click **View** 🔲 ▾, and then click **Large icons**.

Command bar

Library pane

Navigation pane

Details pane

Figure 28   Windows Explorer window

Exploring Files, Folders, and Libraries

Libraries are new in Windows 7 and are virtual folders that display the contents of multiple folders as though the files were stored together in one location. They allow you to access files regardless of which folder they are in. The files are still physically located in different folders, but now they show up in a single window. You can add and remove folders from a library, and you can also create new libraries.

You will explore files, folders, and libraries by using the Music Library as an example.

To Explore Files, Folders, and Libraries

a. In the Navigation pane, if necessary, click the **arrow** ▷ to the left of **Libraries** to expand the folder. The arrow changes to ◢, and a list of Libraries is displayed that correspond to the libraries shown in the Content pane.

b. In the Navigation pane, click **Music**. The Content pane displays all folders in the Music library no matter where they are located.

c. In the Navigation pane, to the left of **Music**, click the **arrow** ▷. The My Music and Public Music subfolders are displayed under the Music folder.

d. Click the **arrow** ▷ to the left of **My Music** and **Public Music**. More subfolders are displayed, and a Sample Music subfolder is displayed under Public Music.

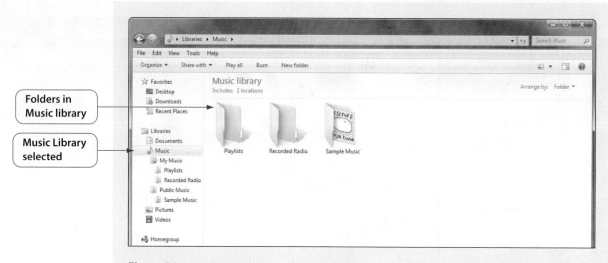

Folders in Music library

Music Library selected

Figure 29 Music Library

e. In the Navigation pane, click **Sample Music**. Several music files are shown in the Content pane that were installed with Windows 7. Click the arrow [▷] to the left of Music to collapse the Music library folder.

f. Look at the address bar near the top of the Windows Explorer window. The address bar displays the path to the folder whose contents are currently displayed. You can use the address bar to navigate back to any of the folders in the path.

g. On the address bar, click the **arrow** [▸] to the right of **Music**. The folders under Music are displayed with Public Music in bold. Point to the **arrow** [▸] to the right of **Libraries**. The folders under Libraries are displayed. Click **Libraries** to return to the Libraries folder.

SIDE NOTE
Expanding and Collapsing Folders
You can also expand and collapse folders by double-clicking the folder name in the Navigation pane.

Working with Folders

Folders and files on your computer work much the same way as folders in a filing cabinet. Folders are commonly used to store related documents. They make it easy to keep related files together so they are easier to find when you need them. If you still receive paper statements, you might place your cell phone bills in one folder and your utility bills in another. Just as you use paper folders to hold related documents, you can create folders on your computer to contain related files. These files include documents, spreadsheets, photographs, songs, and much more. You can also create **subfolders**—which are folders within folders. Program and system files are also stored in folders, but you will be concerned primarily with organizing the files you create. In this section, you will learn how to create, name, move, rename, and delete folders.

Creating and Naming a New Folder

Aidan has already collected numerous files that all employees need. He has put some of these files in folders but wants help to develop a better system of organization. He asks you to use his files as an example when demonstrating how to create folders and organize files.

You suggest creating folders to hold specific types of files, such as documents, pictures, and presentations. The first folder you will create will be on a USB flash drive where you will store all the files for this workshop. If you are not using a flash drive, follow instructions given by your instructor for saving your work.

It is always a good idea to organize related files. You will create a folder called Windows 7 Practice to hold the files used for the exercises in this workshop.

To Create and Name Folders

a. In the Navigation pane, click **Computer**. The Content pane displays the drives connected to your computer. On the menu bar, click View ▦ ▾ , and then click **Large Icons**.

b. Insert your USB flash drive. If an AutoPlay dialog box opens, click **Close** ▭ . After a few moments, the name of your USB flash drive—and assigned drive letter—appears under Computer in the Navigation pane and under the Devices with Removable Storage section in the Content pane.

SIDE NOTE
Using a USB Flash Drive
Additional storage devices are listed under Computer in the Navigation pane and display in the Content pane. USB drives usually display the name of the manufacturer. Your drive may have a different name and drive letter.

USB flash drive

USB drive inserted

Figure 30 Computer window showing USB drive

SIDE NOTE
Computer Window
The Local Disk (C:) refers to the hard drive on your computer. Figure 30 shows a Recovery (D:) drive, a partition on the (C:) drive, installed by the manufacturer containing files to recover your computer if serious problems occur.

c. In the Navigation pane, under **Computer**, click the name of your USB flash drive. Note the contents in the file list.
If your USB flash drive is new, the file list will be empty. If your drive already has files and folders on it, these will be displayed in the file list. As long as there is sufficient storage space available, you will be able to create the folders and subfolders needed for this exercise.

d. In the Navigation pane, right-click the name of your **USB flash drive**, and then click **Rename**. Type your Lastname and press Enter to rename the drive.

e. In the Navigation pane, click the **USB flash drive**.

f. On the command bar, click **New folder** to create a new, empty folder. A New folder icon appears in the Content pane with the words "New folder" highlighted.

g. Type Windows 7 Practice and press Enter to name the new folder. Click anywhere on a blank area to deselect the new folder.

SIDE NOTE
Renaming a USB Flash Drive
You can rename your USB flash drive. This is very useful if you have several drives from the same manufacturer, all with the same name.

h. In the Navigation pane, click the **arrow** ▷ to the left of your USB flash drive, if necessary, and then click the **Windows 7 Practice** folder that you just created. The Content pane will be empty.

i. With the Windows 7 Practice folder selected, click the **New folder** button, type Resort_Documents, and then press [Enter]. Deselect the new folder. Click the **arrow** $\triangleright$ to the left of **Windows 7 Practice**. Notice that the Resort_Documents folder appears in the Navigation pane and the Content pane.

j. Use the same method to create two more subfolders named Resort_Pictures and Resort_Presentations.

k. Create one more folder named Lastname_Snips using your own last name. This folder will be used to store snips that can be submitted to your instructor.

l. Scroll to the bottom of the Navigation pane as necessary, so the four subfolders are visible under the Windows 7 Practice folder.

You will use the Snipping Tool to create a snip of your screen showing the folders listed in both the Navigation pane and Content pane.

To Use the Snipping Tool

a. Click **Start** . Point to **All Programs**, click **Accessories**, and then click **Snipping Tool**. The Snipping Tool window opens.

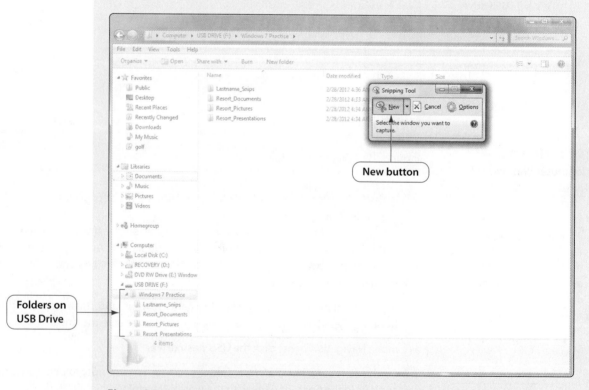

Figure 31 Snipping Tool window

b. Click the **New snip arrow** , and then click **Full-screen Snip**. The snip is displayed. You may need to use the horizontal and vertical scroll bars to see the entire snip.

c. On the menu bar, click **File**, and then click **Save As**. Click the **Save as type arrow**, and then click **JPEG file**. In the File name box, type Lastname_Firstname_w701_ws01_ Folders.

d. In the Save As dialog box, scroll to locate your USB flash drive. If necessary, click the **arrow** ▷ for the flash drive and the **Windows 7 Practice** folder to display all subfolders.

e. Click the **Lastname_Snips** folder, and then click **Save**.

f. Click **Close** to close the Snipping Tool window. You return to Windows Explorer. In the Navigation pane, click **Lastname_Snips**. The Lastname_Firstname_w701_ws01_ Folders snip file appears in the file list.

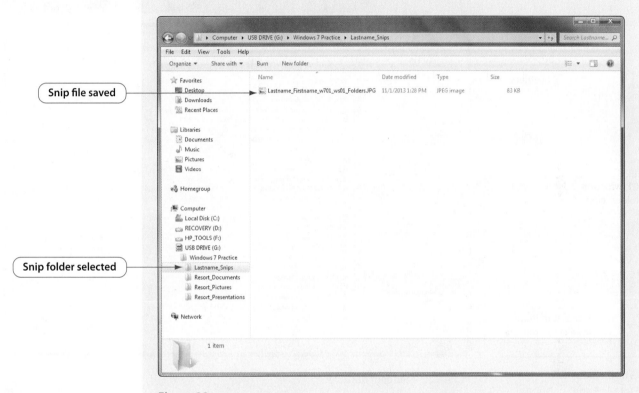

Figure 32   Folders and snip

Copying, Moving, Renaming, and Deleting Folders

As you create more and more files, the original folders that you created may no longer meet your needs. You can move folders to a new location, or copy them so they exist in two or more locations. You can also rename folders if the original name no longer fits, and you can delete folders when they are no longer needed.

In the following exercises, you will copy, move, rename and delete folders.

Copying Folders

The files that Aidan has already accumulated are on your student data disk. You will help organize these files by moving them into the corresponding folders that you just created on your USB flash drive.

To Copy Folders from a CD to a USB Flash Drive

a. With Windows Explorer still open, insert your student data CD. If an AutoPlay dialog box appears, click **Close** [×]. Your CD may display a different name. If the student data files are stored elsewhere, follow your instructor's instructions.

b. In the Navigation pane, click the **arrow** [▷] for your CD/DVD drive, and then click the **arrow** [▷] for Student Data Files. Click the **arrow** [▷] for **01_windows_7_workshop_1**. Select the **01_windows_7_workshop_1** folder in the Navigation pane. Three folders and numerous files are displayed in the file list.

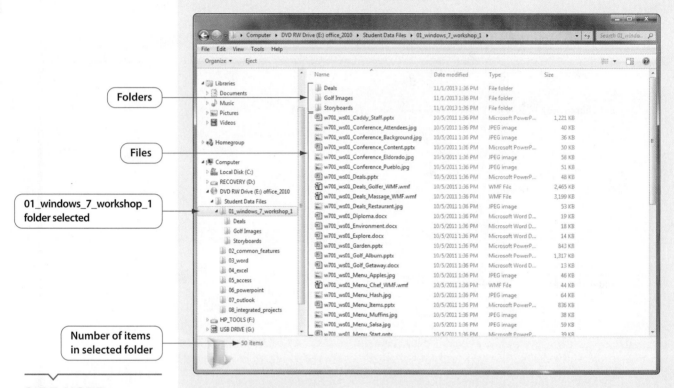

Folders

Files

01_windows_7_workshop_1 folder selected

Number of items in selected folder

Figure 33 Student data files

SIDE NOTE
Details Pane

The Details pane indicates 50 items, which includes the 3 folders and 47 files. Files stored within the 3 folders are not included. To see the contents of the folders, click the folder name in the Navigation pane.

c. If your list looks different, click the **More options arrow** [▼] next to the Change your view button [⊞ ▼] on the right of the command bar, and then click **Details**.

d. In the Navigation pane, if necessary, click the **arrow** [▷] to the left of your USB flash drive to display the folders, and then click the **arrow** [▷] to the left of the **Windows 7 Practice** folder. Be sure your student data files are still displayed in the file list.

At the top of the file list, notice the column headings: Name, Date modified, Type, and Size. Files can be sorted by any of these categories. Currently, the files are sorted by Name as indicated by the upward pointing arrow in the center of the Name column. Folders are listed first, followed by files in alphabetical order. You can reverse this order by clicking anywhere in the Name column heading. The arrow points downward, and folders are at the bottom of the list with files arranged in reverse alphabetical order.

e. Click and drag the **Deals** folder from the file list on top of the **Windows 7 Practice** folder in the Navigation pane.

As you drag, you will see a thumbnail image of the folder attached to the pointer and a message that says you are copying the folder. When the message reads Copy to Windows 7 Practice, release the mouse button. The Deals folder appears under the Windows 7 Practice folder.

f. Click and drag the **Golf Images** folder on top of the **Windows 7 Practice** folder. Repeat this process to copy the **Storyboards** folder to the **Windows 7 Practice** folder. The three folders that were copied appear under Windows 7 Practice in the Navigation pane. You now have seven subfolders—the four you created and the three that were just copied.

Moving Folders

You have two folders related to pictures—Golf Images and Resort_Pictures. Because both folders contain pictures, it would be logical to move the Golf Images folder to the Resort_Pictures folder so all picture files will be in the same place.

To Move Folders

a. In the Navigation pane, in the Windows 7 Practice folder, drag **Golf Images** on top of the **Resort_Pictures** folder. When the message reads Move to Resort_Pictures, release the mouse button. The Golf Images folder is moved to the Resort_Pictures folder and is no longer visible in the Navigation pane.

b. In the Navigation pane, under the Windows 7 Practice folder, click the **arrow** ▷ to the left of **Resort_Pictures** and verify that the Golf Images folder is under the Resort_Pictures folder in the Navigation pane.

c. In the Navigation pane, click **Resort_Pictures** to see the Golf Images folder in the file list.

d. Click the **arrow** ◢ to close the Resort_Pictures folder.

Renaming Folders

As you work with folders you will often find that the name you first assigned to a folder does not work anymore. You can easily rename a folder to maintain the organization that you want. In the next exercise, you will rename the Storyboards folder to match the names of the other folders.

Renaming a Folder
You can rename a folder by right-clicking the name in either the Navigation pane or the Content pane and then clicking Rename.

To Rename a Folder

a. In the Navigation pane, click the **Windows 7 Practice** folder. Six folders should be displayed in the file list.

b. In the file list, right-click **Storyboards**, and then click **Rename**. The folder name is highlighted and is in Edit mode. Type Resort_Storyboards and press Enter. The folder is renamed.

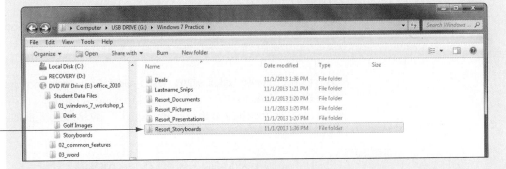

Folder renamed

Figure 34 Renaming a folder

Working with Folders 39

Deleting Folders

There will also be times when you have a folder that contains files you no longer need. Just as you would shred and discard paper files that are outdated, you will want to delete folders that are no longer needed. You will delete the Deals folder that contains image files for special resort promotions that have expired.

SIDE NOTE
Delete Confirmation May Vary

If you are working on your hard drive, your screen will say, Are you sure you want to move this folder to the Recycle Bin?

To Delete a Folder

a. In the file list, right-click **Deals**, and then click **Delete**. When asked **Are you sure you want to permanently delete this folder?**, click **Yes**. Five folders should be visible in the Navigation pane and the file list.

b. In the Navigation pane, click the names of each of the folders. Notice that the Resort_ Documents and Resort_Presentations folders are empty. The Resort_Pictures folder contains the Golf Images folder, and the Resort_Storyboards folder contains storyboard files for various topics related to the resort. The Lastname_Snips folder contains the snip file created earlier.

Working with Files

Many different types of files are stored on your computer. There are operating system files that make Windows run, application files that run the programs you use, and data files that store the information used by those programs. Most of your work will be done with data files such as Word documents, Excel workbooks, PowerPoint presentations, various types of image and sound files, and other types of data files. In this section, you will copy, move, rename, preview, and delete files. You will also compress and expand files and add tags to make searching easier.

Copying, Moving, Renaming, and Deleting Files

The same procedures that you just practiced with folders can also be applied to files. As you create more documents, you will often find that you did not anticipate how your files would need to be organized. Files can be copied or moved to new locations. They can also be renamed or deleted when no longer needed.

Copying and Moving Files

In the following exercise, you will copy files from your student data files to appropriate folders in the Windows 7 Practice folder on your USB flash drive. You will begin by copying one file, and then you will learn how to copy several files at the same time.

To Copy One File

a. In the Navigation pane, click the **01_windows_7_workshop_1** folder. If necessary, click the **arrow** ▷ to the left of the Windows 7 Practice folder on your USB flash drive to display the five subfolders.

b. In the file list, click **w701_ws01_Golf_Getaway**, and drag the file to the **Resort_ Documents** folder in the Navigation pane. A thumbnail, showing this as a Word document, is attached to the pointer, and a Copy to Resort_Documents message appears.

Currently the folders and files in the 01_windows_7_workshop_1 folder are arranged by name. When you want to copy several files of the same type, it is more useful to arrange the files by type.

To Copy Adjacent Files at the Same Time

a. Click the **Type** heading at the top of the column. The upward pointing arrow is now in the Type column, and files are sorted alphabetically by the type of file. Use the scroll bar to see the different types of files in the folder.

b. Move the pointer to the right side of the Type column heading until you see a ⊕ pointer. Double-click to widen the column so all text is visible.

c. Scroll until you see all the files for the type Microsoft Word Document. Click **w701_ws01_ Diploma**. Press and hold ⌈Shift⌉, and then click **w701_ws01_Thanks**. All Microsoft Word Document files are selected, and the Details pane shows that 12 items are selected. You can select any number of adjacent files by using this method.

d. Point anywhere in the selection. Press and hold the left mouse button, and then drag the thumbnails on top of the **Resort_Documents** folder. Notice the number 12 on the thumbnail indicating that you are copying 12 files.

e. Because you already copied the w701_ws01_ Golf_Getaway file to this folder, a Copy File dialog box appears asking you to decide if you want to copy this file again. Because you know the files are identical, click **Don't Copy**.

    Whenever you copy a file to a folder that already contains a file with the same name, the Copy File dialog box appears, giving details—such as size and date modified—of both files and allows you to choose to copy and replace the file or not to copy the file. You also have the option of keeping both files, in which case the file you are copying will be renamed. Usually you will want to keep the most recent version of a file, but there are times when you might want to keep several versions.

f. Scroll until you see all the files for the type Microsoft PowerPoint Presentation. Click **w701_ws01_Caddy_Staff**. Press and hold ⌈Shift⌉, and then click **w701_ws01_ Tournament**. All presentation files are selected. Drag these files to the **Resort_ Presentations** folder in the Navigation pane. Notice the number 12 on the thumbnail indicating that you are copying 12 files.

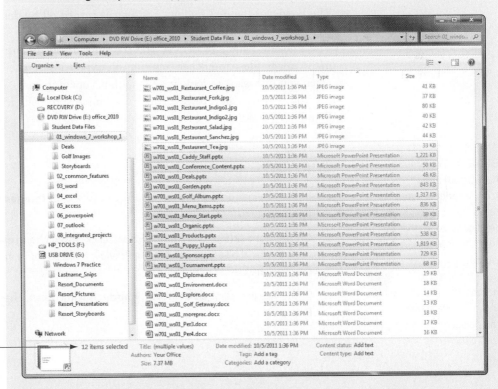

Number of files selected

Figure 35   Presentation files selected

There are times when you will want to copy several files that are not adjacent in the file list. You can do this by selecting files using Ctrl instead of Shift.

To Copy Nonadjacent Files at the Same Time

a. Scroll until all files of the WMF File type are visible in the file list.

b. Click **w701_ws01_Deals_Golfer_WMF**. Hold down Ctrl and click **w701_ws01_Menu_ Chef_WMF** and **w701_ws01_Restaurant_Burger_WMF**. Three files that are not adjacent are selected.

c. Point to any of the selected files. Press and hold the left mouse button, and then drag the thumbnail on top of the **Resort_Pictures** folder in the Navigation pane. The number **3** appears on the thumbnail showing you are copying three files.

Files can easily be moved from one folder to another.

To Move a File

a. In the Navigation pane, click **Resort_Pictures**. The Golf Images folder and the three WMF files are displayed in the file list.

b. In the file list, drag **w701_ws01_Deals_Golfer_WMF** to the **Golf Images** folder.

c. In the Navigation pane, click **Golf Images**, and then verify that the w701_ws01_Deals_ Golfer_WMF file is now in that folder.

Previewing Files

The Preview pane in Windows Explorer is turned off by default. When it is open on the right side of the window, it displays a preview of the file selected in the Content pane. The Preview pane can display the contents of documents, workbooks, presentations, many image files, and other common file types. Using the Preview pane is very helpful when you just want to look at a file without opening it.

You will use the Preview pane to examine some of the files that you copied to the Windows 7 Practice folder.

SIDE NOTE
Additional Files
You may at times see a file called Thumbs.db. These are database files that are created automatically by Windows whenever you have viewed a folder in thumbnail view and then changed to another view later on. You can delete these files or just ignore them.

To Use the Preview Pane

a. In the Navigation pane, if necessary, click the **Golf Images** folder. The file list displays five files.

b. On the right side of the command bar, click **Show the preview pane** 🔲. The Preview pane opens. If necessary, resize the Preview pane so the Name, Date modified, and Type columns are visible in the file list.

c. In the file list, click **w701_ws01_Caddy_Background**. The image is displayed in the Preview pane.

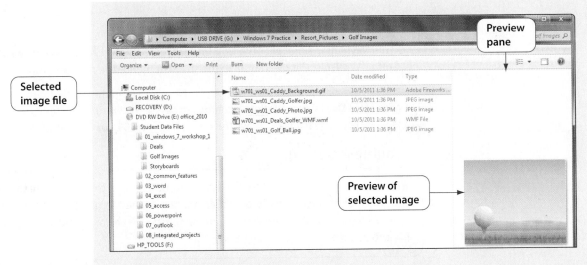

Figure 36 Preview pane open

SIDE NOTE

Changing Your View

You can also preview thumbnails of images and presentations by using the Change your view button to select Extra Large, Large, or Medium icons. Multiple thumbnails can be displayed in the Content pane.

---

d. Click each of the remaining files. Notice that the files with a .jpg extension are displayed but the file with the .wmf extension is not. This type of file is not supported in the Preview pane.

e. Double-click the **w701_ws01_Deals_Golfer_WMF** file. The Paint program opens. **Maximize** the Paint window so you can view the .wmf image. **Close** the Paint window.

f. In the Navigation pane, click **Resort_Presentations**. In the file list, click **w701_ws01_ Menu_Items**. The first slide of the presentation is displayed in the Preview pane.

g. Click the **Vertical Scroll Bar arrow** to view additional slides. Hide the preview pane.

Renaming and Deleting Files

There will be times when you will want to rename and delete files to keep your files organized.

Real World Advice   Naming Files

At one time, file names could only be eight characters long, followed by a period and a three-character extension. This rule made it very difficult to name numerous files and also made them difficult to find again. Now, file names can be much longer— depending on the location, potentially as many as 255 characters. Most likely, you will never want to use file names that long. You may use all letters and numbers on your keyboard, as well as spaces, and some symbols. The following characters may not be used:

$$\backslash \ / \ ? \ : \ * \ " \ > \ < \ |$$

When several people work on the same document, they often add their initials and a date before saving a file and sending it to someone else on the team. That way everyone always knows who made the most recent revision and when it was made.

To Rename and Delete a File

a. In the Navigation pane, click the **Golf Images** folder. Right-click the **w701_ws01_Deals_ Golfer_WMF** file. Click **Rename** on the shortcut menu. The file name is highlighted.

b. You do not want to change the name completely. Click in the highlighted area to the left of the **D** in **Deals**. Press Delete six times to delete the word "Deals" and the underscore. Press Enter. The file now shows the new name—**w701_ws01_Golfer_WMF**.

Troubleshooting

When renaming a file, it is essential that you not change the **file extension**—the three or four letters after the period at the end of the file name that indicate the file type. Windows 7 tries to prevent you from making this error by not highlighting the file extension when you rename a file.

c. Right-click the **w701_ws01_Golf_Ball** file, and then click **Delete**. The Delete File dialog box appears and asks **Are you sure you want to permanently delete this file?**

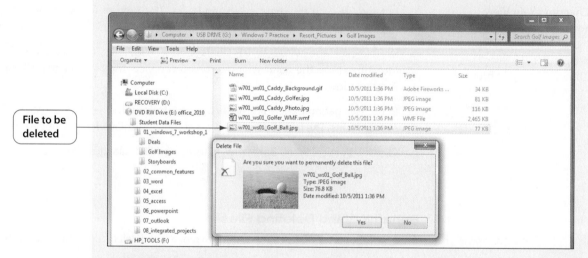

Figure 37 Delete File dialog box

d. Click **Yes**. The file is removed from the list, and four files remain.

Compressing Files to Save Space

One of the main reasons to **compress** folders and files is to reduce their size so they can be sent more quickly as e-mail attachments. Large files containing graphics and videos are often too large to transfer easily or may not transfer at all. Windows 7 allows you to compress a single file or numerous files into a single compressed folder with a .zip extension. Files stored in a compressed folder take up less space and can be transferred more quickly.

You will compress the files in the Resort_Presentations folder. The Details pane will display the size of the files before and after compressing. Some files show little savings while others may show a savings of as much as 80% or more.

To Compress Files

a. In the Navigation pane, click the **Resort_Presentations** folder. Click the **first file** at the top of the file list. Press Shift, and then click the **last file** in the file list. The Details pane indicates that 12 items are selected. If the size of the files is not displayed, click **Show more details**. Notice that the files have a total size of 7.37 MB.

b. **Right-click** anywhere on the selected files. On the displayed shortcut menu, point to **Send to**, and then click **Compressed (zipped) folder**. After a few moments, during which time the files are compressed, a new compressed folder with a zipper icon and a .zip file extension appears in the file list. The folder name reflects the file that you right-clicked and is in Edit mode.

c. Type Compressed_Presentations and then press Enter. The folder is renamed. Look at the Details pane. Notice that the size of the compressed folder is 6.89 MB, which reflects a small savings in space. Other files may show a much greater compression rate.

d. In the file list, double-click the **Compressed_Presentations** folder. Scroll to the far right and notice that the files are listed with the original sizes and compressed sizes. The compression ratio for each file is also listed and shows a range from as low as 1% to a high of 25%.

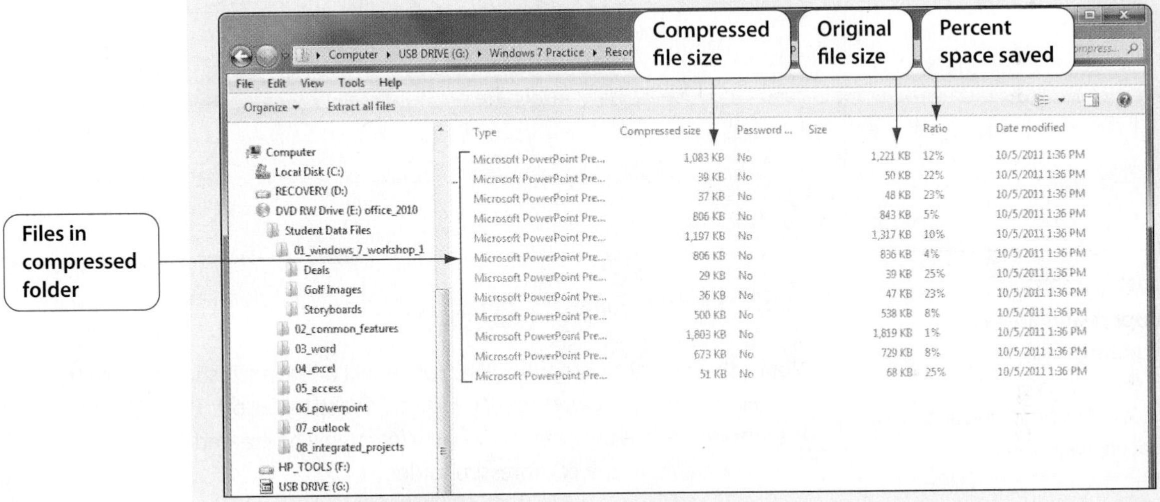

Figure 38 Comparison of file sizes

e. Make sure that the horizontal scroll bar is to the far right of the screen.

f. Open the **Snipping Tool**, and then use the skills you practiced to create a full-screen snip of the window. Save it as a JPEG file in the **Lastname_Snips** folder as Lastname_Firstname_w701_ws01_Compressed, and then **Close** the Snipping Tool window.

Extracting Compressed Files

If you receive a compressed folder from someone, you will need to extract the files so you can view them. When you select a compressed folder in the Navigation pane, an Extract all files command appears on the command bar. When you click this command a dialog box appears and shows you that the files will be extracted to the same location as the compressed folder. This folder will have the same name, but the files will no longer be compressed. You can change the name of the folder and the location to which it will be saved before you continue the extraction process.

To Extract Compressed Files

a. In the Navigation pane, if necessary, click the **arrow** ▷ to the left of **Resort_Presentations**. Click **Compressed_Presentations**. On the command bar, click **Extract all files**. Alternatively, you can right-click the **Compressed_Presentations** folder, and then click **Extract All** on the shortcut menu. The Extract Compressed (Zipped) Folders dialog box opens.

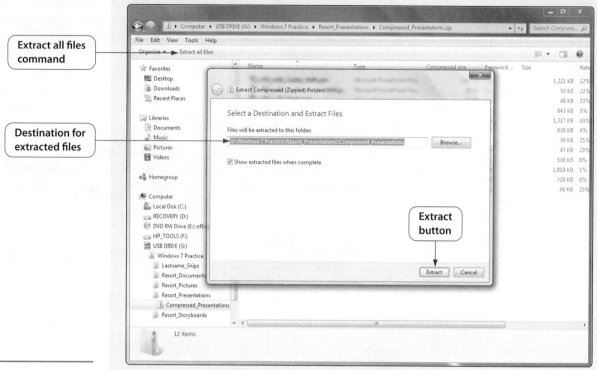

Figure 39   Extract Compressed (Zipped) Folders dialog box

b. Notice the path showing where the folder will be saved. It should show the letter of your USB Flash Drive followed by \Windows 7 Practice\Resort_Presentations\Compressed_Presentations. This indicates that a new folder will be created for the extracted files using the same name as the compressed folder.

c. Make sure the **Show extracted files when complete** check box is selected. Click the **Extract** button. When the extraction process is complete, the Compressed_Presentations folder is selected in the Navigation pane, and the extracted files are displayed in the file list. Close the window showing extracted files.

Adding Tags to Files

Tags are custom file properties that are added to files as keywords to enable you to categorize and organize your files and find the files you need more quickly. First, locate and select the file to be tagged. In the Details pane, click the Tags field and type your text. You can add one or more tags to a file.

To Add Tags to Files

a. In the Navigation pane, click the **Resort_Presentations** folder. In the file list, click the **w701_ws01_Golf_Album** file. The Details pane at the bottom of the window displays properties related to the selected file.

b. Move the pointer to the top of the **Details** pane to display the **Vertical Resize** pointer ⬍, and then drag the top of the **Details** pane to display three lines, if necessary.

c. In the Details pane, to the right of Tags, click **Add a tag**. A box opens in which you can enter your keywords as tags to help locate related files.

d. In the Tags box, type Golf and press →. Type Swimming and press →. Type Camps and click **Save**.

e. In the files list, click **w701_ws01_Sponsor**. In the Details pane, click to the right of Tags. Type Golf and press →. Type Tournament and click **Save**.

Searching for Files

Windows 7 includes powerful search tools that make locating files easy. You have already used the search box on the Start menu to search for a program. In the next section, you will use Windows Explorer to search for files that meet certain criteria.

To Search for Files

a. In the Navigation pane, click your **USB flash drive**, and then click the **Windows 7 Practice** folder. You will only search the files in this folder.

b. On the far right of the address bar, click in the **Search box**. Type the letter g and then in the file list, examine the results of your search. File names, folder names, and file types that begin with the letter "G" are displayed.

   Note that only files that include words that start with "G" and file extensions that begin with "g" are displayed. The Golf_Album file displays along with files that include the word "Garden" or a .gif extension. The Sponsor file does not display because you must expand the search to include tags, text that is a portion of a file name, and text within a file.

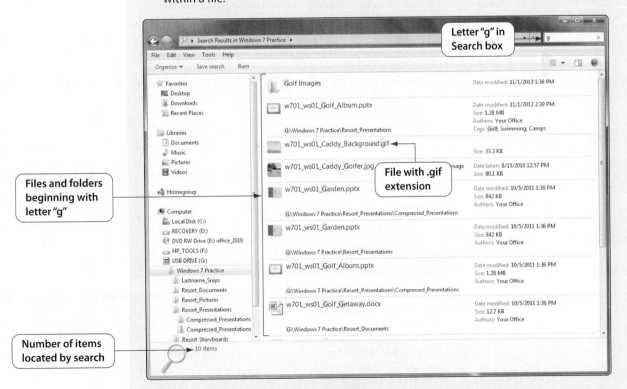

Figure 40   Results of search after typing "g"

c. In the Search box, continue typing olf. Notice that now only files that include the word golf are displayed.

d. At the bottom of the file list, under Search again in, click **File Contents**. Notice that the search results now include the file where you added a tag for Golf.

e. Open the **Snipping Tool**, and then use the skills you practiced to create a full-screen snip of the window. Save it as a JPEG file in the **Lastname_Snips** folder as Lastname_Firstname_w701_ws01_Search and then close the Snipping Tool window.

f. Leave the search open for the next exercise.

If you find that you search for the same group of files over and over again, you will find it useful to save the search results.

To Save a Search

a. On the command bar, click the **Save search** button. In the Save As dialog box, click **Save**. A search folder, named "golf" is saved on your computer under Favorites, not on your USB drive.

If you add more files that meet the search criteria, these will be included when you open the search again. However, it is important to remember that the search will be performed only on files stored in the location specified—in this case the Windows 7 Practice folder on your USB drive. Any time that you want to perform this search again, just click the folder name in the Navigation pane. Your USB drive must be connected to your computer for the search to function properly.

b. Open the **Snipping Tool** and use the skills you practiced to create a **Full-screen Snip** of the window. Save it as a JPEG file in the Lastname_Snips folder as Lastname_Firstname_w701_ws01_Golf and then close the Snipping Tool window.

If you are not working on your own computer, you should delete the search folder just created. You would also do this when the search is no longer needed.

c. In the Navigation pane, right-click "golf" and then click **Remove**. Close Windows Explorer.

d. Submit the Snip files as directed.

If you have been working with folders and files on a USB flash drive, it is essential that you remove the drive properly. If this is not done, you risk losing data that cannot be recovered.

To Remove a USB Flash Drive

a. On the taskbar, in the notification area, click **Show hidden icons** ⬛. A window opens showing additional icons.

b. Locate and click **Safely Remove Hardware and Eject Media** ⬛. Click the command that begins with **Eject** followed by your USB flash drive name. The **Safe to Remove Hardware** message appears, indicating you may remove the USB flash drive.

Concept Check

1. How do you open a program when no shortcuts are available?

2. Discuss three ways to make a window active when multiple programs are open.

3. Where would you place a shortcut to a program used every day? Why?

4. How do you create a new subfolder using Windows Explorer?

5. What are tags, and how are they helpful?

Key Terms

Active window   17
Address bar   12
All Programs   10
Application software   2
Click   2
Command bar   12
Compress   44
Content pane   32
Context-sensitive   3
Desktop   2
Desktop background   4, 26
Details pane   32
Dialog box   13
Double-click   4
Drag   10
File extension   44

File list   32
Gadget   26
Graphical user interface
   (GUI)   2
Hard drive   5
Icon   2
Jump List   6
Library   33
Library pane   32
Maximize   12
Menu bar   12
Minimize   12
Mouse pointer   3
Navigation pane   32
Notification area   5
Operating system   2

Peek   5
Pinned programs area   9
Preview pane   32
Recycle Bin   3
Restore   13
Right-click   3
Screen saver   26
ScreenTip   3
Scroll bar   10
Scroll box   10
Search box   11
Shake   19
Shortcut menu   3
Show desktop button   5
Snip   25
Snipping Tool   25

Start button   5
Start menu   5
Status bar   12
Subfolder   34
System software   2
Tag   46
Taskbar   3
Title bar   12
USB flash drive   5
Wait time   27
Window   12
Windows Aero   2
Windows Explorer   32

Visual Summary

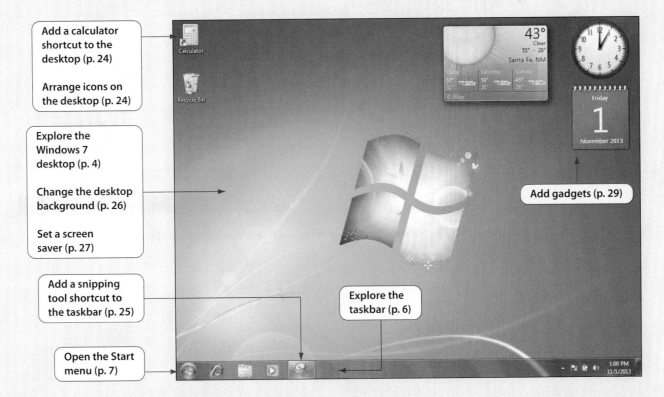

Add a calculator shortcut to the desktop (p. 24)

Arrange icons on the desktop (p. 24)

Explore the Windows 7 desktop (p. 4)

Change the desktop background (p. 26)

Set a screen saver (p. 27)

Add a snipping tool shortcut to the taskbar (p. 25)

Open the Start menu (p. 7)

Explore the taskbar (p. 6)

Add gadgets (p. 29)

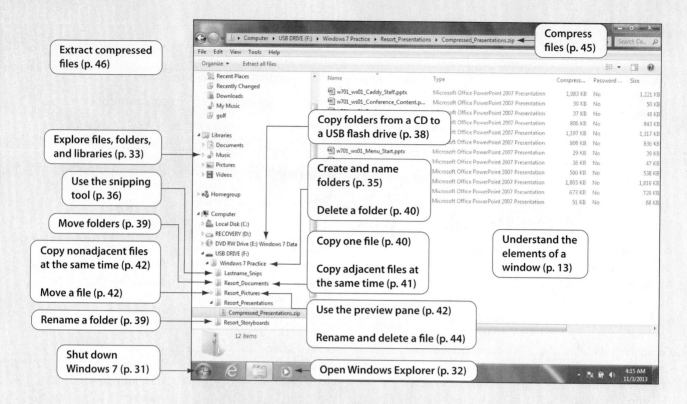

Extract compressed files (p. 46)

Compress files (p. 45)

Copy folders from a CD to a USB flash drive (p. 38)

Explore files, folders, and libraries (p. 33)

Create and name folders (p. 35)

Use the snipping tool (p. 36)

Delete a folder (p. 40)

Move folders (p. 39)

Copy nonadjacent files at the same time (p. 42)

Copy one file (p. 40)

Understand the elements of a window (p. 13)

Move a file (p. 42)

Copy adjacent files at the same time (p. 41)

Use the preview pane (p. 42)

Rename a folder (p. 39)

Rename and delete a file (p. 44)

Shut down Windows 7 (p. 31)

Open Windows Explorer (p. 32)

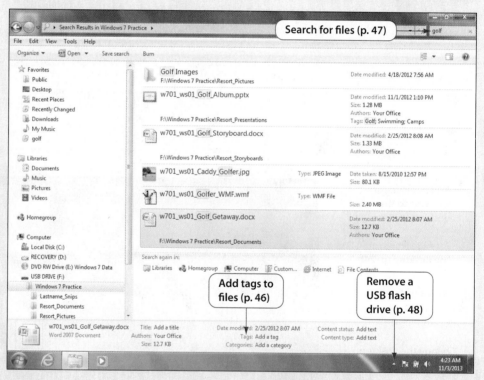

Search for files (p. 47)

Add tags to files (p. 46)

Remove a USB flash drive (p. 48)

Figure 41   Understanding the Windows 7 Desktop and Managing Windows Final

Student data file needed:
No data files needed

You will save your files as:
Lastname_Firstname_w701_ws01_Desktop
Lastname_Firstname_w701_ws01_Background

Personalizing Event Planning Department Computers

Information Technology

Patti Rochelle, corporate event planner at Painted Paradise Golf Resort and Spa, would like you to work with her staff to help them customize their new Windows 7 computers. Because computer screens are sometimes visible to guests, Patti would like to have the desktop background reflect the ambience of the resort. To better meet the needs of her department, she has also asked you to show her staff how to add useful gadgets to the desktop and to add shortcuts for frequently used programs.

a. Turn on your computer and, if necessary, follow any logon instructions required for the computer you are using.

b. If the Snipping Tool is not on your taskbar, click the **Start** button, point to **All Programs**, and click **Accessories**. Right-click **Snipping Tool**, and then click **Pin to Taskbar**.

c. Click the **Start** button, point to **All Programs**, and then click **Accessories**. Right-click **Calculator**, point to **Send to**, and then click **Desktop (create shortcut)**. Right-click an empty place on the desktop. On the shortcut menu, point to **Sort by**, and then click **Name**.

d. Close any Gadgets that may be open on your desktop. In an open area of the desktop, right-click to display a shortcut menu, and then click **Gadgets**. Double-click the **Clock** gadget, double-click the **Calendar** gadget, and then double-click the **Weather** gadget. Close the Gadgets gallery window. Point to the **Weather** gadget, and then click **Options**. In the Select current location box, type Santa Fe and click **Search**. From the displayed list, click **Santa Fe, New Mexico**, and then click **OK** to close the Weather options box. Click the **Larger size** button, and then drag the Weather gadget to the top of your desktop to the left of the clock. (Note: You must be connected to the Internet for the Weather gadget to display information about a specific location.)

e. On the taskbar, click **Snipping Tool**. In the Snipping Tool window, click the **arrow** to the right of the New button, and then click **Full-screen Snip**. In the Snipping Tool window, click the **Save Snip** button. In the Save As dialog box, in the left pane, navigate to your **Lastname_ Snips** folder. Save the snip as Lastname_Firstname_w701_ws01_Desktop. Be sure the Save as type box displays JPEG file. Click **Save**, and then close the Snipping Tool window.

f. Move the mouse pointer to an open area of the desktop, and then right-click. From the shortcut menu, click **Personalize**. Resize the Personalization window so it is centered on the screen with about an inch of the desktop showing on all four sides. (Make note of the current background as you will return to this background at the end of this practice exercise.)

g. At the bottom left of the Personalization window, click **Desktop Background**. If necessary, select Windows Desktop Backgrounds from the Picture location list. Use the vertical scroll bar to display the United States desktop backgrounds, and then click the picture of the stone arch. Click **Save changes** to apply the new background.

h. With the Personalization window still open, click **Screen Saver**. Move the Screen Saver Settings dialog box so the top-left corner is above and to the left of the top-left corner of the Personalization window. Click the **Screen saver arrow**, and then click **Mystify**. Make sure the Wait time shows **10 minutes**.

i. Use the skills you practiced to create a full-screen snip of the desktop. Save the file as Lastname_Firstname_w701_ws01_Background, and then close the Snipping Tool window.

j. In the Screen Saver Settings dialog box, click **Cancel**. In the Personalization window, click **Desktop Background**, and then select the original background. Click **Save changes**, and then close the Personalization window. On the desktop, right-click **Calculator**, on the short-cut menu, click **Delete**, and then **Yes**. On the taskbar, right-click **Snipping Tool**, and then click **Unpin this program from taskbar**. Close the three Gadgets that you added to the desktop.

k. Submit the two Snip files as instructed.

Practice 2

Student data file needed:
01_windows_7_workshop_1 folder

You will save your files as:
Lastname_Firstname_w701_ws01_Files
Lastname_Firstname_w701_ws01_Tags

Organizing Folders and Files for the Event Planning Department

Information Technology

Patti Rochelle would like you to continue working with the events planning staff to help them develop strategies for organizing folders and files. Because employees must often fill in for one another, Patti thinks it would be helpful if her staff could develop a common folder hier-archy. She has asked you to show them how to set up folders that will be useful for the various events that take place at the Painted Paradise Resort.

a. Turn on your computer and, if necessary, follow any logon instructions required for the computer you are using.

b. On the taskbar, click **Windows Explorer**, and then, if necessary, maximize the window. Insert your USB flash drive, and then in the Navigation pane click the flash drive name. Create a new folder named Event_Planning.

c. In the Navigation pane, if necessary, click the **arrow** to the left of the flash drive name to display the contents of the flash drive. Click **Event_Planning**, and then create two sub-folders named Conferences and Weddings. In the Navigation pane, click the **arrow** to the left of the Event_Planning folder so both subfolders are visible.

d. Insert your student data CD. In the Windows Explorer window, navigate to the location where your student data files are stored. Click the **arrow** in front of **01_windows_7_workshop_1** and then select that folder to display the folders and files in the file list.

e. In the Name column, make sure the arrow is pointing up and the files are sorted in ascending order starting with "a" to "z." Click **w701_ws01_Conference_Attendees**, hold down **Shift**, and then click **w701_ws01_Conference_Pueblo**. Drag the five selected files to the **Conferences** folder on your USB flash drive. Select the seven files with the word **Menu**, and then drag these files to the **Weddings** folder on your flash drive.

f. In the Navigation pane, click the **Weddings** folder. In the file list, right-click the file **w701_ws01_Menu_Items**, and then from the shortcut menu, click **Rename**. Change the file name to w701_ws01_New_Menu_Items.

g. Right-click **w701_ws01_Menu_Start**, and then click **Delete**. In the message box, click **Yes**.

h. Use the skills you practiced to create a full-screen snip of the Windows Explorer window. Save it in the **Lastname_Snips** folder as Lastname_Firstname_w701_ws01_Files, and then close the Snipping Tool window.

i. With the Weddings folder still selected, in the file list, click the **w701_ws01_New_Menu_Items** file. In the Details pane, click in the box to the right of the word **Tags**. Type Appetizers and press →. Type Lunch and save the file.

j. Create a full-screen snip of the Windows Explorer window. Save it in the **Lastname_Snips** folder as Lastname_Firstname_w701_ws01_Tags, and then close the Snipping Tool window. Close Windows Explorer.

k. Submit the snip files as instructed.

Student data file needed:

01_windows_7_workshop_1 folder

You will save your files as:

Lastname_Firstname_w701_ps1_Cascade
Lastname_Firstname_w701_ps1_Stacked
Lastname_Firstname_w701_ps1_Shopping

Working with Multiple Windows

Production &
Operations

Elena Frederick owns Second Chances, a consignment shop selling gently used, upscale clothing. She has just hired Katie Snow, who will perform a number of duties including arranging merchandise, assisting customers, and completing sales. Katie will also create a monthly newsletter that will be e-mailed to customers informing them of new acquisitions. She is familiar with Windows 7 but has only worked with one program at a time. She has asked you for a brief refresher on using multiple programs and arranging windows so she will be able to work more efficiently.

a. Open WordPad. If necessary, click Restore Down so the WordPad window is not maximized. Open Windows Explorer and if necessary, click Restore Down. Open Paint and if necessary, click Restore Down. Make Windows Explorer the active window and then, if necessary, change the view to display medium icons. Cascade the windows.

b. Insert your USB flash drive. Create a Full-screen Snip of the screen. Save it in the **Lastname_Snips** folder as Lastname_Firstname_w701_ps1_Cascade and then close the Snipping Tool window.

c. Show the windows stacked. Create a Full-screen Snip of the screen. Save it in the **Lastname_Snips** folder as Lastname_Firstname_w701_ps1_Stacked and then close the Snipping Tool window.

d. Close Paint. Snap the WordPad window to the right side of your screen. Snap Windows Explorer to the left side of your screen. (If your computer is not capable of using the Aero Snap feature, move and size WordPad so it fills the right half of your screen and then move and size Windows Explorer so it fills the left half of your screen.)

e. Insert your student data CD. Locate your 01_windows_7_workshop_1 files. Copy the Deals folder to the Windows 7 Practice folder on your USB flash drive.

f. Click in the WordPad window and type Second Chances Monthly News. Press Enter two times. Click on the w701_ws01_Deals_Shopping file in the Deals folder in Windows Explorer and drag it under the text you just typed in WordPad.

g. Create a Full–screen Snip of the screen. Save it in the **Lastname_Snips** folder as Lastname_Firstname_w701_ps1_Shopping and then close the Snipping Tool window.

h. Close all windows. Do not save the WordPad document. Submit all files as directed.

Student data file needed:

No student data files needed

You will save your files as:

Lastname_Firstname_w701_pf1_Europe

Lastname_Firstname_w701_pf1_Tour

Marketing a Tour for a Travel Agency

Sales & Marketing

You have just been hired by the Let's Go Travel Agency to market a new 14-day European tour that will visit London, Paris, and Rome. Claire Alexander, owner of the agency, wants you to give talks to various groups and organizations around the state to publicize the tour and solicit future travelers. She has asked you to prepare a PowerPoint presentation to use during these meetings as well as a brochure that will be distributed to all attendees. You will be in frequent contact with representatives in the three cities to stay informed about tour details as they evolve. Before you begin, you will design your desktop to help you carry out your job responsibilities efficiently and effectively.

a. Choose a desktop background that is suitable for this assignment. Will you find this background distracting? Will the icons be easy to identify?

b. Select a screen saver, and then set the wait time so it is appropriate for the way you work. Consider how often and for how long you leave your computer.

c. Add shortcuts for the programs that you plan to use regularly. Where should these shortcuts be placed?

d. Add several gadgets that will be useful for this task. Consider the time difference between where you work and the three European cities. Will it be important for you to know about the weather in these locations?

e. Use the Internet to download one picture that represents each city on the tour. Rename the files appropriately, and then compress the three files to a folder named Lastname_Firstname_w701_pf1_Europe. The folder will have a .zip extension.

f. Create a full-screen snip of your desktop. Save it in the Lastname_Snips folder as Lastname_Firstname_w701_pf1_Tour, and then close the Snipping Tool window.

g. Submit the files as instructed.

Student data file needed:

01_windows_7_workshop_1 folder

You will save your files as:

Lastname_Firstname_w701_pf2_Cruise

Lastname_Firstname_w701_pf2_Chef

Improving the Desktop and Creating Order

General Business

Charles Thomas is head chef on the Sail Away cruise line. So far, the line has only one ship, the *SS Nemesis*, sailing out of San Juan, Puerto Rico. The *Nemesis* alternates between cruising the eastern and western Caribbean. On the last cruise, Charles agreed to mentor an intern. He has since regretted that decision. Without his knowledge or permission, the intern went a bit overboard on customizing and personalizing Charles' computer. You have been asked to look at the desktop and make recommendations for restoring it so it will be more professional and less distracting. The intern did not organize Chef Thomas' files as requested, and you have also been asked to preview these files, create appropriate folders, and then move the files where they logically belong.

a. Examine Figure 1 and determine what you would do to improve the appearance and functionality of the desktop.

Figure 1

b. Consider the following:
- Is the background suitable for a chef on a cruise ship?
- Which gadgets would be useful for Charles to have available?
- Is there ever a reason to have two of the same gadget on the desktop?
- Would you want shortcuts to the same program in two different places?

c. Create a desktop that would be more suitable for the work Charles would do as head chef. Consider the background, gadgets, and shortcuts to frequently used programs.

d. Save a snip of your desktop to the Lastname_Snips folder as Lastname_Firstname_w701_ pf2_Cruise.

e. Open Windows Explorer. On your USB flash drive, create a new folder called Cruise_ Data_Files. Open Windows Explorer. Navigate to the **01_windows_7_workshop_1** folder on your student data files CD. Copy all files to the Cruise_Data_Files folder. Do not copy the three folders. Preview all the files. Delete any files that are not related to dining, food, or views of eating areas.

f. Create two or three folders that are appropriate for storing the remaining files. Chef Thomas uses pictures of food on menus in the casual dining venues onboard. He uses other images for publicity brochures. He would like you to create a file structure that will make it easy for him to locate the files he wants quickly.

g. After organizing the files, compress all folders to a zipped folder called Lastname_ Firstname_w701_pf2_Chef.

h. Submit all files as directed.

Common Features of Microsoft Office 2010

Understanding the Common Features of Microsoft Office

PREPARE CASE
Working with the Common Features

General Business

The gift shop at the Red Bluff Golf Club has an array of items available for purchase from toiletries to clothes to presents for loved ones back home. There are numerous part-time employees including students from the local college. Frequently, the gift shop holds training luncheons for new employees. Susan Brock, the manager, is worried about the expense of providing lunch at the trainings. Your first assignment will be to start two documents for a meeting with Susan.

Andrey Kekyalyaynen / Shutterstock.com

You will begin a Word document for meeting minutes and an Excel spreadsheet to add and analyze expenses during the meeting. To complete this task, you need to understand and work with the common features from the Microsoft Office suite.

Student data files needed for this workshop:

 New, blank Word document

 New, blank Excel workbook

You will save your files as:

 Lastname_Firstname_cf01_ws01_Minutes

 Lastname_Firstname_cf01_ws01_Budget

Working with the Office Interface and the Ribbon

When you walk into a grocery store, you usually know what you are going to find and that items will be in approximately the same location, regardless of which store you are visiting. The first items you usually see are the fruits and fresh vegetables while the frozen foods are near the end of the store. This similarity among stores creates a level of comfort for the shopper. The brands may be different, but the food types are the same. That is, canned corn is canned corn.

Microsoft Office 2010 creates that same level of comfort with its Ribbons, features, and functions. Each application has a similar appearance or user interface. Microsoft Office 2010 is a suite of productivity applications or programs. Office is available in different suites for PCs and Macs. Office Home and Student includes Word, Excel, PowerPoint, and OneNote 2010. Office Home and Business includes Word, Excel, PowerPoint, OneNote, and Outlook 2010. Office Professional includes Word, Excel, PowerPoint, OneNote, Outlook, Access, and Publisher 2010. Other suites include Office Standard, Office Professional Plus, Office Professional Academic, and Office for Mac 2011. Each of the applications in these suites can be used individually or in combination with other Office applications. Figure 1 shows the interface for Word 2010.

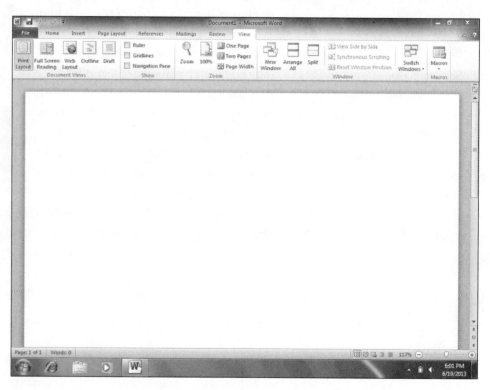

Figure 1 Overview of Office Word 2010 program interface

Microsoft Word is a word processing program. This application can be used to create, edit, and format **documents** such as letters, memos, reports, brochures, resumes, and flyers. Word also provides tools for creating **tables**, which organize information into rows and columns. Using Word, you can add **graphics,** which consist of pictures, clip art, SmartArt, shapes, and charts, that can enhance the look of your documents.

Microsoft Excel is a spreadsheet program. Excel is a two-dimensional database program that can be used to model quantitative data and perform accurate and rapid calculations with results ranging from simple budgets to financial and statistical analyses. Data entered into Excel can be used to generate a variety of charts such as pie charts, bar charts, line charts, or scatter charts, to name a few, to enhance spreadsheet data. The Excel files created are known as **workbooks**, which contain one or more worksheets. Excel makes it possible to analyze, manage, and share information, which can also help you make better and smarter decisions. New analysis and visualization tools help you track and highlight important data trends.

Microsoft PowerPoint is a presentation and slide program. This application can be used to create slide shows for a presentation, as part of a website, or as a stand-alone application on a computer kiosk. These presentations can also be printed as handouts.

Microsoft OneNote is a planner and note-taking program. OneNote can be used to collect information in one easy-to-find place. With OneNote, you can capture text and images, as well as video and audio. By sharing your notebooks, you can simultaneously take and edit notes with other people in other locations, or just keep everyone in sync and up to date. You can also take your OneNote notebooks with you and then view and edit your notes from virtually any computer with an Internet connection or your Windows 7 phone device.

Microsoft Outlook is an e-mail, contact, and information management program. Outlook allows you to stay connected to the world with the most up-to-date e-mail and calendar tools. You can manage and print schedules, task lists, phone directories, and other documents. Outlook's ability to manage scheduled events and contact information is why Outlook is sometimes referred to as an **information management program**.

Microsoft Access is a relational database management program. Access is known as **relational database** software (or three-dimensional database software) because it is able to connect data in separate tables to form a relationship when common fields exist— to offer reassembled information from multiple tables. For example, a business might have one table that lists all the supervisors, their shifts, and which area they supervise. Another table might accumulate data for employees and track which shift they are working. Because the common field in this example, for both database tables are shift hours, a business could use Access to query which employees are working the second shift, who the supervisor is, and produce a report with all their names. Thus, Access is used primarily for decision making by businesses that compile data from multiple records stored in tables to produce informative reports. Many businesses use Access to store data and Excel to model and analyze data by creating charts.

Microsoft Publisher is a desktop publishing program that offers professional tools and templates to help easily communicate a message in a variety of publication types, saving time and money while creating a more polished finished look. Whether you are designing brochures, newsletters, postcards, greeting cards, or e-mail newsletters, Publisher aids in delivering high-quality results without the user having graphic design experience. Publisher helps you to create, personalize, and share a wide range of professional-quality publications and marketing materials with ease.

Starting and Exploring Office Programs and Common Window Elements

There is more than one way to start Office programs. As you become familiar with the various options, you will be able to decide which method is more comfortable and efficient for your personal needs and workflow. Once you start working with these applications, also notice that it is possible to have more than one application open at a time. This is a valuable tool for users. One method for opening any Office program is from the Start menu on the taskbar.

To Start Office Programs

a. Click the **Start** ⊕ button.

b. Click **All Programs**, scroll if necessary, and then click the **Microsoft Office** folder.

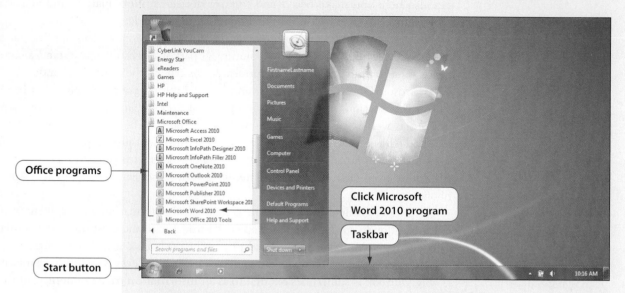

Figure 2 Starting Word from the Start menu

Troubleshooting

If Microsoft Office is not listed on your menu, you can use the Search programs and files input box at the bottom of the Start menu to type keywords to help find items quickly. Type in the application name desired and a list of options will appear. Notice when "word" is the keyword typed, "Microsoft Word 2010" appears at the top of the list.

c. Click the Office program you want to start.

Starting Word and Opening a New Blank Document

A blank Word document is like a blank piece of paper. The insertion point is at the first character of the first line. This provides a clean slate for your document.

To Start Word

a. Click the **Start** button, and then click **All Programs** to display the All Programs list.

b. Click the **Microsoft Office** folder, and then point to **Microsoft Word 2010**.

c. Click **Microsoft Word 2010**. Word will start with a new blank document.

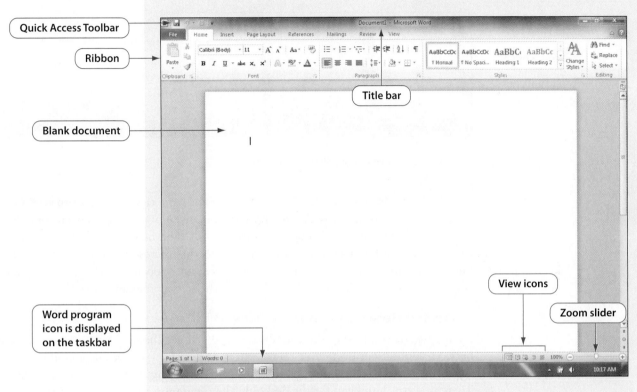

Quick Access Toolbar

Ribbon

Title bar

Blank document

View icons

Zoom slider

Word program icon is displayed on the taskbar

Figure 3 A blank document in Word

Starting Excel and Opening a New Blank Document

A blank spreadsheet is like a blank sheet of columnar paper. The active cell is at the first cell of the first row. This provides a clean slate for your spreadsheet.

To Start Excel

a. Click the **Start** button, and then click **All Programs** to display the All Programs list.

b. Click the **Microsoft Office** folder, and then point to **Microsoft Excel 2010**.

c. Click **Microsoft Excel 2010**. Excel will start with a new blank workbook.

The other Office programs can be opened using the same method. As previously mentioned, more than one application can be opened at the same time. It is possible to switch between any open applications to view their contents. The taskbar contains icons for open applications, as well as any program icons that have been pinned to the taskbar to allow for quick access when starting a program.

Switching Between Open Programs and Files

When moving your mouse pointer over a taskbar icon for an open program, a **thumbnail** or small picture of the open program file is displayed, as shown in Figure 4. This is a useful feature when two or more files are open for the same application. A thumbnail of each open file for that application is displayed, and you simply click the file thumbnail you want to make active.

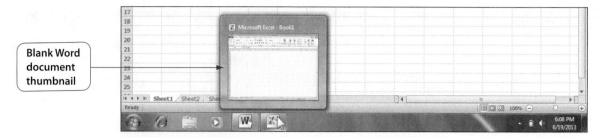

Blank Word document thumbnail

Figure 4 Viewing a thumbnail of Word

When two or more programs are running at the same time, you can also access them through the taskbar buttons. As you move the mouse pointer over each open application, stop and point to the Excel program button ⊞. A thumbnail will appear. If you want to switch to the Excel application file, just click the Microsoft Excel thumbnail or the button—because only one Excel document is currently open. If a different program is active, the program will switch to make Excel the active program.

Switching Between Windows Using [Alt]+[Tab]

As an alternative to using the thumbnails, you can use the keyboard shortcut to move between applications by holding down [Alt] and pressing [Tab]. A small window appears in the center of the screen with thumbnails representing each of the open programs. There is also a thumbnail for the desktop. The program name at the top of the window indicates the program that will be active when you release [Alt].

To Switch Between Applications

a. On the taskbar, point to **Word** 📝 and click.

b. On the taskbar, point to **Excel** ⊞ and observe the thumbnail of the Excel file.

c. Click the **Microsoft Excel - Book1** thumbnail to make sure the Book1 Excel document is the current active program.

d. In the current active cell **A1**, type Budget, and then press [Enter]. In the new cell **A2**, type 1234, and then press [Enter].

Resizing Windows and Workspaces

Office has a consistent design and layout as shown in Figure 5. This is beneficial because once you learn to use one Office program, you can use many of those skills when working with the other Office programs.

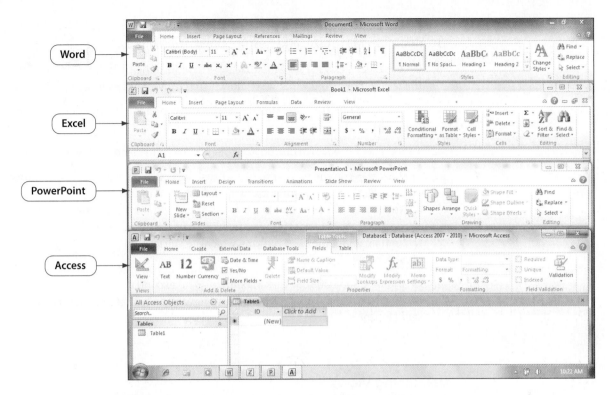

Figure 5 The Ribbons of Word, Excel, PowerPoint, and Access

One feature common among all of the applications is the three buttons that appear in the top-right corner of an application's title bar. The left button is the Minimize button ▭. This button hides a window so it is only visible on the taskbar. The middle button is a toggle button between Restore Down ▭ and Maximize, depending on the status of the window. If the window is at its maximum size, the button will act in a Restore Down capacity by restoring the window to a previous, smaller size. Once a window is in the Restore Down mode, the button toggles to a Maximize button ▭, which expands the window to its full size. Finally, the button on the right is the Close button ▭, which will close a file or exit the program.

These buttons offer another layer of flexibility in the ability to size and arrange the windows to suit your purpose or to minimize a window and remove it from view. The **Maximize** button might be used most often, because it offers the largest workspace. If several applications are opened, the windows can be arranged using the **Restore Down** button so several windows can be viewed at the same time. If you are not working on an application and want to have it remain open, the **Minimize** button ▭ will hide the application on the taskbar.

Excel has two sets of buttons in the top-right corner: the set on the program title bar is for the Excel program, and the set just below that represents the workbook currently open as shown in Figure 6.

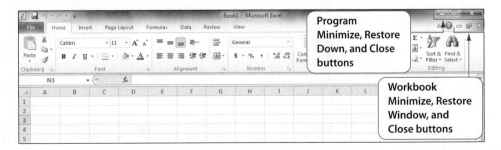

Figure 6 Program and workbook Minimize, Restore Down, Restore Window, and Close buttons

To Minimize, Maximize, and Restore Down the Windows

a. On the Excel title bar, click **Minimize** to reduce the program window to an icon on the taskbar. The Word window will now be the active window in view.

b. On the Word title bar, click **Maximize** to expand the Word program window to fill the screen.

c. Click the **Restore Down** button to return Word to its previous window size.

d. Click Excel on the taskbar to make Excel the active program. On the workbook window, under the Excel set of buttons, click **Restore Window**.

   Notice the workbook window is reduced to a smaller sized window within the Excel window and the three buttons for the workbook now appear on the workbook title bar rather than under the Excel buttons, which are still located in the top-right corner of the Excel window.

e. On the workbook title bar, click **Maximize** to expand the workbook back to the original size. Notice the workbook set of buttons are again located under the Excel window set of buttons.

Switching Views

There are a variety of views in each program. The views provide different ways to display the file within the program. There are five views in Word: Print Layout, Full Screen Reading, Web Layout, Outline, and Draft. The content or file information is the same in the different views; it is merely the presentation of the document information that appears different. For example, in Word, Print Layout shows how the document appears as a printed page. Web Layout shows how the document appears as a web page. Print Layout is the most commonly used view when creating a draft of a document as shown in Figure 7.

SIDE NOTE

Switching Between Views

You can quickly switch between views using the options located on the View tab in the Document Views group, or you can use the View buttons located on the status bar at the bottom-right side of the window.

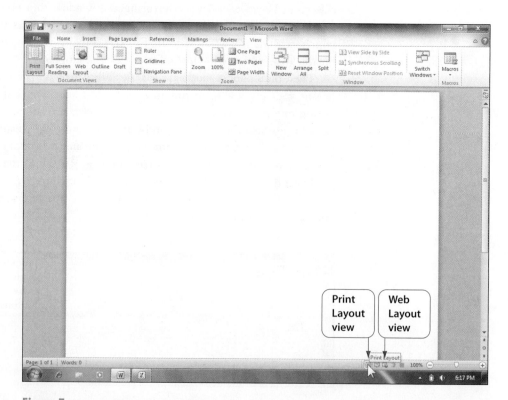

Figure 7 Print and Web Layout views

Zooming and Scrolling

To get a closer look at the content within the program, you can zoom in. Alternatively, if you would like to see more of the contents, you can zoom out. Keep in mind that the Zoom level only affects your view of the document on the monitor and does not affect the printed output of the document, similar to using a magnifying glass to see something bigger—the print on the page is still the same size. Therefore, the zoom level should not be confused with how big the text will print—it only affects your view of the document on the screen. On the right side of the status bar is a slide control that permits zooming in Word from 10% to 500%. The plus and minus propose an easy method, or you can drag the Zoom Slider [⊖——⊕]. In Excel and PowerPoint, the zoom range is from 10% to 400%. When using zoom, sometimes text is shifted off the viewing screen. Depending on the program and the zoom level, you might see the vertical or horizontal scroll bars, or both scroll bars, which can be used to adjust what is displayed in the window. The scroll bars have arrows that can be clicked to shift the workspace in small increments in a specified direction and a scroll box that can be dragged to move a workspace in larger increments.

To Zoom and Scroll in Office Applications

a. On the taskbar, click **Word** [icon]. On the Word title bar, if necessary, click **Maximize** [icon] to expand the Word program window to fill the screen.

b. The insertion point should be blinking on the blank document. Type Word.

c. On the Word status bar, drag the **Zoom Slider** [⊖——⊕] to the right until the percentage is **500%**. The document is enlarged to its largest size. This makes the text appear larger.

d. On the Word status bar, click the **Zoom level** button, currently displaying 500%. The Zoom dialog box opens. You can set a custom Zoom level or use one of the preset options.

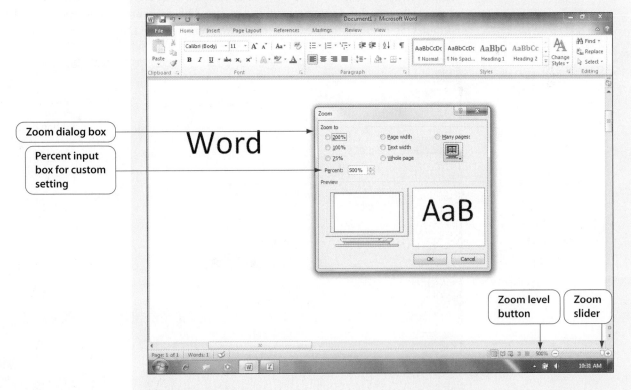

Zoom dialog box

Percent input box for custom setting

Zoom level button

Zoom slider

Figure 8 Zoom dialog box

e. Click **Page width**, and then click **OK**. The Word document is zoomed to its page width.

f. On the taskbar, click **Excel** 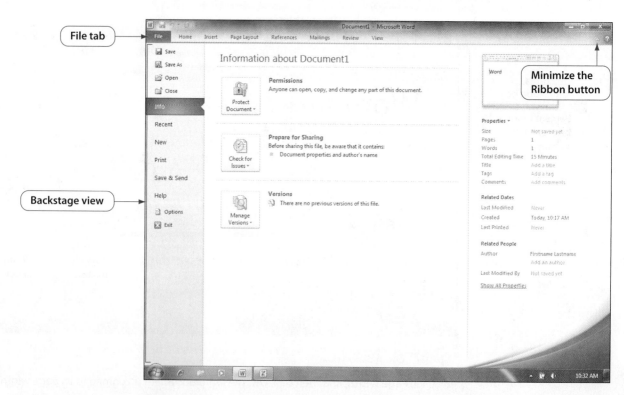. The Excel program should now be displayed as the active window.

g. Click cell **B1** (which is the first row cell under Column B on the worksheet).

h. Type Firstname Lastname, replacing Firstname Lastname with your own name.

i. Press Enter. Text has been entered in cell B1, and cell B2 is now the active cell.

j. On the status bar, notice the Zoom level and click **Zoom Out** ⊖ three times. The Zoom level magnification is now 70% (if you started at 100%).

k. On the horizontal scroll bar, click the **right scroll arrow** ▶ two times and the text is shifted to the left. Some columns may not be visible now.

l. On the horizontal scroll bar, drag the scroll box all the way to the left. The columns should be visible again.

m. Drag the **Zoom Slider** to the right to return the Zoom level to **100%**.

n. On the taskbar, click **Word**. The Word program window is displayed as the active window.

Using the Ribbon

While the tabs, which contain groups of commands on the **Ribbon**, differ from program to program, each program has two tabs in common: the File tab and the Home tab. The File tab is the first tab on the Ribbon and is used for file management needs. When clicked, it opens **Backstage view**, which provides access to the file level features, such as saving a file, creating a new file, opening an existing file, printing a file, and closing a file, as well as program options, as shown in Figure 9. The Home tab is the second tab in each program Ribbon. It contains the commands for the most frequently performed activities, including copying, cutting, and pasting; changing fonts and styles; and other various editing and formatting tools. The commands on these tabs may differ from program to program. Other tabs are program specific, such as the Formulas tab in Excel, the Design tab in PowerPoint, and the Database Tools tab in Access.

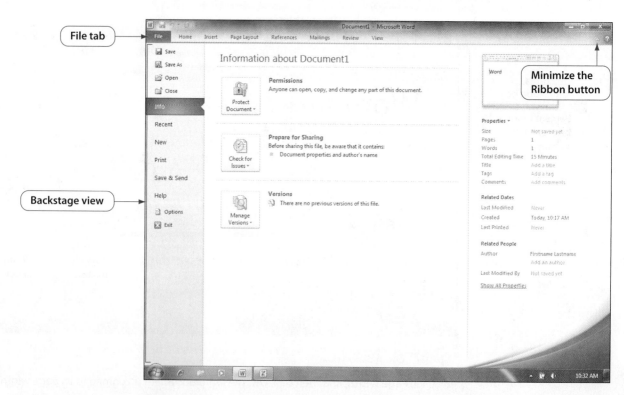

Figure 9 File tab to display Backstage view

Using the Ribbon Tabs

It is possible to enlarge your workspace by minimizing the Ribbon. The **Minimize the Ribbon button**, shown in Figure 9, is located just below the Close button in the top-right corner of the window and directly next to the Help, question mark, button. The Minimize the Ribbon button reduces the Ribbon to a single line and toggles to the Expand the Ribbon button. Click the Expand the Ribbon button to display the full Ribbon again.

To Use Ribbon Tabs

a. Word should be the active application. Click **Maximize** 🔲 to expand the Word program space so the document within the program window fills all of the screen.

b. Click **Minimize the Ribbon** ⌃, and then point to the **Page Layout tab** on the Ribbon. Notice that the Page Layout tab is highlighted but the current tab is still the active tab.

c. Click the **Page Layout tab**. The Page Layout tab Ribbon options are displayed. This tab provides easy access to the page formatting and printing options.

d. Click the **Home tab**. This displays the Home tab options on the Ribbon. If you click in the document again, notice the Ribbon options toggle out of view again. Click **Expand the Ribbon** ⌄ to toggle the Ribbon options into constant view (or alternatively, double-click any of the tab names).

SIDE NOTE

How Buttons and Groups Appear on the Ribbon

If you notice that your Ribbon appears differently from one computer to the next—the buttons and groups might seem condensed in size—there could be a few factors at play. The most common causes could be monitor size, the screen resolution, or the size of the program window. With smaller monitors, lower screen resolutions, or a reduced program window, buttons can appear as icons without labels, and a group can sometimes be condensed into a button that must be clicked to display the group options.

Clicking Buttons

Clicking a button will produce an action. For example, the Font group on the Home tab includes buttons for Bold and Italic. Clicking any of these buttons will produce an intended action. So, if you have selected text that you want to apply bold formatting to, simply click the Bold button and bold formatting is applied to the selected text.

Some buttons are toggle buttons: one click turns a feature on and a second click turns the feature off. When a feature is toggled on, the button remains highlighted. For example, in Word, on the Home tab in the Paragraph group, click the Show/Hide button ¶. Notice paragraph marks appear in your document, and the button is highlighted to show that the feature is turned on. This feature displays characters that do not print. This allows you to see items in the document that can help to troubleshoot a document's formatting, such as when Tab was pressed an arrow is displayed, or when the Spacebar was pressed dots appear between words. Click the Show/Hide button again, and the feature is turned off. The button is no longer highlighted, and the paragraph characters, as well as any other nonprinting characters, in the document are no longer displayed.

Also notice that some buttons have two parts: a button that accesses the most commonly used setting or command, and an arrow that opens a gallery menu of all related commands or options for that particular task or button. For example, the Font Color button A⏷ on the Home tab in the Font group includes the different colors that are available for fonts. If you click the button, the last color used will be the default color applied to selected text. Notice this color is also displayed on the icon and will change when a different color is applied in the document. To access the gallery menu for other color options, click the arrow next to the Font Color button, and then click the alternate color or command option. Whenever you see an arrow next to a button, this is an indicator that more options are available.

It should also be said that the two buttons on your mouse operate in a similar fashion. The left mouse click can also be thought of as performing an action, whether it is to click a Ribbon button, menu option, or to open a document. The right-click (or right mouse button) will never perform an action, but rather it provides more options. The options that appear on the shortcut menu when you right-click change depending on the location of the mouse pointer. For example, right-click an empty area of the status bar and you will see options available for status bar features. All of these status bar options are toggles, meaning you can toggle them on or off—a check mark is displayed for the features currently on. By contrast, if you hover the mouse pointer over text in the Word document and right-click, you will see menu options that apply to text—many of the same options found in the Font group on the Home tab. When a desired option is found on a shortcut menu, simply click the option to apply it. If none of the options meets your needs, click in empty space outside the menu to cancel the shortcut menu.

CONSIDER THIS | **Changes Among Versions of Microsoft Office**

A consistent user interface helps users feel comfortable. In Office 2010, Microsoft removed the Office Button used in Office 2007 and created the File tab and Backstage view. Why do you think the company made this change? Which do you prefer? Are there any future changes you would recommend?

To Work with Buttons

a. If necessary, click **Word** 🔲 on the taskbar to make it the active window, and then click **Maximize** 🔲.

b. Place the mouse pointer over the typed text **Word**, and then double-click to select the text. With the text selected, click the **Home tab**, and then click **Bold** B in the Font group. This will toggle on the Bold command. Notice that the Bold button is now highlighted and the selected text is displayed in bold format.

Bold button toggled on and highlighted

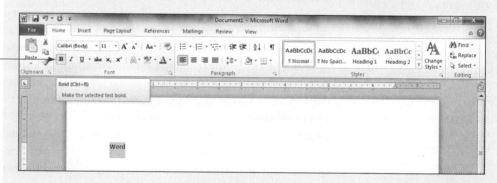

Figure 10 Bold toggled on with text highlighted

c. With the text still selected, press ⌨Backspace once to delete the text Word. Notice that the Bold button is still highlighted, which means any new text typed will be bold.

d. Type Meeting Minutes, and then press ⌨Enter. The insertion point moves to the next line of the document. If you made any typing errors, you can press ⌨Backspace to remove the typing errors and then retype the text.

e. With the insertion point on the second line, click **Bold** B again to toggle it off.

SIDE NOTE
Live Preview Feature
Live Preview, which allows you to see how formatting looks before you apply it, is available for many of the gallery libraries.

f. Position the insertion point to the left of the word **Meeting**, press and hold the left mouse button, drag the mouse until the text in the first line of text is selected, and then release the mouse button when all the text in Meeting Minutes is highlighted.

g. Click the **Home tab**, and then click the **Font Color arrow** A▾ in the Font group. Under **Standard Colors**, point to, but do not click, **Dark Red**. Notice a Live Preview feature that shows how the selected document text will change color. As the mouse pointer hovers over a color, a ScreenTip appears to show the color name.

h. Click **Dark Red**. The selected text should now be bold and dark red.

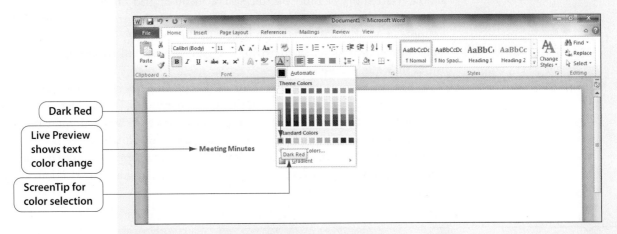

Dark Red

Live Preview shows text color change

ScreenTip for color selection

Figure 11 Live Preview of font color

i. Click below **Meeting Minutes** to move the insertion point to the next line.

Real World Advice Using Keyboard Shortcuts and Key Tips

Keyboard shortcuts are extremely useful because they allow you to keep your hands on the keyboard instead of reaching for the mouse to make Ribbon selections. **Key Tips** are also a form of keyboard shortcuts. Pressing Alt will display Key Tips (or keyboard shortcuts) for items on the Ribbon and Quick Access Toolbar. The **Quick Access Toolbar** is located at the top left of the application window and can be customized to offer commonly used buttons. After displaying the Key Tips, you can press the letter or number corresponding to the Ribbon item to request the action from the keyboard. Pressing Alt again will toggle the Key Tips off.

Many keyboard shortcuts are universal to all Windows programs; you will find they work not only in past versions of Office, but they also work in other Windows software. Keyboard shortcuts usually involve two or more keys, in which case you hold down the first key listed, and press the second key once. Some of the more common keyboard shortcuts are shown in Figure 12.

Keyboard Shortcut	To Do This:
Ctrl + C	Copy the selected item
Ctrl + V	Paste a copied item
Ctrl + A	Select all the items in a document or window
Ctrl + B	Bold selected text
Ctrl + I	Italic selected text
Ctrl + Z	Undo an action
Ctrl + Home	Move to the top of the document
Ctrl + End	Move to the end of the document

Figure 12 Common keyboard shortcuts

Using Galleries and Live Preview

Live Preview lets you see the effects of menu selections on your document file or selected item before making a commitment to a particular menu choice. A gallery is a set of menu options that appear when you click the arrow next to a button which, in some cases, may be referred to as a More button ⏷. The menu or grid shows samples of the available options. For example, on Word's Home tab in the Styles group, the Styles gallery shows a sample of each text style you can select. In this example, the Styles gallery includes a More button that you click to expand the gallery to see all the available options in the list, as shown in Figure 13.

When you point to an option in a gallery, Live Preview shows the results that would occur in your file if you were to click that particular option. Using Live Preview, you can experiment with settings before making a final choice. When you point to a text style in the Styles gallery, the selected text or the paragraph in which the insertion point is located appears with that text style. Moving the pointer from option to option results in quickly seeing what your text will look like before making a final selection. To finalize a change to the selected option, click on the style.

SIDE NOTE
Closing a Gallery
Esc can be used to close a gallery without making a selection, or, alternatively, you can click an empty area, such as the title bar, outside the gallery menu.

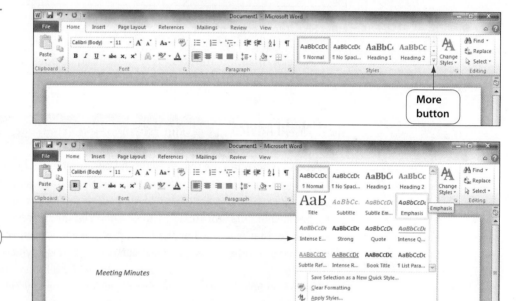

Figure 13 The More button and the Styles gallery

To Use the Numbering Library

a. Click the Home tab, and then click the **Numbering arrow** in the Paragraph group. The Numbering Library gallery opens.

b. Point to, but do not click the number followed by a closing parenthesis.

c. Place the pointer over each of the remaining number styles, and then preview them in your document.

d. Click the number style with the **1)**.
   The Numbering Library gallery closes, and the number 1) is added to the current line of text, which is now indented. The Numbering button remains toggled on when the insertion point is located in a paragraph line where numbering has been applied.

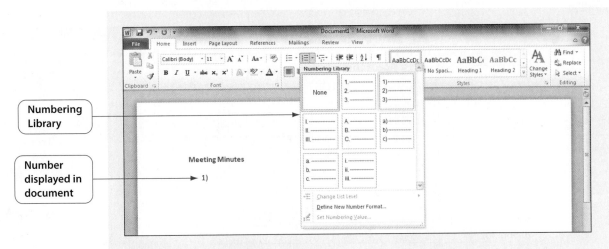

Numbering Library

Number displayed in document

Figure 14 Numbering Library

e. With the insertion point located after the number, type Meeting was called to order at 2:15 pm.

f. Press Enter twice to end the numbered list.

Opening Dialog Boxes and Task Panes

Some Ribbon groups include a diagonal arrow in the bottom-right corner of the group section, called a **Dialog Box Launcher** 🔲 that opens a corresponding dialog box or task pane. Hovering the mouse pointer near the Dialog Box Launcher will display a ScreenTip to indicate more information. Click the Dialog Box Launcher to open a **dialog box**, which is a window that provides more options or settings beyond those provided on the Ribbon. It often provides access to more precise or less frequently used commands along with the commands offered on the Ribbon; thus using a dialog box offers the ability to apply many related options at the same time and located in one place. As you can see in Figure 15, many dialog boxes organize related information into tabs. In the Paragraph dialog box shown in the figure, the active Indents and Spacing tab shows options to change alignment, indentation, and spacing, with another tab that offers options and settings for Line and Page Breaks. A **task pane** is a smaller window pane that often appears to the side of the program window and offers options or helps you to navigate through completing a task or feature.

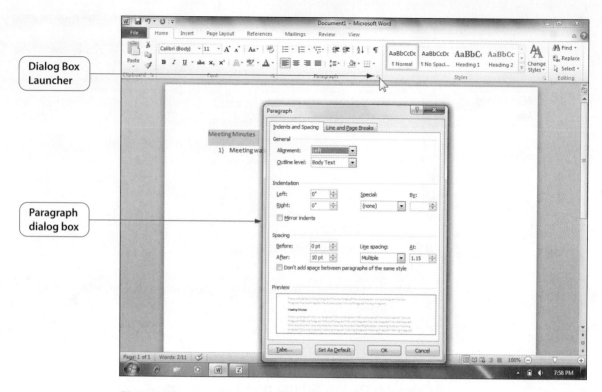

Dialog Box Launcher

Paragraph dialog box

Figure 15 Paragraph Dialog Box Launcher with dialog box overlay

To Open the Format Cells Dialog Box

a. On the taskbar, click **Excel** to make Excel the active program.

b. Click cell **A2**, the first cell in the second row.

c. Click the Home tab, if necessary. The Number group options appear on the Ribbon.

d. Click the **Dialog Box Launcher** in the Number group. The Format Cells dialog box opens with the Number tab displayed.

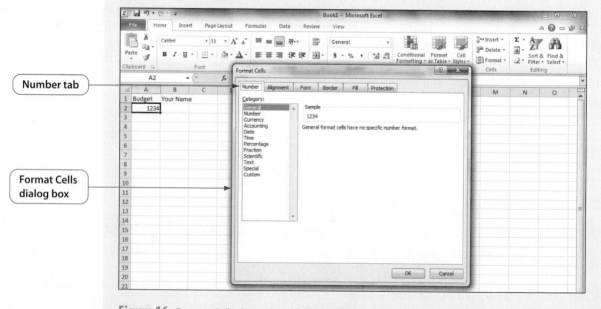

Number tab

Format Cells dialog box

Figure 16 Format Cells dialog box showing the Number tab

e. Under Category, click **Number**. Click the **Use 1000 Separator (,)** check box.

f. Click the **Alignment tab**. Notice, the dialog box displays options that are related to alignment of the text. If you needed to make changes, you could use the check box options or the arrows to display a list of options when appropriate to do so.

g. Click the **Fill tab**, and then click to select **Purple, Accent 4, Lighter 60%**, third row in the eighth column, which will show in the Sample box. Click **OK**. The format changes are made to the number, and the fill color is applied.

Using Contextual Tools

Whenever you see the term "contextual tools," this usually refers to tools that only appear when needed for specific tasks. Some tabs, toolbars, and menus are displayed as you work and only appear if a particular object is selected. Because these tools become available only as you need them, the workspace remains less cluttered.

A **contextual tab** is a Ribbon tab that contains commands related to selected objects so you can manipulate, edit, and format the objects. Examples of objects that can be selected to produce contextual tabs include a table, a picture, a shape, or a chart. A contextual tab appears to the right of the standard Ribbon tabs. For example, Figure 17 shows the Picture Tools Format tab that displays when a picture is selected. The contextual tabs function in the same way as a standard tab on the Ribbon. The contextual tab disappears when you click outside the target object (in the file) to deselect the object. In some instances, contextual tabs can also appear as you switch views.

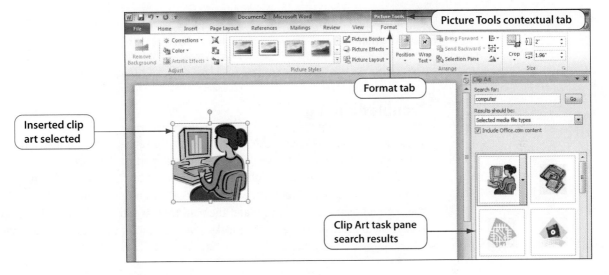

Figure 17 Contextual tab for Picture Tools in Word

Accessing the Mini Toolbar

The **Mini toolbar** appears after text is selected and contains buttons for the most commonly used formatting commands, such as font, font size, font color, center alignment, indents, bold, italic, and underline. The Mini toolbar button commands vary for each Office program. The toolbar appears transparent whenever text is selected and comes into clearer view as you move the pointer towards the toolbar. When you move the pointer over the Mini toolbar, it comes into full view, allowing you to click the formatting button or buttons. It disappears if you move the pointer away from the toolbar, press a key, or click in the workspace. All the commands on the Mini toolbar are available on the Ribbon; however, the Mini toolbar offers quicker access to common commands because you do not have to move the mouse pointer far away from selected text for these commands.

To Access the Mini Toolbar

a. If necessary, on the taskbar, click **Excel** [icon]. Click cell **A3**, the first cell in the third row of the worksheet.

b. Type Expenses.

c. Press [Enter]. Text has been entered in cell A3, and cell A4 is selected.

d. Type FY 2013, and then press [Enter]. The year has been entered in cell A4, and cell A5 is selected.

e. Double-click cell **A3** to place the insertion point in the cell. Double-clicking a cell enables you to enter edit mode for the cell text.

f. Double-click cell **A3** again to select the text. The text appears to be opposite when selected (white text on a black background), and as you move the pointer upwards, the transparent Mini toolbar starts to appear and come into view directly above the selected text.

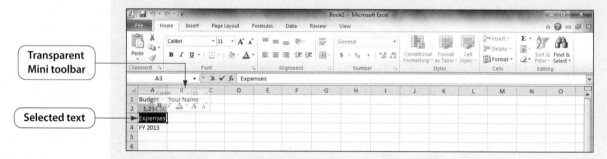

Figure 18 Transparent Mini toolbar and selected text

g. Move the pointer over the Mini toolbar. Now it is completely visible.

Troubleshooting

If you are having a problem with the Mini toolbar disappearing, you may have inadvertently moved the mouse pointer to another part of the document. If you need to redisplay the Mini toolbar, right-click the selected text and the Mini toolbar will appear along with a shortcut menu. Once you select an option on the Mini toolbar, the shortcut menu will disappear and the Mini toolbar will remain while in use (or repeat the previous two steps, then make sure the pointer stays over the toolbar).

h. On the Mini toolbar, click **Italic** [I].

The text in cell A3 is now italicized. The Mini toolbar remains visible allowing you to click other buttons.

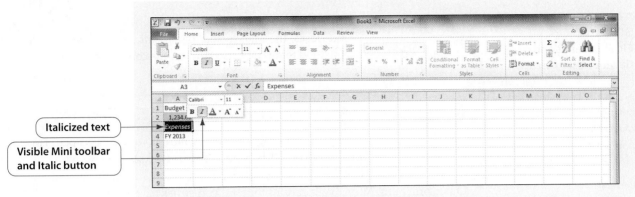

Italicized text

Visible Mini toolbar and Italic button

Figure 19 Cell A3 is now formatted with Italic from the Mini toolbar

i. Press Enter. Cell A4 is selected, and the Mini toolbar disappears.

Opening Shortcut Menus

Shortcut menus are also context sensitive and enable you to quickly access commands that are most likely needed in the context of the task being performed. A **shortcut menu** is a list of commands related to a selection that appears when you right-click (click the right mouse button). This means you can access popular commands without using the Ribbon. Included are commands that perform actions, commands that open dialog boxes, and galleries of options that provide Live Preview. As noted previously, the Mini toolbar opens when you click the right mouse button. If you click a button on the Mini toolbar, the shortcut menu closes, and the Mini toolbar remains open allowing you to continue formatting your selection. For example, right-click selected text to open the shortcut menu *and* the Mini toolbar; the menu contains text-related commands such as Font, Paragraph, Bullets, Numbering, and Styles, as well as other program specific commands related to text.

To Use the Shortcut Menu to Delete Content

a. Right-click cell **A1**. A shortcut menu opens with commands related to common tasks you can perform in a cell, along with the Mini toolbar.

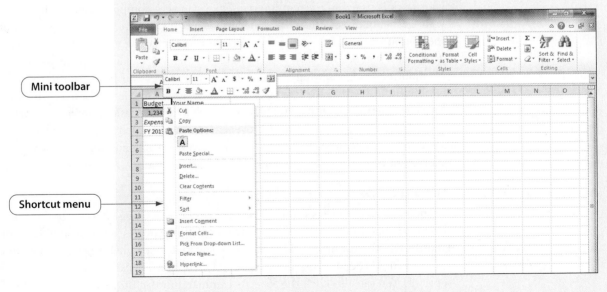

Mini toolbar

Shortcut menu

Figure 20 Shortcut menu and Mini toolbar

Workshop 1

b. On the shortcut menu, click **Clear Contents**.

The shortcut menu closes, the Mini toolbar disappears, and the text in cell A1 is removed. This is one method that can be used to clear the contents of a cell.

SIDE NOTE
Closing Menus and Galleries Using Escape
Esc can be used to cancel or close an unwanted short-cut menu, gallery menu, or Mini toolbar without making a selection.

Manipulating Files in the Office Environment

Creating, opening, saving, and closing files are the most common tasks performed in any Office program. These tasks can all be completed in Backstage view, which is accessed from the File tab shown in Figure 21. These processes are basically the same for all the Office programs. When you start a program, you either have to create a new file or open an existing one. When you start Word, Excel, or PowerPoint, the program opens a blank file, which is ready for you to begin working on a new document, workbook, or presentation. When you start Access, the New tab in Backstage view opens, displaying options for creating a new database or opening an existing one.

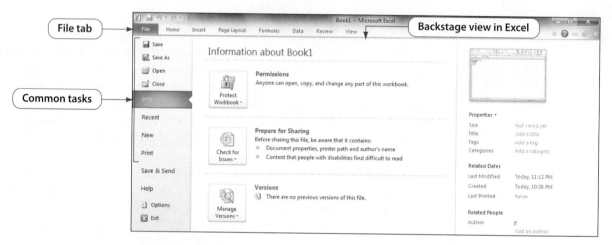

Figure 21 Backstage view in Excel

Working with Files

While working on an Office file, whether creating a new file or modifying an existing file, your work is stored in the temporary memory on your computer, not on the hard drive or your USB flash drive. Any work done will be lost if you were to exit the program, turn off the computer, or experience a power failure without saving your work. To prevent losing your work, you need to save your work and remember to save frequently—at least every 10 minutes or after adding many changes. That saves you from having to recreate any work you did prior to the last save. You can save files to the hard drive, which is located inside the computer; to an external drive, such as a USB flash drive; or to a network storage device. Office has an AutoRecovery feature (previously called AutoSave) that will attempt to recover any changes made to a document if something goes wrong, but this should not be relied upon as a substitute for saving your work manually.

Saving a File

To quickly save a file, simply click Save 🔲 on the Quick Access Toolbar or use the keyboard shortcut Ctrl+S. Backstage view also provides access to the Save command and the Save As command. The first time you save a new file, it behaves the same as the Save As command and the Save As dialog box opens. This allows you to specify the save options. You can also click the Save As command in Backstage view to open the Save As dialog box when saving for the first time, or use the Save As command when you want to save an existing file as a copy or separate version—possibly with a different name. In the Save As dialog box, you name the file and specify the location in which to save it, similar to the first time you save a file. Once you save a file, the simple shortcut methods to save any changes to the file work fine to update the existing file. No dialog box will open to save after the first time—as long as you do not need to change the file name or location as with the Save As command.

The first time a file is saved, it needs to be named. The file name includes the name you specify and a file extension assigned by the Office program to indicate the file type. The file extension may or may not be visible depending on your computer settings. By default, most computers do not display the file extension (only the file name). Use a descriptive name that accurately reflects the content of the document, workbook, presentation, or database, such as "January 2013 Budget" or "012013 Minutes." The descriptive name can include uppercase and lowercase letters, numbers, hyphens, spaces, and some special characters (excluding ? " / | < > * :) in any combination. Each Office program adds a period and a file extension after the file name to identify the program in which that file was created. Figure 22 shows the common default file extensions for Office 2010. File names can include a maximum of 255 characters including the extension (this includes the number of characters for the file path—the folder names to get to the file location). As a reminder, depending on how your computer is set up, you may or may not see the file extensions.

Application	Extension
Microsoft Word 2010	.docx
Microsoft Excel 2010	.xlsx
Microsoft PowerPoint 2010	.pptx
Microsoft Access 2010	.accdb

Figure 22 Default file extensions for Microsoft Office 2010

Real World Advice Sharing Files Between Office Versions

Different Office versions are not always compatible. The general rule is that files created in an older version can always be opened in a newer version, but not the other way around (a 2010 Office file is not easily opened in an older version of Office). With this in mind, maybe the company you work for is using Office 2010 and another company you need to share files with is using Office 2003. The concern is, prior to Office 2007 different file extensions were used. For example, .doc was used for Word files instead of .docx, .xls instead of .xlsx for Excel, and so on. It is still possible to save the Office 2010 files in a previous format version. To save in one of these formats, use the Save As command, and in the Save As dialog box, click the Save as type option near the bottom of the dialog box. From the list, click the 97-2003 format option. If the file is already in the previous format, it will open in Office 2010 and save with the same format in which it was created.

To Save a File

a. On the taskbar, click **Word** to make Word the active program.

b. Click the **File tab**. Backstage view opens with command options and tabs for managing files, opening existing files, saving, printing, and exiting Word.

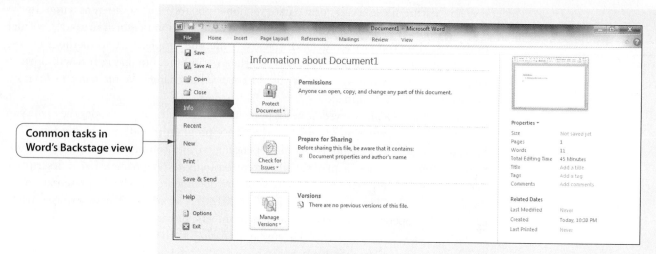

Common tasks in Word's Backstage view

Figure 23 Backstage view in Word

c. Click **Save As**.

The Save As dialog box opens. This provides the opportunity to enter a file name and a storage location. The default storage location is the Documents folder, and the suggested file name is the first few words of the first line of the document.

d. Click the **File name** box, and if necessary, highlight the current suggested file name. Navigate to where you are storing your files, and then type Lastname_Firstname_cf01_ws01_Minutes in the File name box replacing Lastname_Firstname with your last name and first name. This descriptive file name will help you more easily identify the file.

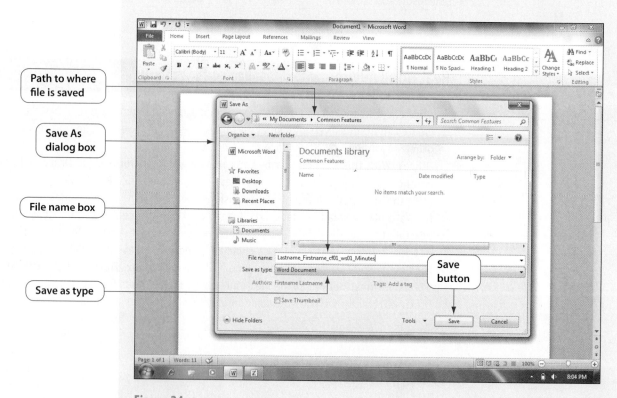

Path to where file is saved

Save As dialog box

File name box

Save as type

Save button

Figure 24 Save As dialog box

e. Click the **Save** button. The Save As dialog box closes, and the name of your file appears on the Word window title bar.

f. Click **Excel** on the taskbar to make Excel the active file, repeat Steps b through e, saving the file you created as Lastname_Firstname_cf01_ws01_Budget.

Modifying Saved Files

Saved files only contain what was in the file the last time it was saved. Any changes made after the file was saved are only stored in the computer's memory and are not saved with the file. It is important to remember to save often—after making changes—so the file is updated to reflect its current contents.

Remember, it is not necessary to use the Save As dialog box once a file has been saved unless you want a copy of the file with a different name or you want to store it in a different location.

To Modify a Saved File

a. Click **Word** on the taskbar to make the Word document the active window.

b. Make sure the insertion point is in the last line, below the numbered text. Type Today's date (the date you are doing this exercise), and then press Enter.

c. On the Quick Access Toolbar, click **Save**. The changes you made to the document have just been saved to the file stored in the location you selected earlier. Recall that no dialog boxes will open for the Save command after the first time it has been saved.

Real World Advice | Saving Files Before Closing

It is recommended that files be saved before closing them or exiting a program. However, most programs have an added safeguard or warning dialog box to remind you to save if you attempt to close a file without saving your changes first. The warning dialog box offers three options. Click Save, and the file will be saved with any new changes. Click Don't Save if you do not want any of the changes added to the file, and the file will close without saving or adding any changes since the last Save command was applied. Click Cancel if you changed your mind about closing the program and want to get back into the file before you close the program. This warning feature helps to ensure that you have the most current version of the file saved.

Closing a File

When you are ready to close a file, you can click the Close command on the File tab in Backstage view. If the file you close is the only file open for that particular program, the program window remains open with no file in the window. You can also close a file by using the Close button in the top-right corner of the window. However, if that is the only file open, the file and program will close.

To Modify and Close a Document

a. With the insertion point on the line under the date in the Word document, type your course number and section, replacing course number and section with the course and section you are in, on this line and press Enter. The text you typed should appear below the date.

b. Click the **File tab** to open Backstage view.

c. Click **Close**. A warning dialog box opens, asking if you want to save the changes made to the document.

d. Click **Save**.

   The document closes after saving changes, but the Word program window remains open. You are able to create new files or open previously saved files. If multiple Word documents are open, only the document you closed will close. The other documents will remain available.

Opening a File

You create a new file when you open a blank document, workbook, presentation, or database. If you want to work on a previously created file, you must first open it. When you open a file, it transfers a copy of the file from the file's storage location to the computer's temporary memory and displays it on the monitor's screen. There is a copy on the drive and in your computer's memory.

When opening files downloaded from the Internet, accessed from a shared network, or received as an attachment in e-mail, you may sometimes run across a file in a read-only format called Protected View, as shown in Figure 25. In **Protected View**, the file contents can be seen and read, but you are not able to edit, save, or print the contents until you enable editing. If you were to see the information bar shown in Figure 25, and you trust the source of the file, simply click the Enable Editing button on the information bar.

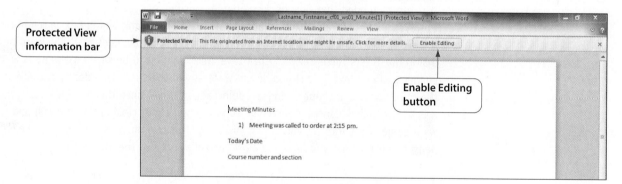

Figure 25 Open document in Protected View

To Reopen a Document

a. In Word, click the **File tab** to display Backstage view.

b. Click **Open**. The Open dialog box is displayed.

c. In the Open dialog box, click the **disk drive** in the left pane where you are saving your files. Navigate through the folder structure, and then click **Lastname_Firstname_cf01_ws01_Minutes**.

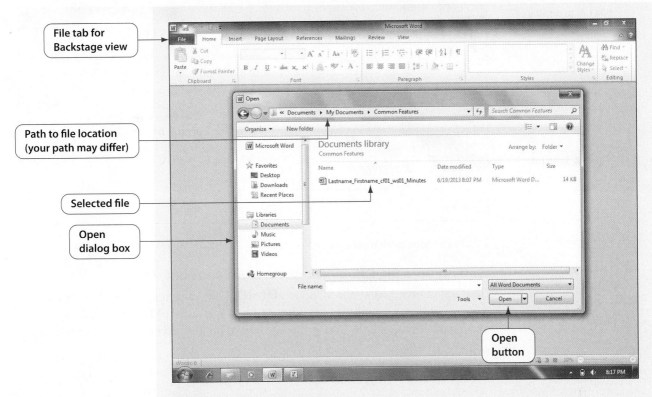

File tab for Backstage view

Path to file location (your path may differ)

Selected file

Open dialog box

Open button

Figure 26 Open dialog box

d. Click **Open**. The file opens in the Word program window.

Sharing Files Using Windows Live SkyDrive

Many times you create files in order to share them with other people. You can share files by attaching the file to an e-mail to send to someone else to read or use. Sometimes you collaborate with others by posting files on a blog. Tools for this can be found on the File tab in Backstage view, on the Save & Send tab.

When a file is sent via e-mail, a copy of the file can be attached, a link can be sent, or you can include a copy of the file in a PDF, XPS, or other file format. The file can also be saved to an online workspace where it can be made available to others for collaboration and review. The Save to Web option on the Save & Send tab in Backstage view gives you access to Windows Live **SkyDrive**, which is an online workspace provided by Microsoft. SkyDrive's online filing cabinet is a free Windows Live service. As of this writing, you are provided with 7 GB of password-protected online file storage. This makes it possible for you to store, access, and share files online from almost anywhere. This personal workspace comes with a Public folder for saving files to share, as well as a My Documents folder for saving files you want to keep private. (As of this writing, SkyDrive is not available for Access.) Figure 27 shows the Save to Web options on the Save & Send tab in Backstage view of Word.

Files saved to an online workspace can be edited by more than one person at the same time. The changes are recorded in the file with each author's name and the date of the change. A web browser is used to access and edit the files, and you can choose who can have access to the files.

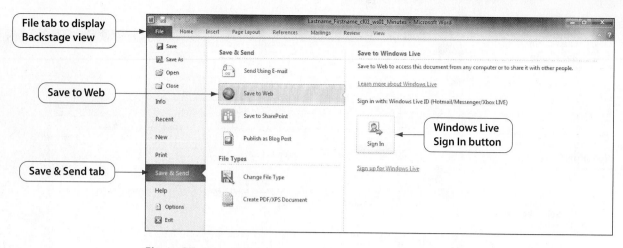

File tab to display Backstage view

Save to Web

Save & Send tab

Windows Live Sign In button

Figure 27 Save to Web options

Setting up a SkyDrive (Windows Live) Account

To use SkyDrive, you need a Windows Live ID. You can sign up for an ID at no cost. After you sign in, you can create new folders and save files into the folders. SkyDrive is a small section of Windows Live. You will need to have Internet access to complete this exercise.

To Set Up and Create a New Document in SkyDrive

a. On the taskbar, click **Internet Explorer** to open Internet Explorer; or alternatively, click the **Start** button, point to **All Programs**, and then click **Internet Explorer** to open the program.

b. In the Address bar, type skydrive.live.com and press Enter.

c. If you already have a Windows Live account, sign in. If not, click the **Sign Up** button on the left side of the page. Follow the steps to set up an account.

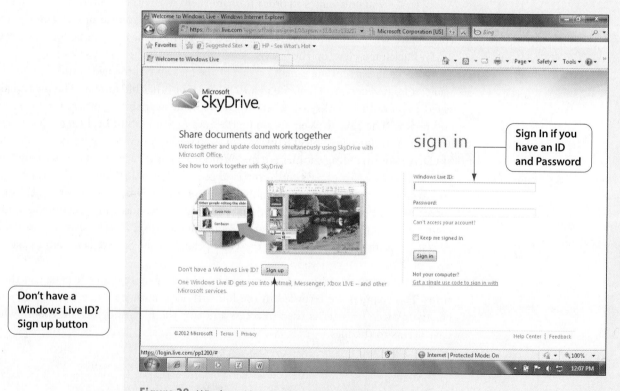

Sign In if you have an ID and Password

Don't have a Windows Live ID? Sign up button

Figure 28 Windows Live sign in or Sign up page

d. Once your ID is created, you can sign in. Once you sign in you will see your SkyDrive with areas on the left side: Files, Documents, and Photos.

e. To create a new document, presentation, or workbook, click the **SkyDrive** button at the top of the screen. On the drop-down menu, click **New Word document**, name the document, and then click **Create**. Type Firstname Lastname in the document, replacing Firstname and Lastname with your own name, click the **File tab**, and then click **Save**.

f. If you want to share this file with others, you need to click the **File tab** and then click **Share**. To add the people you want to share with, in the To: text box type the e-mail address, you can add an optional message, and then click **Send**.

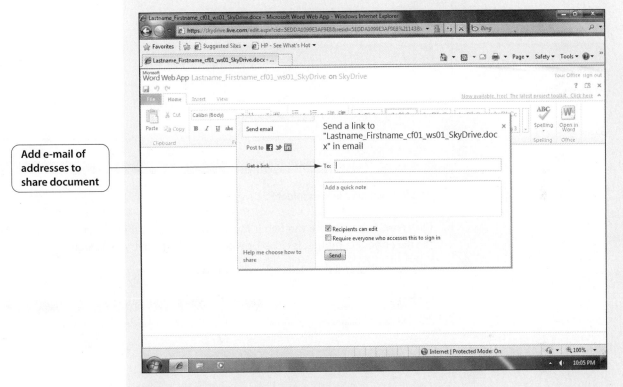

Add e-mail of addresses to share document

Figure 29 Sharing a document in SkyDrive

g. To return to your folders, click the **Close** button in the top-right corner of the document. Your document should appear in the Files list because it was not shared.

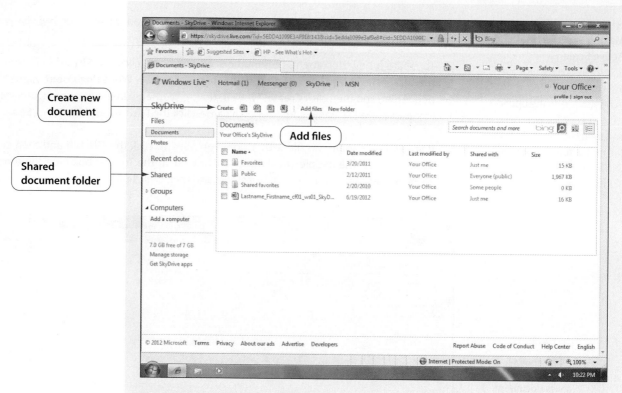

Figure 30 Document in Files folder

h. Click **New folder**. Name the folder **My Documents**, and then press Enter. Make sure the file on your computer is closed, before uploading it in the next step.

i. Click **Add files**, and then select them from your computer.

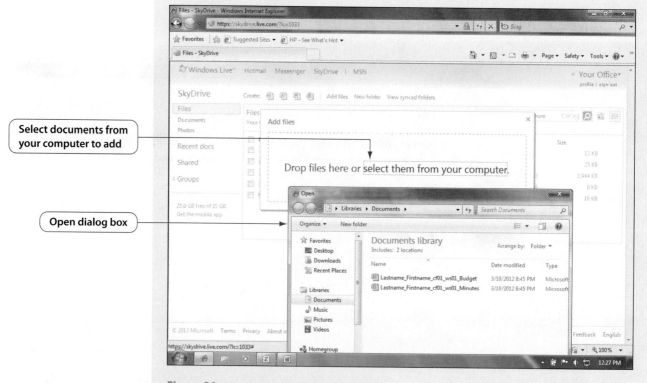

Figure 31 Uploading a file from your computer

j. Navigate to the location where your student files are stored. Select the file **Lastname_Firstname_cf01_ws01_Minutes**, and then click **Open**. The file will upload to your SkyDrive. You will be returned to the My Documents folder with your newly uploaded file.

k. To delete a file from the folder, select the file by selecting the check box, and then click **Delete** from the menu on the right side. If you wish to keep the file on SkyDrive click **No**. Click **sign out** to exit SkyDrive, located in the top-right corner under your sign in name. Close **Internet Explorer**.

Getting Help

If you require additional information about a feature or are not sure how to perform a task, make sure you acquaint yourself with the Office Help button and how to use it. In addition, do not overlook the ScreenTips within the program, which can also offer guidance along the way.

Viewing ScreenTips

ScreenTips are small windows that display descriptive text when you rest the mouse pointer over an object or button. You just need to point to a button or object in one of the Office applications to display its ScreenTip. In addition to the button's name, a ScreenTip might include the keyboard shortcut if one is available, a description of the command's function, and possibly more information. If you press $F1$ while displaying some ScreenTips it will open the Help file to the relevant topic displayed.

To Open Help

a. If necessary, on the taskbar, click **Word** to make Word the active program.

b. Point to **Microsoft Word Help** in the top-right corner of the window. The ScreenTip is displayed with the button's name, its keyboard shortcut, and a brief description.

c. Click the **Home tab**, and then point to the **Format Painter** button in the Clipboard group to display the ScreenTip. With the mouse pointer still over the Format Painter button and the ScreenTip showing, press the $F1$ key and notice that the Help window opens with information on how to use the Format Painter. Scroll down and read through the information. When you are done, click the **Close** button in the top-right corner of the Word Help window.

Using the Help Window

The Help window provides detailed information on a multitude of topics, as well as access to templates, training videos installed on your computer, and content available on Office.com, the website maintained by Microsoft that provides access to the latest information and additional Help resources. To access the contents at Office.com you must have access to the Internet from the computer. If there is no Internet access, only the files installed on the computer will be displayed in the Help window.

Each program has its own Help window. From each program's Help window you can find information about the Office commands and features as well as step-by-step instructions for using them. There are two ways to locate Help topics—the search function and the topic list.

To search the Help system on a desired topic, type the topic in the search box and click Search. Once a topic is located, you can click a link to open it. Explanations and step-by-step instructions for specific procedures will be presented. There is also a Table of

Contents pane, which displays a variety of topics to choose from when exploring various Help subjects and topics. It is organized similar to a book's table of contents. To access a subject or topic, click the subject links to display the subtopic links, and then click a subtopic link to display Help information for that topic.

SIDE NOTE
Help Shortcut
For those who prefer keyboard shortcuts, pressing F1 is the shortcut to access Help.

To Search Help for Information about the Ribbon in Excel

a. On the taskbar, click **Excel** [icon] to make Excel the active program.

b. Click **Microsoft Excel Help** [icon]. The Excel Help window opens.

c. If the Table of Contents is not displayed on the left side of the Help window, click the **Show Table of Contents** button [icon] on the toolbar of the Help window. Scroll down and notice the list of topics. Click the **Charts** topic and notice the subtopics displayed. Click **Charts** again to close the topic.

d. Click in the **Type words to search for** box, and then type ribbon.

e. Click the **Search button arrow**. On the displayed Search menu, notice that options for both the online content—if you are connected to the Internet—and local content from your computer are available in the list.

f. If the computer has Internet access, verify there is a check mark next to **All Excel** in the Content from Office.com list. If you are not connected to the Internet, click **Excel Help** in the Content from this computer list.

g. Click the **Search** button. The Help window displays a list of the topics related to the keyword "ribbon" in the right pane.

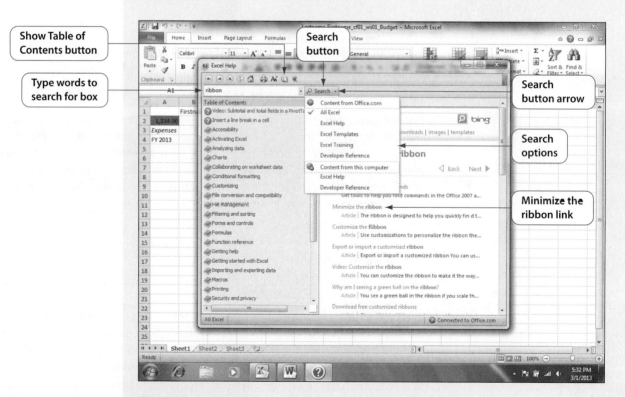

Figure 32 Excel Help

h. Scroll through the list to review the Help topics.

i. Click the **Minimize the ribbon** link from the list of results.

j. Read the information, and then click the links within this topic to explore how Help links work.

k. On the Help window title bar, click **Close** [×] to close the window.

Printing a File

There are times you will need a paper copy, also known as a hard copy, of an Office document, spreadsheet, or presentation. Before printing, review and preview the file and adjust the print settings as needed. Many options are available to fit various printing needs, such as the number of copies to print, the printing device to use, and the portion of the file to print. The print settings vary slightly from program to program. It is advisable that you check the file's print preview to ensure the file will print as you intended. Doing a simple print preview will help to avoid having to reprint your document, workbook, or presentation, which requires additional paper, ink, and energy resources.

To Print a File

a. On the taskbar, click **Word** [W] to make Word the active program.

b. If necessary, open the **Lastname_Firstname_cf01_ws01_Minutes** file.

c. Click the **File tab** to open Backstage view.

d. Click the **Print tab**. The Print settings and Print Preview appears.

e. Verify that the Copies box displays **1**.

f. Verify that the correct printer (as directed by your instructor) appears on the Printer button (your printer choices may vary). If the correct printer is not displayed, click the Printer button arrow, and click to choose the correct or preferred printer from the list of available printers.

g. If your instructor asks you to print the document, click the Print button.

Exiting Programs

When you have completed your work with the Office program, you should exit it. You can exit the program with either a button or a command. You can use the Exit command from Backstage view or the Close button on the top-right side of the title bar. Recall that if you have not saved the final version of the file, a dialog box opens, asking whether you want to save your changes. Clicking the Save button in the dialog box saves the file, closes the file, and then exits the program as long as other files are not open within the same program.

Exiting programs when you are finished with them helps save system resources and keeps your Windows desktop and taskbar uncluttered, as well as prevents data from being accidentally lost.

To Exit Office Applications

a. On the Word title bar, click **Close** [×].
Both the Word document and the Word program close. Excel should be visible again.

b. Click the **File tab** to open Backstage view, and then click **Exit**. If a dialog box opens asking if you want to save the changes made to the workbook, click Don't Save because no changes need to be saved.

c. The workbook closes without saving a copy, and the Excel program closes.

Concept Check

1. Which application would you use to write a memo?

2. Explain the main purpose for using Backstage view.

3. What is the Quick Access Toolbar?

4. Which tab on the Ribbon would you use to change the font settings?

5. What are the advantages of using SkyDrive instead of a USB flash drive?

Key Terms

Backstage view 66
Contextual tab 73
Dialog box 71
Dialog Box Launcher 71
Document 58
Graphic 58
Information management
 program 59
Key Tip 69

Keyboard shortcut 69
Live Preview 70
Maximize 63
Mini toolbar 73
Minimize 63
Minimize the Ribbon button 67
Protected View 80
Quick Access Toolbar 69
Relational database 59

Restore Down 63
Ribbon 66
ScreenTip 85
Shortcut menu 75
SkyDrive 81
Table 58
Task pane 71
Thumbnail 62
Workbook 59

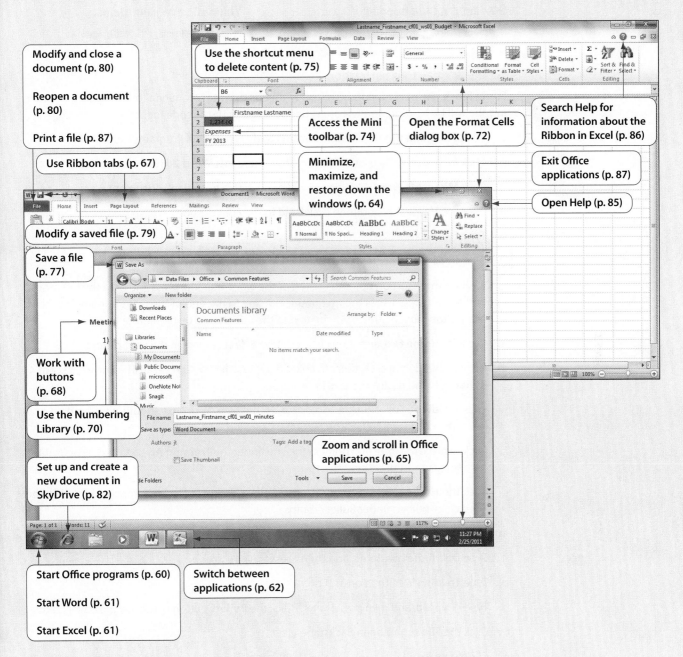

Modify and close a document (p. 80)

Reopen a document (p. 80)

Print a file (p. 87)

Use Ribbon tabs (p. 67)

Use the shortcut menu to delete content (p. 75)

Access the Mini toolbar (p. 74)

Open the Format Cells dialog box (p. 72)

Search Help for information about the Ribbon in Excel (p. 86)

Minimize, maximize, and restore down the windows (p. 64)

Exit Office applications (p. 87)

Open Help (p. 85)

Modify a saved file (p. 79)

Save a file (p. 77)

Work with buttons (p. 68)

Use the Numbering Library (p. 70)

Set up and create a new document in SkyDrive (p. 82)

Zoom and scroll in Office applications (p. 65)

Start Office programs (p. 60)

Start Word (p. 61)

Start Excel (p. 61)

Switch between applications (p. 62)

Figure 33 Working with the Common Features Final

Student data file needed:

New, blank Word document

You will save your file as:

Lastname_Firstname_cf01_ws01_Agenda

Creating an Agenda

Human
Resources

Susan Brock, the manager of the gift shop, needs to write an agenda for the upcoming training she will be holding. You will assist her by creating the agenda for her.

a. Click **Start**, and then click **All Programs** to display the All Programs list.

b. Click **Microsoft Office**, and then point to **Microsoft Word 2010**.

c. Click **Microsoft Word 2010**. Word will open with a new blank document.

d. Click the **Home** tab, and then click **Bold** in the Font group.

e. Type TRAINING AGENDA, and then press Enter.

f. Click **Bold** to toggle the feature off.

g. Position the insertion point to the left of the word Training, press and hold the left mouse button and drag across the text of the first line to the end of the word Agenda, and then release the mouse button. All the text in the line should be highlighted.

h. Click the **Home tab**, and then click the **Text Effects arrow** in the Font group.

i. Point to, but do not click, the fifth color in the fourth row, **Gradient Fill – Purple, Accent 4, Reflection** and notice the Live Preview.

j. Click **Gradient Fill – Purple, Accent 4, Reflection**. Your text should now be bold and have the purple with reflection text effect applied.

k. Click to place the insertion point in the line under the **Training Agenda** text. Type Today's date (the current date), and then press Enter twice.

l. Click the **Home tab**, and then click the **Bullets arrow** in the Paragraph group. Click the filled circle button under Bullet Library.

m. Type Welcome trainees 2:00 pm, and then press Enter.

n. Type Distribute handouts, and then press Enter.

o. Type Training, and then press Enter.

p. Type Wrap-Up, and then press Enter. Click the **Bullets** button to turn off the bullet feature.

q. Click the **File tab** to open Backstage view.

r. Click **Save As**.

s. In the Navigation Pane, navigate to where you are saving your files. In the File name box, delete the existing file name, and then type Lastname_Firstname_cf01_ws01_Agenda.

t. Click **Save**.

u. Click **Close** in the top-right corner of the title bar to close the document and exit Word.

Student data file needed:
cf01_ws01_Banquet

You will save your file as:
Lastname_Firstname_cf01_ws01_Budget_Update

Using the Ribbon for Event Planning

Finance & Accounting

You have been asked to make some changes to the budget spreadsheet for the upcoming book publisher's conference. The publishers will be at the resort for the weekend and will be renting rooms and having a banquet dinner Saturday night. You will be working on a small portion of the banquet budget for the event planning and catering manager. You will need to apply some formatting so the document is not plain.

a. Click **Start**, and then click **All Programs** to display the All Programs list.

b. Click **Microsoft Office**, and then point **to Microsoft Excel 2010**.

c. Click **Microsoft Excel 2010**. Excel starts with a new blank workbook.

d. Click the **File tab** to open Backstage view.

e. Click **Open**.

f. In the Open dialog box, click the disk drive in the left pane where your student data files are located. Navigate through the folder structure, click **cf01_ws01_Budget**, and then click **Open**.

g. If necessary, click the Home tab.

h. Click cell **A1** to make it the active cell. Click **Bold** in the Font group to make the text Banquet Budget bold.

i. Highlight column **B** by placing the mouse pointer over column letter B and clicking when the mouse pointer displays a down arrow over the B. Click the **Accounting Number Format** button in the Number group.

j. Click the **File tab**, and then click **Save As**. In the Save As dialog box, navigate to where you are saving your files, and then type Lastname_Firstname_cf01_ws01_Budget_Update in the File name box. This descriptive file name will help you more easily identify the file.

k. Click **Save**.

l. Click the **File tab**, and then click **Exit**.

Student data file needed:
cf01_ps1_Agenda

You will save your file as:
Lastname_Firstname_cf01_ps1_Agenda_Updated

Adding More Formatting to a Document

Human Resources

Susan Brock, the manager of the gift shop, was very pleased with the training agenda you created. She decided she would like it a little more stylized. You have been asked to add some more custom formatting to the document.

a. Start **Word**, and then open **cf01_ps1_Agenda**.

b. Click the **Page Layout tab**, and then click **Margins** in the Page Setup group.

c. Change the Margins to **Wide**. This will provide space to take notes.

d. Position the insertion point to the left of the words **Training Agenda**, and then drag across the text of the first line to the end of the word **Agenda** to select the text. All the text in the line should be highlighted.

e. Click the **Home tab**, and then click the **Text Highlight Color arrow** in the Font group. Use Live Preview to view the available colors. Select **Turquoise**.

f. Click the **File tab**. Click **Save As** in Backstage view. Navigate to where you are saving your files. Save the updated file as Lastname_Firstname_cf01_ps1_Agenda_Updated.

g. Close the document. Close Word.

Perform 1: Perform in Your Career

Student data file needed:	You will save your file as:
New, blank Excel workbook	Lastname_Firstname_cf01_pf1_Training_Schedule

Creating a Training Schedule

Information Technology

One of the managers you worked for recommended you to Aidan Matthews, chief technology officer of the Red Bluff Golf Club. Aidan has asked you to create a training schedule in Excel for several of the trainings he is planning to schedule. The trainings include Windows 7, Word 2010, Excel 2010, and PowerPoint 2010. The trainings will be offered on Mondays, January 14, January 28, February 4, and February 11, 2013. Each training is three hours in length, with one hour between sessions. The first session starts at 9:00 am. There are two trainings per day. You will create an attractive schedule using features you worked with in this workshop.

a. Start **Excel**. Using the features of Excel, create a training spreadsheet that is attractive and easy to read. Some suggestions follow: Create column headings for the Applications, day and date and row headings for the name of the application. Format the date (under the Number group use the drop-down list to select long date), format the column headings, format a title for the workbook, use bold, colors, etc.

b. Save the file in your folder as Lastname_Firstname_cf01_pf1_Training_Schedule. Close Excel.

Student data file needed:

New, blank Word document

You will save your file as:

Lastname_Firstname_cf01_pf2_Critique

Improving the Look of Files

General Business

Prior to your tenure at the Red Bluff Golf Club, many different students passed through the doors as interns. You have been touted as an expert in how to format documents and spreadsheets. You have been asked to review a spreadsheet and a document and make suggestions on what to do to improve their look. Examine the following figures and answer the statements.

a. Open a new Word 2010 blank document.

b. List five items you would change in the document and why.

c. List five items you would change in the worksheet and why.

d. Save the file as **Lastname_Firstname_cf01_pf2_Critique**. Submit the file as directed.

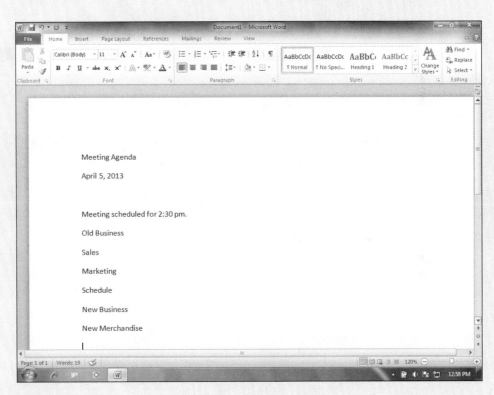

Figure 1 Word document

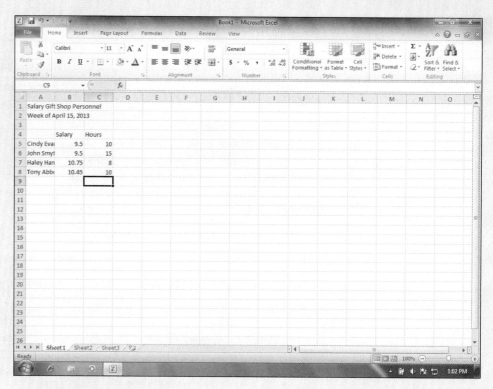

Figure 2 Excel worksheet

WORKSHOP 1

Reviewing and Modifying a Document

PREPARE CASE

Putts for Paws Golf Tournament Memo

General Business

Painted Paradise Golf Resort and Spa sponsors an annual charity golf tournament, with proceeds benefiting a different organization each year. This year, the tournament spotlights the Santa Fe Animal Center. The goal is to raise money for the center as well as to facilitate the adoption of as many animals as possible to loving homes. Your assignment is to review and edit a memorandum to employees of the hotel's event-planning staff. The memo provides a summary of tournament activities and sponsorship opportunities so the staff can answer questions and encourage participation.

photofriday / Shutterstock.com

Student data file needed for this workshop:

 w01_ws01_Putts

You will save your files as:

 Lastname_Firstname_w01_ws01_Putts   Lastname_Firstname_w01_ws01_Putts.pdf

Understanding Business Communication

Sales & Marketing

Each day you spend a great deal of time communicating with others, either orally or in writing. As you converse with others, you want your listeners to understand your meaning and to become engaged in the topic. It is equally important that written communication reflect your objectives and convey your messages exactly as you intend. Excellent communication skills are crucial in the success of a business—so much so that American businesses spend $3.1 billion annually in training people how to better communicate.

Business communication is defined as communication between members of an organization for the purpose of carrying out business activities. Always remember that the way you communicate verbally, and in writing, is often the first and most lasting impression that others have of you. In fact, communication skills are often the factor that sets you apart from others in a company. Its importance cannot be overstated. Often referred to as a *soft skill*, excellent written and oral communication abilities can identify you as one of the most valued employees in a business.

Communication is not a one-way street. It is not a monologue but is, instead, a dialogue. If your message is not interpreted by your audience exactly as you intended, then the communication has failed. Students often spend an inordinate amount of time developing technical skills in software and business operations, but they give too little credence to the importance of understanding the target audience and communicating on a level where both the sender and the receiver can understand each other. Regardless of the message topic, always take time to identify and understand your audience. In this section, you will explore the topic of business communication, identifying standard business letter styles and effective methods of communication.

Using Word Processing Software

Word processing is one of the most often cited reasons to use a computer. People in businesses, schools, and homes use word processing on a daily basis to create documents of all types. You can use word-processing software to create reports, letters, memos, newsletters, flyers, business cards, and many other documents. Within documents, you can include graphics, tables, charts, text boxes, and borders along with text. Obviously, word processing is a very creative application that enables you to work with more than just text. Although you can select from several word-processing software packages with a wide range of capability and cost, you should be aware that Microsoft Word is the leading word-processing program in terms of usage and sales. This textbook provides information on **Microsoft Word 2010**, which is Microsoft's most current version of word-processing software. Although Microsoft Word 2010 is a component of Microsoft Office 2010, you can also purchase it individually. In this section, you will explore the Word interface and learn to create, edit, and print documents.

Opening a Document

When you start Microsoft Word, you will see a blank document. As you work with the document, you will want to save it periodically to a flash drive or hard drive. Later, you can use Word to open the document so that you can edit, format, or print the document.

Real World Advice — Too Many Open Documents

Using Word, you can open multiple documents. When you do, each document is shown as an overlapped Word icon on the Windows taskbar. Unless there is a specific need to have several documents open, perhaps because you want to copy text from one to the other, it is best to work with only one document—or very few—open at a time. That way, you are not overly distracted by multiple Word windows and projects that require your attention.

myitlab
Workshop 1 Training

To Start Microsoft Word

a. Click the **Start** button.

b. Point to **All Programs**. Scroll up or down if necessary, click **Microsoft Office**, and select **Microsoft Word 2010**.

A blank Word document opens. Note the standard components of the Word interface, including the document area, Ribbon, and Quick Access Toolbar.

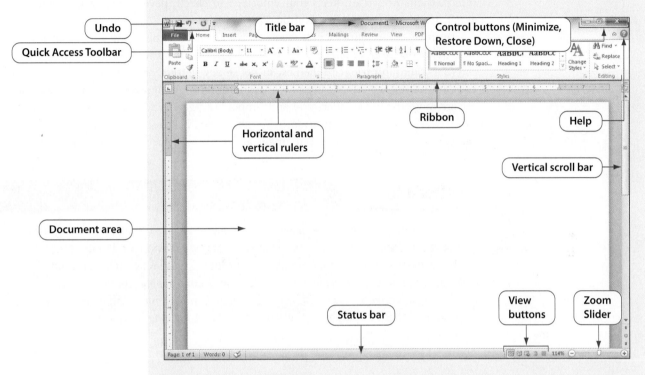

Figure 1   The Word interface

Troubleshooting

If you do not easily find Word in the All Programs list, you can click Start and then type Word in the Search box at the bottom of the Start menu. If Word is installed, you will see it in the list above. Simply click the search result to open Word.

Developing Effective Business Documents

When you talk with others, you get immediate feedback in the form of body language and conversation. Usually, you have an accurate feel for how your message is received, and you are able to elicit responses from your target audience. However, once a word is spoken, it cannot be retracted. Choose your words with care. On the contrary, you can give much more forethought to the selection of words included in written communication. Carefully considering your objectives and your audience, you can craft a well-worded document that achieves your purpose. Remember, though, that a document containing grammatical errors, misspellings, overly informal wording, "techspeak," or inaccurate facts might lead others to consider you careless or noncredible. Written documents can remain in circulation or filed away for a very long time, so you should use utmost care in composing letters, memos, e-mail, or any communication.

Before distributing anything in writing, review it several times, both for grammar, spelling, and proper wording, and to be certain that it communicates your message in a professional manner. If possible, have a trusted colleague provide feedback before you send a letter or memo, especially if the topic is sensitive or likely to be misunderstood. In the absence of body language, it can be difficult for a reader to understand your tone. Humor is especially difficult to convey in written communication. Even the use of upper-case letters and punctuation can mislead a reader and convey an unintended message. Your communication should be concise, with careful attention given to the wording and punctuation. Above all, keep your emotions in check, never airing your frustration or anger in any written communication.

Business documents include many forms of written communication. Some are considered *internal communication,* while others are *external communication.* Examples of written internal communication are memos, in-house newsletters, and e-mail. Effective internal communication can create a better work atmosphere and increase productivity as employees are more likely to understand and support the goals and objectives of the company. Effective external communication, through letters, brochures, reports, and newsletters, can encourage a healthy corporate image and serve to attract and retain customers.

Sales & Marketing

Real World Advice — Preparing Business Correspondence

Before writing any sort of document, you should give ample time to planning it. Ask yourself these questions first. Who is my *target audience*? Do I understand that audience and what they are likely to be looking for in my communication? What is the *purpose* of my document? How can I build *support* for my message? What *information* do I need to include? Though you may find it difficult at times, answering these questions is of utmost importance for every document.

Working with Business Correspondence

Types of business correspondence include letters, memos, resumes, applications, newsletters, flyers, reports, and brochures. You can find a wealth of information, in varying detail, related to these and other major categories of business correspondence, online or in books dedicated to business communication. With just a bit of study, you can learn to compose well-worded documents, including application letters, letters of inquiry, and internal newsletters.

This section of the workshop focuses on the technical aspects of letters and memos. At this point, you should understand the importance of planning a document and understanding your target audience. Now you will look at how to structure a letter and exactly what elements to include.

Real World Advice — Document Formats

Although you may be familiar with generally accepted styles for letters, memos, and even e-mail, always check with your place of employment when creating business documents. Some businesses have specific formats, or branding guidelines, that you should adhere to. For example, a company might require that the company logo be included in all correspondence or that a specific letterhead be used. There may be rules regarding the use of headers and footers. Become familiar with the specifics related to your workplace.

Quick Reference

A business letter should include the following items. Some are required and some are optional, as you will see in the following description. Refer to Figure 2 for a visual summary of letter components.

Heading—This includes the writer's address and the date of the letter. If you are using letterhead, you may not need to include an address.

Inside address—This shows the name and address of the recipient of the letter.

Salutation—This directly addresses the recipient by title and last name. It is followed by a colon, as in "Dear Mr. Durham:".

Subject or reference line—This can replace the salutation if you are not sure who will be receiving the letter. It can also be used in addition to a salutation.

Body—This is the message area, usually including several paragraphs.

Complimentary close—This is the letter ending, usually in the form of "Sincerely yours," although other possibilities include "Respectfully," "Respectfully yours," and "Sincerely." The complimentary close is always followed by a comma.

Signature block—This is most often two to four blank lines after the complimentary close and includes your typed name and title. The blank space above this block is where you sign your name. Whenever possible, include your position or title beneath your typed name.

End notations—This is one or more abbreviations or phrases that have important functions. They include *initials* (capital letters for the writer and lowercase letters beneath for the typist), *enclosures* (usually abbreviated "Enc" or "Encl" and followed by a very brief summary of the enclosure), and *copies* (an indication of any other recipients of the letter, such as "cc: Ms. Jane Clemmons").

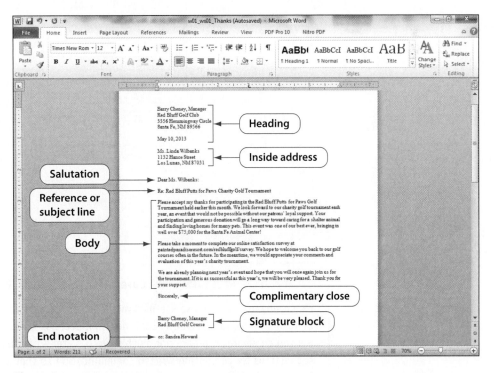

Figure 2   Components of a letter

Much less prescriptive than a letter, a memorandum is intended for internal distribution. It typically includes the word "Memo" or "Memorandum," followed by indication of the memo recipients, the sender of the memo, the memo subject, and the date.

Business letters should conform to an accepted letter style, as shown in Figure 3 and described next.

Block style—The entire letter is left-aligned and single-spaced and includes double-spacing between paragraphs.

Modified block style—The body of the letter is left-aligned and single-spaced. The heading (return address and date) and closing are aligned in the center of the page and there is a double-space between paragraphs.

Semiblock style—This is identical to the modified block style except that each paragraph is indented by 1/2".

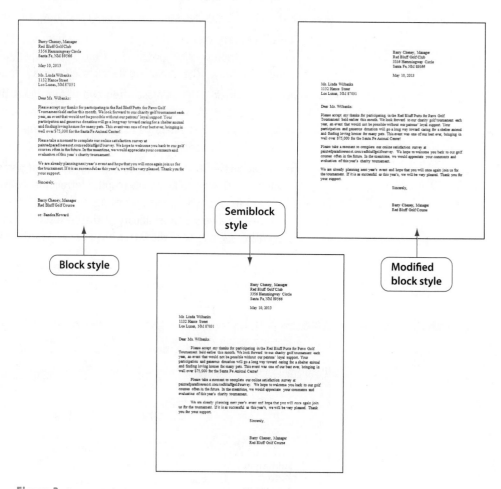

Figure 3 Letter styles

CONSIDER THIS | **Be Careful with Written Words**

Experts have suggested that e-mail messages are like postcards, in that they can be read by anyone involved in their delivery. Letters, memos, and any other form of written communication are not much more private. With that in mind, do you have any suggestions for composing written communication so that as much privacy as possible is maintained?

To Open a Document

a. Click the **File tab**, and then click **Open**. Click the disk drive in the left pane where your student data files are located. Navigate through the folder structure and double-click **w01_ws01_Putts**. A memorandum providing information on the upcoming Putts for Paws golf tournament opens.

b. Read through the memorandum, noting the various elements such as the header and body. You will find one or more misspelled words in the memo, which you will address later in this workshop.

Exploring the Word Interface

Figure 1 identifies elements of the Word interface. You were introduced to several of those items, such as the Quick Access Toolbar, the Ribbon, and the status bar, in the Common Features module. With only slight differences, those items serve a similar purpose in each of the main Office applications: Access, Excel, PowerPoint, and Word.

The Word interface is unique to other Office applications because it presents a large document area on which you can type. You might think of the document area as a piece of paper. As you type, the text automatically wraps from one line to the next. You should not press Enter at the end of each line. Only press Enter at the end of a paragraph or a distinct line, such as a date or salutation. The feature whereby Word automatically wraps text from one line to the next is called **word wrap**. At the end of each line, Word places a **soft return**. The placement of soft returns can change when you format a document with new margins or different text size because the position where a line ends might change.

When you press Enter, such as at the end of a paragraph, you create a **hard return**. Because the placement of a hard return does not change when text is reformatted, a margin or text change could create very awkward line separations in a document with unnecessary hard returns at the end of each line. Although you *cannot* remove soft returns, you *can* delete and insert hard returns. Later in this workshop, you will have a chance to use word wrap and experiment with hard and soft returns.

Because word processing is a keyboard-oriented application, you might want to minimize the time spent moving your hand from the keyboard to the mouse when you make a Ribbon selection. For example, you most often click a Ribbon tab to invoke an action, requiring that you move your hand from the keyboard to the mouse. If, instead, you could simply press a key to make a Ribbon selection, you would save time by not leaving the keyboard. Press [Alt] on the keyboard to display **Key Tips**, shown in Figure 4, then press a corresponding key to select a Ribbon item. Press [Alt] again to remove Key Tips, if you like.

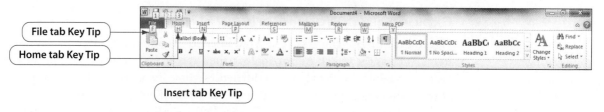

File tab Key Tip

Home tab Key Tip

Insert tab Key Tip

Figure 4 Key Tips

Changing the View

When you work with a Word document, you are likely to see not only the typed area, but top, bottom, left, and right margins. That *view* is called **Print Layout**, which is the default view. A **default** setting is one that is automatically prescribed unless you specify otherwise. You will most often want to view a document in Print Layout view because it shows all margins, headers, footers, graphics, and other features that will be displayed when a document is printed. It gives a close approximation to the way a document will actually appear in print.

Full **Screen Reading view** is much like Print Layout, except that it hides the Ribbon, providing more document space on the screen. If a document has many pages, Full Screen Reading view shows pages side by side, as if they were bound in a book.

To view a document as it would appear as a Web page, you can view the document in **Web Layout view**. When you create a report or lengthy document, you will likely include headings, subheadings, and other levels of detail. When that is the case, you can view the document in **Outline view** to show levels of organization and detail. You can expand or collapse detail to show only what is necessary. Outline view is often used as a springboard for a table of contents or a PowerPoint summary.

Draft view provides the most space possible for typing. It does not show margins, headers, footers, or other features, but it does include the Ribbon.

Showing Nonprinting Characters

Many keys, such as Spacebar, Enter, and Tab, actually insert **nonprinting characters** in a document when you press a key. For example, when you press [Tab], text is indented and a tab "character" is inserted, although the character is not shown when the document is printed. Sometimes called **formatting marks**, nonprinting characters are not displayed on the screen by default, but you can make a selection on the Ribbon to display them if you like.

Choosing to show or hide nonprinting characters is a matter of preference. As you gain experience working with Word, you will probably find that you often want to show nonprinting characters because doing so enables you to troubleshoot the document,

SIDE NOTE
Full Screen Reading View

When a document is shown in Full Screen Reading view, neither the status bar nor the Ribbon is available to select another view from. From Full Screen Reading view, you can change views by pressing [Esc] or clicking Close.

removing unnecessary tabs and spaces and adding others where they are needed. Earlier, you learned that when you press Enter, you actually insert a hard return. If you change the format of the document later, perhaps with different margins or spacing, the presence of hard returns can cause the document's lines to end awkwardly. At that point, if nonprinting characters are displayed, you can simply click before or after any unnecessary hard return and remove the character, returning lines of text to an attractive position (see Figure 5). Only if your document is set to display nonprinting characters can you actually see the hard returns so that you can easily remove them. Similarly, you can insert or remove other nonprinting characters such as tabs or spaces. Figure 5 shows a document with nonprinting characters displayed.

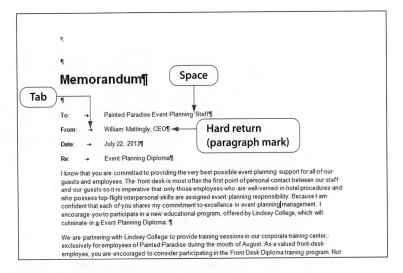

Figure 5 Nonprinting characters displayed

To Change the View and Show Nonprinting Characters

a. Click the **View tab**, and then click **Draft** in the Document Views group.

The Draft selection, along with other document views, is available in two areas within the Word interface. You can change a document view by making a selection in the Document Views group on the View tab or by selecting from options on the right side of the status bar. Document view options on the status bar are always available, regardless of which Ribbon tab is selected, so those selections are usually more convenient to access.

Troubleshooting

When you change the view, the document should be displayed in approximately the same size as before the change. If, however, the document's size changes dramatically so that it is difficult to read, click the View tab and click 100% in the Zoom group, as shown in Figure 6.

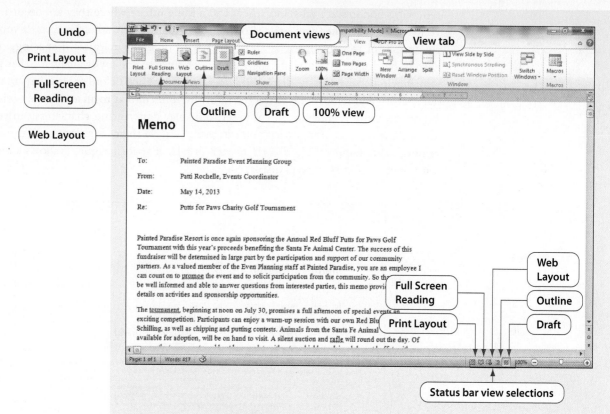

Figure 6 Changing the view

b. Click **Print Layout** in the Document Views group. This view shows a document with all margins displayed.

c. Click the **Home tab**, and then click **Show/Hide** ¶ in the Paragraph group, if necessary, to show nonprinting characters.

Troubleshooting

If nonprinting characters are already displayed, the display will be toggled off when you click Show/Hide. In that case, click Show/Hide once again to display them.

d. Click to place the insertion point before the paragraph mark—hard return—that is displayed just beneath the **Re:** line. Press Delete. The paragraph mark is removed, and the text moves up.

Troubleshooting

If you place the insertion point at the wrong location, the blank paragraph mark will not be deleted when you press Delete. If you make such a mistake, click Undo on the Quick Access Toolbar (see Figure 6) and repeat Step d.

SIDE NOTE
Troubleshooting with Nonprinting Characters
When you click Show/Hide to show formatting marks, you might make the job of troubleshooting a document a little easier. For example, an awkwardly split paragraph might be the result of an unnecessary hard return. Also, if Word identifies an area as grammatically incorrect, it might simply be that you have too many spaces between words. In both cases, with nonprinting characters displayed, you can more easily identify those problems.

Displaying the Ruler

When you work with tabs and indents, you need to specify placement in terms of inches. For example, you might want to place a tab stop 1/2" from the left margin. Or perhaps you plan to indent a quote for a research paper 1" from both the left and right margins. Tabs, indents, and other paragraph settings are covered later in this module, so you may not be familiar with those terms yet. However, you can see that measurement is a necessary element for tabs, indents, and many other settings in Word. The use of a **ruler** can simplify those settings.

Quick Reference Display the Ruler

1. Click the View tab.
2. Click Ruler in the Show group.
   OR
   Click View Ruler at the top of the vertical scroll bar.

SIDE NOTE
Why Zoom?
When you zoom in a document so that the text is larger, it is easier on your eyes, and it may be easier to proofread the document and locate errors that are otherwise not always obvious—such as incorrect word usage or spelling errors. It is important to note that changing the magnification does not actually change the text size of the document when it is printed.

To View the Ruler and Change Zoom Level

a. If a horizontal ruler is not already visible at the top of the document, click **View Ruler**. You can also display rulers when you click the View tab and then Ruler.

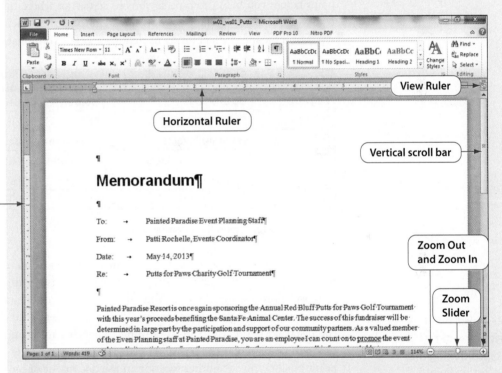

Figure 7 Showing the ruler

b. Click the **View tab**, click **Zoom** in the Zoom group, click **200%**, and then click **OK**.

c. Drag the vertical scroll bar at the right side of the display down, so you can see most of the first two body paragraphs. Locate the word-usage error in the first paragraph of the body of the memorandum. The word "Even" should be "Event." The word is not flagged as a spelling error because it is not misspelled. Instead, it is considered a word-usage error because it is an incorrect word choice for the sentence. Click after the word **Even**, and type **t**.

d. On the status bar, drag the Zoom Slider ⊖━━━▽━━━⊕ to the left to reduce the size of the document to 50%.

Troubleshooting

If you drag the Zoom tab too far to the left, the document might become too small. Just drag the Zoom Slider back to the right slightly until you can read the text comfortably.

e. On the **View tab**, click **Page Width** in the Zoom group to return the document to the largest size possible without the need for the horizontal scroll bar. The Page Width zoom setting provides an optimal size for reviewing and proofing a document.

Moving Around a Document

The **insertion point** is the blinking black bar that indicates the position where the text you type will be placed. You can reposition the insertion point by clicking anywhere in the existing text within a document. You should make a habit of noting the position of the insertion point before you begin to type so you are certain of where text will be placed. If you type text where it is not intended, simply click Undo on the Quick Access Toolbar. You can also reposition the insertion point by using keys and key combinations as indicated in Figure 8.

Keys	Resulting Insertion Point	Keys	Resulting Insertion Point
Page Up	Up one page	**Home**	Beginning of the current line
Page Down	Down one page	**End**	End of the current line
←	Left one character	**Ctrl+Home**	Beginning of the document
→	Right one character	**Ctrl+End**	End of the document
↑	Up one line	**Ctrl+←**	Left one word
↓	Down one line	**Ctrl+→**	Right one word

Figure 8   To reposition the insertion point

Changing the view of text that is shown on screen is not the same as repositioning the insertion point, although confusing the two actions is a common mistake made by beginning word processing students. You can use the horizontal and vertical scroll bars to move the display so that you see other areas of the document, but doing so does not reposition the insertion point. Even after scrolling to another location in a document, newly typed text will be placed at the position of the insertion point. You can only move the insertion point by clicking in another location in the document or by using a keyboard shortcut— several of which are described in Figure 8.

SIDE NOTE
Repositioning the Insertion Point

To move the insertion point, you must *click* in a new location. Simply pointing to a new location does not reposition the insertion point. To position the insertion point farther down in a blank area in the document space, well beneath the last typed line, simply double-click in the desired location. Hard returns will automatically be inserted between previously typed text and the new location of the insertion point.

To Move Around a Document

a. Press Ctrl+End to position the insertion point at the end of the document.

b. Press Ctrl+Home to position the insertion point at the beginning of the document.

c. Click just before the word **Painted** in the first paragraph of the body of the memo. Press Ctrl+→ to place the insertion point before the word **Paradise** in the same sentence.

d. Drag the vertical scroll bar down to show the end of the document.

   Dragging the scroll bar changes the area of the document that is displayed, but it does not physically reposition the insertion point. Note that you do not see the blinking insertion point at the end of the document. Instead, it remains in the same position as where you placed it in Step c—thus you may need to scroll back up to view the first body paragraph if you cannot see the insertion point.

e. Press $\boxed{\text{Ctrl}}$+$\boxed{\text{Home}}$ to move the insertion point to the beginning of the document. The date is incorrect. It should be "May 12, 2013." Click to place the insertion point after the number **4** in the date. Press $\boxed{\text{Backspace}}$, and then type 2. When removing text or nonprinting characters, you can press $\boxed{\text{Backspace}}$ to remove characters to the left of the insertion point, or you can press $\boxed{\text{Delete}}$ to remove characters to the right.

Viewing Backstage

When you click the File tab, you are in Microsoft's **Backstage view**. Backstage view is a collection of common actions and settings that apply to the current document. It is also the location where you can define global settings, such as whether to use the spelling checker automatically or on demand. You will find such actions as print, save, and open in Backstage view. You can view document properties, such as file size and author, and you can set security permissions. Backstage view provides a quick way to open recently accessed Word files and save files to a disk drive or share them online. You can also use Backstage view to close a file and exit Word. Best defined as a collection of common actions, properties, and settings related to an open file, Backstage view is unique to Office 2010. It is not found in earlier Office versions.

To Use Backstage View

a. Click the **File tab**. Backstage view is displayed. The Info option is selected, displaying information about the current document, including file properties and permissions.

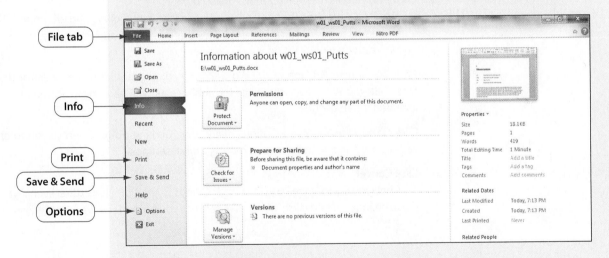

Figure 9 Backstage view

b. On the **File tab**, click **Save & Send**.
   You can send a file through e-mail, save it to the web, or publish it as a blog post. You can also change the file type or even create a PDF file, among other things.

c. On the **File tab**, click **Print**.
   Selecting the Print option displays the document as it will appear when printed. It also enables you to select print options such as the number of copies to print and the page orientation.

d. Click the **Home tab** to return to the document and close Backstage view.

Working with Word Options

Without changing any settings or options, you can use Word as it is configured when installed. However, you might develop preferences regarding the way Word handles spelling errors or grammatical mistakes. Perhaps you want to customize the Ribbon, change the default location where files are saved, or specify different security and privacy settings. These and many other options are available when you click the File tab and then click Options.

Quick Reference — Change Word Options

1. Click the File tab.
2. Click Options.
3. Click a category.

To Work with Word Options

a. On the **File tab**, click **Options**. The Word Options dialog box opens.

Note the categories on the left side, including General, Display, Proofing, and others. Click a category to view related settings that you can confirm or change. Keep in mind that changes to these options are global, not local. For example, if you change the way Word corrects spelling errors, that change not only applies to the current document, but to all others as well. In effect, you are modifying the Word installation, not just the current Word document. For that reason, you might not be allowed to change these Word options if you are working in a computer lab. This workshop will not ask you to change Word options, although you will explore several.

b. Click **Proofing** in the Word Options dialog box.

Word Options in the Proofing group relate to the way spelling and grammatical errors are corrected in all Word documents. Any changes that you make will affect all Word documents you work with on your computer.

c. Click **Customize Ribbon** in the Word Options dialog box. You can select or deselect tabs that you want to include on the Ribbon, as well as indicate commands to be included in tab groups.

d. Click **General** in the Word Options dialog box. General options enable you to change your user name and initials, among other global settings.

e. Click **Cancel**.

When you click Cancel, you return all settings to their previous state, even if you have made changes. If you click OK, all changes that you have made are accepted.

Saving and Closing a Document

You will need to save your work so you can continue to work with a document later. It is a good idea to save a document often so you are less likely to lose a great deal of work if you encounter a power outage or other disruption.

You might consider creating a system of folders on a disk drive to organize your documents and other projects. Then, you can simply navigate to the desired folder and save the document. In theory, a very organized person would create a personal folder structure long before the need arises. The truth is, though, that most of us recognize the need for a folder too late. In fact, it is usually as you are saving a document that you realize that you do not have an appropriate folder to save it in. In that case, you can create a folder for the file as you are saving it.

Saving a Document to SkyDrive

When you save a file, you must specify a location. Usually, that location is a flash drive or perhaps a hard drive. At some point, you will inevitably need a file, only to realize that you do not have the storage device that the file is saved on with you. That can be a very frustrating and costly experience, especially if the file is necessary for a class or for an important task at work. Recognizing the mobile lifestyle of most people today, Microsoft built functionality into Office 2010 that enables you to save files to the Web and open them on any computer, even if that computer does not have Office 2010 installed.

Files that you send to the Web from Word 2010 are saved to a **SkyDrive** account. SkyDrive is essentially Web storage space that Microsoft makes available to you at no cost. When you sign up for SkyDrive storage, you are given access to 7 GB of space in which you can create folders and upload documents, spreadsheets, presentations, and other files. If all you need is extra storage, perhaps for backup and easy retrieval of files from any location, SkyDrive could be your solution. In addition, with the release of Office 2010, Microsoft introduced Web Apps, a feature that not only lets you store files but also enables you to open them in a Web version of Word, PowerPoint, or Excel. The Web Apps version of those applications is limited, missing many of the features that you find in Office 2010 on a local computer, but core editing and formatting elements are included.

If you plan to send files from Word to SkyDrive, you must first have a Windows Live account or sign up for SkyDrive access online. Windows Live is a group of free Microsoft programs designed to assist with e-mail, blogging, and social networking. With a Windows Live ID, you can also access free storage space through SkyDrive. If you do not already have a Windows Live account, you can sign up at skydrive.live.com. Click Sign Up, and complete the required registration. During the registration process, you will create a user name and password that you will later use to upload and retrieve files.

Real World Advice — Creating a Strong Password

As you work with the Internet, perhaps shopping, banking, or taking classes, you will be asked to create a password. When you create a SkyDrive account, you will also create a password. A password should be something that you can easily remember but something that would be difficult for anyone else to guess. The following tips can help you create a strong password.

1. Include at least 14 characters, including letters (both uppercase and lowercase) and numbers.
2. Do not use real words, as software used by ill-intentioned hackers can quickly check every word in the dictionary.
3. Use a passphrase, such as the first letter of every word in a favorite song or poem, combined with numbers that are easily remembered.
4. Do not use personal information, such as your pet's name or a middle name.
5. Use an assortment of keyboard characters, including special characters.
6. Do not use the same password for all of your online activity.

You can access SkyDrive from within a browser when you visit skydrive.live.com, enter your ID and password, and click Sign in. Using your Windows Live ID, you can access your storage space and follow links to upload files directly from your computer. The files do not have to be Microsoft Office files, so you can actually use SkyDrive to store such items as digital pictures.

Probably the best SkyDrive feature, though, is the facility to save a document to SkyDrive from within Word, much as you would save the same document to a hard drive or flash drive. Later, you can access the file from any computer, opening it in the Web Apps version of Word if you do not have access to a full Word version. To save to SkyDrive, click the File tab, click Save & Send, and then click Save to Web. Click Sign In, if necessary, and enter your SkyDrive credentials—user name and password. You can ask Word to remember your account information so that you can skip the Sign in step later. Once you are connected to SkyDrive, you can create a new folder, or double-click to select an existing folder to store your document in.

When signed in to SkyDrive, you can open a file from your storage space when you click File, and then Open in Word. SkyDrive appears as a selection in the Computer area—although it is in a somewhat cryptic form. You can also open a file in Word by accessing SkyDrive through a browser. Double-click the file to open it, and indicate that it should be opened in Word.

Real World Advice | Collaboration in Word 2010

Sales & Marketing

How often have you heard the phrase "It was a team effort"? Although you might not consider the development of a Word document a team effort, Word 2010 simplifies the process of coauthoring so that many business documents and school projects are actually developed jointly. At one time, it was unheard of for more than one person to collaborate on a document. More recently, people began to send Word documents as e-mail attachments, receiving feedback from others in the form of marked-up or edited versions of the documents. The number of iterations of the same document was difficult to organize, to say the least, requiring a great deal of time to sort out and merge back into one master document. Document management systems, like SharePoint, provided a single "shared" document that could be edited by multiple users. The problem was that there was only one shared version of the document, so if someone else had the document for editing, you might be locked out until he or she posted it back. Recognizing the need to collaborate on documents simultaneously, Microsoft included such capability in Word 2010. By sharing files through company networks or on SkyDrive, coauthoring is almost as seamless and natural as authoring a document independently. Multiple authors can edit the same document at the same time, resulting in only one edited copy that is available to all authors for final approval. That is teamwork at its finest!

CONSIDER THIS | Saving to the Web

Part of the usefulness of web storage such as SkyDrive is the convenience with which you can access files from any location. However, as with anything stored online, security and privacy are always a concern. Identify any document types that are not appropriate for online storage. What disadvantages or risks are involved with storing files on SkyDrive or a similar web storage site? Can you identify any ethical concerns associated with online storage of files?

Saving a Document to a PDF File

When you distribute a Word document electronically, you cannot be sure that your recipient has Word installed on their computer. Even if Word is available, many people prefer not to receive Office attachments because of the risk of acquiring a virus. Instead of saving and sending a Word document, you might consider saving the document as a **PDF (Portable Document Format)** file. PDF is a file type that preserves most formatting attributes of a source document regardless of the software in which the document was created. The only software required to read a PDF file is Adobe Reader, which is available as a free download at **www.adobe.com/products/reader/**. Because Adobe Reader enables you to read a PDF file, but not change it, saving a Word document as a PDF file can help ensure its readability on any computer.

Real World Advice   Using PDFs

Sales & Marketing

If you plan to share a Word document for the purpose of collaboration, or teamwork on a project, you will save it as a Word file. That way, others can open and edit the document. However, PDF is the preferred file format to use when sharing a document for informational purposes with a group of people. Some files, including legal documents, are not intended for editing, and in fact would be compromised if they were changed. Unless a user has specialized software, a PDF file cannot be changed, so the likelihood of a user inadvertently modifying a file is minimized. Unlike a Word file, a PDF file can be read regardless of the operating system in use, so compatibility is not an issue when distributing a file in PDF format. When you need to transmit a Word document in a portable, compatible, and secure format, you should save the file as a PDF file.

To Save a Document

a. Click the **File tab** and then click **Save As**.

  The File tab includes both Save and Save As options. As you learned in the Common Features workshop, the first time that you save a file there is no difference in the two options, as both will ask you to specify a location in which to save the file as well as a name for the file. The next time you save the file, you can simply click the File tab and then click Save, saving the file in the same location with the same file name. You can also click Save on the Quick Access Toolbar.

b. Drag the scroll bar up or down in the left pane to locate the disk drive where you save your student projects. Click the disk drive in the left pane.

Quick Access Toolbar Save

Disk drive to save to (yours might be different)

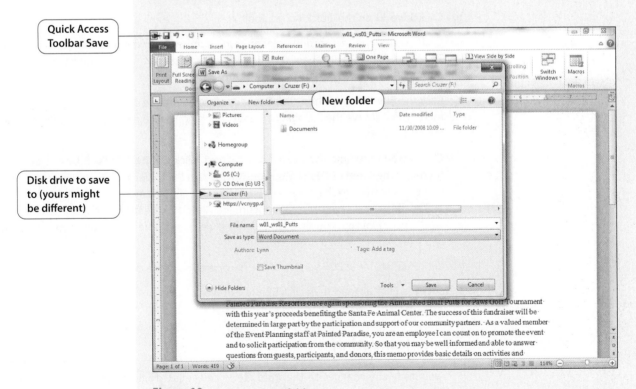

Figure 10   Creating a new folder

c. Click **New folder**, type Word Projects, and then press Enter to create a folder to save your Word projects. With the new folder selected, double-click to select the folder as the destination for the save.

d. Click in the File name box and type Lastname_Firstname_w01_ws01_Putts, replacing Lastname with your own last name and Firstname with your own first name.

Troubleshooting

If the file name is not shaded—selected—when you click in the File name box, you will need to press Delete or Backspace to remove the current file name before typing the required file name.

e. Click **Save**.

f. Click to place the insertion point just before the word **Pro** in the second body paragraph. Type Golf and press Spacebar. You have more specifically identified the type of professional by changing "Pro" to "Golf Pro."

Troubleshooting

If you see any unnecessary spaces, click to the right of the unnecessary space and press Backspace to remove it—or click to the left of the space and press Delete to remove it. If a space is needed, click where the space is to be placed, and press Spacebar as necessary to add a space.

g. Click **Save** 💾 on the Quick Access Toolbar.

h. Click to position the insertion point after the number **30** in the second body paragraph. The date for the charity event recently changed. Press Backspace once to remove the number 0, and type 1 so the date reads **July 31**.

i. Click the **File tab**, and then click **Save**. Because you made some changes to the document, you will save the file again without changing the file name or the location where the file is saved.

j. Click the **File tab**, and then click **Save & Send**. Click **Create PDF/XPS Document**, and then click the **Create PDF/XPS** button. Navigate to the folder you created in Step c. Click in the **File name box**. If necessary, type Lastname_Firstname_w01_ws01_Putts.

The file will be saved as a PDF document. Although the file name is the same as the Word document that you saved in Step i, the file type is different, so the identical nature of the file names is not a problem.

k. Click **Publish**. If the PDF version of the file opens, close the document.

l. Click the **File tab**, and then click **Exit** to exit Word.

Troubleshooting

If you made any changes to the Word file since the last time it was saved, Word will prompt you to save the file before exiting Word.

Opening a File from the Recent Documents List

You will often want to continue working with a document that you saved previously. Word makes opening a recently saved file easy by providing a list of recent files you can select from. By default, Word shows the 20 most recently opened files, but you can change the number of files shown to be more or less than 20.

To Open a Recent File

a. Start **Word**. Click the **File tab**, and then click **Recent**, if necessary.

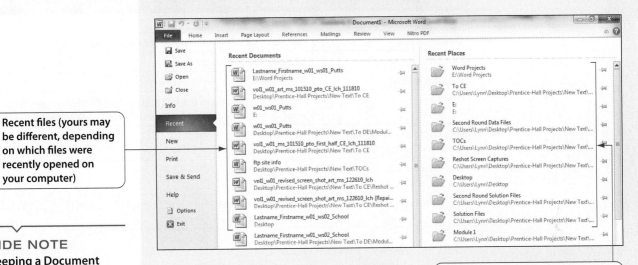

Recent files (yours may be different, depending on which files were recently opened on your computer)

Folders from which recent files were opened (yours may be different)

Figure 11 Opening recent files

b. Click **Lastname_Firstname_w01_ws01_Putts**. Recall that your last name and your first name will be shown instead of Lastname and Firstname. **Lastname_Firstname_ w01_ws01_Putts** should be displayed near the top of the Recent Files list because it is a recently opened document.

Editing a Document

A document is seldom in its final form when you finish typing it. As you look back over a project, you will most likely want to change some wording, add emphasis effects—such as italics and boldfacing—or correct spelling and grammatical errors. The first thing to consider when editing a document is to identify text that you want to change. You can add, delete, copy, move, or format text. You can change the style and add features such as graphics and borders.

Always keep the purpose of the document in mind before making significant changes. A business report is much more bound by rules of tradition—a professional appearance—than is a family newsletter. While you might have fun experimenting with color and unique fonts in a newsletter, you will want to take a more conservative approach to editing a business document.

Selecting Text

Before applying changes to existing text, you must select the text. Selecting text is easy: Simply position the pointer before the text, press the mouse button and hold it, and then drag to highlight, or select, the text. This textbook will refer to such an action as "dragging," not "clicking and dragging." Although you will learn a few shortcuts to selecting text, this

SIDE NOTE
Keeping a Document Recent

You can keep a document in the Recent Documents list no matter how recently it was opened. To do so, open Word, and click the File tab. Click Recent, and then click the pushpin icon to the right of the file that you want to maintain. The pushpin will change direction so that it appears to be pressed in. The document will remain in the Recent Documents list indefinitely or until the pushpin is clicked again to toggle this feature off.

SIDE NOTE
Changing the Number of Recent Files

To change the number of files shown in the Recent Documents list, click the File tab, click Options, and then click Advanced. Scroll down in the list of options, and under Display change the value in Show this number of Recent Documents. Click OK.

always works. The bottom line is that you cannot change an area of text unless you first select it. To deselect text, simply click anywhere.

Although dragging to select text is an option, it is not always the simplest method of selection. For example, it can be difficult to select a single character by dragging because the area of selection is so small. Similarly, selecting an entire 200-page document can be a challenge if you rely solely on dragging to select it. Although it is definitely possible, it would take some time and patience to drag through 200 pages. Figure 12 presents some shortcuts to selecting blocks of text.

To Select	Do This
One word	Double-click the word
One sentence	Press and hold Ctrl while you click in the sentence
One paragraph	Triple-click the paragraph
One document	Press Ctrl + A
One line	Position the pointer in the left margin beside the line to select; when the pointer resembles a white arrow, click to select the line
One character to the left of the insertion point	Press Shift + ←
One character to the right of the insertion point	Press Shift + →
One block of text	Click where the selection is to begin, hold down Shift, and click where the selection is to end

Figure 12   Shortcuts to selection

SIDE NOTE
Select, Then Do
Remember that you must first select text before applying any changes to it. Select text by dragging the mouse to highlight it or by using a shortcut selection method (see Figure 12).

To Edit a Document

a. Locate the second bullet in the middle of the document that begins with **Team of Four**. The charge for a team of four players is listed in error. Select the text **$600**, and then type $550.

b. At the beginning of the document, locate the line beginning with the word **To:**, and then double-click the word **Staff**.

   When you double-click a word, you select the entire word. At that point, you can add character formatting, such as bold, italics, font color, or font size, or you can delete selected text by pressing Delete. You will learn more about character formatting later in this workshop.

Troubleshooting

If the entire paragraph is selected instead of a single word, you triple-clicked instead of double-clicked. Click anywhere, and then double-click the word "Staff" once more.

c. Type Group to replace the word Staff with Group.

   You can replace selected text by simply typing new text. If a block of text is selected, it is immediately replaced with new text that you type.

d. Press Ctrl + Home. Move the pointer into the left margin, just to the left of the word **Memorandum**, to change the pointer to 🢅. Click to select the line of text. When you click in the left margin—the selection area—the entire line to the right of the pointer is selected. Type Memo.

e. Place the pointer anywhere in the first sentence of the first paragraph of the memo body, and then triple-click to select the paragraph.

f. Click anywhere to deselect it.

g. In the first paragraph of the body of the memo, drag to select the words **guests, participants, and donors**. Do not select the comma following the last word in the selection. Type interested parties to replace the existing text with the new wording.

h. If necessary, scroll so that the first two body paragraphs are visible. Click before the word **Painted** in the first line of the first body paragraph. Press and hold Shift, and then click after the words **Indigo 5** in the second body paragraph (after the exclamation point).

    Both paragraphs are selected. Holding the Shift key enables you to click another location to select all text between that location and the initial insertion point.

i. Click to deselect the selection. Press Ctrl+A.

    The entire document is selected. Click anywhere to deselect it.

j. Save the document.

Changing Font Type, Size, and Color

For the most part, word processing is a text-based application, which means that it focuses on the generation of documents containing words and sentences. Its primary purpose is to enable you to create attractive documents that communicate a message. Although you can quickly learn the mechanics of how to select a typeface, or font, you will want to develop skills in preparing business documents—selecting an appropriate font and text style for the project under development. As you progress through this module, you will be presented with tips for creating well-designed business documents.

A **font** is a character design, including such qualities as typeface, size, and spacing. A typeface is a style of printed characters. Typeface, combined with character size and the amount of spacing between characters, makes up a font. You can choose to use the default font, which is the specified font when you begin a new document, or you can select from a number of additional fonts. With experience, you will develop font preferences and will understand that some font selections are better suited for certain document types than are others.

The Font group on the Home tab shows the current font and font size. When you click the Font arrow, a list of fonts is displayed, with each font shown as a sample of the actual font. Theme fonts—described later in this workshop—are shown first, followed by recently used fonts. The remaining fonts are listed in alphabetical order. The current font is highlighted in orange. If you have selected text before viewing the list of fonts, you can hover the mouse over any font selection—without clicking—to see a **Live Preview** of the font's effect. Live Preview is a feature that provides a look at the result of a selection before you actually make the choice. If you like the change, click the font to select it.

A characteristic of a font is the presence or absence of thin lines, or hooks, that end the main strokes of each letter. A **serif font**, such as Times New Roman, includes the decorative strokes that provide a visual connection between characters and words. Because a serif font is easy to read in large amounts of text, it is a good choice for printed material, such as reports and lengthy documents. Newspapers and books almost always use serif fonts for body text. In addition to Times New Roman, other serif fonts include Bodoni and Century Schoolbook.

A **sans serif font**, such as Arial, does not include the ending strokes and appears blockier. The word "sans" means "without" in Latin. A sans serif font, then, is *without* the ending strokes typical of a serif font. A sans serif font is useful for titles, logos, and headings. Web developers prefer the blocky appearance of sans serif fonts for web page readability.

In general, fine details like the ending strokes of serif fonts can disappear or appear too large when displayed within the resolution of a typical web page. Not only does that detract from the web page, but it can cause eye strain as well. If a document is to be shown as a web page, it is almost always formatted in a sans serif font. Common sans serif fonts include Helvetica, Verdana, and Geneva, along with Arial. Figure 13 compares serif and sans serif fonts.

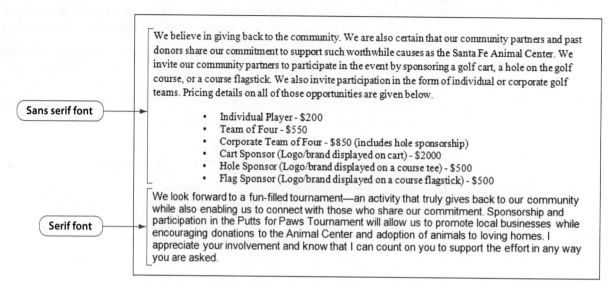

Figure 13 Sans serif and serif fonts

Another characteristic of a font is its spacing. A font is either *monospaced* (sometimes called *fixed width*) or *proportional*. If you consider the way that you would print words, you can envision giving more space to some characters than to others. For example, printing the letter "w" typically requires more space than the letter "l." Giving more physical space to some letters and less to others is an example of proportional spacing. Because proportional spacing is generally considered easier to read, it is found almost exclusively in professionally published printed material and in most business documents. Monospaced text is appropriate for tables and financial reports where text must line up neatly in columns and rows. Figure 14 compares monospaced and proportional font selections.

```
This is an example of a monospaced font. Each character requires the
same amount of space.
```

This is an example of a proportional font. Each character requires only the space that is necessary for display. For example, the letter *m* requires more space than the letter *i*.

Figure 14 Monospaced and proportional fonts

Regardless of which font type you select, you can apply additional attributes, including reducing or increasing the font size and changing the color. All of these options are located in the Font group on the Home tab. Font size is measured in points (abbreviated "pt"), with each point equivalent to 1/72 of an inch. A typical font size is 12 pt, but other sizes are appropriate for other purposes such as conveying a hierarchical structure. For example, you might want to make a report title much larger than the text in the body of the report. You can also change font color, although you should use color sparingly in business documents. One exception to that rule is when developing newsletters or flyers. Both of those projects can be made more attractive by judicious use of color. Text effects enable you to enhance text by adding a shadow, outline, reflection, or glow. Such effects can be very effective in certain documents as you draw attention to headers or text blocks. After selecting text to modify, you can click Text Effects in the Font group (shown in Figure 15) to select an effect.

Real World Advice | Selecting an Appropriate Font for Business Correspondence

With the wide variety of available font selections, you are probably wondering how to select an appropriate font for business correspondence. A short answer is that a serif font at 11-pt to 12-pt size is a good choice for printed material, such as letters, memos, and reports. The accepted standard is Times New Roman 12 pt. You might reduce the font to 11-pt size if you need to get all of your text on one page. Avoid overly ornate or abnormal fonts, such as Comic Sans.

Sales & Marketing

CONSIDER THIS | Going Mobile

If you are like most people, the term "business correspondence" evokes images of business letters or memos. While those written forms of correspondence are very viable ways to communicate, correspondence is also often displayed on a computer screen or mobile phone. Do you think such *mobile* correspondence would be better received in a sans serif font, such as that used by web designers, or should you stay with a serif font that is more traditionally associated with business correspondence? How would the culture of corporate business affect your decision?

Quick Reference | Change Character Formatting

1. Select text to format.
2. Click the Font Dialog Box Launcher.
3. Specify formatting or special effect.
4. Click OK.

To Change Character Formatting

a. Drag to select the words **Annual Red Bluff Putts for Paws Golf Tournament** in the first paragraph of the body of the memo.

b. Click the **Home tab**. The Font group includes several options for character formatting. Click **Bold** B in the Font group to draw the reader's attention to this particular charity event. Click anywhere to deselect the text.

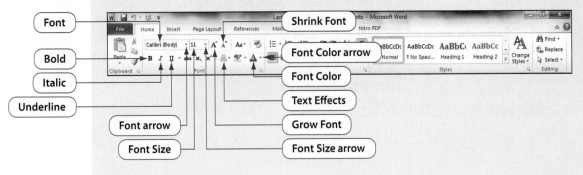

Figure 15 The Font group

c. Select the words **July 31** in the second body paragraph. Click the **Font arrow** in the Font group on the Home tab. Scroll down and position the pointer over **Arial**—without clicking.

Live Preview is a feature that enables you to see how a proposed change would affect selected text before you commit to the change. Before selecting a font, you can see how it would affect a selection.

d. Do not click Arial. Click outside the font list to remove it from view.

e. Scroll up and select the word **Memo**. Click the **Font arrow**, and then click **Times New Roman**.

The heading is now consistent with the other text in the document. Click anywhere to deselect the text.

f. Double-click **To** on the second line of the memo. Move the pointer near the selected area to reveal the Mini toolbar. Click **Bold** on the Mini toolbar. Similarly, select and bold the words **From**, **Date**, and **Re**.

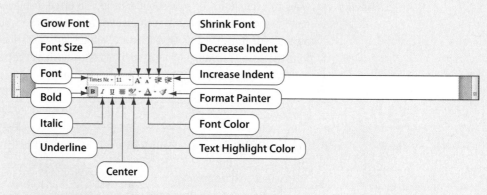

Figure 16 The Mini toolbar

Troubleshooting

If you do not see the Mini toolbar when the pointer is near the selection, right-click on the selected text to reveal the Mini toolbar along with context menu options. Once you click an option on the Mini toolbar, the context menu disappears and the Mini toolbar remains available for the selected text.

g. Drag to select the words **basic details** in the last sentence of the first paragraph of the body of the memo. Make sure that you do not select the space following the word **details**. Click **Underline** [U ▾] in the Font group.

h. Click **Undo** [↶] on the **Quick Access Toolbar** to undo the underline.

When you click Undo once, it enables you to undo the most recent action. If the action that you want to reverse is not the most recent, you can still undo it by clicking Undo repeatedly. Each time you click Undo, an action is reversed, in the order that you performed the steps. You can also select an action to undo when you click the Undo arrow and select the action.

i. Click **Redo** on the Quick Access Toolbar.

When you click Redo, the most recent "undone" action is redone. For example, if you delete a word and then click Undo, the deleted word is once more displayed in the document. If you then click Redo, the word is once again deleted.

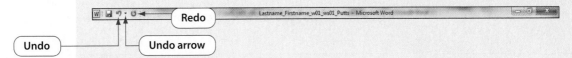

Redo

Undo

Undo arrow

Figure 17 The Quick Access Toolbar

j. Select the word **Memo**. Click the **Font Size arrow**, and click **20**. Click anywhere to deselect the text.

k. In the first body paragraph, select the words **Annual Red Bluff Putts for Paws Golf Tournament**. You decide that the document is more attractive without boldfacing the selected words, so you will remove bold formatting. Click **Bold** in the Font group.

l. Select the text **July 31** in the second paragraph of the body of the memo. You will use the Format dialog box to bold and format the selection.

m. Click the **Font Dialog Box Launcher** in the Font group, and then click **Bold** under Font style. Click the **Underline style arrow**, and click the third selection—a thick dark line. Click **OK**. The date should be bold and thickly underlined.

n. Save the document.

SIDE NOTE
Increasing and Decreasing Font

A quick way to increase or decrease the size of selected text is to click Grow Font or Shrink Font in the Font group on the Home tab or on the Mini toolbar, as shown in Figures 15 and 16.

SIDE NOTE
Using the Font Dialog Box

Selections in the Font dialog box enable you to format text in many different ways. Some of the most commonly accessed settings are also available on the Ribbon's Home tab. However, if you are applying several format effects, especially if those effects are not commonplace—such as superscript, small caps, or a specific underline style—you will appreciate the Font dialog box because it collects all font selections in one easily accessible area. Access the Font dialog box by clicking the Font Dialog Box Launcher on the Home tab.

Adjusting Paragraph Alignment

The way you define a paragraph and the way Word defines a paragraph are likely very different definitions. While a paragraph may be defined as a group of two or more sentences with a common idea or concept, Word defines a paragraph as a hard return—every time you press Enter. By that definition, an empty line with a hard return, or a single line, such as the title of a report with a hard return, is a paragraph. It is important to understand how Word identifies paragraphs, because some formatting settings apply to entire paragraphs. One such setting is alignment.

By default, paragraphs in a Word document are **left-aligned**, which means that lines of text begin evenly on the left, but include an uneven, or ragged, right edge. Left-aligned text is easy to read; therefore, it is the primary form of alignment of paragraphs in letters, reports, and memos. Text that is **right-aligned** is the reverse: Text is aligned on the right with a ragged left edge. Right-aligned text is often used for short lines such as dates, figure captions, and headers. Text that is **centered** places the middle of each line of text precisely in the middle of the page between the left and right margins. Report titles and major headings are usually centered. **Justified** (sometimes called *fully justified*) is an alignment style that spreads text evenly between the right and left margins so that lines begin on the left margin and end uniformly on the right margin. Such alignment can cause awkward spacing as text is stretched to fit evenly between the margins. Newspaper articles are sometimes formatted in justified alignment. An alignment setting applies to all text within the current paragraph.

To Adjust Alignment

a. Drag to select all paragraphs in the body of the memo, starting with the paragraph beginning with **Painted Paradise Resort** and ending at the end of the document.

b. Click **Justify** [≡] in the Paragraph group. Click anywhere in the document to deselect the selection. With the exception of the bulleted text, all paragraphs are evenly aligned on both the left and right margins.

Figure 18 Adjusting alignment

SIDE NOTE
Alignment Shortcuts

Some keyboard shortcuts are worth memorizing. Because you will often change alignment, you should remember that [Ctrl]+[L] left-aligns, [Ctrl]+[R] right-aligns, [Ctrl]+[E] centers, and [Ctrl]+[J] justifies text.

c. Click anywhere on the line containing the word **Memo**, and then click **Center** [≡].

Because the new alignment applies to the entire paragraph—text that ends with a hard return—you do not have to select the entire line of text. Instead, simply clicking within the line of text that identifies the paragraph to be formatted with center alignment.

d. Click **Undo** [↺]. Centering the word **Memo** is not an attractive change and is not an accepted practice in the design of business documents, so you return alignment to left-align.

e. Drag to select all paragraphs in the body of the memo, starting with the paragraph that begins with **Painted Paradise Resort** and ending at the end of the document.

f. Click **Align Text Left** [≡]. Justify is an alignment that is often used in published documents, such as newspapers and magazines, but it is not suitable for a memo. Therefore, you return text to left alignment. Click to deselect the selected area.

g. Save the document.

Sales & Marketing

CONSIDER THIS | Minimize Errors

As you create a document, what are some ways that you could minimize or prevent errors before they occur? Of course, you will want to try to avoid typos and misspellings, but what are some other things you can do to prepare an error-free document?

Checking Spelling and Grammar

By default, Word checks spelling as you type, underlining in red any words that are not found in Word's dictionary. Sometimes, the underlined words are not actually misspelled, but instead are names or technical terms that Word simply does not recognize. In that case, you can ignore the flagged text. Phrases or words that appear to be incorrect grammar, capitalization, or spacing are underlined in green. Occasionally, the underlined text is not an error at all, but is instead part of the document formatting or wording that you prefer to leave as is. Often, the "grammatical error" is simply too many spaces between words. If your document displays nonprinting characters, you can quickly identify and remove any extra spaces. Finally, Word will underline in blue any word-usage errors, such as using the word "bear" instead of "bare." Word may not catch every occurrence of a word-usage, grammatical, or spelling error, so you should carefully proofread the document yourself.

Real World Advice   The Importance of Proofreading

Do not rely too heavily on Word to identify errors in a document. Instead, make it a practice to carefully proofread a document yourself to catch errors that Word might miss. For example, using the word "of" when you intended to use the word "or" is a common mistake—and one that Word would most likely miss. Similarly, you might type "not" instead of "now," which is not a spelling mistake. Only if you manually proofread the document would you be able to correct such word-usage errors. As you proofread, you might also identify alternate wordings that might improve readability. Never print or distribute a document that you have not carefully proofread.

You might not want to take time to visually examine all of the text for underlines that indicate word usage or spelling errors, especially if you are working with a lengthy document. Instead, it would be helpful to rely on Word to present each "error" so that you could specify how, or if, it should be corrected. You can do just that by clicking the Review tab and then clicking Spelling & Grammar in the Proofing group. Word will present each error, as shown in Figure 20, so that you can decide whether to ignore it or change it. As you make those determinations, the underlining that indicates the error is removed.

To Check Spelling and Grammar

a. Right-click the red underlined word in the first paragraph of the body of the memo. Click **promote** in the shortcut menu of suggested correct spellings.

When you right-click a flagged spelling mistake, a shortcut menu is displayed. You can then choose to accept a suggestion or to ignore the error. If none of Word's suggested corrections are appropriate, you can edit the document to correct the misspelling or grammatical mistake.

Troubleshooting

Before you right-click an identified spelling or grammatical mistake, make sure the pointer is on the underlined area. If that is not the case, the displayed shortcut menu might not include selections related to the mistake. Simply right-click the underlined area to display the correct shortcut menu.

SIDE NOTE
Proofing Options

You can specify proofing options by clicking the File tab, clicking Options, and then clicking Proofing. For example, if you prefer that Word does not check your spelling as you type, you can deselect that option.

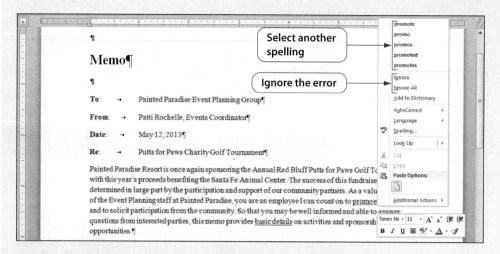

Figure 19 Correcting spelling

b. Click the **Review tab**, and then click **Spelling & Grammar** in the Proofing group. When presented with the first misspelled word (it should be "tournanent"), select the correct spelling from the Suggestions box, and then click **Change**. Word will proceed through the entire document, presenting each error for your consideration. Repeat this process for the two remaining errors.

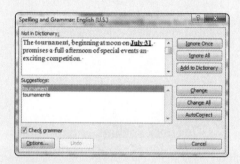

Figure 20 Spelling and Grammar dialog box

c. Click **OK** when the spelling and grammar check is complete.

d. Save the document.

Using AutoCorrect

AutoCorrect is a feature that is similar to a spelling checker, but it serves a slightly different purpose. As you type, you are likely to misspell some of the same words repeatedly. For example, if you type fairly quickly, you might notice that you sometimes type "adn" when you meant to type "and." Similarly, the word "the" is sometimes typed "teh," usually because your fingers move too rapidly. AutoCorrect automatically corrects common mistakes such as these. When you begin a new line or sentence with a lowercase word, Word automatically changes the first letter to uppercase.

The next time you are using Word, try typing "adn" and notice that as soon as you press ⌴Spacebar⌴ after typing, the misspelling is immediately corrected. You can compare

Word's AutoCorrect feature to the cell phone mode that guesses a word that you are attempting to text before you finish the word. If the guess is not correct, you can usually progress to the next guess, and in most cases you can even "teach" the cell phone to recognize the word correctly the next time.

AutoCorrect also enables you to abbreviate words that AutoCorrect will expand. If you often type a company name, for example, you can configure AutoCorrect to replace an abbreviation for the company name with the full company name. You could even configure AutoCorrect to recognize your initials and replace them with your full name. If you type your name often, including your initials as an AutoCorrect entry will save a significant amount of typing. Some symbols are even included in AutoCorrect's list of replacements, such as replacing (c) with ©.

To Use AutoCorrect

a. Click the **File tab**, click **Options**, click **Proofing**, and then click **AutoCorrect Options**.

You will often use the phrase "Painted Paradise Resort and Spa" in documents that you prepare for the resort. Because typing so much text is time consuming and might result in typing errors, you will create an AutoCorrect entry to simplify that process. When you create an AutoCorrect entry, the replacement will not only apply to text that you type in the current document, but to all Word documents that you create on your computer.

b. Type **pp** in the Replace box.

c. Type **Painted Paradise Resort and Spa** in the With box.

Troubleshooting

If the words "Painted Paradise Resort and Spa" are displayed in the With box before you type them, another student might have worked with this exercise before you (at the same computer). Therefore, the AutoCorrect entry has already been created. In that case, simply click OK. Click OK again to close the Options dialog box.

d. Click **Add**, and then click **OK**.

SIDE NOTE
AutoCorrect Entries
If you want to view the list of automatic corrections or add an entry in the AutoCorrect list, click the File tab, click Options, click Proofing, and then click AutoCorrect Options. Scroll through the list to see current corrections.

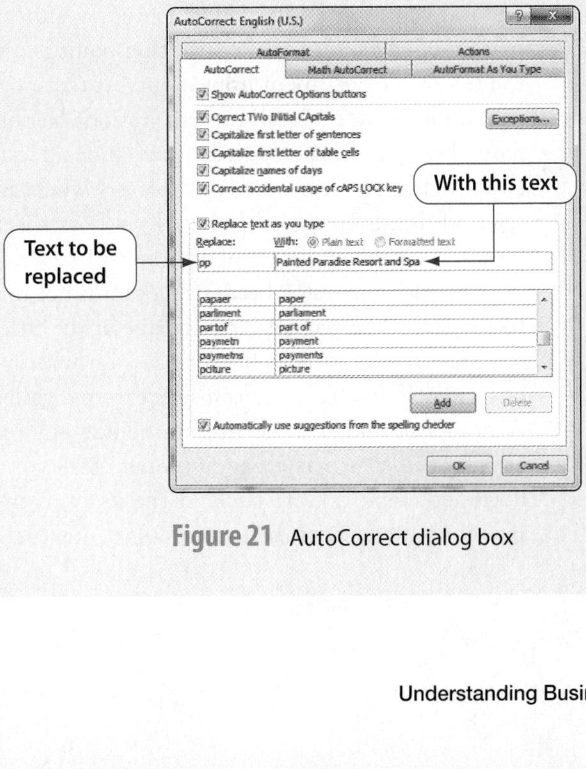

Figure 21 AutoCorrect dialog box

e. Click **AutoCorrect Options**.

You know that you will often use the word "resort" in the documents that you prepare. However, you tend to type quickly, sometimes reversing the order of letters so that you type "resrot." Scroll through the list of replacements to see if the text "resrot" is included as text to be replaced with a correct spelling.

f. If you do not see "resrot" in the replacement list, click in the **Replace box**, and type resrot. Click in the **With box**, and type resort. Click **Add**, click **OK**, and then click **OK** again.

g. Click after the words **Indigo 5!** in the second paragraph of the body of the memo, and press [Spacebar]. Type pp has prepared for you a fun-filled day at the resrot! (Type the word resrot, misspelled as shown.)

As you type the letters pp and press [Spacebar], the text should adjust to show "Painted Paradise Resort and Spa." As you type the word "resrot," the text should adjust to show the word "resort."

h. Because you are most likely in a computer lab, you will remove the two AutoCorrect entries created in this exercise. Click the **File tab**, click **Options**, click **Proofing**, and then click **AutoCorrect Options**. Scroll through the list of AutoCorrect entries, click **pp**, and then click **Delete**. Scroll through the list, click **resrot**, click **Delete**, click **OK**, and then click **OK** again to close the Word Options dialog box.

i. Save the document.

Inserting a Header and Footer

A **header** or **footer** is text or graphics printed in the top or bottom margin of a document. A header appears in the top margin; a footer is in the bottom margin. By default, headers and footers are not included in a document, but you can choose to add them if you like. Probably the most recognizable footer is a page number. A page number footer automatically increases in increments so that all pages are properly numbered. You could include your name as a footer, or perhaps your project title should be displayed as a header. When you specify a header or footer, the item appears on all pages unless you specify that it is only to appear on odd or even pages—or perhaps on all pages except the first page. You can also include headers or footers in only one section of a document. You will learn to create sections in Workshop 2.

You can insert a header or footer by simply double-clicking in the top or bottom margin of a document. The insertion point is displayed in the header or footer area, with the rest of the document grayed out. At that point, you can type text, such as your name, and align it using the alignment options on the Home tab. As you work in a header or footer area, the Ribbon adjusts to include a Header & Footer Tools contextual tab, which is a special tab that is only displayed when an item or object—such as a header—is selected. Items on the tab relate directly to the selected object. In the case of a header or footer, you can choose to include fields like a page number, the file name, or the author. You can indicate that a header or footer is not to appear on the first page, which would be handy if the first page is a cover page or the title page of a report.

You can also insert a header or footer when you click the Insert tab and select Header or Footer. If you like, you can select from a gallery of predesigned header or footer styles. A header or footer style might include colored horizontal lines, and preselected and aligned fields such as a page number. To leave a header or footer area and return to the document text, double-click in the body of the document, or click Close Header and Footer on the Header & Footer Tools contextual tab.

Quick Reference Insert a Header or Footer

1. Click the Insert tab.
2. Click Header (or Footer) in the Header & Footer group.
3. Click Edit Header (or Footer).
4. Type a header or footer, or select a predefined item such as Date & Time or Page Number.
5. Click Close Header and Footer to return to the document, or double-click in the document.

SIDE NOTE
Placement of a Header or Footer

If you want to specify that a header or footer only appears on certain pages, such as odd or even, you can select an option in the Options group of the Header & Footer Tools contextual tab.

To Insert Headers and Footers

a. Click the **Insert tab**, and then click **Footer** in the Header & Footer group. Although you can select from a gallery of footer designs, you will create your own, so click **Edit Footer**.

The document text appears grayed out, and the insertion point is displayed in the footer area. The Ribbon is expanded to include a Header & Footer Tools contextual tab. The contextual tab contains commands related to the currently selected item, which is a footer.

Header & Footer group

Header & Footer Tools contextual tab

Figure 22 Inserting headers and footers

b. Type Painted Paradise Resort and Spa. Press Enter, and then type Internal Communication. Headers and footers are left-aligned unless you specify otherwise. Press Tab once to center an entry. Press Tab again to right-align. You can also change alignment by selecting an alignment option in the Paragraph group on the Home tab.

c. Drag to select both lines of the footer. Click the **Home tab**, and then click **Align Text Right** ≡ in the Paragraph group. With both lines still selected, change the font size to **10** and the font to **Times New Roman**.

d. Double-click in the body of the memo to close the footer and return to the body of the document. You can also click Close Header and Footer to return to the document. Press Ctrl + Home to move to the beginning of the document if the insertion point is not already positioned there.

e. Double-click the top margin to place the insertion point in the header area. Click the **Insert tab**, and then click **Quick Parts** in the Text group. Click **Field**, scroll down the Field names list, click **FileName**, and then click **OK**.

You have included the file name as part of the header, making it convenient to identify the source of the document. You can also include a page number when you click Page Number in the Header & Footer group (on the Header & Footer Tools contextual tab), or you can insert the current date when you click Date & Time. Although you will

SIDE NOTE
Using Quick Parts

The Quick Parts button is located in two places on the Ribbon. With a header or footer open, Quick Parts is found in the Insert group of the Header & Footer Tools Design contextual tab. You can also access Quick Parts in the Text group of the Insert tab.

Deleting a Header or Footer

To delete a header or footer, click Header (or Footer) in the Header & Footer group on the Header & Footer Tools contextual tab. Of course, the insertion point should be positioned in the header or footer in order to display the contextual tab. Otherwise, you can click the Insert tab and then click Header (or Footer). From the subsequent list, click Remove Header (or Footer).

not often include a file name header in a business memo, you are including it here so that your instructor can easily identify the memo as belonging to you.

f. Click the **Header & Footer Tools Design tab**, and then click **Close Header and Footer** in the Close group.

g. Save the document.

Real World Advice — Using Headers and Footers

A primary purpose of headers and footers, especially when used in academic and business reports, is to identify pages as belonging to a particular project. If you include your name, the company name, or a project name in a footer, you will be reminded with each page of the document's origin and purpose. Research papers and books might include page and chapter numbers in a header or footer. Use headers and footers where appropriate to add organization and professionalism to a document.

Inserting and Deleting Text

You will often find it necessary to insert or delete text. By default, Word is configured so that text you type is inserted within existing text. For example, you might notice that you left a word out of a sentence, or that additional text within a sentence would improve readability. Click where you want the new text to be placed and type. Text automatically shifts to make room for the new entry.

You can delete text in several ways. If you click to the right of text that you want to delete, simply press Backspace repeatedly to remove characters one at a time. Pressing Delete also removes text, but it does so for text to the right of the insertion point. You can also select text that you want to remove by dragging to highlight the selection or using any of the selection techniques described in Figure 12, and then pressing Delete. The selected text is deleted.

Be careful when deleting text. The only way to retrieve deleted text is to retype it or to click Undo on the Quick Access Toolbar—if you are quick enough! The Undo action only works if you invoke it fairly quickly after the unwanted deletion. Even then, if you have performed any actions between the time of the deletion and clicking Undo, all actions in between will be undone as well.

Clearing Formatting

Often, it is easier to "do something" than to "undo it." Applying a format, such as bold or underlining, is as simple as selecting text and clicking a command on the Ribbon—or making a selection from the Mini toolbar or the Font dialog box. To remove the formatting, reverse the action by selecting the text and clicking the command again. As you recall, a command that reverses itself when clicked a second time is called a **toggle**. But what if the selected text has several character attributes assigned? If selected text is underlined, italicized, and set at a larger font size than it was originally, you would have to undo several character formats. Word provides a quick fix to clearing one or more formats in the form of the Clear Formatting command. You will find the Clear Formatting option in the Font group on the Home tab, as shown in Figure 23.

To Clear Formatting

a. Click after the words **Painted Paradise Resort** (before the space) in the first paragraph of the body of the memo. Press Spacebar, and then type and Spa. In the same paragraph, select the words **in large part**, and then press Delete. Adjust the spacing between the remaining words, if necessary.

b. Select **July 31**. Click **Clear Formatting** 🔲 in the Font group. All character formatting is removed.

Click to clear formatting

Figure 23 Clearing formatting

c. Because you want to retain the Times New Roman font, you must specify it once more. With **July 31** still selected, click the **Font arrow**, and then select **Times New Roman**.

d. Save the document.

Printing a Document

Backstage view provides options for printing a document. In earlier versions of Word, it was a bit cumbersome to preview a document before printing, because the Print and Preview actions were located in separate areas of the Word command structure. Backstage view brings those actions together, displaying a preview of the document when you click Print. Although you cannot edit a document in print preview, you can take a quick last look before printing.

Exploring Print Settings

When in Backstage view, you can select several options related to printing a document. By default, documents are shown in portrait orientation, where the document is taller than it is wide. Some documents might be better suited for landscape orientation, which is when the document is displayed wider than it is tall. You can easily change the page orientation, as well as other print settings, in Backstage view. For example, you might want to print several copies of a document, or perhaps only certain pages of a current document. Backstage view makes all of those options easily accessible.

Real World Advice   Creating a PDF

Recall that a PDF (Portable Document Format) is a format that makes it possible to send formatted documents and have them appear on a recipient's monitor or printer as they were intended. The data in a PDF file cannot be easily changed. Adobe Reader, free software that is easily downloaded, is required to open a PDF file, but it does not allow changes to the document. In some cases, it might be appropriate to save the document as a PDF file and then deliver it to a recipient electronically. Doing so avoids unnecessary printing. Working with a PDF version of a document that is not printed is more cost-effective and environmentally friendly than using paper.

To Preview and Print a Document

a. Click the **File tab**, and then click **Print**.

Note the preview of the memorandum that is displayed on the right. Options, such as number of copies, orientation, and printer selection, are available in the center section.

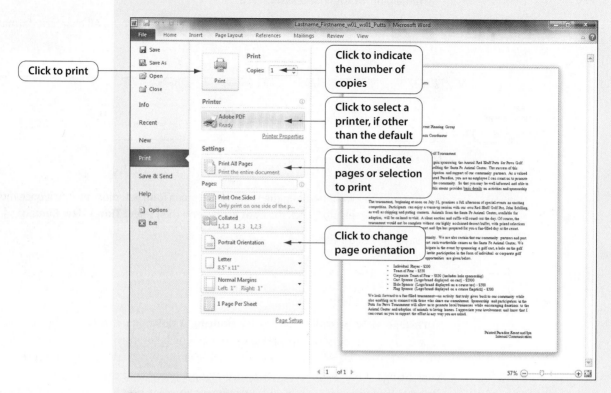

Figure 24 Print settings

b. In the Copies box, increase the number of copies to 5.

c. Click **Print All Pages**, and note that if the document were a multi-page document, you could choose to print only the current page. You could also indicate a selection to print or identify a custom range of pages. Click **Print All Pages** again to close the options list.

d. Click **Portrait Orientation**, and then click **Landscape Orientation** to change the orientation to landscape.

e. Because the new orientation is not attractive, click **Landscape Orientation**, and then **Portrait Orientation** to return to the original orientation. Click the **Home tab** to leave Backstage view and return to the document.

f. Save the document and exit Word.

Concept Check

1. You are applying for a position related to your college major. The application package requires a written letter of application. Who is your target audience? How can you build support for your message, and what information do you need to include?

2. Identify a business document that might require either a header or footer. What header or footer would you include? Is there any reason that a header might not be appropriate on the first page? Provide specific examples.

3. In some cases, a subject or reference line replaces the salutation in a business letter. Why would you choose not to include a salutation? Suggest an appropriate salutation for a case in which you do not have a specific recipient in mind, as in the case of applying for a job. Think of ways that you can avoid being gender specific in your salutation.

4. As you progress through college and into the workforce, you are likely to find occasion to share documents with others who assist in their development. Word 2010 makes it easy to collaborate and share documents online. Although you have not yet worked with online document sharing, can you identify possible advantages and disadvantages to such sharing? Specifically, identify document types that are well suited for sharing as well as those that should not be made available online.

5. You are assigned to the new employee training unit of your company. Your most recent project involves developing training materials for the preparation of Word documents. Provide an itemized list of suggestions regarding font, paragraph alignment, and use of color. Be sure to note any differences in your list when applied to documents developed for electronic display.

Key Terms

AutoCorrect 122
Backstage view 107
Block 100
Business communication 96
Centered 119
Default 102
Draft view 102
Font 115
Footer 124
Formatting marks 102
Full Screen Reading view 102
Hard return 101

Header 124
Insertion point 106
Justified 119
Key Tips 102
Left-aligned 119
Live Preview 115
Microsoft Word 2010 96
Modified block 100
Nonprinting characters 102
Outline view 102
PDF (Portable Document Format) 110

Print Layout 102
Right-aligned 119
Ruler 105
Sans serif font 115
Semiblock 100
Serif font 115
SkyDrive 109
Soft return 101
Toggle 126
Web Layout view 102
Word processing 96
Word wrap 101

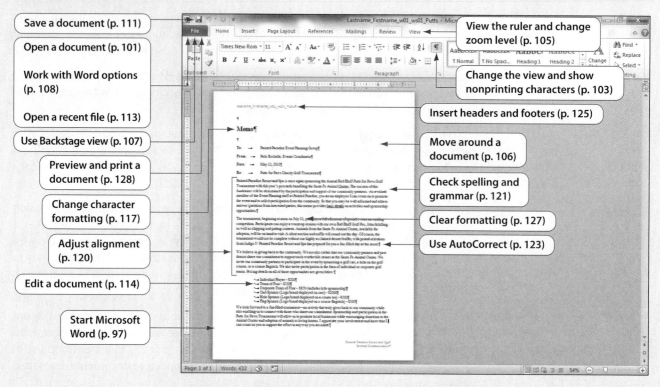

Save a document (p. 111)

Open a document (p. 101)

Work with Word options (p. 108)

Open a recent file (p. 113)

Use Backstage view (p. 107)

Preview and print a document (p. 128)

Change character formatting (p. 117)

Adjust alignment (p. 120)

Edit a document (p. 114)

Start Microsoft Word (p. 97)

View the ruler and change zoom level (p. 105)

Change the view and show nonprinting characters (p. 103)

Insert headers and footers (p. 125)

Move around a document (p. 106)

Check spelling and grammar (p. 121)

Clear formatting (p. 127)

Use AutoCorrect (p. 123)

Figure 25 Putts for Paws Golf Tournament Memo final document

Student data file needed:

w01_ws01_Thanks

You will save your file as:

Lastname_Firstname_w01_ws01_Thanks

Thank You Letter

Customer Service

The Red Bluff Golf Club Putts for Paws Golf Tournament was a tremendous success! Over 80 golfers enjoyed a day on the greens, putting for the Santa Fe Animal Center. You will edit and send a thank you letter to each participant. Before completing a mail merge though (covered in Workshop 4), you will prepare a single letter, making sure all formatting is correct and that there are no misspellings or grammatical mistakes.

a. Start **Word**. Click the **File tab**, and then click **Open**. Navigate to the location of your student files, and then double-click **w01_ws01_Thanks**. A draft of a thank-you letter is displayed. Save the file as Lastname_Firstname_w01_ws01_Thanks.

b. If necessary, click **Show/Hide** ¶ in the Paragraph group to display formatting marks. If the ruler is not already displayed, click the **View tab**, and then select **Ruler** to show the ruler.

c. Press Ctrl+A to select the entire document. Click the **Font arrow** in the Font group, and then scroll to select **Times New Roman**. Press Ctrl+Home to place the insertion point at the beginning of the document, and then change the date to **May 15, 2013**.

d. Click the **Review tab**, and then click **Spelling & Grammar** in the Proofing group. Change any misspelled words as they are presented. If a flagged word is not actually misspelled, ignore the error by clicking Ignore Once. Click **OK**.

e. Proofread the document to make sure you did not overlook any misspellings or incorrect word usage. Correct anything that is out of order. You should find one word-usage error that Word did not identify.

f. Save and close the document. Click the **File tab**, click **Recent**, and then click **Lastname_ Firstname_w01_ws01_Thanks**.

g. Click the **File tab**, and then click **Print**. Note the document preview displayed to the right. What is the name of the printer the document will be sent to if you click Print?

h. Click **Options**, click **Proofing**, and then click **AutoCorrect Options**. Because you often type the manager's name, Barry Cheney, you will make it easy to enter the name. You will create an AutoCorrect entry so that the letters "bc" automatically convert to "Barry Cheney."

i. In the Replace box, type bc. Click in the **With box**, and then type Barry Cheney. Click **Add**, click **OK**, and then click **OK** again.

j. Press Ctrl+End to place the insertion point at the end of the document. Type bc and then press Spacebar. The words "Barry Cheney" are displayed. Press Enter, type Red Bluff Golf Club, and save the document.

k. Scroll to the top of the document. Drag to select **Red Bluff Putts for Paws Golf Tournament** in the first paragraph in the body of the letter. On the Home tab, click **Bold** in the Font group.

l. Drag to select **$75,000** in the same paragraph. Do not select the space following the dollar amount. On the Home tab, click **Underline** in the Font group.

m. Drag to select the URL (web address) in the second paragraph in the body of the letter. Click **Italic** in the Font group, and then click **Undo** on the Quick Access Toolbar to remove the italics. You decide that you do want italics, so click **Redo** on the Quick Access Toolbar.

n. Select the name and address block in the first four lines of the letter. On the Home tab, click **Align Text Right** in the Paragraph group.

o. Click the **File tab**, and then click **Print** to see a preview of the document.

p. Click the **Insert tab**, click **Footer** in the Header & Footer group, and then click **Edit Footer**. So that your instructor can identify your submission, you want to include your name and the file name in the footer. Type your name, and then press Enter. Click **Quick Parts** in the Insert group, click **Field**, scroll down and click **FileName**, and then click **OK**.

q. On the Header & Footer Tools Design tab, click **Close Header and Footer**.

r. Click the **File tab**, and then click **Options**. You will remove the AutoCorrect entry that you created in this exercise. Click **Proofing**, and then click **AutoCorrect Options**. Scroll through the list, select **bc**, click **Delete**, click **OK**, and then click **OK** again.

s. Save the document, and then exit Word.

Problem Solve 1

Student data file needed:

w01_ps1_Club

You will save your file as:

Lastname_Firstname_w01_ps1_Club

Sales & Marketing

Club Memorandum

You have recently been elected secretary of Covington Club, a college service organization. In that position, you make sure club members are kept apprised of volunteer activities that the club supports. Covington Club is coordinating with the campus Women's Center to participate in Caps for Cancer, an effort to provide hats to cancer patients who are dealing with hair loss as a side effect of cancer treatment. You will edit a memorandum to club members, encouraging them to participate in the program.

a. Start Word. Click the **File tab** and then click **Open**. Navigate to the location of your student data files, and then double-click **w01_ps1_Club**. A draft of the memorandum displays. Save the file as Lastname_Firstname_w01_ps1_Club.

b. If necessary, click **Show/Hide** in the Paragraph group to display formatting marks. Double-click **To** in the second line of the memorandum and then click **Bold** in the Font group. Similarly, boldface **From**, **Date**, and **Re**.

c. Click the **File tab**, and then click **Options**. Click **Proofing**. Click **AutoCorrect Options**. In the Replace box, type cc. Click the **With box** and type Covington Club. Click **Add**, click **OK**, and then click **OK** again.

d. Click at the right of the tab arrow in the **To:** line and type cc Members.

e. Click at the right of the tab arrow in the **From:** line and type your first and last name.

f. Click to place the insertion point before the word **As** in the sentence beginning "As you are aware." Press [Enter] twice.

g. Drag to select **room 213C** in the second body paragraph. Click **Underline** in the Font group.

h. Press [Ctrl]+[Home]. Click **Replace** in the Editing group. In the **Find what box**, type hats. Click in the **Replace with** box and type caps. Click **Replace All**, and then click **Close**.

i. Drag to select the word **such** in the second sentence of the second body paragraph. Press [Delete] to delete the word.

j. Double-click **Monday** in the last sentence of the memo. Type Monday, February 5.

k. Press [Ctrl]+[A] to select all memo text. Click the **Font arrow**, scroll down if necessary, and click **Times New Roman**. Click anywhere to deselect the text. Drag to select all text with the exception of the first line (Memorandum). Click the **Font Size arrow** and click **12**.

l. Click the **Review tab**, and then click **Spelling & Grammar**. Correct any words that are actually misspelled. Proofread the document yourself to identify any mistakes Word might have missed.

m. Click the **File tab**, click **Options**, click **Proofing**, and then click **AutoCorrect Options**. Scroll through the AutoCorrect entries and click **cc**. Click **Delete**, click **OK**, and then click **OK** again.

n. Click the **Insert tab**, click **Footer**, and then click **Edit Footer**. Click **Quick Parts** in the Insert group, and then click **Field**. Scroll through the field names, click **FileName**, and then click **OK**. Click the **Home tab**, and then click **Align Text Right** in the Paragraph group.

o. Click the **File** tab, and then click **Print** to preview the document.

p. Save the document, and then exit Word.

 Additional Workshop Cases are available on the companion website and in the instructor resources.

WORKSHOP 2

Creating and Editing a Document

PREPARE CASE
Red Bluff Caddy School Flyer

Sales & Marketing

Each spring, Painted Paradise Resort and Spa sponsors a caddy school that is open to current and aspiring caddies. The four-day event teaches the basics of caddying and provides an opportunity for participants to caddy for a golf tournament.

Your assignment is to create, edit, and format a flyer providing information on the caddy school. You will also create an invitation from a template, which is a predesigned document.

Denise Kappa / Shutterstock.com

Student data file needed for this workshop:

 None

You will save your files as:

 Lastname_Firstname_w01_ws02_School   Lastname_Firstname_w01_ws02_Gift

Creating a New Document

A new blank document is displayed when you start Word. You can then begin to type and edit text for a document. That works well if you are starting Word at the same time that you want to begin a new document. But what if you are closing one document and want to begin a new one? When you complete work on a project, you will want to save it. When you save and close a document without exiting Word, Word remains open but displays a blank gray area instead of the usual white document space. You can then open a new blank document to begin a new project. In this section, you will learn to work with styles, edit text, adjust paragraph and line spacing, include bullets and numbering, and cut, copy, and paste text.

Understanding Word Styles

A **style** is a set of formatting characteristics that you can apply to selected text. Some styles are predefined and are available when you begin Word. You can also create and apply your own styles. Using styles, you can simplify the task of formatting text, and you can be sure that similar elements have the same formatting. When creating a report, for example, you will most likely want all major headings to be formatted identically, with the same font and alignment settings. Simply apply an appropriate style to all headings, and the job is done! Because a style can include any number of formatting options, you can save a great deal of time when you apply a style instead of setting each format option individually, especially if the style includes many complex format settings.

Styles in the Styles group are also known as **Quick Styles**. Related styles in the Quick Styles gallery (Styles group) are designed to work together. For example, Heading 2 style is designed to color coordinate and to look subordinate to the Heading 1 style. So using Quick Styles can help you quickly create a cohesive and attractive document. Additionally, if you use built-in heading styles, Word can automatically generate a table of contents. Based on headings applied through Quick Styles, Word 2010 also generates a Document Map (see Figure 1), which is a convenient way to move rapidly through a lengthy document.

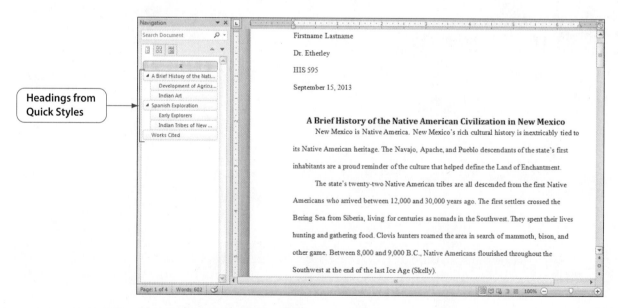

Figure 1   Document Map

Real World Advice | Styles and Organization

Using styles can do more than simplify the task of ensuring consistent formatting throughout a document. If a document is lengthy, with multiple sections or topics, correct selection of styles can help you think more purposefully about the document's organization. For example, by selecting different heading levels for subsequent levels of detail within a document, you will be better able to visualize the structure of the document.

Most styles are considered to be either a *character style* or a *paragraph style*. Character styles set the formatting of font, font size, color, and emphasis—underline, bold, or italics—to individual characters or selections. You can apply a character style to any area of selected text. A paragraph style sets the alignment, spacing, and indentation formatting. Paragraph styles are applied to entire paragraphs. Therefore, to apply a paragraph style, you only need to position the insertion point within a paragraph before selecting the style.

A few styles are neither character nor paragraph, but are instead *linked styles*. A linked style behaves as either a character style or paragraph style, depending on what you select. For example if you click within a paragraph without selecting any specific text and then select the Heading 1 style, the entire paragraph is formatted with both font characteristics, such as font color and size, and paragraph features, such as alignment. However, if you select only one word or a limited amount of text within the paragraph and then apply the Heading 1 style, only the font characteristics are applied. Font color and size may change, but alignment does not.

Even though you have applied a specific style to a paragraph or text selection, you can always change to another style by selecting a new style. You can also modify existing styles, even if you have already applied those styles to elements of your document. When you change a style's formatting options, the new options are immediately applied to all text that has been formatted in that style within the current document. That means that if your research paper includes 10 major headings, all of which you have formatted in a certain style, modifying that style immediately causes all 10 headings to reflect the new settings.

Using the Normal Style

The default style for all new documents is called Normal. Normal style is a paragraph style with specific spacing and formatting characteristics. Although that style might be appropriate for some documents, it will not be the best choice for all documents. You can easily select another style that is more appropriate for either the entire document or for selected text or paragraphs. Normal style formats text at 11-pt Calibri font, left-aligned, and with 1.15 line spacing. It also includes a small amount of additional space between paragraphs.

Workshop 2 Training

To Work with Styles

a. Start **Word**. Save the blank document as Lastname_Firstname_w01_ws02_School on the disk drive where you save your projects.

b. With the Home tab selected, click **Show/Hide** ¶ in the Paragraph group to show nonprinting characters—unless nonprinting characters are already displayed.

Troubleshooting

It is possible that your document was already set to show nonprinting characters. In that case, when you clicked Show/Hide, you "toggled" the setting off instead of on. Simply click Show/Hide again to show nonprinting characters.

c. Type Painted Paradise Resort and press Enter. Type Invites you to participate in a and press Enter.

d. Type Caddy School and press Enter. Type Sponsored by the and press Enter. Type Red Bluff Golf Club and press Enter.

e. Click anywhere in the first line of the document, and then place the pointer over **Heading 1** in the Styles group on the Home tab. Do not click, but move the mouse pointer to another style in the Styles group. Live Preview shows the effect that the style would have on the selected text. To see even more styles, click **More** ▾. Move back to **Heading 1** and click. The Heading 1 style is applied to the selected line.

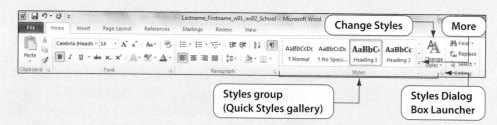

Figure 2   Word Styles

f. Click the **Dialog Box Launcher** ▣ in the Styles group. Double-click the **title bar** of the Styles pane to dock it (make it stationary). If the dialog box was already docked before you double-clicked, you will see no change.

g. Place the pointer over **Heading 1** (the currently selected style) in the Styles pane, and then note the style description that displays. Make sure that you point to Heading 1 in the Styles pane instead of Heading 1 in the Styles group on the Home tab.

h. Click the **Heading 1 arrow**, and then click **Modify**. Because you plan to repeat the Heading 1 style in this document, but with different font and alignment settings, you will modify the style.

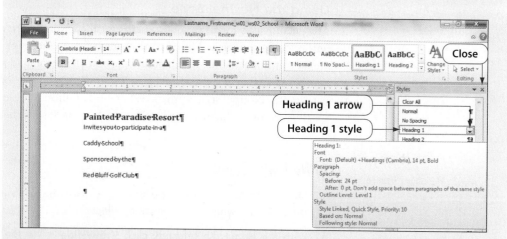

Figure 3   Styles pane

Troubleshooting

If you click the style name instead of the arrow to the right, the style is applied to the selection again without modification. In that case, simply repeat Step h.

i. Click **Center** ▤ in the Formatting section, click the **Font Size arrow**, and then click **18**.

SIDE NOTE
Selecting Font Color

When you click the Font Color arrow in the Font group, you can select from a palette of colors. As you place the pointer over a color, you will see a tip identifying the color selection. Colors are very precisely identified, such as Olive Green, Accent 3, Darker 25%. When working with a document, you might need to match a color precisely, so such specific color identification can be helpful.

j. Click the **Font Color arrow**, and then select the font color **Dark Blue, Text 2, Darker 50%** (row 6, column 4).

k. Click the **Format** button, click **Text Effects**, and then click **Shadow**. Click the **Presets** button, and then under the Outer category, click **Offset Right** (row 2, column 1). Click **Close**. Click **OK**.

l. Click **Close** ☒ to close the Styles pane.

m. Save 🖫 the document.

Quick Reference — Adding the Current Style to the Quick Access Toolbar

Sometimes it is helpful to know what style a paragraph or selection is formatted in. You might think that when you click in a paragraph, you would somehow be informed of the paragraph's style. Unless the style is one of the few that is displayed in the Styles group on the Home tab, however, it is not always easy to quickly determine the style. A fix is to place a Styles list on the Quick Access Toolbar.

1. Click Customize Quick Access Toolbar, and then click More Commands.
2. Click the arrow beside the Choose commands from box, and then select Commands Not in the Ribbon.
3. Scroll through the list, and then click Style.
4. Click Add, and then click OK.

At that point, you can click in any paragraph within the document and see the style of that paragraph in the Styles list box. If you later want to remove the box, just right-click the Styles list box arrow and click Remove from Quick Access Toolbar.

Real World Advice — Creating an Effective Flyer

Sales & Marketing

Creating a flyer is more than simply listing a few facts. Before delving into the design, you should have a clear understanding of exactly what you want the flyer to convey. Create an information checklist on a sheet of paper before attempting to place the information in the flyer. Choose your words wisely, as a flyer is usually brief. Use bold, persuasive, and descriptive words. Keep the flyer clean and effective by using no more than two fonts. You might use one font for headlines and a separate font for the text. Use pictures and graphics if possible. Print the flyer on light paper because light colors showcase a clear, bold font. Understand the value of white space. It is easy to get excited with text, images, and decorative paper, but be careful not to overtax the eye with too much on the page. Finally, place the flyer on a wall and step back to take a good look. If you are distracted by an overabundance of color or graphics, it is a safe bet that your target audience will be also. Of course, always proofread before printing.

Defining a New Style

If a current style has most of the formatting that you want for a particular text selection or paragraph, but you want to adjust it a little, you have learned that you can modify the style. For example, Normal is the default style when you begin a new document, but it does not single-space text. If you prefer to single-space your documents, you can simply modify the Normal style to single-spacing or select another style. Occasionally, however, you cannot find a style that contains even a few of the formatting options that you need for a selection. In that case, you can create a new style.

Deleting a Style

When you no longer need a style, you can delete it. Be careful though—deleting a style will remove its formatting options from any text where the style has been applied.

Real World Advice   Creating a Shortcut Key for a Style

If you often apply a particular style, you might find it cumbersome to continually find and click the style on the Styles pane or in the Quick Styles gallery. Instead, you might want to create a shortcut key combination for the style.

1. Open the Styles pane, and then place the pointer on the style you want a shortcut for.

2. Click the Style's list arrow, and then click Modify.

3. Click Format, and then click Shortcut key.

4. Click in the Press new shortcut key box and type the desired shortcut keys. For example, you might assign Alt+Ctrl+V as a shortcut for the Heading 1 style. If the shortcut combination is not already in use, you can simply click Assign. If you are informed that it is already in use, try another sequence.

5. Click Close, and then click OK.

To Define a New Style and Edit a Document

a. Click the **Home tab**, select the second line, **Invites you to participate in a**, and then click **Center** ☰ in the Paragraph group.

b. Click the **Font Size arrow** in the Font group, and then select **14**. Click the **Font Color arrow** ⊞, and then select **Dark Blue, Text 2, Darker 50%** (row 6, column 4).

c. Click the **Styles Dialog Box Launcher** to open the Styles pane. Click **New Style** ⊞ in the Styles pane. Type Lower Paragraph in the Name box. Make sure **Add to Quick Style list** and **Only in this document** are selected, and click **OK**.

After applying font attributes to text in the flyer, you create a new style based on those settings. You can then apply that style later to other text without redefining the font settings.

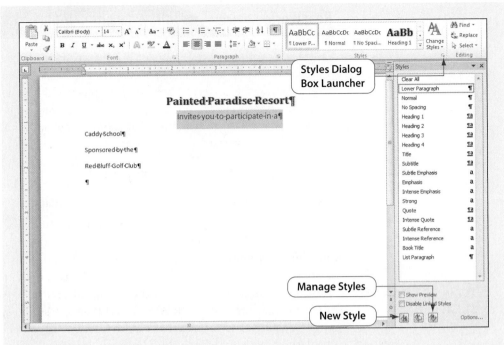

Figure 4   Styles pane

d. Select the last three lines of text: **Caddy School**, **Sponsored by the**, and **Red Bluff Golf Club**. Click **Lower Paragraph** in the Styles pane. Click outside the selected area to see the result.

e. Point to **Lower Paragraph** in the Styles pane box, click the style's **list arrow**, click **Modify**, click **Bold** $\boxed{\text{B}}$, and then click **OK**. When you modify a style, any changes are immediately applied to all text identified with that style, even text that you have typed earlier.

f. Press **Ctrl+End** to place the insertion point at the end of the document, and then click **No Spacing** in the Styles group. Text that you type will be formatted in the No Spacing style.

g. Type the following paragraph, but do not press Enter when you get to the end of a line. Word wrap will automatically move the insertion point to the next line when necessary.

Our goal is to enable you to become the best caddy that you can be! You will learn to take personal responsibility for your time, appearance, knowledge, attitude, and character. Join us for four fun-filled days. We promise that you will be glad you did!

h. Triple-click in the paragraph that you just typed to select it. Although the No Spacing style is appropriate for the spacing of the paragraph, you want to add a few additional formatting features, without modifying the style.

i. Click **Bold** $\boxed{\text{B}}$ in the Font group. Click the **Font arrow**, and then click **12**. Click the **Font Color button** $\boxed{\text{A} \cdot}$—not the arrow—to apply the most recently selected font color to the selection.

j. Press $\boxed{\text{Ctrl}}$+$\boxed{\text{End}}$ to move the insertion point to the end of the document, and then press $\boxed{\text{Enter}}$.

k. Click **Close** $\boxed{\times}$ in the top-right corner of the Styles pane to close it.

l. Save $\boxed{\text{H}}$ the document.

SIDE NOTE
Selecting a Recent Font Color

When you click the Font Color button in the Font group, the most recently selected font color is applied. That comes in handy if you are attempting to precisely match the most recent font color to another text selection.

Regardless of what you write, most likely someone is going to read it. It is critical that you have a clear understanding of your target audience so you can plan your approach and develop the content. Always keep the interest of your audience in mind, and avoid overusing the word "I." You are not writing about yourself or what you think but about your target audience. Remember that knowing your audience lets you refine the subject matter so that it matches your readers' needs. Analyze your audience before you write!

Adjusting Paragraph and Line Spacing

Before considering the topic of paragraph and line spacing, remember that Word defines a paragraph as any text that ends with a hard return. That means that a list of four bulleted items, such as those shown in Figure 5, is actually four separate paragraphs. Similarly, a report title is a paragraph, as is the salutation line in a letter. Even a blank line is considered a paragraph, as indicated by a paragraph mark if nonprinting characters are displayed. Also, recall that unless you specify otherwise, all text in a new document is formatted in Normal style. If you check the formatting options in Normal style (which you can do if you open the Styles pane and hover the pointer over Normal), you will find that Paragraph Alignment is Left, Spacing is 1.15 lines, and Spacing After is 10 pt. To understand that summary and to be able to specify spacing options in a document, you need to understand the concept of paragraph and line spacing.

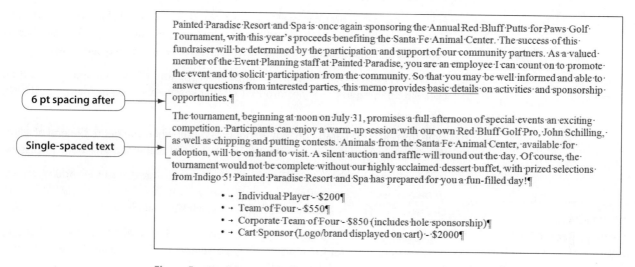

Figure 5   Paragraph and line spacing

Formatting options are generally categorized as *paragraph* formatting or *character* formatting. Character formatting is formatting that is applied only to selected text. For example, when you underline a word, you have applied character formatting. Paragraph formatting is formatting that is applied to entire paragraphs. Generally, paragraph formatting is defined as paragraph or line spacing, tabs, and indents. Figure 5 shows a document with both paragraph and line spacing. Individual paragraphs are single-spaced, but notice the space between paragraphs. It appears that there is more space between paragraphs than there is between lines. In fact, that is the case. In this example, **line spacing** is 1, and **paragraph spacing** is 6 pt after.

Selecting Line Spacing

Before specifying either line or paragraph spacing, remember that such formatting is only applied to currently selected text or to text that you are going to type. If you are creating a document that you know should be double-spaced, you can specify the line spacing before you begin. If you are changing the line spacing for existing text, you can simply click in a paragraph you want to change the line spacing in, or you can select several paragraphs and then apply the new line spacing. Figure 5 shows single-spaced text.

Selecting Paragraph Spacing

Paragraph spacing is the space before and after paragraphs. In most documents, you will find that there is more space between paragraphs than there is within paragraphs (see Figure 5). Remember that line spacing defines space *between lines* in a paragraph, while paragraph spacing is evident *between paragraphs*. Paragraph spacing is measured in points. Technically, a point is 1/72", but you do not need to measure space that closely. Just be aware that paragraph spacing is measured in terms of points, with common settings specified in units of 6. You can identify paragraph spacing *before* or *after*, and making that choice is much like the old adage "Which came first—the chicken or the egg?" Most often, it does not make much difference how you interpret the spacing because either way you are creating space between paragraphs. As a general rule, most spacing is specified *after* a paragraph. Figure 5 shows 6-pt spacing after paragraphs.

To Work with Paragraph and Line Spacing

a. Make sure the ruler is displayed. If it is not, on the View tab click **Ruler**. Press **Ctrl+End** to position the insertion point at the end of the document.

b. Type the following paragraph.

   Caddy School is offered each spring to current and aspiring caddies. We hope you will join us this April for a three-day program designed to introduce caddying basics and to give you an opportunity to caddy for a charity tournament held right here at the Red Bluff Golf Course!

c. Select the last two paragraphs in the document beginning with **Our goal** and ending with **Course!** Click the **Dialog Box Launcher** in the Paragraph group. The Paragraph dialog box enables you to adjust both paragraph and line spacing.

d. In the Paragraph dialog box, under Spacing, click the **After up arrow** twice to increase to **12 pt**. Each time you click the arrow, the spacing value is adjusted by 6. Click **OK**.
   Instead of clicking the arrow, you can simply click in the Spacing Before or Spacing After box and type a value. The value that you type does not have to be a multiple of 6.

e. Press Ctrl+End, press Enter, and then click **Center** in the Paragraph group.

f. Type Red Bluff Caddy School and then press Enter. Type April 3–6, 2013 and then press Enter. Type 8:00–3:00 daily and then press Enter. Type (meeting at the Pro Shop) and then press Enter.

g. Select the last two lines of text beginning with **8:00–3:00** and ending with **(meeting at the Pro Shop)**, and then click **Line and Paragraph Spacing** in the Paragraph group. Click **Remove Space After Paragraph**.

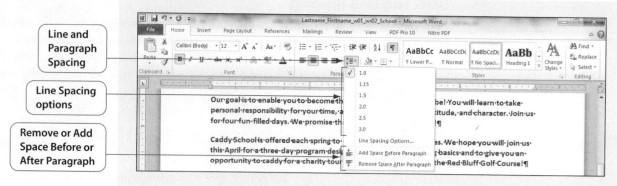

Line and Paragraph Spacing

Line Spacing options

Remove or Add Space Before or After Paragraph

Figure 6   Spacing options in the Paragraph group

h. Press Ctrl+End to move to the end of the document, and then press Enter.

i. Click **Align Text Left** [icon] in the Paragraph group. Type Day 1 – Indoor lecture on basics of caddying and then press Enter. Be sure to leave a space before and after the dash. Type Days 2 and 3 – On the golf course, with instruction from a golf pro and then press Enter. Type Day 4 – Caddying for a tournament and then press Enter.

j. Select the three lines that you just typed beginning with **Day 1** and ending with **tournament**. (Do not select the final paragraph mark.) Click **Line and Paragraph Spacing** [icon] in the Paragraph group, and then click **1.15**. Do not deselect the text.

Real World Advice   How and When to Choose Line Spacing

When you use the Paragraph dialog box to select line spacing, you have more choices than simply single- and double-spacing. You can also select Exactly, At Least, or Multiple. What exactly are those options? *Exactly* enables you to choose a highly precise line spacing that remains fixed at a specified point size. *At Least* lets you specify a minimum line spacing while allowing Word to adjust the height if necessary to accommodate such items as drop caps, which are oversized letters that sometimes begin paragraphs. The At Least setting is used more in desktop publishing than in routine documents. *Multiple* enables you to set line spacing at an interval other than single, double, or 1.5.

Indenting Lines

Some document styles, such as a semiblock letter style, require that the first line of each paragraph be indented from the left margin. Such an indent is called a **first-line indent**. If you have ever created or read a bibliography, which is a list of references included with a research report, you may recall that typically the first line begins at the left margin, but all other lines in a citation are indented. That indent style is called a **hanging indent**. If you have studied methods of writing research reports, you might recall that a lengthy quote is often indented an equal distance from both the left and right margins. Indenting an entire paragraph from the left margin is called a **left indent**. Similarly, indenting from the right margin is a **right indent**. You can easily create indents in a document using either the Paragraph dialog box or the ruler. Figure 7 provides examples of indents.

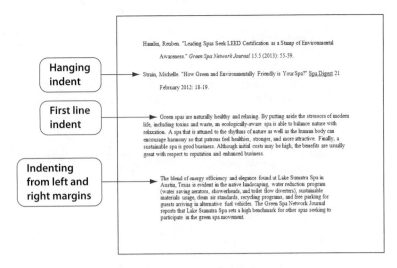

Hanging indent

First line indent

Indenting from left and right margins

Hamlin, Reuben. "Leading Spas Seek LEED Certification as a Stamp of Environmental
   Awareness." *Green Spa Network Journal* 15.5 (2013): 55-59.

Strain, Michelle. "How Green and Environmentally Friendly is Your Spa?" Spa Digest 21
   February 2012: 18-19.

Green spas are naturally healthy and relaxing. By putting aside the stressors of modern
life, including toxins and waste, an ecologically-aware spa is able to balance nature with
relaxation. A spa that is attuned to the rhythms of nature as well as the human body can
encourage harmony so that patrons feel healthier, stronger, and more attractive. Finally, a
sustainable spa is good business. Although initial costs may be high, the benefits are usually
great with respect to reputation and enhanced business.

The blend of energy efficiency and elegance found at Lake Sumatra Spa in
Austin, Texas is evident in the native landscaping, water reduction program
(water saving aerators, showerheads, and toilet flow diverters), sustainable
materials usage, clean air standards, recycling programs, and free parking for
guests arriving in alternative fuel vehicles. The Green Spa Network Journal
reports that Lake Sumatra Spa sets a high benchmark for other spas seeking to
participate in the green spa movement.

Figure 7   Examples of indents

Real World Advice   Tab to Indent

Probably the easiest way to set a first-line indent is to press [Tab] before you begin
to type. By default, that action indents the first line of a paragraph ½" from the
left margin. To remove a first-line indent that you have just set by pressing a [Tab],
simply press [Backspace]. To configure Word to indent each paragraph by default,
open Backstage view, click Options, click Proofing, click AutoCorrect Options, click
the AutoFormat As You Type tab, and then select Set left- and first-indent with tabs
and backspaces.

   Indenting is considered to be paragraph formatting. That means that unless you
are indenting several paragraphs, you do not need to select a block of text. Instead,
simply click within a paragraph to be indented, or select an indent setting before
typing a paragraph. Word provides several tools that enable you to specify indents.
Using the Paragraph dialog box, you can change the left and right indentation of the
entire paragraph. You can also specify a first-line or hanging indent. The Home tab
and the Page Layout tab on the Ribbon each provide quick access to indent buttons.
You can even use the ruler to quickly specify indents.

Quick Reference   Set Paragraph and Line Spacing

1. Click the Home tab.
2. Click the Paragraph Dialog Box Launcher.
3. Adjust Indentation and Paragraph/Line Spacing settings.
4. Click OK.

To Indent Paragraphs

a. If necessary, select the last three paragraphs of text. Click the **Dialog Box Launcher** 🔲 in the Paragraph group, and then under Indentation, click the **Left up arrow** until it displays 1". Click **OK**. Because all three paragraphs are selected, each paragraph—or line in this case—is indented by 1".

Special indents include first line and hanging

Indent entire paragraph from left

Indent entire paragraph from right

Specify the number of inches to indent

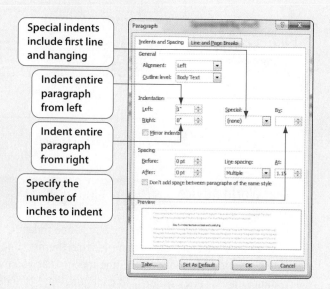

Figure 8   Indenting with the Paragraph dialog box

Troubleshooting

If only one line is indented, you did not have all three selected. Select the remaining lines and repeat Step a.

Troubleshooting

Be sure to change the left indentation to 1" not 0.1". If you make a mistake, simply correct the Left indent setting in the Paragraph dialog box.

b. Place the pointer on the **Left Indent** handle on the ruler.

You will see a tip indicating that the handle is for the left indent. Just above the Left Indent handle is a small shape that represents a hanging indent. Directly above that is a shape representing a first-line indent. On the right side of the ruler, note the small shape that resembles an arrow shape. It represents a right indent. You can drag any of those shapes to set a corresponding indent.

c. Drag the **Left Indent** handle on the ruler to the ½" ruler mark to decrease the left indent. As you drag, notice the vertical guide that moves with you, giving a visual clue as to placement within the document. Keep the text selected.

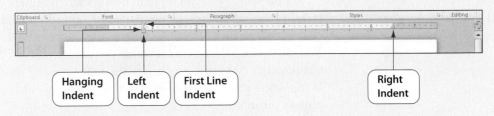

Hanging Indent • Left Indent • First Line Indent • Right Indent

Figure 9   Using the ruler to set indents

Troubleshooting

If you drag a handle other than the Left Indent handle, your text may not line up cleanly at the ½" mark. In that case, click Undo and repeat Step c.

d. Click the **Page Layout tab**, and then in the Indent section of the Paragraph group click the **Indent Left up arrow** to increase the left indent to **0.8"**. Click anywhere to deselect the text.

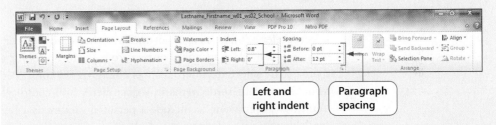

Left and right indent • Paragraph spacing

Figure 10   Using the Page Layout tab to set indents

e. Select the two paragraphs beginning with **Our goal** and ending with **Course!** (after the exclamation point). Click the **Home tab**, and then click **Increase Indent** ⬚. Each time you click an Indent command, the entire paragraph is indented from the left margin by ½".

f. Because the change is not attractive, click **Decrease Indent** ⬚ to return to the original setting. Press Ctrl+End.

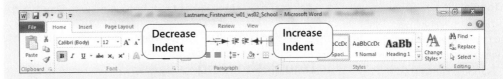

Decrease Indent • Increase Indent

Figure 11   Indenting with the Home tab

g. Save ⬚ the document.

Adding Bullets, Numbers, and Symbols

A document should be easy to read. You want your readers to find it easy to quickly hone in on major points. You might even consider developing an itemized or *bulleted* series of summary points. If your document is outlining steps in a process, you could *number* those steps for better readability. By striking a balance between straight text and bulleted or numbered items, you can produce well-organized documents that get your point across.

Using Word, you can include **bullets** and numbers in any document. If you have standard round bullets in mind, Word can accommodate. But you can also be as creative as you like, selecting check marks, colored boxes, or even symbols for bullets. You can define bullets from personal pictures or clip art. Numbering can occur in various formats. You can even change the font type and color of numbers in a document. If you delete a numbered item, Word will renumber the subsequent items so that they remain consecutive.

With such a wide range of possibilities, you are only limited by the purpose of your document. Business documents are more formal and conservative than other types, but you can still take advantage of a library of standard bullets and numbering schemes.

Selecting Bullets and Numbers

Bullets and numbers precede paragraphs. Remember that the definition of a paragraph is any text that ends with a hard return. When you list items within a document, you type an item and then press Enter. That means that each item in the list is a paragraph. You can then select the list of items and add bullets to the list—or numbers, if the list illustrates a sequential process. If you want to add bullets to text that you are about to type, you can click Bullets in the Paragraph group, type each line, and then click Bullets again to *turn off* bullets.

Defining New Bullets

If you prefer a bullet that is not included in Word's Bullet Library, you can create your own. You can select a symbol or picture for your bullet, or you can change the format of a previously selected bullet, such as changing its color. Perhaps you are using financial terms to describe some items in a document. You could select a dollar sign as a bullet. You might even want to include a personal picture as a bullet. All of those options are available when you define a new bullet.

Inserting Symbols

Symbols are characters that do not usually appear on a keyboard, such as © or ™. Word provides a gallery of symbols that you can select from. Some frequently accessed symbols are considered special characters, such as a nonbreaking hyphen or double opening and closing quotes.

SIDE NOTE
Bullets and Numbering Toggle

The Bullets feature is actually a toggle, as is Numbering, which means that you can click the command once to begin an action, and a second time to end it.

To Insert Bullets, Numbers, and Symbols

a. Select the last three lines of text beginning with **Day 1** and ending with **tournament**.

b. Click the **Bullets arrow** ⊞ ▾.

Troubleshooting

If you click the Bullets *button* instead of the Bullets *arrow*, solid round bullets are immediately applied to each selected paragraph. Because you want to select a different bullet style, click Undo, and then click the Bullets arrow.

c. Click the **star shape**. If you do not see a star shape or cannot identify it, select another bullet shape. Do not deselect the text.

If you had wanted to apply the default bullet style (round black bullet), you could have simply clicked Bullets in the Paragraph group. If you had wanted numbers instead, you would have clicked Numbering. To select from the Numbering Library, which includes not only numbers, but letters and Roman numerals, click the Numbering arrow.

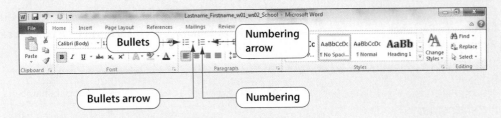

Figure 12   Applying bullets and numbering

d.   With the three bulleted lines selected, click the **Bullets arrow** , and then click **Define New Bullet**.

e.   Click **Font** in the Define New Bullet dialog box. Click the **Font color arrow**, select **Red, Accent 2** (first row, sixth column under Theme Colors), click **OK**, and then click **OK** again.

f.   Click **Undo** to reset the bullet color. You decide that the bullets were more attractive as they were originally formatted.

g.   Press **Ctrl+End**, and then press ⎡Enter⎤. Click **Center** in the Paragraph group. Type **For registration and additional information, contact:** and then press ⎡Enter⎤. Type the following text, pressing ⎡Enter⎤ at the end of each line.

Jorge Cruz, Caddy Master
Red Bluff Golf Club
3355 Hemmingway Circle
Santa Fe, NM 89566

h.   If necessary, be sure to press ⎡Enter⎤ after the last line of text. Select the last four lines of text beginning with **Jorge Cruz** and ending with **Santa Fe, NM 89566**.

i.   Click the **Page Layout tab**, and adjust the Spacing to **0** pt in both the **Before** and **After** boxes in the Paragraph group. Press ⎡Ctrl⎤+⎡End⎤ to place the insertion point at the end of the document.

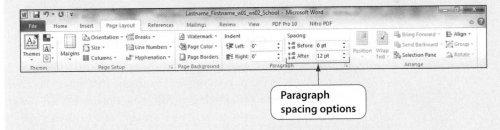

Figure 13   Adjusting paragraph spacing on the Page Layout tab

j.   Type the following text:

Be one of the first 20 to register and receive a Rigid Golf Umbrella. All registrants may also apply for the Pfazz–Tremble Scholarship, a college scholarship awarded to a caddy who is currently enrolled in college and who has caddied for at least one year.

k.   In the Paragraph group, adjust the **Before Spacing** to **6-pt size**. Click the **Home tab**, select the paragraph that you just typed, and then click **Italic** in the Font group. Click **Align Text Left** .

l.   Click immediately after the word **Rigid** to position the insertion point, click the **Insert tab**, and then click **Symbol** in the Symbols group. A few of the most commonly used symbols are shown, but even more symbols are available when you click More Symbols.

m. Click **More Symbols**. The Symbol dialog box opens. Click the **Special Characters tab**, and then click **Trademark**. Click **Insert**, and then click **Close**.

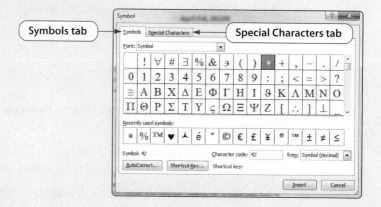

Figure 14   Symbol dialog box

n. Save ⊞ the document.

Real World Advice   Assign a Shortcut Key to a Symbol

If you often use a symbol or special character, you can save time by assigning a shortcut. In the Symbol dialog box, click the Special Characters tab to make sure a shortcut does not already exist for the symbol. Some special characters, but not all, are assigned a shortcut. For example, the shortcut for the copyright symbol is Ctrl+Alt+C. If a shortcut does not exist, click Shortcut Key, and then type a shortcut combination in the Press new shortcut key box.

Cutting, Copying, and Pasting Text

You will seldom create a document that you do not change later. Often, those changes involve moving or copying text from one location to another. Using Microsoft Office, you are not limited to copying within only one document—you can actually collect text in a document and place, or paste, it in an Excel worksheet or a PowerPoint presentation. Or perhaps you need to copy or move a selection from one Word document to another. All of those activities are possible using Word's cut, copy, and paste functions.

The key to the process of cutting and copying is the **Clipboard**, which is an area of memory reserved to temporarily contain text that you have cut or copied. When you **copy** text, you place a copy in the Clipboard, but leave the original text in the same location. When you **cut** text, the text is removed from its original location and placed in the Clipboard. You can then **paste** the text into a document at the insertion point. Usually, you will cut or copy text and then immediately paste it in a new location. That is because the Clipboard typically holds only one item at a time so when you cut or copy another selection, the item replaces whatever may already be on the Clipboard.

If you need to work with multiple selections, you can open the **Clipboard task pane**. With the task pane open, the Clipboard can hold up to 24 selections. The Clipboard task pane shows the most recently cut or copied item first. You can select any selection in the Clipboard task pane and paste it in another location. Remember that unless the Clipboard task pane is open, the Clipboard will only hold one item at a time. Therefore, you must paste a selection before cutting or copying another if the Clipboard task pane is not open.

Figure 15 identifies several methods of cutting, copying, and pasting a selection. Regardless of which method you prefer, the first step is to select what you want to copy or cut. Because the process of cutting, copying, and pasting is universal, you will want to remember shortcuts for those operations—shortcuts that are applicable to many applications, including other Microsoft Office components. The shortcut for copy is $\boxed{Ctrl}+\boxed{C}$, cut is $\boxed{Ctrl}+\boxed{X}$, and paste is $\boxed{Ctrl}+\boxed{V}$. The methods described in Figure 15 are best suited for text that you intend to paste immediately after cutting or copying.

To	Select Text and Then Do This
Copy	• Click Copy in the Clipboard group on the Home tab OR • Right-click the selection and click Copy on the shortcut menu OR • Press $\boxed{Ctrl}+\boxed{C}$
Cut	• Click Cut in the Clipboard group on the Home tab OR • Right-click the selection and click Cut on the shortcut menu OR • Press $\boxed{Ctrl}+\boxed{X}$
Paste	• Click Paste in the Clipboard group on the Home tab OR • Right-click in the position where the insertion should occur, and select a paste option OR • Press $\boxed{Ctrl}+\boxed{V}$

Figure 15 Cutting, copying, and pasting

Real World Advice   Paste Preview

Often, the very next thing that you do after pasting a selection is undo it because it does not give the effect that you intended. For that reason, Word 2010 now includes a **Paste Preview** feature, much like Live Preview, so that you can see the effect of a change before you accept it. After you copy a selection, click the Paste arrow in the Clipboard group. Each of the three Paste Options preview buttons shows the result in a different way. Keep Source Formatting retains the formatting from the *source* document that you copied. A source document is a document from which you copied an item or text. Merge Formatting shows the formatting from the *destination* document, which is the document to which a cut or copied item is pasted. Keep Text Only discards certain things that were present in the source such as images and formatting. Hover the pointer over any preview button to see the effect. When you move the pointer away, the preview disappears. Click the button to accept the change.

CONSIDER THIS | Avoid Plagiarism

You are probably well aware of the wealth of information available online. When completing a paper or a homework assignment, you might be tempted to copy and paste text from the Internet. When do you think such activity is permissible, and when would it be considered plagiarism? How might you detect plagiarism in a document given to you? If you revise a document and fail to recognize plagiarism, should you be held accountable?

Dragging and Dropping Text

If you plan to copy (or cut) and paste text within the same document, and if the beginning and ending locations are within a short distance of each other, you can simply drag text to paste a selection. Such action is very visual in that you must be able to see the selection and watch as you drag it to another area. Simply position the pointer over a selection, so that the pointer is displayed as a white arrow. Then drag the selected text to another location to move it, or press and hold $\boxed{\text{Ctrl}}$ while you drag the selection to copy it. Before you release the button, a small vertical bar will indicate the position where the text will be placed.

To Work with the Clipboard

a. Click the **Home tab**, and then click the **Dialog Box Launcher** ☐ in the Clipboard group.
   The Clipboard task pane is displayed on the left. Although it is not necessary to open the Clipboard task pane unless you plan to cut or copy multiple items before pasting any of them, you view it here simply to illustrate the concept of the Clipboard. As you continue to cut or copy text, the text will be shown in the Clipboard task pane. Until you turn off the computer or otherwise lose power, you can paste any item shown in the Clipboard task pane, regardless of its order. If you do not use the Clipboard task pane, you should immediately paste any text that you have cut or copied.

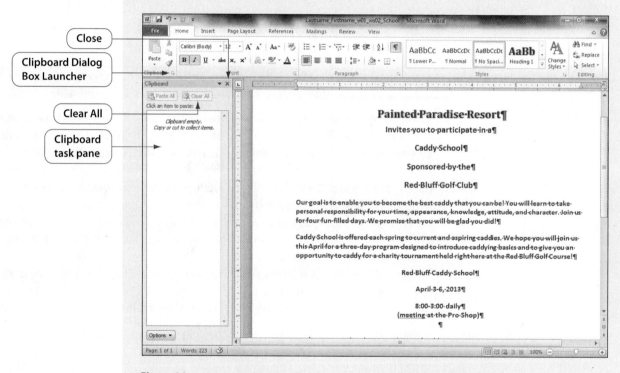

Figure 16 Clipboard task pane

b. Triple-click the paragraph that begins with **Caddy School is offered**. In the Clipboard group, click **Cut**. The selected text is displayed in the Clipboard task pane.

c. Click to place the insertion point just before the word **Our** in the first paragraph. Click **Paste** in the Clipboard group.
   The Paste button is actually a combination of the Paste command and the Paste arrow. When you click the Paste command, the most recently cut or copied item is immediately pasted at the position of the insertion point. When you click the Paste arrow, you can then choose a Paste option, several of which are described later in this section.

Paste button

Cut

Copy

Paste arrow

Figure 17 Clipboard group

d. Double-click the word **basics** in the first paragraph to select it. With the pointer, drag the selection to the left until a small vertical line shows just before the word **caddying**. Release the mouse button.

e. Click to place the insertion point just before the word **caddying**, and then type of followed by a space.

f. Select **Jorge Cruz**, right-click the selection, and then click **Copy** on the shortcut menu. The selection is displayed as the first item in the Clipboard task pane. Select the words **a golf pro** in the second bullet item but do not include the paragraph mark.

g. Hover the pointer over the **Jorge Cruz** text displayed at the top of the Clipboard task pane, click the arrow to the right of the selection, and then click **Paste**.

h. Click **Clear All** in the Clipboard task pane.
   All items are removed from the Clipboard. If you want to remove only one selection, click the arrow beside the item, and click Delete.

i. Click **Close** to close the Clipboard task pane.

j. Save and close the document. Do not close Word.

Working with Templates

A **template** is a document that is used as a starting point for another document. It is a framework into which you can place your own content. A template has very little content of its own, perhaps only headings or very generic sample content. For example, an application letter template contains sample text that you can modify to suit your own situation. An invitation template leaves room for you to compose your own text or to modify existing wording. Obviously, templates can save a lot of time and can jump-start a document if you need a little push. Some templates are located in Microsoft's online site, Office.com. Others are local, which means they are included in a typical Word installation.

Real World Advice Selecting a Template

Some businesses develop templates that are used in-house and that are preferred over certain templates provided by Microsoft. Before using a template obtained online or within an Office application, check to make sure there is not an equivalent or preferred template where you work.

To Work with Templates

a. Click the **File tab**, and then click **New**.
   Word's templates are organized into two categories. Some are local—within Word's built-in collection—and others are found at Office.com.

b. Click **Certificates** in the Office.com Templates area. Click **Gift Certificates**. Click **Gift certificate (Arc design)**, and then click **Download**.

SIDE NOTE
To Work with the Clipboard Task Pane
Working with the Clipboard task pane is simple and intuitive. Click in the document where you want to paste an item that appears in the Clipboard task pane. Hover the pointer over the item in the task pane, click the arrow that is displayed on the right, and then click Paste. The real value of working with the Clipboard task pane is that you can paste any item—even if it is not the most recently collected.

c. Save ⊟ the document as Lastname_Firstname_w01_ws02_Gift. If asked about saving in a new format, click **OK**.

d. Click **Your Logo Here**, on the first gift certificate, and then press ⌈Delete⌉ to remove the logo box.

Troubleshooting

If the logo box is not completely removed, click the dashed border so that it becomes a solid line, and then press ⌈Delete⌉.

e. Select **Company Name**, and then type Red Bluff Golf Club. Select the next three address lines and type

3355 Hemmingway Circle
Santa Fe, NM 89566

f. Select the two address lines that you just typed. On the Home tab, click the **Font arrow** in the Font group, scroll down to select **Arial**, click the **Font size arrow**, and then select **10**.

g. Click after the word **to** on the second line of the gift certificate, and then press ⌈Spacebar⌉—the word **to** will become capitalized. Type $25 meal at Red Bluff Bistro. Click after the word **Number**, press ⌈Spacebar⌉, and type 315.

h. Save ⊟ and close the document. Because you will only need one gift certificate, the remaining two gift certificates in the template will not be filled in.

Troubleshooting

When saving the gift certificate, you may be asked whether you want to also save changes to the template. Click No.

Formatting a Document

You have explored formatting at the character level and at the paragraph level. When you format at the *document* level, you adjust page layout by changing margins, exploring page orientation, centering vertically, selecting a document theme, and changing the background. Especially when working with a lengthy document, knowing how to apply formats that affect an entire document can get a job done quickly and easily.

The group of tools on the Page Layout tab enables you to adjust page characteristics, such as page orientation, margins, page background, and themes. Such settings affect the entire document, so learning to use them properly can make the difference between a polished final product and a document that is not as effective as it could be. In this section, you will explore page layout settings, learn to adjust margins, change page orientation, modify page color and borders, and work with themes.

Changing Page Setup

The page setup of a document includes such settings as margins, orientation, and alignment. When you format a document, you can format the entire document or only a section. For example, even after a document is complete, you might decide that its margins should be adjusted or that the first page should be centered vertically. You might even determine that one or more pages should be oriented in landscape orientation, which is when a page is wider than it is tall. Selections on the Page Layout tab enable you to easily complete all of these tasks.

Changing Page Orientation

A document presented in **portrait orientation** is taller than it is wide. **Landscape orientation** displays pages wider than they are tall. Typically, documents are best suited in portrait orientation. In fact, the default orientation setting is portrait, so unless you specify otherwise, all documents are presented in that fashion.

If you determine that a document would be more attractive in landscape orientation, you can easily make that change. You can even change a small part of a document to another orientation. For example, perhaps you have included a table or a graphic that would be displayed best in landscape orientation. Other pages, however, should remain in portrait. Simply select the item or text to orient differently and select another orientation. The selection will be moved to its own page, but it is displayed in the orientation you selected.

> **CONSIDER THIS** | **Selection of Page Orientation**
>
> Most documents are presented in portrait orientation. However, some might be better suited for landscape orientation. Can you identify any documents that would be more attractive or effective in landscape orientation?

Centering a Page Vertically

When you center a page vertically, you center the text evenly between the top and bottom margins. Knowing how to center a page vertically is a useful skill in developing cover pages for reports. It is also a fairly simple task. Unless you specify otherwise, all pages in a document are centered vertically when you apply that setting. Suppose that you only want the first page of a document to be centered vertically. By indicating that selection, you can center text on the first page only.

Real World Advice — Designing a Cover Page

Although you can develop a cover page by centering a page vertically, you can let Word do the work for you instead. On the Insert tab, click Cover Page in the Pages group. Select a cover style, or click More Cover Pages from Office.com for even more choices.

Changing Margins

Every document has a top, bottom, left, and right **margin**. If you do not specify otherwise, all margins are set at 1". Inevitably, you will find a need to change margins in some documents. You might even want to change margins within a document so that some sections have different margins than others. Word provides a collection of predefined margins you can select from; however, you can easily define custom margins if you need to be more specific.

Real World Advice — Changing Default Margins

If you often change margins from Word's default, you might want to change the default settings to mirror your preferences. On the Page Layout tab, click Margins in the Page Setup group. Click Custom Margins, and select the new margin settings. Then, if desired, click Set As Default to set those margin settings as the default. At that point, each time that you begin a new document in Word 2010, the new margin settings will be in effect.

To Work with Page Layout Settings

a. Open **Lastname_Firstname_w01_ws02_School**.

b. Triple-click the second paragraph in the flyer beginning with **Our goal**. Press Delete to remove the paragraph because you do not think the paragraph is necessary.

c. Click the **View tab**, and then click **Zoom** in the Zoom group. In the Zoom dialog box, click in the **Percent box**, change the value to **50%**, and then click **OK**. By reducing the magnification, you are better able to see the results of changes made to the page layout.

d. Click the **Page Layout tab**, click the **Dialog Box Launcher** in the Page Setup group, and then click the **Layout tab**.

e. Click the **Vertical alignment arrow**, click **Center**, and then click **OK**.

   If you want to vertically center only a selection of text (perhaps one page) instead of the entire document, click the Apply to arrow and click Selected text. The selected text will be centered vertically on a separate page.

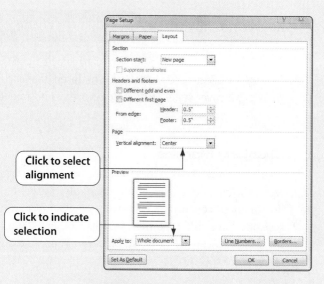

Click to select alignment

Click to indicate selection

Figure 18   Centering a page vertically

f. Click **Orientation** in the Page Setup group, and then click **Landscape**. As you see from the resulting document layout, landscape is not an attractive option. Click **Undo** on the Quick Access Toolbar.

   You can also change orientation in Backstage view. Click the File tab, and then click Print. If the document is already situated in Portrait orientation, that is the selection that will be included in the print settings. In Backstage view, you can select either Portrait or

Landscape orientation. An advantage of using Backstage view to change orientation is that as soon as you select another setting, its effects are displayed in the print preview on the right. If you are not happy with the effect, you can return the selection to its original orientation.

g. Click **Margins** in the Page Setup group.

Preset margins are available from which you can choose. If you do not find a set of suitable margins in a predefined group, you can define your own.

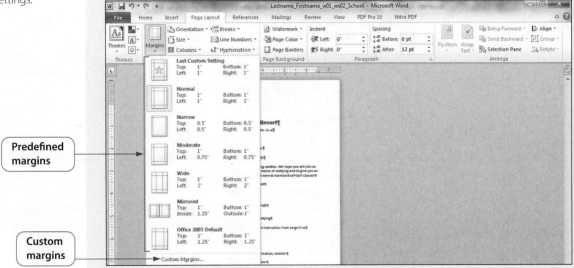

Predefined margins

Custom margins

Figure 19   Selecting margins

h. Click **Custom Margins**. Change the **top** and **bottom margins** to **0.5"**. Left and right margins should remain at 1". Click **OK**.

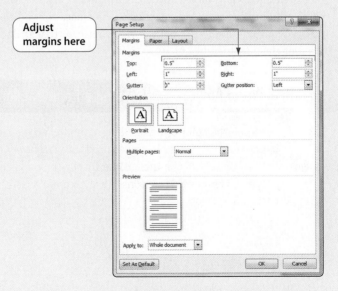

Adjust margins here

Figure 20   Defining custom margins

i. Save 💾 the document.

Changing Page Background

For most documents, a plain white background is effective. Therefore, the default page color for Word 2010 is white. There is no border or graphic on the page. Although you never want to go overboard with color or graphics, there are occasions when some color, borders, or even texture might enhance a document. Page Background settings are included on the Page Layout tab.

Changing Page Color

In limited cases, a change to a more colorful or textured background might better suit the document's purpose and audience. Use your judgment when changing a background hue, as brightly colored documents can be expensive to print—considering the use of color cartridges or toners—and they are most often not necessary or appropriate for business documents. Colored backgrounds might liven up greeting cards, flyers, business cards, or personal stationery, but the background should never overwhelm the text.

Inserting a Watermark

A **watermark** is text or a picture that appears behind document text. A watermark can add interest or identity to a document. For example, documents often include a DRAFT watermark, indicating that they are not in final form. Figure 21 shows a document with a watermark. If you include a watermark, it will only display in Print Layout, Full Screen Reading View, or when the document is printed. Word provides some built-in text and graphics that you can select as a watermark, or you can create your own. You can lighten or wash out a picture or text watermark so that it does not interfere with the readability of the document.

Figure 21 Including a watermark

Adding a Page Border

A page border works especially well in flyers and customized stationery. A page border is a line or graphic that surrounds a page. A page border is most appropriate for one-page documents; seldom is it necessary to include a page border in a multiple-page document.

Adding Borders and Shading

The addition of borders and shading can add emphasis to one or more paragraphs or to the entire document. Although the most frequently used borders are bottom, top, left, right, or outside, Word provides a wide range of additional specialty borders. All are available in the Paragraph group on the Home tab if applying borders to a paragraph, or they are alternatively available in the Page Background group of the Page Layout tab to apply borders to the document page. As you apply a border to a paragraph, you can specify line color and weight. Not limited to single line borders, Word provides a wide range of choices, including double, triple, dashed, zigzag, and various thicknesses. Shading, or background color, is another type of paragraph formatting. Especially when used in conjunction with a border, shading can add definition and draw attention to one or more paragraphs.

Because the use of shading and borders is a type of paragraph formatting, you do not have to select a paragraph to be bordered or shaded. Instead, the selected border or shading is only applied to the paragraph in which the insertion point is positioned. Of course, if the border or shading is to apply to more than one paragraph, you must select all of those paragraphs.

Real World Advice   **Highlighting Text**

Paragraph shading adds background color to one or more paragraphs. If you want to add background color to a smaller selection of text, rather than to an entire paragraph, you can add highlighting by selecting text and clicking the Text Highlight Color arrow in the Font group on the Home tab. Choose a highlight color from the palette.

To Modify a Page Background

a. On the Page Layout tab, click **Page Borders** in the Page Background group, and then click **Shadow**.

b. Click the **Color arrow**, and then select **Dark Blue, Text 2, Darker 50%** (row 6, column 4 under Theme Colors). Click the **Width arrow**, click **1-pt size**, and then click **OK**.

   Borders do not have to be solid lines. You can select from a variety of art borders when you click the Art arrow in the Borders and Shading dialog box.

c. Click **Page Color** in the Page Background group. Place the pointer on any color selection in the color palette without clicking.

   A preview of the selection is displayed. Explore the effect of several colors. For even more color detail, you can click More Colors. If you prefer a gradient or texture fill, click Fill Effects. Other effects include patterns or even pictures.

d. Click **White, Background 1, Darker 15%** (row 3, column 1 under Theme Colors).

e. Click the **Home tab**. Select the caddy school information, beginning with **Red Bluff Caddy School** and ending with **(meeting at the Pro Shop)**.

f. Click the **Borders arrow** ⊞ ▾ in the Paragraph group, and then click **Borders and Shading**.

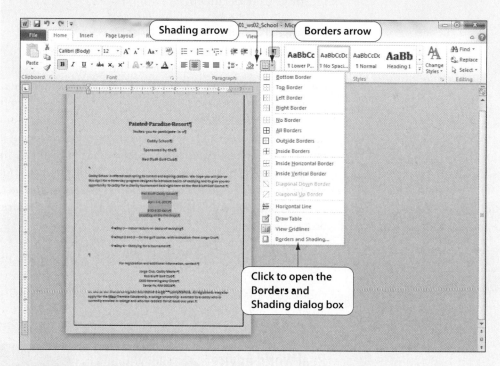

Figure 22   Selecting a border

g. Click **Box**, scroll down the list of line styles, select the **double underline** (seventh from top), and then click **OK**. Do not deselect the text.

h. Click the **Shading arrow** ▥ ▾, and then click **White, Background 1, Darker 35%** row 5, column 1. Deselect the text to see the effect.

i. Click the **Page Layout tab**, and then click **Watermark** in the Page Background group.

   The gallery provides selections from a predefined list or from Office.com. You can also create a custom watermark with text or a picture or you can remove a watermark. Because the flyer must be approved before distribution, you will include a DRAFT watermark.

j. Scroll through the predefined watermarks and click **DRAFT 1**.

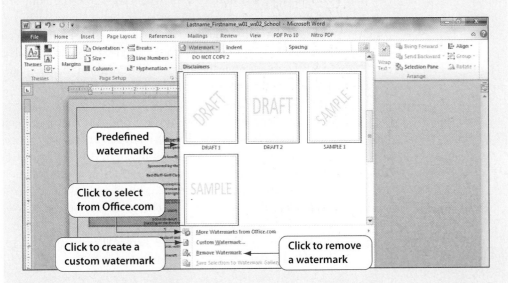

Figure 23 Creating a watermark

k. Click **Watermark**, and then click **Custom Watermark**. Because the watermark is a little too transparent, you will make it more visible. Click to deselect **Semitransparent**, and then click **OK**.

l. Click the **View tab**, and then click **100%** in the Zoom group.

m. Save the document.

Using Themes

A **theme** is a set of design elements that enables you to create professional, color-coordinated documents with minimal effort. Color, fonts, and graphics can be combined to provide a unified look for a document and can even coordinate with other Office applications to create "matching" files. For example, a PowerPoint presentation that includes a certain theme can be matched to a Word document sporting the same color coordination. A company might require a certain theme so that all documents portray a unified, even branded, look.

Sales & Marketing

CONSIDER THIS | **Global Theme**

Businesses today must think globally. The use of technology simplifies worldwide communication and facilitates global marketing. Communicating in so many diverse cultures can be quite a challenge. When creating a theme or common design to represent your business globally, what sorts of considerations are necessary to be effective in a worldwide market?

Themes are located in the Themes group of the Page Layout tab. As you hover the pointer over a theme, you see a live preview of the effect of the theme on document text. With just one click, as you select a theme you can reformat your document.

Even a blank document is based on a theme. If you do not specify otherwise, the default theme, which is called Office, is in place when a new document is created. When you click the Font Color arrow, you will see colors divided into Theme Colors and Standard Colors. The Theme Colors set is actually a group of colors that works well together. You might also have noticed that when you click the Font arrow, a few fonts are listed as Theme Fonts, which are fonts that will coordinate with the color selection and effects of the current theme. Because theme colors are designed to complement one another, it is a good idea to select colors from a single theme's color palette to ensure compatibility.

Each theme identifies one font for document headings and another for body text. Click the Theme Fonts button to see two fonts listed for each theme. One is specified as a headings font, while the other is a body text font. If you like some elements of a theme but want to change others, you can select Theme Colors, Theme Fonts, or Theme Effects in the Themes group of the Page Layout tab and make changes. Each group of coordinated colors you can choose from when modifying a theme is identified by name. For example, the Civic group is comprised of more conservative color choices than is Concourse.

A theme contains four text and background colors, six accent colors, and two hyperlink colors. The colors in the Theme Colors button that you see in the Themes group of the Page Layout tab represent the current text and background colors. When you click Colors, a collection of named color themes is displayed, representing the accent and hyperlink colors for that particular theme.

To Work with a Theme

a. Press Ctrl + Home, click the **Page Layout tab**, and then click **Themes** in the Themes group.

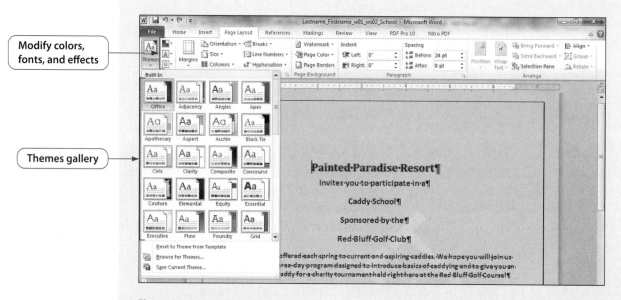

Figure 24   Selecting a theme

b. Scroll through the Themes group, pausing over any theme to view its effect on the flyer. Click **Paper** to apply the theme to the entire document. Font, font color, and effects are modified.

c. Click **Theme Fonts** in the Themes group. Scroll through the font selections, pausing on several to view the effect on the document's font. Click **Foundry**.

d. Click the **Home tab**, and then click the **Font arrow**.
   Note that the headings and body font are not what they were initially. That is because you have selected a different theme.

e. Click the **Font Color arrow**, and then note the different Theme Colors.

f. Save ⊟ the document.

Modifying a Document

You have learned how easy it is to create a document using Word. As you review the document or continue to develop it, you might identify text that should be replaced or items that should be formatted identically. Beyond basic editing, Word enables you to make sweeping changes to a document with very little effort. Such activities as finding certain text or punctuation and replacing them with more appropriate selections, or copying a full package of formatting from one text selection to another, can shorten the time it takes to produce a well-worded and effective document. In this section, you will learn to copy formatting from one selection to another and to find and replace items within a document.

Using Format Painter

Documents that are attractively formatted draw attention to the content and encourage readers' interest. Achieving just the right combination of format settings is not always an easy task, but once done, you will probably want to recreate the same format elsewhere in the same document. Identically formatting similar elements provides consistency and gives a professional feel to the document. The best part is that Word provides an easy-to-use tool for copying formatting—**Format Painter**. Just format one section of text the way you like. You might bold and italicize text, change the font or font size, and adjust the alignment. Perhaps you have just formatted a caption that is to appear under several pictures in a document. Because you want all captions to appear identically, simply select the first caption that is formatted correctly and use Format Painter to copy the formatting to another selection.

To Use Format Painter

a. Select **Caddy School** in the third paragraph of the document. Click the **Home tab**, click the **Font size arrow**, and then select **18**.

b. Click **Text Effects** 🅰▾ in the Font group, and then point to **Shadow**. In the Outer section of the gallery, click **Offset Right** (row 2, column 1 under Outer category).

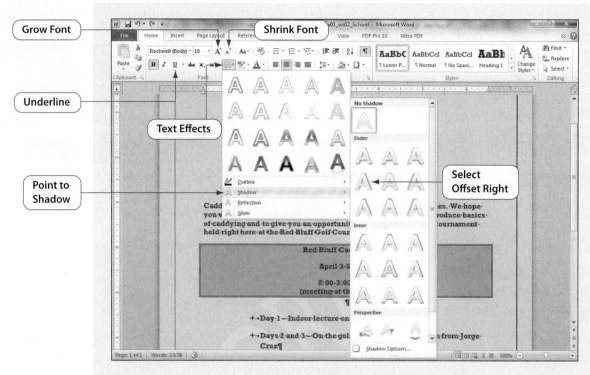

Labels pointing to the figure: Grow Font, Shrink Font, Underline, Text Effects, Point to Shadow, Select Offset Right

Figure 25 Font effects

c. With the text **Caddy School** still selected, click **Format Painter** in the Clipboard group. As you move the mouse pointer over the text in the document, note that it resembles a paintbrush. Drag to select **Red Bluff Golf Club** in the fifth paragraph of the document.

d. Select **Day 1** in the first bullet, but be sure not to select the following space. Click **Underline** [U ▾], and then click **Grow Font** [A˙]. Because you want to apply the same formatting to the other days, you will use Format Painter's multiple-use feature.

e. Double-click **Format Painter**.

    When you double-click Format Painter, you can repeatedly copy the same formatting from one selection to others. When you have completed all formatting, press [Esc] or click Format Painter again.

f. Select **Days 2 and 3**, and then select **Day 4**. The formatting from the first day is copied to all the days. Click **Format Painter** again to turn the feature off.

g. Select **Day 1**. As you view the document, you decide that it would be more attractive if the formatting from Day 1 is also copied to each day's text. Double-click **Format Painter**.

h. Select **Indoor lecture on basics of caddying**. Select **On the golf course, with instruction from Jorge Cruz**. Select **Caddying for a tournament**. Press [Esc] to turn the Format Painter off.

i. Select all three bullet items. Click **Shrink Font** [A˙] twice. The Day 2 and 3 activities wrap unattractively, so you reduce the size of the font for each day.

j. Save [💾] the document.

Finding and Replacing Text

Finding a particular word or phrase and replacing it with another might not seem to be a huge undertaking if you are working with a very short document. But consider the challenge if the document were much longer—like a 400-page dissertation! Perhaps you have consistently misspelled a name, or maybe a meeting date has changed so you need to find the incorrect date and replace it. Especially if the incorrect text appears repeatedly in a lengthy document, you could conceivably save a great deal of time spent locating and retyping, if you simply use Word's **Find and Replace** feature. Occasionally, you might need to locate a word in a document without replacing it. Word's Navigation Pane enables you to do just that.

Using the Navigation Pane to Find Text

The **Navigation Pane** provides a set of related features for getting around in a document and searching for content. New to Word 2010, the Navigation Pane is displayed to the left of an open document. To open the Navigation Pane, select Navigation Pane in the Show group on the View tab. The Navigation Pane is also displayed when you click the Home tab and then Find, or you can press Ctrl+F. If you are looking for a particular word, phrase, graphic, formula, or footnote, the Navigation Pane can help you find the item quickly.

To Find and Replace

a. Press Ctrl+Home to position the insertion point at the beginning of the document. On the Home tab, click **Replace** in the Editing group.

Because you often make the mistake of using the word "Course" instead of "Club" when referring to the Red Bluff Golf Club, you want to find all occurrences of "Course" and replace them, if necessary.

b. Click in the **Find what box**, and then type Course. Click in the **Replace with box**, and then type Club.

You only want to find the word "Course" if it is capitalized as part of the golf course name, not if it is simply used in a sentence. Therefore, you must indicate that the search should match the case of the search term.

c. Click **More**, and then select **Match case**. Click **Replace All** so that you will not be asked to confirm every replacement. One replacement is made. Click **OK**, and then click **Close**.

SIDE NOTE
Caution with Find and Replace

Although the process of finding and replacing characters is fairly straightforward, you should carefully consider each replacement. Before clicking Replace All (instead of Find Next, and Replace), you must be certain that all instances of the found text should be replaced. Replace All does not ask for your confirmation, so it can be a dangerous activity if you have not carefully thought through the possible changes.

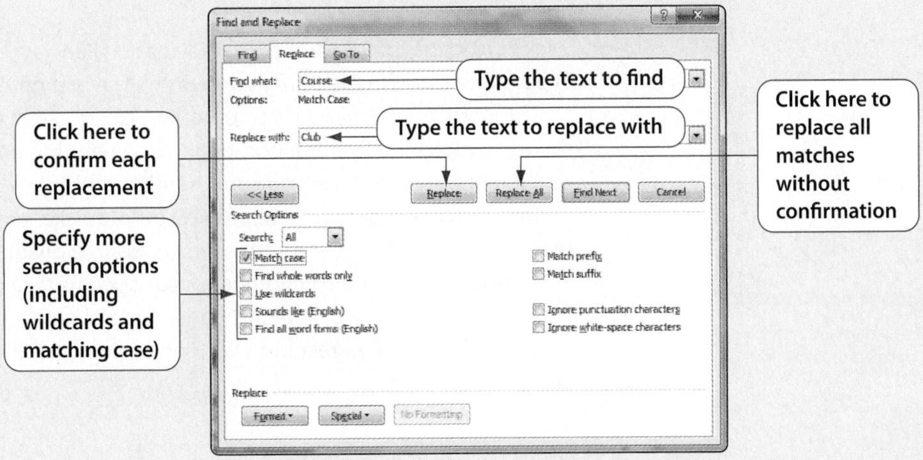

Figure 26 Find and Replace dialog box

d. Press ⌈Ctrl⌉+⌈Home⌉, click **Replace** in the Editing group, and then click the **Find tab**.

The words "caddy," "caddies," and "caddying" appear at various places throughout the flyer. You will use a **wildcard** to find each occurrence of words beginning with "cad," which should identify each of the words listed above. Because you only care that a search result begins with "cad" but know that what follows those letters is irrelevant to your search, you will use the asterisk (*) wildcard.

Wildcards	
Symbol	**Represents**
*	Any number of characters, including none
?	One character
#	One number

Figure 27   Wildcards

You will use the asterisk wildcard because the number of letters following "cad" varies in the search previously described. For example, the word "caddy" includes two additional letters following "cad," while the word "caddying" includes five additional letters. Because wildcard searches are case sensitive (the option to deselect Match Case is unavailable) results will only display words beginning with "cad," not "Cad."

e. Type cad* in the **Find what box**, replacing existing text. Click **Use wildcards**, and then click **Find Next**. The first word containing the text "cad," regardless of what follows, is displayed.

f. Click **Find Next** to view another word beginning with "cad." Continue clicking **Find Next** until the search is complete, click **OK**, and then close the Find and Replace dialog box.

Troubleshooting

> If the Find and Replace dialog box obscures a search result, click the dialog box title bar and drag the box out of the way.

g. Click **Find** in the Editing group. The Navigation Pane appears to the left of the document. Type tournament in the **Search box** of the Navigation Pane, and press ⌈Enter⌉.

The word "tournament" is temporarily highlighted in the flyer to show you where it is found. Because the flyer is a one-page document it is easy to see all matches, but if the document were lengthier, you could scroll through pages to view the results.

Tabs in the Navigation Pane provide even quicker access to search results. If a document includes sections with titles formatted in a heading style (Heading 1, Heading 2, etc.), click the Browse the headings in your document tab to see search results organized by section. You can see resulting pages when you click the Browse the pages in your document tab, and all resulting text when you click the Browse the results from your current search tab.

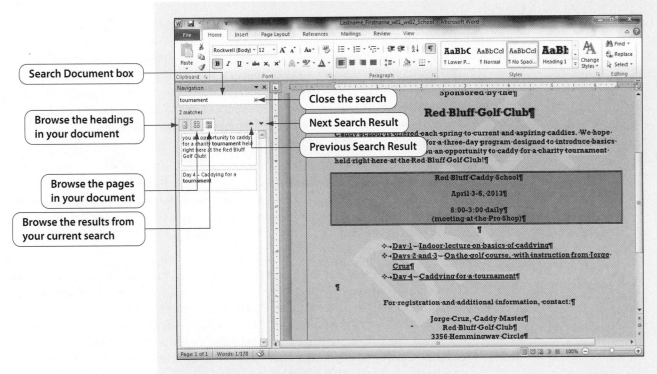

Search Document box

Browse the headings in your document

Browse the pages in your document

Browse the results from your current search

Close the search

Next Search Result

Previous Search Result

Figure 28   Navigation Pane

SIDE NOTE
Navigation Pane Shortcut
Press Ctrl+F to quickly open the Navigation Pane. You can also click the View tab and click Navigation Pane, or you can click Find in the Editing group on the Home tab.

h. Click **Next Search Result** to move to the next result, and then click **Previous Search Result** to return to a previous match.

i. Click **Close** in the Search box to remove highlights and return to where the search began.

j. Close ⊠ the Navigation Pane.

k. Save 🖫 the document.

1. As the secretary of the Student Government Association (SGA), you are summarizing student questions and concerns for a meeting of the SGA and the college president. You plan to provide the college president with a summary so that she can have an idea of what she will be asked to address. How would you structure the document so the president can quickly ascertain the primary concerns? In your response, address such topics as use of headings, bullets, numbers, and page formatting.

2. The use of color and special formatting, such as page and paragraph borders, can add much to a document if used appropriately. It is possible, though, that color and special formatting could be unnecessarily distracting in certain documents. Provide specific examples of documents that would benefit from color and borders as well as those in which such elements should be used sparingly.

3. Your supervisor has asked you to develop a policy for preparing internal company documents. You know that the use of templates, styles, themes, and font choices could be integral components of such a policy. Provide general comments about how you would incorporate any or all of those elements into guidelines for preparing such printed documents as memos, reports, and forms. Include thoughts on whether you would encourage the use of predefined templates and styles or whether you would suggest company-developed items. How could you encourage the use of a unified color choice and a logo in company documents?

4. Whenever possible, you will want to simplify the task of preparing documents by sharing text. If text in one document is to be used in another, you can copy and paste the text. What is the difference between the two methods? Give specific examples of when you would copy and paste text, and when it might be simpler to insert text from a file.

5. The use of styles can better organize a document. Do you agree or disagree with that statement? Elaborate on your response, providing specific rationale for your position.

Key Terms

Bullet 146
Clipboard 148
Clipboard task pane 148
Copy 148
Cut 148
Find and Replace 163
First-line indent 142
Format Painter 161
Gutter 156

Hanging indent 142
Landscape orientation 153
Left indent 142
Line spacing 140
Margin 153
Navigation Pane 163
Paragraph spacing 140
Paste 148
Paste Preview 149

Portrait orientation 153
Quick Styles 134
Right indent 142
Style 134
Symbol 146
Template 151
Theme 159
Watermark 156
Wildcard 164

Visual Summary

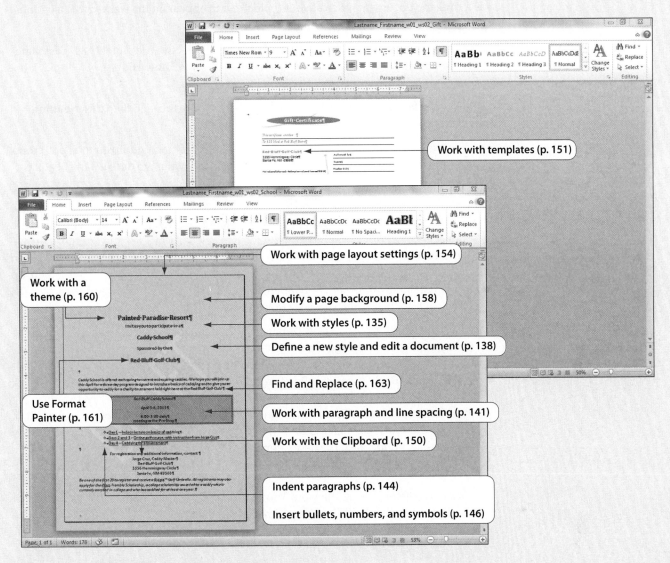

Work with templates (p. 151)

Work with page layout settings (p. 154)

Work with a theme (p. 160)

Modify a page background (p. 158)

Work with styles (p. 135)

Define a new style and edit a document (p. 138)

Find and Replace (p. 163)

Use Format Painter (p. 161)

Work with paragraph and line spacing (p. 141)

Work with the Clipboard (p. 150)

Indent paragraphs (p. 144)

Insert bullets, numbers, and symbols (p. 146)

Figure 29 Red Bluff Caddy School Flyer Final Document

Practice 1

Student data file needed:	**You will save your file as:**
w01_ws02_GolfGetaway	Lastname_Firstname_w01_ws02_GolfGetaway

Women's Golf Getaway

Sales & Marketing

Each fall, the Red Bluff Golf Club hosts a weekend golf getaway for women. The three-day event combines golf lessons, rounds of golf, an evening reception, regional cuisine, and luxury accommodations at the Painted Paradise Resort and Spa. Open to women of all ages, participants receive instruction from two of the top pros in the country. The Women's Golf Getaway program provides instruction for all skill levels and is one of the best attended annual events of the resort.

Painted Paradise Resort and Spa maintains a web site to promote upcoming events, including the weekend golf getaway, so you will prepare a document with event details. You will format the document much as you would like it to appear on the web, so that a designer can easily transfer the information into an online format.

a. Start **Word**. Open **w01_ws02_GolfGetaway**. Save the document as Lastname_Firstname_w01_ws02_GolfGetaway. If necessary, click **Show/Hide** ¶ to display non-printing characters.

b. Select the first line, **Red Bluff Golf Club**. Click the **Home tab**, and then click **Heading 1** in the Styles group.

c. With the first line still selected, click **Center** in the Paragraph group; in the Font group, click the **Font Size arrow**, and then select **22**. Click anywhere to deselect the heading.

d. Click anywhere in the paragraph beginning with **Join us at**. Click the **Dialog Box Launcher** in the Styles group, and then click the **New Style button**. You will create a new style for the body of the document. With the **Name** selected in the Properties area, type Body. Click the **Font arrow**, and then scroll and select **Arial**. Click the **Font Size arrow**, and then click **12**. Click the **Font color arrow** (beside the word **Automatic**), and then click **Dark Blue, Text 2, Darker 50%**. Click **Format**, click **Paragraph**, click the **Left up arrow** repeatedly to change the Indentation value to **0.5"**, click **OK**, and then click **OK** again to close the Create New Style from Formatting dialog box.

e. Select the words **Women's Golf Getaway** in the second sentence, and click **Bold** in the Font group. You will change the Body style to adjust the left indent and to increase spacing before the paragraph. The Body style should be selected in the Styles pane. If it is not selected, click **Body** to select it. Point to the **Body** style, click the **arrow** to the right, click **Modify**, click **Format**, click **Paragraph**, and then click the **Left down arrow** to reduce the indentation to **0**. In the Spacing section, change **After** to **6 pt** and **Before** to **6 pt**. Click **OK**, and then click **OK** again to close the dialog box. The paragraph based on the Body style is adjusted to reflect the new settings.

f. Close the Styles pane.

g. Click immediately before the word **You** that begins the third sentence from the end of the document. Press Enter to begin a new paragraph there.

h. Press Ctrl + End to place the insertion point at the end of the document, and then press Enter twice.

i. Click the **Bullets arrow** in the Paragraph group, and then click the **check mark** in the Bullet Library. Type the following lines, pressing Enter after typing each. A check mark bullet will appear before each line that you type.

Do you love to play golf?

Do you enjoy a resort atmosphere?

Do you feel the need to pamper yourself?

When you press Enter after the last line, another check mark appears. Click **Bullets** in the Paragraph group to remove the check mark. Select all bulleted lines, and then click **Center** in the Paragraph group.

j. Click the **Page Layout tab**, click **Orientation**, and then click **Portrait**. Because you can see that landscape might not be the best orientation for this document, you change the orientation to portrait. Press Ctrl + End to place the insertion point at the end of the document.

k. Press Enter, click the **Home tab**, click the **Font Color arrow**, and then click **Dark Red** (first selection under Standard Colors). Click the **Font Size arrow**, click **18**, and then click **Center** in the Paragraph group. Type Reserve your place today for the and press Enter. Type Women's Golf Getaway!, and then press Enter twice.

l. Click **No Spacing** in the Styles group, type Contact: and then press Enter. Type the following, pressing Enter after each line. When you press Enter after typing the e-mail address, the address will become an underlined link.

Patti Rochelle, Corporate Events Coordinator

Painted Paradise Resort

3566 Hemmingway Circle

Santa Fe, NM 89566

555-555-5656

prochelle@paintedparadiseresort.com

You are reminded that the official name of the resort is "Painted Paradise Resort and Spa." You have been in the habit of abbreviating that title to "Painted Paradise Resort" so you suspect that you have continued that practice in this document. Therefore, you will replace all occurrences of "Painted Paradise Resort" with "Painted Paradise Resort and Spa."

m. Press Ctrl+Home, click **Replace** in the Editing group, click in the **Find what box**, remove any existing text, and then type Painted Paradise Resort. Click in the **Replace with box**, remove any existing text, type Painted Paradise Resort and Spa, and then click **Replace All**. You should see that three replacements were made. Click **OK**, and then click **Close**.

The Red Bluff Golf Club was recently renamed. Previously, it had been the Red Bluff Golf Course. Because you have been accustomed to referring to the golf club by its previous name, you want to quickly check this document to make sure you did not make a mistake with the name. You will find all occurrences of the word *course*.

n. Click **Find** in the Editing group. The Navigation Pane opens on the left. Type Course in the search box, and then press Enter to begin the search. If the word *course* is found, it will be highlighted in the document wherever it occurs. Scroll up or down, if necessary, to see all occurrences, and then replace any that are included in the name of the golf course with the word Club. Close the Navigation Pane.

o. Click anywhere in the first sentence of the first paragraph beginning with **Join us**. Press and hold Ctrl while you click on the sentence to select it. Click **Cut** in the Clipboard group, click immediately before the first sentence in the second paragraph before the word **You**, and then click **Paste** in the Clipboard group to move the selected sentence to that location.

p. Select the first line containing the text **Red Bluff Golf Club**, and then click **Title** in the Styles group to change the style of the selected words.

q. Press Ctrl+End to place the insertion point at the end of the document, press Enter, and then type Painting Your Perfect Getaway. Click anywhere in the colored text that reads **Reserve Your Place Today for the Women's Golf Getaway!**, click **Format Painter** in the Clipboard group, and then drag to select **Painting Your Perfect Getaway**. Because the additional text caused the document to extend over two pages, you will decrease the top and bottom margins to make room for the text on only one page.

r. Click the **Page Layout tab**, click **Margins**, and then click **Narrow**.

s. Click **Margins**, click **Custom Margins**, and then click the **Layout tab**. Click the **Vertical alignment arrow**, click **Center** to align the document vertically, and then click **OK**.

t. Save and close the document.

Student Data file needed:

None

You will save your file as:

Lastname_Firstname_w01_ps1_Minutes

Minutes Template

Sales & Marketing

You are helping coordinate a summer children's robotics camp. The camp provides children an opportunity to design and build basic robots, with teams competing for camp awards. You recorded notes of a recent planning meeting and will organize those notes into meeting minutes for distribution. You will use a template to begin the document.

a. Start Word. Click the **File tab**, and then click **New**. Click **Minutes** from the Office.com Templates area. Click the **Meeting minutes folder**. Click **Meeting minutes**. Click **Download**. Save the file as Lastname_Firstname_w01_ps1_Minutes.

b. Drag to select **Meeting Title** in the first line of the document. Type ACSB Robotics Camp.

c. Click **[MEETING DATE]** and type 01/08/13. Press Tab and **replace [MEETING TIME]** with 9:00 A.M.. Press Tab and replace **[MEETING LOCATION]** with CONF. ROOM 213C.

d. Drag to select **MINUTES** in the second line of the document. Click **Format Painter** in the Clipboard group. Drag to select the date, time, and location that you typed in Step c, effectively copying the formatting to the selection.

e. Click in the box at the right of **TYPE OF MEETING** and type Camp Planning Meeting. At the right of **NOTE TAKER** type your first and last names.

f. In the Agenda topics section, click **[AGENDA TOPIC]** and type CAMP ACTION PLAN. Click in the white space at the right of **DISCUSSION** and type Camps must be publicized well and early. Brochures, registration material, and other publicity are at the printer. Click in the white space underneath **PERSON RESPONSIBLE** and type All. Click in the white space underneath **DEADLINE** and type 02/01/13.

g. Drag to select all remaining lines of text beginning with **TIME ALLOTTED** in the next section and ending at the end of the document. Press Delete to remove the selected area. Press Ctrl+Enter to insert a page break and begin a new page.

h. Type Camp Publicity and press Enter. Select **Camp Publicity**, and click **Heading 1** in the Styles group. Press Ctrl+End.

i. Click the **Font arrow** and click **Arial**. Click the **Font Size arrow** and click **16**.

j. Click the **Page Layout tab**. Click the **up arrow** to change Spacing Before to **12 pt**. Click the **Home** tab, and then click **Line and Paragraph Spacing** in the Paragraph group. Click **1.5**.

k. Type the following paragraph. (The e-mail address that you type will automatically be formatted as a hyperlink.)
Direct all camp publicity through Ms. Janet Mayfield for approval. Her office will assure that material is consistently designed and not duplicative. E-mail Ms. Mayfield at jmayfield@acsb.org for publishing guidelines.

l. Click the **Home tab**, if necessary. Click the **Styles Dialog Box Launcher**. Point to **Heading 1** in the Styles pane and click the **Heading 1 arrow**. Click **Modify**. Click **Center**, and then click **OK**. Close the Styles pane.

m. Click **Replace** in the Editing group. In the **Find what box**, type publicity. Click in the **Replace with box** and type publications. Click **Replace All**. Click **OK**. Click **Close**.

n. Press Ctrl+End. Press Enter. Type Above all, be sure any publications adhere to the following guidelines:

o. Press **Enter**. Click the **Bullets arrow** in the Paragraph group. Click the checkmark bullet. Type the following bulleted items, pressing Enter after each:

Concise and informative

Attractive

Proofread!

Click Bullets.

p. Drag to select the bulleted items you just typed. Click **Line and Paragraph Spacing** in the Paragraph group. Click **1.0**. Click **Decrease Indent** in the Paragraph group so that the bullets are aligned with the left margin.

q. Click in the second sentence of the paragraph beginning **Direct all camp**. Hold down **Ctrl** and click in the sentence to select it. Click **Cut** in the Clipboard group. Click **at the end of the paragraph** (following the period after the word guidelines). Click **Paste** (the button, not the arrow) in the Clipboard group. The sentence that you removed should show at the end of the paragraph.

r. Click the **Page Layout tab**. Click the **Page Setup Dialog Box Launcher**. Click the **Layout tab**. Click the **Vertical alignment arrow**, and then click **Center**. Click **OK**.

s. Click the **Insert tab**, and then click **Footer**. Click **Edit Footer**. Click **Quick Parts** in the Insert group, and then click **Field**. Scroll down and click **FileName**. Click **OK**.

t. Save the document and exit Word.

 Additional Workshop Cases are available on the companion website and in the instructor resources.

In the following cases you will be required to use skills and concepts that you learned in the previous two Workshops. While working with these cases, you need to follow the steps carefully to ensure correct spelling, punctuation, and capitalization.

More Practice

Student data file needed:

w01_mp_LEED

You will save your file as:

Lastname_Firstname_w01_mp_LEED

Production & Operations

Environmental Alliance Sustainable Hotel Information

You have prepared a rough draft of an information sheet for the Santa Fe Environmental Alliance Trade Show, an event that showcases buildings that are Leadership in Energy and Environmental Design (LEED) certified or that otherwise contribute to a more environmentally aware Santa Fe area. Painted Paradise Resort and Spa has recently attained LEED certification, having met a rigorous set of standards for sustainable construction and operation. The information sheet highlights the resort's environmental construction and activities.

Before the document is ready for final distribution, you will modify it so that it includes appropriate headings, paragraph and document formatting, and text emphasis. In addition, you will insure that it is error free.

a. Open **w01_mp_LEED** from your student data files. Save the document as Lastname_Firstname_w01_mp_LEED. Show nonprinting characters.

b. Select the first line, and then apply the **Title** style. Select the second line, and then apply the **Subtitle** style.

c. Click anywhere in the first paragraph of the body of the document, and then create a new style called **Body Paragraph**. The new style should be Verdana font, 10 pt, justified, have line spacing of 1.5 and have 12 pt spacing after paragraphs. Set a first-line indent.

d. Apply the **Body Paragraph** style to the first two paragraphs in the body of the document, and then close the Styles pane.

e. Select the line beginning **Conservation doesn't have to mean deprivation**, set a **0.5"** left and right indent, and Bold the selection.

f. Bold the words **Painted Paradise Resort and Spa** wherever they appear in the document. To do this using Find and Replace, press Ctrl+Home, click **Replace**, and then type Painted Paradise Resort and Spa in the **Find What** box. Type Painted Paradise Resort and Spa in the **Replace With box**. If necessary, click the **More** button to display additional Search Options. Click **Format**, click **Font**, and then click **Bold**. Click **OK**, and then click **Replace All**. Four replacements should be made. Click **OK**, and then close the dialog box.

g. Press Ctrl+End. Bold the line beginning **Become a Fan on Facebook**, change the font size of the selection to **14**, and then center the line. Bold the line containing **Painting Your Perfect Getaway**, change the font size of the selection to **16**, and then center the line.

h. Click after the word **development** in the first paragraph of the body of the document, delete the **comma** and **space**, and then insert an em dash character.

i. Modify the Body Paragraph style to include a font color of **Blue, Accent 1, Darker 25%**.

j. Change the **Building Material** heading to Recycled Building Materials. Change the **Kitchen** heading to Energy-Efficient Kitchen. Bold **Green Roof** and change the font size to **12**. Copy the format of the **Green Roof** heading to all other headings: **Solar Panels, Water Usage and Air Quality, Recycled Building Materials, Energy-Efficient Kitchen,** and **Lighting**.

k. Rearrange the headings and content so they appear in alphabetical order. For example, the first category should be **Energy-Efficient Kitchen**, followed by **Green Roof**, and so on.

l. Change all of the black text to **Blue, Accent 1, Darker 25%**.

m. Click at the beginning of the first body paragraph beginning with **Santa Fe**, and then press Enter twice to add two blank paragraphs after the subtitle.

n. Type the following category within the current list of categories. Make sure the new category is the same format as other groups and alphabetize all categories.
Guest Room Enhancements
Carpeting certified by the Carpet and Rug Institute's Green Label Plus certification systems; chairs and cabinets made with Forest Stewardship Council certified sustainable wood, recycled upholstery fabric, and energy-conserving guest room televisions.

o. Change the margins to **Normal**. Preview the document as it will appear when printed.

p. Because the document ends awkwardly, with only a few lines on the final page, adjust the margins to **Narrow** to better accommodate the text.

q. Use the spelling checker to help correct any errors. Manually proofread the document, making any corrections necessary. **Plyboo** is not misspelled.

r. Insert a left-aligned footer with your first name and last name separated by a space. Check the document for any awkward page endings such as a heading on a page by itself. Insert a **manual page break** (press Ctrl+Enter), if necessary, to correct any problems.

s. Save the document and exit Word.

Problem Solve 1

Student data file needed:
w01_ps1_Romantic

You will save your file as:
Lastname_Firstname_w01_ps1_Romantic

"Romantic Getaway" Gift Basket Welcome Note

Customer Service

Painted Paradise Resort and Spa offers a "Romantic Getaway" package especially designed for couples who want to celebrate their partnership by enjoying a relaxing visit to the resort. The two-night package includes a welcome amenity of champagne, fruit, and favors, delivered upon arrival. Each basket includes a note, welcoming the couple to the resort and inviting them to enjoy all that the resort has to offer them during their stay.

Your supervisor has supplied you with a draft of the welcome note, but it is incomplete. You will add and format text, include bullets where appropriate, create and apply a style, move text, and insure that the document is error free. When complete, the document will be the perfect addition to the welcome package that is planned for those special couples!

a. Open **w01_ps1_Romantic** from your student data files, and then save the document as Lastname_Firstname_w01_ps1_Romantic. Show nonprinting characters.

b. Apply the **Heading 1** style to the title line, **Welcome to the Painted Paradise Resort and Spa!** Also for the first line, change the font color to **Black, Text 1**.

c. Move the insertion point to the beginning of the paragraph that begins **This complimentary gift basket**. Apply a new style named **Body Paragraph** to the paragraph. This style should be 12 pt, single-spaced, with 6 pt spacing before a paragraph and 0 pt spacing after.

d. In addition to the first body paragraph, apply the **Body Paragraph** style to the last two paragraphs in the document.

e. Center the first line of the document, click to place the insertion point at the end of the document, and then add two hard returns. Remember that a hard return will result in a paragraph mark.

f. Type Compliments of Indigo 5 with the **No Spacing** style applied and a hard return at the end.

g. Select a **heart** as a new bullet.

h. Type the following text using the new bullet, with a hard return after each line.
Fruit and champagne
Chocolates
The Best of Indigo 5 Recipe Book
Souvenir letter opener and pen set

i. Click **Bullets** to turn off the bullets. Select the lines that you just typed beginning with **Fruit and champagne** and ending after **Souvenir letter opener and pen set** and increase the indent twice.

j. Bold the first line of the bulleted area—**Compliments of Indigo 5**. Click immediately after the word **hope** in the second sentence of the first paragraph of the document, press Spacebar, and then insert the word that in the sentence.

k. Bold the last sentence in the first paragraph beginning with **Thank you for letting us**.

l. Use the spelling checker to help correct only those items that are actually misspelled or that are grammatically incorrect, if any. Note that the word **Salbarro** is not misspelled.

m. Modify the **Body Paragraph** style to **Lucida Handwriting** font.

n. Copy the format of the text currently shown in **Lucida Handwriting** font to the title line, **Welcome to Painted Paradise Resort and Spa**. Bold the title, center it, and then change the font size to **16**.

o. Select **Compliments of Indigo 5** above the bulleted list at the end of the document, change the font size to **14**, and then change the line spacing for the bulleted items to **1.5** lines.

p. Move the second paragraph so that it is beneath the third paragraph. Make sure the style of the paragraph that you moved is **Body Paragraph**.

q. Insert a blank paragraph before the first paragraph in the body of the document beginning with **This complimentary gift basket**.

r. You will emphasize the resort slogan **paint your perfect getaway** by making sure it is capitalized wherever it occurs. To do so, replace **paint your perfect getaway** with Paint Your Perfect Getaway. Be sure to match case in the **Find and Replace** dialog box and to deselect **Use wildcards** if the setting is selected. Replace all occurrences.

s. Preview the document as it will look when printed.

t. Save the document and exit Word.

Customer
Service

Student data file needed:

w01_ps2_Directions

You will save your file as:

Lastname_Firstname_w01_ps2_Directions

Painted Paradise Resort Concierge Station – Directions to Local Attractions

Guests often ask the concierge staff for directions to the many attractions within driving distance of the resort. The requests are so numerous that you have been asked to prepare a sheet with detailed driving directions to the most popular destinations. The concierge staff can simply hand the directions to a guest upon request. With directions in hand, guests will find it easy to tour the area.

You will work with a document begun by another staff member, enhancing the document for eye appeal and making sure that it is error free. With well-numbered steps and easy-to-read text, the set of directions is sure to get guests where they want to go.

a. Start **Word**, open **w01_ps2_Directions** from your student data files, and then save the document as Lastname_Firstname_w01_ps2_Directions. Show nonprinting characters.

b. Apply the **No Spacing** style to the first two paragraphs in the document, beginning with **Painted Paradise** and ending with **Attractions**. Center and bold the first two lines, and change the font size to **16**.

c. Apply a new style called Attraction to the next three lines of the address information for **The Plaza**. The new style should include bold font and 6 pt spacing before the paragraph.

d. Apply the **Attraction** style to all other addresses of attractions in the document.

e. Use the spelling checker, correcting words that are misspelled and ignoring others. Note that there are no misspellings in the attraction addresses, and **Railyard** should be left as one word, so ignore any suspected errors in this category. After you finish checking the spelling, proofread the document to locate any errors that were not identified.

f. After proofreading the document, you decide to remove the 0 from a mileage indicator if the mileage is measured in tenths. For example, instead of stating a mileage as .20, you prefer .2. Be very careful to only replace mileage measured in tenths. You should not replace a 0 included in a zip code, street address, or a mileage measurement such as 40 miles.

g. Convert the directions to **The Plaza** beginning with **Make a sharp right turn** and ending with **Arrive at The Plaza on the right** into a numbered list. Decrease the indent by one level, and then change the line spacing to **1.5** lines for all the items in the list.

Copy the formatting of the numbered instructions to all other sets of instructions in the document. Remember to use Format Painter's multiple use feature so that you can copy the format repeatedly to all other instructions.

h. Note that although the numbering format copied, each set of instructions does not begin with 1. Instead, the numbering scheme was continued throughout the document. Scroll back to the first step under **Canyon Road**. Click the first number. Click the **Numbering arrow** in the Paragraph group, and then click **Set Numbering Value**. Make sure **Start new list** is selected. Change the value in the **Set value to:** box to **1**, and then click **OK**. Similarly, begin all other directions to area attractions with a value of 1.

i. Click immediately before the word **Make** in the first step under **The Plaza**, and then press [Enter] to insert a new step as number **1**. With the insertion point immediately to the right of **1** type Turn right from the parking deck. Because each set of directions should begin with the same step, you will copy and paste the step repeatedly in the next step.

j. Position the pointer in the left margin beside the new first step under The Plaza. When the pointer resembles a right-directed white arrow, click to select the step. The numeral 1 will not be selected, but the wording will be highlighted. Copy this to the Clipboard, click to place the insertion point immediately before the first word in the first step under **Canyon Road**, and then paste in the copied text. Continue pasting the text as the first step in all remaining groups of directions.

k. Insert a footer with a **Plain Number 2** page number that is centered. Close the footer.

l. Press ⎡Ctrl⎤+⎡Home⎤, and then preview the document as it will appear when printed, ensuring that you preview all four pages.

m. Return the view to **Page 1**. Experiment with the page orientation, selecting the most appropriate from either **Portrait** or **Landscape**.

n. Save the document and exit Word.

Problem Solve 3

Student data file needed:	You will save your file as:
w01_ps3_Pricing	Lastname_Firstname_w01_ps3_Pricing

Homework 3

Memo from Management to the Resort Business Center Informing of New Pricing Table

Finance & Accounting

Brian Paxton, the coordinator of the resort business center, wants your help in designing a memo informing resort staff of pricing changes in the business center. Given recent increases in the cost of business supplies, the center will slightly increase the amount charged for certain services. So that staff and guests are well aware of business center pricing, it is important that the memo accurately convey both the reasoning for the increase and the current prices.

Mr. Paxton has given you a draft of a memo, but it is incomplete. He wants you to include the new pricing table and to proofread the document. You will make improvements to the readability of the text, including styles, formatting existing text, adjusting margins, and replacing text where necessary. As a finished product, the memo will be a polished memo, accurately conveying the intended information to the target audience.

a. Start **Word**, open w01_ps3_Pricing from your student data files, and then save the document as Lastname_Firstname_w01_ps3_Pricing. Show nonprinting characters.

b. Place the insertion point at the very end of the document, and then create a hard return to create a new paragraph. Apply a new style called Item List to the paragraph. The Before paragraph spacing of the new style is 6 pt.

c. Type the following text, pressing ⎡Enter⎤ after each line.
All incoming faxes – $1.00
Local outgoing faxes – $2.00 first page (additional pages – $1.00)
Black-and-white photocopying (single-sided) – $0.20
Black-and-white photocopying (double-sided) – $0.25
Color (each copy) – $1.50
Color paper – $0.25
Transparencies (black-and-white) – $1.25
Transparencies (color) – $2.50
Computer workstation – 10 minutes free (each additional 15 minutes – $5.00)

Note: Press ⎡Spacebar⎤ before and after each dash in the price list, except for the words **single-sided, double-sided, and black-and-white**.

d. Modify the Item List style to apply italic.

e. Apply bullet to all of the lines providing pricing information with a right-facing arrow-head bullet.

f. Bold the text **October 1** in the last sentence of first body paragraph. Change the font for all text beginning with **To:** through the end of the document to Times New Roman with a font size of 12. Do not select the word **Memo** or any text above it.

g. Bold the word **To**. Use Format Painter's multiple-use feature to copy the formatting of the selection to **From**, **Date**, and **Re**.

h. Replace the word **photocopying** throughout the document with **copying**.

i. Change the left and right margins to **1"** and the top and bottom margins to 0.5".

j. Move the insertion point to the end of the last bullet point. Create a hard return to add an additional item on the bulleted list that states Shipping (1–5 lbs.) – $5.00. Be sure when typing **1–5 lbs.** to not insert a space before or after the dash. However, place a space before and after the dash between **(1–5 lbs.)** and **$5.00**. Create another hard return to add another item to the bulleted list. Copy the word **Shipping** to the new bullet line. After the word **Shipping** type (6–15 lbs.) – $10.00. There should be a space between the word **Shipping** and **(6–15 lbs.)**. Create another hard return to add another item to the bulleted list. Paste the word **Shipping** again. (Hint: Ctrl+V is a shortcut for the paste operation.) After the word **Shipping** type (16–30 lbs.) – $15.00. There should be a space between the word Shipping and (16–30 lbs.). Using the same method as the previous step, add one more bulleted item that states Shipping (31 lbs. and up) – $0.60/lb. Preview the document as it will print.

k. Save the file and exit Word.

Perform 1: Perform in Your Life

Student data file needed:

New, blank Word document

You will save your files as:

Lastname_Firstname_w01_pf1_Letter

Lastname_Firstname_w01_pf1_Flyer

Class Reunion Announcement

Sales & Marketing

In this project, you will create a cover letter and a flyer that will be mailed to former classmates who graduated from high school with you. Assume that you have been out of high school for almost 10 years, and you are responsible for getting the word out to others about the event. The cover letter invites classmates to the event to be held at a time and location that is relevant to your high school. The letter should provide general details on the weekend event, while the flyer is much more descriptive and is designed to generate enthusiasm.

Select an appropriate letter style, making sure to include relevant components, such as an address and/or salutation. Although the content is up to you, be sure to include at least two body paragraphs informing your audience of the event and encouraging interest. Design the flyer as a one-page summary, using appropriate color (think school colors!) and tasteful design. The flyer should include contact information for the chair of the planning committee, as well as information on accommodations and any dress requirements. Be sure to mention any monetary charge. Above all, make the flyer fun, eye-catching, and informative.

a. Start **Word** and create a cover letter. Use a letter style of your choice. You will design the content, but keep your audience in mind, providing a general description of the event. Save the document as Lastname_Firstname_w01_pf1_Letter.

b. In the body of the letter, provide a bulleted list, perhaps listing weekend events. Select a bullet that is eye-catching and appropriate. You can use a symbol or picture for a bullet if you prefer.

c. Create a one-page flyer, incorporating design elements that will generate enthusiasm and interest in the event. Save the flyer as Lastname_Firstname_w01_pf1_Flyer.

d. Define **1"** top and bottom margins and **0.75"** right and left margins on the flyer.

e. Include your name as a footer on both the cover letter and the flyer.

f. Use one or more Word styles in the flyer to provide consistency and ease of formatting. Although you will initially apply a Word style, you will adjust the format (without modifying the style itself) to include color or other character formatting.

g. Include at least two different font selections and sizes in the flyer. Use at least one instance of bold and italic formatting in the flyer.

h. Include a page border on the flyer.

i. Because the cover letter and the flyer will be shared with other planning committee members before the documents are finalized, place a DRAFT watermark on each document.

j. Use the spelling checker on both documents, and then proofread them.

k. Save both documents and exit Word.

Perform 2: Perform in Your Career

Student data file needed:

New, blank Word document

You will save your files as:

Lastname_Firstname_w01_pf2_Agenda
Lastname_Firstname_w01_pf2_Minutes
Lastname_Firstname_w01_pf2_Minutes_Unapproved

Meeting Minutes

General Business

You recently were appointed to chair the Ducky Derby Subcommittee at the Stone River Rotary Club where you volunteer. After your first meeting, you offer to develop an agenda for the next meeting. You will also draft a document containing minutes of the previous meeting for review and approval at the meeting. After approval of the minutes, they will be circulated to everyone in the Stone River Rotary Club.

a. Under **Agendas** on Office.com, choose an appropriate agenda template. Remember that this is a formal meeting. Save the document as Lastname_Firstname_w01_pf2_Agenda, and then click **OK** if asked about saving the file to a new format.

b. The following text summarizes the agenda for the upcoming meeting. Using the summary information, prepare a meeting agenda on the template that you opened in the previous step. Format and word the document as you see fit.

Stone River Rotary Club
Meeting Date: August 20, 2013

Meeting Time: 7:30 p.m.

Meeting Type: Ducky Derby Subcommittee

Meeting Leader (or Facilitator): Janet McClernand

Agenda:

1. Call to Order
2. Approval of Minutes from Previous Meeting
3. Action Items
   a. Appoint Festival Committee
   b. Develop Derby Budget
   c. Finalize Charities
   d. Approve Master Schedule of Activities
   e. Select Derby Spokesperson
4. Study/Report Items
   a. Summary of 2011 Festival
   b. Financial Report
   c. Nominating Committee Report
5. Adjournment

c. Remove any unused or unnecessary items from the agenda template such as **Invitees**.

d. Move the **Study/Report Items** section so that it appears before **Action Items**.

e. Include a list of Ducky Derby Subcommittee members before the **Call to Order** section. The committee members are Janet McClernand, Lavinia Fields, Randy King, Michael Summerlin, Marsha Cooper, and Tucker Dodd.

f. Use the spelling checker on the document, and then proofread for errors. Change the top and bottom margins to **2"**, and the left and right margins to **1.5"**. Preview the document as it would print.

g. Include a footer, aligned on the left margin, with your first and last name.

h. Save and close the document. Keep Word open.

i. Open a **blank document**. You jotted down the following summary of the previous Ducky Derby Subcommittee meeting and will now transcribe the notes to a Word document. The minutes will be approved at the upcoming meeting. Save the document as Lastname_Firstname_w01_pf2_Minutes.

Meeting Date: July 18, 2013
Meeting Time: 7:30 p.m.
Meeting Type: Ducky Derby Subcommittee
Attendance: Tucker Dodd, Michael Summerlin, Marsha Cooper, Janet McClernand, and Lavinia Fields
Absent: Randy King

Topics and Discussion:

1. Charity this year: Stone River Advocacy Center, a nonprofit training and development center for adults with developmental disabilities
2. Determination of duck cost: 1 duck is $5, a quack pack is $25, a big quack pack is $50, and a flock of ducks is $100.
3. Prizes are still being identified, but we already have a Honda Civic, a motor scooter, and $1,200 cash. We will continue to seek prizes through July 31.
4. Plans for preliminary promotional activities:
   - Duck Tagging Party, where we will put race numbers on the bottom of 10,000 ducks
   - Kick-Off Party to begin "Duck Season"

- Local newspaper article on partnership with the Stone River Advocacy Center and plans for the Derby
- Development of SR Ducky Derby web site and Facebook page

5. Appointed Nominating Committee to develop slate of officers for next year's Ducky Derby. The Nominating Committee will report at next month's meeting.

6. Ducky Derby Day will be November 9, 2013, at Flat Creek Falls. We will have a maximum of 10,000 ducks ready for purchase and float. Most ducks will be presold before Derby Day.

j. The Word document that you develop for the meeting minutes must include the following:

- Format appropriately using at least two different Word styles of your choosing. In addition, you might want to center the text and/or bold it so that it shows emphasis. Make sure you convey organizational hierarchy in your choices.

- Apply bullets and/or numbers to items, as appropriate.

- Set margins appropriately.

- Proofread and check the spelling of the document.

- Format the text so the document is attractive and easy to read.

- Type your first name and last name as a footer, aligned on the left margin.

- Place a watermark on the minutes to show that they are currently unapproved.

- Preview the document as it will print.

k. Create a PDF copy of the meeting minutes to e-mail ahead of time to committee members. This will allow them to read the minutes before a vote for approval. Name the PDF Lastname_Firstname_w01_pf2_Minutes_Unapproved, save the document, and then close it. Keep Word open.

l. Open **Lastname_Firstname_w01_pf2_Agenda** from the Recent list. You will add another agenda item. The new item is Preview of Ducky Derby Web Site. It should be placed between **Approval of Minutes from Previous Meeting** and **Study/Report Items**, numbered appropriately.

m. Save the document and exit Word.

Perform 3: Perform in Your Career

Student data file needed:
w01_pf3_Plan

You will save your file as:
Lastname_Firstname_w01_pf3_Plan

Cover Letter for a New Business Plan

General Business

You are seeking investors for a new business that you are contemplating. The business, IQ Up, will produce educational toys for toddlers and babies. In order to get the company started, you will need funding. The cover letter template includes areas for such items as the company's mission, target market, and funding sought. As a template, the letter will be easy to modify and quickly distribute to multiple recipients. You will not only personalize the letter for its intended recipients, but you will also format it so that it is attractive and error free.

a. Open **w01_pf3_Plan** from your student data files. The cover letter for a business plan is a generic template. You will replace the items in brackets with the following information. Adjust spacing where necessary and remove all brackets. Save the letter as Lastname_Firstname_w01_pf3_Plan.

Date: October 30, 2013

Name of potential investor: Mr. Jeff Wilhite

Address: 578 W. 51st Street

City, State/Zip: Indianapolis, IN 46201

Name of company: IQ Up

Person referring: Ms. Dale Henderson

What the company does: Produces educational baby and toddler toys

Mission 1: To create memorable moments between parents and children

Mission 2: To produce excellent educational products and software

Mission 3: To encourage early cognitive development in babies and toddlers

Target market: Parents of newborns to toddlers who want to provide an early boost to their children's development and who emphasize the crucial role of education

Amount of money: $30,000

Percentage equity: 5%

Telephone: 203-555-1132

E-mail address: IQBabyCo@ndchi.com

b. Show nonprinting characters. Check the document for spelling errors, and be sure to also manually proofread the document to locate any additional errors.

c. Cut the third paragraph in the body of the letter, and then paste it before the second paragraph. Adjust paragraph marks if necessary.

d. Use the **Find and Replace** feature to find occurrences of the word **company**. Because you feel that you have overused the word in this letter, replace the second occurrence of the word **company** with business.

e. Change the left and right margins to **1.5"** and top and bottom margins to **1"**.

f. Format the threefold mission statement in paragraph 3 of the body of the letter so that each element of the mission statement appears in a bulleted list. Format the bulleted list with a bullet style and indentation of your choice. The fourth paragraph now begins with **Our target market is comprised**. Adjust punctuation and paragraph and line spacing as appropriate to improve the readability of the bulleted items.

g. Right-align the date.

h. Include a left-aligned footer with your first name and last name.

i. Bold **$30,000** and **5%** in the fourth paragraph of the body of the letter.

j. Select the entire letter, and then change the font to **Century Schoolbook** and the font size to **12 pt**.

k. Preview the document as it will appear when printed.

l. Save the document and exit Word.

Perform 4: How Others Perform

Student data file needed:

w01_pf4_Garden

You will save your file as:

Lastname_Firstname_w01_pf4_Garden

Arbor Day Business Letter

Sales & Marketing

You are a volunteer with the Ebersold Botanical Garden in Lebanon, Texas. With Arbor Day approaching, the Botanical Garden is planning a promotion of historical plants and trees. Perfect for school field trips or history lovers, the plants are representative of various eras of American history.

You will finalize a cover letter, informing interested parties of the program. Working from a draft, you will make sure the paragraphs flow well and are in correct format. In addition, you will format paragraphs and develop appropriate styles. Your goal is to produce an attractive, well-formatted document, that is informative, readable, and error free.

a. Start **Word**, open **w01_pf4_Garden** from your student data files. and then save the document as Lastname_Firstname_w01_pf4_Garden.

The letter is from a local plant nursery, introducing a new program that offers seedlings from historical plants. The letter to the Ebersold Botanical Garden offers the seedlings for sale by the garden.

b. Edit the document so that it is in block style. Study the various parts of the letter (recipient address, date, return address, salutation, etc.), and then make any adjustments you find necessary.

c. Create a new style for the paragraphs in the body of the letter. Apply the style to all body paragraphs with the exception of the numbered items. Format the numbered items attractively.

d. The paragraphs are not in logical order. Rearrange them so they flow well.

e. Select an attractive font type and size for the document.

f. Adjust the margins so they adhere to those recommended for a standard business letter.

g. Check the spelling. If you are not certain of whether a word is misspelled, you need to look it up online or in a dictionary.

h. Because the items listed in the numbered list are not sequential items, numbers are not the best choice. Use bullets and indentation of your choice, instead.

i. Make sure the document fits on one page. If it extends over two, adjust the margins, spacing, and/or font size to reduce it.

j. Make any other improvements you think necessary. Save the document and exit Word.

Objectives

1. Use WordArt   p. 184
2. Create SmartArt   p. 190
3. Insert a text box   p. 194
4. Insert graphics   p. 196
5. Insert text from another document   p. 201
6. Set tabs   p. 203
7. Create a table   p. 205
8. Manage the end of a page   p. 214
9. Work with sections p. 215

Including Tables and Objects

PREPARE CASE
Turquoise Oasis Spa Services Publication

Sales & Marketing

The Turquoise Oasis Spa has been recognized as one of the leading spas in the nation. It was rated by *Traveler's Choice* magazine as the third best spa in the nation and was recently awarded accreditation by the Day Spa Group, a nationally recognized accrediting association for spas and wellness groups. The Day Spa Group sponsors a quarterly publication that spotlights leading spas. Turquoise Oasis Spa will be featured in the next issue of the Day Spa publication, *Relax*.

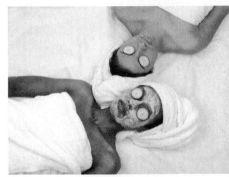

OLJ Studio / Shutterstock.com

You are responsible for collecting information and preparing the article. You want to include information on spa benefits and spa packages, highlighting the spa's unique location, facilities, and treatments. Using Word to create the document, you will include text, graphics, WordArt, and SmartArt. In the process, you will work with tabs, tables, and text from other documents.

Student data files needed for this workshop:

 w02_ws03_Relax

 w02_ws03_Service

You will save your file as:

 Lastname_Firstname_w02_ws03_Relax

 w02_ws03_Spa_Exercises

Including Objects in a Document

When you create a document, you want it to be as effective as possible at reaching the target audience. Suppose you are creating a newsletter with details on an upcoming company picnic. As you develop the newsletter, you decide that a picture or graphic would add spark to the newsletter text, drawing attention to the topic. Maybe a decorative heading would liven it up. Newsletters often sport headlines that are specially formatted with shading, beveled (round-edged) text, or oversized letters. A shaded box with text in it can emphasize or restate an item of interest. Charts and tables can add organization to a document, summarizing and diagramming data. All of those objects enhance a document if used in the right context. An **object** is an item that you can work with independently of surrounding text. You can insert an object, resize it, format it, and even delete it without affecting document text. Word objects include pictures, clip art, WordArt, text boxes, SmartArt, and screenshots. The challenge is to include objects in moderation, always keeping a document's main purpose in mind. In this section you will learn to insert objects into documents and to modify them.

Sales & Marketing

CONSIDER THIS | **Selecting Appropriate Objects**

With the multitude of objects provided by Word, including WordArt, SmartArt, charts, and tables, you should take care to include objects that are appropriate for the documents they appear in. Charts tend to add professionalism as they visually convey business trends. On the other hand, WordArt is more appropriate for banners and informal documents. What types of objects would you consider appropriate for a preschool, a hospital, a media company, or an investment banking firm? Or does the image presented have less to do with the type of object and more about how the object is presented or configured?

Using WordArt

WordArt is a Word feature that modifies text to include shadows, outlines, colors, gradients, and 3-D effects. It also shapes text in waves, curves, and angles. You can format existing text as WordArt, or you can insert new WordArt text into a document. You can also drag WordArt to various places within the document. The Insert tab includes a WordArt command that produces a gallery of WordArt styles you can choose from.

Formatting a WordArt Object

When an object is *selected,* you will see a dashed or solid line surrounding it. You can click outside the selected object to deselect it. The Ribbon displays a **contextual tab** for a selected object, with commands related to the object. For example, a Picture Tools contextual tab is shown for a selected picture or clip art. When WordArt is selected, the Drawing Tools contextual tab is displayed. Other selected objects cause a contextual tab to be displayed with commands related to the object.

The Drawing Tools Format tab that is shown when a WordArt object is selected includes options for modifying WordArt styles, color, and text. A Shape Styles gallery enables you to change the background color, texture, and style of the box surrounding the WordArt selection. You can also change the shape outline and add effects, such as a glow or shadow. To enhance the text of a WordArt selection, select a different WordArt style, or identify a different text style, fill, or outline. There is almost no limit to your creativity when modifying a WordArt selection.

To Create and Format WordArt

a. Start **Word**. Click the **File tab**, and then click **Open**. In the Open dialog box, click the disk drive in the left pane where your student data files are located. Navigate through the folder structure and double-click **w02_ws03_Relax**. Click the **File tab**, and then click **Save As**. In the Save As dialog box, navigate to where you are saving your files, and then type Lastname_Firstname_w02_ws03_Relax replacing Lastname and Firstname with your own name. Click **Save**. If necessary, on the Home tab, click Show/Hide ¶ to display nonprinting characters.

b. Select the first line in the document, **Turquoise Oasis Spa at Painted Paradise**, click the **Insert tab**, and then click **WordArt** in the Text group.

The WordArt gallery presents several styles to choose from. If you position the pointer over a style, a ScreenTip gives the style name.

c. Point to the third style from the left in the last row, and click **Fill - Red, Accent 2, Matte Bevel**.

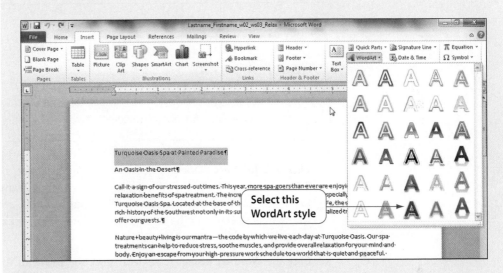

Figure 1 WordArt Gallery

d. With the WordArt object still selected (if it is not, click the object edge to select it as indicated by a solid border), click the **Drawing Tools Format tab**, click the **Shape Styles More** button, and then place the pointer over any style. Live Preview shows the effect of each potential selection.

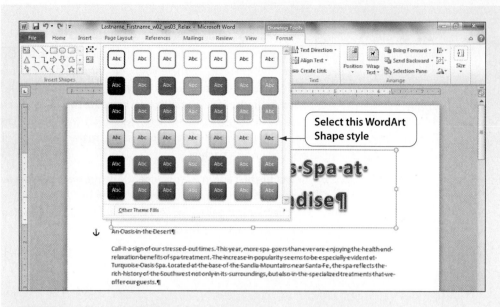

Figure 2 Shape Styles Options

Troubleshooting

If you do not see the Drawing Tools Format tab, the object is not selected. Click anywhere on the WordArt object to select it.

e. Click **Subtle Effect - Orange, Accent 6** (the last selection in the fourth row), click **Text Fill arrow** in the WordArt Styles group, and then click **Orange, Accent 6** (last selection in the first row under Theme Colors). Click **Shape Effects**, point to **Bevel**, and then click **Angle** (first selection in the second row under Bevel). Click outside the WordArt object to see the result.

f. Click the **WordArt object** to select it, click the **Drawing Tools Format tab**, click **Text Effects** in the WordArt Styles group, and then point to **Transform**.

   A gallery of transform effects is displayed. As you move the pointer over each effect, you see a preview of the effect on the selected WordArt object.

g. Click **Chevron Up** (first selection in the second row under Warp). The text slants upward and then down in a chevron effect.

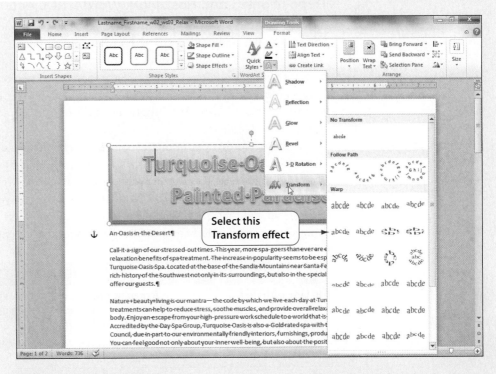

Figure 3 Transform Effects

h. Drag the pink diamond, located near the top-left border of the WordArt object, up slightly to reduce the chevron effect. You can drag the pink diamond up or down to reduce or increase the transform effect.

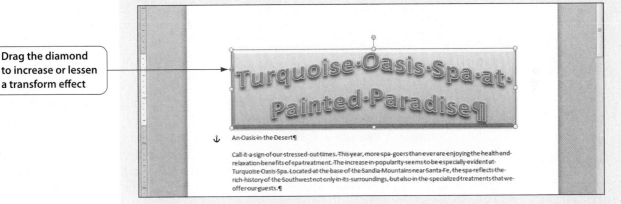

Drag the diamond to increase or lessen a transform effect

Figure 4 Modify a text effect

i. Click in the WordArt object after the word Spa and delete the words **at Painted Paradise**. If the chevron effect loses some shape, drag the pink diamond to adjust the transform effect to your preference.

Troubleshooting

As you edit the WordArt, the chevron effect will temporarily disappear. However, when you click outside the object, the effect will return.

j. Click outside the object to deselect it. **Save** 🖫 the document.

Repositioning and Resizing a WordArt Object

When an object is *selected,* you will see small boxes, or circles, on the border surrounding the object. These are called **sizing handles**. Sizing handles are located in the center and corners of the border surrounding an object and can be used to resize the object. To resize an object, simply drag a sizing handle to increase or reduce the size of the object. If you drag a corner handle, both sides of the object change size simultaneously. To change the font or font size of WordArt, simply select the object, and select font settings in the Font group of the Home tab.

To move WordArt, position the pointer on a border of the selected object so the pointer is a four-headed arrow. Drag the object to a new location. Text wraps around the WordArt object as you move it. The way text wraps around the WordArt is determined by the WordArt object's **text wrap** setting. With a WordArt object selected, you can click the Drawing Tools Format tab and then click Wrap Text in the Arrange group to determine the current text wrap setting and to select another. Text Wrap options are described in Figure 5.

Text Wrap Option	Effect
In Line with Text	A graphic or other object that is positioned directly in the text of a document at the insertion point and responds as another character in the paragraph.
Square	Text wraps on all sides of the object, following the border of an invisible square.
Tight	Text follows the shape, but does not overlap it. If the object is shaped, the text will be also, adhering closely to the object's shape but always an equal distance from the edge.
Through	Text follows the shape, filling any open spaces in the object.
Top and Bottom	Text appears above and below the borders of an object.
Behind Text	The object appears behind the text. Unless the fill color exactly matches the text color, both the object and text will be visible.
In Front of Text	The object appears on top of the text, obscuring the text unless there is no shape fill or the fill is set to semitransparent.

Figure 5   Text Wrap options

You can position a WordArt object within a document, controlling the way text wraps around the object, in a couple of ways. The Arrange group on the Drawing Tools Format tab includes a Position option and a Wrap Text option. The Position option places an object in a preset location within a document (with Square text wrapping). You can place an object in the top, middle, or bottom of a document (situated at the top, middle, or right side horizontally). As you explore options in the Position gallery, you can see the effect of each option on a selected object. Using the Wrap Text command in the Arrange group, you can select any of the text wrapping options in Figure 5.

SIDE NOTE
Rotating WordArt

When a WordArt object is selected, you see a green handle at the top center. Drag the green handle to the right or left to rotate the object. You can also rotate an object using Rotate on the Drawing Tools Format tab in the Arrange group.

Real World Advice   Working with WordArt

Be careful when rotating or resizing WordArt. It is easy to get carried away with the artistic effects of transforming an object. Make sure that such activity does not result in text that is awkward or difficult to read.

To Reposition and Resize WordArt

a. Click the **WordArt object** to select it. Click the **Drawing Tools Format tab**, click **Wrap Text** in the Arrange group, and then point to **Tight**, but do not click. Point to **Square** and note any change. Similarly, explore other options without clicking, to get a preview of the effect on the WordArt selection. Click **Tight**.

b. Click the **arrow** beside **Shape Height** in the Size group to change the size to **0.8**". Change the **Shape Width** to **6.3**".

You can also resize an object by dragging a sizing handle. For more precise sizing, adjust the height and width selections in the Size group.

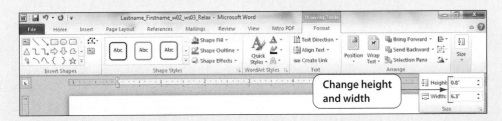

Figure 6   Resizing WordArt

c. Press `Ctrl`+`End` to position the insertion point at the end of the document, and then press `Enter`. Click the **Insert tab**, click **WordArt** in the Text group, and then click **Fill - Orange, Accent 6**, **Warm Matte Bevel** (row 6, column 2). Type A passion for helping people relax. Place the pointer on the **WordArt border** so it is displayed as a four-headed arrow. Click the **border** to select all of the text within the WordArt object. When the surrounding border is solid, you do not have to select all the text before applying a change in format as a change affects all text within the object.

d. Click the **Home tab**, and then change the font to **Verdana** and the font size to **20**. Click the **Drawing Tools Format tab**, click the **Shape Fill arrow** in the Shape Styles group, and then click **Orange, Accent 6, Lighter 80%**. Click **Shape Fill,** point to **Gradient,** and then click **Linear Down** (second from left under Variations). Change the height to **0.5**", click **Wrap Text**, and then select **Top and Bottom**.

e. Place the pointer near a border of the WordArt object so it appears as a four-headed arrow. Drag the WordArt up and release it at the left margin just above the text Join Us at Turquoise Oasis Spa.

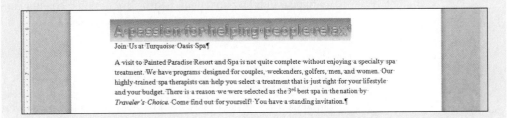

Figure 7   Repositioning WordArt

f. On the Drawing Tools Format tab, click **Align** in the Arrange group, and then click **Align Center**.

The first three options in the Align menu relate to horizontal alignment. The next three options (Align Top, Align Middle, and Align Bottom) relate to vertical alignment on the current page.

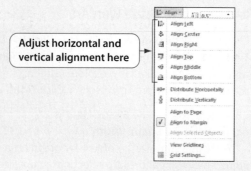

Adjust horizontal and vertical alignment here

Figure 8 Adjusting alignment

Troubleshooting

If you click Align Text (in the Text group) instead of Align, you will not see the selection indicated in Step f. Simply click Align (in the Arrange group).

g. Click before the word **Join** in the line just below the WordArt. Press [Enter] to insert a blank line and open some space beneath the WordArt.

h. Press [Ctrl]+[Home], and then select the first paragraph beneath the WordArt, An Oasis in the Desert. Because the WordArt object is anchored to that paragraph, the WordArt object is also selected.

i. Click the **Home tab**, click **Bold** [B] in the Font group, and then change the font size to **20**.

j. Copy the format of the selected line to **Calm Your Frazzled Nerves**, **Specialty Spa Packages**, **Specialty Spa Massages**, and **Join Us at Turquoise Oasis Spa**.

k. **Save** [💾] the document.

Real World Advice | Using Color and Design Elements

Research shows that the impact of color in a document is significant. Putting a border around a table or paragraph or changing a font color is sure to catch the eye. But be careful, too much color and gaudy design elements can make a document appear unprofessional and garish. Use design elements consistently and sparingly to provide emphasis without being overwhelming.

Creating SmartArt

SmartArt is a visual representation that helps you communicate processes, concepts, or ideas that would otherwise require a great deal of text to describe. Using SmartArt, you can create diagrams such as organization charts, process flows, lists, cycle diagrams, and step-by-step processes. Microsoft Office 2010 includes over 130 SmartArt diagrams in eight categories. When you click SmartArt in the Illustrations group of the Insert tab, you can select from SmartArt categories, including one that enables you to include your own pictures in SmartArt shapes. You can also create process diagrams, relationship charts, and hierarchy designs. You can include your own text in SmartArt shapes, and you can format SmartArt with color, special effects, and font selections. When a SmartArt diagram is selected, the Design and Format tabs are displayed on the Ribbon, offering related options you can select from.

Identifying Types of SmartArt

Using SmartArt saves a great deal of time that would otherwise be spent describing a process or even designing a chart yourself. The built-in SmartArt diagrams enable you to quickly portray a situation or process. You can select from eight categories of SmartArt, as described in Figure 9.

Category	Represents
List	Nonsequential information
Process	Steps in a process or timeline
Cycle	A continual process
Hierarchy	Organization
Relationship	Connections
Matrix	How parts relate to a whole
Pyramid	Proportional, interconnected, or hierarchical relationships
Picture	Arrangements of pictures in a relationship

Figure 9   SmartArt types

Sales &
Marketing

Real World Advice   Designing SmartArt

In selecting and formatting SmartArt, be sure to limit text to key points. A large number of shapes and a great deal of text can detract from the visual appeal and make it more difficult to convey your message. The Trapezoid List is one of the few SmartArt diagrams that can actually handle a large amount of text, so as a rule, be brief and direct when creating SmartArt.

SIDE NOTE
Using the SmartArt Text Pane
You can enter text in SmartArt shapes by typing in the SmartArt Text pane or by typing directly in the shape. Occasionally, a shape may be obscured so you are unable to click it to type text. In that case, use the SmartArt Text pane.

To Create SmartArt and Add Text

a. In the paragraph beginning with **Getting lost is the absolute best way to discover a place**, click at the end of the paragraph. Press [Enter], click the **Insert tab**, and then click **SmartArt** in the Illustrations group. Select **Cycle** from the list of categories, click **Nondirectional Cycle**, and then click **OK**.

Select
Nondirectional
Cycle

Select Cycle
category

Explanation
of selected
SmartArt

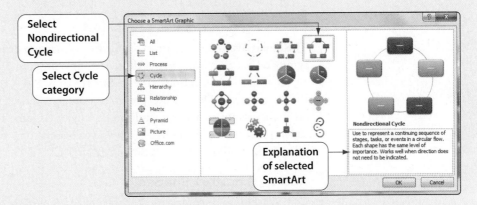

Figure 10   Inserting SmartArt

b. Click beside the first bullet in the SmartArt Text pane. If you do not see a SmartArt Text pane, click the **small rectangular box** on the left border of the SmartArt object. The SmartArt Text pane simplifies the task of typing text in SmartArt shapes.

c. Type Mind. Click beside the second bullet, and type Body. Click beside the third bullet, and type Spirit. You can also enter text in a shape by clicking the shape and typing text. Close ⊠ the SmartArt Text pane.

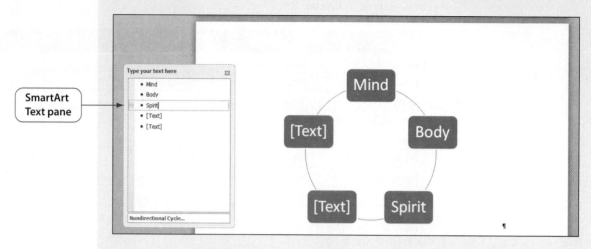

Figure 11   SmartArt Text pane

d. Click one of the two remaining SmartArt shapes that are without text. If the border surrounding the shape is a dashed line, place the pointer on the border of the selected shape, click to change the dashed line to a solid line, and then press Delete to delete the shape. Similarly, delete the remaining shape without text. Click outside the SmartArt graphic to deselect it.

e. Save 🖫 the document.

SIDE NOTE
Deleting SmartArt
To delete a SmartArt object, click to select the border of the SmartArt object and press Delete.

CONSIDER THIS │ SmartArt Applications

In the business world, SmartArt can be extremely effective for traditional business representations such as an organizational chart or process flow map. What other business figures or representations might SmartArt be useful for?

Modifying and Resizing SmartArt

The SmartArt Tools Design tab and the Format tab provide plenty of options for modifying and resizing SmartArt. After creating a diagram, you might want to explore other styles and color selections. If the SmartArt is too large or too small, you will want to resize it. The Design tab provides a SmartArt Styles gallery and a Layouts gallery, with options for enhancing and modifying a diagram. The Format tab is more centered around individual shapes, enabling you to change text and WordArt styles. You can also select a page alignment for a SmartArt object.

Adding SmartArt Shapes

You will seldom be completely satisfied with a SmartArt object immediately after creating it. You will often find that you need to add a shape to the SmartArt diagram to better depict a process. With a SmartArt object selected, click the SmartArt Tools Design tab and click Add Shape in the Create Graphic group. By default, a new shape is added after a selected shape, although you can specify whether the new shape should appear before or after when you click the Add Shape arrow and make a selection.

To Modify SmartArt and Add a Shape

a. Select the **SmartArt object**, click the **SmartArt Tools Design tab,** and then point to a selection in the Layouts group and view the effect on the selected SmartArt. Explore other layouts. Click **More** ▾ for additional selections, and then click **Basic Cycle** (first selection in the first row).

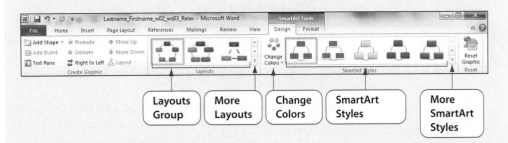

Figure 12   Modifying SmartArt

b. Be sure that none of the SmartArt shapes are selected. If any are selected, click in the white space to the left or right of a shape to deselect a specific shape and select the entire diagram. Click **Add Shape** in the Create Graphic group of the SmartArt Tools Design tab, and then type Emotion. The font size adjusts in each shape to accommodate the new text.

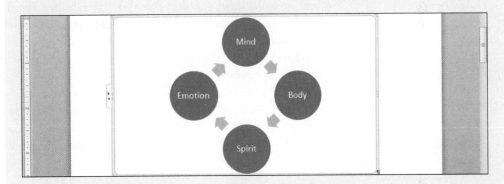

Figure 13   Spa SmartArt

c. Point to any style in the SmartArt Styles group but do not click. Hold the mouse steady to view the effect on the SmartArt diagram. Click **More** ▾ to explore other style options, and then click **Cartoon** (third selection in the first 3-D row).

d. Click in the white area just outside a SmartArt shape to select the entire diagram. Click the **SmartArt Tools Format tab**, and then click the **Height arrow** to reduce the height to **3**".

Troubleshooting

> If a shape within the SmartArt diagram is resized instead of the entire diagram, the shape was selected instead of the SmartArt. Click Undo, click on the white space in the diagram, and make sure that the border surrounds only the diagram, not an individual shape. Then change the size once more.

e. Click the **Emotion shape**. You decide that the shape is unnecessary so you will delete it. If the border around the selected shape is dashed, place the pointer on the border, so it resembles a four-headed arrow [➕], and click. The dashed line becomes solid. Press Delete to remove the shape.

f. If an individual shape is selected, click outside the shape to select the entire SmartArt diagram instead. Click the **SmartArt Tools Design tab**, click **Change Colors** in the SmartArt Styles group, and then point to any selection and view the effect on the SmartArt diagram. Explore other selections. Scroll down and click **Gradient Loop - Accent 6** (fourth selection under Accent 6).

Troubleshooting

> If you do not see the Accent 6 group, scroll further down in the list of color categories.

g. Click the **SmartArt Tools Format tab**, and then change the height in the Size group to **2.8**" and the width to **6**". If the object disappears, scroll up to view the bottom of the preceding page. The diagram should appear there.
  Click outside the SmartArt diagram to deselect it.

h. **Save** 🖫 the document.

Inserting a Text Box

A **text box** is a drawing object that you can place in a Word document and then add text to. It is literally a box, or block, of text that you can format just as you would any other drawing object. You can shade the text box, add a border to it, and add special effects, such as shadows or special fills. A text box can give you control of text because you can limit the space the text can be displayed in. For example, you could set up newsletter columns in text boxes, and even link the text boxes so text flows from one "column" to the next. Projects such as business cards and greeting cards are easily created by using text boxes to limit text to certain areas. When a text box in a document is selected, a Drawing Tools Format tab is displayed on the Ribbon with commands relevant to the text box design and placement.

To Create and Modify a Text Box

a. If necessary, click the Home tab, and click Show/Hide ¶ in the Paragraph group to display nonprinting characters. Press Ctrl+End. Click the **Insert tab**, click **Text Box** in the Text group, and then click **Draw Text Box**. Point to the insertion point at the end of the document and click. A narrow text box is drawn, with an insertion point inside.

b. Click the **Home tab**, and click **No Spacing** in the Styles group to single-space the text. Type Turquoise Oasis Spa and press Enter. Type Painted Paradise Resort and Spa and press Enter. Type 3355 Hemmingway Circle and press Enter. Type Santa Fe, NM 89566.

c. Click the **Drawing Tools Format tab**, and then click **More** ⊽ in the Shape Styles group. Point to a style to view the effect on the selected text box. Explore other styles. Select **Intense Effect - Orange, Accent 6** (row 6, column 7).

Troubleshooting

> If the Shape Styles gallery obscures the text box, you will not be able to see the effect of a shape style until you select a style.

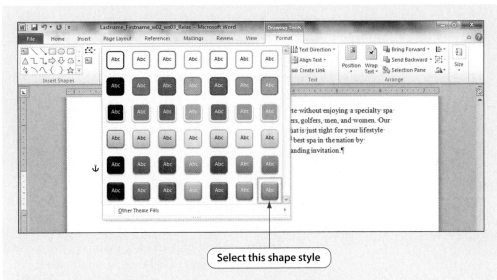

Select this shape style

Figure 14   Modifying a text box

d. Point to a border of the text box so the pointer appears as a four-headed arrow , and then click to make the dashed line solid. Click the **Home tab**, and then change the font size to **14**. The text box expands to accommodate the larger font size.

e. Click the **Drawing Tools Format tab**, click the **Shape Outline arrow** in the Shape Styles group, and then click **Orange, Accent 6, Darker 50%** (tenth column in the last row under Theme Colors). Click **Shape Effects**, point to **Shadow**, and then under Outer click **Offset Diagonal Bottom Right** (the first option in the first row).

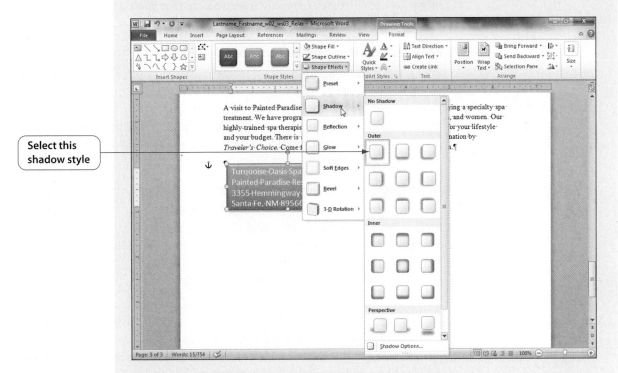

Select this shadow style

Figure 15   Shape Effects

f. Click the **Home tab**, and then click **Center** ≡ to center the text within the text box. Click the **Drawing Tools Format tab**, click **Align** in the Arrange group, and then click **Align Center** to center the text box horizontally. Click the **Width arrow** in the Size group to increase the width to **3.5**".

Troubleshooting

> If only one line within the text box is centered, click the dashed line surrounding the text box to make it solid. Then click the Home tab and click Center.

g. Click outside the text box to deselect it.

h. **Save** 🖫 the document.

Inserting Graphics

Newsletters, business cards, and other specialty documents can be enhanced with the addition of pictures and clip art. For example, when creating a family newsletter, you might want to include a personal picture saved on a disk drive. On occasion, you might identify a clip art image that is perfect for your project. You can place clip art or a picture in a document and then determine how text should wrap around the image. You can also format the graphic with outline styles and artistic effects. You can even crop an image or recolor it to better suit the document.

Inserting a Picture

A **picture** is a photo that is saved on a disk drive. Perhaps you enjoy using a digital camera to take photographs. You can save your photos on a CD or disk drive and then insert a photo into a document. The photo becomes a graphic object that you can manage just as you do other objects, resizing, formatting, and wrapping text as needed. You might locate a picture or graphic image online that you plan to use in a document. Save the graphic to a disk and then insert the image exactly as you would a digital photo.

Moving and Resizing a Picture

When a picture is inserted in a document it is surrounded by a border that includes sizing handles—small squares or circles at the corners and center of each side. To resize the photo, drag a handle. You should always drag a corner handle so the picture is resized proportionally. If you drag a center handle, the picture will be skewed. To move a picture, point to a border (not a handle) so it appears as a four-headed arrow. Drag to move the picture to a new location.

Adjusting Picture Settings and Style

When a picture is selected, the Picture Tools Format tab is displayed on the Ribbon. The Picture Tools Format tab includes options for changing the picture style, adding a border and special effects, cropping the picture, and wrapping text. You can even apply color corrections and add artistic effects.

To Insert and Format a Picture

a. Press Ctrl + Home. Click at the end of the second paragraph ending with environment and press Enter. If nonprinting characters are not displayed, click the **Home tab** and click **Show/Hide** ¶ in the Paragraph group.

b. Click the **Insert tab**, click **Picture**, and then navigate to the location of your student data files. Click **w02_ws03_Service**, and then click **Insert**.

   A picture of a spa service is inserted in the document at the position of the insertion point. The picture is likely to be much too large, but you will correct that. The picture is selected, as you can tell by the border surrounding it. The border includes sizing handles.

c. If necessary, on the View tab, click the Ruler check box in the Show group to display horizontal and vertical rulers. Point to the top-right sizing handle so the pointer appears as a two-headed arrow ⟋. Watching the horizontal ruler, drag the picture toward the center, reducing the picture size, so the right edge is approximately at the 5" mark on the ruler.

Troubleshooting

> If a ruler does not appear when you click the Ruler check box, you removed an existing ruler instead of displaying it. That is because the Ruler check box is a toggle, acting much like a light switch, and you turned *off* a ruler instead of turning it *on*. Simply click the Ruler check box again to display the ruler.

Horizontal ruler

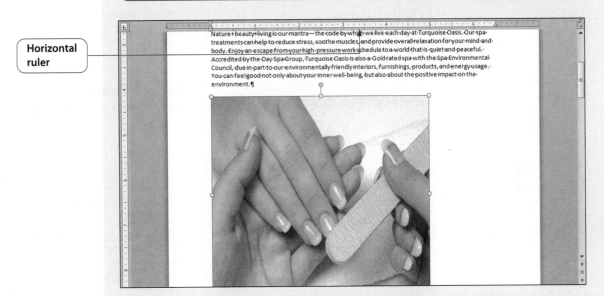

Figure 16   Inserting a picture

d. Click the **Picture Tools Format tab**, and then click the **Height arrow** in the Size group to show **1"**.

As you change height, the width changes also so the picture is not skewed. The height and width specifications in the Size group enable you to more precisely resize a picture.

Troubleshooting

> If the Ribbon does not display the Size group, click the Picture Tools Format tab.

e. On the Picture Tools Format tab, point to a selection in the Picture Styles group. Note the effect on the picture and the tip that displays providing a description of each picture effect. Explore other styles. Click **Soft Edge Rectangle**. Other selections in the Picture Styles group enable you to add a picture effect, border, or picture layout (so you can include text within a picture).

f. On the Picture Tools Format tab, click **Color** in the Adjust group, and then click **Orange, Accent color 6 Light** (the last selection on the right in the third row under Recolor). You can recolor a picture as well as adjust the color saturation and tone.

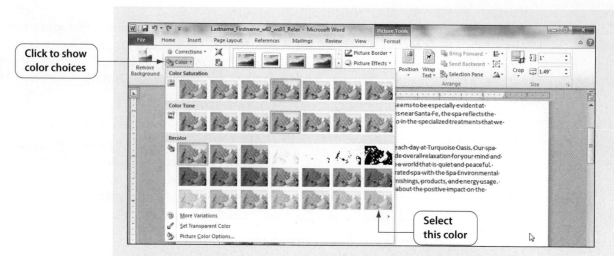

Click to show color choices

Select this color

Figure 17 Coloring a picture

g. Click **Wrap Text** in the Arrange group, and then click **Square**. Text wraps around the picture on the right, in a square fashion. Remove the extra paragraph mark at the right of the picture.

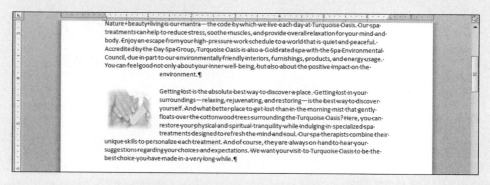

Figure 18 Picture with wrapped text

SIDE NOTE
Delete a Picture
To delete a picture, select the picture and then press [Delete].

h. **Save** 🔲 the document.

Real World Advice | Word and Image Editing

Word 2010 includes image-editing features that at one time were reserved for image-editing software, such as correcting contrast and brightness. You can even add artistic effects, remove a background, and compress a picture to reduce its size within a document. When you compress a picture, the picture's dimensions are not affected, but the file size is made smaller. Especially when disk space is limited, or when you plan to share a document electronically, it might be helpful to reduce a picture's file size. Take advantage of these features if you want to avoid purchasing other image-manipulation software.

Inserting Clip Art

Clip art is a graphic illustration that can be inserted into a Word document. Word provides an extensive collection of clip art for you to select from when developing a document including drawings, audio, video, and photographs. At your request, that collection includes clip art available from Office.com, Microsoft's online gallery of Microsoft Office material, as well as clip art housed locally within Word. Clip art is inserted as a graphic object that can be resized, recolored, and formatted. When a clip art image is selected, the Format tab is displayed, offering many options so you can apply style settings, wrap text, and change alignment. Using the Clip Art task pane, you can indicate a search term. For example, if you are looking for clip art to support a report on a company's financial performance, you could use the search term "dollars" or "money." In addition, you can specify the type of clip art sought—illustrations, photographs, videos, or audio. If you include Office.com content, the search will draw from Microsoft's extensive online clip art library.

To Insert and Format Clip Art

a. Under the heading Specialty Spa Massages, click after the word fatigue at the end of the list of massage benefits, and then press Enter. Click the **Insert tab**, click **Clip Art** in the Illustrations group, and then make sure the **Include Office.com content** check box is selected. If not, click the check box to select it. Click in the **Search for** box, remove any text, and type spa. Click the **Results should be arrow**, select **Illustrations**, deselect all other categories, and then click **Go**.

Enter a search keyword

Specify media type

Include Office.com content

Search results

Figure 19 Searching for clip art

b. Scroll down, if necessary, and click the clip art image described as Woman in towel with toiletries. If you do not see that image, select a similar image. The clip art is placed in the document. **Close** [×] the Clip Art task pane.

Troubleshooting

If instead of clicking the clip art image in the task pane, you click the arrow beside the clip art selection, you will see a menu from which you can click Insert. Doing so places the image in the document just as if you had clicked the clip art.

Click this clip
art image

Figure 20   Selecting clip art

c. Click the **Picture Tools Format tab**, click the **Height box** in the Size group, and type **1.5**,
    replacing the current height with the new dimension. Press ⌐Enter⌐.

    The clip art image is resized. Delete any paragraph marks that might display immedi-
    ately beneath or to the right of the clip art image.

Troubleshooting

If you do not see the Picture Tools Format tab on the Ribbon, the clip art is not
selected. Click the clip art image to select it and display the tab.

d. If necessary, click the clip art to select it. Click the **Picture Tools Format tab**, click **More** ▼
    in the Picture Styles group, and then click **Soft Edge Oval**.

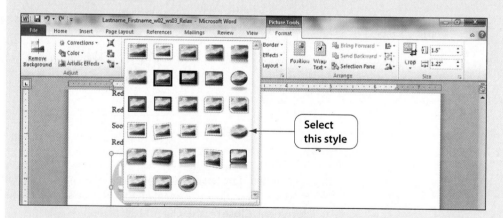

Select
this style

Figure 21   Picture styles

e. On the Picture Tools Format tab, click **Wrap Text** in the Arrange group, and then click
    Tight. Text wraps around the clip art, following the edges in a curved shape. Click out-
    side the clip art to deselect it and see the effect of the text wrap.

f. Select the **clip art**. Click the **Picture Tools Format tab**, click **Artistic Effects** in the Adjust group, and then click **Line Drawing**.

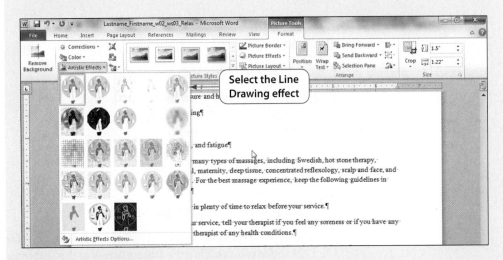

Figure 22 Artistic effects

g. Deselect the clip art.

h. **Save** 🖫 the document.

CONSIDER THIS | **Intellectual Property and the Internet**

Intellectual property is defined as creations of the mind and is protected by copyright, patent, trademark, and industrial design rights. Can intellectual property on the Internet be compromised? Suggest ways intellectual property could be better protected on the Internet.

Real World Advice   Inserting a Screenshot

Word 2010 enables you to easily insert screenshots into a document. A **screenshot** is an image of a window or screen display that you can manipulate as an object, much as you would manage a picture or clip art. Click the Insert tab and click Screenshot in the Illustrations group. You can select from currently open windows (even those that are minimized). You can also click Screen Clipping and drag to select a portion of the currently open window to place that portion within the Word document. You might want to include screenshots if you are preparing an explanatory document where screenshots would help demonstrate a process or illustrate a point. As part of a marketing plan or a research report, you can even include screenshots of websites.

Inserting Text from Another Document

If you can save time spent typing, you should. Word makes it possible to insert text from another document so you do not have to retype it. Not only can you save time by reusing text, but you also minimize typing errors. Suppose you have prepared and saved a document that includes only the company name and address. Because you must often include the company information in other documents, you can simply insert the text from the original document into another document you are working on. That way, you are not required to retype the company name and address, and you do not run the risk of making a typo.

Quick Reference — Inserting Text from Another Document

1. Click the Insert tab.
2. Click the Object arrow in the Text group.
3. Click Text from File.
4. Navigate to the document to include and double-click it.

To Insert Text from Another Document

a. Scroll up and click after the heading **Calm Your Frazzled Nerves**, and then press Enter. Click the **Insert tab**, click the **Object arrow** in the Text group, and then click **Text from File**. Navigate to the location of your student data files and double-click **w02_ws03_ Spa_Exercises**.

Troubleshooting

If you click Object instead of the arrow beside it, you will see an Object dialog box. Close the dialog box, and click the Object arrow instead (in the Text group of the Insert tab). Click Text from File and navigate to the file to include.

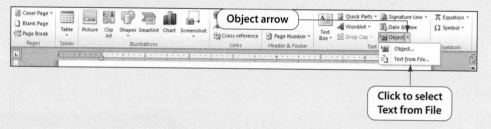

Figure 23   Inserting text from another file

b. Remove any extra paragraph marks beneath the inserted text. **Bold** [B] the numbered headings, including the number preceding the text heading for each (1. Visualize Calmness, 2. Breathe, etc.).

c. Press Ctrl+A to select all text, click the **Home tab**, and then select **Times New Roman** as the font.

d. Deselect the text and **Save** [💾] the document.

Working with Tabs and Tables

Creating columns of data is easy when you use tabs or tables. You will often find it necessary to set data apart in a document so it appears spaced a certain distance from a margin or aligned in columns. Perhaps you are preparing a table of contents. You could type the chapter or topic, and then leave a set amount of space before typing a page number. By setting a right-aligned tab stop, you can be sure all page numbers line up evenly.

Similarly, you can define a table with a set number of columns and rows. Then, just type text in the table cells, or boxes. A table would be appropriate for listing employee names in one column and departments in another. You can select a predesigned table style to draw attention to table text. Although both methods enable you to align text in columns, each has unique features that make it appropriate for various applications. In this section, you will format documents with tabs and you will learn to summarize data in tables within documents. You will also explore ways to manage the end of a page, making sure that each page ends attractively. Finally, you will learn to format text in sections.

Setting Tabs

A **tab** stop is a location where the insertion point will stop when you press $\boxed{\text{Tab}}$. If you do not specify tab stops, the default tab stop is each 1/2". If you press $\boxed{\text{Tab}}$ once, the insertion point stops 1/2" from the left margin. Press $\boxed{\text{Tab}}$ again to stop at 1". Most often, though, you have particular tab stops in mind, so you must set them manually.

You will frequently select from four tab types. A **left tab** aligns text on the left, while a **right tab** aligns text on the right. A right tab stop is appropriate for a table of contents, where page numbers align on the right. A **decimal tab** aligns text on a decimal point, such as a columnar list of student grades, where grades might have varying places to the right of the decimal point. With the grades aligned on the decimal point, they will appear neat and readable. A **center tab** aligns text evenly to the left and right of the tab stop. You can add **leaders** to a tab stop so that a row of dots or dashes is displayed before a tab stop. You have seen dot leaders on restaurant menus where a line of dots precedes each menu price.

When you set a tab stop, it only applies to text that you have yet to type or to paragraphs that you have selected. Therefore, you can set different tab stops for different paragraphs in a document.

Using the Ruler to Set Tabs

In most cases, the easiest way to set a tab stop is to use the ruler. With the ruler displayed, select a tab type. The default tab stop is left, but you can select another type by clicking the tab button to the left of the horizontal ruler. Click the tab button once to select a center tab stop ⊡. Click again to select a right tab stop ⊡, and again to select a decimal tab stop ⊡. After identifying the tab type, simply click the location on the ruler where the tab is to be placed.

You can move a tab stop by dragging it along the ruler. If you want to delete a tab, just drag it off the ruler.

Using the Tabs Dialog Box

Tab stops that you set on the ruler are a rough estimate. For example, if you click to place a left tab stop at the 1" mark, you might instead place it at 1.2", or perhaps at 0.9". If you need more precise tab stops, you can use the Tabs dialog box. If you plan to use tab leaders (dots or dashes that precede a tab stop), you must make that selection in the Tabs dialog box. You can also clear tab stops and set a default tab stop measurement. Open the Tabs dialog box when you click the Paragraph Dialog Box Launcher on the Home tab and click the Tabs button. You can also open the dialog box when you double-click a tab on the ruler.

CONSIDER THIS | **Tabs and Spacing**

Setting tabs enables you to precisely position text in columns. However, you could accomplish the same outcome by pressing the $\boxed{\text{Spacebar}}$ to position items. Do you think that using the Spacebar can position text as precisely as tabs?

Quick Reference / Setting Tabs

1. Click the Paragraph Dialog Box Launcher.
2. Click Tabs.
3. Type a tab stop position.
4. Select an alignment and leader (if necessary).
5. Click Set (or OK, if you are only setting one tab stop).
6. Repeat Steps 3–5, clicking OK when finished.

To Set Tabs

a. Click before the heading **Specialty Spa Packages**, and then press Enter. Click before the new paragraph mark, and type Spa Hours. Press Enter, change the font to **12 pt** size, and then click **Bold** B to remove the bold formatting.

b. If the ruler is not displayed, click the **View tab** and click the **Ruler** check box in the Show group. Point to the **1.5**" mark on the horizontal ruler, and then click to set a left tab stop. Click the **4**" mark to set another left tab stop.

Troubleshooting

If the tab stop is displayed incorrectly on the ruler, drag the tab stop off of the ruler or simply click Undo.

Tab button →

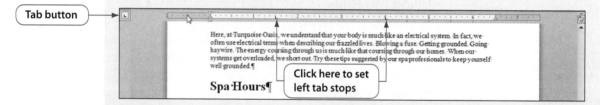

Here, at Turquoise Oasis, we understand that your body is much like an electrical system. In fact, we often use electrical terms when describing our frazzled lives. Blowing a fuse. Getting grounded. Going haywire. The energy coursing through us is much like that coursing through our homes. When our systems get overloaded, we short out. Try these tips suggested by our spa professionals to keep yourself well-grounded.¶

Spa Hours¶

Click here to set left tab stops

Figure 24   Using the ruler to set tabs

c. Press Tab, and then type Monday–Friday (do not leave a space before or after the dash). Press Tab, type 7:00 a.m.–11:00 p.m. (do not leave a space before and after the dash), and then press Enter. Press Tab and type Saturday. Press Tab, type 7:00 a.m.–midnight, and then press Enter. Press Tab, and then type Sunday. Press Tab, and then type 7:00 a.m.–11:00 p.m. Do not press Enter.

d. Point to the left tab stop at the **4**" mark, and then click and drag it back to **3.5**".
   You decide that the tab stop is too far to the right, so you reposition it to the left. However, because you did not select all three lines that were to be affected by the tab adjustment, only the current line moved.

e. Click **Undo**, select the three lines of spa hours, and then drag the 4" tab stop back to 3.5". All three lines are adjusted.

f. If they are not already selected, select the three lines containing spa hours. Double-click either of the **left tabs** on the ruler to open the Tabs dialog box.
   You will specify a dot leader for the space between the days and times. Leaders are attached to the tabs that follow them, so you will adjust the 3.5" tab stop to include a dot leader.

g. Click **3.5**" in the Tab stop position box. If you did not set the tab stop precisely at 3.5", you may not see the exact tab stop. In that case, click the tab stop position closest to 3.5".

SIDE NOTE
Adjusting Tabs for a Selection of Text
Remember that a tab stop only affects text that is typed after the tab stop is set, or text that is selected before the tab stop is set.

h. Select option **2** (dot leader) in the Leader area, and then click **OK**.

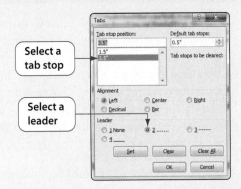

Figure 25 The Tabs dialog box

i. Click outside the selected area. Word may incorrectly indicate a grammatical mistake in the listing of spa hours. If that is the case, right-click the **green underline**, and then click **Ignore Once**. Repeat the process for other incorrectly identified grammatical mistakes.

j. Select the three lines of spa hours. Click the **Home tab**, click the **Paragraph Dialog Box Launcher**, and then click **Tabs**. Type 1 in the Tab stop position box, and then click **Set**. Click **1.5"** in the Tab stop position box, click **Clear**, and then click **OK**. Deselect the text.

k. **Save** 🖫 the document.

Creating a Table

A **table** is a grid of columns and rows. A table is often used to summarize data, such as sales totals for various divisions of a company or enrollment data for college classes. When you find the need to list data in columns and rows within a document, you might consider organizing that data in a Word table.

A table typically includes headings that identify each column and rows that contain data. For example, if you are summarizing sales data for company divisions, the headings in row 1 could be "Division" and "Sales." The table includes two columns. The first row might show "Brunswick Division" and "650,109," indicating that the sales total for the Brunswick Division is $650,109. Data for other divisions is displayed in the following rows. If there are six divisions in the company, the table will include seven rows (one header row and six rows of data).

When you create a table, you specify the number of columns and rows. Often, the number that you indicate turns out to be more or less than what is actually necessary. Adding and deleting columns and rows is a simple task, enabling you to easily change a table structure. You can even merge cells to accommodate long entries or table titles. A table **cell** is the intersection of a column and a row. You will type table data in cells, pressing Tab to move from one cell to the next. Word provides a gallery of table designs to choose from if you want to add energy to a table or make it more noticeable.

The Table Tools Design tab and the Layout tab enable you to change table layout and design, inserting rows and columns, merging cells, sorting table data, changing styles, and modifying table properties. If a table includes numeric data, you can produce summary information, such as a sum or average.

CONSIDER THIS | **Document Tables**

What kinds of data could you summarize in a Word table? Could you use tabs in the document to display the same data just as effectively? Why or why not?

Entering Data in a Table

When you insert a table, Word creates an empty grid of columns and rows. You can enter data in a cell by clicking in the cell and typing. To move to another cell, simply click the cell or press [Tab] (or press →, ←, ↑, or ↓) to move to an adjacent cell. Most often, you will press [Tab] to continue completing the table. As you type in a cell, Word automatically wraps text that reaches the end of the cell, increasing the cell's height (along with all other cells on the row) to accommodate the entry. If you want text to continue to the next line in a cell before you reach the end of the cell, you can press [Enter] to force a hard return.

To Create a Table

a. Point to the first paragraph under the heading **Specialty Spa Packages** after the word fancy!, and click. Press [Enter], click the **Insert tab**, and then click **Table** in the Tables group. A table grid is presented for you to specify the number of columns and rows to include in the table.

b. Drag to highlight three columns and three rows. Click and release the mouse button when the table is a **3x3** matrix. As you drag to indicate the table size, a Live Preview of the table is displayed in the document.

Troubleshooting

If you make a mistake in selecting the number of columns and rows to include, click Undo and repeat the process of inserting a table.

Table grid with 3 rows and 3 columns selected

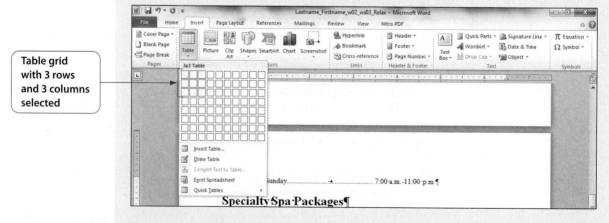

Figure 26   Creating a table

c. Click in the top-left cell of the table.

Note that all three columns are equal width and each row is the same height. If non-printing characters are shown, you will see an end-of-cell mark in each cell and an end-of-row mark at the right side of each row. The Table selector at the top-left corner of the table enables you to select the entire table. You can drag the resize handle in the bottom-right corner of the table to resize the table.

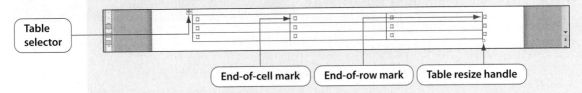

Table selector

End-of-cell mark   End-of-row mark   Table resize handle

Figure 27 A blank table

d. Type Body Package (3 hours). Press ⌷Tab⌷, and then type Oasis Signature Massage. Because several spa services are included in the Body Package, you will list them all within the same cell.

e. Press ⌷Enter⌷. The pointer is positioned on the next line in the same cell. The style is Normal, so there is a large space between lines.

f. Type Oasis Manicure and Pedicure and press ⌷Enter⌷. Type Jade Facial and do *not* press ⌷Enter⌷.

Troubleshooting

If you press ⌷Enter⌷ too many times in the cell so there is a blank line at the end of the cell, click Undo or press ⌷Backspace⌷ to remove the hard return.

g. Press ⌷Tab⌷, type 185, and press ⌷Tab⌧. Type the following text in the remaining two rows of the table. If a cell entry is longer than the cell, as is the case in the description of at least one of the services, do not press ⌷Enter⌷. Let Word wrap the text automatically.

| Soul Package (2 hours) | Oasis Signature Massage

European Cleansing or Gentleman's Facial | 135 |
| Mind Package (4–5 hours) | Oasis Signature Massage

Classic Desert Facial

Oasis Manicure and Pedicure

Paradise Fruit Bar | 465 |

h. Point to the border of any cell so the pointer becomes a two-headed resizing pointer ⟷. You can drag the pointer to resize columns and rows.

i. Point to the top of any column so the pointer appears as a downward black arrow ⬇. At that point, you can click to select the column. Similarly, you can click to the left of a row, when the pointer is a large white arrow ⬈, to select the row.

j. Point just inside the left edge of a cell so the pointer appears as a right-directed black arrow ➤. You can then click to select everything in the cell.

k. Practice selecting columns, rows, and cells. To select the entire table, click the Table selector ⊞ at the top-left corner of the table.

l. **Save** 🖫 the document.

Real World Advice **When to Use Tabs and Tables**

Tabs and tables are similar in that they both enable you to align text in columns. So which method should you use? It depends on the purpose of the document. Tabs are appropriate for quick alignment of data, especially if a dot leader is required. You can align text and numbers with precision, and the tabbed data blends well into the document. A table is best if you think you might need to sort rows or provide summary data. Also, a table can be formatted so it is an eye-catching component, standing out from the rest of the document.

Inserting Columns and Rows

You will seldom develop a table that is perfect the first time. Most often, you will find that you need to add or delete rows or columns after the table is created. As you enter text in the last cell of a table, you can press Tab once more to insert a new row at the end of the table. That method works well for adding a row at the *end* of the table, but what if the new row should be inserted *between* two existing rows? Simply click to position the insertion point in a row that is to appear below the new row, or in a row that is to appear above the new row. Click the Table Tools Layout tab and select Insert Above (or Insert Below) in the Rows & Columns group. Insert a new column in the same way, clicking in a column to the left or right of the desired location of the new column. Then click Insert Right or Insert Left to insert the new column.

To Insert Rows

a. Confirm that the insertion point is at the end of the last cell in the table after **465**. Press Tab to add a new row, and then type Balance Package. Press Tab, and then type One-night hotel accommodation with full breakfast. Press Enter to continue the list of services, and then type Ancient Drumming. Press Enter and type Detoxifying Mud Masque. Press Enter and then type Oasis Manicure and Pedicure. Press Enter and then type $125 spa credit. Press Tab and then type 725.

b. Click in any cell in row 1. You will insert a top row so you can include table headings.

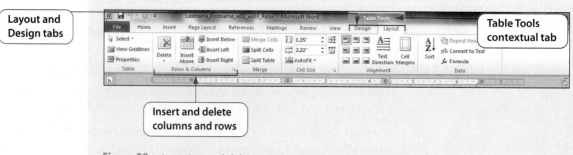

Layout and Design tabs

Table Tools contextual tab

Insert and delete columns and rows

Figure 28 Inserting and deleting columns and rows

c. Click the **Table Tools Layout tab**, and then click **Insert Above** in the Rows & Columns group. A new row is added at the top of the table.

d. Click in the **first cell** of the new row, and then type Spa Package. Press Tab, and then type Services. Press Tab, and then type Price.

New row

Spa·Package¤	Services¤	Price¤	¤
Body·Package·(3·hours)¤	Oasis·Signature·Massage¶ Oasis·Manicure·and·Pedicure¶ Jade·Facial¤	185¤	
Soul·Package·(2·hours)¤	Oasis·Signature·Massage¶ European·Cleansing·or·Gentleman's·Facial¤	135¤	¤
Mind·Package·(4-5·hours)¤	Oasis·Signature·Massage¶ Classic·Desert·Facial¶ Oasis·Manicure·and·Pedicure¶ Paradise·Fruit·Bar¤	465¤	¤
Balance·Package¤	One-night·hotel·accommodation·with·full·breakfast¶ Ancient·Drumming¶ Detoxifying·Mud·Masque¶ Oasis·Manicure·and·Pedicure¶ $125·spa·credit¤	725¤	¤

Figure 29 Table with new row

e. **Save** 🖫 the document.

Deleting Columns and Rows

Deleting a column or row is not the same as deleting the contents of a column or row. To delete *contents*, simply select the row or column and press Delete. The contents are removed, but the row or column remains. You can then enter new data in the row (or column). When you delete a *row* or *column*, both the row or column and its contents are removed. Select the row or column and click Delete in the Rows & Columns group. Choose to delete cells, columns, rows, or the entire table. You can delete multiple rows and columns by selecting them first.

To Delete Rows

a. Position the pointer at the left of the Soul Package row so the pointer appears as a white arrow ⌐. Click to select the row.

b. Click the **Table Tools Layout tab**, click **Delete** in the Rows & Columns group, and then click **Delete Rows**. The Soul Package row is removed because you no longer offer that package.

c. **Save** 🖫 the document.

SIDE NOTE
Selecting Multiple Rows and Columns

To delete adjacent rows and columns, position the pointer at the left of the first row or above the column. When the pointer changes to an arrow, drag to select other rows or columns. To select nonadjacent rows or columns, press Ctrl while you select each row or column.

Formatting a Table

Text that is included in a table can be formatted in a variety of ways. You can align text horizontally or vertically within cells, or apply font attributes such as bold, underline, font color, or font size. You can specify font type and add shading to cells, columns, and rows. Word also provides a gallery of table styles from which you can choose to add color, borders, shading, and other design elements.

Before formatting table text, you must first select it. To select all text in a cell, position the pointer just inside the left edge of the cell and click. To select a row, place the pointer in the left margin beside the row (the pointer will appear as a white arrow) and click. To select a column, click when the pointer appears as a black arrow at the top of the column. To select the entire table, click the Table selector at the top-left corner of the table. You can identify options in the Font group of the Home tab to format selected text (such as bold, font color, etc.), or you can select horizontal alignment in the Paragraph group. You can even apply bullets or numbers to selected text in a table.

Options on the Table Tools Design tab enable you to add shading to selected areas and to apply a style from the Table Styles gallery. Some table styles apply a different color to the first row or to the first column, to set off the header row or column. Others apply alternating color to rows, called banded rows. Still others apply alternating color to columns, called banded columns.

To Format a Table

a. Click at the left of the first row in the table to select it. Click the **Home tab**, click **Bold** [B] in the Font group, and then click **Center** [≡] in the Paragraph group.

b. Click the **Table selector** [⊞] in the top-left corner of the table to select the entire table. Click the **Font arrow**, and then select **Arial**. Point above the last column until a downward black arrow appears [⬇]. Click to select the column, and then click **Center** [≡] in the Paragraph group.

Troubleshooting

> If you do not see the Table selector [⊞], click any cell in the table, and click the Table Tools Layout tab. Click Select in the Table group and click Select Table.

c. Select the **first row**. Click the **Table Tools Design tab**, click the **Shading arrow** in the Table Styles group, and then click **Orange, Accent 6, Darker 25%**—last column in the fifth row under Theme Colors. Click outside the row to see the result.

d. With the pointer to the left of the second row, drag to select the remaining rows. Click the **Shading arrow** in the Table Styles group, and then click **Orange, Accent 6, Lighter 40%**—last column in the fourth row under Theme Colors.

e. Select the **first row**. Click the **Borders arrow** [⊞▾] in the Table Styles group, and then click **Borders and Shading** to open the Borders and Shading dialog box.

Troubleshooting

> If you do not see the Borders and Shading dialog box when you click Borders, you clicked the Borders button instead of the arrow. Click Undo and repeat Step e.

f. Scroll down the Style list, click the first double underline, and then click **OK**. Click outside the selection to see the result.

g. Select the **first two columns**, click the **Layout tab**, and then click **Align Center Left** [≡] in the Alignment group. Text in the first two columns are aligned horizontally and centered vertically at the left side of each cell.

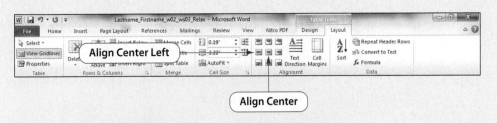

Figure 30   Aligning cells vertically

h. Select the **third column**. Click **Align Center** ▤ in the Alignment group to align text in the center both horizontally and vertically. Select the first row, and then click **Align Center** ▤ to center all text in the row.

i. Select the **second column**, click the **Home tab**, and then click **Underline** ⊔ ▾ in the Font group. Because you do not want the word Services underlined, click just inside the left edge of the cell when the pointer changes to ➔ to select the text. Click **Underline** ⊔ ▾ to remove the underline.

j. Click the **Table Tools Design tab**, and click **More** in the Table Styles group. Point to any table style to see a Live Preview of the style on the selected table. Because you prefer the style that you designed, click outside the gallery to remove it from view.

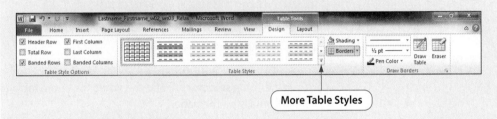

Figure 31   Exploring Table Styles

k. Remove the extra paragraph mark after the table. Click the **View tab**, and then click **One Page** to view the entire table.

l. **Save** ▤ the document.

Modifying Table Properties

When Word creates a table, all columns and rows are of equal width and height. As you enter text in a table cell, Word increases row height to accommodate additional text if necessary. However, columns remain the same width, with text wrapping within a cell if more than one line is required. If you want to change column width or row height, you can drag a row or column border. For more precise resizing, click Properties in the Table group of the Table Tools Layout tab and indicate a measurement for a selected column or row.

Cells can be merged or split. Often as an afterthought, you will find that several cells should be merged to enable a title to extend across the width of a table. Or perhaps a lengthy cell should be split so you can provide more detail in additional cells on the same row. The Table Tools Layout tab includes options for splitting and merging cells.

To Modify a Table

a. Click the **View tab**, and then click **100%** in the Zoom group. Select the first row in the table. Click the **Table Tools Layout tab**, click **Insert Above** in the Rows & Columns group to add a row above the current row, click in the **first cell** of the new row, and then type Turquoise Oasis Spa.

b. Select the row that you just added. Click **Merge Cells** in the Merge group to merge all cells in the row into one cell. The first row is now a title row.

c. Click any cell to deselect the first row. Point to the right border of the third column (beside any row other than the first row). The pointer appears as a double-headed arrow ⊹⊹. Because the Price column seems too wide for its contents, you will reduce the column width. Drag to the left to approximately the **5.5"** position on the horizontal ruler.

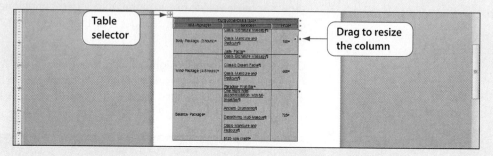

Figure 32 Manually resizing a column

d. Click the **Table selector** ⊞, and then drag the entire table to the right to visually center it horizontally on the page.

e. On the Table Tools Layout tab, click **AutoFit** in the Cell Size group, and then click **AutoFit Contents**. Word determines the best fit for each column and adjusts the widths accordingly.

f. Confirm that the entire table is still selected. If it is not, click the **Table selector** ⊞ to select the table. Click the **Home tab**, and click **Center** ▤ in the Paragraph group. The table is more precisely centered horizontally on the page.

Troubleshooting

If the entire table does not shift toward the center, you might not have the table selected. Click Undo, and then click the Table selector in the top-left corner. Click Center in the Paragraph group of the Home tab.

g. Select **row 1**, right-click the selected row, and then click **Delete Rows**. You are removing the first row because you decide that it is not necessary to identify the spa by name.

h. Click outside the table to deselect it. Click the **View tab**, and then click **One Page** to view the finished table.

i. **Save** ⊟ the document.

Sorting Table Data

You can sort, or rearrange, rows based on the contents of one or more columns. For example, if a table includes last names in column 1, first names in column 2, and college majors in column 3, you can sort the table to place rows in order by last name. Knowing that one or more students might share the same last name, you can sort by both last and first names, so that if the last names are identical, the matching records will then be sorted by first name.

You can sort in alphabetic, numeric, or chronological order in either ascending or descending fashion. A descending alphabetic sort would place records in order from Z to A, while an ascending sort would arrange them from A to Z.

Ordinarily, a table includes a header row with column titles. When you sort rows, you do not want to include the header row. As you begin the sort process, you will indicate that the table includes a header row. That way, Word will sort all rows except the header row, which remains intact as the first row in the table.

To Sort a Table

a. Click the **View tab**, and then click **100%** in the Zoom group. Click any cell in the table.

b. Click the **Table Tools Layout tab**, and then click **Sort** in the Data group.

The Sort dialog box appears. The first column (Spa Package) is correctly assumed to be the sort field. If such were not the case, you could click the Sort by arrow and select another column. The field is a Text field, and the sort order is assumed to be Ascending. If any of those assumptions were not correct, you would change them in the dialog box. Word also correctly assumes that your table includes a header row, as shown by the selected option in the bottom-left corner of the dialog box.

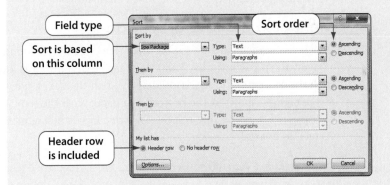

Figure 33 Sorting a table

c. Click **OK**. Click outside the table to deselect it. The Spa Packages are rearranged alphabetically.

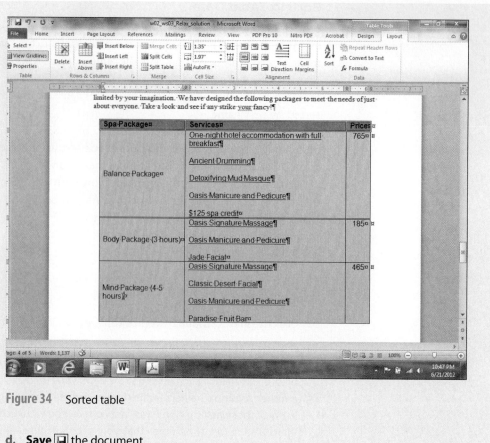

Figure 34 Sorted table

d. **Save** 🖫 the document.

SIDE NOTE
Using Tab Within a Cell

On occasion, you might want to apply a tab to data in a table column. The problem with that is that when you press Tab within a cell, you move to another cell. Instead, press and hold Ctrl while you press Tab.

Managing the End of a Page

When a document includes more than one page of text, there is always a possibility that a page will end awkwardly. You might find that a heading shows at the bottom of a page, with the contents of that section displayed on the next page. Or perhaps only the first line of a paragraph shows at the bottom of a page, with the remainder of the paragraph on the next page. Always be sure to preview a document before printing so you can identify and correct an unattractive page ending.

Inserting a Page Break

Word automatically separates pages according to a standard page size. Occasionally, you will want to insert a page break in a different location than what was suggested by Word. In the case where a heading shows on one page with the remainder of the section on the next, you might want to force a page break immediately before the heading. When typing a report divided into sections or chapters, you will need to insert a page break at the end of each section. That way, each section or chapter begins on a new page. Hold down Ctrl while pressing Enter to insert a page break. You can also click the Insert tab and click Page Break in the Pages group.

Avoiding Orphan and Widow Lines

Orphans and widows are lines that dangle at the beginning or ending of a page. "An orphan has no past and a widow has no future" is a saying that helps define the two. An **orphan** is a line that is alone at the bottom of a page. The rest of the paragraph appears at the top of the next page. A **widow** is a paragraph's last line that is alone at the top of a page. The first part of the paragraph appears at the end of the previous page.

To Work with the End of a Page

a. Press `Ctrl`+`Home`, click the **View tab**, and then click **Two Pages** in the Zoom group. Scroll to view all four pages. Note that page 3 begins awkwardly, with only one line of the tabbed area displaying. Click **100%** in the Zoom group to return pages to full size.

b. Scroll to the bottom of the second page, click before the heading **Spa Hours**, and then press `Ctrl`+`Enter`.

   A page break is inserted. If you are in Print Layout view, with nonprinting characters displayed, you will see the page break.

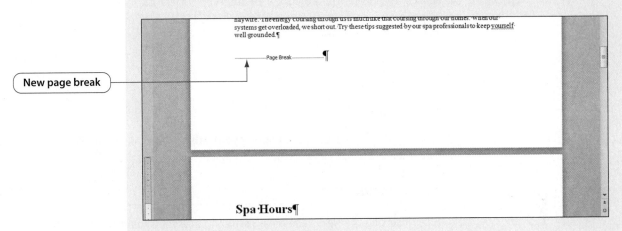

New page break

Figure 35 Inserting a page break

c. Click the **View tab**, and then click **Two Pages**. Check for any more problems with page endings. Because page 4 now ends with the text box too close to the bottom of the page, remove the extra paragraph mark before the heading **Join Us at Turquoise Oasis Spa.**

d. Check all pages for attractive beginnings and endings. Click the **View tab**, and then click **100%** in the Zoom group.

e. Click the **Home tab**, click the **Paragraph Dialog Box Launcher**, and then click the **Line and Page Breaks tab**. Make sure the **Widow/Orphan control** check box is selected. If it is not, click to select it. Click **OK**. By default, Word is configured to avoid orphan and widow lines.

f. **Save** 💾 the document.

SIDE NOTE
Deleting a Page Break
In Print Layout view, with nonprinting characters displayed, you can see a manual page break. To remove the page break, click the page break and press `Delete`.

Working with Sections

A document can be divided into **sections**, which are areas of a document that can be formatted differently. Suppose you are working with a quarterly sales report for your employer, in which you describe sales activities and provide a table of sales data. Although the description is best suited for portrait orientation, you find that the table has more columns than will comfortably fit in that format. The table would be more attractive in landscape orientation. In that case, you simply define a separate section for the table and assign landscape orientation to that section.

Each section can have its own orientation, margins, headers, footers, and any other document format. Options on the Page Layout tab enable you to assign a section break, which divides a document into a new section. When you insert a section break you will see a dotted line with the words "Section Break" if nonprinting characters are displayed. You can insert a Continuous section break, which starts at the position of the insertion point but does not break the page flow. For example, if you are creating a newsletter, you might want the title of the newsletter to be centered horizontally, but all text beneath that point is to be arranged in columns. After centering the title, insert a Continuous section break so the remaining text can be formatted in columns on the same page, without affecting the title. A Next Page section break begins a section on a new page. Perhaps a report's cover sheet should appear in landscape orientation, while the body of the report is in portrait orientation. Simply insert a Next Page section break after the cover page and change the orientation.

To Work with Sections

a. Press Ctrl+Home. Click the **Page Layout tab**, click **Breaks** in the Page Setup group, and then click **Next Page** (do not click Page).

Troubleshooting

After inserting the Next Page break, scroll up and you should see a "Section Break (Next Page)" designation at the top of the cover page (if nonprinting characters are toggled on). If, instead, the designation is shown as "Page Break," you selected "Page" instead of "Next Page," inserting a simple page break instead of a page and section break. Click Undo and repeat Step a.

b. Press Ctrl+Home to place the insertion point at the top of the new page.

Day Spa Group requires that all articles include a cover sheet in landscape orientation, with contact information related to the submission. You will create the cover sheet as the first page in your article.

c. Click the **Home tab**, change the font to **Verdana**, and then confirm that the font size is **20**. Click **Center** ≣ in the Paragraph group, and then click **Bold** B to toggle bold off. Type Turquoise Oasis Spa and press Enter. When you press Enter, the insertion point will not immediately return to the next line. Type At Painted Paradise Resort and Spa and press Enter four times. Type For Submission to Day Spa Group and press Enter four times. Type Irene Kai, Manager.

d. Click the **Page Layout tab**, click **Orientation** in the Page Setup group, and then click **Landscape**. Click **Margins**, and then click **Custom Margins**. Click the **Layout tab**, click the **Vertical alignment arrow**, select **Center**, and then click **OK**. You have vertically centered text on the cover page.

SIDE NOTE
Deleting a Section Break
In Print Layout view, with nonprinting characters displayed, you can see a section break. To remove the section break, click the section break and press Delete.

e. Click **Page Borders** in the Page Background group, and then click **Box**. Click the **Width arrow**, and then select **1 pt**. Click the **Color arrow**, and then select **Orange, Accent 6, Darker 50%**, the last selection in the last row under Theme Colors. Click the **Apply to arrow**, select **This section**, and then click **OK**.

Troubleshooting

If a page border appears around all pages, instead of only the first page, you did not select "This section" as you created the border. Click Undo and repeat Step e.

f. Click the **View tab**, and then click **Two Pages** in the Zoom group.

The first page should be in landscape orientation and the second page should be in portrait orientation. The page border should be on the first page only.

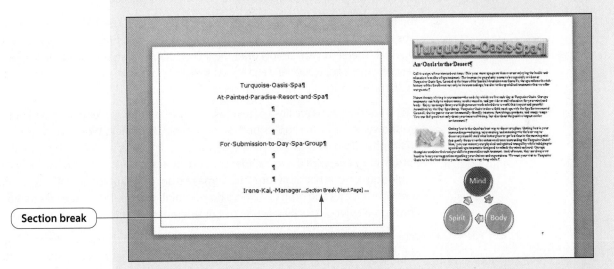

Section break

Figure 36 Section break

g. Click the **View tab**, and then click **100%** in the Zoom group.

h. **Save** 🖫 the document. **Exit** Word.

Sales & Marketing

1. You recently bought a local candy company from its retiring owner. Along with a new location for the store, you plan to increase product awareness, hopefully encouraging new customers and more sales. Along with other selections, you carry a line of 15 truffle flavors. You will spotlight the truffles in a printed listing, available beside the truffle case so customers can get a feel for the choices. Each truffle flavor will be listed and described. For example, you will indicate that a champagne truffle is sweet, with dry fruit notes. As you think about how to design the list, consider whether to organize the truffle descriptions as tabbed items or whether it would be easier to include them in a table. Which would you use and why? As part of your response, provide a diagram of the truffles list with a specific description of the tabbed or table items. You do not need to research truffle flavors—simply give an example of how a listing would appear. If you use a table for the listings, how would it be organized, and how would you make it more attractive? If you use tabs instead, what type of tabs would you use, and where would they be placed?

2. You are including a series of tabbed items in the body of a research report. Having set the tabs on the ruler, and having typed the tabbed text, you find that the tabs are too close together. Therefore, you simply drag the incorrect tab along the ruler to increase the space between the tabs. However, the tabbed text does not shift to accommodate the new tab position. Why not? How would you correct the situation?

3. Widows and orphans are lines of text (usually the beginning or ending of a paragraph) that are shown alone at the top or bottom of a page. By default, Word avoids leaving widow and orphan lines. Even so, you find that a subheading in your report is shown alone at the bottom of a page, with the remainder of the section shown at the top of the next page. How would you correct that situation? If for some reason, you want to "turn off" Word's automatic control of widows and orphans, where do you think you would find the command to do so? Conceptually, would such an action be considered "text" or "paragraph" oriented?

4. Your community is organizing and publicizing a "heritage day" that celebrates the history of the area through exhibits, tours, and storytelling. In preparing promotional material, you have located and inserted a picture. However, the picture is not positioned appropriately, so you attempt to move it to another location within the document. Although the picture moves, it does so in a choppy fashion and does not seem to be included within surrounding text. What might be the problem, and how would you correct it?

5. Especially in persuasive writing, you want to give your audience as much information as possible to make your point. Depending on your readers, the level of detail needed may vary. Using Word's Tables feature, you can summarize a lot of data in an orderly fashion. Is it possible to give too much information? Why or why not?

Key Terms

Cell 205
Center tab 203
Clip art 199
Contextual tab 184
Decimal tab 203
Leader 203
Left tab 203

Object 184
Orphan 214
Picture 196
Right tab 203
Screenshot 201
Section 215
Sizing handle 188

SmartArt 190
Tab 203
Table 205
Text box 194
Text wrap 188
Widow 214
WordArt 184

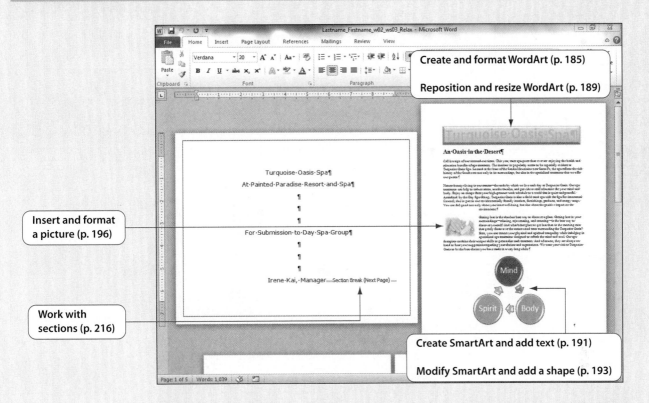

Create and format WordArt (p. 185)

Reposition and resize WordArt (p. 189)

Insert and format a picture (p. 196)

Work with sections (p. 216)

Create SmartArt and add text (p. 191)

Modify SmartArt and add a shape (p. 193)

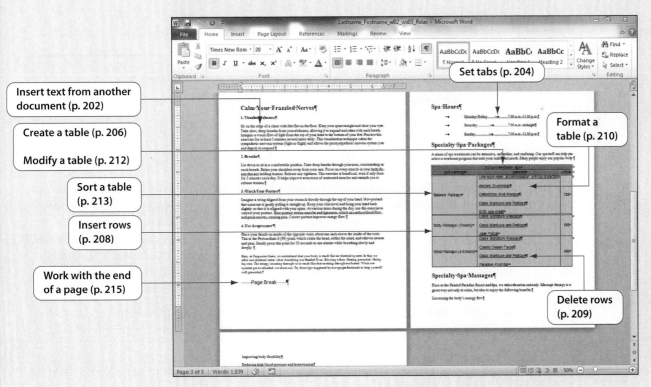

Insert text from another document (p. 202)

Create a table (p. 206)

Modify a table (p. 212)

Sort a table (p. 213)

Insert rows (p. 208)

Work with the end of a page (p. 215)

Set tabs (p. 204)

Format a table (p. 210)

Delete rows (p. 209)

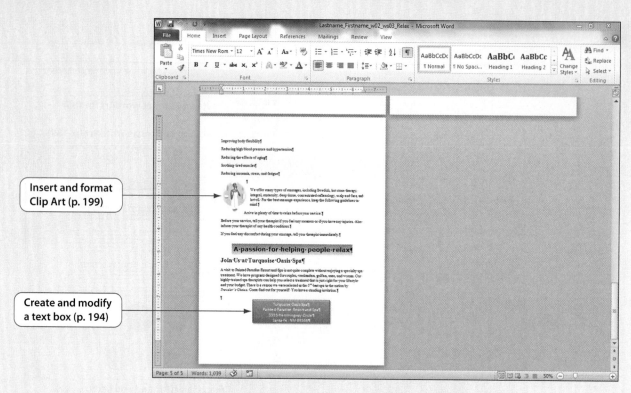

Insert and format Clip Art (p. 199)

Create and modify a text box (p. 194)

Figure 37 Turquoise Oasis Spa Services Publication Final Document

---

Practice 1

Student data files needed:	You will save your file as:
w02_ws03_Spa_Exclusives	Lastname_Firstname_w02_ws03_Spa_Exclusives
w02_ws03_Spa	
w02_ws03_Spa_Table	

Spa Exclusives

Sales & Marketing

The website for Turquoise Oasis Spa includes a link where visitors to the site can register for Spa Exclusives, a program that e-mails reminders of spa specials and product sales. Visitors are asked to indicate an interest category—Fitness, Group Events, Spa Boutique, or Spa Treatments—and to provide an e-mail address. Each month, a targeted flyer is sent by e-mail and also made available as a link on the Spa Exclusives Member web page. This month, you are preparing a flyer that highlights items in the spa boutique. The flyer will be prepared as a Word document and sent as an e-mail attachment. It will also be available at the Painted Paradise Resort and Spa web page.

a. Open **Word**. Open **w02_ws03_Spa_Exclusives**. Save the document as Lastname_Firstname_w02_ws03_Spa_Exclusives. Click **Show/Hide** to display nonprinting characters, if necessary.

b. Press Ctrl+Home. Click the **Insert tab**. Click **Picture**. Navigate to your student data files and double-click **w02_ws03_Spa**.

c. Select **Spa Specials for July 2013**. Click the **Insert tab**. Click **WordArt** in the Text group. Click **Gradient Fill - Blue, Accent 1, Outline - White** (row 4, column 4). Click **Wrap Text** in the Arrange group. Click **Top and Bottom**. Click the **Text Fill arrow** in the WordArt Styles group. Click **Black, Text 1**. Click **Align** in the Arrange group. Click **Align Center**. Delete the blank paragraph mark above the Spa Specials heading.

d. Select the paragraph underneath the WordArt object. Because the WordArt object is anchored to the paragraph, the object will also be selected. Click the **Home tab**. Change the font to **Verdana** and the font size to **14**. Press `Ctrl`+`End`. Press `Enter` twice.

e. Type the following text.

Each month, we spotlight an essence. This month is Lavender. Try the following selections at a special price!

f. Press `Enter` twice. If the horizontal ruler is not displayed, click the **View tab** and click the **Ruler check box**. Click the **Tab button** at the left of the ruler and continue clicking until it displays a Right Tab symbol. Click to place a right tab stop at **6"** on the ruler.

g. Type Lavender Bath Salts and press `Tab`. Type $30 but do not press `Enter`. Click the **Home tab** and click the **Paragraph Dialog Box Launcher**. Click **Tabs**. Click **2** in the Leader group and click **OK**. Press `Enter`. Enter the following three items, pressing `Tab` between each item and its price. Press `Enter` after each item.

Lavender Shower Gel $18

Lavender Lip Balm $3

Signature Lavender Lotion $8

h. Click before the first blank paragraph under the first paragraph beginning with Bring the spa experience. Click the **Insert tab**. Click **Clip Art** in the Illustrations group. Type lavender in the **Search for** box of the Clip Art task pane. Be sure **Include Office.com content** is checked. Click the **Results should be arrow** and deselect all types except **Illustrations**. Click **Go**.

i. Scroll through the results and click the clip art described as "Flowering lavender herb." If you cannot locate the clip art, select another. The clip art is placed in the document and selected. Click **Wrap Text** in the Arrange group of the Picture Tools Format tab. Click **Square**. Change the clip art height to **1.5"**.

j. Click the Picture Tools Format tab, and click **Color** in the Adjust group. Point to **More Variations** and then click **Purple, Accent 4, Darker 25%**. Close the Clip Art task pane.

k. Press `Ctrl`+`End` and press `Enter`. Click the **Insert tab**. Click **Text Box** in the Text group. Click **Draw Text Box**. Click at the location of the last paragraph mark. Change the width of the text box to **6.5"** and the height to **0.8"** in the Size group. Click the **Shape Fill arrow** in the Shape Styles group. Click **Dark Blue, Text 2, Lighter 60%**. Click **Shape Outline** and then click **Black, Text 1**. Click the **Tab button** at the left of the ruler and select a left tab stop. Click **2.5"** on the horizontal ruler to set a tab stop. Click **5"** to set another tab stop.

l. In the text box, type Painted Paradise Resort and Spa and press `Tab`. Type 3355 Hemmingway Circle and press `Tab`. Type (403)555-3892. Press `Enter`. Type www.paintedparadiseresort.com.

m. Click the dashed line surrounding the text box to make it solid. Click the **Home tab**. Click **Center** in the Paragraph group. Click the **Font Color arrow** and click **White, Background 1**.

n. Press `Ctrl`+`End`. Click the **Insert tab**. Click **Footer**. Click **Edit Footer**. Type your first name and last name in the footer area. Click **Different First Page** in the Options group. Click **Close Header and Footer**. Click the **Page Layout tab**. Click **Breaks** and then click **Next Page**. Click **Orientation** in the Page Setup group and click **Landscape**.

o. Type The following items will no longer be carried in inventory, so we are passing along the best price possible. Supplies are limited so place your order now! Press `Enter`. Click anywhere in the paragraph that you just typed. Click the **Home tab**. Click **Center** in the Paragraph group. Press `Ctrl`+`End`. Press `Enter`.

p. Click the **Insert tab**. Click the **Object arrow** in the Text group and click **Text from File**. Navigate to your student data files and double-click **w02_ws03_Spa_Table**.

q. Click any cell of the table to select the table. Click the **Table Tools Design tab**. Click **More** in the Table Styles group. Click **Medium Shading 1 - Accent 1** (row 4, column 2 under Built-In).

r. Right-click the first column. Click **Table Properties** in the shortcut menu. Click the **Column tab**. Click the **Preferred width** check box and type 1.5" in the text box. Click **OK**.

s. Click the **Table Tools Layout tab**. Click View Gridlines in the Table group to display table gridlines, if necessary. Position the mouse pointer on the right edge of the Size column so it appears as a two-headed arrow. Drag slightly to the right so the size shows on one line. Click the **Table selector** to select the entire table. Click **Align Center Left** in the Alignment group. Select the first row. Click **Align Center**.

t. Click in any table cell. Click **Sort** in the Data group. Click the **Sort by arrow** and click **Category**. Click the **Then by arrow** and click **Product**. Click **OK**. Click the **View tab**. Click **Two Pages**. Save the document and exit Word.

Problem Solve 1

Student data file needed:

w02_ps1_Bank

You will save your file as:

Lastname_Firstname_w02_ps1_Bank

Bank Flyer

Sales & Marketing

As an account manager for Midfield Independent Bank, you are working with a marketing campaign to publicize the bank. In this exercise, you will create a flyer as an attractive display of options, bank services, and hours.

a. Start **Word**. Open **w02_ps1_Bank** and then save the document as Lastname_Firstname_ w02_ps1_Bank. If necessary, click Show/Hide to display nonprinting characters. If the ruler does not display, click the **View tab** and then click **Ruler** in the Show group.

b. Select the first line in the document. Click the **Insert tab**. Click **WordArt**. Select **Fill – Olive 3, Accent 3, Powder Bevel** (row 5, column 4). If the box surrounding the WordArt object is dashed, click the border to make it solid. Click the **Home tab** and change the font size to **20**. Click the **Drawing Tools Format tab** and then click **Wrap Text**. Click **Top and Bottom**.

c. Press Ctrl+End to move to the end of the document. Click the **Insert tab** and then click **Table**. Select 4 columns and 4 rows to create a 4x4 table. Type ACCOUNT TYPE in the first cell and then press Tab. Type Basic Savings and press Tab. Type Preferred Savings and press Tab. Type Money Market and press Tab. Complete the table with the following data.

Min. deposit to open:	$100	$1,000	$10,000
Avg. monthly account balance:	$500	$2,500	$10,000
Fee if below required balance:	$5	$12	$16

d. Click the **Table Tools Design tab** and then click **More** in the Table Styles group. Select **Light List – Accent 3** (row 2, column 4 under Built-In). Select the last three rows in the table and change the font size to 9.

e. Select the last three columns on the right, click the **Table Tools Layout tab**, and then select **Align Center** in the Alignment group. Click the **Table selector** to select the entire table. Click the **Table Tools Layout tab** if necessary, click **AutoFit** in the Cell Size group, and then click **AutoFit Contents**. Click the **Home tab** and click **Center** in the Paragraph group.

f. Click to position the insertion point anywhere in the Avg. monthly account balance row. Click the **Table Tools Layout tab** if necessary, and then click **Insert Below** in the Rows & Columns group. A new row is added beneath row 3. Enter the following data in the new row.

Free checks	No	No	Yes

g. Select the first row. Right-click in the selected row and click **Table Properties**. Click the **Row** tab. Click the **Specify height check box** to select it and change the height to **0.5"**. Click **OK**. Position the pointer just inside the first cell in the first row so that it appears as a small black arrow, and click to select the first cell. Click the **Table Tools Layout tab** if necessary, and then click **Align Center** in the Alignment group.

h. Press Ctrl+End to move to the end of the document. Click the **Insert tab** and then click **Text Box** in the Text group. Click **Draw Text Box** and click near the final paragraph mark to create a small box.

i. With the insertion point in the text box, click the **Insert tab** and then click **Clip Art** in the Illustrations group. Remove any existing text in the Search box of the Clip Art pane and type money. Deselect **Include Office.com content**. Click the **Results should be arrow** and limit results to Illustrations. Click **Go**. Select the clip art image representing dollar (U.S.) currency, or select another if the clip art image is not available.

j. With the clip art image selected within the text box, click the **Picture Tools Format tab** if necessary and type 0.5". Press Enter. Close the Clip Art pane. Click **Color** in the Adjust group and select **Olive Green, Accent color 3 Dark** (row 2, column 4).

k. Click near a border of the text box to deselect the clip art and select the text box. Drag the center handle on the right side of the text box to extend the width to approximately 4" on the horizontal ruler. Click before the paragraph mark in the text box. Click the **Home tab** and select the **No spacing** style. Press Enter. Type Free statements. Press Enter. Type Free online banking. Do not press Enter.

l. Select the two lines that you just typed and click **Bullets** in the Paragraph group. Click the **Drawing Tools Format tab**, click **Shape Fill** in the Shape Styles group and select **Olive Green, Accent 3, Lighter 60%**. Click **Shape Effects**, point to **Bevel**, and then select **Circle** (first selection under Bevel).

m. Click **Align** in the Arrange group and then click **Align Center**. Click before the blank paragraph mark between the table and the text box. Click the text box to select it. Click **Wrap Text** and then click **Top and Bottom**. Click outside the text box to deselect it.

n. Click before the blank paragraph mark between the table and the text box. Press Enter twice. Click the **Home tab** and then click **Center** in the Paragraph group. Click **Bold** and change the font size to 18. Type Bank Hours and press Enter.

o. Change the font size to **11** and click **Align Text Left** in the Paragraph group. Click to set a left tab stop at **1.5"** on the horizontal ruler. Click the **Tab selector** twice to select a right tab. Click to set a right tab stop at **5.5"** on the horizontal ruler.

p. Press Tab. If necessary, click **Bold** to toggle bold off. Type Monday-Friday (do not leave a space before or after the dash). Press Tab. Type 8:30 a.m.-6:00 p.m. (do not leave a space before or after the dash). Do not press Enter.

q. Click the **Paragraph Dialog Box Launcher** and click **Tabs**. Click **5.5"** in the Tab stop position box, click **2** in the Leader area, and then click **OK**. Press Enter. Press Tab. Type Saturday and then press Tab. Type 8:30 a.m.-noon. Press Enter and then press Tab. Type Closed Sunday. Press Enter.

r. Click the **View tab** and then click **One Page**. Click the **Page Layout tab** and then click the **Page Setup Dialog Box Launcher**. Click the **Layout tab**. Click the **Vertical alignment arrow** and select **Center**. Click **OK**.

s. Click the **View tab**, and then click **100%**. Click the **Review Tab** and then click **Spelling & Grammar**. Correct any errors and ignore those that are not incorrect.

t. Click the **Insert tab**, click **Footer**, and then click **Edit Footer**. Type your first name and last name. Click **Close Header and Footer**.

u. Click the **File tab** and then click **Print** to preview the document. Save the document and then exit Word.

Objectives

Formatting Special Documents and Using Mail Merge

PREPARE CASE

Turquoise Oasis Spa Newsletter and Research

Sales & Marketing

Research & Development

The Turquoise Oasis Spa is one of the most highly acclaimed spas in the Southwest. Aggressive marketing in local and national publications keeps the spa's name in the forefront, as does a newsletter that you develop and distribute each month. The newsletter is sent to former clients who are maintained on a mailing list, as well as to anyone indicating an interest after visiting the spa's web page. You will use Word to develop the newsletter, formatting text in columns and including graphics. You

Curtis Kautzer / Shutterstock.com

will then develop a cover letter to accompany the newsletter, using Word's mail merge feature to personalize the letter and to produce mailing labels.

As a requirement for a graduate class in resort management, you will edit a research paper on developing a sustainable spa. The Turquoise Oasis Spa is considering an incremental program in which the spa will phase in environmentally appropriate improvements. Your paper will help you better understand the "green" spa movement.

Student data files needed for this workshop: **You will save your files as:**

 w02_ws04_Spa_News   w02_ws04_News   Lastname_Firstname_w02_ws04_Spa_News   Lastname_Firstname_w02_ws04_Spa_Research

 w02_ws04_Wine   w02_ws04_Spa_Research   Lastname_Firstname_w02_ws04_Letter   Lastname_Firstname_w02_ws04_Addresses

 w02_ws04_Letter   w02_ws04_Addresses   Lastname_Firstname_w02_ws04_Merged_Letters   Lastname_Firstname_w02_ws04_Labels

 Lastname_Firstname_w02_ws04_Envelopes

Creating a Newsletter

A **newsletter** is a regular publication that is distributed in print, through e-mail, or as a link on a web page. A newsletter is designed to provide information of interest to a defined group of people. Its main purpose is to convey information in an at-a-glance format, using design techniques that consolidate points so they are quickly understood. Catchy graphics and color add an element of entertainment and hold the interest of a reader.

Newsletters can be designed for internal distribution to employees of a company, or for external communication to customers, clients, or patrons. Clubs, churches, societies, and professional associations use newsletters to provide information of interest to their members. An organization might include news and upcoming events, as well as contact information, for general member inquiries. Often used as a marketing strategy, a regularly scheduled newsletter can be an effective way to draw attention to a company or a cause and to create enthusiasm among clients.

An internal newsletter, distributed to employees, can foster a sense of company pride and ownership as it encourages communication. Not only does an internal newsletter enable management to explain policies and programs, but it can boost morale by recognizing employees for their contributions. Information included in a company newsletter could just as easily be included in a memo, but the vibrancy of the text and the newsletter's columnar format, photos, or graphics that illustrate the contents often hold attention a little longer and might convey a message more effectively. Of course, a newsletter is not private and is not appropriate for a company's critical internal communication, but when used correctly, newsletters can create a better-informed employee base.

Sales & Marketing

Real World Advice — Creating an E-Zine

An e-mail newsletter connects you with people who have expressed a positive interest in your product or service. To keep exposure to your product or service current, you can publish an e-zine (electronic magazine) or an electronic newsletter (delivered via e-mail or available online). You can duplicate the same content from the electronic version to a printed newsletter, and encourage visits to your website by printing a link at the bottom of all pages of the printed newsletter. An electronic newsletter or e-zine also lets you reach customers outside your immediate geographic area, gives you greater exposure, and may open new business channels.

Learning to design an effective newsletter is more than simply mastering the technical techniques required to create a newsletter, such as those that you will learn in this workshop. You should also consider appropriate wording so you make the most of the available space to get your message across. Selecting graphics and placing them where they will be the most effective can draw attention to key points. A consistent color scheme can tie the newsletter together and increase eye appeal.

At first glance, a newsletter gives an impression of your organization or cause. Therefore, you should take plenty of time to plan and organize the content. Of course, you should always be well aware of your audience, but in addition, you should ask yourself what you want to happen as a result of publishing the newsletter. Understanding your purpose helps direct the content and the presentation.

Sales & Marketing

CONSIDER THIS | **Magazine or Newsletter?**

What is the difference between a magazine and a newsletter? How does the audience of a magazine differ from that of a newsletter? How do you think color, length, and size would differ in the presentation of each?

Although this workshop focuses on using Word to create printed newsletters, they can also be distributed through e-mail or made available online. Delivering newsletters electronically has gained acceptance as more people depend on the Internet to gather news on upcoming events. The ideas and strategies for both printed and online newsletters are the same. The only difference is that printed material is slightly more expensive to generate and to distribute. Also, the immediacy of online newsletters is a very attractive feature for getting information out quickly. If your company is promoting a new product or featuring a sale, an online newsletter might be an excellent way to quickly convey that to your customer base.

Sales & Marketing

CONSIDER THIS | **Junk Mail**

Junk mail can litter your mailbox. Junk e-mail can also clutter your inbox. If you create an e-zine or an e-newsletter, how can you keep your e-mail as a valuable resource instead of being perceived as junk mail?

Although you can use Word to create a newsletter, you might consider saving it as a PDF file. PDF is often used as the format for distribution of electronic newsletters because most computers have the ability to display PDF documents, and the recipient is not able to manipulate the text, photos, or content in a PDF document without PDF-editing software. That way, there is little chance that the document could be mistakenly altered or made unreadable.

Regardless of the format—online or printed—a newsletter should communicate information in a way that is easily read and quickly assimilated. Consider the following tips when creating a newsletter.

1. Your newsletter should communicate clearly, consistently, and truthfully. Because it will be distributed widely, the newsletter must contain only accurate information.

2. Check the newsletter for spelling and grammatical errors before distributing it. Although you can use Word to check for errors, always remember to proofread the document yourself to identify any mistakes that Word might miss, such as incorrect word usage or awkward spacing.

3. Whether you publish a newsletter in print or electronically, stick to a firm schedule. You might publish weekly, bi-weekly, monthly, or quarterly, but keep a schedule so you avoid an image of amateurism. If you cannot keep an orderly distribution schedule, it is probably best not to develop a newsletter at all. The accepted wisdom is to publish no fewer than four times a year.

4. Keep the format simple. The purpose of a newsletter is to provide relevant information that a reader can take in at a glance. Always give readers what they want instead of what you think they should have.

5. Focus on the reader. Avoid the use of such words as "we," "us," or "I." Instead, use "you" or "your." A newsletter should contain at least 95% information for the reader and 5% information about your company.

6. Provide a simple way to navigate the newsletter, especially if it spans more than one page. A front page sidebar is a great place for navigational aids, as is a short table of contents.

7. Provide your contact information on every page of the newsletter. At a minimum, that should include your web address, e-mail address, and phone number. Footers and headers are excellent vehicles for that purpose.

8. If an article contains over 300 words, provide an executive summary. People will usually skim over long articles, so the summary will help them absorb the material quickly.

9. Keep a newsletter as short as possible, while still conveying pertinent information. People will usually only glance through the newsletter, so include bold headings and bullet points to make your point more quickly.

10. Provide a simple way to unsubscribe from your newsletter as well as a contact for new subscribers. U.S. law requires that you also provide a physical mailing address.

11. Select a short, to-the-point newsletter title. The title should be uncluttered and does not need to include the word *newsletter*.

Real World Advice   Creating an HTML Newsletter

An HTML newsletter is a document delivered by e-mail that looks very much like a web page. The document is created using HTML, the same coding language used to develop many web pages. The convenience of presenting an HTML newsletter is often matched by improved readership, comprehension, and sales. You can learn to develop an HTML newsletter yourself, but you will probably want to use a distribution service to communicate with your clients. You can even use an all-in-one service to both develop and distribute the newsletter.

Working with Columns

Many newsletters are designed with text in columns. A **column** draws the eye downward, enabling you to scan through information fairly quickly. As text flows from one column to the next, it gives the impression that minimal reading is required, especially if it is punctuated by graphics or a pull quote (an excerpt from the document that is presented in larger typeface in the document, reiterating a point). A section break is a common element in a Word newsletter, enabling you to uniquely format a newsletter heading or an ending line, so the format does not affect other text that may be presented in columns. You can define up to three columns in each section, or page, with those columns of equal width or weighted more heavily on one side or the other.

Formatting in Columns

The Columns option on the Page Layout tab enables you to format an entire document in columns or to specify only a section that is to include columns. Word evenly spaces columns with equal width by default, but you can specify column width in inches if you need to be more prescriptive.

Quick Reference   Formatting Columns

1. Click the Page Layout tab.
2. Click Columns.
3. Select the number of columns, or click More Columns for additional selections.

To Format a Newsletter in Columns

a. Open **w02_ws04_Spa_News** from your student data files. Save the document as Lastname_Firstname_w02_ws04_Spa_News. If necessary, click the **Home tab**, and then click **Show/Hide** in the Paragraph group to show nonprinting characters. Press [Ctrl]+[End].

b. Type Turquoise Trail May & June events. Select the line that you just typed, and then change the font size to **36**. Select the words **May & June**, click the **Font Color arrow**, and then click **More Colors**. Click a pink shade that closely matches the pink flower in the newsletter banner, and then click **OK**.

c. Select the word **events**, change the font to **Lucida Handwriting**, and then change the font size of the selected word to **20**. Click the **Font Color arrow**, click the most recently selected pink color shown under Recent Colors, and then press [Ctrl]+[End].

Turquoise·Trail·May·&·June·*events*¶

Figure 1   Beginning the Spa Newsletter

d. On the Home tab, click the **Border arrow** ⊞▾ in the Paragraph group, and then click **Borders and Shading**. Click the **Color arrow**, and then select the most recent pink color. Click the **Width arrow**, select **1½ pt**, click **Bottom Border** ⊞, and then click **OK**.

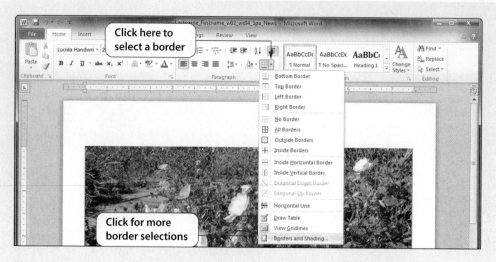

Figure 2   Adding a bottom border

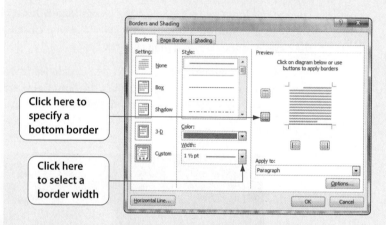

Figure 3   Selecting a border style

e. Double-click just beneath the bottom border to position the insertion point. Change the font to **Lucida Handwriting**, and then change the font size to **8**. Type A publication of Turquoise Oasis Spa, located at Painted Paradise Resort and Spa. Click **Center** [≡] to center the line horizontally. If the text is bold, select the line and click **Bold** [B] to remove the format. Press Enter.

f. Click the **Insert tab**, click the **Object arrow** in the Text group, and then select **Text from File**. Navigate to your student data files, and then double-click **w02_ws04_News**.

g. Click before **Children at the Oasis**. Click the **Page Layout tab**, click **Columns**, and then click **More Columns** to open the Columns dialog box.

   You could select one, two, or three columns from the Columns menu. Selecting More Columns enables you to insert a section break before arranging the text in columns (so only the text after the current position is formatted in columns).

h. Click **Three** in the Presets section. A preview shows three columns of equal width.

i. Click the **Apply to arrow**, select **This point forward**, and then click **OK**. A section break is inserted and all text following the section break is shown in three columns.

j. Click the **View tab**, and then click **One Page**.

   The newsletter text is arranged in three evenly spaced columns. The columns are not balanced, however, as they end unevenly. You will learn to address that problem later in this workshop.

k. **Save** the document.

Figure 4 Formatting columns

Real World Advice — Selecting a Newsletter Title

Sales & Marketing

A good newsletter title invites reading; a bad title can create a negative image before a word is read. How do you select a good title? These tips might help.

Avoid unnecessary words and unnecessary pride of ownership. Words like "the" and "newsletter" create clutter. Using your company name in the title can also clutter and actually yield little, if any, benefit because other areas of the newsletter will undoubtedly draw attention to the company.

Use words that describe the purpose of the newsletter. For example, "*Fort Morgan Preservation*" is more descriptive and appealing than "The Fort Morgan Association Newsletter."

Build visual contrast. Pair words in large type with words in smaller type. Using a different color also adds interest.

Use action words. Consider using words ending in "ing." For example, instead of "Southwest Hiking Association News," consider "Hiking the Southwest." You could set the association name in smaller type underneath the main title.

Use words with news appeal. Words like "alert," "connection," "digest," and "happenings" combined with your company name or purpose can create an attractive newsletter title.

Inserting Drop Cap

A **drop cap** is a design element in which the first letter of a paragraph is shown as a large graphic representation of the character. You often see drop caps in magazines and books. They tend to draw the eye to the beginning of an article, providing interest and eye appeal. A drop cap can be placed in the margin next to the paragraph, or with text wrapped around the character.

To Insert a Picture and Drop Cap

a. Click the **View tab**, and then click **100%** to return the view to normal size. Click before the words **Morning Yoga**. You will insert a graphic to enhance the body of the newsletter.

b. Click the **Insert tab**, click **Picture**, navigate to your student data files, and then double-click **w02_ws04_Wine**. Click the **Picture Tools Format tab**, and change the width to **1"** in the Size group.

c. Click **Drop Shadow Rectangle** in the Picture Styles group (fourth from left). Click **Wrap Text** in the Arrange group, and then select **Tight**. Drag to position the picture approximately as shown.

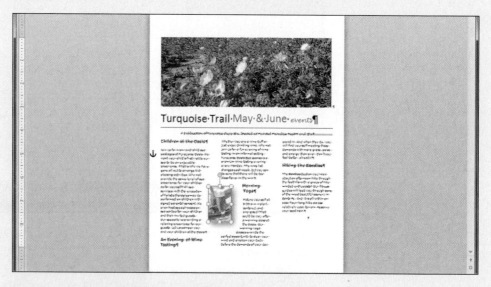

Figure 5   Inserting a picture

d. Click the **View tab**, click **Page Width**, and then click before the word **Join** in the first paragraph of the newsletter body.

e. Click the **Insert tab**, click **Drop Cap** in the Text group. Point to each option, and view the Live Preview of the effect. Click **Dropped**.

   If you need more precision, you can click Drop Cap Options. However, most often, the orientation of the drop cap is appropriate without any additional direction from you. The letter "J" appears in large print at the left of the paragraph, with text wrapped around it.

Figure 6 Inserting a drop cap

f. **Save** 🖫 the document.

Balancing Columns

Columns will seldom end evenly. Although that is not always a problem, you will definitely want to avoid having column headings begin awkwardly at the end of a column, or have only a small amount of text in a column. You can insert a column break to manually align columns in a more even fashion.

To Insert a Column Break

a. Click the **View tab**, and then click **One Page**. The first column ends unattractively, with a heading alone at the end of the column.

b. Click **100%** to return the view to normal size. If the heading, **An Evening of Wine Tasting**, displays near the end of the first column, you will insert a column break before the heading so it begins in a new column. To insert a column break, click before the heading.

c. Click the **Page Layout tab**, click **Breaks**, and then click **Column**. The text wraps much more attractively. If necessary, reposition the picture so all headings are displayed on a single line (with the exception of the "An Evening of Wine Tasting" heading, which requires two lines).

d. **Save** 🖫 and close the document.

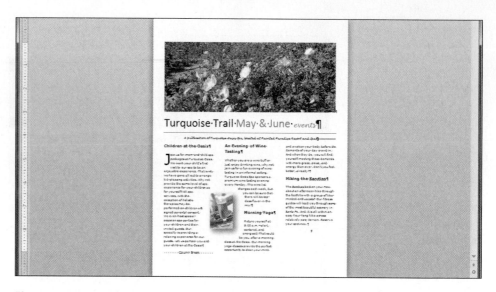

Figure 7 The completed newsletter

Creating a Research Paper

A requirement of most composition classes is that you write a research paper. The very words "research paper" strike fear in the hearts of many college freshmen. Researching a topic might not be the most difficult part of the assignment. Instead, assuring that your paper is in the correct format, according to an identified **style guide**, might be the bigger challenge.

A style guide, or style manual, is a set of standards for designing documents. A style manual is not as concerned with the selection of wording as it is with the standardized documentation of citations and general page characteristics such as margins, spacing, headers, footers, and page numbers. Although it may seem that adherence to a particular style is yet another hurdle to overcome in an already challenging chore of writing a research paper, it is really very helpful. When you follow set rules for citing works (giving credit to the original author), you are less likely to inadvertently plagiarize. Adherence to a style also gives your instructor the ability to work through a paper's ideas and to judge the validity of the work in a consistent manner with other student papers.

Research & Development

Real World Advice   Styles and a Table of Contents

Did you know that if you apply heading styles to headings in your research paper, Word can create a table of contents for you? Using the Table of Contents command on the References tab, you can select from a gallery of styles, or you can open a dialog box from which you can design a custom style. Then if you add or remove additional headings, the table of contents is automatically updated each time you refresh the table of contents.

Research & Development

Real World Advice   What Is Plagiarism?

When writing any sort of paper, you should be very careful not to plagiarize. **Plagiarism** occurs when you present the information, ideas, or phrasing, as worded by another author, as if it were your own. In effect, you mislead others into believing that the original work is your own, when in fact you are theoretically "stealing" it from someone else. Regardless of the writing style guide that you use, you must identify the source of information, and you must identify all quoted material by quotation marks or indentation on the page. You can be charged with plagiarism for the following activities:

- Copying, paraphrasing, or quoting any person or source without giving proper credit
- Claiming another person's published or unpublished work as your own, with or without permission

There is no universally accepted style guide for all writing. Instead, different academic disciplines, and even different journals within a discipline, tend to favor one or another standard style. As you progress through a field of study, you will be required to write papers that adhere to a prescribed style manual. You will find a wealth of information on the various writing style guides both in print and online.

When assigning a research paper, your instructor will identify the preferred writing style. The paper's subject matter is often what determines the style. Some styles are preferred by the social sciences, while others are the choice of humanities or sciences. Each style has unique requirements regarding the treatment of citation of sources, and preparation of a bibliography or title page. Some elements of a writing style even address such topics as when to spell out numerals. For example, should you write the number "thirty-one" or "31"? Is it correct to state "Nineteenth Century," "19th century," or "nineteenth century"? When writing according to a particular style, you will work with a manual indicating preferred treatment of all such variables. The major style guides are MLA, APA, Chicago, and CSE.

MLA (Modern Language Association) style is often used in the humanities, including English, foreign languages, philosophy, religion, art, architecture, and literature. MLA is generally considered simpler and more concise than other styles. It requires brief parenthetical citations that are keyed to an alphabetical list of works cited at the end of a paper. Available for over 50 years, the style is widely followed internationally, including North America, Brazil, China, India, and Japan. The association publishes two manuals, *MLA Handbook for Writers of Research Papers* and *MLA Style Manual and Guide to Scholarly Publishing*.

APA (American Psychological Association) is preferred by the social sciences, including business, economics, communication, justice, education, geography, law, political science, and sociology. Originating in 1929, the style was developed to simplify the communication of scientific ideas in a consistent manner. It focuses on the presentation of technical ideas and research, and is often the required style for the compilation of literature reviews and experiment reports. The association publishes the *Publication Manual of the American Psychological Association*, containing style requirements.

Chicago (University of Chicago) style is primarily concerned with the preparation and editing of papers and books for publication. As such, it is less prescriptive with regard to such items as a title page or an abstract (a summary of the research or paper contents). Since 1906, Chicago has been the recognized standard with regard to American English style, grammar, and punctuation. Offering writers a choice of several different formats, Chicago style only requires that the result is clear and consistent. The *Chicago Manual of Style* provides guidance to writers using Chicago style.

CSE (Council of Science Editors) is the primary style used in the sciences, such as biology, chemistry, computer science, engineering, environmental sciences, geology, math, health sciences, physics, and astronomy. Previously known as CBE (Council of Biology Editors), the association publishes *Scientific Style and Format: The CBE Manual for Authors, Editors, and Publishers*, which provides detailed guidelines for using the CSE style.

Real World Advice | Style Guide Updates

Major research style guides, including MLA, APA, Chicago, and CSE, are not static. New style manuals are published regularly, often with minor changes to style requirements. Although Word incorporates the citation, footnote, and bibliography requirements of the writing style that you indicate, it is possible that the most current style manual requirements are not included. Therefore, you should always refer to a current style manual when preparing a research paper. Do not depend on Word as the final authority.

Research & Development

CONSIDER THIS | Plagiarism?

In 2004, a school board member in Orange County, North Carolina, delivered a commencement speech that sounded strangely familiar to a reporter covering the event. Upon investigation, the reporter found that the speech was identical to one given by Donna Shalala, former U.S. Secretary of Health and Human Services. When confronted, the school board member admitted that he had found the speech by searching the Internet for "commencement speeches." He denied wrongdoing, claiming that the availability of the speech on the Internet made it open for use. What do you think? Was this plagiarism or not? How do you define plagiarism, especially as it concerns the web's open access?

Formatting a Research Paper

Regardless of the writing style in use, a research paper typically includes several standard elements. A title page, copyright page, dedication, table of contents, and a list of illustrations and tables are all possibilities for the front matter (pages preceding the actual report). Different styles require some or all of those parts. The body of the research paper is the typed text, including the report, appropriate citations, headers, and footnotes. At the end of the report is reference material, which could include appendices, a bibliography or references, a glossary, and an index. The body of the report is usually double-spaced, with the exception of indented block quotes which are single-spaced. Footnotes should also be single-spaced.

Pages in a research paper are numbered, with a few exceptions. The title page and dedication do not display page numbers, but they are included in the page count. The front matter is numbered with consecutive lowercase Roman numerals in the bottom center. The remaining pages are numbered with Arabic numerals (1, 2, 3, etc.). The exact placement of page numbers depends upon the writing style in use.

Real World Advice House Writing Style

A house style is a set of writing standards for a specific organization. The purpose of a corporate writing style is to make sure that documents conform to a consistent style and branding. For example, a corporation might prefer that its name is abbreviated in a certain way or that key industry terms are presented consistently. Clients might have a preferred style for their name, as well. A corporate, or house, style might even include a few tips for conducting research. Before assuming a particular style guide, check on the availability of one that might be preferred by your company.

Understanding Research Styles

When writing a research paper according to a particular style such as MLA or APA (which are the two most commonly used in education), you will most likely refer to a style manual for specific guidelines. Before delving into the manual, however, you should be aware of a few basic requirements that will get you started on the right track, even if you do not have a style manual handy.

- Double-space the body of the report, with 1" margins on all sides.
- Always print the report or submit it online as directed by your instructor—never turn in a handwritten paper.
- Use a plain serif or sans serif font—preferably 10–12 pt Times New Roman or Palatino. Acceptable sans serif choices include Arial and Helvetica.
- Place only one space between sentences.
- Page numbers should begin 1/2" from the top of the document.

Real World Advice Turabian Style

Turabian style is very close to Chicago style. In fact, it is often referred to as Chicago/Turabian style. A slight difference is that Chicago style focuses on providing guidelines for publishing in general while Turabian is more concerned with guidelines for student papers, theses, and dissertations that are not necessarily intended for publication. Named for Kate Turabian, the dissertation secretary at the University of Chicago for over 30 years, the style omits some of the publishing details and options that Chicago provides.

To Begin a Research Paper

a. Open **w02_ws04_Spa_Research** from your student data files. Save the document as Lastname_Firstname_w02_ws04_Spa_Research. If necessary, click the Home tab, and then click Show/Hide in the Paragraph group to show nonprinting characters.

The paper is a first draft for research on the sustainable spa industry. A sustainable establishment includes building features and resources that conserve energy and protect the environment. A sustainable spa might use low-flow water fixtures and solar lighting, for example.

b. Review the document for adherence to MLA formatting rules.

Both MLA and APA are well-accepted writing styles in college composition classes. With the exception of page numbering rules and heading alignment, both styles are very similar. Although you will use MLA style for the document in this exercise, a quick review of APA formatting guidelines would enable you to easily format the research paper in APA style. At this point, the research paper is not in acceptable MLA format, but you will correct it in this exercise.

An MLA document should be formatted as follows:

- All lines are double-spaced.
- The first line of each body paragraph is indented 0.5" from the left margin.
- The font should be 10 to 12 pt Times New Roman (or a similar font).
- A right-aligned header is included, with your last name and a page number.
- It is recommended that you include your name, instructor name, class number, and date, left-aligned and double-spaced above the report title.

c. Select all **body paragraphs**, beginning with **Often associated** and ending at the end of the document. Click the **Home tab**, click **Line Spacing** in the Paragraph group, and then select **2.0**.

d. With all of the paragraphs still selected, click the **Paragraph Dialog Box Launcher**, and then click the **Special arrow** under Indentation. Click **First line** to indent the first line of each paragraph 0.5". Click the **Spacing After arrow** to select **0 pt** spacing after each paragraph, and then click **OK**.

e. Click to deselect the paragraphs. Press Ctrl+Home. Change **Firstname** in the first line to your first name and change **Lastname** to your last name.

f. If the ruler is not displayed, click the **View Ruler** button at the top of the vertical scroll bar. Scroll down the document to the top of the second page, and then select the heading **Seeking LEED Certification**. The heading should be aligned on the left margin, so you will remove the left indent.

g. Drag the **First Line Indent marker** on the ruler to the left to align it with the left margin. Similarly, adjust the left indent of the heading **Living in Harmony with Nature**.

h. Click the **Insert tab**, click **Header** in the Header & Footer group, and then click **Edit Header**. Click the **Home tab**, and then click **Align Text Right** in the Paragraph group. You will insert a right-aligned header including your last name and a page number, as required by MLA style.

i. Click the **Design tab**, type your last name, and press Spacebar. Click **Quick Parts** in the Insert group, and then select **Field**. Scroll through the **Field names list**, click **Page**, click **1, 2, 3** in the Format group, and then click **OK**. Click the **Different First Page** check box in the Options group because you do not want the header to display on the first page of the report, and then click **Close Header and Footer** in the Close group.

j. Click the **View tab**, and then click **Two Pages** to view the report. Scroll through the report, noting that it includes four pages, and that the header is displayed on all pages with the exception of the first.

k. **Save** the document.

Real World Advice · Page Numbers

At your request, Word places a page number in a header or footer. The Insert tab includes a Page Number option in the Header & Footer group. Click that option and select a location (or click Format Page Numbers to specify a numbering format or to change a beginning number). You can also begin page numbering from within a header or footer. Click Page Number on the Header & Footer Tools Design tab to find the same options as those found on the Insert tab's Page Number command. Finally, you can click Quick Parts on the Header & Footer Tools Design tab and click Field. Scroll down the list to locate Page, and select a numbering format. To remove a page number, select a page number on any page (in the header or footer), click the Page Number command (on either the Insert tab or the Header & Footer Tools Design tab), and click Remove Page Numbers.

Inserting Citations

Referencing, or citing, is the act of giving credit for ideas and information in your research paper. If you quote someone, use someone else's words or ideas, or include information gleaned from another publication, you must indicate the source of your information. Including a reference to a published or unpublished source, or a **citation**, is necessary whether you use the exact words of the source or whether you paraphrase it. You must always give credit so that you are not in danger of plagiarism.

An *in-text reference* is usually in the form of parenthetical information that you include beside any text that belongs to another writer or that was learned from another resource. The parenthetical reference should be short, in order to minimize interruption of the text itself. It should be placed at the end of a paragraph, if the entire paragraph is borrowed, or at the end of a sentence if the following sentence is your own work or is identified by another citation. The purpose of an in-text citation is to direct the reader to the correct entry in your list of works cited at the end of the research paper or to locate the source in a library. Rules for including citations vary among the writing styles, but generally you are required to list the author or publication name along with a year, with an optional page number.

Real World Advice · Collecting URLs as Citations

When including a web address as an online citation, consider copying the URL and pasting it in the Create Source dialog box. That way, you do not run the risk of making a typo as you transcribe the information. Simply select the URL in the browser Address bar and press Ctrl+C to copy it. Then, paste it (press Ctrl+V) in the Create Source dialog box when indicating the online source.

If a quote or reference to another source includes an author name, the parenthetical citation should only include a page number from the source. For example, "According to Witt, the increase in plant emissions is in no way related to an increase in production (38)," indicates that the information can be found on page 38 of the bibliographic entry for an author named Witt. On the other hand, if the sentence does not include the author name, you should include both the author name and an optional page number (depending on the writing style), as in "The increase in plant emissions is in no way related to an increase in production (Witt 38)."

You are not required to reference information that is assumed to be general knowledge in the field. Neither should you reference text that is your own summary or determination based on your research. The conclusion of a research paper is most often composed of your thoughts and suggestions, so references are seldom included in a paper's conclusion.

CONSIDER THIS | **General Knowledge?**

"General knowledge" is broadly defined. You do not need to cite general knowledge, but you do need to give credit for knowledge from the others' work, therefore you should have a clear definition in mind. How would you define general knowledge?

Word includes reference tools that enable you to accurately include citations, according to one of several writing styles. Allowing Word to format the citations means that you do not have to pay as much attention to learning the minutia of a particular writing style. Although a style guide is handy, it becomes less necessary when Word assists you in the referencing task. The References tab contains several tools that you will become familiar with when formatting a research paper.

Real World Advice   When to Insert a Citation

Although Word simplifies the technical task of citing research, you must know where in the text to place the citation. The task is easier if you place citations in the text as you write the paper. If you wait until the paper is finished, you must backtrack to locate material and position citations. If you have to backtrack, you risk missing a citation and plagiarizing. You should position a reference as close to the source of information as possible, without disrupting the sentence. If you are including a long section of material that comes from one source, do not cite each sentence in the section. Instead, place the reference at the end of the section. Always place a citation outside a quotation and before a punctuation mark that ends a sentence. Finally, if possible, include reference information such as an author's name in the sentence to avoid long parenthetical information.

To Insert Citations

a. Click the **View tab**, and then click **Page Width** in the Zoom group. Press Ctrl+Home, and then click after the word **facilities** but before the period in the sentence in the middle of the second body paragraph. The quoted material came from a journal article that you will reference.

b. Click the **References tab**, click the **Style arrow** in the Citations & Bibliography group, and then select **MLA Sixth Edition**. Click **Insert Citation**, and then click **Add New Source**. Click the **Type of Source arrow**, and then select **Journal Article**. Because your reference will include a volume number and an issue number, you must show more areas than those currently displayed in the dialog box.

c. Click **Show All Bibliography Fields**. Complete the reference as shown next. You must scroll down the listing to locate the Volume and Issue fields. Click **OK**.

Author	Hamlin, Reuben
Title	Leading Spas Seek LEED Certification as a Stamp of Environmental Awareness
Journal Name	Green Spa Network Journal
Year	2013
Pages	55–59
Volume	15
Issue	5

d. Click after the word **resorts** (but before the period) in the first sentence of the first paragraph under the **Seeking LEED Certification** heading, which is located at the top of page 2. Click **Insert Citation**, and then **Add New Source**. Confirm that the **Type of Source** is **Journal Article**. Click **Show All Bibliography Fields** to expand the areas shown. This article has no author. Type the following citation, and then click **OK**.

Title	The Greening of the Spa Industry
Journal Name	LEED News
Year	2013
Pages	58
Volume	68
Issue	4

e. Click after the word **practices** (but before the period) in the second paragraph under the **Seeking LEED Certification** heading. Click **Insert Citation**, click **Add New Source**, and then click the **Type of Source arrow**. Select **Book**, and then enter the information below.

Author	Clairday, Steven
Title	Relax! The Advent of the Ecologically Aware Spa
Year	2009
City	Boston
Publisher	Amber Press

f. Click **OK**. Because the author name is mentioned in the sentence, you will revise the parenthetical citation so it includes a page number, but no author name.

g. Click the **Clairday parenthetical reference** after the word **practices**. Click the **arrow** on the right, and then click **Edit Citation**. Type **48** in the Pages box. Click the **Author**, **Year**, and **Title** check boxes to suppress the display of those items within the citation. Click **OK**.

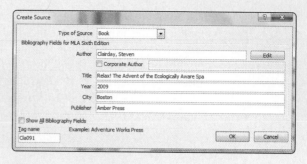

Figure 8 Adding a book citation

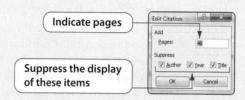

Indicate pages

Suppress the display of these items

Figure 9 Editing a citation

h. Scroll down to the bottom of the second page, and then click after the word **Clairday** (but before the period) in the first sentence of the first paragraph under **Living in Harmony with Nature**. Click **Insert Citation**, and then select **Clairday, Steven**.

Because you are reusing a citation referring to work referenced earlier, you can simply select the citation from the list. However, the sentence in which the reference is included already includes the author name, so you do not need to include the name in the reference. Instead, you will only give the page number.

i. Click the **Clairday citation** that you just added, and then click the **arrow** on the right. Click **Edit Citation**, and then type **30** in the Pages box. Click the **Author**, **Year**, and **Title** check boxes, and then click **OK**.

j. Scroll to the top of page 3, and then click after the quotation mark and before the period in the quote ending with **unhealthy world**. Click **Insert Citation**, click **Add New Source**, and then click the **Type of Source arrow**. Select **Journal Article**, type the following information, and then click **OK**.

Title	Destination Spas
Journal Name	Green Spa Network Journal
Year	2013
Pages	2

k. Click after the word **spa** and before the period in the last sentence of the third page. Click **Insert Citation**, and then click **Add New Source**. Click the **Type of Source arrow**, scroll down the list, and select **Web site**. Type the information shown here, and click **OK**.

Name of Web Page	The Green Spa Industry
Year Accessed	2013
Month Accessed	July
Day Accessed	12
URL	http://www.spanetworknews.com/green

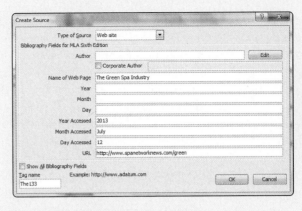

Figure 10   Adding a website citation

l.   **Save** 💾 the document.

Adding Footnotes and Endnotes

Both **footnotes** and **endnotes** are used to direct a reader to a specific source of information referred to in a paper. Footnotes are placed numerically at the foot of the page where a direct reference is made, while endnotes appear in a numerical list at the end of the paper but before a bibliography or works cited page. Footnotes and endnotes are not used as often as they once were because many instructors prefer that you include all references in a works cited or bibliography page. A research paper can appear cluttered if you overuse footnotes or endnotes, but depending on the writing style used and an instructor's preference, you might be required to include them. A general rule of thumb is that if you include footnotes to identify references, you do not need endnotes. Word makes it easy to include footnotes and endnotes, with options on the References tab.

If you use either, should you use footnotes or endnotes? Of course, your instructor's preference should decide the issue, but it would help to understand the differences between the two. Because endnotes are included in one list at the end of the document, they do not add clutter to each page of the paper as footnotes tend to do. Endnotes might even make a paper easier to read because a reader's eyes are not constantly shifting between the text and the bottom of the page. However, if a reader wants to immediately identify a source, he or she might find it easier to glance at a footnote at the bottom of the page for quick information. Footnotes can also be used to make additional comments without including more text in the body of the report. If you do use footnotes or endnotes, do not mix the two. Be consistent and follow through with one or the other throughout a paper.

When you include a footnote or endnote, you place a number or symbol in superscript (slightly elevated from the line) to the right of the source information that you want to reference. The detailed reference is then keyed to the same number or symbol at the end of the page (footnote) or at the end of the document (endnote). If you use footnotes or endnotes, you do not need to include parenthetical information beside the source. Since 1988, however, MLA has recommended parenthetical information instead of footnotes. Parenthetical references are directly tied to a works cited list, which serves as a comprehensive list of all references throughout a paper. A works cited page or a bibliography is a general requirement in university composition classes and is standard practice in the preparation of research papers.

Including a works cited list does not mean that you cannot use footnotes to provide more detailed descriptions of statements or facts in the paper. You might use a footnote to provide an explanation of statistics. For example, a statistic on the number of victims in a natural disaster, or the amount of money given through a government program could be further detailed in a footnote. You might also define or illustrate a concept included in the report, providing a personal comment. Much of business writing is actually persuasive text, where you explain a situation or encourage others to take some action. Using a footnote is a great way to further describe a statistic used in your text without having to incorporate it into the written paragraph. That way, you do not risk muddling the text with overly explanatory text, perhaps losing or diverting the attention of the reader.

If you choose to include footnotes, you should know that most writing styles limit a footnote to only one sentence. In a bibliography, however, each entry consists of three sentences. The first sentence gives the author name, the second is the title statement, and the last describes publication information including publisher and publication date.

Real World Advice Footnotes or Works Cited?

A works cited page is a complete list of sources referenced in the preparation of a paper. Footnotes also identify sources that were referenced in the paper. A source is only listed once in works cited, regardless of the number of times it was referenced. However, if you use footnotes, a footnote is required each time a document is referenced in a paper, possibly yielding several footnotes on the same source. Subsequent references after the first source footnote are abbreviated, but are still required. It is more common to use a works cited page than to include footnotes, which can unnecessarily clutter the body of a report.

Quick Reference Adding a Footnote

1. Click in the position of the footnote (after a period, if at the end of a sentence).
2. Click the References tab.
3. Click Insert Footnote in the Footnotes group.
4. Type footnote text.

To Add and Edit Footnotes

a. Scroll to the second page, and then click after the period after **Washington, DC**, in the first body paragraph. You will add a footnote providing additional information on the LEED program.

b. Click the **References tab**, and then click **Insert Footnote** in the Footnotes group.
   A numeral superscript is placed at the insertion point, a divider is placed at the foot of the current page, and the same superscripted numeral begins the footnote. You will type additional text to make the comment.

c. Type LEED is the primary internationally recognized building certification system for environmental awareness. (Include the period.)

Troubleshooting

If the insertion point is displayed at the end of the document instead of the bottom margin of the current page, you clicked Insert Endnote instead of Insert Footnote. Click Undo and repeat Steps b and c.

d. Scroll to the top of the current page and note the raised numeral 1 at the end of the sentence. Double-click the **footnote number** to move directly to the footnote at the end of the page.

Troubleshooting

If double-clicking the footnote number does not advance you to the footnote at the end of the page, you probably clicked near, but not on, the number. Double-click the footnote number in the body of the report again.

SIDE NOTE
A Footnote Is Not a Footer
A footnote provides further explanation of an item in a paper. It is not the same thing as a footer, which is any text that appears at the bottom of every page in a document, such as a page number.

e. Scroll to the top of page 2, and then drag to select the superscript beside the words **Washington, DC**. Because this is the only footnote you will include in the document, you decide to define a symbol instead of a number for the footnote designator. You will use an asterisk.

f. Click the **Footnotes Dialog Box Launcher**, and then click **Symbol**.

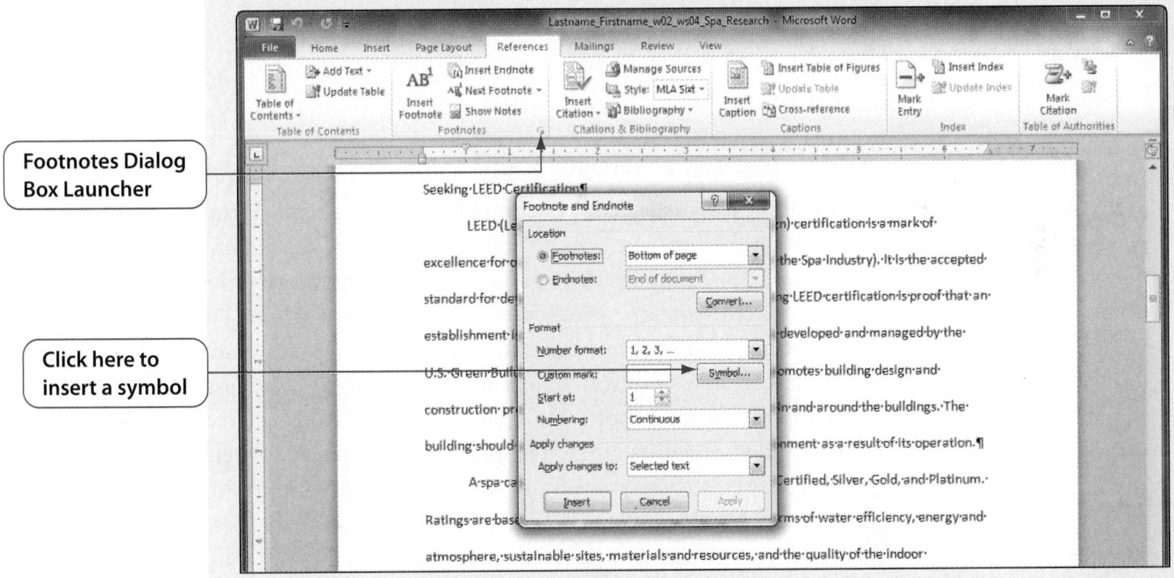

Footnotes Dialog Box Launcher

Click here to insert a symbol

Figure 11   Defining a footnote symbol

g. Scroll up, if necessary, to locate and click the **asterisk symbol**. If you do not see the symbol, click the **Character code box**, and then type 42. Click **OK**, and then click **Insert**. The footnote symbol is changed to an asterisk in both the document reference and in the footnote itself.

Troubleshooting

If the footnote symbol does not change to an asterisk, or is otherwise incorrectly displayed, click Undo and repeat Steps e–g. You can also simply type the character code in the Custom mark box next to the Symbol button in the Footnote and Endnote dialog box.

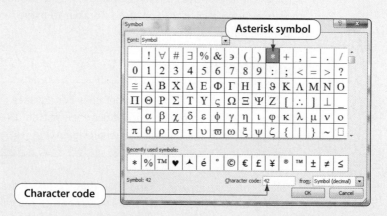

Figure 12   Selecting a footnote symbol

h. Select the **footnote line**, click the **Home tab**, and then change the font size to **9**. You can format footnote text in the same way that you format other text.

i. **Save** 🖫 the document.

Developing a Bibliography or Works Cited Page

A **bibliography** is a list of documents or sources used during research for a paper. Those sources might not have been referenced directly in the paper, but they were helpful as you prepared the document. A bibliography can help others understand the basis of your work and can save them time when conducting similar research. They can use your bibliography as a springboard, perhaps consulting some of the same sources as they continue to study the subject of your research. Although similar to a bibliography, a **works cited** page serves a different purpose. Only those sources that you actually referenced in the paper are included as works cited. The rule is, if you place a parenthetical reference in a paper, there must be a corresponding item in the list of works cited. The major difference is that a bibliography is more inclusive, listing all sources whether they were referenced or not. A works cited page is considered part of the document, continuing the page numbering, whereas a bibliography is a separate component.

   MLA style uses the term "works cited" to refer to the works cited page, whereas APA style prefers "references." Both terms are synonymous. Each is an alphabetical list of works that you have referenced in the body of a research report. Entries are placed in alphabetical order by last names of authors, editors, or by first words of titles. A bibliography is also alphabetized.

Real World Advice — Bibliography Note Cards

Students often find that creating bibliography note cards before writing a research paper can be very helpful. Create a note card for every resource that you locate, listing the information much as you would in an actual bibliography (including author, article name, book or journal title, publication material, etc.). Keep collecting cards until your research is complete. Then, as you compose an outline and write the paper, you will have ready access to your sources. You can also alphabetize the note cards to make it much easier to transfer the material onto an alphabetized bibliography page.

Options on Word's References tab enable you to easily add citations, footnotes, endnotes, bibliographies, and works cited pages. Word prepares the bibliography or works cited page directly from the parenthetical citations that you included when you used the Insert Citation command. Having selected the writing style (MLA, APA, etc.), Word formats all citations and the works cited page appropriately. You can edit the bibliography page to include additional sources or to modify existing ones, if necessary.

Using an Annotated Bibliography

An **annotated bibliography** is a special type of bibliography that compiles references along with a short paragraph summarizing or reviewing the value of the source to the research project. Creating an annotated bibliography gives you a chance to consider several sources, evaluating each to determine its applicability and value to your project. If your instructor requires an annotated bibliography, you should begin preparing the bibliography as you conduct your research, and you should consult relevant writing style rules to ensure adherence to a particular style. For each source, include not only the title and other pertinent publication information, but also a paragraph of 150 words or less that summarizes the article or book as follows:

Purpose or main focus

Target audience for the work

Relevance to the research topic

Features that are unique or that should be helpful

Author credibility and background

Author conclusions and observation

Creating a Bibliography Page

Although a writing style manual (MLA, APA, Chicago, etc.) can be helpful as you develop various parts of a research paper, you can also rely on Word to correctly format bibliography and works cited pages. The Citations & Bibliography group on the References tab includes a Bibliography option from which you can insert a predesigned bibliography or works cited page. You can also choose to insert a bibliography page with no heading or title, so you can manage it more independently. Regardless of which approach you take, you should always confirm the resulting page meets all requirements of the particular style you are following. Just as you would proofread a document instead of relying solely on Word's spelling checker, you should also consult a writing style manual to make sure your document is correct.

When Word creates a bibliography page, it places all citations in a field, which is a unit that is recognized as a single entity. The Citations field is a unit that can be updated if you add more references to the document. In fact, when you click any text on a bibliography page, a content control tab, titled Update Citations and Bibliography, appears at the top of the selected list of citations. If you have included additional citations in the body of the research paper, clicking the content control tab automatically updates the bibliography. You can also change bibliography entries into static text, which removes the field designation and enables you to treat the text as normal, editing and deleting references at will.

To Create a Bibliography Page

a. Press Ctrl+End. Because a bibliography must begin on a new page, you will insert a manual page break so text begins on the following page.

b. Press Ctrl+Enter to insert a page break. If the view is Print Layout with nonprinting characters toggled on, you will see a page break indicator at the end of page 4.

c. Click the **References tab**, and then click **Bibliography** in the Citations & Bibliography group.

   You can then select either Bibliography or Works Cited. The only difference in the selections is the resulting title. All sources that you inserted as you created the research paper will be alphabetically placed under the title Works Cited (or Bibliography, if you made that selection). You can also select Insert Bibliography, which includes all citations, but without a page title.

d. Click **Works Cited**, and then scroll up to view the works cited page, with five entries. The Works Cited title is left aligned above the entries. Click any entry to select the Works Cited field. Note that all entries are shaded, indicating they are considered a single unit. You will also see the content control tab, Update Citations and Bibliography, at the top of the page.

Content control tab

Shaded area indicates the bibliography field

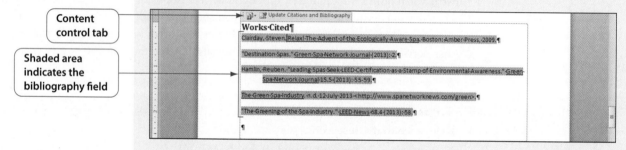

Figure 13   The Works Cited page

e. **Save** the document.

Editing a Bibliography

The only distinction that Word makes between a bibliography and a works cited page is the title. All sources that you have created in the paper are included on the bibliography or works cited page. However, a bibliography actually differs from a works cited page in that it includes all resources, even those that are not cited in the paper. Therefore, the bibliography included with your research paper might not be complete after Word creates it. You will need to edit the page to include other resources that helped you develop the paper.

   In reviewing your research paper, you might determine that one or more citations should be updated or corrected. Perhaps you made a typo when entering the citation. Even if you have already created a bibliography or works cited page, you can edit the citation source and then easily update the bibliography or works cited to include the new information.

To Edit an Existing Source and Update a Bibliography

a. Scroll to the second page and locate the (**48**) reference in the second paragraph. Click the **reference**. A content control surrounds the citation.

b. Click the **arrow** on the right, and then click **Edit Source**.

c. Click the **Year box**, and change the year to 2011. Click **OK**, and then click **Yes** if asked whether to update the master source list and the current document.

d. Press Ctrl+End. Scroll up slightly and note that the Clairday reference includes 2009 as the year. You will update the Works Cited page to reflect the year 2011. Click any reference in the Works Cited page to display the content control.

e. Click the **Update Citations and Bibliography tab**. The works cited list is updated with the new year in the Clairday reference.

f. Click the **Bibliographies** button 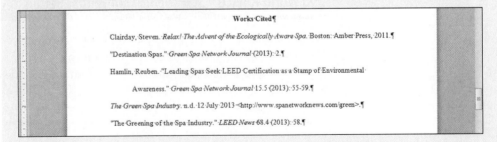 on the left side of the content control tab, and then click **Convert bibliography to static text**.

   The bibliography or works cited page that Word includes is not exactly as required by MLA. Because you must edit the page slightly to accommodate the MLA style, you convert the field to regular, or static, text. After you convert the page, it can no longer be updated automatically if citations are changed, so only convert to static text after all updates are complete.

Troubleshooting

> Even though the bibliography is converted to static text, the Update Citations and Bibliography tab will still appear, and the bibliography will still be selected as a unit when you click any entry.

g. Click the **Home tab**, select all text on the works cited page, including the title, and change the font to **12 pt Times New Roman**. Click **Line and Paragraph Spacing** in the Paragraph group, and then select **2.0** so the page is double-spaced, as required by the MLA style. Click the **Paragraph Dialog Box Launcher**, and make sure Spacing after is **0 pt**.

h. Select the **Works Cited** title, and then on the **Home tab**, click **Center**. Each underlined title should be italicized instead of underlined. Select each title, click the **Underline** button, and then click **Italic**. Click outside the border to deselect the Works Cited entries, and then press Ctrl+End.

Works Cited

Clairday, Steven. *Relax! The Advent of the Ecologically Aware Spa*. Boston: Amber Press, 2011.

"Destination Spas." *Green Spa Network Journal* (2013): 2.

Hamlin, Reuben. "Leading Spas Seek LEED Certification as a Stamp of Environmental Awareness." *Green Spa Network Journal* 15.5 (2013): 55-59.

The Green Spa Industry. n.d. 12 July 2013 <http://www.spanetworknews.com/green>.

"The Greening of the Spa Industry." *LEED News* 68.4 (2013): 58.

Figure 14 MLA format

i. **Save** and close the document.

Creating a Mail Merge Document

The term **mail merge** is a little misleading. The term suggests that the process focuses only on preparing documents for mailing, and although that is a primary application, it is not the only reason you will use the feature. Actually, mail merge simplifies the task of preparing documents that contain identical formatting, layout, and text, but where only certain portions of each document vary. Perhaps you are preparing a document announcing a new product line that you will distribute to many clients. To personalize the announcement, you want to include the client's name and company in the body. The bulk of the announcement is text that will not vary, but the client name and company name should be inserted as if they were part of the original document. You will include a *field* for each bit of variable data in the document, and then simply merge, or copy, data into those fields from a master list of clients and companies.

Obviously, mail merge is the ideal vehicle for generating mailing labels, envelopes, address lists, and personalized letters and handouts. In addition to generating mailings, mail merge can be helpful in the preparation of multiple e-mails and electronic faxes. To succeed, a company needs to maintain a well-informed client base, where each customer is made to feel a part of the success. Word can help you save vast amounts of time in preparing personalized documents that assist in recognizing each customer.

You will work with two files during a mail merge process—the **main document** and the **data source**. In the example given previously, the announcement is the main document. It consists primarily of text that will not change regardless of how many times it is duplicated. The data source contains the variable information, such as specific client and company names. Those items will change each time the announcement is printed or otherwise duplicated. Items in the data source are called **fields**, because their contents will vary.

A field is much like a mailbox. The name on the outside never changes, but the contents change often. For example, the *client name* field is a holding area, much like a mailbox, for actual client names. Similarly, a *company name* field would contain actual company names.

The main document contains not only text that does not change, but also **merge fields**, which are references to the fields in the data source. When the two documents are merged, Word replaces each merge field with data from the data source. Ultimately, the two documents are merged into a third document that is a combination of the main document and the data source. However, if you are merging to the printer, fax, or e-mail, you will not actually create a third document. Also, you can preview the merge before finalizing the process.

Using Mail Merge

Mail merge is a step-by-step process, achieved by using the Mailings tab in Word. Using a task pane and responding to prompts, you indicate the starting document (main document) and the location of the data source. If you are creating mailing labels, you will not have a main document. Instead, you will simply begin with a blank document. Similarly, you do not have to begin with a data source. Instead, you can create a field list during the mail merge process. Of course, it is much more common to use a data source of fields that you can call on for use in more than one merged document. Your Outlook Contacts can also serve as a data source.

Before completing the mail merge, you can preview the document and make changes, if necessary. Although the most common option is to merge to a document, you can also merge to an e-mail. Simply indicate where the text should be sent, enter a subject line, and select a format option. The document will automatically be sent to all e-mail recipients that you indicated earlier in your data source.

Creating a Mail Merge Document

You will use two documents for the mail merge process—the main document and the source data. In this project, the main document is a letter that you will send to spa clients on your mailing list, informing them of the regular newsletter mailings that Turquoise Oasis Spa is beginning. You will first review the letter to familiarize yourself with its content.

To Review the Main Document

a. Open **w02_ws04_Letter** from your student data files, and then save the document as Lastname_Firstname_w02_ws04_Letter. If necessary, click the **Home tab**, and then click **Show/Hide** in the Paragraph group to display nonprinting characters. During the mail merge process, you will replace the bracketed information with data from an address list, which is your data source.

b. Click before the left bracket before **Current Date**, and then press ⌈Delete⌋ 14 times to remove the words and the right bracket, without removing the final paragraph mark.

   You will insert the current date, in the format "August 6, 2013." When you insert the date, you can specify that it be updated automatically, which means that each time the document is opened, it will display the exact date on which the document is opened. The date will change each time the document is opened on another day.

Troubleshooting

If you mistakenly remove the final paragraph mark beside the date, click Undo and repeat Step b.

SIDE NOTE
When to Insert a Date that Updates Automatically

Inserting a date so it is updated each time a document opens may not be appropriate for all documents. It is sometimes important that the date reflect the date of the document preparation, instead of the date the document is opened.

c. Click the **Insert tab**, and then click **Date & Time** in the Text group. The Date and Time dialog box opens.

d. Click the **third selection** from the top, indicating the current date in the format of Month Day, Year, such as August 6, 2013. If necessary, click the **Update automatically check box** to select it, and then click **OK**.

e. Click the **current date** to select the content control, which is indicated by the shaded area. When the date is updated automatically, the Update tab is useful only if you also included the current time in the selected date format and want to update the document to show the current time. Click outside the content control.

Current date, which will be updated each time the document is opened

Fields to be replaced with data from the data source

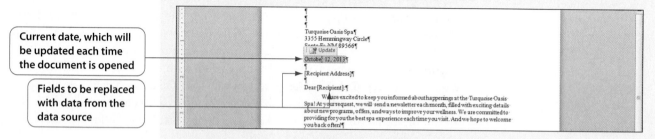

Figure 15   The main document

f. **Save** 🖫 the document.

CONSIDER THIS │ **Use of Formal Titles**

When do you think it is appropriate, or even required, to use formal titles such as Dr., Mr., or Ms. in documents? And when is it better to leave the formal titles off?

Beginning a Mail Merge

Options on the Mailings tab enable you to create a merged document, edit source data, and create envelopes and labels. The basic process of merging a main document and source data is fairly simple, accomplished by responding to a series of prompts and indicating preferences.

To Begin a Mail Merge

a. Navigate to your data files and right-click **w02_ws04_Addresses**. Click **Copy**. Navigate to the location where you save your Word projects, right-click the folder (or disk drive), and click **Paste**. Locate the file that you pasted, right-click it, and click **Rename**. Type Lastname_Firstname_w02_ws04_Addresses and press Enter.

b. Click the **Mailings tab**, and then click **Start Mail Merge** in the Start Mail Merge group.
   From the Start Mail Merge menu, you can work with letters, envelopes, labels, or e-mail messages. Perhaps the simplest way to begin that process is to work with a Mail Merge wizard. A wizard leads you through a process step by step, so you simply respond to prompts to produce a desired result.

c. Click **Step by Step Mail Merge Wizard**. The task pane opens, enabling you to complete the mail merge process one step at a time.

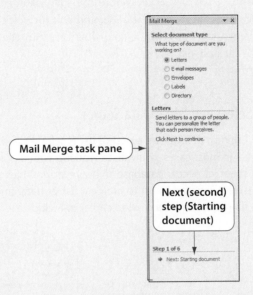

Mail Merge task pane

Next (second) step (Starting document)

Figure 16   The Mail Merge task pane

d. Confirm that **Letters** is selected in the Select document type area, and then click **Next: Starting document**.

e. Confirm that **Use the current document** is selected in the Select starting document area. The document that you indicate is the main document. Although the main document is often the currently open document (as is the case here), you could also indicate that a template is to be used or that you prefer to use a previously saved document.

f. Click **Next: Select recipients**.

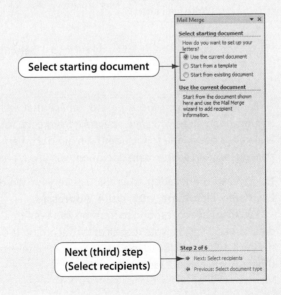

Select starting document

Next (third) step (Select recipients)

Figure 17   Selecting starting document

Selecting a Data Source

A data source is a list of fields that contains variable data. For example, a list of mailing addresses, including names, street addresses, cities, and states, can supply data for a client mailing. A Word table, containing such data, can serve as a data source, as can an Excel worksheet, an Access database, and an Outlook contacts list. By keeping the data source current, you can reuse it countless times in the preparation of documents that require such variable data.

SIDE NOTE
Formatting and Mail Merge

When you merge a document with a data source, formatting is not incorporated. For example, if currency is included in a data source, the number will not carry the currency format over. Instead, you must format it in the merged document as well.

To Select and Edit a Data Source

a. Confirm that **Use an existing list** is selected in the Select recipients area.

In most cases, you will be working with a predefined list—a Word table, Excel worksheet, or Access database. If, however, you have not yet created a data source, you can select *Type a new list* to create a list of data. In this case, the data source is an Access database that was created earlier to include client mailing addresses.

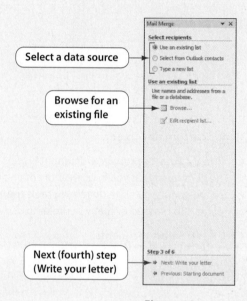

Select a data source

Browse for an existing file

Next (fourth) step (Write your letter)

Figure 18   Selecting a data source

b. Click **Browse**.

Earlier, you copied the Access database that will be used as your data source to the location where you save your Word projects. You will navigate to that location. It is always a good idea to include the main document and the data source in the same storage location so the main document will always have the data source at hand.

c. Navigate to the location where you save your Word projects, and then double-click **Lastname_Firstname_w02_ws04_Addresses**.

You may have to respond to prompts in a Confirm Data Source dialog box before your data source displays. Note that all of the records in the data table are checked, indicating they will each be included in a letter. You can deselect any you do not wish to include. In this case, you will include them all.

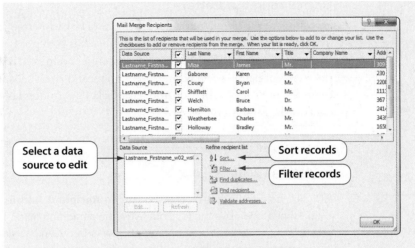

Figure 19   Accessing the data source

d. Click **Sort**.

   The Mail Merge Recipients dialog box includes several selections related to sorting, filtering, and editing the recipient list. You will sort the list by last name.

e. Click the **Sort by arrow**, and then select **Last Name**.

   The default sort order is ascending. Although you will sort by only one field, note that you could also narrow the sort to include secondary fields. For example, you could sort by Last Name and then by First Name (within Last Name).

f. Click **OK**, and then click **Filter**. Suppose that you want to limit the mailing to clients from Iowa. Click the **Field arrow**, scroll down the list, and select **State**. The default comparison operator is **Equal to**, but you can select from others (such as greater than or less than) by clicking the Comparison arrow and making another selection.

g. Type IA in the Compare to box, and then click **OK**.

   Only one record is displayed—Charles Weatherbee, from Des Moines, IA. If you proceeded with the mail merge at this point, the end result would be only one letter, because you have only one client from Iowa.

h. You will include all records, so click **Filter** once more, click **Clear All** to remove the filter, and then click **OK**.

i. Click the **data source file name** in the Data Source box, and then click **Edit**.

   You can edit records, changing data and adding new contacts. You can also remove records. Dana Nye's address has changed.

j. Click the address, **347 Maple Drive**, backspace or delete the current address if necessary, and then type 3213 13th Avenue.

k. Click **New Entry**. Enter data for a new client as follows (pressing the **Tab** key to move to each desired field):

Title:	Dr.
First Name:	Melinda
Last Name:	Abrams
Address 1:	111 Raintree Circle
City:	Santa Fe
State:	NM
Zip	89566

l. Click **OK**, click **Yes** when asked whether to update the recipient list, and then click **OK**.

m. Click **Next: Write your letter**.

Completing the Letter

To complete the letter, you will identify data to be inserted from the data source into the main document. Since the mail merge process is commonly used for preparing mailings, Word is designed to simplify the use of mailing addresses. Although you could work with the recipient name, street address, city, state, and zip as separate fields, Word incorporates them all into a unit called an Address block. The Address block is available with a single click in the Mail Merge wizard.

SIDE NOTE
Manage Address Items Separately

Instead of selecting Address block, you can select More Items if you want to separately manage such items as title, recipient name, street address, city, state, and zip. Selecting Address block includes them all as a unit.

To Insert an Address Block

a. Click before the left bracket beginning **Recipient Address**, and then press Delete 19 times to remove the text, but leave the paragraph mark.

   You should see three paragraph marks between the date and the salutation. The insertion point should be displayed before the second paragraph mark.

b. Click **Address block** in the Write your letter area of the Mail Merge task pane. Confirm that **Insert recipient's name in this format** is checked.

c. From the address formats shown, select **Joshua Randall Jr.** The resulting address block in the letter that you are creating will include only the first and last name of recipients.

d. Confirm that **Insert postal address** is selected, so the entire address including street address, city, state, and zip will be included in the address block.

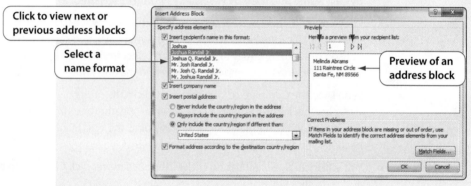

Figure 20   Selecting an address block

e. Click **OK**. A merge field, **AddressBlock**, is inserted in the letter. The field begins and ends with double characters that appear to be left and right facing arrows.

f. Click the **AddressBlock** field and note that the entire field is shaded, indicating that it is now considered a unit.

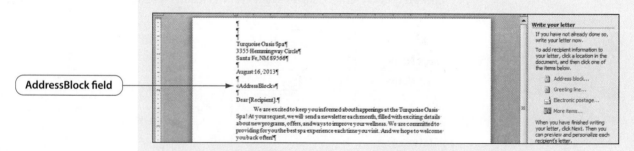

Figure 21   The AddressBlock field

g. Click outside the AddressBlock field to deselect it.

Designing a Salutation Line

A salutation is included in a typical business letter. Although the format can vary slightly, it typically includes a title and a last name, followed by a colon. You can include any fields from the data source in any order, providing for appropriate spacing between each field.

To Design a Salutation Line

a. Click before the left bracket beginning **Recipient**. Remove both brackets and the word **Recipient**, but leave the colon in place. In the task pane, click **More items**, and then click **Title**. Click **Insert**, click **Close**, and then press Spacebar so a space is placed between the title and the last name.

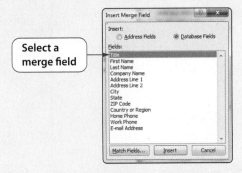

Figure 22   Selecting merge fields

b. Click **More items**, click **Last Name**, click **Insert**, and then click **Close**. The salutation line, with two merge fields, is displayed.

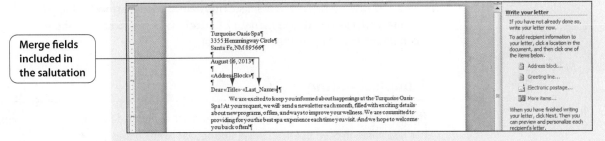

Figure 23   The salutation line

c. Click **Next: Preview your letters**.

Previewing Letters

After so much formatting, you will want to preview the finished result. The Preview step of the mail merge process presents a document with data from the data source in place of the merge fields. In this case, you will see a letter with an address and a salutation instead of the placeholders visible earlier. Before the merge is complete, the preview enables you to check for formatting errors.

To Preview the Merged Document

a. Click the **Next Recipient button** [>>] to view another letter. You can page forward or backward among letters, although each letter is identical with the exception of the address and salutation.

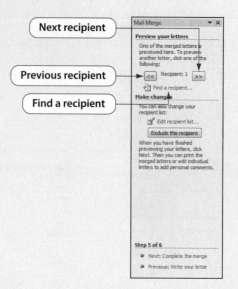

Figure 24   Previewing a letter

b. Click **Find a recipient**. Especially if you are working with a large recipient database, you might want to ensure that a particular recipient is included.

c. Type Gaboree in the Find box. Select **This field**. Click the **arrow** beside **Title**, select **Last Name**, click **Find Next**, and then click **Cancel**. The letter to Karen Gaboree is displayed, confirming that she is in the recipient pool.

Troubleshooting

If Karen Gaboree's letter is not shown, you most likely made a mistake when typing her last name in Step c. Click Cancel and repeat Steps b and c.

d. Select the **two paragraphs** in the body of the letter. Before completing the merge, you can edit the letter, if necessary. You determine that the paragraphs should not be indented.

e. If the ruler is not displayed, click the **View tab**, and then select **Ruler**. Drag the **First Line Indent** marker to the left margin. Confirm that the spacing in the body paragraphs is correct.

Completing a Mail Merge

The last step of the mail merge wizard completes the merge, resulting in a document with one page for each recipient. In this case, since you are sending letters to 10 recipients, the merged document will include 10 pages. The resulting document is separate from the main document and the data source, and as such must be saved as a separate file.

To Complete the Mail Merge

a. Click **Next: Complete the merge**. You can select the Print option to print the letters directly to the printer, or you can choose to edit individual letters so they are compiled into a document that you can save.

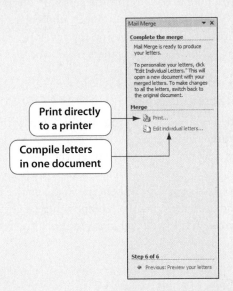

Print directly to a printer

Compile letters in one document

Figure 25   Completing a mail merge

b. Click **Edit individual letters**. The Merge to New Document dialog box enables you to specify whether to print all letters or a subset. In this case, you will print all letters, so the default option **All** is correct as selected. Click **OK**.

Scroll through the letters, noting that each letter is in its own page section, as noted by the Next Page section break dividing each letter from the next. All address and salutation information is unique to the recipient, but the body of each letter is identical. The file name, shown in the title bar, is Letters1, indicating that this is a new document. However, the original main document **Lastname_Firstname_w02_ws04_Letter** also remains open.

c. Save the merged letter, calling it Lastname_Firstname_w02_ws04_Merged_Letters. Close Lastname_Firstname_w02_ws04_Merged_Letters. **Save** and close Lastname_Firstname_w02_ws04_Letter.

Real World Advice   Using an Excel Worksheet as a Data Source

An Excel worksheet, which is a grid of columns and rows, simplifies the maintenance of such items as mailing addresses. For that reason, Excel is a logical choice when creating a table of mailing addresses that you want to use as a data source for a mail merge. When creating the Excel worksheet, do not leave a blank row between the column headings and the mailing records. Also, give column headings recognizable titles such as First Name and Last Name, so that Word is able to connect the fields with its mail merge blocks. When working through the mail merge wizard, you will select an existing list for the data source and navigate to the Excel workbook. Double-click the workbook, and then select the desired worksheet from the resulting Select Table dialog box. At that point, you can edit, filter, and sort records in the Excel data source just as you would with other types, such as an Access or Word table.

Creating Labels and Envelopes

Having created a letter to clients, you will mail it. You can use the same data source that you used for the mail merged letter, placing the address on mailing labels, with one mailing label for each record in the data source. Using Word's Mail Merge feature, you can simply select labels and then specify the label size and type. Additionally, indicate the font and positioning of data to suit the needs of your project.

When you create envelopes, the entire envelope is fed through the printer so the address is printed directly on the envelope. Although mailing labels are probably easier to manage than envelopes, there may be occasions when an envelope is more suitable. Word makes it easy to create envelopes.

Selecting Labels

When creating labels, you should begin with a blank Word document. The Mail Merge feature enables you to select from numerous label types, including mailing, folder, and even name tag labels. Although the most common type of label used is a mailing label, it is by no means the only choice. Labels are listed by manufacturer, with Avery being the most often listed label type in the choice of labels provided by Word. Avery is such a standard that you will often find other label types providing an Avery equivalent number so you can use the label in a Word mail merge process.

To Select Labels

a. Click the **File tab**, click **New**, and then double-click **Blank document**. Click the **Mailings tab**, click **Start Mail Merge** in the Start Mail Merge group, and then click **Step by Step Mail Merge Wizard**.

b. Select **Labels** in the Select document type area. Click **Next: Starting document**. Confirm that **Change document layout** is selected in the Select starting document area, and then click **Label options** in the Change document layout area.

   The mailing labels that you generate will be placed on the blank document. You must indicate the label type.

c. Click the **Label vendors arrow**, and then scroll, if necessary, to select **Avery US Letter**. Scroll through the list of labels to locate and select **5160 Easy Peel Address Labels**. Change any printer information, if necessary, and then click **OK**.

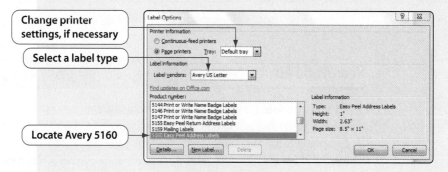

Figure 26   Selecting a label type

Selecting Recipients and Arranging Labels

You can select recipients from a data source just as you learned in the previous section. You can filter the data source so labels are only printed for a certain subset of the data source. You can also edit the data source, deleting, adding, and editing records. Word inserts fields from the data source onto a mailing label, duplicating the fields for each label so each label contains a different recipient.

To Select Recipients and Arrange Labels

a. Click **Next: Select recipients**. Confirm that **Use an existing list** is selected in the Select recipients area, and then click **Browse**. Navigate to the location where you are storing your files, and double-click **Lastname_Firstname_w02_ws04_Addresses**, to select the data source. As you learned previously, you can edit, sort, or filter the records before printing labels.

b. Click **Sort**, click the **Sort by arrow**, and then select **Last Name**. The default sort order is ascending. Click **OK**. The mailing labels will be printed alphabetically by last name. Click **OK**.

c. Click **Next: Arrange your labels**. Confirm that the insertion point is located in the top-left label. Click **Address block** in the Arrange your labels area, click **Joshua Randall Jr.**, and then click **OK**.

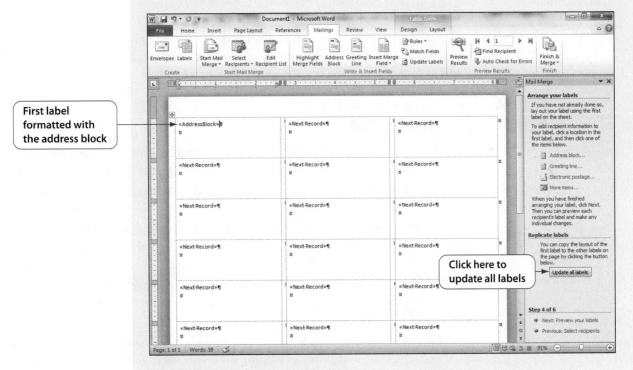

First label formatted with the address block

Click here to update all labels

Figure 27   Arranging mailing labels

d. Click **Update all labels** in the Mail Merge task pane, and then click **Next: Preview your labels**.

e. Click the **View tab**, and then click **One Page** in the Zoom group to see the entire page of labels. Note that all 10 addresses in the data source are included, one on each label.

f. Press $\boxed{\text{Ctrl}}+\boxed{\text{A}}$ to select all mailing labels, click the **Home tab**, and then click **No Spacing** in the Styles group so all text fits more neatly within each label space.

g. Click the **View tab**, and then click **100%** in the Zoom group. Click **Next: Complete the merge**, and then click **Edit individual labels**. Click **OK** to select all records.

   The completed mailing label document is displayed. After positioning a sheet of mailing labels in the printer, you can print the mailing labels. Note that the mailing labels are actually a document that you can save, if you like.

h. Save the mailing labels as Lastname_Firstname_w02_ws04_Mailing. Close the document. Close the original labels document without saving it.

CONSIDER THIS | **Mailing Labels or Envelopes?**

Word allows you to create mailing labels as well as addresses on envelopes. Is there a preference for one over the other? Do you feel any differently when you receive a letter that is addressed on an envelope without a mailing label?

Creating Envelopes

To create an envelope, begin with a new blank document. Using Word's Mail Merge wizard, you will step through the process of creating an envelope. During that process, you can specify font selection and you can adjust the font size.

To Create Envelopes

a. Begin a new blank document. Click the **Mailings tab**, and then click **Start Mail Merge** in the Start Mail Merge group. Click **Step by Step Mail Merge Wizard**.

b. Select **Envelopes** in the Select document type area, click **Next: Starting document**, and then click **Envelope options**.

   The Envelope Options dialog box appears. You can select an envelope type, and you can indicate a font size and type. Options on the Printing Options tab enable you to identify printing methods.

c. The default envelope size is Size 10. Leave the size as is, or click the **Envelope size arrow** to select **Size 10** if it is not displayed. At this point, you could change the font selection or size. Click **OK**.

d. Click **Next: Select recipients**. You will use the same data source you used for the previous exercises. Confirm that **Use an existing list** is selected in the Select recipients area, and then click **Browse**.

e. Navigate to the location where you are storing your files, and then double-click **Lastname_Firstname_w02_ws04_Addresses**. The data source is displayed, with all records selected. You will print an envelope for all recipients. Click **OK**.

f. Click **Next: Arrange your envelope**. Click before the paragraph mark in the delivery address area of the envelope (lower middle), and then click **Address block** in the Mail Merge task pane. The Insert Address Block dialog box appears.

g. Click **Joshua Randall Jr.** to select a recipient name format, and then click **OK**.

h. Click **Next: Preview your envelopes**. Click the left or right arrows in the **Preview your envelopes** section to view the envelopes.

i. Click before the first paragraph mark in the top-left corner of the envelope. You will type a return address. Type Turquoise Oasis Spa and press Enter. Type 3355 Hemmingway Circle and press Enter. Finally, type Santa Fe, NM 89566.

j. Click **Next: Complete the merge**. Click **Edit individual envelopes** (or click **Print** if you want to send the envelopes directly to the printer without first saving the document). Click **OK**.

k. **Save** 🖫 the new document as Lastname_Firstname_w02_ws04_Envelopes and close the document. Close the original envelopes document without saving it, and then exit Word.

1. You are an accountant for the city in which you live. With a CPA and a CMA, which are both professional certifications, you are involved in several professional organizations. You have agreed to edit the newsletter for the Institute of Professional Accountants. You are also planning to attend your high school reunion next month and have been asked to help with the newsletter informing classmates of the activities. How would the two newsletters be similar and how would they differ? How would you use color in each, and what type of graphics (if any) would you select? Provide general suggestions on the preparation of newsletters in professional and informal settings.

2. As a member of the Institute of Professional Accountants, you are preparing the newsletter for mailing. You are aware of Word's mail merge process that can be used to prepare mailing labels. You can quickly print and affix mailing labels to the newsletter for mailing. You have also used Word to print envelopes, a process in which a printer prints the mailing address directly on the envelope. When you receive documents in the mail—some with mailing labels attached and others with your name typed on the envelope—do you feel any differently about one or the other? Is there any difference in your perception regarding the way each is received? On what occasions or for what purposes would an envelope with a typed address be preferred over mass-produced mailing labels?

3. The Student Government Association, of which you are a member, is sponsoring a fall festival to raise money for the local volunteer center. You agreed to develop a newsletter chronicling the festival activities, but you are short on time. Therefore, you check Office.com for a relevant newsletter template that you can modify. To your surprise, when you open the newsletter template that you selected, the newsletter columns are organized in text boxes instead of Word columns. Why do you think the template's designer chose to use text boxes instead of formatting in columns? Can you identify any advantages or disadvantages to using text boxes as columns?

4. One of the first things you are likely to do when you are assigned a research paper or English report is to search online for related information. Recently, your English instructor assigned the task of writing an essay comparing and contrasting Lincoln's "Gettysburg Address" with Martin Luther King, Jr.'s "I Have a Dream" speech. You find an overwhelming amount of information online—even essays that you can buy! At what level is what you draw from online sources considered plagiarism? Although some instances of plagiarism are obvious, others may be grayer, or more indefinite. Provide suggestions regarding how to avoid plagiarism when conducting online research. In your own words, define plagiarism.

5. Your niece is graduating from kindergarten, and you want to present her with a personalized diploma. On such a fun occasion, you want to make the certificate as colorful and child-oriented as possible. What Word features would you use to design the major headings? How would you incorporate color and graphics? Where would you find pictures and clip art appropriate for the diploma? Identify at least one SmartArt diagram style that could serve a purpose in the kindergarten diploma—be specific.

Key Terms

Annotated bibliography 247
APA 235
Bibliography 246
Chicago 235
Citation 239
Column 228
CSE 236

Data source 250
Drop cap 231
Endnote 243
Fields 250
Footnote 243
Mail merge 250
Main document 250

Merge field 251
MLA 235
Newsletter 226
Plagiarism 235
Style guide 234
Works cited 246

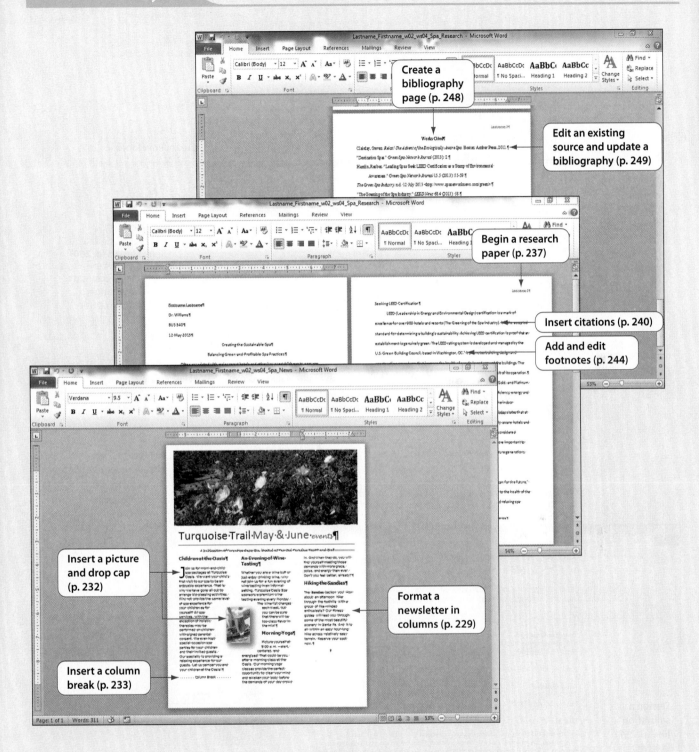

Create a bibliography page (p. 248)

Edit an existing source and update a bibliography (p. 249)

Begin a research paper (p. 237)

Insert citations (p. 240)

Add and edit footnotes (p. 244)

Insert a picture and drop cap (p. 232)

Format a newsletter in columns (p. 229)

Insert a column break (p. 233)

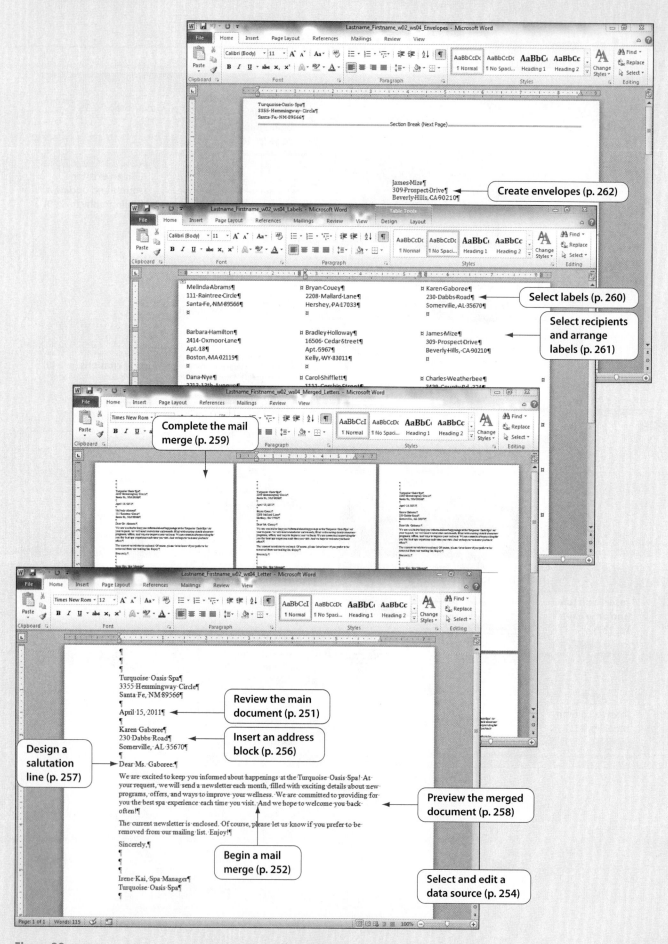

Figure 28   Turquoise Oasis Spa Newsletter and Spa Research Final

Student data files needed:

w02_ws04_Pet_Addresses
w02_ws04_Pet_Spa
w02_ws04_Pet_Text
w02_ws04_Pet
w02_ws04_Pet_Letter

You will save your files as:

Lastname_Firstname_w02_ws04_Pet_Addresses
Lastname_Firstname_w02_ws04_Pet_Spa
Lastname_Firstname_w02_ws04_Pet_Letter
Lastname_Firstname_w02_ws04_Merged_Pet_Letters

Turquoise Oasis Spa Newsletter

Sales & Marketing

The Turquoise Oasis Spa has expanded to include a center for pets—Turquoise Oasis Pet Pals. Guests of the Painted Paradise Resort and Spa often place their pets in the resort's pet lodge, and the spa is capitalizing on that group by offering pet spa services. Pets can enjoy massages, baths, grooming, and pedicures. In addition, Turquoise Oasis Pet Pals offers a full line of pet clothing and grooming accessories in the on-site boutique. The pet lounge affords space for occasional seminars with pet professionals and veterinarians, and provides play space for well-trained dogs. Cats enjoy a dog-free environment for play and grooming services. The new pet center is spotlighted in the summer edition of *Solutions*, the Turquoise Oasis Spa's quarterly newsletter. You will develop the first page of the newsletter in this exercise.

a. Navigate to your data files and right-click **w02_ws04_Pet_Addresses**. Click **Copy**. Navigate to the location where you save your Word projects, right-click the folder (or disk drive), and click **Paste**. Locate the file that you pasted, right-click it, and click **Rename**. Type Lastname_Firstname_w02_ws04_Pet_Addresses. Press Enter.

b. Start **Word**. Open **w02_ws04_Pet_Spa** from your student data files. Save the document as Lastname_Firstname_w02_ws04_Pet_Spa.

c. Click before the first blank paragraph beneath the newsletter banner. If nonprinting characters are not displayed, click the **Home tab**, and then click **Show/Hide** in the Paragraph group.

d. Click the **Page Layout tab**, click **Breaks**, and then click **Continuous**. Click **Columns** in the Page Setup group, and then click **More Columns**. Click **Left** in the Presets group of the Columns dialog box, and then click **OK**. Note that the horizontal ruler displays two uneven columns, with more space in the column on the right.

e. Click the **Home tab**, and then click **Center** in the Paragraph group so text will be centered in the first column. Change paragraph spacing to **0 pt** before and after, and make sure line spacing is 1.15. Click **Bold**, and then change the font size to **18**. Change the font color to **Olive Green, Accent 3, Darker 50%**. Type SUMMER 2013 and press Enter. Type TURQUOISE OASIS SPA and press Enter twice. Change the font size to **14**, and then type the following text, pressing Enter after each line. All text will be centered.

CONTENTS

Turquoise Pet Pals

1

Happenings at the Oasis

2

Desert Splendor Fitness

2

Should I Eat That?

3

Make Time for Children

3

Aromatherapy

4

A Word from the Staff

4

f. Click the **View tab**, and then click **One Page** in the Zoom group. With the entire page displayed, column changes that you make are more evident.

g. Click the **Page Layout tab**, and then click **Breaks**. Click **Column** to insert a column break so the first article appears to the right of the contents.

h. Select all of the text in the first column, beginning with **SUMMER 2013** and ending at the final paragraph mark in the column. Click the **Home tab**, click the **Borders arrow**, and then select **Borders and Shading** from the menu. Confirm that the **Borders tab** is selected. Click **Box** in the Setting area, click the **Color arrow** in the Borders and Shading dialog box, and then click **Black, Text 1**. Click the **Width arrow**, and then select **1 1/2 pt**. Click the **Shading tab**, click the **Fill arrow**, and then select **Light Green** (fifth column under Standard Colors). Click **OK**.

i. Click the **View tab**, and then click **100%**. Press ⌃Ctrl+End, type Turquoise Pet Pals, and press Enter. Click the **Home tab**, and then click **Align Text Left** to begin aligning paragraph text at the left of the column.

j. Click the **Insert tab**, and click the **Object arrow** in the Text group. Click **Text from File**. Navigate to your student data files, and double-click **w02_ws04_Pet_Text**. Text will be placed in the column.

k. Select the **newly added text**. Click the **Home tab**, and then change the font color to **Olive Green, Accent 3, Darker 50%**.

l. Click before the word **Share** in the second paragraph in the right column. Click the **Insert tab**, and then click **Picture** in the Illustrations group. Navigate to your student data files, and then double-click **w02_ws04_Pet**. Click in the **Height box** in the Size group, and change the size to **1.7"**. Click **Wrap Text**, and select **Tight**. Drag the **picture** to the right so it is positioned near the right margin with two lines of the second paragraph appearing above the picture. Other text will wrap around the picture on the left.

m. Click the **File tab**, and then click **Print** to see a print preview.

n. Save and close the document. Keep Word open.

o. Open **w02_ws04_Pet_Letter**. The letter will serve as the main document for a mail merge. It is a cover letter that will accompany the newsletter, inviting spa clients to an open house for Turquoise Oasis Pet Pals.

p. Save the document as Lastname_Firstname_w02_ws04_Pet_Letter.

q. Remove the **Current Date** item, including both brackets but leaving the paragraph mark. The insertion point should be positioned before the second blank paragraph between the inside address and the **Recipient** line. Click the **Insert tab**, click **Date & Time**, and then select the third date format, showing month, day, and year, similar to **April 3, 2013**. Confirm that **Update automatically** is selected, and then click **OK**.

r. Click the **Mailings tab**, click **Start Mail Merge**, and then click **Step by Step Mail Merge Wizard**. Confirm that **Letters** is selected as the document type, and then click **Next: Starting document**.

s. Confirm that **Use the current document** is selected, and then click **Next: Select recipients**.

t. Confirm that **Use an existing list** is selected, and then click **Browse**. Navigate to the location where you are storing your files, and double-click **Lastname_Firstname_w02_ws04_Pet_Addresses**. Click **Sort**. You will sort the letters alphabetically by last name. Click the **Sort by arrow**, select **Last Name**, click **OK**, and then click **OK** again.

u. Click **Next: Write your letter**. Click before the first bracket on the **Recipient** line, and then remove the entire line of text, with the exception of the final paragraph mark. Click **Address block**, click **Joshua Randall Jr.** to select a block style, and then click **OK**.

v. Remove the brackets and the words **Title** and **Last Name** in the line below the address block. Do not remove the colon. The insertion point should be positioned before the colon. Click **More items** in the Mail Merge task pane, select **Title**, and then click **Insert**. Click **Close**, press Spacebar, click **More items**, click **Last Name**, and then click **Insert**. Click **Close**, and then click **Next: Preview your letters**.

w. Click **Next: Complete the merge**, click **Edit individual letters**, and then click **OK**. Note that the resulting merged document includes nine pages, with one letter on each page. Also note that the letters are arranged alphabetically by last name.

x. Save the merged document as Lastname_Firstname_w02_ws04_Merged_Pet_Letters. Save and close all open documents, and then exit Word.

Problem Solve 1

Student data files needed:

w02_ps1_Military

w02_ps1_Labels

You will save your files as:

Lastname_Firstname_w02_ps1_Military

Lastname_Firstname_w02_ps1_Labels

Military Research Report

Research & Development

As a project for your English class, you are required to prepare a research report on the preparedness of young adults for service in the United States Armed Forces. Based on your research, you are to take a position either in support of or in opposition to the recruitment of young adults, ages 18–21. You have developed a very rough draft of the report, in which you make the argument that young adults are not emotionally mature enough to contribute significantly to the military effort. Your report will be submitted to a university committee, which will select several student reports for inclusion in an academic journal. In this exercise, you will edit the report so that it adheres to the MLA writing style. In addition, you will use Mail Merge to prepare mailing labels so that you can mail a copy of your report to each member of the university committee.

a. Start Word. Open **w02_ps1_Military** and then save the document as Lastname_Firstname_w02_ps1_Military. If necessary, click Show/Hide to display nonprinting characters.

b. Press Ctrl+A to select the entire document. Change the font to Times New Roman. Font size should be 12. Click anywhere to deselect the text.

c. With the exception of the heading, select all text in the document. Click the Home tab if necessary, and then click the **Paragraph Dialog Box Launcher**. Change line spacing to double, set paragraph spacing before and after to 0 pt., and select a First line Indent. Click **OK**. Click to deselect the text.

d. Press Ctrl+Home to move to the beginning of the document. Press Enter, press Ctrl+Home again, and left align the new paragraph. Type your first name and last name and press Enter. Type Dr. Peterson and press Enter. Type English 112 and press Enter. Type 19 April 2013. Do not press Enter.

e. Check spelling and grammar, making any necessary corrections. The word premilitary is not misspelled, nor are any researcher names misspelled.

f. Scroll to page 4 and click to place the insertion point just before the period that ends the third sentence in the last paragraph on the page (immediately after the quotation mark). Click the **References tab**, click the **Style arrow** in the Citations & Bibliography group, and then select **MLA Sixth Edition**. Click **Insert Citation**. Click **Add New Source**. Click the **Type of Source arrow**, and then click **Journal Article**. Type the following information but *do not click OK* when you have finished typing.

Author: Friedman, Arthur

Title: Post-Traumatic Stress Disorder and Military Veterans

Journal Name: North American Psychiatric Journal

Year: 2011

Pages: 260–265

g. Click **Show All Bibliography Fields**. Scroll down and type the following information.

Volume: 17

Issue: 1

h. Click **OK**. Because you need to include the page number in the parenthetical citation, click the citation and then click the **citation arrow**. Click **Edit Citation**. Type **265** in the Pages box. Click **OK**.

i. In the same paragraph, click before the period that ends the next sentence (after the quote ending with the words *war veterans*). Insert a **Book** citation. Click in the **Author box** and type Fuller, Martin. Click **Edit** (beside the Author box). The second author's last name is **Sano**, and his first name is **Andrew**. Click **Add**. Click **OK**. Complete the citation with the following information.

Title: Acute and Long-Term Responses to Trauma

Year: 2001

City: Washington D.C.

Publisher: Amber Psychiatric Press

j. Edit the citation to include a page number of 46. In the same paragraph, click before the period at the end of the sentence that ends with *chronic exposure to violence*. Insert a citation to a journal article with the following information. (Remember to click Edit before adding the second author name.)

Author: Brewin, Pamela & Case, Marcella

Title: Analysis of Risk Factors for Post Traumatic Stress Disorder

Journal Name: Journal of Consulting Psychology

Year: 2008

Pages: 270–279

Volume: 29

Issue: 5

k. Edit the citation to include a page number of 275. Click before the period that ends the next sentence and click **Insert Citation**. Click the **Brewin citation**. Click the citation in the paper to select it and then click the **citation arrow**. Click **Edit Citation**. Click to suppress the Author, Year, and Title. Type **275** in the Pages box. Click **OK**.

l. Click the **Insert tab** and then click **Header**. Click **Edit Header**. Type your last name and press Spacebar. Click **Quick Parts**, and then click **Field**. Scroll down and click **Page**. Accept the default settings and then click **OK**. Right align the header. Select the header and change the font to 12 pt Times New Roman. Double-click in the report to close the header.

m. Press Ctrl + End to move to the end of the document. Press Ctrl + Enter to insert a page break. Click the **References tab**, click **Bibliography**, and then click **Insert Bibliography**.

n. Select all text in the bibliography and change line spacing to double. Remove any spacing before or after paragraphs. Change the font to 12 pt Times New Roman. Click before the first citation in the bibliography and press Enter. Click before the new paragraph mark and type **Works Cited**. Center the line. Remove underlining from periodical and journal titles, and format them in italics.

o. Save and close the document.

p. Open a new blank Word document. Click the **Mailings** tab, click **Start Mail Merge**, and then click **Step by Step Mail Merge Wizard**. In the Mail Merge task pane, click **Labels**, and then click **Next: Starting Document**.

q. Click **Label options**. Click the **Label vendors arrow** and select **Avery US Letter**. Select **5162 Easy Peel Address Labels** from the Product number list. Click **OK**. Click **Next: Select recipients**.

r. Make sure **Use an existing list** is selected, and then click **Browse**. Navigate to the location of your student data files and double-click **w02_ws04_Labels**. Click **OK**. Click **Next: Arrange your labels**.

s. Click **Address block**, ensure that Mr. Joshua Randall, Jr. is selected in the format box, and click **OK**. Click **Update all labels**. Click **Next: Preview your labels**. Click **Next: Complete the merge**.

t. Click **Edit individual labels**. Ensure that **All** is selected, and then click **OK**. All labels are merged to a new document. Save the document as **Lastname_Firstname_w02_ps1_ Labels**. Close the document.

u. Close the remaining open document without saving.

Additional Workshop Cases are available on the companion website and in the instructor resources.

MODULE CAPSTONE

More Practice 1

Student data files needed:

w02_mp_Children

w02_mp_Movies

w02_mp_Play

You will save your file as:

Lastname_Firstname_w02_mp_Children

Paradise Kids

Sales & Marketing

Painted Paradise Resort and Spa is a favorite destination for many families and business travelers. Over half of those enjoying the resort's facilities are families, many with children under the age of 13. So parents can enjoy some leisure time apart from the children, Painted Paradise offers activities just for children in an on-site center staffed with resort employees. Children enjoy themed afternoons, movies, crafts, and outdoor activities in the Paradise Kids Resort. A one-page flyer, listing children's activities for each week, is placed in each guest room. You will prepare the flyer for this week, in a two-column style, including graphics and WordArt. Activities will be summarized in a table within the flyer.

a. Open **w02_mp_Children**, and then save the document as Lastname_Firstname_w02_mp_Children. If nonprinting characters are not shown, click the **Home tab**, and then click **Show/Hide**.

b. Press Ctrl+End, change line spacing to **1.0**, and then make sure paragraph spacing after is **0 pt**. Change the font to **Times New Roman**. Set a right tab stop at **6"**. Type September 13, 2013 and press Tab. Type A publication of Painted Paradise Resort and Spa and press Enter. Press Tab, type 3355 Hemmingway Circle, press Space four times, type Santa Fe, NM 89566, and then press Enter. Press Tab, and then type (444)555-4892. Press Enter twice.

c. Change paragraph Spacing After to **12 pt**. Paragraph Spacing Before should be **0 pt**.

d. Click the **Page Layout tab**, click **Breaks**, and then click **Continuous**. Click **Columns**, and then click **Two** to create two columns.

e. Change the alignment to **Center**, and then change the text color to **Dark Blue, Text 2, Darker 50%**. Change the font size to **14 pt**, select **Bold**, and then type Paradise Kids Membership.

f. Create a new style based on the text typed in Step e, called **Topic Heading**, and then press Enter.

g. Select **left alignment** and change the font color to **Black, Text 1** (first row, second column, under Theme Colors). Change font size to **12**. Toggle off the bold setting.

h. Create a new style based on the existing text called Topic Text. Close the Styles pane.

i. Type We invite your child to be a Paradise Kid! As you enjoy the resort, why not make sure your child does the same? The Paradise Kids Club is designed for children aged 4 to 14, offering fantastic indoor and outdoor activities. Children enjoy hiking around the resort property, special movie afternoons, themed parties, and plenty of creative projects. To make sure you don't miss a minute of fun, pick up an application form from the front desk or the Pool Towel Hut.

j. Press Enter, and then type Upon registration, you will receive.

k. Press ⎡Enter⎤. Select a hollow round bullet, and click **Decrease Indent**. Type Paradise backpack and then press ⎡Enter⎤. Type the following items, pressing ⎡Enter⎤ after each bulleted item.

T-shirt

Paradise name tag

Paradise key ring or mug

l. Click **Bullets** to turn off bullets. Select the **first three bulleted items** (making sure not to select the final bulleted item) and change the paragraph Spacing After to **0 pt**. Press ⎡Ctrl⎤+⎡End⎤.

m. Type Participating families also receive 10% off a dinner at Indigo 5. The fun doesn't stop there, though! Children will receive their own Paradise Kids Newsletter with cool news from the crew at Painted Paradise Resort and Spa. With plenty of great surprises, Paradise Kids is the place to be!

n. Press ⎡Enter⎤, click **Topic Heading** in the Styles group, and then type Babysitting Services. Press ⎡Enter⎤, and then click **Topic Text** in the Styles group. Type Painted Paradise offers a babysitting service so parents can enjoy time to themselves. All of our female babysitters are Painted Paradise staff, many who have been with the resort for over 15 years and have a long history of caring for children. The service is free to our guests for the first two hours. After that time, $15 per hour will be added to the room charge.

o. Press ⎡Enter⎤, click the **View tab**, and then click **One Page** to view the display of the newsletter as one page. Click the **Home tab**, click **Topic Heading** in the Styles group, and then type Check Out the September Specials. Press ⎡Enter⎤, and then insert a table with two columns and six rows.

p. Click the **View tab** and then click **100%**. Click the **Layout Selector** in the top-left corner of the table to select the entire table. Click the **Home tab** and then click **Normal** in the Styles group. Click in the **first cell** of the table, and then complete the table as shown here, pressing ⎡Tab⎤ between each entry.

9/3	Water slide
9/7	Star Wars movie time
9/12	Native American art
9/17	Boogie board race
9/22	Guitar Hero competition
9/28	Nature and mountain hike

q. Select the **first table row**, insert a row above, click in the **first cell** of the new row, and then type All events are scheduled from 1:00–3:00.

r. Select the **first row**, and then click **Merge Cells** in the Merge group on the Layout tab. Bold the first row, and then apply a table style of **Light Shading - Accent 5**. Press ⎡Ctrl⎤+⎡End⎤.

s. Press ⎡Enter⎤. Type See You at the Movies and apply Topic Heading style. Press ⎡Enter⎤. Insert text from the file **w02_mp_Movies**. Select the inserted text, and then apply the **Topic Text** style.

t. Press ⎡Ctrl⎤+⎡End⎤. Insert the picture **w02_mp_Play** from your student data files. Change text wrapping to **Square**. Change the picture height to **1.5**. Drag the picture to position it so that it is immediately beneath the Paradise Kids Membership heading and aligned with the left side of the first column.

u. Review the newsletter to make sure that each column ends attractively. Insert a column break, if necessary, to make sure the second column begins with the title **Babysitting Services**.

v. Save the document, and then exit Word.

Problem Solve 1

Homework 1

Student data files needed:

w02_ps1_Coffee
w02_ps1_Coffee_Shop

You will save your files as:

Lastname_Firstname_w02_ps1_Coffee
Lastname_Firstname_w02_ps1_Coffee_Shop
Lastname_Firstname_w02_ps1_Coffee_Shop_Merged

Terra Cotta Brew Coffee Klatch

Sales &
Marketing

Paul Medina, the manager of the Terra Cotta Brew Coffee Shop at Painted Paradise Resort, is beginning a weekly coffee klatch and book club for hotel guests and local residents. The coffee shop has recently expanded its line of gourmet and specialty coffees, and he sees the coffee klatch as a way to introduce the new line and encourage sales. Terra Cotta Brew is located in the hotel lobby, which is an excellent location for walk-through traffic and visibility for the weekly gathering. To introduce the coffee klatch, he has asked you to edit and merge a letter that he has drafted. You already have a mailing list, so you will simply merge the letter with the addresses. He has also asked you to design a table that can be included with the letter, providing details on the new line of coffee carried by Terra Cotta Brew. You will include SmartArt, as well, to depict coffee klatch activity.

a. Navigate to your student data files and right-click **w02_ps1_Coffee**. Click **Copy**. Navigate to the location where you are storing your files, right-click the folder (or disk drive), and click **Paste**. Locate the file that you pasted, right-click it, and click **Rename**. Type Lastname_Firstname_w02_ps1_Coffee. Press Enter.

b. Start **Word**. Open **w02_ps1_Coffee_Shop**, and then save the document as Lastname_Firstname_w02_ps1_Coffee_Shop. Click **Show/Hide** to display nonprinting characters, if they are not already displayed. Click **View Ruler** to display the ruler if it is not already displayed.

c. Click after the second paragraph in the body of the letter, and then press Enter. Place a left tab stop at **1"** on the horizontal ruler, and then set a right tab stop at **5"**.

d. Modify the 5" tab to include a dot leader.

e. Press Tab, and then type Blue Thunder Blend. Press Tab, and then type Smoky, sweet tones. Press Enter.

f. Continue to tab between entries, and type the following.

Sumatra Roast	Creamy tropical and vanilla
Costa Rica Cerro	Citrus and fruit notes
Colombian Organic	Tangy honey-orange

g. Reposition the left tab for the tabbed lines to 1/2".

h. Select the words **fine coffee** in the last paragraph. Drag the selection to the left of the words **great conversation**. Revise the sentence to Enjoy fine coffee and great conversation at the Terra Cotta Brew Coffee Klatch.

i. Click the **Mailings tab**, and then begin a mail merge process to create letters. Indicate that you want to use the current document and that you will use an existing list for addresses.

j. Browse to the location where you are saving your files, and then select **Lastname_Firstname_w02_ps1_Coffee** as the data source. Sort the recipients by last name in ascending order alphabetically.

k. Select the Recipient area in the letter, and then click Address Block. Select **Joshua Randall Jr.** as the format. Include the title and last name in the salutation. Preview your letters.

l. Complete the merge. Select **Edit individual letters**, confirm that **All** is selected, and then click **OK**.

m. Confirm that five letters are included in the merged document, each addressed to a different recipient. Save the document as Lastname_Firstname_w02_ps1_Coffee_Shop_Merged.

n. Save and close any open documents, and then exit Word.

Problem Solve 2

Student data file needed:

w02_ps2_Teen

You will save your file as:

Lastname_Firstname_w02_ps2_Teen

Homework 2

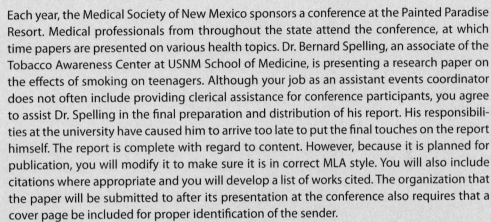

Research & Development

Teens and Smoking

Each year, the Medical Society of New Mexico sponsors a conference at the Painted Paradise Resort. Medical professionals from throughout the state attend the conference, at which time papers are presented on various health topics. Dr. Bernard Spelling, an associate of the Tobacco Awareness Center at USNM School of Medicine, is presenting a research paper on the effects of smoking on teenagers. Although your job as an assistant events coordinator does not often include providing clerical assistance for conference participants, you agree to assist Dr. Spelling in the final preparation and distribution of his report. His responsibilities at the university have caused him to arrive too late to put the final touches on the report himself. The report is complete with regard to content. However, because it is planned for publication, you will modify it to make sure it is in correct MLA style. You will also include citations where appropriate and you will develop a list of works cited. The organization that the paper will be submitted to after its presentation at the conference also requires that a cover page be included for proper identification of the sender.

a. Start **Word**. Open **w02_ps2_Teen**, and then save it as Lastname_Firstname_w02_ps2_Teen. Click **Show/Hide** to display nonprinting characters, if they are not already displayed.

b. Select all of the **document text**, and then change the font to **12 pt Times New Roman**. With the text still selected, double-space the document. Center and bold the first two lines.

c. Scroll through the document, and center the subheadings **The Link Between Smoking and Drinking**, **The Link Between Smoking and Illegal Drugs**, **The Link Between Smoking and Mental Health Disorders**, and **Recommended Changes**.

d. Select all paragraphs within the first section under the major heading, and then apply a first line indent. Similarly, apply a first line indent to other body paragraphs with the exception of the last four paragraphs in the **The Link Between Smoking and Mental Health Disorders** section.

e. Using a square filled bullet, format the last four paragraphs in the **The Link Between Smoking and Mental Health Disorders** section. Decrease the indent until the bullets are at the left margin.

f. Insert a header with Dr. Spelling's last name and the page number, aligned at the right margin. Use the page number default settings.

g. Press Ctrl+Home and press Enter. Press Ctrl + Home again. Type the following three lines of text at the top of page, double-spaced and aligned left. The text should not be bold. Do not type the words Current Date. Instead, insert the current date in the format "August 16, 2013," making sure that the date does not update automatically.

Bernard Spelling, M.D.

Teen Health Medical News

Current Date

h. Click after the word **illness** and before the **period** in the second sentence of the second body paragraph. Click the **References tab**, make sure the style is MLA Sixth Edition, and then add the following journal article citation:

Corporate Author	The National Center on Addiction and Substance Abuse
Title	Teens and Smoking—Identifying the Risks
Journal Name	Cranston Medical School Journal
Year	2012
Pages	50–53

i. Click after the **last sentence** in the second paragraph (after the word Recovery) but before the **period**, and insert the following website citation.

Name of Web Page	Bradford Center
Year	2013
Month	June
Day	18
Year Accessed	2013
Month Accessed	July
Day Accessed	10
URL	http://www.bradfordrecovery.com

j. Click after the word **disorders** and before the **period** at the end of the second sentence in the third paragraph. Insert the following periodical article citation.

Author	Stephenson, Arthur
Title	Nicotine: Hidden Dangers
Periodical Title	ASA Journal
Year	2011
Month	February
Day	21
Pages	19–20

k. In the same paragraph, click after the last sentence after the word **Abuse** but before the **period**. Click **Insert Citation**, and then select the **The National Center on Addiction and Substance Abuse** source. You will edit the citation, however, because there is no need to repeat the center's name in the citation. The page number will be sufficient. Click the **new citation**, and then click the **arrow** on the right. Click **Edit Citation**; suppress the Author, Year, and Title; and make the page number **52**.

l. Click after the word **alcohol** but before the **period** in the third sentence of the first paragraph in the section, **The Link Between Smoking and Drinking**. Insert the following journal article citation.

Corporate Author	Center for Disease Identification and Control
Title	Why Do Smoking Teens Also Drink?
Journal Name	Teen Health Digest
Year	2012
Pages	112–116

m. Click after the first occurrence of the word **use** in the first sentence of the first paragraph in the section, **The Link Between Smoking and Illegal Drugs**. Click **Insert Citation**, and then click **Center for Disease Identification and Control** to insert a predefined source.

n. Click after the word **disorders** and before the **period** in the first sentence of the first paragraph in the section, **The Link Between Smoking and Mental Health Disorders**. Insert the following periodical citation:

Corporate Author	Parents Against Teen Smoking
Title	Dangers of Teen Smoking
Periodical Title	Medical Research News
Year	2013
Month	March
Day	2

o. Click to select the newly inserted parenthetical citation. Because the name of the organization is already stated in the sentence, edit the citation to indicate page 28. Suppress Author, Year, and Title.

p. Cut the last paragraph of the document, and then paste it immediately underneath the **Recommended Changes** heading.

q. Press Ctrl + End, add a new page at the end of the document, and then insert a works cited page. Change the font to 12 pt Times New Roman and center the title Works Cited. It should not be bold. Double-space the works cited page and remove any paragraph spacing after.

r. Click the **Insert tab**, and then in the Pages group, click **Cover Page**. Click **Conservative**, and then change the Company Name to STANFORD RECOVERY CENTER. The document title is Smoking and Teens and the subtitle is Structural, Chemical, and Health Effects. List Dr. Bernard Spelling as the author and include the current date.

s. Select the table shown at the bottom of the cover page. Right-click the selected table, and then click **Delete Table**.

t. Save and close the document, and then exit Word.

Problem Solve 3

Sales & Marketing

Student data files needed:
w02_ps3_Cooking
w02_ps3_Chef

You will save your file as:
Lastname_Firstname_w02_ps3_Cooking

Indigo 5 Cooking School

The Indigo 5 Cooking School is offered every Tuesday afternoon in the Indigo 5 kitchen. The cooking school is very popular with resort guests as well as local residents—so much so that reservations far in advance are required. Cooking school students don aprons and learn to prepare for anything from elegant dinners to informal luncheons. Recipes from the cooking school are included on the Indigo 5 website as well as the in-house cookbook sold at the resort's Painted Treasures Gift Shop. To promote the cooking school and to encourage advance reservation, you will prepare a mailing to past guests and a selected number of local residents. The one-page flyer will include an introduction to the cooking school, registration information, and a sample recipe suitable for home use.

a. Start **Word**. Open **w02_ps3_Cooking** from your student data files, and then save the document as Lastname_Firstname_w02_ps3_Cooking. Show nonprinting characters. Show the ruler if it is not already displayed.

b. Press Ctrl+Home, press Enter, and then press Ctrl+Home again. Insert a WordArt object as **Gradient Fill - Orange, Accent 6, Inner Shadow** (row 4, column 2). Type Indigo 5 Cooking School to replace the title text.

c. Select the WordArt text. Select **Tan, Background 2, Darker 50%** (row 4, column 3) as WordArt Text Fill. Center the WordArt object. Select **Top and Bottom** text wrapping. Click **Text Effects** in the WordArt Styles group, and then point to **Transform**. Select **Deflate** (row 6, column 2 under Wrap).

d. Deselect the WordArt object. Change the page color to **Tan, Background 2** (row 1, column 3), click before the blank paragraph under the WordArt object, and then add a bottom border.

e. Select the first three paragraphs under the bottom border beginning with **You are invited** and ending with **Painted Paradise Resort and Spa**. Change the font size to **16**, and then center the selected paragraphs. Select and bold the words **Cooking School** in the first line of the centered text.

f. Select and center the remaining paragraphs, and then change the font size to **14**. Bold the telephone number. Press [Ctrl]+[End], and then press [Enter]. Click before the first blank paragraph under the contact information, apply a bottom border, and then press [Ctrl]+[End].

g. Select center alignment, and then change the font size to **14**. Type Bring a bit of Indigo 5 home with this award-winning recipe! Insert a continuous section break.

h. Click **Columns**, and then click **Two**. Click the **Home tab**, and then click **Align Text Left**. Type Santa Fe Pasta Salad. Press [Enter]. Change line spacing to **1**, and then remove all paragraph spacing. Change the font size to **11**. Type the following ingredients, pressing [Enter] after each.

1 pound uncooked tri-color pasta

1 cup broccoli florets

1 cup cauliflowerets

1/3 cup grated carrot

6 ounces black olives

2 tablespoons chopped garlic

2 cups mayonnaise

1/3 cup ranch salad dressing

Salt and white pepper to taste

i. Bold the recipe title. Select the last ingredient **Salt and white pepper to taste** and the empty paragraph under the last ingredient, and then change the paragraph spacing after to **6 pt**. Click before the paragraph mark following the last ingredient, and then press [Enter]. Type the following, pressing [Enter] only at the end of each of the three paragraphs.

Cook the pasta al dente using the package directions; rinse with cold water and drain.

Combine the pasta with the broccoli, cauliflower, carrot, olives, and garlic in a large bowl.

Add the mayonnaise and salad dressing. Season with salt and white pepper.

j. Insert the **w02_ps3_Chef** picture. Change text wrapping to **Square**. Change the picture height to **1.5"**. Drag the picture to position it at the top of the second column, aligned at the right margin. The picture should appear just beneath the heading **Bring a bit of Indigo 5 home with this award-winning recipe!**

k. Click at the end of the last ingredient **Salt and white pepper to taste**. Because the columns are not even, insert a column break. Delete one of the extra paragraph marks in the second column, just above the recipe description.

l. If necessary, position the clip art to once again appear at the top right of the second column. View the document on one page. Return the page to **100%**.

m. Insert a text box at approximately 7.5" on the vertical ruler. Change the width of the text box to **5"** and the height to **1"**. Type Don't miss the opportunity to learn from some of the best chefs in the country! Press Enter . Type Indigo 5 looks forward to welcoming you to our kitchen!

n. With all text in the text box selected, click **Align Text** in the Text group, and then click **Middle**. Click Position in the Arrange group and select Position in Bottom Center with Square Text Wrapping (last row, second column). Click the **Home tab**, and then click **Center**. Bold the text, and change the font size to **12**.

o. Click the **Format tab**, and then change Shape Fill to **Orange, Accent 6, Lighter 40%** (row 4, last column). Change Text Fill to **White, Background 1, Darker 50%** (row 6, column 1).

p. Click **Shape Effects** in the Shape Styles group, and then point to **Shadow**. Click **Offset Bottom** under Outer.

q. Deselect the text box.

r. Preview the page as it will appear when printed.

s. Save and close the document, and then exit Word.

Perform 1: Perform in Your Life

Student data file needed:

New, blank Word document

You will save your files as:

Lastname_Firstname_w02_pf1_Resume
Lastname_Firstname_w02_pf1_Cover
Lastname_Firstname_w02_pf1_Companies
Lastname_Firstname_w02_pf1_Merged_Cover
Lastname_Firstname_w02_pf1_Envelopes

Resume and Cover Letter

Sales & Marketing

As you prepare to seek employment, you are aware of the importance of an attractive resume and cover letter. Websites such as www.monster.com provide resume and cover letter tips, and Microsoft provides templates for both documents at http://office.microsoft.com. Using a resume template, you will prepare your resume. You will also prepare a cover letter, providing potential employers with information on your employment goals. Finally, you will create a data source, with addresses of employers, so you can personalize the cover letter.

a. Start **Word**. Click **File**, and then click **New**. Scroll through the Office.com templates, and then click **Resumes and CVs**. Review the resume categories, and then download an appropriate resume template. Save the resume as Lastname_Firstname_w02_pf1_ Resume. Be sure to save it as a document file, not as a template. (Hint: Pay close attention to the Save as type area when saving the document.)

b. Modify the resume document to include information specific to your educational and professional preparation. Enhance the resume in any way you like, keeping in mind the need to present a concise, professional document. Save and close the document.

c. Click **File**, and then click **New**. Scroll through the Office.com templates, and then click **Letters.** Click **Cover Letters**. Review the cover letter templates, identifying one that you can modify to serve as a cover letter for your resume. Download the file and save the document as Lastname_Firstname_w02_pf1_Cover.

d. Personalize the cover letter to include information specific to your job search. For example, you may want to include a sentence in the cover letter similar to "This position is of great interest to me because _____." Because the letter will be the basis for a mail merge document, include a placeholder for the address block and for the salutation. Save the document.

e. Begin a mail merge, using the mail merge wizard. The merge is to produce letters, based on a list of addresses that you will type. In Step 3 of the mail merge wizard, select **Type a new list**. Then click **Create**. Type at least 8 address records using fictional addresses, if you like. Click **OK** when the list is complete. Save as Lastname_Firstname_w02_pf1_Companies.

f. Complete the mail merge, based on the address list, including an AddressBlock and an appropriate salutation, so each letter is individualized. Save the document as Lastname_Firstname_w02_pf1_Merged_Cover.

g. Use mail merge to create envelopes for the employers to whom you are sending the cover letter. Save the document as Lastname_Firstname_w02_pf1_Envelopes. Exit Word.

Perform 2: Perform in Your Career

Student data file needed:

w02_pf2_Counselors

You will save your files as:

Lastname_Firstname_w02_pf2_Counselors

Lastname_Firstname_w02_pf2_NSID

Lastname_Firstname_w02_pf2_NSID_Merged

NSID Scholarships

Sales & Marketing

You are employed as the marketing director for the National Society of Interior Designers (NSID). Your job responsibilities include preparing marketing and educational material to promote the society and to encourage new membership. At one time, becoming an interior designer involved little more than some practical experience and artistic talent. However, the industry has now evolved to include various specialties such as eco-friendly interior design solutions and revitalizing older homes with period design. In response, colleges and universities have redesigned curricula to provide focused training in interior design. NSID has partnered with the Interior Design Educators Group and the National Association of Family and Consumer Sciences to provide scholarship opportunities for interior design students. You will prepare a letter to be sent to high school guidance counselors outlining the various scholarship programs provided by NSID. You will then create a mail merge document, combining addresses from a data source with the letter.

a. Copy **w02_pf2_Counselors** from the student data files to the location where you are saving your files, renaming it Lastname_Firstname_w02_pf2_Counselors. Start **Word** and begin a new document. Save the document as Lastname_Firstname_w02_pf2_NSID. The font should be **11 pt Times New Roman**. In block letter style, type your address as shown here (replacing Firstname and Lastname with your first and last names).

Firstname Lastname, Marketing Coordinator

National Society of Interior Designers

134 Greenfield Street

Fort Worth, TX 76102

b. Insert the current date, so it is updated automatically. You should not simply type the date, but insert it using the Insert tab. The format is Month Day, Year (for example, September 2, 2013).

c. Leave space for a mailing address that will be inserted in the mail merge process. The salutation should include the word Dear, with space left for a recipient's name to be placed during the mail merge process.

d. Compose a letter to guidance counselors encouraging them to inform students of the exciting opportunities in interior design afforded by the National Society of Interior Designers. Remind them that the field of interior design has expanded to include even more specialties, such as "green" design and antique architectural design. Specific scholarships, sponsoring organizations, and award amounts are given next. You should note in your letter that additional information regarding specific requirements for each scholarship is available through the NSID website www.NSIDDesign.com/careers or at (205)555-0088. List the scholarships in the form of a table.

Scholarship	Sponsor(s)	Award
NDFA Scholarship	National Design and Furnishings Association	$1500/semester
Metropolis Design	In Sync Design Professionals	$1500/semester plus all books
Student Design Award Competitions	National Society of Interior Designers	$2000/semester

e. Apply an attractive design style to the scholarship table, or create your own, using shading and bordering. Center the entries in the first row. Insert a row above the first row, merge all cells, and center the text **Interior Design Scholarships**. Resize columns if necessary to provide the best readability and use of space.

f. Design a SmartArt diagram (perhaps a process chart) in the letter to graphically indicate the progression to a career in interior design. Include the following steps, in sequence, in the SmartArt diagram.

Practice your skills at home

Seek an industry contact to shadow

Explore scholarships

Network and market yourself

g. End the letter with a closing paragraph and a complimentary close.

h. Begin the mail merge wizard, and then select **Letters**. You will merge the letter with an existing data source called Lastname_Firstname_w02_pf2_Counselors, that you copied and renamed in Step a (saved with your Word projects).

i. Include first name, last name, and address lines in the merged recipient information. The salutation should include the word Dear followed by a title and last name.

j. The letters should be sorted alphabetically by last name (in ascending order).

k. Save the merged document as Lastname_Firstname_w02_pf2_NSID_Merged. Close the document. Save Lastname_Firstname_w02_pf2_NSID and then exit Word.

Perform 3: Perform in Your Career

Student data file needed:

w02_pf3_Digitalconnection

You will save your file as:

Lastname_Firstname_w02_pf3_Digitalconnection

Kids and Nature—Can They Stay Connected?

Research & Development

You are the managing director of the Copler National Wildlife Refuge, located in Willowee, Florida. The Wildlife Refuge occupies 26,400 acres of wetlands and dry upland habitat. The refuge was created in 1989 under the Endangered Species Act specifically to protect the Florida panther and other endangered plant and animal life indigenous to Florida. The Florida panther is the only cougar species found east of the Mississippi River. The refuge sponsors educational programs and school field trips in an effort to introduce children to the native habitat of Florida and to encourage an appreciation for nature and a desire to conserve our natural resources. For many children, the refuge is a unique opportunity to enjoy the outdoors in a natural setting.

Having been employed at the refuge for a number of years, you have noticed a shift in the interest, attention span, and expectations of newer visitors. Children appear to be more easily distracted and bored with static displays. They crave active exhibits in which they can interact and see results. Recently, you received a call for proposals from the National Science Foundation, which is offering a monetary grant for innovative student learning programs in nature centers. You wonder how you can design a learning program that is built around the learning style of "millennials," those born between 1977 and 1998. To better understand that generation, you have asked your assistant to draft a report on millennials, which you will edit and modify. Because you might be able to include part or all of the report in the NSF proposal, you will make sure that it meets NSF guidelines (as described in the call for proposals that you received) and that all sources are properly cited.

a. Start **Word**, and then open **w02_pf3_Digitalconnection** from your student data files. The rough draft of a research paper needs to be finalized. Save the document as Lastname_Firstname_w02_pf3_Digitalconnection.

b. Select an attractive font for the document. **The Millennial Generation: Learning Styles** is the major heading, with subheadings of **Social and Workplace Expectations**, **Teaching and Mentoring Challenges**, and **General Observations**. Apply appropriate styles to all headings and subheadings.

c. Insert a page number footer at the bottom center of all pages. Center each heading and subheading.

d. Use Find and Replace to find all occurrences of **millennials** and replace it with Millennials. The word **Millennials** is appropriate when referring to the specific generation. It is correctly spelled with two l's and two n's. You should match the case in your search and stop at all occurrences to determine whether action should be taken. Therefore, you will not use Replace All, but rather a combination of **Find Next** and **Replace**. Spell check the document, making any necessary corrections, and ignoring others. The word **key** is used correctly in the sentence in which it is located.

e. Bullet the last four paragraphs of the document under **General Observations**, using a bullet style of your choice. The bulleted items should begin at the left margin.

f. Double-space the entire document, indent each body paragraph with the exception of bulleted items by **1/2"**, and apply appropriate paragraph spacing.

g. Create a citation in MLA style for the statistic given in the last sentence of the second paragraph under **Social and Workplace Expectations**. The source is a book titled Generational Learning Styles by Andrew Keller. It is published by Brennan Publishers located in Boston. The publish date is 2012.

h. Insert a citation following the second sentence of the report. The source is a journal article, by Sarah Belknap titled What Now? How to Bridge the Digital Divide. It is located in the Teaching and Learning Digest on page 15. The journal year is 2013.

i. You mistakenly listed the year for the book citation as 2012. It is actually 2011. Edit the source to make the correction. You will update both the master list and the current document.

j. Check each page to make sure a page does not begin or end awkwardly (perhaps with a heading or only one line of a paragraph displayed). Correct any problems identified.

k. Insert a works cited page at the end of the document, and center the page heading. Double-space the works cited page.

l. Save and close the document. Exit Word.

Student data files needed:

w02_pf4_Fall

w02_pf4_Leaves

You will save your file as:

Lastname_Firstname_w02_pf4_Fall

Gibson Elementary Fall Festival

Sales & Marketing

As a new fourth grade teacher at Gibson Elementary, you are in charge of organizing the school's fall festival. Your homeroom parent, the parent who has volunteered to help with school functions throughout the year, has begun the process of creating a flyer to send home with school children. The flyer provides details on the festival. Because your homeroom parent is unable to complete the flyer, you will edit and modify it. You want to build the flyer around a fall color scheme, and you plan to include graphics to make it fun and eye appealing. At this point, the document is only in the beginning phase. There is much to be done.

a. Start **Word**, and then open **w02_pf4_Fall**. Save the document as Lastname_Firstname_ w02_pf4_Fall.

b. Review the document. Although it is a beginning, you know that it can be much more attractive with color-coordinated elements and some formatting. In addition, you need to include the schedule of events, which is currently missing on the document.

c. Modify the WordArt so it is formatted in a color that coordinates with the fall theme. You can select a different style, include a shape color, and modify the text effects, as you like.

d. Apply a page color and border, if those items fit in to your overall scheme.

e. Add a shape to the SmartArt diagram. The shape should be added under (or after) the last shape. It should be titled Food. Then add a couple of general food categories on the right.

f. Include at least one fall-related photograph or clip art. You will find a photograph in your student data files that you can use, named **w02_pf4_ Leaves**. Wrap text appropriately, and then position the graphic(s) within the flyer. Format the picture, if you like, with a picture style or picture effect.

g. The schedule of activities follows. Using either tabs or a table, arrange the schedule of activities underneath the heading, Schedule of Events. If using a table, you might choose to include the heading within the table itself, removing it from its current location.

Games	Noon–3:00
Scarecrow making	2:00
Pumpkin painting	12:30
Lisa Delray concert	1:30
Face painting	1:00–2:30
Channel Creek Band concert	1:30
Art contest awards	2:45

h. Format the document to make it as attractive as possible. Save and close the document. Exit Word.

Objectives

Understanding and Manipulating Microsoft Excel 2010

PREPARE CASE

Red Bluff Golf Club Golf Cart Purchase Analysis

Finance & Accounting

The Red Bluff Golf Course Pro Shop makes golf carts available to its members for a fee. Recently, the resort has been running out of carts. The time has come for the club to add more golf carts to its fleet of 10. Club manager, Barry Cheney, wants to use Microsoft Excel to analyze the purchase of golf carts by brand, model, price, and financing parameters.

Laura Gangi Pond / Shutterstock.com

Student data file needed for this workshop:

 e01_ws01_Cart_Analysis

You will save your file as:

 Lastname_Firstname_e01_ws01_Cart_Analysis

Excel Worksheets—What If Data and Information Could Speak?

Data play an integral part in supporting businesses. Without data, businesses are not able to determine their effectiveness in the market, let alone their profit or loss performance. In addition, as businesses grow or change, the types of data collected by a particular business is one of the few things that remain relatively static over time. Jobs change, products change, and businesses grow or evolve into different organizations (or even lines of business) based on customer and market demands. However, the data gathered and analyzed is constant. That is, much of the same information is required about customers, vendors, products, services, materials, transactions, and so on. The values may change, but the type of information remains the same.

The problem is that in all that data, there is so much information to decipher. Thus, the data requires processing—categorization, counting, averaging, summarization, statistical analysis, and formatting for effective communication—to reveal information that the data cannot tell you itself. With an application like Excel, it is possible to structure data and to process it in a manner that creates information for decision-making purposes. With the help of Excel, you give the data a voice, a medium through which underlying trends, calculated values, predictions, decision recommendations, and other information can be revealed.

In this section, you will be introduced to spreadsheets, otherwise called **worksheets**. You will learn to create worksheets and to manipulate rows and columns, as well as to navigate in and among worksheets within a workbook. You will learn how to enter data—text, numbers, dates, and times—into a worksheet, and how to use powerful analysis features that enable you to work intelligently in the worksheet environment.

Understand Spreadsheet Terminology and Components

A **spreadsheet** is a powerful computer program with a user interface that is a grid of **rows** and **columns**. The intersection of each row and column is called a **cell**. Cells can contain text, numbers, formulas, or functions. A **formula** is an equation that produces a result and may contain numbers, operators, text, and/or functions. A **function** is a built-in program that performs a task such as SUM or AVERAGE. Both formulas and functions must always start with the equal sign (=).

From balancing an accounting ledger to creating a financial report, many business documents are Excel spreadsheets. Excel spreadsheets are designed to support analyzing business data, representing data through charts, and modeling real-world situations.

Spreadsheets are also commonly used to perform **what-if analysis**. In what-if analysis, you change values in spreadsheet cells to investigate the effects on calculated values of interest.

Spreadsheets are used for much more than what-if analysis, however. A spreadsheet can be used as a basic collection of data where each row is a **record** and each column is a **field** in the record. Spreadsheets can be built to act as a simple accounting system. Businesses often use spreadsheets to analyze complex financial statements and information. Excel has built-in statistical analysis capabilities. Excel can calculate statistical values such as mean, variance, and standard deviation. Excel can even be used for advanced statistical models such as forecasting and regression analysis. Spreadsheet applications *excel* at calculations of most any kind.

Starting Excel

Starting Microsoft Excel 2010 can be accomplished in several ways. In this section, you will learn how to start Excel from the Start menu.

myitlab
Workshop 1 Training

To Start Excel Using the Start Menu

a. Click the **Start** button 🔵.

b. From the Start menu, locate and then click **Microsoft Excel 2010**.

c. If you do not see Microsoft Excel 2010 on the Start menu, click **All Programs**, click **Microsoft Office**, and then click **Microsoft Excel 2010**.

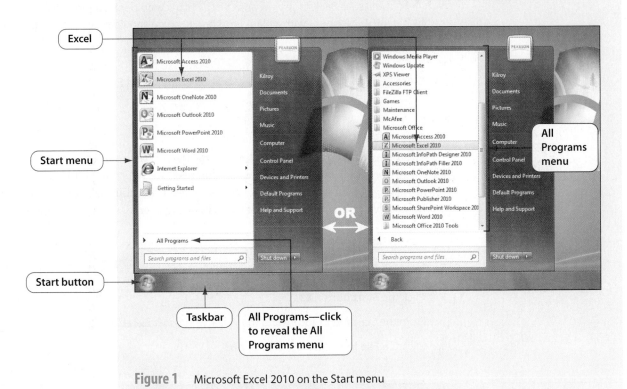

Figure 1   Microsoft Excel 2010 on the Start menu

CONSIDER THIS | **Excel Can Store a Vast Amount of Data**

There are 1,048,576 rows × 16,384 columns = 17,179,869,184 cells in an Excel 2010 worksheet. With so much capacity, some are tempted to use Excel as a database. What other Office application would be better for storing vast amounts of data?

What Is a Workbook?

A **workbook** is a file that contains at least one worksheet. In Microsoft Excel, workbooks have a file extension of .xlsx. By default a new, blank workbook contains three worksheets, identified by tabs at the bottom of the Excel window titled Sheet1, Sheet2, and Sheet3. The active worksheet is Sheet1 by default and is denoted by a white tab with bold letters. Worksheets that are not active are denoted by gray tabs with normal letters. The number of worksheets that can be contained in a workbook is a function of the amount of available memory. The next exercise will show you how to create a blank workbook.

To Create a Blank Workbook

a. Click the **File tab** to enter Backstage view.

b. Click **New** on the menu on the left. Available Templates will appear to the right of the menu. Blank workbook is the default and is shown in the workbook preview pane.

c. Double-click **Blank workbook**. Alternatively, you can click **Create**.
   You will leave Backstage view and see the blank workbook. As previously mentioned, by default, Excel opens with a blank workbook, so you should now have two blank workbooks opened.

d. You are not going to need these two workbooks, so there is no need to save them. Click **Close** [X] two times to close both workbooks and to exit Excel.

Opening a Workbook

As with many tasks in the Windows operating system, there are a number of ways to open an Excel workbook. For the purposes of this text, we will focus on how workbooks are opened using the Ribbon menu, and dialog boxes in Excel itself. Now you will open the workbook that you will use for all of the remaining exercises in this workshop.

To Open an Existing Workbook

a. Click the **Start** button.

b. From the Start menu, locate and then click **Microsoft Excel 2010**.

c. Click the **File tab**, and then click **Open**.

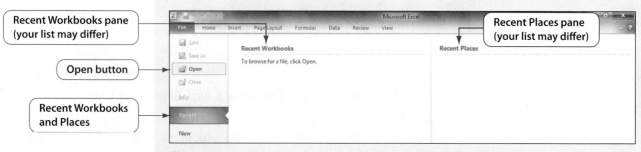

Recent Workbooks pane (your list may differ)

Open button

Recent Workbooks and Places

Recent Places pane (your list may differ)

Figure 2 Open an existing workbook in Backstage view

SIDE NOTE
Recent Workbooks vs. Recent Places

Figure 2 shows the Recent pane in Backstage view. Files recently opened or saved, and the folders where those files are stored, are listed in the Recent Workbooks and Recent Places panes, respectively. Click an item in either pane to open it.

d. Click the disk drive in the left pane where your student data files are located, navigate through the folder structure, click **e01_ws01_Cart_Analysis**, and then click **Open**.

Saving and Renaming a Workbook

Once a workbook has been created or opened, any changes to the workbook will need to be saved. The Save and Save As commands accomplish the same task; however, Save As is useful for saving a copy of a file with a new name. It is also useful for creating a backup of a file or for creating a copy of a workbook when you want to use that workbook as the starting point for another workbook.

To Save and Rename a Workbook

a. Click the **File tab**. Backstage view of the Info menu pane is displayed. The Info pane displays document properties such as file size, create and modified dates, and author.

b. Click **Save As**. In the Save As dialog box, navigate to the location where you are saving your files. In the File name box, type Lastname_Firstname_e01_ws01_Cart_Analysis, replacing Lastname and Firstname with your own name.

c. Click **Save**.

Real World Advice — AutoRecover and Quick Save—Outsmart Mr. Murphy!

Computers are not perfect. While life's imperfections often make things interesting, they are also an opportunity for Murphy's Law: *Anything that can go wrong will go wrong*. However, never fear—AutoRecover and Quick Save are here!

- Excel automatically saves your work at regular intervals. The default is 10 minutes, but you can change this setting in the Options menu on the File tab, in the Save category of the Excel Options dialog box. The automatically saved copies of your work are called AutoRecover files. If your computer shuts down unexpectedly, Office will recognize that the file you were working on was not closed properly and will give you the option of opening the most recent AutoRecover file.

- The Ctrl+S shortcut quickly saves your file to the same location as the last save. Whenever you make a significant change to your file, save it right away using the "quick save" keyboard shortcut.

Cells, Rows, and Columns

A worksheet consists of rows and columns. Each row is numbered in ascending sequence from top to bottom. Each column is lettered in ascending sequence from left to right. The intersection of each row and column is called a cell. Each cell has a default name, generally referred to as a **cell reference**—the combination of its column and row. For example, the intersection of column *A* and row *1* has a cell reference of A1 and the intersection of column *D* and row *20* is cell D20.

Worksheet Navigation

Whether a worksheet is small or extremely large, navigation from one cell to another is necessary to enter or to edit numbers, formulas, functions, or text.

Navigating in a small worksheet is simple—move the mouse pointer over the target cell and click. The border around the cell changes to a thick, black line. That is now the **active cell**. Any information you enter via the keyboard is placed into the active cell. **Worksheet navigation** is simply defined as moving the location of the active cell.

SIDE NOTE
Scrolling
It is important to note that scrolling does not move the active cell, only your view in the document.

Scrolling

When part of a document (or in the case of Excel, a worksheet) is out of view because it is too large to be displayed in the visible application window, use the vertical and horizontal scroll bars to shift other parts of the document into view. The vertical scroll bar is on the right side of the application window, and the horizontal scroll bar is at the bottom of the application window, on the right.

Keyboard Navigation

There are several keyboard shortcuts that may be used to navigate a worksheet in order to change the scope and direction the active cell is moved. Figure 3 contains a description for each of these shortcuts.

Keyboard Navigation	Moves the Active Cell
Enter	Down one row
Shift+Enter	Up one row
→ ← ↓ ↑	One cell in the direction of the arrow key
Home	To column A of the current row
Ctrl+Home	To column A, row 1 (cell A1)
Ctrl+End	To the last cell, highest number row and far-right column, that contains information
End+→ End+← End+↓ End+↑	If the first cell in the direction of the arrow beyond the active cell contains data, to the last cell containing data in the arrow direction before an empty cell If the first cell in the direction of the arrow beyond the active cell is empty, to the next cell in the arrow direction that contains data
Page Up Page Down	Up one screen, down one screen
Ctrl+Page Up Ctrl+Page Down	One worksheet left One worksheet right
Tab Shift+Tab	One column right One column left

Figure 3 Navigation using the keyboard

To Navigate Using the Keyboard

a. Click **Sheet1** to make it the active worksheet, if necessary. Press End+→.
The active cell should be XFD1. Be sure to release End between keystrokes. End does not work like Shift; its effect on other key functions is turned off once another key is pressed. End must then be pressed again to change the function to another key.

b. Press End+↓. The active cell should be XFD1048576.

c. Press End+←. The active cell should be A1048576.

d. Press End+↑. The active cell should be A13, the first nonblank cell in the direction of the pressed arrow key.

e. Press End+↑. The active cell should be A5. Because the active cell was nonblank when you pressed End+↑, the active cell is shifted to the cell before the next nonblank cell in the direction of the pressed arrow key.

f. Press End+↑. The active cell should be A1. Excel searches for the next nonblank cell, and stops at row 1.

g. Press → three times. The active cell is D1.

h. Press ↓ five times. The active cell is D6.

i. Press Home. This keystroke takes you to column A of whatever row contains the active cell at the time of the keystroke. The active cell is now A6.

j. Press End+→. The active cell is the next nonblank cell—D6.

k. To finish, press Ctrl+Home to return to cell A1.

Troubleshooting

The active cell is repositioned using the mouse pointer, arrows, and Page Up and Page Down. Even experienced users often scroll through a worksheet and press an arrow only to be returned to the active cell where they began scrolling.

Using the Go To Command

For large worksheets in particular, the Go To command allows rapid navigation to a specific location. Although the worksheet you are currently working with is not large, knowledge of how to use the Go To dialog box to navigate directly to any cell in the worksheet by specifying a cell reference is a skill that you will find useful.

To Navigate Using the Go To Dialog Box

a. Click the **Home tab**, click **Find & Select** in the Editing group, and then click **Go To**. The Go To dialog box will appear.

b. In the Reference box, type **B25**, and then click **OK**. The active cell is now B25.

c. Click **Find & Select** in the Editing group on the Home tab, and then click **Go To**.
Notice that $A$1 is listed in the Go To box. Excel stores the cell reference of the active cell when Go To was invoked in order to make returning to your original location easier.

d. Select **$A$1** in the Go To box, and then click **OK**.

SIDE NOTE
Quick Access to the Go To Dialog Box
The Go To dialog box can be accessed very quickly using the keyboard shortcut Ctrl+G.

Navigating Among Worksheets

Workbooks often contain more than one worksheet. In the bottom-left corner of the Excel worksheet window are worksheet tabs. Each tab represents a single worksheet in the workbook. Recall that by default, a new workbook contains three worksheets: Sheet1, Sheet2, and Sheet3.

The **active worksheet**, by default, is Sheet1. Recall, the active sheet is readily identifiable because the background color of its worksheet tab is white. To make a different worksheet active, click its worksheet tab. The following exercise shows you how to change the active worksheet.

To Change the Active Worksheet

a. Click the **Sheet2 worksheet tab** in the bottom-left corner of the worksheet window. Sheet2 is now the active worksheet.

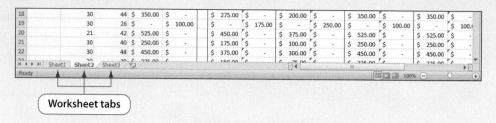

Figure 4   Change the active worksheet

b. Click the **Sheet3 worksheet tab**. Sheet3 is now the active worksheet.

c. Click the **Sheet1 worksheet tab**. Sheet1 is now the active worksheet.

Documentation

Worksheets are often used by people who did not develop them. Even if a worksheet will never be used by anyone other than its builder, best practice dictates that you document a workbook and its worksheets.

A well-documented worksheet is much easier to use and maintain, particularly for a user who did not develop the worksheet. Documentation also helps the developer return to and use the workbook after a long period of time. You may use a worksheet on a regular basis, but over time you may forget how the worksheet actually operates.

Documentation is vital to ensure that a worksheet remains usable. Documentation can take several forms such as file and worksheet names, worksheet titles, column and/or row titles, cell labels, cell comments, or a dedicated documentation worksheet. Many people do not take the time to document adequately because they do not feel it is time spent productively. Some do not feel it is necessary or do not think anyone else will ever use the workbook. For a workbook to be useful, it must be accurate, easily understood, flexible, efficient, *and* documented. While accuracy is most important, an undocumented workbook can later create inaccurate data. Where documentation is concerned, less is *not* more—more is more and is better. A well-structured worksheet is somewhat self-documented in that there are ample titles, column headings, and cell labels. However, a documentation worksheet and comments are created specifically to add documentation to a worksheet and/or workbook.

To Document a Workbook Using a Documentation Worksheet and/or Comments

a. Click the **Sheet3 worksheet tab**. Click cell **A5**. Type today's date in mm/dd/yyyy format and press Enter, or alternatively press Ctrl+;.

b. Click cell **B5**, and then type Lastname, Firstname replacing Lastname, Firstname with your last name and first name.

c. Click cell **C5**, and then type Added comments to key cells.

d. Click the **Sheet1 worksheet tab**.

SIDE NOTE

Insert the System Date

Ctrl+; is a keyboard shortcut that inserts the computer system date into the active cell. Rather than type the current date, assuming the system date is set properly, use this keyboard shortcut to insert it.

e. Click the **Review tab**, click cell **A7**, and then click **New Comment** in the Comments group to create a comment.

f. In the comment box, select the user name text that is automatically inserted into the comment, and then press Delete.

g. Press Ctrl+B to toggle on bold text, type Retail Price, and then press Ctrl+B to toggle off bold text.

h. Press Enter, and then type Commonly known as Manufacturer's Suggested Retail Price, or MSRP. Click on any worksheet cell. Cell A7 now has a red triangle in the top-right corner to indicate the presence of a comment.

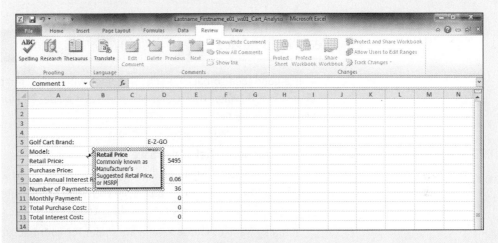

Figure 5   Documenting retail price using a comment

Troubleshooting

All the figures in this text were taken at a monitor resolution of 1024 X 768. Higher or lower resolution will affect the way Excel displays Ribbon options. The order in which groups in the Ribbon are displayed is not affected, however.

i. Click cell **A8**, and then click **New Comment**. Notice cell A8 now has a red triangle in the top-right corner to indicate the presence of a comment.

j. In the comment box, select the user name that is automatically inserted into the comment, and then press Delete.

k. Press Ctrl+B to toggle on bold text. Type Purchase Price, and then press Ctrl+B to toggle off bold text.

l. Press Enter, and then type What must you actually pay to purchase the golf cart?.

m. Click cell **A9**, and then click **New Comment**. In the comment box, select the user name text that is automatically inserted into the comment, and then press Delete.

n. Press Ctrl+B to toggle on bold text, type Annual Interest Rate, and then press Ctrl+B to toggle off bold text.

o. Press Enter, and then type Annual rate of interest in decimal or percentage format, e.g., 5% is entered as 0.05 or 5%.

Do Not Give Mr. Murphy an Opportunity!

Do not get caught by Murphy's Law for computer users: *The probability your program or application will crash is directly proportional to the amount of time since you last saved your file.* Press Ctrl+S often.

p. Click cell **A10**, and then click **New Comment**.

q. In the Comment box, select the user name text that is automatically inserted into the comment, and then press Delete.

r. Press Ctrl+B to toggle on bold text, and then type # of Payments. Press Ctrl+B to toggle off bold text.

s. Press Enter, type Total number of payments over the term of the loan and then click any cell in the worksheet.

t. Click **Save**.

Real World Advice — Back Up Your Workbook!

It is a good idea to back up your workbook when you are about to make significant changes to it, when those changes have been made, and/or when you have finished working for the moment.

To make a backup of your workbook:

1. Click the **File tab**. Click **Save As**.

2. In the Save As dialog box, navigate to the location where you are saving your files. In the File name box, type the name of your file—for example, Your_File_ yyyy-mm-dd, where yyyy-mm-dd is today's date. Click **Save**.

You may want to create a separate folder for your backup files. If possible, it is best practice to store backup files on an entirely different drive. A USB drive is a great option since you can take it with you as an off-site backup.

Save As not only saves a copy of your file, it changes the file Excel has open. Your_File_yyyy-mm-dd will be the open file, and the title bar at the top of the Excel application window will display the new file name. Click **Close** and open your original file before continuing your work.

Enter the location and name of the backup in a documentation worksheet in the original file so others (and you) will know the name of backup files and where they are stored.

Failing to Plan is Planning to Fail

Winston Churchill said, "He who fails to plan, plans to fail." The first step in building a worksheet should be planning. There are several questions that should be considered before you begin entering information:

- What is the objective of the worksheet? Is it to solve a problem? Is it to analyze data and recommend a course of action? Is it to summarize data and present usable information? Is it to store information for use by another application?

- Do you have all of the data necessary to build this worksheet?

- What information does your worksheet need to generate?

- How should the information in your worksheet be presented? Who is the audience? What layout will best present the worksheet information?

- A well-designed worksheet presents information in a clear and understandable way and allows for efficiency in the workbook development process.

Enter and Edit Data

In building and maintaining worksheets, the ability to enter and format data is fundamental. As data is entered via keyboard, the data simultaneously appears in the active cell and in the formula bar. Figure 6 shows the result when a cell is double-clicked to place the insertion point into cell contents. Alternatively, if you click in the formula bar, the insertion point is displayed in the formula bar.

Active cell's contents in the formula bar

Formula bar

Red triangle in upper-right corner of a cell indicates the presence of a comment

Selected cell

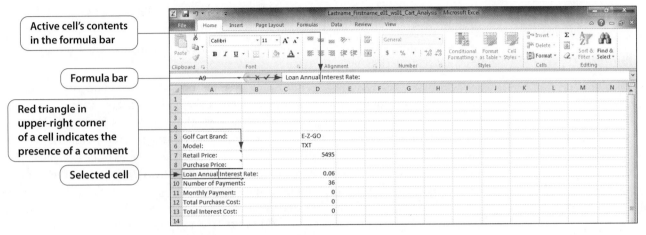

Figure 6 Editing data in a cell

Text, Numbers, Dates, and Times

Text data consists of any combination of printable characters including letters, numbers, and special characters available on any standard keyboard.

Numeric data consists of numbers in any form not combined with letters and special characters other than possibly the period (decimal) and/or hyphen (to indicate negativity). Technically, special characters such as the dollar sign ($) or comma (,) are not considered numeric. They are only displayed for contextual and readability purposes and are not stored as part of a numeric cell value.

In Excel, dates and times are a special form of numeric data. Information entered in a recognized date and/or time format will be converted automatically to an Excel date and/or time value. Figure 7 includes examples of valid dates and times that can be entered into Excel and how they will be displayed:

Enter	Excel Displays	Enter	Excel Displays
December 21, 2012	21-Dec-12	12/21/2012	12/21/2012
December 21, 2012 10 p	12/21/2012 22:00	2012/12/21	12/21/2012
Dec 21, 2012	21-Dec-12	13:00	13:00
21 Dec 2012 10:30	12/21/2012 10:30	1:00 p	1:00 PM

Figure 7 Date/time entry and how Excel displays dates and times

If Excel recognizes a value as a date/time, it will right-align displayed values. If you enter a date or time that is not recognized, Excel treats the information as text and left-aligns it in the cell. By default, Excel left-aligns text data and right-aligns numeric, date, and time data.

How Excel Really Stores Date and Time Data

Date and time information is automatically displayed in a format easily understood by the user, but in Excel, dates and times are actually real numbers in which the value to the left of the decimal place is the number of days since December 31, 1899 (1 = January 1, 1900) and the value to the right of the decimal place is the proportion of 1 day that represents a time value (1.1 = January 1, 1900 + 144 minutes = January 1, 1900 2:24 AM). The advantages of storing date and time values in what is commonly referred to as the 1900 date system are many:

- Sorting a list of dates and/or times is as simple as putting the list in ascending or descending numerical order.

- Since dates and times are real numbers, mathematical manipulation to add to, or subtract from, dates and times is greatly simplified.

- Determining a time span is simply a function of subtracting one date from another, a single calculation.

The vast majority of applications and systems now store date and time values in this manner. The main difference among them is the base date. For example, in DOS, Microsoft's precursor operating system to Windows, the base date is January 1, 1980.

Had all applications and computer systems stored dates as serial numbers, or serial dates, the Y2K bug never would have been an issue when the Western calendar progressed from December 31, 1999, to January 1, 2000. The Y2K bug was the result of a widespread practice in the computer industry, that dated as far back as the 1950s, of storing date values with the four-digit year abbreviated to two digits—1999 was stored as 99, and 2000 would have been stored as 00. The purpose was to save expensive disk space—unlike today, digital media was very expensive and every character consumed precious space. Many information systems sort and process information by date, and since 1999 is greater than 2000 when stored as a 2-digit year, many systems would output incorrect information; it was feared that many systems would fail to operate at all as of January 1, 2000, because date values would not sort properly.

Real World Advice — Do Not Confuse Formatting with Value

Formatting data only changes the way a value is displayed. It does not change the actual value stored in the cell. Special formatting characters such as the dollar sign ($) and the comma (,) are not part of the stored value.

Dates and times may be entered in standard format: mm/dd/yy and hours:minutes:seconds. Excel recognizes information entered in date and/or time formats and converts it to a serial value in the 1900 date system. What is stored is a serial number, and what is displayed is determined by the default or selected date/time format.

To Enter Information in a Worksheet

a. Click the **Sheet1 worksheet tab**.

b. Make sure cell A1 is the active cell. If it is not, press [Ctrl]+[Home].

c. Type Red Bluff Golf Course in cell A1, and then press [Enter]. The active cell is now A2.

d. Type Golf Cart Purchase Analysis in cell A2, and then press [Enter].

e. Type 12/15/2013 in cell A3. Use the format mm/dd/yyyy.

f. Click cell **D8** to make it the active cell, type 5295, and then press ↓ and notice how the ↓ performs the same function as Enter. The values in cells D11, D12, and D13 are automatically recalculated.

g. Click cell **D10**, type 48, and then press Enter. Notice the monthly payment changed from 161.084159 to 124.353229.

h. Click cell **D9**, type 7.77%, and then press Enter. Notice the monthly payment changed from 124.353229 to 128.695525.

Troubleshooting

If the monthly payment is thousands of dollars, you probably entered 7.77. That is actually 777% for calculation purposes. You must enter the percentage, 7.77%, or enter .0777—the decimal equivalent for 7.77%.

i. Click **Undo** ↺ to return the Loan Annual Interest Rate to 0.06.

j. Click the **Sheet3 worksheet tab**, click cell **A6**, and then type today's date in mm/dd/yyyy format. Click cell **C6**, and then type Entered titles and updated data.

k. Click the **Sheet1 worksheet tab**.

l. Click **Save** 💾.

SIDE NOTE
Undo Keyboard Shortcut

The keyboard shortcut Ctrl+Z is a fast and efficient method of performing an Undo ↺.

SIDE NOTE
Use Undo History

If you need to Undo a change in the recent past, but have made other changes since, click the arrow next to Undo ↺ to see a history of changes you have made to your worksheet. Pick the change you would like to Undo from the list.

Text Wrapping and Hard Returns

Excel, by default, places all information in a single line in a cell. Text that is too long to fit in a cell is displayed over contiguous cells to the right, unless contiguous cells contain information. If contiguous cells contain information, then the cell entry is truncated—essentially cut off, at least for display purposes.

A couple of ways to avoid text truncation can be through changing the alignment of a cell in order to wrap words, or by placing hard returns into text to force wrapping at a particular location.

To Wrap or Unwrap Text in a Cell

a. Click the **Home tab**, click cell **A2**, and then click **Wrap Text** in the Alignment group.
The text in cell A2 now wraps so you can see all the text in one cell. Wrap Text has its place, but this sheet title might be better formatted in a manner that allows you more control over the result.

b. Click **Wrap Text** again to unwrap the text in cell A2.

c. Double-click cell **A2**. Either use ← or → to move the cursor or click to position the cursor immediately after **Cart**.

d. Press Delete to remove the space between **Cart** and **Purchase**.

e. Press Alt+Enter to insert a hard return and then press Enter.

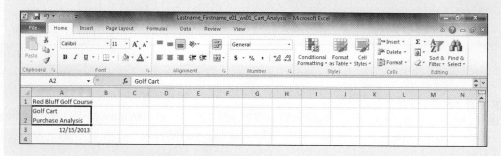

Figure 8 Insert a hard return to control wrap location

f. Click the **Sheet3 worksheet tab**.

g. Click cell **A7**, type today's date in mm/dd/yyyy format, click cell **C7**, and then type Modified titles.

h. Click the **Sheet1 worksheet tab**.

i. Click **Save** 💾.

Manipulate Cells and Cell Ranges

Part of what makes a worksheet an efficient tool is the ability to perform actions that affect many cells at once. A cell **range** is a selection of multiple cells at once. Knowing how to manipulate cells and cell ranges is a vital part of maximizing the efficacy of worksheet usage.

Selecting Cells and Cell Ranges

Using the mouse, multiple cells can be selected simultaneously. Selected cells can be contiguous to each other or they can be noncontiguous. Once multiple cells are selected, they can be affected by actions such as clear, delete, copy, paste, formatting, and many other actions while offering the convenience of performing the desired task only once for the selected cells.

To Select Contiguous and Noncontiguous Cell Ranges

a. Click and hold on cell **D5**. Drag down until cells **D5:D13** are selected—the active cell border expands to include D5:D13, and the background color of selected cells also changes.

b. Press Ctrl+Home. Click and hold cell **A5**. Drag down until cells **A5:A13** are selected.

c. Press and hold Ctrl, click and hold cell **C5**, and then drag to select cells **C5:C13**.

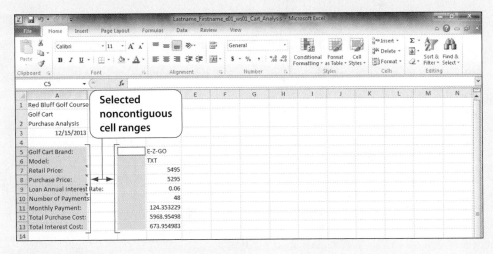

Figure 9 Selecting noncontiguous cell ranges

Quick Reference Selecting Cell Ranges

There are several ways to select a contiguous range of cells:

1. Expand the active cell by dragging the mouse.

2. Select the first cell in the range, press [Shift], and click the last cell in the desired range.

A contiguous range of rows or columns can be selected in the following ways:

1. Click a row or column heading. Drag the mouse pointer across the headings to select contiguous rows or columns.

2. Click a row or column heading. Press [Shift], and then click the last row or column you wish to select.

Once a cell or contiguous range of cells has been selected, you can add noncontiguous cells and ranges by pressing [Ctrl] and using any of the above methods for selecting ranges that do not involve [Shift].

Drag and Drop

As worksheets are designed, built, and modified, it is often necessary to move information from one cell or range of cells to another. One of the most efficient ways to do this is called "drag and drop" and is accomplished entirely with the mouse pointer as shown in the following exercise.

To Drag and Drop Cells

a. Select cell range **D5:D13**. Point to the border of the selected range. The cell pointer changes to a move pointer.

b. Click and hold the left mouse button, and then drag the selected cells to the right one column (column E). A *ghost* range, also referred to as a target range, and range callout are displayed as the pointer is moved to show exactly where the moved cells will be placed.

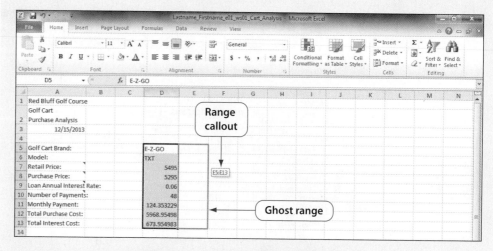

Figure 10   Drag and drop to move a cell range

c.   Drop the dragged cells into column E by releasing the left mouse button. Be careful to drop the range onto the same rows occupied in column D.

d.   Move the cell pointer until it is over the border of the selected range in column E. The cell pointer will change to a move pointer.

e.   Press and hold Ctrl. The move pointer changes to a copy pointer.

f.   Drag the selected range until the ghost range is directly to the left in column D to copy the cells from range **E5:E13** to the range **D5:D13**. Release the left mouse button, and then release Ctrl. Press Ctrl + Home.

g.   Click the **Sheet3 worksheet tab**.

h.   Click cell **A8**, type today's date in mm/dd/yyyy format, click cell **C8**, and then type Added Column E of data.

i.   Click the **Sheet1 worksheet tab**.

j.   Press Ctrl + Home, and then click **Save**.

Cut/Copy and Paste

The same copy and/or move results can be obtained with the copy and paste or cut and paste features. The paste feature presents more options than drag and drop through Paste Options and Paste Special to give you more control of exactly what is placed into the target cells. Drag and drop moves or copies everything in a cell, including formatting. In the next exercise you will learn to use Cut, Copy, and Paste in Excel. Later in this workshop we will learn the advantages of Paste Options and Paste Special.

To Use Cut, Copy, and Paste

a. Select cell range **D5:D13**, and then click **Cut** in the Clipboard group. The solid border around cell range D5:D13 changes to a moving dashed border.

b. Click cell **F5**, and then click **Paste** in the Clipboard group.

c. Click **Copy** in the Clipboard group. The solid border around cell range F5:F13 changes to a moving dashed border.

d. Click cell **D5**, press and hold [Ctrl], and then select cells **G5:H5**.

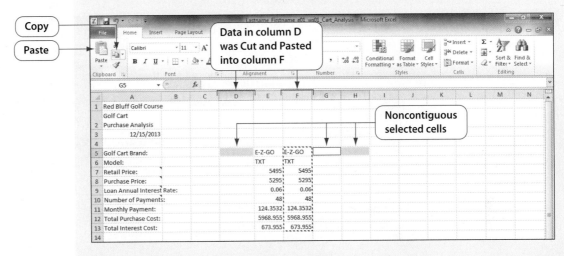

Figure 11 Selection of multiple locations to paste a copied cell range

e. Click **Paste** in the Clipboard group.

f. Press [Esc] to clear the Clipboard and remove the dashed border from around cell range F5:F13.

g. Click the **Sheet3 worksheet tab**.

h. Click cell **A9**, type today's date in mm/dd/yyyy format, click cell **C9**, and then type Added Columns F:H of data.

i. Click the **Sheet1 worksheet tab**.

j. Press [Ctrl]+[Home], and then click **Save** 💾.

Series (AutoFill)

The **AutoFill** feature is a powerful way to minimize the effort required to enter certain types of data. AutoFill copies information from one cell, or a series in contiguous cells, into contiguous cells in the direction the fill handle is dragged. AutoFill is a smart copy that will try to guess how you want values or formulas changed as you copy. Sometimes, AutoFill will save significant time by changing the contents correctly. Other times, AutoFill changes the contents in a way you did not intend—when that happens, the Auto Fill Options button makes options available that may be helpful.

The fill handle is a small black square in the bottom-right corner of the active cell or selected cells border. To engage the AutoFill feature, click and drag the fill handle in the direction you wish to expand the active cell.

To Quickly Generate Data Using AutoFill

a. Select cell **D4**, type Option 1, and then press Enter. You need to add titles to the cart option columns you just created.

b. Select cell **D4**. Point to the fill handle—the tiny square in the bottom-right corner of the active cell—and then click and hold the **handle** once the mouse pointer changes to ⊞. Drag the fill handle right until the border around the active cell expands to include cells **D4:H4**, and then release the left mouse button. Sheet1 will have column titles Option1–Option 5.

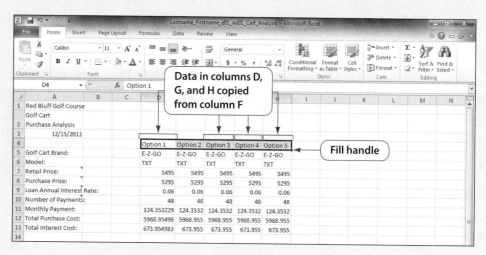

Figure 12 Using AutoFill to generate a series of headings

c. Click the **Sheet2 worksheet tab**. The Analysis of Cart Usage worksheet has some data missing that can be supplied using AutoFill.

d. Select cell **A11**. Click the **fill handle**, drag it down until the border around the cell range expands to include cells **A11:A41**, and then release the left mouse button.

e. Click **Auto Fill Options** ⊞ that has appeared at the bottom right of cell A41. Select **Fill Without Formatting**.

Barry Cheney filled the background color for the first of May because the demand was abnormally high that day. The pink background is specific to May 1st, so you do not want that formatting to be on all the dates. Fill Without Formatting displays all the filled dates as 1900 date system values.

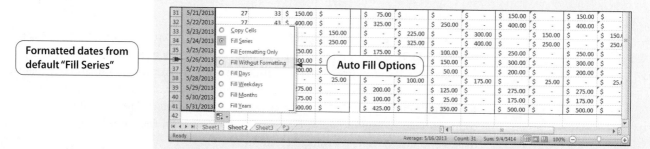

Figure 13 AutoFill and Fill Without Formatting

f. If necessary, select range **A11:A41**. Click the **Home tab**, click the **Number Format arrow** General, and then select **Short Date** on the menu.

g. Select cell range **I3:J3**. Selecting more than one cell sets a pattern—in this case increments of one—for AutoFill to follow.

h. Click and hold the **fill handle**, drag the fill handle to the right until the border around the cell range expands to include cells **I3:M3**, and then release the left mouse button. Notice the AutoFill callout that shows the filled value of each cell as you move the fill handle to the right.

i. Select cell **G9**. Click the **fill handle**, and then drag it right until you have selected cell range **G9:P9**. If you click the Auto Fill Options button, you will see the default option currently displays Fill Series, which is why the cells correctly filled by increments of 1.

j. Click the **Sheet3 worksheet tab**.

k. Click cell **A10**, type today's date in mm/dd/yyyy format, click cell **C10**, and then type **Filled Series**.

l. Click the **Sheet1 worksheet tab**.

m. Press Ctrl+Home, and then click **Save** 💾.

CONSIDER THIS | **More on AutoFill, Anyone?**

You just met Aidan Matthews, the chief technology officer at Painted Paradise Resort and Spa. You explained to him the work you have been completing for Barry. He urged you to explore AutoFill further as it is very flexible and can assist you in many ways. As he reminisced on his time conducting Excel training sessions earlier in his career, he remembered a file he gave trainees to practice AutoFill. If you would like to try some more AutoFill activities, open Aidan's file e01_ws01_Autofill_Practice, and follow the instructions provided in cell comments. When you finish, save the file as **Lastname_Firstname_e01_ws01_Autofill_Practice**.

Modifying Cell Information

Copying and pasting content from one range of cells to another range or more is a highly efficient way to reuse parts of a worksheet. The ranges you just pasted into columns D, F, G, and H contain a lot of information that is calculated using formulas that you do not want to type more than once. However, you do not need five copies of a purchase analysis of an E-Z-GO TXT golf cart.

Changing the contents of cells is as simple as double-clicking the cell to invoke edit mode. The active cell will contain an insertion point. If you want to change part of the content, use the arrow keys or click to position the insertion point at the desired location. If all the cell content is to be replaced, click the cell once to make it the active cell. All cell content will be replaced when you begin typing to enter the new content for the selected cell.

To Modify Worksheet Contents by Changing Copied Information

a. Click cell **E6**, type RXV, and then double-click cell **F6**. Press [Home] to go to the left margin of the cell, type Freedom, and then press [Spacebar] once so the formula bar displays **Freedom TXT**. Press [Enter]. Click cell **G6**, type Freedom RXV. Press [Enter]. Click cell **H6**, and then type The Drive.

b. Click cell **E7**, and then type 5995. Press [Tab] to move to cell **F7**, and then type 6495. Press [Tab] to move to cell **G7**, and then type 7135.

c. Click cell **E8**, and then type 5695. Press [Tab] to move to cell F8, and then type 5995. Press [Tab] to move to cell G8, and then type 6125. Click cell **H8**, and then type 5150. Notice that as you change the values in each of the cells in row 8, Monthly Payment, Total Purchase Cost, and Total Interest Cost are recalculated.

d. Click cell **H5**, type Yamaha, and then press [Enter].

e. Select cell range **F6:G6**, and then click **Wrap Text** in the Alignment group.

f. Click the **Sheet3 worksheet tab**.

g. Click cell **A11**, type today's date in mm/dd/yyyy format, click cell **C11**, and then type Updated cart data.

h. Click the **Sheet1 worksheet tab**.

i. Press [Ctrl]+[Home], and then click **Save** 💾.

Inserting Cells

You want to make the golf cart analysis worksheet easier to read and use by adding some white space. **White space** is part of a document that does not contain data or documentation. While white space does not need to be the color white, the lack of data gives a document visual structure and creates a sense of order in the mind of the worksheet user. For example, white space above and below the titles Loan Annual Interest Rate and Number of Payments visually creates a group of information associated with financing the golf carts.

To Insert Rows in a Worksheet

a. Click cell **A7**, click the **Insert arrow** in the Cells group, and then click **Insert Sheet Rows**. Excel inserts a row above the active cell location and moves all cells at A7 and below down to make room.

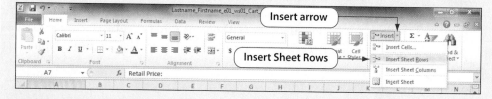

Figure 14   Inserting sheet rows

b. Select cell range **A10:A11**, click the **Insert arrow** in the Cells group, and then click **Insert Sheet Rows**. If you have more than one cell (or row) selected, Excel will interpret the number of rows selected as the number of rows you want inserted.

c. Select cell range **A14:A15**, click the **Insert arrow** in the Cells group, and then click **Insert Sheet Rows**. Press Ctrl+Home.

Troubleshooting

White space was only inserted in column A!
If you click the Insert button instead of the Insert arrow, Excel will default to inserting extra cells only, instead of rows. Inserting rows is often more efficient and less error prone than inserting cells. When inserting white space throughout your data, insert rows.

d. Click the **Sheet3 worksheet tab**.

e. Click cell **A12**, type today's date in mm/dd/yyyy format, click cell **C12**, and then type Created white space.

f. You need more rows in the modifications section of the documentation worksheet. Select rows **14:29** using the row headings, and then click **Insert** in the Cells group.

g. Click the **Sheet1 worksheet tab**.

h. Press Ctrl+Home, and then click **Save**.

Deleting Cells

White space is a good way to visually separate and logically categorize information in a worksheet. However, the old saying, "You can't have too much of a good thing" definitely is not true where white space is concerned. There is too much white space between the headings in column A and the numbers in column D. One way to move the columns of cart information to the left is to delete a few cells.

To Delete Cells, Cell Ranges, and Rows

a. Click cell **B4**, and then click **Delete** in the Cells group. Notice that only the Option numbers in row 5 moved left.

b. Select cell range **B5:B18**, and click **Delete** in the Cells group. The remaining data cell values in rows 5:18 moved left.

c. Click a cell in row **10**. Press and hold Ctrl, and then click a cell in row **15**. Click the Delete arrow in the Cells group.

d. Click **Delete Sheet Rows**, and then press Ctrl+Home.

e. Click the **Sheet3 worksheet tab**.

f. Click cell **A13**, type today's date in mm/dd/yyyy format, click cell **C13**, and then type Relocated data to the left, deleted some blank rows.

g. Click the **Sheet1 worksheet tab**.

h. Press Ctrl+Home, and then click **Save**.

Merge & Center vs. Center Across Selection

The titles in the golf cart analysis worksheet are entered in cells A1:A3. Although they contain the correct information to communicate the purpose of the golf cart analysis worksheet, they might better present that information with some formatting improvements. Titles that identify the general purpose of a worksheet are often at the top and centered above worksheet content. Additionally, they are often displayed in a different, larger font and may be bolded or italicized. Merge & Center ▦ combines selected cells into a single cell and centers the content in the left and/or top cell in the resulting single cell—all other data is lost. Merge & Center can be applied both horizontally and vertically. Center Across Selection erases the borders between cells such that a selected range looks like a single cell, but the original cells remain—the borders between them are removed and the content is centered. Center Across Selection can only be applied horizontally. Additionally, Center Across Selection will never cause a loss of data.

To Merge, Center, and Format Headings

a. Select cell range **A1:G1**, and then click **Merge & Center** in the Alignment group.

b. Select cell range **A2:G3**, and then click **Merge & Center** in the Alignment group. Notice the warning message.

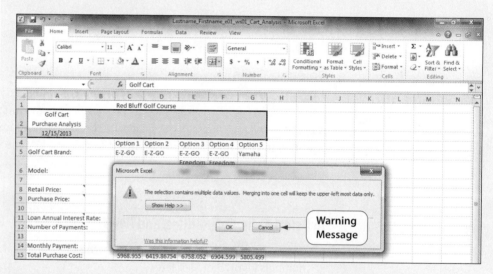

Figure 15   Merge and center a range containing multiple values and data

c. Click **Cancel**; you do not want to lose the data in cell A3.

d. Click the **Alignment Dialog Box Launcher** ⬚. This displays the Alignment tab of the Format Cells dialog box. Click **Center Across Selection** in the Horizontal list box.

e. Click **OK**. Cell A2 content is centered across cell range A2:G2, and cell A3 content is centered across cell range A3:G3.

f. Click the **Sheet3 worksheet tab**.

g. Click cell **A14**, type today's date in mm/dd/yyyy format, click cell **C14**, type Centered titles, and then press Enter.

h. Click the **Sheet1 worksheet tab**.

i. Press Ctrl+Home, and then click **Save** 🖫.

Try this. In the Sheet1 worksheet of the Lastname_Firstname_e01_ws01_Cart_Analysis workbook, select cell range A1:D16. Try to select cell range A1:B9.

Now try to select cell range A2:D16. Try to select cell range A2:B9.

Merge & Center ▣ creates a single cell that can cause problems if you want to select a range of cells that includes only part of the merged cell range.

There are Excel experts who feel Merge & Center should never be used and should not even be a part of Excel. Do you agree?

Manipulate Columns and Rows

By default any worksheet you create has set column widths and row heights. As you build, refine, and modify a worksheet, it is often necessary to add and/or delete columns and rows for formatting and content purposes. Fortunately, Excel makes these activities extremely easy to accomplish.

Select Contiguous and Noncontiguous Columns and Rows

To manipulate columns and rows, you must first indicate which of each you wish to affect by your actions. As with cells and ranges, you can select entire columns, rows, column ranges, and row ranges. You can select noncontiguous columns and rows, and even select ranges of columns and rows at the same time.

Quick Reference | Selecting Columns and Rows

To select an individual column or row, click the heading (letter or number, respectively) in the header.

To select a range of contiguous columns or rows, click and hold the heading at the start of the range you want to select. Then drag the mouse to select additional columns or rows, or click the heading of the column or row at one end of the range you want to select, press and hold [Shift], and then click the heading of the column or row at the other end of the range you want to select.

To select noncontiguous columns or rows, click the heading of the first column or row you want to select. Press and hold [Ctrl], and then click the headings of any additional columns and/or rows you want to select. Contiguous ranges of columns or rows can be part of a noncontiguous range. To use the methods listed above for selecting a range of contiguous columns or rows, simply hold down [Ctrl] during the first step.

To select all cells in a worksheet, place the pointer over the Select All ▣ button and the pointer will change to ⊕; then click the left mouse button. Alternatively, press [Ctrl]+[A].

Inserting Columns and Rows

A selected range is defined as a contiguous set of cells, columns, or rows that are all part of a single contiguous selection. However, how you select columns and rows determines whether they are a single, contiguous range or are considered separate, individual selections.

If you click column C, press and hold [Shift], and click column E, you have created a contiguous selection of columns C:E. All three columns are highlighted as a group. But, if you click column C, press and hold [Ctrl], click column D, and then click column E, you have just selected three individual columns—three individual selections. In this situation, columns C, D, and E are treated by Excel as noncontiguous columns—there is a slight border highlighted between the columns. Whether columns (or rows) are a selected range or are noncontiguous has an effect on how actions such as Insert are applied to a worksheet.

There is still a need to add some white space to the cart analysis worksheet—the columns of information for the different carts are too close together. One way to add white space is to insert a blank column between each column of cart information. Additionally, there is enough definitional difference between the Monthly Payment and the Purchase and Interest totals that some white space to separate them may be advisable. This can be accomplished by inserting a row in the appropriate locations.

To Insert a Column Between Each Column of Cart Data

a. Click the heading for column **D** to select column D, press and hold Shift, and then select column **G**.

b. Click **Insert** in the Cells group. Four contiguous columns were inserted to the right of column C.

c. Press Ctrl+Z to undo the last change. This is not what you wanted.

d. Click on the heading for column **D**, press and hold Ctrl, and then select column **E**, column **F**, and column **G** by clicking on each column heading individually. Notice the white line between each column selection—this is not a selected range of columns, it is four individually selected columns.

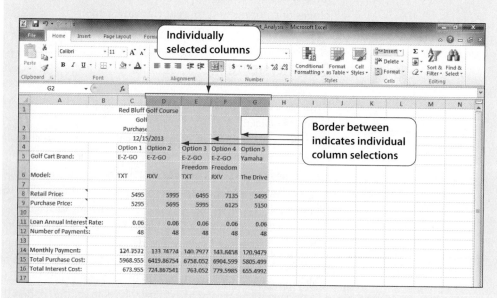

Figure 16 Use Ctrl to select individual columns, rows, cells, or ranges

e. Click **Insert** in the Cells group.
A column has been inserted to the left of each selected column because columns D, E, F, and G were selected as noncontiguous individual columns.

f. Click the heading for row **15**. Press and hold Ctrl, select row **4**, click **Insert** in the Cells group, and then press Ctrl+Home.

g. Click the **Sheet3 worksheet tab**.

h. Click cell **A15**, type today's date in mm/dd/yyyy format, click cell **C15**, and then type Added more white space.

i. Click the **Sheet1 worksheet tab**.

j. Click **Save**.

SIDE NOTE

A Faster Way to Insert

When columns or rows are selected for the purpose of inserting them into the worksheet, you can click the right mouse button and select Insert from the shortcut menu.

Column Width and Row Height

You have inserted columns and rows to add additional white space, but there is still a need to refine the amount of white space in the worksheet. At this point there is too much—the information is spread too far apart.

Column width and row height often need to be adjusted for a couple of reasons. One reason is to reduce the amount of white space a blank column or row represents in a worksheet; the other is to allow the content of cells in a row or column to be displayed properly.

Column width is defined in characters. The default width is 8.43 characters. The maximum width of a column is 255 characters.

Row height is defined in points. A point is approximately 1/72 of an inch (0.035 cm). The default row height in Excel is 15 points, or approximately 1/6 of an inch (0.4 cm). A row can be up to 409 points in height (about 5.4 inches).

To Manually Adjust Column Width and Row Height

a. Select column **D**, press and hold Ctrl, and then select columns **F**, **H**, and **J**.

b. Click **Format** in the Cells group, click **Column Width** from the Cell Size menu, and then type **2** in the Column Width dialog box.

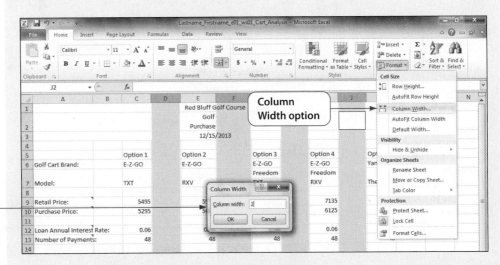

Figure 17 Column Width dialog box

c. Click **OK**, click row **4**, press and hold Ctrl, and then select rows **8**, **11**, **14**, and **16**.

d. Click **Format** in the Cells group, and then click **Row Height** on the Cell Size menu.

e. Type **7** in the Row Height dialog box.

f. Click **OK**, and then press Ctrl + Home.

g. Click the **Sheet3 worksheet tab**.

h. Click cell **A16**, type today's date in mm/dd/yyyy format, click cell **C16**, and then type Resized some rows and columns.

i. Click the **Sheet1 worksheet tab**.

j. Click **Save**.

Changing Column Widths Using AutoFit

Column width and row height can also be adjusted automatically based on the width and height of selected content using the AutoFit feature. The width of columns will be adjusted to allow selected content to fit into the column. Care is required in that data in cells not selected may be truncated or not displayed properly.

To Use the AutoFit Feature to Adjust Column Width

a. Click cell **A7**, press and hold Ctrl, and then select cells **C7**, **E7**, **G7**, **I7**, and **K7**.

b. Click **Format** in the Cells group, and then click **AutoFit Column Width**.

Since AutoFit sizes columns (also notice there is an AutoFit Row Height command, which works in exactly the same manner) to the selected content, columns C and E are too narrow to display most of the numeric data, which is then displayed as a series of number signs (#). Notice also that columns A and B together are too narrow to display the content of cells A12 and A13, so they are truncated on the right.

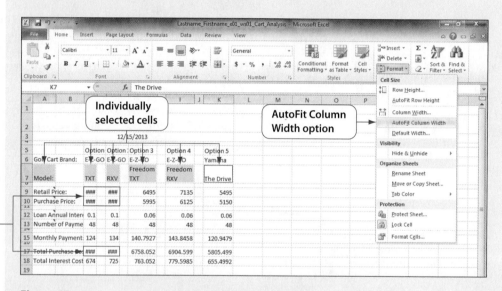

Some columns are too narrow to display all content after AutoFit—### indicates a cell is too narrow to display contents

Figure 18   AutoFit Column Width results for selected cells

c. Select column **A**, press and hold Ctrl, select columns **C**, **E**, **G**, **I**, and **K**, and then click **Format** in the Cells group.

d. Click **AutoFit Column Width** from the Cell Size menu.

Since columns were selected instead of individual cells, the columns are automatically adjusted to the widest content in the column, resulting in no number signs. AutoFit Column Width made the columns wide enough to display seven (7) digits to the right of the decimal place in the Monthly Payment row. That is more than necessary for what is obviously a dollar amount.

SIDE NOTE

There Is an Increase Decimal Button Too

What do you do if you click Decrease Decimal ⌐ too many times? Click Increase Decimal ⌐ as many times as necessary to display the correct number of decimal places.

e. Select cell range **C15:K18**, and then click **Decrease Decimal** in the Number group repeatedly until only two decimal places are visible.

f. Select column **C**, press and hold **Ctrl**, and then select columns **E, G, I,** and **K**. Click **Format** in the Cells group, and then click **AutoFit Column Width** on the Cell Size menu.

Column width can also be set manually. Column A could be a little wider than set by AutoFit Column Width.

g. Place the mouse pointer over the **border** between column A and column B. The pointer should change to ⊞. Click and hold the left mouse button, and then drag the mouse to the right until column A is about 1/4 inch wider. Press Ctrl + Home.

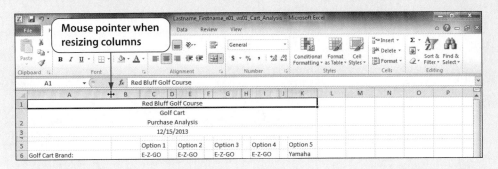

Figure 19   Manually adjust column width

h. Click the **Sheet3 worksheet tab**.

i. Click cell **A17**, type today's date in mm/dd/yyyy format, click cell **C17**, and then type Resized columns using AutoFit.

j. Click the **Sheet1 worksheet tab**.

k. Click **Save** 🖫.

Real World Advice — Fast Ways to Adjust Column Width and Row Height

For small worksheets in particular, you will often want to simply adjust a column width or row height using the content you can see on the screen.

1. Hover the mouse pointer over the column header between two columns. The mouse pointer will change to ⊞.

2. Click and hold the left mouse button and move the mouse left or right to adjust the width of the column to the left of the cursor, or double-click to use the AutoFit feature.

The same procedure can be used to adjust row height.

1. Hover the mouse pointer between two row headers; it should change to ⊞.

2. Click and hold the left mouse button, and then move the mouse up or down to adjust the height of the row above the cursor, or double-click to use the AutoFit feature.

If multiple columns or rows are selected, adjusting width or height for one selected column or row adjusts the width or height for all.

Delete vs. Clear

Worksheet data can be either cleared or deleted—there is a difference. Clearing contents from a cell does not change the location of other cells in the worksheet. Deleting a cell shifts surrounding cells in a direction determined from a prompt. Delete works exactly as you would expect when editing a string of characters or a formula in a cell in edit mode. When you are not in edit mode, pressing Delete clears content, but does not delete the cell(s). This distinction is important because clearing content does not shift the location of other cells in the worksheet, whereas deleting cells does shift worksheet cells.

Deleting rows or columns is very much like deleting cells. Simply click on the row or column header and click Delete in the Cells group.

The golf cart analysis worksheet is formatted well, but after adjusting the width of column A, column B is no longer necessary to avoid truncation of the text in cells A12 and A13. Further, Barry has decided that the E-Z-GO Freedom TXT and the E-Z-GO Freedom RXV are not options to be further considered, so they are to be removed from the analysis. The date in row 3 is not necessary, so you have been asked to delete that content as well.

To Delete Columns and Rows

a. Click and hold the heading for column **F**, and then drag the mouse pointer to the right until columns **F** through **I** are selected. Press and hold Ctrl, and then select column **B**.

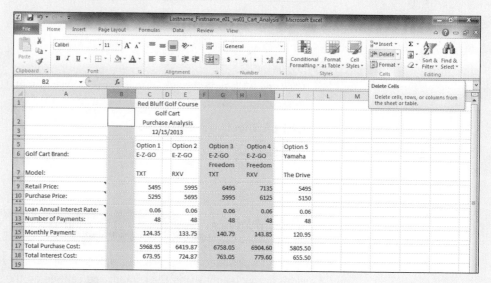

Figure 20   Multiple columns selected for deletion

b. Click **Delete** in the Cells group.

c. Select cell **A3**, and then press Delete.
    You have just cleared the contents of cell A3. Recall that for the cell range that includes the centered date, you used Center Across Selection. Clearing the contents of cell A3 removes the date that was centered across columns A:G because the date is stored in cell A3 where it was initially entered.

d. Select row **3** by clicking on the row heading.

e. Click **Delete** in the Cells group—now you have cleared the date. Also, notice the borders between all cells in row 3 are again visible.

f. Select cell **F4**, and then type Option 3.

g. Click on **Sheet3**, click cell **A18**, type today's date in mm/dd/yyyy format, click cell **C18**, and then type Removed carts no longer under consideration.

h. Click the **Sheet1 worksheet tab**.

i. Press Ctrl+Home, and then click **Save** 🖫.

Inserting Columns That Contain Data

Barry has asked that the analysis include multiple payment schedules for 24, 36, and 48 months of interest for each of the three remaining golf carts in the analysis. The interest rate for 24-month financing is 5.0%, 36-month financing is 5.5%, and 48-month financing is 6.0%. Expanding the analysis to include additional payment schedules is easily accomplished by inserting new columns that have been copied to the Clipboard and then editing the newly inserted columns.

To Expand the Analysis by Reusing and Editing Column Data

a. Select column **B**, and then click **Copy** in the Clipboard group. Right-click the heading for column **B**.

b. Click **Insert Copied Cells** on the shortcut menu. Press [Esc].

c. Repeat Steps a–b one more time.

d. Select column **F**, right-click the heading for column **F**, and then click **Copy** on the shortcut menu.

e. Right-click the heading for column **F**, and then click **Insert Copied Cells** on the shortcut menu. Press [Esc].

f. Repeat Steps d–e one more time.

g. Select column **J**. Right-click the heading for column **J**, and then click **Copy** on the shortcut menu.

h. Right-click the heading for column **J**, and then click **Insert Copied Cells** on the shortcut menu. Press [Esc].

i. Repeat Steps g–h one more time. Press [Esc].

j. Click cell **B11**, type **0.05**, and then press [Ctrl]+[Enter] to apply the change and to keep cell B11 selected. Press [Ctrl]+[C] to copy cell B11 to the Clipboard. Select cell **F11**, press and hold [Ctrl], and then select **J11**. Press [Ctrl]+[V] to paste cell B11 into cells F11 and J11. Press [Esc].

k. Click cell **C11**, type **0.055**, and then press [Ctrl]+[Enter]. Press [Ctrl]+[C]. Click cell **G11**, press [Ctrl], select cell **K11**, and then press [Ctrl]+[V]. Press [Esc].

l. Click cell **B12**, type **24**, and then press [Tab]. Type **36**, and then press [Enter]. Select cell range **B12:C12**, and then press [Ctrl]+[C]. Select cell **F12**, press and hold [Ctrl], select cell **J12**, press [Ctrl]+[V], and then press [Esc].

m. Select column **C**, press and hold [Ctrl], and then select columns **D**, **G**, **H**, **K**, and **L** (be sure to click each column heading rather than drag across). Click **Insert** in the Cells group.

n. Select column **C**, press and hold [Ctrl], and then select columns **E**, **I**, **K**, **O**, and **Q**—you may have to scroll right to access all the columns while still pressing [Ctrl] while scrolling. Click **Format** in the Cells group, and then select **Column Width** from the Cell Size menu. Type **1** in the Column Width dialog box, and then click **OK**.

o. Select cell range **B4:F4**, and then click **Merge & Center** in the Alignment group. Click **OK** when the warning message appears.

p. Repeat Step o for cell ranges H4:L4 and N4:R4. Press [Ctrl]+[Home].

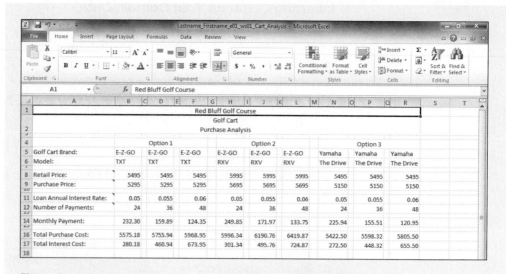

Figure 21 Golf cart analysis with option headings centered and additional payment schedules

q. Click the **Sheet3 worksheet tab**.

r. Click cell **A19**, type today's date in mm/dd/yyyy format, click cell **C19**, and then type Added analysis for 24 and 36 month loans.

s. Click the **Sheet1 worksheet tab**.

t. Press ⌈Ctrl⌉+⌈Home⌉, and then click **Save** 🖫.

Printing Worksheets and Manipulating Workbooks

Worksheets must often be printed for discussion at meetings or for distribution in venues where paper is the most effective medium. Excel has a lot of built-in functionality that makes printed worksheets easy to read and understand. Further, as workbooks grow to include multiple worksheets and evolve to require maintenance, it is necessary to be able to create new worksheets, copy worksheets, delete worksheets, and reorder worksheets.

In this section you will learn to use Excel's print functionality to ensure that your worksheets are usable when presented on paper, and you will learn to create, copy, delete, and reorder worksheets in a workbook.

Preview and Print Worksheets

The golf cart analysis is now ready to distribute as part of a package that will be given to management at the next board meeting. This will require that the analysis be printed on paper with appropriate headings and so forth.

Excel has a great deal of flexibility built into its printing functionality. To appropriately present your work in printed form, it is important that you understand how to take advantage of Excel's print features.

Worksheet Views

In the bottom-right corner of the application window are three icons that control the worksheet view. Normal view 🁣 is what you use most of the time when building and editing a worksheet. Only the cells in the worksheet are visible; print-specific features such as margins and page breaks are not shown.

Page Layout view ▣ shows page margins, print headers, and page breaks. It presents you with a reasonable preview of how a worksheet will print on paper.

Page Break Preview ▣ does not show page margins, but allows you to manually adjust the location of page breaks. This is particularly helpful when you would like to force a page break after a set of summary values and/or between data categories, and force the next part of a worksheet to print on a new page.

Quick Reference Switching Among Worksheet Views

On the right side of the status bar, do the following:
1. Click ▦ for Normal view.
2. Click ▣ for Page Layout view.
3. Click ▣ for Page Break Preview view.

To Switch Among Worksheet Views and Manipulate Page Breaks

a. Click **Page Layout** ▣ on the status bar.

b. Use the **Zoom Slider** [⊖———▯————⊕] on the status bar to adjust the view until two pages are completely visible.

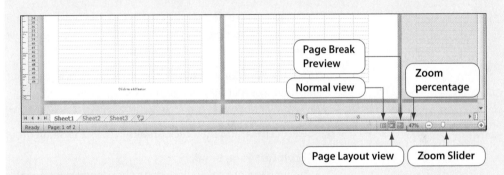

Figure 22 Page Layout view

c. Click **Page Break Preview** ▣ on the status bar. If the Welcome to Page Break Preview dialog box displays, click **OK**.
   Only the part of the worksheet that will print is displayed. A dashed blue border indicates where printing will break from one page to another.

d. Use the **Zoom Slider** [⊖———▯————⊕] to adjust the zoom level to make the pages as large as possible without hiding any data off the visible application window.

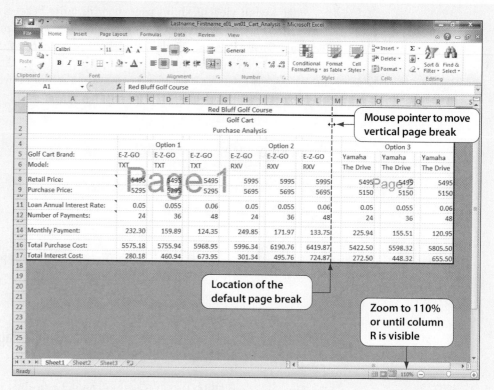

Figure 23   Page Break Preview

e. Point the mouse pointer over the blue page break border. The mouse pointer changes to ↔. Click and hold the left mouse button, and then move the page break to the cell border between columns **G** and **H** to adjust its location.

f. Click the **Page Layout tab** on the Ribbon—not Page Layout on the status bar. Now you need to insert another page break so each of the three golf carts still under consideration will print on a separate page.

g. Select cell **N4**, and then click **Breaks** in the Page Setup group.

h. Click **Insert Page Break**.

Two page breaks are inserted, a horizontal page break above the active cell, and a vertical page break to the left of the active cell. You only want the vertical page break between columns M and N.

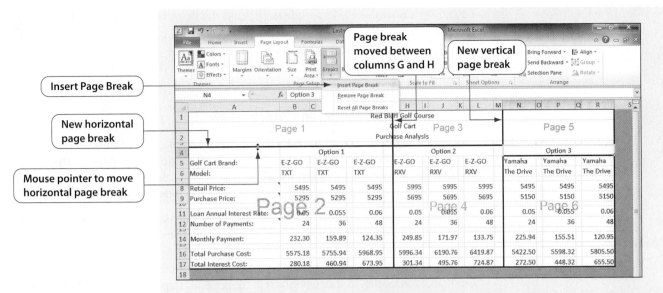

Figure 24 Insert horizontal and vertical page breaks in Page Break Preview

i.   Point to the horizontal page break, and the mouse pointer will change to ↕. Drag the **horizontal page break** off the bottom (or top) of the print area to remove it. There should now be page breaks after column G and after column M.

j.   Click **Normal** ▦ on the status bar. The dotted lines between columns G and H and columns M and N are the page breaks you just created.

     Notice that the titles in rows 1 and 2 will be split between two pages and will not print at all on the third page. You will remove them from the print area.

k.   Click **Page Break Preview** ▦ on the status bar. If the Welcome to Page Break Preview dialog box displays, click **OK**. Point to the top border of the worksheet, and the mouse pointer will change to ↕. Click and hold the left mouse button, and then move the top border down until it is between rows 3 and 4.

l.   Click **Normal** ▦ on the status bar. The dotted lines show the print area and the location of page breaks.

m.   Click the **Sheet3 worksheet tab**.

n.   Click cell **A20**, type today's date in mm/dd/yyyy format, click cell **C20**, and then type Adjusted page breaks.

o.   Click the **Sheet1 worksheet tab**.

p.   Press ⌨Ctrl+⌨Home, and then click **Save** 🖫.

Using Print Preview and Selecting a Printer

Enter Backstage view by clicking the File tab. Select Print on the left menu. The right side of the screen is Print Preview. **Print Preview** presents a facsimile of your document printed. You can use the scroll bar on the right or the paging control on the bottom to view additional pages if your worksheet requires more than one page to print.

Often a computer is connected to a local area network, or LAN. More than one print device can be made available to a computer via a LAN. You must be sure to select the printer/device you want to use from the Printer Status control. The default printer is selected automatically and is usually acceptable. When a different printer is required, click the Printer Status arrow on the right side of the printer status control to see a list of available devices.

Printing a worksheet is as simple as clicking the Print button. If more than one copy is desired, change the number in the Copies box to the right of the Print button. The copy count can be increased or decreased by clicking the arrows or by clicking in the Copies box and entering the number of copies from the keyboard.

To Use Printer Status Control and Print Preview

a. Click the **File tab**, and then click **Print** on the left side menu. If your computer has access to a printer, either via a USB cable or some other direct connection, or through a network, the Printer Status control displays the default printer. Click the **Printer Status control** to determine what print devices are available on your network.

b. The right side of the window is the preview of what will print. Use the scroll bar on the right, or the Next page or Previous page navigation buttons at the bottom to view each page that will print.

   Print Preview is an excellent way to see exactly how your worksheet will look when printed. Examination of your worksheet in the previous step revealed that there is more to be done before this worksheet is ready for printing.

SIDE NOTE
Print Preview

Any time you are going to print any or all of a worksheet, it is important to preview what will print to avoid wasting time and paper.

Print Titles

When a worksheet is too large to print on a single page, it is often difficult to keep track of data from one page to another. Headers, such as those in column A of the golf cart analysis, are only printed on the first page.

Print titles can be included on each printed page so every column and/or row is labeled and easily identified from one page to another.

To Specify Print Titles

a. Click the **Page Layout tab**, and then click **Print Titles** in the Page Setup group. The Page Setup dialog box will appear.

b. On the Sheet tab of the Page Setup dialog box, under Print titles, type **A:A** in the Columns to repeat at left text box.

   Since the golf cart analysis worksheet contains too many columns to print on a single page, you should print at least one column on each page that identifies cell contents in each row—it may seem odd, but the Print Titles feature requires the specification of a range, even when only a single column will be printed, thus the need to enter column A as A:A.

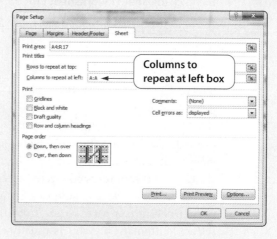

Figure 25   The Sheet tab in the Page Setup dialog box for creating print titles

c. Click **OK**, click the **File tab**, and then click **Print** on the left side menu.

d. In the Print Preview pane, use the scroll bar on the right, or the Next page or Previous page navigation buttons at the bottom, to view each page that will print.

e. Click the **Home tab**. Click the **Sheet3 worksheet tab**.

f. Click cell **A21**, type today's date in mm/dd/yyyy format, click cell **C21**, and then type Specified print titles.

g. Click the **Sheet1 worksheet tab**, and then press Ctrl + Home.

h. Click **Save** 🖫.

Print Headers/Footers

There are often items of information that should be included on a printed document that are not necessary to display in a worksheet. These items might include the following:

- Print date
- Print time
- Company name
- Page number
- Total number of pages
- Filename and location

The print header and footer are divided into three sections: left, center, and right—information can be placed in any section or all sections. Print headers place information at the top of each printed page. Print footers place information at the bottom of each printed page. You may include information in either or both the print header and print footer as deemed necessary.

To Add a Print Header and Print Footer

a. Click **Page Layout** 🔲 on the status bar. If necessary, use the **Zoom Slider** to adjust zoom to 100%.

b. Select **Click to add header** in the top margin of Page Layout view. The Design tab for Header & Footer Tools will appear on the Ribbon.

c. Select the **left section** of the print header, and then click **Current Date** in the Header & Footer Elements group.

d. Select the **center section** of the print header, type Red Bluff Golf Club, press Enter, and then type Cart Purchase Analysis.

e. Select the **right section** of the print header, click **Page Number** in the Header & Footer Elements group, press Spacebar to add a space, and then type of. Press Spacebar to add a space again, and then click **Number of Pages** in the Header & Footer Elements group.

f. Click **Go to Footer** in the Navigation group, or alternatively click **Click to add footer** at the bottom margin of Page Layout view—you may have to scroll down to find it.

g. Select the **left section** of the print footer, and then click **File Name** in the Header & Footer Elements group.

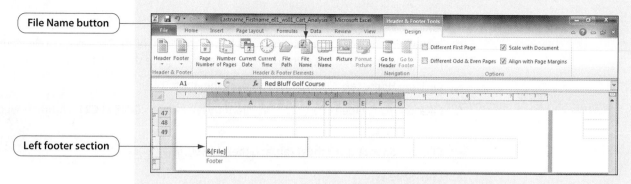

File Name button

Left footer section

Figure 26   Page Layout View—Add information to the page footer

h. Select any cell in the worksheet, press `Ctrl`+`Home`, and then click **Normal** ▦ on the status bar.

i. Repeat Steps a–h for the **Sheet2** and **Sheet3** worksheets.

j. Click the **Sheet1 worksheet tab**. Click the **File tab**, and then click **Print** on the left side menu.

k. Use the scroll bar on the right or the page navigation buttons to view each page that will print. Notice the headers and footers are added.

    Once again, there is still more to be done to the worksheet before printing.

l. Click the **Home tab**. Click the **Sheet3 worksheet tab**.

m. Click cell **A22**, type today's date in mm/dd/yyyy format, click cell **C22**, and then type Added print header and footer.

n. Click the **Sheet1 worksheet tab**.

o. Click **Save** 🖫.

Page Margins

Page margins are the white space that appear at the edges of the printed page. Normal margins for Excel are 0.7 inches on the left and right sides of the page, 0.75 inches on the top and bottom of the page, and 0.3 inches for header and footer, if included.

Margins can be changed to suit conventions or standards for an organization, to better locate information on the page, or to avoid a page break at the last column or line of a worksheet. For the golf cart analysis, there is no need to change page margins.

Quick Reference / Setting Page Margins

Page margins can be changed as follows:

1. Click the File tab.
2. Click Print on the left side menu.
3. Under Settings, the margins control is the second from the bottom.
4. Margins can be set to several preset values: Normal, Wide, or Narrow.
5. Click Custom Margins to reveal the Margins tab in the Page Setup dialog box.

Page margins can also be changed as follows:

1. Click the Page Layout tab.
2. In the Page Setup group, select Margins to reveal the same Margins control as displayed in the File tab, Print menu.

Page Orientation

Worksheets can be oriented to print on paper in one of two ways, **portrait**—the vertical dimension of the paper is longer, or **landscape**—the horizontal dimension of the paper is longer. Landscape is generally used when a worksheet has too many columns to fit into a single page in portrait orientation. Scaling the worksheet to fit all columns on a single page can work in portrait orientation, but if scaling makes the data too small to be readable, landscape orientation is an option to resolve the problem.

To Change Page Orientation

a. Click the **File tab**, and then click **Print** on the left side menu.

b. Click **Landscape Orientation** in the Orientation control—fourth from the bottom under Settings.

c. The right side of the window is the preview of what will print. Use the scroll bar on the right or the page navigation buttons at the bottom to view each page that will print.

d. Use the scroll bar on the right or the page navigation buttons to view each page that will print. Notice there is now quite a lot of white space on the right side of every page.

e. Click the **Home tab**. Click the **Sheet3 worksheet tab**.

f. Click cell **A23**, type today's date in mm/dd/yyyy format, click cell **C23**, and then type Set page orientation to landscape.

g. Click the **Sheet1 worksheet tab**.

h. Click **Save** 🖫.

Scaling

It is not uncommon for worksheets to be too large to print on a single page, or to be so small that they appear dwarfed in the top-left hand corner of the page. Scaling changes the size of the print font to allow more of a worksheet to print on a page or for a worksheet to print larger and use more page space. A printed worksheet that has been scaled to fit a sheet of paper generally looks more professional and is easier to read and understand than a worksheet that prints on two pages that uses only a small part of the second page.

To Change Page Scaling

a. Click the **File tab**, and then click **Print** on the left side menu.

b. Click **Fit All Columns on One Page** in the Scaling control—the bottom control under Settings.

Click the **Sheet2 worksheet tab**. Click the **File tab**, and then click **Print**. Click **Fit All Columns on One Page** in the Scaling control. Click the **Home tab**. Click the **Sheet3 worksheet tab**. Click the **File tab**, and then click **Print**. Click **Fit All Columns on One Page** in the Scaling control. Click the **Home tab**. Click the **Sheet1 worksheet tab**.

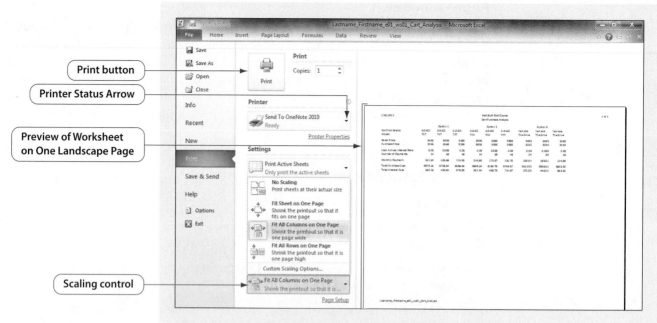

Print button

Printer Status Arrow

Preview of Worksheet on One Landscape Page

Scaling control

Figure 27 Print—Scaling control in Backstage view

SIDE NOTE
Navigate Between Worksheets in a Workbook

- Click the worksheet tab of an inactive worksheet to make it the active worksheet.
  or
- Press Ctrl+PgUp to go to the prior worksheet or Ctrl+PgDn to go to the next worksheet.

c. If your computer is attached to a printer, the Printer Status control displays the default printer. If you want to print to a different printer (if your computer has access to more than one printer), click the **Printer Status arrow** next to the printer name, and then select the desired printer from the list. Click **Print** or submit your workbook file as directed by your instructor.

d. If necessary, click the **Home tab**. Click the **Sheet3 worksheet tab**.

e. Click cell **A24**, type today's date in mm/dd/yyyy format, click cell **C24**, and then type Scaled worksheets to print all columns on one page.

f. Click the **Sheet1 worksheet tab**.

g. Click **Save** 💾.

Manipulate Worksheets and Workbooks

When there are two (or more) worksheets in a workbook, there is a need to navigate between (or among) the worksheets. Worksheets can be added to a workbook, deleted from a workbook, moved within a workbook, or moved to other workbooks. Sheet names are displayed on each sheet's tab at the bottom of the application window, just above the status bar. See Figure 28. The white worksheet tab identifies the active worksheet. Gray worksheet tabs identify hidden worksheets.

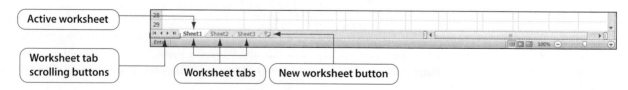

Active worksheet

Worksheet tab scrolling buttons

Worksheet tabs

New worksheet button

Figure 28 Worksheet tabs and navigation controls

SIDE NOTE
Navigate Between Workbooks

In Windows 7, pressing `Windows`+`TAB` reveals a 3D display to rotate through open applications. Hold `Windows` and press `TAB` repeatedly to rotate through open applications—release `Windows` when the desired application is at the front of the rotation.

When a workbook contains a large number of worksheets or when worksheets have very long names, some worksheet tabs may not be visible in the application window. To bring tabs that are not visible into view, use the worksheet tab scrolling buttons to the left of the worksheet tabs.

Name a Worksheet

When worksheets are created, whether among the default three in a new workbook, or the dozens that can be added to a workbook, the default name is "Sheet*n*" where *n* is a sequential integer: if you add a fourth worksheet to a workbook, its default name will be "Sheet4."

The default worksheet names are not particularly descriptive and do nothing to help document the contents or purpose of a worksheet. Worksheets can be renamed by double-clicking the worksheet tab or by right-clicking the worksheet tab and clicking Rename on the shortcut menu. Worksheet names can be up to 31 characters long.

To Navigate Among and Rename Worksheets in a Workbook

a. Double-click the **Sheet1 worksheet tab**. Sheet1 is the active worksheet, and the Sheet1 name in the worksheet tab is highlighted as selected text.

b. Type RBGC_Golf_Cart_Purch_Analysis, and then press `Enter`.

c. Double-click the **Sheet2 worksheet tab**. Sheet2 is the active worksheet, and the Sheet2 name in the worksheet tab is highlighted as selected text.

d. Type RBGC_Golf_Cart_Usage_Analysis, and then press `Enter`.

e. Double-click the **Sheet3 worksheet tab**. Sheet3 is the active worksheet, and the Sheet3 name in the worksheet tab is highlighted as selected text.

f. Type Documentation, and then press `Enter`.

g. Click the **RBGC_Golf_Cart_Purch_Analysis worksheet tab**.

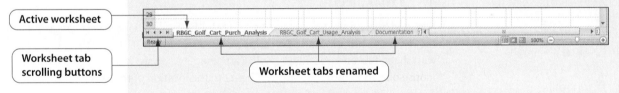

Active worksheet

Worksheet tab scrolling buttons

Worksheet tabs renamed

Figure 29   Worksheet tabs after renaming

h. Click the **Documentation worksheet tab**, click cell **A25**, and then type today's date in mm/dd/yyyy format. Click cell **C25**, and then type Renamed worksheets. Click cell **B32**, and then type RBGC_Golf_Cart_Purch_Analysis. Click cell **B38**, and then type RBGC_Golf_Cart_Usage_Analysis. Click cell **B44**, type Documentation, and then press `Ctrl`+`Home`.

i. Click the **RBGC_Golf_Cart_Purch_Analysis worksheet tab**. Press `Ctrl`+`Home`.

j. Click **Save** 🖫.

Insert or Delete a Worksheet

Manipulating a workbook will occasionally require the creation, or insertion, of new worksheets as well as the deletion of existing worksheets. Inserted worksheets are by default given a name such as "Sheet4", where the digit is one larger than the last digit appended to a worksheet name. An inserted worksheet is automatically the active worksheet. To insert a worksheet, move to the right of the list of worksheet tabs and click Insert Worksheet 🗐.

To delete a worksheet, right-click the tab of the worksheet you want to delete and click Delete in the shortcut menu.

To Insert a Worksheet

a. Click the **Insert Worksheet tab** to the right of the worksheet tabs. You may have to use the worksheet tab scrolling buttons to access the Insert Worksheet tab.

b. Click the **Insert Worksheet tab** a second time.

c. Click **Save**.

First Worksheet button

Last Worksheet button

Previous Worksheet button

Next Worksheet button

Insert Worksheet tab

Figure 30 Two inserted worksheets

Move a Worksheet

The order of worksheets in a workbook can be changed by reordering the worksheet tabs. To move a worksheet, make the target worksheet the active worksheet by clicking on its tab. Click and hold on the worksheet tab, drag the worksheet tab to its new location, and drop it by releasing the mouse button. As a worksheet is dragged, a ▼ will appear between worksheet tabs. This indicates the location where the worksheet will be inserted when the left mouse button is released.

SIDE NOTE
A Fast Way to Copy a Worksheet
Click and hold the target worksheet tab. Press and hold Ctrl, and then drag the worksheet tab to the desired location. The mouse pointer changes to ▯ to show that you are copying. Release the mouse button.

SIDE NOTE
Move Quickly Between Workbooks
To move quickly between two or more open workbooks, press Ctrl+Tab.

To Move a Worksheet

a. Click and hold on the **Sheet2 worksheet tab**. The mouse pointer will change to ▯. Move the mouse to the left until a ▼ appears between the RBGC_Golf_Cart_Purch_Analysis worksheet tab and the RBGC_Golf_Cart_Usage_Analysis worksheet tab. Release the mouse button to move worksheet Sheet2 to the location of the ▼.

b. Click and hold on the **Sheet1 worksheet tab**. The mouse pointer will change to ▯. Move the mouse to the left until a ▼ appears between the RBGC_Golf_Cart_Usage_Analysis worksheet tab and the Documentation worksheet tab. Release the mouse button to move Sheet1 to the specified location.

c. Click **Save**.

Figure 31 Worksheet tabs—Sheet1 and Sheet2 moved

Deleting a Worksheet

Deleting a worksheet is most commonly done to remove unused worksheets from a workbook—recall that a new workbook contains three worksheets by default, and many workbooks do not require three worksheets. Unused worksheets are a form of clutter in a workbook and add unnecessary size to the stored workbook file.

To Delete a Worksheet

a. Click the **Sheet2 tab** to make it the active worksheet tab. Right-click the Sheet2 tab, and then click **Delete** from the shortcut menu.

b. Use the worksheet navigation buttons to locate and click the **Sheet1 tab** to make it the active worksheet. Right-click the Sheet1 tab, and then click **Delete** from the shortcut menu. Click the **RBGC_Golf_Cart_Purch_Analysis tab** to make the first worksheet the active sheet.

c. Click **Save** ⊟. Print or submit your documents as directed by your instructor. Close ⊠ Excel.

1. The instructor in one of your classes distributed a syllabus that includes the following statement: "Late assignments are not accepted unless university policy specifically addresses your situation, such as family tragedy or personal medical malady—both of which require written validation. Computer and network problems are not an excuse, so *back up your work!*" What strategy will you implement to ensure you will not miss a due date owing to a computer or network problem, or because of the loss of a USB drive or other portable storage medium?

2. Often, acceptance into a college requires a specific grade point average (GPA) in a student's first two years of high school coursework. Acceptance into graduate school or a professional school such as law or medical school requires a minimum undergraduate GPA. Many students could make use of a worksheet into which they can enter courses they have taken and the grades they earned, as well as courses they *will* take. The worksheet could then calculate both the current GPA and the GPA that would result from expected grades in future courses. Plan such a worksheet. What data will you need? What calculations will you need to make? How will you structure the worksheet?

3. Although Merge & Center and Center Across Selection result in exactly the same look in your worksheet, they function differently. How are they different? When would you recommend to use one over the other and why?

4. Print titles, page headers, and page footers, if used properly, can make your printed worksheets easier to read and appear more professional. Explain what each does, why, and when you would use them.

5. Page orientation and scaling can be used together when printing your worksheet. What does each do, and how can they be used in tandem to allow you to efficiently print a professional-looking worksheet?

Key Terms

Active cell 289	Formula 286	Row 286
Active worksheet 291	Function 286	Spreadsheet 286
AutoFill 301	Landscape 321	What-if analysis 286
Cell 286	Portrait 321	White space 304
Cell reference 289	Print Preview 317	Workbook 287
Column 286	Range 298	Worksheet 286
Field 286	Record 286	Worksheet navigation 289

Create a blank workbook (p. 288)

Open an existing workbook (p. 288)

Save and rename a workbook (p. 289)

Use Printer Status control and Print Preview (p. 318)

Document a workbook using a documentation worksheet and/or comments (p. 292)

Delete columns and rows (p. 312)

Insert a column between each column of cart data (p. 308)

Expand the analysis by reusing and editing column data (p. 313)

Navigate using the keyboard (p. 290)

Navigate using the Go To dialog box (p. 291)

Enter information in a worksheet (p. 296)

Use Cut, Copy, and Paste (p. 301)

Wrap or unwrap text in a cell (p. 297)

Merge, center, and format headings (p. 306)

Quickly generate data using AutoFill (p. 302)

Use the AutoFit feature to adjust column width (p. 310)

Insert rows in a worksheet (p. 304)

Delete cells, cell ranges, and rows (p. 305)

Drag and drop cells (p. 299)

Manually adjust column width and row height (p. 309)

Select contiguous and noncontiguous cell ranges (p. 298)

Modify worksheet contents by changing copied information (p. 304)

Change the active worksheet (p. 292)

Switch among worksheet views and manipulate page breaks (p. 315)

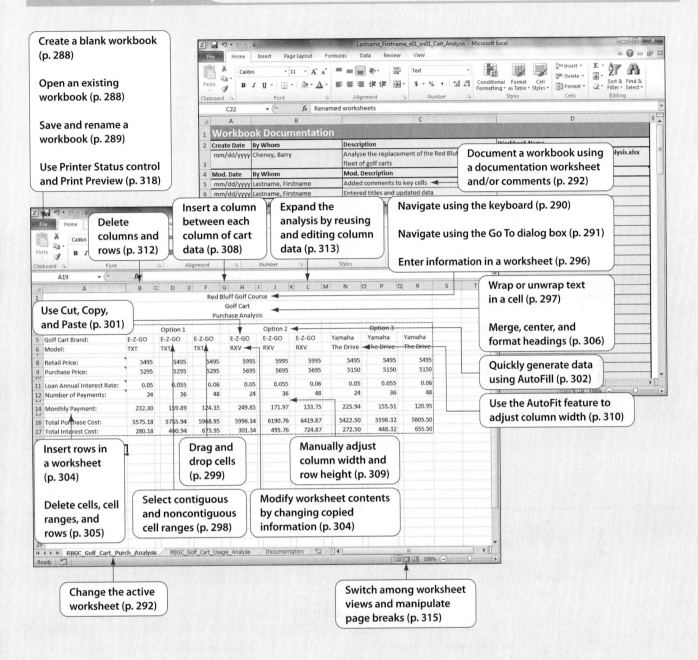

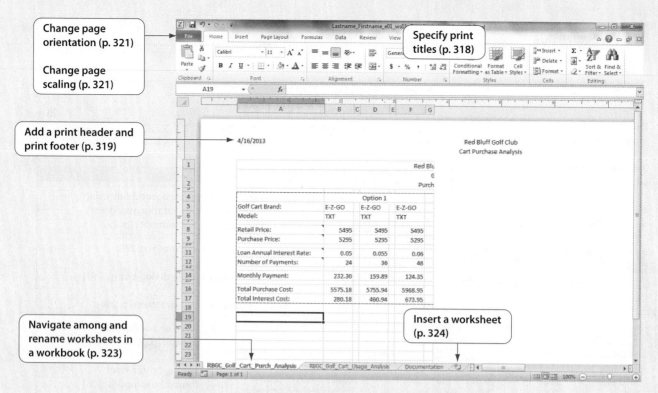

Change page orientation (p. 321)

Change page scaling (p. 321)

Specify print titles (p. 318)

Add a print header and print footer (p. 319)

Navigate among and rename worksheets in a workbook (p. 323)

Insert a worksheet (p. 324)

Figure 32   Red Bluff Golf Club golf cart purchase analysis final

Practice 1

Student data file needed:

e01_ws01_Wedding_Worksheet

You will save your file as:

Lastname_Firstname_e01_ws01_Wedding_Worksheet

Red Bluff Resort Wedding Planning Worksheet

Sales & Marketing

Weddings are becoming an important part of the resort's business. Thus, Patti Rochelle started a worksheet to improve the wedding planning process for her staff. Last year, on average, the resort hosted three weddings per week and has done as many as six in a weekend. The worksheet Patti wants you to finish will allow for changes in pricing to be immediately reflected in the planning process.

You have been given a workbook that includes product/service categories, prices, and an initial worksheet structure in order to help standardize the process and pricing of weddings. You will build a worksheet that calculates the price of a wedding and doubles as a checklist to use as weddings are set up to ensure subcontractors, such as DJs, are reserved in a timely fashion and that all contracted services are delivered.

a. Start **Excel**, click the **File tab**, and then click **Open**. Click the disk drive in the left pane where your student data files are located, navigate through the folder structure, and click **e01_ws01_Wedding_Worksheet**. Click the **File tab**, and then click **Save As**. In the Save As dialog box, navigate to the location where you are saving your files. In the File name box, type Lastname_Firstname_e01_ws01_Wedding_Worksheet, replacing Lastname_ Firstname with your name. Click **Save**.

b. Double-click the **Sheet1 worksheet tab**, type Wedding_Planner, and then press [Enter].

c. Double-click the **Sheet2 worksheet tab**, and then type Documentation as the new name for the worksheet. Press [Enter]. Click cell **B16**, and then type Wedding_Planner. Press [Ctrl]+[Home].

d. Click the **Wedding_Planner worksheet tab**.

e. Type the Value information into the cell indicated as follows:

Data Item	Value	Cell
Wedding Date	6/18/2014	B2
Start Time	4:00 PM	D2
End Time	5:00 PM	G2
Reception Start Time	6:00 PM	D3
Reception End Time	12:00 AM	G3
Total Hours	8	B5
Reception Hours	6	D5
Estimated Guests	125	B7
Ceremony	650	H11
Reception	750	H12
Catering	17	H13
Flowers	1250	H18
Decorations	1500	H19
Photography	1500	H24
Webcast	250	H25
Entertainment Hours Played		
Piano Player (Hours)	1	C28
String Quartet (Hours)	2	C29
DJ (Hours)	4	C32
Discount	-0.05	H33

f. Select cell range **F3:G3**, click the **Home tab**, click **Cut** in the Clipboard group, click cell **H8** to make it the active cell, and then click **Paste** in the Clipboard group.

g. Select cell range **C3:D3**, click **Cut** in the Clipboard group, click cell **H7**, and then click **Paste** in the Clipboard group.

h. Click cell **B3**. Hover over the border of the active cell; when the mouse pointer changes, click and hold the left mouse button, drag cell **B3** to cell **G7**, and then release the mouse button to drop.

i. Select cell range **F2:G2**, press [Ctrl]+[X], click cell **H5**, and then press [Ctrl]+[V].

j. Select cell range **C2:D2**, press [Ctrl]+[X], click cell **H4**, and then press [Ctrl]+[V].

k. Select cell range **A2:B2**, press [Ctrl]+[X], and then click cell **G3** to make it the active cell. Press [Ctrl]+[V], select the column range **G:H**, click **Format** in the Cells group, and then click **AutoFit Column Width**.

l. Press [Ctrl]+[Home]. Hover over the border of the active cell; when the mouse pointer changes to the move pointer, click and hold the left mouse button, and then drag cell **A1** to cell **G1**.

m. Select cell range **B9:C9**, press [Ctrl], and then select cell range **B34:C34**. Click **Merge & Center** in the Alignment group.

n. Select columns **B:C**, click **Format** in the Cells group, and then click **Column Width**. Type **17** in the Column width box, and then click **OK**.

o. Click cell **A27**, click the **Insert arrow** in the Cells group, and then click **Insert Sheet Rows**.

p. Click the header for column **E**. Right-click and select **Delete** from the shortcut menu. In the Cells group, click **Format**, and then click **Column Width**. Type **2** in the Column width text box, and then click **OK**.

q. Select cell range **A5:A35**. Press Ctrl, and then select cell ranges **B10:D10**, **B17:C17**, **B23:C23**, **B28:D28**, **F1:F35**, **G4:G8**, and **G10:H10**; and cells **C5**, **B35**, **G14**, **G21**, **G26**, and **H35**. Press Ctrl+B.

r. Click **Page Layout** on the status bar. Scroll to the bottom of the worksheet and click **Click to add footer**.

s. Click in the left section of the Footer.

t. If necessary, click the **Design tab** under Header & Footer tools. Click **File Name** in the Header & Footer Elements group, and then click a cell in the worksheet. Press Ctrl+Home. Click **Normal** on the status bar.

u. Click the **Documentation worksheet tab**, and then click cell **A5**. Enter today's date in mm/dd/yyyy format. Click cell **B5**, and then type Lastname, Firstname, replacing Lastname, Firstname with your actual name. Click cell **C5**, type Completed Ms. Rochelle's initial work - reorganized worksheet to function better as a checklist, and then press Ctrl+Home.

v. Right-click the **Sheet3 worksheet tab**, and then click **Delete**. Click the **Wedding_ Planner worksheet tab**, select cell range **F1:H35**, click the **File tab**, and then click **Print** from the menu on the left. Under Settings, click the **Print Active Sheets arrow**, and then click **Print Selection**. Click **Print** and/or submit your workbook file as directed by your instructor. On the Wedding_Planner worksheet tab, press Ctrl+Home.

w. **Save** and close the workbook.

Problem Solve 1

Student data file needed:	You will save your file as:
e01_ps1_Spa_Pricing	Lastname_Firstname_e01_ps1_Spa_Pricing

Turquoise Oasis Spa Pricing Analysis

Sales & Marketing

Meda Rodate, the manager of the Turquoise Oasis Spa at Painted Paradise Golf Resort and Spa, wants to review the spa's services and pricing. Several competitors have opened in the area and Meda sees the need for an organized presentation of spa information to facilitate identifying the spa's highpoints and using them to gain a competitive edge.

Meda created a workbook containing three worksheets. One worksheet contains documentation on the dates the workbook and worksheets were created or modified and by whom. Another worksheet contains a list of spa services, current pricing, and a possible 10 percent price increase. The third worksheet contains the hours of operations. Meda has to be out of town for a few days and has asked you to complete the workbook prior to her return. You are to enhance the appearance of the worksheets, edit content, insert comments, and improve overall formatting, making the workbook and its information easier to review and assess.

a. Start **Excel**. Click the **File tab**, and then click **Open**. Click the disk drive in the left pane where your student data files are located, navigate through the folder structure, and then double-click **e01_ps1_ Spa_Pricing** to open the file. Click the **File tab**, and then click **Save As**. In the Save As dialog box, navigate to the location where you are saving your files. In the File name box, type Lastname_Firstname_e01_ps1_ Spa_Pricing, replacing Lastname_Firstname with your name.

b. Double-click the **Sheet1 worksheet tab**, type Spa_Services as the new name for the worksheet, and then press Enter.

c. Double-click the **Sheet2 worksheet tab**, type Spa_Hours as the new name for the worksheet, and then press Enter.

d. Click the **Spa_Services worksheet tab**, click cell **A10**, and then click **Wrap Text** in the Alignment group. Double-click cell **A10** to enter Edit mode and position the insertion point immediately following the word **Treatment**. Press Delete to remove the space. Press Alt+Enter to insert a hard return.

e. Click cell **B4**, click the **Review tab**, and then click **New Comment** in the Comments group. Repeatedly press Backspace until the comment box is cleared of the user name. Press Ctrl+B. Type If two or more services are performed in a single visit, a 15% discount will be given.

f. Click cell **A10**, and then click **New Comment** in the Comments group. Repeatedly press Backspace until the comment box is cleared of the user name. Press Ctrl+B. Type A price will be quoted after a skin assessment. Click cell **A1**. If the comments in cell B4 and A10 are visible, click **Show All Comments** in the Comments group.

g. Double-click cell **A12**, double-click on the word **Special**, and then type Men's.

h. Click cell **D3**, type 12, and press Enter. Verify that the values in column D automatically increased to reflect the additional 2% increase.

i. Right-click the **header** for row 20, and then select **Insert** in the shortcut menu. Click cell **A20**, and then type Seaweed Wrap. Click cell **B20**, type 60, and press Enter

j. Select cell range **D3:D30**. Press Ctrl+C. Select cell range **E3:F3**. Press Enter. Select cell range **E4:F4**, and then click the **Home tab**. Click **Wrap Text** in the Alignment group. Click **Format** in the Cells group, and then select **AutoFit Column Width**.

k. Click cell **E3**, and then type 15. Click cell **F3**, and then type 17. Press Enter.

l. Click the **header** for column E, press and hold Ctrl, and click the **header** for column F. Right-click with the mouse pointer anywhere over the selected columns, and then select **Insert** from the shortcut menu.

m. Click the **column C header**, press and hold Ctrl, and then click the **column E header** and the **column G header**. Right-click the **column G header**, and then select **Column Width** from the shortcut menu. Type 5 in the Column width box, and click **OK**. Click the **column A header**. Right-click the **column A header**, and then select **Column Width** from the shortcut menu. Type 35 in the Column width box, and then click **OK**.

n. Click the **column B header**. Right-click the **column B header**, and then select **Column Width** from the shortcut menu. Type 8 in the Column width box, and then click **OK**.

o. Click the **Page Layout tab**, click **Orientation** in the Page Setup group, and then select **Landscape**. Press Ctrl+Home.

p. Click the **Spa_Hours worksheet tab**. Click cell **B4**, type Hours, and then press Ctrl+Enter. Press Ctrl+B. Select cell range **B4:C4**, click the **Home tab**, and then click **Merge & Center** in the Alignment group.

q. Click cell **A5**. Click and hold the **AutoFill** handle and expand the active cell to encompass cell range **A5:A11**.

r. Click cell **B5**, and then type Closed. Press Ctrl+Enter. Press Ctrl+C. Click cell **B11**, and then press Ctrl+V.

s. Click cell **B6**, type 10:00 am, and then press Ctrl+Enter. Click and hold the **AutoFill** handle and expand the active cell to encompass **B6:B10**. Click the **Auto Fill Options button**, and then select **Copy Cells**.

t. Click cell **C6**, type 8:00 pm, and then press Ctrl+Enter. Click and hold the **AutoFill** handle and expand the active cell to encompass **C6:C10**. Click the **Auto Fill Options button**, and then select **Copy Cells**. Press Ctrl+Home.

u. Click the **Documentation worksheet tab**, and then select cell range **C5:C14**. Click **Wrap Text** in the Alignment group of the Home tab. Click cell **A5**, and then press Ctrl+; to enter today's date. Click cell C5, type Inserted comments, and then press Ctrl+Enter. Click cell **C6**, and then type Added two additional price increase columns. Click cell **B5**, and then type your name in Lastname, Firstname format. Press Ctrl+Home.

v. Click the **Spa_Services worksheet tab**. Click the **Page Layout tab**, and then click **Print Titles** in the Page Setup group. Click the **Header/Footer tab** in the Page Setup dialog box, and then click the **Custom Footer button**. Click in the left section of the Footer dialog box. Click **Insert File Name**, click **OK** in the Footer dialog box, and then click **OK** in the Page Setup dialog box.

w. Click **Save**. Print and/or turn in workbook files as directed by your instructor. Close Excel.

 Additional Workshop Cases are available on the companion website and in the instructor resources.

WORKSHOP 2

Objectives

1. Format cells, cell ranges, and worksheets   p. 334

2. Create information with functions and formulas p. 350

3. Use conditional formatting to assist decision making p. 361

Formatting, Formulas, and Functions

PREPARE CASE
Red Bluff Golf Club Pro Shop Sales Analysis

Sales & Marketing

The Red Bluff Golf Course Pro Shop sells to its members products ranging from golf clubs and accessories to clothing displaying the club logo. In addition, the Pro Shop collects fees for rounds of golf and services such as lessons from golf pro John Schilling.

Manager Aleeta Herriott needs to track Pro Shop sales by category on a day-by-day basis. Sales, at least to some extent, are a reflection of traffic in the Pro Shop and can be used to help determine staffing requirements on different days of the week. In addition, summary sales data can be compared to inventory investments to determine if product mix is optimal, given the demands of clientele.

Each item or service is recorded in the Pro Shop point-of-sale (POS) system at the time of sale. At the end of each day, the POS system produces a cash register report with categorized sales for the day. This is the data source of each day's sales for the worksheet. Aleeta has created an initial layout for a sales analysis workbook, but she needs you to finish it.

Samot / Shutterstock.com

Student data files needed for this workshop:

 e01_ws02_Weekly_Sales

 e01_ws02_Documentation_Template

You will save your file as:

 Lastname_Firstname_e01_ws02_Weekly_Sales

Worksheet Formatting

In Excel, you can easily manipulate cells, cell ranges, and worksheets in a workbook as well as print worksheet information. However, manipulating and printing information is often not enough. To be of value, information must be effectively communicated. Effective communication of information generally requires that the information is formatted in a manner that aids in proper interpretation and understanding.

Some of the most revolutionary ideas in history have been initially recorded on a handy scrap of paper, a yellow legal pad, a tape recorder, and even a paper napkin. Communication of those ideas generally required that they be presented in a different medium and that they should be formatted in a manner that aided others' understanding. The content may not have changed at all, but the format of the presentation is important. People are more receptive to well-formatted information because it is easier to understand and absorb. While accuracy of the information is of utmost importance, what use is misunderstood accurate data? In this section, you will manipulate a worksheet by formatting numbers, aligning and rotating text, changing cell fill color and borders, using built-in cell and table styles, and applying workbook themes.

Format Cells, Cell Ranges, and Worksheets

There are several ways to present information. If different technologies, media, and audiences are considered, a list of more than 50 ways to present information would be easy to produce—the list could include such varied communication methods as books, speeches, websites, tweets, RSS feeds, and bumper stickers. An analysis of such a list, however, would reveal a short list of generic communication methodologies:

- Oral
- Written narrative
- Tabular
- Graphical

Excel is an application specifically designed to present information in tabular and graphical formats. **Tabular format** is the presentation of information (text and numbers) in **tables**—essentially organized in labeled rows and columns. **Graphical format** is the presentation of information in charts, graphs, and pictures. Excel facilitates the graphical presentation of information via charts and graphs based on the tabular information in worksheets. This workshop is focused on formatting information for tabular presentation.

Workshop 2 Training

To Get Started

a. Start **Excel**. Click the **File tab**, and then click **Open** on the menu on the left.

b. In the Open dialog box, click the disk drive in the left pane where your student data files are located, navigate through the folder structure, click **e01_ws02_Weekly_Sales**, and then click **Open**.

c. Click the **File tab**, click **Save As**, and then in the Save As dialog box, navigate to the location where you are saving your files. In the File name box, type Lastname_Firstname_ e01_ws02_Weekly_Sales, replacing Lastname_Firstname with your own name, and then click **Save**.

d. Double-click the **Sheet1 worksheet tab**. Type Weekly_Sales as the new name for the sheet, and then press Enter.

e. Press Ctrl+Home. Click **Save** .

Copying a Worksheet from One Workbook to Another

One way to easily document workbooks is to have a standard documentation template that you can reuse in any workbook. To reuse a documentation template, you will need to copy and insert the documentation template into your workbooks. Copying a worksheet from one workbook into another can be accomplished in just a few steps.

To Copy a Documentation Template from Another Workbook

a. Click the **File tab**, and then click **Open**. In the Open dialog box, click the disk drive in the left pane where your student data files are located, navigate through the folder structure, click **e01_ws02_Documentation_Template**, and then click **Open**.

b. Click **Select All** in the top-left corner of the Documentation worksheet.

c. Press Ctrl+C.

d. Press Ctrl+Tab to switch to Lastname_Firstname_e01_ws02_Weekly_Sales.

e. Click **Insert Worksheet** to the right of the worksheet tabs.

f. Press Ctrl+V.

g. Double-click the **Sheet1 worksheet tab**. You will now update the new documentation worksheet.

h. Type Documentation as the new name for the Sheet1 worksheet, and then press Enter.

i. Click cell **A3**, type 8/25/2013, click cell **B3**, and then type Herriott, Aleeta.

j. Click cell **C3**, and then type Pro Shop weekly sales analysis.

k. Click cell **A5**, and then press Ctrl+; to enter today's date.

l. Click cell **B5**, and then type your name in Lastname, Firstname format.

m. Click cell **B16**, and then type Weekly_Sales to replace and update the sheet name text.

n. Click cell **B17**, type Herriott, Aleeta, click cell **B23**, and then type Herriott, Aleeta.

o. Click cell **B18**, type 8/25/2013, click cell **B24**, and then type 8/25/2013.

p. Click cell **B19**, and then type Analyze weekly Pro Shop sales by item category and subcategory.

q. Click cell **B25**, and then type Analyze a day's sales by subcategory and time.

r. Click the **Weekly_Sales worksheet tab**.

s. Click **Save**. Press Ctrl+Tab to make e01_ws02_Documentation_Template the active workbook. Click to close e01_ws02_Documentation_Template without saving if prompted.

Numbers

Number formatting is probably more important than text formatting in Excel. Through number formatting, context can be given to numbers that makes text labeling unnecessary, such as with a date and/or time value. Most of the world's currencies can be represented in Excel through number formatting. Financial numbers, scientific numbers, percentages, dates, times, and so on all have special formatting requirements and can be properly displayed in a worksheet. The ability to manipulate and properly display many different types of numeric information is a feature that makes Excel an incredibly powerful and ubiquitously popular application in almost all walks of life.

Formats

Numbers can be formatted in many ways in Excel, as shown in Figure 1.

Ribbon Button	Menu Button	Format Name	Example
General ▾	ABC 123	General	1234
General ▾	12	Number	1,234.00
General ▾	🖩	Currency	$1,234.00
$ ▾	🖩	Accounting	$ 1,234.00
General ▾	🖩	Short Date	6/15/2013
General ▾	🕐	Time	6:00:00 PM
%	%	Percentage	7.50%

Figure 1   Common number formats

To Format Numbers

a. Select cell **B6**, and then click the **Number Format arrow** General ▾ in the Number group. A list of formats will appear. Click **Currency**.

b. Select cell range **B20:H25**, and then click **Accounting Number Format** $ ▾ in the Number group. If any of the cells in B20:H25 display number signs (#), click **Format** in the Cells group, and then click **AutoFit Column Width**.

c. Press Ctrl+Home, and then click **Save** 🖫.

Real World Advice — Accounting Number Format vs. Currency Number Format

The Accounting and Currency formats are both intended for the identification and display of monetary values. Characteristics of the Accounting format are as follows:

- The Accounting format always displays negative numbers in parentheses; thus, a consistent right margin space is maintained to accommodate parentheses when needed.
- The currency symbol is aligned with the left side of the cell.
- Zero values are displayed as a dash (—) aligned at the decimal position.
- The decimal place is aligned.

Currency is a more complex format than the Accounting format as shown in Figure 2. The currency format has several formatting options:

- Negative numbers can be identified with a minus sign (–), parentheses, or displayed in a red font color. The red font color option can be combined with parentheses as well.
- The currency symbol is placed directly left of the value and inside the parentheses if they are used to denote negative numbers.
- Zero values are displayed as 0 with zeroes in each decimal place.

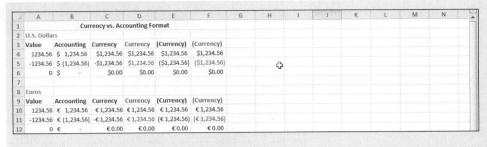

	A	B	C	D	E	F	G	H	I	J	K	L	M	N
1			Currency vs. Accounting Format											
2	U.S. Dollars													
3	Value	Accounting	Currency	Currency	(Currency)	(Currency)								
4	1234.56	$ 1,234.56	$1,234.56	$1,234.56	$1,234.56	$1,234.56								
5	-1234.56	$ (1,234.56)	-$1,234.56	$1,234.56	($1,234.56)	($1,234.56)								
6	0	$ -	$0.00	$0.00	$0.00	$0.00								
7														
8	Euros													
9	Value	Accounting	Currency	Currency	(Currency)	(Currency)								
10	1234.56	€ 1,234.56	€1,234.56	€1,234.56	€1,234.56	€1,234.56								
11	-1234.56	€ (1,234.56)	-€1,234.56	€1,234.56	(€1,234.56)	(€1,234.56)								
12	0	€ -	€0.00	€0.00	€0.00	€0.00								

Figure 2 Accounting and Currency format options

Negative Values and Color

Negative numbers often warrant more than parentheses or a hyphen to call attention to the fact that a value is below zero. The phrase "in the red" is often used to describe financial values that have fallen below zero so, not surprisingly, Excel makes it very easy to display negative numbers in a red font color.

To Display Negative Numbers in Red

a. Select cell range **B20:H25**, click the **Number Format arrow** General in the Number group, and then click **More Number Formats**.

b. Under Category, click **Number**. If necessary, enter 2 in the Decimal places box. Make sure **Use 1000 Separator (,)** is checked.

c. Under Negative numbers, select the red negative number format **(1,234.10)**, and then click **OK**.

   To apply red formatting to the negative number, be sure to select the red version of the negative number format (1,234.10). If any of the cells in B20:H25 display number signs, click Format in the Cells group, and click AutoFit Column Width on the Cell Size menu.

d. Press Ctrl+Home, and then click **Save**.

CONSIDER THIS | Usability and Color-Blindness

Approximately 8–12% of people of European descent are color-blind. This does not mean they cannot see any color, but for about 99% of them, it means they have trouble distinguishing between reds and greens. How should this information affect the way you format your worksheets?

There are several keyboard shortcuts that allow rapid application of specific number formats:

Keyboard Shortcut	Number Format
Ctrl + Shift + ~	General
Ctrl + Shift + 1	Number -1,234.10
Ctrl + Shift + 2	Time hh:mm AM/PM
Ctrl + Shift + 3	Date dd-mmm-yy
Ctrl + Shift + 4 or Ctrl + Shift + $	Currency ($1,234.10)
Ctrl + Shift + 5 or Ctrl + Shift + %	Percentage
Ctrl + Shift + 6 or Ctrl + Shift + ^	Scientific (exponential)

Figure 3   Number format keyboard shortcuts

Dates and Times

Excel stores a date and time as a real number where the number to the left of the decimal place, or the absolute value, is the number of complete days since January 1, 1900, inclusive. The right side of the decimal place is the decimal portion of the day. This kind of date system allows Excel to use dates in calculations. For example, if you add 1 to today's date, you will get tomorrow's date.

While useful for computer systems and applications like Excel, people have not been taught to interpret time in this manner, so unformatted date and time values (those displayed in General format) mean little or nothing. Date and time formatting allows Excel date and time values to be displayed in a fashion that allows proper reader interpretation. A heading that identifies a column as date values gives context to the information, but in the case of date information, without proper formatting, it is for the most part not interpretable by the reader.

To Format a Cell or Cell Range as a Date or Time

a. Select cell **B4**, type 12/1/2013, and then press Ctrl + Enter to accept the data and to keep cell B4 selected.

b. Click the **Number Format arrow** [General ▾] in the Number group, and then click **General**.

   Cell B4 is no longer formatted to display the date you entered in month/day/year format. The number in cell B4 (41609 in this example) is what Excel actually stores for the date you entered.

c. Drag the **fill handle** in cell B4 to the right, until the border around the active cell expands to include cells **B4:H4**, and then release the left mouse button.

   The General formatted number has been copied to each of the cells in C4:H4.

d. Click **Auto Fill Options** 🔡, which appears next to the fill handle. Click **Fill Series** on the Auto Fill Options menu. The numbers in B4:H4 are now incremented by 1 in each cell from left to right.

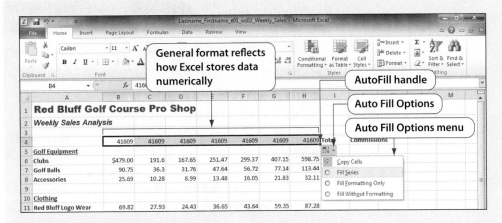

Figure 4   AutoFill and Auto Fill options

e. Click the **Number Format arrow** `General ▾` in the Number group, and then click **Short Date**. If any of the cells in B4:H4 display number signs, click **Format** in the Cells group, and then click **AutoFit Column Width** on the Cell Size menu.

f. Click cell **A1**, and then click **Save** 🖫.

g. Double-click the **Sheet2 worksheet tab** to make Sheet2 the active sheet and to enter edit mode. Type Hourly_Sales_Sunday as the new name for Sheet2, and then press Enter.

h. Select cell range **A6:A7**. Position the mouse over the bottom-right corner fill handle, and then drag the fill handle down to include cells **A6:A28**.

   The series in cell range A6:A7 has been expanded through cell A28. The number series is formatted as General numbers.

i. Click the **Number Format arrow** `General ▾` in the Number group, and then click **Time**. If any of the cells in A6:A28 display number signs, click **Format** in the Cells group, and click **AutoFit Column Width** on the Cell Size menu.

   The default time format includes a value for seconds. This is not necessary and adds clutter in the form of an additional :00 to every time value.

j. With cells A6:A28 still selected, click the **Number Format arrow** `General ▾` in the Number group, and then click **More Number Formats**.

k. In the Category box, click **Time**, if necessary. In the Type box, select **1:30 PM**.

l. Click **OK**.

m. Click the **Documentation worksheet tab**, click cell **B22**, and then type Hourly_Sales_Sunday to document the name change for this worksheet.

n. Press Ctrl + Home, and then click **Save** 🖫.

Excel stores time values as decimal portions of one day as follows:

- 1 = 1 day = 1,440 minutes
- .1 = 144 minutes = 2:24 AM
- .01 = 14.4 minutes = 12:14:24 AM

For this system to work in conjunction with date values, *0* and *1* are displayed as equivalent time values: 12:00:00 AM. However, in reality once a time value increases to 1, the date increments by 1 day and time reverts to 0.

Since a digital watch or cell phone is actually a computer, do you think it handles time in this manner and simply reformats it for your use?

CONSIDER THIS | Could You Use "Excel Time"?

Would you be able to adapt if your digital watch or cell phone showed time the way Excel stores it? Would there be any advantages if time were actually displayed and handled in this format? What about date values?

Cell Alignment

Cell alignment allows for cell content to be left-aligned, centered, or right-aligned on the horizontal axis, as well as top-aligned, middle-aligned, or bottom-aligned on the vertical axis. Certain cell formats align left or right by default. Most number formats align right. Date and time formats align right as well. Most text formatting aligns left by default, and for the most part, horizontal alignment changes will be made to alphabetic content such as titles, headings, and labels.

To Right-Align Text, Increase Indent, and Bottom-Align

a. Click the **Weekly_Sales worksheet tab**. Select cell range **A5:A25**, and then click **Align Text Right** ▤ in the Alignment group.

b. Click cell **A5**, press Ctrl, and then select cells **A10**, **A15**, and **A19**. Click **Increase Indent** ▤ in the Alignment group.

c. Select cell range **I4:J4**, and then click **Align Text Right** ▤ in the Alignment group.

d. If necessary, click **Bottom Align** ▤ in the Alignment group.

e. Click cell **J4**, click **Format** in the Cells group, and then select **AutoFit Column Width** on the Cell Size menu.

f. Press Ctrl+Home, and then click **Save** ▤.

Content Orientation

Sometimes, it is helpful to display information at an angle or even vertically rather than the standard horizontal left to right. This is particularly true for tabular information. When formatting charts and graphs, rotating textual content can be very helpful in presenting information in a space-efficient yet readable manner.

To Rotate Text

a. Select cell range **B4:H4**, and then click **Orientation** in the Alignment group. A menu will appear.

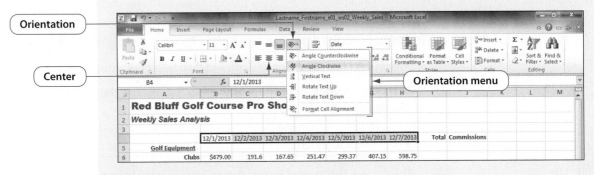

Figure 5 Orientation menu

b. Click **Angle Clockwise** on the Orientation menu, and then click **Center** ▤ in the Alignment group.

c. Press Ctrl+B to bold the dates in B4:H4.

d. Select cell range **B4:H25**, click **Format** in the Cells group, and then select **AutoFit Column Width** on the Cell Size menu in the Cells group.

e. Press Ctrl+Home, and then click **Save** 🖫.

Fill Color

Fill color refers to the background color of a cell. It can be used to categorize information, to band rows or columns as a means to assist the reader to follow information across or down a worksheet, or to highlight extreme values.

Unless you are using fill color to highlight information that is potentially erroneous, it is generally a best practice to use muted or pastel fill colors. Bright colors are difficult to look at for long periods of time and often make reading information in the cell(s) very difficult.

To Change Cell Background Color

a. Select cell range **B4:H4**, press Ctrl, and then select cell range **A5:A25**. Click the **Fill Color arrow** 🖌▾ in the Font group to display the color palette.

b. Under Theme Colors, point to any color in the left column and a ScreenTip will appear identifying the color name. Select **White, Background 1, Darker 15%** (first column, third row).

c. Click cell **A4**, press Ctrl, and then select cells **I4** and **J4**. Click the **Fill Color arrow** 🖌▾ in the Font group. Under Theme Colors, click **White, Background 1, Darker 50%**.

d. Click cell **A9**, press Ctrl, and then select cells **A14** and **A18**. Click the **Fill Color arrow** 🖌▾ in the Font group, and then click **No Fill**.

e. Press Ctrl+Home, and then click **Save** 🖫.

Cell Borders

In the last exercise you changed the background color in a range of cells. When the background color is changed for a range of contiguous cells, the cell borders may no longer be visible. If it would be preferable to have cell borders visible, cell borders can be formatted in a number of ways to make them visible.

To Format Cell Borders

a. Select cell range **B4:J4**, press ⌃Ctrl, and then select cell range **A5:A25**.

b. Click the **Borders arrow** ⊞ ▾ in the Font group, and then click **All Borders** on the Borders menu.

Troubleshooting

> The Borders button may look different in your Excel application window than it does when referenced in this text because the Borders button in the Font group of the Home tab always displays the last border setting applied.

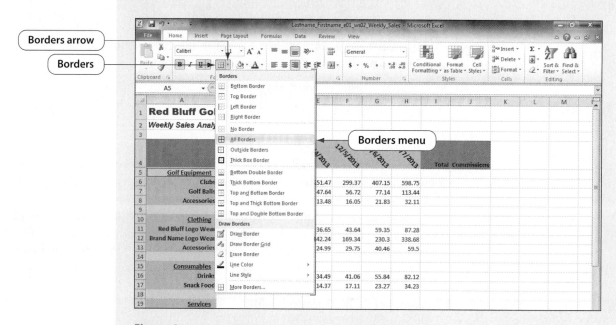

Figure 6   Borders menu

SIDE NOTE
Want to See More of Your Worksheet? Hide the Ribbon

Double-click the Home tab to hide the Ribbon if you would like to see more rows of the Weekly_Sales worksheet. You can double-click the Home tab again to unhide it.

c. Click cell **A5**, press ⌃Ctrl, and then select cells **A10**, **A15**, and **A19**. Click the **Borders arrow** ⊞ ▾ in the Font group, and then click **Thick Bottom Border** on the Borders menu.

d. Select cell range **B9:I9**, click the **Borders arrow** ⊞ ▾ in the Font group, and then click **Top and Bottom Border** on the Borders menu.

e. Select cell range **B14:I14**, press ⌃Ctrl, and then select cell ranges **B18:I18** and **B26:I26**. Click **Top and Bottom Border** ⊞ ▾ in the Font group.

f. Select cell range **B27:I27**, click the **Borders arrow** ⊞ ▾ in the Font group, and then click **Bottom Double Border** on the Borders menu.

g. Press ⌃Ctrl+Home, and then click **Save** 🖫.

Real World Advice   Formatting—Less Is More

Excel offers many formatting options for text and numbers. Be careful to avoid overusing formatting in your worksheets. Too much variety in formatting creates a worksheet that is hard on the eyes, difficult to read, seems haphazard in its design, and conveys a sense that the designer did not have a plan. The following are some suggested guidelines for general formatting:

- Formatting should be done for a reason, not simply for appearances.

- Use no more than three fonts in a worksheet. Use each font for a purpose such as text, numbers, headings, and titles.

- Use color sparingly. Only use color to assist in readability, categorization, or identification purposes. For example, use organization colors for titles, bright colors to call attention to small details, and background colors to separate categories. In particular, where coloration of text and numbers is concerned, treat color as though it is expensive to include.

- When color is used as a background, use calm and soothing pale or pastel colors. Large amounts of bright colors are tiring for the reader and can actually become painful to look at after long periods of time.

- Special characters such as the ($) should be applied only as necessary. The first value in a column of numbers is sufficient to tell the user that column values are monetary. Then values such as subtotals and totals can be formatted with a $ to identify them as a value of importance.

Copying Formats

Developing a worksheet with clarity requires more than just setting a font and font size. Formatting a cell can consist of several steps involving fonts, colors, sizes, borders, and alignment. You gain a significant efficiency advantage by reusing your work. Once a cell is formatted properly, you can apply the formatting properties to a different cell. Copying formats from one cell to another saves a great deal of time and often frustration.

Format Painter ✍ is a tool that facilitates rapid application of formats from one cell to another cell or to a range of cells. To use the Format Painter, simply select the cell that is the source of the format you want to copy, click the Format Painter ✍ in the Clipboard group of the Home tab, and then select the cell or range of cells you want to "paint" with the source cell's formatting.

SIDE NOTE
How to Use the Format Painter Multiple Times
Format Painter ✍ allows you to paint formats from a cell to noncontiguous cells by double-clicking Format Painter ✍. Format Painter will then remain active until you click it again, or press Esc, to toggle it off.

To Use the Format Painter to Copy Formats

a. Select cell **B20**, and then click the **Format Painter** ✍ in the Clipboard group. The mouse pointer will change to ⬚. Select cell range **B16:H17**.

b. Click **Save** 🖫.

Paste Options/Paste Special

When a cell is copied to the Clipboard, there is much more than a simple value ready to be pasted to another location. Formats, formulas, and values are all copied and can be selectively pasted to other locations in a workbook.

Different paste options are shown in Figure 7. Although there are a large number of paste options, most worksheet activities require only a few of these options. Paste, 📋 Paste Formats 📋, and Paste Values 📋 will accomplish most of what you will need to do. The various paste options are also additive, in that you can first paste a value to a copied cell and then paste the format from the copied cell, after which you could paste the formula from the copied cell.

Button	Function	Description
📋	Paste	Pastes all content from the Clipboard to a cell
📋	Formatting	Pastes only the formatting from the Clipboard to a cell
📋	Values	Pastes only the value from the Clipboard to a cell
📋	Formulas	Pastes only the formula from the Clipboard to a cell
📋	Paste Link	Pastes a link (e.g., =A25) to the source cell from the Clipboard to a cell
📋	Transpose	Pastes a range of cells to a new range of cells with columns and rows switched

Figure 7 Paste options

To Use Paste Options and Paste Special to Copy Formats

a. Select cell **B20**, press Ctrl+C to copy cell B20 to the Clipboard, and then select cell range **B11:H13**.

b. Right-click the **selected range**. The shortcut menu will appear, which includes options that are determined by the context of the object that is the focus of the action.

c. Move the mouse pointer over each button on the Paste Options menu and notice what happens in the selected cell range. Click **Formatting** 📋 on the Paste Options menu. Press Esc to cancel further paste options when finished.

d. Select cell **B11**, press Ctrl+C to copy cell B11 to the Clipboard, and then select cell range **B6:H8**.

e. Right-click the **selected range**. The shortcut menu will appear. Point to each button on the Paste Options menu, and notice what happens in the selected cell range.

f. Point to **Paste Special**. The Paste Special shortcut menu in will appear. Select **Formatting** 📋 under Other Paste Options.

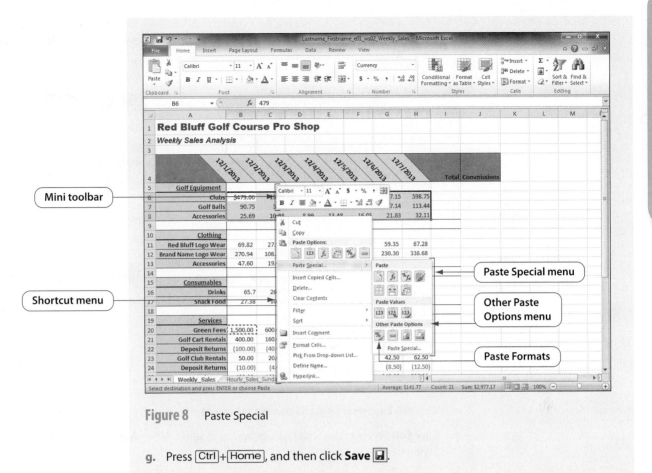

Figure 8   Paste Special

g.   Press `Ctrl`+`Home`, and then click **Save** 🖫.

Built-In Cell Styles

Built-in cell styles are predefined and named combinations of cell and content formatting properties that can be applied to a cell or range of cells to define several formatting properties at once. A built-in cell style can set font, font size and color, number format, background color, borders, and alignment with a couple clicks of the mouse. Built-in cell styles allow for rapid and accurate changes to the appearance of a workbook with very little effort.

To Apply Built-in Cell Styles

a.   Click the **Hourly_Sales_Sunday worksheet tab**. Select cell range **B4:D4**, press `Ctrl`, and then select cell ranges **E4:G4**, **H4:I4**, and **J4:O4**. Each range is a distinct selection. Click **Merge & Center** in the Alignment group.

b.   Click cell **B4**, press `Ctrl`, and then select cell **H4**.

c. Click **Cell Styles** in the Styles group. The Cell Styles gallery menu will appear. Select **20% - Accent2** on the Themed Cell Styles menu.

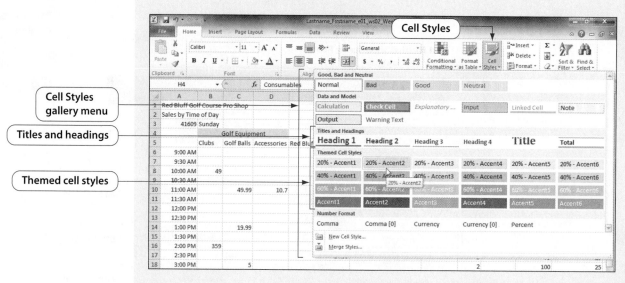

Figure 9   Cell Styles gallery menu

d. Click cell **E4**, press Ctrl, and then select cell **J4**.

e. Click **Cell Styles** in the Styles group, and then select **40% - Accent2** on the Themed Cell Styles menu.

f. Select cell range **A3:B3**, press Ctrl, and then select cell ranges **B4:O5** and **A6:A29**.

g. Click **Cell Styles** in the Styles group. Select **Heading 4** under the Titles and Headings menu. Notice that in cell range B4:O4, the Accent2 cell background colors have not changed.

h. Select cell range **B29:O29**, click **Cell Styles** in the Styles group, and then select **Total** on the Titles and Headings menu.

i. Press Ctrl+Home.

j. Click the **Weekly_Sales worksheet tab**, select cell range **A1:A2**, and then press Ctrl+C.

k. Click the **Hourly_Sales_Sunday worksheet tab**, select cell range **A1:A2**, right-click the selected range, and then click **Formatting** 📋 on the Paste Options menu.

l. Click cell **A3**, click the **Number Format arrow** [General ▼], and then select **Short Date**.

m. Select cell range **B6:O29**, click the **Number Format arrow** [General ▼], and then click **More Number Formats** to display the Format Cells dialog box.

n. Click **Number** under the Category box. If necessary, enter **2** in the Decimal places box. Make sure **Use 1000 Separator (,)** is checked. Select red negative number format **(1,234.10)** in the Negative numbers box. Click **OK**.

o. Press Ctrl+Home. Click **Save** 💾.

SIDE NOTE
Multiple Built-In Styles Can Be Applied to One Cell

Cells are not limited to a single built-in style. Different styles affect different cell elements. The end result of applying multiple styles to a single cell is determined by the order in which the styles are applied.

Table Styles

A **table** is a powerful tabular data-formatting tool that facilitates data sorting, filtering, and calculations. Once a collection of data has been defined as a table by the application of a table style, it has special table properties not available to data simply entered into rows and columns of cells.

A **table style** is a predefined set of formatting properties that determine the appearance of a table. One of the useful features of a table style is the ability to "band" rows and columns. **Banding** is alternating the background color of rows and/or columns to assist in tracking information. Banding can be accomplished manually by changing the background color of a range of cells (a row for example) and then pasting the formatting into every other row. Manually banding a table is a tedious process at best. By applying a table style to a selected range of rows and columns, banding is accomplished in a couple of clicks. Most importantly, table banding is dynamic. If a row or column is inserted into—or deleted from—the worksheet, the banding is automatically updated. If banding is done manually, insertions and deletions require the banding to be manually updated as well.

Tables also allow for calculations in a total row such as summations, averages, or counts for each column in the table. These calculations are possible without table formatting. However, a table makes the calculation simple.

To Apply a Table Style to a Cell Range

a. Right-click the **Hourly_Sales_Sunday worksheet tab**, and then on the shortcut menu, click **Move or Copy**. In the Move or Copy dialog box, under Before sheet, click **Documentation** so the new sheet copy will be positioned before this sheet. Click the **Create a copy** check box at the bottom of the dialog box, and then click **OK**.

b. Double-click the **new worksheet tab**, type Hourly_Sales_Sunday_2, and then press Enter to accept the new tab name.

c. With the Hourly_Sales_Sunday_2 worksheet as the active tab, select cell range **A5:O28**, and then click **Format as Table** in the Styles group. The gallery menu will appear.

d. Select **Table Style Medium 3** in Medium table styles. The Format As Table dialog box appears. Be sure **My table has headers** is checked, and then click **OK**. The Ribbon switches to the Table Tools Design tab.

e. Double-click cell **A5** to edit the cell contents. Double-click cell **A5** again to highlight the Column1 text, and then type Time. Press Ctrl+Enter.

   Cell A5 was titled *Column1* since no column heading existed. *Time* is a more appropriate heading.

f. Click the **Home tab**, click **Cell Styles** in the Styles group, and then select **Heading 4**. Click **Align Text Right** 🔳 in the Alignment group, and then click **Increase Indent** 🔳 in the Alignment group two times.

g. Click the **Filter arrow** 🔽 in the Time column, and then click **Sort Largest to Smallest** on the Filter menu.

   The order of the rows in the table is reversed. The filter next to each column heading in the table in row 5 allows you to sort the entire table by the information in each column.

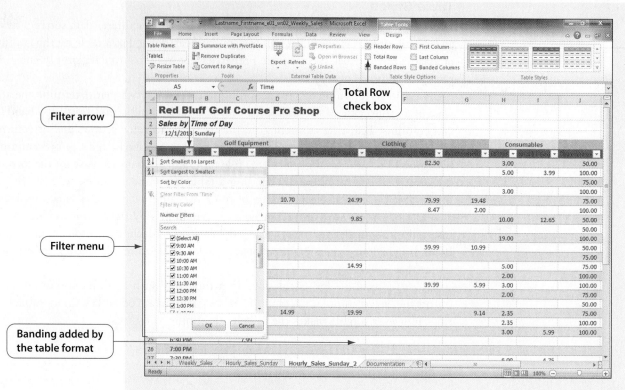

Figure 10   Table Tools Design tab and the Table filter menu

h. Click the **Filter arrow** in the Time column, and then select **Sort Smallest to Largest** to revert to the original order.

i. Click **Sort & Filter** in the Editing group, and then click **Filter** to toggle off data filtering. Since sorting by time or any of the other columns in the table is not really necessary, the Filter arrows can be removed.

j. The table format did not override the font style applied to the header row when you copied formats from the Hourly_Sales_Sunday worksheet. The blue font color is difficult to read on the red background. Select cell **A5**, press [Shift]+[Ctrl]+[→] to select cell range A5:O5. In the Styles group, click **Cell Styles**, and then select **Accent2**.

k. Click the **Table Tools Design tab**, and then check **Total Row** in the Table Style Options group. This adds a special total row that works with the table style to total each column as appropriate.

l. Select row 30 by clicking on the **row 30 header** when the cursor appears as [→]. Right-click the selected row, and then click **Delete** on the shortcut menu to delete the unnecessary total row copied from the Hourly_Sales_Sunday worksheet.

m. Click cell **C7**, and then scroll down until row 5 disappears at the top of the application window.

   Notice what happens to the column headers. As long as the active cell is inside the table, if you scroll down the table column headings of the visible application window, table column headings replace worksheet column headings.

n. Click the **Documentation worksheet tab**, click cell **B28**, and then type Hourly_Sales_ Sunday_2. Click cell **B29**, enter your Lastname, Firstname, click cell **B30**, and then type today's date in mm/dd/yyyy format.

o. Click the **Hourly_Sales_Sunday_2 worksheet tab**.

p. Press Ctrl+Home, and then click **Save** 🖫.

Troubleshooting

Is the Table Tools Design tab not available when you want to select it? Check to make sure the active cell is somewhere in the table you formatted. A worksheet can contain many tables. Excel only makes the Table Tools Design tab available when the active cell is part of a formatted table.

Workbook Themes

A **workbook theme** is a collection of built-in cell styles associated with a theme name. The **default** workbook theme, the theme that is automatically applied unless you specify otherwise, in Excel is the Office theme. Changing the assigned theme is a way to very quickly change the appearance of your worksheet(s). When a different workbook theme is applied, the built-in cell styles in the Styles group on the Home tab change to reflect the new workbook theme. Workbook themes are a way to rapidly change the look of the worksheets in a workbook and are particularly helpful for those who suffer from color-blindness or who do not have a good eye for design. Applying a workbook theme assures a consistent, well-designed look throughout your workbook.

To Change the Workbook Theme

a. Click the **Hourly_Sales_Sunday worksheet tab**, click the **Page Layout tab**, and then click **Themes** in the Themes group. The gallery menu appears.

b. Point to the **Black Tie** built-in workbook theme. Note that any cell that was assigned a Cell Style now reflects the corresponding cell style in the Black Tie workbook theme.

c. If necessary, scroll down using the scroll bar on the right side of the Themes menu, and then click the **Horizon** theme. Some cells, such as cell A1, where color and font were explicitly set, are not affected by a change to the Horizon workbook theme.

d. Click the **Weekly_Sales worksheet tab**. Notice that the background colors that were set using cell formatting are not affected by the new workbook theme.

e. Click the **Hourly_Sales_Sunday_2 worksheet tab**. The table style applied to this worksheet reveals the extent to which a change in workbook theme can change the appearance of a worksheet.

f. Press Ctrl+Home, and then click **Save** 🖫.

Creating Information for Decision Making

New information is most often produced in Excel through the use of functions and/or formulas to make calculations against information in the workbook.

Often, the objective is to improve decision making by providing additional information. In this section, you will manipulate data using functions and formulas and will assist in decision making using conditional formatting to highlight or categorize information based on problem-specific parameters.

What Is a Function?

Functions are one of Excel's most powerful features. A **function** is a small program that performs operations on data. Function syntax takes the form of *functionname* (*argument* 1,…, *argument* n), where *functionname* is the name of the function and the **arguments** inside the parentheses are the variables or values the function requires. In Excel, a **variable** is simply a value in a cell that is referenced in a formula or function. Different functions require different arguments. Some functions do not require any arguments at all—they are commonly referred to as null functions. There are more than 400 functions built in to Excel that can be categorized as financial, statistical, mathematical, date and time, text, and several others—collectively these are referred to, not surprisingly, as **built-in functions**.

Arguments can be entered as letters, numbers, cell references, cell ranges, or other functions.

The power of functions is two-fold:

1. Functions allow you to take advantage of code that has been thoroughly tested to make complex calculations, to access operating system variables, to manipulate strings of text characters, and to make logical decisions.
2. Functions are easily copied and pasted to new locations in your worksheet to facilitate the reuse of code.

Part of what makes functions so useful is the use of cell references as arguments. Cell references enable you to use information from a particular cell or cell range in a function. Recall that a **cell reference** is the combination of a cell's column and row addresses. When a function that includes a cell reference as an argument is copied, the cell reference is changed to reflect the copied location relative to the original location. For example, say a function in cell B26 calculates the sum of cells B1:B25; if you copy the function from cell B26 to cell C26, the function in cell C26 will automatically be changed to summate C1:C25. You copied the function one column to the right, relative to the original location—cell references in the copied function will be relatively adjusted one column to the right.

AutoSum Functions

Of the more than 400 functions built into Excel, the most commonly used are the **AutoSum functions**. Since SUM( ), COUNT( ), AVERAGE( ), MIN( ), and MAX( ) are used so often, Excel makes them more readily available than any other function via AutoSum Σ in the Function Library group on the Formulas tab or in the Editing group on the Home tab. Further, when these functions are invoked using the AutoSum button, Excel inspects your worksheet and automatically includes a range adjacent to the active cell. In general, adjacent cells above are used by default. If there are no adjacent cells above, then adjacent cells to the left are used for the range. Excel does not inspect cell ranges to the right or below the active cell for AutoSum functions.

SUM( )

The **SUM( ) function** produces a sum of all numeric information in a specified range, list of numbers, list of cells, or any combination. Figure 11 contains examples of the different ways in which data can be included in a SUM( ) function.

Type of Data	Function
Numbers	=SUM(1,3,5,7,11,13)
Cell range	=SUM(B3:B25)
List of noncontiguous cells	=SUM(B3,B9,C5,D14)
Combination	=SUM(B3,B9:B15,C12/100)

Figure 11 SUM( ) function variations

To Use the AutoSum SUM( ) Function

a. Click the **Weekly_Sales worksheet tab**, click the **Formulas tab**, and then select cell **H9**.

b. Click the **AutoSum** button in the Function Library group. Excel will try to predict the cell range to sum by examining the cells directly above H9. Since there is numeric information in the three rows above H9, H6:H8 is automatically inserted into the function. This is correct. Press Enter.

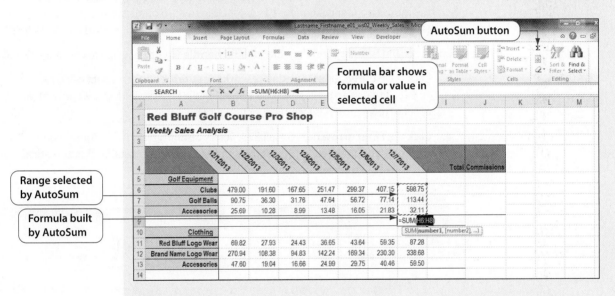

Figure 12 AutoSum SUM( ) function

c. Repeat Step b for cells **H14**, **H18**, and **H26**.

d. Select cell **H9**. Click the **fill handle** to copy cell **H9** directly to the left in cell range **B9:H9**. Click the **fill handle** again and fill to the right through cell **I9**. Click cell **E9**.

   Look at the formula displayed in the formula bar. The relative cell references in the formula were changed when you copied the original formula from cell H9. If any of the cells in B9:I9 display number signs, click Format in the Cells group of the Home tab, and then click AutoFit Column Width on the Cell Size menu.

e. Repeat Step d to copy cell **H14** to cell range **B14:I14**.

f. Repeat Step d to copy cell **H18** to cell range **B18:I18**.

g. Repeat Step d to copy cell **H26** to cell range **B26:I26**.

h. Click the **Formulas tab**, select cell **I6**, and then click **AutoSum** in the Function Library group. Excel tries to predict the cell range to sum and in this case chooses the seven columns to the left of I6, which is correct. Press Enter.

SIDE NOTE

Double-Click AutoSum

Rather than click AutoSum and press Enter, double-click AutoSum—the result is the same, but you get there more quickly. Double-check the resulting formula to make sure the correct range was selected.

i.   Select cell **I6**. Click the **fill handle** to copy cell **I6** to cell range **I7:I8**. Notice the automatic recalculation of the sum in cell I9.

j.   Select cell **I8**. Press `Ctrl`+`C` to place the formula in I8 on the Clipboard. Select cell range **I11:I13**, and then press `Ctrl`+`V` to paste the formula from the Clipboard into the selected cell range.

k.   Select cell range **I16:I17**, press `Ctrl`+`V`, and then select cell range **I20:I25**. Press `Ctrl`+`V` to paste the formula from the Clipboard into the selected cell ranges, and then press `Esc` when finished pasting.

l.   Click the **heading** for column I. Click the **Home tab**, click **Format** in the Cells group, and then select **AutoFit Column Width** on the Cell Size menu.

m.   Click the **Hourly_Sales_Sunday worksheet tab**, and then click the **Formulas tab**.

n.   Select cell **B29**, and then click **AutoSum** Σ in the Function Library group.
     In this case Excel does not predict the summated range properly. The predicted range is outlined with a moving dotted line. Excel predicts range B20:B28. You want to sum the cells that represent all the day's time slots. Point to a top corner of the dotted outline so the mouse pointer changes to ⬉ or ⬈. Drag the top of the summated range upward to encompass B6:B28. The formula displayed in the formula bar should be =SUM(B6:B28).

o.   Press `Ctrl`+`Enter`, and then drag the **fill handle** to copy cell B29 to cell range **C29:O29**.

p.   Click the **Hourly_Sales_Sunday_2 worksheet tab**, and then select cell **B29**.
     Recall that in an earlier exercise you applied a table style to this worksheet. Row 29 is a "Total" row which has formula functionality built into it.

q.   Click the **Filter arrow** next to cell B29. Select **Sum** from the Table Totals menu.
     Excel does not need to predict the summated range for a table. It automatically sums all the rows in the table column.

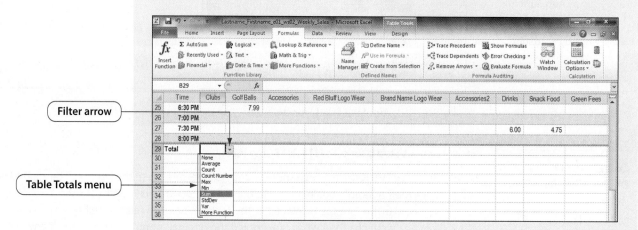

Figure 13   Calculating sum in a table total row

r.   Drag the **fill handle** to copy cell **B29** to cell range **C29:O29**.

s.   Press `Ctrl`+`Home`, and then click **Save** 💾.

COUNT( )

The **COUNT( ) function** returns the number of cells in a range of cells that contain numbers. It can be used to generate information such as the number of sales in a period by counting invoice numbers, the number of people in a group by counting Social Security numbers, and so on.

To Use the AutoSum COUNT( ) Function

a. Click the **Home tab**. Click the **Hourly_Sales_Sunday worksheet tab**, select cell **A30**, type # of Sales, and then press Enter. Select cell range **A29:A30**, click **Align Text Right** ▤ in the Alignment group, click cell **A30**, and then click **Bold** **B** in the Font group.

b. Click the **Formulas tab**, select cell **B30**, and then click the **AutoSum arrow** Σ in the Function Library group. The AutoSum menu will appear. Select **Count Numbers**.

c. Select cell range **B6:B28**. The cell range should be outlined in a moving dotted line and cell B30 should display **=COUNT(B6:B28)**. Press Ctrl + Enter.

d. Use the fill handle to copy cell **B30** to cell range **C30:O30**.

e. Click the **heading** for row 30 to select the entire row, and then press Ctrl + C to copy row 30 to the Clipboard.

f. Click the **Hourly_Sales_Sunday_2 worksheet tab**, click the **heading** for row 30, and then press Ctrl + V to paste row 30 from the Clipboard.

g. Press Ctrl + Home, and then click **Save** 🖫. Rows 29 and 30 in the Hourly_Sales_Sunday and Hourly_Sales_Sunday_2 worksheets should contain matching data results.

AVERAGE( )

The **AVERAGE( ) function** returns a weighted average from a specified range of cells. The sum of all numeric values in the range is calculated and then divided by the count of numbers in the range. Essentially, the AVERAGE( ) function is SUM( )/COUNT( ).

To Use the AVERAGE( ) AutoSum Function

a. Click the **Hourly_Sales_Sunday** worksheet, and then click the **Home tab**.

b. Select cell **A31**, type Average Sale, and then press Ctrl + Enter to accept the changes and keep cell A31 selected. Click **Align Text Right** ▤ in the Alignment group, and then click **Bold** **B** in the Font group.

c. Select cell **B31**, click the **Formulas tab**, click the **AutoSum arrow** Σ in the Function Library group, and then select **Average**.

d. Select cell range **B6:B28**. The cell range should be outlined in a moving dotted line, and cell B31 should display =AVERAGE(B6:B28). Press Enter.

e. Select cell **B31**, and then use the fill handle to copy cell **B31** to cell range **C31:O31**.

f. Click the **heading** for row 31 to select the row. Press Ctrl + C to copy row 31 to the Clipboard.

g. Click the **Hourly_Sales_Sunday_2 worksheet tab**, click the **heading** for row 31, and then press Ctrl + V to paste row 31 from the Clipboard.

h. Press Ctrl + Home, and then click **Save** 🖫.

MIN( ) and MAX( )

An average gives you an incomplete picture. If your instructor stated that the average on the exam is 75%, you do not have any information about the actual score distribution. Everyone in the class may have gotten a C with the low of 71% and high of 79%. Conversely, no one may have gotten a C with half the class getting an A and half getting an F. Both situations could have a 75% average but are very different distributions.

The average should never be relied on without looking at additional statistics that help complete the picture. While many statistics exist to do this, the minimum and the maximum value provide at least a little more insight into the distribution of data by defining the extremes. The **MIN( )** and **MAX( ) functions** examine all numeric values in a specified range and return the minimum value and the maximum value respectively.

To Use the AutoSum MIN( ) and MAX( ) Functions

a.   Click the **Hourly_Sales_Sunday worksheet tab**.

b.   Click the **Home tab**, select cell **A32**, and then type Max. Sale. Select cell **A33**, type Min. Sale, and then select cell **A31**. Click **Format Painter** ☑ in the Clipboard group, and then select cell range **A32:A33**.

c.   Click cell **B32**, click the **Formulas tab**, click the **AutoSum arrow** Σ in the Function Library group, and then click **Max**.

d.   Select cell range **B6:B28**. The cell range should be outlined in a moving dotted line, and cell B32 should display =MAX(B6:B28). Press Enter. Cell B33 should be the active cell.

e.   Click the **AutoSum arrow** Σ in the Function Library group, and then click **Min**.

f.   Select cell range **B6:B28**. The cell range should be outlined in a moving dotted line, and cell B33 should display =MIN(B6:B28). Press Enter.

g.   Select cell range **B32:B33**, and then use the fill handle to copy cell range **B32:B33** to cell range **C32:O33**.

h.   Select the **headings** for rows 32 and 33, and then press Ctrl+C to copy rows 32:33 to the Clipboard.

i.   Click the **Hourly_Sales_Sunday_2 worksheet tab**, click the **heading** for row 32, and then press Ctrl+V to paste rows 32:33 from the Clipboard. Press Ctrl+Home.

j.   Click the **Hourly_Sales_Sunday worksheet tab**. Press Esc.

k.   Press Ctrl+Home, and then click **Save** 🖫.

29	TOTAL	479.00	90.95	25.69	69.82	270.94	47.60	65.70	27.38	1,500.00	400.00
30	# of Sales	3	5	2	4	5	5	13	4	19	12
31	Average Sale	159.67	18.19	12.85	17.46	54.19	9.52	5.05	6.85	78.95	33.33
32	Max. Sale	359.00	49.99	14.99	24.99	82.50	19.48	19.00	12.65	100.00	50.00
33	Min. Sale	49.00	5.00	10.70	9.85	8.47	2.00	2.00	3.99	50.00	25.00
34											
35											

Figure 14   AutoSum AVERAGE( ), MAX( ), and MIN( )

What Is a Formula?

A **formula** allows you to perform basic mathematical calculations using information in the active worksheet (and others) to calculate new values; formulas can contain cell references, constants, functions, and mathematical operators. Formulas in Excel have a very specific syntax. In Excel, formulas always begin with an equal sign (=). Formulas can contain references to specific cells that contain information; a **constant**, which is a number that never changes, such as the value for π; **mathematical operators** such as +, - , *, /, and ^; and functions. Cells that contain formulas can be treated like any other worksheet cell. They can be referenced, edited, formatted, copied, and pasted.

If a formula contains a cell reference, when copied and then pasted into a new location, the cell reference in the formula changes. The new cell reference reflects a new location relative to the old location. This is called a **relative cell reference**. For example, as shown in Figure 15, when the formula in the left column is copied one column to the right and two rows down, the cell references in the formula change to reflect the destination cell relative to the original cell. Consequently, columns A and J are changed to B and K respectively—one column right, and rows 3 and 12 are changed to 5 and 14, two rows down. Note that the column and row numbers of the cells that contain the formulas are not shown in Figure 15. The active cell address does not matter in relative addressing. All that matters is the relative shift in columns and rows from source to destination, and the cell references in the formula.

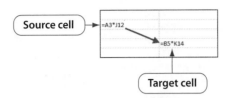

Figure 15 Relative referencing when copying from a source cell to a destination cell

Relative cell references create a powerful opportunity for the reuse of formulas in a well-designed worksheet. You can enter a formula once and use it many times without having to reenter it in each location. Simply copy and paste it to new locations.

Further, relative references are a powerful means by which worksheets adjust formulas to ensure correctness when the structure of the worksheet changes. If a column is inserted to the left of a cell referenced in a formula, or a row is inserted above a cell referenced in a formula, the cells referenced by the formula will be adjusted to ensure the formula still references the same relative locations.

Operators

Excel formulas are constructed using basic mathematical operators very similar to those used in a mathematics class and exactly the same as used in most programming languages. Figure 16 contains the mathematical operators recognized in Excel.

Operation	Operator	Example	Formula Entered in Current Cell
Addition	+	=B4+B5	Assign the sum of B4 and B5 to the current cell
Subtraction	-	=B5-B4	Assign the difference of B4 and B5 to the current cell
Multiplication	*	=B5*3.14	Assign B5 multiplied by 3.14 to the current cell
Division	/	=B5/B4	Assign the quotient of B5 divided by B4 to the current cell
Exponentiation	^	=B4^2	Assign the square of B4 to the current cell

Figure 16 Mathematical operators in Excel

To Use a Formula to Sum Totals

a. Click the **Weekly_Sales worksheet tab**, click the **Home tab**, select cell **B27**, and then type =B9+B14+B18+B26. Press [Ctrl]+[Enter].

b. Press [Ctrl]+[C] to copy cell B27 to the Clipboard.

c. Select cell range **C27:I27**, and then press Ctrl+V to paste cell B27 from the Clipboard. If any of the cells in B27:I27 display number signs, click **Format** in the Cells group, and then click **AutoFit Column Width** on the Cell Size menu.

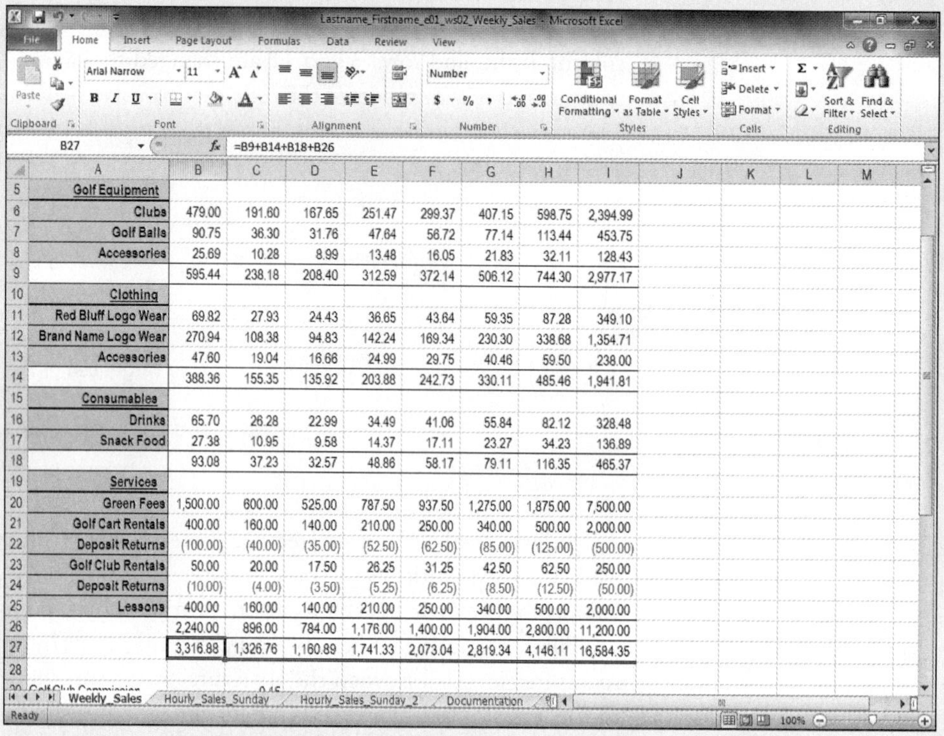

Figure 17   Use of a formula to sum subtotals

d. Press Ctrl+Home, and then click **Save**.

Troubleshooting

Excel allows you to copy formulas from one location to another and adjusts cell references to ensure calculation accuracy. This is not necessarily true when a formula is moved from one location to another, however. If you move a formula by dragging it from one location to another, cell references *do not* change. Be sure you double-check a formula after you move it to ensure it is still producing a correct result.

SIDE NOTE
How to Copy a Formula and Not Change Relative References

To copy a formula from one cell to another and not have relative cell references adjusted, highlight the formula in the formula bar, press Ctrl+C, press Esc, select the destination cell, and press Ctrl+V.

Real World Advice   An Alternative to Typing Cell References

An alternative, and more accurate, method to typing cell references into a formula is to type only the operators and then select the cells from the worksheet. The steps to enter the daily sales total in the Weekly_Sales worksheet would be as follows:

1. Select cell B27.

2. Type =.

3. Click cell B9, and then type +.

4. Click cell B14, and then type +.

5. Click cell B18, and then type +.

6. Click cell B26, and then press Enter.

SIDE NOTE

How to Remember Order of Operations

An old acronym that is often used to remember order of operations is PEDMAS.

- **P** arentheses
- **E** xponentiation
- **D** ivision and/or
- **M** ultiplication
- **A** ddition and/or
- **S** ubtraction

Order of Operations

Order of operations is the order in which Excel processes calculations in a formula that contains more than one operator. Mathematical operations execute in a specific order:

1. Parentheses
2. Exponentiation
3. Multiplication and division
4. Addition and subtraction

Excel scans a formula from left to right while performing calculations using the above order of operation rules. Thus you can control which part of a calculation is performed first by enclosing parts of a formula in parentheses. Portions of a formula enclosed in parentheses are evaluated first, following the previously listed order. Figure 18 contains some examples of the effect of order of operations on formula results.

Formula	Result	Formula	Result
=4-2*5^2	-46	=(5+5)*4/2-3*6	2
=(4-2)*5^2	50	=(5+5)*4/(2-3)*6	-240
=5+5*4/2-3*6	-3	=(5+5)*4/(2-3*6)	-2.5

Figure 18 Order of operations

Golf pro John Schilling is paid a commission on sales. He receives 70% of all lesson fees received by the Pro Shop. Additionally, he must report all tips on a weekly basis for tax purposes. Pro Shop manager Aleeta Herriott is in charge of all golf club sales. She receives a 15% commission on all sales of clubs and a 10% commission on golf balls and accessories.

To Enter Formulas to Calculate Commissions

a. Select cell **J25**, and then type =I25*C33.

b. Select cell **J6**, and then type =I6*C29.

c. Select cell **J7**, and then type =(I7+I8)*C30.

d. Select cell **I6**, and then double-click **Format Painter** in the Clipboard group.

e. Select cell range **J6:J7**, click cell **J9**, and then click cell **J25**.
   Although cell J9 does not contain data, the Format Painter can still be used to change its format. Data, or a formula, entered later will be displayed with the "painted" format.

f. Click **Format Painter** in the Clipboard group to toggle off the Format Painter.

g. Select cell range **J7:J8**. On the Home tab, click the **Merge & Center arrow** in the Alignment group, and then click **Merge Cells** from the menu.
   The merged cell J7 will contain the formatting applied in Step e.

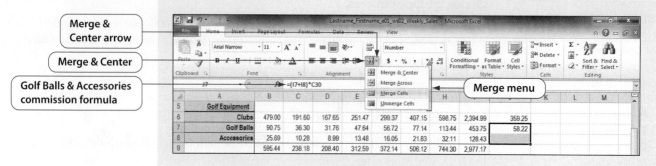

Figure 19   Merge & Center the Golf Balls & Accessories Commission

h.   Press Ctrl + Home, and then click **Save** 🖫.

Real World Advice   Use Parameters, Do Not Hard-Code Numbers in Formulas

Hard-coding means the inclusion of an explicit value in a formula, an actual number—in =H12/60, the number 60 is hard-coded. Excel formulas and functions can include what are called constants. A constant is a number that never changes, such as the number of hours in a day, or the number of minutes in an hour. Hard-coding constants is acceptable. For example, to calculate the area of a circle, if the radius was stored in cell C2, the area could be calculated as =C2^2*3.14 since the value of π never changes.

However, for the majority of values, there is a probability of change. Most numbers, such as tax rates, commission percentages, age limits, and interest rates will potentially change over time. Such values should be treated as parameters. A **parameter** is a special form of variable included in a worksheet for the sole purpose of inclusion in formulas and functions. A value is treated as a parameter by placing it in a cell, giving it a label (which is important for documentation), and referencing the value in formulas and/or functions via its cell address, rather than explicitly typing it into formulas and/or functions.

In Figure 20, the values in rows 29 through 34 are parameters. To use them in a formula you would reference them by cell address. For example, to calculate the commission on the sale of a $1,600 set of golf clubs, if the value of the sale were stored in cell B5, the formula would be =B5*C29, not =B5*0.15 or =1600*0.15. Cell C29 is a parameter—it stores the commission percentage for pro shop golf club sales for use in worksheet calculations.

The elegance of parameters is that the value of a parameter can be changed in its cell, and any of potentially hundreds of formulas that reference that parameter will instantly reflect the change in value. If the value were entered explicitly into each of hundreds of formulas, each formula would have to be changed, one at a time, by hand. Use parameters.

Hiding Information in a Worksheet

A worksheet can contain information that may not be necessary, or even desirable, to have displayed most of the time. This is often true of a list of parameters. It can also be the case that detailed information used to calculate totals can be hidden until such time that the person using the worksheet would like to see it.

Hiding information in a worksheet is relatively simple. Entire worksheet rows and columns can be hidden. Simply select the rows and/or columns to be hidden by clicking on the row or column heading. Right-click with the mouse pointer over the heading or in the selected row(s) or column(s), and click Hide on the shortcut menu that appears.

To Hide and Unhide Rows in a Worksheet

a. Click the heading for row 29, press $\boxed{\text{Shift}}$, and then click the **heading** for row 34.

b. Point to the **selected rows**, and then right-click. Click **Hide** on the shortcut menu.

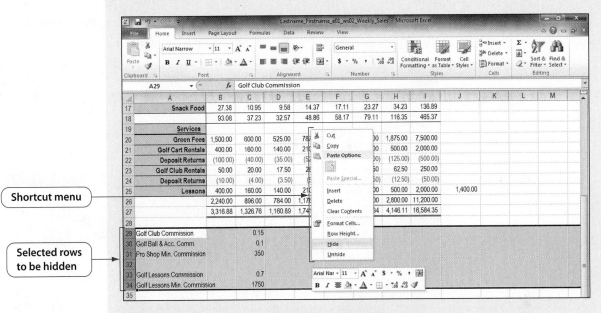

Shortcut menu

Selected rows to be hidden

Figure 20   Hide rows using the shortcut menu

c. Click the **heading** for row 28, press $\boxed{\text{Shift}}$, and then click the **heading** for row 35.

d. Point to the **selected rows**, and then right-click to display the shortcut menu. Click **Unhide**.

e. Press $\boxed{\text{Ctrl}}+\boxed{\text{Z}}$ to undo and leave rows 29:34 hidden.

f. Press $\boxed{\text{Ctrl}}+\boxed{\text{Home}}$. Click **Save** 💾.

Show Functions and Formulas

What is displayed in a cell that contains a function or a formula is the calculated result. The function or formula that generated the displayed value is only visible one cell at a time by selecting a cell and then looking at the formula bar. The keystroke combination $\boxed{\text{Ctrl}}+\boxed{\ \ }$ toggles Show Formulas on and off. When Show Formulas is on, the calculated results are hidden, and functions and formulas are shown in the cells instead whenever applicable.

Show Formulas is very helpful in understanding how a worksheet is structured. It is an essential debugging aid when something in a worksheet is in error. A worksheet that has Show Formulas toggled on can be printed for documentation purposes.

SIDE NOTE

A Faster Way to Show Formulas

Don't want to use the Ribbon to show formulas? Press $\boxed{\text{Ctrl}}+\boxed{\ \ }$ to toggle Show Formulas. (Note: this is the accent mark generally on the same key as the ~, not an apostrophe.)

To View and Print All Formulas in a Worksheet

a. Click the **Formulas tab**, and then click **Show Formulas** in the Formula Auditing group. Cells containing formulas will display the formulas rather than the calculated results.

b. Use the **Zoom Slider** ⊖━━━⊕ on the status bar to move the zoom level so you can view the entire worksheet on the monitor. If necessary, scroll the worksheet to the right to view formulas through column J.

c. Click the **Page Layout tab**, click **Orientation** in the Page Setup group, and then select **Landscape** on the menu.

d. Click the **Width Box arrow** in the Scale to Fit group, and then click **1 page**. This will scale your worksheet to print in the width of a single page.

e. Click the **Height Box arrow** in the Scale to Fit group, and then click **1 page**. This will scale your document to print in the height of a single page.

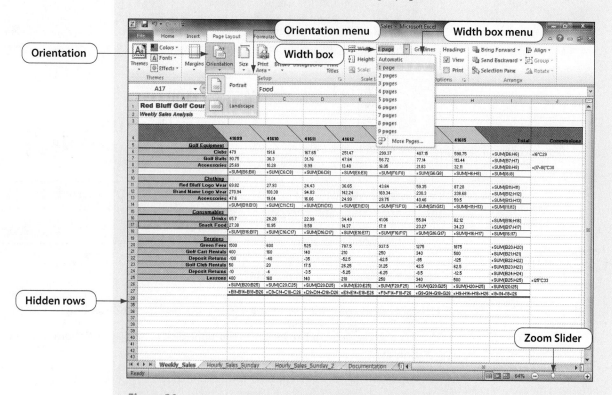

Figure 21   Page orientation, width adjustment, and Zoom control

f. Click **Print Titles** in the Page Setup group, click the **Header/Footer tab** in the Page Setup dialog box, and then click **Custom Footer**.

g. Click in the **Left section** of the Footer dialog box, click **Insert File Name**, click **OK** in the Footer dialog box, and then click **OK** in the Page Setup dialog box.

h. Click the **File tab** to enter Backstage View, click **Print** on the left menu, and then look over the Print Preview of the worksheet displayed on the right side (notice the file name in the footer).

i. Make sure the top button under **Settings** is set to **Print Active Sheets** to ensure you only print the Weekly_Sales worksheet.

j. Make sure you have selected the proper printer under Printer, and then click **Print**.

k. Press Ctrl+` to toggle Show Formulas off and return to the default Normal view.

l. Use the Zoom Slider on the status bar to set the zoom to **100%**.

m. Click **Save**.

Real World Advice — Print Function View for Documentation

You need to document your workbooks. As the worksheets you develop become more complex—use more functions and formulas—the need for documentation increases. Once your worksheet is complete, one vital documentation step is to print a Formula view of your worksheet. If anything ever goes wrong with your worksheet in the future, a Formula view printout may be the fastest way to fix it. Remember, an environmentally friendly documentation option can be to print to PDF. **Portable Document Format (PDF)** was developed by Adobe Systems in 1993 and is a file format that has become a standard for storing files. PDF preserves exactly the original "look and feel" of a document but allows its viewing in many different applications.

Decision Making

As discussed previously, one of the primary purposes of the analysis of information in Excel worksheets is to assist in decision making. People are often influenced by the format by which information is presented. Worksheets can be huge—with thousands of rows and dozens of columns of information. The number of calculated items can be daunting to analyze, digest, and interpret. To the extent Excel can be used to assist the decision maker in understanding information, decision-making speed and quality should improve.

Conditional formatting is one way Excel can aid the decision maker by changing the way information is displayed based on rules specific to the problem the worksheet is designed to address.

Conditional Formatting

Conditional formatting allows the specification of rules that apply formatting to a cell as determined by the rule outcome. It is a way to dynamically change the visual presentation of information in a manner that actually adds information to the worksheet.

Conditional formatting can be used to highlight information by changing cell fill color, font color, font style, font size, border, and/or number format.

To Highlight Above and Below Average Daily Sales

a. Click the **Home tab**, select cell range **B6:H6**, and then click **Conditional Formatting** in the Styles group. Point to **Top/Bottom Rules**, and then select **Above Average** from the menu.

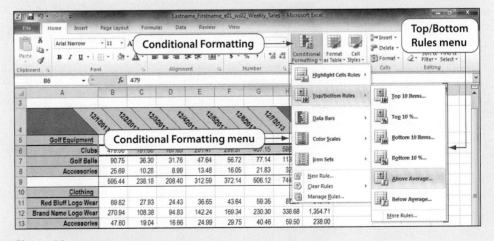

Figure 22   Conditional Formatting menus

b. In the Above Average dialog box, click the **for the selected range with arrow**, select **Green Fill with Dark Green Text**, and then click **OK**.

c. Click **Conditional Formatting** in the Styles group, point to **Top/Bottom Rules**, and then select **Below Average**. In the Below Average dialog box, click the **for the selected range with arrow**, select **Light Red Fill with Dark Red Text**, and then click **OK**.

d. Press Ctrl + C to copy the cell range to the Clipboard.

e. Select cell **B7** and right-click. On the shortcut menu that appears, click **Formatting** 🗋 on the Paste Options menu. This will create a new set of rules for cell range B7:H7.

f. Repeat Step e for cells **B8**, **B11**, **B12**, **B13**, **B16**, **B17**, **B20**, **B21**, **B22**, **B23**, **B24**, and **B25**. Press Esc.

Troubleshooting

Conditional formatting is very sensitive to relative references. Copy and paste very carefully. Be sure to double-check the results of any copy-and-paste activity when conditional formatting is involved. The row of cells that contain conditional formatting is copied to the Clipboard. The row must be pasted from the Clipboard, Paste Formatting 🗋 one row at a time or the conditional formatting rules will be broken.

g. Click the **heading** for row 28, press Shift, and then click the **heading** for row 35. Right-click, and then select **Unhide** on the shortcut menu. You need access to the parameters hidden in rows 29:34.

h. Click cell **J9**, click the **Borders arrow** in the Font group, and then select **Top Border** on the Borders menu.

i. Click **AutoSum** in the Editing group, and then press Ctrl + Enter.

j. Click **Conditional Formatting** in the Styles group, point to **Icon Sets**, and then click **More Rules**.

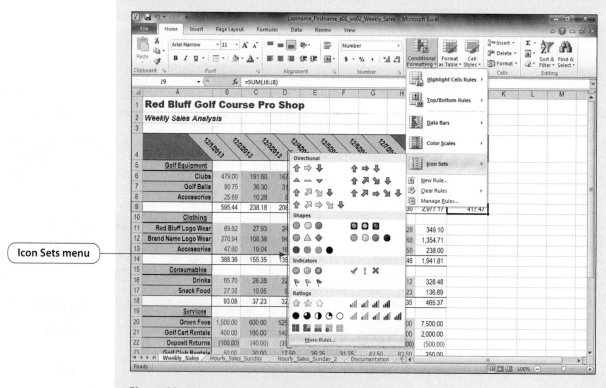

Icon Sets menu

Figure 23   Conditional formatting using icon sets

k. In the New Formatting Rule dialog box, select **Format all cells based on their values** under Select a Rule Type. Click **3 Arrows (Colored)** in the Icon Style box—you may have to scroll up.

l. Under **Icon**, select the **Red Down Arrow** for the bottom Icon box. Select **No Cell Icon** in the bottom Icon box—the Icon Style box will change to Custom, and then select **Number** in both Type boxes.

m. Double-click the top **Value** box. Select cell **C31**—the minimum commission for the Pro Shop manager, and then click **OK**.

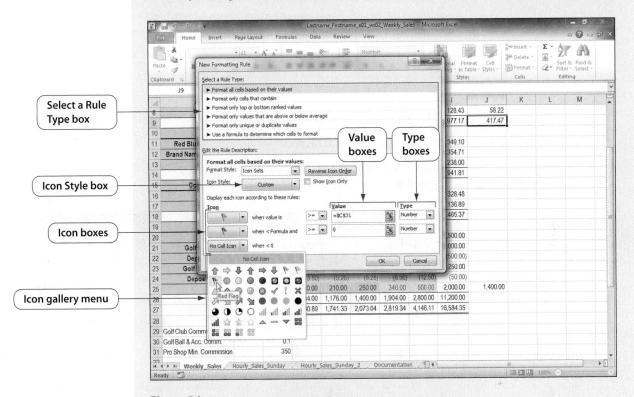

Figure 24   New Formatting Rule dialog box

n. Select cell **J25**, click **Conditional Formatting** in the Styles group, point to **Icon Sets**, and then select **More Rules**.

o. In the New Formatting Rule dialog box, select **Format all cells based on their values** under Select a Rule Type. Click **3 Flags** in the Icon Style box.

p. Under **Icon**, select the **Red Flag** in the middle Icon box—the Icon Style box will change to Custom. Select **No Cell Icon** in the bottom Icon box, and then select **Number** in both Type boxes.

q. Click **Collapse Dialog Box** in the top Value box. The New Formatting Rule dialog box collapses in size, and the Collapse Dialog button toggles to the Expand Dialog button.

r. Click cell **C34**—the minimum commission for the RBGC golf pro. Click **Expand Dialog box** . Click **OK**.

s. Select **rows 29:34** using the row headings. Point to the selected rows, right-click, and then click **Hide** on the shortcut menu.

t. Press Ctrl + Home, and then click **Save** .

Removing Conditional Formatting

Once conditional formatting has been applied to a cell or range of cells, it may be necessary to remove the conditional formatting without affecting other cell formatting or cell contents. Conditional formatting can be removed from a selected cell or cell range, and it can be removed from the entire sheet, depending upon which menu option is chosen.

CONSIDER THIS | **How Might You Use Conditional Formatting?**

Can you think of ways you could use conditional formatting in worksheets to aid personal decisions? Could you use conditional formatting as an aid in tracking your stock portfolio? Monthly budget and expenses? Checking account?

To Remove Conditional Formatting from a Range of Cells

a. Select cell range **B22:H22**, press Ctrl, and then select cell range **B24:H24**.

b. Click **Conditional Formatting** in the Styles group, point to **Clear Rules**, and then select **Clear Rules from Selected Cells**.

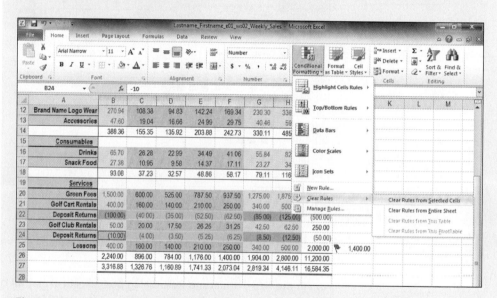

Figure 25   How to clear conditional formatting

Troubleshooting

Did all the conditional formatting in your worksheet disappear? You probably selected Clear Rules from Entire Sheet by mistake. Press Ctrl+Z to undo, and carefully select Clear Rules from Selected Cells.

c. Press Ctrl+Home, and then click **Save** 🖫.

d. To see more of the worksheet, click the **View tab**. Uncheck **Formula Bar** in the Show group, and then double-click the **View tab**.

e. Double-click the **View tab**, and then check **Formula Bar** in the Show group.

f.   Click the **Documentation worksheet tab**, click cell **C5**, and then type Formatted for appearance and clarity. Include punctuation.

g.   Select cell **C6**, and then type Added column and row totals where appropriate. Include punctuation.

h.   Select cell **C7**, and then type Applied cell themes and workbook theme (Horizon). Include punctuation.

i.   Select cell **C8**, and then type Applied conditional formatting to show above and below average daily sales. Applied conditional formatting to indicate commission status. Include punctuation.

j.   Press [Ctrl]+[Home], and then click **Save**. Submit your work as directed by your instructor. Close [x] Excel.

Real World Advice   The Power and Risk of "Machine Decision Making"

Never forget that tools like Excel are decision-making aids, *not* decision makers. Certainly there are highly structured decisions that can be programmed into a worksheet in Excel such that the result is the decision, such as a product mix problem. Excel is more often used for the analysis of information in less highly structured problems. In addition, generally not all factors in a decision can be quantified and programmed into a worksheet. Never forget that Excel and other tools are decision-making *aids*, not decision makers. Computers make calculations; people make decisions.

1. Jon, who works with you in accounting, is creating a new workbook. This workbook will be used to present information to clients outside the department and will form the standard of appearance for all worksheets in the accounting department. Jon's supervisor has asked that the workbook be flexible enough to allow for easy changes to formatting that would affect all worksheets in the workbook with minimal effort. Jon admits he is not very good with formatting. His primary concern at the moment is column headings. What advice would you give Jon to enhance the appearance and readability of column headings while satisfying his supervisor's desire for flexibility and workbook-wide changeability?

2. Your supervisor, Shannon, has asked you to update a financial worksheet because some of the upper-level managers who read it are having difficulty finding information they need—mostly totals and other aggregate data. The worksheet currently contains no special formatting other than the numbers that are all displayed with two decimal places. List five things you could do to make the worksheet more readable for upper-level managers.

3. You have been asked to add a new section of data to a worksheet. The additional data will require the same formatting that is used by other data in the worksheet. There are several ways to set the formatting for the new cells to reflect what is already in place. The most difficult way is to set the formatting manually (changing each cell or cell range). What are two easier ways to set the formatting for the new data?

4. Approximately 99% of color-blind individuals have trouble distinguishing between the colors red and green. For financial worksheets, where green may be used as conditional formatting for positive numbers and red may be used for negative numbers, color-blindness would make such an informational aid difficult. What other things could you do with conditional formatting to ensure color-blind readers have the similar differential formatting as non-color-blind readers?

5. Documentation is a vital part of ensuring that a workbook is usable over time and that the information presented in a workbook will be correct. One of the most powerful capabilities of a worksheet is the creation of new information by aggregating data and by applying various functions to data and ranges of data. The formulas and functions that are used to create new information are not generally of interest to workbook readers, but at times they are very important to people responsible for maintaining and enhancing a workbook. Rebuilding an accidentally deleted or modified formula can be frustrating and time consuming. How would you document the formulas and functions to assist future users in maintaining and enhancing a workbook?

Key Terms

Argument 350
AutoSum function 350
AVERAGE() function 353
Banding 347
Built-in cell style 345
Built-in function 350
Cell alignment 340
Cell reference 350

Conditional formatting 361
Constant 354
COUNT() function 352
Default 349
Fill color 341
Format Painter 343
Formula 354
Function 350

Graphical format 334
Hard-coding 358
Mathematical operator 354
MAX() function 354
MIN() function 354
Order of operations 357
Parameter 358
Portable Document Format (PDF) 361

Relative cell reference 355
SUM() function 350
Table 334, 347
Table style 347
Tabular format 334
Variable 350
Workbook theme 349

Visual Summary

View and print all formulas in a worksheet (p. 359)

Format a cell or cell range as a date or time (p. 338)

Rotate text (p. 341)

Change cell background color (p. 341)

Format cell borders (p. 342)

Use the AutoSum SUM() function (p. 351)

Get started (p. 334)

Format numbers (p. 336)

Highlight above and below average daily sales (p. 361)

Right-align text, increase indent, and bottom align (p. 340)

Use Paste Options and Paste Special to copy formats (p. 344)

Use the Format Painter to copy formats (p. 343)

Copy a documentation template from another workbook (p. 335)

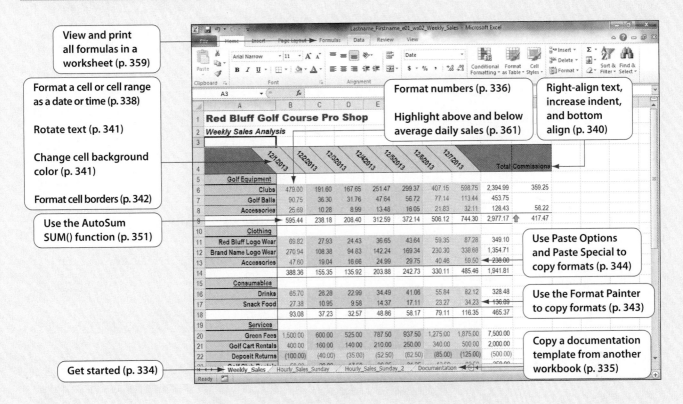

Remove conditional formatting from a range of cells (p. 364)

Use a formula to sum totals (p. 355)

Hide and unhide rows in a worksheet (p. 359)

Display negative numbers in red (p. 337)

Enter formulas to calculate commissions (p. 357)

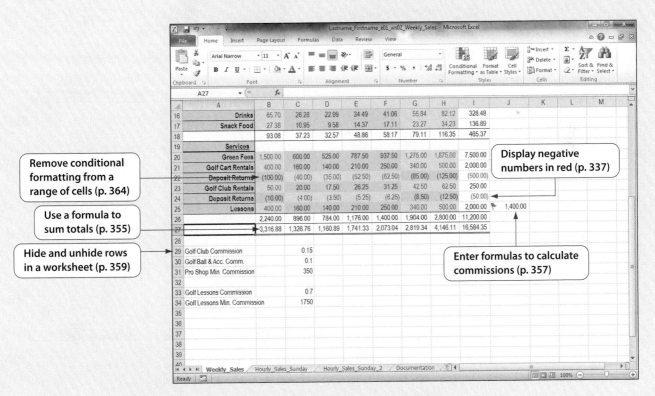

Apply built-in cell styles (p. 345)

Change the workbook theme (p. 349)

Use the AVERAGE() AutoSum function (p. 353)

Use the AutoSum MIN() and MAX() functions (p. 354)

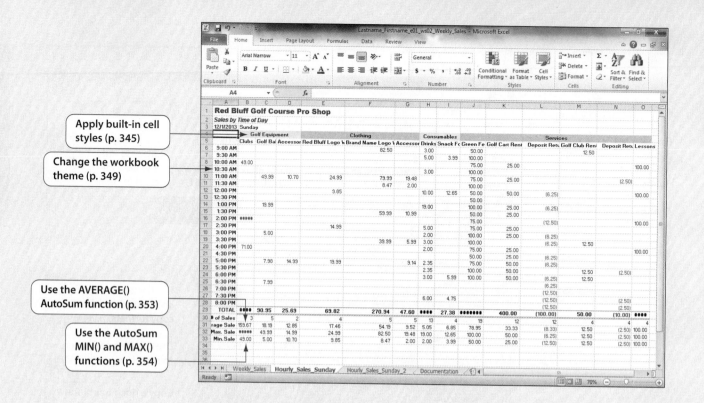

Apply a table style to a cell range (p. 347)

Use the AutoSum COUNT() function (p. 353)

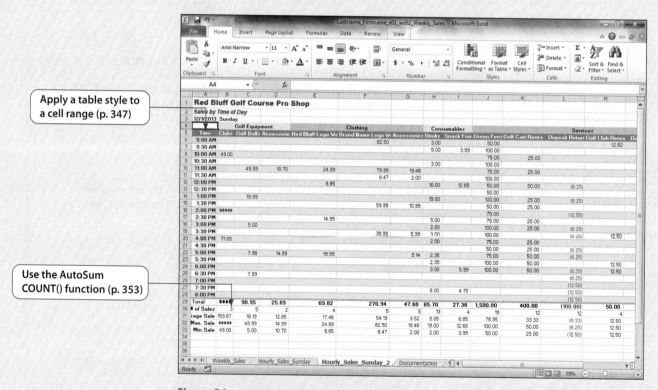

Figure 26 Red Bluff Golf Club Pro Shop Sales Analysis Final

Pro Shop Budget

Finance &
Accounting

After you completed the Pro Shop sales analysis, Aleeta realized the value of the worksheet would be enhanced if sales budget analysis could be added to it. She added the budget figures to the WS2_Practice1 worksheet. You are to use number formatting and conditional formatting to add information to the worksheet that indicates whether or not the WS2_Practice1 data meets budget goals.

a. Start **Excel**, and then open **e01_ws02_ProShop_Budget**. Click the **File tab**, and click **Save As**. In the Save As dialog box, navigate to the location where you are saving your files, and then in the File name box, type Lastname_Firstname_e01_ws02_ProShop_Budget.

b. Click cell **B41**, click the **Formulas tab**, and then click **AutoSum** in the Function Library group. Press Enter.

c. Click cell **B41**, click the **fill handle** in the bottom-right corner of cell B41, and then drag to select the cell range **B41:I41**.

d. Click cell **I37**, click **AutoSum** in the Function Library group, and then press Enter.

e. Click cell **I37**, click on the **fill handle** in the bottom-right corner of cell I37, and then drag to select the cell range **I37:I40**.

f. Click cell **B36**, and then click the fill handle and drag the mouse to the right until cell range **B36:H36** is selected. Next you want to add conditional formatting to cell B9 to identify whether the category sales for each day met budgeted amounts.

g. Click cell **B9**, click the **Home tab**, and then click **Conditional Formatting** in the Styles group. Point to **Highlight Cells Rules**, and then select **More Rules**. In the New Formatting Rule dialog box, under Select a Rule Type, click **Use a formula to determine which cells to format**.

h. Under Edit the Rule Description, in the Format values where this formula is true box, type =B9>=B37. Click **Format**, and then click **Bold** under Font style. In the Color box, click **More Colors**. If necessary, click the **Custom tab** in the Colors dialog box. Set Color model to **RGB**, Red to **0**, Green to **100**, and Blue to **0**. Click **OK**, click **OK** in the Format Cells dialog box, and then click **OK** in the New Formatting Rule dialog box.

i. In the Styles group, click **Conditional Formatting**, point to **Highlight Cells Rules**, and then select **More Rules**. In the New Formatting Rule dialog box, under Select a Rule Type, click **Use a formula to determine which cells to format**.

j. Under Edit the Rule Description, in the Format values where this formula is true box, type =B9<B37. Click **Format**, and then under Color, click **Red**, second from the left in Standard Colors. Click **OK**, and then click **OK** in the New Formatting Rule dialog box.

k. Click the **fill handle**, and then drag the mouse right until cells **B9:I9** are selected. Click **Auto Fill Options**, and then select **Fill Formatting Only**.

l. Repeat Steps g–k for cells **B14**, **B18**, **B26**, and **B27**; and cell ranges **B14:I14**, **B18:I18**, **B26:I26**, and **B27:I27**. Modify the formulas in the Conditional Formatting Rule dialog box to compare each cell to the proper budget figure; for example, for cell B14 the formula for Step i is =B14>=B38.

m. Add Data Bar conditional formatting to the daily totals in row 27 by selecting cell range **B27:I27**. Click **Conditional Formatting** in the Styles group, point to **Data Bars**, and then under Gradient Fill, click **Green Data Bar**.

n. Select cell range **I37:I41**, press Ctrl, and then select cell range **B41:H41**. Press Ctrl+B.

o. Format the budget amounts with two decimal places and a comma separator. If necessary, click the **Home tab**. Select cell range **B37:I41**. In the Number group, click the **Number Format arrow**, and then click **More Number Formats**. Under Category, click **Number**. If necessary, in the Decimal places box, enter **2**. Make sure **Use 1000 Separator (,)** is checked. Click **OK**. If any of the cells in B:I display number signs, select column headings **B:I**, click **Format** in the Cells group, and then select **AutoFit Column Width** on the Cell Size menu.

p. Select cell range **A36:A41**, press Ctrl, and then select cell range **B36:I36**. Press Ctrl+B. In the Alignment group, click **Align Text Right**.

q. To add cell borders to better differentiate individual budget figures from budget totals, select cell range **A41:I41**. Click the **Borders arrow** in the Font group, and then click **Top Border** on the Borders menu. Select cell range **I36:I41**, click the **Borders arrow** in the Font group, select **Left Border** from the Borders menu, and then press Ctrl+Home.

r. Click the **Documentation worksheet tab**, click cell **A5**, and then press Ctrl+; to replace the date format with the current date.

s. Click cell **A9**, and then type today's date in mm/dd/yyyy format.

t. Click cell **B9**, and then type your Lastname, Firstname replacing Lastname and Firstname with your own name.

u. Click cell **C9**, and then type Added budget analysis using daily budgets by category and conditional formatting. Press Ctrl+Home.

v. Click the **Page Layout tab**, click **Print Titles** in the Page Setup group, click the **Header/Footer tab** in the Page Setup dialog box, and then click **Custom Footer**. Click in the **Left section** box, click **Insert File Name**, click **OK** in the Footer dialog box, and then click **OK** in the Page Setup dialog box.

w. Click the **WS2_Practice1 worksheet tab**. Repeat Step v.

x. Click **Save**, and then submit your project as directed by your instructor. Close Excel.

Problem Solve 1

<table>
<tr><td>**Student data files needed:**</td><td>**You will save your file as:**</td></tr>
<tr><td>e01_ps1_Spa_Schedule</td><td>Lastname_Firstname_e01_ps1_Spa_Schedule</td></tr>
<tr><td>e01_ps1_Documentation</td><td></td></tr>
</table>

Spa Schedule

Sales & Marketing

Irene Kai, another manager of the Turquoise Oasis Spa, has exported sales data from a database program into an Excel spreadsheet to facilitate the analysis of services received by a client during a visit to the spa. This spreadsheet is in the initial development stages, but the intention is to keep track of the treatments performed on an individual client during their stay at the resort, the consultant that performed each service, and the treatments that seem most popular. This will allow the staff to review spa usage in a visually appealing layout, notice trends in treatment choices, and improve the scheduling of therapists. In the future it might lead to the mailing of special promotions to regular or high usage customers, a reevaluation of pricing, or the addition or deletion of treatments based on popularity.

Irene has imported the data and created a workbook that will consist of three worksheets. One worksheet contains the clients' names, a list of the dates of service, type of treatment administered, the cost of the treatment, and the consultant that performed that service. A second worksheet has a list of spa therapists and the days of the week and times that each is available.

a. Start **Excel**. Click the **File tab**, and then click **Open**. Navigate to where your student files are located, and then open **e01_ps1_Spa_Schedule**. Click the **File tab**, and then click **Save As**. In the Save As dialog box, navigate to the location where you are saving your files. In the File name box, type Lastname_Firstname_ e01_ps1_Spa_Schedule, replacing Lastname and Firstname with your own name.

b. Double-click the **Sheet1 worksheet tab**. Type Schedule by Date, and then press Enter. Double-click the **Sheet2 worksheet tab**. Type Therapists, and then press Enter.

c. Click the **File tab**, and then click **Open**. Navigate to where your student files are located, and then open **e01_ps1_Documentation**. Click the **Select All button**, and then press Ctrl+C. Press Ctrl+Tab to make Lastname_Firstname_e01_ps1_Spa_Schedule the active workbook. Click the **Documentation worksheet tab**, and then press Ctrl+V. Press Ctrl+Tab to make e01_ps1_Documentation the active workbook, and then click **Close Window**. If prompted, click **No** to delete the Documentation worksheet from the Clipboard. If necessary, press Ctrl+Tab as many times as is necessary to make Lastname_Firstname_e01_ps1_Spa_Schedule the active workbook.

d. Click cell **A3**, press and hold Ctrl, and then click cell **A5**. Press Ctrl+; to insert today's date, and then press Ctrl+Enter. Click cell **B3**, and then type Irene Kai. Click cell **B5**, and type your name in Lastname, Firstname format. Click cell **C3**, and then type Analysis of spa services and sales. Click cell **D3**, and then type Lastname_Firstname_ e01_ps1_Spa_Schedule, replacing Lastname and Firstname with your own name.

e. Click the **Schedule by Date worksheet tab**. Click the **Page Layout tab**, click **Themes** in the **Themes** group, and select **Angles** from the gallery menu.

f. Select cell range **A1:J1**. Click the **Home tab**, and then click **Merge & Center** in the Alignment group. Click **Cell Styles** in the Styles group, and then select **Title** from the gallery menu. Click the **Fill Color arrow** in the Font group, and then select **Turquoise, Accent 3, Lighter 80%** from the gallery menu.

g. Select cell range **A2:J2**. Click **Merge & Center** in the Alignment group. Click **Cell Styles** in the Styles group, and then select **Heading 4** from the gallery menu.

h. Select cell range **A4:J4**, click **Cell Styles** in the Styles group, and then select **Heading 3** from the gallery menu.

i. Click cell **A2**, and then click **Copy** in the Clipboard group. Select cell range **A26:A30**. Right-click on cell **A26**, and then select **Formatting** from the Paste Options shortcut menu. Click **Align Text Left** in the Alignment group.

j. Click cell **A6**, click the Format Painter in the Clipboard group, and then select cell range **A7:A23**.

k. Select cell range **I6:I23**. Click the **Number Format arrow** in the Number group, and then select **Currency**. Click **Decrease Decimal** in the Number group two times.

l. Select cell range **C6:C23**. Click the **Number Format arrow** in the Number group, and then click **More Number Formats**. In the Category box, click **Time** if necessary. In the Type box, select **1:30 PM**. Click **OK**.

m. Select cell **J10**. Press Alt+=, and then select cell range **I6:I9**. Press Ctrl+Enter. Select cell **J13**. Press Alt+=, and then select cell range **I11:I12**. Press Ctrl+Enter. Select cell **J18**. Press Alt+=, and then select cell range **I14:I17**. Press Ctrl+Enter. Select cell **J21**. Press Alt+=, and then select cell range **I19:I20**. Press Ctrl+Enter. Select cell **J24**. Press Alt+=, and then select cell range **I22:I23**. Press Ctrl+Enter.

n. Select cell **C28**, and then type =MAX(J6:J24). Select cell **J24**, click the **Format Painter** in the Clipboard group, and then click cell **C28**.

o. Right-click the **column H header**. Select **Hide** from the shortcut menu.

p. Select cell range **A4:J24**. Click **Format as Table** in the Styles group, and then select **Table Style Medium 4** from the gallery menu. Check **My table has headers** in the Format As Table dialog box, and then click **OK**. Click **Total Row** in the Table Style Options group.

Click the **Home tab**. Click cell **J13**, click the **Format Painter** in the Clipboard group, and then click cell **J25**.

q. Click the **Data tab**, and then click **Filter** in the Sort & Filter group. Click the **Home tab**.

r. Select cell **J10**, press and hold `Ctrl`, and then select cells **J13**, **J18**, **J21** and **J24**. On the Home tab, click **Conditional Formatting** in the Styles group, click **Highlight Cells Rules**, and then select **Greater Than**. Type =C$31 in the Format cells that are GREATER THAN box. Click the **arrow** on the right of the with box, and then select **Custom Format**. If necessary, click the **Font tab** in the Format Cells dialog box. Click **Bold** in the Font style box. Click the **Color arrow**, and select **Turquoise, Accent 3, Darker 50%** from the palette. Click **OK**, and then click **OK** again.

s. Click the **Page Layout tab**, click **Orientation** in the Page Setup group, and then select **Landscape**. Click the **Width Box arrow** in the Scale to Fit group, and then click **1 page**.

t. Click the **Formulas tab**, and then click **Show Formulas** in the Formula Auditing group. Click the **File tab**, and then click **Save As**. Click the **Save as type arrow**, and then select **PDF (*.pdf)**. Uncheck the **Open file after publishing checkbox**. Click **Save,** and then click **Show Formulas** in the Formula Auditing group.

u. Click the **Therapists worksheet tab**. Select cell **C8**, type Monday, and then press `Ctrl`+`Enter`. Click and hold the **AutoFill handle** and expand the active cell to encompass cell range **C8:C14**. Press `Ctrl`+`C`. Click cell **C16**, press and hold `Ctrl`, and then click cell **C24**. Press `Ctrl`+`V`.

v. Click the **Home tab**, and then select cell range **A6:D6**. Click **Cell Styles** in the Styles group, and then select **40%-Accent3** from the gallery menu. Click **Bold** in the Font group. Click **Orientation** in the Alignment group, and then select **Angle Clockwise** in the shortcut menu. Press `Ctrl`+`Home`.

w. Click the **Documentation worksheet tab**. Click cell **C5**, and then type Applied visual formatting. Click cell **C6**, and then type Calculated daily totals. Click cell **C7**, and then type Determined maximum day's sales. Click cell **C8**, and then type Formatted schedule as a table with totals. Click cell **C9**, and then type Finished and formatted the Therapists worksheet. Select cell range **C5:C14**, and then click **Wrap Text** in the Alignment group. Press `Ctrl`+`Home`.

x. Click the **Schedule by Date worksheet tab**. Click the **Page Layout tab**, and then click **Print Titles** in the Page Setup group. Click the **Header/Footer tab** in the Page Setup dialog box, and then click the **Custom Footer** button. Click in the **Left section** of the Footer dialog box. Click **Insert File Name**, click **OK** in the Footer dialog box, and then click **OK** in the Page Setup dialog box. Press `Ctrl`+`Home`.

y. Click **Save**. Print and/or turn in workbook files as directed by your instructor. Close Excel.

MODULE CAPSTONE

Student data file needed:

e01_mp_Beverage_Sales

You will save your file as:

Lastname_Firstname_e01_mp_Beverage_Sales

Beverage Sales/Inventory Analysis

Sales & Marketing

The Painted Paradise Resort and Spa offers a wide assortment of beverages through the Indigo 5 restaurant and bar. The resort must track the inventory levels of these beverages as well as the sales and costs associated with each item. Analyze the inventory and sales data found in the worksheet. There are four categories of beverages: Beer, Wine, Soda, and Water. You also have three inventory figures: Starting, Delivered, and Ending. Resort management wants you to generate an analysis of beverage sales in which you identify units sold of each beverage, cost of goods sold, revenue, profit, profit margin, and appropriate totals and averages.

a. Start **Excel**, and then open **e01_mp_Beverage_Sales**. Save the file with the name Lastname_Firstname_e01_mp_Beverage_Sales, replacing Lastname_Firstname with your own name.

b. Click the **Documentation worksheet tab**, click cell **A3**, and then press Ctrl+; to enter today's date. Click cell **B3**, and then type your Lastname, Firstname. Click cell **C3**, type Formatting More_Practice worksheet, and then press Enter.

c. Type More_Practice in cell **B16**. Type your Lastname, Firstname in cell **B17**. Enter today's date into cell **B18**. Enter a descriptive sentence or two in cell B19 that accurately reflect the activities in this exercise. Press Ctrl+Home. Click the **More_Practice worksheet tab**.

d. Select cell range **A1:K1**, and then click **Merge & Center** in the Alignment group. Apply the **Title** cell style to the selected range. If necessary, on the Home tab, in the Cells group, click **Format**, and then click **AutoFit Row Height**.

e. Select cell range **A2:K2**, and then click **Merge & Center** in the Alignment group. Apply the **Heading 4** cell style to the selected range.

f. Insert a hard return at the specified locations in the following cells—be sure to remove any spaces between the words, and then press Alt+Enter:
   - Between **Starting** and **Inventory** in **C6**
   - Between **Inventory** and **Delivered** in **D6**
   - Between **Ending** and **Inventory** in **E6**
   - Between **Units** and **Sold** in **F6**
   - Between **Cost** and **Per Unit** in **G6**
   - Between **Cost of** and **Goods Sold** in **H6**
   - Between **Sale Price** and **Per Unit** in **I6**
   - Between **Profit** and **Margin** in **K6**

g. Format the height of row 6 to 30, select cell range **A6:K29**, and apply **AutoFit Column Width**. Select cell range **C6:K6** along with cells **B13, B19, B26, B30**, and **B31**. Apply **Align Text Right**.

h. Select cell ranges **C13:K13**, **C19:K19**, **C26:K26**, and **C30:K30**. Add a **Top and Bottom Border** to the selected cell ranges. Select cell range **C31:K31**, and then add a **Bottom Double Border** to the selected range.

i. Select cell range **C7:F31**. Format the selected range as **Number** with a comma separator and zero decimal places. Select cell range **G7:J31**, and then format the selected range as **Number** with a comma separator and two decimal places. If any cells contain a string of pound signs (#), select the columns, and then apply **AutoFit Column Width**.

j. Select cell **F7**. Calculate Units Sold by adding Starting Inventory to Inventory Delivered and subtracting Ending Inventory. Type =C7+D7-E7, and then copy cell **F7** to cell ranges **F8:F12**, **F15:F18**, **F21:F25**, and **F28:F29**. Press ⌐Esc⌐ when done to cancel the target copy cell. If any cells contain a string of pound signs (#), select the column, and then apply **AutoFit Column Width**.

k. Select cell **H7**. Calculate Cost of Goods Sold as Units Sold multiplied by Cost Per Unit. Type =F7*G7, copy cell **H7** to cell ranges **H8:H12**, **H15:H18**, **H21:H25**, and **H28:H29**. If any cells contain a string of pound signs (#), select the column, and then apply **AutoFit Column Width**.

l. Select cell **J7**. Calculate Revenue as Units Sold multiplied by Sale Price Per Unit. Type =F7*I7, and then copy cell **J7** to cell ranges **J8:J12**, **J15:J18**, **J21:J25**, and **J28:J29**. If any cells contain a string of pound signs (#), select the column, and then apply **AutoFit Column Width**.

m. Select cell **K7**. Calculate Profit Margin as (Revenue – Cost of Goods Sold)/Revenue. Type =(J7-H7)/J7, and then copy cell **K7** to cell ranges **K8:K12**, **K15:K18**, **K21:K25**, and **K28:K29**.

n. Select cell range **C13:F13**, press ⌐Ctrl⌐, and then select cells **H13** and **J13**. Click **AutoSum**. If any cells contain a string of number signs (#), select the cells, and then apply **AutoFit Column Width**.

o. Select cell range **C19:F19**. Press ⌐Ctrl⌐, and then select cells **H19** and **J19**. Click **AutoSum**. If any cells contain a string of number signs (#), select the cells, and then apply **AutoFit Column Width**.

p. Select cell range **C26:F26**. Press ⌐Ctrl⌐, and then select cells **H26** and **J26**. Click **AutoSum**. If any cells contain a string of number signs (#), select the cells, and then apply **AutoFit Column Width**.

q. Select cell range **C30:F30**, press ⌐Ctrl⌐, and then select cells **H30** and **J30**. Click **AutoSum**. If any cells contain a string of number signs (#), select the cells, and then apply **AutoFit Column Width**.

r. Select cell **C31**. Calculate the total number of items in Starting Inventory for all categories combined by using the SUM() formula. Type =SUM(C13,C19,C26,C30), and then copy cell **C31** to cell range **D31:F31** as well as cells **H31** and **J31**. If any cells contain a string of number signs (#), select the cells, and then apply **AutoFit Column Width**.

s. Copy cell **K12**, and then from **Paste Options**, paste **Formulas** into cells **K13**, **K19**, **K26**, **K30**, and **K31**. Select cell range **K7:K31**. Format the selected range as **%** with one decimal place. If any cells contain a string of pound signs (#), select the cells, and then apply **AutoFit Column Width**.

t. Select cells **H13**, **J13**, **H19**, **J19**, **H26**, **J26**, **H30**, **J30**, **H31**, and **J31**. Format the selected cells as **Currency**. If any cells contain a string of pound signs (#), select the cells, and then apply **AutoFit Column Width**.

u. Select cell range **F7:F12**. Use conditional formatting to highlight the beer with the highest number of units sold for the week as **Green Fill with Dark Green Text**. Use **Top 10 Items** in Top/Bottom Rules, and then change the number of ranked items to **1**.

v. Repeat Step u with cell ranges **J7:J12**, **F15:F18**, **J15:J18**, **F21:F25**, **J21:J25**, **F28:F29**, and **J28:J29**. Do not use Ctrl to select all the above ranges at the same time; repeat Step u seven times, once for each range.

w. Select cell range **A6:K6**, press Ctrl, and then click cells **A14**, **A20**, and **A27**. Apply **20% - Accent1** in the Themed Cell Styles to the selected cells. Select cell range **A4:B4**, press Ctrl, and then select cell ranges **A6:K6**, **B13:K13**, **B19:K19**, **B26:K26**, **B30:K31**, as well as cells **A14**, **A20**, and **A27**. Click **Bold**.

x. Click the **Page Layout tab**, in the Themes group click **Themes**, and then click **Adjacency** to change the workbook theme to Adjacency.

y. Click **Print Titles**, click the **Header/Footer tab** in the Page Setup dialog box, and then click the **Custom Footer** button. Click in the **Left section** of the Footer dialog box, click **Insert File Name**, click **OK**, and then click **OK** again to close the Page Setup dialog box.

z. Press Ctrl + Home, click **Save**, and then close **Excel**.

Problem Solve 1

Student data file needed:

e01_ps1_Hotel_ Discounts

You will save your file as:

Lastname_Firstname_e01_ps1_Hotel_ Discounts

myitlab grader
Homework 1

Analysis of Hotel Sales Discounts

Finance & Accounting

The Painted Paradise Resort and Spa has 700 rooms. The Paradise Resort and Spa gives discounts to guests who meet certain conditions. First, the Paradise Club discount, a 9% discount applicable to all products and services at the resort, is offered to guests who opt into the resort's rewards program. Another 10% discount, good on hotel rooms and services, is offered to groups who book a large block of rooms. Finally, at the discretion of the resort management, rooms may be charged at a complimentary rate. The resort's management would like to get an idea of how much revenue is lost to discounts on Friday and Saturday nights, the busiest nights of the week.

a. Start **Excel**, and then open **e01_ps1_Hotel_Discounts**. Save the file with the name Lastname_Firstname_e01_ps1_Hotel_Discounts, replacing Lastname_Firstname with your own name.

b. Click the **Documentation worksheet tab**, click cell **A3**, and then press Ctrl + ; to enter today's date. Click cell **B3**, type your Lastname, Firstname, click cell **C3**, and then type Formatting Problem_Solve_1 worksheet.

c. Type Problem_Solve_1 in cell **B16**, and then type your Lastname, Firstname into cell **B17**. Enter today's date into cell **B18**. Enter a descriptive sentence or two in cell B19 that accurately reflect the activities in this exercise.

d. Press Ctrl + Home, and then click the **Problem_Solve_1 worksheet tab**.

e. Apply the **Title** cell style to cell **A1**. Apply the **Heading 4** cell style to cells **A2**, **A12**, **A24**, and **A41**.

f. Apply the **Heading 3** cell style to cells **A3:G3** and **A7**.

g. Change the font in cells **A4:A5** and **A8:A10** to **Dark Blue**, **Text 2**, and **Bold**.

h. Format the range **B8:G10** as **%** with one decimal place.

i. Format cells **A13:G17** as **Table Style Light 9** with the option **My table has headers** checked. On the Table Tools Design tab, check **First Column** in the Table Style Options group. In the Tools group, click **Convert to Range**, and then click **Yes** in response to "Do you want to convert the table to a normal range?"

Convert to Range enables you to apply table formatting for appearance purposes without some of the overhead and restrictions of a table in manipulating data in the range. Of course, you also lose the power of tables for sorting, totals, and so on. Convert to Range should only be used when you are quite certain rows will not be inserted into, or deleted from, the range since the banding of a normal range (if present) would be affected.

j. Format cells **A18:G22** as **Table Style Light 9** with **My table has headers** checked. Check **First Column**, and then convert the table to a normal range.

k. Format cells **A25:H31** as **Table Style Medium 2** with **My table has headers**. Check **First Column** and **Last Column**, and then convert the table to a normal range.

l. Format cells **A33:H39** as **Table Style Medium 2** with **My table has headers**. Check **First Column** and **Last Column**, and then convert the table to a normal range.

m. Format cells **A42:H46** as **Table Style Medium 2** with **My table has headers**. Check **First Column** and **Last Column**, and then convert the table to a normal range.

n. Format cells **B26:G29**, **B34:G37**, and **B43:G45** as **Number** as follows: **(1,234.00)**. Negative numbers should *not* be displayed in red; **2 decimal places** and **Use 1000 Separator (,)** should be checked.

o. Format cells **B30:H31**, **H26:H29**, **B38:H39**, **H34:H37**, **B46:H46**, and **H43:H45** as Accounting.

p. In cell **B26**, enter a formula to multiply the total number of One Double rooms rented on Friday by the Standard Rate for a One Double room. Click **AutoSum**, and then select the cell range **B14:B17**. Edit the formula to multiply the SUM() function by the Standard Rate for a One Double room. Copy the formula to cell range **C26:G26**.

q. Calculate the discount total for the Paradise Club for each room type for Friday night in cell **B27**. Enter a formula to multiply the number of Paradise Club One Double rooms rented on Friday by the Standard Rate for a One Double room by the Paradise Club discount. The result will be a negative number to reflect the discount total. Copy the formula to cell range **C27:G27**.

r. Calculate the following:
- Group discount total for each room type for Friday night in cell range **B28:G28**
- Comp discount total for each room type for Friday night in cell range **B29:G29**
- Gross Sales for One Double rooms for Saturday night in cell range **B34:G34**
- Paradise Club discount total for all room types for Saturday night in cell range **B35:G35**
- Group discount total for all rooms for Saturday night in cell range **B36:G36**
- Comp discount total for all rooms for Saturday night in cell range **B37:G37**

s. Calculate the Paradise Club discounts for Friday and Saturday night for One Double rooms in cell **B43**, and then copy the formula to cell range **B43:G45**—be sure not to copy over any formatting.

t. In cell **H26**, calculate the Total Gross Sales using AutoSum. Copy the formula in cell **H26** to cell ranges **H27:H29**, **H34:H37**, and **H43:H45**—be sure to copy and paste **Formulas** only so the table formatting is not disturbed.

u. In cell **B30**, use AutoSum to calculate Net Sales, the sum of Gross Sales, and all discounts for One Double rooms on Friday. Copy the formula to cell range **C30:H30**—be sure not to copy over any formatting.

v. In cell **B31**, calculate Total Discounts for Friday for One Double rooms by subtracting Net Sales from Gross Sales. Copy the formula to cell range **C31:H31**—be sure not to copy over any formatting.

w. Copy the formulas in cell range **B30:H31** to cell range **B38:H39**.

x. Calculate the total discounts for One Double rooms for the weekend by using AutoSum in cell **B46**. Copy the formula to cell range **C46:H46**—be sure not to copy over any formatting.

y. Bold cell ranges **B31:G31**, **B39:G39**, and **B46:G46**. Apply **AutoFit Column Width** for columns **A:H**, and then insert **File Name** into the **Left section** of the **Custom Footer**.

z. Press Ctrl + Home , click **Save**, and then close **Excel**.

Problem Solve 2

Homework 2

Student data file needed:

e01_ps2_Room_Service

You will save your file as:

Lastname_Firstname_e01_ps2_Room_Service

Room Service Charges Analysis

Sales & Marketing

The Painted Paradise Resort and Spa offers an extensive array of food and drink available for delivery to guests' rooms. For the convenience of in-room delivery, guests pay a premium price for the service. Recently, the resort has asked representatives from both the hotel and the restaurants to start tracking the charges by room type and day of the week. From this information, management hopes to determine what menu items are being ordered and which room types are ordering.

a. Start **Excel**, and then open **e01_ps2_Room_Service**. Save the file with the name Lastname_Firstname_e01_ps2_Room_Service, replacing Lastname_Firstname with your own name.

b. Click the **Documentation worksheet tab**, click cell **A3**, and then press Ctrl + ; to enter today's date. Click cell **B3**, type your Lastname, Firstname, click cell **C3**, and then type Formatting Problem_Solve_2 worksheet.

c. Type Problem_Solve_2 in cell **B16**, type your Lastname, Firstname into cell **B17**, and then enter today's date into cell **B18**. Enter a descriptive sentence or two in cell B19 that accurately reflect the activities in this exercise.

d. Press Ctrl + Home , and then click the **Problem_Solve_2 worksheet tab**.

e. Merge across, but do not center, cell range **B4:C4**, and then apply the **Comma Style (,)** number format to cell range **B7:H20**.

f. Format cell ranges **A4:A23** and **B6:H6** as **Bold** and **Align Text Right**. Select cell ranges **A7:A23** and **B6:H6**, and then set the Fill Color to **White, Background 1, Darker 15%**. Click cell **A6**, and then set the Fill Color to **White, Background 1, Darker 25%**.

g. Place a **hard return** between **Grand** and **Villa** in cell **G6** (remember to remove the space between the two words).

h. Set the width of **column A** using AutoFit Column Width. Set the column width to 12 for columns **B:H**.

i. Calculate the total room service charges for One Double rooms for the week in cell **B14**. Copy the function to cells **C14:G14**.

j. Calculate the average room service charges for One Double rooms for the week in cell **B15**. Copy the function to cells **C15:G15**. Be careful not to include the total room service charges in the average calculation.

k. Calculate the minimum room service charges for One Double rooms for the week in cell **B16**. Copy the function to cell range **C16:G16**.

l. Calculate the maximum room service charges for One Double rooms for the week in cell **B17**. Copy the function to cell range **C17:G17**.

m. Calculate the total room service charges for Sunday in cell **H7**, copy the function to cell range **H8:H22**, and then delete the function from cells **H18** and **H21**. Change the number of decimal places in cell **H22** to **0**.

n. Click cell **I19**, type <-Total, press Ctrl+Enter, apply **Bold**, and then copy it into cell **I20**.

o. Change the Fill Color in cell range **H19:I19** to **White**, **Background 1**, **Darker 15%**. Change the Fill Color in cell range **H20:I20** to **White**, **Background 1**, **Darker 25%**.

p. Calculate the average individual sale in cell **B23**. Divide the total sales for the week by the number of rooms and the number of days in a week. Copy the formula to cell range **C23:H23**.

q. Select cell range **B7:B15**. Use conditional formatting to apply bold if a cell value is greater than or equal to the daily target for One Double rooms—use **Highlight Cells Rules, More Rules**, and then click **Format only cells that contain**.

r. Repeat Step q for cell ranges **C7:C15**, **D7:D15**, **E7:E15**, **F7:F15**, **G7:G15**, and **H7:H15**. Make sure the cell values in each column are compared to the daily target for that column (row 19).

s. Clear conditional formatting from cell range **B14:H14**. Apply the **Total** built-in cell style to cell range **A14:H14**, and then apply **Accounting Number Format** to cell ranges **B14:H17**, **H7:H13**, and **B23:H23**.

t. Apply **Solid Fill Green Data Bars** to cell range **B14:H14**, and then apply **Solid Fill Green Data Bars** to cell range **H7:H14**.

u. Use conditional formatting to put a gold star in cell **H14** if the total room service charges for the week meet or exceed the total Weekly Target. If any cells contain a string of number signs (#), select the column, and then click **AutoFit Column Width**.

v. Change the font in cell **A1** to **Arial Black**, and then make the text color **Dark Red**.

w. Insert **File Name** into the left section of the **Custom Footer** in the Print Titles.

x. Click **Save**, and then close **Excel**.

Problem Solve 3

Student data file needed:

e01_ps3_Housekeeping_Analysis

You will save your file as:

Lastname_Firstname_e01_ps3_Housekeeping_Analysis

myitlab
grader
Homework 3

Housekeeping Staff Performance

Production & Operations

The Painted Paradise Resort and Spa takes great pride in the efficiency of its housekeeping staff. The housekeeping staff at the Painted Paradise Resort and Spa is expected to properly clean a hotel room in an average of 25 minutes and never more than 30 minutes. Management is interested in how long it takes to actually begin cleaning rooms after guests check out. This is referred to as lag time—time when a room cannot be rented. The Painted Paradise Resort and Spa wants guests to be able to check in early at no additional charge as long as there is a room available. By keeping lag time to a minimum, room availability is maximized.

a. Start **Excel**, and then open **e01_ps3_Housekeeping_Analysis**.

b. Save the file as Lastname_Firstname_e01_ps3_Housekeeping_Analysis, replacing Lastname_Firstname with your own name.

c. Click the **Documentation worksheet tab**, click cell **A3**, and then press Ctrl+; to enter today's date. Click cell **B3**, type your Lastname, Firstname, click cell **C3**, and then type Formatting Problem_Solve_3 worksheet.

d. Type Problem_Solve_3 in cell **B16**, and then type your Lastname, Firstname into cell **B17**. Enter today's date into cell **B18**. Enter a descriptive sentence or two in cell B19 that accurately reflect the activities in this exercise.

e. Press Ctrl+Home, and then click the **Problem_Solve_3 worksheet tab**.

f. Apply **Merge & Center** to cell ranges **A24:B24**, **A25:B25**, **A26:B26**, **A27:B27**, **A29:B29**, **C22:D22**, and **E22:F22**.

g. In cell range **C8:F8**, replace the hyphen and any surrounding spaces with a hard return. In cell **B8**, replace the space between **Checkout** and **Time** with a hard return.

h. Apply **AutoFit Column Width** in columns **A:H**.

i. Apply **Merge & Center** in cell range **B7:D7**, and then apply **AutoFit Column Width** to column **B**.

j. Apply **Align Text Right** to cell ranges **A3:A5**, **E3:E4**, **A24:A29**, **C23:F23**, and cells **A8**, **C3**, and **H8**.

k. Center-align the cell range **B8:F8**.

l. Apply the **20%-Accent1** cell style to cells **A2**, **B7**, and **C22**. Apply the **40%-Accent1** cell style to cell **E22**.

m. Apply the **Heading 2** cell style to cell **A2**. Apply the **Heading 3** cell style to cell range **A8:H8** and cells **B7**, **C22**, and **E22**. Apply the **Heading 4** cell style to cell ranges **A3:A5**, **E3:E4**, **A24:A29**, and cell **C3**.

n. Adjust the column width for the following columns:
   - Column **A** to **18**
   - Columns **B:F** to **12**
   - Column **H** to **10**

o. Calculate the following:
   - Room Clean Lag Time in cell **E9** by subtracting the Checkout Time from the Room Clean Start Time. Copy the formula you just created to cell range **E10:E20**. Notice that the cells that contain formulas that subtract one time value from another time value are automatically formatted as time values.
   - Room Clean Duration in cell **F9** by subtracting the Room Clean Start Time from the Room Clean End Time. Copy the formula you just created to cell range **F10:F20**.
   - Total Room Cleaning Time—Lag in cell **D24** by summing all individual Room Clean Lag Time.
   - Total Room Cleaning Time—Duration in cell **F24** by summing all individual Room Clean Duration.

p. Calculate the following:
   - Average Room Cleaning Time—Lag and Duration in cells **D25** and **F25**, respectively
   - Minimum Room Cleaning Time—Lag and Duration in cells **D26** and **F26**, respectively
   - Maximum Room Cleaning Time—Lag and Duration in cells **D27** and **F27**, respectively

q. Calculate the number of Maintenance Issues Reported in cell **C29**. Format cell **C29** as **Number** with zero decimal places.

r. Apply **Conditional Formatting** to the cell range **E9:E20** so Room Clean Lag Times that are greater than the Allowed Average Room Clean Time Lag display cell values in **Red Text**.

s. Apply **Conditional Formatting** to the cell range **F9:F20** so Room Clean Durations that are greater than the Allowed Average Room Clean Time Duration display cell values in **Red Text**.

t. Apply **Conditional Formatting** to change the font color in the following:
- Cell **D24** to **Red Text** if the value in D24 > the value in cell C24
- Cell **D25** to **Red Text** if the value in D25 > the value in cell C25
- Cell **D26** to **Red Text** if the value in D26 > the value in cell C26
- Cell **D27** to **Red Text** if the value in D27 > the value in cell C27
- Cell **F24** to **Red Text** if the value in F24 > the value in cell E24
- Cell **F25** to **Red Text** if the value in F25 > the value in cell E25
- Cell **F26** to **Red Text** if the value in F26 > the value in cell E26
- Cell **F27** to **Red Text** if the value in F27 > the value in cell E27

u. Format the cell ranges **E9:E20**, **D24:D27**, **F9:F20** and **F24:F27** with a green font color.

In earlier exercises you have also applied conditional formatting to display the opposite in green, meaning if D24 > C24, then display D24 in red text; the opposite is that if D24 <= C24, then display D24 with a green font. By formatting all the cells in the conditionally formatted ranges with a green font, you accomplish the same result, but you only have to apply Conditional Formatting once, rather than twice.

v. Apply the **Foundry** workbook theme.

w. Insert **File Name** in the left section of the Custom Footer.

x. Press Ctrl+Home, click **Save**, and then close **Excel**.

Perform 1: Perform in Your Life

Student data file needed:

Blank Excel document

You will save your file as:

Lastname_Firstname_e01_pf1_Grade_Analysis

Grade Analysis

General Business

Most students are concerned about grades and want to have some means of easily tracking grades, analyzing performance, and calculating the current grade (as much as is possible) in every class.

a. Start **Excel**, and then open a blank document. Save the file as Lastname_Firstname_e01_pf1_Grade_Analysis, replacing Lastname_Firstname with your own name.

b. Look in your syllabus or ask your instructor for the grading scale in this course. Your grading scale may also be given by points rather than percentage. Enter the grading scale into Excel, enter points or percentages in one column and the corresponding letter grade in the column just to the right.

c. Look in your syllabus for a list of assignments, exams, and other point-earning activities. Enter the assignments into Excel. For completed assignments, enter the points possible and your score. Be sure to label all data items.

d. Calculate the percentage score for each point-earning activity, and then use conditional formatting to indicate whether you received an A, B, C, or below a C on each assignment.

e. Calculate the possible points earned to date and total points earned to date in the class.

f. Calculate the current overall percentage earned in the class.

g. Calculate the percentage you need to earn on the final examination to achieve an A, B, and C given the points possible to date and points earned to date.

h. Conditionally format the percentage required to achieve an A in the course to visually indicate how hard you may have to study for the final examination.

For example, if you will have to score at least an 80% on the final examination to achieve an *A* in this course, color the cell that contains the points required to achieve an *A* red to show that you have to study pretty hard for the final examination. Use other colors to indicate whether or not you must score less than 80% or less than 70% on the final examination to achieve an *A* in the course. Use parameters to identify the cutoff values for *A*, *B*, and *C*.

i. Repeat Step h for the percentage required to achieve a *B* in the course.

j. Repeat Step h for the percentage required to achieve a *C* in the course.

k. Also add conditional formatting to visually indicate if an *A* is not possible because the percentage required on the final examination to achieve an *A* exceeds 100%.

l. Repeat Step k for the percentage required on the final examination to achieve a *B* in the course.

m. Repeat Step k for the percentage required on the final examination to achieve a *C* in the course.

n. Ask your instructor whether to include any other courses you are currently taking.

o. Insert the **filename** in the left Custom Footer section of the Print Titles on all worksheets in the workbook.

p. Document your work by copying a documentation worksheet from another file and inserting into your workbook. Update the documentation worksheet to reflect your activities in completing this exercise.

q. Press Ctrl+Home, save and close your file, and exit Excel.

Perform 2: Perform in Your Career

Student data file needed:

Blank Excel document

You will save your file as:

Lastname_Firstname_e01_pf2_Time_Tracking

Personal Time Tracking

Human Resources

You have started working as a computer programmer with BetaWerks Software Corporation. The company requires you to track the time that you spend doing different things during the day each week. This helps the company determine how many of your hours are billable to customers. You have several different projects to work on as well as a few training sessions throughout the week. The company pays for one 15-minute coffee break and one 30-minute lunch each day. Any additional time is considered personal time.

a. Start **Excel**, and then open a blank Excel document. Save the file as Lastname_Firstname_e01_pf2_Time_Tracking, replacing Lastname_Firstname with your own name.

b. Create a spreadsheet to track your time for the company this week. The following requirements must be met:

- Your time must be broken down by project/client and weekdays.
- Time not billable to a project should be classified as Unbillable.
- Unbillable time should be broken into at least two categories: Breaks and Work.

c. BetaWerks bills your time spent on each account according to the following rates:

Klemisch Kompany	$250
Garske Advising	$250
United National Distributors	$175
K&M Worldwide	$150
L&H United	$200

d. Set up your worksheet so you can easily calculate the amount of time you spent working on each account, in meetings, in training, and on breaks according to the information below:

- Monday, you spent two hours in a meeting with your development team. This is billable to the BetaWerks Software company as unbillable hours. Following the meeting, you took a 20 minute coffee break. After your break, you spent two hours and 15 minutes working on your project for Garske Advising. After a one-hour lunch, you attended a two-hour training and development meeting. Before heading home for the day, you spent two hours working on the United National Distributors (UND) project.

- Tuesday morning you spent four hours on the Klemisch Kompany project. To help break up the morning, you took a 20-minute coffee break at 10:00. You only had time for a 30-minute lunch because you had to get back to the office for a team-building activity. The activity lasted 40 minutes. To finish the day, you spent a solid four hours working on the Garske Advising assignment.

- Wednesday morning, you spent two hours each on the Garske Advising and Klemisch Kompany projects. Lunch was a quick 30 minutes because you had a conference call with Mr. Atkinson from UND at 1 p.m. The conference call took one hour, and then you spent an additional three hours working on the project.

- Thursday, the day started with a 30-minute update with your supervisor. Following the meeting, you were able to spend two hours on the UND project. After a 15-minute coffee break, you started on a new project for K&M Worldwide for 90 minutes. You took a 45-minute lunch break, and then spent two and a half hours on the Klemisch Kompany project and two hours on your work for L&H United.

- Friday started with a two-hour training and development session about a new software package that BetaWerks is starting to implement, followed by a 15-minute coffee break. After your coffee break, you were able to squeeze in two more hours for L&H United before taking a one-hour lunch. After lunch, you put in four hours on the Klemisch Kompany project before finally going home for the week.

e. Your salary is $100,000/year with benefits. Given two weeks of vacation, you cost BetaWorks $2,000 in salary and benefits/week.

f. Include in your worksheet a calculation of your profit/loss to BetaWorks for the week.

g. Be sure to document your worksheet using a documentation worksheet, comments, and instructions.

h. Insert the **filename** in the left custom footer section of the print titles footer.

i. Press Ctrl + Home, save your file, and then exit Excel.

Perform 3: Perform in Your Career

Student data file needed:

Blank Excel document

You will save your file as:

Lastname_Firstname_e01_pf3_Check_Register

Check Register

Finance & Accounting

You volunteer your time with a local nonprofit, the Mayville Community Theatre. Because of your business background, the board of directors has asked you to serve as the new treasurer and to track all of the monetary transactions for the group.

a. Start **Excel**, and then open a blank document. Save the file as Lastname_Firstname_e01_pf3_Check_Register, replacing Lastname and Firstname with your own name.

b. Create a spreadsheet to track receipts and expenditures that should be assigned to one of the following categories: Costumes, Marketing, Operating and Maintenance, Scripts and Royalties, and Set Construction. Also track the following for each receipt or expenditure: the date, amount of payment, check/reference number, recipient, and item description.

c. Enter the following receipts and expenditures under the appropriate category.

Date	Item	Paid To	Check or Ref. #	Amount
11/1/2013	Starting Balance	N/A		$1793.08
11/2/2013	Royalties for "The Cubicle"	Office Publishing Company	9520	-$300.00
11/2/2013	Scripts for "The Cubicle"	Office Publishing Company	9521	-$200.00
11/5/2013	Building Maintenance—Ticket Office	Fix It Palace	9522	-$187.92
11/8/2013	Patron Donation	N/A	53339	$1,000.00
11/12/2013	Costumes for "The Cubicle"	Jane's Fabrics	9523	-$300.00
11/22/2013	Building Materials for set construction of "The Cubicle"	Fix It Palace	9524	-$430.00
11/30/2013	TV and Radio ads for "The Cubicle"	AdSpace	9525	-$229.18
11/30/2013	General Theater Operating Expenses—November	The Electric Co-op, City Water Works	9526	-$149.98
12/15/2013	Ticket Revenue from "The Cubicle"	N/A	59431	$1,115.50
12/30/2013	General Theater Operating Expenses—December	The Electric Co-op, City Water Works	9527	-$195.13

d. Periodically, money is deposited into the checking account. Include a way to track deposits.

e. Finally, include the running balance and totals by expenditure category. This should be updated any time money is deposited or withdrawn from the account.

f. If the running account balance drops below $1,000 there should be a conditional formatting alert for any balance figure below the threshold.

g. Document the check register using a documentation worksheet, explicit instructions, and comments where helpful.

h. Insert the **filename** in the left custom footer section of the print titles footer on all worksheets in the workbook.

i. Press Ctrl + Home , save your file, and then exit Excel.

Student data file needed:

e01_pf4_Project_Billing

You will save your file as:

Lastname_Firstname_e01_pf4_Project_Billing

Project Management Billing

Human Resources

John Smith works with you at The Excellent Consulting Company. Each week, consultants are required to track how much time they spend on each project. A spreadsheet is used to track the date, start time, end time, project code, a description of work performed, and the number of billable hours completed. At the bottom of the spreadsheet, the hours spent on each project are summarized so clients can be billed. In your role as an internal auditor, you have been asked to double-check a tracking sheet each week. By random selection, Mr. Smith's tracking worksheet needs to be checked this week. Make sure his numbers are accurate, and ensure that his spreadsheet is set up to minimize errors. His worksheet is also badly in need of some formatting for appearance and clarity, and it is completely lacking in documentation.

a. Start **Excel**, and then open **e01_pf4_Project_Billing**. Save the file as Lastname_Firstname_e01_pf4_Project_Billing, replacing Lastname_Firstname with your own name.

b. Make sure all calculated figures are correct—if you subtract Start Time from End Time and multiply the difference by 24, the result is the number of hours between the two times. Do the Client Totals look correct to you? What about the total hours for the week?

c. What formatting changes would make the worksheet more attractive?

d. Are there formatting changes that would make the worksheet easier to understand and to use?

e. Add documentation.

f. Insert the **filename** in the left custom footer section of the print titles footer on all worksheets in the workbook.

g. Press Ctrl + Home, save your file, and exit Excel.

WORKSHOP 3

Objectives

1. Reference cells within formulas or functions   p. 388

2. Create, modify, and use named ranges within formulas or functions   p. 395

3. Understand the syntax of a function   p. 401

4. Introduce common function categories   p. 405

Conducting Excel Analysis Through Functions and Charts

PREPARE CASE
Massage Table Analysis

The Turquoise Oasis Spa currently has a set of two massage tables. Irene, the spa manager, is considering purchasing more tables. Before any decision can be made, an analysis of existing data is needed pertaining to maintenance costs, including the replacement of the thermostats that control the heating unit on the massage tables. Irene has given you the task of completing a spreadsheet started by

Finance & Accounting

Jerko Grubisic / Shutterstock.com

another staff member. This spreadsheet will be used to order replacement parts and track maintenance of the massage tables as well as evaluate purchase decisions.

Student data file needed for this workshop:

 e02_ws03_Spa_Equipment

You will save your file as:

 Lastname_Firstname_e02_ws03_Spa_Equipment

Cell References and Formula Basics

The value of Excel expands as you move from using the spreadsheet for displaying data to analyzing data in order to make informed decisions. As the complexity of a spreadsheet increases, techniques that promote effective and efficient development of the spreadsheet become of utmost importance. Integrating cell references within formulas and working with functions are common methods used in developing effective spreadsheets. These skills will become the foundation for more advanced skills.

A **cell reference** is used when you refer to a particular cell or range of cells within a formula or function instead of a value. When a formula is created, you can simply use values, like =5*5. However, Excel formulas typically refer to a cell or range of cells, like =B4*C4, where cells B4 and C4 contain values to be used in the calculation. The formula now references a cell rather than a value, which is preferable as it improves efficiency should cell data change over time.

Importantly, anyone who uses the spreadsheet can easily view and change the value in the referenced cell. Every time you change the value within a referenced cell, the formula computes a new result. Changing the value in a cell is easier than editing the formula every time a value needs to be changed. Additionally, you can reference the same cell in multiple formulas or functions. Thus, changing the value once in a cell is superior to changing the value multiple times in every formula that uses that value. Cell referencing increases a spreadsheet's flexibility.

There is also another level of cell referencing that Excel uses to offer built-in intelligence for moving or copying formulas to other cell locations within a spreadsheet or workbook. By default, cells are referenced in formulas in a relative manner, where directions for locating the cell are *relative* to where the formula is placed. For instance, the cell referenced is viewed as being two cells to the right and three cells below the cell containing the formula. When you copy the formula to many cells, that reference will remain relative to where the formula resides.

Conversely, there may be circumstances in which you want a cell reference to remain stationary when a formula is copied to other cells. You do not want the reference to be copied or moved *relative* to the original formula location but rather in an *absolute* manner. In this situation, an absolute location is indicated in the formula so that the cell reference does not change as the formula is copied to other cells. It does not matter where the formula is placed, it will continually reference the same absolute referenced cell location.

Real World Advice — Hard-Coding Data within a Spreadsheet

Some users always use numbers in their formulas. Including actual data in a formula, like =5*25, is known as **hard-coding** the values. Hard-coding decreases the ability to easily update data in the spreadsheet and adapt to change. When developing a spreadsheet, build in flexibility and include cells with data and then reference those cells.

To calculate a monthly payment for a loan, the loan amount, loan period, and interest rate are required. In Figure 1, if the loan amount needs to be changed, it is intuitive to change it in cell B2. For example, the user may want to change the loan amount from 10,000 to 20,000 and would simply change it in cell B2. However, because the 10,000 was hard-coded within the formula, you would also need to change it within the formula before the answer would be correct. The model shows a loan amount for 20,000, but the answer is still calculated for a loan of 10,000, as shown in Figure 1. Hard-coding means you must understand the formula and be able to modify it.

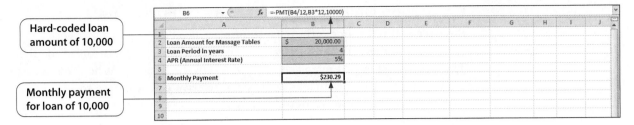

Hard-coded loan amount of 10,000

Monthly payment for loan of 10,000

Figure 1   Hard-coding a formula

As you change the loan amount, the number of years, or interest rate in cells B2, B3, or B4 respectively, the formula automatically recalculates the solution. When the loan is changed in B2 from 10,000 to 20,000, the monthly payment is automatically calculated in B6 as shown in Figure 2. That is, you do not have to change the formula. This approach makes it easier to change the values and thus is more flexible.

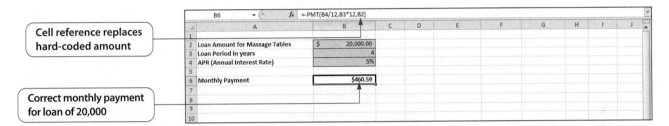

Cell reference replaces hard-coded amount

Correct monthly payment for loan of 20,000

Figure 2   Cell referencing in formula

Not only is it easier to distinguish between data and formulas for editing data, using *relative* versus *absolute* cell referencing allows you to quickly replicate formulas. There is no need to create each formula individually. For example, if a spreadsheet needs to list the prices, you can calculate the total price by multiplying quantity and unit price. Rather than creating a formula multiple times, with relative cell referencing you can create just one formula, then use AutoFill to copy the formula. Excel automatically adjusts the cell references to use the correct cells for the calculation of each product. Figure 3 shows how the formula is automatically adjusted to reference the two cells to the left of the formula after the formula in E5 has been copied down through E16 using AutoFill.

Figure 3   AutoFill to copy formulas

There are three ways in which a cell can be referenced. Mastering cell reference techniques allows you to increase the speed of development of your worksheet. The three ways cells can be referenced in formulas or functions are relative, absolute, and mixed.

Reference Cells within Formulas or Functions

Relative cell reference is the default format when creating formulas with a cell reference position that will automatically adjust when the formula is copied to other cells. Thus, the formula will reference cells *relative* to the location. When you use AutoFill to copy a formula to the right or left, the relative cell reference to the column will change. When you use AutoFill to copy a formula up or down, the reference to the row will change.

For example, assume you are thinking about taking a job where you earn a base amount plus commission on sales. When you start, you earn 10% of sales in addition to your base pay. You have the potential of increasing your commission rate to 15%, 20%, and 25% as you get more experience. Additionally, you have been told that $1,000 in weekly sales is a conservative estimate, an average is $2,000, and $3,000 is really good. You want to see the potential for how much you can make in a week given these numbers. Figure 4 shows the percentages you can earn and three estimates of projected sales. The formula entered in cell B5 was copied down and to the right to show what happens to the cells referenced when they are all relative.

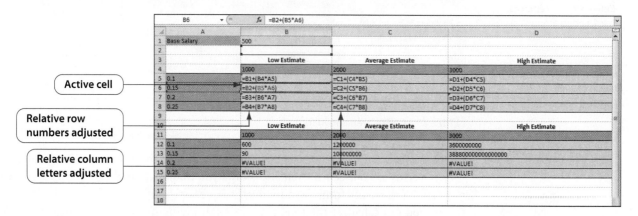

Figure 4 AutoFill with incorrect cell references

Notice the cell reference, B1, in the formula changed to B2, B3, and so forth as the formula was copied downward using AutoFill. Because the formula was only moving down rows, row numbers were adjusted in a relative manner. When it was copied to the right, the B1 changed to a C1 and D1. The formula was being moved across columns and remaining in the same row, so only column letters were adjusted in a relative manner. As the formula was copied to other cells, the relative cell addresses also adjusted, relative to the new location of the formula. In this example, the B1 cell in the formula should stay as B1 regardless of where the formula is copied.

In Figure 5, starting with the formula in cell B5, the cells referenced have dollar signs ($) entered in the formula in B5. A dollar symbol in front of both column and row creates an absolute cell reference to ensure the cell reference location will not change. Placing a dollar symbol in front of only a row number or only the column letter creates a mixed reference to ensure the respective row reference or column reference will not change. The formula in cell B5 was then copied down using AutoFill, and the column of formulas—column B—were copied to the right using AutoFill. Now, you should be able to see that cell B1, which is referenced as an absolute value using $B$1, continues to reference B1. It does not move relative to the formula but stays absolutely where it is referenced. Additionally, the $A5 reference in the formula in cell B5 is relative so the 5 changes to a 6, 7, and 8 as the formula is copied down using AutoFill. The B4 reference in the formula, shown as B$4 in cell B5, is relative so it changes to C and D as the formula is copied to the right using AutoFill.

	A	B	C	D
	C7		f_x =$B$1+(C$4*$A7)	
1	Base Salary	500		
2				
3		Low Estimate	Average Estimate	High Estimate
4		1000	2000	3000
5	0.1	=$B$1+(B$4*$A5)	=$B$1+(C$4*$A5)	=$B$1+(D$4*$A5)
6	0.15	=$B$1+(B$4*$A6)	=$B$1+(C$4*$A6)	=$B$1+(D$4*$A6)
7	0.2	=$B$1+(B$4*$A7)	=$B$1+(C$4*$A7)	=$B$1+(D$4*$A7)
8	0.25	=$B$1+(B$4*$A8)	=$B$1+(C$4*$A8)	=$B$1+(D$4*$A8)
9				
10		Low Estimate	Average Estimate	High Estimate
11		1000	2000	3000
12	0.1	600	700	800
13	0.15	650	800	950
14	0.2	700	900	1100
15	0.25	750	1000	1250
16				
17				
18				

Figure 5   AutoFill with correct cell references

The results of the relative references are shown in the second table of Figure 5 so you can see the formulas in B5:D8 and the corresponding formula results in B12:D15. In Figure 4, the formulas used in B5:D8 resulted in monthly payments that grew exponentially, with some value errors, because the formula in B5 was copied to the rest of the range with relative cell references. Some of the cells in the formulas referred to an empty cell reference or a cell with formulas, which resulted in the #VALUE! math error as shown in Figure 4. The same table has been altered to make some of the references absolute and some relative so the formula correctly references cells after the formula has been copied from B5 to the cell range of B5:D8 as shown in Figure 5.

To Work with Relative Cell Referencing

a. Click the **Start** button 🌀. From the Start menu, locate and then start **Microsoft Excel 2010**.

b. Click the **File tab**, and then click **Open**.

c. In the Open dialog box, click the disk drive in the left pane where your student data files are located, navigate through the folder structure, click **e02_ws03_Spa_Equipment**, and then click **Open**.

d. Click the **File tab**, and then click **Save As** 🖫. The Save As dialog box will appear.

e. In the Save As dialog box, navigate to the location where you are saving your files. In the File name box, type Lastname_Firstname_e02_ws03_Spa_Equipment, replacing Lastname and Firstname with your own name, and then click **Save**.

f. Click the **Documentation worksheet tab**, click cell **A6**, and then press Ctrl+; to input the current date. Press Tab.

g. In cell **B6**, type your first name and last name, and then press Tab.

h. In cell **C6**, type Continuing to develop file, and then press Tab.

i. In cell **D6**, type e02_ws03_Spa_Equipment, and then press Enter.

j. Click the **Insert tab**, and then click **Header & Footer** in the Text group to insert a footer with the file name. Click the **Design tab**, and then click **Go to Footer** in the Navigation group. If necessary, click on the left section of the footer, and then click **File Name** in the Header & Footer Elements group.

k. Click any cell in the spreadsheet to move out of the footer. Click the **View tab**, and then click **Normal** in the Workbook Views group. Press Ctrl+Home.

l. Click the **Thermostats worksheet tab**.

   Notice the worksheet is in Page Layout view so you can see what the layout will be on the printed order form. As you work on the report you will want to ensure everything fits on one page.

m. Click cell **E5**, type =**C5*D5**, and then press Enter.

   The active cell moves to E6, and Excel displays a price value for the HD504 thermostat in cell E5. A similar formula needs to be created for all of the remaining thermostats. While this could be done individually, just like you did in cell E5, Excel allows you to extend the formula to the necessary cells since relative cell referencing will work in addressing the Price column.

n. Click cell **E5**, click the **AutoFill handle** in the lower-right corner of the cell, and then drag down to copy the formula down to cell **E16**.

Troubleshooting

The AutoFill handle is in the lower-right corner of the active cell or range of cells. To select it, hover the mouse pointer over the corner and the pointer will turn to a black plus sign as shown in Figure 6.

Black plus sign cursor on AutoFill

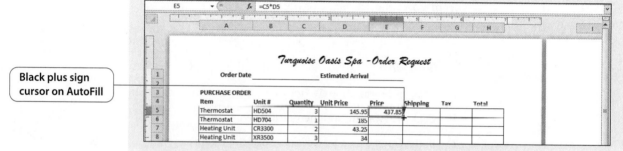

Figure 6 AutoFill handle

SIDE NOTE
Super Quick AutoFill
To copy a large data range using AutoFill, you can hover over the bottom-right corner, where the AutoFill handle is located, and double-click. Excel will attempt to offer the desired result and copy the formula to the bottom of the data set.

o. Click cell **E16**, and then notice that the formula has changed to = C16*D16. It is relative to the formula location—multiplying the two cells that are to the immediate left of the formula.

p. Press Ctrl+` to toggle the Show Formulas feature on. Alternatively, click the **Formulas tab**, and click **Show Formulas** in the Formula Auditing group.

   You should see the formulas displayed on the spreadsheet instead of the results from the formulas. You may need to scroll to the right or left to see all of the columns as they expand in size to accommodate showing the full formulas. In **Show Formulas view**, the cells display the formulas instead of the output, or values.

q. Press Ctrl+` again to toggle back to Normal view.

r. Click **Save** 🖫.

Real World Advice — The Cost Benefit of Documentation

Irene already started the spreadsheet and has asked you to continue development. There is basic information in the workbook including the project details on the Documentation sheet. This is an internal file that few people will see or use, so a lot of detail may not be required.

There are many factors that determine the information required for the documentation on each file, such as your boss, the situation, the number of people working on the project, and who will see the project. In the business world, it is a matter of balance. It would be great to have lots of detail about the spreadsheet, but from a practical viewpoint, the documentation will vary from file to file.

Absolute Cell Reference

Absolute cell references are used when a formula needs to be copied and the reference to one or more cells within the formula should not change as the formula is copied. **Absolute cell reference** refers to the address of a cell, when both the column and row need to remain constant regardless of the position of the cell when the formula is copied to other cells.

To make a cell reference absolute means to *freeze* the reference so Excel does not change the reference when the formula is copied to other cells. Dollar signs within the cell reference are used to let Excel know to keep that reference. For example, a formula =A1*B4 located in C4 has relative cell referencing. If you need to copy that formula to C5:C10, and you need the formula to continue to refer to cell A1, you would change it to =$A$1*B4. The dollar sign before the *A* freezes column A and the dollar sign before the *1* freezes row 1. When the formula is copied to cells in any direction, either left, right, up, or down, the formula reference to cell $A$1 will absolutely stay referenced to the exact cell address of $A$1. The relative reference to cell B4 will move in a relative manner as the formula is copied in the direction of left, right, up, or down. To make a reference absolute, the dollar signs need to be before both the column letter and the row number.

To Work with Absolute Cell References

a. Select cell **G5**.

b. Type =E5*$D$29, and then press [Enter].

This will calculate the tax, based on the current tax rate listed in D29. Since the tax rate is the same for all products, the formula needs to be copied to the other items purchased in the list. The reference to the tax rate cell should not change, but the reference to the price of the item in column E should change.

c. Click cell **G5**, click the **AutoFill handle**, and then extend the formula in G5 down through **G16**.

Notice the formulas in cells G5 through G16 are now identical except the E5 has changed to E6, E7, and so forth. Also, note the numeric results contain more than two decimal points in some cells, and less than two decimal places in other cells. Since this is currency, the cells need to be formatted to eliminate the extra decimals. This will be adjusted and fixed later in this workshop.

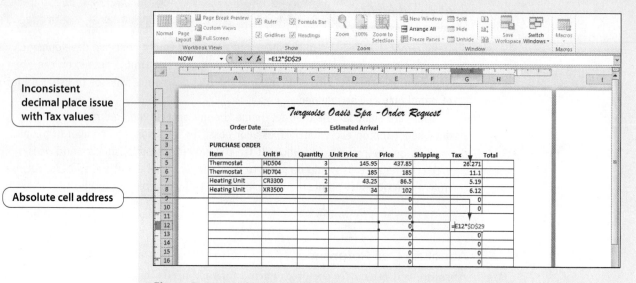

Figure 7 Absolute cell reference

Mixed Cell Reference

Mixed cell references within formulas are less common but can be useful in the development of spreadsheets. Mixed cell reference refers to referencing a cell within the formula where part of the cell address is preceded by a dollar sign to lock—either the column letter or the row value—as absolute and leaving the other part of the cell as relatively referenced.

Recall that a cell reference is composed of two components, the column and the row reference. Cell B10 is referencing column B and row 10. When you want to make a cell reference totally absolute, you insert a dollar sign in front of the column letter so it will not change when the formula is copied into cells to the left or right. Additionally, you would insert a second dollar sign in front of the row number to make it absolute so it will not change when the formula is copied up or down. When you add one dollar sign, but not the other, you have a mixed reference. If you only want to make the column absolute, you only put a dollar sign in front of the column reference. For example, as you copy $B10 to other cells, the B column would remain unchanged in the formula. The row reference, however, would change relative to where the formula was placed. Likewise, if you referenced a cell as B$10, then column B would change when copied to other cells and row 10 would never change.

If you are creating a spreadsheet and developing a formula that will not be copied elsewhere, relative and absolute cell referencing is not an issue. However, you may have data in a table and need to add a column of formulas beside the data that does calculations on each row, or record. In this case you need to incorporate cell referencing. Thus, when you are developing a spreadsheet, you should consider whether you will need to copy a formula or not. Having established the need to copy a formula, you should also establish where the formula will be copied. Remember, the issue revolves around which cell references need to move as you copy the formula and which should remain constant when copied. This thought process, in considering when to use absolute, relative, or mixed, can be broken into four cases.

First, if the formula is not to be copied, using the default of relative cell addressing is the quickest and simplest solution. It really does not matter if you make any of the cell references relative or absolute.

Second, if a formula will be copied only over rows, up or down, the only part of the cell reference that would change is the row number. In this case, it is only necessary to consider whether the row number needs to be relative or absolute. The column would not change. Consequently, it does not matter if you make the column letter relative or absolute.

Third, if a formula is only going to be copied sideways, left or right, the only part of the cell reference that would change is the column letter. The row will not change. Thus, it does not matter if you make the row relative or absolute.

Finally, if a formula is going to be copied both across rows and columns, you must consider both parts of the cell reference. You must consider whether each cell referenced in the formula needs the row and the column reference to remain constant or move relative to the formula.

Real World Advice — **Layout of a Spreadsheet Model**

Think of a spreadsheet as a report. In a report, you have an executive summary first that is then supported with your details. On a spreadsheet, it can be useful to have a section along the top that has the summary data and any text that will guide the user. Along with the summary data you can include the inputs you need for the model. These would include any values, like a tax rate or credit limit, that would be used in calculations. Then, put the data set below the summary or, if necessary, on another sheet. This makes it easy for any user to see the summary data first, at the top of a spreadsheet, then look for supporting data, analysis, and details as needed.

If you need to verify the formula has the correct relative and absolute referencing after it has been copied or moved into other cells within the spreadsheet, a quick and easy verification is to examine one of the cells in edit mode. Best practice dictates following these steps:

1. Double-click a cell containing the formula to enter edit mode.
2. In edit mode, notice the color-coded borders around cells match the cell address references in the formula. Using the color-coding as a guide, verify that the cell(s) are referenced correctly.
3. If the referencing is incorrect, notice which cells are not referenced correctly.
4. Exit out of edit mode by pressing Esc and returning to the original formula.
5. Edit the cell references, and then copy the corrected formula again.
6. Always recheck the formula again to see if your correction worked when copied into other cells or cell ranges.

Repeat this process as needed. Instead of typing the dollar signs within your cell references, F4 is a handy toggle to use. If the insertion point is placed within a cell reference in your formula, press F4 one time and Excel will insert dollar signs in front of both the row reference and column reference. If you press F4 again, Excel places a dollar sign in front of the row number only. Press F4 as needed to toggle through the remaining variations.

Quick Reference — **Using the F4 Key Toggle**

1. Press F4 one time to place a $ in front of both the column and row value.
2. Press F4 a second time to place a $ in front of the row value only.
3. Press F4 a third time to place a $ in front of the column value only.
4. Press F4 a fourth time to remove all $ characters.
5. Press F4 a fifth time to start the sequence again.

For the comfort of the spa's customers, the massage tables have heating components with thermostats to adjust the temperature. The usage and energy costs need to be tracked. This allows the company to determine the true costs for running the business and ensure the business is generating revenue. Irene has requested the model be set to show 30 days so the model can easily be verified. Later it can be scaled to handle the normal life of a thermostat. Because of this, she wants you to use cell referencing as you create formulas in the model.

Real World Advice   Building for Scalability

When you develop a spreadsheet you should consider scalability and accuracy. A good spreadsheet model allows the user to add more data as needed. If you are making a spreadsheet to track your sales staff, you need to consider how many sales staff you may have in the future.

Instead of assuming current conditions will never change, your spreadsheet should be built to accommodate growth. You need to consider a reasonable growth of sales people so you do not have to change the spreadsheet layout and formulas every time the number of sales staff changes. It may make sense, given the size of the company and growth potential, to build in the ability to have up to 10 staff.

While developing the model, use hypothetical data so you can see how the model will look when it has real data. Work on a small scale so you can work out the kinks. It is much easier to see, check, and modify a model that uses 30 records than one that uses 1,000 records.

To Work with Mixed Cell Referencing

a. Click the **Table_Life worksheet tab**, and then click cell **C18**.

b. Type =B18*B9, which is the Usage (minutes) times Energy cost per minute. Press Enter.
   Notice that the reference to cell B18 does not need any dollar signs. You will need to use AutoFill to copy the formula down. The row will change; thus, you need to evaluate the row references in the formula. The B18 cell reference has a row reference of 18, and as you copy the formula down, the row value 18 will change to a 19, 20, and so on. Thus, that reference is relative, and you will leave it as B18 so it remains as relative.

c. Notice that the reference to cell B9 needs one dollar sign. Select just the **B9** in the formula in cell C18. Press F4 until the B9 changes to B$9. Once it appears as B$9 in the formula, press Enter.
   Since you need to extend the formula down, the row will change. Thus, you need to evaluate the row references in the formula. Cell B9 has a row reference of 9. As you copy the formula down, you need the 9 to stay at a constant value as row 9—that is where the Energy cost per minute resides. Thus, the 9 needs to be frozen. You need to put the $ sign immediately on the left of the 9.

d. Click cell **C18** again, click the **AutoFill handle**, and then extend the formula in C18 down through **C31**.

e. Double-click cell **C31** to enter edit mode. Following the best practice, verify that the color borders are around B9 and B31.

	A	B	C	D	E	F	G
7	Current Thermostat Life						
8	Thermostat Usage						
9	Energy cost per minute	$ 0.55					
10	Total Energy Cost						
11	Thermostat age limit		600				
12	Time to change Thermostat?	#NAME?					
13	Average Energy Cost						
14	Median Energy Cost						
15							
16	Heating component usage						
17	Days	Usage	Daily Energy Cost				
18	6/12/2011	48	$ 26.40				
19	6/13/2011	60	$ 33.00		Total Visits		
20	6/14/2011	32	$ 17.60				
21	6/15/2011	12	$ 6.60				
22	6/16/2011	0	$ -				
23	6/17/2011	0	$ -				
24	6/18/2011	0	$ -				
25	6/19/2011	0	$ -				
26	6/20/2011	0	$ -				
27	6/21/2011	0	$ -				
28	6/22/2011	0	$ -				
29	6/23/2011	0	$ -				
30	6/24/2011	0	$ -				
31	6/25/2011	0	=B31*B$9				
32							

Figure 8   Verify AutoFill

f. Press Esc to exit edit mode.

CONSIDER THIS | Relative Addresses

In the exercise, you placed a $ before the 9, but not the B. Would it have been incorrect to place the $ before the B in this particular situation, as in $B$9? Describe a situation where a dollar sign would be optional. Describe a situation where you must use mixed referencing.

Working with Named Ranges

Once you are comfortable working with formulas and cells there is a natural progression to using named ranges and functions. Named ranges are an extension of cell references and provide a quick alternative for commonly used cell references or cell ranges.

Spreadsheet formulas that use cell references such as =C5*C6 may be easy to interpret when simple. However, as the size and complexity of the workbook increases, so does the difficulty and time needed to incorporate cell references in formulas. This is especially the case with workbooks that use multiple worksheets. The use of named ranges enables a developer to quickly develop formulas that make sense.

A **named range** is a set of cells that have been given a name that can then be used within a formula or function. For example, you may not understand =SUM(C4:C20)*B2 until you determine what is in those cells. You can quickly understand the formula if it is written with assigned names you designate. For instance, if you named the range C4:C20 as *Sales* and B2 as *Bonus*, you can write the formula as =SUM(Sales)*Bonus, which is easier to understand.

Creating Named Ranges in the Name Box

Named ranges are easy to create as you develop a spreadsheet. A named range can be either a single cell or a set of cells. Most named ranges are sets of cells used within multiple formulas. The simplest way to name a range is to select the range and use the Name Box to create the name.

You must follow a few rules when naming ranges.

- Names for ranges must start with a letter, an underscore (_), or a backslash (\ ).
- You should use words that provide meaning. If you have a set of numbers representing sales, then name the range *Sales*.
- Do not use spaces when using multiple words. Either put a hyphen or underscore in lieu of a space, or capitalize the first letter of each word in the phrase to avoid using a space. Thus, *Sales_2012* or *NetSales* are both acceptable and convey meaning.
- Do not use names that are Excel words, like function names or conjunctions. Excel will allow you to name a range SUM. However, a formula such as =SUM(SUM) does not convey meaning. Thus, stay away from AND, COUNT, ROW, and other Excel words. They may confuse you, other users, or possibly Excel.
- Whenever using a combination of letters and numbers for named ranges, do not use a combination that creates a reference to a cell. In other words, *Sales2012* is acceptable but *S2012* is not. A cell in column S and row 2012 already exists.

To Create a Named Range Using the Name Box

a. Click the **Thermostats worksheet tab**, and then click cell **D29**.

b. Click in the **Name Box**, which is to the left of the formula bar and should currently display **D29**. The text will be highlighted when you click in the Name Box.

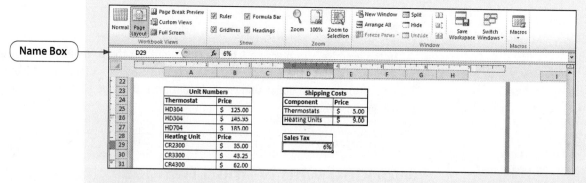

Figure 9 Name Box

c. Type TaxRate replacing the existing cell name.

d. Press Enter.

The Name Box displays *TaxRate* instead of the cell address D29. Now that D29 is named TaxRate, you could use the named range instead of using absolute cell referencing in the formulas in cells G5:G16. Excel does not automatically update cell references already existing in formulas.

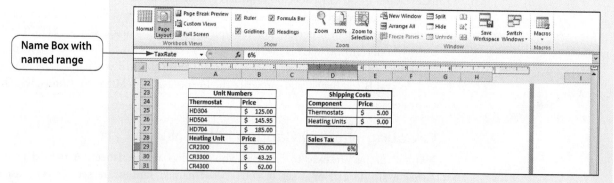

Figure 10 Name Box with named range

e. Click cell **G5**. Notice the formula did not change the $D$29 to TaxRate.

f. Click the **Formulas tab**, click the **Define Name arrow** in the Defined Names group, and then click **Apply Names**. The Apply Names dialog box appears with TaxRate highlighted.

g. Click **OK**. Notice the range of cells G5:G16 now shows the TaxRate named range.

   With named ranges, you can see the listing of current names by clicking on the Name Box arrow. When there are multiple named ranges, you can select one, and Excel will take you to that range with the range cells selected. This is useful when you want to determine the location of the named range.

h. Click the **Name Box arrow** to see the listing of current named ranges, and then click **Thermostat**.

   Notice that the active cell is A24, which is named Thermostat. You will use this named range later as a part of determining the shipping cost in column F.

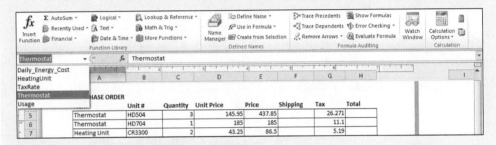

Figure 11 Name Box drop down list

Troubleshooting

If you enter the name in the Name Box and then click onto a new range on the spreadsheet to select another range to name, that will not name the range. Be sure to press ⎡Enter⎤ to finish the process of naming the range. If you name the range incorrectly, you must go to the Formulas tab and click the Name Manager. There, you can delete named ranges or edit and modify them as needed.

Creating Named Ranges from Selections

Using the Name Box is the most convenient method for creating named ranges. This allows for naming ranges as you develop a spreadsheet. At times your worksheet's data will be organized in such a way that the names for your ranges exist in a cell in the form of a heading, either for each row or each column in the data set. Rather than selecting each row or column separately in a time-consuming process, you can use the Create from Selection method.

The Create from Selection method is a process that produces multiple named ranges from the headings in rows, columns, or both from the data set. The key element is to realize that the names for the ranges need to exist in a cell either above the data range for naming columns, or to the left for naming rows. Most commonly, these names are column headers that make for very convenient names for each column of data.

To Create a Set of Named Ranges from Selections

a. Select the range **E4:G16**. This includes the column headers that will be used for the names of each range.

b. Click the **Formulas tab**, and then click **Create from Selection** in the Defined Names group.

The dialog box that appears will have options for top, left, bottom, and right column or rows. Excel will try to guess what you want to use for the names of the ranges. Be sure to include the heading cells in the target selection, and verify that Excel offered the correct checked option in the Create Names from Selection dialog box—and if necessary, select the appropriate option.

c. In the Create Names from Selection dialog box, click the **Top row** check box, make sure all other check boxes are unchecked, and then click **OK**.

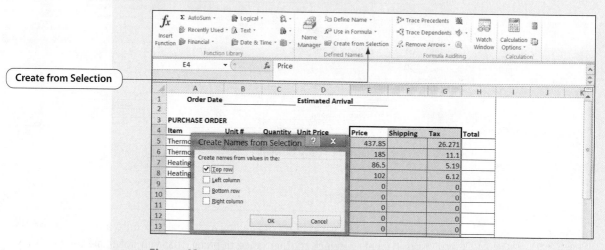

Figure 12 Create Names from Selection dialog box

d. To check the named ranges, click the **Name Box arrow** and you should see the new names—Price, Shipping, and Tax—in addition to previously existing named ranges.

Modifying Named Ranges

As you create named ranges, you may need to make a change to an existing named range. You may also have names that are no longer required and need to be deleted. These kinds of changes need to be made with the Name Manager—which is also found on the Formulas tab—in the Defined Names group.

To Modify a Named Range

a. Click the **Table_Life worksheet tab** to make it the active sheet.

The Table_Life worksheet had some initial named ranges created. It is always wise to check named ranges to determine if they are correct for the current model. Notice, the template will record the number of minutes the massage table heating thermostat is on each day in the Usage column. An employee will enter the data daily. Currently the model will handle two weeks' worth of data. Thus, the named range needs to be modified to include this full column range.

b. If necessary, click the **Formulas tab**, and then click **Name Manager** in the Defined Names group.

c. In the Name Manager dialog box, click the name **Usage**. Notice, under the Refers To column, the range is indicated as =Table_Life!$B$18:$B$20. If needed, you can resize the Refers To column to see the details better by double-clicking the border in the column heading between Refers To and Scope.

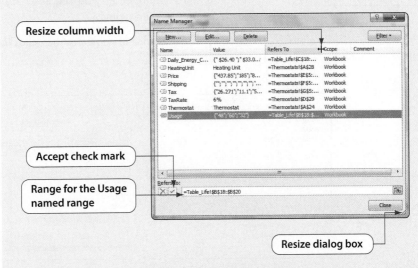

Resize column width

Accept check mark

Range for the Usage named range

Resize dialog box

Figure 13 Name Manager dialog box

d. Click in the **Refers to** box, highlight **20**, and then type **31**. Click **Enter** ☑ to accept the changes and set the new range.

e. In the Name Manager dialog box, click the Name range **Daily_Energy_Cost**, as it also needs modification. In the Refers to box, highlight **20**, and type **31**. Click **Enter** ☑ to set the new range.

f. Click **Close**, and then click **Save** 🖫 to save changes to the workbook.

Using Named Ranges

As you begin creating your own formulas, the usage of named ranges is a simple element within the process. You can use named ranges in formulas like the tax calculation you already applied to column G on the Thermostats worksheet. However, when you want to indicate the range of cells, you simply type in the named range instead of having to select the cells. There are two methods for using named ranges in formulas or functions. First, you can start typing the named range and a drop-down list will appear to show not only function names, but also named ranges. You can select the named range from the drop-down list by using ⬇ and pressing ⎄Tab to select the name (or alternatively double-clicking on the name when it appears in the list). Conversely, if you forget the name of the range, you can press ⎄F3. Pressing ⎄F3 opens a dialog box listing all the available named ranges.

Creating Formulas Using a Named Range

On the Table_Life worksheet, you need to calculate the total minutes for thermostat usage.

To Create a Formula Using a Named Range

a. Click cell **B8**. You need to calculate the total minutes used in this cell.

b. Type =sum. As you start typing, when you see SUM appear in the drop-down list, double-click on it to complete the typing.

c. Press F3. From the Paste name list of named ranges, click **Usage**.

d. Click **OK**.

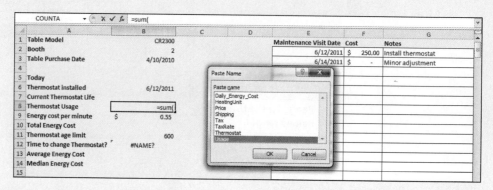

Figure 14   Paste Name dialog box

e. Press Enter to have Excel add the closing parenthesis and accept the formula. Notice, this function now totals the range named Usage.

f. Click cell **B10**, and then type =sum(da.

   Notice, a drop-down list including the Daily_Energy_Cost named range appears. The named ranges appear with the ▦ next to the name of the range in the drop-down list while the functions have ⑨ to the left of the function name.

g. If Daily_Energy_Cost is not highlighted, press ↑ or ↓ until **Daily_Energy_Cost** is highlighted. Press Tab to select that named range and have it inserted into the SUM function.

Symbol representing a named range

Symbol representing a function

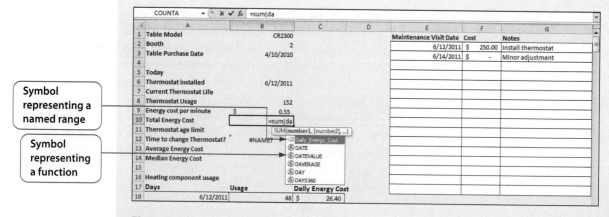

Figure 15   Formula drop-down list

h. Press Enter to finish the formula, and then click **Save** ▦.

Real World Advice — When to Use Named Ranges

Named ranges are useful. However, they can also be overused. Named ranges make it easy to understand formulas, such as =Sales*Bonus and can also be used to select a range of cells quickly. However, you must invest time and effort to create and use the named ranges. If others will not be using the spreadsheet, your time may be better spent. Named ranges have the most value when sets of data are used in multiple formulas or when other users need to understand the construction of the spreadsheet. You should do a mental cost-benefit analysis to ensure it is worth the time and effort. Your decision on when to use named ranges will become easier with practice and experience.

Functions

A **function** is a named calculation where Excel calculates the output based on the input provided. These can be fairly simple such as using a SUM function that adds any cell address range as input. Conversely, functions can be more complex. For example, calculating a monthly loan payment is accomplished by indicating various inputs, known as **arguments**—the loan amount, number of payments, and interest rate. Arguments are any inputs used by a function to compute the solution. As long as you have the correct inputs, Excel will calculate the function.

Understand the Syntax of a Function

Functions are composed of several elements and need to be structured in a particular order. When discussing functions, you need to be aware of the syntax of an Excel function. The **syntax** is the structure and order of the function and the arguments needed for Excel to run the function. If you understand the syntax of a function, you can easily learn how to use new functions quickly. There are a couple of techniques for creating functions once you learn the structure of a function.

Function Structure

Functions have a particular structure and rules for construction. Once learned, you will be able to quickly learn and use any function within the Excel library. The structure, or syntax, for a function consists of the following:

1. =
2. Function name
3. Opening parenthesis
4. Arguments—inputs separated by commas
5. Closing parenthesis

and looks like: =*FunctionName (Arg1, Arg2, ArgN)*

The FunctionName is any function that is in the Excel library. Examples are SUM, COUNT, and TODAY.

With all functions, a pair of parentheses () are required inside which resides all of the inputs, called arguments. An argument is a piece of data that Excel needs to run the function. Some functions, like TODAY(), do not have any arguments. These functions do not need any inputs to be able to generate output. The TODAY() function simply uses the clock on the computer to return the current date. Even though there are no arguments needed, the () parentheses are always included, which helps Excel understand that a function is being used.

Arguments can either be required or optional. The required arguments always come first, before the optional arguments. All arguments are separated with commas. Optional arguments are identified in the ScreenTip or help file with square brackets [ ] around the argument name. You never type the square brackets into the actual construction of the function. They are only used to inform you that the argument is optional.

For example, the PMT function is a handy financial function that calculates a periodic payment, like a monthly car payment, given some standard inputs. When you insert a function by hand, Excel provides a ScreenTip as shown in Figure 16 that offers guidance for the expected arguments needed for any function. The ScreenTip for a PMT function shows PMT(rate, nper, pv, [fv], [type]). The rate, nper, and pv arguments are required, but the [fv] and [type] arguments are optional. Commas are used between the arguments you list.

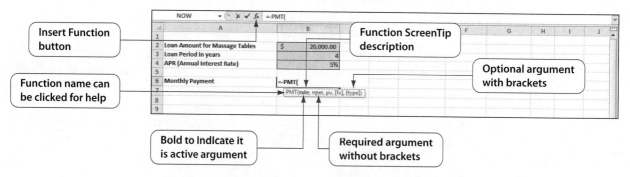

Figure 16 Function ScreenTip

Arguments, like variables in a math equation, need to be appropriate values that are suitable for the function. With Excel, the acceptable values can take six common forms, including other functions, as shown in Figure 17:

Form of Input	Example	Explanation
Numeric value	5	Type the value
Cell reference	C5	Type the cell or range of cells
Named range	SALES	Type the name of the range
Text string	"Bonus"	Type the text with quotes "" so Excel will recognize it as a text string rather than a named range
Function	SUM(C5:C19)	Type a function following the correct syntax of the function name, pair of parentheses, and any arguments
Formula	(C5+D5)/100	Type the formula following correct mathematical formula structure

Figure 17 Function argument Formats

Functions are typically categorized for easy access. The primary categories are shown in Figure 18. Over time, you will develop knowledge of functions that are specific to your needs. For this reason, you must learn where to find functions and the basic syntax. If you learn this, you can quickly learn how to use new functions as the need arises.

Category	Description
Financial	Working with common financial formulas
Logical	Evaluating expressions or conditions as being either true or false
Text	Working with text strings
Date & Time	Working with dates and times
Lookup & Reference	Working with indexing and retrieving information from data sets
Math & Trig	Working with mathematics
Statistical	Working with common statistical calculations
Engineering	Working with engineering formulas and calculations
Cube	Working with data and filtering, similar to pivot tables
Information	Providing data about cell content within a worksheet
Compatibility	A set of functions that are compatible with older versions of Excel

Figure 18 Function Categories

Function Construction with the Function Arguments Dialog Box

There are two common methods for creating functions: through the Function Arguments dialog box and by typing in the function. When you are first developing the skills for using functions in Excel, the Function Arguments dialog box can be very valuable. As you become familiar with specific functions, it will become easier to type in the functions. Even then, the Function Arguments dialog box is also helpful for trouble-shooting.

Creating a function through the Function Arguments dialog box first entails selecting the cell location where you want the results to be displayed. There are two ways to access the Function Arguments dialog box. First, you can use the category buttons in the Function Library group on the Formulas tab. When you select a function from the category, the Function Arguments dialog box opens. The second method is to click Insert Function f_x, which is located between the Name Box and formula bar. When the Insert Function dialog box opens, type or find the desired function and click OK. This will take you to the Function Arguments dialog box for the chosen function.

The Function Arguments dialog box will list the arguments. The arguments in bold are required and listed first. Then, the optional arguments (if any) are listed next but are not bold. To the right of the argument name is the box where you will input the information needed for the argument. On the far right, the result is displayed for that argument once you input information. Below the listing of arguments, you will find a description of the argument currently selected. Finally, at the bottom you will find the formula result and a link that will take you to the Excel Help for the function as shown in Figure 19.

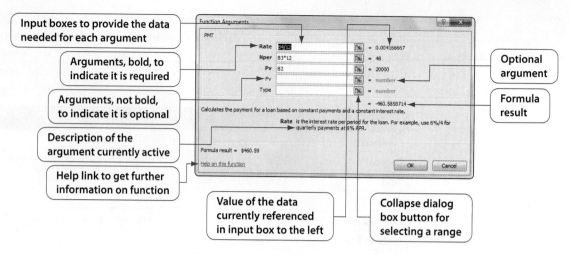

Input boxes to provide the data needed for each argument

Arguments, bold, to indicate it is required

Arguments, not bold, to indicate it is optional

Description of the argument currently active

Help link to get further information on function

Value of the data currently referenced in input box to the left

Collapse dialog box button for selecting a range

Optional argument

Formula result

Figure 19 Function Arguments dialog box

Function Construction with the Formula Bar

Functions can also be constructed without using the Function Arguments dialog box. This is accomplished by typing the equal sign and typing the function name directly into the cell. Excel will still provide guidance using this method. Additionally, as needed, you can always jump into the Function Arguments dialog box to get more assistance.

When you initially type in the beginning of a function name, an AutoComplete listing of functions will be shown from which you can select the appropriate function as shown in Figure 20. The list will automatically reflect changes as you type in more letters. Excel will even display a short description of the function when the function name is highlighted. As the function names appear you can use ⬇, ⬆, ➡, ⬅, or your mouse to move through the listing. To select a function, press Tab or double-click the selected function.

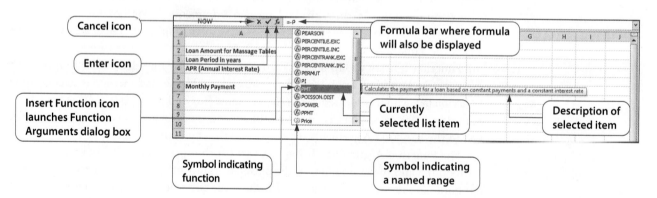

Cancel icon

Enter icon

Insert Function icon launches Function Arguments dialog box

Formula bar where formula will also be displayed

Currently selected list item

Description of selected item

Symbol indicating function

Symbol indicating a named range

Figure 20 Function drop-down list

Once the function is selected, the arguments will be listed in a movable tag to provide a guide. The argument you are currently working on will be displayed in bold. The optional arguments, as stated previously, will be listed but with square brackets [] as shown in Figure 21. If you have entered some of the arguments, you can click on the argument in the movable tag, and Excel will relocate the insertion point to that argument. Finally, you can click the Insert Function button fx any time to switch to the Function Arguments dialog box.

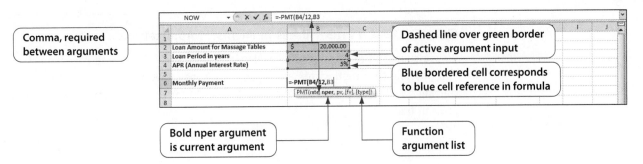

Comma, required between arguments

Dashed line over green border of active argument input

Blue bordered cell corresponds to blue cell reference in formula

Bold nper argument is current argument

Function argument list

Figure 21   Function ScreenTip

Common Functions

Remember, there are hundreds of functions available, although most users will primarily use a small set of very common functions. The following is an explanation of common functions that will provide a strong foundation for building powerful spreadsheets. Learning these functions will also provide the skill set needed for learning additional functions on your own.

Date and Time Functions

Date and Time functions are useful for putting in the current day and time as well as calculating time intervals. This category of functions is based on a serial date system where each day is represented sequentially from a starting point. In Microsoft, that standard is 1/1/1900, which has a serial number of 1. Thus, dates prior to that will not be recognized by the system. Interestingly, when Apple initially made its starting point, it began in 1904. Excel settings can be changed to use the Apple starting point, but it is generally accepted practice to keep the default setting of 1/1/1900 as the starting point. You can only imagine the potential issues when the two different starting points are used in Excel spreadsheets. Common date and time functions are shown in Figure 22:

Date & Time Functions	Usage
NOW()	Will use computer system to give date and time
TODAY()	Will use computer system to give date
DATEDIF(Date1,Date2,Interval)	Will return the time unit specified between two dates, including the two dates (inclusive)
DATE(Year,Month,Day)	Returns the number that represents the date in Microsoft Excel date-time code
DAY(Serial_number)	Returns the day of the month, a number from 1 to 31
MONTH(Serial_number)	Returns the month, a number from 1 to 12
YEAR(Serial_number)	Returns the year of a date, an integer in the range 1900–9999
WEEKDAY(Serial_number, omit [return_number], [Return_type])	Returns a number from 1 to 7 representing the day of the week. Can be set to return 0–6 or 1–7
WEEKNUM(Serial_number, [Return_type])	Returns the week number in the year, which week of the year the date occurs
NETWORKDAYS(Start_date, End_date,[Holidays])	Returns the number of whole workdays between two dates, inclusive; does not count weekends and can skip holidays that are listed

Figure 22   Date and Time functions

Also remember, with a sequential serial date system, you can find any interval in time as well. Time is represented by the decimal portion of a number. The decimal is based on the number of minutes in a day ($24*60=1440$). Thus, a 0.1 decimal is equal to 144 minutes.

There is only a slight difference between the TODAY() and NOW() functions. The key difference is that the TODAY() function simply puts in the date while the NOW() function puts in the date and time. If you think about it, the TODAY() function only works with integer representation of days while the NOW() function uses decimals to include the time in addition to the day. Both functions can be formatted to show just the date, and you can work with time calculations that mix the two functions.

Real World Advice Using NOW and TODAY functions

Be careful using NOW() versus TODAY(), especially when doing date calculations. Both functions use a serial number, counting from 1/1/1900. But, the NOW() function also includes decimals for the time of day while TODAY() works with integer serial numbers. At noon, on 5/1/2013 the NOW() function has the value of 41395.5 while the TODAY() function has a value of 41395.0. If you are using these date functions inside an IF statement, this could change the result if you are comparing a date the user input. It is suggested to use the TODAY() function if a user will be inserting the date into Excel by hand so the hand-typed value will be compared or used in a calculation with the function, eliminating the decimal issue.

To Work with the TODAY Function

a. If necessary, click the **Table_Life worksheet tab** to make it the active worksheet, and then click cell **B5**.

b. Click **Insert Function** f_x beside the formula bar to open the Insert Function dialog box. Click the **Or select a category arrow**, and then click **Date & Time**.

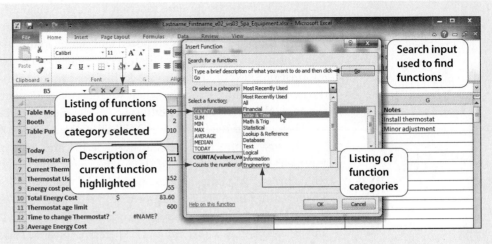

Insert Function to launch Insert Function dialog box

Listing of functions based on current category selected

Description of current function highlighted

Search input used to find functions

Listing of function categories

Figure 23   Insert Function dialog box

c.   In the **Select a function** box, scroll and click **TODAY**. Click **OK**, read the information in the Function Arguments dialog box, and then click **OK** when done.

d.   Click the **Thermostats worksheet tab**, and then click cell **B1**. Type **=NOW**. Notice that as you type each letter, the list of functions decreases the options until only the one you need is listed.

e.   Press [Tab], and the NOW function is selected.

f.   Press [Enter], and Excel adds the closing parenthesis and you see the current date and time.

g.   Right-click cell **B1**, and then click **Format Cells** from the shortcut menu.

h.   If necessary, click the **Number tab**, and then click **Date**. In the Type box list, click the **14-Mar-01** format, click **OK** , and then click **Save** [icon].

SIDE NOTE

Typing Functions and Cell References

Although functions and cell references are typically shown in uppercase, they can be typed in lowercase. Excel converts cell references and function names to uppercase in formulas.

Troubleshooting

Do you get a #NAME? error when you start putting in your function? When creating a function and choosing a function name from the drop-down list, be sure to press [Tab] instead of [Enter]. [Enter] simply enters what you have currently typed and moves to the next cell below. [Tab] moves to the function and inserts it into the cell.

CONSIDER THIS | **Where Did DATEDIF Originate?**

Search the Internet for Excel DATEDIF. Can you find speculation as to why it does not have the same coverage as other Excel functions? If you cannot find any speculation, can you imagine any reasons why?

DATEDIF is a useful date function because it enables you to find the time between two dates. The function can return the time unit as days, months, or years. However, while all the other functions are listed and can be found in Excel help, you will not find any information on the DATEDIF function unless you search the Microsoft site. Since no information exists on it within Excel, this is one function that you must hand type and do the research to understand the syntax (or function arguments). The Function Library will not help. Nonetheless, DATEDIF is one of the more useful date functions.

The syntax of the function is DATEDIF(Date1, Date2, Interval).

The first argument is the starting date in time—the older date—while the second argument is the ending date in time—the newer, more recent date. It may be helpful to remember that time lines are usually depicted as moving left to right, just like you read. So, the earlier date comes first, or to the left. The third argument is the interval that should be used, like the number of months, weeks, or days between the two dates. The unit is expressed as a text value and therefore must be surrounded by quotes for correct syntax. The viable unit value options are shown in Figure 24.

Unit Value	Description
"D"	Returns the number of complete days between the dates
"M"	Returns the number of complete months between the dates
"Y"	Returns the number of complete years between the dates
"YM"	Returns the months remaining, after subtracting completed full years
"YD"	Returns the days remaining, after subtracting the completed full years
"MD"	Returns the days remaining, after subtracting the completed full months and full years

Figure 24 Unit value options

CONSIDER THIS | **Calculating Time**

Since Excel uses the 1900 date system, do you really need to use the DATEDIF function to calculate the difference between days—the "D" unit? What other way could you calculate the difference? What would that formula look like?

To Work with the DATEDIF Function

a. Click the **Table_Life worksheet tab**, and then click cell **B7**.

b. Type =datedif(B6,B5,"D"), and then press Enter .

Notice, you want to determine the age of the current thermostat. The date the thermostat was installed is entered one time. It would not be a function, like TODAY or NOW since these functions would be updated each time the spreadsheet is opened. Thus, the user would type the date into cell B6. Then, you need to find the current age, so the current date is needed in cell B5 also. Rather than type it in each time the spreadsheet is opened, the TODAY function is used to get the current date. The DATEDIF function uses three arguments. The first argument is the date the thermostat was installed, which would be the older date, or the date closest to 1/1/1900. The second argument is the current date, the date furthest from 1/1/1900. The third argument is the units of time to use. In this case, the number of days between the two dates was used, thus the "D" argument.

Figure 25 DATEDIF function

Troubleshooting

Do you get a #NUM! error when you construct a DATEDIF function? The most common error is mixing up the order of the two dates within the function. The first date should be the date that is closest to 1/1/1900. The other common error is actually typing in a date as the argument. Typing 12/3/2000 will be interpreted as division instead of a date. The value must be in serial date format. Thus, it is highly recommended you put the dates in cells and reference the cells in the function. One more possible common error is to neglect putting quotation marks around the last argument for the interval unit.

Math and Trig Functions

The Math and Trig functions are useful for various numerical manipulations. Commonly used math functions are shown in Figure 26. Of the common math functions, the work horse would have to be the SUM function. You can specify values, ranges, and named ranges to be summed. You can indicate multiple ranges and values, separated by commas.

Math and Trig Functions	Usage
SUM(Number1,[Number2],...)	Adds all the numbers in a range of cells
INT(Number)	Rounds a number down to the nearest integer
ABS(Number)	Returns the absolute value of a number, a number without its (negative) sign
RAND()	Returns a random number greater than or equal to 0 and less than 1
RANDBETWEEN(Bottom,Top)	Returns a random integer between the numbers you specify
ROUND(Number,Num_digits)	Rounds a number to a specified number of digits (decimal places)
ROUNDDOWN(Number,Num_digits)	Rounds a number down, toward zero (to a specified number of decimal places)
ROUNDUP(Number,Num_digits)	Rounds a number up, away from zero (to a specified number of decimal places)

Figure 26 Math and Trig functions

The ROUND function is important when you have calculations that result in answers with more decimals than you need in the result. One common occurrence is with calculating money. For the spa, when the order form was being developed, recall that the calculations of the Tax column can and did result in values with three or more decimal places, and in some instances, one decimal place. For currency results, the ROUND function can come to the rescue. It is important to understand that formatting numbers can mask or hide the true values underneath.

To Work with the ROUND() Function

a. Click the **Thermostats worksheet tab** to make it the active tab, and then select the cell range **G5:G16**.

b. Click the **Home tab**, and notice that the **Number Format** General in the Number group is currently set to General format. That is, the values currently have a General format with no specific format.

c. On the Home tab, click the **Number Format arrow** General in the Number group, and then click **Accounting**. Notice the values now show two decimal places. The values have not changed, just how they are displayed has changed.

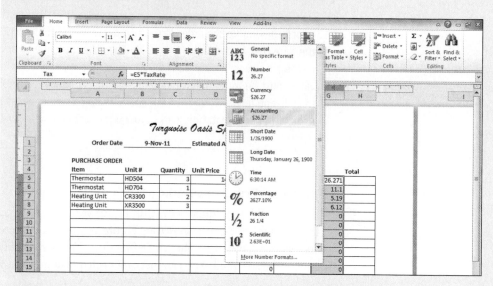

Figure 27 Cell formatting

d. On the Home tab, click the **Number Format arrow** General in the Number group, and then click **General**. Notice the values now show a variable number of decimal places. Now it is time to edit the formula to round the result so the value will have values to the second decimal place and no more.

e. Click cell **G5** to select this cell only.

f. Press [F2] to enter into edit mode for the formula, and then place the insertion point between the = and **E5** within the formula.

g. Type ROUND(.

Notice that as you type, the drop-down list of functions appears and changes as you type the word. It will show the arguments needed and the first argument, number, is bold. This indicates that you are currently working in that section of the ROUND function.

h. Position the insertion point at the end of the formula after **TaxRate** so you can type the last argument of the ROUND function.

Notice that the E5*TaxRate is still a part of the number argument (which is still bold) and is the part of the formula that provides the raw answer. That result is what needs to be rounded.

i. Type a , and notice that the bold shifts from the number argument to the num_digits argument indicating you are ready to put in the number of decimals you want with the result.

j. Type **2**. Type **)** to finish the formula.

As you type in the), notice that the pair of () will turn bold for a moment. This is Excel indicating what it considers to be a pair of () and is a visual cue that you are inserting the function correctly.

SIDE NOTE
Round Instead of Format
Formatting will retain all decimals, an issue with currency. Use ROUND for getting only two decimals.

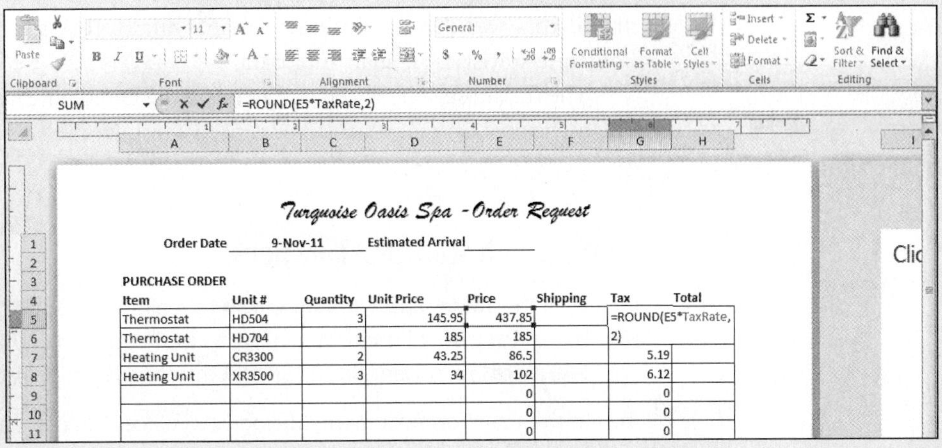

Figure 28   Round function

k. Press Enter, click cell **G5**, hover over the bottom-right corner of the cell, and then double-click to copy the formula using AutoFill for the range **G5:G16**.

l. Select **D5:H16** since the entire range should be formatted the same. Click the **Accounting Number Format** $ ▾ button in the Number group, and then click **Save** 💾.

Statistical Functions

Similar to mathematical functions, statistical functions, as shown in Figure 29, handle common statistical calculations such as averages, minimums, and maximums. Statistical functions are extremely useful for business analysis as they aggregate and compare data. Common descriptive statistics are used to describe the data. The average, median, and mode are common descriptive statistics that help describe the nature of a data set. They help us understand and predict future data.

Statistical Functions	Usage
AVERAGE(Number1,[Number2],…)	Returns the mean from a set of numbers
COUNT(Value1,[Value2],…)	Counts the number of cells in a range that contain numbers
COUNTA(Value1,[Value2],…)	Counts the number of cells in a range that are not empty
COUNTBLANK(Range)	Counts the number of empty cells in a range
MEDIAN(Number1,[Number2],…)	Returns the number in the middle of a set of numbers
MAX(Number1,[Number2],…)	Returns the largest number from a set of numbers
MIN(Number1,[Number2],…)	Returns the smallest number from a set of numbers
MODE(Number1,[Number2],…)	Returns the value that occurs most often within a set

Figure 29   Statistical functions

The AVERAGE function is commonly used in business analysis. It requires only one argument, a set of values. While many use AVERAGE by itself to help understand data, it is important to be careful when using this by itself. For example, if you were looking at the average starting salaries of graduates among universities in order to determine which school to attend, the University of North Carolina would stand out as having enormous average starting salaries for their graduates in 1984. However, further exploration might reveal this was due to Michael Jordan's huge NBA salary. Thus, it is wise to consider multiple statistics in analyzing data.

The thermostat life is being tracked on the Table_Life worksheet. To have a better idea of the usage on a daily basis, the model needs to show the average and the median of the usage.

To Work with Statistical Functions

a. Click the **Table_Life worksheet tab** to make it the active worksheet, and then click cell **B13**. Click **Insert Function** [fx] next to the formula bar. Under Or select a category, click **Statistical**, and then click **AVERAGE** from the function list. Click **OK**.

b. In the Function Arguments dialog box, place the insertion point in the Number1 box, press [F3], and then click **Daily_Energy_Cost**. Click **OK**, and then click **OK** again.

c. Click cell **B14**. Click **Insert Function** [fx]. Under Or select a category, click **Statistical**, and then click **MEDIAN** from the function list. Click **OK**.

d. In the Function Arguments dialog box, the Number1 input box will be active, press [F3], click **Daily_Energy_Cost**, and then click **OK**. Click **OK** to finish the function. Click **Save** [💾].

   Note the current solution for the median and average energy cost. The median is 0 and the average is 5.97. These formulas are using all the cells in the Daily_Energy_Cost range because the cells actually have numbers in every cell. Thus, while the median and average are calculated correctly, the range has 0 values for cells that have no daily energy cost. The functions are using the 0 values in their calculation, resulting in misleading results. The Daily Energy cost formulas need to be changed so they show numbers when there is usage and do not show numbers when there has not been usage. This issue will be addressed later in this workshop.

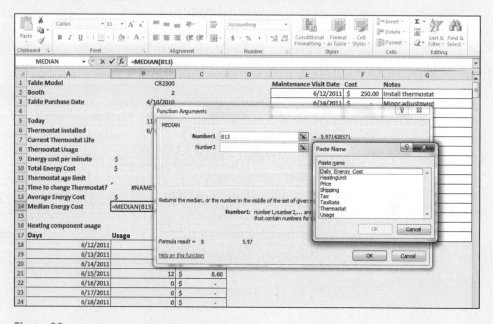

Figure 30 Paste name in function argument

e. Click the **Table_Usage worksheet tab** to make it the active worksheet, and then click cell **B8**. Click **Insert Function** next to the formula bar. Under Or select a category, click **Statistical**, and then click **AVERAGE** from the function list. Click **OK**.

In addition to the Table_Life calculations, the spa has two portable massage tables that the therapists share. Irene wants to track the usage and has started two worksheets that the receptionist will use to check the tables in and out. These two worksheets, Table_Port1 and Table_Port2, are included, but they do not provide any consolidated information. The Table_Usage worksheet will be used to develop statistical information about the table usage based on information logged into the two Table_Port worksheets. Irene wants you to develop the formulas in the simple grid provided for the needed statistics on the Table_Usage worksheet.

f. In the Function Arguments dialog box, place the insertion point in the Number1 box, click to collapse the dialog box, and then click the **Table_Port1 worksheet tab**. Select the range **E4:E23**.

g. Click **Expand Dialog Box** to expand the dialog box and return to the Function Arguments dialog box. Click **OK**.

Notice the formula will include the worksheet name, Table_Port1, with an exclamation mark (!) between the worksheet and the range. Since there is a range E4:E23 on every worksheet, this formula is specifying which worksheet has the range that is to be averaged. So, anytime you are working with a formula that has cells referenced that are on other worksheets, you need to include the worksheet name with an exclamation mark.

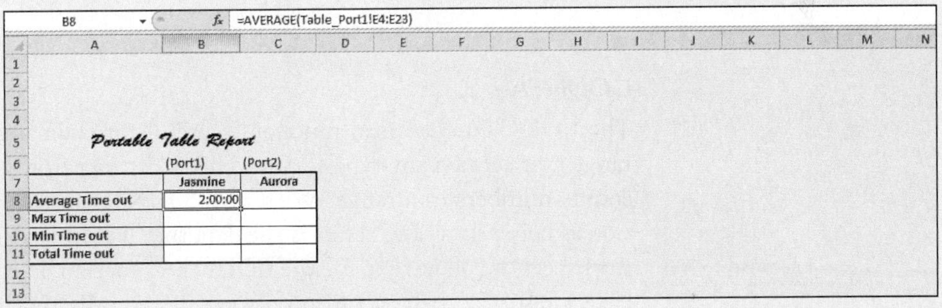

Figure 31 Formula referencing another worksheet

h. Click cell **B9**. Click **Insert Function** next to the formula bar. Under Or select a category, click **Statistical**, and then click **MAX**. Click **OK**.

i. In the Function Arguments dialog box, place the insertion point in the Number1 box, click to collapse the dialog box, and then click the **Table_Port1 worksheet tab**. Select the range **E4:E23**. Click **Expand Dialog Box** to expand the dialog box, and then return to the Function Arguments dialog box and click **OK**.

j. Click cell **B10**. Click **Insert Function** next to the formula bar. Under Or select a category, click **Statistical**, and then click **MIN** from the function list. Click **OK**.

k. In the Function Arguments dialog box, place the insertion point in the Number1 box, click **Collapse Dialog Box** to collapse the dialog box, and then click the **Table_Port1 worksheet tab**. Select the range **E4:E23**. Click **Expand Dialog Box** to expand the dialog box and return to the Function Arguments dialog box. Click **OK**.

l. Click cell **B11**. Click **Insert Function** next to the formula bar. Under Or select a category, click **All**, click **SUM** from the function list, and then click **OK**.

SIDE NOTE
Watch that Function List
Keep an eye on the function list to learn how functions are listed. You might be used to using AVG, but in Excel the function name is AVERAGE.

m. Click **Collapse Dialog Box** ⬚ to collapse the dialog box, click the **Table_Port1 worksheet tab**, and then select the range **E4:E23**. Click **Expand Dialog Box** ⬚ to expand the dialog box and return to the Function Arguments dialog box. Click **OK**.

n. Click the **Insert tab**, and then click the **Header & Footer** button to insert a footer with the file name. Click the **Design tab**, and then click the **Go to Footer** button. If necessary click on the left section of the footer, and then click **File Name** in the Header & Footer Elements group.

o. Click any cell on the spreadsheet to move out of the footer, and then press Ctrl+Home. Click the **View tab**, and then click the **Normal** button in the Workbook Views group.

p. Click the **Table_Port1 worksheet tab**, click the **Insert tab**, and then click the **Header & Footer** button. On the **Design tab**, click the **Go to Footer** button. Click in the left footer section, and then click the **File Name** button in the Header & Footer Elements group.

q. Click any cell on the spreadsheet to move out of the footer, and then press Ctrl+Home. Click the **View tab**, and then click the **Normal** button in the Workbook Views group.

r. Click the **Table_Port2** worksheet tab, click the **Insert tab**, and then click the **Header & Footer** button. Click the **Design tab**, and then click the **Go to Footer** button. Click in the left footer section, and then click **File Name** in the Header & Footer Elements group.

s. Click any cell on the spreadsheet to move out of the footer, and then press Ctrl+Home. Click the **View tab**, and then click **Normal** in the Workbook Views group.

COUNTA

The COUNTA statistical function is useful for counting the number of cells within a range that contain any type of data. This is distinct from the COUNT function that only counts numbers in a range. With the COUNTA function, it does not consider a function as being data. The result is the data that would be counted. Thus, on the Table_Life worksheet, if you were to use the COUNTA function on the Daily_Energy_Cost it would have a result of 4. It would not count all the cells that have formulas, only the values returned. This is different from the AVERAGE function that did use the formulas in the entire range in determining the average daily energy cost.

Using COUNTA is a great way to count the number of records in a data set. With the maintenance for the massage tables, it may be that a technician would visit but not incur any charges. In this case, it would not be correct to simply count the cost column as there may not be a cost. However, the table would have a date for each visit and that could be counted using the COUNTA function.

To Work with the COUNTA() Function

a. Click the **Table_Life worksheet tab**, and then click cell **F19**.

b. Click **Insert Function** 𝑓ₓ next to the formula bar. Under Or select a category, click **Statistical**, and then click **COUNTA** from the function list. Click **OK**.

c. Click **Collapse Dialog Box** ⬚ to collapse the dialog box, and then select the range **E2:E17**.

d. Click **Expand Dialog Box** ⬚ to expand the dialog box and return to the Function Arguments dialog box, click **OK**, and then click **Save** ⬚.

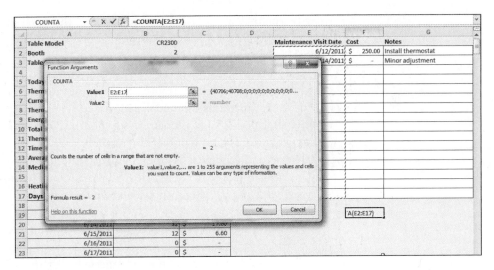

Figure 32 COUNTA function

Financial Functions

Finance & Accounting

Excel has many financial functions available to help businesses make decisions. A foundation for a successful business is generating revenue—any income brought into the business, prior to paying any expenses out—and hopefully yielding net profits. This also applies to personal finances where individuals generate income with the main goal of covering their expenses as they go through life with a net profit to spare. Having a foundational knowledge of financial terms is thus an important element of succeeding in both your personal and professional life. Some common financial terms that you will see and hear or possibly make use of in an Excel spreadsheet are shown in Figure 33.

Financial Term	Definition
APR	The annual percentage rate, an interest rate expressed in an annual equivalent
Compounding interest	A process of charging interest on both the principal and the interest that accumulates on a loan
Interest payment	The amount of a payment that goes toward paying the interest accrued
NPV	The net present value of future investments
Period	The time period of payments, such as making payments monthly
Principal payment	The amount of a payment that goes toward reducing the principal amount
Principal value	The original amount borrowed or loaned
PV	Present value—the total amount that a series of future payments is worth now
Rate (and APR)	The interest rate per period of a loan or an investment
Simple interest	The interest charged on the principal amount of a loan only
Term	The total time period of a loan, typically expressed in years or months
Time value of money	Recognizing that earning one dollar today is worth more than earning one dollar in the future

Figure 33 Financial terminology

One of the most common and useful financial functions in Excel is the PMT function for determining the periodic payment for a loan. The PMT function by default returns a negative value. The function is really calculating an outflow of cash, a payment to be made. Within the financial and accounting industry, an outflow of cash is considered a negative value. In other words, this function assumes you are actually making a payment—taking money out of your pocket to give to someone else, or a negative value. Since some people may be confused seeing the value as negative, the value can be made positive by simply inserting a negative sign prior to the function or placing the absolute value function—ABS()—around the PMT function.

The PMT function uses three required arguments. The first is the **rate**, which is the periodic interest rate. Importantly, the interest rate must be for each period. Most loans are discussed in terms of annual percentage rate (APR), while the period would be a shorter time period such as quarterly or monthly. The APR would need to be divided by 12 to get an equivalent monthly interest rate.

The second argument is **nper**, which is the number of periods or total number of payments that will be made for the loan. Again, many loans are discussed in years while the payments would be monthly. Thus, you will need to determine the total number of periodic payments.

The third, and final, required argument is **PV**, which is the present value of an investment or loan—the amount borrowed that needs to be paid back.

There are other common financial functions that are useful for both personal and business analysis. These are listed below in Figure 34.

Financial Functions	Usage
PMT	Calculates periodic payment for a loan based on a constant interest rate and constant payment amounts
IPMT	Calculates periodic interest payment for a loan based on a constant interest rate and constant payment amounts
PPMT	Calculates periodic principal payment for a loan based on a constant interest rate and constant payment amounts
NPV	Calculates the net present value based on a discount interest rate, a series of future payments, and future income

Figure 34 Financial functions

Within the spa, the managers would like your help analyzing the costs and benefits of purchasing and using equipment. This involves looking at the total cost of purchasing equipment including any interest that may be charged for borrowed money. You then need to look at the revenues generated to determine if they cover the payments and, over time, offer more revenue in than expenses out. Not only does the equipment purchased need to generate enough revenue to cover the total cost, it also needs to generate enough revenue in the short term to make the monthly payments on time. It may not be feasible to try to pay back a loan in six months if the equipment cannot generate enough revenue quickly. Other factors may influence the decision. For example, a longer loan may have lower monthly payments. But, the interest is typically higher for longer term loans. Thus, you need to develop a model that will allow you and the managers to examine various interest rates, principal amounts, and time periods to determine a monthly payment that would work for your business needs.

To Work with the PMT() Function

a. Click the **Table_Purchase worksheet tab** to make it the active worksheet, and then click cell **B6**.

b. Click **Insert Function** f_x next to the formula bar. Under Or select a category, click **Financial**, and then click **PMT** from the function list. Click **OK**.

c. Click in the **Rate** box, and then type B4/12 so you will have the correct interest rate per number of annual payments.

    The division by 12 is to convert an annual rate, which is typically how the loan would be discussed, to months, which is the payment period length. Again, when discussing a loan, it is typical to speak in terms of an APR—the annual percentage rate rather than the period interest rate. Thus a conversion is needed to get the equivalent monthly interest rate.

d. Click in the **Nper** box, and then type B3*12 so the total number of payments for the loan can be calculated, in this case the number of years times the number of months since the payments are on a monthly rate.

e. Click in the **Pv** box, and then type B2.

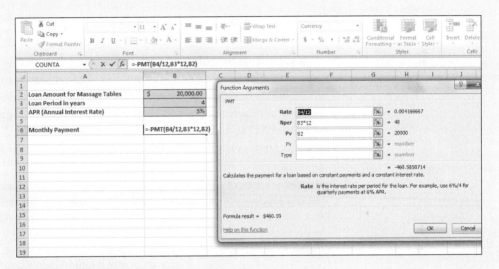

Figure 35   PMT function

f. Click **OK**. Notice the result will be in red with parentheses, which is due to the result being a negative number.

g. Press F2 to enter edit mode. Move the cursor to the right of the = sign and type – (a negative sign), and press Enter. The result is now displayed as a positive number.

h. Click the **Insert tab**, and then click the **Header & Footer** button. Click the **Design tab**, click the **Go to Footer** button, click in the left footer section, and then click the **File Name** button in the Header & Footer Elements group.

i. Click any cell in the spreadsheet to move out of the footer, and then press Ctrl + Home. Click the **View tab**, and then click the **Normal** button in the Workbook Views group. Click **Save** .

Logical Functions

Logical functions are statements, or declarations, that can be evaluated as being either true or false. For example, the statement "the sky is blue" is a declaration that can be evaluated as true. If the statement was "Is the sky blue?" the response would be a yes/no instead of true/false. So, all logical functions are structured around the concept of declaring a position or statement that Excel will evaluate and return as True or False.

The best way to think of a declaration is to think of using comparison symbols like the =, <, >, or >= symbols as shown in Figure 36. When you set up a statement of X>Y, Excel can evaluate that comparison as true or false.

Comparison Operator Symbol	Example	Declarative Clause
<	A < B	A is less than B
>	A > B	A is greater than B
=	A = B	A is equal to B
<=	A <= B	A is less than or equal to B
>=	A >= B	A is greater than or equal to B
<>	A <> B	A does not equal B

Figure 36 Comparison operator symbols

It is possible to create intricate logical statements using the AND and the OR functions that allow you to evaluate multiple logical statements. The IFERROR function can be useful to eliminate an error message that might otherwise confuse the user. The common logical functions and their usage are listed in Figure 37. It is very common to have the AND and OR functions as arguments within an IF statement. The components can incorporate values, cells, named ranges, and even other functions

Logical Functions	Usage
IF	Returns one of two values, depending upon whether the logical statement is evaluated as being true or false
IFERROR	Returns a specified value if a function or formula is showing an error, otherwise it returns the value of the function or formula
AND	Allows multiple logical statements to be evaluated; returns a true result if all of the logical statements are true
OR	Allows multiple logical statements to be evaluated; returns a true result if one or more of the logical statements are true

Figure 37 Logical functions

The most common logical function to learn is the IF function:
IF(Logical_test,[Value_if_true],[Value_if_false])

With this function, you will put in the Logical_test, the declarative equation, as the first argument. Excel will then evaluate it as either true or false. The second argument is the result you want returned in the cell if the expression is evaluated as true. The third argument is the result you want in the cell if the expression is evaluated as false.

Notice that only the expression is required. The last two arguments are optional. If you leave them out, Excel will automatically return the word TRUE or FALSE. However, it is much more common and expected that you will put in something for all three arguments. If you consider the context, logical statement, and results of the IF function, the structure begins to fall into place. Figure 38 has some examples of evaluating a context and constructing the components into a logical IF statement.

CONSIDER THIS | Variations in Constructing Formulas

In Excel, there can be many ways that a formula can be written. Some are more efficient than others. At a minimum, every IF statement can be written two ways. Why? Provide an example with both ways.

Context: Display the word *Good* if the exam score in J10 is better than or equal to the target goal of 80, which is in cell B2. If it is worse than 80, display the word *Bad*.

Example: =IF(J10>=$B$2,"Good","Bad")

Interpretation: If the value of cell J10 is greater than or equal to the value in B2, the text *Good* is displayed. Otherwise, the text *Bad* is displayed.

Context: Display the status of an employee meeting their goal of getting a number of transactions, where transactions are listed in the range of A2:A30 and the target number of transactions are in cell C3.

Example: =IF(COUNT(A2:A30<C3),"Below Goal","Met Goal")

Interpretation: If the count of transactions that are listed in range A2:A30 is below the value in C3 (the target goal for our employee), then the employee did not make their goal and the text *Below Goal* should be displayed. Otherwise, the goal must have been met and the text *Met Goal* should be displayed.

Context: For tracking any projects that have not been completed, check the text in H20 and if it does not say *Complete*, assume the project is not complete and calculate how many months are left when A3 has today's date and A4 has the targeted completion date.

Example: =IF(H20<>"Complete",DATEDIF(A3,A4,"M"),0)

Interpretation: If H20 does not say *Complete* to represent a completed project, calculate the number of months left, based on dates in cells A3 and A4. Otherwise, show a zero.

Context: Determine salary by checking if the employee generated less revenue than their goal, listed in B2. If so, they simply get their base pay. If they do meet their goal or generate more revenue than their goal, they get a bonus, which is a percent of sales added to their base pay. Since this may result in a value that has more than two decimals, the result needs to be rounded to two decimals.

Example: =ROUND(IF(SUM(Sales)<B2,Base,Base+BonusPercent*(Sum(Sales))),2)

Interpretation: The ROUND() function will round the result to two decimals. Inside the ROUND function, the SUM(Sales) functions will sum the range named Sales to give the total sales. The IF statement then indicates that IF the total Sales is less than the value in B2 (the sales goal), provide the value that is in the range called Base (Base pay). Otherwise, the total Sales must be greater than B2 and the pay would be calculated as the Base (Base pay) plus the value in the named range, BonusPercent times the total Sales.

Figure 38 Evaluating IF statements

CONSIDER THIS | What IF There Are Three Options?

An IF statement can handle just two results: true and false. Are most real-world situations that simple? How could you use an IF statement if there are more than two results? It is possible!

As you develop a spreadsheet, there are guidelines to help when developing formulas and functions. Some of the common guidelines include the following:

1. Use parentheses for grouping operations in calculations in order to get the correct order. However, do not overuse parentheses as it quickly adds to the complexity of the formula. For example, use =SUM(Sales) instead of =(SUM(Sales)).

2. Insert numbers without formatting such as 10000. Do not enter 10,000 using a comma. The comma is a formatting element and in Excel is used to separate arguments.

3. Insert currency as 4.34 instead of $4.34 as this will get confusing with relative and absolute cell referencing. Then, format the cell that will contain the result as Accounting or Currency. Recall that an even better practice for functions and formulas is to enter the 4.34 value in a cell and the cell address in the formula.

4. Enter percentages as decimals, such as .04. Then, format the number as a percentage.

5. Logical conditions have three parts—two components to compare and the comparison sign. Do not type >5 when there is no value to evaluate as being greater than 5.

6. Use the negative sign, such as -333 to indicate negative numbers in formulas as opposed to (333).

7. Always put quotes around text unless it is a named range. Also, numeric values do not require quotes unless the number will be used in a textual context and not for a mathematical equation, such as displaying a zip code or telephone number.

Pseudocode is the rough draft of a formula or code. It is intended to help you understand the logic and determine the structure of a problem before you develop the actual formula. When you get a logical statement, especially when it is complex, it is helpful to write it in a manner to focus on the logical aspect of what needs to be accomplished without worrying about the formula syntax or formatting. The proper placement of commas or parentheses will not matter if you do not have a clear plan of the logical intent needed.

The shipping cost varies depending on whether the component is a thermostat or heating unit. So, without worrying about getting the syntax exactly correct when you write the logic of the IF statement in pseudocode, the logical statement is as follows:

IF the component is a thermostat, the shipping cost will be $5.00. Since there are only two items and the item is not a thermostat, the item must be a heating unit. Thus by process of elimination, the shipping will be $9.00.

This could be written again in the following format:

IF(x = Thermostat, Thermostat shipping cost, Heating Unit shipping cost)

This form is closer to the actual syntax but conveys the logic of making your logical test, putting in what will happen if the logical test is true and what will happen if it is false. You can then break it down to the three parts, focusing on the syntax of each argument separately.

The logical test could be stated as either x="Thermostat" or x="Heating Unit". Both could be evaluated as true or false so it does not matter which logical test is used as long as the true and false correspond properly.

To Use the IF() Function

a. Click the **Thermostats worksheet tab**, and then click cell **F5**, the cell in which the shipping cost will be calculated.

b. Click **Insert Function** f_x next to the formula bar. Under Or select a category, click **Logical**, and then click **IF** from the function list. Click **OK**.

c. Click the **Logical_test** argument input box, and then type A5="Thermostat" with quotes so Excel will know that *Thermostat* is a text string and not a named range.

d. Click in the **Value_if_true** argument input box, and then type $E$25*C5.

e. Click in the **Value_if_false** argument input box, type $E$26*C5, and then click **OK**.

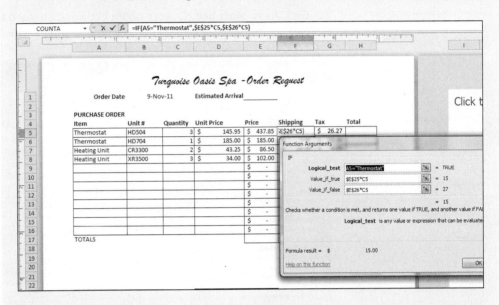

Figure 39   IF function

f. Click the **AutoFill handle** on cell F5, and then drag down to copy the formula to cell **F16**.

g. Click the **Insert tab**, and then click the **Header & Footer** button. Click the **Design tab**, and then click the **Go to Footer** button. Click in the left footer section, and then click the **File Name** button in the Header & Footer Elements group.

h. Click in any cell on the spreadsheet to move out of the footer, and then press [Ctrl]+[Home]. Click the **View tab**, and then click the **Normal** button in the Workbook Views group.

i. Click **Save** 💾.

Adding an IF Function to an Existing Formula

The IF statement can return either text or numbers. It can even mix the data in the same IF statement, returning a value for the true argument and text for the false argument. This can be useful when you are doing other statistics on the results as you saw on the Table_Life worksheet.

The formula in the Daily Energy Cost range on the Table_Life worksheet, C18:C31, is causing a value to be seen for every cell with the average and median calculations. Since these functions will only use numbers, if you change the value to a text string when there is no energy cost, the functions will then be calculated correctly. So, the existing formula needs to be modified to check if there is usage. If there is, then the daily energy cost will be calculated. If there is not any usage, an empty text string will be put in, which will be ignored by the average and median functions in B13 and B14.

To Add an IF Function to an Existing Formula

a. Click the **Table_Life worksheet tab**, and then click cell **C18.**

b. Click the **formula bar**, put your cursor between the = and **B**, type IF(B18>0, move the cursor to the end of the formula and type , ""), and then press Enter.

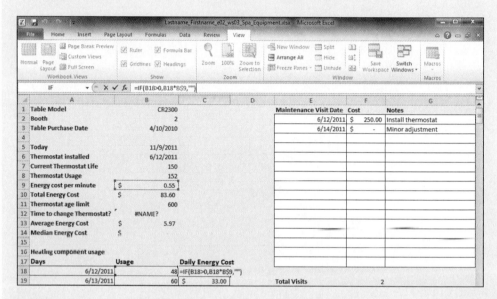

Figure 40   Incorporate an IF function

c. Select **C18**, and using the AutoFill handle, copy the formula down through **C19:C31**. Notice the median and average are being calculated using the four data points rather than including the empty cells. As Usage data are added, the daily energy cost will be calculated with the average and median being updated.

Editing and Troubleshooting Functions

Logical functions dramatically increase the value of a spreadsheet. However, on the path to learning how to use functions, and even as an experienced spreadsheet user, you will still make typing errors during the development of functions. Excel does an excellent job of incorporating cues to help you determine where you have gone astray with a function.

When you make a mistake with a function that prevents Excel from returning a viable result, Excel will provide an error message. While these may seem cryptic initially, they actually can be interpreted. Typically an error message will be prefaced with a number symbol (#). Examples would be #VALUE!, #N/A, #NAME?, or #REF!. Over time you will learn to recognize common issues that would cause these error messages.

Quick Reference — Common Error Messages

1. **#NAME?**—Excel does not recognize text in a formula and believes there is a named range being listed that does not exist. Commonly, this is due to using a text string and forgetting the quotes or mistyping the function or named range.

2. **#REF!**—Excel is showing a reference to a cell range location that it cannot find. This happens often in development when big changes occur like deleting a worksheet. A formula on Sheet2 may have worked originally but when Sheet1 is deleted, the formula on Sheet2 can no longer find the cell on Sheet1 and will replace it with a #REF! error.

3. **#N/A**—This error indicates that a value is not available in one or more cells specified. Common causes occur in functions that try to find a value in a list but the value does not exist. Rather than returning an empty set—no value—Excel returns this error instead.

4. **#VALUE!**—This error occurs when the wrong type of argument or operand is being used, such as entering a text value when the formula requires a number. Common causes can be the wrong cell reference that contains a text value rather than a numeric value.

5. **#DIV/0!**—This is a division by 0 error and occurs when a number is divided by zero or by a cell that contains no value. While it can occur due to an actual error in the design of a formula, it also may occur simply due to the current conditions within the spreadsheet data. In other words, this is common when a spreadsheet model is still in the creation process and data has not yet been entered into the necessary cells. Once proper numeric data does exist, the error will disappear.

When you encounter errors, you should click the Insert Function button f_x and examine the arguments and corresponding values in the Function Arguments dialog box. When something is contained in the argument input box that cannot be evaluated by Excel, it displays an error message to the right of the offending argument input box. Most helpfully, it will also be in red. If Excel can interpret the input information for the argument, it displays the current value(s) to the right. Using the visual clues and values in the dialog box can at the very least aid in guiding you as to where Excel is struggling with the function construction.

On the Table_Life worksheet, there is a function applied by one of the managers, and the function results are displaying an error message. The manager looked at the function and believes the logic is correct. So, your debugging skills are needed.

To Edit a Function with the Insert Function Button

a. Click the **Table_Life worksheet tab** to make it active, and then click cell **B12** and notice that it currently displays the **#NAME?** error.

b. Click the **Insert Function** f_x to the left of the formula bar.

   This will bring up the Function Arguments dialog box. Notice, the Value_if_true and the Value_if_false inputs have error messages to the right. They both are bold and red indicating that there is a name issue. Recall, the #NAME? error is common when you input a text string without using quotes to surround the text. A text string should always have quotes around it unless it is a reference to a function name or named range. Without the quotes, Excel will believe the text is a named range. Excel cannot find a range that has been named Thermostat, Age, Limit, Reached, and so on for all of the individual words typed in the input box; therefore, Excel is confused and letting you know that it has not found a name in the list of named ranges.

c. Click once inside the **Value_if_true** box to enter edit mode.

d. Click in the **Value_if_false** box, and Excel will automatically adjust to add quotes for the text in the Value_if_true box. You should also see the red, bold #NAME? error disappear and be replaced with the appropriate text string for that argument value.

e. With the insertion point now in the Value_if_false argument input box, click in the **Logical_test** input box, and Excel will adjust the Value_if_false box so that quotes appear around the text again. The red #NAME? error is replaced with the appropriate text string value. Click **OK**.

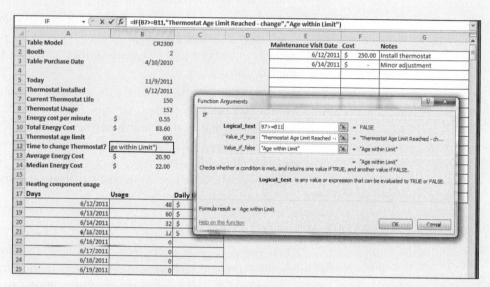

Figure 41   Function corrected

f. Click the **Insert tab**, and then click the **Header & Footer** button. Click the **Design tab**, and then click the **Go to Footer** button. Click in the left footer section of the footer, and then click the **File Name** button in the Header & Footer Elements group.

g. Click any cell in the spreadsheet to move out of the footer, press Ctrl + Home , click the **View tab**, and then click **Normal** in the Workbook Views group.

h. Click **Save** . Submit or print your project as directed by your instructor. Close Excel.

Concept Check

Production & Operations

Finance & Accounting

1. You are the manager of the production department and need to create a spreadsheet to track projections. What differences would exist if this spreadsheet were to be used only by you versus being accessed by other staff employees?

2. You have a spreadsheet that contains performance data for the staff. How would you organize this data considering that it would be data used for annual performance reviews for each staff member? What are some of the ethical considerations to keep in mind when using this data?

3. You are reviewing a spreadsheet for your employee and notice the formula that calculates production costs as =B25*10000, where B25 is the unit cost and 10000 is the estimated production. What is wrong with how this formula has been structured, and what suggestions would you offer to correct the formula to make it more efficient?

4. You have a range C4:C8 that are the number of transactions for each division of your company. The sum of the transactions is in C9. You want a formula in D4:D8 that will figure the percent of transactions for each division. The formula in D4 is =C4/C9, which works for the first division, but when that formula is copied down through D8, errors occur for the other divisions. Why? How would you fix the formula so it could be copied to other cells and work correctly?

5. You are creating a PMT function and you see PMT(rate,nper,pv,[fv],[type]) just below where you are typing. Why is the *nper* bold? Why are there [] brackets around the *fv* and *type* arguments?

Key Terms

Absolute cell reference 391
Argument 401
Cell reference 386
Function 401
Hard-coding 386

Mixed cell reference 392
Named range 395
Nper 416
Pseudocode 420
PV 416

Rate 416
Relative cell reference 388
Show Formulas view 390
Syntax 401

Create a set of named ranges from selections (p. 398)

Work with relative cell referencing (p. 389)

Create a named range using the Name Box (p. 396)

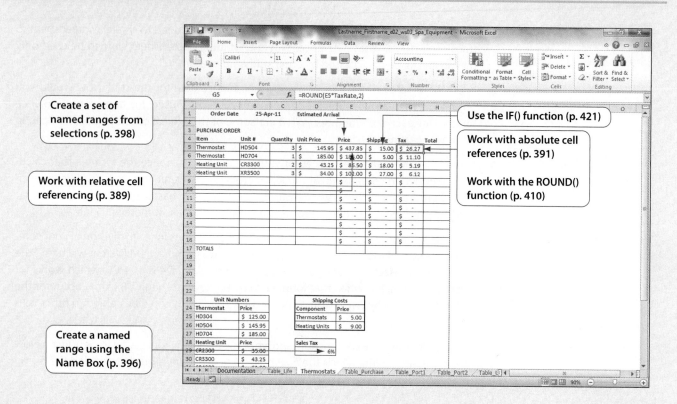

Use the IF() function (p. 421)

Work with absolute cell references (p. 391)

Work with the ROUND() function (p. 410)

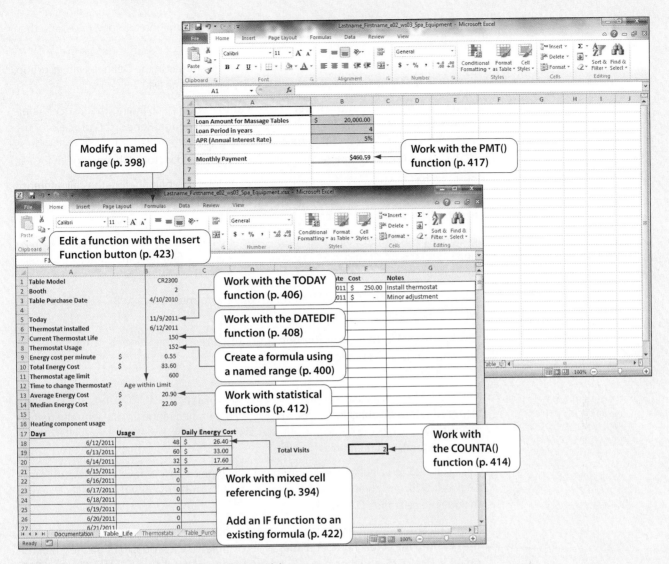

Figure 42 Massage Table Analysis Final Spreadsheet

Practice 1

Student data file needed:

e02_ws03_Bonus

You will save your file as:

Lastname_Firstname_e02_ws03_Bonus

Massage Therapists Bonus Report

Human Resources

Two managers, Irene and Meda, have been discussing a worksheet that would enable them to coordinate the goals for the massage therapists and calculate their pay. The massage therapists have a base pay plus they earn commission for massages along with a bonus. Meda is heading to a conference so they have asked you to make some modifications and complete the worksheet.

a. Start **Excel**, and then open **e02_ws03_Bonus**. A spreadsheet with a partially completed model for bonuses will be displayed. Click the **File tab**, and then click **Save As**. In the Save As dialog box, navigate to where you are saving your files, and type Lastname_Firstname_e02_ws03_Bonus, replacing Lastname and Firstname with your own name.

b. Click cell **J17**.

c.   Click in the **Name Box**. The cell address J17 should be highlighted. Type Bonus, and then press Enter.

d.   Click the **Formulas tab**, and then click the **Name Manager** in the Defined Names group. In the Name Manager dialog box, click **Christy** in the Name list.

e.   Modify the cell range in the **Refers to** box at the bottom, changing the last cell reference from $I$12 to $K$12. Press Enter to accept the change. Repeat this process for the Jason, Kendra, and Pat named ranges, changing the column letter for last cell address from I to K so the named ranges include all the massage data for each massage therapist.

f.   Click cell **B4**, and type =B3*A4. Click to place the insertion point before the cell reference **B3**, and then press F4 twice until the B3 becomes B$3 so column B will be relative and row 3 will be an absolute reference.

g.   Position the insertion point in front of the cell reference **A4**, and then press F4 three times until the A4 becomes $A4 so column A is an absolute reference and row 4 is relative. Press Enter.

h.   Click cell **B4**. Click the **AutoFill handle** to copy the formula down to **B8**. The range B4:B8 will now be selected.

i.   Click the **AutoFill handle** in the bottom-right corner of the selected range, and then copy the range B4:B8 to the right to column K. When finished, the formula will be copied to the range **B4:K8**.

j.   Click cell **F19** to calculate actual Massages given. Type =SUM(Christy). Press Enter. Repeat this formula for cells **F20:F22** replacing the named range Christy with the named range that matches the name in column A of the same row. For example, in cell F20 type =SUM(Kendra), and then press Enter.

k.   Click cell **D25** to calculate the Commission Pay. Type =C19*C25, and then press Enter. Click cell **D25**, and then double-click the **AutoFill handle** to copy the formula down to include the cell range **D25:D28**.

l.   The bonus is earned if the therapist generated actual revenue equal to or greater than the goal and the actual number of massages completed was equal to or greater than the goal. Click cell **E25**, and then type =IF(D19*G19=1,"Yes","No"). Press Enter. Click cell **E25**, and then double-click the **AutoFill handle** to copy the formula down to include the cell range **E25:E28**. This formula takes the met revenue goal value and multiplies it by the met massages goal value. The formulas in both of these columns yield a numeric value of zero for no and a value of 1 for yes, thus multiplying these two numbers together will only yield a value of 1 if both goals are met—represented by 1. Any met goal represented by a zero will yield a zero since multiplying any number times zero results in zero.

m.   Click cell **F25**, and then type =IF(E25="Yes",Bonus,0). Press Enter. Click cell **F25**, and then double-click the **AutoFill handle** to copy the formula down to include the cell range **F25:F28**.

n.   Click cell **G25**, and then type =B25+D25+F25. Press Enter, click cell **G25**, and then double-click the **AutoFill handle** to copy the formula down to include the cell range **G25:G28**.

o.   Click the **Insert tab**, and then click the **Header & Footer** button. Click the **Design tab**, and then click the **Go to Footer** button. Click in the left footer section, and then click the **File Name** button in the Header & Footer Elements group.

p.   Click in any cell on the spreadsheet to move out of the footer, press Ctrl+Home, click the **View tab**, and then click the **Normal** button in the Workbook Views group.

q.   Click **Save**.

Student data file needed:

e02_ps1_Car_Rental

You will save your file as:

Lastname_Firstname_e02_ps1_Car_Rental

Express Car Rental

Sales & Marketing

Jason Easton is a member of the support/decision team for the San Diego branch of Express Car Rental. He created a worksheet to keep track of weekly rentals in an attempt to identify trends in choices of rental vehicles, length of rental, and payment method. This spreadsheet is designed only for Jason and his supervisor to try and find weekly trends and possibly use this information when marketing and forecasting the type of cars needed on site. The data for the dates of rental, daily rates, payment method, and gas option have already been entered.

a. Start **Excel**. Navigate to where your student files are located, select **e02_ps1_Car_Rental**, and then save the file as Lastname_Firstname_e02_ps1_Car_Rental.

b. Rename worksheet Sheet1 as RentalData and Sheet2 as Documentation.

c. On the RentalData worksheet, in cell F12, enter the appropriate date formula to determine the length of rental in days.

d. Copy this formula to the range **F13:F38**.

e. Set the name range for C12:C38 to Memberships and F12:F38 to DaysRented.

f. In cell F6, enter the formula to calculate the average number of days for rentals. Format this result as a number with 1 decimal place.

g. In cell F7, enter the formula to calculate the Median length of rental in days. Format this result as a number with 0 decimal places.

h. In cell F9, enter the formula to calculate the number of rentals that had a Gold Membership.

i. In cell I12, enter the formula to calculate the discount that would apply to any rental that had a Gold Membership. Make sure to reference the cell with the discount. Gold Memberships get a discount applied to the rental fee that is the daily rate times the days rented. Rentals with no Gold Membership have a discount of 0. Format the cell with Accounting Number Format.

j. Copy the formula in I12 down to the range **I13:I38**.

k. In cell J12, enter a formula to determine the total cost based on the number of days the vehicle was rented and the discount indicated in cell I12. Format the cell with Accounting Number Format.

l. Copy the formula in J12 to the range **J13:J38**.

m. Format the range J12:J38 with Accounting Number Format and 2 decimal places.

n. In cell L12, enter the correct formula to determine the total cost with insurance if the customer chose that option as indicated in column K. Be sure to reference cell B7 in this formula. Format that cell with Accounting Number Format.

o. Copy the formula in L12 to the range **L13:L38**.

p. On the RentalData worksheet, merge and center the range **A1:L1**. Apply the **Title** style to the same range, and then use the Fill Color option to change the cell background color to **Dark Blue, Text 2, Lighter 60%**.

q. Merge and center the range **A2:L2** and **A3:L3**. Apply the **Heading 4** style to each range.

r. Apply the **Heading 4** style to the labels in the range **A11:L11**. Apply **Wrap Text** to this range.

s. Change the orientation of the RentalData sheet to landscape, and within the Page Setup, change the scaling to fit to 1 page wide by 1 page tall.

t. On the Documentation worksheet insert the appropriate content in cells D3, A5, B5, and C5. Wrap the text in cell C5.

u. Print preview the RentalData sheet. If all columns fit on one page, print the sheet if your instructor requests a copy.

v. Save the workbook.

 Additional Workshop Cases are available on the companion website and in the instructor resources.

WORKSHOP 4

Using Charts

Sales & Marketing

PREPARE CASE

Turquoise Oasis Spa Sales Reports

The Turquoise Oasis Spa managers, Irene and Meda, are pleased with your work and would like to see you continue to improve the spa spreadsheets. They want to use charts to learn more about the spa. To do this Meda has given you a spreadsheet with some data, and she would like you to develop some charts. These charts will provide knowledge about the spa for decision-making purposes.

Alfred Wekelo / Shutterstock.com

Student data files needed for this workshop:

 e02_ws04_Spa_Sales

 e02_ws04_Couple

You will save your file as:

 Lastname_Firstname_e02_ws04_Spa_Sales

Designing a Chart

With Excel you can organize data so it has context converting data into meaningful information. **Data visualization** is the graphical presentation of data with a focus upon qualitative understanding. It is central to finding trends and supporting business decisions. Even basic charts are at the heart of data visualization. Charts enlighten you as you compare, contrast, and examine how data changes over time. Learning how to work with charts means not only knowing how to create them but also realizing that different knowledge can be discovered or emphasized by each type of chart.

While it may seem simple to create a pie chart or bar chart, there are many considerations in creating your charts. A well-developed chart should provide context for the information, without overshadowing key points. You should create charts that use accurate, complete data and your objective should be to provide a focused, clear message. There are three primary objectives businesses have in charting: data exploration, hypothesis testing, and argumentation.

Using the **data exploration objective**, you simply manipulate the data, and try to evaluate and prioritize all the interpretations or messages. There may be a need to create multiple charts, using a variety of data sources, layouts, and designs as you interpret the data. In this case, examine the data and let the charts tell a story.

Using the **hypothesis testing objective**, you may have some ideas or hypotheses about the data. Maybe you believe that a certain salesperson performs better than the others. Or maybe you believe that certain types of massages are more popular with particular types of customers. Charts can visually support or refute a hypothesis.

Using the **argumentation objective**, you have a position you want the data to visually support. You will need to select a specific and appropriate chart layout, use the necessary data, and design a chart that conveys your message clearly and unambiguously. Further, you have an ethical obligation to accurately represent the data. Misrepresenting data can result in lawsuits, loss of your job, or even cost lives.

Regardless of the objective, just a small set of data allows you to create a variety of charts, each offering a different understanding of the data. In this workshop, you will start with understanding concepts for creating a chart in Excel, and understand which type of chart will depict the information in the best and most efficient manner.

Exploring Chart Characteristics—Types, Layouts, and Styles

When you decide to represent data visually, you need to make some initial decisions about the basic design of the chart. These initial decisions include the location of the chart, the type of chart, the general layout and style, and what data you will be using. These elements can be set initially and modified later. Best practice dictates that you first consider and develop the basic design of the chart.

Regardless of the location or type of chart, the process of creating a chart starts with the organization of the data on the spreadsheet. The typical structure is to have labels across the top of the data, along the left side of the data, or both. While the labels do not have to be directly next to the data, it helps when selecting data and making your chart. The data may have been brought in from an external data source, like Access. The data may need to be filtered, calculated, or reorganized prior to creating a chart.

When ready to create a chart, select the cells that contain both the label headings and the data. Rarely do people create a perfect chart the first time. Initially, you may start a chart, work with it for a while, and then realize a different chart type would better convey the information. Fortunately, there is flexibility when designing charts. Thus, if you change your mind, you can modify the chart or simply start over.

Navigating a Chart

If a chart is an object within a worksheet, you can select the outer edge of a chart. When you do, this activates the largest component of the chart—the chart area. It will be highlighted on the border while the middle of the sides and the corners will have light, small dots used to signal resizing handles for the chart. The border edge can also be used to move the entire chart to a new location within the spreadsheet.

When a chart is selected, the data used in creating the chart will be highlighted in the worksheet, offering a visual cue of the associated data. This is the data that is being used within the chart. In a pie chart, the purple border surrounds the data that represents the legend labels. The range with a blue border is the data that represents the data series for the pie slices. A **data series** is a set of data to be charted. A **data point** is an individual piece of data in a data series. There can be multiple data series in some chart types.

Subcomponents of the chart can also be selected, such as the background, various text elements, and even the individual chart elements themselves. Click components to make them active, and adjust specific items through either the Ribbon options or by right-clicking to display the shortcut menu to see available options. In the pie chart constructed on the TableUse worksheet, the various components, like the chart background and the plot area, are easy to see because they use textured backgrounds.

While navigating through a chart, the Ribbon displays the Chart Tools contextual tabs, which include the Design, Layout, and Format tabs. These are specific tabs associated with formatting and adjusting chart elements. Click anywhere outside the chart border area, and this group of tabs disappears. Click anywhere within the chart, and this group of contextual tabs reappears.

Documentation in a worksheet is an internal document that details changes made to that workbook. This helps others to understand who made changes in the past and is an internal document that only a few people will see or use. You will also want to practice safe file-development procedures by saving the file often, and creating backups as needed.

Real World Advice **First Impressions**

First impressions are important with charts. You want the audience to receive the correct message during the initial moments. If the audience is distracted by the look and feel of the chart, they may stop looking for the message in the chart or extend the chaotic personality of the chart to the presenter. Thus, the chart can become a reflection upon you and your company.

Workshop 4 Training

To Update Documentation and Navigate a Chart

a. Start **Excel**.

b. Click the **File tab**, and then click **Open**. In the Open dialog box, click the disk drive in the left pane where your student data files are located, navigate through the folder structure, and then double click **e02_ws04_Spa_Sales**.

c. Click the **File tab**, click **Save As**, and then in the Save As dialog box, navigate to the location where you are saving your files. In the File Name box, type Lastname_Firstname_e02_ws04_Spa_Sales, replacing Lastname and Firstname with your own name, and then click **Save**.

d. If necessary, click the **Documentation worksheet tab** to make it the active worksheet, click cell **A6**, and then press Ctrl+; to input the current date. Click cell **B6**, and then type your first name and last name.

e. Click the **Insert tab**, and then click the **Header & Footer** button in the Text group. Click the **Design tab**, and then click the **Go to Footer** button. Click in the left footer section, and then in the Header & Footer Elements group click **File Name**.

f. Click any cell on the spreadsheet to move out of the footer, press Ctrl+Home, click the **View tab**, and then click **Normal** in the Workbook Views group.

g. Click the **TableUse worksheet tab** to view the pie chart on this worksheet, and then click **Save**.

h. Click the **outer border edge** of the chart to select the chart and display the Chart Tools contextual tabs.

i. Click the **Layout tab**. If necessary, click the **Chart Elements arrow** in the Current Selection group, and then choose **Chart Area**. The Chart Elements box indicates that the Chart Area is the current selection.

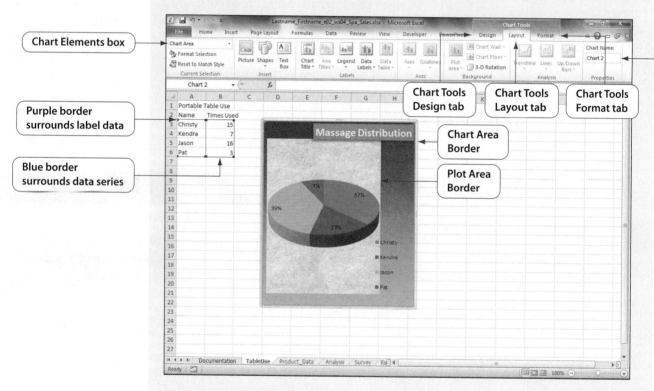

Figure 1 Navigating through a chart

j. With the border currently selected, click the **chart title** area. Notice the border appears around the chart title indicating it is the active component. The Chart Elements box in the Current Selection group will change to display Chart Title.

k. Click the **pie chart**. Notice the pie becomes the active component. You can then select individual pie slices by clicking the desired pie slice. The Chart Elements box reflects the current selection.

l. Click the **green pie slice**. With the green slice as the active component, right-click the green slice to display the shortcut menu that contains options available for that component.

Troubleshooting

> If you clicked on a pie slice and the percentage label displays a border with corner handles around it, then you have clicked on that element accidentally. You should click one more time on the pie slice, but not on any of the text labels.

m. Click the **Chart Elements arrow** in the Current Selection group, and then click **Plot Area**. It now becomes the active component with circle handles displayed on the four corners. These can be used to resize the plot area or change the background.

n. Click **Save** 🖫. Click cell **A1**. Notice that the Chart Tools tabs have disappeared.

CONSIDER THIS | **Misleading Charts**

Charts are supposed to frame information. But, have you ever seen a chart in a newspaper, online article, or magazine that would lead the viewer to an incorrect assumption or conclusion? Look for a chart that is misleading, discuss the context and possible incorrect conclusions that could be made, and consider the ethical aspect of the creator for that chart.

Quick Reference / Working with Chart Objects

It is possible to navigate through a chart using some of the guidelines below:

1. Click the chart edge to activate the Chart Tools group of tabs.
2. Click chart objects to select individual chart components.
3. Click again to select subobjects of any larger chart object.
4. Click another chart outside of an object or press Esc to deselect an object.
5. Use the Chart Elements list to select object components.
6. Use border corner handles to resize selected objects.
7. Click the border edge, and drag to move a chart object.

Chart Locations

When developing a chart, consider the chart location, as this might affect the flexibility of moving and resizing your chart components. There are two general locations for a chart—either within an existing worksheet or on a separate worksheet referred to as a chart sheet.

Creating Charts in an Existing Worksheet

Placing a chart within a worksheet can be very helpful, allowing you to display the chart beside the associated data source. When comparing charts side by side, placing the charts on the same worksheet can also be handy. Additionally, placing a chart within the worksheet may offer easy access to chart components when copying and pasting components into other applications.

Your manager, Irene, would like you to work with some data. Irene would like the data organized and presented in an effective graphical manner to aid in the analysis of the data so it is more informative.

To Create a Chart in an Existing Worksheet

a. Click the **Product_Data worksheet tab**, and then select the range **A3:I13** to use the data for creating a chart. Do not include the Totals in column J.

b. Click the **Insert tab**, and then click **Column** in the Charts group to display a gallery menu for column chart options.

c. Click **Clustered Column** under 2-D column. Notice the chart appears on the currently active spreadsheet and shows colored borders surrounding the associated data linked to the chart.

d. Click the **chart border** and notice that the cursor appears as a four-way arrow. Be careful not to click the corners or middle areas of the border that are designated by small handles and used for resizing the chart. Drag the border to move the chart to the right of the data so the top-left chart corner is approximately in cell L3. Click **Save**.

Modifying a Chart's Position Properties

Charts created within the worksheet will appear as objects that "float" on top of the worksheet. It should be noted that the default property settings resize the chart shape if any of the underlying rows or columns are changed or adjusted. However, it is possible to change the setting to lock the size and position of the chart so it does not resize or move when columns or rows are resized, inserted, or deleted.

To Modify the Chart Position Properties on a Worksheet

a. On the Product_Data worksheet, make sure the **border edge** of the chart is still selected. Right-click the **border edge** of the chart, and then click **Format Chart Area**.

b. In the Format Chart Area dialog box, click **Properties** to display the Properties settings.

c. Click **Move but don't size with cells**, and then click **Close**. Click **Save**.

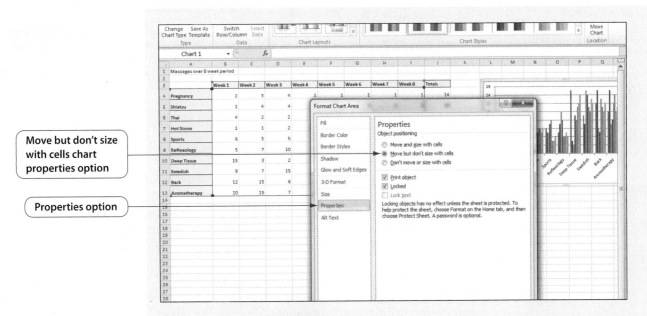

Move but don't size with cells chart properties option

Properties option

Figure 2 Format Chart Area dialog box

The chart size will not be resized if the width or height of the columns or rows underneath are changed or adjusted but will move along with the cells that it is sitting over. From here, you can easily move the chart by dragging the border, or you can resize the chart by clicking and dragging the corners.

Placing Charts on a Chart Sheet

A chart can also be created on a separate sheet. Having the chart on a separate chart sheet can make it easier to isolate and print on a page. A **chart sheet** is a worksheet with a tab at the bottom similar to other worksheets. However, the sheet replaces the cell grid with the actual chart. This is useful when you want to create a set of charts and easily navigate between them by sheet tab names rather than hunting for them on various worksheets. Additionally, the data associated with the chart will be on a different worksheet.

To Create a Chart in a Chart Sheet

a. Click the **Product_Data worksheet tab**, select the range **A4:A13**, hold down Ctrl, and then select **J4:J13** to create a pie chart showing the distribution of massage totals over the eight-week period.

b. Click the **Insert tab**, click the **Pie** button in the Charts group, and then under the 2-D Pie category, click **Pie**. The chart will be inserted on the worksheet so you will need to move it to a chart sheet.

c. If necessary, click the **Design tab** on the Chart Tools contextual tab, and then click **Move Chart** in the Location group. The Move Chart dialog box is displayed.

d. Click the **New sheet** option. In the New sheet box, clear the existing name and type MassagePie. Click **OK**. Notice that you now have a new chart sheet tab in your workbook file. This chart sheet is exclusively for the chart and will not have the normal spreadsheet look and feel.

e. Right-click on the **MassagePie worksheet tab**. Select **Tab Color**, and then choose **Red, Accent 2** as the tab color.

SIDE NOTE
Moving a Chart Between a Chart Sheet and a Worksheet
The Move Chart button on the Chart Tools Design tab is the only simple method for transferring a chart from a worksheet to a chart sheet. It acts as the toggle for moving between a worksheet and a chart sheet.

f. Click the **Insert tab**, and then click the **Header & Footer** button in the Text group. Click the **Custom Footer** button. In the left section, click **Insert File Name** 📄.Click **OK**. Click **OK** again.

g. Click **Save** 💾.

Chart Types

The next thing you will need to do is decide what chart type to use. Each chart type conveys information differently. The chart type sets the tone for the basic format of the data and what kind of data is included. Thus, it helps to become familiar with the types of charts that are commonly used for business decision making and for presentations. Always consider which type is appropriate for the message you are trying to convey.

Pie Charts

Pie charts are commonly used for depicting parts of the whole such as comparing staff performance within a department or comparing the number of transactions of each product category within a time period.

For a pie chart you need two sets of data, the labels, and a set of corresponding values that make up the pie similar to the data selection made in the TableUse sheet to indicate the percentage of times each person used the portable massage table. Note that the data can be described as a percentage of the whole as in the chart.

The questions you have will influence what textual data you will include in any chart. If you are exploring a use fee, then having the percentage would indicate which therapist would be contributing the most fees, and the actual numbers may not be a crucial element. When you create a chart, examine it to see if it answers your questions.

Line Charts

Line charts help convey change over a period of time. These are great for exploring how data in a business, such as sales or production, changes over time. Line charts help people to interpret why the data is changing and to make decisions about how to proceed. For example, when a doctor examines a heart rate on an electrocardiogram, he or she is looking at data over time to see what has been happening. The doctor wants to determine if there are issues, and then make decisions on whether the patient should go home, be given medications, or have surgery.

To create a line chart, you need to have at least one set of labels and at least one set of corresponding data. It is possible to have multiple sets of numbers, each set representing a line on the chart. For example, you may want to examine the number of massages given on a weekly basis. Each week would be a point on the line that is created. Each massage type would be a separate line on the chart.

To Create a Line Chart

a. Click the **Revenue worksheet tab**, select cell **A5**, hold down Ctrl, and then press A to select the entire data set, including the labels.

b. Click the **Insert tab**, click the **Line** button in the Charts group, and then under 2-D Line click **Line**.

c. With the chart still selected, click the **border edge** of the chart (not the corner), and then drag to move the chart to the right of the data set so the top-left corner is over cell G4.

d. Position the mouse pointer over the bottom-right corner of the chart until the pointer changes to ⤢, and then drag to resize the chart so the bottom-right corner is over cell N19. Click **Save** 💾.

Troubleshooting

If you end up with a chart that looks dramatically different than what you would expect, check the colored borders around the linked data set. It is very common to select all the data in a table when the intention was to grab part of the data. If too much data was selected, you can delete the selected chart by pressing Delete. Alternatively, you could select the corner of a colored link data border and drag the border to adjust the set of data. The blue-border data is displayed in the chart. When that border is adjusted, the associated label data is automatically adjusted accordingly. The chart is also automatically adjusted so changes can be immediately seen.

Column Charts

Column charts are useful for comparing data sets that are categorized, like departments, product categories, or survey results. Column charts are also useful for showing categories over time where each column represents a unit of time. Column charts are good for comparisons both individually, in groups, or stacked. Column chart data can easily allow for grouping of data so comparisons of the groups can occur.

For the Survey data, it would be useful to show the overall satisfaction rating by massage type to determine if there are differences in satisfaction based on the massage. To do this, the data has to be summarized and organized before a chart can be constructed. The types of massages need to be listed, and the corresponding average for each type needs to be calculated.

To Create a Column Chart

a. Select the **Survey** worksheet, and then select range **D4:D55**. Hold down Ctrl, and then press C to copy the data.

b. Click cell **F1**, hold down Ctrl, and then press V to paste the range.

c. Select the **Data tab** on the ribbon, and click **Remove Duplicates**.

d. In the Remove Duplicates dialog box, click the **My data has headers** check box, then click **OK**. Click **OK** again. It will find and remove 41 duplicates, leaving 10 unique values.

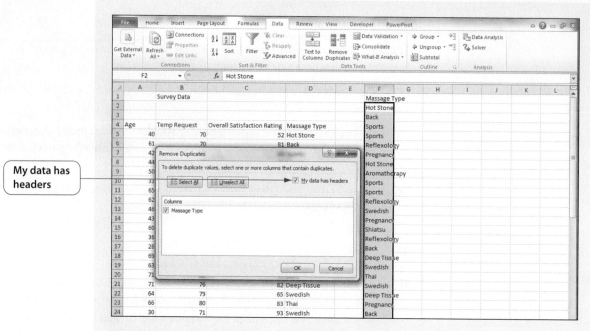

Figure 3 Remove duplicates

e. Select cell **G2**, type =AVERAGEIF($D$5:$D$55,F2,$C$5:$C$55), and then press ⌊Enter⌋.

f. Select cell **G2**, click the **AutoFill handle** in the lower-right corner of the cell, and then drag down to copy the formula down to cell **G11**. With the range **G2:G11** still selected, on the **Home tab**, click the ⌊ , ⌋ icon to format as comma style.

g. Select the range **F2:G11**. Click the **Insert tab**, click **Column** in the Charts group, and then click **Clustered Column** within the 2-D Column options. Notice the chart shows the average ratings for each massage type on the x-axis.

h. With the chart still selected, if necessary click the **Layout tab**, and then select the **Chart Name** text box in the Properties group. Change the name of the chart to Survey Rating, and then press ⌊Enter⌋.

i. If necessary, click the **Design tab** on the Chart Tools contextual tab, and then click **Move Chart** in the Location group.

j. Click the **Object in** option. In the **Object in** drop-down list, select **Feedback**, and then click **OK**.

k. Click the **border edge** of the chart (not the corner), and then drag to move it until the top-left corner is in cell A1.

l. Select the **Survey worksheet tab**, and then select range **F2:G11**. Hold down ⌊Ctrl⌋, and then press ⌊X⌋ to cut the range.

m. Select the **Feedback worksheet tab**, and then select cell **J2**. Hold down ⌊Ctrl⌋, and then press ⌊V⌋ to paste the range.

n. On the Survey worksheet tab, if necessary, click the **bottom-right corner**, and then resize the chart so the bottom-right corner is over cell H16. Click **Save** ⌊🖫⌋.

Even though all the data is used to show every massage type, you do not have to use all the data. If the goal is to examine the data and extract a portion of the information, like the fact that several massage types have low or high average ratings, it may be better to only show a few massage types rather than flood the audience with too much information. Showing a subset of massage types may help to emphasize particular ratings.

In determining how to proceed once the data has been initially examined, start developing hypotheses and questions. For example, it may be that Shiatsu and Thai massages are very new and need to be marketed more. Develop questions, and then use the data to determine the validity of the questions and make strategic decisions.

Bar Charts

Bar charts are useful for working with categorical data. The data is categorized in groups and are similar to column charts, except that the bars are horizontal representations of the data rather than vertical. Like column charts, bar charts can depict a single piece of data, can be grouped sets of data, and even be stacked.

Because bar charts typically use groups and sum data, stacked bar charts can be useful when you want to see how the individual parts add up to create the entire length of each bar. For example, with the product data, you may want to compare each type of massage, summing revenue or counting sales for each type of massage. The x-axis would be number of massages or revenue. While it is the same data as used for the line chart, it conveys information about an output without the emphasis on time that is inherent with the line chart.

While bar charts are often viewed as simply being column charts turned on their sides, there is a particular bar chart that does use time values on the x-axis. It is a **Gantt chart**, which shows a project schedule where each bar represents a component or task within the project. The breakdown of tasks is useful for scheduling. Gantt charts are commonly used with project management. Gantt charts can be complex, showing start times, end times, the sequence of tasks, and people assigned to each task. A basic Gantt chart can be created that is informative and helps a team successfully complete a project.

To Create a Bar Chart

a. Click the **Gantt worksheet tab**, and then select the range **A4:D9** to include both the data and the labels.

b. Click the **Insert tab**, click **Bar** in the Charts group, and then under 2-D Bar click the **Stacked Bar**.

c. Click the **Layout tab** on the Chart Tools contextual tab, and then click the **Chart Name** text box in the Properties group. Name the chart Gantt, and then press Enter.

d. Click any **blue data bar** within the chart corresponding with the Series "Start Date" so it is selected. Right-click a blue data bar, and then choose **Format Data Series**. Select **Fill**, and then choose the **No Fill** option.

e. Click **Border Color** in the left pane, and then choose the **No Line** option.

f. On the Chart Tools Layout tab, click the **Chart Elements** arrow, and then choose **Vertical (Category) Axis**.

g. In the Axis Options of the Format Axis dialog box, click the **Categories in reverse order** check box, and then click **Close**.

h. On the Chart Tools Layout tab, click the **Charts Elements** arrow, and then choose **Plot Area**. On the top of the Plot Area, click the **upper-right corner**, and then resize the plot area down so there is room for the dates, which are now on the top of the chart area, to be displayed correctly when the following steps are applied.

i. On the Chart Tools Layout tab, click the **Charts Elements** drop-down list, choose **Horizontal (Value) Axis**, then click **Format Selection**.

j. In Axis Options in the Format Axis dialog box, for the Minimum, select the **Fixed** option, and then change to 41400. For the Maximum, select Fixed and change to 41500. This component will be explained in further detail later in the chapter.

k. In Axis Options, for the Major Unit, select the **Fixed** option, and then change 200 to 50.

l. Select **Alignment**, and then change the custom angle to -50 degrees so the dates can be seen. Click **Close**.

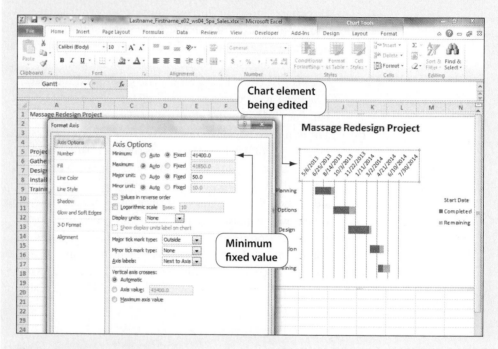

Figure 4 Formatting a bar chart's axis

m. With the chart still selected, click the **border edge** of the chart (not the corner), and then drag so the top-left corner is over cell A11.

n. Click the **bottom-right corner**, and resize the chart until the bottom-right corner is over cell G29. Click **Save**.

The resulting Gantt chart depicts the time for each task in the project. For each bar, the task is set up with the amount completed and the amount that is remaining. The tasks are staggered to show the relation of each task to the other.

Scatter Charts

Scatter charts, also called scatter plots, are a particular type of chart that convey the relationship between two numeric variables. This type of chart is very common as a statistical tool depicting the correlation between the two variables. The standard format is to have the x-axis data on the far-left column and the y-axis data in a column on the right side.

The data for a scatter plot could be categorical, such as survey response and age. This can provide some knowledge for analysis, but it can also be confusing when you first see the resultant chart, as shown in Figure 5.

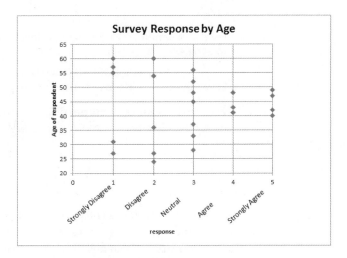

Figure 5 Categorical scatter plot

More typical is having the two sets of data being on the line of a continuum, such as age and the time the person has been on Facebook, as shown in Figure 6. With this chart, the data is on a continuum along the x-axis and y-axis rather than in categories. For the spa, the managers have data from a survey showing the requested temperature of the room used for massages and the age of the customer. With this data, you would have a wider range of temperatures and of ages, producing a more traditional scatter plot. This data may reveal important information as to what temperature is typically requested by different age groups.

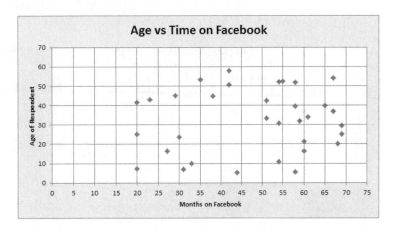

Figure 6 Scatter plot with continuous data

To Create a Scatter Chart

a. Click the **Survey worksheet tab** to make it active, and then select the range **A4:B55** to include the data and labels for Age and Temp Request.

b. Click the **Insert tab**, click **Scatter** in the Charts group, and then click **Scatter with only Markers**.

c. With the chart still selected, click the **border edge** of the chart (not the corner), and then drag to move it to the right of the data so the top-left corner is over cell E4.

d. Click the **Chart Tools Layout tab** and in the Chart Elements drop-down list, select the **Vertical (Value) Axis**, and then click the **Format Selection** button.

e. For the Minimum, click the **Fixed** option, and then change the value for the minimum from 0 to **60**. Click **Close**.

Notice the resulting scatter plot has a slight upward trend as the age of the customer increases. This knowledge may lead to decisions that help provide better customer service.

f. Click the **bottom-right corner** of the chart, and then resize the chart until the bottom-right corner is over cell L20. Click **Save** 🖫.

Area Charts

An **area chart** is a variation of a stacked line chart that emphasizes the magnitude of change over time and visually depicts a trend. The area chart stacks a set of data series and color-izes each area that is created. This type of chart has a nice visual characteristic because each colored layer changes, growing or shrinking, as it moves across time periods. Thus, with an area chart, the x-axis is typically a time sequence. The area chart could also use categories instead of time on the x-axis where each layer again is showing the individual contribution to the area; thus, it is a quantitative chart that shows growth or change in totals.

To Create an Area Chart

a. Click the **Product_Data worksheet tab**, and then select the range **A3:I13** to include the data and labels.

b. Click the **Insert tab**, click **Area** in the Charts group, and then under 2-D Area click **Stacked Area**.

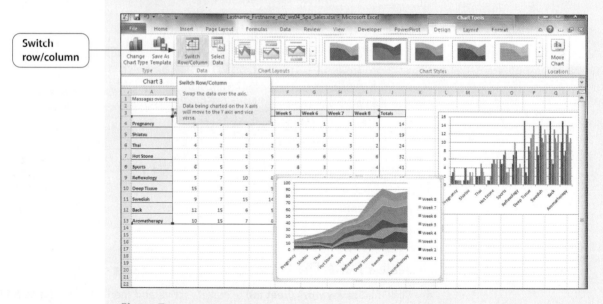

Figure 7 Stacked area chart

c. Click the **Design tab**, and then click **Switch Row/Column** in the Data group so the data will have the weeks as the x-axis scale.

d. If necessary, click the **Design tab** on the Chart Tools contextual tab, and then click **Move Chart** in the Location group.

e. Click the **Object in** option. In the **Object in** drop-down list, select **Massage**, and then click **OK**.

f. With the chart still selected, click along the **border edge** of the chart (not the corner), and then drag to move the chart so the top-left corner is over cell A1.

g. Click the **bottom-right corner**, and then resize the chart so the bottom-right corner is over cell H16.

h. Click **Save** .

Quick Reference / Chart Selection Guide

The common types of charts and their usage are listed below:

1. Pie—Great for comparing parts of a whole
2. Line—Shows changes within a data series; used a lot with time as the x-axis
3. Column—Compares data vertically; can incorporate a time element and groups
4. Bar—Compares data horizontally; stacked bar can show progress, growth
5. Scatter—Used for correlations, exploring the relationship between two variables
6. Area—Used to highlight areas showing growth over time or for categories; a variation of a line chart

Chart Layouts, Styles, and Data

While the default chart settings are pleasant visually, you can still improve the look and feel of the chart. The chart layouts are clustered on the Design tab within the Chart Tools, in the Chart Layouts group. Excel provides a great deal of variety in arranging the components on a chart. This includes placement of the titles and legends as well as the display of information such as the data point values.

Chart styles are a variation of chart layouts. Where chart layouts focus on location of components, styles focus more on the color coordination and effects of the components. The chart styles are located on the Design tab within the Chart Tools group of tabs, in the Chart Styles group. The choices mix color options with shadows and 3-D effects to create a variety of templates. You can also start with a template then adapt it for individual tastes.

Chart data is the underlying data for the chart and labels. There can be many reasons for modifying data, and it can be accomplished through various methods. For example, if the data needs to be swapped between the data points and the axis data, you can use the Ribbon.

One helpful component of creating charts in Excel is that you may create the chart and then realize a need to correct some data errors. Because the chart is tied to data on the spreadsheet, changes are automatically reflected in the linked chart. This is extremely useful if you have a model that is using some calculations that are then used in a chart. You can do what-if analysis by changing the inputs and see the corresponding changes on the chart.

A second problem is when the chart has too much information, making it difficult to get a clear picture. The initial charts may guide you to look at a smaller subset of data rather than all the data at once. The line chart on the Product_Data worksheet is one that is pretty chaotic, and it should be broken down a bit so it uses less data.

A third problem can occur when creating a chart and then discovering a need to add additional data to the chart. If the new data is adjacent to the existing data, it is a simple process to expand the existing data series. This is achieved by resizing the borders around the data series after activating the chart. If the data is on another sheet or location, it is advisable to relocate the new data so it is adjacent to the current data to simplify resizing the current data series borders.

To Work with Layouts, Styles, and Data

a. Click the **Product_Data worksheet tab**, and then click the **border edge** of the column chart. The data is overwhelming with eight weeks and ten types of massages.

b. With the chart selected, click the **bottom-right edge** of the blue border that surrounds the range B4:I13, and then drag it so it is over **B4:E7**. This reduces the types of massages to four, and reduces the weeks from eight to four.

c. Click the **Massage worksheet tab**, and then click the **border edge** of the area chart (inside the chart border). It may help visually to reduce the amount of data used. However, the data is on another sheet so a different method needs to be used to adjust the data set.

d. If necessary, click the **Design tab**, and then click **Select Data**. In the Chart data range box, select **I**, type **E** so the range will be =Product_Data!$B$3:$E$13, and then click **OK**. Click **Save** 🖫.

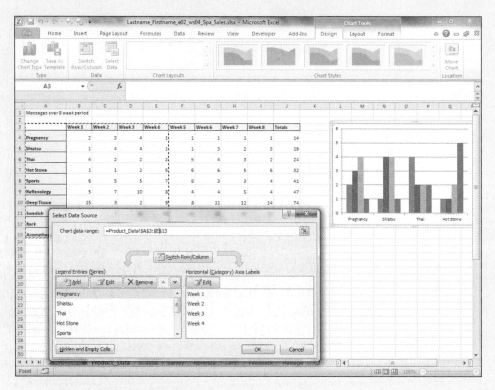

Figure 8 Select data source

e. Click **Save** 🖫.

Laying Out a Chart

As you have seen, a chart can help answer questions or may even generate more questions. This helps move toward the understanding of information, which can also lead to better decision making. Creating these initial charts to explore data is quick, efficient, and informs the user.

When presenting a chart to others, the context of the chart is of utmost importance. Without context, your audience will try to guess the context. You need to provide meaning.

Providing context means providing textual guidance to the audience. The audience will see the pie chart, but you need to inform them more about the data. This includes putting in titles, labels, and any miscellaneous objects that provide textual guidance. These components are found on the Layout tab within the Chart Tools.

Inserting Objects

If you work for a company, it would be useful to insert the company logo into any chart that is used outside the company. After all, marketing occurs everywhere. It may also be useful to use images to help convey the tone of the presentation. This can be accomplished with an image inserted into the chart.

To Insert Objects into a Chart

a. Click the **MassagePie worksheet tab** containing the pie chart.

b. Select the **chart**, click the **Layout tab**, and then click **Picture** in the Insert group. In the Insert Picture dialog box, click the **disk drive** in the left pane where your student data files are located, navigate through the folder structure, and then click **e02_ws04_ Couple**. Click **Insert**.

c. With the picture as the active object, click the **Format tab**, change the Shape Height to 1", and then press [Enter]. Drag the image to position it in the bottom-left corner of the chart.

d. Click the **edge** of the chart to select the chart and deselect the picture. Click the **Layout tab**, click the **Shapes** button in the Insert group, and then under Basic Shapes click **Oval**. Click once in the **top-right corner** of the chart area. Type Massage Distribution into the shape.

e. With the shape still selected, click the **Format tab**, click the **More** [▾] button in the Shape Styles group to display the Shape Styles gallery. Click **Subtle Effect – Black, Dark 1** from the first column, fourth row down. You decide you do not like this style and undo it by pressing [Ctrl]+[Z].

f. If the border surrounding the shape is a dashed line, click the surrounding border once so the border line surrounding the shape is solid. Click the **Home tab**, click the **Font Size arrow** in the Font group, and then select **16** to change the font size.

g. Click the **Format tab**, and then change the Shape Height in the Size group to 1" and the **Shape Width** to 2". Press [Enter].

h. Click the **border** of the shape, and then drag the shape to the top-right corner of the chart area. Click the **edge** of the chart sheet to deselect the shape. Click **Save** [💾].

Working with Labels

Labels are another crucial element needed to provide context in charts. The labels include the chart title and axes titles, the legend, and the labels for the data. All these elements should work cohesively to convey a complete picture of what the chart is trying to convey to the audience.

Titles for the Chart and Axes

Chart and axes titles are input easily through the Layout tab within the Chart Tools contextual tabs. The Labels group has all the elements for inserting and positioning the labels. Labels can be set within the chart or they can reference cells on the spreadsheet for easy updating.

To Work with Titles

a. Click the **Revenue worksheet tab**, and then click the **line chart** to display the set of Chart Tools tabs. Click the **Layout tab**, click **Chart Title** in the Labels group, and then click **Above Chart**.

b. Select the **Chart Title text**, if necessary, and type Revenue – June 2012. Press Enter to apply the changes to the title above the chart.

c. On the Layout tab, click the **Axis Titles** button in the Labels group, point to **Primary Horizontal Axis Title**, and then click **Title Below Axis**.

d. With the x-axis title selected, type Date, and then click the **edge** of the chart to apply the title change and deselect the component.

e. On the **Layout tab**, click the **Axis Titles** button in the Labels group, point to **Primary Vertical Axis Title**, and then click **Vertical Title**.

f. With the y-axis title selected, type Revenue. Notice the typed text appears in the formula bar, but the component still displays the text **Axis Title**. Press Enter, or alternatively click the **edge** of the chart to apply the title change.

g. Click the **Gantt worksheet tab**, and then click the **border edge** of the bar chart below the line charts to make it the active chart.

h. Click the **Layout tab**, click **Chart Title** in the Labels group, and then click **Above Chart**. Notice the title is the active component.

i. Click in the **formula bar**, type =, click cell **A1**, and then press Enter. The bar chart now reflects the text contained in cell A1 on the worksheet. Click **Save** .

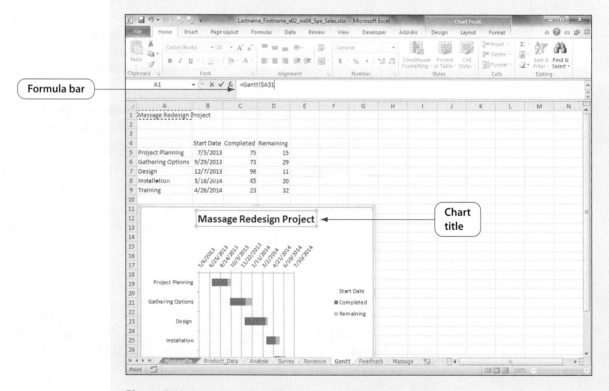

Figure 9 Formula bar with chart title

Sales &
Marketing

You are presented with a chart titled "2012 Sales Report" and the x-axis is showing 20, 30, 40, and so on for the scale. What is this report depicting? Is it the number of sales transactions—number sold—or the revenue for 2012? Are the 20, 30, and 40 the actual numbers or in hundreds or thousands? What context should there be to make certain the audience knows? Should the term "Sales" ever be used without qualifying whether it is sales revenue or sales volume?

Working with the Legend and Labeling the Data

The legend is an index within a chart that provides information about the data. With some charts the legend is automatic and adds context. With other charts, such as pie charts, it is possible to incorporate the legend information beside each pie slice. When the parts are labeled on the chart, the legend is not needed and can be removed. This is accomplished by clicking on the Legend button on the Layout tab and choosing None. If the legend is missing, go to the same location and simply add the legend to the chart using any of the various options listed.

Labels can also be added alongside the data on the chart. This is quite informative as it moves the information from a legend to the data. This can be a visually useful addition. The data labels can be added, moved, or removed through the Data Labels button on the Layout tab.

To Work with Legends and Labeling

a. Click the **MassagePie worksheet tab**, and then, if necessary, click the **border edge** of the chart to display the Chart Tools contextual tabs.

b. Click the **Layout tab**, click **Legend** in the Labels group, and then click **None**. Notice that the legend disappears from the chart and the chart enlarges to fit the space.

c. Click the **Layout tab**, click **Data Labels**, and then click **More Data Label Options**. The Format Data Labels dialog box is displayed.

d. Under Label Options, click the **Category Name** and **Percentage** check boxes. Leave the other options **Value** and **Show Leader Lines** selected, and then click **Close**. Click outside of the chart. Notice the data labels are now showing the massage type, the value, and the percentage represented by each pie slice. Click **Save** 🖫.

Modifying Axes

The x-axis and y-axis scales are automatically created through a mathematical algorithm within Excel. However, sometimes the scale needs to be modified as you have already seen. For example, when the numbers are spread out a bit, a significant gap can exist near 0. In this case, you can modify the scale to start at a more appropriate number instead of 0—the standard minimum value for Excel.

Additionally, when you need to compare two or more charts, the scales must be consistent. Any time you put charts side by side, you need to also make sure your x-axis and y-axis scales are the same. Your audience may not realize otherwise and make incorrect assumptions or decisions.

Lastly, the axis data could be jammed together, making it difficult to read. In this situation, you would be able to modify the layout of the scale by adjusting the alignment of the data. The data on the axis can be vertical, horizontal, or even placed at an angle.

For these elements and more, you work through the Layout tab in the Axes group. Choose the Axes button, and at the bottom of all the gallery menus for Labels and Axes buttons, there is always a choice for more options. These additional options will provide a dialog box that offers more choices beyond the most common options offered on the gallery menu, options such as formatting the background fill, border color, styles, and number formats, as well as many others.

To Work with Axes

a. Click the **Feedback worksheet tab**, and then click cell **K2**. The heights of the columns vary across the chart but may show the data better sorted. On the Home tab, click **Sort & Filter**, and then click **Sort Smallest to Largest**.

b. Click the **border edge** of the column chart. Click the **Legend** to select it, and then press Delete.

c. On the Layout tab, click **Chart Title**, and then click **Above Chart**. Type Massage Satisfaction Score, and then press Enter.

d. Click the **y-axis vertical numbers**, so that component is selected. Looking at the y-axis scale, the scale goes up to 100, and the lowest bar column is around 70. The minimum scale can be changed to enhance the different average ratings.

e. Click the **Layout tab**, click the **Chart Elements** arrow, check that the Vertical (Value) Axis is the current selection, and then click **Format Selection**. For the minimum click the **Fixed** option, and then change the value to 50.

SIDE NOTE
The Quick Right-Click
Remember, if you select a component, such as the y-axis, right-click over the selected area and choose a format option from the menu to quickly get the dialog box that pertains to the selected component.

SIDE NOTE
Update the Fixed Option
The Fixed option within a chart eliminates the automatic adjustment of the scaling on the x- or y-axis. If you change the data, you may need to adjust the Fixed minimum or maximum for the scale.

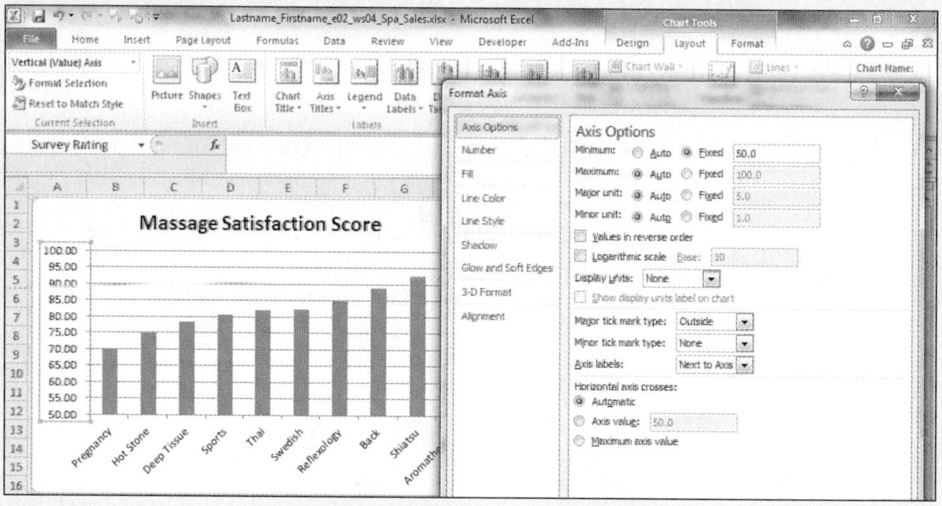

Figure 10 Format Axis options

f. Click **Close**, click on a cell to deselect the chart, then click **Save**.

Changing Gridlines

Gridlines are the lines that go across charts to help gauge the size of the bars, columns, or data lines. In Excel, the default is to display the major gridlines (the gridlines at the designated label values) and not to display the minor gridlines (the gridlines between the label values). If the chart is a line or column chart, it puts in the horizontal major gridlines while the bar chart puts in vertical major gridlines. The default is a good starting point, but personal preferences can dictate which lines to display.

The Format Axis dialog box is handy for manually setting the axis options for consistency between a set of charts. Under the Axis Options, the default Excel setting is Auto. To change and adjust these units, change the Auto option to Fixed, then adjust the corresponding fixed value. If the source data for the chart is changed, the scale will remain fixed (and will not automatically be updated); therefore, any fixed values may also need to be reevaluated as source data changes.

To Work with Gridlines

a. Click the **Revenue worksheet tab**, and then click the **border edge** of the line chart.

b. Click the **Layout tab**, click the **Gridlines** button, point to **Primary Vertical Gridlines**, and then click **More Primary Vertical Gridlines Options**. The Format Major Gridlines dialog box is displayed.

c. If necessary, click **Line Color**, and then click **Solid line**. Click the **Color arrow**, and then under Theme Colors, click **Dark Blue, Text 2**.

d. Click **Close**.

e. If necessary, click the **Layout tab**, click **Axes** in the Axes group, point to **Primary Horizontal Axis**, and then click **More Primary Horizontal Axis Options** to open the Format Axis dialog box.

f. On the left side, click **Alignment** to display the Alignment options.

g. Under the Text layout section, click in the **Custom angle** box, and then type **-55** degrees.

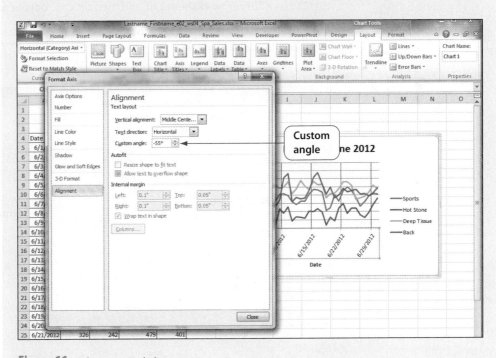

Figure 11 Adjust vertical alignment

h. Click **Close**.

Analysis with Trendlines

Excel has a few tools that can help analyze data within a chart. The Analysis group is on the Layout tab within the Chart Tools contextual tabs. One of the most common analysis tools is the trendline. A **trendline** is a line that uses current data to show a trend or general direction of the data. Data, however, can have a variety of patterns. For scatter plots that explore how two variables interact, a linear trend may be seen. For example, as the price for Oreo cookies drop, we would expect sales of milk to increase because everyone knows a glass of milk is the perfect companion for dunking cookies.

If data fluctuates or varies a great deal, it may be more desirable to use a moving average trendline. Instead of creating a straight line based on all the current data, the moving average trendline uses the average of small subsets of data to set short trend segments over time. The moving average trendline will curve and adjust as the data moves up or down.

The trend or pattern of the data may suggest or predict what will happen in the future. For linear trends, the predicted data can be charted using the Linear Forecast Analysis feature and the current trend of the data.

The trendline for the Survey worksheet data indicates older customers may desire a warmer room than younger customers. This may lead the staff to adjust the room temperature prior to a customer arriving. The staff could predict the desired temperature based on the age of the customer. The data suggests a correlation between age and room temperature. This could help improve customer satisfaction. Again, you may want to consider other demographics—characteristics—of the customers that allow for providing a customized and personalized service that will build customer loyalty and repeat business. It is easier to retain existing customers than find new customers.

To Insert a Trendline

a. Click the **Survey worksheet tab**, and then click the **border edge** of the chart to select it.

b. Click the **Layout tab**, click **Trendline** in the Analysis group, and then click **Linear Trendline**. Click **Save** 🖫.

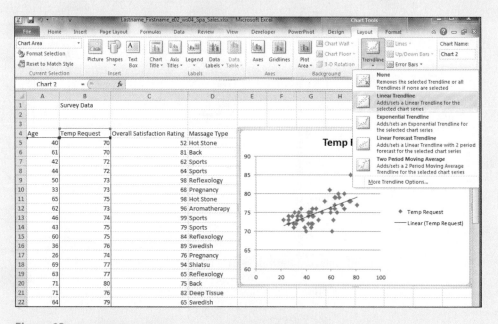

Figure 12 Insert linear trendline

Quick Reference — Chart Trendlines

The following is a listing of the types of trendlines available within Excel.

1. Linear trendline—Adds/sets a linear trendline for the selected chart series, like weather temperature and sales of iced tea
2. Exponential trendline—Adds/sets an exponential trendline for the selected chart series, such as financial growth of an investment
3. Linear Forecast trendline—Adds/sets a linear trendline with a two-period forecast for the selected chart series, like predicting sales growth for the next two months
4. Two-Period Moving Average trendline—Adds/sets a two-period moving average trendline for the selected chart series, such as showing the trends of daily weather temperature

Real World Advice — The Timing of Trends

Sales & Marketing

Trends show patterns over time. When looking at hourly sales at a restaurant, it becomes important to look at more than one day's worth of hourly sales to obtain a better understanding of the trend. Charting multiple days reveals any trends and consistent patterns. For example, maybe it is discovered that on Friday and Saturday hourly sales are consistently higher than other days of the week. This would suggest a need for scheduling more people to work on those days. If only one day had been charted, or even just one week, the overall weekly trends may have been missed or interpreted incorrectly.

Editing and Formatting Charts

When formatting a chart it is important to have a plan in mind as to the overall layout and look and feel. With a well thought-out plan, it will be easy to apply the desired adjustments to the components with regard to position, color, and emphasis. Typically, you can either create a unique layout or modify one of Excel's many layouts. Either way, being able to make formatting changes is easy and a very useful and powerful way to convey information. In this section, you will explore various ways to format a chart.

Colorizing Objects

Working some color into charts can be helpful from a marketing perspective. To change the colors of objects within the chart, simply select the item and use the Format tab within the Chart Tools contextual tabs. Excel offers options that allow changing the interior color as well as the border color. When examining the properties of any component within a Properties dialog box for that component, you will typically see options on the left side indicating Fill, Line Color, Line Style, and so on. These are formatting and color options. Keep in mind, while it is possible to spruce up charts with color, it is also possible to overdo it.

To Work with Formatting and Color

a. Click the **Revenue worksheet tab**, and click the **border edge** to select the line chart.

b. Click the **Format tab**, and change the **Shape Height** in the Size group to 4" and the **Shape Width** to 6". Press Enter.

c. On the Format tab verify that the Chart Elements box in the Current Selection group is displaying Chart Area. If necessary, click the **Chart Elements arrow**, and then click **Chart Area**.

d. Click the **Shape Fill** button in the Shape Styles group, and then select **Olive Green, Accent 3, Lighter 80%**.

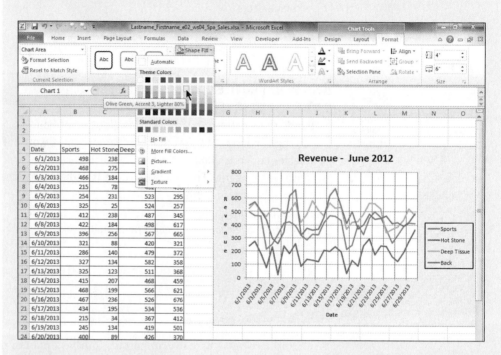

Figure 13 Shape fill with color

e. Click the **Chart Elements arrow** in the Current Selection group, and then click **Legend**.

f. On the **Format tab**, click the **Shape Outline** button in the Shape Styles group, and then click **Black, Text 1** to apply a black border to the legend.

g. On the **Format tab**, click the **Shape Outline** button again, point to **Weight**, and then click the **1½ pt** weight line. Click **Save** 💾.

Working with Text

Whether the text is in a text box, title, legend, or axis scale you can format the text using one of two methods. For some stylish formatting of text, use the Format tab and select the buttons from the Ribbon. This is where you would select WordArt Styles or Shape Styles. However, to change font characteristics such as font type or size, you can do this from the Home tab or by right-clicking the selected text and using the Mini toolbar options.

To Format Text Within a Chart

a. Click the **Survey worksheet tab**, and then click the **chart title** once to make it active. Verify the border surrounding the title component is a solid line and not a dashed line. If necessary, click the **title border edge** again to make the surrounding border solid.

b. Type Temperature Survey, and then press Enter to apply the change.

c. With the title still selected, click the **Format tab**, click the **Text Fill arrow** in the WordArt Styles group, and then click **Dark Red**.

d. Click the **Home tab**, click the **Font arrow**, and then scroll as necessary to locate and click **Garamond**. Click **Save** 🖫.

Exploding Pie Charts

The traditional pie chart is a pie with all the slices together. Preset options offer a pie chart with a slice pulled slightly away from the main pie or you can manually move a slice outward creating an exploded pie chart. This technique allows for highlighting a particular part of the pie. To explode a pie slice, simply click to select the correct pie slice and then drag it away from the rest of the pie.

To Explode a Pie Slice in a Pie Chart

a. Click the **TableUse worksheet tab**, and then click the **pie** in the chart to select it. Notice the circle handles at the corners of all the pie slices.

b. Click the **green pie slice** so the handles are only around that one slice.

c. With the one slice selected, click and drag to move the slice to the left away from the pie, and then release the mouse button. The green slice is now separated and highlighted as an important component within the chart.

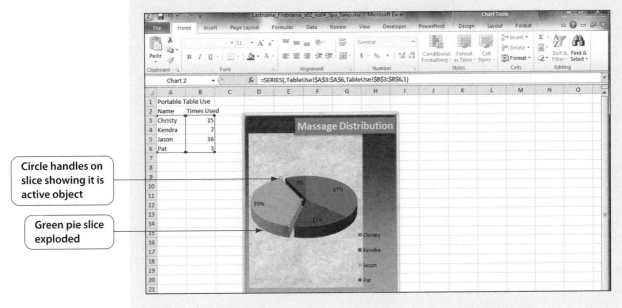

Figure 14 Explode pie slice

3-D Charts and Rotation of Charts

The 3-D effect and rotation of charts is something that should be used conservatively. The effect can be done well, or it can be abused, resulting in a chart that goes overboard and distracts from the intended message. You can choose the 3-D effect when starting to develop a chart. Additionally, options are available to rotate the 3-D effect, giving the chart a crisp, distinctive look. The 3-D Format and rotation options are found in the Format dialog box. The 3-D format can be applied to a variety of objects. The 3-D Rotation setting is intended for the chart area only.

The pie chart doesn't have a lot of marketing appeal currently. Adding some depth to the pie will help accentuate the graph. Then, you will apply formatting to add a little pop to the chart.

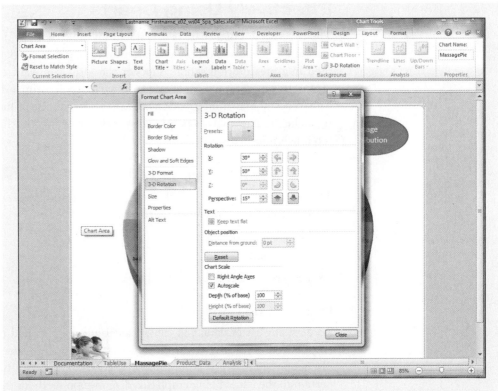

Figure 15 3-D rotation options

The 3-D options can be reset as needed by clicking the **Reset** button in the Format Chart Area dialog box. The 3-D effect becomes more dramatic if you include some color changes to the chart area, particularly to the walls and floor.

e. Click the **Layout tab**, click the **Chart Elements arrow** in the Current Selection group, and then click **Series 1**.

f. Click **Format Selection** in the Current Selection group to display the Format Data Series dialog box. Select 3-D Format, and change the Bevel Top setting to be **Cool Slant**.

g. Click **Close**, and then press Esc to deselect the chart.

h. Click **Save** 💾.

Quick Reference Formatting Options for Chart Objects

Below are format options for charts and their descriptions:

1. Number—Format data as currency, date, time, and so on.
2. Fill—Fill the background of a component with a color, picture, or pattern.
3. Border Color—Set the color of the border for a component.
4. Border Styles—Set the thickness and type of border for a component.
5. Shadow—Add shadowing effect to a component.
6. Glow and Soft Edges—Add glow and edge effects to a component.
7. 3-D Format—Add 3-D effects to component.
8. Alignment—Align text direction for a component, such as left, top, vertical, or horizontal.

Effectively Using Charts

The effectiveness of a chart is dependent on the chart type, the layout, and formatting of the data. Charts should provide clarity and expand the understanding of the data. Charts used in a presentation should support the ideas you want to convey. The charts should highlight key components about an issue or topic being addressed in the presentation. Providing too much information on a chart can confuse or hide the issue being discussed. It can be difficult to get a point across if the chart is confusing, cluttered, or packed with too much information.

Strategic Statements with Charts

The same data can be viewed through various perspectives, emphasizing different parts of information. Charts typically do three things:

- Support or refute assertions
- Clarify information
- Help the audience understand trends

Emphasizing Data

As with any set of data, you can reasonably expect to find multiple ideas that could be emphasized. Typically within a business, one to three key issues might be chosen for discussion. The idea is to eliminate any extraneous data from the chart that does not pertain to the issues being emphasized. Common methods can be employed to emphasize the idea in the chart. When using a single chart, highlight a particular data set within the chart to help focus attention to a key point. Depending on the chart type, the emphasis may be depicted differently as shown in Figure 16.

Single Chart Types	Common Emphasis Methods
Pie chart	Explode a pie slice
Bar/Column	Use an emphasizing color on the bar/column
Line	Line color, weight, and marker size
Scatter	Adding a trendline

Figure 16   Emphasis methods for single chart types

Another way of emphasizing information on a chart is to create a chart that uses two types of charts. This is useful when you have a clustered column chart, where data has been grouped in columns but you also want to show the average of each group. Rather than have the average of the group shown as yet another column in the cluster, it is possible to have the averages of each cluster depicted as a line chart that overlays the clustered columns. This is an effective method for comparing clusters of data. The technique requires combining all the data together into one chart, then taking a specific subset of data and converting it to a second chart type.

To Combine Two Chart Types

a. Click the **Product_Data worksheet tab**, click cell **K3**, and then type Average. Click cell **J3**, click the **Home tab**, in the Clipboard group click **Format Painter**, and then click cell **K3** to apply the same cell border formatting to the new cell heading.

b. Click cell **K4**, and then type =AVERAGE(B4:I4). Press Enter.

c. Click cell **K4**, and then double-click the **AutoFill handle** to extend the formula in K4 down through **K13**.

d. Select the range **A3:I13**, then hold down Ctrl and select range **K3:K13** so both ranges are selected, excluding the totals column.

e. Click the **Insert tab**, click **Column** in the Charts group, and then click **Clustered Column**.

f. Click the **Format tab**, select the **Shape Height** box, and then type 4". Select the **Shape Width** box, and then type 7". Press Enter. Notice on the chart that the last series in the legend is Average. Click the **border edge** of the chart, and then drag to reposition the chart so the top-left corner is over cell L15.

g. Click the **Format tab**, click the **Chart Elements arrow** in the Current Selection group, and then click **Series** "**Average**" to select that series as the active component within the chart.

h. Click the **Design tab**, click the **Change Chart Type** button in the Type group, click **Line**, and then click the **Line with Markers**. Click **OK**.

i. Click the **Format tab**, click the **Chart Elements arrow** in the Current Selection group, and then click **Series** "**Average**." Click **Format Selection** in the Current Selection group to display the Format Data Series dialog box.

j. In the Format Data Series dialog box, click **Line Color**, click **Solid line**, click the **Color arrow**, and then click **Black, Text 1**.

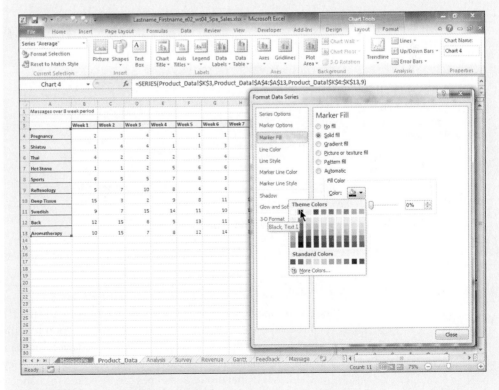

Figure 17 Combining two chart types

k. In the Format Data Series dialog box, click **Line Style**, and then in the **Width** box, select **2.25 pt** and type **3.5**. Click **Close**. Notice the Average data for the clusters is clearly shown with a thick black line. The line representing the average for each cluster helps clarify the information trend. Click **Save** 💾.

Sparklines

Sparklines are small charts that are embedded into a spreadsheet, usually beside the data to facilitate quick analysis of trends. A sparkline can be used within a spreadsheet to give an immediate visual trend analysis, and it adjusts as the source data changes.

The sparkline can graphically depict the data over time through either a line chart or a bar chart that accumulates the data. For example, for the spa, the number of massages given each week, shown by massage type, could have sparklines that show the trend over time.

To Work with Sparklines

a. On the Product_Data worksheet, right-click **column A**, and then click **Insert**. Right-click the new **column A**, and then click **Column Width**. In the **Column width** box type **25** to expand the width setting. Click **OK**.

b. Select the cell range **A4:A13**. This is the target cell range to create a set of sparklines showing the trend over time for each of the massage types.

c. Click the **Insert tab**, and then in the Sparklines group click the **Line** button to display the Create Sparklines dialog box.

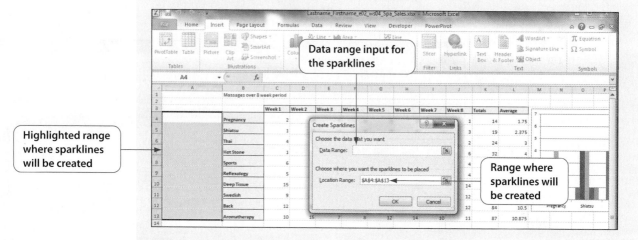

Figure 18 Creating a sparkline

d. In the Create Sparklines dialog box, in the Data Range input box, click **Collapse Dialog Box** 📊, and then select the range **C4:J13**.

e. To the right of the input box, click **Expand Dialog Box** 📊, and then click **OK**.

The Sparklines appear in column A and display the trend over the eight-week period for each massage type. The sparklines are grouped together by default so if any one cell in the group is selected, an outline is displayed surrounding the entire set—in this case the cell range A4:A13. When changes are applied, they will be applied for all the sparklines in that group. Sparklines can be edited to change colors or to display markers on the highest or lowest points.

f. If necessary, select the range **A4:A13**.

g. Click the **Design tab**, click the **Sparkline Color** button in the Style group, and click **Dark Red** to change the line color.

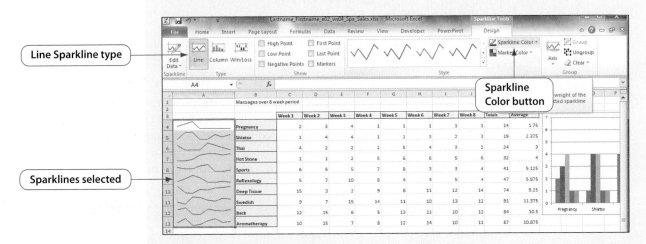

Figure 19 Sparkline Tools Design tab

h. Click the **Design tab**, and then click to select **Markers** in the Show group to display the data markers on the sparklines. Click **Save** 🖫.

Quick Reference / Working with Sparklines

Using the following process will help in the development of sparklines:

1. Select any cell within the Sparklines group to display the Sparkline Tools.
2. Ungroup sparklines using the Ungroup button on the Design tab.
3. Group sparklines using the Group button on the Design tab.
4. Change colors using the Sparkline Color button on the Design tab.
5. Choose to show high or low points using the Show group options on the Design tab.

Data Bars, Color Scales, and Icon Sets

Data bars are graphic components that are overlaid onto data in worksheet cells. They are a mixture of conditional formatting, sparklines, and charts. In addition to data bars, there are color scales and icon sets that work the same way. All three are visual cues that aid in understanding and interpreting data. The graphic component is added to a cell and interprets a set of data in a range giving color codes or images that help a spreadsheet user gain a quick understanding of the data.

These Excel components are found on the Home tab in the Styles group as gallery menu options on the Conditional Formatting button. The data bars can be applied as a one-color solid fill or a gradient fill from left to right as the numerical value gets bigger. With the Color Scales, the color shifts as the numerical values change. A low score could be red, while a high score could be green. The icon sets provide images to indicate the good/bad or positive/negative rating to the value. This technique can be employed with scores, ratings, or other data where the user would want to do a visual inspection to see a relative scale on the data. With the spa, the survey data includes an overall satisfaction rating. Using these visual cues would enable a manager to glance through the data and quickly distinguish the lowest or highest scores.

To Work with Data Bars

a. Click the **Survey worksheet tab**, and then select the cell range **C5:C55** to select the **Overall Satisfaction Rating** data. Since the data represents a collection of scores, where low scores are bad and high scores are good, it would be useful to have a color scale.

b. Click the **Home tab**, click **Conditional Formatting** in the Styles group, point to **Color Scales**, and then click **Green – Yellow – Red Color Scale.** Click outside the range.

Notice the lower numbers are red while the high numbers are green. Using this technique it is possible to scan through the data to get a sense that there are not many low satisfaction scores and there is a higher incidence of high scores.

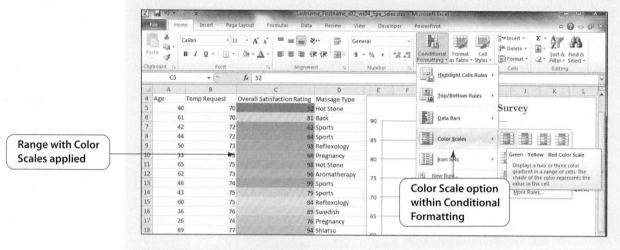

Figure 20 Color scales on data

c. Click **Save** 🖫.

Recognizing and Correcting Confusing Charts

The process of working with and creating visually appealing charts with clear messages involves recognizing when you have a confusing chart. It is possible to have too much information, ambiguous information, or even inappropriate chart types for the data. Irene has included a worksheet that contains questions the managers want to explore with charts. Irene has requested that you take a look at the charts a previous staff member started. They need to be updated and set up as a set of coordinated charts that allow for flexibility in analysis.

The Sales column chart was supposed to address the question of highlighting massage data over the eight-week period. However, there is so much information that it is difficult to get a clear picture of any particular highlights. Additionally, it appears the scaling is off. Examining the data shows the chart includes the totals—making the y-axis scale ineffective. Changing this and focusing on only a few weeks and a few massage types can accentuate some details about the data. It was shown earlier how a subset of data can be used to narrow the scope of data depicted in a chart. Another method will accomplish the same thing while allowing even more flexibility. If a filter is applied to the data it will be possible to change which massage types are shown in the set of charts.

To Correct an Overloaded Chart

a. Click the **Analysis worksheet tab**, and then select **A5** so one cell within the data is selected. Click the **Home tab**, in the Editing group click the **Sort & Filter** icon, and then select **Filter**.

b. On cell **A3**, select the drop-down list, and then uncheck **Shiatsu**, **Sports**, and **Swedish**. Click **OK**.

c. Right-click the column chart border, and then select **Format Chart Area**. For the Fill, select **Solid Fill**, and then choose **Dark Blue, Text 2, Lighter 80%** as the Fill Color. Click **Close**.

d. Click the **Layout tab**, click **Chart Title**, and then choose **Above Chart**. Type Sales by Massage Type, and then press Enter.

e. On the Layout tab, click **Axis Titles**, **Primary Vertical Axis Title**, and **Rotated Title**. Type Number of Transactions, and then press Enter.

f. Click the **Format tab**, change the Chart Element to **Chart Area**, then change the Shape Height in the Size group to **4"** and the Shape Width to **6"**. Press Enter.

g. With the chart selected, use the sizing handles of the blue box outlining the chart data to change data in the chart to B7:E12.

h. Click **Save**.

Troubleshooting

If you click on the chart to see the source data associated with the chart and only see some of the data selected with a blue border, a chart component might have been clicked by mistake instead of the full chart area. To get the data set associated with the entire chart, click the Format tab and change the Chart Element to Chart Area. Data associated with the selected component will be highlighted with a colored border.

Correcting a Line Chart

The second analysis question explores sales over time. The line chart shows the time period as the legend rather than the x-axis. The chart did not include all the labels. Additionally, it would help to have a target number of massages integrated into the chart to enhance analysis.

To Correct a Line Chart

a. Click the **border edge** of the Sales line chart below the data to select it.

b. Click the **Design tab**, and then click **Select Data** in the Data group.

c. In the Select Data Source dialog box, under the Horizontal (Category) Axis Labels, click the **Edit** button. The number labels need to be changed to reference the names of the massage types.

d. In the **Axis label range** box, click **Collapse Dialog Box**, and then select the cell range **A4:A13**. Click the **Expand Dialog Box** button, and then click **OK**. This will place the massage type names along the x-axis; however, the desired result would be to switch the legend week labels with the massage types.

e. Still in the Select Data Source dialog box, click the **Switch Row/Column** button to make the legend list the massage types and the x-axis labeled by weeks. Click **OK**.

f. Click the **Format tab**, change the Shape Height in the Size group to 4″ and the Shape Width to 6″. Press Enter.

g. Right-click on the chart border, and then select **Format Chart Area**. For the Fill, select **Solid Fill**, and then choose **Dark Blue, Text 2, Lighter 80%** as the Fill Color. Click **Close**.

h. Click the **Layout** tab, click **Chart Title**, and then choose **Above Chart**. Type Sales Transactions Over Time, and then press Enter.

i. Select cell **A14**, and then type Weekly Target. Select cell **B14**, type 10, and then press Enter. Select **B14** again, and then using the AutoFill Handle, copy that value over to C14:I14.

j. Click the edge of the line chart, and then click the **Layout tab** to ensure the Chart Area is selected in the Chart Elements box. In the source data for the chart, drag the **bottom-right corner** of the blue border in the data area down so it includes row 14 and the range selected is **B4:I14**.

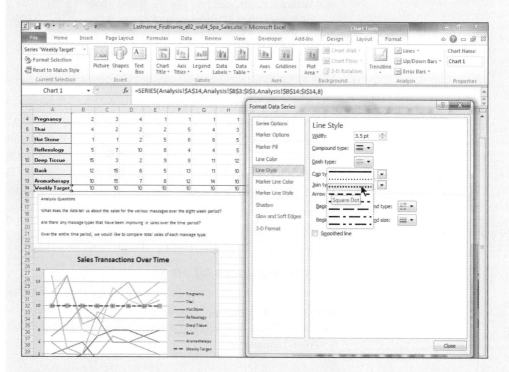

Figure 21 Add target line

k. On the Line chart, click the line for the **Weekly Target data** so that the data series is selected. Click the **Layout tab**, and in the Current Selection group, verify that Series "Weekly Target" is showing in the Chart Elements box, and then click **Format Selection**.

l. For **Line Style**, change the Width to **3.5pt**. Change the Dash Type to the third type, the square dot dashed line.

m. For the **Line Color**, change the color to **Red**. Click **Close**.

n. Click **Save**.

Changing the Chart Type and Legend

Finally, the Sales Comparison chart was an attempt to compare totals by week. The line chart does have totals, but the x-axis is showing the totals for each massage type labeling them numerically since no labels have been set up. Secondly, the chart does not really allow comparison of the massages for the entire time period. A doughnut chart would be more appropriate.

To Change Chart Type and Legend

a. Click the **border edge** of the Total Sales line chart.

b. Click the **Design tab**, click **Change Chart Type** in the Type group, and then under the Pie category click **Pie**. Click **OK**.

c. Click the **Design tab**, and click **Select Data** in the Data group to display the Select Data Source dialog box. Under Horizontal (Category) Axis Labels, click the **Edit** button so the legend can be changed.

d. With the insertion point in the Axis label range input box, select the range **A4:A13** (do not include the weekly target), and then click **OK**. This will put the massage types as the legend. Click **OK** to close the Select Data Source dialog box.

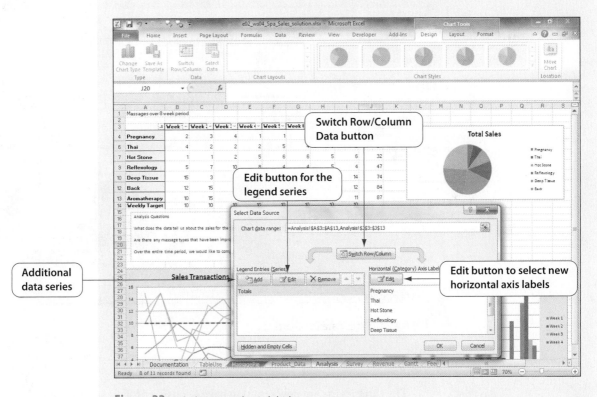

Figure 22 Edit horizontal axis label

e. Click the **Layout tab**, click the **Data Labels** button, and then click **More Data Label Options**.

f. In the Format Data Labels dialog box, under Label Options, click to select **Percentage** so both Value and Percentage are shown (as well as Show Leader Lines). Click **Close**. Press [Esc] to deselect the chart.

The pie chart now allows a comparison of the massage types over the entire time period. By including both the percentage and the value, it provides more complete information for the decision makers.

g. Click the **Format tab**, change the Chart Elements setting to **Chart Area**, then change the Shape Height in the Size group to 4" and the Shape Width to 5". Press ⌷Enter⌷.

h. In the Shape Styles group, select **Shape Fill**, and then choose **Dark Blue, Text 2, Lighter 80%** as the Fill Color.

i. Click the **Title** so it is selected. In the formula bar, type Distribution by Massage Type, and then press ⌷Enter⌷.

j. Arrange the three charts side by side. The upper-left corner of the line chart should be over A24 with the column chart next to it and the pie chart to the right of the column chart.

k. Select the **A3** drop-down list, and then uncheck all the items except for Back, Hot Stone, and Reflexology. Click **OK**.

l. Click **Save** ⌷.

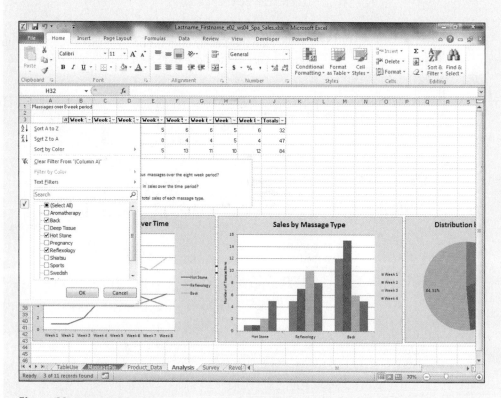

Figure 23 Filter data for charts

The three charts are now set up to have a consistent look and feel. The drop-down filter allows quick analysis of a subset of massage types. The current view of three massages allows detection of a dip in Back massages in weeks three and four even though overall, they have a higher count than some of the other massages. The Hot Stone massages have been going through an increase over the eight weeks. These charts provide more information to the decision maker and may lead to other questions to determine why there was a dip in sales and how this can be prevented in the future. With the filter, it is easy to explore various massage types at one time.

Quick Reference — Common Charting Issues

These are common issues you should try to avoid in the development of charts.

1. Not enough context; users do not understand the chart.
   - Add titles to x-axis and y-axis.
   - Add a chart title that conveys context of time and scope.
   - Add data labels to show percentages or values of chart elements.
2. Too much information is on the chart.
   - Use a subset of the data, rather than all the data.
   - Summarize the data so it is consolidated.
3. Incorrect chart type is used.
   - Choose a type more appropriate, such as a line chart for trends.
4. Chart has issues with readability.
   - Check the color scheme to ensure text is readable.
   - Check font characteristics such as font type or font size.
   - Move data labels, and remove excess information.
   - Resize the overall chart to provide more area to work.
   - Check the color scheme and formatting so it is professional and does not hide chart information or text.
5. Information or labeling is misleading.
   - Check the scaling to ensure it is appropriate and labeled for the correct units.
   - Consider the following wording: Does "Sales" mean the number of transactions or the total revenue?

Preparing to Print and Copy

Printing charts is basically the same as printing any portion of a spreadsheet. If printing a chart sheet, select the chart sheet and go through the normal printing process and adjust print options as you would for a spreadsheet. The chart will be a full-page display. If the chart is on a regular spreadsheet, it will be printed if you choose to print everything on the spreadsheet. In this case, the chart will be the size you developed on the spreadsheet. This is convenient when you want to print some tables or other data along with the chart. Finally, if you want to print just the chart on the spreadsheet, select the chart first, then choose the print option to Print Selected Chart to print only the current chart.

Another useful technique when exploring data through charts is the ability to create static copies of the chart that can be used to compare with later versions. You can, in essence, take a picture of a chart that will not retain the underlying data. Maybe after exploring changes to the chart, a second or third static picture is taken to use for chart comparisons. The process of creating a picture of the chart is to select the chart, copy it, then use the Paste Special option and paste it as a picture. When pasting as a picture, there are multiple picture format options such as a PNG, JPEG, or GIF file.

To Create a Chart Picture

a. Click the **Analysis worksheet tab**, and then click the **border edge** of the Sales by Massage Type column chart.

b. Click the **Home tab**, click **Copy** in the Clipboard group, and then press Esc or click outside the chart (on the worksheet) to deselect the chart.

c. On the Home tab, click the **Paste arrow**, and then click **Paste Special** to display the Paste Special dialog box.

d. Click **Picture (GIF)**, and then click **OK**.

   The picture will be inserted and can be resized or moved as needed. The picture can even be used in another application like Word or PowerPoint if you do not want to link between files.

e. Using the border of the picture, move the picture so the top-left corner is over cell L3, and then resize it so the bottom-right corner is over Q21. It is ready to be used in other applications or compared to other similar charts that are created.

f. Click **Save** 🔲, and then close Excel.

Concept Check

1. Describe a scenario where you would want to use a line chart.

2. You want to compare the revenue that each of your departments has generated as a portion of total revenue. What type of chart would you choose and why?

3. You have transaction data pertaining to three types of gasoline sold at the gas station. List questions that you might explore and the type of chart that would help answer those questions.

4. List the ways in which context for a chart is provided.

5. What ethical issues arise when creating charts?

Key Terms

Area chart 444
Argumentation objective 432
Bar chart 441
Chart sheet 437
Column chart 439
Data bars 461

Data exploration objective 432
Data point 433
Data series 433
Data visualization 432
Gantt chart 441
Hypothesis testing objective 432

Line chart 438
Pie chart 438
Scatter chart 442
Sparkline 460
Trendline 452

Visual Summary

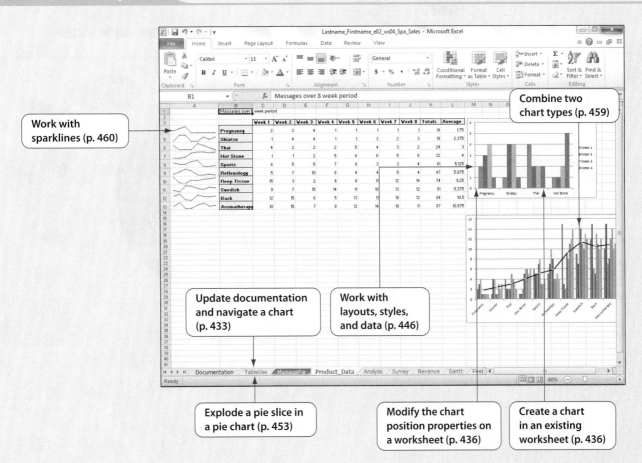

Work with sparklines (p. 460)

Combine two chart types (p. 459)

Update documentation and navigate a chart (p. 433)

Work with layouts, styles, and data (p. 446)

Explode a pie slice in a pie chart (p. 453)

Modify the chart position properties on a worksheet (p. 436)

Create a chart in an existing worksheet (p. 436)

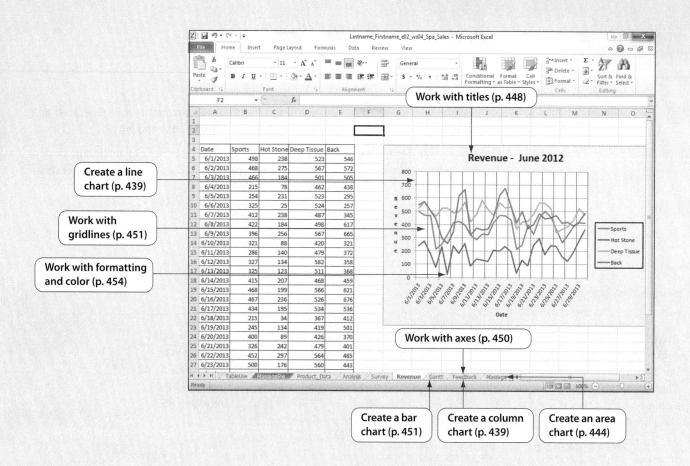

Work with titles (p. 448)

Create a line chart (p. 439)

Work with gridlines (p. 451)

Work with formatting and color (p. 454)

Work with axes (p. 450)

Create a bar chart (p. 451)

Create a column chart (p. 439)

Create an area chart (p. 444)

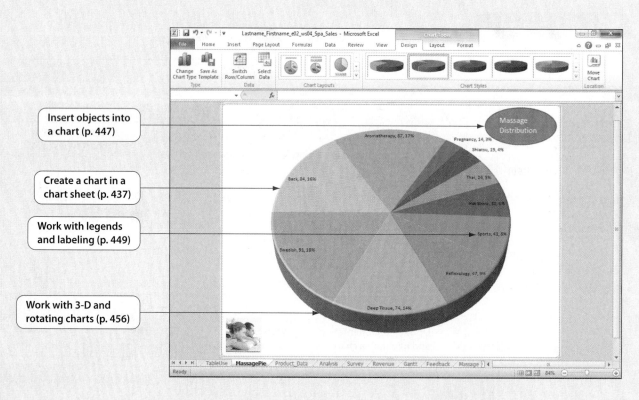

Insert objects into a chart (p. 447)

Create a chart in a chart sheet (p. 437)

Work with legends and labeling (p. 449)

Work with 3-D and rotating charts (p. 456)

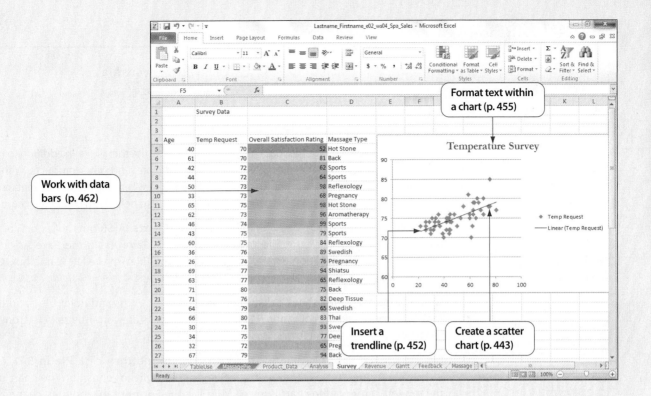

Format text within a chart (p. 455)

Work with data bars (p. 462)

Insert a trendline (p. 452)

Create a scatter chart (p. 443)

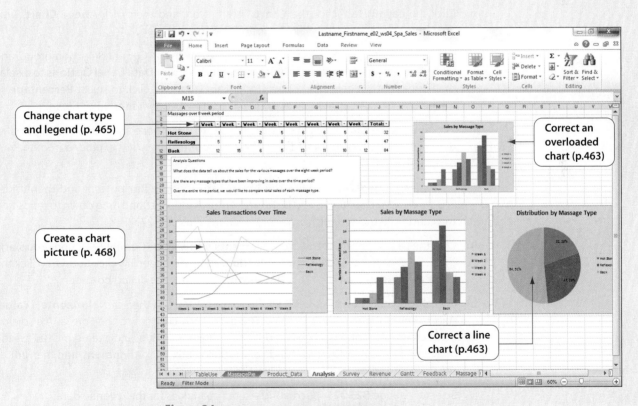

Change chart type and legend (p. 465)

Correct an overloaded chart (p.463)

Create a chart picture (p. 468)

Correct a line chart (p.463)

Figure 24 Turquoise Oasis Spa sales final reports

Student data file needed:

e02_ws04_Therapist_Charts

You will save your file as:

Lastname_Firstname_e02_ws04_Therapist_Charts

Therapist Product Sales Report

Sales &
Marketing

The managers have pulled together data pertaining to sales by the therapists. In addition to massages, the therapists should also promote skin care, health care, and other products. With the monthly data, the managers want a few charts developed that will enable them to look at trends, compare sales, and provide feedback to the therapists. You are to help them create the charts.

a. Start **Excel**, and then open **e02_ws04_Therapist_Charts**. A Summary Report for the month is displayed. Click the **File tab**, and then click **Save As**. In the Save As dialog box, navigate to the location where you are saving your files. In the File Name box, type Lastname_Firstname_e02_ws04_Therapist_Charts.

b. On the **Summary worksheet**, select the range **B12:J12**, press and hold ⌃Ctrl, and then make a second selection of range **B17:J17** so two ranges are currently selected, one for the labels and one for the Totals.

c. Click the **Insert tab**, click **Pie** in the Charts group, and then click **Pie in 3-D**. Click the **border edge** of the chart, and then drag to the right to reposition the chart until the top-left corner of the chart is in cell M1. Click the **Format tab**, and then change the Shape Height to 4" and the Shape Width to 6". Press ⏎Enter.

d. Click the **Layout tab**, click the **Chart Title** button, and then click **Above Chart**. Type Therapist Transactions for the Month, and then press ⏎Enter.

e. On the Layout tab, click the **Chart Elements arrow** in the Current Selection group, and then click **Series 1**. Click **Data Labels**, and then click **More Data Label Options** to display the Format Data Labels dialog box. Under Label Options, click to select **Percentage** so the percent is included along with **Value** and **Show Leader Lines**. Click **Close**.

f. Click the **Pie** (be careful not to click the label text). Click once again on the **red pie slice** to select the one slice. Click and drag the **slice** to the right so it is exploded from the rest of the pie.

g. Select the range **A20:J24**, click the **Insert tab**, click the **Bar** button, and then under 2-D Bar click **Stacked Bar**. Click the **border edge** of the chart, and drag down to reposition the chart until the top-left corner of the chart is in cell A27.

h. Click the **Layout tab**, click the **Chart Elements arrow** in the Current Selection group, and then click **Plot Area**. Click **Format Selection**, and then under Fill, click **Solid fill**. Click the **Color arrow**, and then click **Tan, Background 2**. Leave the dialog box open.

i. Click the **Layout tab**, click the **Chart Elements arrow**, and then click **Horizontal (Value) Axis** to select the x-axis in the chart. The dialog box changes to the Format Axis dialog box. Under Axis Options, click **Fixed** for the Minimum value, and then type 100 for the minimum fixed value. On the left side of the dialog box, click **Alignment**, and then adjust the **Custom angle** to 40 degrees. Click **Close**.

j. Select the range **B25:J25** for creating a set of sparklines for the revenue data.

k. Click the **Insert tab**, and then click the **Line** button in the Sparklines group to display the Create Sparklines dialog box.

l. To the right of the Data Range box, click **Collapse Dialog Box**, and then select the range **B21:J24**. Click **Expand Dialog Box**, and then click **OK**. Click on any cell outside of the sparklines to deselect the sparklines.

m. Click the **Insert tab**, and then click the **Header & Footer** button. Click the **Design tab**, and then click the **Go to Footer** button. Click in the left footer section, and then click the **File Name** button in the Header & Footer Elements group.

n. Click any cell on the spreadsheet to move out of the footer, and then press Ctrl+Home. Click the **View tab**, and then click the **Normal** button in the Workbook Views group.

o. Click **Save**.

Problem Solve 1

Student data file needed:

e02_ps1_ExpressCar

You will save your file as:

Lastname_Firstname_e02_ps1_ExpressCar

Express Car Rental Data

Finance & Accounting

Thomas Reynolds is the corporate buyer for vehicles put into service by Express Car Rental. Tom has the option to buy several lots of vehicles from another rental agency that is downsizing. He wants to get a better idea of the nationwide figures for rentals by vehicle type. The corporate accountant has forwarded Tom a spreadsheet containing rental data for last year. Tom wants to use this summarized data but feels that embedding charts will provide a quicker analysis and more visual manner to the Chief Financial Officer at their meeting next week.

a. Start **Excel**. Navigate to where your student files are located, select **e02_ps1_ExpressCar**, and then save the file as Lastname_Firstname_e02_ps1_ExpressCar.

b. Rename the worksheet currently identified as Sheet1 to Annual_Data and the one identified as Sheet2 to Documentation.

c. On the Documentation worksheet insert the appropriate content in cells D3, A5, B5, and C5. Wrap the text in cell C5. Change the worksheet names in B16 and B21 to match the renamed worksheets from Step b.

d. On the Annual_Data worksheet merge and center cell **A1** across the range A1:O1, the cell **A2** across the range A2:O2, and the cell **A3** across the range A3:O3.

e. On the Annual_Data worksheet in cell **H5**, enter the formula to calculate the semiannual total for cars rented in the Green Collection. Copy this formula to the range **H6:H10**.

f. On the Annual_Data worksheet in cell **O5**, enter the formula to calculate the annual total for cars rented in the Green Collection. Copy this formula to the range **O6:O10**.

g. Using the data on the Annual_Data worksheet, create a 3-D pie chart of the annual sales total for the six car types. Reposition the chart below the monthly data.

h. On the 3-D pie chart insert the title, Annual Sales, above the chart. Adjust the data labels on the pie chart to include the auto type, percent, and position the label information outside of the chart. Set bold and change the font size of the labels to **8**. Delete the legend.

i. On the pie chart explode the segment of the chart that represents the auto type with the lowest annual sales.

j. Create a **Clustered 2-D Bar** chart with markers using the fourth quarter (Oct, Nov, Dec) sales data. Reposition the chart below the data range. Insert the title, Quarter 4 Sales, above the chart.

k. Change the bar chart to a line chart with markers. The legend should be the months of the fourth quarter and the horizontal axis should be the auto types.

l. On the line chart add major vertical grid lines. Change the background color of the line chart, including the plot area, to **Orange, Accent 6, Lighter 80%**.

m. Change the font of the titles of the pie and line chart to **Arial Black** and the font size to **18**.

n. Create a 3-D clustered column chart using the data for the first quarter (Jan, Feb, Mar) for all auto types on the Annual_Data worksheet. The legend should be the months of the year, and the primary horizontal axis should be the auto types.

o. Move the 3-D column chart from the Annual_Data worksheet to a separate sheet, and name that sheet 3D_Column. Reposition the 3D_Column worksheet after the Annual_Data worksheet.

p. Increase the data used to create the 3-D column chart to include the first six months of figures by adjusting chart data range to **$A$4:$G$10**.

q. On the 3-D column chart switch the row/column data. This will make the auto types the legend and the months the primary horizontal axis. Insert the title, Semi-Annual Sales, above the chart, and then insert the vertical axis title, Autos Rented, to the left of the vertical number axis.

r. Adjust margins of the Annual_Data worksheet to have a top and bottom margin of .75 and a left and right margin of .25. Change the orientation to Landscape. Change the view to Page Layout. In the Scale to Fit group, change Width to 1 page. If necessary, adjust the position and size of the two charts to fit on the same page as the monthly data.

s. Insert the file name Lastname_Firstname_e02_pf4_ExpressCar into the left footer section for all worksheets.

t. Save the file, and submit it as directed by your instructor.

 Additional Workshop Cases are available on the companion website and in the instructor resources.

MODULE CAPSTONE

More Practice

Student data file needed: **You will save your file as:**

e02_mp_Restaurant_Sales   Lastname_Firstname_e02_mp_Restaurant_Sales

Restaurant Marketing Analysis

Sales & Marketing

The restaurant receives data on a daily basis that can be used for analysis to gauge its performance and determine needed changes. The restaurant is considering entering into a long-term agreement with a poultry company and getting a new refrigeration unit to store the chicken. The restaurant also ran a marketing campaign for its Chicken Caliente because a chef recently modified the dish. Management would like you to analyze some trends with the restaurant's chicken dishes, see if the marketing is working for the new dish, and explore an amortization table for the refrigerator loan.

a. Start **Excel**, and then open **e02_mp_Restaurant_Sales**. Click the **Documentation worksheet tab**. Save the file as Lastname_Firstname_e02_mp_Restaurant_Sales.

b. Click in cell **A6**, and then press Ctrl+: to input the current date. Click cell **B6**, and then type in your first name and last name.

c. Click the **Summary worksheet tab**, and then click cell **C2**. Type =TODAY(), and then press Enter.

d. You need to consolidate the weekly quantity sold on the Summary sheet.
   - Click cell **C28**, type =, and then select the **Week1 worksheet tab**. Click cell **C5**, and then press Enter.
   - Click cell **D28**, type =, and then select the **Week2 worksheet tab**. Click cell **C5**, and then press Enter.
   - Click cell **E28**, type =, and then select the **Week3 worksheet tab**. Click cell **C5**, and then press Enter.
   - Click cell **F28**, type =, and then select the **Week4 worksheet tab**. Click cell **C5**, and then press Enter.
   - Select range **C28:F28**, click the **AutoFill handle**, and then drag down through row 35 to copy those four formulas for the remaining cell range **C29:F35**.

e. You also need to summarize the data to calculate the totals and average for each item.
   - Click cell **F5**, type =SUM(C28:J28), and then press Enter.
   - Click cell **G5**, type =SUM(C17:J17), and then press Enter.
   - Click cell **H5**, type =AVERAGE(C28:J28), and then press Enter.
   - Select range **F5:H5**, click the **AutoFill handle**, and then drag down through row 12 to copy those three formulas for the remaining cell range **F6:H12**.

f. Click cell **D5**, type =E5*F5, and then press Enter. Click cell **D5**, click the **AutoFill handle**, and then drag to copy the formula down through cell **D12**.

g. Click cell **L17**, type =IF((C28-C17)/C17>=$N$14,1,0), and press Enter. Click cell **L17**, click the **AutoFill handle**, and then drag down to copy the formula through **L24**. Use the AutoFill feature across to column O so the formula is copied into the range **L17:O24**.

h. Click cell **T17**, type =SUM(L17:S17), and then press Enter. Click cell **T17**, click the **AutoFill handle**, and then drag down to copy the formula through cell **T24**.

i. Click cell **A17**, type =IF(T17=MAX($T$17:$T$24),"TopPerformer",""), and then press Enter. Click cell **A17**, click the **AutoFill handle**, and then drag down to copy the formula through cell **A24**.

j. Select the range **A28:A35**. Click the **Insert tab**, and then click **Line** in the Sparklines group. To the right of the Data Range box, click **Collapse Dialog Box**, select the range **C28:J35**, click **Expand Dialog Box**, and then click **OK**. Click the **Design tab**, and then click the **Markers** check box in the Show group to toggle this feature on.

k. Select range **B27:F35** so you can create a growth chart for chicken sales by type of dish.

- Click the **Insert tab**, click **Bar** in the Charts group, and then click **Stacked Bar** (first row, second column).
- Click the **Layout tab**, click the **Chart Title** button in the Labels group, click the **Above Chart** option, type Chicken Sales – Accumulative, and then press Enter.
- Click the border edge and then drag to reposition the chart so the top-left corner falls in cell **A37**. Click near the **right border chart edge**, and then when the resize cursor appears click and drag to the right to resize until the right chart edge fills column E.
- Click the **Layout tab**, and then click the **Format Selection** button in the Current Selection group.
- Under Fill, click the **Solid fill** option, click the **Color** button, click **Orange, Accent 6, Lighter 40%** (fourth row, last column), and then click **Close**. Press Esc to deselect the chart.

l. Select range **B27:F35** so you can create a line chart showing the Caliente dish sales.

- Click the **Insert tab**, click **Line** in the Charts group, and then click **Line** (first row, first column).
- Click the **border edge**, and then drag to move the chart so the top-left corner is over **G37** (across from the previous chart). Click near the right border chart edge when the resize cursor appears, and then click and drag to the right to resize until the right chart edge fills column N.
- Click the **Design tab**, and then click **Switch Row/Column** in the Data group.
- Click and drag the **top-left corner** of the blue border that surrounds the linked data range **C28:F35** until the border only surrounds the range **C33:F35**.
- Click the **Layout tab**, and then click **Format Selection** to change the chart area background.
- Under Fill, click the **Solid fill** option, click the **Color** button, and then click **Orange, Accent 6, Lighter 40%**. Leave the dialog box open.
- Click the **Layout tab**, click the **Chart Elements arrow** in the Current Selection group, and then click **Series "Chicken Caliente"**.
- On the left side of the Format Data Series dialog box, click **Line Color**. Under Line Color, click **Solid line**, click **Color**, and then click **Red**.
- On the left side of the Format Data Series dialog box, click **Line Style**, and then change the Width to 4.25 pt. Leave the dialog box open.
- Click the **Layout tab**, click the **Chart Elements arrow** in the Current Selection group, and then click **Vertical (Value) Axis**. Under the Axis Options, click the **Fixed Minimum** option, and then adjust the minimum value by typing 20.0. Click **Close**.
- Click the **Layout tab**, click **Chart Title** in the Labels group, click **Above Chart**, and then type Caliente - New Recipe Promotional Sales. Press Enter. If necessary, widen the title so the text is on one line. Press Esc twice, and then press Ctrl+Home.

m. Click the **Loan worksheet tab**. Click cell **C7**, type =-PMT(C6/12,C5*12,C4), and then press [Enter]. Note: Be sure to type a minus sign between the equal sign and the PMT function name.

n. On the Loan worksheet tab, add the following formulas for the amortization table:

- Click cell **B12**, and then type =C4 since the beginning balance in the first month is the loan amount. Press [Enter].
- Click cell **B13**, type =F12, and then press [Enter] since the beginning balance for the remainder of this column is the ending balance from the previous month. Click to select **B13** again, and then double-click the **AutoFill handle** to copy the formula down through the range **B14:B131**.
- Click cell **C12**, type =$C$6/12*B12, and then press [Enter].
- Click cell **D12**, type =IF(B12<$C$7,B12+C12,$C$7), and then press [Enter]. This will check the balance, and if it is less than the normal monthly payment, the payment will be the balance plus the interest for that month. If the balance is greater than the payment, the normal payment will be made.
- Click cell **E12**, type =D12-C12, and then press [Enter]. This is the amount of the payment that goes towards reducing the principal loan amount.
- Click cell **F12**, type =B12-E12, and then press [Enter]. This will give the ending balance for the month.
- Select the range **C12:F12**, and then double-click the **AutoFill handle** to copy the formulas down through the range **C13:F131**.

o. Select the range **C12:C131**, click in the **Name Box**, type Interest, and then press [Enter].

p. Click cell **C9**, type =SUM(Interest), and then press [Enter] so the total interest is calculated. Notice the total interest paid on $15,000 for 10 years is $4,091.79. If you change the number of years from 10 to 5 in cell C5, the total interest paid would be $1,984.11—a lot less interest to pay.

q. Select all worksheets, and then insert the file name Lastname_Firstname_e02_mp_ Restaurant_Sales into the left section of the footer.

r. Press [Ctrl]+[Home]. Click **Save**, and then close Excel.

Problem Solve 1

Student data file needed:

e02_ps1_Hotel_Survey

You will save your file as:

Lastname_Firstname_e02_ps1_Hotel_Survey

Customer Service

Hotel Marketing Survey

The hotel periodically surveys guest satisfaction prior to the guest leaving. You need to chart this data. The hotel is also considering hiring a company to complete a comprehensive customer satisfaction and marketing research analysis. This project would require a loan of $50,000 to be paid in quarterly payments over one year. The manager would like a simple amortization schedule for this loan.

The Survey_Q10 worksheet contains a set of recent customer survey data in A23:J98. The respondents marked their rating for the question asking for the likelihood they would return. A response of 1 indicates no intention of returning, and a response of 10 indicates a high likelihood of returning. Above the data, you need to create summary information and a chart of all the scores.

a. Start **Excel**, and then open **e02_ps1_Hotel_Survey**. Click the **Documentation worksheet tab**. In A6, press Ctrl+: to input the current date. Save the file as Lastname_Firstname_ e02_ps1_Hotel_Survey. Click cell **B6**, and then type your first name and last name.

b. Click the **Survey_Q10 worksheet tab**. Click cell **B8**, and then enter a COUNTA formula that ignores blank cells while counting the number of "x"s for the choice 1, in range A24:A98. Calculate a similar COUNTA formula in cells B9:B17 using the appropriate range corresponding to the Score number.

c. With the scores tallied, create a Clustered Cylinder column chart showing the count by score. In creating the chart, develop the following:
   - Position the top-left corner of the chart over cell G2.
   - Resize the chart to have a height of 3.5" and width of 6".
   - Change the Chart background to **Orange, Accent 6, Lighter 80%**.
   - Insert a chart title above the chart that displays Plans to Return, and then move the chart title to the top-left corner of the chart area. Remove the chart legend.
   - Add a text box that states 10 - Definitely will on the first line and 1- Definitely will not on the second line. Make the text box .5" high and 1.5" wide, and then position it in the top-right corner of the chart area.
   - Change the columns for 7, 8, 9, and 10 to **Olive Green, Accent 3, Darker 25%**.
   - Change the columns for 4, 5, and 6 to **Yellow**.
   - Change the columns for 2 and 3 to **Red**.
   - Change the Chart Area 3-D Rotation to a 15 degree Perspective. (*Hint*: Click the **Format Selection** button and appropriate option from the resulting dialog box, and then uncheck the Right Angle Axes to adjust perspective value.)
   - Change the Vertical (Value) Axis to a Fixed Major unit of 5.0.

d. Click the **Satisfaction worksheet tab**, select cell ranges **A4:A9** and **E4:F9**, and then create a **3-D Clustered Column** chart for the Quality of Service. Develop the chart with the following elements:
   - The chart should cluster the age groups by Restaurant and Hotel only providing a group of Restaurant data and a second group of Hotel data. If necessary, apply the **Switch Row/Column** button.
   - Position the top-left corner of the chart over cell H2.
   - Make the chart 7" wide and 3" high.
   - Create a chart title above the chart that says Quality of Service by Age Group.
   - Change the properties of the chart to **Don't move or size with cells**.

e. Select the ranges **A15:A49** and **C15:C49**, and then create a **Scatter with only Markers** scatter chart for the Overall Satisfaction. Develop the chart with the following elements:
   - Position the top-left corner of the chart over cell E20.
   - Make the chart 4" high and 8" wide.
   - If necessary, create a chart title above the chart that states Overall Satisfaction.
   - Modify the Vertical scale so it starts at minimum of 3 and only goes up to 10 maximum.
   - Modify the Horizontal scale so it starts at minimum of 20.
   - Add primary vertical gridlines and major gridlines. If necessary, apply the **Switch Row/ Column** button.
   - Change the properties of the chart to include the **Don't move or size with cells** option.

f. Select the cell range **B16:B49**, click in the **Name Box** to name the cell range, type TotalBill, and then press Enter.

g. Click cell **B11**, and then create a formula that will provide the average bill amount for cell range **TotalBill**.

h. Click cell **B12**, and then create a formula that will provide the minimum bill amount for cell range TotalBill.

i. Click cell **B13**, and then create a formula that will provide the maximum bill amount for cell range **TotalBill**.

j. Click the **Name Box arrow**, click **TotalBill** to select the TotalBill cell range, hold down Ctrl , add the cell range **B11:B13** to the selection, and then apply the **Accounting** format with two decimal places.

k. Click the **AdLoan worksheet tab**, click cell **C4**, and then create a formula that will use the loan amount (or present value) in C1, number of payments in C2, and the annual interest rate in C3 to calculate the quarterly payment amount for the loan.

l. Click cell **B9**, and then add a cell reference to the beginning Loan Amount. Then, for cells B10:B12 add a cell reference of a beginning balance that should reference the ending balance cell for the previous quarter's Ending Balance.

m. Click cell **C9**, and then add a cell reference with an absolute reference to the Quarterly Payment amount. Use the AutoFill feature to copy the formula cell reference to the cell range **C10:C12**.

n. Click cell **D9**, and calculate the interest charged, which is the quarterly Annual Interest Rate times the Beginning Balance. Use the AutoFill feature to copy this formula down to **D10:D12**.

o. Click cell **E9**, and calculate the principal amount of the quarterly payment. This would be the total payment minus the interest charged for that quarter. Use the AutoFill feature to copy this formula down to **E10:E12**.

p. Click cell **F9**, and calculate the ending balance, which is the Beginning Balance minus the Principal. Use the AutoFill feature to copy this formula down to **F10:F12**.

q. Click the **Documentation worksheet tab**. Hold Shift , and then click on the **AdLoan worksheet tab**. This will select all the tabs as a group, and you will see **[Group]** appear in the title bar at the top of the window. Click the **Insert tab**, and then insert the file name Lastname_Firstname_e02_ps1_Hotel_Survey into the left footer section. Click out of the footer, and then return to Normal view. Press Ctrl + Home , right-click one of the worksheet tabs, and then click **Ungroup Sheets**.

r. Click **Save**. Close Excel.

Problem Solve 2

Sales & Marketing

Student data file needed:	You will save your file as:
e02_ps2_Advertising	Lastname_Firstname_e02_ps2_Advertising

Resort Advertising Review

The resort has been investing in advertising using different advertising media. When customers book travel to the resort, they reference how they learned about the resort, which could include magazine ads, radio ads, the Internet, or referrals of past customers. Data that shows this advertising has been gathered on the Advertising worksheet. You will develop charts for an upcoming presentation that will discuss a marketing strategy.

The Magazines worksheet contains cost and inquiry data for four magazine ads. The ads were placed into one monthly issue of each magazine. Each customer contact is an inquiry. If the customer actually booked business, it is a sale. You will create charts to compare performance of the magazines.

a. Start **Excel**, and then open **e02_ps2_Advertising**. Click the **Documentation worksheet tab**. In A6, press Ctrl+: to input the current date. Save the file as Lastname_Firstname_ e02_ps2_Advertising. Click cell **B6**, and then type your first name and last name.

b. Click the **Advertising worksheet tab**.

   The data in the cell range A4:D8 shows transactions that came from advertising for specific travel packages to the resort. Some totals need to be developed using this data.

   - In cell **B9** create a formula that will sum the Romance transactions in B5:B8, then use the AutoFill feature to copy the formula to **C9:D9**, for Golf and Relax travel packages.

   - In cell **E5**, create a formula that will sum all the transactions generated from the Magazine ads, in range **B5:D5**.

   - In cell **F5**, create a formula that will determine the cost per transaction using the Cost table that shows the total Magazine costs in C12 and the total number of packages generated by the magazine ad, found in cell E5.

   - Select the range **E5:F5**, and then use the AutoFill feature to copy these formulas down to **E6:F8** for the other advertising types.

c. Using the range A4:D8, create a 2-D Bar, Stacked Bar chart grouping the packages by Advertising Type. As you develop this chart include the following:

   - Position the chart so the top-left corner is over H3.

   - Change the width of the chart to be 5" and the height to be 3".

   - Create a chart title above the chart that says Resort Package Advertising Results.

   - Create an axis title below the horizontal axis, and then type # of Packages Sold.

   - Create an axis title for the vertical axis, rotate the title, and then type Advertising Type.

   - Adjust the scaling for the horizontal axis so the maximum is 25.

d. Using all the monthly data in A20:D44, create a 2-D Line chart that will show the three magazine types, Travel, Business, and Health, over time.

   - Position the top-left corner of the chart over cell F20. Make the width of the chart 8" and the height 3".

   - Create a chart title using the **Centered Overlay Title** style, and then type Advertising Results by Magazine Type 2011-2012.

   - Change the Shape Fill color of the Chart Title text box to **Orange**.

   - Create an axis title for the vertical axis, rotate the title, and then type # of Transactions.

e. Click the **Magazines worksheet tab**, and then in cell **C17** create a sum formula that will total all the transactions for Spaaaah for Month 1 through Month 6. Use the AutoFill feature to copy the formula down from C17 to **C18:C20**.

f. In cell **F17**, use the DATEDIF function to calculate the number of days between the Start Date of Advertising using an absolute reference to cell C14 and the Date of Last Inquiry for Spaaaah, in cell E17. Use the AutoFill feature to copy the formula in F17 down through **F18:F20**.

g. In cell **G17** create a formula that will find the cost per inquiry, given the cost of advertising in B17 and the total number of Spaaaah inquiries in C17. Round the formula to two decimal places. Use the AutoFill feature to copy the formula down from G17 to **G18:G20**.

h. In cell **H17** create a formula that will find the cost per number of sales, given the cost of advertising in B17 and the total number of Spaaaah sales in D17. Round the formula to two decimal places. Use the AutoFill feature to copy the formula down from H17 to **H18:H20**.

i. In cell **I17** create a formula that will find the number of inquiries per day using the number of inquiries in C17 over the number of total days that the inquiries were being received in F17. Round the formula to two decimal places. Use the AutoFill feature to copy the formula down from I17 to **I18:I20**.

j. In cell **B7** create a formula that will determine the percentage of inquiries for Spaaaah that occurred in Month 1, given the Month 1 data in B2 and the number of Spaaaah inquiries in C17. Use the AutoFill feature to copy the formula in B7 down to **B8:B10**, and then copy the formulas in B7:B10 over to **C7:G10**. Be sure to check your formula in G10 to ensure you have it correct. (*Hint*: Assess if cell references need to be absolute or relative.)

k. Select **B7:G10**, and then add a conditional formatting **Gradient Fill Blue Data Bar**. This will indicate the effectiveness over time of the advertising.

l. Select **A16:A20** and **C16:D20**, and then create a **2-D Column, Clustered Column** chart on the worksheet. As you develop the chart include the following:
   - Position the top-left corner over cell A22.
   - Change the width to 6.5" and the height to 3.5".
   - Create a chart title above the chart, and then type Inquiry vs Transactions by Magazine.
   - For the Travel Zone data point that represents the highest # of Sales from Inquiries, change the column color from red to green.

m. Select **A16:A20** and **H16:H20**, and then create a **Clustered Bar in 3-D** chart on the worksheet. As you develop the chart include the following:
   - Position the top-left corner over cell G22.
   - Change the width to 6.5" and the height to 3.5".
   - Create a chart title using the **Centered Overlay Title** style, and then type Average Cost per Transaction.
   - Change the alignment for the vertical axis to have a custom angle of –45 degrees.
   - Show the data labels for the bars. Format the data labels to be bold and to have a font size of 14.
   - For the data point that represents the best—lowest—Cost/Sale, change the column color from blue to green.
   - Delete the legend.
   - Change the chart area background fill color to **Aqua, Accent 5, Lighter 80%**.

n. Insert the file name Lastname_Firstname_e02_ps2_Advertising into the left footer section for all worksheets.

o. Press Ctrl+Home and then ungroup the worksheets. Click **Save**. Close Excel.

Problem Solve 3

my it lab grader
Homework 3

Sales & Marketing

Student data file needed:	You will save your file as:
e02_ps3_Hotel_Occupancy	Lastname_Firstname_e02_ps3_Hotel_Occupancy

Hotel Occupancy Analysis

Painted Paradise Resort and Spa would like to review the occupancy and profitability of the various rooms in the hotel with the data on the Occupancy worksheet. Further, Painted Paradise is developing a VIP club that will provide rewards based on points earned. The points are earned based on the guest's usage of the different areas within the resort. The hotel manager has asked you to analyze the potential points program using the data on the Villa worksheet. After your analysis, management may want to change some of the point levels and values. Thus, all of your formulas must be updated appropriately if those values changed.

a. Start **Excel**, and then open **e02_ps3_Hotel_Occupancy**. Save the file as Lastname_Firstname_e02_ps3_Hotel_Occupancy Click the **Documentation worksheet tab**. In A6, press Ctrl+: to input the current date. Click cell **B6**, and then type in your first name and last name.

b. Click the **Villa worksheet tab**, click cell **I14**, and then calculate the Resort Points for the customer.

If the customer has a combined total of five or more Golf and Spa activities as shown in D4, found in columns F and G, then they earn Resort points. If the customer does not have a total of five or more activities, they will earn zero Resort points. Resort points are calculated by taking the Spa activities times the Spa Resort Points plus the Golf activities times the Golf Resort Points. Pay attention to constructing the formula so cell references can be automatically filled down the column for all the customers. (Note: If a green error triangle appears in the top-left corner of the cell after a formula is applied, it often occurs if reference cells are not adjacent. Click the arrow next to the Error Checking options icon that appears next to the selected cells, and then click **Ignore Error**.)

c. In cell **J14** calculate the Hotel Points by multiplying the Villa Points per Night for the customer by the Number of Nights the customer stayed. The formula should be constructed so it can be automatically filled down the column for all the customers.

d. In cell **K14**, use functions to create a formula that will determine the Gift Shop Points earned.

The formula should check to determine if the customer has purchased more than the Gift Shop Minimum, in which case they will earn points based on the Gift Shop Point Percentage of their total Gift Shop purchases. If a customer's purchases are less than the minimum, the customer would earn zero points. Since the calculation may give a result with decimal points, add a ROUND function to round the results to 0 decimals. The formula should be constructed so it can be automatically filled down the column for all the customers.

e. Click **L14**, and then calculate the Total Points by adding the Resort Points, Hotel Points, and Gift Shop Points for the first customer.

f. Copy all formulas in I14:L14 to **I15:L32**, so points are calculated for all customers.

g. For the Total Points range, L14:L32, use Conditional Formatting to add a **Gradient Fill Green Data Bar**.

h. Click the **Occupancy worksheet tab**, and then calculate the following:
- Select the cell range **B11:G18**. Click the **Create from Selection** option on the Formulas tab to create named ranges for each room type and usage data.
- In cell **B19** create a Total formula that will add up all the rooms used for the One Double week days found in range B12:B18.
- In cell **B20** calculate the average daily occupancy for the One Double room type in range B12:B18.
- Copy the formulas in the range B19:B20 to the range **C19:G20**, so the total and average for each room type is calculated. Remember to update the named ranges in these formulas.

Be sure to click the Top row option when defining the named ranges—an example of the result will be the range B12:B18 will be a named range of One_Double defined by the heading in cell B11.

i. In **B6** calculate the Revenue for the One Double room type in B19, times the Average Room Rate in B5.

j. In **B7** calculate the Gross Profit, which is the Revenue in B6 times the profit Margin in B4.

k. Use the AutoFill feature to copy the formulas in the range B6:B7 right across the table to fill the range **C6:G7**. Widen all the columns as necessary to display all data.

l. Using the ranges **A2:G2** and **A7:G7**, create a 2-D Pie chart showing a comparison of Gross Profit by room type. For the chart, make the following changes:
- Add data labels with the percentages showing, but not the values.
- Select the **red piece** of pie that has 23%, and then pull it away from the rest of the pie so it is emphasized.
- Add or adjust a chart title above the chart that says Comparison of Gross Profit by Room Type.

- Resize the chart to have a height of **3**" and width of **6**".
- Position the top-left corner of the chart over cell I2.

m. Select the ranges **A2:G3** and **A20:G20**, and then create a **Clustered Bar, 2-D Bar** chart showing the Average Occupancy clustered with the Number of Rooms for each room type.

n. For this second chart, make the following changes:

- Change the Chart Layout to **Layout 3**.
- Add data labels—using the **Outside End** option.
- Move the chart to a chart sheet that is named Room Utilization, and then, if necessary, move the Room Utilization chart sheet to position it after the Occupancy sheet.
- Add or adjust a chart title above the chart so it states Average Room Utilization by Room Type.
- Change the chart area background to **Tan, Background 2, Darker 10%**.
- Change the plot area background to **Tan, Background 2**.
- Add a custom footer to insert a file name footer in the left footer section.

o. Insert the file name Lastname_Firstname_e02_ps3_Hotel_Occupancy into the left footer section for all remaining worksheets—Documentation, Villa, and Occupancy.

p. Save your file. Close Excel.

Perform 1: Perform in Your Life

Student data file needed:

Blank Excel workbook

You will save your file as:

Lastname_Firstname_e02_pf1_Investment_Portfolio

Personal Investment Portfolio

Finance & Accounting

You have started working and realize the importance of paying off current debt, managing expenses, and preparing for your retirement. You need to start paying down school loans and thinking about investing for the future. You want to start a spreadsheet that you can use to track some stock investments.

Either use the data provided for the stock below, or choose current stock data from the Internet per your instructor's preference. If using the Internet, use one of several known stock sites that provide historical data such as finance.yahoo.com.

Company	Nobel Energy, Inc
Ticker	NBL
Date	Closing Share Price
1/2/2008	72.58
4/1/2008	87.00
7/1/2008	73.87
10/1/2008	58.82
1/2/2009	48.93
4/1/2009	56.75
7/1/2009	61.12
10/1/2009	65.63
1/4/2010	73.94
4/1/2010	76.40
7/1/2010	67.06
10/1/2010	81.48
1/3/2011	91.10

a. Open a new, blank Excel workbook. Save it as Lastname_Firstname_e02_pf1_Investment_Portfolio.

b. Start with a worksheet named Investment and with one stock. Create labels showing the name of the stock and the tracking information such as the account name and ticker symbol.

c. Create a table that will track investments into the stock. You would track the following data:
   - Date of investment
   - The investment amount
   - The share price on date of purchase
   - The number of shares purchased, which is the investment divided by the share price
   - Add a column that will show the accumulated total number of shares purchased.

d. Next, the stock activity needs to be tracked on a quarterly basis. Create a table that will record quarterly activity including the following:
   - A Quarter column labeling the first date of each quarter
   - A Value column showing the current overall value of your investment at the start of the quarter—this would be the share price times the number of shares you possess
   - A Quarterly Investment column showing total amount invested in that quarter—this would be the quarterly investment, the money you invested each quarter based on your investments table
   - A Total Investment column that records the total amount invested to date—accumulated
   - A Total Growth column of the investment to date—this would be the total value minus the total investment
   - A Total Growth % column that records the percentage growth for that quarter—this is the current total growth divided by the total investment
   - A Qtrly Growth column that calculates the growth of the investment minus the total investment from the previous quarter
   - A Qtrly Growth % column that calculates the percentage growth for the quarter—this is the current total quarterly growth divided by the total investment

e. To test the worksheet, put in either the data provided or use the quarterly data from the Internet for a chosen stock.

f. Create an appropriate chart that will track the quarterly growth percentage over time.

g. Insert the file name Lastname_Firstname_e02_pf1_Investment_Portfolio into the left footer section of the worksheet.

h. Save your work, and then close Excel.

Perform 2: Perform in Your Career

Student data file needed:

Blank Excel workbook

You will save your file as:

Firstname_Lastname_e02_pf2_Loan_Amortization

Loan Amortization

Finance & Accounting

You are doing some consulting for the owners of a small business who want spreadsheets created so they can track loans. They would like to track the payment of the loans by splitting up the monthly payment into the amount going to interest and the amount going to principal. They would like to incorporate extra payments and then determine the total interest paid over the life of the loan. Finally, they would like to track their progress on the repayment.

a. Open a new, blank Excel workbook. Save it as Lastname_Firstname_e02_pf2_Loan_Amortization. Create a spreadsheet that calculates the monthly payment for a standard loan based on the time period, loan amount, and interest rate. Your calculations should be set up so the time period, loan amount, and interest rate can easily be changed. Then, the spreadsheet should track the monthly payment for the loan in a table format. You can assume the loan is for three years. At a minimum, this amortization table should include the following:

   - The beginning balance for each time period
   - The interest charged for the month
   - The payment that month
   - The amount of the payment that would go toward the principal
   - The ending loan balance after the principal has been paid
   - In addition to the standard monthly payment, also calculate the total amount of interest paid if the owner pays off the loan with no extra payments.

b. In conjunction with the loan payment, create a table that can then be used to create a chart that demonstrates that the total amount of interest charged for a loan that goes up as the number of years to repay the loan goes up. Have the table tie into the interest rate and loan amount used for the above calculations.

c. Create a second amortization table that would allow the owner to make an additional payment that would go toward the principal during any month. Allow flexibility so the owner could change the amount of the extra payment any month. At a minimum, this amortization table should include the following:

   - The beginning balance for each time period
   - The interest charged for the month
   - The payment that month
   - The amount of the payment that would go toward the principal
   - The extra payment made that month
   - The ending loan balance after the principal has been paid

d. Create summaries of the two amortization tables to show the total interest for the first payment schedule and the second payment schedule if the owner pays an amount greater than the standard monthly payment.

e. Create a chart showing the total interest paid with the two plans: paying the minimum payment and then paying more than the minimum payment.

f. Insert the file name Lastname_Firstname_e02_pf2_Loan_Amortization into the left footer section of the worksheet.

g. Save and close your file.

Perform 3: Perform in Your Career

Student data file needed:

e02_pf3_Tolerance_Charts

You will save your file as:

Lastname_Firstname_e02_pf3_Tolerance_Charts

Manufacturing Tolerance Analysis

Production & Operations

You have started a job with a manufacturer for components used in medical instrumentation. One of your duties is to get data about the components coming off the manufacturing floor so you can determine the quality of the components. Your task is to analyze measurements of a small silicon tube that is used to give medicines intravenously. When the machines get out of alignment over time they need to be adjusted.

The width of the tubing is within tolerance if the width is within 0.025 centimeters of the target diameter of 0.3 centimeters. Thus, if the tubing is between 0.275 and 0.325 in diameter, it is good quality. Otherwise, it is out of tolerance and the machinery needs adjusting. The spreadsheet will compare the sample to the target diameter of the tube, determine how much it is off from the specification, then chart the sample data over time to see if the machine is still aligned or needs to be adjusted up, down, or be totally recalibrated.

a. Start **Excel**, and then open **e02_pf3_Tolerance_Charts**. Save the file as Lastname_ Firstname_e02_pf3_Tolerance_Charts.

b. On the Tolerance_Data worksheet you will find 30 samples taken from the line over the past 30 days. Each sample is taken from the manufacturing line daily. So Sample 1 is the part that was pulled on day 1. Sample 10 was pulled on day 10. The width in centimeters is taken of the tube diameter. Add formulas to the new columns to calculate the data to determine the error—the difference between the actual diameter and the required, or specified, diameter of the tubing—and then determine if the diameter is wider than the specification or narrower than the specification.

c. You should determine some base statistics of the diameter of the samples. Determine the minimum, maximum, and average diameter of the samples in the provided cells.

d. A table has been started that will tally the results of the error analysis so you can determine how many samples were out of tolerance. Add formulas to complete the table as follows:
   • Add a function for the total number of samples that had widths that were wider than the allowable tolerance.
   • Add a function for the total number of samples that had widths that were narrower than the allowable tolerance.
   • Add a function for total number of samples that were within the tolerance.

e. As a part of the table, targets have been set to determine when the machine needs to be adjusted. It is the goal that 25 or more of the samples overall will be within the tolerance. Add a function to the Note column cells to test if the Low and High Totals are greater than the Target, and place a note to Check Machine if totals for the High or Low categories exceed target; otherwise, the Note cell can remain blank. If the count for the OK do NOT exceed the target, place a note to Check Machine, otherwise it can be blank.

f. To help visualize the samples, chart the error measurement over time. Consider the following as you create the chart:
   • Review and adjust the axis scales if needed.
   • Create textual guidance with titles and text so the chart is self-explanatory.
   • Keep the chart professional as it may be printed with a report that is given to the manufacturing team.

g. A second chart should be created that compares the counts of OK, High, and Low relative to the total counts. This chart should also be professional.

h. Insert the file name Lastname_Firstname_e02_pf3_Tolerance_Charts into the left footer section for the worksheet.

i. Save your work, and then close Excel.

Student data file needed:

e02_pf4_BMI_Analysis

You will save your file as:

Lastname_Firstname_e02_pf4_BMI_Analysis

BMI Health Analysis

Research & Development

A state health agency wants to examine health data on college students starting with the body mass index (BMI). The agency has provided a file with a dataset of average BMI numbers for males and females from 1952 through 2011. In addition to looking at that data, the agency has some current data and wants to be able to work with current clients to analyze their health condition using the BMI. You have been hired to look at the data, correct some issues, and create some new components on the spreadsheet.

The BMI is calculated using the height (in inches) and the weight (in pounds). The formula for BMI is as follows:

Weight/Height^2 * 703

For example, if a client weighs 120 pounds and is 5 foot 6 inches tall, their BMI would be 120/66^2 * 703=19.37.

The BMI has categories as follows:

- Underweight less than 18.5
- Normal 18.5 or greater and less than 25
- Overweight 25 or greater and less than 30
- Obese 30 or greater

a. Start **Excel**, and then open **e02_pf4_BMI_Analysis**. Save the file as Lastname_Firstname_e02_pf4_BMI_Analysis.

b. Click the **Historical worksheet tab**. The historical data, showing average BMI numbers for males and females, has been collected. The agency wants to see the trend of average BMI index numbers for males and females over the entire time period. However, the chart that has been created does not depict the trend over time. Add an additional chart to offer a trend analysis. The new updated chart should consider the following:

- The chart should be a more appropriate chart type that would show the trend over time for males and females.
- The chart should have clear titles, including for the x-axis and y-axis.
- The chart should have a professional, business look so it can be used by the state agency in a presentation.
- Adjust the scales and create gridlines that help convey the context as appropriate.

c. Click the **Donor worksheet tab**. The agency has included a copy of current raw survey data. The data includes the ID, Height, Weight, and Gender of the respondent. The agency would like to use this data to create a few charts. It would like to compare the numbers of males in each BMI category to the total number of females surveyed to determine the percentage of males in each category compared to females. You should sort and regroup the data as needed so the agency can easily tally the number of males and the number of females in separate tables that also include a column to calculate BMI. This summary data should be organized so you can create the two charts.

- The two charts should have a similar look and feel and be arranged side by side for comparison.
- The charts should be an appropriate type that allows comparison of the pieces as a part of the whole.
- The charts should be formatted to look professional in preparation for being in a brochure.

d. The agency would also like a simple input table to act as a calculator to determine the BMI for any client along with a table that uses formulas to calculate BMI index values that could be printed and used as a reference in the office when a computer is not handy. These two elements should be on the Donor worksheet.

- The BMI calculator should use cells where the client's Height and Weight information is inputted and the BMI is calculated.
- The BMI table should show a range of heights in inches down the side and a range of weights along the top. The ranges should be reasonable for typical adults. The ranges would not have to handle extreme heights or weights.
- The BMI table should also include color scaling so the higher BMI values are white and the low values are green.
- The table should provide guidance, but it does not have to be to the exact pound. The table should be a reasonable size that could fit on a normal sheet of paper and be readable.

e. Insert the file name Lastname_Firstname_e02_pf4_BMI_Analysis into the left footer section for all worksheets.

f. Save your work, and then close Excel.

WORKSHOP 1

General
Business

Objectives

1. Understand what Access is   p. 490

2. Maneuver in the Navigation Pane   p. 493

3. Understand what a table is   p. 497

4. Manually navigate a database   p. 504

5. Understand what a query is   p. 506

6. Understand what a form is   p. 512

7. Understand what a report is   p. 515

8. Be able to back up a database   p. 518

9. Be able to compact and repair a database   p. 519

Understanding the Four Main Database Objects

PREPARE CASE
Red Bluff Golf Club Putts for Paws Charity Tournament

The Red Bluff Golf Club is sponsoring a charity tournament, Putts for Paws, to raise money for the Santa Fe Animal Center. An intern created a database to use to run the tournament but did not finish it before leaving. You have been asked to finish the database to track the participants who enter the tournament, the orders they have placed, and the items they have purchased.

Kati Molin / Shutterstock.com

Student data files needed for this workshop:

 a01_ws01_Putts   a01_ws01_Participant

You will save your file as:

 Lastname_Firstname_a01_ws01_Putts

Understanding Database Basics and Tables

Businesses keep records about everything they do. If a business sells products, it keeps records about its products. It keeps records of its customers, the products it sells to each customer, and each sale. It keeps records about its employees, the hours they work, and their benefits. These records are collected and used for decision making, for sales and marketing, and for reporting purposes. A **database** is a collection of these records. The purpose of a database is to store, manage, and provide access to these business records.

In the past, many databases were paper-based. Paper records were stored in files in file cabinets. Each file would be labeled and put in a drawer in a file cabinet. Elaborate filing schemes were developed so that one record could be located quickly. This was highly labor-intensive and error prone. Today while most businesses use automated databases to store their records, you still see the occasional paper-based system. For example, your doctor's office may still use paper files for patient records.

Data are facts about people, events, things, or ideas, and they are an important asset to any organization as data allow companies to make better business decisions after converting it into useful information. **Information** is data that has been manipulated and processed to make it meaningful. For example, if you saw the number 2,000 out of context, the number has no meaning. If you are told that 2,000 represents the amount of an order in dollars, that piece of data becomes meaningful information. Businesses can leverage meaningful information to gain a competitive advantage, for example, by providing discounts to those who order more expensive items. An automated database management system, such as Microsoft Access, makes that possible.

Databases are used for two major purposes; for operational processing and for analytical purposes. In operational or transaction-based databases, each sale or transaction that a business makes is tracked. The information is used to keep the business running. Analytical databases are used for extracting data for decision-making. The data in these databases are summarized and classified to make information available to the decision makers in the firms.

Automated databases provide many advantages over paper databases. The information in the databases is much easier to find in automated form. The information can be manipulated and processed more rapidly. Automated databases can be used to enforce accuracy and other quality standards. In today's fast-paced world, a business needs to manipulate information quickly and accurately to make decisions. Without today's automated databases, a business cannot compete.

What Is Access?

Access is a relational **database management system (DBMS)** program created by Microsoft. It provides a tool for you to organize, store, and manipulate data, as well as to select and report on data.

Microsoft Access stores data in tables. Similar data are stored in the same table. For example, if you are storing data about participants in an event, you would include all the participants' names, addresses, and telephone numbers in one table.

The power of a relational database system comes with the ability to link tables together. A separate table of purchases for the tournament can be linked with the participant table. This allows users to easily combine the two tables; for example, the tournament manager would be able to print out the participants with a record of their tournament purchases.

SIDE NOTE
Do Not Confuse a DBMS with a Database

Access is a DBMS—it is software—whereas a database is a collection of data. You could use paper files to manage your Putts for Paws database, but you have chosen to use the Access DBMS software instead.

Real World Advice — Why Use Microsoft Access?

There are many database management system (DBMS) software packages available. Why should you use Access?

- Access is an easily available DBMS. It is included with many Microsoft Office suites, which makes Access very attractive to businesses.

- Access is a relational DBMS. What you learn about Access is transferable to other relational DBMSs.

- Access allows for easy interaction with other products in the Microsoft Office suite. You can export data and reports into Word or Excel. You can also import from Excel and Word into Access.

- Access is often used as a stand-alone DBMS, meaning a DBMS used by a single user. Even if a company uses another DBMS for many users, you can easily link to that database with Access. You can use Access queries to output the data you need to interact with other MS Office applications to perform tasks such as mail merges.

What Are the Four Main Objects in a Database?

Access has four main database **objects**: tables, queries, forms, and reports. A **table** is the database object that stores data organized in an arrangement of columns and rows. A **query** object retrieves specific data from other database objects and then displays only the data that you specify. Queries allow you to ask questions about the data in your tables. You can use a **form** object to enter new records into a table, edit or delete existing records in a table, or display existing records. The **report** object summarizes the fields and records from a table or query in an easy-to-read format suitable for printing.

Access objects have several views. Each **view** gives you a different perspective on the objects. For example, the **Datasheet view** of a table shows the data contents within a table. Figure 1 shows Datasheet view of a participant table. **Design view** of a table shows how fields are defined. Depending on the object, other views may exist. Figure 1 shows a toggle button ⬚ you can use to switch between Datasheet view and Design view. Figure 2 shows how a participant table would appear in Design view. In Datasheet view, you see the actual participants and their related information. In Design view, you see how the information is defined and structured. Figure 1 shows the charity event participant table. Each row contains corresponding pieces of data about the participant listed in that row. Each row in Access is called a **record**. A record is all of the data pertaining to one person, place, thing, or event. There are 17 participant records in the table. The second participant is John Trujillo.

Each column in Access is called a **field**. A field is a specific piece of information that is stored in every record. LastName is a field that shows the participant's last name. As you go across the table rows, you will see fields that represent the participant's first name and address.

Creating a New Database and Using Templates

When you create a new database, you can design it yourself starting with an empty database. If you take this approach, you develop the tables, fields, and the relationships among the tables. This requires you to decide what information you want to keep in your database, how this information should be grouped into tables, what relationships you need, and what queries and reports you need.

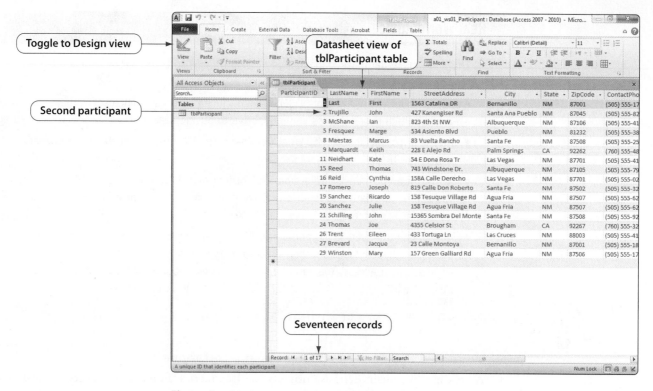

Figure 1 Datasheet view of tblParticipant table

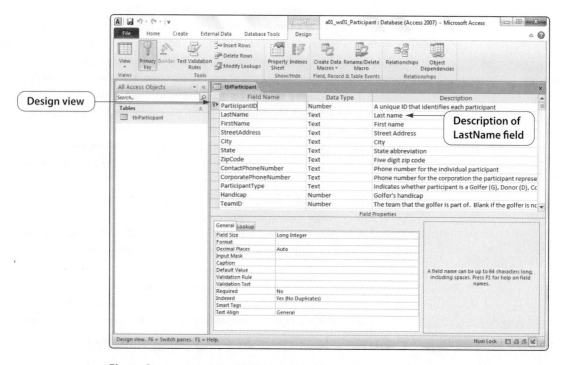

Figure 2 Design view of tblParticipant table

The other option in creating a new database is to start with a prebuilt template. A **template** is a structure of a database with tables, fields, forms, queries, and reports. Templates are professionally designed databases that you can either use as is or adapt to suit your needs. You can download a wide variety of templates from Microsoft's website Office.com. Microsoft provides sample database templates used for managing Assets, Contacts, Issues & Tasks, Non-profit, and Projects.

Templates are created by Microsoft employees or other users. Microsoft then allows users to rate the template so you can see what others have found useful. You can also download sample databases to experiment with. The difference between a template and a sample database is that a sample database has presupplied data, whereas a template is empty except for the structure and definitions. One of the popular databases among Access users is Microsoft's Northwind database, which has sales, customer, and employee data for a fictitious company named Northwind Traders.

For the tournament, the intern created an empty database and defined tables specifically for Putts for Paws. You will work with the database that has already been created. You need to open Access to get started.

myitlab

Workshop 1 Training

To Start Access

a. Click the **Start** button 🌐. From the Start menu, locate and then start **Microsoft Access 2010**.

Troubleshooting

If you do not see a folder called Microsoft Office, look for Microsoft Access 2010 in the list of available programs. Access may also be on the Start menu if it has been opened before. If you still do not see it, type Access in the Search programs and files box.

In Access you have the options of opening a blank database, opening an already existing database, or creating a new database from a template. If you start with a blank database, you will need to define your tables and fields. Microsoft provides several templates with tables and fields already defined to help you create a database.

Maneuvering in the Navigation Pane

An intern started the database for the Putts for Paws charity event. You will open the database, explore it, and make changes to it.

To Open a Database

a. Click the **File tab**, and then click **Open**.

b. In the Open dialog box, click the disk drive in the left pane where your student data files are located. Navigate through the folder structure and click **a01_ws01_Putts**, and then click **Open**. Access opens the database.

c. Click the **File tab**, and then click **Save Database As**. In the Save As dialog box, navigate to the location where you are saving your files. In the File name box, type Lastname_Firstname_ a01_ws01_Putts, replacing Lastname_Firstname with your own name. Click **Save**.

d. Click **Enable Content** in the Security Warning.

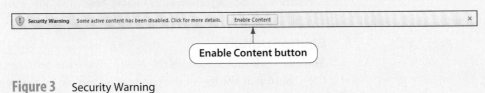

Enable Content button

Figure 3 Security Warning

Why Does Access Give You a Security Warning About Your Database?

Access displays a security warning asking you whether you trust the content of the database. If you download files from the Internet or get them from an unknown source, they may contain viruses. Until you tell Access that you trust this content, Access disables features that might allow the virus to infect your computer.

- Make sure you run a virus scan on any file before you say it should be trusted. You do not want to trust content that you are unsure about.

- You can click Enable Content to trust the content for a single use.

- To trust a database permanently, you can store it in a trusted location. Depending on your computer and operating system, certain locations are predefined as trusted. Click File, click Options, click Trust Center, and then select Trust Center Settings for the Access Trust Center where you can add other locations to the trusted locations.

Ways to View the Objects in the Navigation Pane

When you open a database, Access displays the **Navigation Pane** on the left side as shown in Figure 4. This pane allows you to view the objects in the database. The standard view in the Navigation Pane shows all objects in the database organized by object type. You can see that the database has three tables: tblItem, tblOrder, and tblOrderLine. There is one query, one form, and one report.

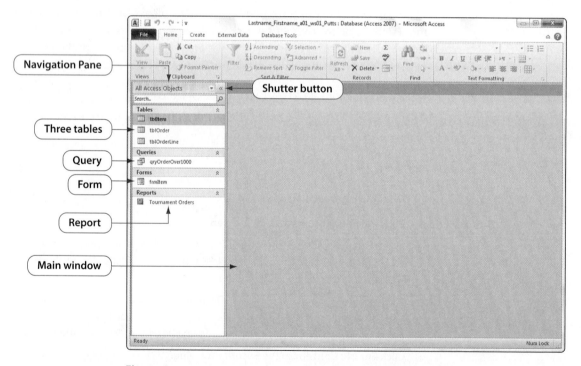

Figure 4   Opening screen for Lastname_Firstname_a01_ws01_Putts

Shutter Button

You can work in Access with the Navigation Pane open or closed. The Shutter Bar Open/Close button at the top of the pane opens and closes the pane.

To Open and Close the Navigation Pane

a. Click the **Shutter Bar Close** button ⧏ to close the Navigation Pane. Access closes the pane, allowing for a larger working space in the database, but leaves the Navigation Pane on the side of the window for when you need it.

b. Click the **Shutter Bar Open** button ⧐ to open the pane again.

Customizing the Navigation Pane

While the default view of the Navigation Pane is all objects such as tables, queries, forms, and reports, organized by object type, you have several choices of views.

To Customize the Navigation Pane

a. Click the **Navigation Pane arrow** ⊙ to display the Navigation Pane view options. The default view is displayed, which is Object Type and All Access Objects.

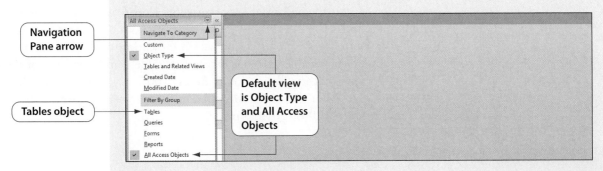

Figure 5   Navigation Pane options (default view)

b. Click **Tables**.

Only the three tables are displayed in the Navigation Pane. When you have many objects in a database, it helps to restrict objects that are shown in the Navigation Pane.

c. Click the **Navigation Pane arrow** ⊙ again, and then click **Tables and Related Views**. The objects are organized by tables. Any query, report, or form related to that table is listed with the table.

Figure 6   Tables and related views in Navigation Pane

Using the Search Box

Currently, there are only a few objects in your database. However, as you work with a database, more objects may be added as you develop reports and queries. As a result, to help you find objects, Access provides a Search box.

To Search for an Object

a. In the Search box at the top of the Navigation Pane, type Order. Access searches for and displays all objects with the word **Order** in their name.

b. Click the **Clear Search String** button to see all objects again.

c. Click the **Navigation Pane arrow** again. Click **Object Type**, click the **Navigation Pane arrow**, and then select **All Access Objects**. This returns you to the default view, which is what will be used throughout this module.

File Extensions in Access

A **file extension** is the suffix on all file names that helps Windows understand what information is in a file and what program should open the file. However, Windows automatically hides these extensions so you often do not notice them. Access 2007 and Access 2010 both use the file extension .accdb indicating that databases created in the two versions are compatible with one another. The file name at the top of the window in Figure 7 shows that the file version is Access 2007–2010. Be careful not to confuse DBMS with the database. The DBMS software you are using is Access 2010, but the database is in Access 2007–2010 format.

To View a File Extension

a. Click the **File tab** to display Backstage view. Under **Information about Lastname_Firstname_a01_ws01_Putts**, you see that the file extension is .accdb.

b. Click the **Home tab**.

File tab to get to Backstage view

File stored in Access 2007–2010 format

File extension is .accdb

Figure 7 Backstage view showing file extension

Quick Reference File Extensions in Access 2002, 2003, 2007, and 2010

Extension	Description	Version of Access	Compatibility
ACCDB	Access database files.	2010 and 2007	Cannot be opened in Access 2002-2003.
ACCDE	Access database files that are in "execute only" mode. Visual Basic for Applications (VBA) source code is hidden.	2010 and 2007	Cannot be opened in Access 2002-2003.
ACCDT	Access database templates.	2010 and 2007	Cannot be opened in Access 2002-2003.
MDB	Access 2002-2003 database files.	2003 and 2002	Can be opened in Access 2007 and 2010. Access 2007 and 2010 can save files in this format.
MDE	Access database files that are in "execute only" mode. Visual Basic for Applications (VBA) source code is hidden.	2003 and 2002	Can be opened in Access 2007 and 2010. Access 2007 and 2010 can save files in this format.

Introducing Tables

Tables store data organized in an arrangement of columns and rows. For illustration, think about the charity event, Putts for Paws. There are many ways participants and companies can participate in the event and help the charity. For example, a participant can play in the event, a company can pay for a foursome to play in the event, or it can sponsor various items such as a cart, hole, or flag. As a result, Painted Paradise needs to keep a record of the available options and what corporations or participants have purchased as shown in Figure 8.

ItemID	ItemDescription	QuantityAvailable	AmountToBeCharged	Notes
G1	Golfer – one	100	$200.00	
TEAM	Golfers – team of four	10	$550.00	
CTEAM	Golfers – corporate team of four	10	$850.00	Includes hole sponsorship
CART	Cart sponsor	40	$2,000.00	Logo or brand displayed on cart
HOLE	Hole sponsor	18	$500.00	Logo or brand displayed on hole
FLAG	Flag sponsor	18	$500.00	Logo or brand displayed on flagstick

Figure 8 Data in the tblItem table

As mentioned previously, the power of a relational database comes when you link tables. The tblItem table shown in Figure 8 contains information about items that a participant or corporation can buy to support the charity, including the items available, a description, the quantity available to be sold, the amount that will be charged for the item, and notes about the item. However, you cannot see who has ordered these items. That additional information becomes available when you use relationships to look at other tables.

Import a Table

Recently, a colleague compiled a list of participants in an Access table in another database. You will begin your work for Putts for Paws by importing this participant table from the Participant database into your database. **Importing** is the process of copying data from another file, such as a Word file or Excel workbook, into a separate file, such as an Access database.

To Import an Access Object

a. Click the **External Data tab**, and then click **Access** in the Import & Link group. The Get External Data – Access Database dialog box is displayed.

Figure 9 External Data tab

b. Click **Browse**, navigate to your student data folder, and then select the **a01_ws01_ Participant** database. Click **Open**, and then click **OK**. Access opens the Import Objects dialog box.

Troubleshooting

If you do not see the Import Objects dialog box, you may have chosen Access from the Export group on the Ribbon rather than from the Import & Link group.

c. If necessary, click the **Tables tab**. Click **tblParticipant**, and then click **OK**. Access displays the message: All objects were imported successfully.

d. Click **Close** at the bottom of the dialog box.

e. Double-click **tblParticipant** in the Navigation Pane to open the table.
   Access opens the table. You may not see exactly the same number of columns and rows in your table because how much of the table is visible is dependent on how large your Access window is. You can change the size of the Access window by using your mouse to resize it or by clicking the Maximize button ▣ to maximize the Access window.

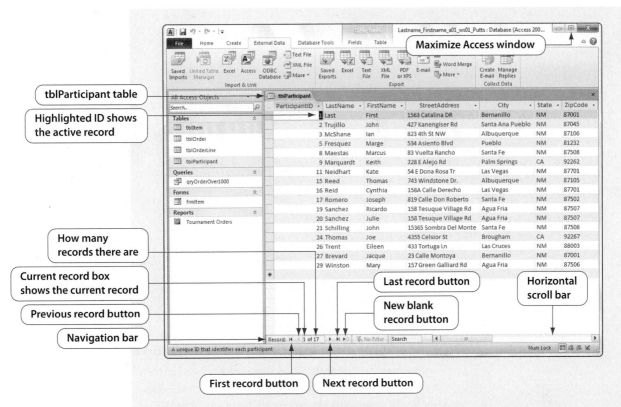

tblParticipant table

Highlighted ID shows the active record

How many records there are

Current record box shows the current record

Previous record button

Navigation bar

Maximize Access window

Last record button

New blank record button

Horizontal scroll bar

First record button

Next record button

Figure 10   Imported tblParticipant table

Real World Advice   What Should You Name Your Tables?

You want to use a name that is easy to understand. While Access allows you to give any name you want to a table, the name tblParticipant follows a standard naming convention:

- Use a name that starts with *tbl*. That allows you to distinguish tables from queries at a glance.
- Follow that with a name that is descriptive. You want it to be easy to remember what is in the table.
- Make the name short enough that it is easy to see in the Navigation Pane.
- You can use spaces in table names (e.g., tbl Participant), but avid Access users avoid them because it makes advanced tasks more difficult.
- You can use special characters in names. Some people use underscores where a space would otherwise be, such as tbl_Participant.

Navigate Through a Table

Carefully examine the tblParticipant table. Each row of data contains information about the participant listed in the LastName field. There are 17 participant records in the table with the second record being John Trujillo. You will change the name in the record for the first participant to your name.

To Change the First Record to Your Name

a. If necessary, click the **First record** button ⊮ to return to the first participant.

b. Press ⎡Tab⎤ to move to the LastName column.

c. Replace Last in the first record of the LastName column with your last name.

d. Press ⎡Tab⎤ to move to the next column, and then replace First with your first name in the FirstName column.

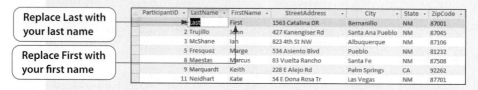

Replace Last with your last name

Replace First with your first name

ParticipantID	LastName	FirstName	StreetAddress	City	State	ZipCode
	Last	First	1563 Catalina DR	Bernanillo	NM	87001
2	Trujillo	John	427 Kanengiser Rd	Santa Ana Pueblo	NM	87045
3	McShane	Ian	823 4th St NW	Albuquerque	NM	87106
5	Fresquez	Marge	534 Asiento Blvd	Pueblo	NM	81232
8	Maestas	Marcus	83 Vuelta Rancho	Santa Fe	NM	87508
9	Marquardt	Keith	228 E Alejo Rd	Palm Springs	CA	92262
11	Neidhart	Kate	54 E Dona Rosa Tr	Las Vegas	NM	87701

Figure 11   Replace Last and First with your name

Navigate Through a Table with the Navigation Bar

At the bottom of the table, Access provides a **Navigation bar** that allows you to move through the table. You can move record by record, skip to the end, or if you know a specific record, jump to that record. The highlighted ID shows the active record. When you open the table, the first record is active.

Examine the various parts of the Navigation bar as shown in Figure 10. The Current Record box shows which record is active and how many records are in the table. There are four arrow buttons in the Navigation bar that you can use to move between records.

To Navigate Through the Table Using the Navigation Bar

a. Click the **Next record** button ▶ to move to the second record. The **Current Record** box changes to show **2 of 17**. Access highlights the first name of participant John Trujillo.

b. Click the **Next record** button ▶ to move to the third participant. The **Current Record** box changes to show **3 of 17**.

c. Click the **First record** button ⊮ to return to the first participant.

d. Click the **New (blank) record** button ▶⁎ to go to the first blank row. Alternatively, you could click in the ParticipantID field of the first blank row.

  The first blank row at the end of the table is the **append row**. This row allows you to enter new records to the table. Notice that Access displays an asterisk in the **record selector** box (the small box at the left of the record) to indicate that it is the append row. When you type information here, you create a new participant record. Whenever you add a participant, you want to make sure you are in the append row so you are not changing the information for an existing participant. You will add a participant to this empty row.

Append row

Asterisk in the record selector box

Figure 12 Append a new record

e. Make sure that the append row (blank row) is selected and that the record selector box contains an asterisk. In the ParticipantID field, type 30. Press Tab to get to the next field. In the LastName column, type Fox.

Alternatively, you can press Enter after typing text in a field to move to the next field. Also, notice that when you start typing, the record indicator changed from an asterisk to a pencil. The pencil means that you are in edit mode. The record after Fox now becomes the new append row. Press Enter, and then in the FirstName column, type Jeff.

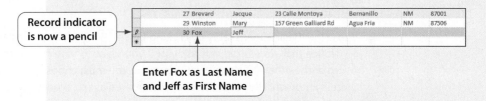

Record indicator is now a pencil

Enter Fox as Last Name and Jeff as First Name

Figure 13 Enter participant Fox into the append row

f. Continue entering the data for Jeff Fox using the following information:

StreetAddress	1509 Las Cruces Drive
City	Las Cruces
State	NM
ZipCode	88003
ContactPhoneNumber	(505) 555–8786
CorporatePhoneNumber	(leave blank)

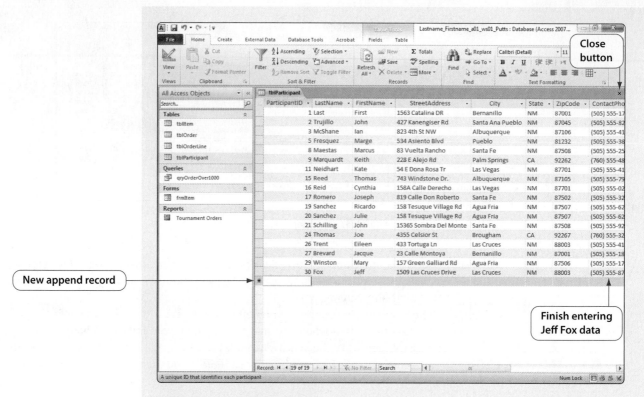

Figure 14 Finish entering Jeff Fox data

g. Close the tblParticipant table by clicking **Close** ☒. Keep Access and the database open. Notice that Access did not ask you if you want to save the table. Access is not like Word or the other Office applications where you must choose an option to save the file. Access automatically saves the data you entered as you type it.

Real World Advice — Break Compound Fields into Their Parts

You might wonder why the name field and address fields are divided into multiple fields. Would it not be easier to have a single field for Name and a single field for Address? It might be easier for data entry, but it is much more difficult for reporting.

- Break names into first name and last name fields. That means you can sort on people alphabetically by last name, and if two people have the same last name, you can perform a secondary sort by first name.

- Break addresses into fields such as StreetAddress, City, State, and ZipCode. This allows reporting by state, city, or other fields.

- For other fields, consider whether you might want to report on smaller parts of the field. For example, for PhoneNumber in some applications, you might want to report on AreaCode. However, that would be rare, and so you usually use just one field.

Differences Between Access and Excel

An Access table looks similar to an Excel worksheet. Both have numbered rows of data and columns with labels. In addition, in both applications the columns are called *fields* and both allow you to manage data, perform calculations, and report on the data. The major difference between the two applications is that Access allows multiple tables with relationships between the tables, thus the term *relational database*. For example, if you are keeping track of participants and the items that they order, you create a table of participants and another table of orders. In Excel, you would have to repeat the participant information on each order.

When you look at Access, you notice that several tables are used for an order. Why use multiple tables for a single order? Figure 15 shows how an order would look in Access and in Excel. The Excel version has to repeat the participant's information on multiple lines. This leads to problems:

- Data redundancy—With repetition, you create redundant information. John Trujillo bought a cart and a team, so in Excel you have two lines. You would have to repeat the address information on both records. It is not efficient to enter the address information twice.

- Errors—Redundant information leads to errors. If the address needs to be changed, you have to look for all records with that information to make sure it is fixed everywhere.

- Loss of data—Suppose that John Trujillo orders just one item. If you deleted the ordered item, it would mean deleting all the information about him as well as the order.

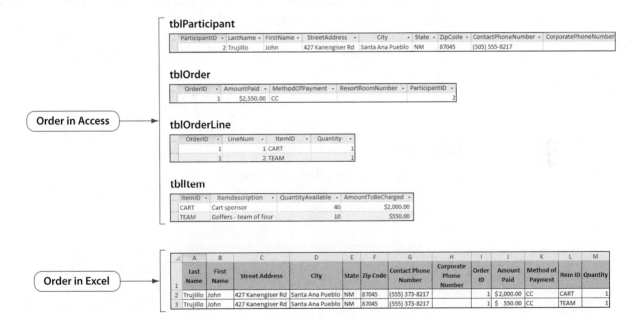

Figure 15   John Trujillo's order in Access and in Excel

Because Access and Excel have so many common functionalities, many people use the tool that they are more confident using. If you prefer to use both, however, you can easily switch by exporting your data from Access to Excel or from Excel into Access. You can also use one tool for most uses and import your data into the other when you need to.

Discovering a Database (Manual Query)

Before you explore the database using Access queries, you will explore the database manually. This will give you an understanding of what Access can do. Patti Rochelle, the events coordinator at Painted Paradise, wants to send follow-up letters to those participants that have booked a corporate team for the Putts for Paws charity event. She asks you which participants have booked a team. First, you have to discover how a team is indicated in the database. Teams are items that participants can order, so you will start in the tblItem table.

To Manually Navigate a Database

a. In the Navigation Pane, double-click **tblItem**.

Access opens tblItem in Datasheet view. Explore the data, and you will notice that a corporate team is indicated as CTEAM.

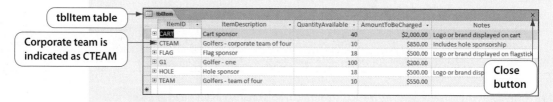

Figure 16   tblItem table

b. **Close** ⊠ the tblItem table.

Next you need to determine which orders include CTEAM. Orders are composed of data from tblOrderLine and tblOrder.

c. Double-click **tblOrderLine** to open the table.

Scan for orders that include CTEAM. There are two, OrderID 4 and OrderID 11.

d. **Close** ☒ the tblOrderLine table.

e. Double-click **tblOrder** to open the table and find OrderID 4 and 11.

You need to find which participants placed these orders. Access uses common fields to relate tables. tblParticipant and tblOrder have ParticipantID in common. You find that the ParticipantID for OrderID 4 is 5 and for OrderID 11 is 19.

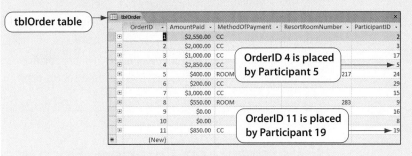

Figure 17   tblOrder table

f. **Close** ☒ the tblOrder table.

g. Double-click **tblParticipant** to open the table.

Scan for the participants that match the two ParticipantIDs you identified earlier, 5 and 19. You find that OrderID 4 was placed by ParticipantID Marge Fresquez. In addition, OrderID 11 was placed by ParticipantID Ricardo Sanchez.

Figure 18   tblParticipant table

h. **Close** ☒ the tblParticipant table.

SIDE NOTE
Knowing Your Data

It is important to know what data is in your database. While Access will do the hard part of matching tables on common fields and finding the results, you still need to tell it what fields you want and where the fields are located.

You now can tell Ms. Rochelle which participants have booked corporate teams and the address that the follow-up should be sent to. However, it may seem like a lot of work to find out who booked the corporate teams. Access queries make this task easier.

While Access allows you to leave several tables open at the same time, it is a good idea to get into the habit of closing a table when you are done with it.

- First, there are many Access functions that use a table that cannot be completed while the table is open. If you close the table, you no longer risk running into this problem.

- Second, closing tables makes it less likely that you will accidently change the wrong table.

- Third, each table open requires more memory for Access. With larger tables, Access could be slowed down by having multiple tables open.

Understanding Queries, Forms, and Reports

You have explored tables, the first of the four main objects in Access. As mentioned previously, the other three objects are queries, forms, and reports. Each object provides a different way to work with data stored in tables. A query is used to ask questions about your data. A form is primarily used to enter data into your database or display data in your database. Reports are used to provide professional looking displays of your tables that are suitable for printing. In this section, you will work with queries, forms, and reports within your database.

Introducing Queries

A query is a way to ask questions about your data. For our charity golf tournament, you can use queries to get answers to questions such as "What is Ian McShane's phone number?" "What has John Trujillo ordered?" "What orders are over $1,000?"

You can also conduct more complex queries such as calculating a score given a player's strokes and their handicap.

One of the strengths of Access is the ability to ask such questions and get answers quickly. You traced who ordered corporate teams earlier in the workshop. That was difficult because you had to keep track of fields such as ParticipantID in one table and then look them up in another table. By using queries, Access will match common fields in the tables and trace the order for you.

You will look at two different views of queries in this workshop:

- *Datasheet view* shows the results of your query.

- *Design view* shows how the query is constructed. It shows the tables, fields, and selection criterion for the query.

Creating a Query Using a Wizard

Access provides wizards to help you with tasks. A **wizard** is a step-by-step guide that walks you through tasks by asking you questions to help you decide what you want to do. Once you have some experience, you can also do the task yourself without a guide. You would like to know which participants are from Bernanillo, New Mexico. You will use the Query Wizard to create the query getting all participants, and then you will modify the query design to select those from Bernanillo.

To Create a Query with a Wizard

a. Click the **Create tab**, and then click **Query Wizard** in the Queries group.

Figure 19 Create tab on the Ribbon

Access displays the New Query dialog box and asks you what kind of query you want.

Troubleshooting

If this is the first time that you have used this wizard, Access may tell you that the feature is not currently installed and ask if you want to install it. Reply Yes and wait while Access configures this wizard.

b. If necessary, click Simple Query Wizard. Click **OK**.

Access asks you which fields you want. You have choices of tables or queries as the source for your fields. Your database has four tables to select as a source. You will choose only one table. You could choose fields from multiple tables, but that is not necessary in this query.

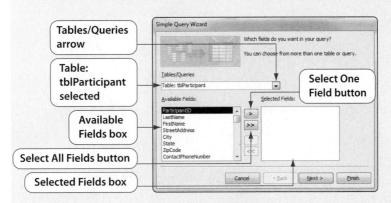

Figure 20 Select tblParticipant

c. Click the **Tables/Queries arrow** to see available field sources. Select **Table: tblParticipant** as the source of your fields.

The dialog box has two list boxes. The box on the left shows you all available fields from this table or query. The box on the right shows you all the fields that you have selected for this query. You use the buttons between the two list boxes to move fields from one box to the other. Selecting a field and clicking the One Field button ▸ moves that field from the Available Fields box to the Selected Fields box. Clicking the All Fields button ▸▸ moves all fields.

d. Click **LastName** under Available Fields, and then click the **One Field** button ▸ . Access moves the LastName field to the Selected Fields box.

e. Click **FirstName**, and then click the **One Field** button ▸ .

f. Click **City**, and then click the **One Field** button ▸ .

Your field list in the right box should be in the following order: LastName, FirstName, and City.

Troubleshooting

If you accidently add the wrong field to the Selected Fields box, select the field, and use the One Field Back button $\boxed{<}$ to place it back in the Available Fields box.

If you select the fields in the wrong order, Access does not have a way to reorder the fields. It is best to place them all back to the Available Fields box using the All Fields Back button $\boxed{<<}$ and then select them again in the right order.

g. Click **Next** to continue to the next page of the wizard. In the What title do you want for your query? box type **qryParticipantBernanillo**.

h. Click **Open the query to view information**, and then click **Finish**.

Access shows you the results of your query. Once you have created this query, the name is displayed under All Access Objects in the Navigation Pane.

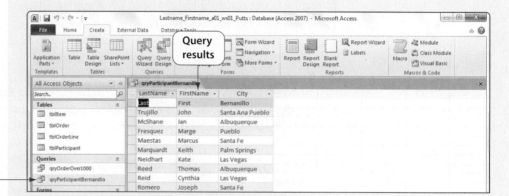

Figure 21 Results of your query

i. Click **Save** $\boxed{\blacksquare}$ to save the query, and then close the query.

Query results are a recordset with records and fields created at **run time**, which means that it is created each time you run the query. This run time table is referred to as a **recordset**. The method to create the query is saved but not the actual results. That means that if you add a participant who meets the query criteria to the participant table, the next time you run this query, that participant will appear in the results of this query.

Real World Advice Naming Your Queries

Access will allow you to give your query any name you want. There are two important considerations:

• You want to remember what a query does, so make the name as descriptive as possible. A query named *tblParticipant Query* will probably have no meaning for you in a few days. It will be easier to remember that *qryParticipantBernanillo* shows participants from Bernanillo.

• When you are looking at field sources, you often have a choice between tables and queries. Starting all your tables with *tbl* and all your queries with *qry* makes it easy to distinguish what you are choosing.

Real World Advice | Using Wizards in Access

Access wizards are shortcuts to building objects, such as reports and forms. They select fields, format the data, and perform calculations. After the wizard does the initial formatting, you can modify the resulting report or form to get exactly what you want.

Selecting a Value Using Design View

The Query Wizard uses a question-and-answer dialog box to create a query. The other method of creating a query is using Design view. Design view goes behind the scenes of the data and shows you the detailed structure of an Access object.

To Switch to Design View of a Query

a. Right-click **qryParticipantBernanillo** in the Navigation Pane.

b. Select **Design View** from the shortcut menu.

Access opens the Design view of your query. The Query Tools Design tab is open on the Ribbon. The left side of the screen shows the Navigation Pane. The top half of the screen shows the **query workspace**, which is the source for data in the query. In this case, the source is the table tblParticipant. The bottom half is called the **query design grid**. It shows which fields are selected in this query: LastName, FirstName, and City.

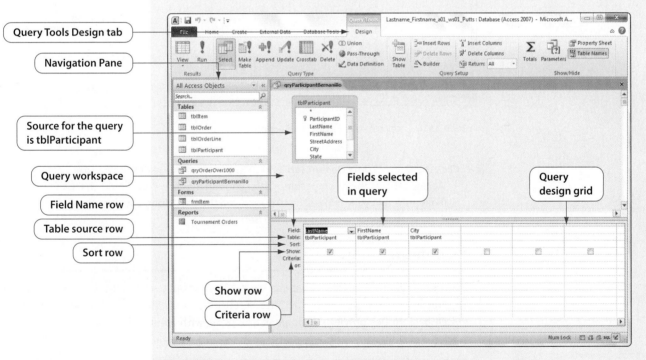

Figure 22   Design view for qryParticipantBernanillo

Selecting Values in a Query

Each row in the design grid shows information about the field. The top row is Field name. The next row shows the table or source for this field. The Sort row allows you to specify the order of records shown in your query results by setting one or more sort fields. The Show row is a check box that specifies whether the field is shown in the table of query results. The Criteria rows allow you to select certain records by setting conditions for the field contents. You are going to change this query to see which participants are from Bernanillo. You will do that by adding selection criteria.

To Select a Criterion in a Query

a.   Click the **Criteria cell** in the City column.

b.   Type Bernanillo in the cell.

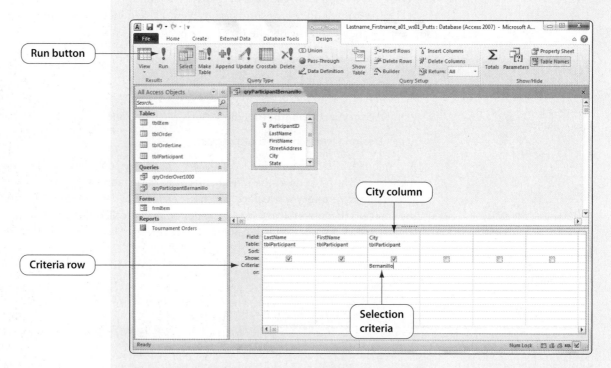

Figure 23   Enter criteria in a query selection

c.   Click the **Query Tools Design tab**, and then click **Run** in the Results group.
        Access returns the query results. When you run a query, you should check the results to make sure that they make sense. You wanted the participants with a city of Bernanillo, and the participants shown are only in Bernanillo.

Troubleshooting

If your query results are not what you expect (two records should display), you made an error in entering your selection criteria. Click the View button on the Home tab to switch back to Design view. Compare your criteria with Figure 23. Make sure that you spelled *Bernanillo* correctly and that it is in the City column.

Quick Reference   Selection Criterion in a Query

When you typed *Bernanillo* in the criteria, you asked Access to select those participants that had a City equal to Bernanillo. The equal sign is implied, though you can enter it if you wish. Figure 24 shows other operators that can be entered in the selection criterion.

Operator	Meaning	Description
=	Equal to	Selects the records where the field value is equal to the value provided. If no operator is used, equal to is assumed.
<	Less than	Selects the records where the field value is less than the value provided.
>	Greater than	Selects the records where the field value is greater than the value provided.
< =	Less than or equal	Selects the records where the field value is less than or equal to the value provided.
> =	Greater than or equal	Selects the records where the field value is greater than or equal to the value provided.
< >	Not equal	Selects the records where the field value is not equal to the value provided.
Between	Between	Selects the records where the field values listed are within the two values. For example, between 1 and 7 is true for any value between 1 and 7 (includes the value of 1 and the value of 7).

Figure 24   Common selection criterion

Printing Query Results

If you want to print your query results, you can do this from the File tab. Printing tables is done the same way.

To Print a Query

a. Click the **File tab** in the Ribbon to display Backstage view.

b. Click **Print**, and then click **Print Preview** to see what the results would look like if printed.

c. If your instructor asks you to print your results, on the **Print Preview tab** click **Print**. In the Print dialog box, select the correct printer, and then click **OK**.

d. On the **Print Preview tab**, click **Close Print Preview**.

e. Click **Save** in the Quick Access Toolbar.

f. **Close** the qryParticipantBernanillo query.

Troubleshooting

If you accidently closed Access instead of just the query, open Access the same way you did at the beginning of the workshop. Click the File tab, and then click the name Lastname_Firstname_a01_ws01_Putts to open the database again.

Introducing Forms

A form provides another interface to a table beyond the table in Datasheet view. In corporate databases, end users of a database computer system often use forms to enter and change data. You can also use forms to limit the amount of data you see from a table. In a personal database, you can create forms for entering data if you wish.

Forms have three views:

- **Form view** shows the data in the form. This is the view you use to enter or change data. You cannot change the form design in this view.

- **Layout view** shows the form and the data. Some of the form design such as field lengths and fonts can be changed in this view. The data cannot be changed.

- Design view shows the form design but not the data. Any aspect of the report design can be changed. The data cannot be changed.

Creating a Form

You want to create a form to make it easier to enter a participant. There are different types of forms that can be created. The default form shows one participant at a time and has each field clearly labeled.

To Create a Form

a. Click **tblParticipant** in the Navigation Pane, click the **Create tab**, and then click **Form** in the Forms group.

b. Click **Save** 🖫 to save the form. In the Save As dialog box, type frmParticipant as the Form Name, and then click **OK**.

Access creates a form. Notice that the form displays the same Navigation bar that you had in the table. That is because a form is a data entry or display tool for the table. You can use it to navigate through your table. The form is created in Layout view, which allows you make minor changes to the design.

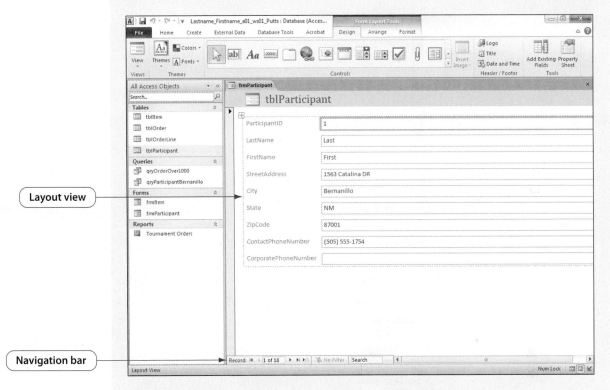

Figure 25 Form in Layout view

c. Click the title of the form **tblParticipant**, and then click in the field again to get an insertion point. Replace the old title with Participant form Lastname_Firstname, replacing Lastname and Firstname with your own name.

d. Press Enter, and then click **Save** 🖫 to save your form.

Entering Data via a Form

Jackie Silva has asked to register for the tournament. You will use your newly created form to add her to the participant table. It is very important that you navigate to the append row so you enter her information into a blank form. If you see data about a participant in the form, you will be replacing that participant with Jackie Silva instead of adding a new participant.

To Enter Data Using a Form

a. Click the **View arrow** in the Views group, and then click **Form View**. This view allows you to use the form to enter data into the table.

b. Click the **New (blank) record button** ▶＊ on the Navigation bar. If you see a participant's name in the form, try again. This will be record 19 of 19 in the Navigation bar.

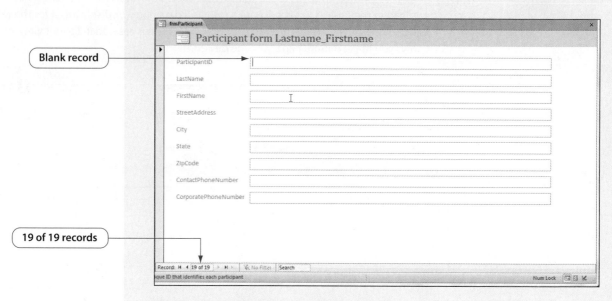

Figure 26   Blank append record

c. Type the following information into the form. Press ⎡Enter⎤ or ⎡Tab⎤ to move to each field.

ParticipantID	31
LastName	Silva
FirstName	Jackie
StreetAddress	1509 Main Street
City	Santa Ana Pueblo
State	NM
ZipCode	87044
ContactPhoneNumber	(505) 555–3355
CorporatePhoneNumber	Leave blank

d. **Close** ✕ the form. The participant data you entered in the form is saved to the table.

e. Double-click **tblParticipant** under Tables on the Navigation Pane.

f. Click the **Last Record** button ▶ on the Navigation bar. Verify that Jackie Silva has been added to your table.

g. **Close** ✕ the table.

SIDE NOTE
Saving in Access

Unlike Word and Excel, Access saves your data as it is entered. Unless you notice while you are typing, you cannot undo an inserted record once you have moved to the next record. Typing over the data in another record means that you lose the data that was there.

CONSIDER THIS | **Adding Data Directly into a Table vs. Adding Data via a Form**

You have added two participants to your table. Earlier, you added a row to the table and added Jeff Fox. Now, you have added Jackie Silva via a form. Which was easier for you? Why would most companies use forms to enter data?

Introducing Reports

A report provides an easy-to-read format suitable for printing. A sample report is shown in Figure 27. As you can see, the report has page headers (the column headings) and a footer. You can easily provide column totals. When printing data for management presentations, you usually use a report rather than a query. The source of data for a report can be a table or query.

Reports have four views:

- **Report view** shows how the report will look in a continuous page layout.

- **Print Preview** shows how the report will look on the printed page. This view allows you to change the page layout.

- Layout view shows the report and the data. Some of the report design such as field lengths and fonts can be changed in this view.

- Design view shows the report design but not the data. Any aspect of the report design can be changed.

Tournament Participants by City Lastname_Firstname			
City	LastName	FirstName	ContactPhoneNumber
Agua Fria			
	Sanchez	Julie	(505) 555-6243
	Sanchez	Ricardo	(505) 555-6243
	Winston	Mary	(505) 555-1756
Albuquerque			
	McShane	Ian	(505) 555-4149
	Reed	Thomas	(505) 555-7943
Bernanillo			
	Brevard	Jacque	(505) 555-1828
	Last	First	(505) 555-1754
Brougham			
	Thomas	Joe	(760) 555-3227
Las Cruces			
	Fox	Jeff	(505) 555-8786
	Trent	Eileen	(505) 555-4101
Las Vegas			
	Neidhart	Kate	(505) 555-4103
	Reid	Cynthia	(505) 555-0247

Monday, April 22, 2013	Page 1 of 1

Figure 27 An Access report

Creating a Report Using a Wizard

The report feature in Access allows us to easily design reports that can serve management purposes and look professional. You will create a report listing the participants in the database. You will use the Report Wizard to create the report.

The Report Wizard starts similarly to the Query Wizard in selecting fields for the report. After that the wizard asks questions about report formatting that were not part of the Query Wizard.

You want to create a list of participants entered in the tournament with their contact phone numbers. You will group all the participants from a single city in a single group. You will print the participants in alphabetic order within each group.

To Create a Report Using a Wizard

a. Click the **Create tab**, and then click **Report Wizard** in the Reports group. Click the **Tables/Queries arrow**, and then click **Table: tblParticipant**.

b. Using the **One Field button** ⟩ move these fields to the Selected Fields box: **LastName**, **FirstName**, **City**, and **ContactPhoneNumber**.

c. Click **Next**. The wizard asks if you want to add grouping levels.

d. Click to select **City**, and then click the **One Field** button $\boxed{>}$ to group by City. When you make this selection the box on the right of the dialog box shows a preview of what the report grouping will look like.

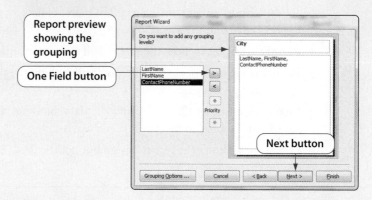

Figure 28 Add grouping levels

e. Click **Next**.

The wizard asks what sort order you want. You always want to put your report in some order that makes it easy to read and understand. Otherwise a report with a lot of information is difficult to understand. In this report, you will list participants alphabetically.

f. In the 1 box, click the **arrow**, and then select **LastName**. If necessary, make sure that the sort order is **Ascending** (alphabetical from A to Z).

g. In the 2 box, click the **arrow**, and then select **FirstName**.

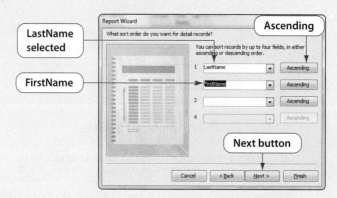

Figure 29 Add sorting

h. Click **Next**. If necessary, change the layout to **Stepped** and the orientation to **Portrait**.

i. Click **Next**. In the What title do you want for your report? box, type Tournament Participants by City as the title for your report.

j. Click **Finish**.

Access displays the report in Print Preview. You notice that the ContactPhoneNumber heading is not fully shown. You can fix that easily in Layout view.

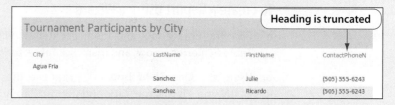

Figure 30 Report in Print Preview

k. Right-click anywhere on the report, and then click **Layout View** from the shortcut menu. Click the heading of the **ContactPhoneNumber** column.

l. Point to the **left border** of the selected heading until the Horizontal Resize pointer displays ⟷.

m. Drag to the left until you can see the entire column heading.

n. Double-click the **title** of the report. At the end of the report title after **City**, add Lastname_Firstname using your own name.

o. Click **Save** 🖫 to save the report.

Notice that the City data is a line above the data in the other columns. That is because the participants are grouped by city. Within City, participants are sorted alphabetically.

CONSIDER THIS | **Grouping vs. Sorting**

Grouping arranges records together by the value of a single field. Sorting puts the records within a group in a specific order based on field values. When would you choose to sort your records, and when would you group before sorting?

Printing a Report

You can print reports the same way that you printed a query earlier using the File tab. You can also take advantage of Print Preview to print a report. You are currently in Layout view and need to change to Print Preview. You will use the button on the status bar to switch views.

To Print a Report

a. Click **Print Preview** 🔍 to change to Print Preview. Alternatively, you could change to Print Preview using the button on the Ribbon as you have done before. Your report should look like Figure 27.

b. If your instructor directs you to print the report, click **Print** in the Print group, and then click **OK**.

c. Click **Close Print Preview**. **Close** ☒ the report.

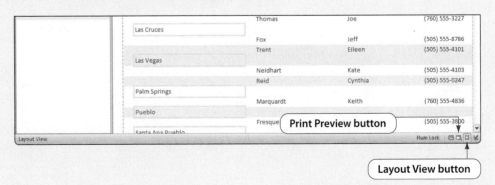

Figure 31   Switch view using the status bar

Backing Up Your Database

A **backup database** is an extra copy of your database that you can use to protect yourself from accidental loss of your database. Backups can help in cases of accidental deletion of data. You can return to the backup copy if you accidently delete the real database. It may not be as current as your real database, but it may save you from having to recreate the whole database. If you store the backup on another storage medium, it can also help in cases of hardware failure (such as a hard drive crash).

In Access, you make backups by using the Back Up Database command, which is available in the **Backstage view** on the Save & Publish tab. If you make multiple backup copies, you will want to give them different names. The backup feature appends the current date to the suggested file name. That allows you to easily distinguish various versions of the backups. You can be sure that you are getting the most recent one.

If you ever need a backup, simply return to the most recent copy that you have and start working with that file. You can copy it to the name of the file you want to work with.

To Back Up a Database

a. Click the **File tab**, and then click **Save & Publish**. Access displays Save Database As options in the right pane.

b. Under Advanced, click **Back Up Database**, and then click **Save As**. The Save As dialog box appears with a suggested file name that has the date appended.

c. Navigate to the drive and folder where you want to store your backup. Change the file name if necessary, and click **Save**.

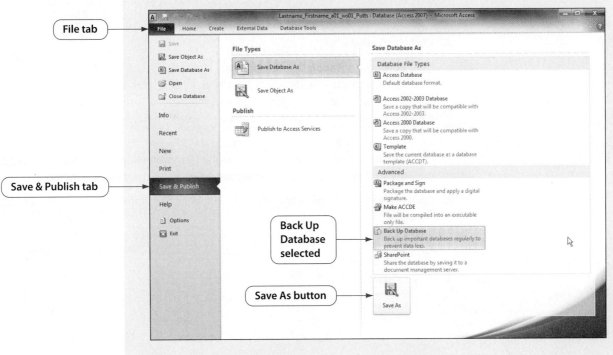

File tab

Save & Publish tab

Back Up Database selected

Save As button

Figure 32   Make a backup copy

CONSIDER THIS | Backups

What would you lose if your PC's hard drive crashed? Do you have copies of school work, photographs, or music? You may never need one, but which would be worse: making unnecessary backups or losing all your files?

Compact and Repair

While you work on an Access database, the size of the database file increases. When you delete a record or object or if you make changes to an object, Access does not reuse the original space. Access provides a compacting feature that makes more efficient use of disk space. **Compacting** rearranges objects to use disk space more efficiently and releases the now unused space. If you do not compact your database, its size can get very large quickly. The compact option also looks for damaged data and tries to repair it.

You have two options for compacting: (1) you can perform a single Compact and Repair Database action at any time, or (2) you can select Compact on Close. If you select Compact on Close, Access automatically compacts your database anytime you close it. Both options are available through Backstage view.

To Compact a Database

a. Click the **File tab**.

b. Click **Compact & Repair Database**.

    Access compacts your database, fixes it if necessary, and returns you to the Home tab. On a small database such as Putts for Paws, this action is very fast. On a larger database with many changes made, there may be a noticeable delay.

c. Click the **File tab**, and then click **Options**.

    By default, Compact on Close is turned off. Many professionals like to turn on Compact on Close so they do not need to remember to compact the database themselves.

d. Click **Current Database in the left pane**. Under Application Options, click the **Compact on Close** check box.

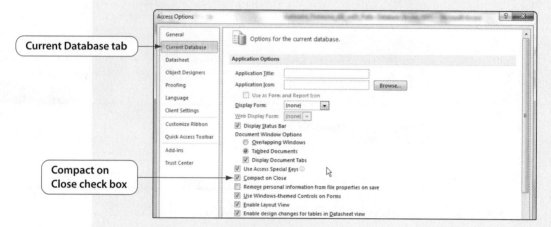

Current Database tab

Compact on Close check box

Figure 33   Select Compact on Close

e. Click **OK** to turn this option on. Access warns you that the option will not take effect until you close and reopen the database.

f. Click **OK**, and then **Close** ![close icon] Access.

Concept Check

1. You want to report on customers and orders. You expect to create several different reports from this data. Is Access or Excel most appropriate? Why?

2. For marketing purposes, you need to create a database identifying potential customers or prospects. Suggest names for the following tables:

   Potential customers or prospects

   Salesperson who identified the prospect

   Territory that each salesperson covers

3. You work in the human resources department. Your employee table needs to contain the employee's name, date that the employee was hired, expected retirement date, and emergency contact. Suggest field names for these fields.

4. For your human resources database, you need to list all those employees who are expected to retire in 2015. How would you get this list of employees?

5. Patti Rochelle, the events coordinator at Painted Paradise, wants to share the names of the charity tournament participants with the Santa Fe Animal Center. Would a report or a query be more appropriate? Why?

Key Terms

Append row 500
Backstage view 518
Backup database 518
Compacting 519
Data 490
Database 490
Database management system (DBMS) 490
Datasheet view 491
Design view 491
Field 491
File extension 496

Form 491
Form view 512
Importing 498
Information 490
Layout view 512
Navigation bar 500
Navigation Pane 494
Object 491
Print Preview 515
Query 491
Query design grid 509
Query results 508

Query workspace 509
Record 491
Record selector 500
Recordset 508
Report 491
Report view 515
Run time 508
Table 491
Template 492
View 491
Wizard 506

Visual Summary

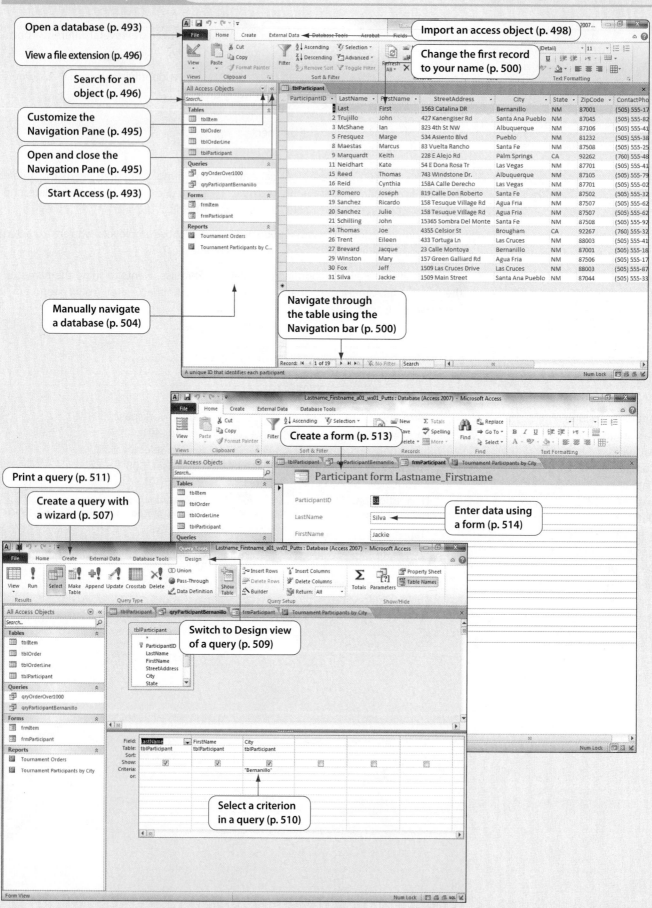

Open a database (p. 493)

View a file extension (p. 496)

Search for an object (p. 496)

Customize the Navigation Pane (p. 495)

Open and close the Navigation Pane (p. 495)

Start Access (p. 493)

Manually navigate a database (p. 504)

Import an access object (p. 498)

Change the first record to your name (p. 500)

Navigate through the table using the Navigation bar (p. 500)

Print a query (p. 511)

Create a query with a wizard (p. 507)

Create a form (p. 513)

Enter data using a form (p. 514)

Switch to Design view of a query (p. 509)

Select a criterion in a query (p. 510)

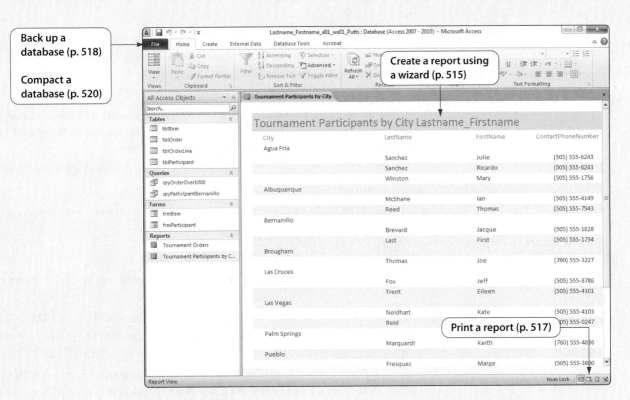

Back up a database (p. 518)

Compact a database (p. 520)

Create a report using a wizard (p. 515)

Print a report (p. 517)

Figure 34 Putts for Paws Charity Tournament Participants Final Database

Practice 1

Student data files needed:

a01_ws01_Painted_Treasures
a01_ws01_Products

You will save your file as:

Lastname_Firstname_a01_ws01_Painted_Treasures

Painted Treasures Gift Shop

Sales & Marketing

The Painted Treasures Gift Shop sells many products for the resort patrons. These include jewelry from local artists, Painted Paradise Linens, products from the resort's restaurant, and spa products. You will create a database that stores the gift shop's products. You will create a form to enter products and an inventory report.

a. Open and modify your database.

1. Start **Access**, and then open **a01_ws01_Painted_Treasures**.

2. Click the **File tab**, and then select **Save Database As**. In the Save As dialog box, navigate to where you are saving your files and then type Lastname_Firstname_a01_ws01_Painted_Treasures, replacing Lastname and Firstname with your own name. Click **Save**.

3. In the Security Warning, click **Enable Content**.

4. Click the **External Data tab**, and then click **Access** in the Import & Link group.

5. In the Get External Data – Access Database dialog box, click **Browse**, navigate to your student data files, and then select **a01_ws01_Products**. Click **Open**, and then click **OK**.

6. In the Import Objects dialog box, select **tblProduct**, click **OK**, and then click **Close**.

b. Create a query to find the clothing products.

1. Click the **Create tab**, and then click **Query Wizard** in the Queries group. Click **Simple Query Wizard**, and then click **OK**.

2. Select **Table: tblProduct** as the source of your fields.

3. In this order, select the **ProductID**, **Category**, **ProductDescription**, **Color**, **Size**, and **Price** fields and move them to the Selected Fields box. Click **Next**, click **Detail (shows every field of every record)**, and then click **Next**.

4. Under What title do you want for your query?, type qryProductsClothingType.

5. Click **Modify the query design**, and then click **Finish**.

6. Type Clothing in the Category Criteria cell, and then click **Run** in the Results group.

7. Save and close the query.

c. Create a form to enter new products.

1. Click **tblProduct** in the Navigation Pane, click the **Create tab**, and select **Form** in the Forms group.

2. Click **Save**, and then in the Save As dialog box, type frmProduct. Click **OK**.

3. In Layout view, select the form title, and then change the title of the form to Products Form Lastname_Firstname using your own name. Save the form.

4. Click the **Form Layout Tools Design tab**, click the **View button arrow** in the Views group, and then select **Form View**. Click **New (blank) record**, and then enter the following product in the blank append record:

ProductID	42
ProductDescription	Polo Shirt
Category	Clothing
QuantityInStock	35
Price	30.00
Size	L
Color	Blue

5. Close the form.

d. Create an inventory report.

1. Click the **Create tab**, and then select **Report Wizard** in the Reports group.

2. Click the **Tables/Queries arrow**, and then click **Table: tblProduct**.

3. Select the fields in the following order: **Category**, **ProductDescription**, **Color**, **Size**, and **QuantityInStock**. Click **Next**.

4. Under Do you want to add any grouping levels?, double-click **Category** and **ProductDescription**. Click **Next**.

5. In the 1 box, click the **arrow**, and then select **Color**. In the 2 box, click the **arrow**, and then select **Size**. Click **Next**.

6. Change the Orientation to **Landscape**, and then click **Next**.

7. Type Inventory Report as the title for your report, and then click **Finish**.

8. Switch to Layout view, and then at the end of the report title add Lastname_ Firstname, making it Inventory Report Lastname_Firstname using your own name. Fix the report columns as necessary.

9. **Save** and close the report, and then close the database.

Student data files needed:

a01_ps1_Planner

a01_ps1_Planner_Items

You will save your file as:

Lastname_Firstname_a01_ps1_Planner

Event Management

Production & Operations

Beth Rakes runs an event planning service. She is moving towards using Access to manage her business more effectively. In one database, she tracks clients, events, and menus that each client has booked. In another she has many decorations reserved for events. She has hired you to consolidate the databases and make some additional changes which will improve the database's functionality.

a. Start Access, and then open **a01_ps1_ Planner**. Save the file as Lastname_Firstname_ a01_ps1_Planner replacing Lastname_Firstname with your own name. In the Security Warning bar, click **Enable Content**.

b. Import tables from the Access database **a01_ps1_Planner_Items**, selecting the **tblEventItems** and **tblDecorations**. Do not save the import steps.

c. Open **tblClients**, and then change the First Name and Last Name in record **25** to Your Name.

d. Client Colorado Rojas moved to 725 Second Avenue (same city). Update his record.

e. Select tblDecorations. On the Create tab, click **Form** in the Forms group to create a form to enter decorations, and then save it as frmDecorations_initialLastname. Change the title of the form to Decorations Form_initialLastname, replacing initialLastname with your own initial and last name.

f. Due to customer demand Beth has added Red and White balloons to the available Decorations. Enter the following data into frmDecorations:

DecorID	DecorItem	Color	Category	Quantity	Price	ExtendedPrice
AutoNumber	Balloons	Red	Miscellaneous	12	1.99	Automatically calculated
AutoNumber	Balloons	White	Miscellaneous	12	1.99	Automatically calculated

g. Beth wants to be able to retrieve information on events and menus.

- Use the Query Wizard to create a query. The query results should list **LastName**, **FirstName**, **EventName**, **EventDate**, **MenuType**, and **CostPerPerson**.
- Run your query. Save your query as qryEventMenus_initialLastname.
- If your instructor directs you to print your results, print your query.

h. Mid-priced meals are the most popular. Beth wants a query that will return all the Menu Choices that are between 15 and 20 dollars.

- Use the Query Wizard to create a query. The query results should list **MenuType**, **CostPerPerson**, and **ServiceType**.
- Run your query. Save your query as qryMidPriceMeals_initialLastname.
- In Design view for **qryMidPriceMeals_initialLastname**, select all meals with CostPerPerson Between 15 and 20. Sort by **CostPerPerson** in Ascending order. Run the query.
- If your instructor directs you to print your results, print your query.

i. Create a report showing **EventDate**, **EventName**, **StartTime**, **EndTime**, **Location**, **TotalAttendees** and **Rate**. Do not add grouping levels. Sort by **EventDate** and **EventName**. Change the Orientation to **Landscape**. Name your report Events Report and then modify the report title to end with your initialLastname. Fix the report columns as necessary. If your instructor directs you to print your results, print your report.

j. Save and close the database.

 Additional Workshop Cases are available on the companion website and in the instructor resources.

WORKSHOP 2

Gathering Data into a Database

PREPARE CASE

Red Bluff Golf Club Putts for Paws Charity Tournament Database

Finance & Accounting

The Red Bluff Golf Club is sponsoring a charity tournament, Putts for Paws, to raise money for the local pet shelter. You are modifying a database for the tournament that tracks money being raised from the event. The scope of this database is limited to tracking monies. Thus, in this instance, you are not tracking whether a participant is a golfer, volunteer, or other role. Anyone can donate money in the form of hole sponsorship or other donation item. You will

Vatikaki / Shutterstock.com

want to track monies derived from corporate sponsorship. You will bring in data for the event from various sources including Excel worksheets and text files.

Student data files needed for this workshop:

 a01_ws02_Putts

 a01_ws02_Putts_Golfers

 a01_ws02_Putts_Contacts

 a01_ws02_Putts_Volunteers

a01_ws02_Putts_Donors

You will save your files as:

 Lastname_Firstname_a01_ws02_Putts

 Lastname_Firstname_a01_ws02_Putts_Donors

Inserting Data into a Database

In designing a database, you will develop the tables, fields, and relationships of the tables. In order to manage the golf tournament, you will need to keep track of participants, the corporations that participate, the tee times, and the items each of the participants purchase. Each of these will be a table in your database. In this section, you will load tables from already existing databases and from Excel worksheets, in addition to creating two tables.

Database Design

Database design can be thought of as a three-step process:

1. Identify your entities—they become the tables.
2. Identify the attributes—they become the fields.
3. Specify the relationships between the tables.

An **entity** is a person, place, item, or event that you want to keep data about. You decide that you need to keep track of participants including golfers, donors, and corporate representatives. You need a participant table to track these people. A single participant is an instance of the participant entity and will become a record in the participant table.

An **attribute** is information about the entity. For example, for each participant you will want to keep information, such as name and address. These attributes will become the fields in your table.

A **relationship** is an association between tables based on common fields. The power of Access comes when you relate tables together. For example, you can relate participants to orders that the participants place.

Later in the workshop, you will look more closely at designing a database. While you explore the database tables and data, think about these general principles or steps to follow.

1. Brainstorm a list of all the types of data you will need.
2. Rearrange data items into groups that represent a single entity. These groups will become your tables.
3. If one item can have several attributes, such as a credit card number, expiration date, name on a card, and a security code, then put it into one group. In this example, it would be a group named credit card.
4. Break each attribute into the smallest attributes; they will become the fields. Give each attribute a descriptive name. For example, split addresses into street, city, state, and zip code.
5. Do not include totals, but do include all of the data needed so the calculation can be done in a query. For example, include the price of an item and the quantity ordered so the total cost can be calculated.
6. Remove any redundant data that exists in multiple groupings. For example, do not repeat customer name in both the customer grouping and the sales grouping.
7. Ensure common fields connect the groupings. For example, make sure that there is a common field between the customer grouping and the sales grouping so they can be connected. Later in this workshop, you will learn more about common fields.

You start with the participant entity, which is the tblParticipant table. You notice that it contains the fields shown in Figure 1 to track the participants in the tournament.

Field Name	Data Type	Maximum Length	Description
ParticipantID	Number—Long Integer		A unique ID that identifies each participant
LastName	Text	25	Last name
FirstName	Text	20	First name
StreetAddress	Text	35	Street address
City	Text	25	City
State	Text	2	State abbreviation
ZipCode	Text	5	Five digit zip code
ContactPhoneNumber	Text	14	Phone number for the individual participant
CorporatePhoneNumber	Text	12	Phone number for the corporation the participant represents

Figure 1 Fields for tblParticipant

Illustrating some of the basic principles, notice that the participant's name is split into two fields and the address is split into four fields. Why should you do this? When you have fields such as name or address that are composed of several smaller fields, you should split them into their component parts. This allows for more flexibility for reporting. For example, often a report is needed in alphabetic order by last or first name. You could not do this if you had stored the first and last name combined in the same field. Further, a field named "name" is confusing, leading to inconsistent data such as nicknames and incomplete names. This also allows us to report or query on just part of the field such as which participants are from a particular state.

CONSIDER THIS | **Street Address Components**

Street addresses contain two parts, the number and street name. While some databases split these apart, this is not necessary for most business uses. What are some businesses that benefit from separating these?

Real World Advice   First and Last Names

Painted Paradise is a U.S. company with guests who primarily use a first name followed by a last name. However, not all cultures around the world break names into first and last. For example, Korean names are designated as family name followed by given name. Designing database fields to accommodate all of the different cultures in the world is challenging. Always keep in mind the typical name for the database, but try to design it in such a way that other naming practices can fit into the database. Because businesses today are global, designing a database sensitive to all global cultures is difficult but important.

To Open a Database

a. Click the **Start** button 🌀. From the Start menu, locate and then start **Microsoft Access 2010**.

b. Click the **File tab**, and then click **Open** to display the Open dialog box.

c. In the Open dialog box, click the disk drive in the left pane where your student data files are located. Navigate through the folder structure and click **a01_ws02_Putts**.

d. Click **Open**. Access opens the database.

e. On the File tab, click **Save Database As**. In the Save As dialog box, navigate to the location where you are saving your files. In the File name box, type Lastname_Firstname_ a01_ws02_Putts, replacing Lastname_Firstname with your own name. Click **Save**.

f. Click **Enable Content** in the Security Warning bar.

g. Double-click the **tblParticipant table** to open it.
   When you open the tblParticipant table, it opens in Datasheet view. In Datasheet view, you can see the information about the participants.

h. If necessary, click the First record button ⏮ in the Navigation bar to return to the first participant.

i. Press Tab to move to the LastName column.

j. Replace **Last** in the first record of the LastName column with your last name and then press Tab to move to the next column. Replace **First** with your first name in the FirstName column.

Replace Last and First with your actual name

Figure 2   Datasheet view of tblParticipant table

k. Click the **Home tab**, click the **View arrow** in the Views group, and then click **Design View**.
   When you switch to Design view, you see the structure of the fields and the field properties.

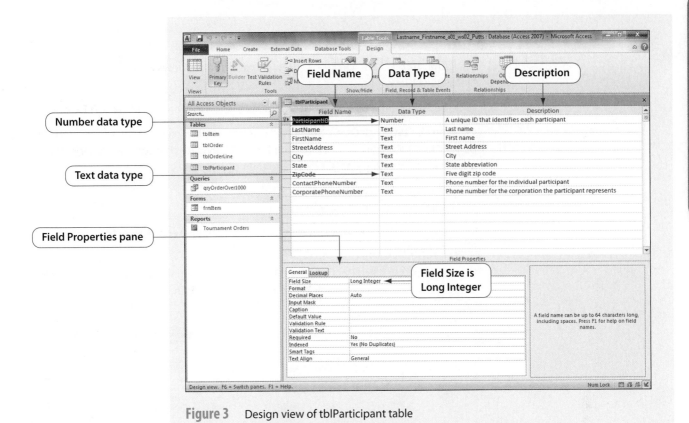

Figure 3   Design view of tblParticipant table

The upper pane of Design view has three columns: Field Name, Data Type, and Description. The Field Name is the column label in Datasheet view. **Data types** are the characteristic that defines the kind of data that can be entered into a field, such as numbers, text, or dates. The data type tells Access how to store and display the field. Number and Text are the two most common data types. In this table, you can see that one field is stored as a **Number data type**. That means that the data can only contain numeric data. The **Text data type** allows any text and numeric characters to be stored. Street Address is Text data type, as a street address in this database can contain numbers, letters, and special characters. The third column, Description, helps the user discern the meaning of the field.

The Field Properties pane in Design view gives more information on how the data is stored, entered, and processed. If your insertion point is on ParticipantID, you can see that the Field Size is Long Integer.

Importing Data from Other Sources

Painted Paradise has had different employees collecting data in different ways. Luckily, the applications within the Microsoft Office suite work together. This allows you to easily move data between Excel and Access. After importing the data, you will be able to further analyze and refine the table structure for the database. Even though other employees have kept track of the roles that each participant plays, remember that the scope of this database does not include tracking the participants' roles in the event. You are only tracking corporate involvement.

Copying and Pasting

Only a few golfer participants were entered into the tblParticipant table. Some others were put in an Excel worksheet. You will copy and paste them from Excel into your Access table.

To Copy and Paste Data from Excel

a. Click the **Home tab**, click the **View arrow** in the Views group, and then click **Datasheet View**.

b. Click the **Start** button ⊕. From the Start menu, locate and then start **Microsoft Excel 2010**.

c. Click the **File tab**, click **Open**, and in the Open dialog box, click the disk drive in the left pane where your student data files are located. Navigate through the folder structure and click **a01_ws02_Putts_Golfers**, and then click **Open**.

d. In Excel, drag to select **cells A1** through **I9**. Click the **Home tab**, and then click **Copy** 📋 in the Clipboard group to copy these cells.

e. On the Windows taskbar, click **Access**, and then click the **record selector** at the beginning of the append row.

f. On the Home tab, click **Paste** in the Clipboard group to paste the golfers into Access. In the warning dialog box, click **Yes** to paste the records in to the table.

New golfers added to table

Figure 4   New golfers at the end of the tblParticipant table

Troubleshooting

If you accidently click in a single cell of the append row and try to paste there, you get the error message "The text is too long to be edited." It appears that you are trying to paste all the data into one cell and Access will not let you continue. If this happens, click OK, indicating that you do not want to put all the text into the one cell.

After that it may be difficult to exit that row and click in the record selector column. It appears you are trying to paste an invalid row and Access will not let you continue. You will get an error message saying "Index or primary key cannot contain a Null value." When you click OK and try to recover, the message will reappear. If this happens, click [Esc] indicating that you do not want to keep that record.

g. **Close** ☒ the tblParticipant table, leaving Access open.

Real World Advice Copying and Pasting from Excel into Access

Copying and pasting requires that the columns be exactly the same in Excel and Access. There cannot be missing columns or columns in different orders. You cannot paste fields that are nonnumeric into numeric fields. If you have any doubt about the files being compatible, use import to append the data to the table.

Use Copy and Paste when:

- You started in Access and exported the data into Excel, made additions, and now want to put it back into Access. That way you know that the columns are the same.

- You are copying and pasting the contents of a field from Excel into Access, such as a street address.

Importing a Worksheet

Access allows you to import an entire worksheet or a smaller portion of a worksheet into a table. This is quite useful as Excel is so frequently used in organizations. Excel column headings are frequently imported as field names.

The golf club has been keeping corporate contacts for the event in an Excel worksheet. You will import this Excel worksheet into your tblParticipant table.

To Import an Excel Worksheet

a. On the Windows taskbar, click **Excel**. **Close** ⊠ the Golfers worksheet.

b. Click the **File tab**, and then click **Open**. In the Open dialog box, click the disk drive in the left pane where your student data files are located. Navigate through the folder structure, click **a01_ws02_Putts_Contacts**, and then click **Open**.

   Notice that the contacts data looks like the tblParticipant table in many ways. However, the corporate phone number immediately follows the participant's name rather than being at the end of the record as it is in the Access table. An import from Excel into an existing Access table is ideal for this type of import because as long as the columns have the same name, Access will match up the columns, skipping any missing column. You cannot copy and paste the way you did earlier because the columns are not arranged the same.

CorporatePhoneNumber immediately follows FirstName

Figure 5 Contact data in Excel

c. **Close** ⊠ Excel.

d. In Access, click the **External Data tab**, and then click **Excel** in the Import & Link group.

e. In the Get External Data – Excel Spreadsheet dialog box, click **Browse**, navigate through the folder structure where your student data files are located, click **a01_ws02_Putts_Contacts**, and then click **Open**.

f. Select **Append a copy of the records to the table**. Click the **arrow**, and then select **tblParticipant**. Click **OK**.

   Access starts the Import Spreadsheet Wizard, which displays worksheets and ranges in the Excel workbook.

g. Make sure **Show Worksheets** is selected and the **Corporate contacts** worksheet is highlighted.

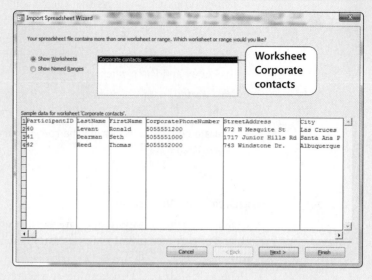

Figure 6   Worksheet to be imported

h. Click **Next**.

Access displays the next page of the wizard. This shows that Access found the column headings in Excel and matched them to the field names in Access.

i. Click **Next**. Click **Finish**, and then click **Close**.

j. In the Navigation Pane, double-click the **tblParticipant table** to open the table.

Your table has the three corporate contacts added. The contacts were imported and because the field names in Access matched the Excel column headings, the fields were rearranged to match the Access table order.

SIDE NOTE
Tables Are Ordered by Primary Key

When you added the contacts, Access added them in the middle of the table. That is because Access orders tables by the primary key. These records had lower keys than some records already in the table.

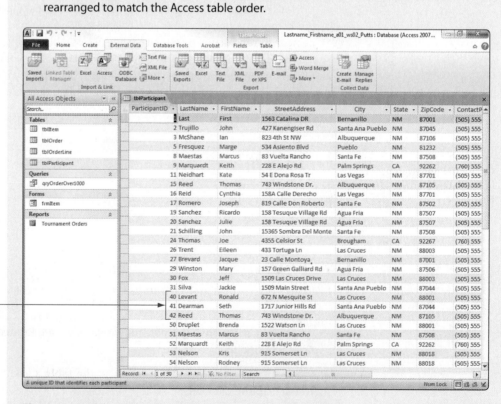

Figure 7   Corporate contacts imported into tblParticipant table

k. **Close** ✕ the tblParticipant table.

Importing from a Named Range

Access allows you to import a smaller portion of a worksheet known as a named range into a table. A named range is a set of cells that have been given a name that can then be used within a formula or function. This part of the worksheet can then be referenced in formulas or charts by name rather than by cell address or range address.

The golf club has been keeping information about the volunteers for the event in an Excel worksheet. This worksheet contains other information about volunteering that you will not need. The contact information for the volunteers has been named VolunteersNamesAddress.

To Import a Named Range

a. Click the **Start** button 🎯. From the Start menu, locate and then start **Microsoft Excel 2010**.

b. Click the **File tab**, click **Open**, and then in the Open dialog box click the disk drive in the left pane where your student data files are located. Navigate through the folder structure and click **a01_ws02_Putts_Volunteers**, and then click **Open**.

   Notice the Volunteers worksheet contains the volunteer information as well as other data. The volunteer information has been given the name VolunteersNamesAddress.

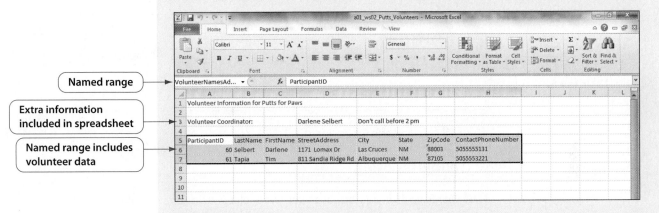

Named range

Extra information included in spreadsheet

Named range includes volunteer data

Figure 8   Volunteers file with extra information

c. **Close** ✕ Excel.

d. In Access, click the **External Data tab**, and then click **Excel** in the Import & Link group. Access displays the Get External Data – Excel Spreadsheet dialog box.

e. Click **Browse**, navigate through the folder structure, click **a01_ws02_Putts_Volunteers**, and then click **Open**.

f. Select **Append a copy of the records to the table**, click the **arrow**, and then select **tblParticipant**.

g. Click **OK**. Click **Show Named Ranges**.

   One named range, VolunteerNamesAddress, is displayed and highlighted in the list box.

h. Click **Next**. Access tells you that it found your column headings in Excel and matched them to the field names in Access.

i. Click **Finish**, and then click **Close**.

Importing from a Text File

Access enables you to import from text and Word files. Typically these files would have been organized in tables. In Word, these tables will have actual rows and columns. In text files, the tables are implied by the separation of the columns. This separation is done by delimiter characters. A **delimiter** is a character that separates the fields. A typical delimiter is a tab or comma. The rows in the text tables will be imported as records into your Access table.

The golf course has been keeping information about the donors for the event in a text file. You want to import that data into your Access database.

To Import from a Text File

a. Click the **Start** button 🔵. From the Start menu, locate and then start **Notepad**. If necessary, point to All Programs, and then click Accessories to find Notepad.

b. Click **File**, click **Open**, and in the Open dialog box, click the disk drive in the left pane where your student data files are located. Navigate through the folder structure and click **a01_ws02_Putts_Donors**, and then click **Open**.

     Notice that there are three donors in this file. The fields are separated by (unseen) tabs.

Troubleshooting

> Your columns may not line up the way Figure 9 shows them lining up. This happens because Notepad does not save Font. It does save tabs so you do not need to worry about any display differences.

File tab →

Three donors in text file →

Figure 9   Donors text file in Notepad

Troubleshooting

> If your Save As dialog box does not show folders, click Browse Folders at the bottom of the dialog box.

c. Click **File**, and then click **Save As**. In the Save As dialog box, navigate to the location where you are saving your files. In the File name box, type Lastname_Firstname_a01_ws02_Putts_Donors, replacing Lastname_Firstname with your own name. Click **Save**, and then **Close** ❎ Notepad.

d. In Access, click the **External Data tab**, and then click **Text File** in the Import & Link group. Access displays the Get External Data – Text File dialog box of the Import Text Wizard.

e. Click **Browse**, and then click the disk drive in the left pane where you are saving your student data files. Navigate through the folder structure, click **Lastname_Firstname_a01_ws02_Putts_Donors**, and then click **Open**.

f. Click **Append a copy of the records to the table**. Click the **arrow** to select **tblParticipant**, and then click **OK**. Access recognizes that this data has columns that are delimited (separated by tabs or commas.)

g. Click **Next**. Select the **Tab** delimiter, and click the **First Row Contains Field Names** check box.

h. Click **Next**, and then click **Finish**.

    Access responds with an error message. This says that Access is unable to append all the data to the table and that one record was lost because of key violations. The first field in your table is a primary key that must be unique. Apparently one of the donors has a ParticipantID that was already used in the Access table.

i. Click **Yes**, and then click **Close**.

j. Double-click **tblParticipant** to open it in Datasheet view.

k. Click the **Start** button ⬤. From the Start menu, locate and then start **Notepad**.

l. Click **File**, click **Open**, and in the Open dialog box, click the disk drive in the left pane where you are saving your files. Navigate through the folder structure and click **Lastname_Firstname_a01_ws02_Putts_Donors**. Click **Open**. There are three donors in the file that have ParticipantIDs of 30, 33, and 34.

Participant ID 30 used for Luis Ortiz →

```
ParticipantID   LastName      FirstName        StreetAddress      City        State    ZipCode  ContactPhoneNumber|
30              Ortiz         Luis        1801 Brilliant Sky Dr   Santa Fe    NM       87508    (505) 555-1722
33              Ramirez       Alice       124 Nana Lou St.        Avondale    CO       81022    (719) 555-9247
34              Victor        Lisa        988 Elguitarra Rd       Santa Fe    NM       87507    (505) 555-2757
```

Figure 10   Donor text file

m. Compare the donor data in the text file to the records in the tblParticipant table. Notice ParticipantID 30 has been used twice, once for Jeff Fox and once for Luis Ortiz. You talk to the person keeping records of donors and discover she meant to type 32 for Luis Ortiz.

n. In Notepad, select the text **30** and type **32**.

Change 30 to 32 →

```
ParticipantID   LastName      FirstName        StreetAddress      City        State    ZipCode  ContactPhoneNumber
32              Ortiz         Luis        1801 Brilliant Sky Dr   Santa Fe    NM       87508    (505) 555-1722
33              Ramirez       Alice       124 Nana Lou St.        Avondale    CO       81022    (719) 555-9247
34              Victor        Lisa        988 Elguitarra Rd       Santa Fe    NM       87507    (505) 555-2757
```

Figure 11   Change ParticipantID from 30 to 32

o. **Close** ⬛ Notepad, and save the file. On the taskbar, click **Access**, and then **Close** ⓧ the tblParticipant table.

p. Repeat the import Steps d–h. This time Access says that two records could not be imported. This makes sense because two donors were already imported.

q. Click **Yes**, and then click **Close** ⬛. Double-click **tblParticipant** to open the table and verify that the records for Luis Ortiz, Alice Ramirez, and Lisa Victor were imported.

r. **Close** ⓧ the tblParticipant table.

Manual Data Entry

If the data does not already exist in another form, you can type the data directly into Access. There are two methods: entering data directly into the table or entering the data in a form.

Entering Data Using Datasheet View

When you open a table in Datasheet view, you can type data directly into the table. You want to enter a new order. You will need to enter data into tblOrder and the details of the order in tblOrderLine. The order to enter is your own; you are entering the tournament as a golfer.

To Enter Data in Datasheet View

a. In the Navigation Pane, double-click **tblOrder**, click in the **AmountPaid column** of the append row, and then enter 200.

    As you type the 200, a pencil icon ✏ appears in the record selector on the left. The pencil icon means that this record is actively being modified. Additionally, the OrderID was filled in with 12. This happens because the field has a data type of AutoNumber, which means that Access assigns the next highest number.

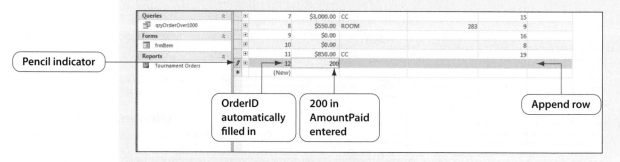

Figure 12   Enter 200 in AmountPaid

b. Press Tab to continue filling in the record with a MethodOfPayment of CC, leave the ResortRoomNumber empty, and type 1 in ParticipantID.

c. Press Tab to go to the next record. The pencil icon disappears. Unlike Word and Excel, Access immediately saves the data change.

d. **Close** ✕ the tblOrder table.

e. In the Navigation Pane, double-click **tblOrderLine**, click in **OrderID** of the append row, and then type 12.

f. Press Tab to continue filling in the record with LineNum 1, ItemID G1, and Quantity 1.

g. **Close** ✕ the tblOrderLine table.

Real World Advice · Undoing in Access

Access immediately saves the changes you make to data. There is very limited undo/redo functionality in Access. If the Undo button 🔄 is dimmed, you cannot undo the change you made.

- Typically you can undo a single typing change even if you have gone on to the next record. However, if you made several changes to different records, you cannot undo more than the changes to the last record.
- If you have made changes to several fields in a single record, you can click Undo to undo each of them.
- You can also press ESC to stop editing a record and revert to the record as it was before you started changing the record.
- If you make an error, you can press ESC to get you out of the error.

Because of the limited undo features, do not count on undoing your changes. You will often find that you cannot undo. For example, when you delete a record or records, you cannot undo the delete.

Design changes are not saved until you save the object you changed. Thus, you can undo design changes until you save.

Removing Data

You can delete records from a table. These are permanent deletions and cannot be undone. Golfer Kate Neidhart needs to withdraw from the tournament.

To Delete Data in Datasheet View

a. In the Navigation Pane, double-click **tblParticipant** to open it in Datasheet view.

b. Click the **record selector** for record 7, Kate Neidhart, ParticipantID 11. Access selects the row.

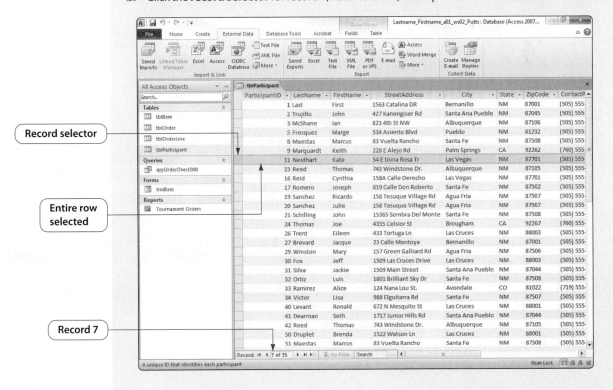

Figure 13   Delete Kate Neidhart record

c. Right-click in this row, and then select **Delete Record**. Because you cannot undo a delete, Access asks if you are sure you want to delete this record.

d. Click **Yes**. Access removes this record.

Troubleshooting

> If you do not get the Access confirmation message asking if you are sure you want the deletion to occur, the confirmation message may be turned off. If you would like to turn it back on, on the File tab click Options, and then click Client Settings. Scroll down to find the Confirm section under Editing, and click the Document deletions check box.

You can also delete individual fields from a table. These are also permanent deletions and cannot be undone. You decide that you will create a table for corporations involved with the tournament, tblCorporate, and that the CorporatePhoneNumber will be a part of that table. Thus, you will not need CorporatePhoneNumber for each tblParticipant record, and you will delete that field. You can delete a field in either Design view or Datasheet view. In Datasheet view, you can see the contents of the field that you are deleting, which gives you an extra check on whether you really want to delete the field.

To Delete a Field in Datasheet View

a. Scroll to the right to find the CorporatePhoneNumber column. Move the mouse pointer in the column heading until it changes to a black down arrow and click so the entire column is highlighted. Make sure that you selected CorporatePhoneNumber and not ContactPhoneNumber.

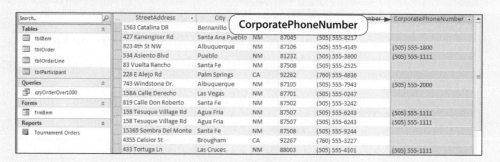

Figure 14 Select the CorporatePhoneNumber column

b. Click the **Home tab**, and then click **Delete** in the Records group.

Because you cannot undo a delete, Access asks, "Do you want to permanently delete the selected field(s) and all the data in the field(s)? To permanently delete the field(s), click Yes." Because you are in Datasheet view, you can glance at it and make sure this is data you want to delete.

c. Click **Yes**. Access deletes the column.

d. **Close** ☒ the tblParticipant table.

Troubleshooting

If when you clicked in the column heading you accidently double-clicked and then clicked Delete, Access blanked out the field name rather than deleting the column. This put you in edit mode, ready to rename the field. Press Esc to cancel edit mode and try again.

Understanding Tables and Keys

Now that you have imported data into the tblParticipant table, you need to further examine and evaluate how the tables have been set up. Tables represent entities or people, places, things, or events that you want to track. Each row represents a single person, place, and so on. To identify that entity, you use a primary key field. A **primary key** field is a field that uniquely identifies the record; it can be any data type, but it should be a field that will not change. For example, a person's name is not a good primary key for two reasons. First of all, it is not unique—several people may have the same name—and second, a person's name could change. If you define a primary key for a table, the field cannot be blank.

In this section, you will create a table from scratch, minimize file size, facilitate quick data entry, minimize errors, and encourage data consistency as shown in Figure 15.

Goal	Example
Minimize file size	If a field is an integer that is always less than 32,767, use Integer rather than Long Integer to define the field.
Facilitate quick data entry, including removing redundant data	Store a state abbreviation rather than the state name spelled out.
Minimize errors	Use the Date/Time data type for dates and not a Text data type. Access will then only accept valid dates (and not 2/31/2013, which is invalid).
Encourage data consistency	Use a Yes/No check box rather than having the word Yes or No typed into a text field where misspellings could occur.

Figure 15 Table design goals

Creating a Table in Design View

You want to keep track of corporations who are involved with the tournament. You do not have a source so you will need to design and create the table. You will use Design view to enter fields, data types, and descriptions.

Data Types

Data types are the characteristic that defines the kind of data that can be entered into a field, such as numbers, text, or dates. The data type tells Access how to store and display the field.

Quick Reference — Data Types

Data Type	Description	Examples
Text	Used to store textual or character information. Any character or number can be entered into this type of field. You should store any data that will never be used in calculations—such as a Social Security number—as text, not a number. There is an upper limit of 255 characters that can be stored in a Text field.	Names, addresses
Memo	Used to capture free text. Can store up to 1 gigabyte of characters, of which you can display 65,535 characters in a control on a form or report. This is a good data type to use if you need more than 255 characters in one field.	Comments
Number	Used for numeric data.	Quantity
Date/Time	Used to store a date and/or time.	Start time
AutoNumber	Used for keys. Access generates the value by automatically incrementing the value for each new record to produce unique keys. For example, it would set the value as 1 for the first record, 2 for the next, and 3 for the third.	ProductID
Currency	A numeric value that is used for units of currency. It follows the regional settings preset in Windows to determine what the default currency should be. In the United States, the data is displayed with a dollar sign and two decimal places.	Salary
Yes/No	A checked box where an empty box is no, and a checked box is yes.	EntryPaid
Hyperlink	Text or combinations of text and numbers stored as text and used as a hyperlink address.	CompanyWebsite
Calculated	A field calculated from other fields in the table. A calculated field is read-only as it performs a calculation on other data that is entered.	GrossPay (calculated based upon HoursWorked and HourlySalary)
Lookup Wizard	Displays either a list of values that is retrieved from a table or query, or a set of values that you specified when you created the field.	ProductType (giving a list of valid types)
Attachment	Attached images, worksheet files, documents, charts, and other types of supported files to the records in your database, similar to attaching files to e-mail messages.	EmployeePhoto
OLE Object	Use to attach an OLE Object, such as a Microsoft Office Excel worksheet, to a record. An OLE object means that when you open the object, you open it in its original application such as Excel. It allows cross-application editing.	SalarySpreadsheet

Real World Advice Number or Text?

Any character can be used in a text field. However, if you are expecting the field to have only numbers, you should only store it in a text field if the numbers will never be used in a calculation. If you store numbers as text, you cannot use them in calculations. Conversely, if you improperly store numeric text as a number, Access will remove any leading zeros. For example, you would not add zip codes together, so a zip code should be stored as text. A person living in Boston might have a zip code of 02108. If you stored the zip code as a number, Access would convert this to 2108.

Field Size

Field size indicates the maximum length of a data field. Whenever you use a Text data type, you should determine the maximum number of text characters that can exist. That number would then be the field size. For example, a state abbreviation can only be two characters long, so the size for this field should be 2. If you allow more than two characters, you are likely to get a mix of abbreviations and spelled-out state names. Limiting the size will limit errors in the data. There is an upper limit of 255 characters for a Text field. If you need more than 255 characters, use the Memo data type.

For numeric fields, the type defines the maximum length or value. You should use the number size that best suits your needs. For example, if a value in a field is always going to be a whole number and never going to be above 32,768, then Integer is the best field size. If the number is currency, you should use the Currency data type instead of Number.

Quick Reference Number Field Sizes

Field Size	Description
Integer	For integers that range from −32,768 to +32,767. Must be whole numbers. Integers cannot have decimal places.
Long Integer	For integers that range from −2,147,483,648 to +2,147,483,647. Long Integers cannot have decimal places. (AutoNumber is a long integer.)
Decimal	For numeric values that contain decimal places. Numbers can be negative or positive. For numeric values that range from −9.999... × 10^{27} to 9.999... × 10^{27}.
Single	For very large numbers with up to seven significant digits. Can contain decimal places. Numbers can be negative or positive. For numeric floating point values that range from −3.4 × 10^{38} to +3.4 × 10^{38}.
Double	For very large numbers with up to 15 significant digits. Can contain decimal places. Numbers can be negative or positive. For numeric floating-point values that range from −1.797 × 10^{308} to +1.797 × 10^{308}.
Byte	For integers that range from 0 to 255. These numbers can be stored in a single byte.

You determine that your corporation table, tblCorporate, should contain the company name, address, and phone number.

To Create a Table Design

a. Click the **Create tab**, and then select **Table Design**.

Access opens a blank table in Design view. You will enter each field in the appropriate row.

b. Type CompanyName for the Field Name. Press Tab to move to the Data Type column.

Notice that Text is the default data type, so you do not need to make a selection to keep Text for this field. For other data types, click the arrow and select the data type. Alternatively, you can type the first letter of the data type, and it will appear, such as "N" for Number.

c. Press Tab to move to the Description column, and then type Company name.

d. In the Field Properties pane, type 50 in the Field Size box.

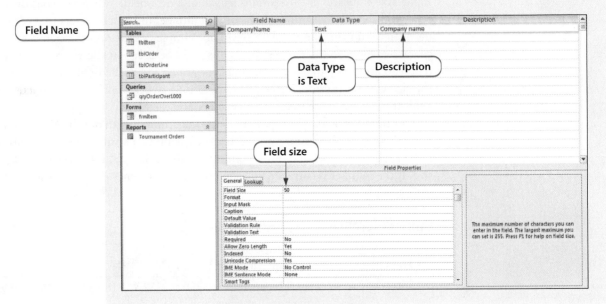

Figure 16   First field in the tblCorporate table

e. Continue defining the table with the following information, being sure to enter maximum length in the Field Size box.

Field Name	Data Type	Description	Maximum Length
CompanyName	Text	Company name	50
StreetAddress	Text	Company's street address	40
City	Text	Company's city	40
State	Text	State abbreviation	2
ZipCode	Text	Zip code either 5- or 9-character format	10
PhoneNumber	Text	Phone number with area code	14

Figure 17   Table fields

f. **Save** 🖫 the table, naming it tblCorporate, and then click **OK**. In the warning message that asks if you want to create a primary key, click **No**. You will define a key later.

Input Masks

Access provides a way to consistently enter data, called **input masks**. For example, phone numbers can be typed (555) 555-5555, 555-5555, or 555-555-5555. An input mask defines a consistent template and provides the punctuation. Access also has a wizard that creates automatic masks for Social Security numbers, zip codes, passwords, extensions, dates, and times. You can also create your own custom masks. Input masks can affect how data is stored.

The characters used when defining input masks are shown in the Quick Reference table.

Quick Reference — Characters Used in Masks

Character	Interpretation
0	Must enter a number
9	Can enter a number
#	Can enter a number, space, or plus or minus sign; if not entered, Access enters a blank space
L	Must enter a letter
?	Can enter a letter
A	Must enter a letter or number
a	Can enter a letter or number
&	Must enter a character or a space
C	Can enter a character or space
.	Decimal point
,	Comma separating thousands in numbers
:	Colon as time or other separator
-	Dash as date or other separator
/	Slash as date or other separator
>	All characters following are converted to uppercase
<	All characters following are converted to lowercase
!	Characters are filled from left to right
\	The character immediately following will be entered in the field. This is used when a standard character is to be automatically inserted.
" "	One or more characters enclosed in double quotation marks will be entered in the field. This is used when standard characters need to be inserted.

To Create an Input Mask

a. With the PhoneNumber field selected, in the Field Properties pane, click in the **Input Mask** box.

b. Click the **Build** button ⊞ to start the Input Mask Wizard. If necessary, select Phone Number.

c. Click **Next** to start the phone number Input Mask Wizard.

    Access suggests the format !(999) 000-0000. This means that area code is optional and will be enclosed in parentheses. The rest of the phone number is required and will have a dash between the two parts.

d. Click **Next** to accept the format.

e. Access asks if you want to store the symbols with the data. Select **With the symbols in the mask, like this**.

f. Click **Next**, and then click **Finish**.

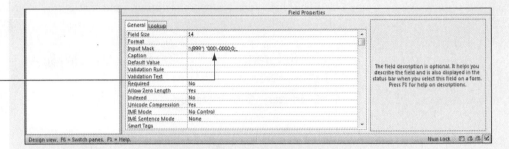

Input mask

Figure 18 Finished input mask

g. Save 🖫 the table design. Click the **Home tab**, click the **View arrow** in the Views group, and then click **Datasheet View**.

h. Notice that the columns are not wide enough for the entire heading text to show. Move your mouse pointer to the border between **CompanyName** and **StreetAddress** until it becomes the Horizontal resize ⟷ symbol. Double-click the **border** to widen the column.

i. Double-click the **border** after the StreetAddress and PhoneNumber headings to widen the columns.

j. Click in the **append row for CompanyName**, and then type Tesuque Mirage Market. Press Tab to move to StreetAddress.

k. Continue entering the records as follows. Notice that the phone number mask that you entered means that you do not need to type the parentheses and dashes in the PhoneNumber field.

CompanyName	StreetAddress	City	State	ZipCode	PhoneNumber
Tesuque Mirage Market	8 Tesuque Mirage Rd	Santa Fe	NM	87506	5055551111
Hotel Playa Real	125 Madison Avenue	Santa Fe	NM	87508	5055551800
Bouzouki Museum	716 Camino Cercano	Santa Fe	NM	87505	5055551200
McDoakes Restaurant	2017 High St	Santa Fe	NM	87501	5055551000
Benson & Diaz	1953A Piazza Pl, Suite 101	Santo Domingo	NM	87052	5055552000

l. **Close** ☒ the tblCorporate table, and reply **Yes** to save the layout.

Formatting

In a table design, you can define a Format field property that customizes how data is displayed and printed in tables, queries, reports, and forms. The **Format** property tells Access how data is to be displayed. It does not affect the way that the data is stored. For example, you can specify that currency fields are displayed in dollars (e.g., $1,234.56) in American databases or in euros (e.g., €1,234.56) in European databases. Formats are available for Date/Time, Number, Currency, and Yes/No data types. You can also define your own custom formats for Text and Memo fields.

Quick Reference — Format Field Property

Data Type	Format	Example
Date/Time	General Date	11/9/2013 10:10:10 PM
	Long Date	Wednesday, November 9, 2013
	Medium Date	9-Nov-13
	Short Date	11/9/2013
	Long Time	10:10:10 PM
	Medium Time	10:10 PM
	Short Time	22:10
Number and Currency	General Number	Display the number as entered.
	Currency	Follows the regional settings preset in Windows. In the United States: $1,234.56. In much of Europe: €1,234.56.
	Euro	Uses the euro symbol regardless of the Windows setting.
	Fixed	Displays at least one digit after the decimal point. In Decimal, you choose how many fixed digits to show after the decimal point.
	Standard	Use the regional settings preset in Windows for thousands divider. 1,234 in the United States; 1.234 in much of Europe.
	Percent	Multiply the value by 100 and follow with %.
	Scientific	Use standard scientific notation, for example, $4.5 * 10^{13}$.
Yes/No	Check Box	A check box.
	Yes/No	Yes or No display options.
	True/False	True or False display options.
	On/Off	On or Off display options.

To Define a Date Field

a. In the Navigation Pane, right-click on **tblOrder**, and select **Design View**.

b. In the first blank row, in the Field Name column, type OrderDate and then enter a Data Type of Date/Time and Description of Date order was placed.

c. Click in the **Format** box in the Field Properties pane.

d. Click the **Format arrow**, and then select **Short Date**.

Notice that the Property Update Options button appears. Clicking it would display an option to change the format of OrderDate wherever else it appears. Because it does not appear anywhere else yet, you do not need to click the button.

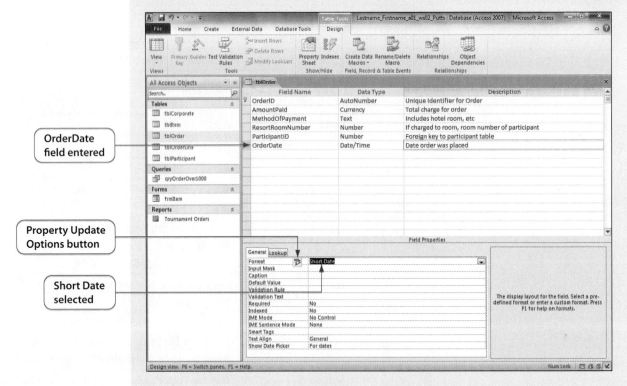

OrderDate field entered

Property Update Options button

Short Date selected

Figure 19   Adding a Short Date field

e. **Save** the table design. Click the **Home tab**, and then click the **View** button in the Views group to switch to Datasheet view.

The orders were placed on May 4, 2013, but no date was entered.

f. For the first order, in the OrderDate field type May 4, 2013. Press ↓ to move to the next record. Notice that Access changes the display to 5/4/2013, the short date display.

g. For the second order, type 05/04/2013. Press ↓ to move to the next record. Again Access changes the display.

h. For the next order, type May 4 13. Press ↓ to move to the next record. Once again Access changes the display to 5/4/2013.

i. Continue typing May 4 13 for all the orders.

j. **Close** the tblOrder table.

It is important to keep in mind that this only affects the display of the field. The stored format is the same for any date field. This allows multiple people to enter dates in many formats, but each date is displayed in the format that was selected for the field. (Access actually stores dates in a floating-point number format that indicates how many days before or after December 30, 1899, the date is. December 29, 1899, is -1; December 30, 1899, is 0; December 31, 1899, is +1; November 6, 2000, is 36836.)

CONSIDER THIS | **Database Design Principles**

Some principles for database design are shown in Figure 15. How do field sizes, formatting, and input masks facilitate these principles? When do you use a format? When do you use an input mask?

Understanding and Designating Keys

Each table should have a field that uniquely identifies each of the records in the table. This field is called the primary key. If you know the primary key, you know exactly what record you want. Another type of key is a **foreign key**. A foreign key is the primary key of one table stored in a second table. The primary and foreign keys form the common field between tables that allow you to form a relationship between the two tables.

Primary Keys

Each row of a table represents a single person or item. The primary key field is the field that says which person or item it is. It uniquely identifies the record. Remember that a primary key field should be a field that has values that will not change. When you define a primary key for a table, the field cannot be blank. A common way of defining a primary key is to use a field specifically designed to identify the entity. This is an arbitrary **numeric key** that is assigned to represent an individual item, such as CustomerID or ProductID. A numeric key is often assigned an AutoNumber data type that Access will fill as the data is entered. Instead of using a numeric key, you can also use an already existing field that uniquely identifies the person or item such as Social Security number.

CONSIDER THIS | **Social Security Number as a Primary Key**

While Social Security number seems like the perfect primary key, it is seldom used. What privacy concerns might arise in using Social Security numbers? Are there other issues that might arise with using Social Security numbers?

Real World Advice Do You Need a Primary Key?

While Access does not require a primary key for every table, you almost always want to give the table a primary key. What are the advantages of having a primary key?

- It helps organize your data. Each record is uniquely identified.
- Primary keys speed up access to your data. Primary keys provide an index to a record. In a large table, that makes it much faster to find a record.
- Primary keys are used to form relationships between tables.

Foreign Keys

A foreign key is a column in a table that stores a value that is the primary key in another table. It is called foreign because it does not identify a record in this table—it identifies a record in another (foreign) table. For example, you have two tables, tblParticipant and tblOrder, in your database. You want to know which participants have placed certain orders. The primary key for your Participant table is ParticipantID. You can add a field called ParticipantID to the Order table that indicates which participant placed the order. ParticipantID is foreign key in the tblOrder table; it identifies the participant in the tblParticipant table. Figure 20 illustrates this relationship. Foreign keys do not need to be unique in the table. Participants can place several orders.

You will use the ParticipantID to form a relationship between the two tables later in this workshop.

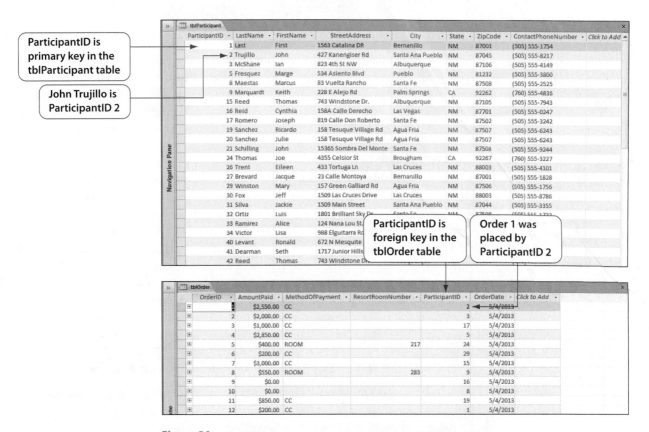

Figure 20   Relationship between tblParticipant and tblOrder tables

Composite Keys

Sometimes, two fields are needed to uniquely identify a record. In that case, both fields are used to create the key and are called a **composite key**. For example, a university might identify a class by subject area and course number. The university could have classes Math 101, Math 102, and MIS 101. It takes both subject and course number to identify a single course. The combination of the two fields is called a composite key.

A typical use of a composite key is on an order form. Figure 21 shows a paper form that the golf tournament organizers used before they used Access. To store the items that have been ordered, a composite key can be made combining the order number with the line number of the order form. You notice that this composite key is used for orders in the golf tournament database.

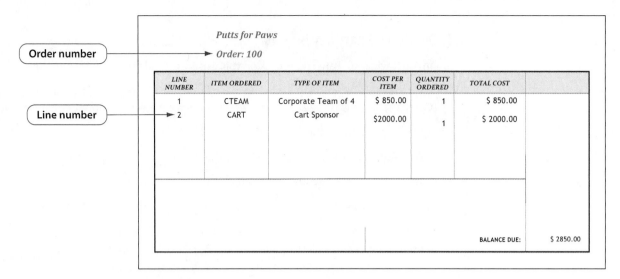

Figure 21   Composite key on a paper order form

To Find a Composite Key

a. In the Navigation Pane, right-click the **tblOrderLine** table, and then click **Design View**. Notice that there are two fields marked as a key: OrderID and LineNum.

b. **Close** ☒ the tblOrderLine table.

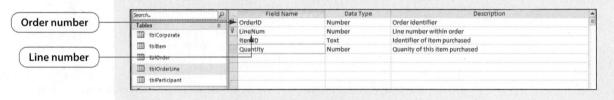

Figure 22   Composite key in the tblOrderLine table

Natural vs. Numeric Keys

Sometimes your data will have a unique identifier that is a natural part of your data. When that is true, you can use the field as a **natural primary key**. If you already identify orders by order number, that would make a good primary key.

The important point is that the natural primary key is a value that will not change. You might start by thinking that telephone number is a natural way to identify a customer. But people change their telephone numbers. When the natural key might change, it is better to use an arbitrary unique number to identify the customer. When natural keys do exist, they are favored over numeric keys.

You can use the data type AutoNumber for the primary key. In that case, Access will automatically assign a unique value for every record. You can also define a key as numeric, and fill the key values yourself.

You decide that you need to create a numeric primary key for your tblCorporate table named CorporateID. You will let Access automatically create the key by using an AutoNumber data type.

To Define a Primary Key

a. In the Navigation Pane, right-click on **tblCorporate**, and then click **Design View**.

b. Click the Table Tools **Design tab**, and then click **Insert Rows** in the Tools group. Because CompanyName was the active field, Access enters a blank row above CompanyName.

c. Type CorporateID as the Field Name column.

d. Select **AutoNumber** as the Data Type. The field size is set to Long Integer.

e. Type Unique corporate identifier in the Description column.

f. Select the CorporateID row by clicking the **record selector** to the left of the field.

g. On the Table Tools Design tab, click **Primary Key** in the Tools group to make CorporateID a primary key. Access places a key icon in the record selector bar.

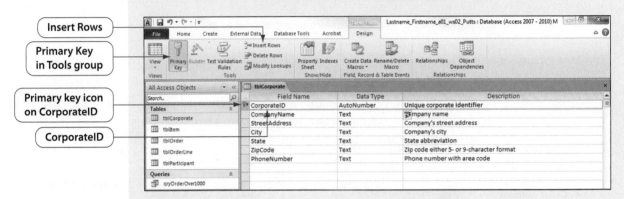

Figure 23   Defining a primary key

h. **Save** 💾 your table design. Click the **Home tab**, and then click **View**. Notice that Access has populated the CorporateID field with automatic numbers.

i. **Close** ✕ the tblCorporate table.

Real World Advice — Read Your Error Messages

The error message "Index or primary key cannot contain a Null value" is one example of an error message that Access gives when you make changes to an Access database that would break the rules you set up in your design. You should read the error message carefully to understand what it is telling you.

If you get the error message "Index or primary key cannot contain a Null value," that means that one of your records has no entry in the primary key field. Look for that record, and enter the primary key. Often the issue is that you accidently entered data in the append record. If you do not want that record to be created, press Escape to cancel the addition of the record.

Understanding Relational Databases

One of the benefits of Access comes when you add relationships to the tables. This allows you to work with two or more tables in the same query, report, or form. For your tournament database, when you relate tables together, you can ask such questions as "What golfers are playing for the Tesuque Mirage Market?" "Did the market agree to purchase any other items?" "Have they paid for those items yet?"

Relationships in a relational database are created by joining the tables together. A **join** is created by creating a relationship between two tables based upon a common field in the two tables, as shown in Figure 24. The tblParticipant table has a field (column) named ParticipantID. tblOrder also has a field named ParticipantID. When you create the relationship, Access will match the ParticipantIDs between the two tables to find those participants that placed an order. Looking at the table, you can mentally join the two tables to see that John Trujillo has placed an order for $2,550. When Access runs a query, it uses an existing join to find the results. In this section, you will form relationships between tables, create a report, and check to make sure the relationships you are creating between tables make sense.

ParticipantID in tblParticipant

ParticipantID in tblOrder

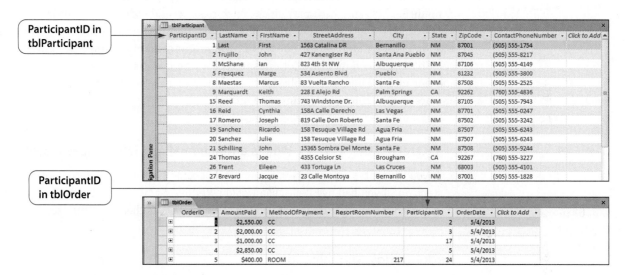

Figure 24 Tables joined between primary and foreign keys

Understanding Basic Principles of Normalization

When you work with tables in Access, you want each table to represent a single item and have data only about that entity. For example, you want a tblParticipant table to have data about participants and nothing else. You do not want to have data about the corporation they represent or the order they placed. You want the data about the participant to be in the participant table and no data about any other item in the tblParticipant table as shown in Figure 24. There is no data that is not about the participant in the tblParticipant table. This is why you deleted the CorporatePhoneNumber field earlier in the exercise.

Entities, Entity Classes, and Attributes

Recall that an entity is a person, place, or item that you want to keep data about. The data you keep about an entity are called attributes. An entity is generally stored in a single table in a relational database. The attributes form the fields or columns of the table. **Normalization** is the process of minimizing the duplication of information in a relational database through effective database design. If you know the primary key of an entity in a normalized database, each of the attributes will have just one value. When you normalize a database, you will have multiple smaller tables, each representing a different thing.

There will be no redundant data in the tables. A complete discussion of normalization is beyond the scope of this workshop, but the following sections will give you an idea of why you normalize your tables.

Figure 25 shows a nonnormalized view of tblParticipant. Suppose John Trujillo places two orders, Order 1 for $2,550 and Order 2 for $500. You can easily fill in his name and address. However, when you get to the order fields, you cannot fill in the attributes with just one value. You want to enter Order 1 for Order ID and Order 2 for Order ID. You want to enter $2,550 for AmountPaid and $500 for AmountPaid. But you only have one field for each.

Participant ID	Last Name	First Name	Street Address	Other Address Fields	Order ID	Amount Paid
2	Trujillo	John	427 Kanengiser Rd		??????	????

Figure 25 Nonnormalized tblParticipant Table

For each record's ParticipantID, you do not have a single value for OrderID and AmountPaid because each participant may make several orders. You could have a column for OrderID1 and OrderID2. But, how many columns would you make? What if this was for a grocery store where one transaction might contain hundreds of items? Any time you do not know how many columns to repeat, the table is not normalized and you need another table. Thus, this table does not fit the principles of normalization. It has two entities in the table: participants and orders.

CONSIDER THIS | **Why Is a Nonnormalized Table Undesirable?**

If you have a table as shown in Figure 25, you could simply enter a record for each item. So, if you had five items, you would enter five records in the table. What kind of redundancy does that create? If you used this method, is there a primary key?

Redundancy Minimization

Figure 26 shows a nonnormalized view of the tblOrder table. In this case, when you know the OrderID, you do know the value of each field.

OrderID	Amount Paid	Method of Payment	Last Name	First Name	Address	Other Address Fields
1	$2,550.00	CC	Trujillo	John	427 Kanengiser Rd	
12	$500.00	CC	Trujillo	John	427 Kanengiser Rd	

Figure 26 Nonnormalized tblOrder Table

However the table has redundant data. **Redundancy** is when data is repeated several times in a database. All of the data about John Trujillo is repeated for each order he makes. That means that the data will need to be entered multiple times. Beyond that, if the data changes, it has to be changed in multiple places. If his address or phone number changes, it will need to be changed on all his order records. Forgetting to change it in one place will lead to inconsistent data and confusion. Again, this table is not normalized because it contains data about two different entities: participant and orders.

In a normalized database, redundancy is minimized. The foreign keys are redundant, but no other data about the entity is repeated.

Understanding Relationships

To make the database normalized, you need to have two tables: one for participants and one for orders. How then do you form a relationship between them? A table represents an entity—or the nouns—in the database. The relationship represents the verb that connects the two nouns. In our example, your two nouns are "participant" and "order." Is there a relationship between these two nouns? Yes. You can say that a participant places an order.

Once you determine that there is a relationship between the entities, you need to describe the relationship. You do that by asking yourself two questions starting with each entity in the relationship:

- Question 1 (starting with the Participant entity): If you have one participant, what is the maximum number of orders that one participant can place? The only two answers to consider are one or many. In this case, the participant can place many orders.

- Question 2 (starting with the Order entity): If you have one order, what is the maximum number of participants that can place that order? Again, the only answers to consider are one or many. An order is placed by just one participant.

The type of relationship where one question is answered "one" and the other is answered "many" is called a one-to-many relationship. A **one-to-many relationship** is a relationship between two tables where one record in the first table corresponds to many records in the second table. One-to-many is called the cardinality of the relationship. **Cardinality** indicates the number of instances of one entity that relates to one instance of another entity.

Using the Relationships Window

Access stores relationship information in the Relationships window as shown in Figure 27.

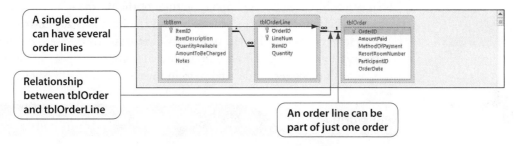

A single order can have several order lines

Relationship between tblOrder and tblOrderLine

An order line can be part of just one order

Figure 27   Relationships window

To Open the Relationships Window

a. Click the **Database Tools tab**.

b. Click **Relationships** in the Relationships group.

   The Relationships window opens. The window shows tables and the relationships between those tables. Notice the join line between tblOrder and tblOrderLine. There is an infinity symbol on the line next to tblOrderLine. The infinity symbol indicates that a single order can have several order lines. There is a "1" on the line next to tblOrder. The "1" indicates that an order line can be on just one order. Access indicates a one-to-many relationship in this way, putting a "1" on the one-side of the relationship line and an infinity symbol on the many-side.

Relationship Types

The relationship between tblParticipant and tblOrder is a one-to-many relationship. There are other types of relationships. Consider the relationship between tblOrder and tblItem. There is a relationship: an item can be on an order. What is the cardinality? You need to ask yourself the two questions to determine the cardinality:

- Question 1 (starting with the Order entity): If you have one order, what is the maximum number of items that can be part of that order? You care only about two answers: one or many. In this case, the order can contain many items. For example, a golfer could buy an entry into the tournament and a T-shirt.

- Question 2 (starting with the Item entity): If you have one item, what is the maximum number of orders that that item can be part of? Again, the only answers to consider are one or many. Obviously you want more than one person to be able to order an entry to the tournament. Therefore, you say that an item can be on many orders.

With both answers being many, this is a many-to-many relationship. A **many-to-many relationship** is a relationship between tables in which one record in one table has many matching records in a second table, and one record in the related table has many matching records in the first table. Because these two tables in the charity database do not have a common field, in Access this kind of many-to-many relationship must have an additional table in between these two. This intermediate table is referred to by several synonymous terms: "intersection," "junction," or "link table." You will look at this later in the workshop.

A one-to-one relationship occurs when each question is answered with a maximum of one. A **one-to-one relationship** is a relationship between tables where a record in one table has only one matching record in the second table. In a small business, a department might be managed by no more than one manager, and each manager manages no more than one department. That relationship in that business is a one-to-one relationship.

There are three types of relationships: one-to-many, many-to-many, and one-to-one. The relationship type is based upon the rules of the business. In the charity golf tournament, the relationship between the order and the item is many-to-many, but in another business it might not be. For example, consider a business that sells custom-made jewelry where each item is one of a kind. In this case, an item can appear on just one order. Thus, the relationship between order and item in that business would be one-to-many.

Real World Advice Use of One-to-One Relationships

When you have a one-to-one relationship, you could combine the two tables into a single table. A single table is simpler than two tables with a relationship between them.

- You could keep the two tables separate when the two tables are obviously two different things like manager and department. You might want to keep private information about the manager in the manager table. Additionally this would be easier to change if business rules change and multiple managers might manage the same department.

- You should combine the two tables when there are just a few attributes on one of the tables. For example, suppose you only wanted to keep the manager's name in the manager table with no other information about the manager. Then you might consider the manager's name to be an attribute of the department.

Create a One-to-Many Relationship

Consider the relationship between tblParticipant and tblOrder. This is a one-to-many relationship. To form a relationship between two tables, you need the tables to have a field in common. The easiest way to accomplish this is to put the primary key from the one side in the table on the many side. In this case, this means that you use the ParticipantID from the one side table and add it as a field to the tblOrder table. The field that you add to the many side is called a foreign key because it is a key to another (foreign) table. ParticipantID is already a field on the many-side table, so you can use it to form the relationship.

Quick Reference / Creating a One-to-Many Relationship in Access

Creating a one-to-many relationship in Access takes three steps:

1. Make sure the two tables have a field in common. Use the primary key from the one-side, and add it as a foreign key in the many-side table.

2. Form the relationship in the Relationships window. This is done by connecting the primary key of the one-side table to the foreign key of the many-side table.

3. Populate the foreign key by adding data to the foreign key in the many-side table.

Forming the Relationship

Because the tables already have a field in common, you can form the relationship. You will connect the primary key of the one-side table to the foreign key on the many-side table.

To Form a Relationship

a. Click **Show Table** in the Relationships group, click **tblParticipant**, and then click **Add**.

b. Click **Close** to close the Show Table dialog box. Drag the **tblParticipant** table in the Relationships window to appear below the other tables. Resize **tblParticipant** so all fields show.

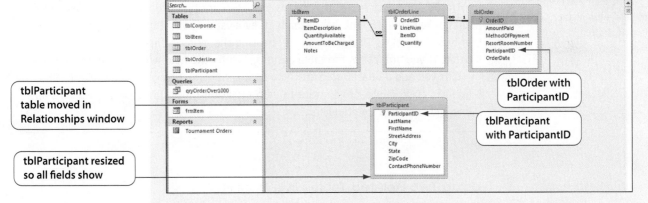

tblParticipant table moved in Relationships window

tblParticipant resized so all fields show

tblOrder with ParticipantID

tblParticipant with ParticipantID

Figure 28   Move the table in the Relationships window

c. Drag the primary key, **ParticipantID**, from tblParticipant to **ParticipantID** in tblOrder. Alternatively, you could drag from ParticipantID in tblOrder to ParticipantID in tblParticipant.
Access displays the Edit Relationships dialog box. Notice that Access calls the relationship a one-to-many relationship. This is because the relationship is between a primary key and a foreign key.

d. Click **Enforce Referential Integrity** to select it, and then click **Create**. Later in the workshop you will look further at what referential integrity accomplishes.

SIDE NOTE
Adding Tables to the Relationships Window
You can also add tables to the Relationships window by clicking on a table in the Navigation Pane and dragging it to the Relationships window.

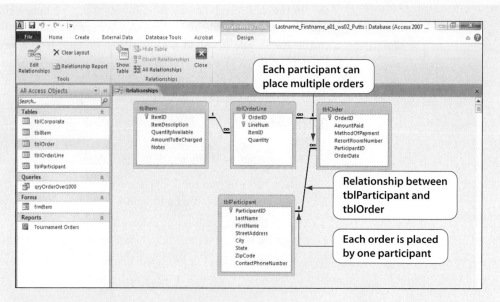

Figure 29 tblParticipant and tblOrder relationship

e. **Close** ☒ the Relationships window, and then click **Yes** to save changes to the layout of the relationships.

Troubleshooting

If you get the error message "The database engine could not lock table 'tblParticipant' because it is already in use by another person or process," this means that the tblParticipant table is still open. Close the table, and try again to form the relationship. You should get in the habit of closing tables when you are done with them.

If you get the error message "Relationship must be on the same number of fields with the same data type," this means that the data types for the primary key and the foreign key are different. For example, they must be both Numeric and Long Integer or both Text. Make sure that you are creating the relationship between the correct fields. If you are, check the table designs, and fix the field with the wrong data type.

If you add a relationship that you do not want, right-click on the relationship line and click Delete. If you want to edit a relationship, right-click the relationship line and click Edit Relationship.

Using Two Related Tables in a Report

The reason you created a relationship is to join two tables in queries, reports, and forms. You will create a simple report showing participants and their orders.

To Create a Report From Two Tables

a. Click the **Create tab**, and then click **Report Wizard** in the Reports group.

b. In the Report Wizard dialog box, click the **Tables/Queries arrow**, and then select **Table: tblParticipant**. Select the **LastName** field, and then click **One Field** >. Select the **FirstName** field, and then click the **One Field** >.

SIDE NOTE
Tables in the Relationships Window

Do not add a table multiple times to the Relationships window. If you do, delete both versions of the table and start over. If you hide the second version of the table instead, it never really disappears. If you ever need to delete the relationship, you must unhide the hidden table and delete both.

c. Click the **Tables/Queries arrow**, and then select **Table: tblOrder**. Select the **OrderID** field, and then click **One Field** $>$. Select the **AmountPaid** field, and then click **One Field** $>$.

Troubleshooting

If you clicked Next instead of selecting the tblOrder fields, you can go back a step in the wizard by clicking Back.

d. Click **Next**.

Access shows you a preview of how your report will look if you group the participants by tblParticipant. Access uses the *one* side of a one-to-many relationship as the default for the grouping. This is the grouping you want.

e. Click **Next**. The wizard asks if you want more grouping levels; however, you do not want any other grouping levels.

f. Click **Next**.

g. Use the arrow to select **OrderID**. Ascending sort order is already selected. Click **Next**.

The wizard asks you to choose a layout for your report. You will accept the default layout.

h. Click **Next**.

i. Title your report Participants and Orders_initialLastname, where initial is your first initial and Lastname is your last name.

j. Click **Finish**.

Access connects the participants and orders in a report.

k. If your instructor directs you to print the report, click **Print** in the Print group, and then click **OK**. Click **Close Print Preview**, and then close your report.

Create a Many-to-Many Relationship

Unless you are connecting a common field such as a foreign key to the same foreign key in a different table, Access cannot form a many-to-many relationship with a single relationship. Instead you need to make two one-to-many relationships to represent the many-to-many relationship. As stated before, tblOrder and tblItem have a many-to-many relationship. An order can have many items on it. Each item can be on many orders. To form this relationship, a new table, tblOrderLine, needs to be added. Both tblOrder and tblItem are related to the new table. The third table is called a junction table. A **junction table** breaks down the many-to-many relationship into two one-to-many relationships.

Figure 30 Relationship between tblOrder and tblItem with tblOrderLine

Look at the relationship between tblOrder and tblOrderLine. It is a one-to-many relationship with orders having many order lines but each order line on just one order. There is also a relationship between tblOrderLine and tblItem. It also is a one-to-many relationship with each order line having just one item but an item able to be on many order lines as shown in Figure 31.

OrderID 4 has two order lines, one with an item of a corporate team, and one with a cart. By traveling left to right across the three tables, you see that OrderID 4 has many items on it. OrderID 6 has one line, an entry to the tournament. By traveling from right to left across the three tables, you see that an entry to the tournament can be on many orders. Hence the junction table tblOrderLine forms a many-to-many relationship between tblOrder and tblItem.

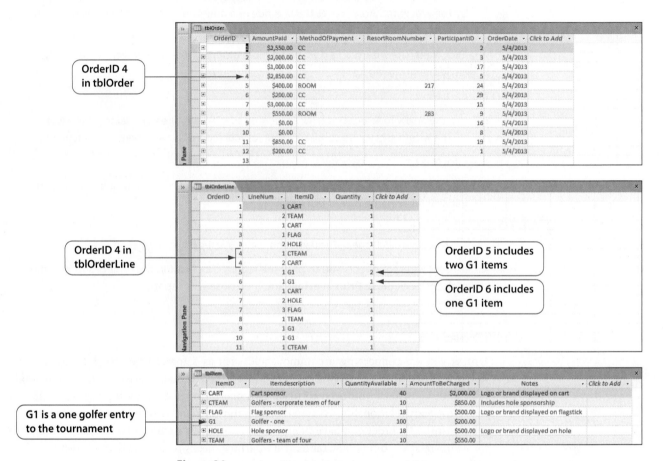

Figure 31   Data in tblOrder, tblOrderLine, and tblItem

tblOrderLine has foreign keys to tblOrder and tblItem. This allows the relationships to be formed. Notice that the relationship between tblOrder and tblOrderLine is formed with OrderID in tblOrder joined to OrderID in tblOrderLine. Similarly the relationship between tblItem and tblOrderLine is formed from ItemID in tblItem to ItemID in tblOrderLine.

The junction table, tblOrderLine, has one field beyond the key fields: Quantity. This indicates the quantity of each item on the order. As shown in Figure 31, OrderID 5 included two entries to the tournament.

Forming a New Many-to-Many Relationship

Consider the relationship between your new table, tblCorporate, and tblParticipant. There is a relationship: a participant can represent a corporation. A participant can be a golfer for a corporation, the corporate representative, or a donor. What is the cardinality? You need to ask yourself the two questions to determine the cardinality:

- Question 1 (starting with the Corporate entity): If you have one corporation, what is the maximum number of participants that can represent that corporation? You care only about two answers: one or many. In this case, the corporation could be represented by many participants. A corporate team might have four golfer participants.

- Question 2 (starting with the Participant entity): If you have one Participant, what is the maximum number of roles that Participant can represent for the corporation? Again, the only answers to consider are one or many. A Participant could be a golfer representing the corporation and also be a corporate representative.

Quick Reference — Creating a Many-to-Many Relationship in Access

Creating a many-to-many relationship in Access takes four steps:

1. Create a junction table. Create a primary key that will be a unique field for the junction table, and add two foreign keys, one to each of the many-to-many tables.
2. Determine if there are any fields that you want to add to the junction table beyond the keys.
3. Form two relationships in the Relationships window. This is done by connecting the primary key of one of the original tables to the appropriate foreign key of the junction table. Repeat for the second of the original tables. The junction table is on the *many* side of both relationships.
4. Populate the junction table.

Create a Junction Table

Because the relationship between tblCorporate and tblParticipant is many-to-many, you need a junction table. Recall that the junction table breaks down the many-to-many relationship into two one-to-many relationships. In this case the junction table will indicate the role that the participant has for the corporation. The primary key for the junction table will be ParticipantRoleID, an AutoNumber. You will have two foreign keys, the CorporateID and the ParticipantID. You will also add a field that describes the role of the participant. Because the table represents roles, you call it tblParticipantRole.

To Create a Junction Table in Table Design

a. Click the **Create tab**, and then click **Table Design** in the Tables group.
   Access opens a blank table in Design view. You will enter each field in the appropriate row.

b. In the Field Name, type ParticipantRoleID. Press Tab to move to the Data Type column. Click the **arrow**, and then select the data type of **AutoNumber**.
   Alternatively, you can type the "A," and "AutoNumber" will appear. Notice that Field Size in the Field Properties pane defaults to Long Integer.

c. Press Tab to move to the Description column, and then type Primary key for tblParticipantRole.

d. Click **Primary Key** in the Tools group to make the field the primary key.

e. Press Tab to move to the next field. Continue filling in the table with the following information, being sure to enter maximum length in field size.

Field Name	Data Type	Maximum Length	Description
ParticipantRoleID	AutoNumber	Long Integer	Primary key for tblParticipantRole
CorporateID	Number	Long Integer	Foreign key to tblCorporate
ParticipantID	Number	Long Integer	Foreign key to tblParticipant
Role	Text	40	Role that this participant fills for the corporation

f. **Close** ☒ the table, replying **Yes** to saving the changes. Name the table tblParticipantRole and then click **OK**.

Create Two One-to-Many Relationships

The many-to-many relationship will turn into two one-to-many relationships between each of the original tables and the junction table. The rule is that the junction table is on the many side of the two relationships. But you can ask yourself the two questions to determine the cardinality:

- Question 1 (starting with the Corporate entity): If you have one corporation, what is the maximum number of participant roles that can represent that corporation? You care only about two answers: one or many. In this case, the corporation could be represented by many participants. A corporate team might have four golfer participants.

- Question 2 (starting with the ParticipantRole entity): If you have one ParticipantRole, what is the maximum number of corporations that the participant can represent? Again, the only answers to consider are one or many. A ParticipantRole is for a single participant.

Thus tblCorporate to tblParticipantRole is a one-to-many relationship with Corporate on the *one* side.

You can ask the same questions between tblParticipant and tblParticipantRole.

To Form Two Relationships to the Junction Table

a. Click the **Database Tools tab**, and then click **Relationships** in the Relationships group.

b. Click the **Relationship Tools Design tab**, and then click **Show Table** in the Relationships group. Select **tblCorporate**, and then click **Add**. Select **tblParticipantRole**, and then click **Add**.

c. **Close** the Show Table dialog box. Drag the **tables** in the Relationships window so there is some space between the tables to form the relationships.

d. Drag the primary key **ParticipantID** from tblParticipant to **ParticipantID** in tblParticipantRole. Alternatively, you could drag from ParticipantID in tblParticipantRole to ParticipantID in tblParticipant.

e. Access displays the Edit Relationships dialog box. Click **Enforce Referential Integrity** to select it, and then click **Create**.

f. Drag the primary key **CorporateID** from tblCorporate to **CorporateID** in tblParticipantRole.

g. Access displays the Edit Relationships dialog box. Click **Enforce Referential Integrity** to select it, and then click **Create**.

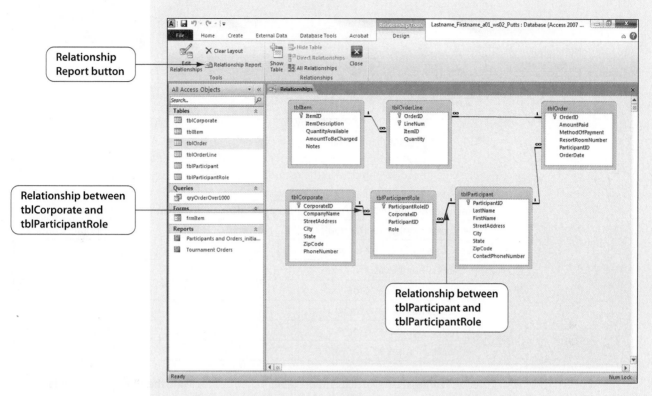

Relationship Report button

Relationship between tblCorporate and tblParticipantRole

Relationship between tblParticipant and tblParticipantRole

Figure 32   Completed Relationships window

h. Click **Relationship Report** in the Tools group to create a report on your relationship. **Save** the report, accepting the name **Relationships for Lastname_Firstname_a01_ws02_Putts**, and then click **OK**.

i. Submit your files as instructed by your instructor. **Close** the Relationship report.

j. **Close** the Relationships window, and then click **Yes** to save changes to the layout of the relationships.

Populate the Junction Table

To complete the many-to-many relationship, you need to populate the junction table.

To Populate the Junction Table

a. Double-click **tblParticipantRole** to open the table in Datasheet view.

b. Click in the **CorporateID append row**. Enter a CorporateID of **1**, a ParticipantID of **5**, and a Role of Corporate Contact. Access automatically numbers ParticipantRoleID as 1.

c. Because the last field is not totally visible, place your pointer in the border on the right of the Role column heading. When your pointer is a double-headed arrow, double-click the **border** to resize the column. Repeat for each field.

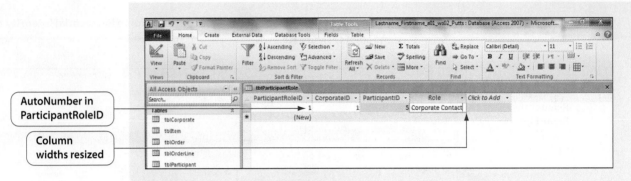

AutoNumber in ParticipantRoleID

Column widths resized

Figure 33 tblParticipantRole columns resized

d. Enter the following data in the records as follows:

ParticipantRoleID	CorporateID	ParticipantID	Role
let Access number as 1 for you	1	5	Corporate Contact
let Access number as 2 for you	1	5	Golfer
let Access number as 3 for you	1	26	Golfer
let Access number as 4 for you	2	1	Golfer
let Access number as 5 for you	2	3	Golfer
let Access number as 6 for you	2	54	Corporate Contact
let Access number as 7 for you	2	54	Golfer

e. **Close** ☒ the tblParticipantRole table, saying **Yes** to saving the change in the table layout.

One-to-One Relationships

One-to-one relationships in Access are formed very similarly to one-to-many relationships. You can put a foreign key in either table and establish the relationship by dragging with the primary key in one table joined to the foreign key. You can also make both tables have the same primary key.

Understanding Referential Integrity

Referential integrity is a set of rules that Access uses to make sure that the relationships you are forming between records in your tables make sense. Recall that when you created the relationship between tblParticipant and tblOrder you told Access to enforce referential integrity.

Referential integrity means that Access will enforce the following rules when you define the fields in Design view:

- The field on the one side of the relationship is unique on the table. You must either use the primary key of the one side in the relationship or a field that you have set to be unique.

- You cannot add a foreign key value in the many side that does not have a matching primary key value on the one side.

- The matching fields on both sides of the relationship are defined with the same data types. For example, if the primary key is numeric and Long Integer, the foreign key must be numeric and Long Integer too. (For purposes of relationships, an AutoNumber primary key is considered Long Integer.)

If these rules are violated, when you try to form the relationship, Access will give you the following error message: "Relationship must be on the same number of fields with the same data type."

Double-check how you defined the relationship between tblParticipant and tblOrder.

To Check and Test Referential Integrity

a. Click the **Database Tools tab**, and then click **Relationships** in the Relationships group. The Relationships window is displayed. The relationship was formed between ParticipantID in tblParticipant and tblOrder.

b. **Close** the Relationships window.

c. Right-click **tblParticipant**, and then click **Design View**. Notice that ParticipantID is defined as Number and Long Integer. **Close** ☒ tblParticipant. Right-click **tblOrder**, and then click **Design View**. Click the ParticipantID field. Notice that ParticipantID is defined as Number and Long Integer.

Referential integrity means that Access will also enforce rules when you work with the data in the tables. You cannot enter a value in the foreign key field on the *many* side table that is not a primary key value on the *one* side table. For example, you cannot add a participant to a team that does not exist. However, you can leave the foreign key unfilled, indicating that this participant is not part of a team.

d. Click the **Home tab**, and then click the **View** button to change to **Datasheet View** for tblOrder.

e. Scroll down to the last record in the table, and then scroll right. In ParticipantID, type 70 and then press ⎡Enter⎤ twice.

Access responds with the error message "You cannot add or change a record because a related record is required in table tblParticipant." That is, you cannot add an order to participant 70 because there is no participant 70.

f. Click **OK**, and then change the ParticipantID for the last order back to 1. Press ⎡Enter⎤ twice. ParticipantID 1 is a valid participant so you can make that change.

g. **Close** ☒ the tblOrder table.

CONSIDER THIS | **Why Enforce Referential Integrity?**

You can decline to enforce referential integrity on a relationship. What are the pros and cons of having Access enforce referential integrity? What are the pros and cons of declining to enforce referential integrity?

If you enforce referential integrity, you cannot delete a record from the *one*-side table if matching records exist in the *many*-side table.

To Understand Relationships Between the One- and Many-Side Tables

a. In the Navigation Pane, double-click **tblParticipant** to open it.

b. Click the **record selector** of the second row, John Trujillo.

c. Click the **Home tab**, and then click **Delete** in the Records group.

Access responds that "The record cannot be deleted or changed because table 'tblOrder' includes related records." That means John Trujillo has placed an order.

d. Click **OK**.

e. **Close** ☒ the tblParticipant table.

f. **Close** ☒ the database and Access.

You also cannot change the primary key value in the *one*-side table if that record has related records.

Quick Reference / Referential Integrity

Access enforces the following rules on defining a relationship with referential integrity:

1. The primary key field on the *one* side of the relationship must be unique in the table.
2. The foreign key values on the *many* side of the relationship must exist as the primary key field for a record on the *one* side of the relationship.
3. The matching fields on both sides of the relationship are defined with the same data types.

Access enforces the following rules on data changes when referential integrity is enforced:

1. You cannot enter a value in the foreign key field on the *many*-side table that is not a primary key on the *one*-side table. However, you can leave the foreign key unfilled, indicating that this record is not in the relationship.
2. You cannot delete a record from the *one*-side table if matching records exist in a *many*-side table (unless Cascade Delete has been selected for the relationship, in which case all the matching records on the many side are deleted).
3. You cannot change a primary key value in the *one*-side table if that record has related records in the *many* side (unless Cascade Update has been selected for the relationship, in which case all the matching records on the many side have their foreign key updated).

Cascade Update

When you ask Access to enforce referential integrity, you can also select whether you want Access to automatically cascade update related fields or cascade delete related records. These options allow some deletions and updates that would usually be prevented by referential integrity. However, Access makes these changes and replicates (cascades) the changes through all related tables so referential integrity is preserved.

If you select Cascade Update Related Fields when you define a relationship, then when the primary key of a record in the one-side table changes, Access automatically changes the foreign keys in all related records. For example, if you change the ItemID in the tblItem table, Access automatically changes the ItemID on all order lines that include that item. Access makes these changes without displaying an error message.

If the primary key in the *one*-side table was defined as AutoNumber, selecting Cascade Update Related Fields has no effect, because you cannot change the value in an AutoNumber field.

Cascade Delete

If you select Cascade Delete Related Records when you define a relationship, any time that you delete records from the *one*-side table, Access automatically deletes all related records in the *many*-side table. For example, if you deleted a tblParticipant record, all the orders made by that participant are automatically deleted from the tblOrder table. Before you make the deletion, Access warns you that related records may also be deleted.

CONSIDER THIS | **Should You Cascade Delete Related Records?**

Should you cascade delete related records? Consider a customer who has made many orders. If the customer asks to be removed from your database, do you want to remove his or her past orders? How do you think the accountants would feel?

Concept Check

1. If you wanted to create a table listing all your suppliers of products, what would be a good table name? What would be a good primary key? What data type should this key have?

2. If you have an Excel worksheet of customers, how could you move the customer data to Access? How would you decide between various ways to move the data?

3. What data types would you use for the following fields: price, phone number, street address, zip code, and directions for using a product?

4. In a university database, you have tables for students and classes. What kind of relationship is the relationship between student and class? What would you do in Access to create this relationship?

5. How many times can the number "4" appear for the ParticipantID field in the tblParticipant table? Why? How many times can the number "4" appear in the ParticipantID field in the tblOrder table? Why?

Key Terms

Attribute   528
Cardinality   555
Composite key   550
Data type   531
Delimiter   536
Entity   528
Field size   543
Foreign key   549

Format   547
Input mask   545
Join   553
Junction table   559
Many-to-many relationship   556
Natural primary key   551
Normalization   553
Number data type   531

Numeric key   549
One-to-many relationship   555
One-to-one relationship   556
Primary key   541
Redundancy   554
Relationship   528
Text data type   531

Visual Summary

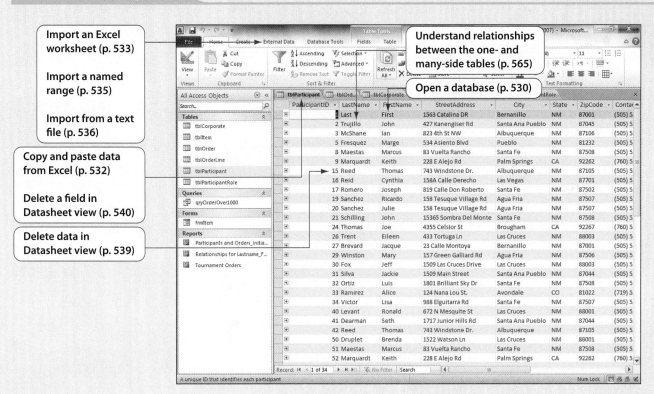

Import an Excel worksheet (p. 533)

Import a named range (p. 535)

Import from a text file (p. 536)

Copy and paste data from Excel (p. 532)

Delete a field in Datasheet view (p. 540)

Delete data in Datasheet view (p. 539)

Understand relationships between the one- and many-side tables (p. 565)

Open a database (p. 530)

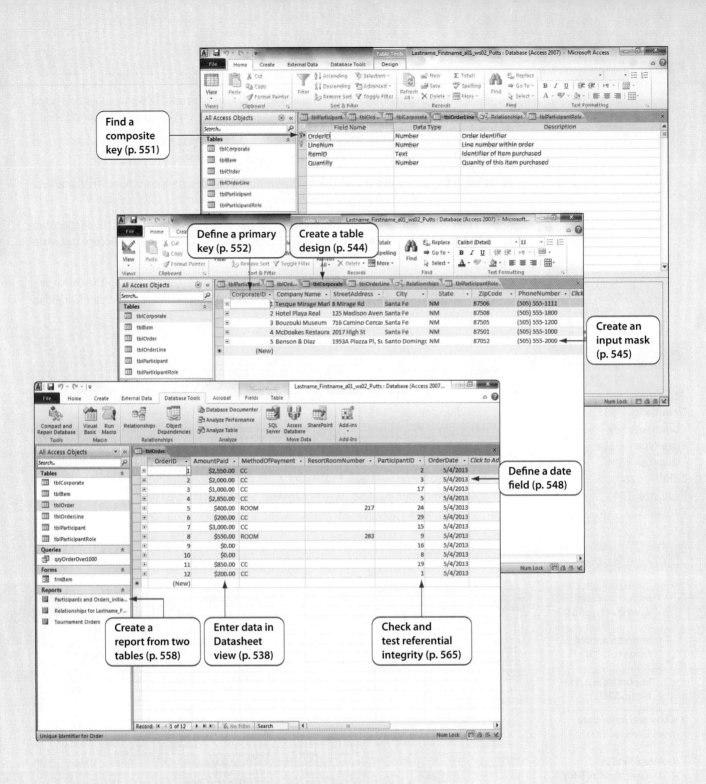

Find a composite key (p. 551)

Define a primary key (p. 552)

Create a table design (p. 544)

Create an input mask (p. 545)

Define a date field (p. 548)

Create a report from two tables (p. 558)

Enter data in Datasheet view (p. 538)

Check and test referential integrity (p. 565)

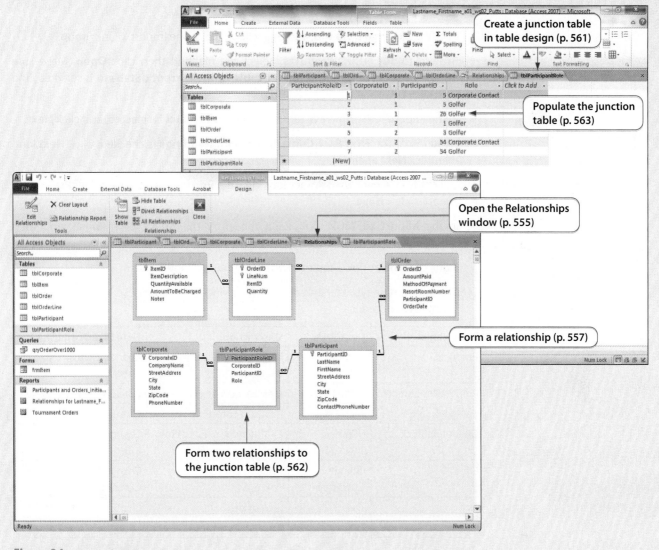

Figure 34   Putts for Paws Charity Tournament Imported Data Final Database

Student data files needed:

a01_ws02_Painted_Treasures

a01_ws02_Products

a01_ws02_Customers

You will save your file as:

Lastname_Firstname_a01_ws02_Painted_Treasures

Painted Treasures Gift Shop

Sales & Marketing

The Painted Treasures Gift Shop sells many products for the resort patrons including jewelry, clothing, and spa products. You will create a database of customers and their purchases.

The three tables that you need are customers, purchases, and products. What are the relationships between these three tables? You will need to add a junction table between the two tables with a many-to-many relationship.

a. You will start by importing an Excel file into Access and changing the field definitions.

- Start **Access**, and then open **a01_ws02_Painted_Treasures.**

- Click the **File tab**, and then click **Save Database As**. In the Save As dialog box, navigate to where you are saving your files, and then type Lastname_Firstname_a01_ws02_Painted_Treasures.

- Click **Save**.

- In the Security Warning bar, click **Enable Content**.

- Click the **External Data tab**, and then click **Excel** in the Import & Link group.

- **Browse** to **a01_ws02_Products**. Select the file, and then click **Open**. Make sure **Import the source data into a new table in the current database** is selected, and then click **OK**.

- In the Import Spreadsheet Wizard, note that **tblProduct** is selected, and click **Next**.

- Be sure that the **First Row Contains Column Headings** is checked. Click **Next**, and then click **Next** again.

- Select **Choose my own primary key**, click the **Primary Key arrow**, select **ProductID**, and then click **Next**.

- In the **Import to Table** box, keep the entry tblProduct, click **Finish**, and then click **Close**.

- Right-click **tblProduct**, and then open it in **Design view**.

- Change the data types as shown in the following table. Enter descriptions and change field sizes as noted.

Field Name	Data Type	Description	Field Size/Format
ProductID	Number	Unique identifier for product	Change Field Size to Long Integer
ProductDescription	Text	Description of product	Change Field Size to 40
Category	Text	Product category	Change Field Size to 15
QuantityInStock	Number	Quantity of product in stock	Change Field Size to Integer
Price	Change to Currency	Price to charge customer	Change format to Currency
Size	Text	Size of product	Change Field Size to 10
Color	Text	Color of product	Change Field Size to 15

- Save the table. Access tells you that some data might be lost because you are making fields shorter in length. Accept this by clicking **Yes**. Close the table.

b. Create the tblCustomer table in Design view.

- Click the **Create tab**, and then click **Table Design**. Access opens a blank table in Design view.

- Fill in the fields.

Field Name	Data Type	Description	Field Size
CustomerID	AutoNumber	A unique ID that identifies each customer	Long Integer
LastName	Text	The customer's last name	25
FirstName	Text	The customer's first name	20
StreetAddress	Text	Street address	40
City	Text	City address	25
State	Text	State abbreviation	2
ZipCode	Text	Five-digit zip code	5
ResortHotelRoom	Text	Leave blank if not guest	6

- Highlight the **CustomerID row** by clicking the record selector to the left of the field. Click **Primary Key** to make CustomerID the primary key.

- Save your table design, naming it **tblCustomer**. Click **OK**. Close your table.

- Click the **External Data tab**, and then click **Excel** in the Import & Link group.

- Click **Browse**. Click the disk drive in the left pane where your student data files are located, navigate through the folder structure, click **a01_ws02_Customers**, and then click **Open**.

- Click **Append a copy of the records to the table**. If necessary, click the **arrow** to select **tblCustomer**, and then click **OK**.

- Click **Next** twice, and then in the Import Spreadsheet Wizard dialog box, keep the entry table **tblCustomer**. Click **Finish**, and then click **Close**.

- Double-click **tblCustomer** to open it in Datasheet view.

- In the first record in the table, change the LastName and FirstName to your last name and first name. Close tblCustomer.

c. Create relationships between your tables.

- Click the **Database Tools tab**.

- Click **Relationships** in the Relationships group, and then click **Show Table**, if necessary.

- Add all four tables in the order **tblCustomer**, **tblPurchase**, **tblPurchaseLine**, and **tblProduct** to the Relationships window, and then close the **Show Table** dialog box.

- Drag the primary key **CustomerID** from tblCustomer to **CustomerID** in tblPurchase.

- Click **Enforce Referential Integrity**, and then click **Create**.

- Drag the primary key **PurchaseID** from tblPurchase to **PurchaseID** in tblPurchaseLine. Click **Enforce Referential Integrity**, and then click **Create**.

- Drag the primary key **ProductID** from tblProduct to **ProductID** in tblPurchaseLine. Click **Enforce Referential Integrity**, and then click **Create**.

- Click **Relationship Report** and save it, accepting the name **Relationships for Lastname_Firstname_a01_ws02_Painted_Treasures**. Close the report.

- Close the Relationships window, and then click **Yes** to save the relationships.

d. Create a report of the customers, purchases, and products.

- Click the **Create tab**, and then click **Report Wizard** in the Reports group.

- In the Report Wizard dialog box, click the **Tables/Queries arrow**, and then select **Table: tblCustomer**. Select the **LastName** and **FirstName** fields.

- Click the **Tables/Queries arrow**, click **Table: tblPurchase**, and then select **PurchaseDate**.

- Click the **Tables/Queries arrow**, click **Table: tblPurchaseLine**, and then select **Quantity**.

- Click the **Tables/Queries arrow**, click **Table: tblProduct**, click **ProductDescription**, and then click **Next**.

- Accept grouping by tblCustomer and then by PurchaseDate by clicking **Next**.

- You do not want any other grouping levels, so click **Next**.

- Click the **arrow** to sort your report by ascending **ProductDescription**, and then click **Next**.

- Change the Orientation to **Landscape**, and then click **Next**.

- Title your report Customer and Purchases_initialLastname and then click **Finish**.

- Close Print Preview, close the report, and then exit Access.

Student data files needed:

a01_ps1_Planner2
a01_ps1_Planner2_Decorations

You will save your files as:

Lastname_Firstname_a01_ps1_Planner2

Event Management

Information
Technology

Sue Morris has a small event planning business. She recently decided to transfer her company's data to a database. While she has started on the database, she is too busy to finish it so she has hired you to complete the implementation.

a. Create your Event database.

- Start **Access**, and then open **a01_ws02_Planner2**.

- Click the **File tab**, and then click **Save Database As**. In the Save As dialog box, navigate to where you are saving your files, type Lastname_Firstname_a01_ws02_Planner2, replacing Lastname_Firstname with your own name, and then click **Save**.

- In the Security Warning bar, click **Enable Content**.

- Double-click **tblClients** in the Navigation Pane to open the table.

- In record **25**, change **First Name** and **Last Name** to Your Name.

b. Sue wants to ensure certain data is entered correctly so you will make changes to the field definitions.

- Change to **Design view**.

- Click the **Phone** field, and then in the Field Properties pane, click in the **Input Mask** box.

- Click the **Build** button to start the Input Mask Wizard. If necessary, select **Phone Number** and click **Next**. Click **Next** to accept the format. Select **With symbols in the mask, like this**, click **Next**, and then click **Finish**.

- Click the **State** field, and then in the Field Properties pane, change **Field Size** to 2.

- Click the **ZipCode** field, and then in the Field Properties pane, change **Field Size** to 5.

- Close the table, click **Yes** to save the definitions, and then click **Yes** to the warning message.

c. Import the decorations from data stored in a text file.

- Click the **External Data tab**, and then click **Text File** in the Import & Link group.

- **Browse** to a01_ws02_Planner2_Decorations. Select the file, and then click **Open**. Make sure **Import the source data into a new table in the current database** is selected, and then click OK.

- Make sure that **Delimited** is selected and then click **Next**.

- Make sure that **Comma** is selected and then click **Next**.

- Click **Next**.

- Select **Choose my own primary key** and make sure **Field1** is selected. Click **Next**.

- In the **Import to Table** box, type tblDecorations, click **Finish**, and then click **Close**.

- Right-click **tblDecorations** and then open it in **Design View**.

- Make the following changes to the field names, data types, descriptions, and Field Size:

Current Field Name	New Field Name	Data Type	Description	Field Size
Field1	DecorationID	Number	A unique identifier for the decoration	Long Integer
Field2	Decoration	Text	Decoration label	35
Field3	Color	Text	Decoration color	30
Field4	Category	Text	Type of decoration	35

- Close the table, click **Yes** to save the definitions, and then click **Yes** to the warning message.

d. Sue wants to be able to record the decorations that are being reserved for each event. This creates a many-to-many relationship between events and decorations. Create a junction table in Design view.

- Click the **Create tab**, and then click **Table Design**. Access opens a blank table in Design view.

- Fill in the following fields (in this order):

Field Name	Data Type	Description	Field Size
EventID	Number	The primary key from tblEvents	Long Integer
DecorationID	Number	The primary key from tblDecorations	Long Integer
NumberReserved	Number	The number of decorations reserved	Long Integer

- Click the record selector to the left of the field **EventID**. Click **Shift** and click the record selector to the left of **DecorationID**. Click **Primary Key** to make a composite key using **EventID** and **DecorationID**.

- Save the new table as tblEventDecoration. Click **OK**. **Close** your table.

e. Create relationships between your tables.

- Click the **Database Tools tab**.

- Click **Relationships** in the Relationships group.

- Click **Show Table** in the Relationships group, click **tblEventDecoration**, and then click **Add**. Click **Close**.

- Move the tables as necessary to give yourself room to create relationships.

- Drag the primary key **ClientID** from tblClients to **ClientID** in tblEvents. Click **Enforce Referential Integrity**, and then click **Create**.

- Drag the primary key **EventID** from tblEvents to **EventID** in tblEventDecoration. Click **Enforce Referential Integrity**, and then click **Create**.

- Drag the primary key **DecorationID** from tblDecorations to **DecorationID** in tblEventDecoration. Click **Enforce Referential Integrity**, and then click **Create**.

- Click **Relationship Report** and save it, accepting the name **Relationships for Lastname_Firstname_a01_ws02_Planner2**. Click **OK** and close your report.

- If your instructor directs you to print the relationships, print your relationship report.

- **Close** the Relationships window, and then click **Yes** to save the relationships.

f. Sue has one order to put into tblEventDecoration.

- Double-click **tblEventDecoration** to open it.

- Enter the following data:

EventID	DecorationID	NumberReserved
3	7	4
3	9	40
3	17	4

- Close your table.

g. Sue wants to be able to retrieve information on events and decorations. Create a report from a query for her use.

- Click the **Create tab** and then click **Query Wizard** in the Queries Group. Select **Simple Query Wizard**, and then click **OK**.

- Click the **Tables/Queries arrow**, and then select **Table: tblClients** as the source of your fields. In the Available Fields box, select fields **LastName** and **FirstName.**

- Click the **Tables/Queries arrow**, and then select **Table: tblEvents**, In the Available Fields box, select fields **EventName** and **EventDate**.

- Click the **Tables/Queries arrow**, and then select **Table: tblDecorations**. In the Available Fields box, select fields **Decoration** and **Color**.

- Click the **Tables/Queries arrow**, and then select **Table: tblEventDecoration**. In the Available Fields box, select **NumberReserved**.

- Click **Next**. Accept **Detail (shows every field of every record)** and click **Next**.

- Type qryEventDecorations_initialLastname as the title of your query.

- Click **Finish**.

- If your instructor directs you to print your results, print your query.

- Close your query.

- Click the **Create tab**, and then select **Report Wizard** in the Reports group.

- Click the **Tables/Queries arrow**, and then select **Query: qryEventDecorations_initialLastname**.

- Select all fields and move them to the Selected Fields box. Click **Next**.

- Accept the default view and click **Next**.

- Accept the default grouping and click **Next**.

- In the 1 box, click the **arrow**, and then select **Decoration**. Click **Next**.

- Change the orientation to **Landscape**. Click **Next**.

- Under "What title do you want for your report," type Event Reservations as the title for your report, and then click **Finish**.

- Switch to Layout view, and then type Lastname_Firstname at the end of the report title, making it **Event Reservations Lastname_Firstname**.

- The NumberReserved column is barely visible. Move the other fields to the left and resize them as necessary, so that you can make that column wider.

- If your instructor directs you to print your results, print your report.

- Save and close the report, and then close Access.

 Additional Workshop Cases are available on the companion website and in the instructor resources.

MODULE CAPSTONE

More Practice 1

Student data files needed:	You will save your file as:
a01_mp_Recipe	Lastname_Firstname_a01_mp_Recipe
a01_mp_Recipe_Preparation	
a01_mp_Recipe_Ingredients	

Indigo 5 Restaurant

Production & Operations

Robin Sanchez, the chef of the resort's restaurant, Indigo 5, wants to keep track of recipes and the ingredients that they include in an Access database. This will allow her to plan menus and get reports and queries on the ingredients that are needed. Ingredients have already been stored in Excel worksheets and can be imported from Excel into Access. The dish preparation instructions can be cut and pasted from Excel. Other data will need to be entered. Complete the following tasks:

a. Start **Access**, and then open **a01_mp_Recipe**. Save the file as Lastname_Firstname_a01_mp_Recipe, replacing Lastname_Firstname with your own name. In the Security Warning bar, click **Enable Content**.

b. Create a new table in Design view. This table will store specific recipe items.

   • Add the following fields, data types, and descriptions. Change field sizes as noted:

Field Name	Data Type	Description	Field Size
RecipeID	Text	The recipe ID assigned to each menu item (primary key)	6
RecipeName	Text	The recipe name	30
FoodCategory	Text	The food category	15
TimeToPrepare	Number	Preparation time in minutes	Integer
Servings	Number	The number of servings this recipe makes	Integer
Instructions	Memo	Cooking instructions	

   • Designate **RecipeID** as the primary key. Save the new table as tblRecipes and then close the table.

c. Create a form to enter recipes. Select **tblRecipes**, click the **Create tab**, and then click **Form** in the Forms group. Save the form as frmRecipes_initialLastname, replacing initialLastName with your own initial and last name.

d. Enter the following data into frmRecipes_initialLastname in Form view:

RecipeID	RecipeName	FoodCategory	TimeToPrepare	Servings
REC001	Chicken Soup	Soup	45	8
REC002	Black Beans	Beans	90	6

e. Start **Excel**, and then open **a01_mp_Recipe_Preparation**. For each recipe, copy the **Cooking Instructions** from the Excel worksheet and paste the recipe instructions into the Access field **Instructions**. Save the form, and close Excel.

f. Import Excel file **a01_mp_Recipe_Ingredients**, appending it to **tblIngredients**. Use the **Ingredients** worksheet. There are headers in the first row of this worksheet. Do not save the import steps.

g. Create a new table in Design view. This table will serve as the junction table between the tblIngredients and tblRecipes tables.

- Add the following fields, data types, and descriptions (in this order). Change field sizes as noted:

Field Name	Data Type	Description	Field Size
RecipeIngredientID	AutoNumber	The recipe ingredient ID automatically assigned to each recipe ingredient (primary key)	
RecipeID	Text	The recipe ID from tblRecipes (foreign key)	6
IngredientID	Number	The ingredient ID from tblIngredients (foreign key)	Long Integer
Quantity	Number	The quantity of the ingredient required in the recipe	Double

- Assign **RecipeIngredientID** as the primary key.
- Save the new table as tblRecipeIngredients.

h. Close the table and form.

i. Open the **Relationships** window and add all three tables to the window.

- Create a one-to-many relationship between **RecipeID** in tblRecipes and **RecipeID** in tblRecipeIngredients. Enforce referential integrity. Do not cascade update or cascade delete.
- Create a one-to-many relationship between **IngredientID** in tblIngredients and **IngredientID** in tblRecipeIngredients. Enforce referential integrity. Do not cascade update or cascade delete.
- Save the relationships, and then close the Relationships window. If your instructor directs you to print the relationships, print your relationship report.

j. Enter the following data into tblRecipeIngredients (in this order):

RecipeIngredientID	RecipeID	IngredientID	Quantity
(Let Access assign)	REC001	7	6
	REC001	9	2
	REC001	16	2
	REC001	17	2
	REC001	6	4
	REC002	10	1
	REC002	16	1
	REC002	17	1
	REC002	21	1
	REC002	18	3
	REC002	20	1

k. Use the Query Wizard and the data in tblRecipes, tblRecipeIngredients, and tblIngredients to create a query that displays the ingredients for each dish. The query results should list **RecipeName**, **Quantity**, **Ingredient**, and **Units**. This will be a **Detail** query. Sort by **RecipeName**. Run your query. Adjust the width of the query columns as necessary. Save your query as qryRecipeIngredients_initialLastname. If your instructor directs you to print the query, print your results.

l. Create a report with the source **qryRecipeIngredients_initialLastname** using the Report Wizard. Select all fields. Group by **RecipeName**, and then sort by **Ingredient**. Name your report Recipe Ingredients Report and then modify the report title to end with your initialLastname. Fix the report columns as necessary. If your instructor directs you to print the report, print your results.

m. Close the database.

Problem Solve 1

Homework 1

Production & Operations

Student data files needed:

a01_ps1_Hotel
a01_ps1_Hotel_Guests
a01_ps1_Hotel_Reservations
a01_ps1_Hotel_Rooms

You will save your file as:

Lastname_Firstname_a01_ps1_Hotel

Hotel Reservations

The main portion of the resort is the hotel. The hotel wants to store information about hotel guests, reservations, and rooms. You will design tables, import data from Excel, and create relationships. Then you will be able to create queries and reports from the data. Complete the following tasks:

a. Start **Access**, and then open **a01_ps1_Hotel**. Save the file as Lastname_Firstname_a01_ps1_Hotel, replacing Lastname_Firstname with your own name. In the Security Warning bar, click **Enable Content.**

b. Import tables from the Access database **a01_ps1_Hotel_Guests**, selecting the **tblGuests** table. Do not save the import steps.

c. Open **tblGuests**, and then change the name in record **25** to Your Name.

d. Create a new table in Design view. This table will store reservations.

- Add the following fields, data types, and descriptions (in this order). Change field sizes or formats as noted:

Field Name	Data Type	Description	Field Size/Format
ReservationID	AutoNumber	A unique identifier for the reservation	Long Integer
GuestID	Number	The guest ID from tblGuests (foreign key)	Long Integer
RoomNumber	Text	The room number from tblRooms (foreign key)	30
CheckInDate	Date/Time	The date the guest will check in	Short Date
NightsStay	Number	How many nights the guest will stay	Integer
NumberOfGuests	Number	The number of guests on this reservation	Integer

- Assign **ReservationID** as the primary key.
- Save the new table as tblReservations.

e. Import **a01_ps1_Hotel_Reservations** from Excel, using the **tblReservations** worksheet and appending it to **tblReservations**. The Excel column headers match the Access field names so you can use them.

f. Select **tblReservations**, click the **Create tab,** and then click **Form** in the Forms group to create a form to enter reservations, and then save it as frmReservations_initialLastname, replacing initialLastname with your own initial and last name.

g. Enter the following data into the append record in frmReservations_initialLastname:

ReservationID	GuestID	RoomNumber	CheckInDate	NightsStay	NumberOfGuests
AutoNumber	25	105	4/20/2014	8	1

h. Create a new table in Design view. This table will store information about the hotel rooms.
   - Add the following fields, data types, and descriptions (in this order). Change field sizes as noted:

Field Name	Data Type	Description	Field Size
RoomNumber	Text	The resort's room number or name (primary key)	30
RoomType	Text	The type of room this is	20

   - Assign **RoomNumber** as the primary key.
   - Save the new table as tblRooms.

i. Import **a01_ps1_Hotel_Rooms** from Excel, using the **Rooms** worksheet and appending it to **tblRooms**. Look to see whether there are column headings that match the Access field names.

j. Open the **Relationships** window, and then create a relationship between **GuestID** in tblGuests and **GuestID** in tblReservations. Enforce referential integrity. Do not cascade update or cascade delete.

k. Create a one-to-many relationship between **RoomNumber** in tblRooms and **RoomNumber** in tblReservations. Enforce referential integrity. Do not cascade update or cascade delete. If your instructor directs you to print the relationships, print your relationship report.

l. Use the Query Wizard to create a query. The query results should list **GuestID**, **GuestFirstName**, **GuestMiddleInitial**, **GuestLastName**, **CheckInDate**, **NightsStay**, and **RoomType**. This query should show every field of every record.

m. Save your query as qryMyReservations_initialLastname. Run the query.

n. In Design view for **qryMyReservations_initialLastname**, select the guest with **GuestID = 25**. Sort by **CheckInDate**. Run the query. If your instructor directs you to print the query, print your results.

o. Create a report showing **ReservationID**, **CheckInDate**, **NightsStay**, and **RoomType**. View by tblRooms and sort by **CheckInDate** and **ReservationID**. Name your report Reservations Report and then modify the report title to end with your initialLastname. Fix the report columns as necessary. If your instructor directs you to print the report, print your results.

p. Close the database.

Student data files needed:

a01_ps2_Hotel_Staffing
a01_ps2_Hotel_Staff

You will save your file as:

Lastname_Firstname_a01_ps2_Hotel_Staffing

Human
Resources

Hotel Staffing Database

The hotel general manager needs a human resource database to store information on employees, the areas they work in, and the hours they are scheduled to work. The database will have three new tables: tblHotelAreas, tblEmployee, and tblSchedule.

a. Start **Access**, and then open **a01_ps2_Hotel_Staffing**. Save the file as Lastname_Firstname_a01_ps2_Hotel_Staffing, replacing Lastname_Firstname with your own name. In the Security Warning bar, click **Enable Content.**

b. Create a new table in Design view. This table will store employees.

   • Add the following fields (in this order). Where necessary, you decide upon data types and field sizes.

Field Name	Data Type	Description	Field Size/Format
EmployeeID	AutoNumber	A unique identifier for the employee (primary key)	
AreaID	Number	The area ID from tblHotel-Areas (foreign key)	Long Integer
FirstName	Pick appropriate type	The employee's first name	30
LastName	Pick appropriate type	The employee's last name	30
StreetAddress	Pick appropriate type	Home street address	40
City	Pick appropriate type	City	30
State	Pick appropriate type	State abbreviation	Pick appropriate size
ZipCode	Pick appropriate type	Zip code (5 digit)	Pick appropriate size
Phone	Pick appropriate type	Home phone number	14
HireDate	Pick appropriate type	Date employee was hired	Short Date
JobTitle	Pick appropriate type	Employee job title	30

   • Make sure you have assigned the most appropriate field to be the primary key.
   • Define an input mask for the phone number. Use a mask of **(555) 555-5555** with a place holder of "_" and save with the symbols in the mask.
   • Save the new table as tblEmployee.

c. Import **a01_ps2_Hotel_Staff** from Excel, using the **Employee** worksheet and appending it to **tblEmployee**. Change the name of the last employee to Your Name.

d. Create a new table in Design view. This table will store hotel areas.

   • Add the following fields, data types, descriptions, and field sizes (in this order):

Field Name	Data Type	Description	Field Size
AreaID	AutoNumber	A unique identifier for the area	Long Integer
AreaName	Text	The name of the area	30

   • Make sure you have assigned the most appropriate field to be the primary key.
   • Save the new table as tblHotelAreas.

e. Import **a01_ps2_Hotel_Staff** from Excel, using the **Area** worksheet and appending it to **tblHotelAreas**.

f. Create a new table in Design view. This table will store information about an employee's schedule.

- Add the following fields, data types, descriptions, and field sizes/formats (in this order):

Field Name	Data Type	Description	Field Size/Format
ScheduleID	AutoNumber	A unique identifier for the schedule (primary key)	Long Integer
ScheduleDay	Date/Time	The day the schedule applies to	ShortDate
StartTime	Date/Time	Starting time for the shift	MediumTime
HoursScheduled	Number	Number of hours on shift	Integer
EmployeeID	Number	The person being scheduled	Long Integer

- Make sure you have assigned the most appropriate primary key. Save the new table as tblSchedule.

g. Import **a01_ps2_Hotel_Staff** from Excel, using the **Schedule** worksheet, and appending it to **tblSchedule**.

h. Open the **Relationships** window, create a one-to-many relationship between **EmployeeID** in tblEmployee and **EmployeeID** in tblSchedule. Enforce referential integrity. Do not cascade update or cascade delete.

i. Create a one-to-many relationship between **AreaID** in tblHotelAreas and **AreaID** in tblEmployee. Enforce referential integrity. Do not cascade update or cascade delete. If your instructor directs you to print the relationships, print your relationship report.

j. Create a form for **tblEmployee**. Notice that Access automatically includes the related records from tblSchedule at the bottom of the form. Save the form as frmEmployeeSchedule_initialLastname.

k. Using **frmEmployeeSchedule_initialLastname**, find your employee record, and add a new schedule for yourself to work on January 3, 2014, starting at 8 am and working for 8 hours.

l. Create a schedule query listing **AreaID**, **AreaName**, **FirstName**, **LastName**, **ScheduleDay**, **StartTime**, and **HoursScheduled**. Run your query, and then save it as qryCoffeeShop-Schedule_initialLastname.

m. In Design view for qryCoffeeShopSchedule_initialLastname, select only the data from **AreaID 4**. Run the query. If your instructor directs you to print the query, print your results.

n. Create a report from qryCoffeeShopSchedule_initialLastname. Select the fields **FirstName**, **LastName**, **ScheduleDay**, **StartTime**, and **HoursScheduled**. View by **tblSchedule**. Group by **ScheduleDay**. Access defaults to ScheduleDay by Month. Click on **Grouping Options**, and then change the **Grouping Intervals** to **Day**. Sort by **StartTime** and **LastName**, and then change to **Landscape** orientation.

o. Name your report CoffeeShopSchedule and then move and adjust the width of the report columns to make them readable. Modify the report title to end with your initialLastname.

p. If your instructor directs you to print the report, print your results. Close the database.

Homework 3

Production &
Operations

Student data file needed:

a01_ps3_Hotel_Event

You will save your file as:

Lastname_Firstname_a01_ps3_Hotel_Event

Group Reservations Case

Patti Rochelle, corporate event planner, wants to be able to track group reservations with the conference rooms that are booked for the event. You want to track conference rooms, groups, and events.

A group can book several events. Each event is booked by just one group.

Each event could take multiple conference rooms. Conference rooms can be booked for several events (on different days.) You will need a junction table for this relationship.

a. Start **Access**, and then open **a01_ps3_Hotel_Event**. Save the file as Lastname_Firstname_a01_ps3_Hotel_Event, replacing Lastname_Firstname with your own name. In the Security Warning bar, click **Enable Content**.

b. Create a new table in Design view. This table will store conference rooms.
   • Add the following fields (in the following order). Where necessary, you decide upon field names, data types, and field sizes.

Field Name	Data Type	Description	Field Size/Format
Choose the best name from the following list: Conference Room ID ConfRoomID ConferenceRoom	AutoNumber	A unique identifier for the conference room	Long Integer
RoomName	Pick an appropriate type	The name of the conference room	40
Choose the best name from the following list: Conference Room Capacity Conf Room Capacity Capacity	Pick an appropriate type	The capacity of the conference room	Integer

   • Make sure you have assigned the most appropriate field to be primary key.
   • Save the new table as tblConfRooms.

c. In this order, enter the following rooms into the table:

RoomName	Capacity
Musica	500
Eldorado	100
Pueblo	25

d. Create a new table in Design view. This table will store groups.
   • Add the following fields, data types, and descriptions (in the following order). Where necessary, you decide upon data types.

Field Name	Data Type	Description	Field Size
GroupID	AutoNumber	A unique identifier for the group (primary key)	Long Integer
GroupName	Pick an appropriate type	Group name	40
ContactFirstName	Pick an appropriate type	Contact person first name	30
ContactLastName	Pick an appropriate type	Contact person last name	40
ContactPhone	Pick an appropriate type	Contact phone number	14

- Define an input mask for contact phone number. Use a mask of **(555) 555-5555** with a place holder of "_" and save with the symbols in the mask.
- Make sure you have assigned the most appropriate primary key. Save the new table as tblGroup.

e. Create a new table in Design view. This table will store events.
  - Add the following fields, data types, and descriptions (in the following order). Where necessary, you decide upon data types.

Field Name	Data Type	Description	Field Size/ Format
EventID	AutoNumber	A unique identifier for the event (primary key)	Long Integer
EventName	Pick an appropriate type	The name of the event	40
EventStart	Pick an appropriate type	Starting date for the event	Short Date
EventLength	Pick an appropriate type	Length of the event (in days)	Integer
GroupID	Number	The Group ID from tblGroup (foreign key)	Long Integer

- Make sure that you have assigned a primary key. Save the new table as tblEvent.

f. Create a new table in Design view. This table will serve as the junction table between tblConfRooms and tblEvent.
  - Add the following fields, data types, and descriptions (in the following order). Where necessary, you decide upon field names and data types.

Field Name	Data Type	Description	Field Size/ Format
ReservationID	AutoNumber	A unique identifier for the conference reservation (primary key)	Long Integer
EventID	Number	The Event ID from tblEvent (foreign key)	Long Integer
ConfRoomID	Number	The Conference Room ID from tblConfRooms (foreign key)	Long Integer
Choose the best name from the following list: ReservationDate Date of Reservation ShortDate	Pick an appropriate type	Reservation date	Short Date
DaysReserved	Number	Number of days reserved	Integer

- Make sure that you have assigned a primary key. Save the new table as tblConfRes.

g. Open the **Relationships** window.

- Create a one-to-many relationship between the correct field in tblGroup and the correct field in tblEvent. Enforce referential integrity. Do not cascade update or cascade delete.

- Create a one-to-many relationship between the correct field in tblEvent and the correct field in tblConfRes. Enforce referential integrity. Do not cascade update or cascade delete.

- Create a one-to-many relationship between the correct field in tblConfRooms and tblConfRes. Enforce referential integrity. Do not cascade update or cascade delete. If your instructor directs you to print the relationships, print your relationship report.

h. Enter the following data into the appropriate tables (in the following order)—you may need to determine keys along the way:

Group:	Benson & Diaz Law Group
	Contact: Mary Williams (505) 555-1207
Benson & Diaz's Event:	Company Retreat
	Start Date: 2/17/2013
	Length of Event: 2 days
Benson & Diaz's Reservation of the Pueblo Room:	
	Date: 2/17/2013
	Number of Days: 2 days

Group:	Dental Association of Nova Scotia
	Contact: Your Name (902) 555-8765
Dental Association's Event:	Annual Meeting
	Start Date: 2/17/2013
	Length of Event: 5 days
Dental Association's Reservation of the Eldorado Room:	
	Date: 2/17/2013
	Number of Days: 2 days
Dental Association's Reservation of the Pueblo Room:	
	Date: 2/20/2013
	Number of Days: 2 days

Group:	Orchard Growers of the United States
	Contact: Will Goodwin (212) 555-7889
Orchard Growers' Event:	Annual Meeting
	Start Date: 2/17/2013
	Length of Event: 2 days
Orchard Growers' Reservation of the Musica Room:	
	Date: 2/17/2013
	Number of Days: 5 days

i. Create a query using **RoomName** from tblConfRooms, and **ReservationDate** and **DaysReserved** from tblConfRes. Save your query as qryEldoradoRoom_initialLastname, replacing initialLastname with your own initial and last name. Specify the room named **Eldorado**, sort by **ReservationDate**, and then run the query. Adjust the width of the query columns as necessary. If your instructor directs you to print the query, print your results.

j. Use data in four tables to create a query about the Dental Association of Nova Scotia. The query results should list **GroupName**, **EventName**, **EventStart**, **EventLength**, **RoomName**, **ReservationDate**, and **DaysReserved**. Save your query as qryDentalAssociation_initialLastname, replacing initialLastname with your own initial and last name. Select the group named **Dental Association of Nova Scotia**, sort by **ReservationDate**, and then run the query. If your instructor directs you to print the query, print your results.

k. Create a report from **qryDentalAssociation_initialLastname**. Select all fields. Accept the default grouping by GroupName and then by all tblEvent fields. Sort by **RoomName** and **ReservationDate**. Select **Landscape orientation**. Name your report Dental Association Booking. Adjust the width of the report columns as necessary. Modify the report title to end with your initialLastname. If your instructor directs you to print the report, print your results.

l. Close the database.

Perform 1: Perform in Your Life

Student data file needed:	You will save your file as:
Blank database	Lastname_Firstname_a01_pf1_Organization

Track Events for Your Organization

Production & Operations

Pick an organization that you belong to. You want to track the members of the organization, events, and member attendance at the events. Because a member can attend many events and an event can be attended by many members, you will need a junction table. You will start by creating three tables, the relationships between the tables, and reports on attendance.

Next, you will decide on one other table that makes sense for your organization, define that table, and relate it to one of the already existing tables.

a. Start **Access**, click the **New tab**, and then click **Blank database**. Browse to where you are storing your data files, and name your database Lastname_Firstname_a01_pf1_Organization, replacing Lastname_Firstname with your own name. Click the **Create** button to create the database.

b. Design a table to store members. Choose appropriate fields that would describe the members of your organization.
   - Assign a field to be primary key, and then make it **AutoNumber**. For all fields, enter appropriate data types, descriptions, field sizes, and masks. Save your table as tblMember.

c. Enter yourself and a friend into the table. Enter as many other members as you wish.

d. Design a table to store events. Use the following fields: EventID, EventName, EventDate, and PlaceName. You may add other fields as appropriate.
   - Assign EventID to be primary key, and then make it an AutoNumber. Enter appropriate data types, descriptions, and field sizes. Save your table as tblEvent.

e. Enter two events that you attended into the table. Enter as many other events as you wish.

f. Design a junction table to relate members and attendance at events. Use the following fields: EventID and the primary key of your member table.
   - EventID is a foreign key and should be Number, Long Integer. Enter an appropriate description.
   - Use the primary key of your member table as a foreign key in this table. Enter an appropriate type and description.

- Create a composite primary key using both EventID and the primary key from your member table.
- Save your table as tblAttendance.

g. Create relationships as appropriate for the tblMember, tblAttendance, and tblEvent tables.

h. Enter the following data into tblAttendance:

EventID	MemberID
Use the EventID for the first event	Your primary key in the member table
Use the EventID for the first event	Your friend's primary key in the member table
Use the EventID for the second event	Your primary key in the member table

i. Create a report on Events using **EventName**, **EventDate**, and **PlaceName**. Sort by **EventDate**. Name your report Event Report and then modify the report title to end with your initialLastname. If your instructor directs you to print the report, print your results.

j. Create a query on Events including **EventName**, **EventDate**, and **PlaceName**. Save the query as qryEventName_initalLastname and then modify the query design to select the EventName for the first event. Run the query. If your instructor directs you to print the query, print your results.

k. Create a report on event attendance. Use **EventName**, **EventDate** from tblEvent and member's name. Group the report by **Event**. Sort the report by **LastName** and **FirstName**. Name your report Event Attendance and then modify the report title to end with your initialLastname. If your instructor directs you to print the report, print your results.

l. Determine one additional table that would make sense for your organization to keep data in.

m. Design this table and the appropriate fields. Make sure to assign a primary key.

n. Enter data into the new table. Create relationships between this new table and your existing tables as appropriate. Ask yourself the two questions to determine the relationships. If your instructor directs you to print the relationships, print your relationship report.

o. Create a report showing data from your new table and data from another table that it is related to. If your instructor directs you to print the report, print your results.

p. Close the database.

Perform 2: Perform in Your Career

Student data file needed:

Blank database

Blank database You will save your file as:

Lastname_Firstname_a01_pf2_PetStore

Pet Store

Sales & Marketing

A pet store owner wants to create a database for the store. The database needs to include information about animals and the breeds of the animals. An animal is of one breed. The pet store can have many animals of each breed.

The pet owner will want to keep records of the purchases and the customers that bought each animal. You will need to decide what tables you need to record purchases and customers. You will also need to decide what relationships you want to create.

a. Start **Access**, click the **New tab**, and then click **Blank database**. Browse to where you are storing your data files, and name your database Lastname_Firstname_a01_pf2_PetStore, replacing Lastname_Firstname with your own name. Click **Create** to create the database.

b. Design a table to store breeds. Use the following fields: BreedID, AnimalType, BreedName, MaximumSize (in pounds), LengthOfLife (in years).

 • Assign **BreedID** to be primary key with the AutoNumber data type.

 • For all fields, enter appropriate data types, descriptions, and field sizes. Save your table as tblBreed.

c. Enter the following data into the table (in this order):

BreedID	AnimalType	BreedName	MaximumSize	LengthOfLife
1	Dog	Akita	110	12
2	Dog	Papillon	9	15
3	Cat	Devon	7	18
4	Cat	Birman	10	19
5	Chinchilla	Silver Mosaic	1	15

d. After entering those five breeds, pick another breed and add it to the table.

e. Design a table to store animals. Use the following fields: AnimalID, DateOfBirth, Price, Weight, Color, Sex, and BreedID.

 • Assign **AnimalID** to be primary key with the AutoNumber data type.

 • BreedID is the foreign key to tblBreed.

 • For all fields, enter appropriate data types, descriptions, and field sizes.

 • Save your table as tblAnimal.

f. Enter the following data into tblAnimal (in this order):

AnimalID	DateOfBirth	Price	Weight	Color	Sex	BreedID
1	6/17/2012	$125.00	28	White	M	1
2	6/17/2012	$125.00	30	White	M	1
3	7/25/2012	$610.00	4	Tan	F	2
4	8/7/2012	$610.00	3	White	F	2
5	8/7/2012	$550.00	3	White	M	2
6	5/10/2012	$225.00	2	Blue	F	3
7	5/10/2012	$225.00	2	Gray	M	3
8	6/26/2012	$150.00	2	White	F	4
9	7/17/2012	$125.00	2	Gray	M	4
10	8/18/2012	$ 30.00	1	Silver	F	5

g. After adding those 10 animals, add another animal that is of the breed you entered for the tblBreed table.

h. Open the **Relationships** window. Create a one-to-many relationship between BreedID in tblBreed and BreedID in tblAnimal. Enforce referential integrity. Do not cascade update or cascade delete.

i. Determine the tables that the store owner would need to keep store customers and their purchases.

 • Design these tables and the appropriate fields. Make sure to assign primary keys.

 • Create relationships between these new tables and your existing tables as appropriate. Ask yourself the two questions to determine the relationships. Add foreign keys as appropriate. If your instructor directs you to print the relationships, print your relationship report.

j. Enter the appropriate customer and purchase data to capture the following events:
- You bought the chinchilla with AnimalID = 10 yesterday.
- A friend bought the Birman cat with AnimalID = 9 and the Akita with Animal ID = 1 today.

k. Create a report showing animals by breed. Show **AnimalType**, **BreedName**, **AnimalID**, **DateOfBirth**, and **Price**. Select correct groupings and sort orders. If your instructor directs you to print the report, print your results.

l. Create a query to find out who purchased AnimalID = 10. Show **Customer name** (FirstName and LastName), **AnimalID**, **AnimalType**, and **BreedName**. If your instructor directs you to print the query, print your results.

m. Create a report showing the animals purchased on all dates. Group and sort appropriately. If your instructor directs you to print the report, print your results.

n. Close the database.

Perform 3: Perform in Your Career

Student data file needed:

Blank database

You will save your file as:

Lastname_Firstname_a01_pf3_Music

Independent Music Label

Production & Operations

The owner of an independent music label needs to keep track of the groups, musicians, and their music. You have been asked to create a database for the label.

The label owner would like to be able to get a list of groups with all musicians, get a list of groups with albums, select an album and see all songs in the album, and select a group and see their albums with all songs in each album.

You will need to design tables, fields, relationships, queries, and reports for the label.

a. Start **Access**, click the **New tab**, and click **Blank database**. Browse to where you are storing your data files, and name your database Lastname_Firstname_a01_pf3_Music, replacing Lastname_Firstname with your own name. Click **Create** to create the database.

b. Design your tables.

c. At this point the label has three groups signed up. Enter the following data (in this order):
- Clean Green, an Enviro-Punk band. The members of the group are Jon Smith (vocalist and guitar) and Lee Smith (percussion and keyboard). The group has two albums:
  - Clean Green with the following songs:

    Esperando Verde

    Precious Drops

    Recycle Mania

    Don't Tread on Me
  - Be Kind to Animals with the following songs:

    It's Our Planet Too

    Animal Rag

    Where Will We Live?

- Spanish Moss, a Spanish Jazz band. The members of the group are Hector Caurendo (guitar), Pasquale Rodriguez (percussion), Perry Trent (vocals), and Meredith Selmer (bass). The group has one album:
  - Latin Latitude with the following songs:

    Attitude Latitude

    Flying South

    Latin Guitarra

    Cancion Cancion

  - Your band. You decide on your band members, albums, and songs.

d. Create your relationships. If your instructor directs you to print the relationships, print your relationship report.

e. Create a report showing all groups and the type of group, with all musicians. If your instructor directs you to print the report, print your results.

f. Create a report showing all groups, the group type, and their albums. If your instructor directs you to print the report, print your results.

g. Create a query to select an album from your band and see all songs in the album. If your instructor directs you to print the query, print your results.

h. Create a query to select your band and see all your albums with all songs in the albums. If your instructor directs you to print the query, print your results.

i. Close the database.

Perform 4: How Others Perform

Student data file needed:	You will save your file as:
a01_pf4_Textbook	Lastname_Firstname_a01_pf4_Textbook

College Bookstore

General Business

A colleague has created a database for your college bookstore. He is having problems creating the relationships in the database and has come to you for your help. What problems do you see in his database design? He has three tables in his database: one for sections of courses, one for instructors, and one for textbooks, as shown in Figures 1, 2, and 3.

a. Open the a01_pf4_Textbook database and resave as Lastname_Firstname_a01_pf4_Textbook. You do not need to make changes to this database but you will want to look at the database in more detail than is shown in the figures.

b. Are there any errors in the way that fields are defined or named in the tables? List your errors by table.

c. Are there any errors in the way that tables are named or defined?

d. He wants to define these relationships. How would you want to define the relationships? What errors are there in the database that would make it difficult to define the relationships?
  - An instructor can teach many sections; a section is taught by just one instructor.
  - A section can have many textbooks; a textbook can be used in many sections.

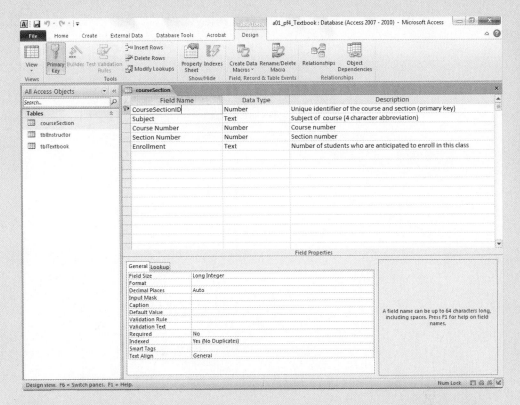

Figure 1   Table design for courseSection

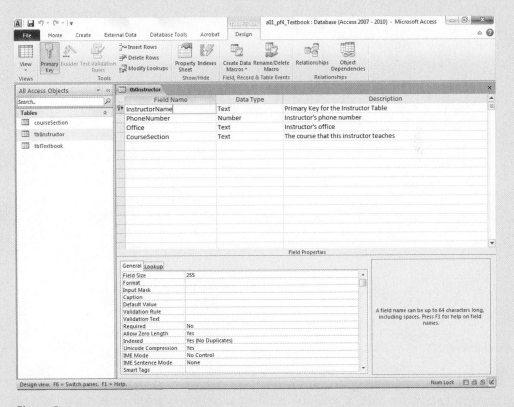

Figure 2   Table design for tblInstructor

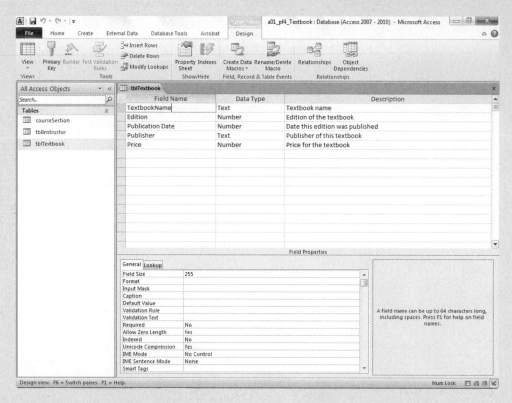

Figure 3 Table design for tblTextbook

WORKSHOP 3

Accessing Information from an Access Database

PREPARE CASE

Turquoise Oasis Spa

The Turquoise Oasis Spa has been popular with resort clients. The owners have spent several months putting spa data into an Access database so they can better manage the data. You have been asked to help show the staff how best to use the database to find information about products, services, and customers. For training purposes, not all the spa records have been added yet. Once the staff is trained, the remaining records will be entered into the database.

General Business

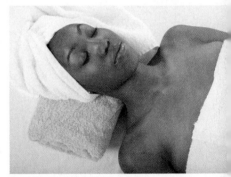

Dewayne Flowers / Shutterstock.com

Student data file needed for this workshop:

 a02_ws03_Spa

You will save your file as:

 Lastname_Firstname_a02_ws03_Spa

Work with Datasheets

Datasheets are used to view all records in a table at one time. Each record is viewed as a row in the table. Records can be entered, edited, and deleted directly in a datasheet. When a table becomes so large that all the records and fields are no longer visible in the datasheet window without scrolling, the Find command can be used to quickly find specific values in a record. In this section, you will find records in a datasheet as well as modify the appearance of a datasheet.

Find and Replace Records in the Datasheet

The Navigation bar allows you to move to the top and bottom of a table or scroll to a specific record; however, this can be inefficient if your table is large. To manage larger tables, Access provides ways for you to quickly locate information within the datasheet. Once that information is found, it can then be easily replaced with another value using the **Replace command**.

If you do not know the exact value you are looking for because you do not know how it is spelled or how someone entered it, you can use a wildcard character. A **wildcard character** is used as a placeholder for an unknown part of a value or to match a certain pattern in a value. For example, if you know the value you are looking for contains the word "market" you can use a wildcard character at the beginning and end such as *market*.

Finding Records in a Table

In Datasheet view, you can use the **Find command** to quickly locate specific records using all or part of a field value. For this project, a staff member found a book left by one of the guests. A first name was printed on the inside of the book cover. They remember helping a gentleman named Guy who said he was from North Carolina, but they are not certain of his last name. You will show them how to use the Find command to quickly navigate through the table to search for this guest.

Workshop 3 Training

SIDE NOTE
Spelling Counts

Spelling counts in Access, so if you enter a search item and Access cannot find it, your search value may be spelled wrong.

To Find Records in the Datasheet

a. Click the **Start** button. From the Start menu, locate and then start **Microsoft Access 2010**. Click the **File tab**, and then click **Open**. In the Open dialog box, click the disk drive in the left pane where your student data files are located, navigate through the folder structure, and then click **a02_ws03_Spa**. Click **Open**.

b. Click the **File tab**, and then click **Save Database As**. In the Save As dialog box, browse to where you are saving your files, change the file name to Lastname_Firstname_a02_ws03_Spa replacing Lastname and Firstname with your own name, and then click **Save**. In the Security Warning, click **Enable Content**.

c. Double-click **tblCustomer** to open the table.

d. Add a record at the end of the table with your First name, Last name, Address, City, State, Phone and E-mail Address. Press Tab until the record selector is on the next row and your record has been added to the table.

e. On the Navigation bar, click **First Record** to go to the first record in the table. Click the **Home tab**, and then click **Find** in the Find group to open the Find and Replace dialog box.

f. Replace the text in the Find What box with Guy. Click the **Look In arrow**, and then select **Current document**.

592   **Module 2**   Microsoft Office Access 2010

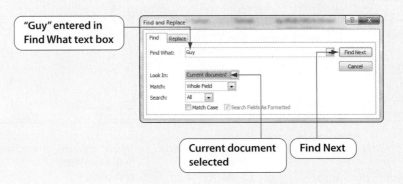

"Guy" entered in Find What text box

Current document selected

Find Next

Figure 1 Find and Replace dialog box to find all "Guy" records

g. Click **Find Next**. Access highlights the first record found for Guy Bowers from Derby, North Carolina (NC).

h. Click **Find Next** again to check for more records with Guy. When Access is done searching and cannot find any more matches, you will see the message "Microsoft Access finished searching the records. The search item was not found." Click **OK**, and then click **Cancel** to close the Find and Replace dialog box.

i. **Close** ☒ the table.

Troubleshooting

If you did not get the results shown here, go back and carefully check the settings in the Find and Replace dialog box. In particular, check the setting for Match Case to make sure it is not checked. When Match Case is checked, the search will be case sensitive. Also check to make sure the Look In box shows Current document. If the Look In box shows Current field, Access will only look in the field selected, which may not be the field that contains the value you are looking for.

Finding and Replacing Data in a Datasheet

Not only can you find records using the Find command, but you can also replace records once you find them with the Replace command. In a large table, it is helpful to locate a record using the Find command, and then replace the data using the Replace command.

For this project, the receptionist receives a notice from Erica Rocha about her upcoming marriage. The receptionist wants to go through the database and find any records related to Erica and change her last name to her married name, Muer. You will show the receptionist how to find Erica in the database and replace her last name of Rocha with Muer.

To Find and Replace Records

a. Double-click **tblCustomer** to open it. Click the **Home tab**, and then click **Find** in the Find group to open the Find and Replace dialog box.

b. In the Find and Replace dialog box, click the **Replace tab**. In the Find What box, type Rocha and then in the Replace With box, type Muer.

c. Click the **Look In arrow**, and then select **Current document**. Leave all other options as they are.

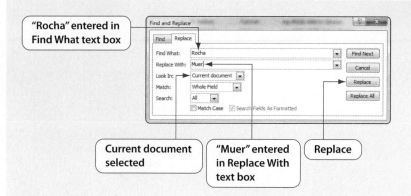

"Rocha" entered in Find What text box

Current document selected

"Muer" entered in Replace With text box

Replace

Figure 2   Find and Replace dialog box options

d. Click **Find Next**. Notice the first record found has the last name Rocha, but the first name is Emily. Click **Find Next** again. Notice this is the record for Erica Rocha. Click **Replace**. Click **OK** when you get the message Microsoft Access has finished searching the records. The Last Name should now be Muer instead of Rocha. Click **Cancel** to close the Find and Replace dialog box.

e. **Close** ⊠ the table.

Using a Wildcard Character

A wildcard character is used as a placeholder for an unknown part of a value or to match a certain pattern in a value. A wildcard character can replace a single character or multiple characters and text or numbers as shown in Figure 3.

Wildcard character	Example
*	To match any number of characters; to search for a word that starts with "ar" you would enter **ar***
#	To match any single numeric character; to search for a three digit number that starts with "75" you would enter **75#**
?	To match any single character; to search for a three letter word that starts with "t" and ends with "p" you would enter **t?p**
[ ]	To match any single character within the brackets; to search for a word that starts with "e," contains any of the letters "a" or "r," and ends with "r," you would enter **e[ar]r** and get "ear" or "err" as a result
!	To match any single character *not* within the brackets; to search for a word that starts with "e," contains any letter other than "a" or "r," and ends with "r," you would enter **e[!ar]r** to get anything except "err" or "ear"
-	To match any range of characters in ascending order (a to z); to search for a word beginning with "a" and ending in "e" with any letter between "b" and "t" in between, you would enter **a[b-t]e**

Figure 3   Wildcard characters

For this project, the staff is looking for products with the word "butter" in the name so they can put together a weekly promotion for all these products. You will show them how to use a wildcard character to find the products.

To Use a Wildcard Character to Find a Record

a. Double-click **tblProduct** to open the table.

b. In the first record, click in the **ProductDescription** field. Click the **Home tab**, and then click **Find** in the Find group to open the Find and Replace dialog box. Replace the text in the Find What box with *butter*. Click the **Look In arrow**, and then click **Current field**.

Figure 4 Find records with "butter" in the ProductDescription field

c. Click **Find Next**. The first record found is for ProductID P018 Cocoa Body Butter. Click **Find Next** again to find the record for ProductID P021 Lemon Body Butter.

d. Click **Find Next** again until Access has finished searching the records. When Access is done searching and cannot find any more matches, you will see the message "Microsoft Access finished searching the records. The search item was not found." Click **OK**, and then click **Cancel** to close the Find and Replace dialog box.

e. **Close** ☒ the table.

SIDE NOTE
I Cannot See the Highlighted Record

If Access highlights a record in the table and you cannot see it, you may have to drag the Find and Replace dialog box to another area of the screen.

Apply a Filter to a Datasheet

A **filter** is a condition you apply temporarily to a table or query. All records that do not match the filter criteria are hidden until the filter is removed or the table is closed and reopened. A filter is a simple technique to quickly reduce a large amount of data to a much smaller subset of data. You can choose to save a table with the filter applied so when you open the table later the filter is still available.

You can filter a datasheet by selecting a value in a record and telling Access to filter records that contain some variation of the record you choose, or you can create a custom filter to select all or part of a field value.

Filtering by Selection

When you **filter by selection**, you select a value in a record and Access filters the records that contain only the values that match what you have selected. For this exercise, a customer came into the spa and stated that she was from Minnesota and had previously been a spa customer but was just browsing today. She left her glasses on the counter and the staff wants to return them to her. You will help the staff members find all customers from Minnesota to see if they can find the customer's name.

To Select Specific Records Using a Selection Filter

a. Double-click **tblCustomer** to open the table, locate the first record with an address in the state of Minnesota (MN), and then click in the **State** field. Click the **Home tab**, click **Selection** in the Sort & Filter group, and then choose the **Equals "MN"** option.

Access displays three records where all states are MN for Minnesota. Toggle Filter in the Sort & Filter group allows you to go back and forth between viewing the filtered records and all the records in the table. To remove the filter, click Toggle Filter in the Sort & Filter group. To show the filter again, click Toggle Filter in the Sort & Filter group.

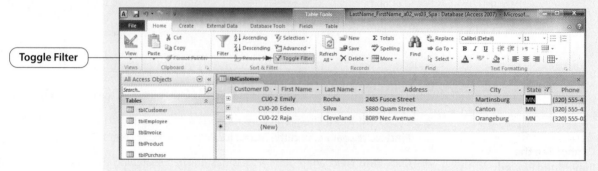

Figure 5   Filtered table for all records containing a state of MN

b. The filter is temporary unless you choose to save it with the table or query. If you do save it, the next time you open the table or query, you only have to click Toggle Filter to see the records from the state of Minnesota. To save the table with the filter, click **Save** 🖫 on the Quick Access Toolbar. **Close** ☒ the table.

c. Double-click **tblCustomer** to open the table. Click the **Home tab**, click **Toggle Filter** in the Sort & Filter group to see the filtered records. **Close** ☒ the table.

SIDE NOTE
How to Clear a Filter
To delete a filter from the table, click Advanced in the Sort & Filter group, and select Clear All Filters.

Using a Text Filter

Text filters allow you to create a custom filter to match all or part of the text in a field that you specify. For this exercise, the staff wants to create a mailing of sample products but cannot send the products to customers with a post office box. You will help the staff find all customers who have P.O. Box as part of their address.

To Select Specific Records Using a Text Filter

a. Double-click **tblCustomer** to open the table. Select the entire **Address** column by clicking the column name. Click the **filter arrow** in the column heading, point to **Text Filters**, and then on the submenu, click **Begins With**.

b. In the Custom Filter box, type **P** and then click **OK**.

Access retrieves the nine records where the addresses contain a P.O. Box number. Notice that Toggle Filter in the Sort & Filter group is selected and the Filtered indicator in the Navigation bar is highlighted. You can toggle between the filtered table and the whole table by clicking on either Toggle Filter or the Filtered indicator.

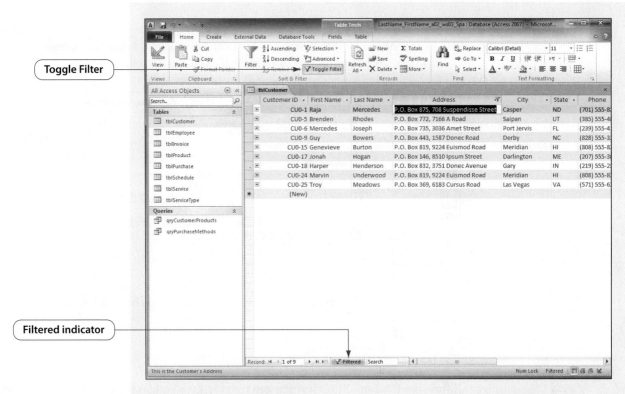

Toggle Filter

Filtered indicator

Figure 6   Results of the filter

c. Click **Save** 💾 on the Quick Access Toolbar to save the table with the new filter applied. **Close** ⊠ the table.

Modify Datasheet Appearance

You can change the appearance of your datasheet by changing the font type, font size, column widths, and background colors to make it more readable. By changing the font size and column width of a table or query, you can often include more data on one page or see all the data in a particular field.

Changing the Look of a Datasheet

For this exercise, the manager is upset because the font is too small and she cannot see all the field headings in the invoice table. You will show her how to make the text larger and the column wider.

SIDE NOTE
The Invoice Table
The Invoice table tracks the balance due from a customer, not necessarily the total amount of charges incurred because some charges are billed directly to the customer's room.

SIDE NOTE
Alternate Method for Changing Column Width
You can also drag a column border to adjust the column's width.

To Change Font Size, Column Width, and Alternating Row Colors

a. Double-click **tblInvoice** to open the table.

b. Click the **Home tab**, click the **Font Size arrow** $\boxed{11 \quad \blacktriangledown}$ in the Text Formatting group, and then click **14** to make the font size larger.

c. Point to the **right border** of the first field name (InvoiceNumber) and double-click. This resizes the column to best fit the data. Repeat this action for all the columns.

d. Click the **Home tab**, click the **Alternate Row Color arrow** in the Text Formatting group, and then under Theme Colors select **Olive Green, Accent 3, Lighter 40%**. The rows will still be alternating colors, but will be changed to olive green.

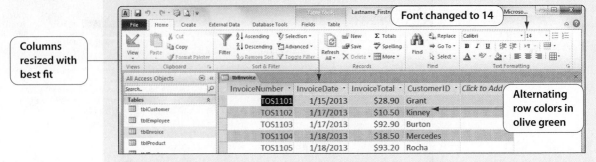

Figure 7   Modified table

e. Close the table, and then when prompted to save the changes, click **Yes**.

Queries

While the Find and Filter features can quickly help you find data, a query can be created for data that you may need to find again in the future. If you recall, the Simple Query Wizard is used to display fields from one or more tables or queries with the option to choose a detailed or summary query if working with more than one table. The Simple Query Wizard does not provide the opportunity to select data criteria.

Queries can also be created in Query Design view, which not only allows you to choose the tables and fields to include in the query, but also allows you to select criteria for the field values, create calculated fields, and select sorting options.

In this section, you will create and define selection criteria for queries, create aggregate functions and calculated fields as well as sort query results.

Run Other Query Wizards

Two other query wizards, the Find Duplicates and Find Unmatched query wizards, allow you to find duplicate records or identify orphans by selecting criteria as part of the wizard steps. An **orphan** is a foreign key in one table that does not have a matching value in the primary key field of a related table.

Quick Reference   Crosstab, Find Duplicates, and Find Unmatched Queries

In addition to the Simple Query Wizard, there are three additional query wizards available to make quick, step-by-step queries.

1. **Crosstab:** Used when you want to describe one field in terms of two or more other fields in the table. Example: summarizing information or calculating statistics on the fields in the table.
2. **Find Duplicates:** Used when you want to find records with the same specific value. Example: duplicate e-mail addresses in a customer database.
3. **Find Unmatched:** Used when you want to find the rows in one table that do not have a match in the other table. Example: identifying customers who currently have no open orders.

Creating a Find Duplicates Query

The Find Duplicates Query Wizard finds duplicate records in a table or a query. You select the fields that you think may include duplicate information, and the Wizard creates the query to find records matching your criteria.

For this exercise, the spa receptionist sends out mailings and reminders to its customers throughout the year. She wants to be able to prevent multiple mailings to the same address to help reduce costs. You will show her how she can use a Find Duplicates query to check for duplicate addresses.

To Find Duplicate Customer Information

a. Click the **Create tab**, and then click **Query Wizard** in the Queries group. Access displays the New Query dialog box and lists the different queries you can select.

b. Select **Find Duplicates Query Wizard**, and then click **OK**.

c. Select **Table: tblCustomer** as the table to search for duplicate field values, and then click **Next**.

d. Under Available fields, click **CustAddress**, and then click the **One Field** button [>]. Access moves the CustAddress field to the Duplicate-value fields list. This is the field you think may have duplicate data. Click **Next**.

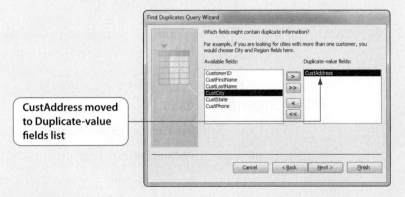

CustAddress moved to Duplicate-value fields list

Figure 8   Select the field that may have duplicate data

e. Click the **All Fields** button [>>] to move all available fields to the Additional query fields list in order to display all the fields in the query results. Click **Next**.

f. Under "What do you want to name your query?", type qryDuplicateCustomers_initialLastname, replacing initialLastname with your own first initial and last name, and then click **Finish**. The query should have two records with the same address.

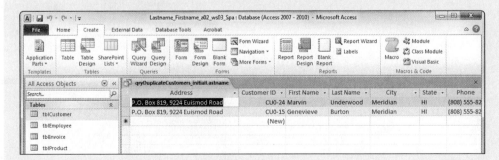

Figure 9   Results from the Find Duplicates query

g. **Close** [×] the query.

Creating a Find Unmatched Query

The Find Unmatched query is designed to find records in a table or query that have no related records in a second table or query. This can be very helpful if you are looking to contact inactive customers or mail a notice to past clients who are still listed in the database. The wizard uses the primary key from the first table and matches it with the foreign key in the second table in order to determine if there are unmatched records. If a one-to-many relationship exists between the two tables, then the wizard will join the two correct fields automatically.

For this project, spa management would like to identify customers who have used the spa's services in the past but do not have a current appointment. This means a record for the customer would be listed in the customer table but not in the schedule table as shown in Figure 10.

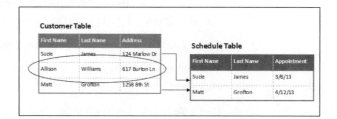

Figure 10 Tables in a Find Unmatched query

Notice Allison Williams is a past customer so she is listed in the customer table, but she does not have an appointment scheduled in the schedule table. Her record would be found in a Find Unmatched query comparing the customer and schedule tables.

To Find Unmatched Records

a. Click the **Create tab**, and then click **Query Wizard** in the Queries group.

b. Select **Find Unmatched Query Wizard**, and then click **OK**.

c. Select **Table: tblCustomer**, and then click **Next**. This is the table you think has past customers with no upcoming appointments.

d. Select **Table: tblSchedule**, and then click **Next**. This is the table that has customers with upcoming appointments you want to compare to the main tblCustomer table.

e. Under Fields in 'tblCustomer', verify **CustomerID** is selected and under Fields in 'tblSchedule', verify **Customer** is selected. This is the common field that the wizard will use to compare the tables. Click **Next**.

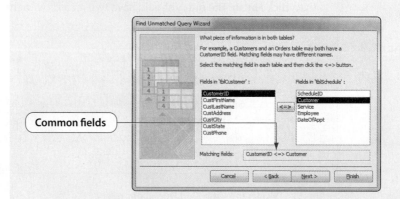

Figure 11 Compare the two tables using their common field

Troubleshooting

The wizard will try to match the primary key field and the foreign key field if there is a one-to-many relationship between the two tables. If there is not a one-to-many relationship, you can select the matching fields manually and use the `<=>` button to confirm the match. The matching fields will then appear at the bottom of the window in the Matching fields box.

f. Click the **All Fields** button `>>` to add all the fields to the Selected fields list. Click **Next**.

g. Under "What would you like to name your query?", type qryCustomersWithoutAppointments_ initialLastname, replacing initialLastname with your own first initial and last name, and click **Finish**. You should see the names and e-mails of three customers who do not currently have appointments at the spa, including yourself. **Close** `×` the query.

Create Queries in Design View

The query wizards work by prompting you to answer a series of questions about the tables and fields to display and then creating the query based upon your responses. Alternatively, you can use Design view to manually create queries. The query window in Design view allows you to specify the data you want to see by building a **query by example**. A query by example provides a sample of the data you want to see in the results. Access takes that sample of data and finds records in the tables you specify that match the example. In the query window, you can include specific fields, define criteria, sort records, and perform calculations. When you use the query window, you have more control and more options available to manage the details of the query design than with the Simple Query Wizard.

When you open Design view, by default, the Show Table dialog box opens with a list of available tables and queries to add. You can either select a table name and click Add, or you can double-click the table name. Either way the table will be added to the query window. If the Show Table dialog box is closed, you can drag a table or query from the Navigation Pane to the query window to add it to the query.

The next step in building your query is to add the fields you want to include from the various tables selected to the query design grid. There are a number of ways to add fields to the query design grid as shown in Figure 12.

Action	Description
Drag	Once you click the field name, drag it to any empty column in the query design grid.
Double-click field name	Double-click the field name to add it to the first empty column in the query design grid.
Select from drop-down list	Click in the first row of any empty column, click the selection arrow, and select the field name from the list.
Double-click the title bar	Double-click the title bar for the table with the fields you want to add and all the fields will be selected. Drag the fields to the first empty column.
Click, Shift, Click	Click on a field name, press and hold down the Shift key, and click another name to select a range of field names. Drag the selected fields to the query design grid.

Figure 12 Methods to add fields to a query design grid

If you add a field to the wrong column in the query design grid, you can delete the column and add it again, or you can drag it to another position in the grid.

All fields that have values you want included in a query—either for the criteria or to show in the results—must be added to the query design grid. For example, you may want to find all customers from New Mexico, but not necessarily show the state field in the query results. You can use the Show check box to indicate which fields to show in the results and which fields not to show.

Real World Advice — Increasing Privacy Concerns

There are many instances where the person running the query does not have the right to see confidential information in the database. An example of this is Social Security numbers. Although companies are doing away with this practice, many existing databases still use Social Security numbers as a unique identifier. You can include a Social Security number in query criteria, but uncheck the Show box so the actual value does not show in the query results.

Creating a Single-Table Query

A single-table query is a query that is based on only one table in your database.

For this exercise, the manager of the spa needs your help to print out a price list for all the products. She only wants to see the product description, size, and price for each product, and she wants to see all the records. You will show her how to add only the fields she wants to the query.

To Create a Single-Table Query

a. Click the **Create tab**, and then click **Query Design** in the Queries group to open the query window with the Show Table dialog box.

b. In the Show Table dialog box, click **tblProduct**, and then click **Add**. Click **Close** to close the Show Table dialog box.

c. Double-click **ProductDescription** to add it to the first column of the query design grid. Repeat for **Price** and **Size**.

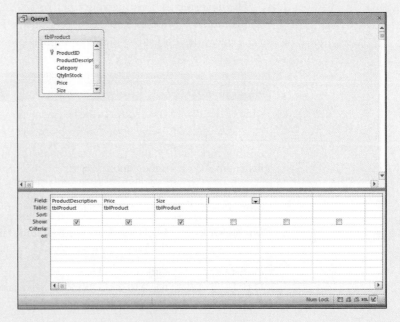

Figure 13   Fields from tblProduct added to the query design grid

Troubleshooting

> If you cannot see the query design grid at the bottom of the query design window, use the pointer ⊞ to drag the top border of the grid up.

d. Click the **Query Tools Design tab**, and then click **Run** in the Results group to run the query. You should have 25 records showing the ProductDescription, Price, and Size fields.

e. Click the **Home tab**, click the **View arrow** in the Views group, and then click **Design View**. To move the Size field to the left of the ProductDescription field, click the **top border** of the Size field to highlight the column. Again pointing to the top border of the field, drag the **Size field** to the left of the ProductDescription field. Click **Run** in the Results groups to run the query again. The query will still have 25 records, but the field order will be Size, ProductDescription, and Price.

f. Click **Save** 🔲 on the Quick Access Toolbar. In the Save As dialog box, type qryProductPriceList_initialLastname, replacing initialLastname with your own first initial and last name, and then click **OK**. **Close** ⨯ the query.

Real World Example The Importance of Knowing Your Data

Many times databases are shared by many users. Different people may enter data differently causing errors or inconsistency. Inconsistent data entry can affect the validity of query results. By misspelling a value or abbreviating a value that should be spelled out, a query may not find the record when it searches using criteria. You must know what your data looks like when you create queries. A quick scan of the records, or using Find with a wildcard for certain values, may help you find misspellings or other data entry errors before you run your query.

Having some idea of what the query results should look like will also help make sure your query has found the right record set. For example, if you query all customers from New Mexico and think there should be a dozen, but your query shows 75, you should check your table records and your query criteria to see why there might be such a big discrepancy from what you expected.

Viewing Table Relationships

A multiple-table query retrieves information from more than one table or query. For Access to perform this type of query, it must be able to "connect" tables using a common field that exists in both tables.

If two tables do not have a common field, Access will join the two tables by combining the records, regardless of whether they have a matching field. This is called the multiplier effect. For example, if one table has 100 records and another table also has 100 records, and if these two tables do not have a common field, all records in the first table will be matched with all records in the second table for a total of 10,000 records!

You can view how your tables are related in the Relationships window. The lines connecting the tables represent relationships. The field that the line is pointing to in each table represents the common field between the tables. It is helpful to understand how tables are related before you try and create a multiple table query.

To View Table Relationships

a. Click the **Database Tools tab**, and then click **Relationships** in the Relationships group. Click the **Shutter Bar Open/Close** button ⟦«⟧ to hide the Navigation Pane and display the whole Relationships window. Take a moment to study the table relationships.

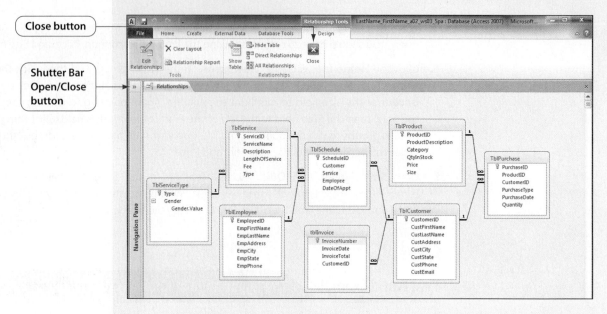

Close button

Shutter Bar Open/Close button

Figure 14 Spa Database table relationships

b. Click the **Relationship Tools Design tab**, and then click **Close** in the Relationships group to close the Relationships window. Click the **Shutter Bar Open/Close** button ⟦»⟧ to show the Navigation Pane again.

Real World Advice   Which Tables to Choose?

You should only select the tables you need when creating a query in the query window. Access treats all the tables selected as part of the query when it executes the query, which means unnecessary tables added to the query may cause performance problems. Best practice is to do the following:

- Understand the table structure and relationships before you construct your query—refer to the Relationships window often.

- Only choose those tables you need data from.

- If no data from a table is needed, do not add the table. The exception to this rule is if a table is required to link the many-to-many relationship together. In other words, no table will be left unconnected and tables can be added to create that connection.

Creating a Query from Multiple Tables

All tables added to a query should be connected by relationships and have a common field. For this project, the staff would like to see one table that includes the services scheduled for each employee. tblEmployee includes the employee names, and tblSchedule lists the services scheduled for each employee. You will create a query that combines the two tables into one query.

To Create a Query from Multiple Tables

a. Click the **Create tab**, click **Query Design** in the Queries group, click **tblEmployee**, and then click **Add**. **Close** the Show Table dialog box.

b. Double-click **EmpFirstName** and **EmpLastName** in that order to add the fields to the query design grid.

c. Click the **Query Tools Design tab**, and then click **Run** in the Results group. Notice there are 14 employee records.

d. Click the **Home tab**, click the **View arrow** in the Views group, and then click **Design View**. From the Navigation Pane, drag **tblSchedule** to the query window. Click the **Query Tools Design tab**, and then click **Run** in the Results group to run the query again.

   Scroll through the table and notice there are 53 records in the query results now. Employee names have been matched up with each scheduled service but you cannot see any information about the services because no fields from that table have been added.

e. Click the **Home tab**, click the **View arrow** in the Views group, and then click **Design View**. In the tblSchedule table, in the following order, double-click **Service**, **DateOfAppt**, and **Customer** to add the fields to the query design grid. Click the **Query Tools Design tab**, and then click **Run** in the Results group to run the query.

   Notice there are 53 records again for each service scheduled, but now the detail for those services are included in the query because you added the fields to the query design grid.

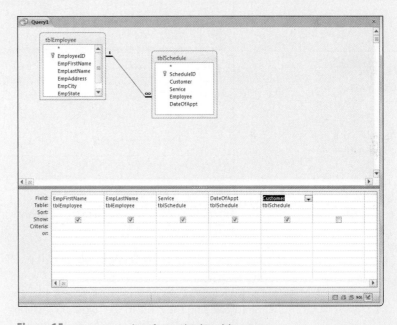

Figure 15   Query window for multiple-table query

f. Click **Save** 💾 on the Quick Access Toolbar, under Query Name type qryEmployeeSchedule_ initialLastname replacing initialLastname with your own first initial and last name, and then click **OK**. **Close** ⊠ the query.

Correcting the Multiplier Effect

When two tables without a common field are used in a query, you will see the multiplier effect. For this exercise, someone in the spa wanted to find out all the products that were purchased by each customer, so they created a multiple table query using two tables without a common field. One table has 25 records and the other has 26, so the multiplier effect caused the query result to have 650 records! You will run their query and then fix it so the information they want can be found.

To Correct a Multiplier Effect

a. Double-click **qryCustomerProducts** to run the query. Notice there are 650 records because every customer name is matched up with every product.

b. Click the **Home tab**, click the **View arrow** in the Views group, and then click **Design View**. Notice there is no relationship between tblProduct and tblCustomer. On the Navigation Pane, drag **tblPurchase** into the query window. Now there should be relationships between all three tables.

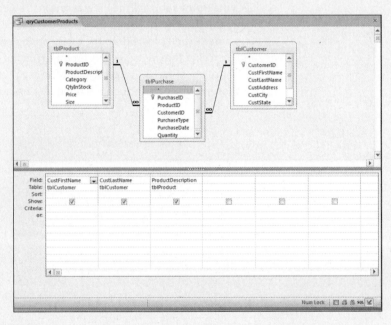

Figure 16 Three tables added to the query window, all with relationships

c. Click the **Query Tools Design tab**, and then click **Run** in the Results group to run the query.

   Notice there are now only 27 records that the tables all connect with relationships. Simply adding the table in the middle to establish the many-to-many relationship gets rid of the multiplier effect.

d. Click the **File tab**, click **Save Object As**, under Save 'qryCustomerProducts' to, type qryCustomerProducts_initialLastname replacing initialLastname with your own first initial and last name, and then click **OK**. Click the **Home tab**, and then **Close** ☒ the query.

SIDE NOTE
Looks Do Not Matter
Where the tables are laid out in the query window will not affect how the tables are related or added to the query. You can even move the tables by dragging the title bar of each table to a new location. If it is hard to see how the tables are related, move the table windows until the relationship lines are untangled.

Define Selection Criteria for Queries

Database programs, including Access, provide a robust set of selection criteria that you can use to make your queries well focused. You can use the different kinds of operators described in Figure 17 to choose criteria for one or more fields in one or more tables.

Using a Comparison Operator

Comparison operators compare the values in a table or another query to the criteria value you set up in a query. The different comparison operators, descriptions, and examples are shown in Figure 17. Comparison operators are generally used with numbers and dates to find a range or a specific value. Equal to and Not equal to can also be used with text to find an exact match to criteria. For example, to find all states that are not NY you could enter < >"NY" for the state criteria.

Operator	Description	Example
=	Equal to	=100
< =	Less than or equal to	<=100
<	Less than	<100
>	Greater than	>100
> =	Greater than or equal to	>=100
< >	Not equal to	< >100

Figure 17 Comparison operators

For this project, the manager of the spa wants to see all products $10 and under so she can plan an upcoming special on the spa's lower-priced products. You will show her how to use a comparison operator in a query to find those products.

To Use a Comparison Operator in a Query

a. Click the **Create tab**, click **Query Design** in the Queries group, click **tblProduct**, and then click **Add**. Click **Close** to close the Show Table dialog box.

b. In the following order, double-click **ProductID**, **ProductDescription**, **Size**, **Category**, **QtyInStock**, and **Price** to add the fields to the query design grid.

c. Click in the **Criteria** row for the **Price** field and type <=10.

d. Click the **Query Tools Design tab**, and then click **Run** in the Results group to run the query. The results should show six records all with prices $10 or less.

e. Click **Save** 🖫 on the Quick Access Toolbar, under Query Name type qryLowPriceProducts_ initialLastname replacing initialLastname with your own first initial and last name, and then click **OK**. **Close** ✕ the query.

SIDE NOTE
Formatting Criteria

In query criteria, text is identified by quotation marks around it and dates with # in front of and at the end of the date. For example, 1/1/16 would appear as #1/1/16#. Access adds the necessary quotation marks and pound signs, but it is a good idea to double check.

Hiding Fields That Are Used in a Query

For a field to be used in a query, it must be added to the query design grid. If you just want to use the field to define criteria but do not want to see the results of that field in the query, it cannot be removed from the query design grid, but it can be hidden from the results.

For this project, the manager is happy with the results of the Low Price Products query you created previously, but she would like to post a list of the products without the prices so she can advertise the list as all under $10. You tell her that is possible by using the Show check box in the query design grid.

To Use a Field Value in a Query but Not Show the Field in the Results

a. Click the **Create tab**, click **Query Design** in the Queries group, click **tblProduct**, and then click **Add**. Click **Close** to close the Show Table dialog box.

b. Double-click **ProductID, ProductDescription, Size, Category, QtyInStock**, and **Price** in that order to add them to the query design grid.

c. Click in the **Criteria** row for the Price field, type <=10, and then click the **Show** check box to remove the check mark in the Price field.

d. Click the **Query Tools Design tab**, and then click **Run** in the Results group to run the query. The results should show the same six records you found in the previous query, but without the price field showing.

e. Click **Save** 🔲 on the Quick Access Toolbar, under Query Name type qryTenAndUnder_ initialLastname replacing initialLastname with your own first initial and last name, and then click **OK. Close** ✕ the query.

Using the AND Logical Operator

When you create a query, you can select criteria for one field or for multiple fields. If you use multiple criteria, then you must also use **logical operators** to combine these criteria. Logical operators are operators that allow you to combine two or more criteria. For example, if you want a record selected when both criteria are met, then you would use the AND logical operator, but if you want a record selected if only one of the criteria is met, then you would use the OR logical operator. For an even more advanced query, you can combine the AND and the OR logical operators.

When you want to specify multiple criteria, and all criteria must be true for a record to be included in the results, then the AND logical operator is used, and the criteria must be in the same Criteria row in the query design grid. Access will look at the first field in the query design grid for criteria and continue moving from left to right looking for criteria. When criteria are in the same row, all criteria must match for the record to be included in the query results. For this project, you want to help the manager narrow down a sales strategy. She is trying to determine which customers place phone orders for products over $10.

To Use the AND Logical Operator

a. Click the **Create tab**, click **Query Design** in the Queries group, and then double-click **tblProduct, tblPurchase**, and **tblCustomer** to add the tables to the query window. Click **Close** to close the Show Table dialog box.

b. In the following order, double-click **PurchaseType** from tblPurchase, **ProductDescription** and **Price** from tblProduct, and **CustFirstName** and **CustLastName** from tblCustomer to add them to the query design grid.

c. Click in the **Criteria** row for the PurchaseType field, type Phone, and then for the Price field type >10.

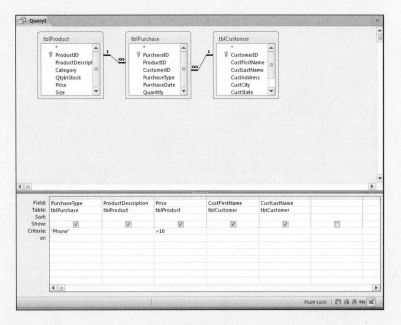

Figure 18 Criteria added for the PurchaseType and Price fields

d. Click the **Query Tools Design tab**, and then click **Run** in the Results group to run the query. The results show five records, with Phone as the Purchase Type and a price greater than $10.

e. Click **Save** on the Quick Access Toolbar, under Query Name type qryPhoneAndTen_ initialLastname replacing initialLastname with your own first initial and last name, and then click **OK**. **Close** the query.

Using the OR Logical Operator

When you want to specify criteria in multiple fields, and at least one of the criteria must be true for a record to be included in the results, then the OR logical operator is used, and the criteria must be in different Criteria rows in the query design grid. Access will look at the first field in the first Criteria row for criteria and continue moving from left to right, then it will start at the left again on the next criteria row which is labeled "or". For this exercise, you want to help the manager find all customers who make purchases either by phone or online.

To Use the OR Logical Operator

a. Click the **Create tab**, click **Query Design** in the Queries group, and double-click **tblProduct**, **tblPurchase**, and **tblCustomer** to add the tables to the query. Click **Close** to close the Show Table dialog box.

b. Double-click **PurchaseType** from tblPurchase, double-click **ProductDescription** from tblProduct, and then double-click **CustFirstName** and **CustLastName** from tblCustomer in that order to add them to the query design grid.

c. Click in the **Criteria** row for the PurchaseType field, type Phone. In the **or** row just below the Criteria line in the PurchaseType field, type Online.

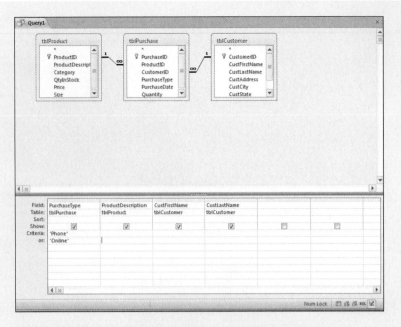

Figure 19 Two criteria added for PurchaseType

d. Click the **Query Tools Design tab**, and then click **Run** in the Results group to run the query. The results should show 12 records, all with Phone or Online as the purchase type.

e. Click **Save** 🔲 on the Quick Access Toolbar, name the query qryPhoneOrOnline_ initialLastname replacing initialLastname with your own first initial and last name, and then click **OK**. **Close** ☒ the query.

Combining the AND and OR Logical Operators

There may be times when you want to use two logical operators, AND and OR, at the same time. Depending on the desired results, you may have to use one or both Criteria rows. If you use both Criteria rows and put criteria in two fields on each row, then Access treats it like two AND logical operators and one OR logical operator. For this project, the manager wants you to find all phone purchase types for products over $10 or all online purchase types for products under $10.

SIDE NOTE
Sometimes Order Does Not Matter
The order that you add tables to the query window will not affect the results of your query. However, the order you add the fields to the query design grid will affect the results.

To Combine the AND and the OR Logical Operator

a. Click the **Create tab**, click **Query Design** in the Queries group, and then double-click **tblProduct**, **tblPurchase**, and **tblCustomer** to add the tables to the query. Click **Close** to close the Show Table dialog box.

b. Double-click **PurchaseType** from tblPurchase, double-click **ProductDescription** and **Price** from tblProduct, and then double-click **CustFirstName** and **CustLastName** from tblCustomer in that order to add them to the query design grid.

c. Click in the **Criteria** row for the PurchaseType field, type Phone and then in the same **Criteria** row for the Price field, type >10. In the **or** row below the Criteria row, type Online for the PurchaseType field, and then in the same **or** row, type <10 for the Price field.

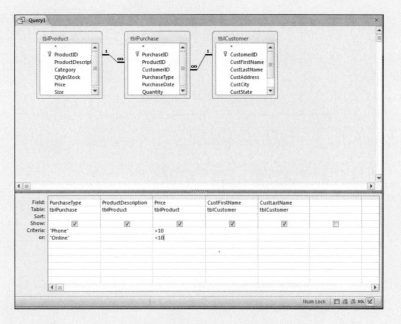

Figure 20 Two Criteria rows added for PurchaseType and Price

d. Click the **Query Tools Design tab**, and then click **Run** in the Results group to run the query. The results should show seven records, all with Phone purchase types with prices greater than $10 or Online purchase types with prices less than $10.

e. Click **Save** 🖫 on the Quick Access Toolbar, name the query qryPhoneAndOnline_ initialLastname replacing initialLastname with your own first initial and last name, and then click **OK**. **Close** ☒ the query.

Combining Multiple AND and OR Logical Operators

You cannot always use two rows for the OR criteria when you combine both logical operators. In cases like this, the word "or" can be used for two criteria used in the same field and the same Criteria row. For this project, the manager of the spa wants you to find all phone and online purchase types for products over $10. If you put the purchase type criteria on two rows and the price of >10 in one row, your results will show all records with phone purchase types over $10 *or* Online purchase types of any amount. Remember, Access moves from left to right on the first Criteria row so it will treat "Phone" and >10 as AND criteria and then move to the next row, which it will consider OR criteria.

To Combine Multiple AND and OR Logical Operators

a. Click the **Create tab**, click **Query Design** in the Queries group, and then double-click **tblProduct**, **tblPurchase**, and **tblCustomer** to add the tables to the query. Click **Close** to close the Show Table dialog box.

b. In the following order, double-click **PurchaseType** from tblPurchase, **ProductDescription** and **Price** from tblProduct, and **CustFirstName** and **CustLastName** from tblCustomer to add them to the query design grid.

c. Click in the **Criteria** row for the PurchaseType field, type Phone, and then in the **Criteria** row for the Price field, type >10. In the **or** row for the PurchaseType field, type Online.

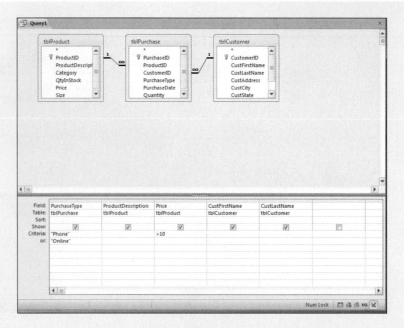

Figure 21 AND and OR criteria added to the query design grid

d. Click the **Query Tools Design tab**, and then click **Run** in the Results group to run the query. Notice the results are all Phone purchase types with prices over $10 or all Online purchase types, regardless of the price. The manager wants to see Phone or Online purchase types over $10, so this is not correct.

e. Click the **Home tab**, click the **View arrow**, and then click **Design View**. In the **or** row for the PurchaseType field, delete Online. Click in the **Criteria** row for the PurchaseType field, and change the criteria to Phone or Online. (*Hint*: make sure you do not include quotation marks and your criteria matches Figure 22.) Click the **Query Tools Design tab**, and then click **Run** in the Results group to run the query again. The results should now show Phone or Online purchase types that are over $10.

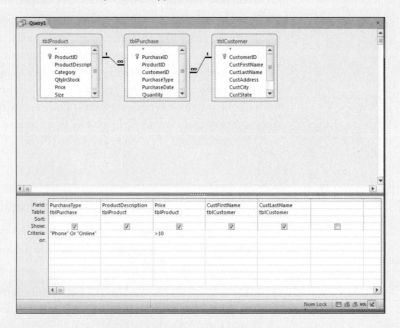

Figure 22 OR criteria in one row with AND criteria

f. Click **Save** 🖫 on the Quick Access Toolbar, under Query Name type qryPhoneOrOnlineOverTen_initialLastname replacing initialLastname with your own first initial and last name, and click **OK**. **Close** ✕ the query.

Combining Operators and Multiple Criteria

The more criteria added to your query means the more difficult it will be to see if you have the correct results. With multiple criteria, it is good practice to add one criterion, run the query to make sure you are getting the correct results, and then continue adding criteria one at a time.

For this project, the spa manager would like to see all of her high-end services listed by price and then service type, and she would like to break down the criteria as follows: Hands & Feet or Body Massage services $50 or more, Facial or Microdermabrasion services over $55, Beauty or Waxing services over $45, and all Botanical Hair & Scalp Therapy services.

To Combine Operators and Multiple Criteria

a. Click the **Create tab**, click **Query Design** in the Queries group, and double-click **tblService** to add the table to the query window. Click **Close** to close the Show Table dialog box.

b. In the following order, double-click **Fee**, **Type**, and **ServiceName** to add the fields to the query design grid.

c. Click in the **Criteria** row for the Fee field, type >55, and then in the **Criteria** row for the Type field type Facial or Microdermabrasion.

d. Click the **Query Tools Design tab**, and then click **Run** in the Results group to run the query. The results should show six records with Facial or Microdermabrasion for the Type field, and all values in the Fee field should be greater than $55.

e. Click the **Home tab**, click the **View arrow** in the Views group, and then click **Design View**. In the **or** row for the Fee field, type >=50, and for the **or** row for the Type field type "Hands & Feet" or Body Massage. Click the **Query Tools Design tab**, and then click **Run** in the Results group to run the query again.

   The query results should show 19 records with types Facial or Microdermabrasion that have fees greater than $55, and records with types Hands & Feet or Body Massage that have fees greater than or equal to $50.

Troubleshooting

If you enter the value Hands & Feet in the Type field without quotation marks, then Access will add those quotation marks for you. In this case, Access evaluates the ampersand character (&) as separating two values, so it will put the quotation marks around the word "Hands" and around the word "Feet" so it will look like "Hands" & "Feet". This is different than having the quotations around the whole phrase, which is what you want it to look like. In this case you should put the quotation marks around the phrase in order for it to look like "Hands & Feet".

f. Click the **Home tab**, click the **View arrow** in the Views group, and then click **Design View**. Click in the third Criteria row for the Fee field, type >45, and then in the **Criteria** row for the Type field, **type** Beauty or Waxing. Click the **Query Tools Design tab**, and then click **Run** in the Results group to run the query again.

   The results should show 23 records with types Facial or Microdermabrasion that have fees greater than $55, records with types Hands & Feet or Body Massage that have fees greater than or equal to $50, and records with types Beauty or Waxing that have fees greater than $45.

SIDE NOTE
Wider Columns

If you cannot see all the text you are entering in a column on the query design grid, you can point to the right border of the column selector bar and double-click to best fit the data. This is similar to making a column wider in Datasheet view.

g. Click the **Home tab**, click the **View arrow** in the Views group, and then click **Design View**. Click in the fourth Criteria row for the Type field and type "Botanical Hair & Scalp Therapy", Click the **Query Tools Design tab**, and then click **Run** in the Results group to run the query again.

The results should show 25 records with types Facial or Microdermabrasion that have fees greater than $55, records with types Hands & Feet or Body Massage that have fees greater than or equal to $50, records with types Beauty or Waxing that have fees greater than $45, and all Botanical Hair & Scalp Therapy types.

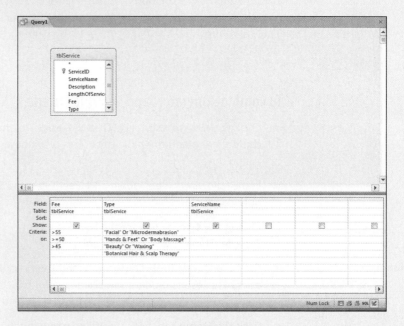

Figure 23 All criteria added to query design grid

h. Click **Save** 💾 on the Quick Access Toolbar, name the query qryHighEndServices_ initialLastname replacing initialLastname with your own first initial and last name, and then click **OK**. Close ⊠ the query.

Using Special Operators

Special operators are used to compare text values using wildcards (LIKE) or to determine whether values are between a range of values (BETWEEN). Commonly used special operators are shown in Figure 24.

Operator	Description
LIKE	Matches text values by using wildcards
BETWEEN	Determines if a number or date is within a range
IN	Determines if a value is found within a set of values

Figure 24 Special operators

The BETWEEN special operator will return results that include and fall between the criteria you enter. If you recall, when working with dates as criteria, a # in front of and at the end of each date is required to identify the numbers as dates and not a string of text.

For this project, the manager of the spa would like you to find all weekday services scheduled from Monday, January 14, through Friday, January 18, 2013, along with the customer who is scheduled for that service.

To Use the BETWEEN Special Operator

a. Click the **Create tab**, click **Query Design** in the Queries group, and then double-click **tblSchedule** and **tblCustomer** to add the tables to the query. Click **Close** to close the Show Table dialog box.

b. Double-click **Service**, **Employee**, and **DateOfAppt** from tblSchedule, and then double-click **CustFirstName** and **CustLastName** from tblCustomer in that order to add them to the query design grid.

c. Click in the **Criteria** row for the DateOfAppt field and type Between 1/14/13 and 1/18/13.

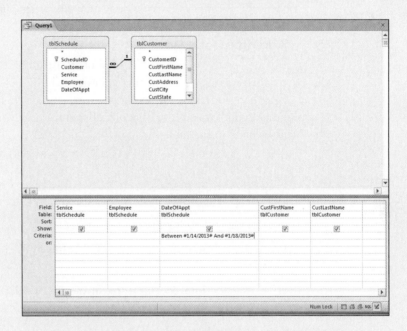

Figure 25   Criteria added for DateOfAppt

SIDE NOTE
Formatting Criteria

While it is a good habit to remember to put the pound signs around a date or the quotation marks around text, if you forget, Access will add them for you.

d. Click the **Query Tools Design tab**, and then click **Run** in the Results group to run the query. The results should show 31 records all with a date between January 14 and January 18, 2013.

e. Click **Save** 💾 on the Quick Access Toolbar, under Query Name type qryWeekdayDates_ initialLastname replacing initialLastname with your own first initial and last name, and then click **OK**. **Close** ✕ the query.

Create Aggregate Functions

Aggregate functions perform arithmetic operations, such as calculating averages and totals, on records displayed in a table or query. An aggregate function can be used in Datasheet view by adding a total row to a table, or it can be used in a query on records that meet certain criteria.

Adding a Total Row

If you need to see a quick snapshot of statistics for a table, you can use the total row. The **total row** is a special row that appears at the end of a datasheet that enables you to show aggregate functions for one or more fields. For this project, you will help the manager quickly find a total for all invoices listed in the invoices table and a count of the number of invoices in the table.

To Add a Total Row to a Datasheet

a. Double-click **tblInvoice** to open the table.

b. Click the **Home tab**, and then click **Totals** in the Records group to add a total row to the table.

c. Click in the **Total row** under the InvoiceTotal field, click the **arrow**, and then select **Sum**. Click in the **Total row** under the CustomerID field, click the **arrow**, and then select **Count**.

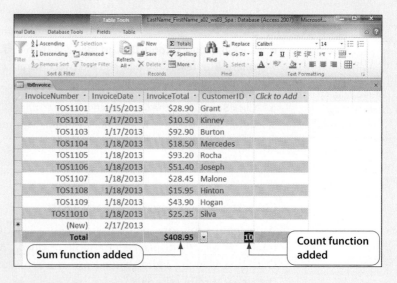

Figure 26   Sum and Count added to the Total row

d. Click the **File tab**, click **Save Object As**, in the Save 'tblInvoice' to text box type tblInvoiceTotals_initialLastname replacing initialLastname with your own first initial and last name, and then click **OK. Close** ✕ the table.

Using Aggregate Functions in a Query

Aggregate functions can be used in queries to perform calculations on selected fields and records. One advantage to using aggregate functions in queries, rather than just a total row, is that you can group criteria and then calculate the aggregate functions for a group of records. By default, the query design grid does not have a place to enter aggregate functions, so the total row must be added from the Query Tools Design tab. Each column or field can calculate only one aggregate function, so to calculate multiple functions on the same field, the field must be added to the grid multiple times.

For this project, you have been asked to come up with a statistical summary of the spa's product prices. The manager would like to see how many products are offered, what the average product price is, and the minimum and maximum product prices.

To Use Aggregate Functions in a Query

a. Click the **Create tab**, click **Query Design** in the Queries group, and double-click **tblProduct** to add the table to the query. Click **Close** to close the Show Table dialog box.

b. Double-click **Price** four times to add the field four times to the query design grid.

c. Click the **Query Tools Design tab**, and then click **Totals** in the Show/Hide group to add a total row to the query design grid.

d. In the first Price column, click in the **Total** row, click the **arrow**, and then select **Count**. In the second Price column, in the **Total** row, click the **arrow**, and then select **Avg**. Repeat for the next two **Price** columns selecting **Min** for the third column and **Max** for the last column.

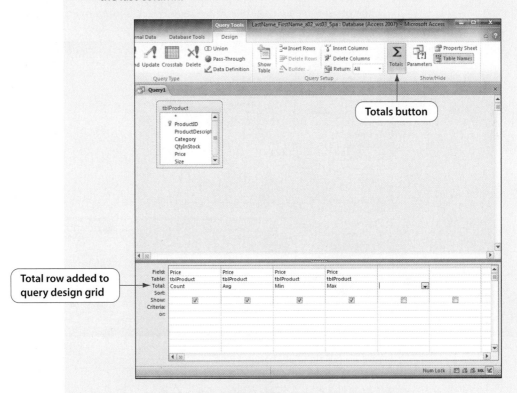

Figure 27   Aggregate functions selected for each column

e. Click the **Query Tools Design tab**, and then click **Run** in the Results group to run the query. Because this is an aggregate query and you are calculating one statistic per column, there will only be one record in the results.

Figure 28 Aggregate query results

Changing Field Names

The field names assigned in an aggregate query can easily be changed either before or after the query is run. However, you must keep the field name in the query design grid so Access knows what field to perform the calculation on. For this project, you will change the names of the fields in the aggregate query you just created.

To Change the Field Names in an Aggregate Query

a. Click the **Home tab**, click the **View arrow** in the Views group, and then click **Design View**.

b. Click in the **Field** row of the first column, and then press Home to move the insertion point to the beginning of the field name. Type Count of Products:. Do not delete the field name Price. The colon identifies the title as separate from the field name. Repeat for the other three fields and type Average Price:, Minimum Price:, and Maximum Price:.

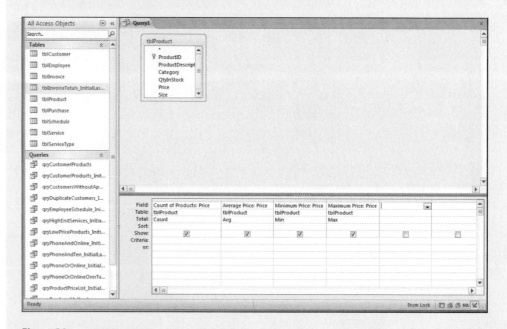

Figure 29 Field titles changed

c. Click the **Query Tools Design tab**, and then click **Run** in the Results group to run the query. Resize the columns to see the complete column names.

d. Click **Save** on the Quick Access Toolbar, under Query name type qryProductStatistics_initialLastname replacing initialLastname with your own first initial and last name, and then click **OK**. **Close** ✕ the query.

Creating Calculations for Groups of Records

Not only can you find statistics information on selected records using aggregate functions in a query, or for all records using the total row, you can also calculate statistics for groups of records. Creating a group to calculate statistics for works the same way as an aggregate query but must include the field to group by. The additional field will not have a statistic selected for the total row, but instead have the default Group By entered in the total row.

For this exercise, you will help the spa manager find the same product price statistics you calculated previously but this time grouped by product category.

To Create a Group Calculation

a. Click the **Create tab**, click **Query Design** in the Queries group, and then double-click **tblProduct** to add the table to the query. Click **Close** to close the Show Table dialog box.

b. Double-click **Category** to add it to the query design grid, and then double-click **Price** four times to add the field four times to the query design grid.

c. Click the **Query Tools Design tab**, and then click **Totals** in the Show/Hide group to add a total row to the query design grid.

d. In the first Price column in the **Total** row, click the **arrow**, and then select **Count**. In the second Price column in the **Total** row, click the **arrow**, and then select **Avg**. Repeat for the next two **Price** columns selecting **Min** for the third column and **Max** for the last column. Notice that the Category Total row displays Group By so the statistics will be grouped by each category type.

e. Click the **Query Tools Design tab**, and then click **Run** in the Results group to run the query.

f. Click the **Home tab**, click the **View arrow** in the Views group, and then click **Design View**.

g. Change the titles for the Price fields to the following: Number of Products, Average Price, Minimum Price, and Maximum Price. **Run** the query again. Resize the columns to best fit the data.

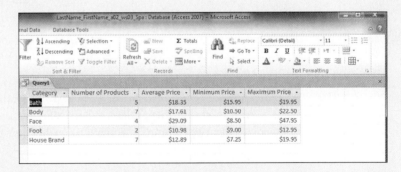

Figure 30 Query results with field titles changed

h. Click **Save** 💾 on the Quick Access Toolbar, under Query Name type qryPriceStatisticsByCategory_initialLastname replacing initialLastname with your own first initial and last name, and then click **OK**. **Close** ☒ the query.

Troubleshooting an Aggregate Query

Caution should be used when using aggregate functions. Forgetting to add a function in the total row can cause a large number of records to be retrieved from the database, or a combination of records that do not make any sense. You must carefully select which field should have the Group By operator in the total row; many times only one field will use Group By. Combining search criteria and aggregate functions in a single query can make the query complex. It also makes troubleshooting more difficult if the query does not work. When in doubt, set all your criteria in one query and then use the aggregate functions in another query based on the query with the criteria. This way, you can first verify that your criteria worked and then concentrate on the aggregate function results.

For this exercise, the manager tried to create an aggregate query to calculate the total number of items and average number of items purchased by different methods—phone, online, and in person. The results made no sense, and she has asked you to help her figure out why.

To Troubleshoot an Aggregate Query

a. Double-click **qryPurchaseMethods** to open the query. Notice the results in the second and third columns are exactly the same, when the intent was to have one column contain a total and the other column contain an average.

b. Click the **Home tab**, click the **View arrow** in the Views group, and then click **Design View**. Look at the second column, Quantity, and notice the Total row shows the Group By operator instead of a function. Change this to **Sum**.

c. Rename the second and third column field titles to Total Quantity and Average Quantity.

d. Click the **Query Tools Design tab**, and then click **Run** in the Results group to run the query. Resize the columns to best fit the data.

e. Click the **File tab**, click **Save Object As**, and then under Query Name type **qryPurchaseMethods_initialLastname**, replacing initialLastname with your own first initial and last name, and then click **OK**. **Close** ☒ the query.

Formatting a Calculated Field

An aggregate query may give you the correct results but the formatting may not be what you expected. Query fields must be formatted in the query design grid using the Field properties sheet. For this project, the manager does not want to see decimal places for the Average Quantity column, so you will show her how to change the formatting of that field.

To Change the Formatting of a Calculated Field

a. Double-click **qryPurchaseMethods_initialLastname** to open the query. Click the **Home tab**, click **View**, and then click **Design View**.

b. Click the **Average Quantity: Quantity** column. Click the **Query Tools Design tab**, and then click **Property Sheet** in the Show/Hide group.

c. Click in the **Format** box, click the **arrow**, and then select **Fixed**. Click in the **Decimal Places** box, and then type 0.

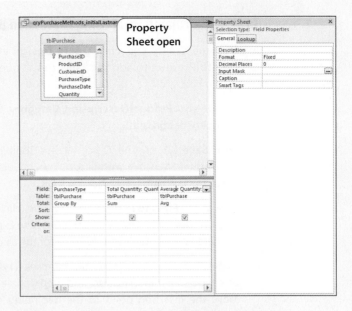

Figure 31 Property sheet open with changes

d. **Close** ⊠ the property sheet, and then run the query again. The results should be formatted with no decimal places.

e. Click the **File tab**, click **Save Object As**, under Query Name type qryPurchaseMethodsNoDecimals_initialLastname replacing initialLastname with your own first initial and last name, and then click **OK**. **Close** ⊠ the query.

Create Calculated Fields

In addition to statistical calculations using aggregate functions, you can also perform an arithmetic calculation within a new query field. The result of the calculated field is displayed each time you run the query. However, this new field is not part of any other table.

A calculated field can be added to a query using the fields in the query or even fields in another table or query in the database. The calculation can use a combination of numbers and field values, which allows you flexibility in how you perform the calculation. For example, you can multiply a product price stored in the table by a sales tax rate that you enter into the calculation.

Building a Calculated Field Using Expression Builder

Expression Builder is a tool in Access that can help you format your calculated fields correctly. The builder provides a list of expression elements, operators, and built-in functions. The capabilities of Expression Builder range from simple to complex.

For this exercise, you will help the spa manager create a query to show what the value of her inventory is using the Quantity in Stock and Price fields for each product.

To Add a Calculated Field Using Expression Builder

a. Click the **Create tab**, click **Query Design** in the Queries group, and then double-click **tblProduct** to add the table to the query. Click **Close** to close the Show Table dialog box.

b. Double-click **ProductDescription**, **Category**, **QtyInStock**, and **Price** to add the fields to the query design grid.

c. Click **Save** 🖫 on the Quick Access Toolbar, and then under Query Name, type **qryProductInventory_initialLastname** replacing initialLastname with your own first initial and last name, and then click **OK**.

d. Click in the **Field** row in the fifth column, click the **Query Tools Design tab**, and then click **Builder** in the Query Setup group. The Expression Builder dialog box opens, which is where you will build your formula for the calculation.

e. Under Expression Categories, double-click **QtyInStock** to add the field to the expression box, type * for multiplication, and then double-click **Price** under Expression Categories. Move the insertion point to the beginning of the expression, and then type Total Inventory:. Click **OK** to save the expression and add it to the query design grid.

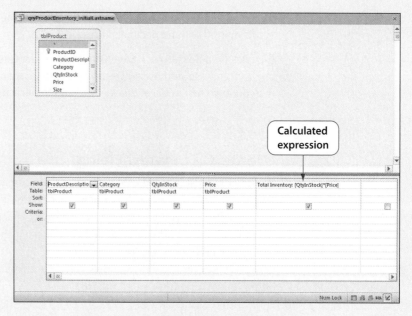

Figure 32   Design grid with calculated expression added

SIDE NOTE
Expression Box

When working with multiple tables in Expression Builder, Access puts the table name in front of the field name with an exclamation mark. If you are using a single table, however, the table name is optional and will not be added by default.

Troubleshooting

When you click Expression Builder to create a calculated field, and you do not see your field names listed in the Expression Categories box in the middle of the dialog box, it may be that the query has not been saved yet. If the query is not saved, then the field names will not appear and you will have to type them in the Expression Builder manually instead of clicking them to select them. It is good practice to save your query first, and then open the Expression Builder to create a calculated field.

f. Click the **Query Tools Design tab**, and then click **Run** in the Results group to run the query. Resize the Total Inventory column to best fit the data. The results should show 25 records with a new column titled Total Inventory that multiplies the QtyInStock by the Price fields.

g. **Close** ☒ the query, and then click **Yes** when prompted to save changes.

Sort Query Results

Sorting is the process of rearranging records in a specific order. By default, records in a table or query are sorted by the primary key field. You can change the sorting of a table in a query, which will not affect how the data is stored, only how it will appear in the query results.

Sorting by One Field

To sort records, you have to select a **sort field**, or a field used to determine the order of the records. The sort field can be a Text, Number, Date/Time, Currency, AutoNumber, Yes/No, or Lookup Wizard field as shown in Figure 33. A field may be sorted either in ascending order or descending order.

Type of Data	Sorting Options
Text	Ascending (A to Z); Descending (Z to A)
Numbers (including Currency & AutoNumber)	Ascending (lowest to highest); Descending (highest to lowest)
Date/Time	Ascending (oldest to newest); Descending (newest to oldest)
Yes/No	Ascending (yes, then no values); Descending (no, then yes values)

Figure 33   Methods for sorting data

If you have numbers that are stored as text—phone numbers, Social Security numbers, zip codes—then the characters 1–9 come before A to Z in the appropriate order sorted as alphanumeric text.

A table may be sorted by a single field in Datasheet view. When a table is sorted using a single field, a sort arrow will appear in the field name so you can see that it is sorted. For this project, you will show the spa manager how to sort the tblProduct table by category.

SIDE NOTE
Alternative Method to Sorting Fields

Alternatively, you can select the field to be sorted and click Ascending or Descending on the Home tab in the Sort & Filter group.

To Sort by a Single Field

a. Double-click **tblProduct** to open the table.

b. Click the **selection arrow** in the field name next to Category, and then click **Sort A to Z**. This will sort the Category field in ascending order.

c. **Close** ☒ the table, and then click **Yes** when prompted to save the changes.

Sorting by More Than One Field

You can also sort by multiple fields in Access. The first field you choose to sort by is called the **primary sort field**. The second and subsequent fields are called **secondary sort fields**. You can sort multiple fields from the datasheet by selecting all the fields at one time and using the buttons on the Ribbon, but there are some restrictions. First, the fields must be next to each other and the sort is executed left to right; that is, the leftmost field is the primary sort field, the next field is a secondary sort field, and so on. Secondly, you can only sort in ascending or descending order for all fields, you cannot have one field sorted in ascending order and another in descending order. Because of all the restrictions, it is more efficient to create a query and sort by multiple fields using Design view.

Using Design view to sort records allows you to sequence the fields from left to right in an order that makes sense for your desired sort results and allows you to combine ascending and descending sorts. You can also sort in an order different than left to right by adding a field multiple times and clearing the Show check box. For this exercise, you will show the staff how to sort the tblSchedule table by Employee, then Date, and then Service by creating a query from the table and setting up the sort options.

To Sort a Query by Multiple Fields

a. Click the **Create tab**, click **Query Design** in the Queries group, and double-click **tblSchedule** to add the table to the query. Click **Close** to close the Show Table dialog box.

b. Double-click the **tblSchedule title bar**, and then drag all the fields to the query design grid.

c. Click at the top of the **Employee** field to highlight it and then drag it to the first column of the query design grid in front of ScheduleID. Drag the **DateOfAppt** field to the second column after the **Employee** field, and then drag the **Service** field to the third column after the **DateOfAppt** field.

d. Click the **Sort** row for **Employee**, click the **selection arrow**, and then click **Ascending**. Click **Ascending** for both the **DateOfAppt** and **Service** fields.

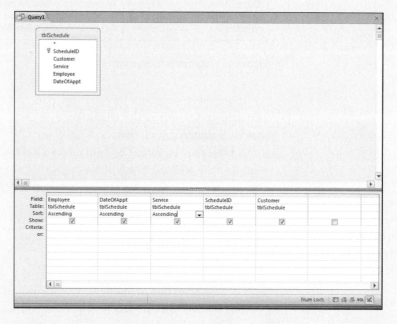

Figure 34   Sort options selected

e. Click the **Query Tools Design tab**, and then click **Run** in the Results group to run the query. The table should be sorted by Employee, then Date, then Service.

f. Click **Save** 💾 on the Quick Access Toolbar, name the query qryEmployeeAppointments_ initialLastname replacing initialLastname with your own first initial and last name, and then click **OK. Close** ❌ the query.

Rearranging the Sort Order

For this exercise, the manager would like a query similar to the one created previously, but she would like it to show employees' first and last names. She would also like it to sort by employee last name and then employee first name, but have the first name show first in the query results. You will show her how to use two tables to create this query and how to add a field multiple times to the query design grid to sort fields one way but display them another way.

To Sort a Query by Multiple Fields in a Different Sort Order

a. Click the **Create tab**, click **Query Design** in the Queries group, and then double-click **tblSchedule** and **tblEmployee** to add the tables to the query. Click **Close** to close the Show Table dialog box.

b. Double-click **EmpFirstName**, **EmpLastName**, and then **EmpFirstName** again from tblEmployee to add the fields to the query design grid. Double-click **DateOfAppt**, **Service**, and **Customer** in that order from tblSchedule to add the fields to the query design grid.

c. Click the **Sort** row for EmpLastName, click the **selection arrow**, and then click **Ascending**. Click the **Sort** row for the second EmpFirstName in the third column, click **Ascending**, and then select **Ascending** for both the DateOfAppt and Service fields. Click the **Show** check box under the second EmpFirstName field in the third column to clear it.

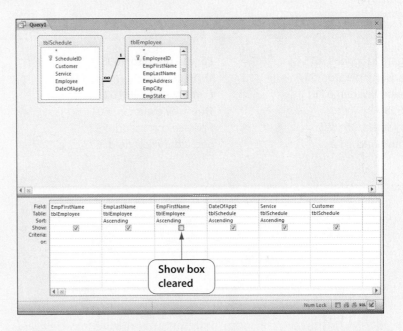

Figure 35   Sort options selected and EmpFirstName Show check box cleared

d. Click the **Query Tools Design tab**, and then click **Run** in the Results group to run the query. The results should show 53 records sorted by employee last name, first name, date, and service. Notice that Alex Weaver comes before Joseph Weaver in the sort.

e. Click **Save** 🖫 on the Quick Access Toolbar, name the query qryEmployeeSort_initialLastname replacing initialLastname with your own first initial and last name, and click **OK**. **Close** ☒ the query. **Exit** Access.

1. You applied a filter to a table to find specific records. The next time you opened the table, Toggle Filter did not show your filtered records. What did you do wrong?

2. You used the Find command to search for someone's first name, which you are sure is in the table. The results keep coming up with nothing. What option could be preventing Access from finding the record you are looking for? What else could you do to find the record?

3. When is there an advantage to finding one record at a time and replacing a value compared to using Replace All?

4. What is the difference between the Find Duplicates Query Wizard and the Find Unmatched Query Wizard? Give an example of when you would use each.

5. Why should you only add the tables you are going to use to a query?

6. What is the multiplier effect, and how can you prevent it from happening?

7. Using logical operators allows you to create powerful queries. When do you put criteria for different fields in the same row in the query design grid? When do you put the criteria for different fields in different rows? How can you combine AND and OR criteria in the same query?

8. Why would you add the same field multiple times to the query design grid?

Key Terms

Aggregate functions 615
Comparison operator 607
Expression Builder 621
Filter 595
Filter by selection 595
Find command 592

Logical operator 608
Orphan 598
Primary sort field 623
Query by example 601
Replace command 592
Secondary sort field 623

Sort field 623
Sorting 623
Special operator 614
Text filter 596
Total row 616
Wildcard character 592

Visual Summary

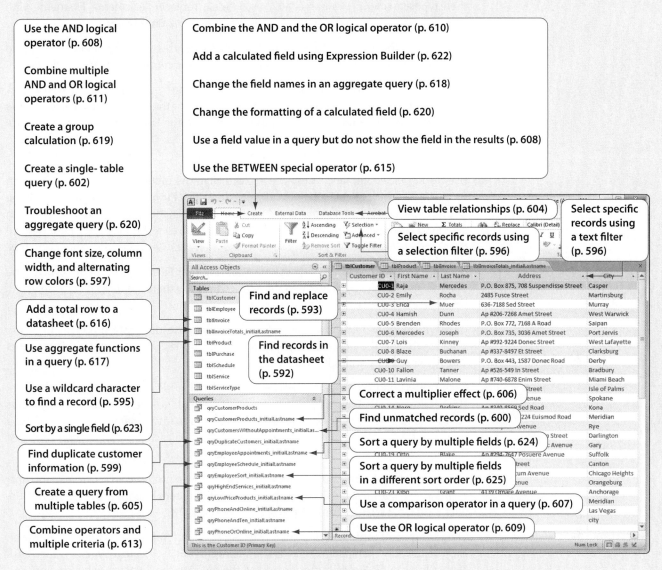

Combine the AND and the OR logical operator (p. 610)

Add a calculated field using Expression Builder (p. 622)

Change the field names in an aggregate query (p. 618)

Change the formatting of a calculated field (p. 620)

Use a field value in a query but do not show the field in the results (p. 608)

Use the BETWEEN special operator (p. 615)

Use the AND logical operator (p. 608)

Combine multiple AND and OR logical operators (p. 611)

Create a group calculation (p. 619)

Create a single-table query (p. 602)

Troubleshoot an aggregate query (p. 620)

Change font size, column width, and alternating row colors (p. 597)

Add a total row to a datasheet (p. 616)

Use aggregate functions in a query (p. 617)

Use a wildcard character to find a record (p. 595)

Sort by a single field (p. 623)

Find duplicate customer information (p. 599)

Create a query from multiple tables (p. 605)

Combine operators and multiple criteria (p. 613)

View table relationships (p. 604)

Select specific records using a text filter (p. 596)

Select specific records using a selection filter (p. 596)

Find and replace records (p. 593)

Find records in the datasheet (p. 592)

Correct a multiplier effect (p. 606)

Find unmatched records (p. 600)

Sort a query by multiple fields (p. 624)

Sort a query by multiple fields in a different sort order (p. 625)

Use a comparison operator in a query (p. 607)

Use the OR logical operator (p. 609)

Figure 36 Turquoise Oasis Spa Final

Practice 1

Student data file needed:

a02_ws03_Spa2

You will save your file as:

Lastname_Firstname_a02_ws03_Spa2

Turquoise Oasis Spa

Production & Operations

The Resort is considering hosting a large convention and is trying to sign a multiple-year contract with an out-of-town group. The Spa is being asked to provide information about the services, products, and packages it offers. All the information can be found in the database, but it needs to come together in a coherent fashion. You have been asked to answer a number of questions about the spa and provide information to help answer those questions. You will also look for discrepancies or mistakes in the data and correct them as necessary.

a. Start **Access**, and then open **a02_ws03_Spa2**. Click the **File tab**, and then click **Save Database As**. In the Save As dialog box, navigate to where you are storing your files, and then type Lastname_Firstname_a02_ws03_Spa2, replacing Lastname_Firstname with your own name. Click **Save**. In the Security Warning, click **Enable Content**.

b. Double-click **tblCustomer** to open the table. Add a new record with your First Name and Last Name, your Address, your City, your State, your Phone, and your E-mail Address.

c. Use the Find command to find Spa customers who come from as far away as Alaska. Click the **First Record**, and then click in the **State** column for the first record. Click the **Home tab**, and then click **Find** in the Find group. Type AK in the Find What box, and then click **Find Next** until Access finishes searching the table. Click **OK**, and then click **Cancel** to close the dialog box. Notice that the Alaska address selected is really a city in Hawaii.

d. Use the Replace command to replace AK with HI in the table. Click in the **State** column for the first record. Click the **Home tab**, and then click **Find** in the Find group. Click the **Replace tab**, and type AK in the Find What box. Type HI in the Replace With box, and then click **Find Next**. When Customer ID CU0-21 is selected, click **Replace**. Click **Find Next** to check for any more similar errors. Click **OK**, and then click **Cancel** to close the dialog box.

e. Click the **arrow** on the **State** field column, point to **Text Filters**, select **Begins With**, type H in the State begins with box, and then click **OK**. Verify there are three records selected. Save and close the table.

f. Create a query to find how many customers purchase duplicate products. Click the **Create tab**, and then click **Query Wizard** in the Queries group. Click **Find Duplicates Query Wizard**, and then click **OK**.

g. Click **Table: tblPurchase**, and then click **Next**. Double-click **ProductID**, and then click **Next**. Click the **All Fields** button to add all the fields to the Additional query fields column, and then click **Next**. Under "What do you want to name your query?" type qryDuplicateProducts_initialLastname replacing initialLastname with your own first initial and last name, and then click **Finish**. Close the query.

h. Create a query to find out which employees currently do not have any customer appointments at the Spa. Click the **Create tab**, and then click **Query Wizard** in the Queries group. Click **Find Unmatched Query Wizard**, and then click **OK**.

i. Click **Table: tblEmployee**, and then click **Next**. Select **Table: tblSchedule**, and then click **Next**. Verify that Matching fields shows **EmployeeID <=> Employee**, and then click **Next**. Click the **All Fields** button to add all the fields to the Selected fields column, and then click **Next**.

j. Name the query qryEmployeesWithoutAppointments_initialLastname, replacing initialLastname with your own first initial and last name, and then click **Finish**.

k. Click the **Home tab**, click the **View arrow** in the Views group, and then click **Design View**. Click the **Sort** row for the EmpLastName field, click the **sort arrow**, and then click **Ascending** to sort the query in ascending order by Last Name. Click the **Query Tools Design tab**, and then click **Run** in the Results group to run the query. Close the query, and then click **Yes** when prompted to save the changes.

l. Create a query to list the Spa's services by Type, Name, Description, and Fee. Click the **Create tab**, and then click **Query Design** in the Queries group. Double-click **tblService** and **tblServiceType** to add the tables to the query window. Click **Close** to close the Show Table dialog box.

m. In the following order, from tblServiceType double-click **Type**, and from tblService double-click **ServiceName, Description**, and **Fee** to add the fields to the query design grid. Click the **Sort** row for the Type field, select **Ascending**, and then for the Fee field, select **Descending**. Click the **Query Tools Design tab**, and then click **Run** in the Results group to run the query.

n. Double-click the **border** between the ServiceType and ServiceName field names to best fit the data. Repeat for all the columns. Click **Save** on the Quick Access Toolbar, name the query qryServicesAndFees_initialLastname replacing initialLastname with your own first initial and last name, and then close the query.

o. Create a query to find how much each customer spent on their product purchase, including 8% sales tax, but only if the purchase was a quantity greater than 1. Click the **Create tab**, click **Query Design** in the Queries group, and add **tblProduct** and **tblPurchase** to the query window. Click **Close** to close the Show Table dialog box. From tblProduct, double-click **ProductDescription** and **Price**, and from tblPurchase double-click **Quantity** and **CustomerID** in that order to add the fields to the query design grid.

p. Click in the **Criteria** row for Quantity and type >1. Click **Save** on the Quick Access Toolbar, name the query qryTotalPurchase_initialLastname replacing initialLastname with your own first initial and last name, and click **OK**.

q. In the fifth column, click in the **Field** row, click the **Query Tools Design tab**, and click **Builder** in the Query Setup group. Double-click **Price** to add it to the expression, type *, double-click **Quantity** to add it to the expression, type *, and then type 1.08. Click at the beginning of the expression, type Total Purchase with tax:, and then click **OK**.

r. Click the **Sort** row for the Quantity field, click the **selection arrow**, and then click **Ascending**. Click the **Query Tools Design tab**, and then click **Run** in the Results group to run the query.

s. Click the Home tab, click the **View arrow**, and then click **Design View**. Click the Total Purchase with tax field, click the **Query Tools Design tab**, and then click **Property Sheet** in the Show/Hide group. Click the **Format arrow**, and then select **Currency**. Click the **Decimal Places arrow**, and then select **2**. Close the property sheet, click the **Query Tools Design tab**, and then click **Run** in the Results group to run the query. The Total Purchase with tax field should be formatted with currency and two decimal places.

t. Close the query, and then click **Yes** when prompted to save the changes.

u. Create an aggregate query to find the average, minimum, and maximum fee for each type of service the spa offers. Click the **Create tab**, click **Query Design** in the Queries group, and add **tblService** to the query window. Click **Close** to close the Show Table dialog box. Double-click **Type** one time, and double-click **Fee** three times in that order to add the fields to the query design grid. Click the **Query Tools Design tab**, and then click **Totals** in the Show/Hide group to add the Total row to the query design grid.

v. Click in the **Total** row, for the first Fee column, click the **arrow**, and then click **Avg**. For the second Fee column select **Min**, and for the third Fee column select **Max**. Click in the **Sort** row in the Type field, click the **arrow**, and then select **Ascending**. Click the **Query Tools Design tab**, and then click **Run** in the Results group to run the query.

w. Click the **Home tab**, and then click **View** to return to Design view. Change the names of the three Fee columns to Fee Average, Minimum Fee, and Maximum Fee in that order. Click the **Query Tools Design tab**, and then click **Run** in the Results group to run the query.

x. Double-click the **border** between the Service Type and Fee Average field names to best fit the data. Repeat for all the columns.

y. Click **Save** on the Quick Access Toolbar, name the query qryFeeStatistics_initialLastname replacing initialLastname with your own first initial and last name, and click **OK**. Close the query. Exit Access.

Student data file needed:

a02_ps1_Baseball

You will save your file as:

Lastname_Firstname_a02_ps1_Baseball

Baseball Academy

Production & Operations

Matt Davis is a retired baseball player who runs the Baseball Academy, an indoor baseball facility for middle school, high school, and college players. He offers lessons as well as practice times for individuals and teams. Due to his growing clientele and increased record keeping needs, Matt wants all his records in a database. While he has already set up a database, he now needs to take the database to the next level of performance by improving his ability to get specific data out of the database. He has hired you to create the queries he will need to get this information.

a. Start **Access** and open **a02_ps1_Baseball**. Save the database as Lastname_Firstname_a02_ps1_Baseball replacing Lastname_Firstname with your own name.

b. Open **tblMember** and add a new record with your first name, last name, address, city, state, zip code of 87594 and phone. Create a filter to show only those members who have a zip code of **87594**. Save and close the table.

c. Modify **tblPayments** so the font type is **Arial** and the font size is **14**. Format the column widths appropriately. Save and close the table.

d. Create a find duplicates query that will show members who have the same address. Show all the fields in the query results. Name the query qryDupAddresses_initialLastname. Close the query.

e. Create a find unmatched query that will return the first name, last name, address, city, state, zip, and phone of anyone who is listed as a member in **tblMember** but has not made a payment. Name the query qryNonPayment_initialLastname. Save and close the query.

f. Create a query which will return the member's **last name**, **first name**, **amount**, and **payment date**. Sort the query in ascending order first by last name then by first name. Name the query qryPayments_initialLastname.

g. Add a total row to show total payments made. Save and close the query.

h. Create a query which returns all the employees who are considered **instructors**. Include employee **first name**, **last name**, and **position**. Sort them by salary (highest to lowest but do not show the salary in the result). Name the query qryInstructors_initialLastname. Save and close the query.

i. Create a query to calculate employee salaries with a 3% raise. Include the employee's **last name**, **first name**, and **salary**. The new calculated field should be called SalaryWithRaise.

j. Format the new field as currency and sort the results by SalaryWithRaise from highest salary to lowest. Name the query qryRaises_initialLastname.

k. Adjust the column widths as necessary. Include total payroll before and after the raises at the bottom of the table. Save and close the query.

l. Create a query which returns the sum, average, minimum and maximum of all the employee salaries. Name the query qrySalaryStats_initialLastname. Save and close the query.

m. Create a query that includes the **last name**, **first name**, **scheduled date**, and **fee** for any lesson between June 1, 2014 and June 30, 2014 which is greater than or equal to $250. Name the query qryBigJuneFees_initialLastname. Save and close the query.

n. Save and close the database. Submit your files as directed by your instructor.

Additional Workshop Cases are available on the companion website and in the instructor resources.

WORKSHOP 4

Maintaining and Presenting Data

PREPARE CASE

Turquoise Oasis Spa's New Database

The Turquoise Oasis Spa has a database with customer, employee, product, and service information for easier scheduling and access. An intern created the database, and the manager and staff members are struggling to use the database to its fullest capacity. You have recently been hired to work in the office of the spa and you have knowledge of Access, so the manager has asked for your help in maintaining the records and creating forms and reports to help better use the data in the database.

Production & Operations   Sales & Marketing

Zadorozhnyi Viktor / Shutterstock.com

Student data files needed for this workshop:

 a02_ws04_Spa3

 a02_ws04_Spa_Image

You will save your files as:

 Lastname_Firstname_a02_ws04_Spa3

 Lastname_Firstname_a02_ws04_Theme

 Lastname_Firstname_a02_ws04_pdfEmployeeSchedule

Maintain Records in Tables

Data may be updated directly in the table where it is stored. When updating data in a table, you will be in Datasheet view. Datasheet view shows all the fields and records at one time, which provides all the information you need to update your data, unlike in a form or query, where some of the fields or records may not be in view.

Compare Navigation and Edit Modes

As you may recall, you can navigate from record to record or field to field in a database using the Navigation bar, or in Navigation mode by using Tab, Enter, Home, End, ↑, ↓, ←, and →. **Navigation mode** allows you to move from record to record and field to field using keystrokes. To update data in a table, you must be in Edit mode. **Edit mode** allows you to edit, or change, the contents of a field as shown in Figure 1. To switch between Navigation mode and Edit mode, press F2.

Keystroke	Navigation Mode	Edit Mode
→ and ←	Move from field to field	Move from character to character
↑ and ↓	Move from record to record	Switch to Navigation mode and move from record to record
Home	Moves to the first field in the record	Moves to the first character in the field
End	Moves to the last field in the record	Moves to the last character in the field
Tab and Enter	Moves one field at a time	Switches to Navigation mode and moves from field to field
Ctrl+Home	Moves to the first field of the first record	Moves to the first character in the field, same as Home
Ctrl+End	Moves to the last field of the last record	Moves to the last character in the field, same as End

Figure 1 Keystrokes used in Navigation mode and Edit mode

SIDE NOTE
Look for the Blinking Insertion Point

When you can see the blinking insertion point in a field, you are in Edit mode. When the text of a field is selected and highlighted, you are in Navigation mode.

Editing a Table in Datasheet View

Datasheet view shows all the records and fields at one time, which is one advantage to using it to update your records. Another advantage is the ability to see all the records in the table, which gives you a perspective on the data you are entering. For this exercise, the staff has received a note from a customer who has changed their phone number. You will show the spa staff how to change that customer's record in the Customer table.

Workshop 4 Training

To Edit a Record in a Table in Datasheet View

a. Click the **Start** button . From the Start menu, locate and then start **Microsoft Access**. Click the **File tab**, and then click **Open**. In the Open dialog box, click the disk drive in the left pane where your student data files are located, navigate through the folder structure, click **a02_ws04_Spa3**, and then click **Open**.

b. Click the **File tab**, and then click **Save Database As**. In the Save As dialog box, navigate to where you are saving your files, and then type Lastname_Firstname_a02_ws04_Spa3, replacing Lastname_Firstname with your own name, and then click **Save**.

c. In the Security Warning bar, click **Enable Content**.

d. Double-click **tblCustomer** to open the table.

e. Locate the customer with the Customer ID CUO-12 and Last Name Hinton.

f. Click in the **Customer ID** field, and then press ⎯Tab⎯. You are now in Navigation mode, and the First Name field should be highlighted.

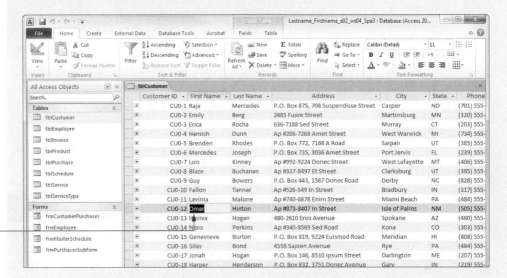

First name highlighted in Navigation mode

Figure 2 Table in navigation mode

g. Continue pressing ⎯Tab⎯ until the Phone field is highlighted. Press ⎯F2⎯ to switch from Navigation mode to Edit mode. Notice the insertion point is at the beginning of the Phone field and the first character is highlighted. Type 5055552923 to enter the new phone number. Because the field is already formatted as a phone number, it is not necessary to enter parentheses or dashes.

h. Press ⎯Tab⎯ to switch to Navigation mode and move to the next field.

i. **Close** ⨉ the tblCustomer table.

Maintain Records in Forms

A form is an object in Access that you can use to enter, edit, or view records in a table. A simple form allows you to see records one at a time rather than as a group in Datasheet view.

When you create a form from two tables that have a one-to-many relationship, the first table selected becomes the **main form** and the second table you select becomes the **subform**. A form with a subform allows you to see one record at a time from the main form and multiple records in Datasheet view from the other related table. Because you only see one record at a time or one record and a datasheet, navigation tools become important when you are working with forms as you cannot see all the records at one time.

Real World Advice | Data Overload!

You may be asked to create a database for someone else that is not familiar with how a database works or even how the computer works. Your role is to make their job as easy as possible so they can get their work done with as few errors as possible.

Looking at a database table with hundreds or thousands of records in Datasheet view can be very intimidating to some people. Trying to keep track of the record or field you are in can be more difficult as the table grows larger and larger. Often seeing one record at a time in a form can eliminate data entry errors and allow the user to focus on the information for that particular record.

Navigate Forms

You navigate records in a form the same way you navigate a table, using the Navigation bar to move from record to record. As a reminder, the Navigation bar has a number of buttons to use for navigation as shown in Figure 3.

Button	Description	What it does
◄	First record	Moves to the first record in the table
►	Last record	Moves to the last record in the table
◄	Previous record	Moves to the record just before the current record
►	Next record	Moves to the record just after the current record
►*	New (blank) record	Moves to a new row to enter a new record

Figure 3   Navigation buttons on the Navigation bar

Navigating a Main Form

Within each record, you can use a combination of Tab, Home, Ctrl, End, and the arrow keys to move from field to field as shown in Figure 4.

Keystroke	What it does
Tab	Moves from field to field within a record; at the last field in a record, it moves you to the first field in the next record
Home	Moves to the first field of the current record
Ctrl+Home	Moves to the first field of the first record of the table
End	Moves to the last field of the current record
Ctrl+End	Moves to the last field of the last record of the table
Arrow keys	Move up or down a field of the current record

Figure 4   Different navigation methods for forms

For this exercise, you will show the spa staff how to navigate the form frmEmployee, which you can use to view employees one record at a time.

To Navigate a Single-Table Form

a. Double-click **frmEmployee** to open the form.

b. Click **Last record** ▶| to go to the last record of the table.

c. Click **First record** |◀ to return to the first record in the table.

d. Click **Next record** ▶ to go to the next record in the table.

e. Click **Previous record** ◀ to go back to the previous record in the table.

f. **Close** × the frmEmployee form.

Navigating a Form with a Subform

When navigating forms with a subform, the Navigation bar buttons at the bottom of the main window are used to navigate the records in the main form, and a second Navigation bar at the bottom of the subform datasheet is used to navigate the records in the subform.

The same navigation keystrokes listed in Figure 4 are still available; however, they work a little differently when a subform is included, as shown in Figure 5.

Keystroke	What it does
Tab	Moves from field to field within a main record. At the last field in a record, it moves to the first field in the subform. At the last record in the subform, it moves to the first field in the next record of the main form.
Home	From the main form, moves to the first field of the current record. From the subform, moves to the first field of the current record in the subform.
Ctrl + Home	From the main form, moves to the first field of the first record. From the subform, moves to the first field of the first record in the subform.
End	From the main form, moves to the last field of the current record in the subform. From the subform, moves to the last field of the current record in the subform.
Ctrl + End	From the main form, moves to the last field of the last record of the subform. From the subform, moves to the last field of the last record of the subform.
Arrow keys	Move up or down a field in the current record in either the form or subform.

Figure 5   Different navigation methods for subforms

For this exercise, you will show the spa staff members how to navigate the form frmCustomerPurchases that shows one customer at a time with all their recent product purchases displayed in a subform.

To Navigate a Multiple-Table Form with a Subform

a. Double-click **frmCustomerPurchases** to open the form.

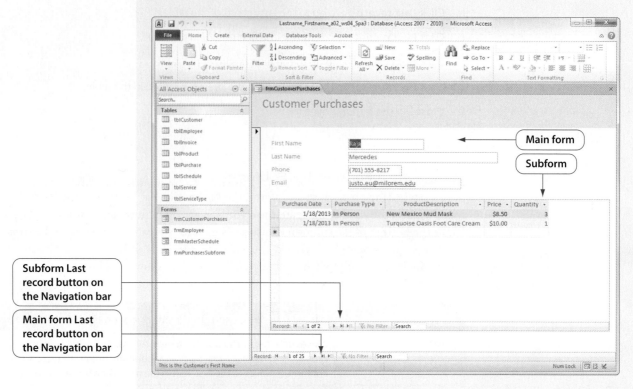

Figure 6 Form with a subform in Datasheet view

b. Click **Last record** ▶| on the subform Navigation bar to highlight the last record in the subform.

c. Click **Last record** ▶| on the main form Navigation bar to go to the last record in the table.

d. Click **Previous record** ◀ repeatedly on the main form to go to record 20 with the customer name Eden Silva.

e. Click **Next record** ▶ in the subform to go to the next record in the subform.

f. **Close** ⊠ the form.

Navigating a Split Form

A **split form** is a form created from one table, but it has a Form view and a Datasheet view in the same window. You can view one record at a time at the top of the window, and see the whole table in Datasheet view at the bottom of the window. This kind of form is helpful when you want to work with one record at a time and still see the big picture in the main table. In a split form, there are buttons on the Navigation bar to move only from record to record, and each record shown at the top is the record highlighted in the datasheet at the same time. You cannot highlight a different record in the form part and the datasheet part at the same time.

For this exercise, you will show the spa staff how to navigate the form frmMasterSchedule, which shows the schedule as a form and a datasheet in the same window.

To Navigate a Split Form

a. Double-click **frmMasterSchedule** to open the form.

b. Click **Last record** ▶ on the Navigation bar to highlight the last record in both the form and the datasheet.

c. Click the record in the datasheet with Schedule ID S046. The record will be highlighted in the datasheet and also shown at the top in Form view.

d. **Close** ⊠ the form.

Use the Find Command with a Form

Finding data in a form is similar to finding data in a datasheet and uses the same Find command. Because you only see one record at a time with a form, using Find can be a quick way to find a record with a specific value in a field and prevents you from having to scroll through all the records in the table one at a time in Form view.

Finding an Exact Match in a Form

When you are looking for a specific value in a field, you are looking for an exact match. For this exercise, a staff member has asked you to search the employee table to find any employees who may live in Las Vegas so they can try to set up a carpool with them. You will show the staff member how to use a form to look for that information.

To Search for an Exact Match

a. Double-click **frmEmployee** to open the form. Press ⎀Tab⎀ to move to the City field in the first record.

b. Click the **Home tab**, and then click **Find** in the Find group to open the Find and Replace dialog box.

c. In the Find What box, type Las Vegas. In the Look In text box, click **Current field**, and then click **Find Next**. Move the Find and Replace dialog box to see all the fields for the current record. The first record with Las Vegas as a value in the City field will be shown.

Figure 7   Find and Replace dialog box

d. Continue to click **Find Next** until Access gives you the message "Microsoft Access finished searching the records. The search item was not found." Click **OK**, and then click **Cancel** to close the Find and Replace dialog box.

e. **Close** ⊠ the form.

We have become accustomed to using tabs in our browsers, and we tend to have many tabs open at one time. In fact, it makes our work more efficient so we do not have to keep opening and closing those windows. Unfortunately, Access does not work the same way. Every time you open an object in Access it opens in a new window with a tab. Those tabs, however, do not work the same way as tabs in our browser. While websites can be updated when they are open in a tab on our desktop, Access objects cannot be updated and saved while they are open. It is therefore a good idea to close an object when you are done working with it, and then reopen it again later when you need it.

Update Table Records Using Forms

Just as you can update data in a datasheet, you can also update data in a form. Remember, a form is just another way to view the data in the table, so when you see a record, you are seeing the record that is actually stored in the table. Nothing is actually stored in the form.

To make changes to data in a form, you must be viewing the form in Form view. You can also add a record to a table using the form. Using the Navigation bar you can go directly to a new record.

Quick Reference   Updating Tables

Data can be edited in tables, queries, or forms. There are advantages and disadvantages to each method. The table below will help you decide the most appropriate place to edit data.

Method	Advantages	Disadvantages	Typical Situation to Use
Tables	All the records and fields are visible in the datasheet.	The number of records and/or fields in the datasheet can be overwhelming.	A user familiar with Access needs to add a record quickly to a smaller table.
Queries	There may be fewer records and/or fields in the datasheet, making the data more manageable. A form can be based on a query rather than a table.	Not being able to see all the records and/or fields, you may inadvertently change related data in the fields you can see. Not all queries are editable, such as aggregate queries.	A user familiar with Access needs to see and modify appointments booked for a particular day.
Forms	Being able to view one record at a time can make the data seem more manageable.	Not all fields may be included in a form. If fields are missing, some data may mistakenly be left out of a record. Provides view of only one record at a time.	A user unfamiliar with Access needs to add data to a large table with many records.

Adding Records

When you add a record to a form, you are actually adding the record to the table it will be stored in. The form will open in Form view, which is the view that allows you to edit the data. Just like in a datasheet, new records are added at the end of the table, which means you must go to a blank record to enter new data. For this exercise, you will use the frmEmployee form to add your name to the list of employees in the tblEmployee table.

To Add a New Record in a Form

a. Double-click **frmEmployee** to open the form. On the Navigation bar, click **New (blank) record** ▶.

New (blank) record button

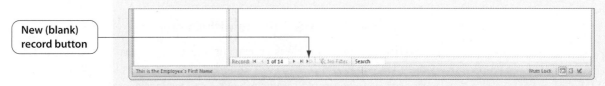

Figure 8 frmEmployee open

b. Type your First Name, Last Name, Address, City, State, and Phone in the new record. **Close** ⨯ the form.

c. Double-click **tblEmployee** to open the table and to see that your record was added. **Close** ⨯ the table.

Editing Records

When you edit a record in a form, you are actually editing the record in the table it is stored in. Changes to data are saved automatically but can be undone while the table or form is open by using the Undo button ↺▾ or by pressing Esc just after the change is made while still in Edit mode.

For this exercise, you are asked to update the tblEmployee table with recent changes. Mary Murphy has recently changed her phone number but it has not been changed in the table yet. You will show the staff how to find her record using a form and update her phone number.

To Edit Records Using a Form

a. Double-click **frmEmployee** to open the form. Press Tab to move to the **Last Name** field. Click the **Home tab**, click **Find** in the Find group, and then in the Find What box type Murphy. Click **Find Next**.

b. When the record for Mary Murphy is displayed, click **Cancel** to close the Find and Replace dialog box, and then press Tab to go to the Phone field. Change Mary's phone number to 5055551289.

c. **Close** ⨯ the form.

Deleting Records

Records can be deleted from a single table without additional steps if the table is not part of a relationship. If the table is part of a relationship, referential integrity has been enforced, and the cascade delete option has not been chosen, a record cannot be deleted if there are related records in another table until those records have also been deleted.

For example, if you want to delete a customer from tblCustomer, and that customer has appointments in tblSchedule, then the appointments for the customer have to be deleted from the tblSchedule before the customer can be deleted from the tblCustomer. This prevents leaving a customer scheduled in one table without the corresponding customer information in another table.

For this exercise, the spa manager would like you to remove Peter Klein from tblEmployee because he has taken a new job and is leaving the spa. You explain to her that if he has any appointments scheduled in tblSchedule those will have to be removed first. She tells you that rather than removing those records she would like to give those appointments to Alex instead. By changing the name to Alex, those appointments will no longer be linked to Peter, and Peter will be able to be deleted from tblEmployee.

CONSIDER THIS | **Delete with Caution**

Deleting records in a table is permanent. Once you confirm a deletion, you cannot use the Undo button. This is very different than programs like Excel or Word. Can you think of ways you could safeguard your data from accidental deletion?

To Delete a Record in a Form

a. Double-click **frmEmployee** to open the form. Click the **Home tab**, click **Find** in the Find group, and then in the Find What box type Peter. Click **Find Next**, and then click **Cancel** to close the Find and Replace dialog box.

b. Click the **Home tab**, click the **Delete arrow** in the Records group, and then click **Delete Record**. Access displays a message saying "The record cannot be deleted or changed because table 'tblSchedule' includes related records." Click **OK**.

c. Double-click **tblSchedule** to open the table. Press Tab to move to the Employee field for the first record. Click the **arrow** next to Peter, and then click **Alex**.

d. Click the **Home tab**, click **Find** in the Find group, and then in the Find What box type Peter. Click **Find Next**. Click the **arrow** next to the name, and then click **Alex**. Click **Find Next**, and then repeat for all three records that have Peter listed as the Employee. Click **Cancel** to close the Find and Replace box.

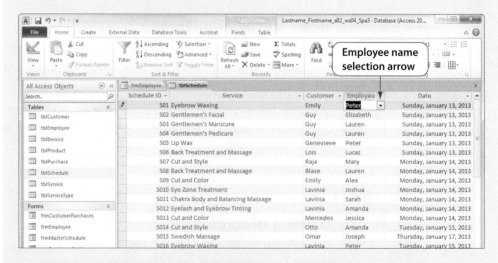

Figure 9 Replacing employee name using selection arrow

e. **Close** ⊠ the table. On the form, make sure the record showing is for Peter. Click the **Home tab**, click the **Delete arrow** in the Records group, and then select **Delete Record**. Click **Yes** to confirm the deletion.

f. **Close** ⊠ the form.

Create a Form Using the Form Wizard

Recall that the Query Wizard walks you through the steps in order to create a query, asking you questions and using your answers to build a query that you can then make changes to if necessary. The Form Wizard works in a similar fashion, walking you through step-by-step to create a form from one or more tables in your database.

Unlike creating a simple form using the Form button on the Create tab, when you create a form using the wizard, it opens automatically in Form view ready for you to enter or edit your records. To make changes to the form, you have to switch to either Layout view or Design view.

Different Form Views

Form view is only for viewing and changing data, so to make any changes to the form you need to switch to either Layout view or Design view. Layout view allows you to make changes to the form while viewing the data at the same time. The effects of your changes can be viewed right away. Design view is a more advanced view that allows you to change the properties or structure of the form. Data is not shown while you are in Design view.

Both Layout view and Design view work with controls. A **control** is a part of a form or report that you use to enter, edit, or display data. There are three kinds of controls: bound, unbound, and calculated. A **bound control** is a control whose data source is a field in the table, such as the customer name. An **unbound control** is a control that does not have a source of data, such as the title of the form. A **calculated control** is a control whose data source is a calculated expression that you create. Every field from the table is made up of two controls: a label and a text box. The text box and label are shown in both the Layout View and the Design View in Figure 10. A **label** may be the name of the field or some other text you manually enter and is an unbound control. A **text box** represents the actual value of a field and is a bound control. When you add a text box to a form, the label is automatically added as well. However, a label can be added independently from a text box.

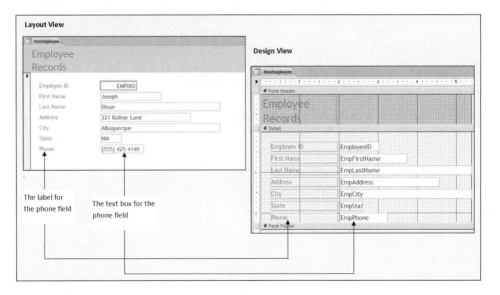

Figure 10 Text box and label controls in Layout view and Design view

For this exercise, the manager of the spa wants the staff to be able to enter and update customer information easily. She thinks it would be much easier to enter data in a form rather than in Datasheet view. You agree with her and offer to help set up the form.

To Create a Single Table Form in Design View

a. Click the **Create tab**, and then click **Form Wizard** in the Forms group. The Form Wizard dialog box opens.

b. Click the **Tables/Queries arrow**, and select **Table: tblCustomer**. Click the **All Fields** button ⟩⟩ to add all the available fields to the Selected Fields box, and then click **Next**.

c. Verify that **Columnar** is selected as the form layout, and then click **Next**.

d. Under **What title do you want for your form?** type frmCustomerInput_initialLastname, replacing initialLastname with your own name. Verify that **Open the form to view or enter information** is selected, and then click **Finish**.

   The form opens in Form view so you can immediately start adding or editing records. The form name is also displayed in the Navigation Pane.

SIDE NOTE
Alternative Method to Add a Label
You can either expand the footer area and then add the label, or you can add the label and the footer will automatically expand to fit what you add.

e. Click the **Home tab**, click the **View arrow** in the Views group, and then click **Design View**. Notice the Form Footer at the bottom of the form window. Click the **Form Design Tools Design tab**, and then click **Label** Aa in the Controls group. Point to the Form Footer area, and then when your mouse pointer changes to ^{+}A, click and drag your pointer to draw a label control wide enough to fit your first initial and last name in the top-left corner of the Form Footer section. In the new label, type your **First Initial** and **Last Name**.

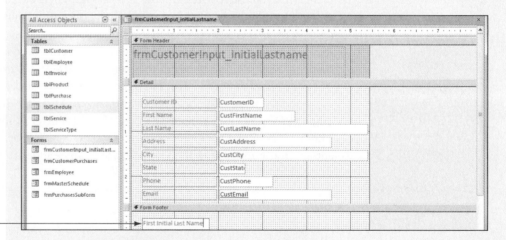

Control added in Form Footer

Figure 11 Form in Design view

f. Click the **Form Design Tools Design tab**, click the **View arrow** in the Views group, and then click **Form View**. Verify that your initial and last name has been entered in the bottom-left corner of the form.

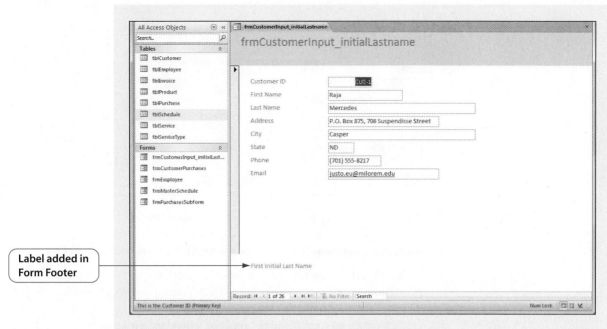

Label added in
Form Footer

Figure 12   Form with first initial and last name added

g. **Close** ☒ the form, and then click **Yes** to save the changes.

Creating Subforms (Multiple-Table Forms)

There may be times when you want to create a form using two tables. Before you can use two tables in a form, you must make sure there is a one-to-many relationship between the tables. Access will automatically use the common field between the tables to create the form.

The main form will display the first table one record at a time just like a single table form. This is the "one" record in the one-to-many relationship. The subform will be displayed as a datasheet below the main form record. This will display the "many" records in the one-to-many relationship.

For this project, you will help the staff create another form that shows each customer in the main form and the customer's scheduled appointments in the subform.

To Create a Subform

a. Click the **Create tab**, and then click **Form Wizard** in the Forms group. The Form Wizard dialog box opens.

b. Click the **Tables/Queries arrow**, and then click **Table: tblCustomer**. Click the **All Fields** button ⟩⟩ to add all the available fields to the Selected Fields list.

c. Click the **Tables/Queries arrow**, and then select **Table: tblSchedule**. Click the **All Fields** button ⟩⟩ to add all the available fields to the Selected Fields list, and then click **Next**.

d. Verify that **by tblCustomer** is selected and that **Form with subform(s)** is selected, and then click **Next**.

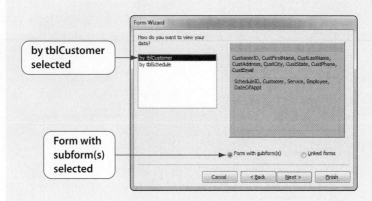

by tblCustomer selected

Form with subform(s) selected

Figure 13   Form options are selected

e. Verify that **Datasheet** is selected for the subform layout, and then click **Next**.

f. Under "What titles do you want for your forms?" in the Form field, type frmCustomerSchedule_initialLastname, replacing initialLastname with your own initial and last name. In the Subform field, type frmCustomerSubform_initialLastname, verify that **Open the form to view or enter information** is selected, and then click **Finish**.

   The form opens in Form view so you can immediately start adding or editing records. The form and subform names are shown in the Navigation Pane.

g. Click the **Home tab**, click the **View arrow** in the Views group, and then click **Design View**. Scroll to the bottom of the form to see the Form Footer. Click the **Form Design Tools Design tab**, click **Label** Aa in the Controls group, and when your mouse pointer changes to ^+_A, click and drag your pointer to draw a label control wide enough to fit your first initial and last name in the top-left corner of the Form Footer section. In the new label, type your First Initial and Last Name.

h. Click the **Form Design Tools Design tab**, click the **View arrow** in the Views group, and then click **Form View**. Verify that your name has been entered in the bottom-left corner of the form.

i. **Close** $\times$ the form, and then click **Yes** to save the changes.

Creating a Split Form

A split form is created from one table and displays each record individually at the top of the window and then again as part of the whole table datasheet in the bottom of the window. This type of form gives you the advantage of seeing each record and the whole table in one place.

For this exercise, the manager would like to see each customer's record individually along with all the records from the customer table. You will show her how to create a split form from the customer table.

To Create a Split Form

a. Click **tblCustomer** one time in the Navigation Pane to select the table, but do not open it.

b. Click the **Create tab**, click **More Forms** in the Forms group, and then select **Split Form**. A window will open with the split form for the customer table.

c. Click the **Form Layout Tools Design tab**, click the **View arrow**, and then click **Design View**. Click **Label** $\boxed{Aa}$ in the Controls group, when your mouse pointer changes to $\boxed{{}^+_A}$, click and drag your pointer to draw a label control wide enough to fit your first initial and last name in the top-left corner of the Form Footer section. In the new label, type your First Initial and Last Name.

d. Click the **Form Design Tools Design tab**, click **View arrow** in the Views group, and then click **Form View**. Verify that your name has been entered in the bottom-left corner of the form.

e. Click **Save** $\boxed{\text{日}}$ on the Quick Access Toolbar, under Form Name type frmCustomerSplit_initialLastname, replacing initialLastname with your own first initial and last name, and then click **OK**. **Close** $\boxed{\times}$ the form.

Customize Forms

While creating a form using the wizard is quick and efficient, there may be times you will want to change how the form looks or add things to the form after you have created it. Formatting, like colors and fonts, can easily be changed. Controls can also be added to a form to include additional fields or labels with text. Pictures and other objects can also be added to a form to make the form more visually appealing.

Modify a Form's Design

Oftentimes, forms are customized to match company or group color themes, or other forms and reports already created by a user. Customizing forms can make them more personal and sometimes easier to use.

Colors, font types, and font sizes are just a few of the formatting changes you can make to an existing form.

Changing the Form Theme

By default, Access uses the Office theme when you create a form using the Form Wizard. Even though there is not a step in the wizard to select a different theme, you can change it once the form has been created. A **theme** is a built-in combination of colors and fonts. By default, a theme will be applied to all objects in a database: forms, reports, tables, and queries. However, you can select to apply a theme to only the object you are working with or to all matching objects. You can also select a theme to be the default theme instead of Office.

Because the form is displayed in Form view, once it is created, the first step is to switch to Layout view to make changes to the form itself. Changing the theme will not only change the colors of the form but also the font type and size and any border colors or object colors added to the form. Once a theme is applied to the form, the colors and fonts can be changed independently of the theme, so you can combine the colors of one theme and a font of another.

For this exercise, the manager of the spa would like to make the customer input form look more like the colors in the spa. You will show her how to change the theme, the colors, and the fonts for the form. The theme will only be applied to the form and not to all the objects.

SIDE NOTE
Point to See

To see the names of each of the themes, point to them to display the ScreenTip. Live Preview will allow you to see what the theme will look like before you apply it to the object. The themes are in alphabetical order.

To Change the Theme of Your Form

a. Double-click **frmCustomerInput_initialLastname** to open the form. Click the **Home tab**, click **View arrow**, and then click **Layout View**.

b. Click the **Form Layout Tools Design tab**, and then click **Themes** in the Themes group to open the Themes gallery. Scroll to find **Solstice** under Built-In themes, right-click the **theme**, and then click **Apply Theme to This Object Only**.

c. Click the **Form Layout Tools Design tab**, and then click **Colors** in the Themes group. Scroll down and click the color scheme **Elemental**.

d. Click the **Form Layout Tools Design tab**, and then click **Fonts** in the Themes group. Scroll down and click the Font theme **Paper**.

New font based on font theme

New header color based on color theme

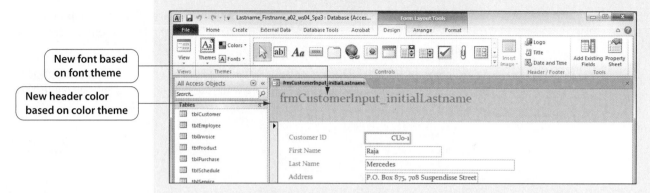

Figure 14   Form with custom formatting

e. Click **Save** 🖫 on the Quick Access Toolbar to save the form.

Saving a Custom Theme

If you put together a combination of fonts and colors you like, you can save that combination as a custom theme. That custom theme can then be used for other objects in Access, like forms, reports, and tables.

For this exercise, you will show the manager how to save the theme from frmCustomerInput_initialLastname as a custom theme so she can apply it to other objects.

To Save a Custom Theme

a. If necessary, double-click **frmCustomerInput_initialLastname** to open the form. Click the **View arrow**, and then select **Layout View**. Click the **Form Layout Tools Design tab**, and then click **Themes** in the Themes group. Click **Save Current Theme**.

b. In the Save Current Theme dialog box, navigate to where you are saving your files and type Lastname_Firstname_a02_ws04_Theme in the File name box, replacing Lastname_Firstname with your own last name. Click **Save**.

c. Click the **Form Layout Tools Design tab**, and then click **Themes** in the Themes group. Point to the second theme shown under the In this Database section of the gallery and notice your saved theme is listed as Solstice used by frmCustomerInput_initialLastname.

d. **Close** ☒ the form.

Real World Advice — Saving Custom Themes

By default, all themes are saved in the Document Themes folder (C:\Users\ username\AppData\Roaming\Microsoft\Templates\Document Themes). If you save a custom theme in the default folder, then it will appear as a custom theme in the Themes gallery. If you save the theme in a different folder, you can select Browse for Themes and look for the saved theme in your Documents folder. You can change where you save the theme, but if another person wants to use that theme for one of their documents, they may not be able to find it if it is saved somewhere other than the default folder. One purpose of saving themes is to have them available for a unified look among various documents, and because you may not be the person creating all the documents, you may want to save the theme somewhere that everyone can find it.

Applying a Custom Theme

If a custom theme is applied to only one object when it is created and saved, then it can be applied to other objects in the database at another time. If **Apply Theme to This Object Only** is not selected when applying the theme to a new object, then the theme will be applied to all objects in the database.

For this exercise, you will show the manager how to apply the theme from frmCustomerInput_initialLastname to the other objects in the database.

To Apply a Saved Theme to All Objects

a. Double-click **frmCustomerPurchases** to open the form. Click the **Home tab**, click the **View arrow**, and then select **Layout View**. Click the **Form Layout Tools Design tab**, click **Themes** in the Themes group, and then select **Solstice used by frmCustomerInput_ initialLastname**.

b. **Close** ☒ the form. Double-click **frmEmployee** to open the form. Notice the Theme is Solstice used by frmCustomerInput_initialLastname.

c. **Close** ☒ the form.

Resizing and Changing Controls

Controls can be resized to make the form more user friendly. When you create a form using the wizard, the order that you choose the fields in the wizard step is the order the fields are added to the form. Once the form is created, you may decide the fields should be in a different order. When you click on a control in Layout view, an orange border appears around the control. When you select a subform control, an orange border appears around the control and a layout selector appears in the top-left corner. The **layout selector** allows you to move the whole table at one time. Once the control is selected you can move it or resize it. You can also change its appearance by adding borders or fill color.

For the following exercise, you will work with the spa staff to rearrange the controls on the Customer Schedule form to make it easier for data entry.

SIDE NOTE
Selecting Different Controls

There are two controls for each field—the label and the text box. The name of the field shows in the label, while the value of the field shows in the text box.

SIDE NOTE
Limited Visibility

If you cannot see the whole subform, use the scroll arrow on the right side of the window to scroll down the form.

To Change Controls on a Form

a. Double-click **frmCustomerSchedule_initialLastname** to open it.

b. Click the **Home tab**, click **View**, and then click **Layout View**. Click the **Last Name** text box and an orange border appears around the control. Point to the right border of the control and drag it to the left so it lines up with the right border of the First Name text box above.

c. Click the **Address** text box, and then drag the right border to the right until it lines up with the right border of the City text box below.

d. Use the scroll bar on the Navigation bar of the subform to scroll to the right to see all the fields. Resize each column to best fit the data. Drag the right border of the subform to the right so that all fields are visible.

e. Double-click the **form title**, select the existing text, which by default is the name of the form, and type Customer Schedule. Press Enter when you are done typing.

f. Click the **Customer ID** label, press and hold Shift, and then click the **Customer ID** text box to select both controls. Press Delete to delete both controls from the form.

g. Click the subform label **frmCustomer**, and then press Delete to delete it from the form.

h. Click the **Phone** label, hold down Shift, click the **Phone** text box, the **Email** label, and the **Email** text box.

i. Point to any of the selected controls. When the mouse pointer changes to 🔲, drag all four controls up and to the right until they are right next to the First Name and Last Name controls.

j. Click the **subform** datasheet to select it. Click the **Layout Selector** ⊞, and then drag it up and to the left so it is just under the State controls.

k. Click the **title** of the form to select it. Click the **Home tab**, click **Bold** 🅱 in the Text Formatting group, click the **Font size arrow** 11 ▾ in the Text Formatting group, and then select **28**.

l. Click the **First Name** text box, hold down Shift, and then click the **Last Name** text box. Click the **Home tab**, and then click **Bold** 🅱 in the Text Formatting group.

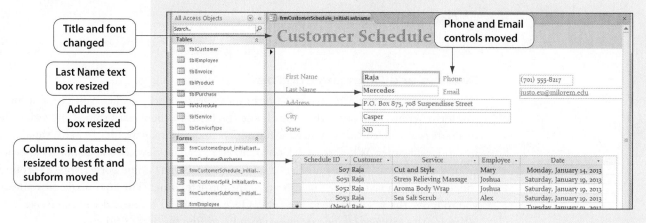

Title and font changed

Last Name text box resized

Address text box resized

Columns in datasheet resized to best fit and subform moved

Phone and Email controls moved

Figure 15 Formatted form and subform

m. Click **Save** 💾 on the Quick Access Toolbar to save the form.

Adding a Picture to the Form

Pictures can be added to forms to make them more appealing. When a picture is added to a form, then the same picture will appear for every record in the table. A different picture cannot be added for each record. A picture can be inserted in the header, footer, or the detail area of the form where the record values are shown. For this exercise you will insert a picture in the detail area of the form to make it more personal for the spa.

To Insert a Picture on the Form

a. Click the **Home tab**, click the **View arrow**, and then click **Layout View**. Click in a blank area of the detail area of the form to select it. If a text box or label is selected, then the Insert Image button will not be available to use.

b. Click the **Form Layout Tools Design tab**, click **Insert Image** in the Controls group, and then click **Browse**.

c. In the Insert Picture dialog box, navigate to where your student files are located, click **a02_ws04_Spa_Image**, and click **OK**. With the image control pointer, click in the form detail to insert the picture. Click the **Layout Selector** and move the picture under the Email text box. With the top-left corner of the picture under the left border of the Email text box, point to the bottom-right corner of the picture and drag the corner until the picture fits between the Email text box and the subform.

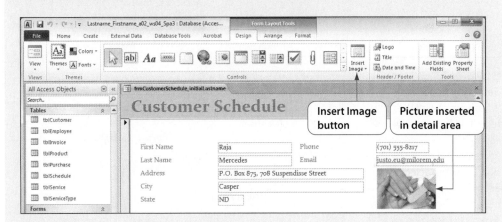

Figure 16 Picture inserted in detail area.

d. **Close** ⊠ the form and click **Yes** to save the changes.

Print Forms

Not only can you see one record at a time using a form, but you can also print one record at a time. Printing a form can be useful if you need only one record's information, or if you want to use a form for other people to manually fill in the information.

Printing a Record from a Form

For this project, the spa manager would like you to print a record for a particular customer from the customer form. You will show her how to preview the form first and then send it to the printer.

To Preview and Print a Record from a Form

a. Double-click **frmCustomerInput_initialLastname** to open it. Click the **Home tab**, click the **View arrow**, and then click **Layout View**.

b. Double-click the **title**, select the **text**, and change it to Customer Record.

c. Click the **Address** text box, and then drag the right border to the right until it is lined up with the Last Name and City text boxes.

d. Click the **File tab**, click **Print**, and then click **Print Preview**. Notice all the records will print in Form view.

e. Click **Last Page** ▶| on the Navigation bar to go to the last record. Notice in the Navigation bar that the number of pages for the printed report will be seven.

f. Click the **Print Preview tab**, and then click **Close Print Preview** in the Close Preview group.

g. Using the Navigation bar, advance through the customer records to find the record for Jonah Hogan.

h. Click the **File tab**, select **Print**, and then click **Print**. In the Print dialog box, in the Print Range section, click **Selected Record(s)**. Click **OK** to print the record if instructed to do so.

SIDE NOTE
Selecting Records

When you view all the records in Print Preview, you cannot choose Selected Record(s) in the Print dialog box. To choose Selected Record(s) you must have one record showing in Form view when you click Print.

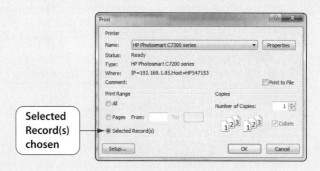

Selected Record(s) chosen

Figure 17 Print one record as a form

i. **Close** ☒ the form, and click **Yes** to save the changes.

Use the Report Wizard

While a report and a form may look similar, a form is a method for data entry and a report is a formatted printout of that data. A report can be created from either a table or a query. Reports may be based on multiple tables in a one-to-many relationship using a common field to match the records. The "one" record from the first table in the relationship will be shown first (similar to a main form), while the "many" records from the second table will be displayed as detailed records in the **subreport** (similar to a subform).

Create a Report Using the Report Wizard

The Report Wizard will walk you through step by step to build your report. You will choose the table or query to base the report on, and choose the fields to include in the report. You will have the option to group the data in your report. A **group** is a collection of records along with introductory and summary information about the records. Grouping allows you to separate related records for the purpose of creating a visual summary of the data. Groups can be created with data from individual tables or from multiple tables.

For example, a report grouped by the primary table containing customer records would show all the selected fields for a customer, and then would list that customer's individual appointments from the secondary table below the customer's record.

Within a report you can also sort using up to four fields in either ascending or descending order. Once a report is created using the wizard, it will open in Print Preview. Print Preview provides a view of the report representing how it will look when it is actually printed and provides you with printing options such as orientation, margins, and size. The current date and page numbers are added, and you can navigate the report in this view using the Navigation bar. To make any changes to the report, you can switch to Layout view using the View button.

Creating a Single Table Report

A report can be created using one table or multiple tables. A single table report is a report created from one table. Any or all of the fields can be selected, and the report can be created from a table or query. For this project, the spa manager would like to have a report to help the staff with scheduling. The report will be a list of employee names and phone numbers so the staff can contact each other if necessary.

To Create a Single Table Report Using Report Wizard

a. Click the **Create tab**, and then click **Report Wizard** in the Reports group.

b. Click the **Tables/Queries arrow**, and then select **tblEmployee**.

c. Double-click **EmpFirstName**, **EmpLastName**, and **EmpPhone** from the Available Fields list. Click **Next**.

d. You will not add any grouping levels to this report, so click **Next**.

e. Click the **Sort arrow**, select **EmpLastName**, and then click **Next**.

f. Verify that **Tabular** layout and **Portrait** orientation are selected, as well as **Adjust the field width so all fields fit on a page**. Click **Next**.

g. Under "What title do you want for your report?", type rptEmployeeList_initialLastname, replacing initiallastname with your own first initial and last name, and then click **Finish**.

h. Click the **Print Preview tab**, and then click **Close Print Preview** in the Close Preview group. Click the **Report Design Tools Design tab**, click **Label** $\boxed{Aa}$ in the Controls group, and then when your mouse pointer changes to $\boxed{{}^+_A}$, click and drag your pointer to draw a label control wide enough to fit your first initial and last name in the top-left corner of the Report Footer section. In the new label, type your First Initial and Last Name.

i. Click the **Report Design Tools Design tab**, click the **View arrow** in the Views group, and then click **Report View**. Verify that your name has been entered in the bottom-left corner of the report.

j. **Close** $\boxed{\times}$ the report, and then click **Yes** to save the changes.

Creating a Multiple Table Report

Similar to other objects created using more than one table, a multiple-table report must use tables that have a common field. The first table chosen for the report becomes the primary table, and the next and subsequent tables chosen become the secondary tables.

In this exercise, the manager would like a report that will show each employee's name and their upcoming appointments. This way the staff members can help coordinate their services for a guest who may be seeing more than one staff member in a day.

SIDE NOTE
It Is a Matter of Order
The order you add the fields in the Report Wizard is the order the fields will appear on the report.

To Create a Multiple Table Report Using Report Wizard

a. Click the **Create tab**, and then click **Report Wizard** in the Reports group.

b. Click the **Tables/Queries arrow**, and then select **Table: tblEmployee**. Double-click **EmpFirstName** and **EmpLastName** in the Available Fields list.

c. Click the **Tables/Queries arrow**, and then select **Table: tblSchedule**. Double-click **Service, DateOfAppt**, and **Customer** from the Available Fields list. Click **Next**.

d. Verify that **by tblEmployee** is highlighted to view the data by Employee, and then click **Next**.

e. Double-click **DateOfAppt** to group by the date. Click **Grouping Options**, and then under Grouping intervals, select **Normal**. Click **OK**, and then click **Next**.

f. Click the **Sort arrow**, select **Customer**, and then click **Next**.

g. Verify that **Stepped** is selected under Layout, and then click **Landscape** under Orientation. Verify that **Adjust the field width so all fields fit on a page** is checked. Click **Next**.

h. Under "What title do you want for your report?", type rptEmployeeSchedule_initialLastname, replacing initialLastname with your own first initial and last name, and then click **Finish**. The report will open in Print Preview.

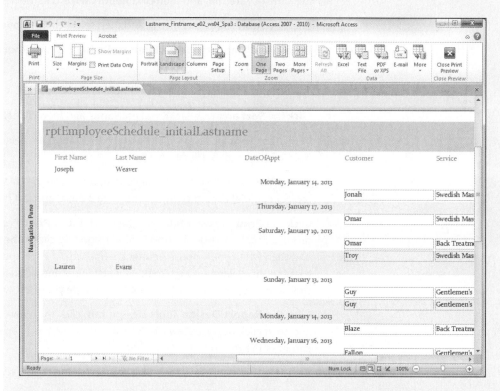

Figure 18 Report open in Print Preview

i. Click the **Print Preview tab**, and then click **Close Print Preview** in the Close Preview group. You should see the report in Design view.

j. Click the **Report Design Tools Design tab**, click **Label** $\boxed{Aa}$ in the Controls group, and then when your mouse pointer changes to $\boxed{{}^+_A}$ click and drag your pointer to draw a label control wide enough to fit your initial and last name in the top-left corner of the Report Footer section. In the new label, type your First Initial and Last Name.

k. Click the **Report Design Tools Design tab**, click the **View arrow**, and then click **Report View**. Verify that your name has been entered in the bottom-left corner of the report.

l. **Close** $\boxed{\times}$ the report, and then click **Yes** to save the changes.

Looking at Different Report Views

You have seen a report in Print Preview when the Report Wizard is done creating the report, which is the view that shows you exactly what the report will look like when it is printed. Print Preview adds the current date and page numbers in the page footer at the bottom of each page. Each type of view has its own features as shown in Figure 19.

View name	What the view is used for
Print Preview	Shows what the printed report will look like
Layout view	Allows you to modify the report while seeing the data
Report view	Allows you to filter data, or copy parts of the report to the Clipboard
Design view	Allows you to change more details of the report design, or add other controls that are only available in Design view

Figure 19 Different view options for a report

In the following exercises, you will show the spa staff members what a report looks like in the different views and how to switch from one view to another. This will be helpful in case they are trying to work on a report and click on a view that they have not worked with in the past.

Looking at Layout View

Layout view allows you to change basic design features of the report while the report is displaying data so the changes you make are immediately visible. You can resize controls, add conditional formatting, and change or add titles and other objects to the report in Layout view. In this exercise, you will view a report in Layout view.

To Look at a Report in Layout View

a. Double-click **rptEmployeeSchedule_initialLastname** to open it.

b. Click the **Home tab**, click the **View arrow** in the Views group, and then click **Layout View**. Notice the orange border around the first Customer field.

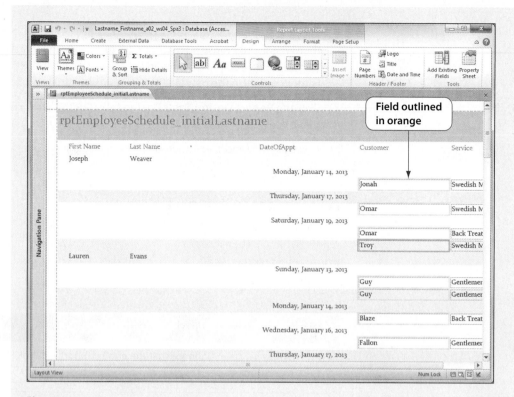

Figure 20   Report in Layout view

SIDE NOTE
Page Numbers

Notice that the date and page number are in the page footer, but the page number shows Page 1 of 1. The actual number of pages will not be calculated until you switch to Print Preview.

c.   Scroll to the bottom of the report.

Looking at Report View

Report view provides an interactive view of your report. In Report view, you can filter records or you can copy data to the Clipboard. There will be no page breaks shown in Report view, so the number of pages at the bottom will show Page 1 of 1. In this exercise, you will just look at the report in Report view.

To Look at a Report in Report View

a.   Click the **Report Design Tools Design tab**, click the **View arrow** in the Views group, and then click **Report View**.

b.   Scroll to the bottom of the report.

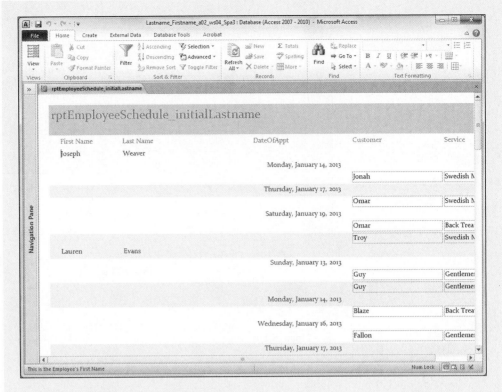

Figure 21 Report in Report view

Looking at Design View

Design view offers more options for adding and editing controls on a report, as well as options not available in any of the other views. In this exercise, you will look at a report in Design view.

To Look at a Report in Design View

a. Click the **Home tab**, click the **View arrow** in the Views group, and then click **Design View**. Data in Design view is not visible; only the controls in each section of the report are.

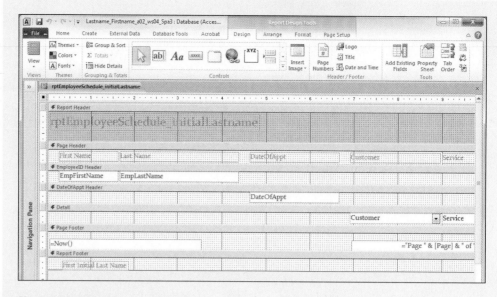

Figure 22   Report in Design view

b. **Close** ☒ the report.

Customize a Report

Reports created by the wizard can be easily customized after they have been created and saved. Themes can be applied to just the report or the whole database to change the colors, fonts, or both. Controls, bound and unbound, can be added or modified on the report to make room for more information or to rearrange the information already there.

In order to break a report into smaller sections, subtotals or groups may be added. Additional sorting options may also be applied or modified.

Conditional formatting may also be applied in order to highlight fields that meet certain criteria.

Use and Customize Access Themes

By default, Access uses the Office theme when you create a report using the Report Wizard just like when you create a form with the Form Wizard. However, even though there is not a step in the wizard to select a different theme, you can change it once the report has been created.

Applying a Theme

Changing the theme will not only change the colors of the report, but also the font type, size, and any border colors or object colors added to the report. Once a theme is applied to the report, the colors and fonts can be changed independently of the theme, so you can combine the colors of one theme and a font of another.

As you recall, by default, a theme will be applied to all objects in a database: forms, reports, tables, and queries. However, you can select to apply a theme to only the object you are working with or to all matching objects. For the following exercise, you will change the theme of the Employee schedule report.

To Apply a New Theme to the Report Only

a. Double-click **rptEmployeeSchedule_initialLastname** to open it. Click the **Home tab**, click the **View arrow** in the Views group, and then click **Layout View**.

b. Click the **Themes arrow** in the Themes group, right-click **Composite**, and then click **Apply Theme to This Object Only**. The Theme should only be applied to the report and no other objects in the database.

c. **Close** ☒ the report.

Modify a Report's Design

Controls, as defined in the section on forms, are also used in reports. A control can be a text box or another object that has been added to the form, either by the wizard or manually in Layout or Design view.

Moving, Resizing, and Formatting Report Controls

Controls can be moved or resized to make the report more readable. When you create a report using the wizard, the order that you choose the fields in the wizard step is the order the fields are added to the report. Once the report is created, you may decide that the fields should be in a different order. When you click on a control in Layout view, an orange border appears around the control. Once the control is selected you can move it or resize it. You can also change its appearance by adding borders or fill color.

For this exercise, you will change the rptEmployeeSchedule schedule report to make it look more like what the manager expected. You will move the date, service, and customer name fields below the employee name, change the title, and change the formatting.

To Move, Resize, and Format a Control in a Report

a. Double-click **rptEmployeeSchedule_initialLastname** to open it. Click the **Home tab**, click the **View arrow** in the Views group, and then click **Layout View**.

b. Click the **DateOfAppt** text box control to select it, and then drag the field to the left so it is just slightly indented under the employee name. If necessary, drag the right border of the control to make the whole date visible.

c. Click the **First Name** label, press and hold ⇧Shift, click the **Last Name** label and the **DateofAppt** label, and then press Delete.

d. Click the **Customer label**, press and hold ⇧Shift, and then click the **Customer** text box, the **Service label**, and the **Service** text box. Point and click on any field to drag all the controls to the left, just next to the date field.

e. Click the **Service** text box. Drag the right border of the text box to the right to fit all the service description. Scroll to the bottom of the report to make sure the longest service description is visible. Click the **Service label**, and then press Delete.

f. Click the **Service** text box, press and hold ⇧Shift, and then click the **Customer** text box. Click the **Report Layout Tools Format tab**, click **Shape Outline** in the Control Formatting group, and then select **Transparent**.

g. Click the **First Name** text box, press and hold ⇧Shift, and then click the **Last Name** text box. Click the **Report Layout Tools Format tab**, click **Shape Fill** in the Control Formatting group, and then select **Light Blue 3** under Standard colors. Click **Bold** B in the Font group.

h. Double-click the **title**, select the **text**, type Employee Schedule, and then press Enter.

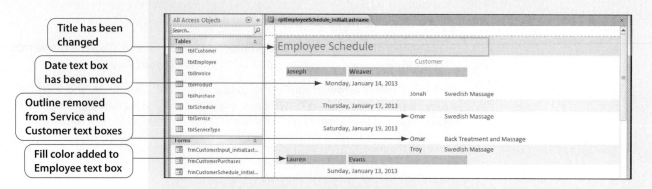

Title has been changed

Date text box has been moved

Outline removed from Service and Customer text boxes

Fill color added to Employee text box

Figure 23 Formatted report in Layout view

i. **Close** ⊠ the report, and then click **Yes** to save the changes.

Enhancing a Report with Conditional Formatting

In the previous section, you changed the colors and fonts of fields. You can also change the fonts and colors of fields only when certain conditions are met in the field. This is called **conditional formatting**. If a field value meets the conditions you specify, then the formatting will be applied. This is a useful tool to automatically highlight sales numbers on a report if they meet a certain threshold, or to highlight students, grades when they exceed a certain limit.

To apply conditional formatting, you must select the field value in the field to which you want the formatting applied. You can select a different font color and font effects for the formatting.

For this exercise, the spa manager would like you to create a report and apply conditional formatting to all services currently scheduled that are over $100. These customers usually get some special treatments like complimentary coffee and tea, and the staff would like to be able to easily see which customers will get this service.

To Apply Conditional Formatting to a Report Field

a. Click the **Create tab**, and then click **Report Wizard** in the Reports group.

b. Click the **Tables/Queries arrow**, and then select **Table: tblSchedule**. Double-click **DateOfAppt**, **Customer**, and **Service** in the Available Fields list.

c. Click the **Tables/Queries arrow**, and then select **Table: tblService**. Double-click **Fee** from the Available Fields list, and then click **Next**.

d. Verify that **by tblSchedule** is highlighted, and then click **Next**. You will not add any grouping to this report, so click **Next**.

e. Click the **Sort arrow**, click **DateofAppt**, and then click **Next**. Verify that **Tabular** is selected under Layout and **Portrait** under Orientation. Verify that **Adjust the field width so all fields fit on a page** is checked. Click **Next**.

f. Under "What title do you want for your report?", type rptHighFees_initialLastname, replacing initialLastname with your first initial and last name, and then click **Finish**. The report will open in Print Preview.

g. Click the **Print Preview tab**, and then click **Close Print Preview**. Click the **Home tab**, click the **View arrow** in the Views group, and then select **Layout View**.

h. Double-click the **title**, select the **text**, type High Service Customers, and press Enter.

i. Click in the **Fee** text box, click the **Report Layout Tools Format tab**, and then click **Conditional Formatting** in the Control Formatting group.

j. Click **New Rule**. Verify that **Check values in the current record or use an expression** is highlighted. Find the three condition text boxes. The first should display **Field Value Is**. Click in the second condition box and select **greater than**. In the third condition text box, type 100.

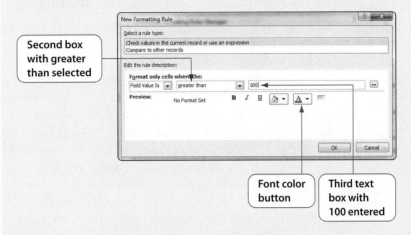

Figure 24 New Formatting Rule dialog box

k. Below the condition text boxes, select the formatting. Click **Bold** B, click the **Font color arrow**, and then click **Dark Red**. Click **OK**, verify that your rule states Value >100, and then click **OK**.

All values greater than $100 in the Fee field should be bold and highlighted in dark red.

l. Click the **Home tab**, click the **View arrow** in the Views group, and then click **Design View**. Click the **Report Design Tools Design tab**, click **Label** Aa in the Controls group, and when your mouse pointer changes to ⁺A, click and drag your pointer to draw a label control wide enough to fit your name in the top-left corner of the Report Footer section. In the new label, type your First Initial and Last Name.

m. Click the **Report Design Tools Design tab**, click the **View arrow**, and then click **Report View**. Verify that your name has been entered in the bottom-left corner of the report.

n. Scroll through the report to make sure all your data is visible. Click the **Home tab**, click the **View arrow**, and then click **Layout View**. If necessary, resize and move text boxes so all data can be seen.

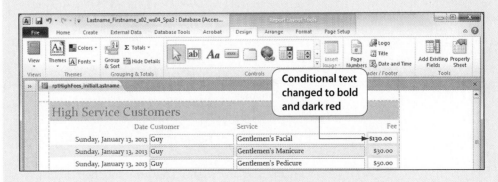

Figure 25 Report with resized fields and conditional formatting applied

---

SIDE NOTE

Delete Conditional Formatting

You can delete a conditional formatting rule by clicking the Report Layout Tools Format tab in Layout view, click the field that has the conditional formatting applied, click Conditional Formatting in the Control Formatting group, and then click the rule you wish to delete and click Delete Rule.

Troubleshooting

If the DateOfAppt text box shows ######## instead of the date, the field is not wide enough to display the whole date. Switch to Layout view, click the DateOfAppt text box, and drag the right border to the right to make the control wider. Then move and resize other text box controls as needed.

o. **Close** ⊠ the report, and then click **Yes** to save the changes.

Applying Grouping and Sorting

The Report Wizard gives you the opportunity to sort and group records, but sometimes seeing the report changes your mind about what and how to group and sort. You can change the sorting and grouping options from either Layout or Design view. Groups are added to a section of the report called the **group header**. Calculations performed on a group in a report are added to a section called the **group footer**. A report may have one or more group headers, group footers, both, or neither.

In Layout view, you will use the Group, Sort, and Total pane to select the sort fields and grouping fields for a report. This is done after the report has been created by the Report Wizard.

For this exercise, the spa manager would like a report that shows appointment dates and services scheduled for those dates. You will show her how to create the report, and then you will make some changes to it until she likes how the information is presented.

To Add Group and Sort Fields to a New Report

a. Click the **Create tab**, and then click **Report Wizard** in the Reports group.

b. Click the **Tables/Queries arrow**, and then select **Table: tblSchedule**. Double-click **DateOfAppt**, **Service**, **Customer**, and **Employee** from the Available Fields list. Click **Next**.

c. Click the **One Field Back** button ⟨ to remove the Service grouping level. Click **DateOfAppt**, and then click the **One Field** button ⟩ to add the date as a grouping level. Click **Grouping Options**, and then under Grouping intervals select **Normal**. Click **OK**, and then click **Next**.

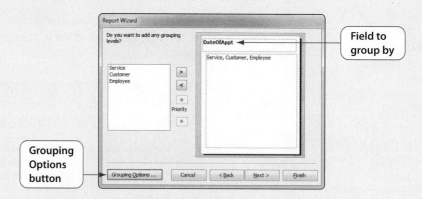

Figure 26   Report Wizard grouping step

d. Click the **Sort arrow**, select **Service**, and then click **Next**.

e. Select **Stepped** layout and **Portrait** orientation. Verify that **Adjust the field width so all fields fit on a page** is selected. Click **Next**.

f. Under "What title do you want for your report?", type **rptAppointments_initialLastname** replacing initialLastname with your own first initial and last name, and then click **Finish**. Click the **Print Preview tab**, and then click **Close Print Preview**.

g. Click the **Report Design Tools Design tab**, click **Label** $\boxed{Aa}$ in the Controls group, and then when your mouse pointer changes to $\boxed{^{+}_{A}}$, click and drag your pointer to draw a label control wide enough to fit your name in the top-left corner of the Report Footer section. Click in the new label you just added, and then type your First Initial and Last Name.

h. Click the **Report Design Tools Design tab**, click the **View arrow** in the Views group, and then click **Report View**. Verify that your name has been entered in the bottom-left corner of the report.

i. Click the **Home tab**, click the **View arrow** in the Views group, and then click **Layout View**. Click the **DateOfAppt** text box, click the **Report Layout Tools Format tab**, and then click **Align Text Left** $\boxed{\equiv}$ in the Font group. Drag the right border of the **DateOfAppt** text box to line up with the left border of the Service text box. All the date values should be visible.

j. Click the **Service** text field, and then drag the left border to the left to make the control wider so all the text can be displayed. Scroll down to the appointments scheduled on Friday, January 18, 2013, and then confirm that the Microdermabrasion Treatment (6 sessions) is showing.

k. Double-click the **title**, select the text, and then type Daily Appointments.

l. Click the **Report Layout Tools Design tab**, click **Group & Sort** in the Grouping & Totals group, and notice the Group, Sort, and Total pane that opens at the bottom of the report.

m. Click on the line that displays **Sort by Service**, and then click **Delete** $\boxed{X}$ on the far right of the line. This will delete the sort that was added in the Report Wizard.

n. Click **Add a group** in the Group, Sort, and Total pane, and then select **Employee**.

o. Click the **Employee** text box, and then drag it to the left until it is under the month name in the date. Click the **Employee** label, press and hold $\boxed{Shift}$, click the **DateOfAppt** label, and then press $\boxed{Delete}$.

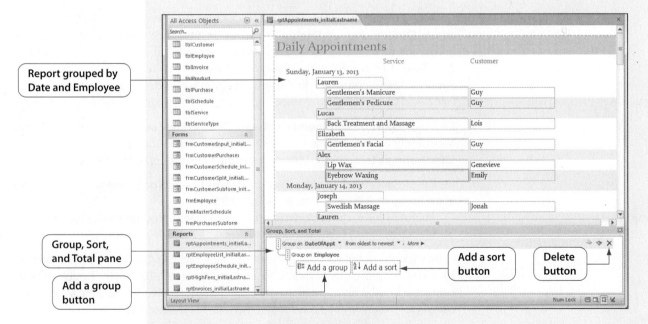

Report grouped by Date and Employee

Group, Sort, and Total pane

Add a group button

Add a sort button

Delete button

Figure 27   New grouping added to report

p. **Close** ⊠ the Group, Sort, and Total pane. **Close** ☒ the report, and then click **Yes** to save the changes.

Adding Subtotals

Subtotals can be added to a report to calculate totals for smaller groups of records. In Layout view, the subtotal is added in the Group, Sort, and Total pane when selecting or modifying groups and sorts for the reports.

For this exercise, the spa manager would like a report that shows all invoices grouped by date and subtotaled for each date.

To Add Subtotals to a Report

a. Click the **Create tab**, and then click **Report Wizard** in the Reports group.

b. Click the **Tables/Queries arrow**, and then select **Table: tblInvoice**. Double-click **InvoiceDate**, **CustomerID**, **InvoiceNumber**, and **InvoiceTotal** from the Available fields list. Click **Next**.

SIDE NOTE
Alternate Method
Another way to add a field to the grouping levels is to double-click it.

c. Click the **One Field Back** button ⌊ < ⌋ to remove the CustomerID grouping level. Click **InvoiceDate**, and then click the **One Field** button ⌊ > ⌋ to add the date as a grouping level. Click **Grouping Options**, and then under Grouping intervals select **Normal**. Click **OK**, and then click **Next**.

d. Click the **Sort arrow**, select **CustomerID**, click the second **Sort arrow**, select **InvoiceNumber**, and then click **Next**.

e. Select **Stepped** layout and **Portrait** orientation. Verify that **Adjust the field width so all fields fit on a page** is selected. Click **Next**.

f. Under "What title do you want for your report?", type rptInvoices_initialLastname, replacing initialLastname with your first initial and last name, and then click **Finish**.

g. Click the **Print Preview tab**, and then click **Close Print Preview** in the Close Preview group. Click the **Report Design Tools Design tab**, click **Label** ⌊Aa⌋ in the Controls group, and then when your mouse pointer changes to ⌊⁺A⌋, click and drag your pointer to draw a label control wide enough to fit your name in the top-left corner of the Report Footer section. Click in the new label you just added, and then type your First Initial and Last Name.

h. Click the **Report Design Tools Design tab**, click the **View arrow**, and then click **Report View**. Verify that your name has been entered in the bottom-left corner of the report. Click the **Home tab**, click the **View arrow** in the Views group, and then click **Layout View**.

i. Click the **InvoiceTotal** text box. Click the **Report Layout Tools Design tab**, click **Totals** in the Grouping & Totals group, and then click **Sum**.

Subtotals for each InvoiceDate group will show under the InvoiceTotal details. A grand total will show at the bottom of the report.

j. Right-click one of the subtotal controls, and then click **Set Caption**. A control label will be added next to each subtotal amount that says InvoiceTotal Total. Double-click the **control**, select the **text**, and then type Invoice Subtotal. Repeat the same steps to set a caption for the grand total control, and then change the text to Invoice Total.

Totals button

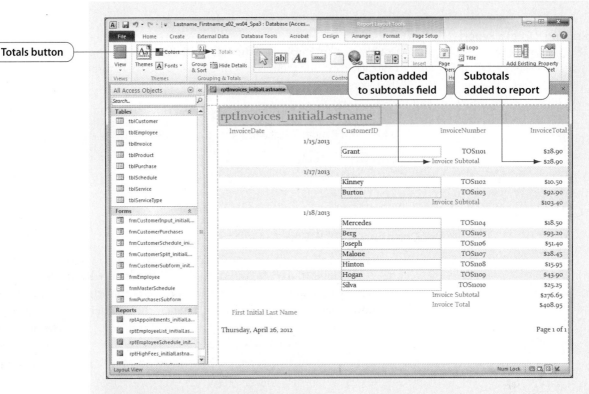

Figure 28   Report with subtotals added

k.   Double-click the **title**, select the **text**, and then type Invoice Amounts. **Close** ✕ the report, and then click **Yes** to save the changes.

Print and Save a Report as a PDF File

Reports are formatted printable documents of your data, so the final result of a report will usually be a printout. If not printed, then the report may be shared with other people electronically. When you send a report to someone electronically, they have to have the same program in which the report was created in order to open the report. To avoid this problem, you can save a report as a PDF file, which can be read by Adobe Reader, a free program that you can download from the Internet.

Printing a Report

To print a report, you will access the Print dialog box from the File tab to select your printing options. Before you print, it is always a good idea to view the report in Print Preview to make sure it looks the way you want. Viewing the report in Layout view and Report view does not show you page breaks and other features of the report as it will look when actually printed. In Print Preview, you have many options to make design changes to your report before you send it to the printer. You can change the margins and orientation, and you can select how many pages, if not all, you want to print.

For this exercise, you will show the staff members how to print the employee schedule report so they can hang it up in the break room.

SIDE NOTE
Print Options
The Print dialog box allows you to print the whole report or a range of pages in the report.

To Print a Report

a. Double-click **rptEmployeeSchedule_initialLastname** to open the report. Click the **File tab**, click **Print**, and then select **Print Preview**. Navigate through the pages to make sure the records fit on the pages correctly.

b. Click the **Print Preview tab**, and then click **Print** in the Print group.

c. Under Print Range, select **All**, and then click **OK**.

d. **Close** [×] the report.

Creating a PDF File

If you need to distribute the report electronically, you also have the option to save the report as an Adobe PDF file. An **Adobe PDF file** is usually smaller than the original document, easy to send through e-mail, and preserves the original document look and feel so you know exactly what it will look like when the recipient opens it. For this exercise, you will show the staff how to create a PDF file of the employee schedule so it can easily be e-mailed to the staff each week. The correct terminology for saving a report as a PDF file format is to "publish" the report. When you are saving the report as a PDF you will see the option to Publish, not to Save or Print.

To Save a Report as a PDF File

a. Double-click **rptEmployeeSchedule_initialLastname** to open the report. Click the **File tab**, and then click **Save & Publish**.

b. Click **Save Object As**. Under Database File Types on the right, click **PDF or XPS**. Click **Save As**.

c. In the Publish as PDF or XPS dialog box, locate the folder where you are saving your files, and in the File name box type Lastname_Firstname_a02_ws04_pdfEmployeeSchedule, replacing Lastname_Firstname with your first name and last name. Click **Publish**.

d. The report will open as a PDF file in Adobe Reader. **Close** [×] Adobe Reader to return to Access. **Close** [×] the report, and then **Close** [⊠] Access.

Concept Check

1. What is the difference in editing and entering data in a form versus a table? When is it better to enter data in a form? When is it better to enter data directly in a table? What about a query? Are there times when editing data in a query can be useful?

2. What is the difference between a main form and a subform? What is a split form? When would you use each of these?

3. What view will you see when the Form Wizard is done creating the form? What is the difference between Layout view, Form view, and Design view?

4. What are controls? What is the difference between a label control and a text box control?

5. What is the difference between sorting and grouping in a report?

6. What is the difference between Report view, Print Preview, Layout view, and Design view when you are creating a report? Which view will show you the most accurate picture of what your printed report will look like?

7. What is conditional formatting, and when would you use it?

8. What is a PDF file, and why would you want to save your report as a PDF? What software do you need to read a PDF file? How can you get this software?

Key Terms

Adobe PDF file 664
Bound control 641
Calculated control 641
Conditional formatting 658
Control 641
Edit mode 632
Group 650

Group footer 660
Group header 660
Label 641
Layout selector 647
Main form 633
Navigation mode 632
Split form 636

Subform 633
Subreport 650
Subtotals 662
Text box 641
Theme 645
Unbound control 641

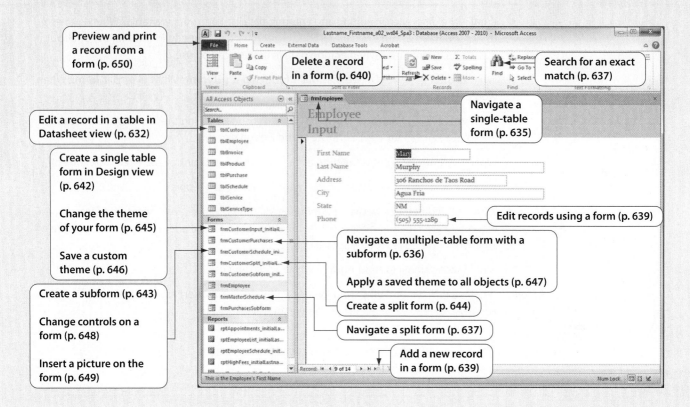

Preview and print a record from a form (p. 650)

Delete a record in a form (p. 640)

Search for an exact match (p. 637)

Navigate a single-table form (p. 635)

Edit a record in a table in Datasheet view (p. 632)

Create a single table form in Design view (p. 642)

Change the theme of your form (p. 645)

Save a custom theme (p. 646)

Edit records using a form (p. 639)

Navigate a multiple-table form with a subform (p. 636)

Apply a saved theme to all objects (p. 647)

Create a subform (p. 643)

Change controls on a form (p. 648)

Create a split form (p. 644)

Navigate a split form (p. 637)

Insert a picture on the form (p. 649)

Add a new record in a form (p. 639)

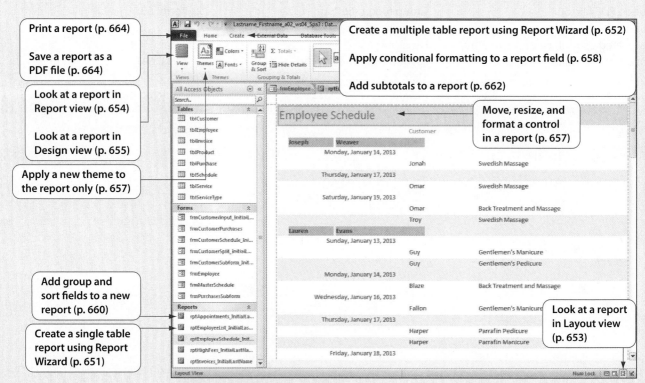

Print a report (p. 664)

Save a report as a PDF file (p. 664)

Create a multiple table report using Report Wizard (p. 652)

Apply conditional formatting to a report field (p. 658)

Add subtotals to a report (p. 662)

Look at a report in Report view (p. 654)

Look at a report in Design view (p. 655)

Move, resize, and format a control in a report (p. 657)

Apply a new theme to the report only (p. 657)

Add group and sort fields to a new report (p. 660)

Create a single table report using Report Wizard (p. 651)

Look at a report in Layout view (p. 653)

Figure 29   Turquoise Oasis Spa's Final New Database

Student data file needed:

a02_ws04_Spa4

You will save your file as:

Lastname_Firstname_a02_ws04_Spa4

Turquoise Oasis Spa

General Business

The spa has just redecorated the staff lounge and has added bulletin boards and even a computer for the staff members to check their appointments and sign in and out. The manager would like to create reports to post on the bulletin boards with schedule and service information, as well as make the database as easy to use as possible. You will help create some of the reports as well as forms to make the database easy for data entry and maintenance.

a. Start **Access**, and then open **a02_ws04_Spa4**.

b. Click the **File tab**, and then select **Save Database As**. In the Save As dialog box, browse to where you are saving your files, type Lastname_Firstname_a02_ws04_Spa4, and then click **Save**.

c. In the Security Warning bar, click **Enable Content**.

d. Create a form that will allow employees to edit their personal information as well as their upcoming appointments:

- Click the **Create tab**, and then click **Form Wizard** in the Forms group.

- In the Form Wizard dialog box, click the **Tables/Queries arrow**, and then select **Table: tblEmployee**. Click the **All Fields** button to add all the fields to the Selected Fields list.

- Click the **Tables/Queries arrow**, and then select **Table: tblSchedule**. Double-click **Customer**, **Service**, **Employee**, and **DateOfAppt** to add the fields to the Selected Fields list. Click **Next**.

- Verify that the data will be viewed **by tblEmployee**, and then click **Next**.

- Verify that **Datasheet** is selected as the layout for the subform, and then click **Next**.

- Name the form frmEmployeeSchedule_initialLastname, replacing initialLastname with your first initial and last name, name the subform frmSubform_initialLastname, and then click **Finish**.

- Click the **Home tab**, click the **View arrow**, and then select **Design View**. Click the **Form Design Tools Design tab**, click **Label**, and then draw a label in the left side of the Form Footer for the main form section. Type your First Initial and Last Name in the label box.

- Click the **Form Design Tools Design tab**, and then click **View** to go to Form view. On the Navigation bar, click **New (blank) record**, and then add your First Name, Last Name, Address, City, State, and Phone. On the Navigation bar, click **First record** to return to the first record in the table, and then click in the **Last Name** field.

- Click the **Home tab**, and then click **Find** in the Find group. In the Find What text box, type Rodriguez and then click **Find Next**. When you find the record for Brenda Rodriguez, click **Cancel**.

- Click the **Home tab**, click the **Delete arrow** in the Records group, and then click **Delete Record**. Click **Yes** when prompted to delete the record.

- Click the **Home tab**, and click **View** to go to Layout view. Double-click the **title**, select the text and type Employee Schedule.

- Click the **Last Name** text box, and then drag the right border of the text box to line up with the right border of the First Name text box.

- Click the **subform** label, and then press Del to delete the control. Click the **Subform** and using the layout selector, drag it to the left so it is right below the Phone label.

- Click the **Employee** heading in the subform datasheet, and then press `Del` to delete the field. Click the **subform** control, and then drag the right border to the right until you can see all the fields in the subform. Click the **Date** heading in the subform datasheet, and then drag it to the left of the Customer field. Resize all the columns to best fit the data.
- Close the form, and then click **Yes** when prompted to save the changes.

e. Create a report to show a list of customers and their purchases.

- Click the **Create tab**, and then click **Report Wizard** in the Reports group.
- In the Report Wizard dialog box, click the **Tables/Queries arrow**, and then select **Table: tblCustomer**. Double-click **CustFirstName** and **CustLastName** to add the fields to the Selected Fields list.
- Click the **Tables/Queries arrow**, and then select **Table: tblProduct**. Double-click **ProductDescription** to add the field to the Selected Fields list. Click the **Tables/ Queries arrow**, and then select **Table: tblPurchase**. Double-click **PurchaseType**, **PurchaseDate**, and **Quantity** to add the fields to the Selected Fields list. Click **Next**.
- Verify that the data will be viewed by **tblCustomer**, and then click **Next**.
- Double-click **ProductDescription** to add it as a grouping level, and then click **Next**.
- Click the **Sort arrow**, click **PurchaseDate**, and then click **Next**. Select a **Stepped** layout and **Portrait** orientation, and then click **Next**.
- Name the report rptCustomerPurchases_initialLastname, replacing initialLastname with your first initial and last name, and then click **Finish**.
- Click the **Print Preview tab**, and then click **Close Print Preview** in the Close Preview group. Click the **Report Design Tools Design tab**, click **Label**, and then draw a label in the left side of the Report Footer section. Type your First Initial and Last Name in the label box.
- Click the **Report Design Tools Design tab**, click the **View arrow**, and then select **Layout View**.
- Click the **Date** text box, and then drag the left border to the left until the date is visible. Move the Date text box to the left until it lines up under the First Name field.
- Click the **ProductDescription** label, press and hold `Shift`, click the **PurchaseDate** label, click the **PurchaseType** label, and then press `Del` to delete the controls.
- Click the **ProductDescription** text box, and then drag the right border to the right until the whole field is visible.
- Double-click the **title**, select the **text**, and then type Customer Purchases. Click the **Report Layout Tools Design tab**, click **Colors** in the Themes group, and then select **Elemental**. On the **Report Layout Tools Design tab**, click **Fonts** in the Themes group, and then select **Technic**.
- Click the **Report Layout Tools Design tab,** click **Group & Sort** in the Grouping & Totals group to open the Group, Sort, and Total pane. Click **Group on ProductDescription**, and then click **Delete** to delete the group.
- In the Group, Sort, and Total pane, click **Add a group**, and then select **PurchaseType**. Click the **PurchaseType** text box, and then drag it to just below the customer's first name and just above the date.
- Click the **Quantity** label and **Quantity** text box, and then drag the left edge so the text and numbers are visible.
- In the Group, Sort, and Total pane, click **Add a sort**, and then select **ProductDescription**. Close the Group, Sort, and Total pane.
- Click the **PurchaseType** text box. Click the **Report Layout Tools Format tab**, click **Conditional Formatting** in the Control Formatting group, and then click **New Rule**. In the second box, select **equal to**, and then in the third text box type Online. Click **Font color**, and then select **Purple**. Click **OK**, and then click **OK** again.

- Click the **PurchaseType** text box. Click the **Report Layout Tools Design tab**, click **Totals** in the Grouping & Totals group, and then select **Count Records**. Select the **PurchaseType** text box, press and hold Shift, and then click the **subtotal** text box. Click the **Report Layout Tools Format tab**, click **Shape Outline**, and then select **Transparent**.
- Right-click the **Subtotal** text box, and then select **Set Caption**. Replace the text in the caption box with Orders.
- Scroll to the bottom of the report. Click the **Grand Total** text box, and then move it under the product description. Right-click the **Grand Total** text box, and then select **Set Caption**. Replace the text in the caption box with Total orders.
- Close the report, and then click **Yes** when prompted to save the changes.

Problem Solve 1

Student data file needed:	You will save your files as:
a02_ps1_Clothing_Sales	Lastname_Firstname_a02_ps1_Clothing Sales Lastname_Firstname_a02_ps1_rptPriceCategories

Clothing Sales

IT
Information Technology

Wanda Robinson runs a home business selling designer clothing and has started using an Access database to keep her records. The database has been created and is now able to retain data. Wanda wants to have some forms and reports created to make dealing with the data easier. She has hired you to develop the necessary forms and reports.

a. Start **Access** and open **a02_ps1_Clothing_Sales**. Save the database as Lastname_Firstname_a02_ps1_Clothing_Sales, replacing Lastname_Firstname with your own name. In the Security Warning bar, click **Enable Content**.

b. Open **tblCustomer** and add a record with the CustomerID 16, your Last Name, First Name, Address, City, State, and Zip.

c. Create a split form to show all the product information from tblProduct except for Product ID. Change the title of the form to Product Information and save the form as frmProductInfo_initialLastname.

d. Apply the theme **Trek** to the form only. Add your first initial and last name to the form footer. Save and close the form.

e. Use the Form Wizard to create a form that will display the customer's **last name**, **first name**, and all their purchase information. Include **product description**, **price**, **size**, and **color** on the subform. Keep all other default options. Name the form frmCustOrders_initialLastname and the subform frmProductSubform_initialLastname.

f. Resize the columns in the subform so all the product information fits and resize the subform. Change the title of the form to Customer Orders. Add your first initial and last name to the form footer (on frmCustOrders_initialLastname). Save and close the form.

g. Use the Report Wizard to create a report to summarize each customer's purchases. Include **last name**, **first name**, **product description**, **price**, and **quantity**. (*Hint*: this information will come from three different tables.) Use the default options and save the report as rptCustSummary_initialLastname.

h. Resize and move the fields as necessary for the best fit. Add a total quantity for each customer and make it **Bold** and **Red** to stand out. Add your first initial and last name to the report footer. Change the title of the report to Customer Summary. Save and close the report.

i. Use the Report Wizard to create a report that will group all the products of the same price together and will show the product description and category. Keep the default options and name the report rptPriceCategories_initialLastname.

j. Resize and move the fields as necessary for the best fit. Change the **Price** field to show 2 decimal places.

k. Add your first initial and last name to the report footer. Change the title of the report to Product by Price. Save and close the report.

l. Create a pdf file from the **rptPriceCategories**. Save the file as Lastname_Firstname_a02_ps1_rptPriceCategories.

m. Save and close the database. Submit your files as directed by your instructor.

 Additional Workshop Cases are available on the companion website and in the instructor resources.

Student data files needed:

a02_mp_Recipes

a02_mp_Recipes_Logo

You will save your files as:

Lastname_Firstname_a02_mp_Recipes

Lastname_Firstname_a02_mp_pdfRecipes

Indigo 5 Restaurant

Production & Operations

Robin Sanchez, the chef of the resort's restaurant, Indigo 5, has started a database to keep track of recipes and the ingredients that the restaurant includes. Right now there are no forms, queries or reports created for this database, so the information available is very limited. You will help create some queries as well as forms for data entry and reports for the daily management of the food preparation.

a. Start **Access** and open **a02_mp_Recipes**. Save the file as Lastname_Firstname_a02_mp_Recipes. In the Security Warning bar, click **Enable Content**.

b. Click the **Create tab**, click **Form Wizard**, and add all of the fields from **Table: tblRecipes**. Include **IngredientID**, **Quantity**, and **Measurement** from **Table: tblRecipeIngredients**. View the form **by tblRecipes** and show the subform as a Datasheet. Save the form as frmRecipe_initialLastname and save the subform as frmRecipeSubform_initialLastname. Switch to **Design View**. Click the **Form Design Tools Design tab**, click **Label**, and then add a label to the form footer with your first initial and last name.

c. Switch to **Layout View**, and change the title of the form to Recipe Input. Click the **Form Layout Tools Format tab**, change the title font to font size 28, and apply **Bold**.

d. Delete the **subform** label and move the subform to the left under the Instructions label. Delete the **Subcategory.Value** label and text box. Move the remaining controls and the subform up to fill in the blank space. Resize all the columns to best fit the data.

e. Click the **Form Layout Tools Design tab**, click in the form body, click **Insert Image**, click **Browse**, navigate to your student data files, and locate **a02_mp_Recipes_Logo**. Insert the image to the right of the Recipe information. Resize the image as necessary to fit above the Instructions text box.

f. Switch to **Form View**. Click in the Recipe Name text box, click the **Home tab**, click **Find**, and locate the record for the Recipe Name Pasta Napolitana. Change the Quantity for the IngredientID Honey to 1.

g. Click the **New (blank) Record** button on the Navigation bar and enter the following data into frmRecipe_InitialLastname:

Recipe Name	Food Category ID	Subcategory	Prep Time (minutes)	Servings	Instructions
Avocado Salsa	Appetizer	Vegetarian	10	6	Peel and mash avocados. Add cayenne pepper, salt, chopped onion, and chopped tomato. Add lime juice and mix well. Refrigerate for at least 4 hours.

Enter the following data into the subform:

IngredientID	Quantity	Measurement
Avocado	2	whole
Tomato	1	cup
Cayenne pepper	.5	teaspoon
Salt	.5	teaspoon
Onions	1	cup
Lime juice	3	tablespoons

Close the form and save the changes.

h. Click the **Create tab**, click **Query Design** and then add **tblRecipes**, **tblRecipeIngredients**, and **tblIngredients**. Include the **RecipeName**, **Ingredient**, and **Quantity**, in the results. Add criteria to the **Ingredient** field so only recipes that contain cumin or paprika are selected. Sort in **Ascending** order by Quantity. Run the query and adjust the width of the query columns as necessary. Save your query as qryCuminOrPaprika_initialLastname. Close the query.

i. Click the **Create tab**, click **Query Wizard**, and create a Find Unmatched Query to find foods in **Table: tblIngredients** that are not used in any recipes in **tblRecipeIngredients**. The **IngredientID** will be the common field between the tables. Include all the available fields. Save the query as qryUnusedIngredients_initialLastname. Sort in Ascending order by **IngredientID**. Save and close the query.

j. Use the Query Wizard to create a **Find Duplicates Query** to find food categories that may be duplicated in **Table: tblRecipes**. Show the **RecipeName**, **TimeToPrepare**, and **Servings** in the results. Sort in **Ascending** order by **FoodCategoryID**. Save the query as qryMultipleFoodCategories_initialLastname. Close the query.

k. Click the **Create tab**, click **Query Design**, and then add **tblRecipes** and **tblFoodCategories**. Include **RecipeName**, **TimeToPrepare**, and **FoodCategory** in the results. Add criteria to the TimetoPrepare field to find all recipes that take less than 30 minutes to prepare. Add criteria to the FoodCategory field to find all recipes that are listed as soup or pizza. The results should show all recipes that take less than 30 minutes to prepare or are listed with the category of soup or pizza. Sort the query in **Ascending** order by **TimeToPrepare**. Adjust the column widths as necessary. Save the query as qryTimeOrCategory_initialLastname. Close the query.

l. Click the **Create tab**, click **Query Design** and add **tblRecipes**, **tblRecipeIngredients**, and **tblIngredients**. Include **RecipeName**, **Ingredient**, **Quantity**, **Measurement**, and **RecipeID** from tblRecipeIngredients in the results, in that order. Sort in **Ascending** order by **RecipeID**. Adjust the column widths as necessary. Save the query as qryRecipeIngredients_initialLastname. Close the query.

m. Click the **Create tab**, click **Report Wizard** and from tblRecipes add the fields **RecipeName**, **Instructions**, **TimeToPrepare**, and **Servings**; and from qryRecipeIngredients_initialLastname add the fields **Ingredient**, **Quantity**, and **Measurement**, in that order. View your report **by tblRecipes**. Group by **RecipeName**. Sort in **Ascending** order by **Ingredient**. Accept all other default settings and name the report rptRecipes_initialLastname.

n. Switch to Layout view, and move the **Ingredient**, **Quantity**, and **Measurement** text boxes to the left under the Instructions field. Delete the **Ingredient**, **Quantity**, and **Measurement** labels. Make the **Prep Time** and **Servings** labels wider so the text is visible. Move the **Servings** text box to the right under the Servings label. Change the title to Recipes.

o. Resize the Ingredient text box and Quantity text box so all the text is visible. Apply conditional formatting to the **Prep Time** field so it is **Bold** and **Red** if the Prep Time is greater than 15.

p. In Design view, click **Label** and add your first initial and last name in the report footer. Click the **File tab**, click **Save & Publish** and **Save Object As**, click **PDF or XPS**, and click **Save As**. Navigate to the folder where you are saving your files, type Lastname_Firstname_ a02_mp_pdfRecipes, and click **Publish**. Close the Adobe Reader window, close the report, and then save all the changes.

q. Click the **Create tab**, click **Report Wizard**, and from tblRecipeIngredients add the fields **IngredientID**, **Quantity**, and **Measurement**; and from tblRecipes add **RecipeName**, in that order. View your data **by tblRecipeIngredients** and add grouping by **RecipeName**. Accept default options and name the report rptIngredientCount_initialLastname. Insert your first initial and last name in a label in the report footer.

r. Switch to Layout view, click the **Report Layout Tools Design tab**, click **Group & Sort**, and delete the grouping by **RecipeName**. Click **Add a group** and add a grouping by **IngredientID**. Move the **IngredientID** text box to the left margin, under the **RecipeName** label. Click the **IngredientID** text box. Click the **Report Layout Tools Format tab**, and click **Align Text Left**. Delete the **RecipeName**, **IngredientID**, **Quantity**, and **Measurement** labels.

s. Change the title to Ingredient List. Click the **IngredientID** text box, click the **Report Layout Tools Format tab**, click **Shape Outline**, and make the border transparent. Click **Shape Fill** and change the shape fill to **Red**, **Accent 2**, **Lighter 80%**.

t. Click the **Quantity** text box. Click the **Report Layout Tools Design tab**, click **Totals**, and then click **Sum** to add subtotals. Right-click the **subtotal** text box, select **Set Caption**, and change it to Total. Click the **subtotal** text box and on the **Report Layout Tools Format tab**, click **Align Text Right** to change the alignment. Delete the **grand total** text box. Make the **RecipeName** text box wide enough to fit all the text for every record.

u. Close the Group, Sort, and Total pane. Close the report and save your changes. Close Access.

Student data files needed:	You will save your files as:
a02_ps1_Hotel	Lastname_Firstname_a02_ps1_Hotel
a02_ps1_Hotel_Image	Lastname_Firstname_a02_ps1_pdfGuestCharges

Hotel Reservations

Sales & Marketing

A database has been started to keep track of the hotel reservations with guest information, reservation information, and additional room charge information. There are no reports, forms, or queries built yet, so the staff feels like the database is not easy to use. You will create reports, forms, and queries to help the staff better manage the data in the database.

a. Start **Access** and open **a02_ps1_Hotel**. Save the database as Lastname_Firstname_a02_ ps1_Hotel. In the Security Warning bar, click **Enable Content**.

b. Open **tblGuests** and add a new record with your Last Name, First Name, Address, City, State, ZipCode, and Phone. Close the table.

c. Create a query using **tblReservations** to calculate the average rate, the minimum rate, and the maximum rate for each **DiscountType** of the rooms that are currently reserved. Rename the fields Average Rate, Minimum Rate, and Maximum Rate. **Sort** the query in **Descending** order by **DiscountType**. Resize the columns to best fit the data. Save the query as qryDiscountTypeStatistics_initialLastname. Close the query.

d. Use the **Form Wizard** to create a form to enter guest information as well as reservation information. Add all fields from both tables EXCEPT **GuestID**. The data should be viewed by **Guest information** first, and the subform should be in **Datasheet** layout. Accept all other default options and name the form frmGuestReservations_initialLastname and the subform frmGuestSubform_initialLastname.

e. Change the form **title** to Guest Reservations. Change the theme to **Black Tie**. Make the title font size **28** and **bold**.

f. Delete the **subform** label. Insert **a02_ps1_Hotel_Image** into the form body to the left of the subform so that the top border of the image lines up with the top border of the subform and the image width is reduced to fit in that position.

g. Resize the column widths in the subform datasheet and scroll to the right as required to see all the fields. Find the record for Elaine Foley. Add a new reservation from the information below.

CheckInDate	1/25/2014
Nights Stay	3
# of Guests	2
Crib	No
Handicapped	No
RoomType	Double (1 king bed)
RoomRate	$289
DiscountType	None

h. Add your first initial and last name to the form footer. Close the form and save the changes.

i. Create a query to find all guests who may not have reservations. Include the fields **GuestLastName**, **GuestFirstName**, **Address**, **City**, **State**, and **ZipCode**. Sort the query by **GuestLastName** in **Ascending** order. Name the query qryGuestsWithoutReservations_initialLastname.

j. Change the Font size of the query results to 14, change the **Alternate Row Color** to **Brown**, **Accent 6**, **Lighter 60%**, and **AutoFit** all the columns. Close the query and save the changes.

k. Create a query that will calculate the total due for each guest based on the number of nights they have stayed and the room rate for each guest. Select only guests who checked in between **December 1, 2013** and **December 31, 2013**. The results should show the **GuestFirstName**, **GuestLastName**, **NightsStay**, and **RoomRate**, in that order.

l. Save the query as qryDecemberRoomCharges_initialLastname. Name the new field TotalRoomCharge. Sort the query in Ascending order by **GuestLastName**. **AutoFit** the new column. Close the query and save the changes.

m. Use the Report Wizard to create a report to show all room charges incurred for each guest (not including the charge for their room). Add the **GuestFirstName**, **GuestLastName**, **ChargeCategory**, and **ChargeAmount** to the report. View the report by the **Guest Name**. Sort by **ChargeAmount** in ascending order. Accept all other default options and name the report rptRoomCharges_initialLastname.

n. Add a subtotal to the **Amount** field, set a caption, and change the caption to Total Charges. Left align the subtotal text box. Add conditional formatting to the subtotal text box to highlight in **Red** and **Bold** all subtotals that are over $200.

o. Resize the **Category** text box to fit on one page. Resize the **page number** control to fit on one page. Change the title to say Room Charges by Guest.

p. Add your first initial and last name to the report footer. Save and close the report.

q. Save the report as a PDF file and name it Lastname_Firstname_a02_ps1_pdfGuestCharges.

r. Create a split form from **tblReservations**. Name the form frmReservationSplit_ initialLastname. Change the title to Reservations.

s. Close the form and close Access.

Problem Solve 2

Student data files needed:
a02_ps2_Hotel2
a02_ps2_Changes_Image

You will save your files as:
Lastname_Firstname_a02_ps2_Hotel2
Lastname_Firstname_a02_ps2_Theme

More Hotel Reservations

Sales & Marketing

A database has been started to keep track of the hotel reservations with guest information, reservation information, and additional room charge information. There are no reports, forms, or queries built yet, so the staff feels like the database is not easy to use. You will create reports, forms and queries to help the staff better manage the data in the database.

a. Start **Access** and open **a02_ps2_Hotel2**. Save the database as Lastname_Firstname_ a02_ps2_Hotel2. In the Security Warning bar, click **Enable Content**.

b. Open **tblGuests** and add a new record with your Last Name, First Name, Address, City, State, ZipCode, and Phone. Close the table.

c. Use the Form Wizard to create a form that will allow the staff to enter Room Charges for each guest during their stay. Include the **GuestLastName**, **GuestFirstName**, **City**, **State**, **ChargeCategory**, and **ChargeAmount**. View the data by **tblGuests** . The sub form should be in Datasheet layout. Accept all other default options and name the form frmGuest RoomCharges_initialLastname and the subform frmGuestSubform_initialLastname.

d. **Delete** the subform label. Change the title to Guest Room Charges. Change the font size to **28** and the font to **Bold**. Resize the title as necessary.

e. Add your first initial and last name to a label in the form footer.

f. Insert **a02_ps2_Charges_Image** to the form body to the left of the subform.

g. Align the top of the image with the top of the subform and resize the image to fit between the edge of the form and the left border of the subform. Close and save the form.

h. Create a query to count the number of times a RoomType has been reserved. Include the average **RoomRate** for each RoomType. Sort the query in ascending order by **RoomRate**. Change the field names to Number of Reservations and Average Room Rate. Resize the column widths. Save the query as qryRoomStatistics_initialLastname. Close the query.

i. Create a query to find Guests that have reservations but do not have any room charges. Include the **GuestID**, **NightsStay**, **CheckInDate**, and **RoomType** in the results. Sort the query in ascending order by **CheckInDate**. Save the query as qryGuestsWithoutRoom Charges_initialLastname. Close the query.

j. Create a query to find guests with multiple room charges. Include **ReservationID**, **ChargeCategory**, and **ChargeAmount** in the results. Sort the query in ascending order by **ReservationID**. Save the query as qryMultipleRoomCharges_initialLastname. Close the query.

k. Create a query to find all guests who have reservations in 2014 and who are staying more than two nights. Include **GuestFirstName**, **GuestLastName**, **CheckInDate**, **NightsStay**, and **NumberOfGuests**. Sort in ascending order by **CheckInDate**. Save the query as qry2014And2_initialLastname. Close the query.

l. Create a query to find all guests who have reservations in 2013 with more than three guests or all guests who are staying three or more nights regardless of their check-in date. Include **GuestFirstName**, **GuestLastName**, **CheckInDate**, **NightsStay**, and **NumberOfGuests**. Sort in ascending order by **GuestLastName**. Save the query as qryGuestRelations_initialLastname. Close the query.

m. Create a query to find all guests who are checking in sometime in April 2014 and are staying between two and four nights. Include **GuestFirstName**, **GuestLastName**, and **NightsStay** in the results. Sort in ascending order by **CheckInDate**. Save the query as qryAprilReservations_initialLastname. Close the query.

n. Use the Form Wizard to create a form to enter new Guest information including reservation information. Add all the fields except **GuestID**. Accept all other default options, name the form frmGuestInput_InitialLastname, and name the subform frmSubform_initialLastname.

o. Change the title of the form to Guest Input. Apply the **Angles** theme to all the objects in the database. Change the font theme to **Concourse**. Save the custom theme to your student folder as Lastname_Firstname_a02_ps2_Theme. Add your first initial and last name to the form footer. Close the form and save the changes.

p. Use the Report Wizard to create a report for all guests with their reservation information. Include **GuestFirstName**, **GuestLastName**, **CheckInDate**, **NightsStay**, **NumberOfGuests**, **RoomType**, and **RoomRate**. View the data by tblReservations. Group the report by **CheckInDate** with normal date grouping options. Sort in ascending order by **GuestLastName**. Accept all other default options and name the report rptGuestReservations_initialLastname.

q. Change the report title to Guest Reservations. Insert your first initial and last name in a label in the report footer. Move or resize all necessary fields so all the text is visible. Highlight any **NightsStay** that is more than two nights in **Dark Red** and **Bold**.

r. Close the report and save the changes. Close Access.

Problem Solve 3

myitlab grader
Homework 3

Student data files needed:	You will save your files as:
a02_ps3_Hotel3	Lastname_Firstname_a02_ps3_Hotel3
a02_ps3_Hotel_Image	Lastname_Firstname_a02_ps3_pdfRoomTypes

Additional Hotel Reservations

Sales & Marketing

A database has been started to keep track of the hotel reservations with guest information, reservation information, and additional room charge information. There are no reports, forms, or queries built yet, so the staff feels like the database is not easy to use. You will create reports, forms, and queries to help the staff better manage the data in the database.

a. Start **Access** and open **a02_ps3_Hotel3**. Save the database as Lastname_Firstname_a02_ps3_Hotel3. In the Security Warning bar, click **Enable Content**.

b. Open **tblGuests** and add a new record with your Last Name, First Name, Address, City, State, Zipcode, and Phone. Close the table.

c. Create a query to calculate the total room charges per guest. Use the **GuestID** and the **ChargeAmount** fields. Rename the field RoomCharges. Sort in **Descending** order by **RoomCharges**. Resize the **RoomCharges** field. Save the query as qryTotalRoomCharges_initialLastname and close the query.

d. Create a query to calculate the total amount due for each guest who had reservations in December 2013, including room rate and room charges. Include **GuestLastName**, **GuestFirstName**, **NightsStay**, **RoomRate**, and **RoomCharges**. Save the query as qryTotalDue_initialLastname.

e. Add a new calculated field to the query to calculate each guest's total amount due based on the room rate, the number of nights they stayed, and room charges. Name the new field TotalDue. Sort the query by **GuestLastName** in **Ascending** order. Save the changes and close the query.

f. Use the Report Wizard to create a report showing the **TotalDue** for each guest. Include all the fields from qryTotalDue_initialLastname. Do not add a grouping level. Sort by **TotalDue** in descending order. Accept all other default options and name the report as rptTotalDue_initialLastname.

g. Add your first initial and last name in the report footer. Change the title to Guest Total Charges. Highlight in **Dark Red** and **Bold** all NightsStay between three and five nights. Adjust all the label sizes to see the headings. Save and close the report.

h. Use the Report Wizard to create a report with the **RoomDescription**, **RoomRate**, **DiscountType**, **NightsStay**, and **CheckInDate**. View the data **by tblRoomTypes**, do not add a grouping level, and sort by **CheckInDate** in ascending order. Accept all other default options and name the report rptRoomTypes_initialLastname.

i. Add your first initial and last name to the report footer. Change the title to Room Types. Remove the outline around the DiscountType text box.

j. Calculate the number of reservations for each RoomRate. Add a caption and change it to Number of reservations. Resize the calculated field so the caption is visible. Add the fill color **Blue**, **Accent 1**, **Lighter 60%** to the field.

k. Calculate the average night stay for each RoomDescription. Add a caption and change it to Average Night Stay. Add the fill color **Blue**, **Accent 1**, **Lighter 60%** to the field.

l. Add a new sort by **RoomDescription** and move it above the group on **RoomID**. Resize the width of all the labels so all text is visible. Save and close the report.

m. Publish the report as a PDF file. Save the file as Lastname_Firstname_a02_ps3_pdfRoomTypes.

n. Use the Form Wizard to create a form to enter room charges along with the charge details. Include **RoomChargeID**, **GuestID**, **ChargeCategory**, **ChargeAmount**, and **Purchase**. View the form **by tblRoomCharges** and view the subform in a tabular layout. Accept all other default options, name the form frmRoomCharges_initialLastname, and name the subform frmRoomSubform_initialLastname.

o. Add your first initial and last name to the form footer. Change the title to Room Charges. Insert **a02_ps3_Hotel_Image** to the right of the main form detail with the top border of the image lined up with the top border of the GuestID text box and the bottom border of the image lined up with the bottom border of the Amount text box.

p. Delete the **frmRoom** label. Change the theme for just the form to **Austin**. Save and close the form and close Access.

Student data file needed:

Blank database

You will save your file as:

Lastname_Firstname_a02_pf1_Schedule

Class Schedule

General Business

One way to stay organized during the semester is to keep track of your schedule. You will create a database of all your classes and grades. The database should track the class information, your personal schedule, and the location of the class. In order to use this for more than one semester, you will keep each of those data in separate tables.

Once the tables are created, you will set up forms to make data entry easier, run queries to get more information, and create reports to help you manage your schedule. You will start by adding data from your current schedule. Assume the current semester is Fall 2012 and the previous semester is Spring 2012.

a. Start **Access**. Click **Blank database**. Browse to find where you are storing your data files and save your database as Lastname_Firstname_a02_pf1_Schedule. Click the **Create** button to create the database.

b. To keep track of class information, design a table that includes fields for the Class Number, Class Description, Credits Offered, and Professor name. Assign an appropriate primary key and save the table as tblClasses.

c. Add the class information for your classes from last semester, or fictitious classes if necessary. Add at least six classes to the table.

d. To keep track of your class locations, design a table that includes fields for the Building Number, building Name, and Campus the building is located on. Assign an appropriate primary key and save the table as tblBuilding.

e. Add the location of the classes you entered in Step c. Include at least three different locations.

f. To keep track of your schedule, design a table that includes fields for the Class Number, Semester, Meeting Days, Meeting Time, Location, Midterm Grade (as a number), and Final Grade (as a number). Resize all the column widths so all text is visible. Assign an appropriate primary key and save the table as tblSchedule.

g. Enter last semester's schedule, or a fictitious one, that includes at least six classes in at least three different locations. The classes and locations should be the ones entered in tblClasses and tblBuildings.

h. Create relationships as appropriate for tblSchedule, tblClasses, and tblBuilding.

i. You would like to be able to enter all your class and schedule information at one time. Create one form that will allow you to enter all the information. Save the form as frmSchedule.

j. Use the form to enter a new record for this semester. You should enter all the information except your grade. Add a new theme to the form, change the title to something more meaningful than the form name, then save and close the form.

k. You would like to see each class individually as well as all the class records at once. Create a form that will show you this view of the data. Save the form as frmClasses.

l. You want to find out what your average midterm grade and average final grade was each semester. Even though there are only grades entered for one semester, create a query to perform this calculation.

m. Rename the fields to something more meaningful and format the fields to show only two decimal places. Sort the query by Semester in descending order. Save the query as qryAverageGrades.

n. You want a schedule of last semester's classes only. Create a query that will show you last semester's classes, the instructor, and where and when it occurred. Save the query as qrySchedule.

o. Create a report that will show you last semester's schedule organized by each day. Sort it in order of class time.

p. Make sure all the fields print on one page of the report and that all the fields are visible. Add your first initial and last name in the report footer. Save the report as rptSchedule.

q. You want to know how to schedule your weekends. Create a query to see whether you have classes after 9 a.m. on Friday. Save the query as qryFridayClasses.

r. You also want to know your average grade for your classes between midterm and final. Create a query to calculate the average grade in each class. Sort the query by an appropriate field. Save the query as qryGrades.

s. You want to print a report to show your parents your grades by class for the semester, including the average grade. Create a report that shows the Class Number, Description, Credits, Midterm, Final, and Average Grade for each class. Sort by an appropriate field. Resize all labels so all the text is visible. Change the title to something more appropriate. Save the report as rptGrades.

t. Add your first initial and last name in the report footer. Highlight all average grades over 90. Save and close the report.

u. Close Access.

Perform 2: Perform in Your Career

Student data file needed:	You will save your file as:
a02_pf2_Fitness	Lastname_Firstname_a02_pf2_Fitness

Fitness Center

Sales & Marketing   Production & Operations

A new fitness center has opened and is developing a database for keeping track of members. So far the fitness center has two tables for Membership information and Member information, and another table with Roster Information. It has no queries, forms, or reports created, so the center has asked you to help answer some questions with queries, make data entry easier with forms, and print some reports for reference.

a. Start **Access** and then open **a02_pf2_Fitness**. Save the file as Lastname_Firstname_a02_pf2_Fitness. In the Security Warning bar, click **Enable Content**.

b. Open each table and familiarize yourself with the fields. Open the Relationships window and note how the tables are related.

c. The staff wants to be able to enter all new member and membership information in the database at one time. Create a form that will allow them to enter the member records and the related membership records for a new member. Insert your first initial and last name in the form footer. Save the form as frmMemberInput.

d. Using frmMemberInput, enter yourself as a member. Use your actual name and address; all other information can be fictitious. Change the title to something more meaningful.

e. The staff wants to know how old each member is (in whole numbers) as of the date they joined the club. This will help them plan age appropriate activities. Create a query to calculate the age of each member as of the date they joined the club. *Hint:* when you subtract one date from the other you get a total number of days, not years. Save the query as qryMemberAge.

f. The manager wants to know which membership types are creating the most revenue and are the most popular. Create a query to calculate the total number of each membership type and the total fees collected for each membership type. Format the query so the manager will understand exactly what each field represents. Save the query as qryMembershipStatistics.

g. The manager would like to know if any membership types have not been applied for. Find any membership types that are not assigned to a current member. Save the query as qryInactiveMemberships.

h. The staff likes to celebrate birthdays at the club. Assume the current year is 2013. Everyone born in 1974 will turn 40 this year and the staff would like a list of all those members along with their actual birthdays so they can quickly see who is celebrating a birthday each day. Save the query as qry1973Birthdays.

i. The staff likes to see each member's data as an individual record while still being able to view the whole table of data. Create a form that will allow the staff to view the data this way. Save the form as frmMemberRecords.

j. The staff needs a master list of members with their membership information. Create a report that will show the relevant information so the staff knows who is a current member and what kinds of membership each person has. Insert your first initial and last name in the report footer. Save the report as rptExpirationDates.

k. Modify rptExpirationDates so the records are grouped by the month of the expiration date. Highlight the expiration date field with a color so it stands out from the other fields.

l. The staff needs a list of members with the facilities their membership gives them access to. Create a report so the staff can quickly locate a member's name and determine which facilities they are allowed to access. Save the report as rptFacilities.

m. Change the report theme, change the report title to something other than the name of the report, save the report, and close the report.

n. Close Access.

Perform 3: Perform in Your Career

Student data file needed:	You will save your files as:
a02_pf3_Internships	Lastname_Firstname_a02_pf3_Internships
	Lastname_Firstname_a02_pf3_pdfCompanySchedule

Internship Coordinator

General Business

You take a job with an organization that matches students from Indiana schools to internship opportunities. The database you use keeps track of the companies that offer internships, the potential intern's information, and interview information dates for the interns.

You are often called upon to add new records to the table, find information for a company or intern, and provide reports for your staff. Currently there are no reports, forms, or queries, so you will have to build them from the existing data.

a. Start **Access** and then open **a02_pf3_Internships**. Save the file as Lastname_Firstname_a02_pf3_Internships. In the Security Warning bar, click **Enable Content**.

b. Open each table and familiarize yourself with the fields. Open the Relationships window and note how the tables are related.

c. Create a form to enter data for new interns and their upcoming interviews. Save the form as frmInterns and the subform as frmInternSubform.

d. Add your name as a new intern with one interview date and company of your choice.

e. You are scheduling for January and March and need to know which students already have interviews scheduled for those months, as well as the interview date and company the interview is with. Save the query as qryJanuaryOrMarch.

f. Indiana University Purdue University Indianapolis (IUPUI) would like to know which of its students have interviews with Del Monte Foods Company or MMI Marketing and when those interviews are scheduled. Save the query as qryIUPUI.

g. Your boss wants to know the total number of interns in the database from each university. Create a query with descriptive field names and sorted appropriately to provide this information. Save the query as qrySchoolCount.

h. In the past there have been problems with interns being scheduled more than once with the same company, or scheduled for interviews on the same day. You need to find all students who have multiple interviews scheduled to check for conflicts. Save the query as qryMultipleInterviews.

i. Your boss has asked for a master list of all interns who have interviews scheduled. He would like to be able to look up a student in the report to see when their interview is and who the interview is with. Save the report as rptInterviewsScheduled.

j. You need a report that counts and highlights how many interviews are scheduled each month. The report should also show the interview date and intern information. Save the report as rptInterviewDates.

k. When a company comes to interview, you need to quickly find who the interview is with. Create a report that will provide a master list of interviews that allows you to quickly see who is interviewing with each company and on what date. Save the report as rptCompany Schedule.

l. Save rptCompanySchedule as a PDF file so you can easily e-mail it to your boss and name it Lastname_Firstname_a02_pf3_pdfCompanySchedule.

m. You would like to stay one step ahead of your boss. Create two more queries that may be helpful in analyzing the database information. Name the queries something descriptive so your boss will know what information is provided.

n. Close Access.

Perform 4: How Others Perform

Student data file needed:

a02_pf4_Lessons

You will save your file as:

Lastname_Firstname_a02_pf4_Lessons

Music Lessons

General Business

You have just taken a new job in a music store and one of your responsibilities is to manage the music instructors and their students. A database has been created, but as you run the queries you notice they are either missing data or have wrong results. Answer the following questions about each of the objects as completely as possible:

a. Open rptListOfTeachers. Why is the image repeated after each record? How could the image have been added to the report so it would not repeat like that?

b. Open qryGuitarPianoAndBeginners. The query is supposed to show all teachers who are teaching piano or guitar and are taking new students. Why are other records in the results? Switch to Design view and explain how you would correct the query criteria to show the correct results.

c. Open qryLessonTimes. The query is supposed to show the average lesson length for each teacher. Instead, the query shows different lesson times for each teacher. What is wrong with this query and how can you fix it to show the average lesson length for each teacher?

d. Open rptLessonList. Can you tell what the report is grouped by and sorted by without looking at the Group, Sort, and Total pane? Describe how you would change the grouping to group by Instrument.

e. Open qryInstrumentList. The query was supposed to find all teacher names, student names, and the instrument the student plays. Instead there are over 200 records. What happened and why did this happen? How can you fix the query so it will provide the information you really want?

f. Open frmStudents. This form was created to see only one student at a time. Why is it showing one student and the whole student table? How was this form created? How would you create the form with only one student record at a time?

WORKSHOP 1

Sales & Marketing

Objectives

1. Describe how to communicate and present with a purpose for an intended outcome   p. 684

2. Open, display, and navigate through a presentation in various views   p. 685

3. Edit slides by modifying text   p. 690

4. Manipulate slides   p. 697

5. Understand the difference between a theme and a template   p. 701

6. Modify slide layouts   p. 706

7. Use the Research pane to check spelling   p. 708

8. Save a presentation in a variety of formats, and select appropriate printing for a presentation   p. 709

Communicating with Presentations

PREPARE CASE

The Red Bluff Putts for Paws Golf Tournament Presentation

The Red Bluff Golf Club hosts a tournament each year to benefit the Santa Fe Animal Center. Golf pro John Schilling speaks at community meetings, such as the Community Club and Women's Business Council, to gather sponsors and golfers. He asked you to assist him with the Putts for Paws tournament this year. Your first assignment is to review and update the PowerPoint presentation he uses during his speeches. This persuasive presentation provides basic information, such as the time, date, and cost of the tournament, as well as sponsorship opportunities and special events.

sattahipbeach / Shutterstock.com

Student data files needed for this workshop:

 p01_ws01_Sponsor   p01_ws01_Sponsor_Theme

You will save your files as:

 Lastname_Firstname_p01_ws01_Sponsor

 Lastname_Firstname_p01_ws01_Sponsor_Show

 Lastname_Firstname_p01_ws01_Sponsor_PDF

Understanding the Purpose of PowerPoint

Presentations are everywhere. In fact, you have probably seen many presentations in your life and even may have been responsible for developing some presentations. In presentations, visual aids such as marks on a whiteboard, a test tube full of bubbling liquid, or computer slide shows, support the speaker. Microsoft Office PowerPoint 2010 is a software application that enables you to efficiently build professional quality presentations.

In many cases presentations are displayed on large screens for audiences; however, there are many creative ways to use PowerPoint. Kiosks, for example, are common in public locations such as malls, banks, hotels, zoos, or museums, and can display self-running PowerPoint presentations that provide information or display advertisements. In fact, posters and billboards can be designed using PowerPoint. It is a versatile tool that improves communication. In this section, you will explore PowerPoint and learn how to communicate with a purpose.

Communicating with PowerPoint Presentations

PowerPoint presentations are tools that help you communicate with your audience. Slides add interest and variety to your presentation. Because of the visual nature of the slides, your audience is able to grasp more information. PowerPoint slides can help you tell your story 25–40 percent faster. Well-built presentations organize thoughts, stimulate interest, clarify and substantiate your message, and reinforce what you say.

Presenting with a Purpose for an Intended Outcome

Every presentation begins with planning. Start by defining the purpose of your presentation. Be specific, and use action words as you list objectives. Determine the outcome you expect from the audience.

With your goals and objectives clearly defined, turn your attention to your audience. What are they expecting to gain from your presentation? What do they already know about the topic? Why are they interested? How will you connect with them as individuals? Thinking about your audience not only prepares you for the actual presentation, but it helps you effectively plan the content, flow, and conclusion of your visual materials, including your slides and handouts.

Real World Advice Defining Your Target Audience

Defining your **target audience** is important to effectively plan your presentation. Asking yourself a few starting questions can help identify your audience.

- Why were you invited to speak?
- Why is the topic important to the audience?
- What do they know about the topic? How will they use the information?
- How large is the audience? What is the physical layout of the presentation room? How long are you expected to speak?

Informing Your Audience

Generally, the purposes of your presentations fall into three major categories. The first, an informational presentation, provides facts and figures to your audience. A fiscal report in business is an example of an informational presentation. The slides in a fiscal report may detail the expenditures and income generated by a business, and perhaps use charts and tables to organize the information for the audience. Another example of an informational presentation is a museum kiosk, giving information about artists, their methods, and the history of the artwork. Yet another example is a class lecture, where objectives, concepts, examples, and questions for discussion are organized. When you provide information to your audience, you need to know what they already know about the topic and how you can support their needs.

Persuading Your Audience

The second purpose of a presentation is to persuade your audience. While this type of presentation may contain elements such as facts and figures, your main objective will be to try and appeal to members of the audience in order to persuade them to do what you want them to do. Sales and political presentations are examples of persuasive presentations. Whenever you try to generate support for an idea, fund a proposal, or get people to change their beliefs about something, you are making a persuasive presentation. For this type of audience you need to know their expectations, biases for or against the topic, and how you relate to them on a personal level.

Preparing Your Audience

The third purpose of a presentation is to prepare your audience. In this case you may be preparing them for bad times, such as layoffs, or you may be preparing them for good times by cross-training them to do a different type of job. You will include important information and also help them to understand the circumstances they will encounter. When you prepare your audience, you need to know what their expectations are, what they know about the topic, what biases they have, and how you relate to them on a personal level.

CONSIDER THIS | **Are There Mixed Purposes?**

Can a presentation have a mixture of purposes? Or, if you begin with the purpose of persuading an audience, is it possible to also inform them? What role do your biases have in the purpose? Can an informational presentation really be devoid of persuasion? If you are preparing an audience, are you also informing them?

Opening a PowerPoint Presentation and Working with the PowerPoint Window

As the tournament manager working with the golf pro at the Painted Paradise Golf Resort and Spa, you will open and modify a persuasive presentation previously created for the Red Bluff Putts for Paws Golf Tournament. This presentation will be given by the golf pro to civic groups in the community in order to gather financial sponsorship for the tournament. Golfers will also be encouraged to register as individuals or teams for the event. The golf pro has asked you to update the slides for the current year, including adding information about additional events. You begin by reviewing the slide show from the previous year.

Workshop 1 Training

SIDE NOTE
Saving Files

By saving the file with a different name, you will have the original in case you need to begin the exercise again.

Save a presentation often as you are working on it. Save the file after completing each section.

To Orient Yourself with PowerPoint

a. Click the **Start** button. From the Start menu, locate and then start **Microsoft PowerPoint 2010**. Click the **File tab**, click **Open**, and then click the disk drive in the left pane where your student data files are located. Navigate through the folder structure, and double-click **p01_ws01_Sponsor**. Click the **File tab** again, and then click **Save As**. In the Save As dialog box, navigate to where you are storing your files, and then type Lastname_Firstname_p01_ws01_Sponsor, replacing Lastname and Firstname with your own name, and then click **Save**.

b. Click each **tab** on the Ribbon, and then review the tools on the Ribbon, noting that the available buttons change and will fit a wide variety of needs as you continue to learn about PowerPoint.

c. Click the **Outline tab** in the left pane, and then observe how the pane changes. The **Outline tab** enables you to concentrate only on the text content of the slide presentation. The **Slides tab** and the Outline tab enable you to move quickly between slides by clicking on the slide you want to view. Use the scroll bar on the right side of the pane to move up or down through the slides.

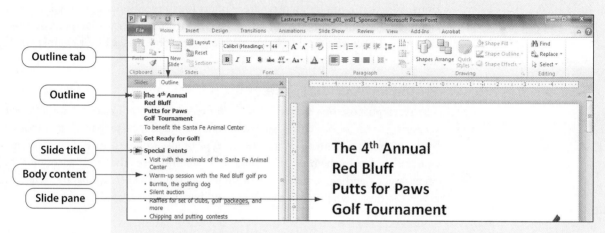

Figure 1   The Outline tab

d. Click the **Slides tab**, and then click the thumbnail image for **Slide 2**. The Slides tab displays thumbnail views of the slides in the presentation. When a slide is selected, it is displayed in the Slide pane.

e. Point to each of the areas on the **status bar** at the bottom of the window.

You will note the number of the current slide, the total number of slides, and the theme used to create the slide show on the left side of the status bar. On the right side of the status bar are buttons for changing the views of the slide show.

f. Drag the **Zoom Slider** to increase the magnification of the slide in the Slide pane to approximately **150%**. Click the **Zoom Out** button on the Zoom Slider until the slide is at **30%** magnification. Click the **Fit slide to current window** button to maximize the slide in the Slide pane.

g. Drag the **border** between the Slides tab and the Slide pane to the left to increase the size of the Slide pane, and then drag the **border** between the Slide pane and the Notes pane at the bottom of the window up.

h. Click the **Previous Slide arrow** to return to the first slide. The Previous Slide and Next Slide arrows are used to move between the slides in Normal view.

i. Click in the **Notes pane,** and then type Introduction – Name and job title. Press Enter to move to the next line, and then type Purpose – Introduce you to the opportunities for sponsorship of the Putts for Paws Golf Tournament.

The Notes pane contains the speaker's notes for each slide in the presentation. These notes are not seen by the audience when the presentation is displayed. As the presenter, you can print the notes with the slides for preparation or practice.

j. **Save** the presentation.

Displaying a Presentation in Normal, Slide Sorter, Reading, and Slide Show Views

PowerPoint can display slides in a variety of views. Each view has a purpose, and the available tools change as you switch between views. **Normal view** is used to edit the slides. **Slide Sorter view** provides options for rearranging slides and reviewing transitions. In Slide Sorter view, you see thumbnails of each of the slides. **Reading view** displays the slides, one at a time, offering tools such as the title bar Minimize, Maximize/Restore, and Close buttons, and navigation buttons for moving between slides. **Slide Show view** is used to display the presentation to an audience. The Normal view, Slide Sorter view, and Reading view are accessed using the View tab. The Slide Show view is accessed on the Slide Show tab. All of the views are available on the view buttons on the status bar.

To Display a Presentation

a. Click the **Slide Sorter** button 🔳 on the status bar. Slide 1 is highlighted with a light orange border because it was the slide selected in the previous view. Thumbnails of all six slides in the presentation are displayed.

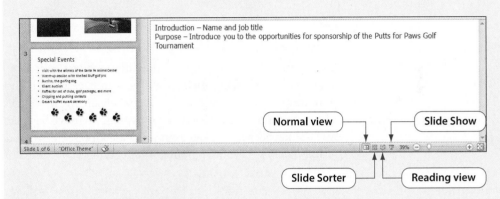

Figure 2   PowerPoint view buttons

b. Click the **View tab**, click **Zoom** in the Zoom group, select **50%**, and then click **OK**. The thumbnails become smaller, which is useful for displaying more slides in a large slide show.

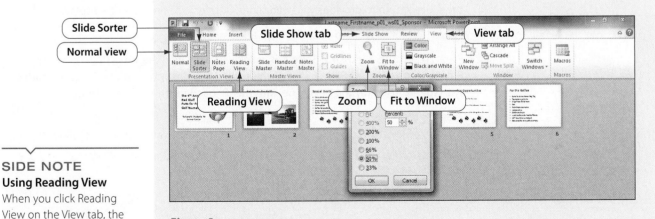

Figure 3   Slide Sorter view

c. Click **Fit to Window** in the Zoom group. This causes the slides to be displayed as large as possible in this view.

d. Click **Slide 5**. The light orange highlighting indicates this slide is selected.

SIDE NOTE
Using Reading View

When you click Reading View on the View tab, the first slide of the presentation is displayed. When you click Reading View on the status bar, the slide displayed in the Slide pane is displayed in Reading view.

SIDE NOTE
Using the Menu

The menu in Reading view enables you to navigate through the slides, preview and print the slides, copy and edit slides, display the slides full screen, and end the show in Reading view.

e. Click **Normal** in the Presentation Views group. Slide 5 is now displayed in the Slide pane.

f. Click **Reading View** on the status bar. Slide 5 is displayed.

g. Click **Next** 🔲 on the status bar to view Slide 6. The Next and Previous buttons on the status bar make it easy to navigate through the slide show in Reading view.

h. Click **Menu** 🔲 on the status bar, and then click **Edit Slides**. Slide 5 is displayed in the Slide pane.

i. Click **Slide Show** 🔲 on the status bar. Slide 5 fills the screen because it was the slide selected when you clicked Slide Show. If a different slide was highlighted, then that slide would have been displayed. Keep the slide show running as you move to the next section.

Troubleshooting

If you need to exit a presentation while it is displayed in Slide Show view, press $\boxed{\text{Esc}}$. This returns you to Normal view.

Navigating in Slide Show View

Most often, when you give a presentation, you will display the slide show in Slide Show view, advancing each slide after you have spoken about the contents of the slide. PowerPoint offers many methods for advancing the slides and returning to previous slides. Some people prefer to use the mouse to move between the slides, yet others like to use the keyboard. You can even purchase a presenter remote control that frees you from standing close to your computer while giving your presentation.

To Display and Navigate Through a Slide Show

a. Click the **left mouse** button to advance to the next slide in the presentation. Right-click, point to **Go to Slide**, and then click **5 Sponsorship Opportunities**.

b. Right-click again, and then click **Previous**. Using the mouse you can advance through the slides, return to previously viewed slides, or select specific slides to display.

c. Press $\boxed{\uparrow}$ on the keyboard. This displays Slide 3.

d. Press $\boxed{\text{N}}$ on the keyboard. Slide 4 is displayed as it was the next slide in the show. Press $\boxed{\text{P}}$ to return to Slide 3. These letter keys enable you to move between slides with the "N" used for the next slide, and the "P" used for the previous slide.

e. Press $\boxed{\text{Enter}}$.
   The display changes to Slide 4. Enter enables you to advance to the next slide.

For the Golfers

- Santa Fe Animal Center Bag Tag
- Tournament golf shirt
- All golf fees for 18 holes
- Cart
- Hole-in-one cash prize
- Longest drive
- Closest to the pin
- Lunch buffet at the Red Bluff Bistro
- 19th hole Dinner at Indigo 5
- Dessert buffet at awards ceremony

Slide displayed in Slide Show view

Menu displayed due to right-click

Slide numbers and titles

Figure 4 Slide Show view

SIDE NOTE
Navigating with the Keyboard Arrows
The up and down arrow keys can be used to move between slides. The right and left arrow keys can also be used, with the left arrow returning you to the previous slide and the right arrow displaying the next slide in the presentation.

f. Press Backspace.
   Slide 3 is displayed again. Backspace returns you to the previous slide.

g. Press Spacebar to display Slide 4. Many people like to use the Spacebar to advance through their presentations because it is a large button that is easy to find in a darkened room.

h. Use your favorite method to advance to the end of the presentation. When you reach the end of the presentation, a black screen alerts you that you are at the end. Any of the methods for moving to the next slide will return you to Normal view at the end of the slide show. The slide that was selected when you started the slide show in the Slide pane will be displayed.

Quick Reference / Navigating the Slide Show

There are many options for navigating through the slide show:

1. To advance to the next slide, press either N, Enter, Page Down, →, ↓, or Spacebar.
2. To return to a previous slide, press either P, Page Up, ←, ↑, or Backspace.
3. To display a black blank slide, press B or period.
4. To display a white blank slide, press W or comma.

Modifying a Presentation to Increase Effectiveness

One of the many advantages of PowerPoint is that it enables you to quickly update or modify a presentation. This means that presentations can be recycled and personalized for the current audience. For instance, your sales presentation may have the basic information about your products, but for each customer you visit, you may wish to update the slide show to include the customer name and date. You may also want to move the slides around so the most relevant products are at the beginning of the presentation. In this section you will edit slides, make adjustments to the font, and manipulate the slides.

Editing Slides

As you continue with the Red Bluff Putts for Paws Golf Tournament presentation, you will modify a slide show from a previous year to reflect a new date, add text to a slide, and delete text.

To Modify a Slide Show

a. Click **Slide 4** on the Slides tab to display it in the Slide pane.

b. Select the text **July 31, 2010**, and then type June 12, 2013 to indicate that the next tournament is on June 12.

c. Click the **Next Slide arrow** ⬇ until Slide 6 is visible in the Slide pane. Click in front of **All golf fees for 18 holes**, type Goodie bag sponsored by Pro Sports of Santa Fe and press Enter.

   You may notice that the size of the text automatically changes to accommodate all of the text within the text placeholder. The **placeholder** is a container for text or graphics and is used to position objects on the layout.

d. Click **Previous Slide** ⬆ until Slide 3 is visible in the Slide pane, select the text **Burrito, the golfing dog**, and then press Delete. Save the presentation, but keep it open.

Troubleshooting

When you delete text, sometimes you do not delete the line break. This may leave a blank line in the middle of the text block. Press Backspace twice to delete the extra space, if necessary.

Modifying Text

The **content** of your presentation, especially the text, is a very important element of your slide show. You must ensure the accuracy of your words. People remember and believe more of what they see on the screen than what they hear. Making retractions or corrections after a presentation is difficult, so review your content carefully.

As you use PowerPoint, you will make a lot of decisions. You will decide how to group content items. You will select fonts for the text elements. You will align the text and organize it on the slide. You will edit your content to improve the layout of slides.

After a discussion on font selections, you will continue to modify the Putts for Paws presentation to improve the readability of the slides. You will also align the text to better organize the information.

Understanding Print-Friendly and Screen-Friendly Fonts

Typography, the art of selecting and arranging text on a page, is an interesting topic for in-depth study. Understanding some basic concepts enables you to produce slides that are easy to read. People read printed pages and screen pages differently, which affects the choices you make for the fonts in your slide show.

Real World Advice Readability Is Key!

Readability is the most important aspect of a presentation. If possible, project your slides and stand at the far back of the room. Can you still read everything easily? What if you had vision problems? Anything that is too small to read should be adjusted prior to displaying the slide show to your audience. A common occurrence in the business world is presentations that contain financial information or other numbers that are small and hard to read. A solution to the problem is to summarize the numbers on the slides and provide the complete data in handouts.

Printer-friendly fonts have characteristics that make them easy to read on paper. They are usually printed in black ink on a white page giving them high contrast, which improves the readability of the text. Serif fonts are considered formal, business-like, and powerful. Often **serif fonts**, such as Times New Roman, are used for large blocks of text. The serifs, or small lines at the ends of the letters, provide guidelines for the eye to follow as the text is read. These fonts move the eye quickly across the page. Black-and-white printing is also less expensive than printing with color.

Figure 5 Serif and sans serif fonts

Screen-friendly fonts are easy to read on the screen, help protect the eyes, and reduce stress. Because of the resolution of the text on displayed slides, fonts on slides must maintain their integrity at great size. **Sans serif fonts**, such as Veranda and Trebuchet, were designed specifically for screens. "Sans" means "without" in Latin, so sans serif fonts do not have small lines at the ends of the letters. Sans serif fonts give the text a casual, modern feel. The serif font Georgia is also a good screen-friendly font. You will often find the title of slides displayed in a serif font, while the content of the slide is set to a sans serif font. Screen-friendly fonts have an additional perk; you can use color without additional expense. Be aware that you must still select colors that have a good amount of contrast to make the text easy to read. Avoid color combinations that are hard on the eyes, such as a red background with turquoise text. Select two or three colors to use consistently throughout your presentation. Later you will learn about PowerPoint themes that enable you to use colors consistently. Remember that your goal is to have people read your slides.

Making Font Selections

Generally, you will design slides with a sans serif font for the majority of the text, occasionally using a serif font for emphasis. Text should be a mixture of upper and lowercase characters, even for headings. It is more difficult to read text that is written in all capitals. You should avoid hyphenation of words on your slides when possible. Tracking between the parts of hyphenated words is difficult when the slide is projected. It is a good idea to use bold for emphasis instead of italic, which can be hard to read, or underscored text, which is confused with hyperlinks.

Importantly, you must also decide the font size. Your goal is to have your slides read. Text that is too small frustrates the audience. Slide titles are set in a larger font than the body of the slide. The minimum font size you should use for the body text is 18 point. Of course, larger is better!

Providing an Appropriate Amount of Text on a Slide

As you create content for your slides, think like a headline writer, striving for the fewest words possible to convey your point. For instance, replace "Our goal is to increase sales by 55% in the coming year," with "Goal—Increase sales 55%." Use bullet points rather than complete sentences. Remove repetitive words, replacing them with a heading. Rather than placing a number-rich table on a slide, summarize the numbers. Focus your audience by covering one major point or concept per slide.

A worthwhile rule of thumb is the **Rule of 6's**. This rule calls for a maximum of six words per line, and six lines per slide, not including the title. The rule ensures that your slides are readable. Do not fret if you occasionally have more words on a line. This is a guideline. Your goal is to put the absolute essence of your message on your slides. You want the audience to interact with you—not spend all of their time reading the screen. Remember that the slide show is a visual aid, meant to *support* your presentation.

Continuing with the Putts for Paws presentation, you will change the font on a slide and shorten some text items.

To Make Font Adjustments

a. Click **Slide 1** on the Slides tab.

b. Select the text **To benefit the Santa Fe Animal Center**, click the **Home tab**, and then click the **Font arrow** in the Font group. Click **Georgia**.

   Notice that the words "Santa" and "Fe" now appear on different lines. Because these words are related, it is best to keep them together.

c. Click **Decrease Font Size** [A˅] in the Font group once, and then confirm that the words are on the same line.

d. Click **Italic** [I] in the Font group. The italic of Georgia is very screen-friendly when used with a small number of words.

e. Click **Slide 3** on the Slides tab, and then select the text **Warm-up session with the Red Bluff golf pro**. Shorten the statement by typing Warm-up with the golf pro.

f. Click **Slide 5** on the Slides tab, and then review the text. Notice that some words are repeated and are somewhat redundant. Select the text **on the course**, and then press ⌈Delete⌋. Be sure to delete both instances of the words "on the course".

Troubleshooting

If you select the space to the right of the words you want to delete, the next bullet point is also deleted, and the text jumps up to the position of the deleted text. Press ⌈Enter⌋ to recreate the bullet and move the text into the correct position.

g. Select the text **Logo/brand displayed** under the **Hole Sponsor** heading, and then type Corporate signage. Avoid using repetitive phrases whenever possible.

h. Select the text **displayed** under the **Flag Sponsor** heading, and then type waving.

Aligning Text

Text that is appropriately aligned provides organization to the text and enables your audience to read the material faster. On the Home tab, the Paragraph group contains options to Align Text Left, Center, Align Text Right, and Justify. Most of the body text you type on slides should be left-aligned. People begin reading at the left side of the page and are comfortable with this alignment. Center alignment is sometimes used in headings and slide titles. It is difficult to read large amounts of text that is centered, so it is a good idea not to center the slide body text. Right alignment is used for emphasis or artistic reasons, and with limited amounts of text. Often right alignment is a solution to placing captions close to photographs that are on the right side of the slide. Justified alignment produces a block with both the left and right margins aligned. Extra spaces are automatically added between the words to achieve the alignment of the margins. This works well for quotations that are longer than one line.

To Align Text

a. Click **Slide 1** on the Slides tab.

b. Select the title text **The 4ᵗʰ Annual Red Bluff Putts for Paws Golf Tournament**, click the **Home tab**, and then click **Center** ▤ in the Paragraph group.

   The text is centered within the text placeholder. Notice that the placeholder is not centered on the slide. This was a design decision made to balance the head of the golf club with the text on the slide.

c. Select the text **To benefit the Santa Fe Animal Center**, and then click **Align Text Right** ▤ in the Paragraph group. The text aligns with the right edge of the placeholder.

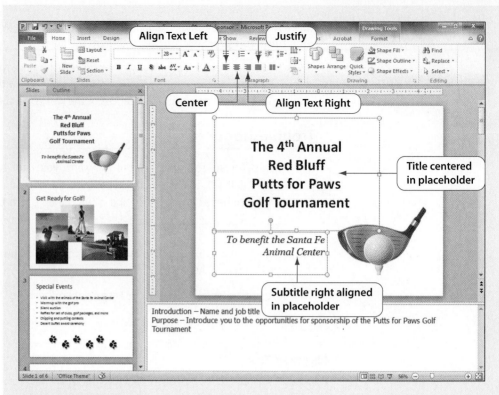

Figure 6 Aligning text

d. Click **Slide 2** on the Slides tab, and then click somewhere on the title of the slide. Click **Center** ≡ in the Paragraph group. Alignment is applied to the entire line when you click on just a portion of the line.

e. Click **Slide 4** on the Slides tab, select the **four lines** of text beginning with **Date** and ending with **Cost**, and then click **Center** ≡ in the Paragraph group.

   Notice that the colons after "Date," "Time," " Format," and "Cost" are now misaligned. After careful consideration, you realize that the words are not required.

f. Select **Date:** and then press ⌷Delete⌷. Repeat this step to remove the words **Time:,** **Format:,** and **Cost:.** Be careful to delete only the word "Cost" and the colon—not the entire line.

Using Text Hierarchy to Convey Organization

As you develop the content of your presentation, you will quickly see that there are relationships between the pieces of information. You will want to group information together and perhaps provide a title so your audience sees the information in an organized way. This helps them to remember your key points.

Text hierarchy can be shown using bullets or numbers. Bullets are used to group items. In PowerPoint, you can select different bullet symbols using the Bullets arrow in the Paragraph group. You can even customize the bullet symbol by changing the color or size. Many people select custom bullet symbols from the Wingdings font because of the graphic nature of the symbols. Numbers are used for sequential steps that need to appear in a specific order. The format of numbers can be changed between Roman numerals, Arabic numerals, and letters. The color and size of the numbers can also be adjusted. You can also change the starting number for the list.

Text hierarchy continues with indenting subitems on a slide. The first bulleted point may have three or four characteristics, which are indented and have a different bullet character. The Paragraph group contains the commands to increase and decrease the indention of the items.

To Apply Text Hierarchy and Bullets

a. On Slide 4, select the three lines of text beginning with **Individual Player - $200**. Click the **Home tab**, and then click the **Bullets arrow** in the Paragraph group.

b. Click **Bullets and Numbering**.

c. Click **Customize**, and then click the **Font arrow**. Select the **Wingdings** font.

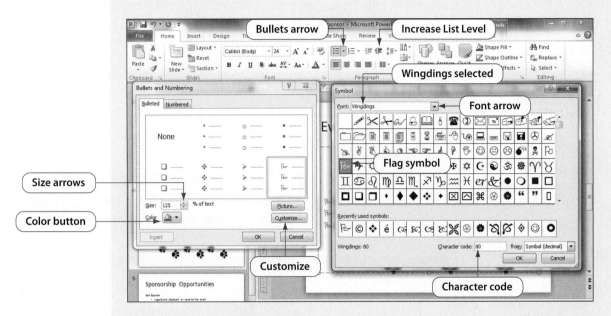

Figure 7 Custom Wingdings bullets

d. Click the **flag symbol** (Character code 80), and then click **OK**.

e. Click the **Color** button in the Bullets and Numbering dialog box, and select **Red, Accent 2** from the palette. Notice that all of the bullet symbols in the dialog box are now displayed in this color.

Troubleshooting

Point to a color on the palette, and a ScreenTip will appear giving the name of the color. Be careful to note that lightened and darkened versions of colors exist—for example, Red, Accent 2, Lighter 60%. You may need to have your slide match the color of a brochure design by an outside marketing company. The marketing vendor informs you the brochure color is Red, Accent 2. The lightened versions are not the same as the nonlightened version.

f. Click the **up Size arrow** repeatedly to increase the size of the symbol to **125%** of the text, and then click **OK**.

g. Click **Slide 6** on the Slides tab, click after the word **Cart**, and then press Enter.

h. Type Contests. Select the next three lines of text, and then click **Increase List Level** in the Paragraph group. The types of contests that will be played are grouped together and indented.

i. Click before the word **Lunch**, and then type Food. Press Enter, select the three lines of text beginning with **Lunch**, and then click **Increase List Level**.

Using the Format Painter

The **Format Painter** enables you to quickly select the text format from already format-ted text and apply it to other text within the presentation. Select the text you want to copy the format from, and then on the Home tab, click Format Painter on the Clipboard group, and then select the text you want to format. For multiple instances of applying the format, such as on different slides, double-click Format Painter, which keeps it turned on as you select the text to format. When you have finished formatting all of the text, click Format Painter again to toggle it off.

Previously, you centered the title for Slide 2. You will now use the format of that text to center the other titles in the presentation.

To Use the Format Painter

a. Click **Slide 2** on the Slides tab, and then select the title of the slide.

b. Click the **Home tab**, and then double-click **Format Painter** in the Clipboard group. You will notice a paint brush icon on the pointer to indicate that the Format Painter is active.

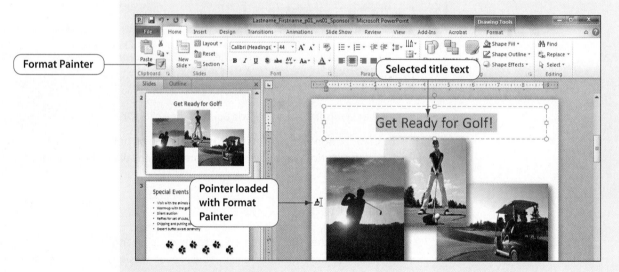

Figure 8 The Format Painter

c. Click **Slide 3** on the Slides tab, and then drag across the **title**. The title is centered. Continue centering the titles on the remaining slides in the presentation by displaying each slide in the Slide pane and then dragging across the title.

d. Click **Format Painter** in the Clipboard group to return to the normal pointer.

Manipulating Slides

PowerPoint features tools that make it easy to add, modify, and delete content on the slides. It goes further by providing tools that enable you to manipulate the slides themselves. You can add new slides at any point in the presentation. The layout of the slides can be changed to provide better balance. You can delete unwanted slides. In addition, moving slides from one position in the show to another is as simple as a drag-and-drop operation.

You may have noticed some problems with the Putts for Paws presentation, such as no contact information. In addition, one slide does not have a real purpose in the presentation, and the organization of the slide show does not convey the most important information at the beginning of the presentation.

Real World Advice   Provide Contact Information

It is always a good idea to have contact information at the end of the presentation. Audience members will contact you to learn more about your topic and suggest that others, with similar interests, contact you.

Adding a New Slide

The number of slides you can add to a presentation are seemingly endless, but keep in mind that your audience will appreciate a concise presentation with a clear message. Slides can be added anywhere in the presentation. Select the slide prior to where you want to insert a new slide, and on the Home tab, click New Slide in the Slides group. The new slide is added after the selected slide. If you want to put a slide prior to the first slide, click above Slide 1 on the Slides tab, and then click New Slide in the Slides group on the Home tab.

Real World Advice   Planning the Number of Slides

Plan to display a new slide every 2 to 3 minutes during your presentation. In a 20- to 30-minute presentation, this is a total of 10 slides. This guideline keeps you on track with timing your presentation as you plan for and deliver your speech.

With the exception of the title slide at the beginning of the presentation, every time you insert a new slide using the New Slide button, it will default to the layout of the previous slide. Most of the time this is what you will want, but in some cases you may want to use a different layout. The New Slide arrow enables you to select a new layout as you insert a new slide.

To Add Slides

a. Click **Slide 6** on the Slides tab, click the **Home tab**, and then click **New Slide** in the Slides group. The thumbnail slide appears at the bottom of the Slides tab, and the slide with empty placeholders is displayed in the Slide pane.

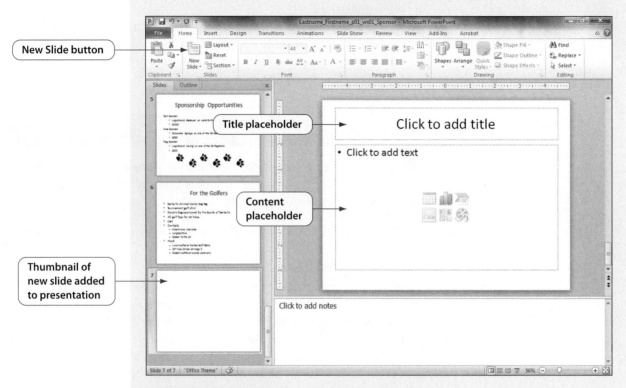

Figure 9 Adding a slide

b. Click the **title** placeholder text, and then type Contact Us.

c. Click the **content** placeholder text, type Your Name and then press Enter.

d. Type Tournament Manager and then press Enter.

e. Type Phone: 505-555-1345 and then press Enter.

f. Type E-mail: followed by Your e-mail address and then press Enter. E-mail addresses are automatically converted to hyperlinks by PowerPoint.

g. Type John Schilling and then press Enter.

h. Type Golf Pro and then press Enter.

i. Type Phone: 505-555-1387 and then press Enter.

j. Type E-mail: jschilling@paintedparadiseresort.com and then press Enter. By pressing Enter, the e-mail address is converted into a hyperlink, but an additional bullet was added to the slide. Press Backspace twice to remove it.

Troubleshooting

To apply the hyperlink, you must press Enter or the Spacebar at the end of the e-mail address.

Changing the Slide Layout

Changing the layout of a slide can improve its readability. You can group similar information together. For example, you have listed yourself and John Schilling on the slide, but by changing the layout, you can ensure that your audience links the information.

The **slide layouts** are provided as part of the theme applied to the presentation. The Putts for Paws presentation currently uses the Office theme, which provides nine slide layouts. Some themes offer more layouts, while others offer less. Most themes contain a title slide, with placeholders for the title and subtitle, and a slide for title and content. Often you will find a blank slide that enables you to place elements where you wish.

You can change the layout of the slide either before you add information or afterward. Placeholders indicate the types of information you can place on the slide. Content slides not only have placeholders for text, but also for graphic elements, such as pictures, clip art, tables, charts, and media clips. The size of placeholders can be adjusted by dragging the **sizing handles** that appear when you click in the content area.

To Change Slide Layouts

a. If necessary, click Slide 7. Click the **Home tab**, click **Layout** in the Slides group, and then select **Two Content**. This layout gives you two columns, but all of the information you typed is in the first column.

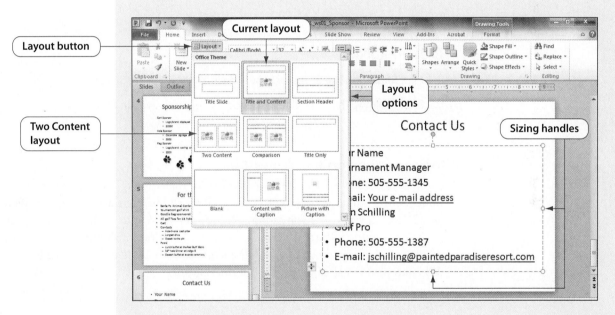

Figure 10   Selecting a layout

b. Select **John Schilling's information**, and drag it to the right column. His e-mail address is now shown on two lines, so further adjustment is needed.

c. Select John's title **Golf Pro**, **Phone: 505-555-1387**, and **E-mail: jschilling@ paintedparadiseresort.com**, but not his name, and then click **Decrease Font Size** in the Font group. Select just the e-mail address **jschilling@paintedparadiseresort.com**, click the **Font Size arrow**, and then click **16**.

d. Select John's **phone text**, and then click **Format Painter** in the Clipboard group. Drag across your title **Tournament Manager**, **Phone: 505-555-1345**, and the word **E-mail:**. Select John's e-mail address **jschilling@paintedparadiseresort.com**, click **Format Painter**, and then drag across your **e-mail address**.

Troubleshooting

> Remember that you do not have to use the Format Painter to change the format of the text. You can always change the formats individually using the tools in the Font and Paragraph groups.

e. Click **your name**, and then click **Bullets** :≡ ▾ in the Paragraph group to remove the bullet. Click **Center** in the Paragraph group to center your name in the text placeholder.

f. Select **your name**, and then click **Format Painter** ✒ in the Clipboard group. Drag across **John's name**. When you click Format Painter just once, the next text you drag across is changed, and the pointer returns to normal when you release the mouse button.

Deleting Slides

On occasion you will delete unneeded slides from your presentation. The slide or slides you want to delete are selected in the Slides tab, and then you press Delete. If you delete a slide by mistake, click Undo to return it to the slide show in the original position. After looking at the Putts for Paws presentation, you decide to delete the second slide as it does not really provide the audience with additional information.

To Delete a Slide

a. Click **Slide 2** on the Slides tab. The slide is displayed in the Slide pane.

b. Press Delete . The next slide in the sequence is displayed in the Slide pane.

Moving Slides on the Slides Tab

Often after reviewing a slide show, you realize that the organization of the presentation would benefit from moving some slides. In PowerPoint there are two ways to do this. You can use the Slides tab, or you can use Slide Sorter view to drag slides to new positions.

The flow of the Putts for Paws presentation can be improved by moving the Event Information slide into position after the title slide. You will also move the For the Golfers slide into position after the Event Information slide.

To Rearrange Slides on the Slides Tab

a. Drag **Slide 3** on the Slides tab upward so a line appears between Slide 1 and Slide 2. Release the mouse button and the Event Information slide will be moved.

b. Drag **Slide 5** on the Slides tab upward so a line appears between Slide 2 and Slide 3. Release the mouse button and the For the Golfers slide appears as Slide 3.

Moving Slides Using Slide Sorter View

Many people prefer to use Slide Sorter view to rearrange slides because you can view more slides at one time than when using the Slides tab. Slide Sorter view is available by clicking the View tab and then clicking Slide Sorter in the Presentation Views group, or by clicking Slide Sorter on the status bar at the bottom of the window.

Using Slide Sorter view, you will move the Sponsorship Opportunities slide into position after the For the Golfers slide. This will show the audience that there is more than just individual opportunities for golfers by offering them opportunities to sponsor part of the event for advertising purposes.

To Rearrange Slides in Slide Sorter View

a. Click **Slide Sorter** on the status bar.

The slide thumbnails are now shown in rows. Notice the small numbers at the bottom-right corner of each slide that indicate their order.

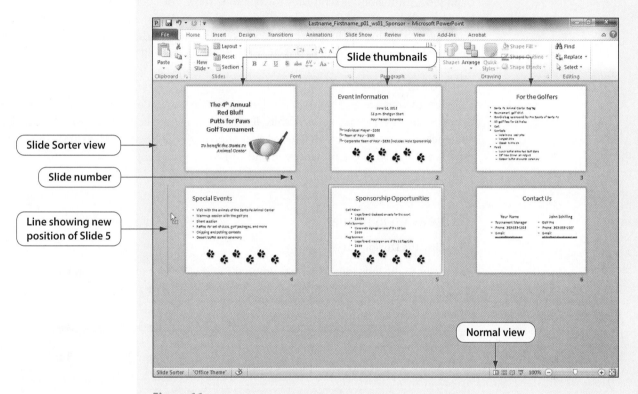

Figure 11 Moving slides in Slide Sorter view

b. Drag the thumbnail for **Slide 5** until you see a vertical line before Slide 4, and then release the mouse button. The Sponsorship Opportunities slide is now the fourth slide in the presentation.

c. Click **Normal** on the status bar. You should now have the title slide, Event Information, For the Golfers, Sponsorship Opportunities, Special Events, and Contact Us slides shown in this order on the Slides tab.

Understanding the Difference Between a Theme and a Template

PowerPoint enables you to concentrate on the message you are trying to convey to your audience and build your presentation around that message. **Design themes** and templates add visual interest to your message. Background, color, and font selections are included as part of the design themes, which can easily be applied to your slide show. PowerPoint has 40 built-in themes, with more available online at Office.com. In some cases, you may want to build your own theme. Many businesses have a standard corporate theme that makes their presentations recognizable and professional. Themes can be used in the various Microsoft applications, so you can apply a theme to a Word document or Excel worksheet that matches the theme of the presentation. Themes can be applied at any time during your work on the presentation, but they will override other formatting changes, so it is best to apply them as you begin working on the presentation.

Like themes, **templates** contain background, color, and font selections, but they may also include sample content, slide transitions, and slide layouts. Many people use templates to guide them in creating presentations. For example, built-in templates are available for project status reports, training, quiz shows, and photo albums. Templates are selected as you begin a new PowerPoint presentation.

Both themes and templates are starting places for the design of your presentation. As you apply design themes or templates to your slide show, consider your purpose, audience, and message. You can modify the colors, font selections, and theme effects to fit your needs. You will apply a theme to the Putts for Paws presentation and then modify it. The theme was created by the marketing department at the resort for the golf course.

Applying a Design Theme

Design themes are available on the Design tab in PowerPoint. You will briefly look at the design themes that are available. Rather than using the built-in themes, the design theme for the Red Bluff Golf Club will be applied to the Putts for Paws slide show. It will give consistency to the presentation and add to its visual appeal.

To Use a Design Theme

a. Click the **Design tab**.

b. Point to the individual **theme thumbnails** in the Themes group, pausing momentarily so Live Preview displays the theme on the slide in the Slide pane.

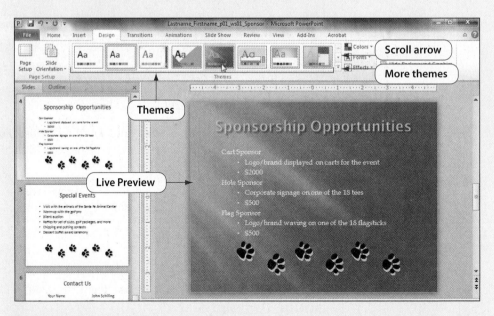

Figure 12 Using design themes

c. Click the **scroll arrow** in the Themes group to display additional themes. Point to the **slide thumbnails** to preview them on the slide.

d. Click **More** ⊡ in the Themes group, and then preview additional themes.

e. Click **Browse for Themes**, navigate to the disk drive where your data files are located, click **p01_ws01_Sponsor_Theme**, and then click **Apply**. This external theme was created especially for the golf tournament.

Troubleshooting

The p01_ws01_Sponsor_Theme file is located in the same folder as the other files for the textbook.

f. Click each of the **slides** on the Slides tab to review the changes made by applying the theme.

   In this theme, the font for the headings is Aharoni, while the body text font for the content is Georgia. The footer, containing the name of the golf course at the bottom of the slide, is a graphic element made with WordArt. The colors used for the theme are clean and crisp, with green suggesting the golf course, and red used to tie in the name of the course.

Modifying a Theme

There are times when you will not be able to find a design theme that fits your preferences. In this case, you can select a theme and then modify it. You can change the theme colors, fonts, and effects. When you change the theme elements, the changes can affect the entire presentation. This saves you time and effort over changing elements individually on each slide. In some cases, you will also want to make adjustments to one or two slides.

   You decide to review your choices for theme fonts. You are looking for a modern, clean font combination. As you may have noticed, the Aharoni font used for the headings is very bold but a little difficult to read. The number 4 on the first slide also appears to be smaller than the rest of the text in the title. The Georgia font used for the body text is a little too formal for your tastes.

To Modify Theme Fonts

a. Click **Slide 1** on the Slides tab, if necessary, to display it in the Slide pane.

b. Click the **Design tab**, click **Fonts** in the Themes group, and then point to each **font** on the list to view the Live Preview of the title slide. As you view each font group, notice the change to the number 4 on the title slide.

c. Click **Create New Theme Fonts** at the bottom of the Fonts gallery.

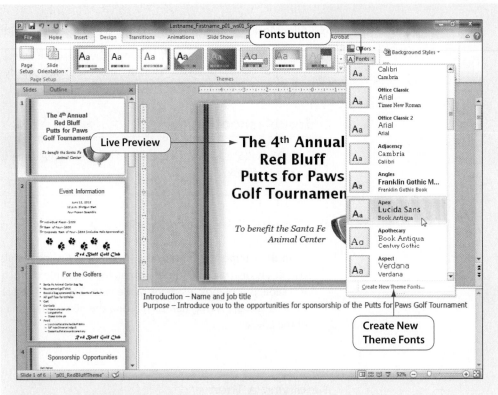

Figure 13 Modifying theme fonts

d. Click the **Heading font arrow**, and then click **Arial**.

e. Click the **Body font arrow**, and then click **Calibri**.

f. Select the text in the **Name** box, and then type Lastname Firstname Red Bluff Font, replacing Lastname Firstname with your own name.

Figure 14 Creating a font group

g. Click **Save**.

h. Click each **slide** in the slide show to review the changes you have made.

   The number 4 on Slide 1 now appears to be the same size as the rest of the heading. The fonts have changed on all of the slides to match your new font group.

Using Color Strategically

There are many aspects to consider when using color in a presentation. Color can be used to emphasize important elements and to organize the message. Colors are also associated with emotions or qualities, with different colors suggesting various things in different parts of the world. For instance, in the American culture, black is associated with death, but in the Chinese culture, the color associated with death is white. Carefully consider your audience, objectives, and message as you make your selections for color in your presentation.

Real World Advice — Color Associations

When using color in presentations be mindful of common color associations. People may think of danger or excitement, for example, when using red; whereas blue can mean calm and tranquility, and yellow can mean cheerfulness or optimism.

As you select the colors for the presentation, it is best to choose the background color first, and then place high contrast colors on top of it. Be careful the colors do not clash. For instance, a medium blue background and red text almost vibrates because the colors clash. Select a maximum of three or four colors to use in a presentation, and keep the colors consistent throughout the presentation. Use the brightest colors as accents in areas needing the most attention.

You will change the color of the title and subtitle text to coordinate with the color scheme of the theme.

To Modify Theme Colors

a. Click the **Home tab**, and then click **Slide 1** on the Slides tab. Select the title text **The 4th Annual Red Bluff Putts for Paws Golf Tournament**. You will only change the color of the font on this one slide, so you select just the text you want to change.

b. Click the **Font Color arrow** in the Font group, and then click **More Colors** in the gallery.

c. Click the **Custom tab**. Modify the color numbers at the bottom of the dialog box as follows:
   - Red: **0**
   - Green: **150**
   - Blue: **0**

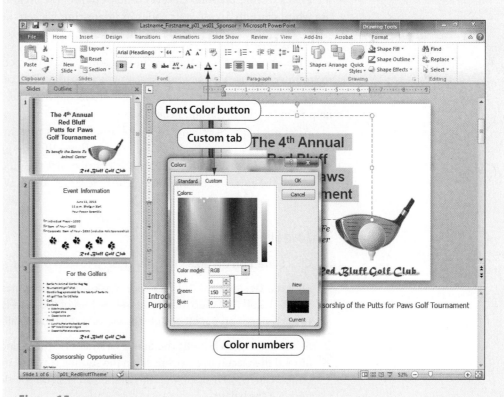

Figure 15 Selecting font colors

d. Click **OK**, and then click outside of the text placeholder. The color of the title has changed to green.

e. Select the subtitle text, **To benefit the Santa Fe Animal Center**, click the **Font Color arrow** ▲ ⁃, and then click **Dark Green** in the Recent Colors section of the gallery.

Modifying a Slide Layout

Various design principles apply to slides and serve as useful guidelines as you make adjustments to your presentations. The **KISS principle** is one of the most important: Keep It Short and Simple. While other common variations for the acronym "KISS" exist, the principle serves you well when preparing presentations by using simplicity to focus attention on the topic. Your audience should be able to read and comprehend your slide in less than 10 seconds. This means that they can quickly read the revealed slide and turn their attention back to you.

Aim to design slides with a path the eye can naturally follow. Keep in mind that people who read English are used to beginning at the top left of the page and reading to the lower right. While it may be interesting to place the titles of the slides in the bottom-right corner, it may also be very confusing to your audience without some additional clues such as font size, emphasis, or color changes.

Strive to make some important element on each slide dominant while achieving a sense of balance with the remaining elements on the slide. In the Putts for Paws presentation, the golf club graphic is quite dominant, and therefore needs to be balanced by the title placeholder position. The dominant element can be the title, a quotation, a graphic—such as a chart, clip art, or picture—or a portion of the text. Look at the slides in your presentation and think about the purpose of each slide. The dominant element should reflect the purpose of the slide.

Planning the Use of White Space

White space, which is not always white, is space on the slide without text or graphics. It serves as a resting place for the eye. It helps to provide organization to your slides. You can use white space to divide your slides in interesting ways to keep your audience involved.

Moving Slide Content

Slide placeholders, the containers for text and graphic elements, can be moved and resized to improve the use of the white space on your slides. You can also manipulate the placeholders to suggest a relationship between items on the slide. Placeholder adjustments can help to move the eye around the slide.

After applying the theme to your Putts for Paws presentation, you notice some areas where text overlaps the background. You will modify the placeholders to move the text into the white areas of the slide. You also notice that the Red Bluff Golf Club text in the bottom-right corner is redundant on the title slide, so you will remove it from that slide.

To Move Slide Content

a. Click **Slide 1** on the Slides tab, if necessary, to view the title slide of the presentation.

b. Click the **Design tab**, and click **Hide Background Graphics** in the Background group. The Red Bluff Golf Club graphic at the bottom of the slide is removed, but you can see that it remains on the other slides by viewing the thumbnail slides on the Slides tab.

c. Select the text **To benefit the Santa Fe Animal Center**, and then drag the dotted line around the placeholder to reposition the subtitle closer to the golf club graphic.
   You can move placeholders anywhere you wish on the slide. This text was moved to improve the balance.

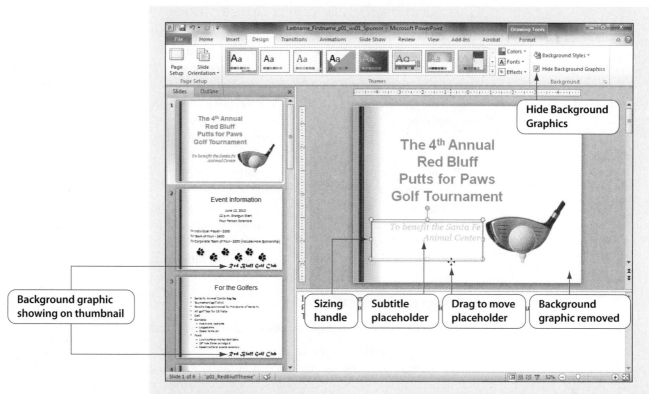

Figure 16 Moving slide content

d. Click **Slide 2** on the Slides tab, and then click anywhere in the body text.

e. Drag the **left sizing handle** to the right to move the text off of the green background.

The text in the last line breaks, leaving an orphaned word on the following line. This provides too much white space for the line and requires additional adjustment. The orphaned word, "Sponsorship," should appear on the same line as "Hole," if possible. You will increase the placeholder size and move "Sponsorship" to the previous line.

f. Drag the **right sizing handle** to the right side of the slide. There is enough room for the word **Sponsorship** on the line.

g. Click the **title** placeholder. Drag the **left sizing handle** to the right to move it off of the green background, and then drag the **right sizing handle** to the right edge of the slide. When you move placeholders, you should be consistent so centering works.

h. Adjust the body text and title placeholders on **Slides 3**, **4**, and **5** so the text is no longer on the green background graphic. Drag the right sizing handle to the right edge of the slide as you did in Step g.

i. Click **Slide 6** on the Slides tab, click the **body text on the left**, press and hold ⎡Shift⎤, and click the **body text on the right**.

Both placeholders are selected. When you select multiple placeholders, you can move the elements together, preserving their alignment. You will move the placeholders down and to the right.

j. Drag a **border** on one of the selected placeholders to the right so the edge of the right-hand placeholder is at the edge of the slide.

A four-pointed arrow will appear when you point to and drag the line. This arrow indicates that you are moving the placeholder.

k. Drag the bottom sizing handle of one of the placeholders up. You have decreased the size of the placeholder, providing room for you to move the placeholders down.

l. Drag a border of one of the selected placeholders down to move the contact information more toward the central portion of the slide.

Checking the Spelling in a Presentation

Keep in mind that accuracy in both the content as well as spelling and grammar is important. Remember that a small mistake on paper looks a whole lot worse when displayed on a big screen. PowerPoint notifies you of words that are not in the Microsoft dictionary by displaying a red, squiggly line under such words. You can immediately change the spelling when the line appears or check the spelling of the entire document as you complete the presentation. It is best not to depend on the spelling feature alone. For instance, on the fifth slide in the presentation, the word "dessert" is misspelled as "desert." Because "desert" is a word in the dictionary, it is not flagged as having incorrect spelling.

There are a couple of strategies for proofreading your presentation that will help you find errors. First, read each and every word of every slide out loud. Second, review your presentation, reading every word from the last slide to the first, in reverse order. Both of these strategies slow you down and remove the natural tendency to read words into the text that are not really there.

You will check the spelling in the entire presentation, making adjustments as needed.

To Review the Presentation

a. Click **Slide 1** on the Slides tab, and then click the **Review tab**.

b. Click **Spelling** in the Proofing group.
    The slides are reviewed and the first instance of a misspelled word is highlighted. The Spelling dialog box appears with suggestions for the correct spelling. You can select the correct spelling from the Suggestions list, retype the word in the Change to box, click to Ignore the spelling error as you might do if a proper name is flagged as an error, or Add the word to the dictionary.

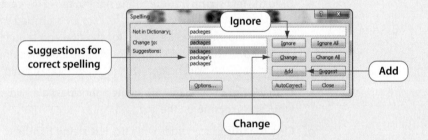

Figure 17   Checking the presentation spelling

c. Click **Change** to accept the spelling packages. PowerPoint reports that the spelling check is complete.

d. Click **OK**.

e. Click **Slide 6** on the Slides tab, and then begin reading the slides in the Slide pane in reverse. Pay attention to the e-mail addresses, making sure they are correct. When you read Slide 5, change the spelling of "desert" to "dessert." Some words will pass the spelling check, when in reality they are not the correct word for the phrase. Continue checking the rest of the slides in the presentation.

Using the Research Pane

PowerPoint provides access to other tools that can help you as you prepare presentations. The Research pane, opened by clicking Research in the Proofing group on the Review tab, provides access to a variety of reference books, research websites, and business and financial sites. You could use this pane to find and review information posted on the Internet by the Santa Fe Chamber of Commerce.

One of the reference books available on the Research pane is a **Thesaurus**. You notice that the word "sponsor" is used three times on Slide 4, and you would like to view other words that have a similar meaning.

To Use the Thesaurus

a. Click **Slide 4** on the Slides tab, select the word **Sponsor** in the Cart Sponsor heading, and then click **Research** in the Proofing group of the Review tab.

b. Click the **Resource** box arrow, and then click **Thesaurus: English (U.S.)**. Possible word substitutions are displayed.

c. Click **Champion** in the result list. The Thesaurus reports alternative words for "Champion." After reviewing these words, you decide not to use them and want to return to the list of words generated by the word **Sponsor**.

d. Click **Back** [←] to return to the **Sponsor** Thesaurus listing.

e. Point to **Patron** in the Thesaurus listing, click the **arrow** that appears on the right, and then click **Insert**. The word **Patron** will only be applied to the first sponsorship opportunity because it is a more expensive sponsorship.

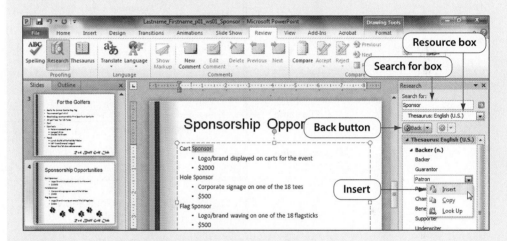

Figure 18 Using the Research pane

f. **Close** [X] the Research pane. **Save** [💾] the presentation.

Saving a Presentation

PowerPoint has many options for saving a presentation to fit different needs. So far you have been saving your presentation in a format that can only be opened with PowerPoint 2010 or 2007. Because not everyone has the most recent version of the software, one of the options is to save the file as a previous version.

You may also want to save the file so it opens directly in Slide Show view. **PowerPoint Show** is convenient because you do not have to open the software and then click the Slide Show button, or click the Slide Show tab and then click From Beginning. It is more professional looking to start the presentation without fumbling with additional clicks. It is important to note that when you have displayed all of the slides, the normal PowerPoint application appears so the slide show can be modified.

Another option you have is to save the file for distribution on a website, via **PowerPoint PDF** (Portable Document Format). When a file is saved as a PDF file it does not open in PowerPoint but rather in the Adobe Reader application. This means that you cannot use PowerPoint to update a PDF file. Be sure to always save the file in PowerPoint format too.

You will save the Putts for Paws presentation as a PowerPoint Show and as a PowerPoint PDF file. Each one will be named differently so you can observe the differences between them.

To Save in Different File Formats

a. Click the **File tab**, and then click **Save As**.

b. Click **Save as type** to display the Save options, and then click **PowerPoint Show**.

c. Click **File name**, and then change the file name to Lastname_Firstname_p01_ws01_Sponsor_Show. Navigate to the location where you store your project files.

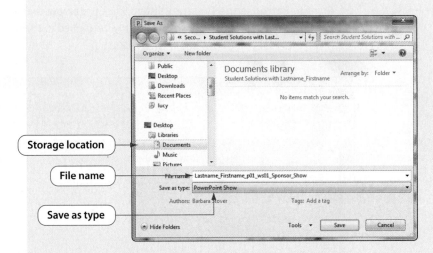

Figure 19 Saving a PowerPoint Show

d. Click **Save**. The file is saved in PowerPoint Show format, and the Normal PowerPoint view is displayed.

e. Click the **File tab**, and then click **Save As**. Navigate to the location where you store your project files.

f. Click **Save as type**, and then click **PDF**.

g. Click **File name**, and then change the file name to Lastname_Firstname_ p01_ws01_Sponsor_PDF.

h. Click **Save**. The file is published in PDF format and displayed. Close the Adobe Reader window.

i. Open the folder where you store your PowerPoint projects. You should now see the three files saved as a result of this exercise.

j. Double-click the **Lastname_Firstname_p01_ws01_Sponsor_Show** file. Click through each slide of the presentation. This is a good time to double-check the presentation for correctness. Close the presentation after reviewing the slides.

k. Open the folder where you store your PowerPoint projects, and then double-click the **Lastname_Firstname_p01_ws01_Sponsor_PDF** file.

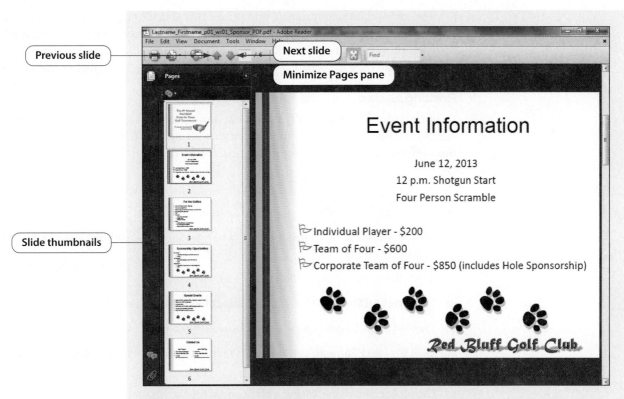

Figure 20 Viewing a PDF presentation

Troubleshooting

Adobe Reader is required to view the PDF version of the file. It can be downloaded for free from www.adobe.com. When you open the PDF version by double-clicking on the file name, it will automatically load Adobe Reader and then the presentation.

l. Advance through each of the slides using the navigation buttons. When you have reviewed the slides, close the Adobe Reader application window.

Previewing and Appropriate Printing of a Presentation

Many audiences will request a copy of your presentation for future reference. Many speakers make the PDF version available on a website as an eco-friendly option. Other speakers will make hard copies of the most important slides in the presentation to distribute after the presentation. For other audiences, handouts with thumbnail versions of the slides are appropriate. The presentation can also be printed in outline format, so the audience has the text from the presentation but not the slide graphics, tables, or pictures. You can print the presentation as Notes Pages, which prints the slides and the notes in the Notes pane, so you can have a copy to use as your speaker notes. The decision to print or not depends upon the audience description and the purpose of the presentation.

CONSIDER THIS | **When Should You Pass Out the Handouts?**

Should you pass out the handouts before you begin the presentation or at the end? Describe a situation where it would be good to hand them out prior. Is there any reason why it may be distracting for the audience to have printed versions of the slides during a presentation? List some reasons for waiting until the end of the presentation.

The rule of thumb for printing is to print as few sheets as possible to conserve resources. It is important to use the preview function of PowerPoint to review the potential printout prior to printing the slide show. Keep in mind that it is more economical to print in black and white than color, especially if you are planning to use a copier to make additional copies.

Printing Slides

Printing each slide individually is time consuming and not generally necessary. At times, one or two slides may contain information that is important. You will print Slides 2 and 4 from the presentation to share with the marketing director.

To Print Selected Slides

a. Open the **Lastname_Firstname_p01_ws01_Sponsor** file, click the **File tab**, and then click the **Print tab**.

b. Select the printer name as directed by your instructor.

c. Click **Print All Slides arrow**, and then select **Custom Range**.

d. Type 2,4 in the **Slides** box. Be sure to include the comma.

e. Click the **Next Page arrow** ▶ in the Preview pane. Each slide is displayed, one slide per page.

f. Click **Color**, and then click **Pure Black and White**.

g. If your instructor directs you to submit a printed copy, click **Print** after reviewing the Preview pane.

h. Click the **Home tab** to return to the presentation in Normal view.

Printing Handouts

As you print handouts for your audience, you have many style choices to make. You can print one to nine slides per page, determining whether they are sequential either horizontally or vertically. You can choose to frame the slides, scale them to fit the paper, and select high-quality printing.

You will print a copy of your entire presentation to use in a discussion you will have with the golf pro, John Schilling. He will give the presentation at various times during the next month and should review the slides. You will preview a few options before printing the final document.

To Print Handouts

a. Click the **File tab**, and then click the **Print tab**. Click **Custom Range**, and then click **Print All Slides**.

b. Click **Print Layout**, which displays the words Full Page Slides, and then click **6 Slides Horizontal**. The slides are displayed on a single sheet of paper, with Slide 1 next to Slide 2, and so on down the page.

c. Click the **Print Layout arrow** again, and then click **6 Slides Vertical**. The slides are again displayed on a single sheet of paper, but this time, Slide 2 is below Slide 1, and so on across the page.

d. Click the **Print Layout arrow** again, and then click **3 Slides**. You decide to print this version so John can take notes during your discussion.

SIDE NOTE
Printing Handouts with Note Lines

Many audiences like to use the 3 Slides handout to take notes during the presentation. With this presentation, copies could be printed on both sides, and only one page per audience member would be needed.

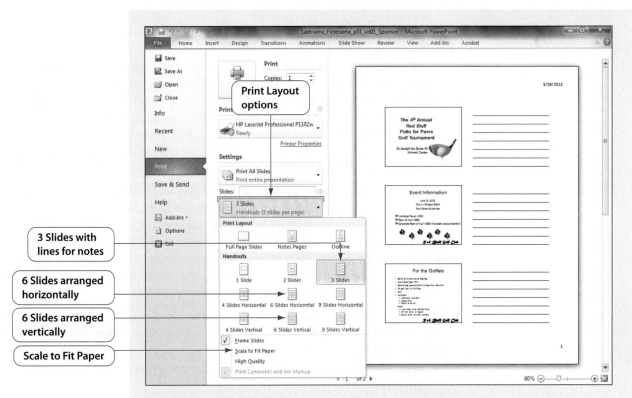

3 Slides with lines for notes

6 Slides arranged horizontally

6 Slides arranged vertically

Scale to Fit Paper

Figure 21   Printing handouts

e. Click the **Print Layout arrow** again, and then click **Scale to Fit Paper**. The size of the slides will increase, making them more readable.

f. If your instructor directs you to submit a copy of the document, click **Print**.

g. Click the **Home tab** to return to the presentation in Normal view.

Printing the Outline

For some audiences, an outline of the presentation is sufficient. The outline displays the headings and body text on the slides, but not the graphics. You will print an outline to use as a reminder sheet when you talk to potential sponsors and players. You want to accurately discuss the perks for the golfers, describe the special events, and recall the costs for participation.

To Print an Outline

a. Click the **File tab**, and then click the **Print tab**.

b. Click the **Print Layout arrow**, and then click **Outline**.

The content of the slides is displayed on two pages. You decide that you do not need to have the title slide information or the Contact Us slide, so you will set a range for the Slide numbers 2 to 5.

c. Type **2-5** in the Slides box, and then click the **Next Page** ▶ button, if necessary, to view the outline. Review the Preview of the print document.

d. Click **Print** if your instructor directs you to submit a copy of the document.

e. Click the **Home tab**, if necessary, to return to the presentation in Normal view.

f. Click the **File tab**, and then click **Close**. Exit PowerPoint.

1. As an intern at a busy engineering firm, you have been asked to research different options for phone communications. The engineers all have company-issued cell phones, but they are rather dated and some need to be replaced. You have gathered your data, and now are preparing a presentation to deliver to the managers of the various departments. Define your intended purpose for this audience of 10 people. Will you be informing the audience, persuading them, or preparing them? Is there a possible secondary purpose for your presentation?

2. You have been interested in astronomy for many years. Ms. Weiler, a 7th grade science teacher, asked you to deliver a presentation to her students. She requested that you focus your speech on celestial objects that students might be able to identify without a telescope or binoculars. You know the students will be tested on the material after your presentation, because you also had Ms. Weiler as a science teacher and you know her style. Define your intended purpose for this classroom audience of approximately 30 people. Do you have a possible secondary purpose?

3. Your supervisor gave you a presentation that he created and asked for your input. You notice that his slides are rather wordy. The following statements came from three different slides.

   • In this past year, we have experienced an amazing growth in our production, with an increase of 25%.

   • The complete satisfaction of our customers is our main goal for the coming quarter.

   • The corporate office is asking us to document the number of items that we produce, that fail quality control testing, and that are shipped.

   How would you shorten the statements to maintain their meaning but to have them comply with the Rule of 6's?

4. As you prepare your PowerPoint presentation for Ms. Weiler's class, what design decisions will you make? Describe some suitable themes that you might want to have for the presentation. Discuss the fonts you would select for this slide show. What color decisions would you make?

5. Return to the scenario of finding suitable phones for the engineering firm. Your presentation ended up being 25 slides long. You have decided not to print all of the slides. Consider the types of information that might be in such a presentation, and describe the slides you might print for audience use. When would you pass the handouts to the members of this audience?

Content 690
Design theme 701
Font groups 703
Format Painter 696
KISS principle 706
Normal view 687
Outline tab 686
Placeholder 690
PowerPoint PDF 709

PowerPoint Show 709
Printer-friendly fonts 691
Reading view 687
Rule of 6's 692
Sans serif fonts 691
Screen-friendly fonts 691
Serif fonts 691
Sizing handles 699
Slide layout 699

Slide Show view 687
Slide Sorter view 687
Slides tab 686
Target audience 684
Template 702
Text hierarchy 694
Thesaurus 709
White space 706

Visual Summary

Orient yourself with PowerPoint (p. 685)

Display and navigate through a slide show (p. 688)

Save in different file formats (p. 710)

Print selected slides (p. 712)

Print handouts (p. 712)

Print an outline (p. 713)

Modify theme fonts (p. 703)

Make font adjustments (p. 692)

Modify theme colors (p. 705)

Use the Thesaurus (p. 709)

Move slide content (p. 706)

Review the presentation (p. 708)

Align text (p. 693)

Apply text hierarchy and bullets (p. 695)

Display a presentation (p. 687)

Rearrange slides on the Slides tab (p. 700)

Modify a slide show (p. 690)

Delete a slide (p. 700)

Add slides (p. 698)

Use the Format Painter (p. 696)

Change slide layouts (p. 699)

Use a design theme (p. 702)

Rearrange slides in Slide Sorter view (p. 701)

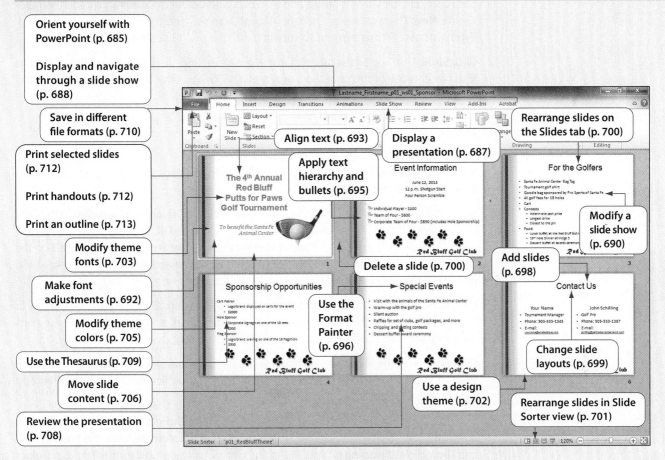

Figure 22 Red Bluff Putts for Paws Golf Tournament Final Presentation

Practice 1

Student data file needed:

p01_ws01_Products

You will save your files as:

Lastname_Firstname_p01_ws01_Products
Lastname_Firstname_p01_ws01_Products_PDF

Gift Shop Product Line Presentation

Human Resources

The Painted Treasures gift shop manager requested your assistance in improving a presentation that she will make to the staff to introduce them to some new products for the shop. You will modify and reorganize the slides, apply a theme to the presentation, make minor modifications to the theme, and proofread the slides. You will print handouts of the slides to distribute to the staff for taking notes during the presentation, and you will save the file in PDF format so it can be posted on the resort's training website.

a. Start **PowerPoint**, and then open **p01_ws01_Products**. Click the **File tab**, and then click **Save As**. In the Save As dialog box, navigate to where you are saving your files, and then type Lastname_Firstname_p01_ws01_Products, replacing Lastname and Firstname with your own name.

b. Click the **Outline tab**, and then review the information on the slides.

c. Click the **Slides tab**, click **Slide 1** on the Slides tab, and then click the **Design tab**.

d. Click the **Angles** theme—fourth from the left—in the Themes group, click **Slide 2** on the Slides tab, and then evaluate the fonts. You decide that these fonts are difficult to read and need adjustment.

e. Click the **Design tab**, click **Fonts** in the Themes group, and then click **Horizon**.

f. Click **Colors** in the Themes group, and then click **Solstice**. Click **Colors** again, and then click **Create New Theme Colors**. Click the **Accent 2 arrow**, and then select **Aqua, Accent 1**. Type Lastname Firstname New Solstice in the Name box. Click **Save**.

g. Click **Slide 1** on the Slides tab, click the **Home tab**, and then click **New Slide**. Click the title placeholder of the new slide, and type Our Goals. Click the body placeholder and type the following:

  • Introduce our new product lines

  • Increase sales by 18%

  • Have fun!

  Select the text you just typed, click **Numbering** in the Paragraph group, click the **Font Size arrow**, and then click **32**.

h. Select the words **Our Goals** on Slide 2, and then click the **Dialog Box Launcher** in the Font group. Click **All Caps** to remove the check mark, and click **OK**. Click the **Font Size arrow**, and then click **40**. Double-click **Format Painter** in the Clipboard group, click **Slide 3** on the Slides tab, and then drag across the title. Continue to click on each of the following slides and format the titles. Click **Format Painter** when all of the titles have been formatted.

i. Click **Slide 1** on the Slides tab, and then select the **title text**. Click the **Font Size arrow** in the Font group, and then click **44**. Select the **subtitle text**, and then click **Increase Font Size** until the font size **20** is reached.

j. Click **Slide 4** on the Slides tab, and then select the text **Comfort**, **Beauty**, and **Style**. Click **Bold** in the Font group to remove the bold formatting. Click **Center** in the Paragraph group, click the **Font Size arrow**, and then click **32**.

k. Select the text on the right side of the slide, click the **Bullets arrow** in the Paragraph group, and then click **Bullets and Numbering**. Click **Customize**, click the **Font arrow**, and then click **Wingdings**. Type 203 in the Character code box, in the from box select **Symbol (decimal)**, if necessary, and then click **OK**. Click **OK**, and then click **Bold** to remove the bold formatting.

l. Click **Next Slide** to advance to Slide 5. Select the **second line** of body text, press and hold ⌃Ctrl, and then select the **fourth** and **sixth line**. Click **Increase List Level** in the Paragraph group. Select all of the **body text**, click the **Font Size arrow** in the Font group, and then click **24**.

m. Click **Next Slide** to advance to Slide 6. Click **Anna** to view the placeholder. Drag the **right sizing handle** to the left so the placeholder does not cover the jewelry photograph. Select the **jewelry items**, including the bulleted items under each type, and then click **Increase Font Size** until the font size of **20** is reached.

n. Click **Slide 7** on the Slides tab, and then select the **body text**. Click **Bold** in the Font group to remove the bold formatting, click the **Font Size arrow**, and then click **24**. Click **Increase List Level** in the Paragraph group.

o. Click **Slide 3** on the Slides tab, click **Layout** in the Slides group, and then select **Two Content**. Select the text beginning with **Ask** and continuing through **Suggest additional items based on purchase**, and then drag the text to the placeholder on the right. Select the **text** in the left placeholder, and then click **Center** in the Paragraph group. Click **Increase Font Size** in the Font group once to change the font to size **28**. Drag the **top sizing handle** of the left placeholder down to visually balance the text, click **Ask**, and then drag the sizing handle on the right side of the placeholder to the right side of the slide.

p. Select the **two questions** on Slide 3, and then click **Increase List Level**.

q. Drag **Slide 3** on the Slides tab to the end of the slide show. Click **Slide 4** on the Slides tab, and drag it to the **Slide 3** position.

r. Click the **Review tab**, and then click **Spelling** in the Proofing group. Click **Ignore** for any proper names that are reported as misspelled. Click **Change** when "Avocado" is reported. Click **OK** when the spelling check is complete.

s. Click the **Slide Show tab**, and then click **From Beginning**. Press [Enter] to advance through the slides, click the **File tab**, and then click **Save** to save the presentation.

t. Click the **File tab**, and then click **Save As**. Click the **Save as type arrow**, and then click **PDF**. Type Lastname_Firstname_p01_ws01_Products_PDF as the file name, and then click **Save**. Review the slides after the file is published. Close the Adobe Reader application.

u. Click the **File tab**, and then click the **Print tab**. Click the **Print Layout arrow** (which displays the words Full Page Slides), and then click **3 Slides** in the Handouts group. Click **Next Page** and **Previous Page** to review the document. Click the **Color arrow**, and then click **Grayscale**. Click **Print** if your instructor directs you to submit a printed copy.

v. Click the **Home tab**, if necessary, to return to the presentation in Normal view. Click the **File tab**, and then click **Close**. Exit PowerPoint.

Problem Solve 1

Student Data File Needed

p01_ps1_Employment

You will save your files as:

Lastname_Firstname_p01_ps1_Employment
Lastname_Firstname_p01_ps1_Employment_Show

Employment Opportunities Presentation for College Students

Human Resources

Sales & Marketing

The Director of Human Resources at Painted Paradise Golf Resort and Spa has prepared a presentation to be shown to local college students informing them about job opportunities at the resort. The presentation contains the information that the Director would like to include but has not yet been formatted. You have been asked to review the presentation and make it more visually appealing. You will apply a theme to the presentation, make minor modifications to the theme, modify and reorganize the slides, and proofread the slides. You will also save the file as a PowerPoint Show so it opens directly in Slide Show view.

a. Start **PowerPoint**. Open **p01_ps1_Employment**. In the Save As dialog box, navigate to where you are saving your files and then type Lastname_Firstname_p01_ps1_Employment.

b. Click the **Design tab**, and then click the **Apothecary** theme in the Themes group. You like the appearance of this theme but want the colors to reflect the tones of the desert surrounding the resort.

c. Click **Colors** in the Themes group, and then click **Hardcover**. These theme colors are more suitable.

d. Click **Slide 2**, and observe the fonts used for the title and body content. Click **Fonts** in the Themes group, and then click **Office Classic 2** to make the text easier to read.

e. Add a New Slide after Slide 2, using the **Title and Content layout**. Type Types of Jobs in the title placeholder. In the body placeholder, type the following:

- Year round:
- Golf club, spa, housekeeping
- Seasonal:
- Counselors, lifeguards, food service
- On call:
- Catering, baby-sitting, instructors

f. Select lines two, four, and six of the text you just typed and then **Increase List Level** one time.

g. Select the title text on Slide 3, increase the font size to **36**, and then apply **Bold**. Use the Format Painter to apply the same format to the title on each of the slides except the title slide. Do not forget to format the title on Slide 2.

h. Click **Slide 4,** select the second level bullets, and increase the font size to **24**.

i. Click **Slide 5,** select the placeholder on the right. Drag the sizing handle on the left side of the placeholder to the left so the left side of the placeholder almost touches the right side of the picture.

j. Click **Slide 6**, select the second level bullets, and increase the font size to **24**. Add the following bullets to the end of the text in the placeholder:
    • Display merchandise attractively
    • Possess excellent communication skills

k. Select the last line of text on Slide 6, and then drag it to the beginning of the list so that it is the first indented bullet under the words Retail Attendant.

l. Click **Slide 8**, and notice there is too much text on the left side of the slide. Click the **Home tab**, click **Layout**, and then click **Two Content**. Select and cut the four lines of body text from **Housekeepers** through **Performers**, and then paste them in the placeholder on the right. Remove any extra bullets, if necessary.

m. Click **Slide Sorter** view on the status bar. Drag **Slide 2** to the end of the presentation. Move **Slide 5** after **Slide 3**.

n. Click **Normal** view on the status bar. Click **Slide 8**, and select the text box at the bottom of the slide. Drag the sizing handles on the left and right sides of the text box to line up with the gray background. Increase the font size to **20**, and then center align the text within the text box.

o. Click the **Review tab**, and then click **Spelling**. Correct any misspelled words. Proofread each slide carefully. Correct any errors that you may find.

p. Save the presentation. Save the presentation again as a PowerPoint Show, with the file name **Lastname_Firstname_p01_ps1_Employment_Show**.

q. Close the presentation and submit your files as directed by your instructor.

 Additional Workshop Cases are available on the companion website and in the instructor resources.

WORKSHOP 2

Objectives

1. Develop an effective presentation with consideration to the audience and content   p. 720

2. Use story-boarding to plan a presentation   p. 722

3. Develop presentation content   p. 723

4. Create a presentation from a template   p. 725

5. Use slide footers, slide numbers, and special symbols   p. 726

6. Use Outline view and reuse slide content   p. 728

7. Insert and modify clip art, photographs, and WordArt for slide content and backgrounds   p. 732

8. Create shapes and lines   p. 739

9. Create a table in a presentation   p. 745

10. Create a chart in a presentation   p. 749

11. Use SmartArt graphics in a presentation   p. 753

Applying and Modifying Text and Graphics

Human Resources

PREPARE CASE

The Red Bluff Caddy School Presentation

The Red Bluff Golf Club is sponsoring a caddy school. You will create the first-day presentation for training. The audience will be people 18–25 years old who are interested in learning about golf and who want to be caddies at the Golf Club. You will create an outline, add appropriate graphics, and modify the presentation before passing it along to John Schilling, the golf pro, for final approval.

Patricia Hofmeester / Shutterstock.com

Student data files needed for this workshop:

 p01_ws02_Caddy_Storyboard

 p01_ws02_Caddy_Staff

 p01_ws02_Caddy_Photo

 p01_ws02_Caddy_Ball

 p01_ws02_Caddy_Golfer

 p01_ws02_Caddy_Background

You will save your file as:

 Lastname_Firstname_p01_ws02_Caddy_School

Creating a Presentation for Effective Communication

According to David A. Peoples, author of *Presentations Plus*, "Ninety-five percent of how well your presentation is going to go is determined before you even start." Planning your presentation is of the utmost importance. Allow approximately four hours of planning time for each hour of presentation time. Clear thinking about what your objectives are, the type of content you will include, and the composition of the audience will assist you in creating a slide show that is a true visual aid. In this section you will create storyboards, develop content, and use special characters as you prepare a presentation.

Organizing and Defining the Purpose, Scope, and Audience of a Presentation

As you define your objectives for the presentation, be specific. Ask such questions as:

- What is your purpose? To persuade? Inform? Prepare?
- Why is the topic important?
- Why should the audience be interested?
- What is in it for the audience?
- What do you expect the audience to do after your presentation?

Use sticky notes to brainstorm the possible main ideas for your presentation. Do not try to edit these ideas in the early stages; just generate ideas. When you reach a point where no more ideas come to mind, then begin eliminating some of the ideas. Your goal is to focus your presentation on two to five main ideas. Translate these ideas into action verb objectives, such as "update our computer systems," or "increase workflow by 15%." The objectives will determine the content of the presentation, determine the scope or level of detail, and enable you to give an effective presentation.

With the objectives clearly stated, continue to add sticky notes to develop the subtopics of the presentation. These subtopics will likely become the titles on your slides and will make the content of your presentation meaningful because they directly relate to the objectives. Consider the order of the subtopics, and try to provide organization so you can lead your audience through the presentation and into achieving the purpose you have defined.

Real World Advice — Pecha Kucha Presentations

Pecha Kucha, pronounced *"pe-CHALK-cha,"* is a unique format for presentations, first used in Tokyo, Japan, in 2003. This type of presentation automatically displays 20 slides, for 20 seconds each, during which the presenter speaks. This causes speakers to concisely edit their comments, so they are completed within a time frame of six and a half to seven minutes. While this trend in presentations began with architects, it has spread worldwide, and now Pecha Kucha Nights cover topics such as travels, art work, business, and research.

Considering the Target Audience

Figuring out the characteristics of an audience enables you to produce a presentation that is worthwhile to the audience and achieves your objectives. Many characteristics can help you to shape your presentation. Consider these questions:

- Why are they listening to your presentation?
- What are the attitudes they have about your topic?

- What do they know about the topic?
- What are the constraints? Are they political? Financial? Knowledge-based?
- How will they use the information you present?
- What are the demographics of the audience? Number of people? Location of the presentation? What technical equipment is available? A microphone? Computer? Projector?
- What is the size of the audience? Is it small and intimate? Or is it large and formal?

Clearly, there are many things to consider, but knowing your audience will enable you to streamline your presentation, customize the materials, and feel more comfortable as you deliver the presentation.

Describing Your Audience's Needs

Audiences come to presentations asking "What's in it for me?" Your presentation should focus on meeting this need while addressing what you want them to know. As you describe the audience's needs, answer these questions:

- What do they want to hear?
- What do they need to know?
- What are the potential benefits to the audience?
- What questions might they have?

Another consideration is to determine what the audience members are doing before and after your presentation. Are they listening to another speaker? Are they about to go home or return to their desks? Have they had lunch? Understanding their frame of mind enables you to better prepare to meet their needs.

CONSIDER THIS | How Many Audiences Do You Really Have?

Will you have only one target audience or multiple audiences in your presentation? Should you plan your presentation around all the different potential audiences or just your main target audience?

Understanding Commonality with Your Audience

Understanding the relationships you have with the audience and the relationships they have with each other helps you to set the tone for your presentation. You may find yourself making a presentation to your superiors, in which case you will want to make suggestions related to the topic so they can make an informed decision. Another audience might be made up of your peers or team members. You will want to engage these audience members by having them share their experiences or expertise. Use "we" language, such as "We can improve our customer service by responding to calls within 1 minute." Special interest groups expect you to focus on their concerns as they relate to your topic.

Anticipating Audience Expectations

Audiences anticipate that you have expertise in your topic area. This may call for concentrated study so you have a complete knowledge of the subject matter. This additional study can add significant time to your preparation for the presentation. The audience will ask you questions. Anticipating their questions and adding them to the planning of the presentation helps the audience to understand your topic more clearly.

Audiences who are interested in your topic are concerned with what additional information you can provide. For this kind of presentation you can focus on teaching them about your topic. Other audiences may not be quite as interested and need to be involved in some way with your presentation. Group work or discussions are often the key in this situation. Still other audiences will be uninterested in your presentation but forced to attend. With this group, strive to entertain them, while remaining true to the purpose and objectives of your presentation.

Understanding Your Audience's Interaction with the Presentation

The expectation of most audiences is that your topic will be presented with few surprises, cover points A through D, and end on time. Planning for interaction should extend well beyond the standard question-and-answer period. Creatively develop activities that draw the audience into the presentation. Use a variety of visual aids, including PowerPoint slide shows, to explain concepts. A pair of binoculars can support the idea of looking forward. A giant clock can signify the importance of time management. Bring in a widget that everyone can hold. Pass out specially made fortune cookies, with questions about your topic for the audience to consider. Keep in mind that people remember much more when visual aids are used in the presentation.

As you plan for organization in your presentation, begin by telling the audience what you are going to discuss. Remember that first impressions do count. Capture the attention of the audience by establishing common ground. Often, presentations outline the objectives or major topic areas first. Next, follow through and talk about each and every item you said you would discuss. Finally, review what you have discussed with them as a summary of the presentation. Finish strong with a call to action that supports your purpose for the presentation.

Real World Advice   Everyone Needs a Roadmap

You can help to organize the thinking of your audience by providing a roadmap of your presentation. It can be a bulleted list of items you will discuss or a graphic depiction of where the presentation will go. Place the roadmap in the beginning of the slide show, and then do a short recap at the end of the slide show to remind the audience of the important parts of the presentation.

Storyboarding the Presentation

Storyboards are conceptual drawings of what will appear on your slides. Being an artist is not a prerequisite to using storyboards to plan your presentations. Quick drawings suffice and remind you of elements you want to include. This is especially important as you select clip art or pictures, and create tables, graphs, or charts.

Generally, storyboards are composed of three panels: content, layout, and visual elements. Each slide in the presentation is represented, beginning with the title slide and continuing with the introduction. The content slides contain the key topics and subtopics of the presentation, followed by a case study and discussion, which serves as the summary.

Reviewing a Storyboard

Storyboards can be used as a communication device between the person who will give the presentation, possibly your supervisor, and the person who will be creating the presentation. Storyboards help you to understand what is critical in the presentation and to come to an agreement on the scope of the slide show.

You will open the storyboard for the Caddy School Presentation and review the plan. The storyboard is a Microsoft Word document.

To Examine a Storyboard

a. Click the **Start** button 🌐 on the taskbar. Click **Computer**. Navigate to the location where your student data files are stored. Double-click the Word document **p01_ws02_Caddy_Storyboard**.

b. Scroll down the document, making note of the content, layout, and visual elements planned for each slide. Notice the progression from introductory material, to the agenda and learning objectives, to actual training on the procedures and responsibilities.

c. Scroll to page 3 of the document. The audience members for this presentation are people who are interested in working as caddies. Notice the pay rate information included in the storyboard. This is important information for workers.

d. Continue to scroll down the page, noting the Tools of the Trade slide, which emphasizes expectations for caddies. The case study at the end of the presentation will be used to summarize the Caddy School introduction.

e. **Close** [×] Word.

Developing the Presentation Content

Text and graphics guide the audience through the content of the presentation. Keep in mind that the PowerPoint slide show is a supporting character to your presentation. You are the focus of the audience. The text should be thoroughly edited to include only the main points or key terms. Complete sentences, with the exception of quotations, should be avoided as slide content. Think like a headline writer, distilling the content down to the essence of the topic. You want the audience to read and understand your slide in less than 10 seconds. People also like numbers in presentation content, such as "Four Hot Tips" or "Three Steps to Success." This helps you to organize content in a way that the audience will recall.

You have probably heard a picture is worth a thousand words, and in fact, media elements such as clip art, photographs, video, audio, charts, and graphics make a significant difference in your presentation. Media can be used to summarize, demonstrate, inject humor, clarify, and reinforce what has been said.

Using Anecdotes and Quotations

Anecdotes and quotations support your message and can be used either as an opening or closing statement. They give your presentation credibility. They can convey a startling fact or statistic. Anecdotes, such as stories in the news or experiences you have had, help you connect to your audience by explaining a situation. Quotations that relate to the subject can add humor to your presentation. Be sure to attribute the quotation to the proper person.

Encouraging Audience Participation

One of the reasons why people enjoy giving presentations is to make a connection with the members of the audience. Encouraging audience participation is an important part of your planning. This is one place where the evaluation of the audience comes into play. In a large group environment, you will use different strategies than in a conference room meeting. Remarkably, games are very engaging, and audience members become very active when a simple prize is offered. Asking questions of your audience helps to keep them on their toes and gives you feedback. Be sure to not put someone on the spot or make them feel uncomfortable. If you have enough time, small group discussions can add a new dimension to your presentation. As with everything else involved with presenting, planning is the key in successful audience participation.

Including Quantitative and Statistical Content

When presenting data, you should resist the urge to put all of the numbers on the screen. If it is necessary for the audience to have all of the numbers, provide handouts. Just as you edited the text content of your presentation, critically review the numerical data and pull out the important numbers, such as the totals, for your slide.

Converting the numbers into a graph often enhances your slide show. It provides information related to trends or quantitative information. The graph can organize the information in a new way. The picture will last longer in the minds of the audience members. The graph can add interest and color to your presentation.

As you create graphs for your presentation, make sure they convey the information clearly. Critically view the graphs and determine if the point you wish to make is evident. As you select the type of chart, consider these characteristics:

- **Pie chart**—Parts make up a whole, usually contains percentages
- **Bar or column chart**—Compare items in rank or changes over a period of time
- **Line chart**—Changes over time, frequency, or relationship between items

Using Appropriate Media

Good media choices, including graphics, audio, and video, stimulate interest, help you clarify important points, and reinforce what has been said. Poor media choices confuse the audience and distract them from your purposes.

As you select media, consider the length of your presentation and the technology available in the presentation room. Consider these questions:

- Does the media element completely support your objectives?
- Is the media element clear enough to see and understand?
- Will you have a good Internet connection for loading a web page or a YouTube video?
- Do you want to devote 3–8 minutes to a video?

Respecting Copyrights

As you select the content for your presentation, it is important to be respectful of copyrights. **Copyrights** include the rights to reproduce, distribute, create derivative works, perform, and display intellectual property. Many people believe that everything on the Internet is copyright free, but it is not. Works that you create, such as photographs, poems and other writing, music, and video, are copyrighted to you automatically as soon as they are in a fixed format. You have the right to post them on the Internet, sell the work to another party, or display them in any way you see fit. If someone uses your materials without your permission, you have a legal path to follow if you want to protect your copyrights.

Copyright law and the Digital Millennium Copyright Act of 1998 address many aspects of how media elements are protected. A good rule of thumb is to seek permission before using copyrighted elements in your PowerPoint slide shows. Using the Internet, it is easy to research and request permission to use these elements. Often permission to use the elements is granted without cost or restriction, and sometimes you make a direct connection with the person that created the item. In some cases, the copyright holder will request a citation or attribution recognizing their contribution.

Real World Advice   Citing Sources

Depending on the presentation's purpose and audience, you should consider citing the sources you used in creating your presentation. Citation formats, such as APA (American Psychological Association), MLA (Modern Language Association), or the *Chicago Manual of Style,* may be recommended by your instructor or supervisor. You can learn more about the formats on the websites for each:

- **APA**—www.apa.org
- **MLA**—www.mla.org
- **The *Chicago Manual of Style*** —www.chicagomanualofstyle.org

Creating a New Presentation from a Template

PowerPoint templates enable you to focus on the content of your presentation by providing professional-looking designs. Templates, like themes, contain slide backgrounds, color schemes, and font selections. In some cases, templates also contain sample content or unique slide layouts. Templates are applied to new slide shows and can be modified as needed.

You will begin your work on the Red Bluff Golf Club Caddy School presentation by selecting and applying a template to a new PowerPoint presentation.

Using a Template to Create a New Presentation

PowerPoint contains a number of built-in templates for a variety of applications. Additional templates can be downloaded for free from Office.com. You can also find free templates by completing an Internet search for "free PowerPoint templates." The Training template you will use in this workshop contains some very interesting effects that will ensure that your audience is engaged during your presentation. The colors are fresh and inviting. The overall look is very consistent. This template works well in training situations because it contains the elements normally presented in training, including an overview, topic coverage, a case study, and a conclusion with a summary. You will create a presentation based on the Training template available in the Sample templates.

To Create a Presentation with a Template

a. Click the **Start** button. From the Start menu, locate and then start **Microsoft PowerPoint 2010**. Click the **File tab**, and then click the **New tab.**

   There are a number of templates available on the New tab. To see the Office.com Templates, you need an Internet connection. Some of the template options shown are for other software applications such as Word and Excel.

b. Click **Sample templates**, and then click each of the template thumbnails to view them in the Preview pane.

c. Click **Training**, and then click **Create**.

   The template opens with slides arranged in sections, detailed notes, and some interesting animations. You will review the current presentation to see if it fits your needs. Keep in mind that this presentation will be viewed by young adults who are interested in becoming caddies.

d. Click the **Slide Show tab**, and then click **From Beginning**. Advance the slides, reviewing the effects and content of the slides. When you have completed the slide show, return to Normal view.

e. Click each slide on the Slides tab, and review the notes provided.

Notice that the slides are divided by section headers that help to organize the presentation. The section headers can be expanded or collapsed by clicking the arrow next to the section name.

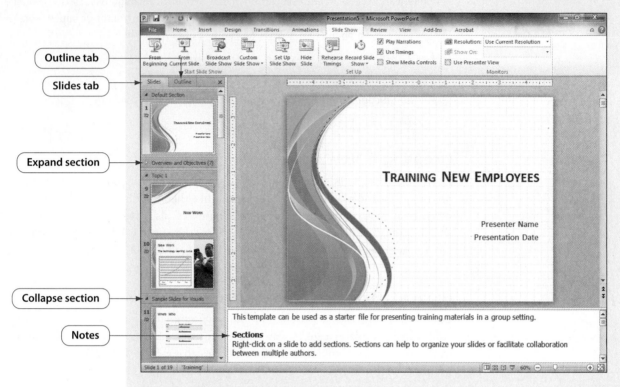

Figure 1 The Training template

f. Click the **File tab**, and then click **Save As**. In the Save As dialog box, navigate to the location where you are saving your files. In the File name box, type Lastname_Firstname_p01_ws02_Caddy_School. Click **Save**.

You will base the Caddy School presentation on this template, adding and deleting slides, using Outline view, selecting graphics, and creating other content. The storyboard reminds you of the content you want to have in the presentation, and the template provides the design.

Inserting Slide Footers and Slide Numbers

Custom **slide footers** can be displayed on slides. Footers often contain the name of the company, the company slogan, or copyright notices. Slide numbers can also be displayed in the footer of slides.

Inserting Footers

The footer in this workshop contains the name of the golf club, Red Bluff Golf Club. You will modify the presentation by placing footers on the content slides but not the title slide.

To Add Slide Footers

a. Click **Slide 2**, click the **Insert tab**, and then click **Header & Footer** in the Text group.

The Header and Footer dialog box opens. There are two tabs in this dialog box, Slide and Notes and Handouts. You will focus on the Slide footer.

b. Click the **Footer** check box, and then type Red Bluff Golf Club in the box. This portion of the footer will appear at the bottom-center portion of the slide.

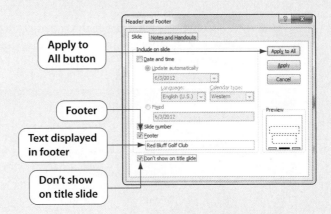

Figure 2 Applying slide footers

c. Click the **Don't show on title slide** check box, and then click **Apply to All**.

The footer is applied to all but the title slide. The title slide will contain the name of the golf club, and a footer would detract from the overall design of the title slide.

Inserting Special Symbols

Special **symbols**, from various fonts, are characters not available on a standard keyboard that can be inserted into text placeholders in PowerPoint. The Insert function enables you to add symbols to your presentation that do not appear on your keyboard. Perhaps the most commonly inserted character is the copyright symbol. Other characters include the trademark symbol, currency signs for different countries, and accents and letters from languages. For instance, the acute accent strokes over the letters "e," in the word "résumé," are available in the Symbol dialog box.

Using the Symbol Dialog Box

The Symbol dialog box displays the available special characters for the selected font. Symbols you have used recently are displayed at the bottom of the dialog box, and you can click these to reuse the symbols in your current presentation. Use the scroll bar on the right side of the dialog box to see additional symbols. The character code is the unique number given to the symbol and can be typed into the box.

You will update the title slide of the Caddy School presentation to include a new title, your name, and a copyright notification.

To Insert a Symbol

a. Click **Slide 1**, select the title **Training New Employees**, and then type Red Bluff Golf Club Caddy School. Drag the **sizing handle** on the left side of the placeholder to the right until the words "Caddy School" appear on the second line of the placeholder.

b. Select the text **Presenter Name**, and then type your first and last name.

c. Select the text **Presentation Date**, click the **Insert tab**, and then click **Symbol** in the Symbols group.

d. Click the © copyright symbol, which is character code 00A9, click **Insert**, and then click **Close.** The symbol is placed at the insertion point. You will complete the copyright statement.

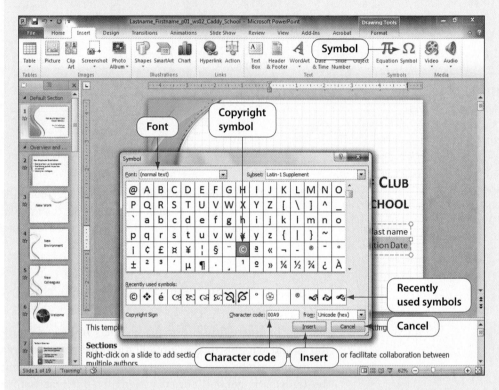

Figure 3 Adding a symbol

e. Type the current year followed by a comma and a space. Then type Painted Paradise Golf Resort and Spa. For example: ©2013, Painted Paradise Golf Resort and Spa.

f. Select the text of the **copyright notice**, and then click the **Home tab**. Click **Decrease Font Size** A˅ in the Font group until the text fits on one line below your name.

Using Outline View

The Outline tab displays the titles and bullet points of the slides in the presentation. It is easy to add, modify, and delete text content in this view. You can also move the slides by dragging them into new positions on the Outline tab.

You will notice that some of the slides appear to be blank on the Outline tab, when in fact they are not. Outline text is drawn from the title and content placeholders. Not all slides in the Caddy School presentation contain these placeholders. To make modifications to these slides, you use the Slides tab.

Promoting, Demoting, and Moving Outline Text

Commands to modify the outline of the presentation are available on the Home tab. There you can make font and paragraph selections. You will use the Paragraph group commands as you update the Caddy School presentation in Outline view.

To Use the Outline Tab

a. Click the **Outline tab**. If necessary, drag the **border** between the Outline and the Slide pane to increase the amount of text you can see in the outline. Minimizing the size of the slide enables you to focus more on the outline content.

b. Click the **Slide 2 icon** on the Outline tab, and then press Delete. Click **Yes** to respond to the warning regarding deleting the slide.

   You deleted Slide 2 because you will be creating a new slide with the learning objectives later in the presentation. You have decided that you will grab the attention of the audience with the Overview slides, and then present the agenda and objectives. Keep in mind that the template is just a suggestion and that you can make your own sequencing and design decisions as you create your presentation.

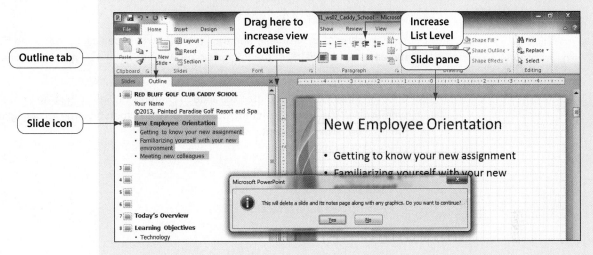

Figure 4 The Outline tab

c. Click **Slide 7,** and then on the Outline tab select the **bulleted text**. Type the following, pressing Enter after each line except the last line:
   - Describe procedures
   - List responsibilities
   - Identify tools of the trade
   - Review the rules of golf

Troubleshooting

Do not worry about the graphics you see in the Slide pane at this time. They will be modified later in the workshop.

d. Click the **Slide 11 icon**, and then drag it to position **8**.

e. Click the **Slide 9 icon**, and then press Delete. Click **Yes** to respond to the warning regarding deleting the slide.

f. Click the **Slide 8 icon**, click the **Home tab**, and then click **New Slide** in the Slides group. Click **Layout** in the Slides group, and then click **Title and Content**. A new slide is added to the Outline tab.

g. Type Procedures and Responsibilities on the new slide you created in Step f and then press Ctrl+Enter. You have created a title for the slide and moved the insertion point to the content area of the slide.

Troubleshooting

If you add an extra slide by mistake, select the slide icon and press Delete.

h. Type Arrive on time and then press Enter. Type 30 – 40 minutes before shotgun starts and then click **Increase List Level** in the Paragraph group. Press Enter. The subtext has been demoted in the outline.

i. Type 20 minutes before scheduled normal rounds and press Enter.

j. Type Look your best and then click **Decrease List Level** in the Paragraph group. Press Enter. The text has been promoted in the outline.

k. Type Maintain pace of play and then press Enter.

l. Type Preserve course quality and then press Enter. Type Pick up trash and then click **Increase List Level** in the Paragraph group. Press Enter. Type Rake bunkers and then press Enter. Type Repair any divots.

m. Click the **Slide 12 icon**, and drag the slide to position **11**. Select the title text, and then type Tools of the Trade. Select the **bulleted text**, and then type the following, pressing Enter after each line except the last line:
- Good attitude!
- Cleaning towel for clubs and golf balls
- Divot repair tool
- Pencils, tees, and scorecards
- USGA Rules

SIDE NOTE
Pressing Tab in Outlines
Pressing Tab increases the list level in the outline, and pressing Shift+Tab decreases the list level.

Reusing Slide Content

Slides from other slide shows can be imported into your current slide show. Reusing slides saves you time. You can reuse the slides that you currently have available on your computer, or use Slide Libraries that are stored on a server. People with access to the server can share the slides in Slide Libraries, which is a more efficient and accurate way to build content.

Reusing Slides

Another presentation created as an introduction to the staff of the Painted Paradise Golf Resort and Spa contains a slide with information about the golf club. You will **reuse slides** from the presentation to list the members of the golf club staff in the Caddy School presentation.

To Reuse Slides

a. Click the **Slides tab** in the left pane. On the Slides tab, click **Slide 12**, and then click the **New Slide arrow**.

b. Click **Reuse Slides**. The Reuse Slides pane opens on the right side of the window.

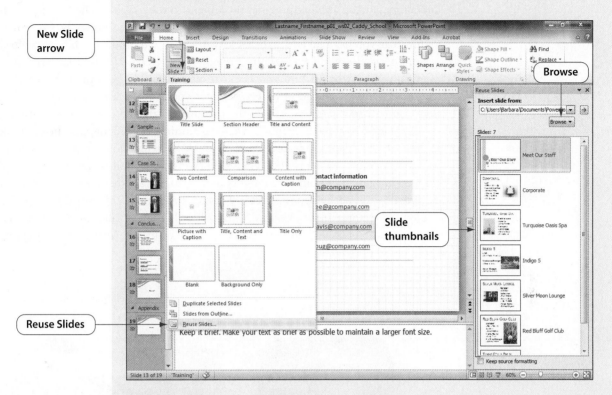

Figure 5   Reusing slides

c. Click **Browse**, and then click **Browse File**. Navigate to where your student data files are located, click **p01_ws02_Caddy_Staff**, and then click **Open**.

   Slide thumbnails are displayed in the Reuse Slides pane. As you point to each thumbnail, it increases in size so you can review the information on the slide. The title of each slide is listed beside the thumbnail.

d. Click the slide thumbnail for the **Red Bluff Golf Club**.

   The slide is inserted into the current Caddy School presentation as Slide 13, complete with the photograph from the original slide show. The bullets were also transferred.

e. **Close** ☒ the Reuse Slides pane. Select the **title** of the slide, and then type Who's Who.

f. Click **Slide 12**, and then press ⌨Delete⌨.

Selecting and Using Appropriate Graphics

Graphics, in the form of clip art, photographs, charts, graphs, and SmartArt, are valuable assets in presentations. Graphics convey information visually and can evoke a greater understanding of a concept. They add interest to the presentation.

There are some basic ground rules you should consider when selecting graphics. Foremost, the graphics must support your message; otherwise, they will distract and confuse your audience. The graphics should be clear and consistent in design with your presentation. Once again, your audience evaluation comes into play. The graphics should be consistent with the expectations of your audience. For instance, a business audience attending your presentation on policy changes would not appreciate the use of cartoon clip art. Likewise, complex charts and graphs would be incomprehensible to an audience of children.

Graphics can come from a variety of sources. PowerPoint accesses the Office **Clip Art**, as well as Office.com to provide high-quality clip art and photographs. You can even find animated clip art that provides movement to the graphic. The Internet is also a rich resource for graphics, but bear in mind that copyright laws do apply. Of course, photographs that you have taken and other artwork that you produce can be downloaded onto a computer and used in PowerPoint presentations. Keep in mind that large graphic files can load very slowly, dragging down the responsiveness of your presentation and making it more difficult to e-mail or otherwise share your presentation with others. In this section, you will add graphics, a table, a chart, and SmartArt to your presentation.

There are two types of graphics, **vector graphics** and **bit-mapped graphics,** as shown in Figure 6. Bit-mapped images are stored as pixels, in individual dots of color arranged in a grid to represent the image. Photographs are an example of bit-mapped images. Scaling bit-mapped images larger sometimes results in pixelation, and the edges of items in the image become ragged and undefined. Vector graphics are made up of shapes. Clip art files are an example of vector graphics. Generally vector graphics are smaller in file size because of the way information is stored. Vector graphics can also be resized without becoming pixelated.

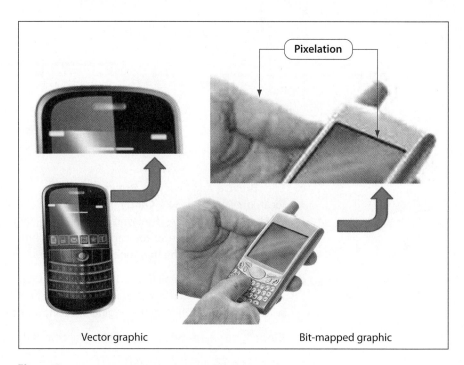

Vector graphic   Bit-mapped graphic

Figure 6   Vector and bit-mapped graphics

Inserting Clip Art and Pictures

Clip art and pictures are inserted into PowerPoint presentations in two ways. By clicking icons on the content placeholders on the slides, you can add graphics. You can also use commands on the Insert tab to place graphics on the slides.

Inserting Graphics

The template included photographs that suggest a business environment. You will modify the current graphics in the Caddy School presentation to represent golf, rather than business.

To Insert a Photograph and Clip Art

a. Click **Slide 11**, click the **photograph** of the man with the laptop, and then press Delete. The content placeholder, with multimedia icons, is displayed on the slide.

b. Click **Insert Picture from File** 🖼 in the content placeholder. Navigate to where your student data files are located, click **p01_ws02_Caddy_Photo**, and then click **Insert**. The photograph appears on the slide, replacing the placeholder.

c. Click **Slide 7**, click the **photograph**, and then press Delete.
   This photograph was not originally placed on the slide with a placeholder, so none appears at this time. You will insert a clip art graphic on this slide.

d. Click the **Insert tab**, and then click **Clip Art** in the Images group.
   The Clip Art pane opens on the right side of the window. This pane enables you to search for media files by specifying the types of files you want to use.

e. Type golf tee in the Search for box, click the **Results should be arrow**, and then click **Illustrations** and **Photographs** to select them, if necessary. Click **Videos** and **Audio** to deselect them, if necessary. Click outside of the pane to hide the options, click **Include Office.com content**, and then click **Go**.

Troubleshooting

You must have an Internet connection to access the Office.com graphics. Further, online content changes over time. Thus, an image you see today may not be available tomorrow.

f. Click the **black-and-white golf ball and tee** illustration.
   It may take a few seconds for the image to appear on your slide. It will be displayed in the center of the slide with sizing handles around it.

g. Drag the **graphic** to the right so it does not overlap the text, but do not resize it at this time. **Close** ✖ the Clip Art pane.

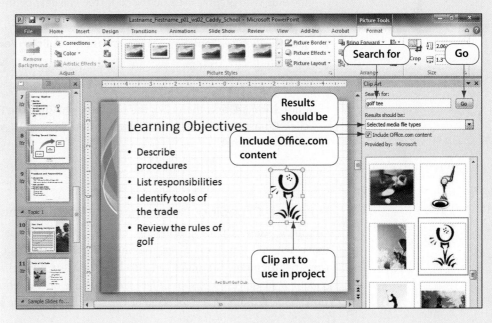

Figure 7   Clip Art pane

h. Click **Slide 5**. Right-click the photograph.

One of the advantages of using a template is that if the pictures are already formatted, you can change them and retain the effects. You will change the photograph on Slide 5 to reflect golf using the Change Picture option on the menu.

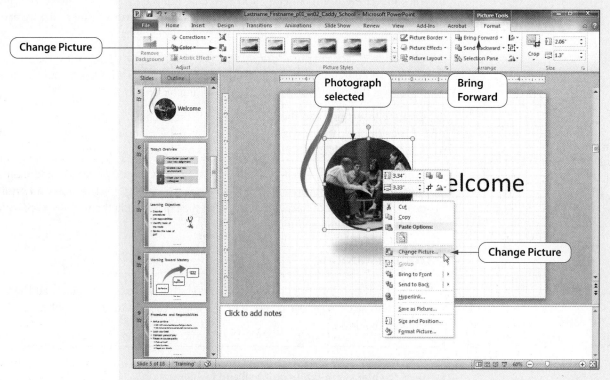

Figure 8   Change picture

i. Click **Change Picture**, click **p01_ws02_Caddy_Ball**, and then click **Insert**.

The photograph automatically adjusts, replacing the previous photograph. Look closely at the picture and you will see a faint white swirl over the picture. This comes from the blue swirl graphic used on this slide. You will change the layering of the graphics to place the swirl behind the photograph.

j. Click the **Pictures Tools Format tab**, and then click **Bring Forward** in the Arrange group.

k. Click **Slide 13**, and then right-click the photograph. Click **Change Picture**, click **p01_ws02_Caddy_Golfer**, and then click **Insert**. The photograph appears on the slide.

l. Click **Slide 14**, and then click the photograph. Click the **Picture Tools Format tab**, click **Change Picture** in the Adjust group, click **p01_ws02_Caddy_Golfer**, and then click **Insert**.

Resizing, Cropping, Rotating, and Flipping Graphics

Graphics, such as photographs and clip art, are easily manipulated using PowerPoint tools. You can resize an object, making it fit the slide. You can crop unwanted portions from photographs. Graphics can also be rotated or flipped to improve the design of the slide. For instance, faces should face the audience or the center of the slide whenever possible. This reinforces the message of the slide, making the audience feel like the person agrees with what is being said on the slide. If you find the perfect graphic but the person faces the edge of the slide, you can flip the image. A note of caution is that if there are words on the slide, such as on a sign in the background, these will also flip and be disconcerting to the audience.

In this portion of the workshop, you will improve the graphics. You will resize a clip art object, crop an area away from a photograph, and flip a graphic.

To Modify Graphics

a. Click **Slide 7**, and then click the clip art **golf ball and tee** graphic.

Sizing handles, displayed around a selected graphic, enable you to resize the graphic and move it around the slide. The corner sizing handles increase or decrease the size of the graphic when dragged, while retaining the proportions of the graphic. The side sizing handles increase or decrease the width or height of the graphic. Be careful not to distort the graphic when using these handles. During sizing actions, the pointer will be a two-pointed arrow ⟷.

Point to the middle of the object with the mouse, and a four-pointed arrow pointer ✥ indicates that you can drag the graphic to a new location on the slide.

b. Click the **Picture Tools Format tab**, and then drag the **bottom-left sizing handle** to the left, increasing the size of the clip art object to about twice the original size.

Notice that the size of the graphic in inches is displayed in the Size group of the Format tab. You will use the Size group to resize the graphic.

c. Click the **Dialog Box Launcher** 🔲 in the Size group on the Picture Tools Format tab. If necessary, click **Lock aspect ratio** to select it. Under Size and rotate, click the **Height spin arrow** to change the height to **4"**. The width of the graphic changes automatically to maintain the proportions of the object.

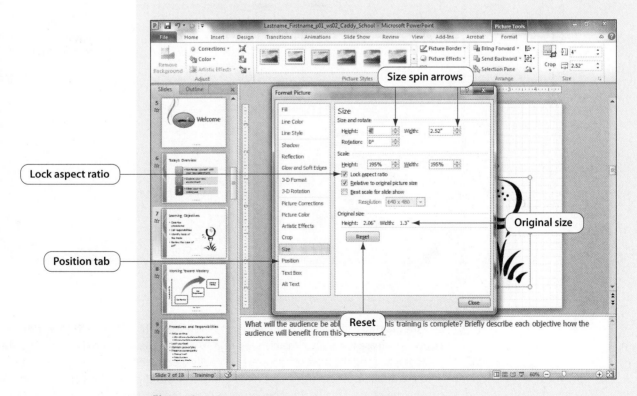

Figure 9   Formatting a picture

Troubleshooting

If you make an error in sizing the photograph and want to return to the original size, click Reset in the Format Picture dialog box.

d. Click the **Position tab** in the left pane of the Format Picture dialog box. You can modify the placement of the graphic on the slide using this tab of the dialog box.

e. Click the **Horizontal spin arrow** to move the graphic to **6.5"** from the top-left corner. Click the **Vertical spin arrow** to move the graphic to **2.5"** from the top-left corner. Click **Close**.

f. Click **Slide 11**, click the **photograph**, and then click the **Picture Tools Format tab**. You will crop some of the grass in the foreground of the photograph.

g. Click **Crop** in the Size group. **Cropping handles** appear at the edges of the photograph to enable you to cut away portions of the graphic that you do not need.

The corner cropping handles crop the vertical and horizontal sides of the photograph at one time. The side cropping handles enable you to crop from one direction.

h. Drag the **bottom-middle cropping handle** up until the handle is just below the feet of the caddy. The gray area below the cropping handle is the area you will delete from the image.

i. Click the **Dialog Box Launcher** [icon] in the Size group of the Picture Tools Format tab, and then in the Format Picture dialog box, click the **Crop tab** in the left pane. Click the Crop position **Height spin arrow** to change the position to **3.5"**.

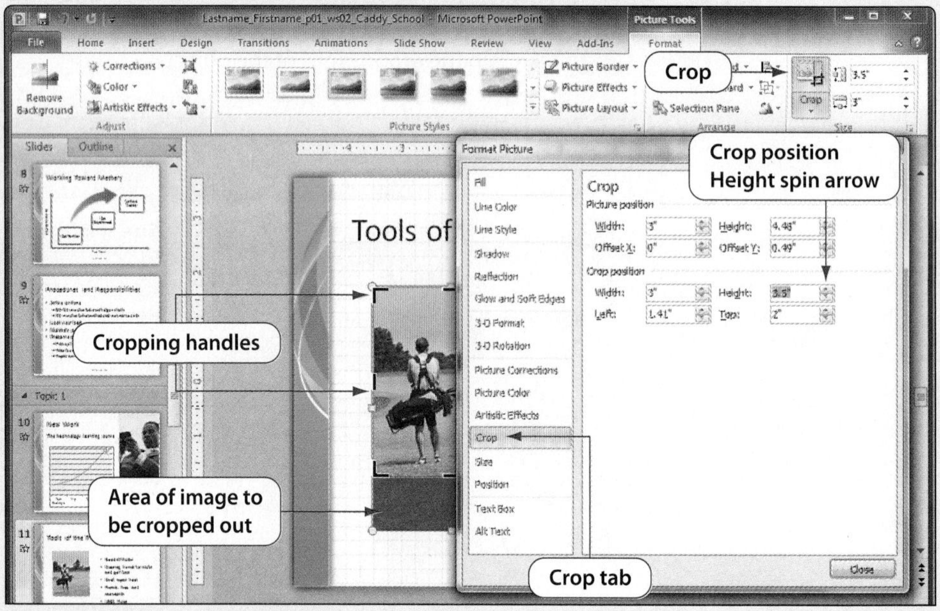

SIDE NOTE
Cropping Handles

Cropping handles enable you to remove portions of photographs that do not add to the message of the graphic, focusing your audience to a more important part of the image.

Figure 10   Cropping a photograph

j. Click the **Size tab** in the left pane of the Format Picture dialog box. Click the **Scale Width spin arrow** to increase the scale of the picture to **120%**, click **Close**, and then click outside of the photograph. Using the Scale option, you can modify the size of the image by percentages.

The cropped portion of the graphic is removed from the slide. This action does not change the original graphic file, but once you save the file, the cropped portion will be permanently removed from the slide.

k. Click **Slide 13**, and then click the **photograph**. On the Format tab, click **Rotate** in the Arrange group, and then click **Flip Horizontal**. The golfer is now facing the center of the slide, which focuses the attention of the audience to the slide.

l. Drag the **rotation handle** to the right to tilt the photograph. Drag the **photograph** to the right so both the top-right and bottom-right corners are off the slide. Images arranged in unusual ways can add interest to the slide.

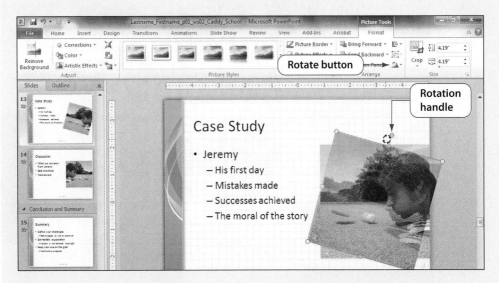

Figure 11 Rotating a graphic

m. Click **Slide 14**, and then click the **photograph**. On the Format tab, click **Rotate** in the Arrange group, and then click **Flip Horizontal**. Drag the **rotation handle** to the left. Press → on the keyboard to move the top and bottom right corners of the photograph off of the slide, and then click outside of the photograph.

Changing the Color of Graphics

PowerPoint contains sophisticated tools for modifying images. Using the Corrections tool on the Format tab of the Picture Tools, you can improve the brightness, contrast, and sharpness of images. The Color tool enables you to change the color of a picture to better match your presentation's color scheme or to improve the quality of the image. Artistic Effects make the picture appear as if it were sketched or painted.

You will **recolor**, or alter the color, of the golf ball and tee clip art to reflect the color scheme of the template. You will change the **color tone**, or the color temperature, of a photograph to add more blue to the image.

To Recolor Graphics

a. Click **Slide 7**, and then click the **golf ball and tee** graphic. Click the **Picture Tools Format tab**, and then click **Color** in the Adjust group. Point to the images in the Recolor gallery and preview the color choices; then click **Aqua, Accent color 5 Light** to apply the color to the image.

The color scheme selected for the template or design theme affects the colors presented in the Recolor gallery. Light and dark accent colors from the scheme appear with various black-and-white, sepia, and washout options.

b. Click **Slide 12**, and then click the **photograph**. Click the **Picture Tools Format tab**, and then click **Color** in the Adjust group. Point to the images in the **Color Tone** group, and then observe that as the Temperature (in Kelvin) goes down, more blue is apparent in the photograph. As the temperature is increased, the yellow tones are enhanced.

Figure 12 Color tones

c. Click the thumbnail for **Temperature: 4700 K**.

The Kelvin scale describes the color temperature of photographs, with the lower numbers on the scale being blue or cooler colors and the higher numbers representing the warmer colors of yellow, red, and orange. Regular daylight color temperature, as you would see outdoors on a clear day, is 5,000 to 6,500 on the Kelvin scale.

Modifying the Picture Style of Graphics

Picture Styles enable you to add preset effects to your graphics. Options include frames, shadows, and unusual shapes. It is a good idea to keep the styles consistent throughout the presentation.

You will use Picture Styles to frame the photographs in the Caddy School presentation, and then you will change the color of the borders to blend with the design theme.

To Apply a Picture Style

a. Click **Slide 5**, and then click the **photograph**. Click the **Picture Tools Format tab**, click **More** in the Picture Styles group, and then point to the **style thumbnails** shown in the gallery and observe Live Preview. The name of the style appears as you point to each thumbnail.

b. Click **Metal Oval** to apply that style to the photograph.

This style gives the photograph a 3-D appearance, but you would like to have it blend more with the colors of the template for consistency. You will change the color of the border.

c. Click the **Picture Border arrow** in the Picture Styles group. Point to various color chips under Theme Colors, and then click **Aqua, Accent 5, Darker 25%**.

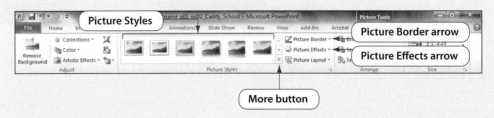

Figure 13 Applying a border

d. Click **Slide 7**, and then click the clip art of the **golf ball and tee**. Click the Picture Tools **Format tab**, if necessary, and then click **More** ⏷ in the Picture Styles group.

As you point to the style options, look at Live Preview on the slide. Frames do not really add to the graphic.

e. Click **Drop Shadow Rectangle**, the fourth thumbnail on the first row. This style adds an interesting shadow effect to the shapes in the graphic.

f. Click **Slide 11**, and then click the **photograph**. Click the **Picture Tools Format tab**, click the **Picture Border arrow** in the Picture Styles group, and then click **Aqua, Accent 5, Darker 25%**. Click the **Picture Border arrow** again, point to **Dashes**, and then click **More Lines**. Click the **Width spin arrow** to increase the Line Style Width to **3 pt**. Click **Compound type**, and then select the second option, **Double**.

g. In the Format Picture dialog box, click the **Shadow tab** on the left pane, click the **Presets** button, and then select **Offset Diagonal Bottom Left**—the third thumbnail in the first row of the Outer group. Click the **Size spin arrow** to increase the size to **102%**, click the **Blur spin arrow** to increase the blur to **6 pt**, and then click **Close**.

h. Click the **Home tab**, and then click the **photograph**, if necessary to select it. Double-click the **Format Painter** ✑ in the Clipboard group. Click **Next Slide** ⬇ twice, and then click the photograph on **Slide 13**. Click **Next Slide** ⬇ again, and then click the **photograph** on Slide 14. Click **Format Painter** in the Clipboard group again to return to the normal pointer.

The photographs now have the same style applied, which adds consistency to your presentation.

Creating Shapes and Lines

Lines and shapes increase understanding of your slides by creating focal points and explaining concepts. Add an arrow to a slide, and the audience will look where it is pointing. Lines and shapes also add color and interest. Text boxes, also considered shapes, enable you to label objects. As you add shapes to your slides, keep in mind that the objects should remain consistent with the other graphics and colors in the presentation.

Applying Shape Styles

PowerPoint contains a wide range of shapes in the Illustrations group on the Insert tab. When you select a shape from the gallery, a crosshair pointer enables you to drag the shape onto the slide. Sizing handles appear on selected shapes so you can change the shape or rotation of the object you have drawn. Shapes can be filled, stacked, aligned, and grouped.

You will modify the shapes on a slide in the Caddy School presentation to better fit your message. The objects you create will demonstrate the rankings caddies can achieve at the Red Bluff Golf Club.

To Apply Styles to Shapes

a. Click **Slide 8**, click next to the **Projects Worked On** text, and then press ⟨Delete⟩ to remove the placeholder. Click in front of the **Time Spent** text, and then press ⟨Delete⟩. You will create text boxes with different words for these parts of the diagram.

b. Click the **Insert tab**, and then click **Shapes** in the Illustrations group. Click **Text Box** 🖾, the first shape in the Basic Shapes group in the gallery. The pointer changes into an insert text box pointer ↓.

c. Move the pointer below the **horizontal line** and click. A small rectangle representing the text box appears. Type More Responsibility in the text box. You will move the text box and align it so it is centered under the line.

d. Drag the **right sizing handle** to the right until it lines up with the point of the arrow on the horizontal line. Drag the **left sizing handle** to the left until it lines up with the corner of the horizontal and vertical line. Drag the **text box** up or down as necessary to place it below the horizontal line.

   As you drag the sizing handles, you notice a dotted alignment guide that helps you align the text box with the ends of the lines. The text is left-aligned in the text box. You will center the text under the line.

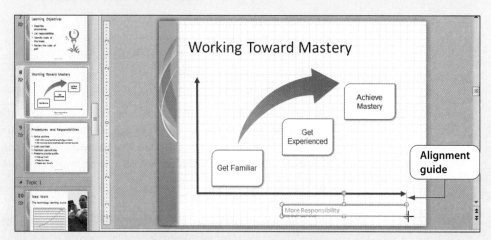

Figure 14   Adding and adjusting text boxes

e. Click the **Home tab**, if necessary, and then click **Center** 🔳 in the Paragraph group. Click **Bold** B in the Font group, click the **Font Color arrow** A ·, and then click **Aqua, Accent 5, Darker 50%**.

f. On the Home tab, click **Shapes** in the Drawing group and then click **Text Box** 🖾 in the Recently Used Shapes group. If you don't see a Shapes button in the Drawing group, click **More** ⊽ in the Shapes gallery.

   You can add shapes from the Insert tab or the Home tab. When you have used a shape, it is shown in the Recently Used Shapes group so you can find it quickly.

g. Click below the slide title, and then type More Money, Better Assignments. This text will be rotated to follow the vertical arrow in the diagram.

h. Click the **Drawing Tools Format tab**, click **Rotate** 🔄 in the Arrange group, and then click **Rotate Left 90°**. Drag the **border** of the text box to the left side of the vertical arrow on the diagram, aligning the bottom of the text box with the corner of the horizontal and vertical arrows. Drag the **top sizing handle** of the text box to the top of the arrow.

i. Click the **Home tab**, and then click **Center** 🔳 in the Paragraph group. Click **Bold** B in the Font group, and then click **Font Color** A ·. The color was loaded into the Font Color button by the actions you took in Step e, so you did not have to reselect the color.

j. Click the **Get Familiar** graphic, press and hold ⌈Shift⌋, and then click the **Get Experienced** graphic and the **Achieve Mastery** graphic. Press ⌈Delete⌋. You have decided to use a different shape for the Caddy School diagram.

k. Click **Shapes** (or More ⌈▾⌋) in the Drawing group on the Home tab and then click **Oval** in the Basic Shapes group. Click below the large arrow, near the middle of the slide. An oval with a default size appears. Type Intermediate Caddy.

  The text will wrap and probably not fit in the oval. Do not worry, you will adjust this later. You are using the largest amount of text so you can consistently create shapes that will be the same size and hold all of the text.

l. Drag the **right sizing handle** to the right until the words "Intermediate Caddy" appear on two lines.

  You will now edit the shape by changing the fill and outline. Later you will copy this shape to create the other shapes. It is easiest to make all the changes to one shape first and then copy it.

m. Click the **Shape Fill arrow** in the Drawing group, and then click **Aqua, Accent 5, Lighter 80%**. The words in the text box disappear because they are white.

n. Click **Font Color** ⌈▲▾⌋ in the Font group. The words reappear in the same color as used previously for text boxes.

o. Click **Shape Effects** in the Drawing group, and then point to **Shadow**. Click **Offset Diagonal Bottom Right** in the Outer group.

p. Click **Copy** ⌈▤⌋ in the Clipboard group on the Home tab. Click **Paste** in the Clipboard group twice. Two additional ovals appear on the slide. Select the **text** in the top oval, and then type Captain Caddy. Drag the **oval shape** to the right but not beyond the point of the horizontal arrow. Select the text **Intermediate Caddy**, and then type Trainee in the shape. Drag the **oval shape** to the left of the Intermediate Caddy shape but within the line pointing upward.

  You have three shapes that are identical in size and color. This ensures a consistent look to the diagram. Later you will arrange the shapes on the slide.

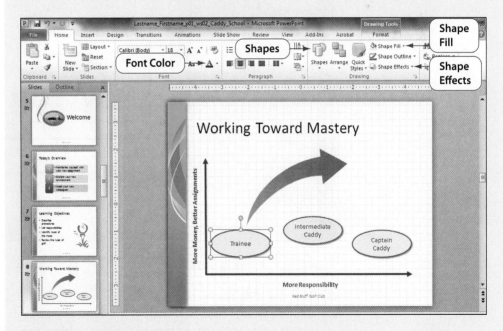

Figure 15   Adding shapes

Arranging Shapes

PowerPoint has tools that enable you to precisely arrange the shapes you create. You can reorder items that are stacked to bring other shapes forward or send them backward. You can group objects so they are treated as one object. You have already rotated shapes on the slide. You can also align two or more shapes in relation to the other selected shapes.

You will align the three oval shapes on the Working Toward Mastery slide. "Trainee" will appear closest to the corner of the horizontal and vertical arrows. "Intermediate Caddy" will appear in the center, and "Captain Caddy" will appear to the right. You will begin by selecting all of the ovals and aligning them evenly on a horizontal plane of the slide. You will then arrange them vertically on the slide.

To Align Shapes

a. Click the **Trainee** shape, and then press and hold Shift. Click the **Intermediate Caddy** and the **Captain Caddy** shapes to select them. All of the shapes must be selected in order to align them.

b. Click **Arrange** in the Drawing group on the Home tab, point to **Align**, and then click **Distribute Horizontally**. The three shapes now have an equal distance between them.

c. Click **Arrange** again, point to **Align**, and then click **Align Bottom**.
   All three shapes are now on the same vertical line. If the shapes are not within the vertical and horizontal arrows on the diagram, drag them into position.

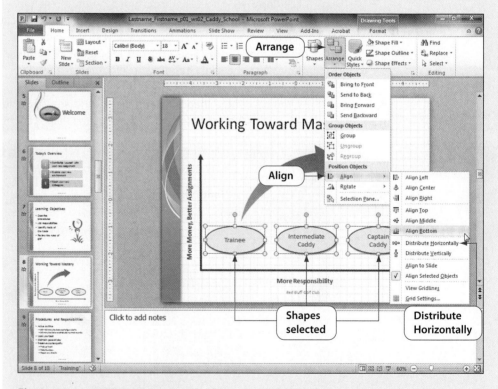

Figure 16   Arranging shapes

d. Click the **slide background** to deselect the shapes, and then click the border of the **Captain Caddy** shape. You want to show this as an elevated position. Press the ↑ on the keyboard until the shape is just below the large arrow. The shape moves up, while maintaining the horizontal distance between the shapes.

Troubleshooting

If you do not see a solid line around the shape, you will not be able to move it. Click the border of the shape to activate a solid line.

e. Select all **three shapes** again while pressing Shift, and then click **Arrange**. Point to **Align**, and then click **Distribute Vertically**. The shapes now have equal distance between them on the vertical plane of the slide.

Inserting WordArt

Just as shapes can be filled in and modified with effects, text can be enhanced with the use of **WordArt**, which is text that has been enhanced with color, outlines, shadows, and special effects. Used for small amounts of text, WordArt adds color and interest to your presentation.

Inserting WordArt

You will add WordArt to two slides in the Caddy School presentation. You decide that the Welcome slide (Slide 5) is rather boring and needs more visual energy. You also decide to enhance the word "Questions" on Slide 17.

To Insert WordArt

a. Click **Slide 5**, and then click the **border** of the text box containing the word **Welcome**. Press Delete to remove the text box from the slide. You will replace the text box with a WordArt graphic.

b. Click the **Insert tab**, and then click **WordArt** in the Text group. Click **Gradient Fill - Blue, Accent 1**— the fourth thumbnail in the third row. Type Welcome in the text box. The size of the text box expands to accommodate the word.

SIDE NOTE
Keep It Short and Simple
As you add shapes and WordArt to your slides, be sure to maintain a balance on the slide. White space should be balanced with the number and size of shapes. Avoid overdoing the use of WordArt, as it can detract from your message.

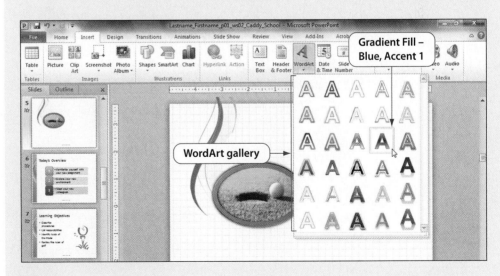

Figure 17   WordArt gallery

c. Click the **border** of the WordArt, click the **Home tab**, click the **Font Size arrow** in the Font group, and then click **80**. Drag the **text box** to the right of the picture.

d. Click **Arrange** in the Drawing group, point to **Align**, and then click **Align Middle**, placing the WordArt in the exact center of the slide. Click **Arrange**, point to **Align** again, and then click **Align Right**. This two-step process aligns the WordArt to the center of the slide vertically, and then aligns it to the right side of the slide horizontally.

e. Click **Slide 17**, select the text **Questions?**, and then click the **Drawing Tools Format tab**.

f. Click **More** ⊽ in the WordArt Styles group to view the gallery. Click **Fill - White, Gradient Outline - Accent 1**—the first thumbnail of the third row. You have converted the text into WordArt.

g. Click the **border** of the WordArt, click the **Home tab**, click the **Font Size arrow** in the Font group, and then click **66** to increase the size of the text. Notice that Font commands can be used on WordArt text.

Applying a Picture as a Slide Background

While templates and design themes often include background images, you can apply your own image to the background of a slide. It is important to remember that text on top of the background must still be easy to read. You will remove the background picture of the template and apply an appropriate picture to the background of a slide.

To Modify a Background

a. Click **Slide 10** and then click the **Design tab**. You will hide the current background on the slide, and then place a more appropriate photograph in the background.

b. Click the **Dialog Box Launcher** ⊠ in the Background group, and then click the **Hide background graphics** check box.

The background changes significantly. This is because the template was based on another slide show. This will not affect your presentation.

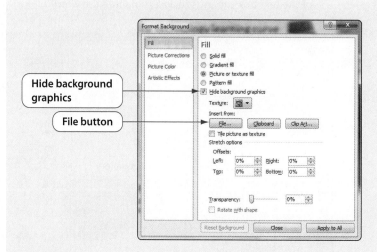

Figure 18   Applying a background to a slide

c. Click the **File** button under Insert from, and then navigate to where your student data files are located and click **p01_ws02_Caddy_Background**. Click **Insert**, and then click **Close**.

The background adjusts to fill the background of the slide. You will delete the extra graphics currently on the slide.

d. Click the **photograph** of the man, press ⌧Delete⌧, click the **edge of the chart**, press ⌧Delete⌧, click the **star** shape, and then press ⌧Delete⌧.

e. Select the **title**, and type The Schedule. Click in front of the text **The technology learning curve**, and press ⌧Delete⌧ to remove the entire placeholder. You have now prepared the slide for the next part of the workshop.

Creating a Table

Tables, which are organized grids of information arranged in rows and columns, relate bits of information together in a way that is meaningful to audiences. Short phrases, single words, and numbers can be placed in the cells of a table. You can even place graphics, such as photographs or clip art, in the cells. The table can be created as a media object directly from the icon on the content placeholder, or the Insert tab can be used to develop the table. Once you have created the table you can change the style, apply table effects, and change the layout. Table cells can be split or merged.

Real World Advice   Using an Excel Worksheet as a Source

Often the data you need to convey in a presentation are already available in an Excel worksheet. You can copy the information from Excel and paste it onto a PowerPoint slide. Options you have for pasting include the following:

• Using the styles of the slide

• Keeping the source formatting from the worksheet

• Linking the information so changes in the worksheet will be reflected in the presentation

• Inserting the information as a picture

• Keeping the text only, and losing all of the worksheet grid

You can also create the table in PowerPoint, and then paste the information from the worksheet into the table.

Inserting a Table

You will create a table to explain the weekly golf schedule in the Caddy School presentation. You will modify the table to fit your needs.

To Insert a Table

a. Click the **Insert tab**, and then click **Table** in the Tables group. Click **Insert Table** 🔲 below the squares on the menu.

b. Increase the Number of columns to **8**, increase the Number of rows to **5**, and then click **OK**.

Figure 19   Inserting a table

SIDE NOTE
Creating a Table
To create a table, you can drag across cells on the Insert tab's Table menu, select Insert Table to use a dialog box, click Draw Table to draw the table cells, or click the Insert Table icon in the content placeholder on the slide.

c. Type Caddy in the first cell, and then type the abbreviations for the days of the week beginning with Monday in each of the cells on the top row of the table.

d. Click in front of the word **Caddy**, and then click the **Table Tools Layout tab**. Click **Select** in the Table group, click **Select Row**, and then click **Center** ☰ in the Alignment group.

e. Type Captain in the second cell of the first column. Click in the cell below. Type Intermediate in the third cell of the first column, and then type Trainee in the fourth cell of the first column. Some of the words are broken in the middle so the words fit the cell. Do not worry about that at this time.

f. Continue to fill in the table as follows:

Caddy	Mon.	Tues.	Wed.	Thurs.	Fri.	Sat.	Sun.
Captain	8 AM	10 AM	8 AM	10 AM	8 AM	7 AM	7AM
Intermediate	Noon	8 AM	Noon	8 AM	Noon	8 AM	8 AM
Trainee	8 AM	Noon	8 AM	Noon	8 AM	9 AM	9 AM

SIDE NOTE

Navigating in a Table

As you move from cell to cell, press Tab to move from the left to the right. Press Shift + Tab to move from right to left. You can also use the arrow keys on the keyboard to move around the table.

Changing the Table Style

Table Styles provide options for color in the table. The Table Style Options, on the Table Tools Design tab, enable you to specify treatment for the various rows in the table. The Header Row command affects the first row of the table where the column headers appear by applying a stronger color to the background of the cells and displaying the words in a bold font. Banded Rows or Banded Columns highlight the rows or columns with different colors. This assists your audience as they read the information in the table. You can apply styles to the Total Row, First Column, and Last Column to highlight totaled information in your table. You can also change the color of individual cells on the table after applying a table style by using the Shading tool. You will continue to work with the schedule to enhance its appearance.

To Modify a Table Style

a. Click anywhere on the table, and then click the **Table Tools Design tab**. Click **More** ▾ in the Table Styles group. Point to the **thumbnails** in the gallery to view Live Preview on the slide, and then click **Themed Style 1 - Accent 3** in the top row of the Best Match for Document group.

   The green colors of the table coordinate with the green of the background graphic. You will continue to modify the table design by applying a fill color to the caddy rank cells.

b. Select the **cells** containing the caddy ranks: **Captain**, **Intermediate**, and **Trainee**. Click the **Shading arrow** in the Table Styles group, and then click **Olive Green, Accent 3**.

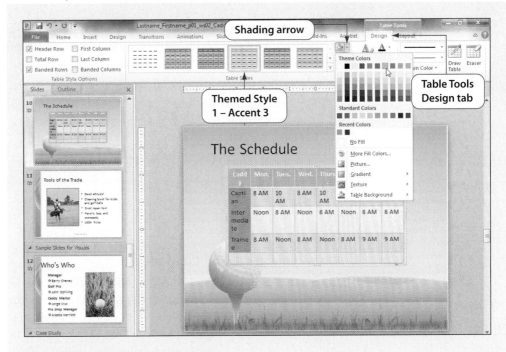

Figure 20   Modifying the table style

Applying Table Effects

Table Effects further enhance a table by providing visual effects such as cell bevels, table shadows, and reflections. Cell bevel effects can make the cells appear in 3-D. Often you will see cell bevels applied to the column or row headers to differentiate them from the rest of the table. Keep in mind the KISS—Keep It Short and Simple—principle, and apply table effects in a way that improves the table. The shadow and reflection effects are applied to the entire table when selected. You will update the Caddy School Schedule table with Table Effects.

To Modify Table Effects

a. Click the **Table Tools Design tab**. Select all of the **cells** in the top row of the table, click **Effects** in the Table Styles group, and then point to **Cell Bevel**. Click **Circle** after pointing to the thumbnails to view Live Preview. This adds dimension to the cells, making the table more interesting.

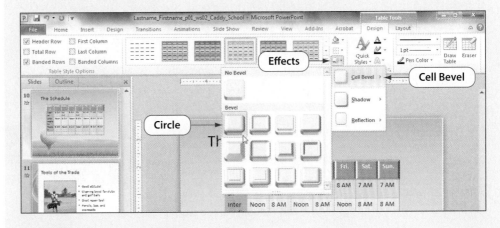

Figure 21   Selecting table effects

b. Select the **cells** containing the caddy ranks. Click **Effects** ⊡ in the Table Styles group, point to **Cell Bevel**, and then click **Cool Slant**. This effect mimics the effect of the column heading cells.

c. Select the **second through fourth rows** of the table. Click the **Table Tools Design tab**, click the **Borders arrow** in the Table Styles group, and then click **All Borders**. Adding a border to the cells in the table enables your audience to differentiate between the cells of the table.

d. Click a **cell** in the table, and then click **Effects** ⊡ in the Table Styles group. Point to **Shadow**, and then click **Offset Diagonal Bottom Right**. The shadow helps maintain consistency with the other graphics in the presentation.

Changing the Table Layout

Often after working on a table, you decide to change the layout. The Layout tab on the Table Tools tab enables you to make such changes as adding rows and columns to the table. You can also delete unnecessary rows or columns. Cells of the table can be merged into a single cell. A single cell can be split into multiple cells. The Layout tab contains Alignment tools that enable you to align the contents of the cells horizontally and vertically in the cells. You can also change the direction of the text and modify the width of the cell margins.

You will add a row to the table, below the column heading row, and merge cells in this row. You will delete the extra row at the bottom of the table.

To Modify a Table Layout

a. Click the **Captain cell** in the table, and then click the **Table Tools Layout tab**. Click **Insert Above** in the Rows & Columns group. A new row is placed between the column headings and the table data.

b. Select the **cells** under Mon. through Thurs. on the second row of the table. Click **Merge Cells** in the Merge group, type Weekday Rates and then click **Center** ▤ in the Alignment group. The cells are merged to show that the cells below are all related to the weekday rates.

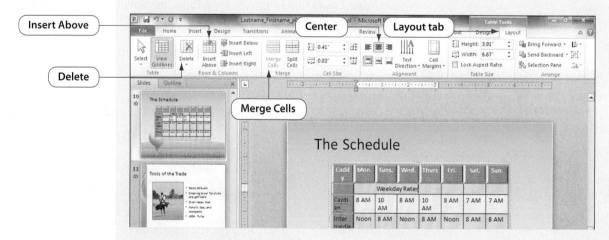

Figure 22   Modifying the table layout

You may be wondering why you did not press Delete on the keyboard to delete the row. Delete removes the information from the cell, but leaves the cell in the table. The Delete tools, in the Rows & Columns group, remove the row or column. If information was in the row or column you deleted, it would also be deleted.

c. Select the **cells** under Fri. through Sun. on the second row of the table. Click **Merge Cells**, type Weekend Rates and then click **Center** ☰ in the Alignment group.

d. Click a **cell** in the last row of the table, and then click **Delete** in the Rows & Columns group. Click **Delete Rows**. The extra row of the table is not needed.

e. Click the cell containing the **Intermediate** caddy rank. Click the **Table Column Width arrow** in the Cell Size group to increase the size until the word **Intermediate** fits on a single line.

   You will adjust the column widths under the days of the week to fit the table on the slide.

f. Select the **column headers** for the days of the week. Click in the **Table Column Width** box in the Cell Size group, type 1, and then press Enter.

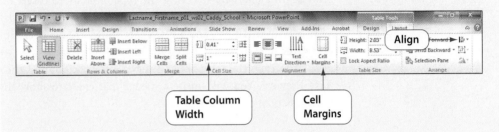

Figure 23   Modifying column width

g. Select the entire **top row** of the table, click **Cell Margins** in the Alignment group, and then click **Wide**. The size of the cells containing the headers seems to have increased, but in reality a wider margin was put around the words.

h. Select the word **Caddy** in the table, and then drag it to the first cell of the second row. This improves the balance of the table. With the word **Caddy** selected, click the **Home tab**, click **Font Color** in the Font group, and then click **White, Background 1**.

i. Click the **Table Tools Layout tab**, click **Align** in the Arrange group, and then click **Align Center**.

Troubleshooting

> If the cell seems extra tall, you may have included the paragraph break in the selection of the word. Click after the word "Caddy," and press Delete to remove the paragraph break.

Creating and Inserting Charts

Just as pictures can tell a story in your presentations, **charts** of numeric data assist your audience in grasping your message. Charts can be persuasive tools in presentations, giving your audience the essence of the problem and the solution. Large amounts of numbers are often difficult to read on the screen, but they can be distilled into charts that describe the real meaning of the data. The message of the chart should stand out as a single statement.

PowerPoint has tools that enable you to enter the data into a worksheet window and then create a chart. A wide variety of chart types are available. After the chart is created you can edit the data and modify the characteristics of the chart including the design, layout, and format.

As you create charts, it is important to critically evaluate them to ensure that the information is correct and that they make sense. Often just switching the data in the rows and columns gives a whole new meaning to the graph. Ask yourself these questions:

- What is the one thing I am trying to convey with this chart?
- What is the core information to be included?
- Does the chart add to the message of the slide? Is it easy to read?

Entering Data

You begin a chart by selecting the type of chart to insert onto a slide. The type of chart relates to the type of data you have. For instance, pie charts are used to show proportions that add up to 100%, and a line chart shows trends over a period of time.

After selecting the chart type, a worksheet table window opens and displays default data. You type the category and series information, and the chart appears on the slide in Live Preview. You will create a stacked bar chart to show the pay rate information in the Caddy School presentation.

To Insert a Chart

a. Click the **Home tab**, and then click **New Slide**. The new slide is inserted after Slide 10 and contains the original background of the template.

b. Type Pay Rates in the title placeholder. This title will be used instead of a chart title.

c. Click **Insert Chart** in the content placeholder. Click **Stacked Column in 3-D** in the gallery, and then click **OK**.

   The worksheet opens with the Live Preview of the default data. The categories represent the columns, and the series provide the numeric data.

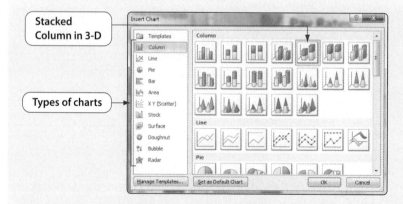

Figure 24   Inserting a chart

d. Type the following information into the worksheet, over the existing data:

	Captain	Intermediate	Trainee
Average Tips	35	25	15
Weekday	35	25	25
Weekend	45	35	30

The final row of the default worksheet is unneeded, so you will delete it.

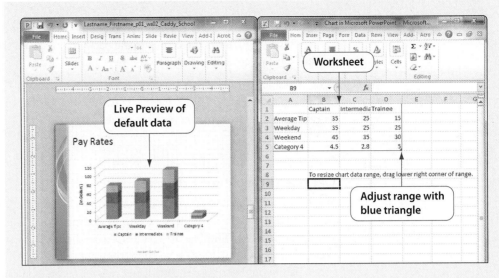

Figure 25 Inserting chart data

e. Drag the **bottom-right corner** of the range—the blue triangle—up so only the four rows used in the worksheet are selected. **Close** [X] the worksheet window. Review the chart to ensure that the data is correct.

    The chart seems to say that the weekend rates are just over $100. It is difficult to determine the pay rate for the individual caddy ranks. This chart clearly needs some modification.

Changing the Chart Type

Usually, confusion with a chart occurs because the wrong choice was made for a chart type or the axes are not correct. PowerPoint makes it easy for you to experiment with the various types of charts to improve the message of your chart.

    As you reviewed the chart, you noticed each of the caddy ranks are shown as a part of the rates. A better display for the slide would be to show the ranks with all of the rates grouped for each rank on bars, rather than stacked. You will change the chart type to make the purpose of the chart more evident.

To Modify the Chart Type

a. Click the **chart**, and then click the **Chart Tools Design tab**.

    The Design tab enables you to change the type of chart, the layouts, and the styles. You will experiment with these tools.

b. Click **Change Chart Type** [icon] in the Type group, click the **Bar** type in the left pane, and then select **Clustered Bar in 3-D**. Click **OK**.

    The 3-D effect is consistent with other graphics in your presentation. The chart now shows that the Trainees make a similar rate to the Intermediate ranked caddies on weekdays, and that the Captain caddy rank makes more money than each of the other ranks, regardless of the day of the week. The color combinations do not work well with your overall presentation, so you will use Chart Styles to improve the chart.

Figure 26 Changing the chart type

c. Click **More** ☰ in the Chart Styles group, and then click **Style 27**.

This style matches the colors on the background of the slide, providing consistency, but the bars are a little dark. You will view another style.

d. Click **More** in the ☰ Chart Styles group, and then click **Style 31**. This lighter overall color makes it easier to see the individual bars. Review the chart to ensure that it makes sense and fits with the color scheme of the presentation.

Changing the Chart Layout

The Chart Layout tab contains tools for adding descriptive labels to the chart, which can increase your audience's understanding of the material. The horizontal and vertical axes should be labeled. The legend enables the audience to match the bars with the caddy ranks. Data labels enable you to show the value of each of the bars on the table. This is beneficial if you do not use the gridlines in your chart. You can also display the Data Table that you used to place the numeric data into the chart if necessary.

You will add an axis title to the numbers at the bottom of the chart. A chart title is unnecessary because there is a descriptive title on the slide. You will experiment with the data labels and the legend.

SIDE NOTE
Adding Number Formats with Excel

The worksheet that opens when you create a chart can be modified using the normal Excel tools. Those modifications will be reflected in your chart in PowerPoint.

To Modify the Chart Layout

a. Click the **chart**, and then click the **Chart Tools Layout tab**.

b. Click **Axis Titles** in the Labels group, and then point to **Primary Horizontal Axis Title**. The gallery shows the location of the title on the slide with an orange block on the thumbnail.

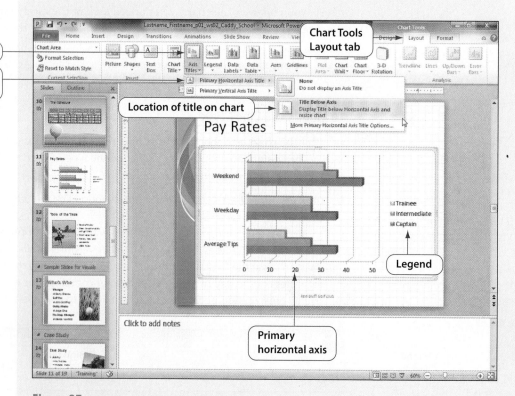

Figure 27 Modifying the chart layout

c. Click **Title Below Axis** on the Primary Horizontal Axis Title gallery, and then type (In Dollars). This indicates that the numbers at the bottom of the chart are in dollar format, rather than millions or billions.

d. Click **Legend** in the Labels group, and then click **None**.

   This turns off the legend, and the chart loses its focus and purpose. You will continue to experiment with the placement of the legend.

e. Click **Legend** in the Labels group, and then click **Show Legend at Top**. This provides some balance to the chart, but you will continue to experiment. Click **Legend** again, and then click **Show Legend at Bottom**. This final placement increases the importance of the numeric data and provides balance to the chart.

f. Click **Data Labels** in the Labels group, and click **Show**. Numbers appear at the end of each bar, reporting the pay, but this is a little distracting. You decide to not show the data labels. Click **Data Labels**, and then click **None**.

Formatting Chart Elements

Individual elements on the chart, such as the series bars, axes, legend, and gridlines, can be selected and modified using the Format tab on the Chart Tools tab. You can change the Shape Styles, and manipulate the shape fill colors, outline colors, and shape effects.

You decide to change the shape fill for the Trainee series and the outline color of the gridlines. When you select one data point in a category, such as the Trainee bar for the Weekend, all of the Trainee bars are selected because they are in the same series.

To Format Chart Elements

a. Click the **chart**, if necessary, to select it, click the **Chart Tools Format tab**, and then click one of the **Trainee bars**. All three Trainee bars are now selected.

b. Click **More** ▼ in the Shape Styles group, and then click **Subtle Effect - Aqua, Accent 5**.
   This shape style appears brighter with a gradient fill. The legend on the chart changed to reflect this new color choice.

c. Click one of the **Intermediate bars**. All three bars are selected. Click the **Shape Fill arrow** in the Shape Styles group, and then click **Olive Green, Accent 3, Lighter 60%**. The change in color adds interest to the chart and makes it easier to see the Intermediate rank.

d. Click one of the **Captain bars**, click **More** ▼ in the Shape Styles group, and then click **Intense Effect - Aqua, Accent 5**. The chart coordinates in color with the overall scheme of the template.

Creating a SmartArt Graphic

SmartArt graphics add color, shape, and emphasis to the text in your presentations. Specialty graphics such as list, hierarchy, process, pyramid, and cycle charts are pre-formatted using your color scheme for use in your slide shows. The gallery contains a number of versions for each chart type. As you review the different SmartArt graphics, you will see a wide range of graphic types. For instance, Process graphics show a sequence of steps, while Cycle graphics represent a circular flow of stages or tasks. Hierarchy and Relationship graphics show how items relate, such as you might find on an organizational chart for a company.

Using SmartArt

The agenda gives you an opportunity to effectively use SmartArt. You will create a new slide to replace Slide 6 in the Caddy School presentation. This slide will show the agenda for the day in a SmartArt graphic. You will begin by selecting the SmartArt graphic from the gallery.

To Create a SmartArt Graphic

a. Click **Slide 7** and then click the **Home tab**. Click **New Slide** in the Slides group to insert a new slide after the Learning Objectives slide, click **Layout** in the Slides group, and then click the **Title and Content** thumbnail.

b. Click the title **placeholder**, and then type Today's Agenda. Click **Insert SmartArt Graphic** in the content placeholder. The gallery of SmartArt graphics opens.

c. Click **List**, click **Segmented Process** in the gallery, and then click **OK**.

   This graphic will provide an interesting change from the normal bullet points used on slides. It will also be more colorful than a bullet point list. The SmartArt Tools tab opens with many options for modifying the design or format of the graphic.

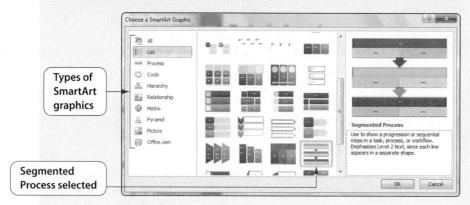

Figure 28   Adding SmartArt

Troubleshooting

You can reset the graphic to the beginning version at any time by clicking Reset Graphic on the SmartArt Tools Design tab.

Adding Text to the Diagram

Just as you have used the Outline tab to focus your attention on the content of your presentation, the SmartArt Text pane enables you to quickly place the text into the graphic, concentrating on the content. You can add additional bullet points at the end of the graphic by pressing Enter. Use the arrow keys or click the bullet points to move within the Text pane. You can move the bullet text up and down on the graphic using tools on the Design tab. The bullet points can be promoted or demoted as needed.

You will place the text on the SmartArt graphic using the Text pane. You will then move the text to reflect a change in the schedule.

To Add Text to a SmartArt Graphic

a. Click **Text Pane** in the Create Graphic group on the SmartArt Tools Design tab if necessary. You will use the Text pane to quickly add the information to the SmartArt graphic.

b. Type Meet and Greet in the Text pane. Press ⬇ on the keyboard to move to the next bullet point in the Text pane, and then type Morning — What is it all about? Press Shift + Tab to decrease the indent in the outline.

c. Press ⬇ to move to the next bullet point, and then type Lunch Buffet — Red Bluff Bistro. Press Shift + Tab to decrease the indent in the outline.

d. Press the ⬇ to move to the next bullet point in the Text pane, and then type Afternoon — Golf Rules Review. Do not press Enter.

e. Press Delete until all of the extra bullet points are removed.

The schedule has undergone a change, and the Meet and Greet activity has been moved to before lunch. You will move the bullet text in the Text pane.

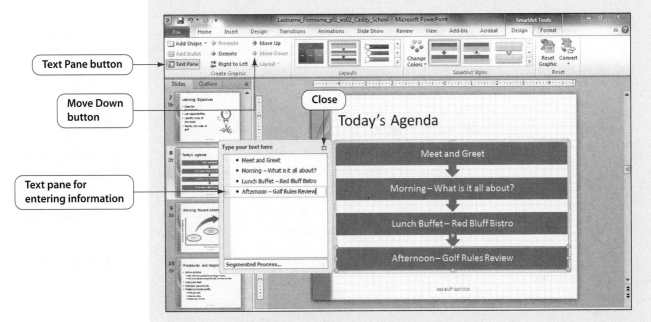

Figure 29   Adding text to a SmartArt graphic

f. Click **Meet and Greet** in the Text pane, and then click **Move Down** in the Create Graphic group. Close the Text pane by clicking **Close** ☒ in the Text pane.

Applying SmartArt Styles

SmartArt Styles enable you to change the appearance of the shapes and colors of the graphics. You can test the options by viewing a Live Preview as you point to the gallery thumbnails.

You will experiment with the SmartArt Styles to make the graphic more interesting.

To Apply a SmartArt Style

a. Click **More** ⏷ in the SmartArt Styles group on the SmartArt Tools Design tab. Point to the thumbnails in the gallery and observe Live Preview.

Options for style changes include Best Match for Document and 3-D. Both options use the template colors. This helps to maintain consistency with the rest of the presentation.

b. Click **Cartoon** in the 3-D group. This effect adds dimension to the graphic and gives a professional feel to the presentation despite the name of the style.

Changing SmartArt Theme Colors

The colors used in SmartArt graphics are based on the colors in the theme or template used for the presentation. Choices for coloring the graphics include Primary Theme Colors, Colorful combinations, and Accent color options. You can also recolor the individual shapes using the Shape Fill and Shape Outline tools on the SmartArt Tools Format tab. Shape effects, such as shadows and bevels can be applied to the individual shapes.

You will modify the colors in the graphic using the template colors option and change the fill color of the luncheon agenda item.

To Modify SmartArt Colors

a. Click **Change Colors** in the SmartArt Styles group on the SmartArt Tools Design tab. Point to the **thumbnails** in the gallery to view the results in Live Preview.

b. Click **Gradient Range - Accent 5** in the Accent 5 group.

Each of the shapes is a slightly different shade of the accent color. You decide to experiment with changing the color of the Lunch Buffet shape.

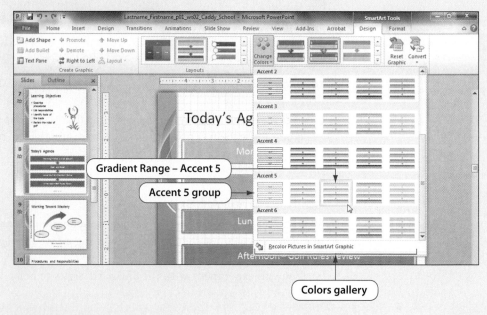

Figure 30   Modifying SmartArt colors

c. Click the **Lunch Buffet - Red Bluff Bistro shape**, and then click the **SmartArt Tools Format tab**.

d. Click the **Shape Fill arrow** in the Shape Styles group, and then click **Aqua, Accent 5, Lighter 60%**.

   This light color clearly shows a change in the schedule, but the text is difficult to read. You will modify the text color.

e. Select the text **Lunch Buffet - Red Bluff Bistro**, and then click the **Home tab**. Click the **Font Color arrow** in the Font group, and then click **Aqua, Accent 5, Darker 50%**. This color keeps the color scheme consistent while making the text more readable.

Changing SmartArt Layouts

As with many things, when you design slides, your first choice may not always turn out as you might wish. After you have placed text into a SmartArt graphic, you can modify the layout to display the information in a different way. As you select the layout, color choices you have made are retained.

   You will change the layout of the SmartArt graphic to make it more interesting.

To Modify a SmartArt Layout

a. Click the **SmartArt Tools Design tab**, and then click **More** ⊽ in the Layouts group.

b. Click **Vertical Curved List**. This layout suggests golf balls with the white circles, and it continues to have a flowing feeling that matches the template.

c. The presentation work is complete, but some slides remain from the template that you did not use. On the Slides tab, click **Slide 6** (Today's Overview), and then press Delete. Click **Slide 16** (Summary), press Shift, click **Slide 17 (**Resources), and then press Delete to remove these slides from the presentation. Click **Slide 17** (Appendix), and then press Delete.

d. Click the **Slide Show tab**, and then click **From Beginning**. View each slide in the presentation. **Save** 🖫 the presentation, and then exit PowerPoint.

1. As you prepare for a presentation, what questions would you ask the organizer of the event about the audience? How would the answers change your plans for your presentation?

2. You have been asked to speak to a physical education class at the local junior high school (grades 6–8) about your hobby of skateboarding. Describe the template and types of graphics you will use to reach this audience. How might you use charts and tables in this presentation?

3. Your supervisor has asked you to compare three laptop computers that the department is considering. A presentation will be given to upper management so they can decide which computers fit the needs of the department. How will you present the technical information about the computers? What role will charts play in your presentation?

4. You are working on a presentation with a coworker that will be given to new employees at your company. What are common types of information that the presentation should contain, and how would you present it in interesting ways? Prepare a storyboard for four of the slides in the presentation.

5. How would you prepare for a Pecha Kucha presentation on your favorite hobby? List three concepts that are very important in this type of presentation.

Key Terms

Bit-mapped graphic 732
Chart 749
Clip Art 732
Color tone 737
Copyrights 724
Cropping handles 736

Pecha Kucha 720
Picture Style 738
Recolor 737
Reuse slides 730
Slide footer 726
SmartArt graphic 753

Storyboard 722
Symbols 727
Table 745
Vector graphic 732
WordArt 743

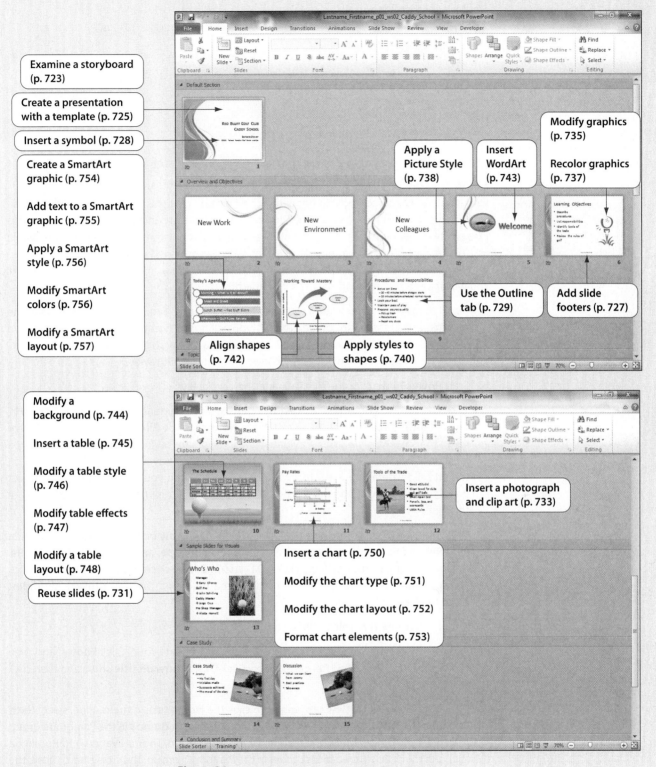

Figure 31 Red Bluff Caddy School Final Presentation

Student data files needed:

p01_ws02_Conference_Storyboard
p01_ws02_Conference_Template
p01_ws02_Conference_Content
p01_ws02_Conference_Attendees
p01_ws02_Conference_Eldorado
p01_ws02_Conference_Pueblo
p01_ws02_Conference_Background

You will save your file as:

Lastname_Firstname_p01_ws02_Conference

Corporate Event Planning at the Painted Paradise Golf Resort and Spa

Sales & Marketing

Patti Rochelle asked you to assist her with a presentation that she will deliver to various business clients who anticipate using the Painted Paradise Resort and Spa for conferences. This presentation will highlight the outstanding service that Patti and her staff provide, while assisting the audience in planning their event. Patti has provided you with a bare-bones presentation that contains slide titles and some content. She has also given you a storyboard. You will use a template to prepare the presentation.

a. Start **Word**, and then open **p01_ws02_Conference_Storyboard**, and review the planned presentation. In this storyboard, you will notice that the template is specified in the first Layout block. The footer is also specified, along with the reuse slide show name. Close the Word document when you have completed your review.

b. Start **PowerPoint**, click the **File tab**, and then click **New**.

c. Click **New from existing**, and then navigate to your student data files and click **p01_ws02_Conference_Template**. Click **Create New**, click the **File tab**, and then click **Save As**. In the Save As dialog box, navigate to where you are saving your files, and then type Lastname_Firstname_p01_ws02_Conference, and click **Save**. Read the Notes pane on the title slide, detailing the design of the template. When you have read the text, select it and press Delete. Drag the **border** of the Notes pane down to increase the display of the slide.

d. Click **Slide 1**, click the **Home tab**, click the **New Slide arrow** in the Slides group, and then click **Reuse Slides**. In the Reuse Slides pane, click **Browse**, and then click **Browse File**. Navigate to your student files, click **p01_ws02_Conference_Content**, and then click **Open**. In the Reuse Slides pane, right-click on a slide, and then click **Insert All Slides**. Close the Reuse Slides pane.

e. Click the **Outline tab**, select **Slide 1**, and then press Delete.

f. Click the **Insert tab**, and click **Header & Footer** in the Text group. Click **Footer**, and then type Painted Paradise Golf Resort and Spa. Click **Don't show on title slide**, and then click **Apply to All**.

g. Click **Slide 3** on the Outline tab, and then click the **Home tab**. In the outline, select **Patti Rochelle—Corporate Event Coordinator**, and then click **Bullets** in the Paragraph group to remove the bullet. Select the **three names** (Lesa Martin, Thomas Vance, and Rosalinda Hill), and then click **Increase List Level** in the Paragraph group. The storyboard shows the bullet scheme for this slide, with the supporting staff indented.

h. Click **Slide 8** on the Outline tab, and then select **Patti Rochelle** in the outline. Click **Bullets** in the Paragraph group to remove the bullet, and then click **Bold** in the Font group. Click the **Font Size arrow**, and then select **32**.

i. Click the **Slides tab**, and then click **Slide 2**. Select the **quotation**, and then click the **Drawing Tools Format tab**. Click **More** in the WordArt Styles group, and then click **Gradient Fill - Red, Accent 6, Inner Shadow**. On the **Home tab**, click the **Font Size arrow**, and then select **32**.

j. Click the **Insert tab**, click **Picture** in the Images group, navigate to your student data files, click **p01_ws02_Conference_Attendees**, and then click **Insert**. Click the Picture Tools Format tab, click **Shape Height** in the Size group, type 2.5, and then press Enter. Drag the **photograph** to the left side of the slide, placing it above the footer. Click **Rotate** in the Arrange group, and then click **Flip Horizontal**.

k. Click **Slide 3**, click the **Insert tab**, and then click **Clip Art** in the Images group. Use the search word planning to search for Illustrations, including Office.com content. Click an appropriate graphic for a business presentation. The storyboard calls for a "couple planning." Drag the **clip** to the bottom-right corner of the slide, and resize the graphic if necessary. Close the Clip Art pane.

l. Click **Slide 4**, and then click the **Home tab**. Click **Layout** in the Slides group, and then select **Two Content**. Click in **The Eldorado Room** text, and then click **Bullets** in the Paragraph group to remove the bullet. Click in **The Pueblo Room** text and remove the bullet.

m. Click the **Insert tab**, and then click **Picture**. Click **p01_ws02_Conference_Eldorado**, and then click **Insert**. Click **Shape Height** in the Size group, type 2, and then press Enter. Click **Crop** in the Size group, and drag the **upper-center cropping handle** down to above the ceiling lights in the photograph. Click the **slide background**. Select the **picture** again, click **More** in the Picture Styles group, and select **Reflected Perspective Right**. Move the photograph under **The Eldorado Room** heading with the left side of the border near the edge of the white space. The storyboard shows both of the photographs at a perspective angle facing each other.

n. Click the **Insert tab**, and click **Picture**. Click **p01_ws02_Conference_Pueblo**, and then click **Insert**. Resize the photograph so it is the same size as the other. Click **Reflected Perspective Right** in the Pictures Styles group, and then click **Picture Effects**. Point to **3-D Rotation**, and then click **3-D Rotation Options**. Type 15 for the X rotation, 7 for the Y rotation, and 0 for the Z rotation. Click **Close**. Move and resize the photographs as necessary to balance them on the slide.

o. Click **Slide 5**, click the Home tab, click **Layout** in the Slides group, and then click **Blank**. Click the **Design tab**, click **Hide Background Graphics** in the Background group, click **Background Styles**, and then select **Format Background**. Click **Picture or texture fill**, click **File**, click **p01_ws02_Conference_Background**, and then click **Insert**. Click **Close**. The storyboard for this slide shows the table is inserted on the screen of the background, as if it were being displayed during a presentation in the conference room.

p. Click the **Hotel/Conference Room Rates** text box, and press Delete. Click the **Insert tab**, click **Table**, and then select **3 columns** and **7 rows**. Drag the **sizing handles** on the table to cover the white space on the screen in the photograph. Click the **Table Tools Layout tab**, select the **first row** of the table, and then click **Merge Cells**. Type Hotel/Conference Room Rates. Select the **text**, click **Center** in the Alignment group, click the **Home tab**, and then increase the font size to **28**.

q. Complete the table as follows:

Rooms Booked	Conference Room	Rate
10 – 30	Eldorado	$2,500
	Pueblo	$1,500
31 – 60	Eldorado	$2,000
61 – 90	Eldorado	$1,500
91+	Eldorado	Free

r. Click the **Table Tools Layout tab**, select the **Conference Room** text, and then type **2.1** in the Table Column Width box in the Cell Size group. Select **all of the cells** in the table, click **Center Vertically** in the Alignment group, and then click **Center** in the Alignment group. Select the **cell** containing 10–30 and the **cell below it**, and then click **Merge Cells** in the Merge group.

s. Click the **Table Tools Design tab**, and then click **Banded Rows** to deselect it. Select **all of the rows** containing the information in the table (not the table title), click the **Borders arrow** in the Table Styles group, and then click **All Borders**.

t. Click **Slide 6**, and then click **Insert Chart** in the content placeholder. Click **Exploded pie in 3-D**, and then click **OK**. Complete the worksheet as follows:

	Percentage
Keynote Speaker	10
Banquet, Meals, Snacks	30
Conference Room	10
Entertainment	10
Registration	3
Technology	5
Other	32

u. Close the Chart worksheet window. Click **More** in the Chart Layouts group, and then click **Layout 6**. Click **More** in the Chart Styles group, and then click **Style 10**. Click the **Chart Tools Layout tab**, click **Chart Title** in the Labels group, and then click **None**. If necessary, drag the **chart sizing handles** to increase the size of the chart until "Other" appears on the legend.

v. Click **Slide 7**, click **Insert**, and then click **Shapes**. Click the **5-Point Star** in the Stars and Banners group, and then click on the **left side** of the content placeholder to create a star. Click the **Drawing Tools Format tab**, and then type **0.7** in the Shape Height box and the Shape Width box. Click the **Shape Fill arrow**, and then click **Orange** in the Standard Colors group. Right-click the **star shape**, click **Copy**, right-click to the left side of the content placeholder, and then click **Paste** four times (for a total of five stars). Drag **each star** away from the other stars so they do not overlap but are run vertically on the slide. Press and hold ⟨Shift⟩ and click **each star**. Click the **Drawing Tools Format tab**, click the **Align** button, and then click **Align Left**. Click the **Align** button again, and then click **Distribute Vertically**. Click the **Group** button, click **Group**, and then drag the group to align it beside the content placeholder. The storyboard specifies the five stars being on the left side of the white space on the slide.

w. Click **Insert SmartArt Graphic** in the content placeholder, click **Cycle** in the categories list, select **Text Cycle**, and then click **OK**. Click **Text Pane** in the Create Graphic group, and then type the following:

- Planning
- Facilities
- Catering
- Management
- Technology

x. Close the Text pane. Click **More** in the SmartArt Styles group, and then click **Polished** from the 3-D group. Drag the **sizing handles** to increase the size of the SmartArt graphic so it fits the space better.

y. Click the **Review tab**, and then click **Spelling** in the Proofing group. Correct any misspelled words, and then proofread the slide show.

z. Click the **Slide Show tab**, and then click **From Beginning**. Review the slides. Save the presentation, and then exit PowerPoint.

Problem Solve 1

Student Data Files Needed

p01_ps1_Destination_Storyboard
p01_ps1_Destination_Template
p01_ps1_Destination_Album
p01_ps1_Destination_Bouquet

You will save your files as:

Lastname_Firstname_p01_ps1_Destination

Planning Your Destination Wedding Seminar

Sales & Marketing

Painted Paradise Golf Resort and Spa is the perfect place for a destination wedding. Corporate Event Planner, Patti Rochelle, has several wedding planners on her staff. She would like to hold quarterly seminars to help brides-to-be plan for their special day. Seminars will be held on a Saturday morning and will feature a continental breakfast. Each seminar will begin with a presentation outlining the benefits of holding a wedding at Painted Paradise Resort. A storyboard for the presentation has already been created. You will use a template, add text, a suggested budget and time line, and add other finishing touches to the presentation. The audience also will include prospective grooms as well as parents of the couples. After the presentation, everyone attending will tour the resort to look at the various venues available for both the ceremony and the reception.

a. Start **Word**. Open the Word document storyboard file **p01_ps1_Destination_Storyboard**, and review the planning for the presentation. Continue to scroll down the storyboard and note that you will be using a chart to give the attendees an idea of how the average wedding budget might be allocated. You also will include a suggested time line using a SmartArt graphic. Toward the end of the presentation, you will reuse pictures from an album. The final slide provides contact information so that brides can make appointments to meet with a wedding consultant and discuss individual needs. Close Word.

b. Start **PowerPoint**. Click the **File tab**, and then click **New**. Click **New from existing**, navigate to where your student data files are located, and then click **p01_ps1_Destination_Template**. Click **Create New**. Review the Notes pane on the title slide of the template, then after you have read the text in the Notes pane, select and delete the text. Reduce the size of the Notes pane. Save the presentation as Lastname_Firstname_p01_ps1_Destination.

c. Click the **title placeholder** on Slide 1, and then type Planning Your Destination Wedding. Type Painted Paradise Golf Resort and Spa in the subtitle placeholder, select the text, and then change the font size to **22.**

d. Click the **Outline tab**, and create the following slides and content:

Slide 2 Layout: Title and Content	**Title:** What We Provide… **Body:** Personal wedding consultant Picturesque wedding location Marriage officiant (if requested) Variety of reception themes Three- or four-tiered wedding cake
Slide 3 Layout: Title and Content	**Title:** Special Wedding Themes **Body:** Beautiful Beginnings Wedding Classic White Wedding Chic and Natural Wedding Desert Rose Wedding Mexican Garden Wedding
Slide 4 Layout: Title and Content	**Title:** Intimate or Traditional?
Slide 5 Layout: Title and Content	**Title:** Sample Budget $20,000
Slide 6 Layout: Title Only	**Title:** Suggested Timeline
Slide 7 Layout: Title and Content	**Title:** Contacts **Body:** Patti Rochelle Corporate Event Planner prochelle@paintedparadiseresort.com Lesa Martin Certified Wedding Planner lmartin@paintedparadiseresort.com Phone: 505-555-1489 **(Indent titles and e-mail addresses)**

e. Click the **Slides tab**, and then click **Slide 2**. Click the **Insert tab**, click **Header & Footer** in the Text group, and then select the **Footer** check box. Type Weddings in Paradise. In the Header & Footer dialog box, click **Don't show on title slide**, and then click **Apply to All**.

f. Click **Slide 3**, click the **Insert tab**, and then click **Picture** in the Images group. Navigate to the location of your student data files. Click **p01_ps1_Destination_Bouquet,** and then click **Insert**. Click the **Picture Tools Format tab**, click the Size group **Dialog Box Launcher**, click **Lock aspect ratio** to select it if necessary, and then decrease the height to **75%**. Click **Close**. Click **Soft Edge Rectangle** in the Pictures Styles group. Drag the picture to the bottom right corner of the slide. Click the **Design tab**, and then click **Hide Background Graphics** to remove the original picture from the slide.

g. Click **Slide 4**, and then click **Insert Table** in the content placeholder. Change the number of columns to **3** and the number of rows to **4**, and then click **OK**. Type the following in the table:

Wedding Type	Guests	Room
Small	Up to 50	Pueblo Room
Medium	50 to 250	Eldorado Room
Large	250 to 500	Musica Room

h. Make the following changes to the table on Slide 4:

Click the **Table Tools Design tab**, and then click the **Medium Style 2 – Accent 4** Table Style.

Click **Banded Rows** in the Table Style Options group to remove the banded row formatting. Click the **Table Tools Layout tab**, and then change the Table Size Height to **4"**.

Select all of the cells in the table, and then click **Center** in the Alignment group. With the text selected, click **Center Vertically** in the Alignment group. Click the **Home tab**, and increase the font size to **24**.

Drag the table down so the top edge is in line with the bottom of the picture in the right corner.

i. Click **Slide 5**, and then click **Insert Chart** in the content placeholder. Click **Pie in 3-D**, and then click **OK**. Type the following information into the chart worksheet:

	Amount
Reception	13,500
Wedding Gown	2,500
Hair & Makeup	400
Groom's Attire	300
Photography	2,000
Miscellaneous	1,300

j. **Close** the chart worksheet. Make the following changes to the chart:

Click the **Chart Tools Design tab**, click **More** in the Chart Styles group, and then click **Style 6**. Click **Layout 6** in the Chart Layouts group.

Click the **Chart Tools Layout tab**, click **Chart Title** in the Labels group, and then click **None**.

k. Click **Slide 6**, and then click the **Insert tab**. Click **SmartArt** in the Illustrations group, click the **Process** category, click **Staggered Process**, and then click **OK**. Click the **SmartArt Tools Design tab**, click **Text Pane** in the Create Graphic group, and then type the following information:

| 12 months |
| Set date, reserve venue, begin guest list **(indent this line)** |
| 9 months |
| Buy dress, alert guests, select officiant **(indent this line)** |
| 6 months |
| Select invitations, photographer, flowers **(indent this line)** |
| 3 months |
| Finalize guests, mail invitations, write vows **(indent this line)** |

l. Close the Text pane. Click **Change Colors** on the SmartArt Tools Design tab, and then click **Transparent Gradient Range – Accent 4**. Click **More** in the SmartArt Styles Group, and then click **Polished** in the 3-D group. Click the **SmartArt Tools Format tab**, and then click **Size**. Change the width of the SmartArt to **8.5"**.

m. Click **Slide 6**, click the **Home tab**, and then click the **New Slide arrow**. Click **Reuse Slides**, click **Browse**, and then click **Browse File**. Select **p01_ws02_Destination_Album**, and then click **Open**. In the Reuse Slides pane, click **Slides 2** to **7** in succession. Select the slides just added on the Slides tab, click the **Design tab**, and then click **Hide Background Graphics** to remove the image in the upper right corner. Close the Reuse Slides pane.

n. Click the **Review tab**, and then click **Spelling** in the Proofing group. Correct any misspelled words (click **Ignore** for "officiant"), and then proofread the slide show.

o. Click the **Slide Show tab**, and then click **From Beginning**. Review the slides. Save the presentation and close PowerPoint. Submit your files as directed by your instructor.

 Additional Workshop Cases are available on the companion website and in the instructor resources.

MODULE CAPSTONE

Student data files needed:

p01_mp_Deals_Storyboard	p01_mp_Deals_Dancing
p01_mp_Deals_Start	p01_mp_Deals_Massage
p01_mp_Deals_Theme	p01_mp_Deals_Shoppers
p01_mp_Deals	p01_mp_Deals_Manicure
p01_mp_Deals_Restaurant	p01_mp_Deals_Reservations
p01_mp_Deals_Hands	p01_mp_Deals_Massage_WMF
p01_mp_Deals_Dining	p01_mp_Deals_Golfer_WMF

You will save your files as:

Lastname_Firstname_p01_mp_Deals

Lastname_Firstname_p01_mp_Deals_PDF

Painted Paradise Golf Resort and Spa Special Deals

Sales & Marketing

The Painted Paradise Golf Resort and Spa along with the Red Bluff Golf Club offer special deals to families and couples. The special deals include various services such as golf, spa treatments, lodging, and meals. They are designed to persuade people to come to the resort and enjoy a perfect getaway. The deals are described in PowerPoint presentations that are sent via e-mail as PDF files to people on the distribution list.

You will create a graphic-rich presentation to feature the Last Minute Deal, the Two Perfect Days Deal, and the Girl's Camp (for Grownups). You will use a theme, modify the colors and font of the theme, and reuse slides. WordArt will appear on a slide to provide interest. You will also develop a table to detail the options for the Girl's Camp. You will use symbols in the presentation and set up the footer. Something you will notice in this project is that there is more text than you might normally use in a slide show. This is because you will not be "delivering" this presentation, but rather depending on your audience members to read it on their computers. You will carefully check the spelling and proofread the document before saving the file as a PowerPoint PDF file.

a. Start **Word** and open **p01_mp_Deals_Storyboard**, and then review the plans for this presentation. Notice the placement of the quotation on the title slide and the drawing of the Wingdings symbol used in front of the source for the quotation. The data for the bar chart is shown at the bottom of page 1. You will move the text on many of the slides that were reused, so study the layouts on those slides. This presentation is meant to persuade the audience to take advantage of the specials. The final slide provides contact information and an engaging photograph of a reservations representative. Close the Word document.

b. Start **PowerPoint**, and open **p01_mp_Deals_Start**. Type your name in the slide title placeholder, and the course name, the course number, and today's date in the content area of the first slide. **Browse for Themes**, navigate to your student data files, and then apply the **p01_mp_Deals_Theme** theme. Click the Design tab, and change the theme fonts to **Horizon**. Save the file as **Lastname_Firstname_p01_mp_Deals**.

c. Insert a title slide layout, and type Special Deals for You from the Painted Paradise Golf Resort and Spa as the presentation title. Change the font size to **44**. Add A passion for helping people relax as the subtitle. Modify the subtitle font to italic and align it to the right.

d. On Slide 2, add the **Rectangle** shape, **2"** in height and **5"** in width, to the top-right area of the slide. Make the following changes to the shape:

- Type The time to relax is when you don't have time for it in the shape. Press ⌈Enter⌉, and type Sidney J. Harris.
- Select the **quotation text**, apply the WordArt style **Fill - White, Outline - Accent 1**, and then increase the size of the font to **32**.
- Insert the Wingdings symbol with a character code of **122** in front of the name Sidney. Align the author's name to the right.
- Add an **Offset Diagonal Bottom Left** shadow to the shape.

e. Create a new theme colors palette by changing the theme color Text/Background - Light 2 setting to **Blue, Text 2, Darker 50%**. Save the Theme Colors as Lastname Firstname Special Deals Colors.

f. Reuse all slides from the **p01_mp_Deals** file, adding them to the current presentation. Click the **Insert tab**, apply footers to all of the slides except the title slide. Click **Date and time**, click **Fixed**, and replace the default date with Offers good through August 30. Click Footer, and then type Reserve now at www.paintedparadiseresort.com.

g. Click the Outline tab and make the following modifications:

- Delete the **Resort Special Deals** slide (Slide 3).
- Drag **Slide 6** to position **4**.
- Drag **Slide 7** to position **6**.
- Add Poppable Pastries and coffee in-room breakfast at the bottom of the feature list on Slide 8. Drag the **Poppable Pastries** line into position above the Lunch line. Select the **Wine and cheese** line, and drag it below the Lunch line.

h. Click the Slides tab, add a new **Title and Content** slide after Slide 3. Type Example of Savings in the title placeholder. Insert a **Stacked Column in 3-D** chart, and then complete the worksheet as follows:

	Normal Pricing	Last Minute Deal 1	Last Minute Deal 2
Room	575	500	500
Spa Treatment	230	200	
Golf	250		215
Meals	120	104	104

i. Continuing your work on the chart, click the Chart Tools Design tab, and switch the rows and columns in the chart by clicking Select Data and making the change in the Select Data Source dialog box. Move the legend to the top of the chart. Edit the data by adding the following column to the end of the worksheet:

Last Minute Deal 3
500
200
215
104

j. Change the layout of Slide 3 to Two Content. Add a clip art photograph, including the Office.com content, using the search word **massage**. For your reference, the image is included in the student data files with a file name of p01_mp_Deals_Massage_WMF. Modify the photograph as follows:

- Resize the photograph to a height of **2.9"**.
- Drag it into position at the bottom-right side of the white space of the slide.
- Apply the **Soft Edge Rectangle** Picture Style.

Use the search word **golfer**, and then insert a photograph of a woman with a golf club. For your reference, the image is included in the student data files with a file name of p01_mp_Deals_Golfer_WMF. Modify the photograph as follows:

- Resize the photograph to a height of **2.9"**.
- Drag the **photograph** above the massage photograph.
- Apply the **Soft Edge Rectangle** Picture Style.
- Select the **body text placeholder**, and then align the text to the middle of the slide. If the right column content text placeholder is visible, delete it.

k. Insert the photograph **p01_mp_Deals_Restaurant** on Slide 5, and then modify the photograph as follows:

- Resize the photograph to a height of **3.3"**.
- Drag the **photograph** to the bottom-right corner of the slide, just inside of the background colored bar.
- Click the **Soft Edge Rectangle** Picture Style.

l. Insert the photograph **p01_mp_Deals_Hands** on Slide 6, and then modify the photograph as follows:

- Alter the color to **Gold, Accent color 4 Light**.
- Resize the photograph to a height of **5.9"**.
- Drag the **photograph** to the left side of the slide.
- Apply the **Soft Edge Oval** Picture Style.
- Drag the **left sizing handle** of the body text placeholder to place the text to the right of the photograph.

m. Insert and modify the following photographs on Slide 7:

- Insert **p01_mp_Deals_Dining**, resize the photograph to a height of **2.5"**, and then move the photograph to the lower-left side of the white space.
- Insert **p01_mp_Deals_Dancing**, resize it to a height of **2.5"**, and then modify the Color Tone to **Temperature: 4700 K**. Move the photograph next to the dining photograph.
- Insert the **p01_mp_Deals_Massage** photograph, resize it to a height of **2.5"**, and then move the photograph to the right of the couple dancing photograph.
- Apply the **Soft Edge Rectangle** Picture Style to the couple dining photograph. Use the Format Painter to apply the style to the other two photographs, and then select **all three photographs** and distribute them horizontally.

n. Insert the photograph **p01_mp_Deals_Shoppers** on Slide 8, and then modify it as follows:

- Resize the photograph to a height of **3.5"**.
- Remove the background of the photograph using Remove Background in the Adjust group of the Picture Tools Format tab, and then drag the **sizing handles** so the photograph will include all of the shopping bags and the heads of the women. If necessary use the **Mark Areas to Keep** tool to select additional areas to include in the photograph.
- Align the photograph to the **Center** and then to the **Bottom**.
- Change the Color Saturation to **200%**.

o. On Slide 9, insert the **Registered Sign** normal text symbol with a character code of **00AE** after the word "Poppable," and then modify the symbol's font effect to **Superscript**. Change the text **Poppable**© **Pastries** to the font color **Orange, Accent 1, Darker 25%** and the style to **Italic**.

p. Continuing with Slide 9, insert the photograph **p01_mp_Deals_Manicure**, and then modify as follows:

   • Resize the photograph to a height of **2.3"**.

   • Apply the **Soft Edge Rectangle** Picture Style.

   • Drag the **photograph** to the bottom-right side of the white space on the slide.

q. Add a new slide after Slide 9. Type The Girl's Camp Deal in the title placeholder. Add a table to the slide with **2 columns** and **6 rows**. Type the following information in the table:

Number of Guests	Cost per Guest
2	$500
3	$450
4	$400
5	$350
6	$300

Modify the table as follows:

   • Resize the table to a height of **4.5"** and a width of **4.5"**.

   • **Center** and then **Center Vertically** in the Alignment group.

   • Apply the **Medium Style 2 - Accent 3** style to the table.

   • **Align Center** using the Arrange group on the Layout tab.

r. Add a new Title and Content slide. Click the Outline tab, type Make Your Reservations Today! in the title placeholder. Press Ctrl+Enter, and type the following three lines of text:

   • Phone: 505-555-1876

   • Online: www.paintedparadiseresort.com/specials

   • E-mail: reservations@paintedparadiseresort.com

s. Continuing with Slide 11, insert the photograph **p01_mp_Deals_Reservations**. Resize the photograph to a height of **3.8"**, drag it to the bottom-right side of the white space on the slide, and then change the picture style to **Soft Edge Rectangle**.

t. Review the slides, carefully proofreading each item and making necessary corrections. Check the spelling. Save the presentation. Then, save the file in PDF format, using the Minimum size option, as Lastname_Firstname_p01_mp_Deals_PDF. Review the presentation in the Adobe Reader window, and then close the window. Close the presentation.

Student data files needed:

p01_ps1_Restaurant_Storyboard   p01_ps1_Restaurant_Coffee

p01_ps1_Restaurant_Template   p01_ps1_Restaurant_Celebration

p01_ps1_Restaurant_Fork   p01_ps1_Restaurant_Tea

p01_ps1_Restaurant_Indigo1   p01_ps1_Restaurant_Sanchez

p01_ps1_Restaurant_Indigo2   p01_ps1_Restaurant_Burger_WMF

p01_ps1_Restaurant_Salad

You will save your files as:

Lastname_Firstname_p01_ps1_Restaurant

Lastname_Firstname_p01_ps1_Restaurant_Show

myitlab
grader
Homework 1

Restaurant Choices at the Painted Paradise Golf Resort and Spa

Sales & Marketing

There are many choices the guests can make for meals and snacks on the grounds of the Painted Paradise Golf Resort and Spa. You will create a presentation that describes the options. The presentation will be shown on computer screens throughout the resort, in places such as elevators and waiting areas. The presentation will also be a part of the in-room advertising done through the TV. You can expect the audience to watch the presentation for just a short amount of time, so the text content will be minimal. You will use a template that has the timing already set up for advancing the slides every five seconds.

a. Start **Word** and open **p01_ps1_Restaurant_Storyboard**, and then review the plans for the presentation. Note that the theme calls for a black background and white font. Photographs of food will draw the audience into the presentation and suggest that there are many good opportunities for meals at the resort. The presentation will also provide information to the audience about when the restaurants are open. Notice that the footer changes on the restaurant slides. Close the Word document. Start **PowerPoint**, and open **p01_ps1_Restaurant_Template**. Review the Notes pane on the title slide of the template, and then select and delete this **text** when you have read it. Reduce the size of the Notes pane. Save the presentation as Lastname_Firstname_p01_ps1_Restaurant.

b. On Slide 1, add the photograph **p01_ps1_Restaurant_Fork** as the slide background.

c. Continuing with Slide 1, enter the text Painted Paradise Golf Resort and Spa Restaurants in the title placeholder. Format the shape with the fill color of **Black, Background 1**. Change the size of the title placeholder to a height of **3.2"** and a width of **4.5"**. Align the title placeholder in the middle and to the right.

d. Add a new slide with a layout of **Title and Content**. Type Indigo 5 in the title placeholder. Insert the photograph **p01_ps1_Restaurant_Indigo1** in the content placeholder. Resize the photograph to a height of **6.2"**, and then reposition it, if necessary, to create balance with the title.

e. Add a new slide with a layout of **Text Right - Content Left**. Type Indigo 5 in the right text placeholder, press [Enter], and then type the following eight lines of text:

Fine dining

Southwestern specialties

Fresh seafood

Artisan salads

Handmade breads

French pastries

Organic fruits and vegetables

Local wines

f. Continuing with Slide 3, change the font size of the text **Indigo 5** in the placeholder on the right to **60**. Apply a **Bold** style. Apply customized bullets to the list you just typed, using the Wingdings font character code **157**. Insert the photograph **p01_ps1_Restaurant_Indigo2** in the left placeholder. Change the height of the graphic to **6.5"**. Reposition the graphic so that the top-left corner aligns with the **4"** mark to the left of 0 on the horizontal ruler and the **3.5"** mark above 0 on the vertical ruler. Add the footer Open from 11 AM to 10 PM only on this slide.

g. Add a new **Title and Content** slide after Slide 3. Enter the text Red Bluff Bistro in the title placeholder. Search for a Clip Art photograph using the keyword burger from Office.com. For your reference, the image is included with the student data files with the file name p01_ps1_Restaurant_Burger_WMF. Change the height of the graphic to **6.3"**, and then move it into a balanced position.

h. Add a new slide with the **Text Left - Content Right** layout after Slide 4. Type Red Bluff Bistro in the left text placeholder. Change the font to bold. Press ⎡Enter⎤ and type the following four lines of text (without bold) below the words Red Bluff Bistro:

Specialty burgers and sandwiches

Organic salads

Microbrewery beers

Daily specials

i. Continuing with Slide 5, apply customized bullets to the list you just typed, using the Wingdings font character code **156**. Insert the photograph **p01_ps1_Restaurant_Salad** into the right placeholder. Change the height of the graphic to **5.75"**. Reposition the graphic so that the top-left corner aligns with 0 on the horizontal ruler and 3" mark above 0 on the vertical ruler. Add the footer Open from 7 AM to 7 PM only on this slide.

j. Add a new **Title and Content** layout slide. Enter Terra Cotta Brew in the title placeholder. Insert the photograph **p01_ps1_Restaurant_Coffee** into the content placeholder. Change the height of the graphic to **3.6"**. Reposition the graphic so that the top-left corner aligns with the **3"** mark to the left of 0 on the horizontal ruler and the **1.5"** mark above 0 on the vertical rule. Insert a text box at **0.25"** mark to the left of 0 on the horizontal ruler and the **1"** mark above 0 on the vertical ruler and type the following three lines of text:

Featuring Poppable Pastries

House-roasted coffees

Gourmet ice cream

k. Modify the text and photograph as follows:

- Apply customized bullets to the text you just typed, using the Wingdings font character code **155**.
- Increase the size of the font to **28**. If necessary, drag the **text** onto the slide and resize the text box so each feature is listed on one line.
- Select the text and the photograph. On the Drawing Tools Format tab, first **Align to Slide**, and then align the elements to the middle.
- Insert the **Registered Sign** normal text character code **00AE** after the word **Poppable**. Change the character to superscript.
- Add the footer Open 24 hours a day only on this slide.

l. Add a new **Title and Content** layout slide. Enter Silver Moon Lounge in the title placeholder. Insert the photograph **p01_ps1_Restaurant_Celebration** into the content placeholder, resize the photograph to a height of **4"**, and then drag the **photograph** toward the top of the slide, leaving room for a text box underneath it. Insert a **text box** below the photograph, and then add this text to the slide on a single line: Microbrewery beers Local wines Cocktails Light snacks.

m. Continuing with Slide 7, immediately in front of Microbrewery insert the Wingdings symbol character code **154** and press [Spacebar]. Copy and paste the symbol and the space immediately to the left of **Local, Cocktails, and Light** leaving a space on both sides of the symbol. Click in front of the symbol before the word **Cocktails**, and press [Enter] (press [Backspace] if you see a duplicated symbol). Change the font size of the text in the text box to **32**. Change the width of the text box to **7.2"** in width. Center the text for the entire text box.

n. Select the **text box** and the **photograph**. Distribute the text box and the graphic vertically. Align them again using **Align Center**, and then move them to the right to improve the balance. Add the footer Open from 11 AM to 2 AM only on this slide.

o. Add a new **Title and Content** slide. Type Turquoise Oasis Spa in the title placeholder. Insert the photograph **p01_ps1_Restaurant_Tea** into the content placeholder, and then resize the photograph to **4.2"** in height. Drag the photograph to the right side of the slide. Insert a text box between the title and the photograph, and then type the following three lines of text:

Specialty tea blends

Organic fruits

Finger sandwiches

- Increase the font size to **28**.
- Apply customized bullets to the text you just typed, using the Wingdings font character code **155**.
- Resize the text box to a width of **4"**. Align the **text box** and **photograph** to the middle of the slide.
- Add the footer Open from 8 AM to 7 PM only on this slide.

p. Add a new **Two Content** layout slide after Slide 8. Type Chef Robin Sanchez Welcomes You in the title placeholder. Insert the photograph **p01_ps1_Restaurant_Sanchez** in the left content placeholder. Change the height of the graphic to **5"** and reposition it on the left side of the slide. Add a table to the right content placeholder, setting the number of columns to **2** and the number of rows to **6.** Type the following information in the table:

Restaurant	Hours of Operation
Indigo 5	11 AM to 10 PM
Red Bluff Bistro	7 AM to 7 PM
Terra Cotta Brew	24 hours a day
Silver Moon Lounge	11 AM to 2 AM
Turquoise Oasis Spa	8 AM to 7 PM

Modify the table as follows:

- Increase the width of the table size to **4.5"**.
- Align the table to the middle of the slide.
- Apply the **Medium Style 2** style to the table.

q. On Slide 3, select the word **Indigo**, double-click **Format Painter**, and then apply the format to the titles on Slides 2, 4, 6, 7, and 8. (Hint: Do not forget to single-click Format Painter when done.) On Slide 7, reduce the font size of the text **Silver Moon Lounge** to **54**. On Slide 8, reduce the font size of the text **Turquoise Oasis Spa** to **54**.

r. Review the presentation, checking the spelling. View the slide show. The slides change automatically, so you do not have to click between slides. Save the presentation.

s. Save the presentation as a PowerPoint Show, with a file name of Lastname_Firstname_ p01_ps1_Restaurant_Show. Close the presentation.

Student data files needed:

p01_ps2_Menu_Storyboard
p01_ps2_Menu_Start
p01_ps2_Menu_Items
p01_ps2_Menu_Apples

p01_ps2_Menu_Salsa
p01_ps2_Menu_Hash
p01_ps2_Menu_Muffins
p01_ps2_Menu_Chef_WMF

You will save your file as:

Lastname_Firstname_p01_ps2_Menu_Training

Wait Staff Training

Human Resources

Chef Robin Sanchez worked up some great new recipes for the Indigo 5 restaurant at the Painted Paradise Resort and Spa. The servers need training so they can accurately describe the new dishes to the guests. You have been asked to create a PowerPoint presentation which reviews some important practices for the wait staff and introduces them to the new menu items.

The chef prepared some slides for you to use in your presentation, but she requested that you create additional slides with guest service information. The chef requested that handouts also be made available so the staff can have the information for future reference.

a. Start **Word** and open **p01_ps2_Menu_Storyboard**, and then review the plans for this presentation. The audience, the servers for the restaurant, need to be able to recognize the new menu items as they come out of the kitchen, so they are pictured on the slides along with information about the ingredients. Notice the table shows the name of the item, the cost, and additional wine or food that complements the choices. The Reasons People Don't Return slide is really meant to drive home the point that poor service is the main reason that guests do not return to the restaurant. Close the Word document.

b. Start **PowerPoint**, and open **p01_ps2_Menu_Start**. Type your name, course name, course number, and today's date in the placeholders. Apply the **Austin** theme, and then make the following changes to the theme colors:

- Text/Background - Light 2 to **Orange, Accent 3, Darker 50%**
- Accent 2 color to **Orange, Accent 3, Lighter 40%**
- Name the New Theme Colors Lastname Firstname Wait Staff Training.
  Save the presentation as Lastname_Firstname_p01_ps2_Menu_Training.

c. Insert a title slide layout, and then enter the title New Menus and More with a subtitle of Winter Season Training. Center both the **title** and the **subtitle**.

d. Create the following slides:

Layout	Title	Body content	
Two Content	5-Star Service	Smile Greet guests quickly Listen carefully Make eye contact Be courteous	Be knowledgeable Up-sell wine, appetizers, dessert Be a problem solver Show gratitude
Title and Content	The Key to Success		
Title and Content	Reasons People Don't Return		
Title and Content	Our New Items		

e. After Slide 6, reuse Slides 2–5 from **p01_ps2_Menu_Items**.

f. Click the **Outline tab**, and increase the list level of the ingredients listed on Slide 7 (Apple and Cheese Baguettes). Change the bullets for the ingredients to **Filled Round Bullets**. Repeat this step with the ingredient lists for Slides 8–9. Repeat this step on Slide 10 for the three restaurants where Poppable Pastries are available.

g. On Slide 7, insert the **p01_ps2_Menu_Apples** picture, and resize the picture to **3"** in height. Insert the following pictures on the slides, and resize as shown. Select and align the picture and the text block to the middle on each slide.

Slide Number	Photograph file	Height
Slide 8	p01_ps2_Menu_Salsa	3.1"
Slide 9	p01_ps2_Menu_Hash	2.9"
Slide 10	p01_ps2_Menu_Muffins	3"

h. Move **Slides 3–5** to the end of the slide show. Move **Slide 3** (Our New Items) to just before Slide 8.

i. Add a new slide, with the **Title and Content** layout, after Slide 2. Enter James Beard said… in the title placeholder. Enter Food is our common ground, a universal experience. in the body placeholder. Include the punctuation. Remove the bullet, and then apply italics to the font. Apply the **Fill - Brown, Text 2, Outline - Background 2** WordArt style to the quotation, and then increase the font size of the quotation to **36**.

j. On Slide 3, search for a clip art illustration (include Office.com content) of a **chef**. For your reference, the image is included with the student data files, with the file name of p01_ps2_Menu_Chef_WMF. Make the following adjustments to the clip art:
- Recolor the illustration to **Brown, Accent color 5 Light**.
- Resize the illustration to **4.5"** in height.
- Resize the body placeholder on the left, so the text fits beside the illustration.
- Center the **body text** in the placeholder. Align the **text placeholder** and the **graphic** in the middle.

k. On Slide 7, insert the registration symbol (character code **00AE** in the normal text font) immediately after the word **Poppable** (no space between the word and the symbol). Alter the font of the symbol to **superscript**.

Module Capstone

l. Add a table with **3** columns and **5** rows to Slide 8. Type the following information in the table:

Item	Price	Up-sell Item
Apple and Cheese Baguettes	8.95	Chardonnay wine
Roasted Onion Salsa and Chips	6.95	Sangria, suggest Southwestern Crab for entrée
Sweet Potato Hash with Duck Eggs	12.95	Organic Fruit Cup
Poppable Pastries	$1 or 3 for $2.50	Freshly brewed coffee

m. Continuing with the table on Slide 8, make the following changes to the table:
   - Decrease the size of the Price column to a width of **1.3"**.
   - Resize the table to **8.3"** in width. Align the **table** in the center of the slide.
   - Change the Table Style to **Medium Style 1 - Accent 5**.

n. On Slide 9, insert a **5-Point Star**, move the shape next to the title on the right, and then make the following changes to the shape:
   - Resize to **1.75"** in height and **2.08"** in width.
   - Change the Shape Style to **Intense Effect - Green, Accent 1**.
   - Enter text by typing 5, and increase the font size to **48**.
   - Apply the WordArt Style **Fill - Light Orange, Accent 2, Warm Matte Bevel** to the number.
   - Select both body text placeholders, and then move the placeholders down on the slide to balance the placement of the star and the text placeholders.

o. On Slide 10, add the SmartArt graphic **Block Cycle** to the body content. Enter the following text:

   5-Star Service

   Happy Guests

   Bigger Tips

   Alter the SmartArt graphic as follows:
   - Remove the extra text shapes.
   - Change the colors to **Colorful Range - Accent Colors 3 to 4**.
   - Change the SmartArt Style to **Polished**.

p. Add a **Pie** chart to Slide 11, and then type the following information into the chart worksheet:

	%
Bad Service	30
Poor Food	25
Location	15
Price	5
Atmosphere	5
Not Sure	20

Make the following changes to the chart:

- Change the Chart Layout to **Layout 2**.
- Change the Chart Style to **Style 26**. Set the Chart Title to **None**.
- Move the **Legend** to the left side of the chart.
- Add a text box to the bottom-left side of the chart (0.4" in height and 2.5" in width), and then type in the text Source: Restaurant Survey 2011. Change the font size to **11**.

q. Add the Left Arrow shape to Slide 11, and then make the following changes to the arrow shape:

- Rotate the **arrow** and point it toward the 30% slice of the pie chart.
- Change the Shape Fill to **Orange, Accent 3, Darker 50%**.
- Add the text This is You! Change the font to **bold** and **italic**. Change the font size to **16**. Modify the size of the arrow to a height of **0.9"** and a width of **1.7"**.

r. Move Slide 11 into position **9**.

s. Review the spelling of the presentation. Review each slide. Save the presentation. Print only **Slide 8** (Our New Items) as a **Full Page Slide**. Close the presentation, and then exit PowerPoint.

Problem Solve 3

Student data files needed:

p01_ps3_Organic_Storyboard   p01_ps3_Organic_Sanchez
p01_ps3_Organic_Start   p01_ps3_Organic_Gardener
p01_ps3_Organic_Theme   p01_ps3_Organic_Symbol
p01_ps3_Organic

You will save your file as:

Lastname_Firstname_p01_ps3_Organic_Food

Homework 3

Sales & Marketing

Organic Food Restaurant Presentation

Chef Robin Sanchez enjoys developing recipes using organic foods. She knows that they are healthy, and she wants to spread the word while promoting Indigo 5 in the community. She will be speaking at the Garden Festival in a few weeks and asked for your assistance in producing a slide show. The chef has an organic kitchen garden on the grounds of the Painted Paradise Resort and Spa where she grows many of the herbs and vegetables she uses in her signature dishes at Indigo 5. She buys other organic foods from local sources, including chicken, farm-raised trout, and fruit. The chef has included a simple recipe using organic foods in the presentation and would like to have that single slide printed as a handout for the audience.

a. Start **Word** and open **p01_ps3_Organic_Storyboard**, and then review the plans for this presentation. In this storyboard, the placement of the graphic elements should be noted. Two slides on page 2 show clip art that is placed partially off the slide. Text box shapes are used in a number of slides to contain additional information. Only one slide contains a footer, but it is very important because it is on the handout slide and provides a subtle advertisement for Indigo 5. Close the Word document.

b. Start **PowerPoint**, open **p01_ps3_Organic_Start**, and then type your name, course name, course number, and today's date. Browse for and apply the **p01_ps3_Organic_Theme** theme, and then save the presentation as Lastname_Firstname_p01_ps3_Organic_Food.

c. Reuse all of the slides from the **p01_ps3_Organic** file.

d. Insert a new Title and Content slide after Slide 2. In the body placeholder, type The garden suggests there might be a place where we can meet nature halfway. Press Enter, and then type Michael Pollan. Remove the bullets from the text. For the quotation text only make the following changes.

- Set the font size to **54**.
- Apply the WordArt Style of **Fill – Olive Green, Accent 3, Outline - Text 2**.
- Fill the text with **Tan, Background 2, Darker 90%**.
- Center the **quotation text**.

e. Align the text **Michael Pollan** to the right. Insert the symbol with the character code of **123** from the Wingdings font immediately in front of the text **Michael Pollan**—no space between text and symbol. Align all of the text on the slide to the middle. Delete the **title** placeholder. Adjust the height size of the body placeholder to **5.9"**, and align it in the **middle** of the slide.

f. On Slide 4, insert the photographs **p01_ps3_Organic_Sanchez** and **p01_ps3_Organic_Gardener**. Resize the photograph heights to **3.2"**, and then adjust their placement to achieve balance on the slide. Apply the **Drop Shadow Rectangle** Picture Style to both photographs.

g. On Slide 5, insert the **p01_ps3_Organic_Symbol** picture at the bottom. Set Corrections to **Brightness: 0% (Normal) Contrast: +40%**. Inside a new text box, type Certified by the USDA as meeting the requirements for the National Organic Program. Resize the **text box** so that text fills three lines. Select the **symbol** and the **text box**, and select to align selected objects, if necessary. Align the elements to the middle, group the elements, drag the group to the lower portion of the white space on the slide, and then align in the center. See the storyboard for visual clarification if needed.

h. Insert a new slide after Slide 5. Enter Conventional versus Organic as the slide title. Insert a table into the body placeholder with **2** columns and **4** rows. Enter the following information:

Conventional Gardeners	Organic Gardeners
Chemical fertilizers	Natural fertilizers, manure, compost
Insecticides	Beneficial insects, traps
Herbicides	Crop rotation, hand weed, mulch

i. Continuing with the table, modify it as follows:

- Change the Table Style to **Dark Style 2 - Accent 3/Accent 4**.
- Add **borders** to all cells of the table.
- Increase the size of the table by adjusting the height to **4.3"**.
- Select the **column headings**, and then increase the font size to **28**.
- Select the **remaining rows** of the table, and then increase the font size to **20**.
- Align the text in the table cells to the middle.

j. On Slide 7, insert a clip art **photograph** of asparagus, using the search word asparagus and search photographs only, including from Office.com. Resize the photograph to **3.75"** in height. Move it to the bottom-right corner of the slide, overlapping some of the background. See the storyboard for visual clarification if needed. Remove the background from the photograph using Remove Background in the Adjust group of the Picture Tools Format tab, and then increase the size of the space until all of the asparagus is shown within the photograph.

k. On Slide 8, insert a clip art **photograph** of lettuce on the slide. Use the search words organic lettuce and search photographs only, including from Office.com. Flip the image horizontally, and then remove the background color as you did in the previous step. Resize it to **4.1"** in height, and then change the Color Tone to **Temperature: 5900K**. Move it to the bottom-right corner of the slide, as shown on the storyboard. Increase the list level for the second, third, and fourth lines of the body content.

l. Add a **Line chart** to Slide 9. Enter the following information in the chart worksheet:

	Growth by Percentage
2000	1.2
2001	1.4
2002	1.6
2003	1.9
2004	2.2
2005	2.5
2006	2.9
2007	3.2
2008	3.6
2009	3.7

Modify the chart as follows:

- Apply **Layout 1** to the chart.
- Remove the legend.
- Remove the Primary Vertical Axis Title.
- Adjust the width of the chart to **4.5"**.
- Move the chart into the bottom-right corner of the white space.

m. On Slide 9, insert a new text box, and then type Source: The Organic Trade Association's. Press Enter, and continue entering 2010 Organic Industry Survey. Decrease the Font Size to **14**, right-align the text, and then move it into a position below the bullet points at the very bottom of the white space.

n. Add a new slide with the title Organic Roasted Cauliflower. Add the SmartArt graphic **Segmented Process**. Change the colors to **Colored Outline - Accent 3** in the Accent 3 group. Enter the information shown here. (Note: All of the information is at the same level, without any subcategories.)

- Cauliflower
- Onion
- Garlic
- Olive Oil
- 450 for 20 Minutes
  Modify the graphic as follows:
- Click after **450** and insert character code **00B0** from the Calibri font.
- Change the Shape Width of the graphic to **6.5"**.
- Use the **SmartArt Tools Format tab** to distribute the graphic horizontally on the slide.

o. Add a footer to Slide 10 that reads Chef Robin Sanchez, Indigo 5, Painted Paradise Golf Resort and Spa. Increase the font size to **14**, and then modify the color to **Tan, Background 2, Darker 90%**. Increase the width of the footer so the text appears on one line, and then center the **footer** on the page.

p. On Slide 11, center the **body text**. Change the first two lines to a font size of **40** and **bold**.

q. Review the slide show for accuracy. View the slides in Slide Show view. Save the presentation. Print only **Slide 10** (Organic Roasted Cauliflower) as a **Full Page Slide**. Close the presentation and exit PowerPoint.

Perform 1: Perform in Your Life

Student data file needed:

p01_pf1_Family_Storyboard

You will save your files as:

A hand-drawn storyboard with your first and last name at the top of the pages.

Lastname_Firstname_p01_pf1_Family

Lastname_Firstname_p01_pf1_Family_Show

My Family Presentation

IT

Information Technology

In this project, you will create a slide show based on your family using the skills you have learned in this module. You have many options on the organization of this presentation. You could focus on each member of your family on individual slides. You could highlight past generations of your family. You may decide to base the slide show on yourself, discussing family members as a supporting cast. Plan to include between 10 and 15 slides. Use the file p01_pf1_Family_Storyboard to draw some thumbnails and plan the content of your slides.

Select an appropriate template, changing the colors or fonts. Create an Outline with the titles and body content for your slides. Change the slide layouts as needed to accommodate the information on the slides. Slide footers should include your name and the slide number. Pay attention to the graphic details of this presentation, selecting appropriate digital photographs you may have, clip art, and shapes to assist you in telling your family story. Use SmartArt creatively, perhaps to develop a family tree. Use a chart in your presentation, as well as a table. Apply WordArt to text, remembering to use it for emphasis and not for large amounts of text.

You will print an outline of the presentation, so you will know what is on each slide as you speak to the audience. You will save the presentation in PowerPoint Show format so it is easy to start.

a. Start **PowerPoint**, select a **template**, and then save the presentation as Lastname_Firstname_p01_pf1_Family.

b. Modify the colors or fonts of the template appropriately.

c. Create 10–15 slides, with titles and body content.

d. Modify the layouts of the slides appropriately. Add footers to every slide (except the title slide) that contain your name and the slide number.

e. On the title slide, include your name and a copyright notice with the copyright symbol.

f. Apply WordArt to text within the presentation.

g. Add photographs, clip art, and shapes to slides in the presentation.

h. Create a SmartArt graphic on a slide.

i. Create a table on a slide, to describe some aspect of your family.

j. Create a chart on a slide.

k. Check the spelling throughout the presentation. Ignore the spelling of proper names, and correct any other misspelled words. Review each slide in the full-screen view.

l. Save the presentation. Save the presentation again as a PowerPoint Show named Lastname_Firstname_p01_pf1_Family_Show. Print an Outline of your presentation. Close the presentation and exit PowerPoint.

Student data file needed:

p01_pf2_Health_Storyboard

You will save your files as:

A hand-drawn storyboard with your first and last name at the top of the pages.

Lastname_Firstname_p01_pf2_Health_Careers

Lastname_Firstname_p01_pf2_Health_Show

Career Day

General Business

As the Administrative Manager of the American Health Group, you have been asked to discuss health care careers during the Fall Career Expo at the local high school. Your audience will be mainly 9th and 10th graders who are deciding what careers they wish to pursue. Your presentation will discuss at least five options in the health care field. Consider nurses, doctors, specialists, medical records personnel, phlebotomists, EMT workers, psychologists, eye care professionals, dentists, geriatric caregivers, and other health care careers as you prepare the presentation. You will deliver the presentation to about 30 people at one time, in a classroom situation. You will need to do enough research to adequately present the material. Use the file p01_pf2_Health_Storyboard to draw some thumbnails and plan the content of your slides.

a. Start **PowerPoint**, select a theme, and then save the presentation as Lastname_ Firstname_p01_pf2_Health_Careers.

b. Modify the colors or fonts of the template appropriately.

c. Create 10–15 slides, with titles and body content.

d. Modify the layouts of the slides appropriately. Add **footers** to every slide (except the title slide), which contains your name, the slide number, and the current date.

e. On the title slide, include your name and a copyright notice with the copyright symbol.

f. Apply **WordArt** to text within the presentation.

g. Add photographs, clip art, and shapes to slides in the presentation.

h. Create a **SmartArt** graphic on a slide.

i. Create a table on a slide, to either describe each career path or compare the career paths.

j. Create a chart on a slide.

k. Type notes in the Notes pane that reflect your research for this project.

l. Check the spelling throughout the presentation. Ignore the spelling of proper names, while correcting any other misspelled words. Review each slide in the full-screen view.

m. Save the presentation. Save the presentation again as a PowerPoint Show named Lastname_Firstname_p01_pf2_Health_Show. Print an outline of your presentation, close the presentation, and then exit PowerPoint.

Student data file needed:

p01_pf3_Garden

You will save your files as:

Lastname_Firstname_p01_pf3_Garden

Lastname_Firstname_p01_pf3_Garden_Show

Lastname_Firstname_p01_pf3_Garden_PDF

Organizing a Community Garden

Sales & Marketing

As an active volunteer in your community, you have been working as the manager of the Let's Grow! Community Gardens, which provides gardening space for people to use for food and flowers throughout your town. You are in charge of three gardens. Each year, in the spring, you visit civic groups to encourage their members to get involved with the gardens, whether as a gardener or as a sponsor. You talk to groups as small as 15 people and as large as 100 people. You will update a PowerPoint slide show to support you as you give your presentation.

a. Open **p01_pf3_Garden**, and then review the slide show. Retain the current theme, but alter the colors to suggest a greener, healthier garden. Name the Custom Colors Lastname Firstname Garden Colors. Save the presentation as Lastname_Firstname_p01_pf3_Garden.

b. On Slide 1, add a copyright notice, with the copyright symbol, the current year, and your name.

c. On Slide 2, improve the display of the mission statement with spacing and font changes.

d. On Slide 3, use WordArt to enhance the quotation. Remove the background from the slide, and then add an appropriate clip art illustration or photograph to the slide.

e. On Slide 4, apply the Rule of 6's to the text. Change the layout to Two Content, and then add a clip art photograph to the slide. Apply a Picture Style to the photograph, and then alter the color as needed to enhance the slide.

f. On Slide 5, using the data provided, create a Stacked Column in 3-D chart. Provide a title of Community Gardens Income, and a legend on the right side of the chart. Delete the data table after creating the chart.

g. Improve the appearance of the table on Slide 6, adjusting the alignment of the numbers, selecting an appropriate Table Style, and then applying Table Styles options. Align the table in the middle of the slide.

h. Apply the Rule of 6's to Slide 7.

i. On Slide 8, place the text into an appropriate SmartArt graphic.

j. Add a footer to all slides but the title slide, containing your name and the current year.

k. Review the slide show. Check the spelling throughout the presentation. Save the presentation. Save the presentation as a PowerPoint Show, named Lastname_Firstname_p01_pf3_Garden_Show. Save it again as a PDF presentation, named Lastname_Firstname_p01_pf3_Garden_PDF. Print the presentation with three slides per page for handouts.

Student data file needed:

p01_pf4_Puppy_U

You will save your files as:

Lastname_Firstname_p01_pf4_Puppy_U
Lastname_Firstname_p01_pf4_Puppy_Show
Lastname_Firstname_p01_pf4_Puppy_PDF

Puppy U

Human Resources

Recently you have been in charge of supervising the veterinary technicians at the Pet Care Clinic. Josie Yancey, an experienced vet tech, is planning a puppy training course that she is calling Puppy U. She prepared a PowerPoint presentation to show at the orientation class. She asked you to review the presentation and improve it.

The audience will be families, some with children as young as 7. The puppies will not be there the night of the orientation. The basic commands, procedures, and equipment are discussed in the slide show. This presentation is informational so the families are prepared when they bring their puppies to class.

a. Open **p01_pf4_Puppy_U**, review the presentation, and then save the presentation as Lastname_Firstname_p01_pf4_Puppy_U.

b. Consider the theme, color scheme, and font. What changes would you recommend? Update the presentation to reflect your thinking.

c. Apply the Rule of 6's to the slides, and then modify the List Level as needed in the bullet lists.

d. What other topics make sense to include? Could any of the slides be deleted? Add or remove slides, but carefully plan to cover the same content or add additional content.

e. How could you make this presentation more attractive to people? Add items that will enhance the presentation, including SmartArt, WordArt, and personal digital photographs if you happen to have a dog. Evaluate the content of the presentation to determine if you can display the same information in a chart or table.

f. Review the slide show. Check the spelling throughout the presentation. Save the presentation. Save the presentation again as a PowerPoint Show, named Lastname_Firstname_p01_pf4_Puppy_Show. Save it again as a PDF presentation, named Lastname_Firstname_p01_pf4_Puppy_PDF. Print the presentation with six slides per page for handouts.

Objectives

1. Apply and modify transitions and animations   p. 786

2. Create hyperlinks within a presentation   p. 791

3. Apply and modify multimedia objects   p. 798

4. Create a PowerPoint photo album   p. 804

5. Create a custom slide show   p. 810

6. Save a presentation in multiple formats   p. 813

Applying and Modifying Multimedia

Sales & Marketing

PREPARE CASE

Introduction to the Turquoise Oasis Spa Presentation

The Turquoise Oasis Spa and Salon manager, Meda Rodate, asked you to create a presentation to send to people who make inquiries about the spa. This presentation is to introduce people to the spa by showing photographs of the spa, detailing the treatments, and giving other useful information for first-time spa guests. The presentation will be distributed on CD or via a PDF e-mail link. Custom slide shows will be developed from the presentation for specific clients, such as brides, who want to enjoy the spa prior to their wedding.

holbox / Shutterstock.com

Student data files needed for this workshop:

 p02_ws03_Spa_Info

 p02_ws03_Spa_Recording

 p02_ws03_Spa_Music

 p02_ws03_Spa_Video

 p02_ws03_Spa_S1

 p02_ws03_Spa_S2

 p02_ws03_Spa_S3

 p02_ws03_Spa_S4

 p02_ws03_Spa_S5

 p02_ws03_Spa_S6

 p02_ws03_Spa_S7

 p02_ws03_Spa_Theme

 p02_ws03_Spa_Meda

You will save your files as:

 Lastname_Firstname_p02_ws03_Spa_Info

 Lastname_Firstname_p02_ws03_Spa_Album

 Lastname_Firstname_p02_ws03_Spa_Custom

 Lastname_Firstname_p02_ws03_Spa_Video

 Lastname_Firstname_p02_ws03_Spa_Presentation_CD_Folder

 Lastname_Firstname_p02_ws03_Spa_Word

Applying and Modifying Multimedia in a Presentation

Multimedia, with elements such as audio and video, enhance presentations. They enable you to make your point in a more engaging way. Multimedia objects break up the presentation. They can explain concepts in a way that appeals to people with different learning styles. Multimedia can also add entertainment value to your presentation while maintaining a professional appearance.

> **CONSIDER THIS** | **Beyond Presentations**
>
> With the help of multimedia, a PowerPoint presentation can be used as a marketing tool. Have you seen a PowerPoint presentation used in a nontraditional way? Describe the situation and the way the presentation was used.

Multimedia objects are applied in a variety of ways in PowerPoint. Simple transitions and animations of the slides and content can engage the audience. Hyperlinks enable you to move through the presentation in nonsequential slide order or to use the resources of the World Wide Web. Buttons and triggers enable you to start multimedia actions. Sounds and recorded narrations enhance slide shows that are self-playing in kiosks or on CDs. Movies can be embedded into presentations to engage your audience.

As always, use caution when applying multimedia to your slide shows. Remember that you are the focus of the presentation, and the multimedia should support you and your message. Too much multimedia also tires your audience. Remember the KISS principle: **K**eep **I**t **S**hort and **S**imple!

In this section, you will apply multimedia to your presentations.

Using Transitions and Animations

PowerPoint has some powerful tools for creating multimedia within the presentation. **Transitions** are defined as the visual and audio elements that occur as the slides change. The transitions add a very professional quality to your presentations. **Animations** refer to the movement of elements, such as text and graphics, on a slide.

Transitions and animations have many settings, with opportunities to apply multiple actions to a slide. Consider the purpose of the slide, and select the elements that support the message. It is important that you maintain consistency with the transitions and animations within the presentation. Suppose you want to build interest in a product. You may decide to list the individual components of the product, one by one, and then make the big reveal at the end of the slide. This animation method works well if you want to focus the attention of the audience on one bullet point at a time.

Transitions can also be used to automatically advance the slides after a set amount of time. As you know, most of the time, slides are advanced by clicking the mouse button or pressing a key. Slides that you want to play on a **kiosk**—which is a computer system that provides information to people in nontraditional places such as museums, grocery stores, or banks—should have automatic transitions. You have the option to make each of the slides advance after a set amount of time, as indicated on the Transitions tab.

Real World Advice — Recording Slide Advancement Timings

You also have the option to record timings on the Slide Show tab. To record the timings, the slide is shown full screen in Slide Show view, and when you advance the slide, the length of time spent on the slide is recorded. Some presenters use this feature by viewing each page and reading the slide out loud before advancing to the next slide. You probably will not want to use this method to advance the slides if you are personally giving the presentation, because it is hard to maintain the same rhythm, and you may want to speed up or slow down based on audience reaction. You do not want your presentation jumping ahead of you or lagging behind!

Applying Effective Transitions

Slide transitions can take many forms in a presentation. The Transitions tab contains the options that are applied to the slides. The slides can enter from any side of the window. Other transition effects cause the slide to fade onto the screen or off of the screen. Sounds can be applied to the transitions. You can modify the length of time it takes for the transition to occur, and also determine the action, such as a mouse click, that causes it to occur. If you want to have a self-playing presentation, such as one that might be displayed in a kiosk, you use the Transitions tab to set up the changing of the slides.

Workshop 3 Training

To Apply Transitions

a. Start **PowerPoint**, click the **File tab**, and then click **Open**. Click the disk drive in the left pane where your student data files are located. Navigate through the folder structure, and double-click **p02_ws03_Spa_Info**. Click the **File tab** again, and then click **Save As**. Navigate to the disk drive and folder where you will store your project files, type Lastname_Firstname_p02_ws03_Spa_Info as the file name, and then click **Save**.

b. Click the **Slide Show tab**, and then click **From Beginning**. Navigate through the slides, exit the presentation, and then click **Slide 2** on the Slides tab.

   The presentation fits the needs of Meda Rodate, but it can use some more visual interest. You will add slide transitions to the presentation.

c. Click the **Transitions tab**, and then click **Fade** in the Transition to This Slide group. Notice the automatic preview as you select the transition.

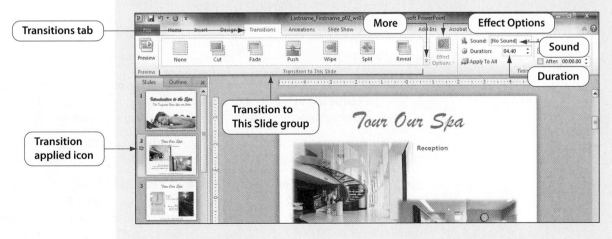

Figure 1   The Transitions tab

SIDE NOTE
Remember to Save!

As you work through the project, be sure to save your project often. If you stop in the middle of the project, save the file and reopen it when you return to the project.

d. Click **Reveal** in the Transition to This Slide group.

You observe the slide changing in a different way for the transition you have selected. Notice the Reveal transition took longer to complete than the Fade transition.

e. Click **More** ▾ in the Transition to This Slide group, and then in the Exciting group, click **Honeycomb**. While this transition is very dynamic, it would be distracting to use on every slide.

f. Click **More** ▾ in the Transition to This Slide group, and then in the Dynamic Content group, click **Rotate**.

You decide that this transition is professional looking. You will apply it to all of the slides in the presentation, except the title slide.

g. Select **Slides 2** through **13** on the Slides tab, and then click **Rotate**.

Troubleshooting

To select multiple slides, click the first one in the range, and then press and hold ⎇Shift while clicking the last slide in the range.

h. Select **Slides 2** through **8** on the Slides tab, click **Effect Options**, and then click **From Bottom**. Slides 9–12 will use the default Effect Option of From Right.

i. Select **Slide 13** on the Slides tab, click **Effect Options**, and then click **From Top**.

Different groups of slides can have different **effect options** that determine the way the transition enters the screen. In this case you selected slides that will be treated differently from the rest to transition. You will review the slide show with the new transitions.

j. Click the **Slide Show tab**, and then click **From Beginning**. Navigate through the slides, and then exit the presentation when you have reviewed each transition.

Editing Transitions

As you work with transitions, you may want to change settings you have made. For instance, in the project you are working on, you may decide that the transitions need to occur more quickly, or you could modify the effects applied to the individual slides.

Keep in mind that you should have some consistency in the way the transitions occur. In your project, you selected a single transition type, but then applied different effect options to the transitions on different slides. You will modify the speed of the transitions and add a sound to some of the slide transitions.

To Modify Transitions

a. Click **Slide 2**, click the **Transitions tab**, click the **Sound arrow**, and then click **Chime**.

A gentle chime sound is placed on the transition. You may have noticed that as you pointed to other sounds, they played. This is a good way to preview a sound.

b. Click **Slide 6**, and then add the **Chime** sound to this slide. You are only adding the sound to selected slides rather than all of the slides to signal that these slides have a new focus.

c. Click **Slide 13**, click the **Sound arrow**, and then click **Other Sound**. Navigate to the student data files, click **p02_ws03_Spa_Recording**, and then click **OK**.

Meda provided you with a greeting that you have added to the slide. After adding the sounds to the slide show, you will review the show. Be sure to turn the sound on so you can hear the effects. At this time, **Click photo to listen to Meda** does not work. You will change that later.

d. Click the **Slide Show tab**, and then click **From Beginning**. Navigate through the slides, and then exit the presentation when you have reviewed each transition. You notice that the length of time it takes for the transition to complete is a little long, even though it is only 2 seconds.

e. Select **Slides 2** through **13** on the Slides tab. Click the **Transitions tab**, type **1** in the **Duration box** in the Timing group, and then review the slide show in Slide Show view, noticing the quicker transitions. Press [Esc] at the end of the slide show to return to Normal view.

Quick Reference | Previewing Slide Transitions

In addition to navigating through the slides to see and hear the transition effects, you can preview the transition from the current slide. Click Preview on the Transitions tab. The display will show the previous slide and demonstrate the transition effect. Only a few seconds of the slide will be previewed, so audio files may stop abruptly during the preview.

Animating Objects for Emphasis

Animations affect the individual objects on the slide. Bullet points, other text, and graphics can be timed to appear on the slide in different ways. The three major animation groups are Entrance, Emphasis, and Exit. In the **Entrance animation** the action happens as the object enters the slide, and in the **Exit animation** the action occurs as the object leaves the slide. The **Emphasis action** is applied to the object after it is displayed on the slide. Another animation option is to set up a motion path to move the object. This is useful if you want to move a single object, such as a car or plane, across the screen.

Animations can be started in one of three ways. You can start the animation by clicking the mouse. The animation can be set up to play with any previous action on the slide. You can also set up the animation to play after another animation. You can set the **duration**, or length of time an animation effect takes to play, in parts of a second. You can also **delay** the action causing it to play after a certain number of seconds. When you select a content placeholder, you have the choice to apply the effect to the text as One Object, All at Once, or By Paragraph. The One Object option treats all of the text in the box as a single animation. The All at Once animation may appear to be the same as the One Object animation, but with different animation types, such as the Fly In, it will be more evident. The By Paragraph animation applies the action to elements of the placeholder object one at a time.

CONSIDER THIS | **Appropriate Animations**

Using animations that support your presentation is a skill that you develop. Can you describe a presentation where you have seen appropriate, engaging animations used? Can you describe a situation where animations were overdone or poorly done?

You can combine animations so an element has an entry, emphasis, and exit animation, but this can be very distracting to the audience and slow down the flow of the presentation. Select the animations carefully, while keeping in mind the important points being made by the slide. Emphasize those points.

You will apply animations to the tour slides, making the photographs appear one after the other. This will give the feeling of walking through the spa.

SIDE NOTE
The Pitfalls of Too Much Animation

While animation adds interest to your presentation, beware of adding too much animation to your slides. Audiences lose focus if there is too much activity going on at one time. Likewise, they can be lost if the animation is annoying and repeated. Plan the length of the animations so you do not have to wait for slide items to appear on the screen.

To Animate Objects

a. Click **Slide 2**, and select the **Reception photograph** and the **Reception text box**. On the Animations tab, click **Fade** in the Animation group.

Two small buttons with the number 1 indicate that the same animation has been applied to both of the objects. You will now select the Timing for the animation.

Troubleshooting

Depending on the size of your window, you may not see the Animation group. Click the Animation Styles button to display the Animation gallery. Click Fade in the Entrance group of the Animation gallery.

Troubleshooting

Click the photograph, press and hold Shift, and then click the Reception text box to select both objects.

b. With the photo and the text placeholder selected, click the **Start arrow** in the Timing group. Click **With Previous**, click the **Duration** box, and then type **1.30**. In the Preview group, click **Preview** to view the animation.

Notice that the numbers indicating the animation have changed to 0. This is because the animation occurs as the slide is displayed. You will see a difference when you animate the Changing Rooms text and photograph in the next step.

Figure 2   The Animations tab

c. Select the **Changing Rooms photograph** and **Changing Rooms text placeholder**. Click **Fade**, click the **Start arrow**, and then click **With Previous**. Click the **Duration box**, and then type **1.30**. Click the **Delay** box, and then type **1.30**.

The numbers on the Changing Rooms objects are zero, indicating that they are triggered by the display of the slide. The slide displays for 1.30 seconds without the Changing Rooms photograph and text. After the short delay the photograph and text will appear gradually over a period of 1.30 seconds. This gives the audience a chance to look at the Reception photograph and then turn their attention to the Changing Rooms photograph.

You will continue setting up the animations for the tour portion of the slide show using a special tool, the Animation Painter. The Animation Painter button is a toggle and works in the same way as the Format Painter. You click it to turn it on for a single use, and it turns off automatically after you click an item. You can double-click it to turn it on for multiple uses, and then click it again to turn it off.

d. Select the **Reception photograph**, and then double-click **Animation Painter** in the Advanced Animation group. Click **Slide 3** on the Slides tab, and then click the **Showers photograph**. Click **Slide 4** on the Slides tab, click the **Couples Massage Room photograph**, and then click the **Couples Massage Room text**. Click **Slide 5** on the Slides tab, click the **Facial Treatment Room photograph**, and then click the **Facial Treatment Room text**. Click the **Animation Painter** to return the mouse pointer to normal.

     You may have wondered why the text on Slide 3 was not selected. Both descriptions are in the same text block. You want to treat them as individual elements, so you will set the animations up for this part in a different way.

e. Click **Slide 2**, click the **Changing Rooms photograph**, and then double-click the **Animation Painter**. Click **Slide 3**, and then apply the animation to the **Sauna photograph**. Click **Slide 4**, and apply the animation to the **Private Jacuzzi photograph** and **text**. Click **Slide 5**, and apply the animation to the **Pedicure Treatment Room photograph** and **text**. Click the **Animation Painter** to return the pointer to normal.

Troubleshooting

> If the Animation Painter is not available when you try to revert to the normal pointer, press Esc to toggle it off.

f. Click **Animation Pane** in the Advanced Animation group, click **Slide 3** in the Slides pane, and then select the text **Showers**, **Private**, and **Wheelchair accessible**. Click the **Fade** animation, and then click **Play** in the Animation Pane to observe the action.

     The Showers text appears after both photographs are displayed. You will alter the animation by moving the text up in the Animation Pane.

g. Click **Up Reorder** at the bottom of the Animation Pane, moving all three text items up. Click **Play** again, noticing that now the text is displayed after the photograph rather than with it.

h. Click the **Start arrow** in the Timing group, and then select **With Previous**. This will display this portion of the text when the Showers photograph appears.

     The Animation Pane gives you a roadmap of the order of the animation of the objects on the slide. The zero means that the action will start as soon as the slide is displayed. Additional numbers indicate that the objects will animate *after* the slide is displayed. The order of the items in the pane gives you an idea of which items will occur first. The yellow bars to the right of the object names show the length of time allotted to the animation and when it will begin. Place the pointer over the icon on the left to see the animation name and the start action. Point to the yellow bar and a ScreenTip gives you the start time and end time of the animation. You can drag the yellow bar to increase or decrease the time. Keep in mind that this can change any duration or delay settings you may have made in the Timing group.

i. Select the text **Sauna**, **Therapeutic heat**, **Zoned heating**, and **Ocean sounds**. Click **Fade**, click the **Start arrow**, and then click **With Previous**. Click the **Duration box**, and then type **1.30**. Click **Play** in the Animation Pane to observe the action.

j. Click the **Slide Show tab**, click **From Beginning**, and then click through the first five slides to review the animations. Press Esc to return to Normal view. **Close** X the Animation Pane and save the slide show.

Creating Hyperlinks

Hyperlinks are objects, such as text or graphics, that provide a path to additional resources. Hyperlinks serve two purposes in PowerPoint. You can hyperlink to slides that are not in the normal progression of the slides. You can also provide hyperlinks to

Internet resources, such as e-mail and the web. With a presentation distributed on CD or as a PDF file, this gives the audience an opportunity to interact with the presentation.

You will begin by setting links from Slide 8, where the treatments are listed, to the slides later in the presentation that contain the appropriate information. You will also create a hyperlink back to Slide 8 so the audience can select another treatment. Later you will hide the slides so the only way to view them is to click the hyperlink.

Linking to Other Slides

Objects of all types can be set as hyperlinks in the slide show. This means that a graphic or text can link to a different slide. When you link text, it will contain the underscore that most people associate with a hyperlink. As with hyperlinks on the web, a ⌖ is displayed to indicate a hyperlink as the slide show is displayed if the mouse pointer hovers over the link.

It is important that you provide a way back to the original slide so you do not leave your audience at a dead-end in the presentation. Again, a graphic or text object can be used to link back to the original slide.

To Create Slide Hyperlinks

a. Click **Slide 8** on the Slides tab. Select the text **Manicure and Pedicure**, click the **Insert tab**, and then click **Hyperlink** in the Links group to display the Insert Hyperlink dialog box.

b. Click **Place in This Document** in the Link to group. Click **11. Manicures and Pedicures** in the Select a place in this document list. Click **ScreenTip**, and then type Check out our manicures and pedicures. Click here! in the Set Hyperlink ScreenTip box, and then click **OK**. Click **OK** in the Insert Hyperlink dialog box, click **Slide Show** ▾ on the status bar, and then click the hyperlink to test it.

    The slide changes and you notice there is not a way to return to Slide 8. You will create an Action Button graphic to hyperlink back to the treatment list slide later in this project.

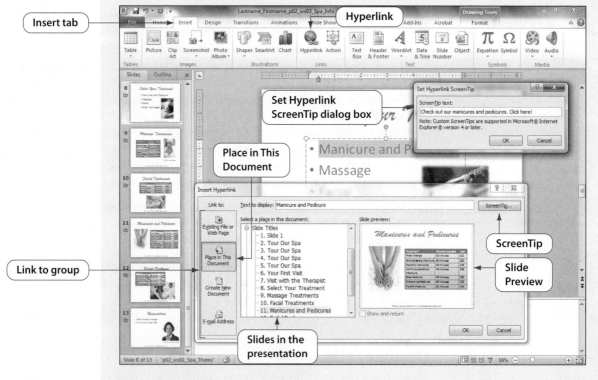

Figure 3 Setting up slide hyperlinks

c. Press Esc to return to Normal view of Slide 11.

d. Click **Slide 8**, select the **Massage** text, click the **Insert tab**, click **Hyperlink**, and then click **9. Massage Treatments** in the Select a place in this document list. Click **ScreenTip**, and then type Our massages will relax you. in the Set Hyperlink ScreenTip dialog box. Click **OK**, and then click **OK** again to close the Insert Hyperlink dialog box.

e. Select the **Facial** text, click **Hyperlink**, and then click **10. Facial Treatments** in the Select a place in this document list. Click **ScreenTip**, and then type Our facials will have you looking younger. in the Set Hyperlink ScreenTip dialog box. Click **OK**, and then click **OK** again to close the Insert Hyperlink dialog box.

f. Select the **Bridal Packages** text, click **Hyperlink**, and then click **12. Bridal Packages** in the Select a place in this document list. Click **ScreenTip**, and type Options for the bride and groom. in the Set Hyperlink ScreenTip dialog box. Click **OK**, and then click **OK** again to close the Insert Hyperlink dialog box.

g. Click the **Slide Show tab**, and then click **From Beginning**. As you view the slides, check each hyperlink to make sure it goes to the correct slide, and then right-click the **slide** and click **Last Viewed** to return to Slide 8 after checking each hyperlink.

As you continue through the slides, you notice that the treatment slides are repeated. These slides will be hidden in a later step in this project.

h. Press Esc to return to Normal view.

Linking to Websites

Two types of hyperlinks, to a web page or an e-mail address, link the audience to these Internet resources. An active Internet connection is required in order for these links to work. When someone clicks a hyperlink to a web page, the default browser opens and the page is displayed. When the e-mail hyperlink is clicked, the default e-mail application opens.

To Set Up Internet Links

a. Click **Slide 13**, click at the end of the phone number, and then press Enter. Type E-mail:. Press Enter, click the **Insert tab**, click **Hyperlink**, and then click **E-mail Address** under Link to. Type mrodate@paintedparadiseresort.com in the **Text to display** box. Type the e-mail address again in the E-mail address box. PowerPoint automatically adds "mailto:" in front of the address. Click the **Subject** box, and then type Important Request from the Spa Presentation. Click **OK**.

In setting up a Subject line, you are giving Meda a way to recognize that e-mail has been generated from the presentation. The e-mail address is displayed as a hyperlink. It is too wide for the placeholder so it wraps to the next line. You will decrease the size of the font to make the e-mail address fit on one line.

Troubleshooting

If the computer automatically capitalizes the "m" in mrodate, that is acceptable.

Figure 4 Setting up e-mail hyperlinks

SIDE NOTE
Dealing with Hyperlinks
Hyperlinks should always appear on a single line. If the viewers do not need to see the address, create descriptive text to use instead of the URL. The viewers will click on the text and the appropriate application will open.

b. Select the **e-mail address text**, click the **Home tab**, type **24** in the **Font Size** box, and then press Enter. You realize that the bullets are unnecessary. Select all of the **content text**, and then click **Bullets** ⌐ in the Paragraph group to remove the bullets.

c. Click at the end of the text, and then press Enter twice. Click the **Insert tab**, click **Hyperlink**, and then under Link to, click **Existing File or Web Page**. Type **www.paintedparadiseresort.com** in the Address box. The same text fills the Text to display box and PowerPoint adds "http://" in front of the Address and the Text to display. Click **ScreenTip**, and then type **Visit our website!** in the Set Hyperlink ScreenTip dialog box. Click **OK**, and then click **OK** again. Select the **website text**, click the **Home tab**, type **24**, if necessary in the **Font Size** box, and then press Enter.

You will adjust a few things on this slide to give a more professional appearance to the information. You will center the text and then apply an animation to it.

d. Select all of the **text** in the content placeholder. Click **Center** ☰ in the Paragraph group, click the **Animations tab**, and then click **Fade**. Click the **Start arrow**, click **With Previous**, and then increase the **Duration** to **2.0** seconds.

e. Click the **Slide Show tab**, click **From Current Slide**, and then click the **hyperlinks** on Slide 13 to make sure they start the correct Internet resource—the default browser or e-mail application. Close each application after it opens. Press Esc to return to Normal view.

Adding Action Buttons

Action Buttons are special shapes, predefined to include actions that help you navigate through slides. The buttons are available in the Shapes gallery on the Insert tab. The actions include moving to a previous slide or the next slide, skipping to the first or last slide of the presentation, playing a sound or movie, opening a document, or opening a Help feature.

You will add Action Buttons to your presentation to return to Slide 8 from each of the treatment slides. You will modify the shape by changing the colors to better blend with your presentation.

To Add and Modify Action Buttons

a. Click **Slide 9**. Click the **Insert tab**, click **Shapes** in the Illustrations group, and then click **Action Button: Back or Previous** ◁ at the bottom of the Shapes gallery. Click the bottom-right corner of the slide to place the graphic. It is possible that your Action Button is not completely on the slide at this point. You will move, recolor, and resize it in the next step. Click the **Hyperlink to arrow**, click **Last Slide Viewed**, and then click **OK** in the Action Settings dialog box, as you want the button to return the user to Slide 8.

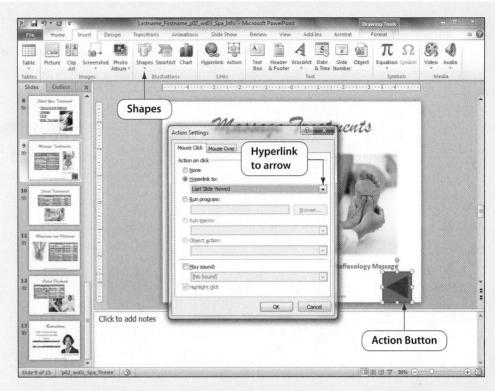

Figure 5 Action Buttons

b. Click the **Drawing Tools Format tab**, and then in the Size group, type **0.5"** in the **Shape Height** box and the **Shape Width** box. Click **Align** in the Arrange group, and then click **Align Right**. Click **Align** again, and then click **Align Bottom**. The button aligns to the bottom-right corner of the slide.

c. Click the **Shape Fill arrow** in the Shapes Styles group, and then select **Aqua, Accent 5, Lighter 80%**.

d. Right-click the **Action Button**, and then click **Copy**. Click **Slide 10**, right-click on the slide, and then click **Use Destination Theme** in the Paste Options. Repeat the pasting of the Action Button on **Slides 11** and **12**.

e. Click **Slide 8**, and then click **Slide Show** on the status bar. Click each **link**, and then click the **Action Buttons** on the resulting slides to ensure they work correctly. Press ⌐Esc¬ to return to Normal view.

SIDE NOTE
Last Slide Viewed or Previous Slide?

The Last Slide Viewed option in the Action Settings dialog box returns you to the slide you just viewed. The Previous option takes you to the slide preceding the slide you are currently viewing.

Hiding Slides

There are a number of reasons why you might want to hide slides in a presentation. In this project, you want to hide the treatment detail slides unless the person viewing the presentation clicks on a hyperlink. In other cases, you may want to anticipate questions your audience might have and place some hidden slides within your presentation to reveal if they ask these questions.

You will hide Slides 9–12 in the presentation. They will open only if someone clicks a link on Slide 8. With the Back buttons you set up, they can return to Slide 8 to view other treatments.

To Hide Selected Slides

a. Select **Slides 9** through **12** on the Slides tab, click the **Slide Show tab**, and then click **Hide Slide**. The number of the slide on the Slides tab now has a line through it to indicate it is not visible.

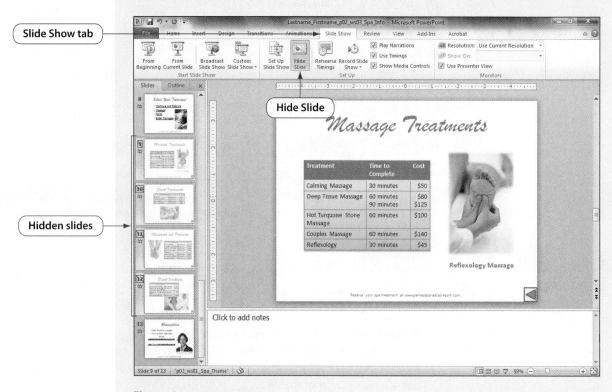

Figure 6   Hiding Slides

b. Click **Slide 8**, and then click **From Current Slide** in the Start Slide Show group on the Slide Show tab. Click each **link**, and then click **Action Button: Back or Previous** ◁ to return to Slide 8. Press Enter to proceed to the next visible slide. Right-click on the slide, point to **Go to Slide**, and then click **(9) Massage Treatments** to display the hidden slide. Press Esc to return to Normal view.

   Notice that the presentation skips from Slide 8 to Slide 13 and does not display the hidden slides. Hidden slides are only hidden from the normal progression through the slides. They are accessed via links or using the Go to Slide menu when you right-click on a slide during a slide show.

Using a Trigger

Triggers are set on objects that already contain animation; this enables you to create movement, reveal additional objects, play a sound or movie, or emphasize objects. The trigger object can be a graphic or text, and it must be clicked in order for the animation to occur.

In your project, Meda begins speaking as soon as Slide 13 is displayed. This can be disconcerting for people to suddenly hear someone speaking when they did not expect it. You will change the transition and apply a trigger to Meda's photograph to play her recorded message when someone clicks the photograph.

Real World Advice   Making Sound Choices

When working on a slide show, consider the audience as you add audio to your presentation. Will they view your presentation in a quiet location where sound would not be appreciated, such as in the office or library? Also consider the likelihood they will have speakers, or a headset, and that the sound will be turned up so they can hear your sounds. If you are making the presentation in person, make sure the sounds you select add to the value of the presentation.

To Add a Trigger

a. Click **Slide 13**. Click the **Transitions tab**, click the **Sound arrow** in the Timing group, and then click **No Sound** to remove the sound from the transition.

b. Click the **Insert tab**, and then click **Shapes**. Click the **Oval** shape, and then drag an oval over Meda's face. You will animate the oval to play the recording Meda made and later hide it behind her photograph.

c. Click the **Animations tab**, and then click **Appear** in the Animation group. It does not matter which animation effect you use for this oval, there just must be an effect applied to the shape.

d. Click **Animation Pane** in the Advanced Animation group, if necessary, to display it. Click the **arrow** to the right of the oval name in the Animation Pane, and then click **Effect Options**.

Figure 7   Adding a trigger

e. Click the **Sound arrow** on the Effect tab, and then click **p02_ws03_Spa_Recording.wav**.

Troubleshooting

If the recording is not on the list, click Other Sound, and navigate to the file on the disk drive.

f. Click the **Timing tab**, and then click **Triggers**. Click **Start effect on click of** to select it, and then click the **Start effect on click of arrow**. Click **Picture 4**, and then click **OK**. The recording begins to play as a preview of the animation.

g. Click the **oval**, if necessary, to select it. Click the **Drawing Tools Format tab**, click the **Send Backward arrow**, and then click **Send to Back**. The sizing handles may continue to be displayed, but they will go away when you click elsewhere on the slide.

h. Click **Slide Show** 🖵 on the status bar. Click **Meda's photograph** to listen to her message, press ⎋Esc⎋ to return to Normal view, and then **Close** ✕ the Animation Pane.

Inserting Audio

There are many audio options available in PowerPoint. As you have already seen, audio files can be added to transitions and animations. Audio can be inserted into presentations, complete with a player, so the audio can be started or paused as needed. Another audio option is to record a narration for your slide presentation.

Real World Advice   Should You Really Add Sound?

Keep in mind that audio can add significantly to the size of the presentation file, so use it sparingly. Large files are often difficult to e-mail to someone because of limits on the size of their e-mail boxes. Also, remember that some people may not have speakers or headsets, so audio should support the message rather than deliver it.

Inserting Sounds

As with other elements you add to your presentation, sounds are inserted using the Insert tab. Sounds can be found and added as Clip Art from Office.com, or audio files, such as MP3 or WAV files. As the audio is added, a player with a Play button is automatically added to the slide. With the player selected, you can modify the way the sound is played, either having it play automatically when the slide is displayed, or when the Play button is clicked. You can also set the audio to play across slides so a background song continues to play as the user advances the slides. Audio can be looped so it continues to play until it is stopped. The audio file can be set to fade in at the beginning of the playback and fade out at the end. If the file is too long, it can be trimmed.

New to PowerPoint 2010 is the ability to add bookmarks to both audio and video files. Bookmarks enable you to mark sections of the file so you can jump to a certain point in the file before starting the playback. This is useful if you want to focus on a part of the audio file during a presentation as a sound bite, but also have the entire file available if you decide to play the complete file for the audience.

To set the mood for the spa presentation, you will play a short musical file on the first slide. It will start automatically and not require a player. You will trim the file to create a smaller presentation file. You will also adjust the volume, so it is a gentle, soft musical interlude.

To Insert an Audio File

a. Click **Slide 1**, click the **Insert tab**, click the **Audio arrow** in the Media group, and then click **Audio from File**.

b. Navigate to the location of the student data files, click **p02_ws03_Spa_Music**, and then click **Insert**. Click **Play/Pause** ▶ on the player controls to listen to the song.

   The player opens in the middle of the slide. Because you will not be using the player, its current position is not important. You will begin by trimming the audio clip.

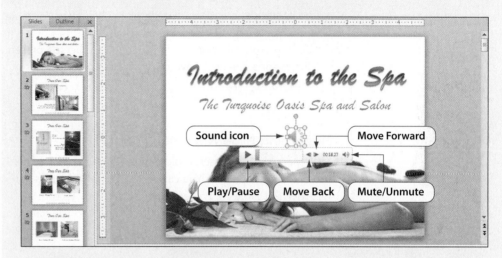

Figure 8 Adding audio and the player controls

c. Click the **Audio Tools Playback tab**, click **Trim Audio** in the Editing group, and then type 00:27.500 in the End Time box. Press Tab, click **OK**, and then click **Play/Pause** ▶ to listen to the current clip. You notice that it ends rather abruptly, but you will fade it in and out so it will not be as evident.

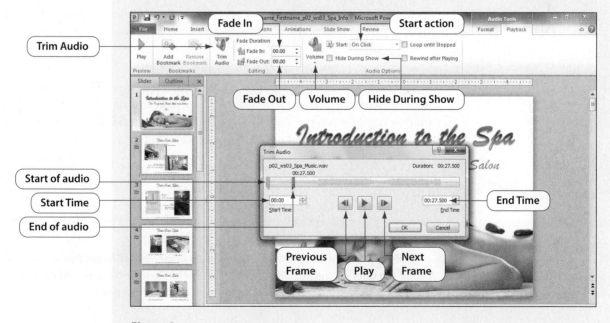

Figure 9 Trimming audio

d. Type 05.00 in the **Fade In** box in the Editing group, and then type 05.00 in the **Fade Out** box. Click **Play/Pause** ▶ to hear the fade in and out effect. You will change the volume so the overall playback is quieter.

e. Click **Volume** in the Audio Options group, click **Medium**, and then click **Play/Pause** ▶ to listen to the final editing of the song. You will now set up the options so the song plays automatically when the presentation is opened and hide the player.

f. Click the **Start arrow** in the Audio Options group, click **Automatically**, and then click the **Hide During Show check box**. Now you will test the audio in Slide Show view.

g. Click **Slide Show** 🖳 on the status bar. You may continue through the slide show or press Esc to return to Normal view.

The audio clip is a nice introduction to the spa presentation by setting the mood. If someone does not have their speakers on, they do not lose any information by not hearing the clip.

Recording Slide Narration

Slide narration is a useful addition to presentations where you will not be making the presentation in person. You can record the narration as you view the slides using a simple recorder available in PowerPoint, or you can record the narration in a different sound software application, such as Audacity, and add the narration to the slides as a part of the transitions or animations as you did with the audio files earlier.

Real World Advice   **Recording Narration and Slide Advances**

The Slide Show tab contains options for setting up the slide show with timed advancement of the slides as well as recorded narration. If you will not be giving the presentation in person, this method works well. The slides are displayed full screen as you record your presentation. You record the narration and advance each slide. When you have reached the end of the slide show, you will be asked if you want to retain the timings. This method of preparing a presentation works well for distance learning, sales presentations, and kiosks.

Slides 6 and 7 contain notes for you to record as narration. The computer you use will need a microphone so you can record the notes. You will modify the sound object so the narration begins when the slide is displayed, and the player does not show on the slide. If you do not have a microphone, read the procedure, but skip the steps.

To Record Narration

a. Click **Slide 6**. Drag the **border** between the Slide pane and the Notes pane up, until you can see both paragraphs of text in the Notes pane.

b. Click the **Insert tab**, click the **Audio arrow**, and then click **Record Audio**.

Read through the text on the Notes pane before you begin to record the sound. It will save you some time and let you experiment with the inflections of your voice.

Troubleshooting

> The Record Audio tool will only be available if you have a built-in or plugged in microphone. Skip the Record Narration steps if you do not have a microphone available.

c. Drag the **Record Sound dialog box** up, if necessary, so you can see the notes. Click **Record**, and then begin reading the notes into the microphone. Click **Stop** when you have completed the reading. Click **Play** to review the recording.

Troubleshooting

> If you would like to re-record the audio, click Cancel, and then repeat Step b and Step c.

d. Type Slide 6 Recording in the Name box. Click **OK** to save the recording to the slide.

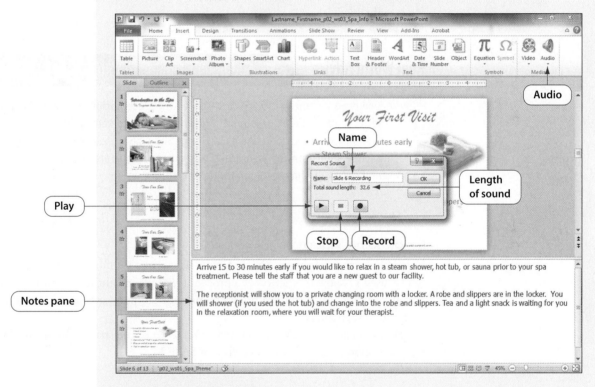

Figure 10 Recording narration

e. Click the **Speaker** that appeared in the center of the slide. Click the **Audio Tools Playback tab**.

f. Click the **Start arrow** in the Audio Options group, click **Automatically**, and then click the **Hide During Show check box**.

g. Click **Slide 7** on the Slides tab, click the **Insert tab**, click the **Audio arrow**, and then click **Record Audio**.

h. Click **Record**, and then begin reading the notes into the microphone. Click **Stop** when you have completed the reading. Click **Play** to review the recording. Type Slide 7 Recording in the Name box, and then click **OK**.

i. Click the **Speaker** 🔊 that appeared in the center of the slide. Click the **Audio Tools Playback tab**. Click the **Start arrow**, click **Automatically**, and then click **Hide During Show**.

j. Click **Slide 6**, and then click **Slide Show** 🖵 on the status bar. Review **Slide 6** and **Slide 7**. Press Esc to return to Normal view. Readjust the Notes pane so it takes less space.

Inserting Video

In some cases, video is the only way to explain a concept to your audience. At other times, you may want to use video to emphasize something on the slide. Videos can come from a variety of sources. You can embed a video file that you have on your disk drive, show a YouTube or other Internet-based video, or add a Clip Art animation.

Keep in mind that when you add video to your presentation, you are significantly adding to the size of the file. You may also notice that the slide is slow to display if a large file is embedded.

Real World Advice — Embedding or Linking to Video

Audience engagement is the key to a successful presentation. Using a video, game, or other activity to break up a presentation can help to keep your audience engaged. If you cannot insert a video due to the large file size, consider placing a hyperlink to the video source on the web. Make sure you have an Internet connection in your presentation environment if you are linking to the web.

Embedding Video

Video clips are engaging to the audience. They provide movement on the screen. They can be used to show live action of a procedure, as you might do in training. You can creatively use video to introduce products, provide support to your sales staff, and present customer testimonials.

You will add a Clip Art animation to Slide 13 of the spa presentation. You will then replace a photograph with a video clip on Slide 11.

Real World Advice — Using YouTube as a Resource

YouTube is a good resource for video clips of all sorts. When you select a YouTube video, it is smart to watch—and listen to—the entire video to decide if it is appropriate for your audience. Select videos that support your message and are worth the time you invest in showing them to your audience. The latest viral video, which is extremely popular due to people sharing it over the Internet, when added to an otherwise serious presentation only detracts from your message and leaves your audience wondering what you were thinking.

To Add Video to Slides

a. Click **Slide 13**, click at the end of the **phone number**, and then press Enter twice. This will give you some room to add a Clip Art animation of a telephone.

b. Click the **Insert tab**, click the **Video arrow** in the Media group, and then click **Clip Art Video**. Type office telephone in the **Search for** box. Click the **Results should be arrow**, and then click **Videos** to select only this type of media file. Click **Include Office.com content**, if necessary, and then click **Go**.

c. Click the **image** of the purple telephone to insert it onto the slide. Drag it into position under the line that begins with **Phone**, and then center it.

Clip Art video

Figure 11   Adding a video clip

d. Click **Slide Show** on the status bar, and then observe the video animation. Press Esc to return to Normal view. While this is a subtle animation, it does call attention to the phone number and supports the message of the slide. **Close** X the Clip Art pane.

e. Click **Slide 11**, click the **photograph**, and then press Delete. You will replace the photograph with a short video.

f. Click the **Insert tab**, click the **Video arrow**, click **Video from File**, and then in the Insert Video dialog box, click the disk drive in the left pane where your student data files are located. Navigate through the folder structure and double-click **p02_ws03_Spa_Video**.

g. Click the **Video Tools Format tab**, type 3.5 in the Video Width box in the Size group, and then press Enter. Click **Crop** in the Size group, and then drag the **middle-right sizing handle** in slightly to remove the green bar on the right side of the video. Deselect the video by clicking on the white space of the slide, and then click the video to select it. Drag the video to the left beside the table, click **Align** in the Arrange group, and then click **Align Middle**.

h. Click the **Video Tools Playback tab**, click the **Start arrow**, and then click **Automatically**. Click **Loop until Stopped**, and then click **Hide While Not Playing**.

i. Click **Slide Show** 🖵 on the status bar, and then review the slide. Press Esc twice when you have finished watching the video, and then **Save** 🖫 the presentation.

Creating Useful Photo Albums

The **Photo Album** feature of PowerPoint is an efficient way to insert a large number of photographs into a slide show just by selecting the photographs you want to include in the presentation. You do not have to individually insert, resize, or arrange the pictures on the slides. This saves you time and effort, and produces a professional looking album of photographs.

It is important to note that when you use the Photo Album feature in PowerPoint, a new file will be generated. The Photo Album is not added into the current open presentation. Once the album has been created, the slides can be reused in other slide shows. In this section, you will create and modify a Photo Album.

Real World Advice　　Using a Photo Album in Business

Most people turn to PowerPoint's Photo Album feature when they have a lot of vacation or family photographs to make into a presentation, but photo albums also have uses in the business world. Consider these ideas:

- Product catalog, showing the items and a short description
- Project history album, showing photographs of different stages towards completion of a project, such as a building project
- Owner's manual, showing photographs of important parts of the machinery
- Training manual, showing a group of figures with comments
- Testimonials from satisfied customers with photographs of them enjoying the product
- Meet the staff album, showing photographs of everyone on the staff with their names and other important information

Working with Photo Albums

Available on the Insert tab, the Photo Album button opens a dialog box that enables you to select the photographs from a storage location, such as a disk drive or USB drive. Once the photographs are in the album, you can preview them in the dialog box and change the rotation, brightness, and contrast. You can change the order of the photographs. Text can be added to the slide at this stage or added with text boxes after the presentation has been created. You can modify the layout of the pictures on the page, specify the shape of the frames around the photographs, and apply a theme.

Continuing with the spa workshop, you will create a photo album that will introduce members of the spa staff. You will later combine these album slides with the slides from the spa presentation.

Selecting Photographs

The most efficient way to select the photographs for the album is to group all of the pictures in a single folder. It makes it easier to select the ones you need. For instance, in the photo album you will create in this workshop, the photographs you will use begin with the same code and name, p02_ws03_Spa_S. If necessary, later you can update a photo album and add more photographs, using the Edit Photo Album feature.

| **Using Social Networking Photographs**

Given the popularity of social networking sites, such as Facebook, what pictures could be found of you on the Internet? Is it ethical to use a picture from one of these sites without permission? Are there times where it would be illegal?

You will create a small photo album with photographs of the members of the staff. It will be added to the spa presentation later.

To Select Photo Album Photographs

a. Click the **Insert tab**, and then click **Photo Album** in the Images group.

b. Click **File/Disk** and navigate to the student data file storage location. Select all seven of the files beginning with **p02_ws03_Spa_S1** through **p02_ws03_Spa_S7**, and then click **Insert**.

Troubleshooting

You can select the files either by pressing Ctrl while clicking each file name or by clicking the first file name, pressing Shift, and clicking the last file name.

c. Click each **file name** in the Pictures in album box to see a preview of the file.

The files are not in the correct order. You will arrange them in a later part of the project. One of the photos is displayed sideways. You will correct that in the next part of the project as well.

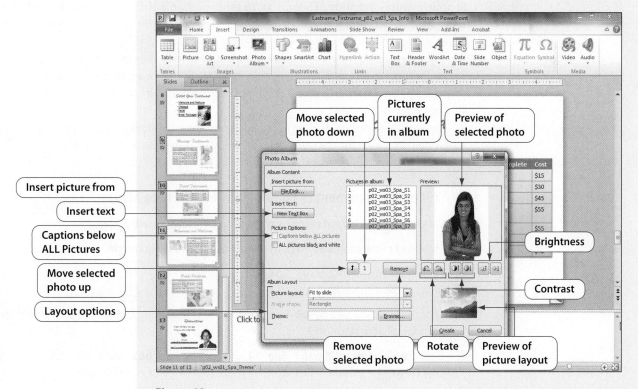

Figure 12 Creating a photo album

Modifying Photographs

Once imported into a photo album, photographs can be modified with some simple tools. They can be rotated in 90-degree increments, either clockwise or counterclockwise. The contrast and brightness of the photographs can be adjusted in the Photo Album dialog box. You can also specify that all pictures be converted to black-and-white in the photo album without changing the original picture color.

When the photo album is created, you will be able to make more sophisticated adjustments, such as altering the color temperature and color tone. You will adjust the brightness and contrast of a photograph, and rotate one of the photographs.

To Modify the Photographs with the Photo Album Tools

a. Click **p02_ws03_Spa_S2** in the Pictures in album box, and then click **Rotate 90 degrees Clockwise** once.

Troubleshooting

> If you selected the wrong button and the woman is now displayed upside down, continue clicking the button until she is in the correct orientation.

b. Click **p02_ws03_Spa_S3** in the Pictures in album box, click **Decrease Brightness** twice, and then click **Increase Contrast** twice.

Arranging Photographs

There are a number of layouts to select from when creating a photo album in PowerPoint. A picture can fill the slide, be placed in the middle of the slide, or you can have two or four pictures per slide. There is an option to place a title on each of the slide pages, regardless of the number of photographs on the slide. You can also choose from seven frame shapes that will hold the photographs.

Photographs can be moved in the photo album with the arrow buttons at the bottom of the Pictures in album box. If you will be placing two or more photographs on a slide, you can also control which photograph appears on the right or left by the order in which you place the file names.

You have decided to display four photographs per slide, with a title. You will specify a rounded rectangle for the frame shape. You will move the files into the correct order.

To Alter the Arrangement of Photographs in the Photo Album

a. Click the **Picture layout arrow**, and then click **4 pictures with title**.

b. Click the **Frame shape arrow**, and then click **Rounded Rectangle**.

c. Click the file name **p02_ws03_Spa_S5**, and then click **Up** multiple times to move the photograph into position 1.

d. Click the file name **p02_ws03_Spa_S7**, and then click **Up** multiple times to move the photograph into position 3.

e. Click the file name **p02_ws03_Spa_S2**, press Shift, click **p02_ws03_Spa_S3**, and then click **Down** multiple times, to move these two files to the end of the list.

Inserting Text

Text can be added to slides in two ways from the Photo Album dialog box. You can add text boxes that you will later fill with text or you can add **captions**, which are text boxes that describe the photographs. The default captions will be the names of the files and not something you want the audience to see, so do not forget to update the captions if you use them. If you later decide you do not want to use the text boxes, they can be replaced with other objects or deleted.

You will add captions to all of the pictures, and you will add text boxes to a few of the slides.

To Add Text to a Photo Album

a. Click **p02_ws03_Spa_S6** in the Pictures in album list, and then click **New Text Box**. The box appears in the list under the photograph file name. Click **Up** ⬆ multiple times to move the text box to the first position in the album.

b. Click **p02_ws03_Spa_S7** in the Pictures in album list, and then click **New Text Box**.

c. Click **p02_ws03_Spa_S3** in the Pictures in album list, and then click **New Text Box**.

d. Click the **Captions below ALL pictures check box** under Picture Options.

Selecting a Theme

Just as you can add themes to a presentation, you can add a theme to a photo album. The Microsoft Office themes that are stored on your computer during the installation of Office 2010 are available. You can also use themes that you have created.

The theme for the Introduction to the Spa presentation is available in your student data files. You will apply the theme to your photo album to maintain consistency with the spa presentation, because you will be reusing slides from the album in the spa presentation.

To Use a Theme in a Photo Album

a. Click **Browse** in the Photo Album dialog box, navigate to the student data files, click **p02_ws03_Spa_Theme**, and then click **Select**.

   You have completed the steps in the Photo Album dialog box. You will create the photo album.

b. Click **Create**. Click the **Slide Show tab**, and then click **From Beginning**. Review the slides in the Photo Album presentation, and then press ⎋Esc to return to Normal view. Click the **File tab**, click **Save As**, and then navigate to where you are saving your files. Type Lastname_Firstname_p02_ws03_Spa_Album as the file name, and then click **Save**.

   The first slide of the photo album contains a title and the name of the person logged on the computer. The subsequent slides contain the photographs of the staff members with text boxes for adding content to the slides. All of the photographs are formatted with the rounded rectangle frame shape.

Editing a Photo Album

As you can see, it is quick work to select photographs and place them on slides using the Photo Album feature of PowerPoint. Depending on selections you make, you may need to edit the slides. Once the photo album has been created, the slides can be modified using the normal PowerPoint tools. You can resize and move the photographs, modify the appearance of the photographs, and add text.

After reviewing the slides, you realize that you did not include Meda Rodate in the staff photo album. You will return to the Photo Album dialog box to add her photograph. You will also add text to the presentation in Normal view.

To Add Text and Edit the Photo Album

a. Click the **Insert tab**, click the **Photo Album arrow**, and then click **Edit Photo Album** to open the Edit Photo Album dialog box.

b. Click **File/Disk**, and then click **p02_ws03_Spa_Meda**. Click **Insert**. With p02_ws03_Spa_Meda selected, click the **Up arrow** ⬆ to move the photograph into position **3**. The third position is the third picture position. That is, the third position does not include the text box at the top of the list. You now have too many text boxes on the final slide, so you will remove the extra ones.

c. Click the last **text box** in the Pictures in album box, click **Remove**, and then continue to remove any extra text boxes until only one appears in the third group.

d. Click **Update** to display the revised photo album.

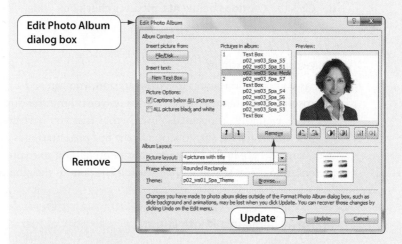

Figure 13   Updating a photo album

e. Click **Slide 2**, select the file name **p02_ws03_Spa_Meda**, and then type Meda Rodate, manager. Replace the text **p02_ws03_Spa_S5** with Kelly Masters, receptionist. Replace the text **p02_ws03_Spa_S1** with Irene Kai, manager.

f. Click the title placeholder, and then type What Our Guests Say:. Select the words **Text Box**, and type "… the receptionist made me feel very welcome and helped me to relax before my day of beauty." Press ⏎ Enter twice, leaving a blank line before typing the next testimonial. Type "The manager helped me to plan a wonderful girls spa day, prior to my wedding. We felt really pampered."

You will balance and resize the photographs to make them more consistent. Notice that Irene's name is quite small. You will crop part of the photograph and increase the size. You will align the photographs on the slide.

g. Click **Irene's photograph**, and then click it again.

This selects the photograph. If you double-click, it selects both the photograph and the text box, but you want to select only the photograph. You should see lines through the sizing handles when the photograph is properly selected.

h. Click the **Picture Tools Format tab**, and then click **Crop** in the Size group. Drag the **top cropping handle** down on Irene's photograph until it is just above her hair. Click **Crop** again to hide the cropping handles. Click away from the photograph, and then click it again, displaying only the outer sizing handles. Type 3.1 in the Shape Height box of the Size group, and then press Enter. Drag Irene's photograph up on the slide. Click the testimonials text box, press Shift, and then click **Irene's photograph**. Click the **Picture Tools Format tab**, click **Align** in the Arrange group, and then click **Align Center**.

i. Click **Slide 3**. Select the **Text Box text**, and type "Christy helped release the stress in my back so I could enjoy my wedding day." Press Enter twice, leaving a blank line before typing the next testimonial. Type "Jason made me feel so relaxed with a hot stone massage." Press Enter twice again, and type "Kendra was a wonderful masseuse!" Click the **title** placeholder, and then type Our Guests Talk About Our Therapists:.

j. Select the text **p02_ws03_Spa_S7**, and then type Christy Istas. Select the text **p02_ws03_Spa_S4**, and then type Jason Niese. Select the text **p02_ws03_Spa_S6**, and type Kendra Mault.

   Now that the text objects are on Slide 3, you will align the objects on the slide. You will place the photographs in a line under the title, and move the text below the photographs. You will then increase the size of the text placeholder to modify the size of the text.

k. Drag **Kendra's photograph** next to the photograph of Christy. Drag the **text** placeholder down towards the bottom of the slide. Drag **Jason's photograph** next to Kendra's. Select all **three photographs**. Click the **Picture Tools Format tab**, click **Align** in the Arrange group, and then click **Align to Slide**, if necessary to select it. Click **Align** again, and then click **Distribute Horizontally**. Click **Align** again, and then click **Align Middle**. Click the **text box**, and then drag the **right sizing handle** to the right edge of the slide. Drag the **left sizing handle** to the left edge of the slide. Click the **Drawing Tools Format tab**, click **Align** in the Arrange group, and then click **Align Bottom**. Click the **Home tab**, and then click **Center** in the Paragraph group. The objects are now nicely balanced.

l. Click **Slide 4**. Select the **p02_ws03_Spa_S2** text, and then type Leslie Dixon. Select the **p02_ws03_Spa_S3** text, and then type Susan Hemmerly. Select the **Text Box** text, and then type ". . . my hands were beautiful as Mike slipped the wedding ring on my finger." Press Enter twice, leaving a blank line before typing the next testimonial. Type "The couples manicure/pedicure was great! We felt like we were floating on air as we walked down the aisle." Press Enter twice, leaving a blank line before typing the next testimonial. Type "The girls in my wedding loved the manicure/pedicure as part of the bachelorette party. What a great idea!" Click the **title** placeholder, and type What Our Guests Say:. With the text in place, you will move the objects on the slide for better balance.

m. Drag **Leslie's photograph** below Susan's. Select **Leslie** and **Susan's photographs**. Click the **Picture Tools Format tab**, click **Align**, and then click **Align Selected Objects**. Click **Align** again, and then click **Align Center**. If necessary, drag the photographs down so they are below the title placeholder. Click the **testimonials text box**. Drag the **top-center sizing handle** in the text box up to balance the text with the photographs. Drag the **right sizing handle** in the text box to the edge of the photographs.

Creating a Custom Slide Show

A **custom slide show** is a subset of slides in a larger presentation. Perhaps you do not need all of the slides in a presentation because your audience has different characteristics or needs. Using the Custom Slide Show feature, you can select just the slides you want to display. Another advantage of creating custom slide shows is that you can display the slides in a different order than in the original slide show.

Customizing a Slide Show

All of the slides that you will need in a custom slide show must be in the same slide presentation. You cannot select slides from different presentations. Because you want to use slides from both the photo album and the Introduction to the Spa presentation, you will save the spa presentation with a new name, and reuse the slides from the photo album.

Once the slides are combined into the same presentation, you will build the custom show. Only certain slides will be selected. You will also modify some parts of the new spa presentation so it functions more efficiently.

To Create Custom Slide Shows

a. Click **Lastname_Firstname_p02_ws03_Spa_Info** on the taskbar. Click the **File tab**, and then click **Save As**. Type Lastname_Firstname_p02_ws03_Spa_Custom in the File name box, and then click **Save**.

b. Click **Slide 12**. Click the **Home tab**, click the **New Slide arrow**, and then click **Reuse Slides**. Click **Browse** in the Reuse Slides pane, and then click **Browse File**. Navigate to where you saved **Lastname_Firstname_p02_ws03_Spa_Album**, and double-click the **file name**.

c. Click the **Keep source formatting check box** at the bottom of the Reuse Slides pane to select this option. Click each of the **last three slides** in the Reuse Slides pane to add them to the presentation. **Close** ❎ the Reuse Slides pane.

d. Click the **Slide Show tab**, click **Custom Slide Show** in the Start Slide Show group, and then click **Custom Shows**. Click **New** in the Custom Shows dialog box. Type Bridal Presentation in the Slide show name box.

e. Click **1. Slide 1** in the Slides in presentation box, press and hold ⎙Shift⎙, and then click **7. Visit with the Therapist**. Click **Add**. Click **(11) Manicure and Pedicures**, press and hold ⎙Shift⎙, and then click **16. Reservations**. Click **Add**, click **OK**, and then click **Close**.

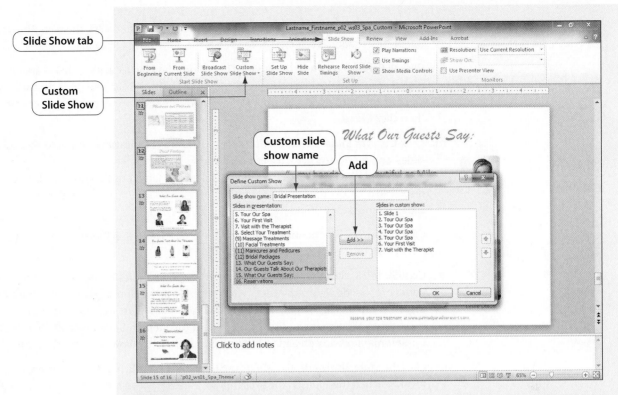

Slide Show tab

Custom Slide Show

Figure 14 Creating a custom slide show

f. **Save** 🖫 the presentation. You have created the presentation, and you will now display it as a custom slide show.

g. Click the **Custom Slide Show arrow** on the Slide Show tab, and then click **Bridal Presentation**. Navigate through the presentation, noting that the slide with the prices for the bridal packages does not show and that there are no transitions on the slides that were reused from the photo album.

Because you created a new presentation for the custom Bridal Presentation show, you can make changes to the slides. You will add transitions to Slides 13, 14, and 15. You will also unhide Slide 12.

h. Click **Slide 13** on the Slides tab, press and hold [Shift], and then click **Slide 15** to select the three slides. Click the **Transitions tab**, click **Rotate** in the Transition to This Slide group, click **Effect Options**, and then click **From Left**.

Troubleshooting

If you do not see Rotate in the Transition to This Slide group, click More, and then click Rotate in the Dynamic Content group.

i. Right-click **Slide 12** on the Slides tab, and then click **Hide Slide**. This reverses the hiding of the slide so it will be viewable in the regular progression of the slides.

j. Click the **Slide Show tab**, and then click **Custom Slide Show**. Click **Bridal Presentation**, and then review each slide. Press [Esc] to return to Normal view.

Did you notice the Previous button on the Bridal Packages slide? If you clicked it, it returns to the Visit with the Therapist slide. You decide to move a slide in the custom slide show to improve the flow of information.

Creating Useful Photo Albums   811

k. Click **Custom Slide Show** on the Slide Show tab, and then click **Custom Shows**. The Bridal Presentation is selected because it is the only show. Click **Edit**.

l. Click **9. Bridal Packages** in the Slides in custom show box. Click the **down arrow** in the dialog box, multiple times, to move the slide into position 12. The Bridal Packages slide will be displayed right before the slide with information on reservations. Click **OK**, and then click **Close**.

m. Click **Custom Slide Show**, and then click **Bridal Presentation**. Navigate through the slides, and then press Esc to return to Normal view.

    Although the Bridal Packages slide is still in the same position on the Slides tab, it is displayed after the testimonial slides in the custom slide show. You notice that the new slides are missing the footer.

n. Click **Slide 13**, click the **Insert tab**, and then click **Header & Footer** in the Text group. Click **Footer** to select it. Click **Apply to All**.

o. Click **Slide 13**, click the **footer**, and drag the sizing handles to the right and to the left edges of the slide. Select the **text** in the footer. Click the **Home tab**, click the **Font Color arrow**, and then click **Aqua, Accent 5, Darker 25%**. Adjust the placement of the photographs to allow room for the footer. Repeat this step on **Slides 14** and **15**. Adjust the **testimonial text box** on Slide 14 upwards as needed to allow room for the footer.

p. Click the **Slide Show tab**, click **Custom Slide Show**, click **Bridal Presentation**, and then review each of the slides in the presentation. Press Esc to return to Normal view. Click the **Slide Show tab** again, click **From Beginning**, review each of the slides in the presentation, and then press Esc to return to Normal view.

    Did you notice that the Bridal Packages slide appears in the normal progression of the slides? This is because you removed the Hide feature from the slide. After reviewing the presentation, you decide to create another custom slide show to focus on the facilities and staff. This slide show will not contain the hyperlink slide or the slides with the prices.

q. Click the **Slide Show tab** if necessary, click **Custom Slide Show**, and then click **Custom Shows**. Click **New**, and then type Facilities-Staff Presentation in the **Slide show name** box. Click **1. Slide 1** in the Slides in presentation box, press Shift, and then click **7. Visit with the Therapist**. Click **Add**, click **13. What Our Guests Say:**, press Shift, and then click **16. Reservations**. Click **Add**, click **OK**, and then click **Close**.

r. Click **Custom Slide Show**, and then click **Facilities-Staff Presentation**. Click through each slide, and then press Esc to return to Normal view.

    You decide to create one more custom slide show, this time just focusing on the facilities.

s. Click **Custom Slide Show**, and then click **Custom Shows**. Click **New**, and then type Spa Facilities. Select **1. Slide 1** through **5. Tour Our Spa**, and then click **Add**. Select **16. Reservations**, click **Add**, click **OK**, and then click **Close**.

t. Click **Custom Slide Show**, and then click **Spa Facilities**. Review each slide, press Esc to return to Normal view, and then save the presentation and close it. PowerPoint should continue running for the next exercises.

    Now, with a single presentation, you have three customized presentations to share with different audiences. The presentation can be used with guests who are new to the spa. Meda can also use the presentation when she wants to introduce people to the spa but not discuss the cost of the treatments. The Spa Facilities custom show can be used for guests who have visited a spa before but who have not been to the Turquoise Oasis Spa and Salon.

Saving and Sending a Presentation

PowerPoint can save your presentation files in a variety of formats and expedite sending them via e-mail to other people. The file can be sent as a PowerPoint attachment, a PDF file attachment, an XPS file attachment, or a fax. You can save your presentation to the web using a Windows Live account or to a SharePoint server to which you have access, so audience members can view it with a web browser. You can also set up the presentation to be broadcast to remote viewers by sending them a link so they can view the slides on the web in real time as you display them. This method requires a Windows Live account. Slides can be stored in a slide library or SharePoint site so other people can access and update the presentation.

Using the Save & Send tab on the File tab, you can also save the presentation in different types of file formats. You can save the presentation in PowerPoint Presentation format, or save it in PowerPoint 97–2003 format. You can save it as an OpenDocument Presentation, which provides an XML-based file format that can be accessed by other software. The presentation can be saved in PDF or XPS format. These file formats retain the fonts, formatting, and images exactly as you created them in PowerPoint, and the content cannot be easily changed. You can create a video with automatic timings to advance the slides, which can then be burned to a DVD or uploaded to the web. You will have a choice of display sizes as you create the video. The display sizes will affect the size of the file. You can package the presentation for distribution on CD, which includes a player so the viewer can watch the presentation whether they have PowerPoint on their computer or not.

Using the Create Handouts option on the Save & Send tab, you can create Word documents with the slides and notes. This enables you to make modifications in layout and format to the handouts. You can also add additional content to the handouts. When you use this option to create the handouts, changes you made to the slide presentation will automatically update the handout.

Saving and Sending a Presentation via E-mail

You have a number of options to select from when you use the Send Using E-mail option on the Save & Send tab. You can attach the PowerPoint file in its native format (.pptx) to an e-mail message. You can e-mail a link to a shared location on a server so others can view it and make modifications. The file can be saved in PDF format and attached to an e-mail message. You can do the same for an XPS file. Both of these formats "lock in" the presentation, making it difficult to modify. The file can be sent as an Internet fax if you have a fax service provider.

You will save and send the Spa Introduction presentation in PDF format to yourself via e-mail so you can see the result. Keep in mind that the various formats create files of different sizes. Generally a PDF file is smaller than an XPS file. Both of these types are smaller than the PowerPoint format of .pptx. Consider the content of the presentation as you select the file type. PDF and XPS files do not enable internal hyperlinks to other slides, play audio or video, or display slide transitions or animations. If these things are necessary for your presentation, you need to send the file in PowerPoint format.

To Send the Presentation as PDF

a. Click the **File tab**, and then click **Open**. Navigate to the location where you store your completed PowerPoint files, and then double-click **Lastname_Firstname_p02_ws03_Spa_Info**.

b. Click the **File tab**, and then click **Save & Send**. Send Using E-mail is selected by default. Click **Send as PDF**. After a short wait the Outlook e-mail window opens.

Troubleshooting

PowerPoint will try to open your Outlook e-mail account when you use Save & Send. If your account is not set up, you may not be able to complete this step. Ask your instructor for additional information.

c. Type your e-mail address in the To box. Type your instructor's e-mail address in the Cc box. Select the **Subject** text, which is the file name, and then type Enjoy this introduction to the Spa from Firstname Lastname, placing your name in the subject line. Click in the **Message** box, and then type I am sending you this file in PDF format. It is a smaller file, but you won't be able to hear the audio or see animations. Press [Enter], and then type Enjoy! Press [Enter] again, and then type your first and last name.

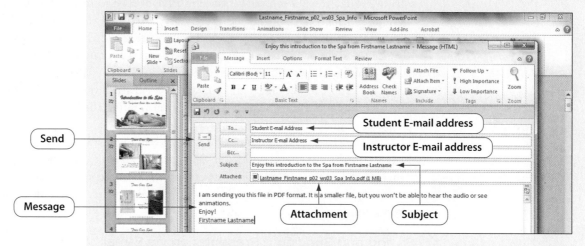

Figure 15 Sending a presentation as a PDF

d. Click **Send**. Click **Start**, and then open **Outlook**. If a message is shown in the Outbox, click **Send/Receive**. Wait a short period of time, and then click **Send/Receive** again. Remember that e-mail is not instant mail, and depending on your network connection, the message may take some time to come to your e-mail box. When the message arrives, click on it, and then click the **attachment link**. Adobe Reader opens, and the presentation is displayed in PDF format.

e. Click the **arrow** to advance the slides. Notice the speaker icon replaces audio. There are no transitions. Click a **hyperlink** on the Select Your Treatment slide. It will not link to the hidden slides because those slides were not saved as part of the PDF file. Click the **e-mail hyperlink** for Meda and an e-mail message window opens. Close the window without sending a message to Meda.

f. **Close** ☒ Outlook, and then close the Adobe Reader window.

Saving a PowerPoint Presentation as a Video

PowerPoint videos display the slides with all of the features that you build into the slide. The animations, transitions, audio, and video work as they do in the normal Slide Show view. Be aware that hidden slides are not part of the video and that hyperlinks do not work. Once you have created the video, it can be distributed via DVD, the Internet, or e-mail.

Saving a presentation as a video provides an opportunity to create the presentation in three different formats and with different overall file sizes. You can create the video for computers and high-definition (HD) displays, such as you might find in the resort waiting areas. Video for computers and high-definition monitors is displayed at 960 × 720 pixels and requires the most storage space. For the Internet or DVD video, the file is displayed at 640 × 480 pixels, which is a commonly used size for a web page. The file is stored as a Windows Media Video (WMV) and can be played using Windows Media Player. The smallest format is 320 × 240 pixels, for display on portable devices, such as the Microsoft Zune. In the smallest format, it may be difficult to read the text on the screen, so plan accordingly and bump up the size of the font in the presentation.

CONSIDER THIS | Mobile Devices

The Send & Save page specifically names the Microsoft Zune portable device. Are there other mobile devices or phones that might be compatible? Why is the Microsoft Zune the only one mentioned? How popular is the Microsoft Zune?

You will create a video in the Internet & DVD size. Because the slides were not set up to automatically advance, you will use the timings provided on the Create a Video pane to advance the slides.

To Save a PowerPoint Video

a. Click the **File tab**, click **Save & Send**, and then click **Create a Video**.

b. Click the **Computer & HD Displays arrow**, and then click **Internet & DVD**.

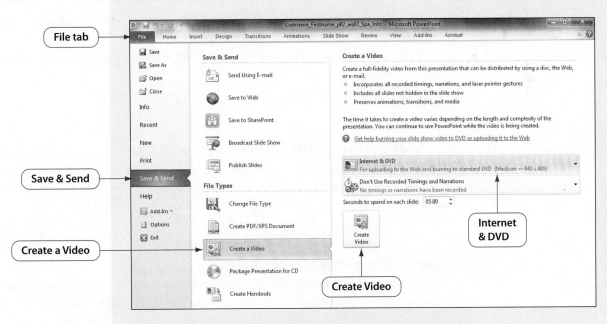

Figure 16 Creating a video of a presentation

c. Click **Create Video**. The Save As dialog box will open. Type Lastname_Firstname_p02_ ws03_Spa_Video in the File name box, and then click **Save**.

The video will be processed and stored in the location where you save your project files. This process can take quite a bit of time. Notice the status bar at the bottom of the window reports that it is creating a video. Wait until it is finished before proceeding to the next step.

d. Click **Start**, and then click **Computer**. Navigate to the storage location for your project files, and then double-click the **file** you just saved to open and play it.

The slides advance automatically after five seconds of display. If media elements are on the slide, such as the music on the first slide, those elements will completely play before the five-second counter begins. If you have slides with a lot of text, you may have to increase the time the slides are displayed before creating the video so people can read the whole slide before it advances.

Troubleshooting

If the Windows Media Player dialog box appears, click the Recommended Settings check box so that the video will play.

e. Close the **Windows Media Player** and the **Computer** window with the file listing to return to the Lastname_Firstname_p02_ws03_Spa_Info presentation.

The video of the nine slides in the presentation requires almost 8.5 MB of storage space. This file would be difficult to e-mail to some audience members who have limits on their e-mail Inbox storage space.

Real World Advice Video Considerations

As you consider the size limitations that some people have on their e-mail Inbox, you may turn to YouTube as an alternative storage location for the video. You could then provide a link to the YouTube video in the e-mail message that you send to your intended audience.

CONSIDER THIS | YouTube Privacy

If you use YouTube as a storage location for presentation video, privacy can become a concern. In what circumstances would YouTube be an appropriate storage location? What type of a presentation video should not be placed on YouTube?

Packaging a Presentation for CD

When you create a CD presentation, you put together a player and the presentation. This means that someone who does not have PowerPoint can still play your presentation on his or her computer. If you are giving a presentation where you are not sure of the equipment you will have available, you should burn a package presentation on CD so you will have a backup plan. CD presentations contain all of the slides, transitions, animations, media elements, and hyperlinks that are in the original presentation.

You will create a new directory on your storage location for the CD package presentation. You will package the presentation for CD. This folder would be placed on a CD that you could distribute to your potential clients. When they put the CD in their computer, it would automatically begin playing the presentation.

To Create a CD Presentation

a. Click the **File tab**, click **Save & Send**, and then click **Package Presentation for CD**.

b. Click **Package for CD**. The Package for CD dialog box opens.

c. Type Spa Presentation in the Name the CD box on the Package for CD dialog box, and then click **Copy to Folder**.

d. Type Lastname_Firstname_p02_ws03_Spa_Presentation_CD_Folder in the Folder name box on the Copy to Folder dialog box. Click **Browse**, navigate to the location where you are saving your projects, and then click **Select** when you are in the correct location. Click **OK** on the Copy to Folder dialog box. When asked if you want to include linked files in your package, click **Yes**. An additional message indicating that comments, revisions, and ink annotations will not be included in the package may appear and disappear. If necessary, click **Continue** if you see the message and it does not disappear automatically.

The folder opens with three files: the PowerPoint presentation, an AUTORUN application, and a PresentationPackage folder. You would copy the entire folder you created to a CD so all of the necessary elements are available.

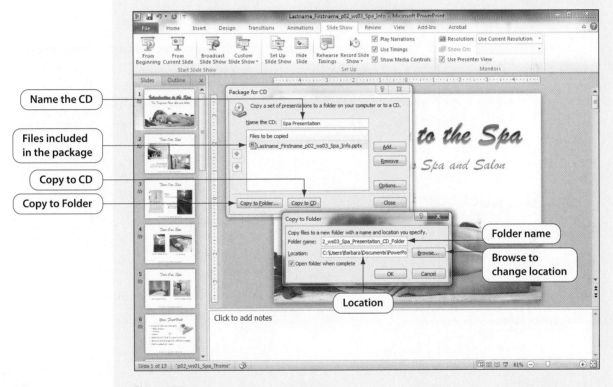

Figure 17 Creating a CD presentation

e. Close the folder window, and then click **Close** on the Package for CD dialog box.

Creating Handouts in Word Format

PowerPoint creates handouts by showing the slides in full-slide format or thumbnail format. There are times when you might want to have the handouts in Word format so you can manipulate them using Word. For instance, you may want to add additional content to the handouts or change the layout. You could also use this document as a beginning point for creating training materials, with details of procedures, for the audience to take with them after viewing a presentation.

You will create a Word document that contains thumbnails of the slides and the notes. You will add your name and today's date to the first page of the document. Do not print the document unless directed by your instructor.

To Create Handouts

a. Click the **File tab**, and then click **Save & Send**. Click **Create Handouts** under File Types, and then click **Create Handouts**.

The Send to Microsoft Word dialog box shows five options. You can place notes or blank lines next to the slides or below them. You can also send only the outline to Word. In this dialog box, you have the option to paste the slides into the Word document or to use the Paste Link option, which creates linked slides in the Word document that are updated if the original slides in PowerPoint are altered at a later time.

b. Click **Notes next to slides**, and then click **OK**. It takes a bit of time to render all of the slides in the document.

A new Word document will open on your desktop. You may have to click the application on the taskbar to view the file. It will take a little time for the document to completely render. The first several slides do not have notes. Notice that the hidden slides are also shown in the Word document.

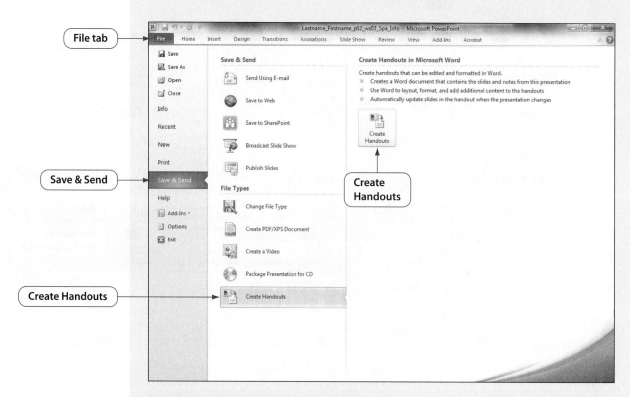

Figure 18   Creating Word handouts

c. Scroll down the document until you see **Slide 6**. Notes were on that slide as well as Slide 7. Scroll back to the top of the document. Click in front of **Slide 1** and type your first and last name and today's date. Press Enter.

d. Click the **File tab** (in the Word window), and then click **Save As**. Navigate to the location where you save your project files, and then type Lastname_Firstname_p02_ws03_Spa_Word for the File name. Click **Save**, exit Word, and then exit PowerPoint.

Concept Check

1. Your supervisor, Larry Houck, has asked you to add some pizzazz to a quarterly report presentation that he created. His intended audience for the presentation includes his boss and the upper management of the company. What types of transitions or animations might you use to engage this audience? Discuss your reasons.

2. As a volunteer at a local animal shelter, you have decided to photograph all of the animals that are up for adoption and create a presentation to persuade people to support the shelter by adopting or making donations. Describe how you would use the Photo Album feature of PowerPoint to create the presentation. How would you distribute the presentation to people who might adopt or make a donation?

3. Continuing with your work on the animal shelter presentation, you decide you want to add some audio to the presentation. What kinds of sounds would you use? How would this audio improve the delivery of your message? Would this change your distribution plans? If so, how?

4. Larry, your supervisor, asked you to create a presentation comparing three laptop computers that the department is considering purchasing. You have decided to add hyperlinks to the websites of the three companies on which you have focused your research. What are some key points to keep in mind for using these hyperlinks? What kind of internal hyperlinks (to slides within the presentation) might you use?

5. Knowing that video can really engage an audience, you have decided to use a YouTube video in your presentation on skateboarding that you will give to students at the local junior high. What are some considerations you must make when adding YouTube video to your presentation?

Key Terms

Action Buttons 794
Animation 786
Caption 807
Custom slide show 810
Delay 789

Duration 789
Effect option 788
Emphasis action 789
Entrance animation 789
Exit animation 789

Hyperlink 791
Kiosk 786
Photo album 804
Transition 786
Trigger 796

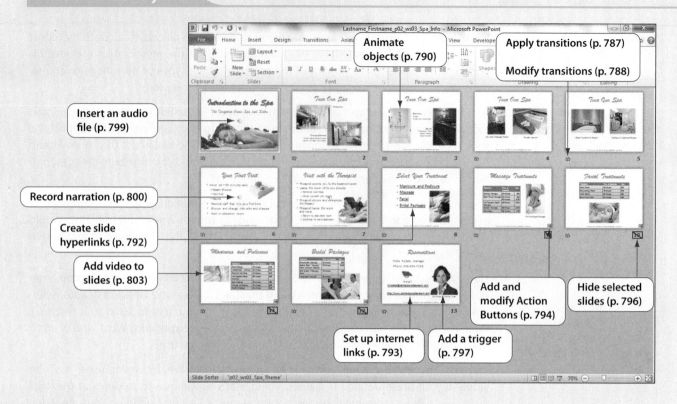

Insert an audio file (p. 799)

Record narration (p. 800)

Create slide hyperlinks (p. 792)

Add video to slides (p. 803)

Animate objects (p. 790)

Apply transitions (p. 787)

Modify transitions (p. 788)

Add and modify Action Buttons (p. 794)

Hide selected slides (p. 796)

Set up internet links (p. 793)

Add a trigger (p. 797)

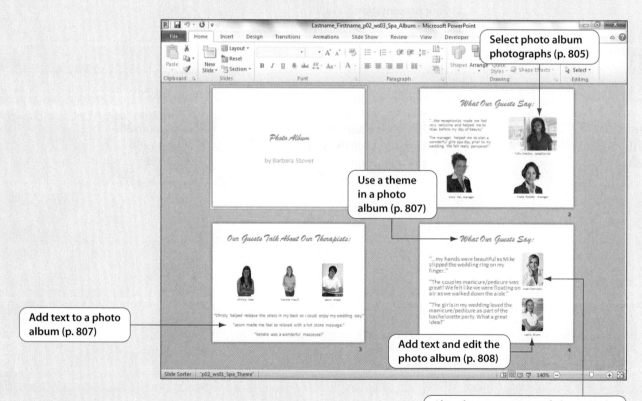

Select photo album photographs (p. 805)

Use a theme in a photo album (p. 807)

Add text to a photo album (p. 807)

Add text and edit the photo album (p. 808)

Alter the arrangement of photographs in the photo album (p. 806)

Modify the photographs with the Photo Album tools (p. 806)

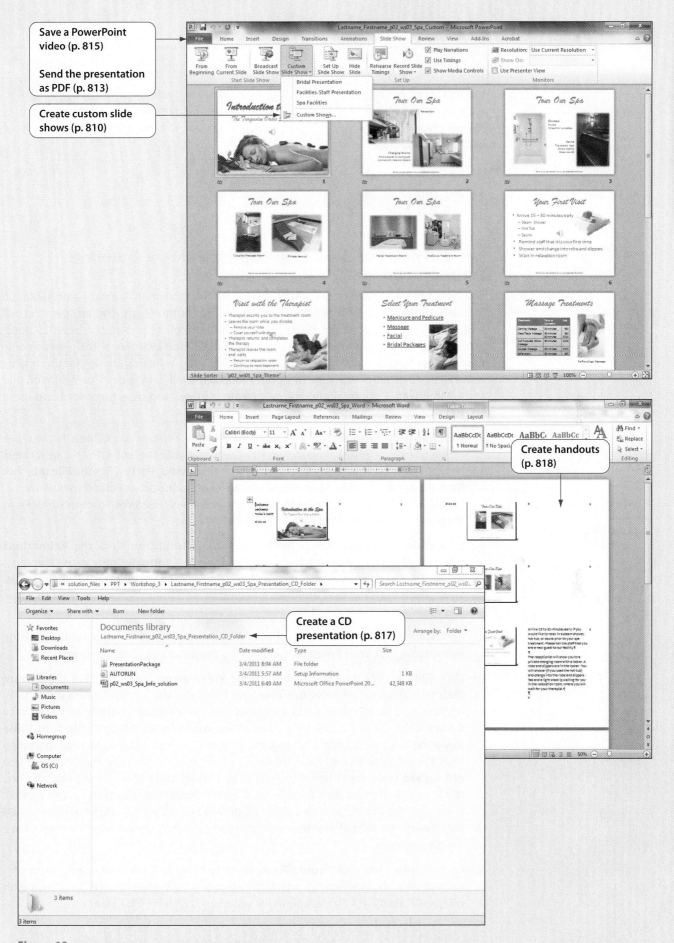

Save a PowerPoint video (p. 815)

Send the presentation as PDF (p. 813)

Create custom slide shows (p. 810)

Create handouts (p. 818)

Create a CD presentation (p. 817)

Figure 19 The Turquoise Oasis Spa and Salon Final Presentations

Student data files needed:

p02_ws03_Party

p02_ws03_Party_P1

p02_ws03_Party_P2

p02_ws03_Party_P3

p02_ws03_Party_P4

p02_ws03_Party_P5

p02_ws03_Party_P6

p02_ws03_Party_Theme

You will save your files as:

Lastname_Firstname_p02_ws03_Party

Lastname_Firstname_p02_ws03_Party_Album

Lastname_Firstname_p02_ws03_Party_Document

The Painted Paradise Golf Resort and Spa Catering Presentation

Sales & Marketing

You have been asked by Patti Rochelle, the resort event planner, to create a presentation focusing on the catering options available for parties at the resort. The presentation will emphasize the professionalism of the staff, the efficiency of the service, the beautiful decorations, the facilities and furnishings, and the excellent food available at the resort. People who are planning a wedding reception, bridal luncheon, rehearsal dinner, family or class reunion, or other party will view this presentation. You will take a basic presentation and embellish it with a photo album you will create. You will add slide transitions and use a YouTube video.

a. Start **Microsoft PowerPoint 2010**. Click the **File tab**, and then click **Open**. In the Open dialog box, click the disk drive in the left pane where your student data files are located. Navigate through the folder structure and click **p02_ws03_Party**. Click the **File tab**, click **Save As**, and then navigate to where you are saving your project files. Type Lastname_ Firstname_p02_ws03_Party as the file name, and then click **Save**. Review the slides in the presentation by clicking each slide on the Slides tab.

b. Click **Slide 2**, and then select the text **Wedding Reception**. Click the **Animations tab**, click **More** in the Animation group, and then click **Brush Color** in the Emphasis group. Click the **Start arrow** in the Timing group, and then click **After Previous**. Select **each bulleted text element** individually, and then apply the same animation and timing.

c. Click **Slide 3**, select the **table**, and then click **Float In** in the Animation group. Click the **Start arrow**, click **With Previous**, type 3 in the **Duration** box, and then press Enter.

d. Click **Slide 4**. Click the **Insert tab**, click the **Video arrow**, and then click **Video from Web Site**. Open an **Internet browser**, and then type www.youtube.com in the URL/ Address box. In the search box type wedding reception table sizes, and then click **Search**. Click the link to the video titled **Decorating for Wedding Receptions Table Sizes**; the video is 2:23 minutes long. If that video is not on the list, select another video from the list. Click **Share** below the video player, click Embed, and then click the **Use old embed code** check box. Right-click the **embed code** (the box with highlighted HTML code in it), and then click **Copy**. Click the **PowerPoint button** on the taskbar. Right-click the **box** in the Insert Video From Web Site dialog box, click **Paste**, and then click **Insert**. You will not see the video until you view the slide in Slide Show view. **Save** the presentation.

e. Click the **Insert tab**, click **Photo Album**, and then click **File/Disk**. Navigate to where your student data files are located, and then select all of the photographs beginning with **p02_ws03_Party_P1**. The last file in the group ends with P6. Click **Insert**.

f. Click **p02_ws03_Party_P6** in the Pictures in album list, and then move it to **position 3**. Move **p02_ws03_Party_P3** to **position 6**. Click the **Picture layout arrow**, and then click **2 pictures with title**. Click the **Frame shape arrow**, and then click **Center Shadow Rectangle**. Click **Captions below ALL pictures**. Click **Browse**, locate the student data files, and then click **p02_ws03_Party_Theme**. Click **Select**, click **Create**, and then save the photo album as Lastname_Firstname_p02_ws03_Party_Album.

g. Select both **photographs** on Slide 2 of the photo album. Press → seven times to balance the photographs in the white space of the slide.

h. Click **Slide 3**. Drag the photograph of the **woman server** up to align with the top of the other photograph. Drag the **photographs** to balance within the white space on the slide. Click the **Insert tab**, click **Text Box**, and then click below the woman server photograph. Type Our friendly servers will keep your party flowing smoothly, whether you choose table, cocktail, or buffet service. Drag the **middle-right sizing handle** to move the text box to the left so the text fits below the woman server photograph.

i. Click **Slide 4**. Drag the **wedding cake photograph** onto the white space. Drag the **buffet food photograph** down to align with the bottom of the wedding cake photograph. Click the **Insert tab**, click **Text Box**, and then click above the buffet food photograph. Type From a luscious buffet of beautifully arranged appetizers, to the wedding cake of your dreams, our chefs strive to produce the highest-quality foods. Drag the **text box** to resize and align it with the top of the wedding cake photograph.

j. Save and close the photo album. Click the **Party presentation** on the taskbar, if necessary, to view the window.

k. Click **Slide 4**. On the **Home tab**, click the **New Slide arrow**, and then click **Reuse Slides**. Click **Browse** in the Reuse Slides pane, and then click **Browse File**. Navigate to the location where you store your project files, and then click **Lastname_Firstname_ p02_ws03_Party_Album**. Click **Open**, click **Slides 2**, 3, and **4**, and then close the Reuse Slides pane.

l. Click **Slide 5**, and then click the title placeholder. Type Select Linens. Select the caption placeholder for the photograph p02_ws03_Party_P1, and then type Striped Linens on White. Select the caption placeholder for the photograph p02_ws03_Party_P2, and then type White Linens on Dark Mocha.

m. Click **Slide 6**, and then click the title placeholder. Type Select the Type of Service. Select the p02_ws03_Party_P6 caption placeholder, and type Table Service with 1 Server for 2 Tables. Select the p02_ws03_Party_P4 caption placeholder, and type Cocktail/ Appetizer Service.

n. Click **Slide 7**, and then click the title placeholder. Type Select the Menu. Click the p02_ ws03_Party_P5 caption placeholder, and then type Cakes Made to Order. Click the p02_ ws03_Party_P3 caption placeholder, and then type Luncheon Buffet.

o. Click **Slide 8**. Click after **Web:,** type a space, click the **Insert tab**, and then click **Hyperlink**. Under **Link to**, click **Existing File or Web Page**, type www.paintedparadiseresort.com in the Address box, and then click **OK**. Click after **E-mail:,** type a space, and then click **Hyperlink**. Click **E-mail Address**, and then type prochelle@paintedparadiseresort .com in the Text to display and E-mail address boxes. Type Party Planning Request in the Subject box, and then click **OK**.

p. Click the **Slide Show tab**, click the **Custom Slide Show arrow**, click **Custom Shows**, and then click **New**. Type Short Party Presentation in the Slide show name box. Click **Slide 1**, press Ctrl , and then click **Slide 2** and **Slide 8**. Click **Add**, click **OK**, and then click **Show**. Review the slides. Press Esc to return to Normal view.

q. Save the presentation. Click the **Slide Show tab**, and then click **From Beginning**. Review each of the slides, proofreading carefully.

r. Click the **File tab**, and then click **Save & Send**. Click **Send Using E-mail**, and then click **Send as Attachment**. Type your e-mail address in the To box. Type your instructor's e-mail address in the Cc box. Select the **Subject** text, and then type Planning a Party. In the message box, type This presentation introduces you to planning a party. The Painted Paradise Golf Resort and Spa has solutions for your party planning needs. Press Enter twice, type your first and last name, and then click **Send**. Open **Outlook**, and then click **Send/Receive** if necessary. Wait a few moments and retrieve your e-mail. Double-click the **attachment** to open the presentation.

s. If necessary, click Enable Editing. Click the **File tab**, click **Save & Send**, and then click **Create Handouts**. Click **Create Handouts**, click **Blank lines below slides**, and then click **OK**. Click the **Word** document on the taskbar, and then review the pages. Click before the words **Slide 1**, and then type your first and last name and the current date. Press Enter, save the document as Lastname_Firstname_p02_ws03_Party_Document in your project storage location, and then close the document.

t. Close the presentation and exit PowerPoint.

Problem Solve 1

Student Data Files Needed:

p02_ps1_Activities
p02_ps1_Activities_Music
p02_ps1_Activities_Thomas

You will save your files as:

Lastname_Firstname_p02_ps1_Activities
Lastname_Firstname_p02_ps1_Activities_Video

Resort Activities Presentation

Customer
Service

Many guests come to the Painted Paradise Golf Resort and Spa to take advantage of the world class golf course and to relax around the pool. Lately, a number of guests have inquired about other activities such as tours and classes. Thomas Vance has been appointed Activities Coordinator. He asked you to help create a presentation that can be used to inform guests of activities available during their stay. You will begin with a file created by Thomas, and then add transitions, sounds, and narration. The file will be saved as a video which will be played on screens in numerous locations around the resort and will be available on TVs in rooms. You will also create an e-mail message with the file attached as a PDF file.

a. Start **Microsoft PowerPoint 2010**. Click the **File tab**, and then click **Open**. In the Open dialog box, click the disk drive in the left pane where your student data files are located. Navigate through the folder structure, click **p02_ps1_Activities**, and then click **Open**. Click the **File tab**, click **Save As**, and then navigate to where you are saving your project files. Type Lastname_Firstname_p02_ps1_Activities as the file name, and then click **Save**. Review the slides in the presentation by clicking each slide on the Slides tab.

b. Click **Slide 1**, and then click the **Insert tab**. Click the **Audio arrow**, and then click **Audio from File**. Navigate to the location of the student data files, click **p02_ps1_Activities_Music,** and click **Insert**. Click the **Audio Tools Playback tab**, click **Trim Audio**, and then type 1:00 in the **Start Time box**. Type 1:15 in the **End Time** box, and then click **OK**. Type 02.00 in the **Fade In** duration box and 02.00 in the **Fade Out** duration box. Click **Automatically** in the Start box in the Audio Options group. Click **Hide During Show** in the Audio Options group.

c. Select all **slides** on the Slides tab. Click the **Transitions tab**, and then click **More** in the Transition to This Slide group. Click **Conveyor** in the Dynamic Content group. Click the **Effect Options arrow**, and then click **From Left**. Type 1.25 in the **Duration box**.

d. Click **Slide 2**, and then drag the border between the Slide pane and the Notes pane so you can see all of the note text. Click the **Insert tab**, click the **Audio arrow**, and then click **Record Audio**. Type Introduction in the Name box, and then click **Record**. Read the information in the Notes pane. Click **Stop** when you have finished reading, and then click **OK** to save the narration on the slide. Click the **speaker** on the slide, if necessary, click the **Audio Tools Playback tab**, and then click **Automatically** in the Start box of the Audio Options group. Click **Hide During Show** in the Audio Options group. Drag the border of the Notes pane to return it to its original size.

e. Click **Slide 10**, place the insertion point after the phone number, press **Enter** and type E-mail: tvance@paintedparadiseresort.com Press **Enter** and type Web: www.paintedparadiseresort.com Select the e-mail hyperlink text, click the **Insert tab**, and then click **Hyperlink**. Type Tour and Class Information Request in the Subject box. Click **ScreenTip**, and then type E-mail Thomas for more information Click **OK** twice to close both dialog boxes. Select the Web hyperlink text, click **Hyperlink** on the **Insert tab**, and then click **Existing File or Web Page**. Click **ScreenTip**, type Visit our website for more information, and then click **OK**. Type www.paintedparadiseresort.com in the **Address box**, and then click **OK**.

f. Click **Picture** on the Insert tab, navigate to file location for the student data files, and then double-click **p02_ps1_Activities_Thomas**. Click the **Shape Height box** on the Picture Tools Format tab, type 2.4, and press **Enter**. Click **More** in the Picture Styles group, and then click **Reflected Rounded Rectangle**. Drag the picture below the website address. Click **Align** in the Arrange group, and then click **Distribute Horizontally**.

g. Click the **Animations tab**, and then click **More** in the Animation group. Click **Bounce**. Click **With Previous** in the Start box in the Timing group. Type 1.0 in the Duration box in the Timing group.

h. Click the **Slide Show tab**, and then click **From Beginning**. Review each slide. Test the hyperlinks on the final slide. Return to Normal view. Close the e-mail and browser windows that were displayed as you tested the hyperlinks. Save the presentation.

i. Click the **File tab**, click **Save & Send**, click **Send Using E-mail**, and then click **Send as PDF**. If a dialog box opens asking if you want a transcript of the recording, click No. Type your e-mail address into the **To** box of the e-mail window. Type your instructor's e-mail address into the **Cc** box. Select the **Subject** and type Resort Activities Presentation Click in the message area and type this message:

Hello,

I am attaching the Resort Activities Presentation to this message. These activities should be fun for the resort guests.

Your name (replace this with your first and last name)

Click **Send**. Some Outlook set-ups require you to open Outlook and then click Send/Receive. Do this if it is necessary. Wait a few moments and retrieve your e-mail. Review the attachment.

j. Click the **File tab**, click **Save & Send**, and then click **Create a Video**. Click the Computer & HD Displays arrow, and then click Internet & DVD. Click Create Video, type Lastname_Firstname_p02_ps1_Activities_Video in the File name box, and then click Save. Watch the status bar and wait until the video is rendered. This may take a few minutes. Navigate to the location where you save your project files, and then double-click on the **Lastname_Firstname_p02_ps1_Activities_Video** file to open and review it. Close the video window and the presentation. Submit your files as directed by your instructor.

 Additional Workshop Cases are available on the companion website and in the instructor resources.

WORKSHOP 4

Objectives

1. Create a custom template using the Slide Master   p. 828

2. Customize notes and handout masters   p. 836

3. Create a presentation based on a custom template   p. 841

4. Import an outline into a presentation   p. 842

5. Use slide sections to organize a presentation   p. 843

6. Use proofing tools   p. 844

7. Create and navigate comments in a presentation   p. 845

8. Create and use speaker notes   p. 847

9. Mark presentations as final and apply a password   p. 849

10. Develop skills in delivering presentations   p. 851

Customizing, Collaborating, and Presenting

PREPARE CASE

Creating a Corporate Identity Template

Finance & Accounting

The management of the Painted Paradise Golf Resort and Spa understand the importance of developing a corporate identity recognizable by employees and the public. You have been asked to create a professional PowerPoint template that will be used in the Turquoise Oasis Salon as the beginning point for slide shows. The specifications from management include developing a color theme, font theme, custom page layouts, and a copyright notice in the footer. The color scheme is to reflect the scenery of the resort. Many of the things you already know about developing slides will be used as you create the template. Once the template is finished, you will collaborate with the salon manager, Irene Kai, to create a quarterly report using the template. You will assist her in creating speaker notes, and develop a template for handouts. You will also work with Irene to prepare her for the actual presentation to the board of directors, giving her advice on overcoming presentation nervousness, being prepared, and engaging the audience.

Andreka / Shutterstock.com

Student data files needed for this workshop:

 p02_ws04_Salon_Outline

 p02_ws04_Salon_Comments

You will save your files as:

 Lastname_Firstname_p02_ws04_Salon_Template

 Lastname_Firstname_p02_ws04_Salon_Presentation

 Lastname_Firstname_p02_ws04_Salon_Update

 Lastname_Firstname_p02_ws04_Salon_Notes

 Lastname_Firstname_p02_ws04_Delivery

Creating a Corporate Identity with a Custom Template

Corporations throughout the world take pride in their **corporate identity**. Visual identities are carefully crafted to make products recognizable. Logos, color schemes, and fonts are used for years to ensure that customers identify with the product. Think about how you can recognize one soft drink can from another just by looking at the colors on the can. People visiting foreign countries are often surprised to recognize the golden arches of McDonald's.

Real World Advice — How Logos Change

Changing a corporate logo is always a risky and expensive proposition. Will the customers recognize the new logo as belonging to a product they know and trust? It is interesting to see how logos evolve over time. Perform an Internet search on the keywords "logos over time" to see how your favorite brands might have changed their logos.

Corporate identities are normally developed by the marketing group of a company. They conduct market research, costs analysis, and other studies to build the identity. They hire professional designers to produce pieces of the overall identity, such as the logo, with guidance from studies. They develop guidelines for the use of the corporate materials, often specifying the exact placement of the logo on a page, or the exact color numbers for the colors used in advertising. Each branch of the organization is expected to use the identity to create consistency and present a unified public view of the company.

CONSIDER THIS | Google Doodles

Google regularly changes its logo to honor people, holidays, or events. Look at www.google.com/logos for examples of logos. What do you think of this as a marketing tactic? Do you think that the audience is confused by it?

This workshop focuses on building a template for a presentation. The template can be reused so an identity emerges over time. It is also somewhat secure because most casual PowerPoint users do not know how to modify a template. In this section, you will modify a slide master, the handout master, and the notes master.

Modifying the Slide Master

Templates are based on the **slide master**. The slide master is a special template slide that details fonts, placement of footers, background colors, and other characteristics for the presentation. The slide master also contains layouts for the template. You can add new layouts, delete layouts, and modify the existing layouts. For instance, if you wanted the title of the slides to appear along the bottom of the slides, you would move the title placeholder to the location on the slide master.

The slide master tools are available on the View tab. While you are working on the slide master, all of the other PowerPoint tools are available. When you have completed your work with the slide master, it is very important that you close Slide Master view before you begin to populate your presentation with information. Otherwise, the information you add to the slides becomes a part of the template.

Modifying the Slide Master Theme

A theme adds color and font consistency to a normal presentation. By setting up the colors and fonts in Slide Master view, you customize the template. You can add background colors, textures, or pictures to all of the slide layouts or to individual slide layouts. It is easier to set up the background for all of the slides using the slide master, but keep in mind that anything you put on the slide master is locked in on the slide layouts and cannot be changed without changing the slide master. For instance, if you put a shape on the slide master, it will appear in the same location on every slide layout.

You will begin this project by opening the slide master and adding background colors to the slide master.

Workshop 4 Training

To Modify the Slide Master Theme

a. Start **PowerPoint**. Click the **File tab**, and then click **Save As**. Type Lastname_Firstname_p02_ws04_Salon_Template as the filename. Click **Save as type**, click **PowerPoint Template**, navigate to the location where you store your project files, and then click **Save**.

   PowerPoint will try to save the template in the Microsoft Templates folder on the computer. Be sure to change the storage location, so your template is located with your project files.

b. Click the **View tab**, and then click **Slide Master** in the Master Views group.

   The Slide Master tab appears with the slide master and the layout slides. You will begin by adding a background to the slide master.

Slide Master tab

View tab

Figure 1   Slide Master tab

SIDE NOTE
Using the Theme Slide Master
The default slide layout when Slide Master view opens is the Title Slide Layout. You can apply different elements to each of the layouts or apply them to the theme slide master. It is more efficient to make global changes on the theme slide master.

c. Click the **Office Theme Slide Master**, which is the first thumbnail in the left pane that appears larger than the other thumbnails. Click **Colors** in the Edit Theme group, and then click **Flow**.

   You are basing your color choices on the Flow color scheme, but you will modify some of the accent colors. These accents will suggest the colors in the landscape of New Mexico.

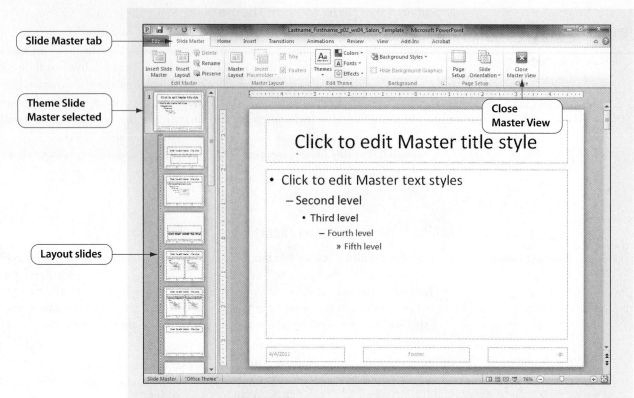

Slide Master tab

Theme Slide Master selected

Layout slides

Close Master View

Click to edit Master title style

• Click to edit Master text styles
  – Second level
    • Third level
      – Fourth level
        » Fifth level

Figure 2   Slide Master view

d. Click **Colors**, and then click **Create New Theme Colors**. Click the **Accent 1 arrow**, and then click **More Colors**. Type **198** for **Red**, **29** for **Green**, **16** for **Blue**, and then click **OK**.

e. Click **Accent 2**, and then click **More Colors**. Type **238** for **Red**, **192** for **Green**, **146** for **Blue**, and then click **OK**.

f. Click **Accent 5**, and then click **More Colors**. Type **253** for **Red**, **114** for **Green**, **9** for **Blue**, and then click **OK**.

   With the color scheme modified, you will now focus your attention on the font selection. Font groups can also be associated with corporate identities. You will select new theme fonts.

g. Type Lastname_Firstname_Salon_Colors in the Name box, and then click **Save**.

Figure 3 Edit theme colors

h. Click **Fonts** in the Edit Theme group, and then click **Create New Theme Fonts**. Click the **Heading font arrow**, and then scroll down and click **Tahoma**.

Troubleshooting

> If you do not have the Tahoma font, select another sans serif font, such as Arial or Calibri.

i. Click the **Body font arrow**, and then click **Century Gothic**. Type Lastname_Firstname_Salon_Fonts in the Name box, and then click **Save**.

   With the font selections made, you will turn your attention to the effects. The effects enable you to make selections that determine the format of graphic elements.

j. Click the **Effects arrow**, and then click **Executive**.

   Now you have set the theme properties. You will modify the master title text style to be shadowed.

k. Select the text **Click to edit Master title style**, click the **Home tab**, and then click **Text Shadow** [s] in the Font group.

   You have decided to apply some simple WordArt to the titles of the slides.

l. Select the title placeholder, if necessary. Click the **Drawing Tools Format tab**, click **More** in the WordArt Styles group, and then click **Gradient Fill – Red, Accent 1**, **Outline – White** in the fourth row, fourth column. Click the **Text Fill arrow** in the WordArt Styles group, and then click **Light Turquoise**, **Background 2**, **Darker 75%**.

   The title text on the slide master layouts is now finished. You will modify the background color of the slide master to a textured graphic.

m. Click the **Slide Master tab**, click **Background Styles** in the Background group, and then click **Format Background**. Click **Picture or texture fill**, and then click the **Texture arrow**. Click **Granite** in the third row, second column of the gallery. Click **Picture Color** in the left pane, and then click **Recolor Presets**. Click **Turquoise, Accent color 3 Dark** in the second row, fourth column, and then click **Close**.

You now realize the footers seem to have disappeared into the granite background. You will change the color of the footers to make them more evident. You notice the other text will also be hard to read, but you will solve this problem in a later step of this workshop.

n. Click the footer date placeholder at the bottom left of the slide, press Shift, and then click the footer and slide number placeholders. Click the **Home tab**, click the **Font Color arrow**, and then click **White, Background 1** at the top-left corner of the Theme Colors palette. Click **Bold** B in the Font group.

Customizing Slide Master Layouts

Eleven slide layouts are provided by default in Slide Master view. You can add additional layouts and delete ones that will not be needed. Each layout can be renamed. You will delete unnecessary layouts in the salon template.

The individual slide master layouts contain various placeholders. You can add, delete, and move placeholders in the slide master layouts. You can add graphic shapes, which you will do in this workshop, so you can read the text more easily. You can also add footers to each of the layouts or apply the same footer to all of the layouts. You will add a single footer to all of the slides.

You also realize that the black text will be hard to read on the background you have selected. You will create boxes to hold the text that coordinate with the background colors.

To Delete Slide Master Layouts

a. Scroll to the bottom of the slide master layouts in the left pane, click **Vertical Title and Text Layout**, click the **Slide Master tab**, and then click **Delete** in the Edit Master group. The slide layout is removed and the previous slide layout (Title and Vertical Text Layout) in the pane is selected. You will delete the Title and Vertical Text Layout next.

Troubleshooting

Point to the slide layout in the left pane to view the names of the layouts.

b. Press Delete. The Title and Vertical Text Layout slide layout is deleted. Continue deleting the following layouts:
   - **Picture with Caption Layout**
   - **Content with Caption Layout**
   - **Blank Layout**
   - **Title Only Layout**
   - **Comparison Layout**
   - **Section Header Layout**

   This leaves four slides in the left pane: the Office Theme Slide Master, Title Slide Layout, Title and Content Layout, and Two Content Layout.

When you are working with the footers in Slide Master view, you are setting up the formats for the footers, rather than setting up the actual text of the footer. The text will be placed in the footers when you create a new presentation based on the template and insert the footers.

To Modify Slide Master Layouts

a. Click the **Office Theme Slide Master** thumbnail. Click the **slide number footer** placeholder on the right side of the slide, and then press $\boxed{\text{Delete}}$ to delete the entire placeholder. Click each of the **layouts**, and then delete the slide number footer placeholder on the right side of the slide layouts.

b. Click the **Office Theme Slide Master** thumbnail. Click the **center footer**, click the **Drawing Tools Format tab**, and then type **5"** in the Shape Width box. Click **Align**, and then click **Align Right**. Click the **left footer**, type **4.5"** in the Shape Width box, click **Align**, and then click **Align Left**.

c. Click the **Title Slide Layout** in the left pane. Click the **Insert tab**, click **Shapes** in the Illustrations group, and then click the **Rounded Rectangle** in the Rectangles group. Drag a **large rectangle** on the Title Slide Layout. Click the **Drawing Tools Format tab**, click the **Send Backward arrow**, and then click **Send to Back**. Type **6"** in the Shape Height box and **9.5"** in the Shape Width box. Click **Align**, click **Align Center**, click **Align**, and then click **Align Middle**.

This is obviously not a color you want to use as a background color. It would be very difficult to read text placed on this red background.

d. Click the **Shape Fill arrow** in the Shape Styles group, and then click **Light Turquoise, Background 2** at the top of the Theme Colors gallery. Click the **Shape Effects arrow**, point to **Preset**, and then click **Preset 1** in the gallery.

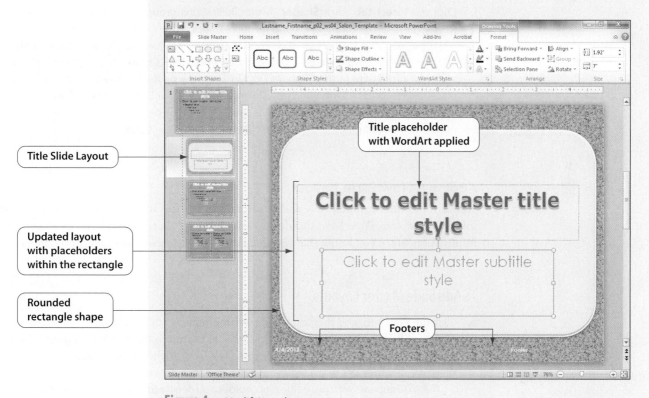

Figure 4   Modifying a layout

e. Click the **Title and Content Layout** in the left pane. Click the **Insert tab**, click **Shapes,** and then click the **Rounded Rectangle** in the Rectangles group. Drag from just outside of the top-left corner of the title placeholder to just outside of the bottom-right corner of the title placeholder to create the rounded rectangle shape.

f. Click the **Insert tab**, click **Shapes** in the Illustrations group, and then click the **Rounded Rectangle**. Drag from the top-left corner of the **body text** placeholder to the bottom-right corner of the placeholder.

   You will use the formatting created for the Title Slide Layout to change the colors on the Title and Content Layout. The Format Painter will enable you to do this easily. You will then send the rectangles to the back.

g. Click the **Title Slide Layout** in the left pane, and then click the **Rounded Rectangle**. Click the **Home tab**, double-click **Format Painter**, click the **Title and Content Layout** in the left pane, and then click the **Rounded Rectangles** to apply the formatting. Click **Format Painter** to return the pointer to normal.

h. Click the title rounded rectangle shape, click the **Drawing Tools Format tab**, click the **Send Backward arrow** in the Arrange group, and then click **Send to Back**. Click the body placeholder rectangular shape, click the **Send Backward arrow**, and then click **Send to Back**. You notice the first bullet in the body text is on the edge of the rectangle. Click the **left sizing handle** for the text placeholder (not the rounded rectangle), and then drag it slightly to the right so the bullet appears within the rounded rectangle. If necessary, drag the **top sizing handle** down so the body text is on the background shape.

i. Click the **Title and Content Layout**, click the edge of the **title** rounded rectangle to select it, right-click the rectangle, and then select **Copy**. Click the **Two Content Layout**, click the **title** placeholder, click the **Home tab**, and then click **Paste** in the Clipboard group. On the Drawing Tools Format tab, click the **Send Backward arrow**, and then click **Send to Back**.

j. Click the **Insert tab**, click **Shapes** in the Illustrations group, and then click **Rounded Rectangle**. Drag a **rectangle** around the left content placeholder. Click the **title** rounded rectangle, click the **Home tab**, click **Format Painter**, and then click the **left rectangle**. Click the **left rectangle shape** (not the placeholder), click **Copy** in the Clipboard group, and then click **Paste** in the Clipboard group. Drag the **pasted shape** to cover the right placeholder. Click the **Drawing Tools Format tab**, click the **Send Backward arrow**, and then click **Send to Back**. Send the rounded rectangle to the back on the other placeholder. Adjust the content placeholders so the bullets are within the shapes.

Adding a New Slide Layout

Just as slides can be added to regular slide shows, you can insert additional slide layouts into the template. You have decided to add a layout that will contain Irene's contact information, since you know that she always uses this type of slide in her presentations.

To Add Slide Master Layouts

a. Click the **View tab**, and then click **Slide Master** in the Master Views group, if necessary. Click the **Slide Master tab**, and then click **Insert Layout** in the Edit Master group. Click **Rename** in the Edit Master group, select the text in the Rename Layout dialog box, and then type Contact Information Layout. Click **Rename**.

   The slide appears with just a title placeholder. You decide to create a rounded rectangle like the one on the title slide to hold the contact information. You will copy the shape from the Title Slide Layout, and then add placeholders to the Contact Information Layout.

b. Click the **Title Slide Layout** in the left pane, right-click the **Rounded Rectangle shape**, and then click **Copy**. Click the **Contact Information Layout** in the left pane, right-click the **slide**, and then click **Use Destination Theme** under Paste Options. Click the **Drawing Tools Format tab**, click the **Send Backward arrow**, and then click **Send to Back**.

c. Drag the **title** placeholder to the top of the rectangle shape.

d. Click the **Slide Master tab**, click the **Insert Placeholder arrow** in the Master Layout group, and then click **Text**. Drag a **rectangle** under the title placeholder that fills the remaining portion of the slide.

Placing Text on the Slide

In some cases, the text that will appear on slides will be consistent between presentations. For instance, the template you have been working on will always be used by Irene Kai for presentations related to the salon. To save time, you can place and format text in the template that will always be displayed when the template is opened. It is important to note that this must be done with Slide Master view closed; otherwise, the text that you add will be placeholder text that will not be displayed on the slide.

You will add the name of the salon and the slogan to the title slide. You will make some minor adjustments to the fonts.

To Add Text to a Slide Layout

a. Click the **Slide Master tab**, click **Close Master View**, and then on the status bar, click **Normal** view ▣, if necessary.

b. Click the **title** placeholder text in the Slide pane, and then type Turquoise Oasis Salon. Select the **text** you just typed, and then click **Increase Font Size** A˙ one time.

c. Click the **subtitle** placeholder text, and then type A passion for helping people relax. Select the **text** you just typed, and then click **Decrease Font Size** A˙ one time.

d. Click the Home tab, click the **New Slide arrow**, and then click **Contact Information Layout**. Click the title text placeholder, and then type Irene Kai, salon manager in the title placeholder.

e. Click the **first bullet text**, type Appointments and then press Enter. Type Phone: 505-555-7329 and then press Enter. Type E-mail: appointments@paintedparadiseresort .com and then press Enter. Type Questions/Concerns and then press Enter. Type Phone: 505-555-7328 and then press Enter. Type E-mail: ikai@paintedparadiseresort.com. Select both occurrences of the **Phone** and **E-mail text**, four bulleted items in all. Click the **Home tab**, if necessary, and then click **Increase List Level** ▤ in the Paragraph group.

Troubleshooting

If the appointments e-mail address is not on a line by itself, click after the word E-mail and press Shift + Enter.

Saving a Template

When you have completed all of the modifications to the slide master, it is important to remember to close Slide Master view. If you forget to do this and save the file, other presentations that you create with this template will open in Slide Master view. It is also important to remember that when you set the file type to template, PowerPoint will try to save the template file in the **Templates folder**, which is the default storage location for templates on the computer. To transport the template between computers, you must change the file storage location after you have selected the template type in the Save As type box.

You closed Slide Master view in the previous steps of the workshop and are now ready to save the presentation. You will first check to see that all of the layouts are available on the template.

To Save the Template

a. Click the **Layout arrow** in the Slides group.

Notice that you have layouts for a Title Slide, Title and Content, Two Content, and Contact Information Layout. They may be shown in a different order.

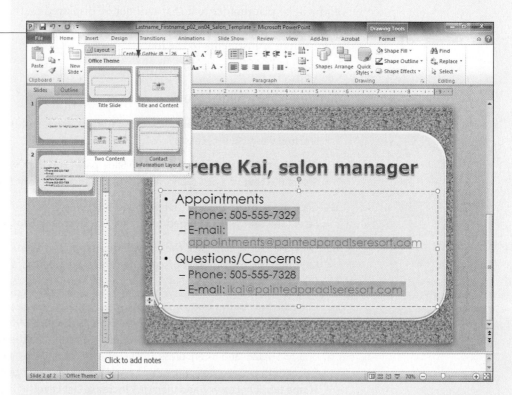

Figure 5 Finished layouts

b. Click the **File tab**, and then click **Save As**. Confirm that the Save As type is **PowerPoint Template**. Confirm that the storage location points to where you store your project files. Click **Save**, and then respond **Yes** if a Confirm Save As dialog box appears.

Customizing the Notes Page Master

Many corporations, businesses, and organizations have guidelines for materials that are printed. They may require things such as a copyright notice or privacy statement. Others will expect you to use a standard format for all documents. The speaker notes can be customized so certain things will appear on the printed document in the **notes master**. The notes master determines the layout of elements, such as the slide thumbnail and note placeholder, on the speaker notes pages.

By default, the notes printed from PowerPoint contain headers and footers. They include a space for a customized header, along with the current date at the top of the page, a space for a customized footer, and the page number at the bottom. The default items can be removed from the notes or modified in placement and text. A graphic of the slide appears above the notes in standard layout, but that can be modified as needed. The size of the text can be increased or decreased, and fonts can be edited on the notes pages.

Modifying the Headers and Footers

You modify the headers and footers through the View tab, using Notes Master view. Using Notes Master view, you have access to the other tabs within PowerPoint so you can modify fonts, for example.

You will modify the header and footer on the notes master to customize the areas for the Turquoise Oasis Salon. You will do this on the template, so the customization is available in each presentation that Irene creates using the template. Later you will apply the template to the presentation in order to update it.

To Customize the Notes Master Header and Footer

a. Click the **View tab**, and then click **Notes Master** in the Master Views group.

b. Click the **Header** box, type Turquoise Oasis Salon, and then press ⏎. Type Irene Kai, manager.

c. Click the **Footer** box, and then type Confidential, All Rights Reserved. Type a space, and then type the current year. Select the **footer text**, click the **Home tab**, and then change the font size to **14**.

d. Click in front of the **page number** on the right-bottom placeholder, and then type Slide. Leave a blank space between the word and the page number symbol. Select the **text** in the slide number footer, click the **Home tab**, and then change the font size to **28**.

This footer will print the number of the slide. The larger font will more easily enable Irene to keep track of where she is in the presentation.

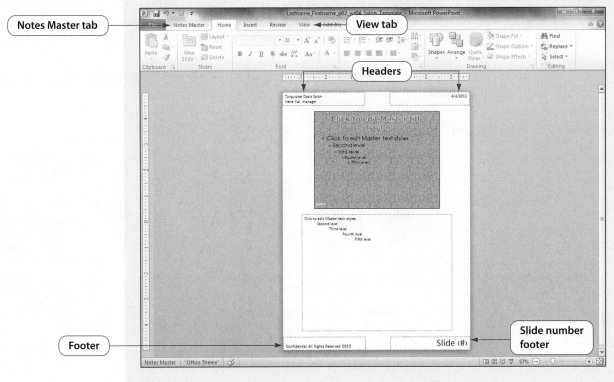

Figure 6   Notes master

Modifying Slide and Notes Placeholders

Many people do not realize that you can change the slide image and the notes placeholder of the notes page. If you make the image smaller, there is more room for notes. You can also change the font size in the notes placeholder, so the text is easier to read as a presenter. If you like your pages in landscape orientation, you can change the orientation on the notes master.

To Customize the Notes Master Layout and Notes Placeholders

a. Click the **slide image**, and then drag a **corner sizing handle** toward the center of the image. The image should be about a fourth of the page, in height. Drag the **slide image** to the left side of the page, under the Header text box.

b. Click the **border** of the notes placeholder, and drag the **center-top sizing handle** to just below the slide image. Drag the **left sizing handle** toward the left to increase the size of the notes area. Drag the **right sizing handle** toward the right to increase the size of the area and to balance the area on the page.

c. Select all of the text in the notes placeholder. Click the **Home tab**, if necessary, and then change the Font Size to **16**. Now it will be easier to read the text.

d. Click the **Insert tab**, click **Shapes**, and then click the **Line shape**. Press ⌈Shift⌉, and drag a **horizontal line** next to the slide image. Right-click the **line**, and then click **Copy**. Right-click again, and then under Paste Options, click **Use Destination Theme**. Paste the **line** three times so there are a total of five lines. Drag the **lines** onto the page, if necessary, and then roughly place them next to the slide image. Select all of the **lines**, click the **Drawing Tools Format tab**, click **Align**, and then click **Distribute Vertically**. Click **Align** again, and then click **Align Right**.

   These lines will be used for last minute notes that Irene might want to write on the printouts. She may want to note the name of the contact person for the presentation, or list pertinent information that she wants to work into the presentation. For instance, she may talk to someone in the audience prior to the presentation and want to include his or her name and a short story about that person.

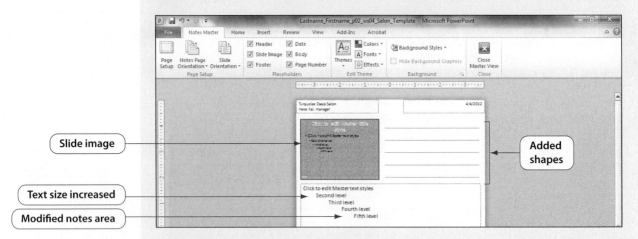

Figure 7   Modifying placeholders

e. Click the **Notes Master tab**, click **Close Master View**, and then save the template.

Customizing the Handout Master

Just as you can customize the notes master, you can make changes to the **handout master**, which determines the layout of elements, such as the header and footer, on the handout pages. In this case, the corporate office may be even more vigilant about changing the printouts as these are handed directly to audience members.

Handouts pages are good places to list contact and company information. You might also be required to place a copyright notice on the page. Using Handout Master view you can specify whether the handouts will be printed in portrait or landscape orientation. It is interesting to note that you cannot move or modify the slide placeholders in a handout master.

Modifying the Headers and Footers

You will add Irene's contact information to the header, and place a standard copyright notice on the handouts. You will also move the page number to the top of the slide and include the word "Page" next to it. You will remove the date placeholder.

To Customize the Handout Headers and Footers

a. Click the **View tab**, and then click **Handout Master** in the Master Views group.

b. Click the **Header**, type Irene Kai, Turquoise Oasis Salon, and then press [Enter]. Type ikai@paintedparadiseresort.com. Select the **text**, click the **Home tab**, change the font to **Century Gothic**, and then change the font size to **16**.

c. Click the **Handout Master tab**, click **Date** in the Placeholders group to deselect it, click the **page number footer**, and then drag it to the position that the date placeholder occupied in the top-right corner. Click in front of the page number symbol, and then type Page:. Be sure to leave a space after the colon.

   You notice the header box with Irene's contact information is oddly spaced, and the page placeholder is larger than needed. You will modify both placeholders to improve the layout.

d. Click the **page** placeholder, and then drag the **left sizing handle** to the right so the placeholder fits the text. Click the **header** placeholder, and then drag the **right sizing handle** to the right until the contact information fits on two lines. Drag the **bottom** of the placeholder down so the text fits within the placeholder.

e. Click the **footer** placeholder, click the **Insert tab**, click **Symbol**, select the **copyright symbol**, and then click **Insert**. Click **Close**. Type the current year followed by a comma and a space, and then Painted Paradise Golf Resort and Spa, Inc. Select the **text**, click the **Home tab**, click **Center** in the Paragraph group, and then increase the font size to **16**. Drag the **right sizing handle** of the placeholder to the right side of the page.

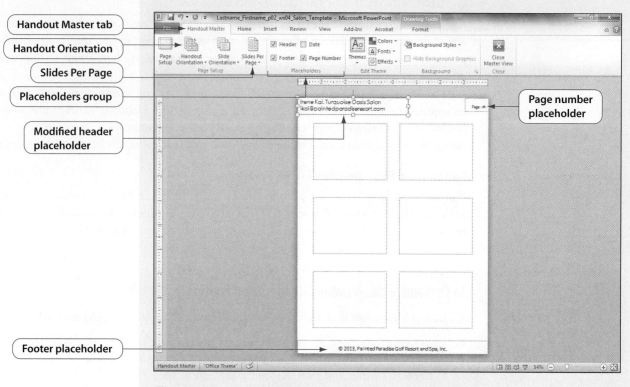

Handout Master tab

Handout Orientation

Slides Per Page

Placeholders group

Modified header placeholder

Footer placeholder

Page number placeholder

Figure 8 Modifying the handout master

f. Click the **Handout Master tab**, click **Slides Per Page** in the Page Setup group, and then click each of the **slide numbers** to review the layouts and make sure that none of the header or footer text conflicts with the slides.

Setting Up the Page

Some people prefer to see handout pages in a landscape orientation, while others prefer portrait. You can change the orientation of the pages as well as the slide images. For the most part, slides are displayed in a 4:3 ratio, making them wider than they are tall. For this reason, you will generally display the slides in landscape orientation to avoid distorting them. Selecting a portrait or landscape handout orientation makes no difference in the size or shape of the slide images, so it becomes a matter of personal preference.

Real World Advice   Printing Handouts

When using handouts for your presentation, it is important to have a good idea of how they will supplement your message. Of course, you want to print handouts that are valuable tools for the audience, and you probably want to avoid printing those that do not contribute information. This helps you to be more environmentally conscious because you are not using printing resources, such as paper and ink, for unnecessary handouts. You should also consider when to distribute the handouts. Do you want the audience members to use them for supplemental notes during your presentation? Are you distracted by people turning the pages or rustling the paper? There are many considerations you should make before printing handouts.

After a discussion with Irene, you will set the handout orientation to landscape. You will also make a final check of the printouts using the two slides that were added to the template presentation.

To Print Handouts and Notes

a. On the **Handout Master tab**, click **Handout Orientation** in the Page Setup group, and then click **Landscape**. If placeholder adjustments are needed to keep the text within the placeholder, make those adjustments.

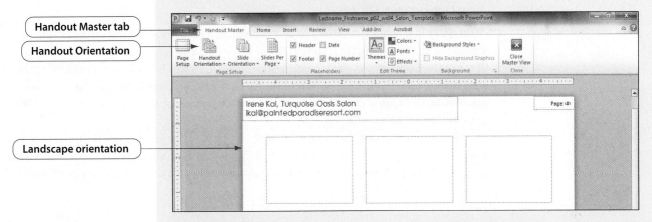

Handout Master tab

Handout Orientation

Landscape orientation

Figure 9　Printing handouts and notes

b. Click **Close Master View**. Click the **File tab**, click **Print**, and then click **Full Page Slides**. Click **2 Slides** in the Handouts group, review the preview, and then click **Print** if your instructor requests a copy of the printout.

c. Click the **File tab**, and click **Print**, if you printed the handouts in Step b. Click **2 Slides**, and then click **Notes Pages**. Click **Next Page** and **Previous Page** at the bottom of the Preview pane to review the printing. Click **Print** if your instructor requests a copy of the printout.

　　The page is displayed in landscape orientation, matching the orientation setting you made for the handout pages. On the notes pages, the slide image is to the left of the lines you put in for last-minute notes. Because there were no speaker notes on the slide, none are displayed on the printout.

d. Click the **File tab**, and then click **Save As**. Confirm that the Save As type is **PowerPoint Template**. Confirm that the storage location points to where you store your project files. Click **Save**, respond **Yes** if a Confirm Save As dialog box appears, and then close the template but leave PowerPoint open to continue with the next steps of the workshop.

Using a Custom Template

Custom templates are accessed in the same way that you use other templates. Begin a new PowerPoint presentation, and select the template. As you add slides, the layouts that are a part of the template are available on the Home tab.

　　You will create a new presentation based on the salon template.

To Create a Presentation Based on a Template

a. Click the **File tab**, click **New**, and then click **New from existing**. Navigate to the location where your project files are stored. Click **Lastname_Firstname_p02_ws04_Salon_ Template**, and then click **Create New**.

The content slides appear with the content that you typed in the template. You will immediately save the file as a PowerPoint presentation.

b. Click the **File tab**, click **Save As**, and then navigate to the storage location where you store your project files. Type Lastname_Firstname_p02_ws04_Salon_Presentation for the File name. The Save As type should default to PowerPoint Presentation. Click **Save**. You are now ready to add the varying content to your slide show.

Importing an Outline

Sometimes it is more convenient to add content to a slide show by importing it from a file created in another application such as Word or Notepad as opposed to starting from scratch. If the outline was created using heading styles, the slides will be created with the hierarchy of data reflected in the outline. If the outline does not have heading styles applied, each item on the outline will appear on a different slide. Content created on the Outline tab of Word flows into the PowerPoint slides very well.

Irene created an outline in Word that she would like for you to include in the presentation. You will import the outline and set the layout for each slide. You will make modifications to the imported text to improve the consistency with the PowerPoint presentation.

To Use a Word Outline

a. Click **Slide 1** on the Slides tab, click the **New Slide arrow** on the Home tab, and then click **Slides from Outline**. Navigate to the location of the student data files, click **p02_ws04_Salon_Outline**, and then click **Insert**.

The slides flow into the presentation, but they are difficult to read. The layouts were not applied to the outline slides as they were imported. You will apply the layouts to the slides.

Figure 10   Importing a Word outline

b. Select **Slides 2** through **10** on the Slides tab, click **Layout** in the Slides group of the Home tab, and then click **Title and Content**. With the slides selected, click the **Home tab**, and then click **Reset** in the Slides group.

The text is now placed and formatted in the rectangle shapes you created in the slide master layouts. Now you will modify the text so it matches the slides created in the slide master.

c. Click **Slide 2** on the Slides tab. Evaluate the placement of the text. Use the sizing handles to move the text block down. Click **Slide 4** on the Slides tab, select the **title text**, and then click **Decrease Font Size** until the title fits on one line. Review each of the slides and make similar adjustments as needed. Click **Slide 8** on the Slides tab, remove the bullet from the quotation, and then adjust the text placeholder. Remove the bullet from the quotation on **Slide 9**, and then adjust the text placeholder.

SIDE NOTE
Using Reset
The Reset button in the Slides group of the Home tab enables you to quickly apply the template settings to slides.

Using Slide Sections

Slide sections are organizational tools for use on the Slides tab. You can place section titles between groups of slides and then collapse or expand the sections. This means that you can see sections you want to work with, while minimizing sections you do not need to see. This is very beneficial for large slide shows, saving you time as you search for a slide.

You will assign sections to the slides and experiment with collapsing or expanding the sections.

To Assign Slides to Sections

a. Click between Slide 2 and Slide 3 on the Slides tab. Click the **Home tab** if necessary, click **Section** in the Slides group, and then click **Add Section**.

The section was added and all subsequent slides were placed in the section. You will name the section.

b. Click **Section**, and then click **Rename Section**. Type Solutions and then click **Rename**.

c. Right-click between Slide 5 and Slide 6 on the Slides tab, and then click **Add Section**. Right-click **Untitled Section**, click **Rename Section**, and then type Inspire Employees. Click **Rename**.

d. Right-click between Slide 6 and Slide 7. Click **Add Section**, right-click the section, and then rename the section Financial Success. Click **Rename**. Add a section called Feedback between Slide 7 and Slide 8. Add a section called Future between Slide 9 and Slide 10. Right-click the first section named **Default Section**, and then rename it Introduction.

e. Click **Section** in the Slides group, and then click **Collapse All**. Click the **arrow** next to the Section titled Solutions to expand it.

When slide sections are collapsed, you cannot select slides in the Slides tab. With the section expanded, you see three slides in the Solutions section.

f. Click the **arrow** next to the Solutions section title. The section collapses. Click the **Feedback section title arrow**. This section expands.

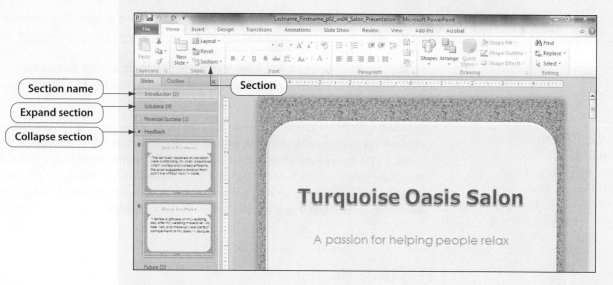

Figure 11   Slide sections

g.   Click **Section** in the Slides group, and then click **Expand All**.

Using Proofing Tools

Proofing documents, especially for spelling, is one of the most important final steps in the preparation of your presentation. Small errors look a whole lot worse when displayed on a giant screen. PowerPoint provides three **proofing tools**: Spelling, Research, and Thesaurus.

You are already aware of the interactive spelling check that occurs—squiggly red lines under misspelled words that appear as you type on slides. However, some words that are flagged are spelled correctly. When you are completing the project, it is a good idea to use the Spelling tool to check the entire document. Sometimes you miss the flag of the interactive spelling check, so a final run-through will help you find any problems.

The Thesaurus pane provides you with alternative word choices. As you read each slide, think about whether you are using a particular word or phrase too much. Select the word in the content area and click Thesaurus to display words with similar meanings.

The Research tool enables you to check facts and develop your ideas for the presentation. References available on the Research pane include the Encarta Dictionary; English, French, and Spanish Thesauruses; Internet research sites such as Bing; and business and financial websites. For your project, you decide to research some ways to inspire employees, as outlined on Slide 6.

To Use the Research Pane

a.   Click the **Review tab**, click **Research** in the Proofing group, and then type Inspire Employees in the Search for box of the Research pane. Click the **arrow** next to the word Bing, and then click **All Research Sites**.

A staggering number of sites were found that contained the words "Inspire Employees." You will view one site to get some ideas.

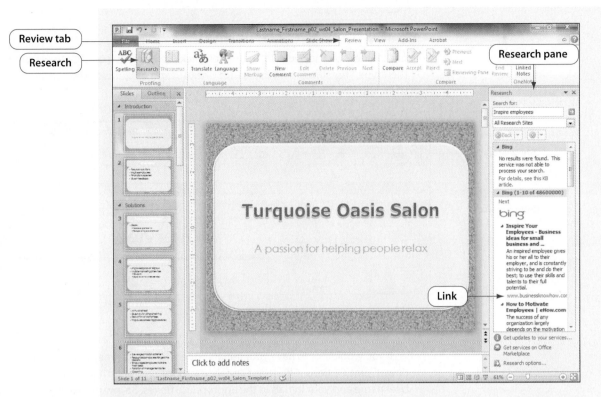

Figure 12 Using the Research tool

b. Click the **expand arrow** next to Bing, if necessary, to view the results. Click the link with the first site listed in the results. Maximize the browser window if necessary to view the site. Review the information, and then close the browser window.

c. **Close** ✕ the Research pane and save the presentation.

Collaborating with Others on a Presentation

In business, collaborating effectively with your coworkers is a valuable skill. Microsoft Office provides many methods for collaboration through its application packages. PowerPoint enables you to place comments on slides so when you share the file with others, they can understand your thinking. If you displayed the slides in Slide Show view, the comments would not appear. In this section, you will use PowerPoint's collaboration tools.

> **CONSIDER THIS** | **Working as a Team Member**
>
> Teamwork is common in today's corporate world. You may collaborate on a presentation as a team member. What challenges would you anticipate while working on a presentation in a team? How could you overcome those challenges?

Creating Comments

Comments are short notes explaining your thoughts. They appear in comment boxes that look like sticky notes. The comment icons contain the initials of the person who wrote the comment, if they have personalized their Microsoft Office options. When you open a comment, the full name of the person is displayed at the top of the comment note along with the date the comment was written.

You will add comments to the presentation, asking Irene for some additional content.

To Add Comments to the Presentation

a. Click **Slide 2** on the Slides tab, and then click the **Review tab**. Click **New Comment**, and then type This slide could use a nice photograph of some of your employees. Be sure to include the period at the end of the sentence.

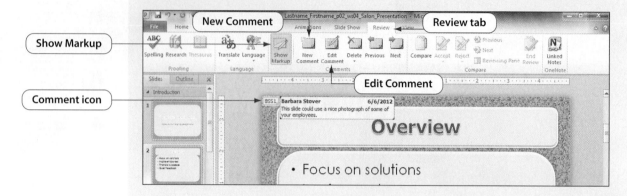

Figure 13   Creating comments

If you would like to have your initials appear in the comment, you can personalize the PowerPoint Options. Click the File tab, click Options, and then type your name for the User name and your initials in the appropriate boxes. Be aware that in a lab, you may not have access to the PowerPoint Options. Also, if you change the User name in a lab, you will want to change it back to the original setting before you leave the computer.

b. Click **Slide 9** on the Slides tab, and then click **New Comment**. Type Irene, can we get a photograph from Jacquie's wedding?

You will update the presentation to include the actual footer text before sending the presentation to Irene.

c. Click the **Insert tab**, and then click **Header & Footer**. Click the **Date and time check box** to select it, and then click **Fixed**. You will replace the contents of this box. Type the current year followed by a comma and a space. Continue by typing Painted Paradise Golf Resort and Spa, Inc. Click the **Footer** to select it, and then type Conscious Rejuvenation at the Turquoise Oasis Salon. Click **Don't show on title slide** to select it, and then click **Apply to All**.

You may have noticed that you cannot access the symbols while viewing the Header & Footer dialog box. You will modify the footer, return to the Header & Footer dialog box, and then apply the modification to all slides.

d. Click in front of the year on the footer shown in the Slide pane. Click the **Insert tab**, click **Symbol** in the Symbols group, and then click the **copyright symbol** ©—character code **00A9** in the normal text font. Click **Insert**, click **Close**, and then click **Header & Footer** again. Notice the copyright symbol is now in front of the date in the footer in the dialog box. Click **Apply to All**.

e. **Save** 🔲 the presentation. Close the presentation but keep PowerPoint open to continue with the next steps of the exercise.

Navigating Comments

When a file is returned to you with comments, the comment icons will appear on the slides. You can click each slide in the presentation and search for the icons, but this takes time. Instead you can use the Comments group on the Review tab to move to the next comment or the previous comment. You can also edit comments and delete comments in this group.

You sent the file to Irene for her review. She sent it back to you with her comments. You will review the changes she made to the file and the comments she added.

To View and Delete Comments

a. Click the **File tab**, click **Open**, and then navigate to the location of the student data files. Double-click **p02_ws04_Salon_Comments**, click the **File tab**, click **Save As**, navigate to the location of your project files, and then type Lastname_Firstname_p02_ws04_ Salon_Update. Click **Save**.

   The presentation that Irene modified is displayed. She added photographs and shapes to the slides. She also placed some comments on the presentation.

b. Click the **Review tab**, and then make sure **Show Markup** in the Comments group is selected. The first comment icon is in the top-left corner of Slide 1. Click the **comment icon** to open the comment.

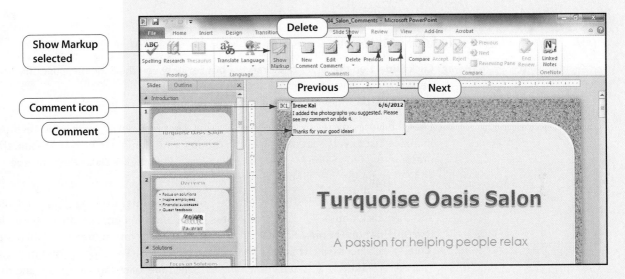

Figure 14   Reviewing comments

c. Click **Next** in the Comments group. This comment mirrors the one you put in your own file earlier. Click **Next** again to see Irene's next comment, and then continue reviewing the comments.

d. Click **Slide 2** on the Slides tab, click the **comment icon**, and then click **Delete** in the Comments group. Because the comment has been addressed, you decide to delete it. Click **Slide 9** on the Slides tab, click the **comment icon**, and then press Delete. Now the comments that you added to the file are deleted.

e. Click **Slide 4**, click the **Insert tab**, and then click **Clip Art** in the Images group. Type cell phone in the Search for box, and then click the **Results should be arrow**. Select only **Videos** in the media file type list, click **Go**, and then click the image of **three cell phones** in a row. Once the image appears on the slide, drag it below the text, and then adjust the size by dragging a corner sizing handle out. **Close** ⊠ the Clip Art pane. You have now completed the adjustments requested by Irene, so you will delete all of the remaining comments.

f. Click the **Review tab**, and then click the **Delete arrow** in the Comments group. Click **Delete All Markup in this Presentation**, click **Yes** when asked to confirm the deletion of all comments and ink annotations in this presentation, and then save the presentation.

Creating Speaker Notes

Speaker notes, displayed in the Notes pane of the PowerPoint window, enable you to write the words you will say during the presentation and store them with the actual presentation. You can later print the notes for reference during the presentation, or if you are using a dual display screen system you can show the audience the slides, while you view the notes in Presenter view.

There are some tips you should consider while creating speaker notes. Avoid writing complete sentences. This will help keep you from reading word for word from the notes. Organize the notes with numbers or letters in outline format. Use the Save & Send feature on the File tab to create handouts and send the slides to Microsoft Word, selecting to put the notes on the side of the slide pictures or below the slides. Having a picture of the slide on the notes enables you to stay on track during the presentation. By converting the presentation file to Word, you can then modify the font size of the notes, making it larger and easier to read in a darkened room.

You will create some speaker notes in the salon presentation. You will then create a Word document with the notes.

To Add Speaker Notes

a. Click **Slide 1** on the Slides tab. Drag the **border** between the Slide pane and the Notes pane upward, so you have more room to type notes.

   The slide becomes smaller, but is still clear enough for you to read.

b. Click the **Notes pane**, and then type Introduce yourself. Press Enter, and then click **Increase List Level** in the Paragraph group of the Home tab. Type Name and then press Enter. Type Salon Manager and then press Enter. Click **Decrease List Level**, and then type Quarterly report on the salon successes.

c. Click **Slide 2** on the Slides tab. Select the **body text content** on the slide, right-click, and then click **Copy**. Right-click the **Notes pane**, and then under Paste Options click **Use Destination Theme**. Click at the end of the text **Focus on solutions**, and then press Enter. Click **Increase List Level**, and then type Goals. Press Enter, and then type Successful solutions we have implemented. Select the following three lines, and then click **Increase List Level** twice.

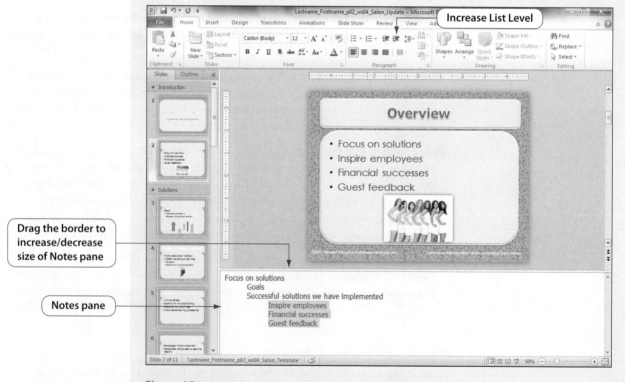

Figure 15 Creating speaker notes

d. Continue adding the following notes to the Notes pane on each slide noted:

Slide 3	Focused on increasing profits
	Realized that employee turnover caused:
	    Expense
	        New employee search
	        Hiring expenses
	    Guest loyalty issues
	    Training period

Slide 4	Salon product display makeover Mobile marketing extremely successful On low-booked days—increased walk-ins by 25%
Slide 5	Goal—reduce turnover to zero for a 6-month period Stylists enjoyed the visit of John Barrett, New York City salon in Bergdorf Goodman Cut costs to stylists Made better use of their time

Slide 6	Worked to develop the employees
	    Recognized
	    Encouraged
	    Offered management training hands-on
	    One-on-one coaching

Slide 7	Because of new salon product display, profits skyrocketed Feature national salon brands and our own Select products Salon treatment profits are up due to hiring of new stylist, Marcee Wood
Slide 10	Increase length of time between employee turnovers Improve communications Continue guest stylist visits Project 15% growth of salon product sales over the next 12 months

e. **Save** 🖫 the presentation. Click the **File tab**, click **Save & Send**, click **Create Handouts**, and then click **Create Handouts**. Click **Notes next to slides**, and then click **OK**. Click the **Word** application when it appears on the taskbar. It takes a few moments for the slides to render in the Word document.

f. Select the **Notes column** in the Word document by clicking above the Slide 1 Notes column when the ↓ is displayed. Click **Grow Font** A˙ in the Font group of the Home tab twice. The size of the font increases, making it easier to read.

g. Click the **File tab** in the Word document, click **Save As**, and then navigate to the location of your project files. Type Lastname_Firstname_p02_ws04_Salon_Notes as the file name, and then click **Save**.

h. **Close** ❎ the Word document window.

Protecting Presentations

The use of passwords protects presentations from being accessed by unauthorized people. This keeps others from opening and modifying the documents. On a shared server or a SharePoint site, you may want to use this feature when you have completed the presentation. Accessed through the Info tab on the File tab, you can mark the file as final and make it read-only. This makes the presentation viewable, but does not allow modifications. You may also encrypt the presentation with a password. People who do not have the password cannot view or modify the presentation. You can also restrict the permission of people so they cannot edit, copy, or print the presentation. An invisible Digital Signature can be added to the presentation, ensuring the integrity of the document.

You will protect a presentation with a password. You will then open a presentation that requires a password. You will mark a presentation as final.

To Encrypt a Presentation with a Password and Mark as Final

a. In the Lastname_Firstname_p02_ws04_Salon_Update presentation, click the **File tab**, click **Info**, and then click **Protect Presentation**. Click **Encrypt with Password**, and then read the caution message. Very carefully type salon for the password. The password will appear as dots in the Password box. Click **OK**, type the same password again, and then click **OK**.

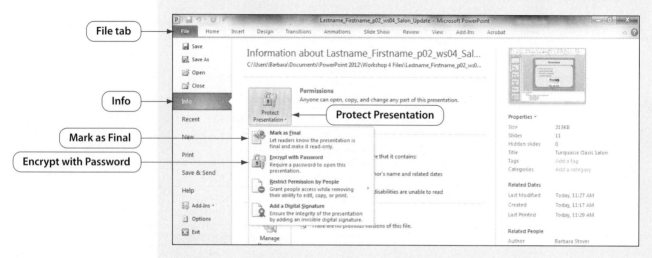

Figure 16 Protecting presentations

b. Save and close the presentation, keeping PowerPoint open.

c. Click the **File tab**, click **Open**, and then navigate to the storage location of your project files. Double-click **Lastname_Firstname_p02_ws04_Salon_Update**, type the password salon in the Password box, and then click **OK**.

The presentation opens, and you can make edits to the slides. You will need to share the password with anyone who will be editing or displaying the presentation.

d. Click the **Slide Show tab**, click **From Beginning**, and then review each slide, carefully proofing. Return to Normal view.

e. Click the **File tab**, and then click the **Info tab** if necessary. Click **Protect Presentation**, and then click **Mark as Final**. Click **OK** to respond to the warning message "This Presentation will be marked as final and then saved." Click **OK** to the explanation note after reading it.

f. Click the **Home tab**.

Notice the yellow bar across the top of the window. Notice the Ribbon is not visible above the yellow bar. The file has been marked as final, but edits are still possible if someone ignores the warning and clicks Edit Anyway.

g. Close the presentation, and then exit PowerPoint.

Delivering a Presentation

At some time in your career, you will probably be asked to make a presentation. For some people, this causes great anxiety, while for others it seems natural to speak in front of the crowd. You hear all kinds of advice about giving presentations. In the long run, it is a skill you build over time, and the real key is practice.

Once you have completed the slides for the presentation, you should practice using them. Project the presentation with the actual equipment you will use, if possible, and practice using the speaker notes, advancing the slides, and looking out into the imaginary audience. You may feel a little funny talking out loud to an empty room, but saying the actual words and hearing them will help to make them flow off your tongue more easily during the real presentation. It is a good idea to enlist a few people to watch a practice session and ask for their honest feedback. They can make you aware of verbal and nonverbal distracters, such as excessively clearing your throat, jingling change in your pocket, and talking too softly. They may also suggest improvements to the content of your presentation. If you do not have people to help you practice, record yourself with a video or audio recorder so you can review the practice session.

In this section, you will explore methods for preparing and delivering a presentation.

Overcoming Presentation Nerves

Rest assured, even the most accomplished presenter occasionally suffers from presentation nerves. Most people are nervous in the few minutes leading up to being introduced and in the minutes just after the presentation has begun. There are many things you can do to lessen the effects of the anxiety. Remember to breathe. Take full breaths, filling your lungs and breathing out through your mouth. Even during your presentation, taking a full breath gives you time to straighten out your thoughts, relax, and give the audience a little break. It is like adding white space to your presentation. Smile at your audience. Nod your head. Use hand gestures. These physical movements help to relax your body and reassure your mind that you are in control.

Be kind to yourself and use positive words and thoughts to calm your nerves. Remind yourself that you are prepared. You have your materials at hand. Your speech has been polished through practice. For the most part, audiences want you to succeed and will support you if you make a genuine effort.

Real World Advice **Memorizing Your Presentation**

You may have observed presenters who do not seem to have any notes at all. They may have given the speech so many times it comes to mind naturally, or they may have memorized what they want to say. There is a difference between memorizing the presentation and memorizing the outline. If you are comfortable with the material, memorizing the outline will not only help to keep you on track during the presentation but also enable you to choose the actual language you use on the fly. If specific things need to be said during a presentation, then memorizing it is the best way to deliver all of the parts. This takes some time and practice to accomplish, and in some cases, the delivery may seem "canned."

Last minute changes or accidents add stress to the presentation. As you prepare, think about the possible problems and try to frame emergency actions. You will be ready for the unexpected if you have previously thought about it. If something unexpected does happen, evaluate whether you can do anything about it. If you can, do it. If you cannot, do not overreact to the situation. The audience may not even know that the widget you were supposed to hold up did not arrive on time or that you are wearing your travel clothes because your luggage went to a different city. Good presenters do not let internal or external forces ruin their presentations.

To Review Speaking Fears

a. Open a blank PowerPoint presentation, type the title Delivering Speeches in the title placeholder, and then your name in the subtitle placeholder. List **five fears** that people might have about delivering a speech in the content placeholder on Slide 2.

b. Classify each of the fears as Internal or External.

c. Develop one or two methods for minimizing each of the fears.

d. Save the document in your project files location with the file name Lastname_Firstname_p02_ws04_Delivery.

Being Prepared

From bandages to extension cords to multiple versions of your presentation (USB flash drive, computer hard drive, and CD/DVD), you can never be too prepared for a presentation. As discussed in the previous section, practice is the best way to arrive prepared for your speech. Arrive 15 minutes to an hour prior to the presentation. If at all possible, you should check the seating arrangements, lighting, audio equipment, handouts, laser pointers, and the projection equipment prior to the presentation. If you bring your own presentation equipment, make sure you have all of the cords to plug the projector into your computer and into the wall. Be sure you have the cord for the computer, even if you have a fully charged battery. You might need a long extension cord. It is a good idea to bring an extra bulb for the projector. A book light might be a handy tool to use for reading your notes if the room will be darkened. Another consideration is what you have on the background of your desktop because the audience may see this displayed on the screen at some point. Be sure that the background is appropriate for a public view.

Walking around the room prior to the presentation gives you a feel for how you might be able to move and engage the audience during the speech. Find out where the light switch is and how to work the microphone if you will be using one. Decide where you will place your computer, the projector, other visual aids, and handouts. If possible, place the projector, focus it on the screen, and test it prior to the audience arrival. Better yet, open your presentation and have it queued to the first slide, so the audience does not see you fumble through your folders looking for the PowerPoint file. This gets you off to a running start and adds professionalism to your presentation.

Real World Advice   Displaying a Presentation

If at all possible, avoid displaying your presentation from a USB flash drive. These devices slow down animations, crash easier, and introduce other problems. If possible, copy the presentation from the USB flash drive onto the desktop computer, and launch the desktop version before your speech. Remember to delete the desktop version after your speech if you are using someone else's computer.

Presenters are a little like airline flight attendants. They need to know where the emergency exits are, the location of the restrooms, and where the refreshments are served. They need to know when the presentation should begin and end. The presenter is viewed as the leader during a speech, so take charge.

Another aspect of being prepared centers around your appearance. You will be more confident if you are comfortable in your clothing. Do not wear a hat during your presentation unless it is part of the speech, and then remove it as soon as your point is made. For instance, you might be playing the role of a coach, complete with a ball cap and whistle. As soon as you have blown the whistle, catching the attention of the audience, remove the cap for a more professional appearance. Make a last minute stop in front of a mirror before your presentation. Check your smile. No spinach between your teeth? Check your hair. Check to make sure all zippers are secured. Give yourself a thumbs-up and head out to meet the audience.

To Create a Checklist

a. After Slide 2, insert a **Title and Content** slide to the presentation, and then title it Presentation Checklist. In the content box, create a checklist of 10 to 12 items that you should have when you arrive at a presentation. Apply **Bullets** ⌄ to the list, if necessary.

b. After Slide 3, insert three additional **Title and Content** slides to the presentation and title them Scenario Reactions. React to the following scenarios by listing what you would do if they happened during your presentation. Insert your answer to the first question on Slide 4, your answer to the second question on Slide 5, and your answer to the third question on Slide 6. Apply **Numbering** ⌄ to each answer as **1.**, **2.**, and **3.**

   1. You are about four minutes into delivering your presentation. The bulb on the projector burns out. What would you do?

   2. During the luncheon prior to your speech, you spilled coffee on your clothing. What would you do?

   3. As you were coming to the stage, you heard thunder in the distance. About 10 minutes after you began your speech the lights went out. What would you do?

Engaging Your Audience

From shaking hands and introducing yourself to audience members prior to the presentation, until you have completed your speech, you should strive to engage your audience and make a connection. Your enthusiasm for the topic should draw the audience into your presentation. You should speak with confidence and humility.

Make eye contact with audience members. If possible, look directly at the person who introduced you or arranged for you to speak, and mention their name in the first few sentences you speak. Then, turn your head to the other side of the audience, make eye contact with someone else, and continue speaking. You should maintain eye contact for one to three seconds per person. Do not focus on just the front row, but also look to the middle and back of the crowd. It is important that you do not face the projection screen and give your presentation with your back to the audience. Avoid standing in front of the screen, where you will be blinded by the projector light and mask the presentation content from the audience. Use a laser pointer or the annotation tools in PowerPoint to focus the attention of the audience on specific parts of the slide.

Real World Advice   Using a Wireless Mouse

Many presenters use a wireless mouse or remote presenter device to control the slide show during the presentation. This enables them to walk around the room and connect with the audience. You may have seen presentations where the speaker seemed to be hiding behind the podium, when in reality they were stuck there by a wired mouse.

If at all possible, leave the lights on in the presentation room. This enables you to see the audience, discourages dozing, and increases the interactivity. If the projector is not powerful enough to use with all of the lights on, try to shut off just the lights closest to the projector.

Use natural gestures during your speech. Avoid putting your hands in your pockets or behind your back, crossing your arms, or wringing your hands. If possible, move toward the audience during your presentation. Occasionally take a step to one side or the other, but avoid pacing. Do not look at your feet.

Your voice is a tool during the presentation. Be interested enough in what you are saying that you do not use a monotone voice to deliver the message. If you find yourself falling into a monotone voice, take a deep breath. Also, many speakers have problems with the speed at which they speak. Presentation nerves make them talk faster. When giving a presentation, slow down. This helps your voice to take on a lower pitch, which projects authority and power. The volume of your speech is something you can check during your presentation preparations, or you can ask your audience if they can hear you. Practice helps you learn how to project your voice so it is clear. You might want to take a bottle of water with you to the podium to moisten your throat during nonspeaking portions of your presentation when others are talking.

CONSIDER THIS | **Using a Microphone**

Most people hesitate to use a microphone, but some people cannot project their voices well enough to be heard. What are some situations where you should use a microphone if you have that option?

Another aspect of engaging your audience is the question-and-answer portion of the presentation. Many speeches end with "Are there any questions?" It is more advisable to ask "What questions can I answer?" Make the assumption that people in the audience will have questions. As an audience member asks a question, make eye contact and listen to the full question. Rephrase the question to help clarify it and to give you some time to frame your response. This also makes sure the audience heard the question you are about to answer. Be honest and sincere in your reply, and try to involve the whole audience with your response. It helps to think about possible questions your audience might ask prior to the presentation, so you have an answer in mind.

To Practice Your Presentation Skills

a. Use the **Delivering Speeches** slides you developed in the last two exercises and practice presenting the material while looking in a mirror. Do you seem friendly? Sincere? Knowledgeable?

b. If possible, record your voice while practicing the presentation, and then review the recording, evaluating whether you have nervous habits, such as clearing your throat, that need to be addressed.

c. Practice the speech one more time in front of a mirror, or if possible, use a video camera to record your practice. Evaluate your performance. Were you speaking clearly? Did you need to use the notes in order to explain or expand on the points made on the slides?

d. After Slide 6, insert a **Title and Content** slide to the presentation, and then title it Evaluation. Write a short evaluation of your practice sessions, and then apply **Bullets** for each comment, if necessary.

Introducing Your Presentation and Providing a Roadmap for Your Audience

As you begin your presentation, you should let the audience know your purpose and provide them with an overview of your presentation. You may have a slide or two that lays out the points you will make at the beginning of your presentation. You should prepare the audience for any unusual activities you have planned, such as group work or a game.

Your initial comments should focus on gaining the attention of the audience members. Each person has many distractions from their own life or job that they bring to your presentation, such as a difficult meeting they had with their boss. You need to draw them into your agenda. Have a clear preview sentence memorized so it is easy to state. For instance, you might say, "I would like to tell you why sales are down this quarter, and propose a plan for improvement."

Your roadmap might be organized in a variety of ways. You may break up the topic into patterns such as past, present, and future. You might present your topic as steps that need completion before the next step occurs. You might use a pro-and-con approach with the topic. It is easier to keep the attention of the audience if they have some idea of where they are in the presentation.

To Get Started with a Speech

a. After Slide 7, insert a **Title and Content** slide to the presentation, and then title it **Attention Getters**. List **four ways** that you could gain the attention of your audience at the beginning of your presentation, and then apply **Bullets** ▤ ˅ to each new thought.

b. After Slide 8, insert three additional **Title and Content** slides to the presentation, and then title them **Roadmaps**. Consider the following three topics, and then develop a general roadmap plan for each.

1. The spa is rolling out a new customer relationship management electronic system. This system records past treatments and products the customer has purchased, and provides additional information about the customer, such as phone number, e-mail address, and how often they visit the spa.

2. The salon is reorganizing and undergoing construction for a new area.

3. The lead masseur is retiring, and you have been asked to speak about the person at the retirement luncheon.

c. **Save** 🖫 the file, and then close the presentation but keep PowerPoint open.

Annotating Slides

As you make your presentation, you may want to emphasize certain points on your slides. You have probably seen presenters use laser pointers for this purpose. If you decide to use a laser pointer, keep in mind that "dancing" the pointer all over the screen is very distracting. Try to point to the area you want to emphasize, and then turn off the pointer, rather than move it back and forth over the area. Generally your audience will see the location and focus on it very quickly.

Quick Reference — A Built-in Laser Pointer

PowerPoint 2010 includes a "built-in" laser (mouse) pointer. In Slide Show view, hold Ctrl and then hold down the left mouse button as you move the pointer.

PowerPoint goes one step better by enabling you to **annotate**, or make notations or marks on the slides during your presentation. You can use an arrow to point to objects, or a pen or highlighter to make long-lasting notations on the slides. You can even select the color of the ink or highlighter. When you close PowerPoint, a warning message will ask whether you want to save the annotations with the file or not. Just like so many other things, it is important to practice using the mouse to draw on the slides prior to using the tool in front of an audience.

To Use Annotation Tools

a. Start **PowerPoint**, if it is not already open. Click the **File tab**, click **Open**, and then navigate to the location of your project files. Double-click **Lastname_Firstname_p02_ ws04_Salon_Update**, type salon when the Password dialog box appears, click **OK**, and then click **Edit Anyway** in the yellow bar.

b. Click the **Slide Show tab**, and then click **From Beginning**. Right-click on the first slide, point to **Pointer Options**, point to **Ink Color**, and then select the dark blue color in the first row—Background 2.

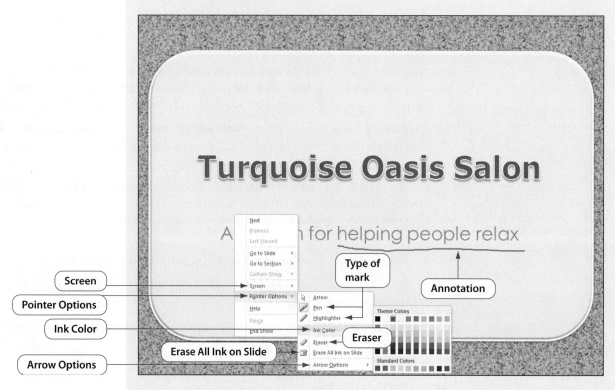

Figure 17   Annotating presentations

c. Drag an underline below the slogan **A passion for helping people relax**.

Troubleshooting

When the pen annotation tool is being used, the left mouse button no longer advances the slides. You can press Enter, the letter "N," or [↑] to advance.

d. Press Enter to advance to the next slide. Right-click and point to **Pointer Options**, point to **Ink Color**, and then click **Accent 2**. Draw an oval around the word **solutions**.

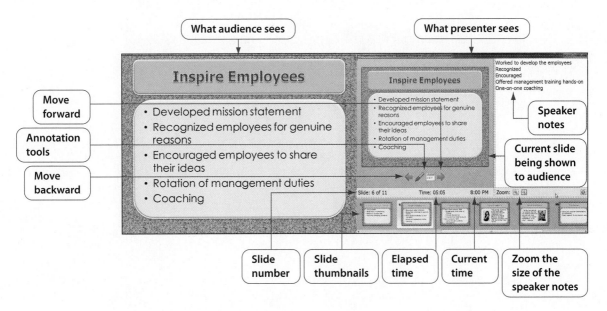

e. Right-click the slide, point to **Screen**, and then click **Show/Hide Ink Markup**. Repeat this step to display the markup again.

f. Right-click the slide, point to **Pointer Options**, and then click **Arrow**.

    Now you can use the mouse to advance through the slides and the arrow to point to parts of the slide. Note that the arrow automatically turns off after a short period of time and turns on when you move the mouse.

g. Press Esc to return to Normal view, and then click **Keep** when you see the warning **Do you want to keep your ink annotations?** Click **Slide 1** on the Slides tab, and then confirm the ink is still visible.

h. Click the **ink annotation** on Slide 1 to select it, and then press Delete. Slide annotations that have been kept can be manipulated in Normal view.

i. **Save** 🖫 the file, close the presentation, open the file again, type the password salon, and then click **OK**. Click **Slide 2** on the Slides tab, and then confirm the ink annotation is still visible. You can save annotations for future use or to distribute with a slide show you are sending out.

j. Close the presentation, and then exit PowerPoint.

Displaying the Presentation in Presenter View

If your computer can be attached to two monitors, PowerPoint can display the speaker notes on one monitor, usually the laptop, and the presentation slides on the second monitor while in **Presenter view**. As shown in Figure 18, the computer displays the speaker notes on the right side. A status bar enables you to view the slide number you are on, the elapsed time of the presentation, and the current time. Icons on the window enable you to move forward and backward through the presentation. Annotation tools are easily accessed in the window. Slide thumbnails are shown at the bottom of the window. You can click the thumbnail to jump directly to the slide you want to display.

    Click Use Presenter View on the Slide Show tab to begin the process of configuring PowerPoint to use Presenter view. The second monitor will be detected, and you can select which monitor will be the speaker notes monitor. After completing a presentation in this format, you will need to return the settings to normal.

Figure 18   Presenter view

Concluding Your Presentation

The conclusion of the speech is one of the most important parts, because you can encourage the audience to fulfill the purpose of your presentation. You should review the roadmap and remind the audience of the content. You can summarize the main points, or ask the audience what they have learned. You can tell a story that emphasizes the content. You can emphasize the importance of action and the benefits the audience members will gain.

In most cases, the conclusion of a presentation includes a question-and-answer period. You should set up some time limits so everyone knows when the Q&A will end. Be concise and brief with your answers, and resist the urge to argue with the person who asks a question or challenges you. Admit if you cannot answer the question, and offer to get back to the person at a later time with the answer.

Real World Advice   When to Accept Questions

Some presenters encourage audience members to participate in the presentation by asking questions or making comments as they think of them. Other presenters prefer to have the audience members hold their questions until the end of the presentation. The size of the audience and the environment of the presentation will help you decide which tactic to use. Keep in mind that questions during your presentation may distract you or the audience and keep you from making all of your points. Regardless of when you accept questions, be sure to repeat the question or paraphrase it so the audience can clearly hear what the question was. This also gives you a chance to frame your response!

When your time is up, thank the audience for their attention. If they applaud, acknowledge the response. Some presenters ask the audience to fill out an evaluation form. This can offer you valuable insight into the pluses and minuses of your presentation. After the presentation, be available to speak with members of the audience. Thank the people who arranged for you to speak. Reward yourself for a job well done.

Concept Check

1. Joanne, a coworker in your department, asked for your help on a template she is working on for the upcoming sales meeting. She will be discussing the new product line with the sales people in hopes of motivating them. She does not understand why the text she is typing in the placeholders on the slide master is not showing up when she creates a new presentation. What is the problem?

2. You have been working on a template for your company that will be used by all of the sales people when they visit customers in the field. The sales people want to create their own customized presentations so they can add the name of the customer and other information to the slide show. What kinds of information would you include on a template for this use?

3. Joanne is back with more questions about the template she is creating (she clearly needed to take this course). Whenever she creates a new presentation with the template, it always opens in Slide Master view. What is the problem?

4. Steve Michaels, the VP of production at your company, requested your input into a presentation he plans to present to the board of directors. He wants feedback on the design of his slides, and he wants you to write some of the text of his presentation. What PowerPoint tools will you use to provide the feedback and text?

5. The board of directors meeting is today, and Steve is in the hospital. You have been asked to make his presentation. You have never made a speech to the board, and you are becoming increasingly nervous. What would you do to control your nerves before the presentation? Once you get into the board room, how will you engage the members of the board and get them to agree to the proposal Steve was making?

Key Terms

Annotate 856
Comments 845
Corporate identity 828
Handout master 839

Notes master 836
Presenter view 857
Proofing tools 844
Slide master 828

Slide sections 843
Speaker notes 847
Template 828
Templates folder 835

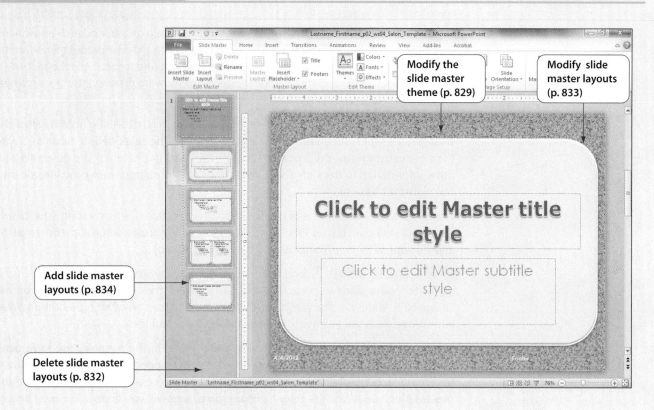

Modify the slide master theme (p. 829)

Modify slide master layouts (p. 833)

Add slide master layouts (p. 834)

Delete slide master layouts (p. 832)

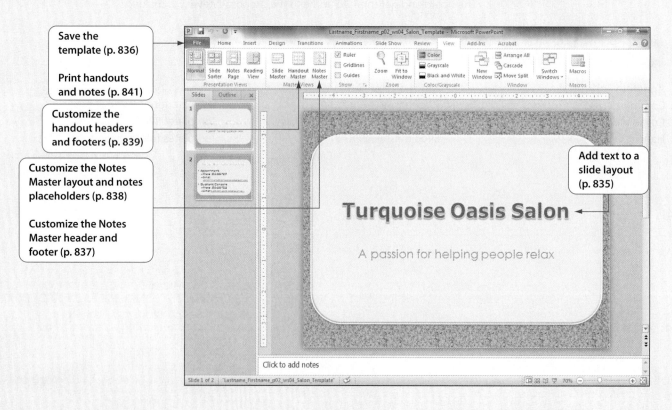

Save the template (p. 836)

Print handouts and notes (p. 841)

Customize the handout headers and footers (p. 839)

Customize the Notes Master layout and notes placeholders (p. 838)

Customize the Notes Master header and footer (p. 837)

Add text to a slide layout (p. 835)

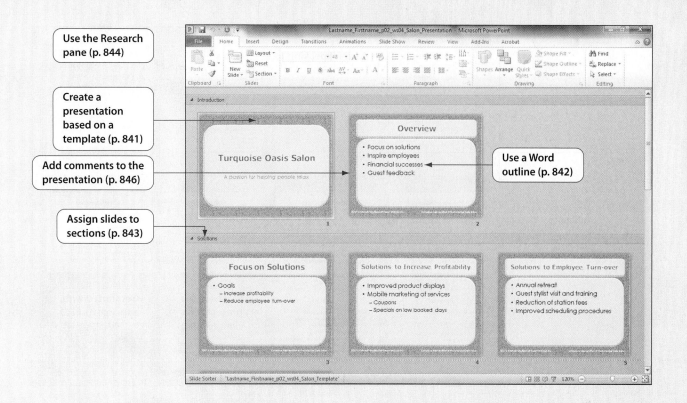

Use the Research pane (p. 844)

Create a presentation based on a template (p. 841)

Add comments to the presentation (p. 846)

Assign slides to sections (p. 843)

Use a Word outline (p. 842)

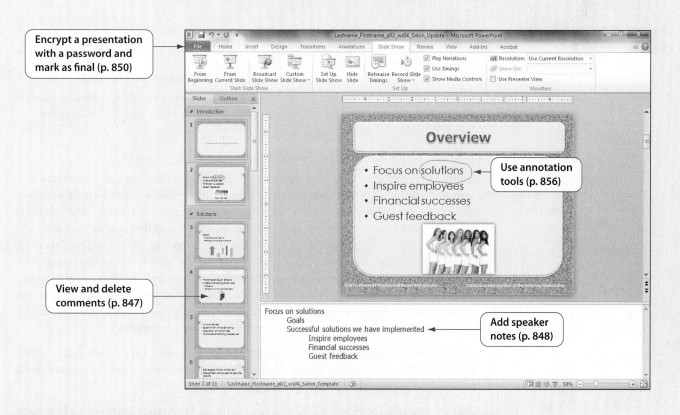

Encrypt a presentation with a password and mark as final (p. 850)

Use annotation tools (p. 856)

View and delete comments (p. 847)

Add speaker notes (p. 848)

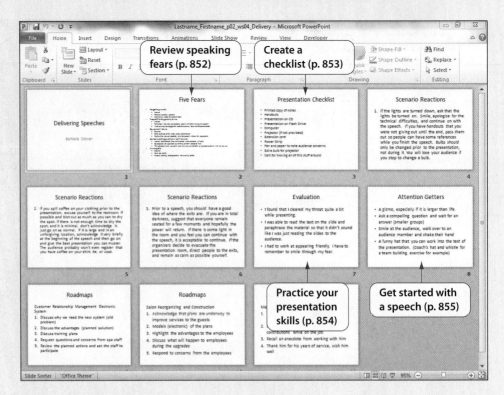

Figure 19 The Salon Manager's Quarterly Report Final Presentations

---

Student data files needed:

p02_ws04_Wedding
p02_ws04_Wedding_Sample

You will save your files as:

Lastname_Firstname_p02_ws04_Wedding_Template
Lastname_Firstname_p02_ws04_Wedding_Test

The Wedding Memory Template

Customer Service

Weddings and receptions are common events at the Painted Paradise Golf Resort and Spa. The wedding planner, Ellie Gold, prepares photographs of the preparations for each wedding, and presents a PowerPoint CD to each couple as a memento of their special day. She takes photographs of the cake, the buffet tables, the decorations and flower arrangements, and includes a short personalized message telling the couple how much she enjoyed working with them on their plans for the wedding and reception. Ellie asked you to create a template that she could reuse as she prepares these presentations. She provided you with a sample presentation with just a few slides to give you an idea of what she needs. You will use this presentation to test the template you develop. After reviewing her presentation, you decide to use many of the same design elements that are in the sample slide show.

a. Start **PowerPoint**. Navigate to the student data files, and then open **ps02_ws04_ Wedding**. Type your name in the placeholder provided, and then type your course information in the body content placeholder.

b. Click the **File tab**, click **Save As**, click **Save as type**, and then click **PowerPoint Template**. Navigate to the location where you store your project files, type Lastname_Firstname_ p02_ws04_Wedding_Template in the File name box, and then click **Save**.

c. Click the **View tab**, click **Slide Master**, and then click the **slide master** thumbnail at the top of the left pane. Click **Background Styles**, click **Format Background**, click **Picture or texture fill**, and then click **Texture**. Select **Parchment** in the fifth column, third row. Type 15% in the Transparency box, and then click **Close**.

d. Click **Fonts** in the Edit Theme group, and then click **Apothecary**. Select the text in the title placeholder, on the Home tab click the **Font Color arrow**, and then select **Red, Accent 2, Darker 50%**. Select all of the text in the body content placeholder of the slide master, click the **Font Color arrow**, and then select **Red, Accent 2, Darker 25%**.

e. Click the **Insert tab**, click **Header & Footer**, and then click **Footer** to select it. Type Painted Paradise Golf Resort and Spa in the Footer box, click **Don't show on title slide**, and then click **Apply to All**. Click the footer placeholder that contains the text you just typed. Drag the **left sizing handle** to the left until it touches the date placeholder. Drag the **right sizing handle** to the right until it touches the slide number placeholder. Select the **footer text** on the slide master, click the **Home tab**, click the **Font Color arrow**, and then apply **Red, Accent 2, Darker 25%**.

f. Click the **Section Header Layout** in the left pane, and then press Delete. Delete the following layouts:

- **Comparison Layout**
- **Title Only Layout**
- **Blank Layout**
- **Content with Caption Layout**
- **Picture with Caption Layout**
- **Title and Vertical Text Layout**
- **Vertical Title and Text Layout**

g. Click the **Title Slide Layout** in the left pane. Click the **Insert tab**, click **Shapes**, and then click the **Line** shape. Starting at the left edge of the title placeholder, just below the placeholder, drag a straight line (press Shift while dragging) about halfway across the slide. Click the **Drawing Tools Format tab**, and then type 3.5" in the Shape Width box. Click **Shape Outline** in the Shape Styles group, and then select **Red, Accent 2, Lighter 40%**. Click **Shape Outline** again, point to **Weight**, click **More Lines**, and then type 4 in the Width box. Click **Compound type**, click **Double**, and then click **Close**. Right-click the line shape, and then click **Copy**. Right-click on the slide, and then under Paste Options, click **Use Destination Theme**. Drag the line you just pasted to the right so it lines up with the right edge of the title placeholder.

h. Click the **Insert tab**, click **Text Box**, and then click between the two lines you just placed on the slide. Right-click the **text box**, and then click **Edit Text**. Click the **Insert tab**, click **Symbol**, click the **Font arrow**, and then click **Wingdings**. Type 205 in the Character code box, and then click **Insert**. Type 212 in the Character code box, click **Insert**, and then click **Close**. Select both symbols, click the **Home tab**, click the **Font Color arrow**, and then select **Red, Accent 2, Darker 50%**. Click the **Font Size** box, and then type 32. Press Shift, and then click each of the lines you created to select the lines and the symbols. Click the **Drawing Tools Format tab**, click **Align**, and then click **Distribute Horizontally**. Click **Align** again, and then click **Align Middle**. Click **Group** in the Arrange group, and then click **Group**. Using the arrow keys, move the lines and symbol between the title placeholder and the subtitle placeholder.

i. Right-click the **lines/symbol group** you created, and then click **Copy**. Click the **Title and Content Layout** in the left pane, right-click on the slide, and then under Paste Options, click **Use Destination Theme**. Drag the group to a position between the title and body content placeholders. Click the body content placeholder, click the **Drawing Tools Format tab**, drag the **top sizing handle** down until the Shape Height box reports that the shape is close to 4.6". Do not type the number in the Shape Height box as the bottom will move, rather than making room at the top for the graphic. Press Shift, and then click the **lines/symbol group** and the title placeholder. Click **Align** in the Arrange group on the Drawing Tools Format tab, and then click **Distribute Vertically**. Click just the **lines/symbol group**, click **Align**, and then click **Align Center**.

j. Right-click the **lines/symbol group**, and then click **Copy**. Click the **Two Content Layout** in the left pane, right-click, and then under Paste Options, click **Use Destination Theme**. Click the left body content placeholder, press Shift, and then click the right body content placeholder. Click the **Drawing Tools Format tab**, type 4.6 in the Shape Height box, and then press Enter. Press the [↓] five times to move the body content placeholders down the slide slightly. Drag the lines/symbol group between the title placeholder and the body content placeholder. Click **Align**, and then click **Align Center**. With the title placeholder selected, press Shift and click one body content placeholder. Click **Align**, and then click **Distribute Vertically**. Click the left body content placeholder, press Shift, and then click the right body content placeholder. Click **Align**, click **Align Selected Objects**, click **Align** again, and then click **Align Bottom**.

k. Click the **Title Slide Layout** in the left pane, select the text in the title placeholder, and then type Name of Couple. Select the subtitle text, click the **Home tab**, and then click **Italic** in the Font group. Click the **Font Color arrow**, and select click **Red**, **Accent 2**, **Darker 25%**. Click the **Font Size** box, and then type 24. Click **Align Text** in the Paragraph group, and then click **Middle**.

l. Click the **Slide Master tab**, and then click **Close Master View**. Click **New Slide** on the Home tab, click **Layout**, and then click **Title Slide**. Click the subtitle text, and type Date of Wedding. Press Enter, and then type Painted Paradise Golf Resort and Spa. If the footer is displayed on the title slide, click **Header & Footer** on the Insert tab, confirm that **Don't show on title slide** is selected, and then click **Apply to All**.

m. Click the **File tab**, click **Save As**, and confirm that the Save As type is **PowerPoint Template**. Navigate to the location where you store your project files, confirm that the File name is **Lastname_Firstname_p02_ws04_Wedding_Template**, and then click **Save**. Confirm to save the file by clicking **Yes**, click the **File tab**, and then click **Close**.

n. Click the **File tab**, click **New**, and then click **New from existing**. Select the template file **Lastname_Firstname_p02_ws04_Wedding_Template**, and then click **Create New**. Click **Slide 2** on the Slides tab, click the **New Slide arrow** on the Home tab, and then click **Reuse Slides**. Click **Browse** in the Reuse Slides pane, and then click **Browse File**. Navigate to the location of your student data files, and then click **p02_ws04_Wedding_Sample**. Click **Open**, right-click one of the slides in the Reuse Slides pane, and click **Insert All Slides**. Close the Reuse Slides pane.

o. Click the **File tab**, click **Save As**, and navigate to the location where you store your project files. Type Lastname_Firstname_p02_ws04_Wedding_Test as the File name, and then click **Save**. You will now make some minor adjustments to the sample. Click **Slide 2** on the Slides tab, and then press Delete. The subtitle text seems to have disappeared. Drag over the subtitle text on Slide 2 to select it (there are two lines of subtitle text), click the **Font Color arrow**, and then select **Red**, **Accent 2**, **Darker 25%**. Click **Slide 3** on the Slides tab, and then select the text **The Eldorado Room**. Click **Bullets** to remove the bullet. Click **Slide 6** on the Slides tab, and then remove the bullet from the text **Hydrangeas accented with roses**.

p. Click the **Slide Show tab**, click **From Beginning**, and then review each of the slides. Click the **File tab**, click **Save**, close the presentation.

Student Data Files Needed

p02_ps1_Review
p02_ps1_Review_Outline
p02_ps1_Review_Background

You will save your files as:

Lastname_Firstname_p02_ps1_Review_Template
Lastname_Firstname_p02_ps1_Review_Test

Restaurant Training Template

Production & Operations

Chef Robin Sanchez would like to send her staff presentations in PDF format to help them review rules and procedures of basic culinary skills used in the restaurants at Painted Paradise Golf Resort and Spa. Topics will include food safety, sanitation, knife skills, plate presentation, and much more. Robin has given you a picture that she wants to use on the title slide and has asked you to create a template with theme colors that will blend well with the image. She wants the presentation to be professional and have an easily recognizable identity that can be reused for all topics. You will create the template, as well as a specialized handout master that includes information that Robin would typically add to handouts. After the template is complete, you will test it using an outline Robin has given you.

a. Start **PowerPoint**. Navigate to the student data files, open **ps02_ps1_Review**, and then type your name in the placeholder provided. Type your course information in the body content placeholder. Click the **File tab**, click **Save As**, click **Save as type**, and then click **PowerPoint Template**. Navigate to the location where you store your project files, type Lastname_Firstname_p02_ps1_Review_Template in the File name box, and then click **Save**.

b. Click the **View tab**, click **Slide Master** in the Master Views group, scroll to the top of the slide layouts in the left pane, and then click the **Office Theme Slide Master**.

c. Click **Colors** in the Edit Theme group, and then click **Median**.

d. Click **Background Styles** on the Slide Master tab, click **Format Background**, and then click **Gradient fill**. Select the **Linear** type. Click the **Direction arrow** and select **Linear Diagonal – Top Left to Bottom Right**. Click the **Angle arrows** to set the angle to **60°**. Click the **Gradient Stop 1 marker**, click **Color**, and then select **Brown, Text 2, Lighter 60%**. Set the **Gradient Stop 2 marker** to a **Position** at **50%** and **Color** of **Tan, Background 2**. Click **Close**.

e. Click **Fonts** in the Edit Theme group. Click **Create New Theme Fonts**, click the **Heading font arrow**, and then click **Lucida Sans**. Click the **Body font arrow**, and then click **Tahoma**. Select the text in the Name box, and then type Lastname_Firstname_Review_Fonts. Click **Save**.

f. Click each of the following layouts in the left pane and press Delete:
    - **Section Header Layout**
    - **Comparison Layout**
    - **Content with Caption Layout**
    - **Picture with Caption Layout**
    - **Title and Vertical Text Layout**
    - **Vertical Title and Text Layout**

g. Select the **date placeholder** on the theme slide master, and then press **Delete**. Repeat this step with the **page number placeholder**. Remove the date placeholder and the page number placeholder from all remaining slide layouts.

h. Click the **Insert tab**, and then click **Header & Footer**. Click **Footer** to select it, and then type Chef Robin Sanchez, Painted Paradise Golf Resort and Spa. Click **Don't show on title slide**, and then click **Apply to All**. On the footer containing the text you just typed, drag the left and right sizing handles until they are in line with the left and right edges of the content placeholder. Select the text in the footer placeholder, and then click the **Home tab**. Increase the font size to **16**.

i. Select the **Title Slide Layout**. Click the **Slide Master tab**, click **Background Styles** in the Background group, and then click **Format Background**. Click **Picture or texture fill**, click **File**, and then navigate to the location of the student data files. Click **p02_ws04_ Review_Background**, click **Insert**, and then click **Close**.

j. Click **Close Master View**, and then click **New Slide** on the Home tab. Click **Layout**, and then click **Title Slide**. Click the subtitle placeholder, and type Presented by Chef Robin Sanchez. Select the text and change the font color to **Black, Text 1, Lighter 15%**.

k. Click the **View tab**, and then click **Handout Master**. Click the **left header placeholder**, and then type Chef Robin Sanchez. In the **date placeholder**, type Date of Presentation and a blank space, and then type the numeric date. In the **footer placeholder**, type Painted Paradise Golf Resort and Spa. In the **page number placeholder**, type Page and a blank space in front of the bracket before the number sign. Click **Slides Per Page** in the Page Setup group, and then click **6 Slides**. Click **Close Master View**.

l. Click the **File tab**, and then click **Save**. Click the **File tab**, and then click **Close** to exit the template.

m. Click the **File tab**, click **New**, and then click **New from existing**. Navigate to the location of your project files, if necessary, and then click **Lastname_Firstname_p02_ps1_ Review_Template**. Click **Create New**, click the **File tab**, click **Save As**, navigate to the location where you store your project files, and then type Lastname_Firstname_p02_ ps1_Review_Test in the File name box. Click **Save**.

n. Click **Slide 2**, and then click the **New Slide arrow** on the Home tab, and then click **Slides from Outline**. Navigate to the location of your student data files, click **p02_ps1_Review_ Outline**, and then click **Insert**.

o. Click **Slide 2**, and then type Food Safety in the title placeholder. Select the title text, increase the font size to **54**, and then apply **Bold** formatting.

p. Click the **Insert tab**, click **Header & Footer**, and then click **Footer** to select it. Click **Don't show on title slide**, if necessary to select it, and then click **Apply to All**.

q. Click **Slide 7**, and then click the **Review tab**. Click **New Comment**, and then type Robin, I would suggest adding a concluding slide to end the presentation.

r. Click the **Slide Show tab**, and then click **From Beginning**. Review each slide. Save the presentation. Close the presentation and exit PowerPoint. Submit your files as directed by your instructor.

 Additional Workshop Cases are available on the companion website and in the instructor resources.

MODULE CAPSTONE

Student data files needed:

p02_mp_Vacation   p02_mp_V8
p02_mp_V1   p02_mp_V9
p02_mp_V2   p02_mp_V10
p02_mp_V3   p02_mp_V11
p02_mp_V4   p02_mp_V12
p02_mp_V5   p02_mp_V13
p02_mp_V6   p02_mp_V14
p02_mp_V7

You will save your files as:

Lastname_Firstname_p02_mp_Vacation_Template
Lastname_Firstname_p02_mp_Vacation_Presentation
Lastname_Firstname_p02_mp_Vacation_Album
Lastname_Firstname_p02_mp_Vacation_CD_Folder

Planning a Family Vacation at the Painted Paradise Resort Presentation

Sales & Marketing

Anthony Oskins, the manager of the Painted Paradise Resort Hotel, is interested in marketing to families who might want to spend a vacation at the resort. The recreational facilities, including the golf course, spa, and water park, make this an attractive destination for all members of the family. The restaurants at the resort make it convenient and cost-effective to feed the family. Anthony asked you to create a template and develop a sample presentation to advertise the benefits of a Painted Paradise vacation. You will create a template that appeals to kids and parents. You will develop a template for handouts as a part of the main template. You will develop a photo album of photographs from around the resort. Hyperlinks will be added to a slide. You will add transitions and animations to the slides, along with audio. The presentation will be packaged as a CD because Anthony intends to mail out the full presentation along with other marketing pieces about the resort. He also requested that you deliver the presentation at his next staff meeting, so you will create some speaker notes and make some planning comments on the slides.

a. Start **PowerPoint**. Navigate to the student data files, and then open **p02_mp_Vacation**. Type your name, course name, course number, and today's date on the slide. Save the file as a template in your project storage location with the file name Lastname_Firstname_p02_mp_Vacation_Template.

b. Change to **Slide Master** view, and select the **Office Theme Slide Master** thumbnail. Apply the **Waveform** color group to the template, and then apply the **Horizon** font group. Set the background texture to **Water droplets**, increase the transparency to **50%**, and then change the title color to **Dark Blue, Text 2**. Apply a **Text Shadow** to the title. Change the body text color to **Blue, Accent 1, Darker 50%**. On the slide master, remove the date and slide number footers. Adjust the size of the remaining footer placeholder so it stretches to the sides of the slide and its text within the placeholder is centered. Change the color of the footer text to **Blue, Accent 1, Darker 50%**.

c. Change to **Handout Master** view. In the header placeholder type Painted Paradise Golf Resort and Spa. On the next line of the header type The Destination for Your Next Vacation! Delete the date placeholder. Align the header placeholder in the center of the page, and center the text within the placeholder. In the footer placeholder type All Offers Subject to Availability. On the second line of the footer, type E-mail reservations@painted paradiseresort.com or phone 505-555-1792. Adjust the footer placeholder until all of the text on the second line appears on one line. Adjust the page number placeholder so it is not within the footer placeholder. Type Page in front of the symbol for the page number and include a space. Click **Close Master View** on the Handout Master tab. Save the template to your project storage location. Close the template.

d. Create a presentation based on the template. Save the file to your project file storage location as Lastname_Firstname_p02_mp_Vacation_Presentation. Add a title slide and type Fun for the Whole Family! in the title placeholder. In the subtitle placeholder, type The Destination for Your Next Vacation. On the second line type The Painted Paradise Golf Resort and Spa. Change the subtitle font color to **Blue**, **Accent 2**, **Darker 25%**, and then change the font to **Italic**. Adjust the size of the subtitle placeholder to a **Shape Width** of 7.9". Align the subtitle placeholder so it is centered on the slide.

e. Create a new Photo Album using the following photographs.

- **p02_mp_V1**
- **p02_mp_V2**
- **p02_mp_V3**
- **p02_mp_V4**
- **p02_mp_V5**
- **p02_mp_V6**
- **p02_mp_V7**
- **p02_mp_V8**
- **p02_mp_V9**
- **p02_mp_V10**
- **p02_mp_V11**
- **p02_mp_V12**
- **p02_mp_V13**
- **p02_mp_V14**

Move picture **4** to position **1**. Move pictures **5** and **6** into positions **3** and **4**. Move pictures **11**, **12**, and **13** into positions **6**, **7**, and **8**. Move picture **14** to position **9**. Remove the pictures in positions **7** and **8**. Change the Picture layout to **2 pictures with title**. Change the Frame shape to **Simple Frame**, **White**. Save the album as Lastname_Firstname_p02_mp_Vacation_Album. Close the file.

f. On the **Lastname_Firstname_p02_mp_Vacation_Presentation** file, reuse slides 2–7 of the **Lastname_Firstname_p02_mp_Vacation_Album**. Type the following titles on each slide:

Slide number	Title
3	Whether You Bike or Hike...
4	Golf with the Kids or Grandma...
5	Swim, Sun...
6	Spa, or Just Laugh Together
7	Catch a Snack or Dine
8	Affordable Luxury

g. On Slide 8, with **Align to Slide** selected, select **both photographs**, and then align them to the middle of the slide. Insert a **text box** below the photographs. Type Suites and Double-Queen Bed Rooms Provide You with Options. Increase the size of the font to 28. Align the text box in the center of the slide, and then move it to balance it with the rest of the elements on the slide.

h. Insert a new **Comparison layout** slide after Slide 6. Type the title Painted Paradise is Your Destination! In the left column heading placeholder, type Family of 4 Deal - 3 Nights. In the right column heading placeholder, type Large Family Deal - 4 Nights. Type the following text in the body placeholders:

• Double-Queen Bed Room	• Family Suite—Sleeps 8
• Round of Golf for 2	• Round of Golf for 4
• Spa Package for 2	• Spa Package for 4
• Access to Water Park	• Access to Water Park
• Family Service Meal at Indigo 5	• Family Service Meal at Indigo 5
• Breakfast at Red Bluff Bistro each morning	• Breakfast at Red Bluff Bistro each morning
• $595	• $895

i. Add a new **Content with Caption layout** slide after Slide 9. Place photograph **p02_mp_V13** in the right body content placeholder. Increase the height of the photograph to 6". Adjust the placement of the photograph so it is on the slide. Increase the Color Saturation of the photograph to **200%**. Apply the **Simple Frame**, **White** Picture Style to the photograph, and then type Make Your Reservations Today in the title placeholder. Center the text in the placeholder, and then increase the Font Size to 28. In the left content placeholder, type www.paintedparadiseresort.com. On the next line, insert the e-mail address hyperlink of reservations@paintedparadiseresort.com with a subject line of Family Deal Reservation. Type 505-555-1792 on the following line. Press Enter twice, and then type Anthony Oskins, manager. Select all of the text in the placeholder, and increase the Font Size to 16. Center the text in the placeholder, change the line spacing to 2.5, and then drag the **sizing handles** to accommodate the e-mail address on one line. Align the title placeholder and the content placeholder so they are centered in relationship to each other and balanced with the photograph.

j. Select **Slides 2** through **10** on the Slides tab, apply the **Fly Through** transition to the group, and then set the duration of the transition to **1.00**.

k. Apply animations to the slides as follows:

Slide Number	Element to Animate	Animation	Timing
3	Title	Zoom	Start With Previous, Duration 1.00
4	Title	Zoom	Start With Previous, Duration 1.00
5	Title	Zoom	Start With Previous, Duration 1.00
6	Title	Zoom	Start With Previous, Duration 1.00
7	Title	Split (Effect Option – Vertical Out)	Start With Previous, Duration 1.00
7	Both column headings	Split (Effect Option – Vertical Out)	Start After Previous, Duration 1.00
7	Both content columns	Float In	Start After Previous, Duration 0.75
8	Title	Zoom	Start With Previous, Duration 1.00
9	Title	Zoom	Start With Previous, Duration 1.00
9	Two photographs and text box	Split (Effect Option – Vertical Out)	Start With Previous, Duration 1.00, Delay 1.00
10	Title	Zoom	Start With Previous, Duration 1.00
10	Hyperlinks, phone number, and manager name	Float In	Start After Previous, Duration 0.50

l. On Slide 2, insert the Clip Art Audio named **Xylo Beat** from Office.com content. Set the Audio Options to start the audio **Automatically**, hide the player during the show, and **Loop until Stopped**. Add the same audio to Slide 10, with the same audio options.

m. Add the footer The Place for Your Next Family Vacation – www.paintedparadiseresort .com to all of the slides except the title slide.

n. Review each slide in the presentation in Slide Show view. Save the presentation, package the presentation for CD distribution, and then name the folder Lastname_Firstname_ p02_mp_Vacation_CD_Folder.

o. On Slide 2, add a comment, by typing This presentation will be given to the marketing staff under the direction of Anthony Oskins. They are interested in seeing the template that was developed to market the vacation deals available at the resort. Press Enter twice, and then type Don't forget: Computer, power supply, extension cords, projector.

p. Add a speaker note to Slide 2:
  • My purpose is to show you the template developed to market the family vacation deals.
  • Most people equate vacation to being around water.
  • Template developed with a water theme.
  • Audio is upbeat and cheerful.
  Add a speaker note to Slide 3:
  • The next few slides show the fun families can have at the resort.
  • The photos contain white borders to appear as if they were vacation photographs.
  Add a speaker note to Slide 7:
  • Example of two deals offered recently by the resort.
  • This would be changed as needed.
  • Single slide change, quick, easy, fast turnaround time.
  Add a speaker note to Slide 10:
  • Final slide is a contact slide.
  • Hyperlinks work and the e-mail link sends a message to the reservations department with the subject of "Family Deal Reservation".
  • What questions do you have for me?

q. Prepare to print handouts with **2 Slides** per page. Review each page of the handout. Notice that page 2 contains the comment that was written on Slide 2. Print the handout if your instructor requests that you turn in a printout.

r. Save and close the presentation file, and then exit PowerPoint.

Problem Solve 1

Homework 1

Student data files needed:

p02_ps1_Bridal
p02_ps1_Bridal1
p02_ps1_Bridal2
p02_ps1_Bridal3
p02_ps1_Bridal4
p02_ps1_Bridal5

p02_ps1_Bridal6
p02_ps1_Bridal7
p02_ps1_Bridal8
p02_ps1_Bridal9
p02_ps1_Bridal10
p02_ps1_Bridal_Outline

You will save your files as:

Lastname_Firstname_p02_ps1_Bridal_Template
Lastname_Firstname_p02_ps1_Bridal_Presentation
Lastname_Firstname_p02_ps1_Bridal_Album
Lastname_Firstname_p02_ps1_Bridal_Video

The Wedding Catering Presentation

Sales & Marketing

Ellie Gold, the wedding planner for the Painted Paradise Golf Resort and Spa, and Robin Sanchez, the chef for the resort, are participating in an upcoming Bridal Fair where brides shop for and plan their weddings. You will create a presentation video that will be displayed on a computer screen in a booth. The presentation's main audience will be brides, but a secondary audience of mothers, fiancés, and bridesmaids should be considered. You will develop a template for the presentation, and create and use a photo album to insert graphics into the presentation. An outline will provide some content. You will include transitions and animations to engage the audience in the presentation. A comment, placed on a slide, will remind Ellie and Robin of the equipment they will need. You will create the video in a small format so you can get approval for it, before creating the larger video file.

a. Open **p02_ps1_Bridal**, and then type your name, course information, and today's date. Save the file as a template in your project files location as Lastname_Firstname_p02_ps1_Bridal_Template.

b. On the Office Theme Slide Master change the Colors to **Opulent**. From this color group, select **Create New Theme Colors** for the **Hyperlink**, using the color **Lavender, Text 2, Darker 75%**. Set the **Followed Hyperlink** to **Lavender, Text 2, Darker 50%**. Name the new theme colors Lastname_Firstname_Bridal_Colors.

c. Create **New Theme Fonts** with **Brush Script MT** for the **Heading font** and **Arial Narrow** for the **Body font**. Name the font group Lastname_Firstname_Bridal_Font.

d. Format the background for all layouts using **Gradient fill** and **Type** set to **Shade from title**. Set Gradient Stop 1 at **Position 0%** in **Gold, Accent 4, Lighter 40%**. Set Gradient Stop 2 at **Position 35%** in **Gold, Accent 4, Lighter 80%**.

e. Set the title font color to **Lavender, Background 2, Darker 90%**. Set the body content font color to **Lavender, Background 2, Darker 75%**. Select the first bullet point, and then customize the bullet to Wingdings symbol **152**, in the color **Lavender, Background 2, Darker 50%**. Select the remaining bullet points, and then customize them to Wingdings symbol **153**, **75%** of the text size, and in the color **Lavender, Background 2, Darker 50%**.

f. Click the **Title Slide Layout**, select the subtitle text, and then change the font color to **Lavender, Background 2, Darker 50%**. On the line below the subtitle text, insert Wingdings symbols **151** and **150**.

g. Delete the Section Header Layout, Title and Vertical Text Layout, and Vertical Title and Text Layout. Delete the date and slide number footer from each of the remaining layouts. Select the **footer text**, change the color to **Lavender, Background 2, Darker 75%**, and then change the font to **Arial Narrow**, size **18**.

h. Click the **Content with Caption Layout**, and select the placeholder on the right side of the slide. Drag the **left sizing handle** to the right so the placeholder is **4.5"** wide. Select the two placeholders on the left, and then change the **Shape Width** of the placeholders to **4"**. Select the **title text**, and then increase the size of the font to **32**. Select the body text placeholder, and then increase the size of the text to **20**.

i. Close the Master view. Save the template in your project storage location. Close the template.

j. Create a new presentation based on the template you just built. Save the file as Lastname_Firstname_p02_ps1_Bridal_Presentation.

k. Create a photo album with the following photographs:

- **ps02_ps1_Bridal1**
- **ps02_ps1_Bridal2**
- **ps02_ps1_Bridal3**
- **ps02_ps1_Bridal4**

- **ps02_ps1_Bridal5**
- **ps02_ps1_Bridal6**
- **ps02_ps1_Bridal7**
- **ps02_ps1_Bridal8**

Move the photographs until they appear in this order in the Pictures in album box:

- **ps02_ps1_Bridal8**
- **ps02_ps1_Bridal2**
- **ps02_ps1_Bridal1**
- **ps02_ps1_Bridal3**

- **ps02_ps1_Bridal6**
- **ps02_ps1_Bridal4**
- **ps02_ps1_Bridal5**
- **ps02_ps1_Bridal7**

Remove the photograph **p02_ps1_Bridal3**. Select **1 picture with title** for the Picture layout, and use **Center Shadow Rectangle** for the Frame shape. Save the photo album as Lastname_Firstname_p02_ps1_Bridal_Album and then close it.

l. In the **Lastname_Firstname_p02_ps1_Bridal_Presentation**, import the outline **p02_ps1_Bridal_Outline**. Select **Slide 2**, and then reuse the photograph content slides from **Lastname_Firstname_p02_ps1_Bridal_Album**.

m. Select **Slides 3** through **9**, and then apply the transition **Reveal**, with a **Duration** of **4.00**. Advance the slides automatically after **5.00** seconds. Select **Slides 2** and **10**, and then apply the transition **Reveal**, with a **Duration** of **2.00**. Advance the slides automatically after **7.00** seconds.

n. On Slide 2, change the layout to **Content with Caption**. Select the **body content text**, and then drag it into the placeholder on the right. If a blank line appears under **Floral matched**, delete it. Align the **text** to the middle of the placeholder, and then align the placeholder with **Distribute Vertically**. Delete the placeholder under the title text, and insert the photograph **p02_ps1_Bridal9**. Resize the photograph to **5"** in height. Apply the **Drop Shadow Rectangle** Picture Style to the photograph, **center** the title text within the placeholder, and then increase the font size to **40**. Select the title placeholder and the photograph, and align them with **Distribute Vertically** to the slide, and **Align Center** to the selected objects. Select the words **Food**, **Décor**, and **Custom Cakes**, and then change their font to **Bold**.

o. Continuing with Slide 2, select the words **Food**, **Décor**, and **Custom Cakes**. Apply the **Float In** animation, starting **After Previous**, with a **Duration** of **1.00**. Select the bullet points related to the **Food heading**, and apply the **Shape** animation using the **Diamond** effect, starting **After Previous**, with the **Duration** of **1.00**. Apply the same animation to the remaining two groups of body content.

p. Type the following titles on the slides, increasing the font size to **54** for each title:

Slide Number	Title
3	Table Décor
4	Table Service for up to 500
5	Appetizer Service
6	Buffets
7	Custom Cakes with Fresh Flowers
8	Custom Cakes with Lace
9	Custom Cakes in Many Flavors

q. Select Slide 10. Increase the font size of the title to **54**. Select the text **Painted Paradise Golf Resort and Spa**, and then set a hyperlink to the URL/address http://www .paintedparadiseresort.com. Press Enter to create a new bullet point, and then set a hyperlink to an e-mail address with the text to be displayed as E-mail the Wedding Planner. Set the e-mail address to be egold@paintedparadiseresort.com and type a subject of Wedding Inquiry. Insert a **Heart** shape in the bottom-right corner of the slide, measuring **4"** in height by **3.3"** in width. Fill the heart shape with photograph **p02_ps1_ Bridal10**, and then apply an **Offset Diagonal Bottom Right** shadow to the graphic.

r. Insert a footer, and then type www.paintedparadiseresort.com. The footer should appear on all slides.

s. On Slide 1, type this comment:

Don't forget this equipment!

DVD player

Computer monitor

3 extension cords

Laptop

DVD of presentation

t. Review the presentation in **Slide Show** view. Save the presentation. Using **Save & Send**, create a video for **Internet & DVD**, using the **Recorded Timings and Narrations**. Name the video file Lastname_Firstname_p02_ps1_Bridal_Video and then save it to your project storage location. Wait until the movie has been rendered, review it, and then close the presentations.

Problem Solve 2

Student data files needed:

p02_ps2_Mobile
p02_ps2_Mobile_Cellphone_WMF
p02_ps2_Mobile_Outline
p02_ps2_Mobile_People_WMF

You will save your files as:

Lastname_Firstname_p02_ps2_Mobile_Presentation
Lastname_Firstname_p02_ps2_Mobile_Notes

Sales & Marketing

Mobile Restaurant Marketing Pitch Presentation

As an avid cell phone user, you have become aware of mobile marketing. You can sign up for special offers and deals that are for cell phone users only. You have been thinking about the implications of this type of marketing for the Painted Paradise Golf Resort and Spa, and have been asked to make a presentation at the next meeting of the board of directors. You will use the slide master tools to create backgrounds on different slide layouts for consistency in the presentation, but you will not create an actual template. You have created an outline of important points, which you will import into the presentation. You have found an interesting YouTube video to embed in the presentation. Transitions and animations will be used in the slide show. You will create speaker notes to use during your persuasive presentation. The handout master will be modified to produce customized handouts of some of the key slides of the presentation.

a. Open **p02_ps2_Mobile**, and then type your name, course information and today's date. Save the file as a PowerPoint presentation in your project files location as Lastname_ Firstname_p02_ps2_Mobile_Presentation.

b. Using Slide Master view, select the **slide master thumbnail** at the top of the left pane. Insert **Clip Art** using the Search term cellphone. (Notice that in this case it is spelled as one word.) Modify the settings in the Clip Art pane so only photographs are searched and include **Office.com** content. Select the **image of the cell phone being held up on a blue background**. For your reference, the image is included with the project starting materials, with the file name **p02_ps2_Mobile_Cellphone_WMF**. Remove the blue background from the photograph using the Picture Tools Format tab. Crop any extra white space. Move the cell phone into position in the bottom-left corner of the slide. Arrange it in back of all objects on the slide. Select the body content placeholder, and drag the **left sizing handle** to the right to move the content away from the photograph. Delete the slide number placeholder. Move the footer placeholder under the body content placeholder, and then increase the footer placeholder size so it is the same width as the body content placeholder. Select the title placeholder, body content placeholder, and the footer placeholder, and then **Distribute Vertically**. Type Mobile Marketing at the Painted Paradise Golf Resort and Spa in the footer placeholder. Place the footer on all slides except the title slide.

c. Select the **Title Slide Layout** in Slide Master view, and then select the title placeholder. Alter the size of the title placeholder to **3.2"** in height and **5"** in width. Select the subtitle placeholder, and then alter the size to **1.5"** in height and **5"** in width. Delete the slide number placeholder and the date placeholder if it is visible. Select the title and subtitle placeholders. Align the selected objects to the center, and then drag them to the right of the photograph above the footer. Align the title and subtitle placeholders to the slide by **Distributing Vertically**.

d. Select the **Title and Content Layout**, and then delete the date and slide number placeholders. Delete all of the layouts except Title Slide, Title and Content, and Hidden Slide Student Info. Close Slide Master view, and then save the presentation.

e. Import the outline named **p02_ps2_Mobile_Outline** into the presentation. Select **Slide 2**, and then change the layout to **Title Slide**. Add your name to the subtitle placeholder. Adjust the size of the font if necessary to attractively space the subtitle.

f. Select **Slides 3** through **9**, and then apply the **Title and Content** layout. If the footer you set up is not on the slide, use **Header & Footer** on the Insert tab to apply it to all of the slides except the title slide.

g. Select **Slide 5**, and then hide the background graphic. Insert a **Clip Art** photograph of **two people using a cell phone**, using the search word cellphone from the **Office.com** content. For your reference, the image is included with the project starting materials with the file name **p02_ps2_Mobile_People_WMF**. Resize the photograph to a width of **4"**, and then align it to the middle on the left edge of the slide.

h. Select **Slide 6**, insert a **rectangle** shape over the screen of the phone. Change the Shape Fill to **Black**, **Text 1**. Add the text Indigo 5 Specials Lunch: Sweet Potato Hash Dinner: Prime Rib w/Potato.

i. Select **Slide 8**, and delete the empty body content placeholder. Open a browser window, navigate to www.youtube.com, and then search for mobile marketing. Review a few of the videos, select one, and then use the old embed code to embed it onto the slide. Position the video box on the right side of the slide.

j. Select **Slide 9**, and insert the following **hyperlinks**:
- Mobile Marketing Association
  - www.mmaglobal.com
- mobiThinking
  - www.mobithinking.com
- Mobile Marketer
  - www.mobilemarketer.com
- Direct Marketing Association
  - www.the-dma.org

Remember to type a space after the last hyperlink to format it as a hyperlink.

k. Select **Slides 2** through **9**, and then apply the **Push** transition with the Effect Option of **From Top**. Select **Slide 5**, and then animate each bullet point so each appears when the mouse button is clicked. Keep the last two points in the same animation because they are related. Select **Slide 6**, animate the **Text Messaging group** so it appears with a mouse click, and then animate the **Social Media group** to appear with a mouse click.

l. Add the following speaker notes to the presentation:

Slide	Note
2	Introduce self, title, role in Marketing department
3	Discussion focus - mobile marketing, essential questions to ask ourselves
4	Show examples of the types of mobile devices, ask if anyone else has any to show
5	Click to show each bullet, discuss: 24/7 customer attention Market trends About 55 billion text messages are sent every day
6	Text messaging can be used to update guests on specials or offer coupons Social media, accessed through mobile devices can also be used Example - the chef could tweet about a new dessert or dinner entrée
7	Customers want information that is relevant to them Security of data is very important Keep it short and simple, small screen, short bursts of information Provide way to elect not to receive future messages
9	Lots of good information in these resources Also included on handout Go to Mobile Marketing Association to show site What questions do you have for me?

m. Select **Slide 2**, and then create a new comment as follows:

Bring cell phone, iPad, and PDA

Check Internet connection

n. Switch to **Handout Master** view. Type Mobile Marketing Presentation and your name in the header placeholder, placing your name on the second line of the placeholder. In the date placeholder, type Date of Presentation in front of the numeric date. In the footer placeholder, type your e-mail address. In the page number placeholder, type Page in front of the parentheses before the number sign. Close **Master view**. Set up the printing of handouts, two per page for Slides 5, 6, 7, and 9, and then print the handouts if requested by your instructor.

o. Review the presentation, and then save the presentation. Create Word handouts with notes next to slides for you to use during your presentation, type Confidential at the top of the document, and then save the Word document as Lastname_Firstname_p02_ps2_ Mobile_Notes. Close the Word document and the PowerPoint presentation.

Student data files needed:

p02_ps3_Cook	p02_ps3_Cook7
p02_ps3_Cook1	p02_ps3_Cook_Outline
p02_ps3_Cook2	p02_ps3_Cook_Fork
p02_ps3_Cook3	p02_ps3_Cook_Knife_WMF
p02_ps3_Cook4	p02_ps3_Cook_Hat_WMF
p02_ps3_Cook5	p02_ps3_Cook_Garlic_WMF
p02_ps3_Cook6	

You will save your files as:

Lastname_Firstname_p02_ps3_Cook_Template
Lastname_Firstname_p02_ps3_Cook_Presentation
Lastname_Firstname_p02_ps3_Cook_Album

Sales & Marketing

Indigo 5 Cooking School

The chef, Robin Sanchez, along with her sous chef, Matt Andretti, and pastry chef, Michael Benoit, decided to offer cooking classes on Tuesday afternoons in the Indigo 5 kitchen. Guests of the resort, as well as local residents, will spend a few hours learning how to cook soup, pasta, fish, bread, and desserts. You will create the PowerPoint presentation the chef will deliver to various audiences. For the most part, the audiences will be viewing the presentation for entertainment, but Robin would like to also advertise the classes and persuade people to participate.

You will begin the project by creating a template. You will import an outline that the chef has provided. A photo album will provide an inside look at the Indigo 5 kitchen. You will add transitions to the slides. Some slides will be hidden. Links between the slides will provide nonsequential viewing of the slides. A graphic will be used to return you to previous slides. A slide footer, added to the slide master, will contain the web address for the restaurant. You will customize the handout master, so it includes the contact information necessary to register for the courses.

After completing the presentation, you will print selected slides as handouts.

a. Open **p02_ps3_Cook**, and then type your name, course information, and today's date. Save the file as a **PowerPoint Template** in your project files location as Lastname_Firstname_p02_ps3_Cook_Template.

b. Open **Slide Master** view. If necessary, set the design theme to **Office Theme**. Click the **theme slide master** thumbnail. Set the background style to **Style 6** so the slides will appear to be stainless steel, the surface of much of the equipment in the Indigo 5 kitchen. Create a **New Theme Color** group named Lastname_Firstname_Cook_Colors. Change the Hyperlink color to **Black**, **Background 1**, **Lighter 35%**. Change the Followed Hyperlink color to **Black**, **Background 1**, **Lighter 50%**. Select **Solstice** as the font group, select the body content placeholder, and then fill the shape with **White**, **Background 1**. Customize the bullets to Wingdings Character code **118**, using the color **Black**, **Text 1**, **Lighter 50%**. Set up the footer placeholders by changing the color of the footer text to **Black**, **Text 1**, **Lighter 15%**, and then select and remove the slide number footer. Select the remaining footer placeholders and distribute them horizontally. Delete the following layouts:

- Section Header Layout
- Title and Vertical Text Layout
- Vertical Title and Text Layout

c. Close Slide Master view, and then open the **Handout Master**. In the header placeholder, type Indigo 5 Cooking School. Type Chef Robin Sanchez on the second line. Remove the date placeholder, center align the header placeholder on the page, and then center the text within the placeholder. In the footer placeholder, type rsanchez@paintedparadiseresort.com. Type 505-555-1964 on the second line. Close the Master view.

d. Save the template to your project files location, and then close the template. Create a new presentation based on the template file you just created, and then save the new file to your project files location with the filename Lastname_Firstname_p02_ps3_Cook_Presentation.

e. Create a photo album using the following photographs:

- **ps02_ps3_Cook1**
- **ps02_ps3_Cook2**
- **ps02_ps3_Cook3**
- **ps02_ps3_Cook4**
- **ps02_ps3_Cook5**
- **ps02_ps3_Cook6**
- **ps02_ps3_Cook7**

  Move **ps02_ps3_Cook4** to position **1**. Move **p02_ps3_Cook7** to position **6**. Add a text box at position **2**. Set the Picture layout to **2 pictures with title**, and then set the Frame shape to **Simple Frame**, **Black**.

  Alter the slides in the Photo Album as follows:

- On Slide 2, select the title placeholder, and then type Meet Our Chefs. Type Chef Robin Sanchez in the text box. Type Pastry Chef Michael Benoit on the second line and Sous Chef Matt Andretti on the third line. Change the font size to **24**, and then apply bullets to the text.

- On Slide 3, select the title placeholder, and then type The Finest Ingredients Prepared in Our Commercial Kitchen.

- On Slide 4, select the title placeholder, and then type Learn the Secrets.

- On Slide 5, select the title placeholder, and then type Learn from Us!

  Save the photo album in your project files location with the name of Lastname_ Firstname_p02_ps3_Cook_Album. Close the photo album.

f. Reuse the photograph slides from the photo album in the **Lastname_Firstname_p02_ ps3_Cook_Presentation** file. Import the outline **p02_ps3_Cook_Outline**. Reset the imported slides to pick up the template formatting. Delete Slide 9, as you will add the contact information to a slide with photographs. Move **Slide 6** (Indigo 5 Cooking School) to position **2**. Move **Slide 7** (Classes this Month) to position **4**. Hide **Slides 9**, **10**, and **11**, insert a **footer**, and then type www.paintedparadiseresort.com. Type Chef Robin Sanchez for a Fixed Date footer, and then apply the footer to all slides except the title slide.

g. On **Slide 4**, create a **hyperlink** on the words **Chop Chop** to the same document, accessing **Slide 9**. Create a **hyperlink** for the **One Night Stand** text to **Slide 10**. Create a **hyperlink** for the **Santa Fe Secrets** text to **Slide 11**. Insert the photograph **p02_ps3_Cook_Fork** in the white space on the slide. Increase the size of the photograph to **3.5"** in height. Align it to the **Middle** and to the **Right** so it lines up with the right edge of the slide. Apply the **Simple Frame**, **Black** Picture Style.

h. On **Slide 9**, insert a **Clip Art illustration** of a **chef knife** from the **Office.com** content. For your reference, the image is included with the project starting materials, with the file name **p02_ps3_Cook_Knife_WMF**. Adjust the graphic to a height of **3"**. Align it to the right and bottom of the slide just above the footer. Change the color to **Grayscale**. With the graphic selected, set a **hyperlink** to **Slide 4**.

i. On **Slide 10**, insert a **Clip Art illustration** of a **chef hat** from the **Office.com** content. For your reference, the image is included with the project starting materials, with the file name **p02_ps3_Cook_Hat_WMF**. Adjust the graphic to a size of **2.5"** in **height**. Align it to the right and bottom of the slide just above the footer. Change the color to **Grayscale**. With the graphic selected, set a **hyperlink** to **Slide 4**.

j. On **Slide 11**, insert a **Clip Art illustration** of **garlic** from the **Office.com** content. For your reference, the image is included with the project starting materials, with the file name **p02_ps3_Cook_Garlic_WMF**. Adjust the graphic to a size of **2.5"** in **height**. Align it to the right and bottom of the slide just above the footer, and then change the color to **Grayscale**. With the graphic selected, set a hyperlink to **Slide 4**. If necessary, remove any extra blank spaces at the bottom of the bullet list.

k. Select **Slides 2** through **11**, apply the **Pan** transition to the slides, set the Effect Option **From Top**, and then set the **Duration** to **1.00** seconds.

l. On **Slide 3**, select the **photograph**, and align it center and middle. Select the text place-holder, and then adjust the size to **2.5"** in height. Align the text placeholder center and bottom. Select the **names**, and then set an entrance animation of **Wipe** to the names. Select the Effect Option **From Top**, and then start the effect **On Click**.

m. On **Slide 7**, select both **photographs** and change the size to **4.7"** in **height**. Distribute them horizontally to the slide, and then align them in the middle. Insert a **text box** under the photograph of the **male chef**, and type mbenoit@paintedparadiseresort.com. Fill the text box shape with **White**, **Background 1** color. Select the **photograph** and the **text box**, and then align the selected objects with center alignment. Insert a **text box** under the photograph of the female chef, and type rsanchez@paintedparadiseresort.com. Fill the text box shape with **White**, **Background 1** color. Select the **photograph** and the **text box**, and then align the selected objects with center alignment. Select both **text boxes**, and align the selected objects to the top (the top of one object will be even with the top of the other object). If the photographs are not balanced, distribute them horizontally, and then distribute the text boxes horizontally. If necessary, move the text boxes above the footers. Select the e-mail address **mbenoit@paintedparadiseresort. com**, and then insert a **hyperlink** to the same address with the subject line of Cooking School Reservation. Repeat this action with the **rsanchez@paintedparadiseresort.com** e-mail address.

n. Review the slide show testing each of the hyperlinks on Slide 4 and returning to the slide using the graphic hyperlink. Set up the print function for four slides per page (horizontal) handouts, printing only Slides 2, 4, 7, and 8. Preview the print out, and then check it for the header and footers. Print the document if requested by your instructor. Save and close the presentation.

Perform 1: Perform in Your Life

Student data file needed:

Blank, PowerPoint document

You will save your files as:

Lastname_Firstname_p02_pf1_Reunion
Lastname_Firstname_p02_pf1_Reunion_Word
Lastname_Firstname_p02_pf1_Reunion_Video
Lastname_Firstname_p02_pf1_Reunion_CD_Folder

High School Reunion Presentation

Sales & Marketing

As a member of the reunion planning committee for your high school class, you will be creating a PowerPoint presentation to show your classmates' current photographs. For this project, you are only to create a small number of slides to use as an example of how a presentation for your entire class would look. You want to share this idea with the committee before you spend a lot of time producing the presentation. You will use PowerPoint's Photo Album feature with appropriate photographs and text. This presentation will be displayed as a self-running presentation. As a money-making resource to help defray the costs of the reunion, you will offer copies of the presentation for sale on CD. The audience for this presentation is composed of people your age who attended your high school.

a. Start **PowerPoint**, start a new presentation, and then start the Photo Album feature of PowerPoint.

b. Create the photo album based on a group of 10–20 photographs. Add text boxes and captions to the slides. Apply a theme, keeping in mind that you can alter the colors of the theme to reflect your school colors after you have created the photo album.

c. After creating the photo album, save it as Lastname_Firstname_p02_pf1_Reunion.

d. On the title slide of the photo album, add a graphic or photograph that ties the presentation with your high school. The title slide should also contain a copyright notice, with the copyright symbol, the year, a comma, and your name. The high school website address/URL should appear somewhere on the title slide as a hyperlink.

e. Add text to the text boxes you included as you created the photo album. Modify the captions of the photographs to include the name of the people in the photograph.

f. Apply transitions to the slides.

g. Add animations to elements on the slides.

h. Modify the theme as needed for colors or fonts.

i. Create speaker notes on each slide with the names of the people pictured and a short snippet of information about the person, such as where they live now and if they are married with children.

j. Create a Word document that contains a thumbnail of the slides and the speaker notes. Save the Word document as Lastname_Firstname_p02_pf1_Reunion_Word. Add narration to the slides, using the speaker notes you created.

k. Save the presentation after you have made the modifications listed here.

l. Save the presentation as a video for Internet or DVD distribution, with the file name Lastname_Firstname_p02_pf1_Reunion_Video.

m. Save the presentation for CD in a folder named Lastname_Firstname_p02_pf1_Reunion_CD_Folder.

Perform 2: Perform in Your Career

Student data file needed:

Blank, PowerPoint document

You will save your files as:

Lastname_Firstname_p02_pf2_HIPAA_Template
Lastname_Firstname_p02_pf2_HIPAA
Lastname_Firstname_p02_pf2_HIPAA_Show
Lastname_Firstname_p02_pf2_HIPAA_Word
Lastname_Firstname_p02_pf2_HIPAA_Narrated

HIPAA Training

Human Resources

As the administrative manager of the American Health Group, you are responsible for training the staff. One issue that must be covered with employees is the Health Insurance Portability and Accountability Act of 1996. You will create a presentation that reviews the type of information covered under the act after completing Internet research for information on HIPAA. Your audience will be medical workers and staff members such as receptionists, records managers, and insurance processors. You may have new employees as part of the audience, but for the most part, this is refresher training. Most of the time, the presentation will be given to groups of 10 to 12 people during coffee meetings that normally last about 30 minutes. In some cases, people will view the slides on their own at their desks, so you will narrate a version for distribution to these people.

a. Start **PowerPoint**, and then create an appropriate template for the topic and audience. You should make adjustments to the background, colors, fonts, and other design elements of the presentation. Modify the handout master to include a header with your name, the current date, and American Health Group. Save the template to your project files folder, with the name Lastname_Firstname_p02_pf2_HIPAA_Template. Close the template file.

b. Begin a new presentation, using the template, based on your research into the types of information that are covered by HIPAA. Name this file Lastname_Firstname_p02_pf2_HIPAA. Be sure to provide an introduction and roadmap, and a conclusion to your presentation. Keep the Rule of 6's in mind as you place content on the slides.

c. Add appropriate transitions to each of the slides.

d. Animate text elements on slides so they appear individually, allowing you to focus the attention of the audience on one point at a time.

e. Create speaker notes for all or most slides.

f. In an appropriate location, include a hyperlink to the external website www.hhs.gov, with the display U.S. Department of Health and Human Services.

g. Embed an appropriate YouTube video related to HIPAA in the presentation.

h. Create a custom slide show that does not contain the YouTube video.

i. Add comments to the title slide describing how you would prepare for this presentation. Provide a checklist of items that you should remember to take with you to the presentation.

j. Add comments to the introduction/roadmap slide describing what you will do during the presentation to engage the audience.

k. Carefully proofread the presentation, and then save the presentation. Save the presentation again as a PowerPoint Show so it opens without opening PowerPoint first. Name this file Lastname_Firstname_p02_pf2_HIPAA_Show.

l. Print handouts with three slides per page and lines for notes. Create a Word document that contains a thumbnail of the slides and the speaker notes to use in the next step. Name the Word document Lastname_Firstname_p02_pf2_HIPAA_Word.

m. Narrate the slides, using the speaker notes you created in Step e. Save this presentation as Lastname_Firstname_p02_pf2_HIPAA_Narrated.

Perform 3: Perform in Your Career

Student data files needed:	You will save your files as:
p02_pf3_Garden_Outline	Lastname_Firstname_p02_pf3_Garden_Template
p02_pf3_Garden_Photo1	Lastname_Firstname_p02_pf3_Garden
p02_pf3_Garden_Photo2	Lastname_Firstname_p02_pf3_Garden_Album
p02_pf3_Garden_Photo3	Lastname_Firstname_p02_pf3_Garden_Show
p02_pf3_Garden_Photo4	
p02_pf3_Garden_Photo5	
p02_pf3_Garden_Photo6	
p02_pf3_Garden_Photo7	
p02_pf3_Garden_Photo8	
p02_pf3_Garden_Photo9	

Let's Grow Community Garden Report to Board Presentation

General Business

It has been a successful year for the Let's Grow Community Garden project, in which you have been participating. You need to make a report to the members of the executive board, and you plan to focus on the newest garden. There are six board members, but other people who are interested in the project will attend the meeting where you will give your presentation. The board is interested in the success of the North garden and is expecting to see some of the results. For this presentation, you will create a template, import an outline, create a photo album, and apply transitions and animations to the slides. You will create a handout for this presentation after modifying the handout master.

a. Start **PowerPoint**, and then create an appropriate template for the Let's Grow Community Garden report. Design the title slide with a background image that is different from the other layout slide backgrounds. Only include layouts in the template that you will use in the presentation. Save the template file as Lastname_Firstname_p02_pf3_Garden_Template.

b. Create a handout master, which includes the following information, in an appropriate font and size:
   • Left Header: Let's Grow Community Gardens
   • Right Header: Your name
   • Left Footer: Copyright symbol, the year, and Let's Grow, Inc.
   • Right Footer: Your e-mail address
   Save the handout master as a part of the template.

c. Create a new presentation based on the template, and then save the presentation as Lastname_Firstname_p02_pf3_Garden.

d. Import the outline file **p02_pf3_Garden_Outline**, and then select appropriate slide layouts for the information on the slides. Use Reset to change the text formatting to the template settings.

e. Create a photo album using the photographs provided and any personal photographs you might have that relate to the garden theme. Select a layout for the photo album that has two or more photographs per slide. Use text where appropriate, and then name the photo album Lastname_Firstname_p02_pf3_Garden_Album.

f. Reuse the slides from the photo album in the original presentation. Make adjustments to the slides to integrate them into the message of the presentation.

g. Apply transitions to each of the slides, and then apply animations to the text elements on the slides so bullet points are introduced with a click.

h. Locate an audio file of birds chirping in the Office.com Clip Art and insert it on the title slide of the presentation. Hide the playback controls, and then have the audio file play until the slide is advanced.

i. Using the Internet, research the topic of community gardens. Provide a slide with five website hyperlinks that would be useful to the audience.

j. Embed a YouTube video that highlights a community garden.

k. Create a custom slide show named Let's Grow Board that only includes the slides created by importing the outline and the photo album. In other words, the hyperlink slide and the YouTube video slide will not be visible in this custom slide show. You have checked out the location of the board meeting and found that an Internet connection is not available, but you also expect to give this presentation at a local school and want to use the resources for that presentation.

l. Create a handout of the hyperlink slide only.

m. On the title slide, place a comment that lists all of the equipment and auxiliary items, such as a basket of produce from the garden, that you might need for the presentation.

n. Save the presentation, and then save the presentation as a PowerPoint Show named Lastname_Firstname_p02_pf3_Garden_Show.

Student data files needed:

p02_pf4_Yoga
p02_pf4_Yoga_Background

You will save your files as:

Lastname_Firstname_p02_pf4_Yoga_Comments
Lastname_Firstname_p02_pf4_Yoga_Template
Lastname_Firstname_p02_pf4_Yoga_New
Lastname_Firstname_p02_pf4_Yoga_CD_Folder

The Yoga for You Presentation

Sales & Marketing

The local yoga studio, 2 Yogis, wants to advertise to the community through a PowerPoint presentation to be shown at an upcoming fitness event. Maddie Wollman asked you to review the presentation that she created and comment on it. She worked hard to put this presentation together, using a template, animations, transitions, an audio file, a photo album, and an interesting YouTube video. Her target audience includes people who are interested in being fit and reducing the stress in their lives. She expects the potential students to be in the age range of 15 to 50 years old. She knows they will only stop by her booth for a few moments, and she needs to quickly catch their attention and engage them.

a. Start **PowerPoint**, and then open the file **p02_pf4_Yoga**. When you open the file, you will see a Security Warning bar. Click **Enable Content** to continue, and then save the file with your project files with the file name Lastname_Firstname_p02_pf4_Yoga_Comments.

b. Review the presentation in Slide Show view. You may have to watch it multiple times to evaluate the content and design.

c. On each slide, place a comment with ideas for improvement of the slide content or design. You may also mention the positive elements on the slides. Save the presentation.

d. Start a new **PowerPoint file**, and then create a new template for the presentation. The photograph used as a background for the title slide, **p02_pf4_Yoga_Background**, has been provided in the data files if you want to use it. Save this template as Lastname_Firstname_p02_pf4_Yoga_Template.

e. Start a new **PowerPoint file** using the template you created. Reuse the slides from p02_pf4_Yoga to create the presentation content, and then save the file as Lastname_Firstname_p02_pf4_Yoga_New.

f. Modify the content and design of the presentation to improve it.

g. Save the file, and then package it for CD distribution under the folder name of Lastname_Firstname_p02_pf4_Yoga_CD_Folder.

Objectives

1. Identify the components of the Outlook window   p. 884
2. Describe the basics of e-mail   p. 885
3. Manage contacts p. 904
4. Manage the calendar p. 911
5. Manage tasks and notes   p. 923

Communicating with E-mail, and Managing Contacts, Calendars, and Tasks

PREPARE CASE

Managing Corporate Event Planning Using Outlook

Production & Operations

Patti Rochelle is the busy corporate event coordinator for the Painted Paradise Golf Resort and Spa. Potential clients, along with clients who have already scheduled their events, contact her via e-mail on a daily basis. She must respond promptly and maintain accurate records so the events proceed smoothly. She manages a calendar to make sure there are no schedule conflicts. Using the task and notes functions in Outlook she makes sure that all aspects of the event are remembered and acted upon. In this workshop, you will take on the role

Andresr / Shutterstock.com

of Patti Rochelle in the communication and planning for the event requested by the Mid-Valley Producers. Using your own e-mail address and that of your instructor, you will send e-mail and manage contacts. You will develop a functioning calendar and record tasks and notes.

Student data files needed for this workshop:

 o01_ws01_Planning_Rates

 o01_ws01_Planning_Patti

 o01_ws01_Planning_Lesa

You will send e-mail messages with the subject lines of:

 Lastname_Firstname_o01_ws01_Planning

 Lastname_Firstname_o01_ws01_Planning_Reply

 Lastname_Firstname_o01_ws01_Planning_Group

 Lastname_Firstname_o01_ws01_Planning_Forward

You will print the following documents:

 RE: Lastname_Firstname_o01_ws01_Planning_Reply _Printout

 Planning Contacts

 Planning Calendar Details

 Planning Calendar Memo

 Planning Tasks Memo

 Planning Notes

Introduction to Outlook and E-mail

Outlook, a part of the Microsoft Office 2010 suite of software, enables you to communicate with others and to effectively plan your activities. Think of Outlook as a personal assistant, keeping track of all types of information, from e-mail to contacts, to schedules and tasks. Outlook extends your use of Microsoft Office by sharing information with the other applications. For instance, your Outlook contact list can be used to perform a mail merge in Word. Documents you create in Word or Excel can easily be sent to someone using the Outlook e-mail component. In this section, you will send, receive, and print e-mail messages.

Identifying the Components of the Outlook Window

Outlook contains four major components to assist you in a variety of ways. Each component contains a Ribbon and toolbars that provide access to commands. Panes display information. Buttons for each of the major components are available at the bottom of the **Navigation Pane**. The Navigation Pane contains folders, calendars, or categories for organizing information for each of the components.

my**it**lab

Workshop 1 Training

To Review the Components of Outlook

a. Click **Start** 🌏 on the Windows taskbar, point to **All Programs**, and then click **Microsoft Office**. Click **Microsoft Outlook 2010**.

b. Initiate a network connection in order to send and receive e-mail. This will vary depending on the computer setup. Your instructor will provide you with information on how to make the connection in the computer lab.

c. Maximize 🔲 the Outlook Today window, if necessary.

   If this is the first time you have used Outlook, the Outlook Today window may appear blank. You will find more information in this view as you complete more of the workshop activities.

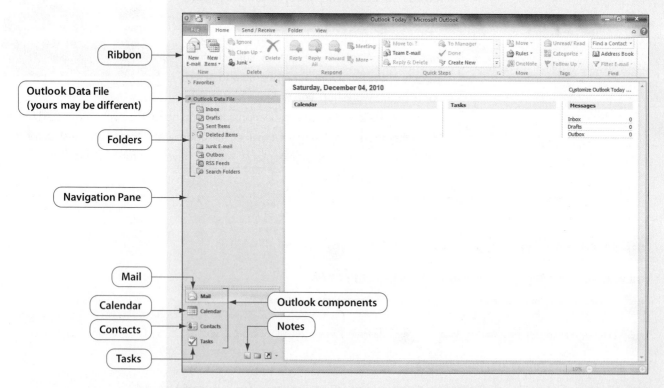

Figure 1   The Outlook Today window

Troubleshooting

If you do not see the Outlook Today window, click Outlook Data File at the top of the Navigation Pane. Depending on the configuration of your account, you may see your e-mail address in place of the words "Outlook Data File."

d. Click **Calendar** in the Navigation Pane, and then observe the changes made to the window. The Ribbon and the panes in the window change based on the component of Outlook that you have selected.

e. Click **Contacts**, and then review the window. Click **Tasks**, and then notice the changes to the window. Click **Mail**, and then observe the changes. Each of these components will be discussed in detail later in the workshop.

Describing the Basics of E-mail

Electronic mail, e-mail for short, is conceptually the same as writing a postcard and sending it through the U.S. Postal Service. E-mail has one very significant advantage, e-mail messages are delivered almost instantly anywhere in the world via the Internet. U.S. Postal Service mail is sometimes referred to as "snail mail" because by comparison it is much slower. Keep in mind that although e-mail messages are delivered quickly, just like the regular postal mail, the recipient has to go to his or her e-mail box to retrieve messages, so there can be a delay in the communication.

All e-mail systems work basically the same way. A **mail client**, with Outlook being an example, enables you to compose, send, and receive e-mail messages. Outlook sets up a connection with a **mail server** on the Internet. The mail server is a special-purpose computer that functions as the post office and enables you to receive your incoming messages and to deliver the messages you send. The mail server, whether on your campus computer network or at your Internet service provider, provides private mailboxes to people authorized to use its services. The mail server receives messages 24 hours a day and stores the messages until the user logs on to retrieve them.

To use the mail server, you must have an account on the server. Check with your instructor or campus help desk for information on how to log on to the campus mail server. You will gain access to your account through the use of a user name and password. Your **user name** is a unique word that identifies you to the mail server. The **password**, a secret word or group of characters, works in combination with your user name to protect your account from unauthorized use by others.

When you log on to the mail server, outgoing mail is uploaded from your computer to the server, where it is sent to the intended recipient's mail server. New mail, stored on the mail server, is downloaded by default into the Outlook **Inbox** folder on your computer. You can read the messages, reply to them, forward them, move them to other folders, and delete them using the Mail component of Outlook.

CONSIDER THIS | Should You Be Monitored?

Employers regularly monitor e-mail. Colleges and universities have the legal right to do so as well. For the sake of strong First Amendment and academic freedom notions, some institutions do not monitor e-mail. Does your educational institution monitor your e-mail? If it does not now, how would you know if it started in the future?

Managing the Inbox

The e-mail component, as shown in Figure 2, contains panes, folders, and tools for managing e-mail. The Navigation Pane contains folders for storing your messages. The Inbox is the default, personal folder for receiving e-mail. Additional folders can be added to the Navigation Pane. Other folders, created by Outlook, enable you to store drafts of unsent messages, keep copies of sent messages, and delete messages from the message list.

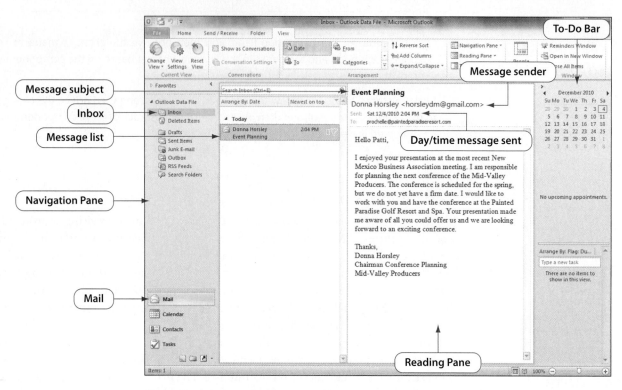

Figure 2   The Mail component

The message list provides information about the e-mail you receive. You will see the subject of the message, the sender's name, the day/time the message was sent, and whether you have viewed the message and replied to it. You can categorize messages with color codes. You can also mark messages for follow-up at a later time, automatically adding them to your Tasks list in Outlook. You can drag messages into folders to effectively manage your Inbox mail.

The **Reading Pane** displays the text of a selected message, appointment, contact, or task depending on the selected component of Outlook. You can move the Reading Pane to the right or bottom of the window, or you can turn it off. If you turn it off, you view a message by double-clicking it in the message list so it is then displayed in a new window.

SIDE NOTE
Arrows Help You Manage Layouts

The right-pointing arrow opened the Navigation Pane. When the pane is open there is a left-pointing arrow ⬲ at the top. This arrow can be used to quickly minimize the pane. Other arrows expand or collapse folders.

To Manage Inbox Layout

a. Click **Mail** in the Navigation Pane, and then click the **Inbox** folder. Click the **View tab**, click **Navigation Pane** in the Layout group, and then click **Minimized**. The Navigation Pane shrinks to the left side of the window. Click the **right-pointing arrow** ⬳ at the top of the Navigation Pane to return it to Normal view.

b. Click **Navigation Pane** in the Layout group again, and then click **Favorites** to hide it in the Navigation Pane. You will use the account folders to manage Outlook.

c. Click **Reading Pane** in the Layout group, and then click **Bottom**. The messages you select will be displayed at the bottom of the window.

d. Click **To-Do Bar** in the Layout group, and then click **Minimized**. With this pane minimized, you have more space for displaying messages.

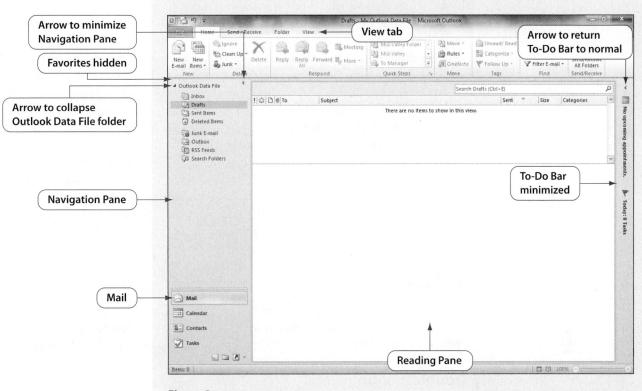

Arrow to minimize Navigation Pane

Favorites hidden

Arrow to collapse Outlook Data File folder

Navigation Pane

Mail

View tab

Arrow to return To-Do Bar to normal

To-Do Bar minimized

Reading Pane

Figure 3 Manage layouts

Managing Mail Folders

The way you process your postal service mail is very similar to the way you handle mail in Outlook. You bring it in from the mailbox and read it at your leisure. Some of the mail is junk mail, which you immediately throw away. Other important mail is filed with your important papers. And some mail you want to share with others in your household; you leave it on the kitchen table to reread at a later time. Still other pieces of mail are read and then discarded.

E-mail is very similar. Your mail arrives in your Inbox. You will receive unsolicited messages, which can be filtered automatically and sent to the Junk E-mail folder as they are received. Important messages that you receive can be moved into folders so they can be retrieved more quickly when needed. Messages that you delete from the Inbox are stored in the **Deleted Items folder** until you permanently delete them. The Deleted Items folder serves as a recycle bin for e-mail.

Real World Advice — Legitimate E-mail Sometimes Is Flagged as Junk

The Junk E-mail filter is set to Low by default in Outlook. This places only the most obvious junk messages into the **Junk E-mail folder**. The Microsoft Research team developed the rules for classifying junk e-mail, but the system is not infallible. In some cases, junk e-mail makes it into your Inbox folder. In other cases, legitimate e-mail gets placed into the Junk E-mail folder. It is a good idea to regularly review your Junk E-mail folder for legitimate messages. If you find a message of value, you can add the sender to the Safe Senders list, so their messages will not be treated as junk e-mail.

You can create folders in any of the default folders in the Navigation Pane. Folders can contain subfolders so a hierarchical filing system can be set up. For instance, you may have a folder called Events, and within that folder, you will have additional folders for each of the upcoming events. You can move messages from one mail folder to another following the same method used in Windows Explorer; that is, drag a message to move it into a new folder.

The purpose of the Outlook default folders can be inferred from their names. The **Outbox folder** contains all of the messages you have written, but not yet uploaded to the mail server. When you connect to the server, these messages are automatically transferred to the server. Once the message is sent, it is automatically moved to the **Sent Items folder**, which maintains a copy of the e-mail you have sent. Messages will remain indefinitely in the Inbox and Sent Items folder unless you move or delete them, in which case they will be moved to the Deleted Items folder. If you close Outlook while you are in the midst of creating an e-mail message, Outlook saves the unfinished message in the **Drafts folder**. You can also save messages that you are composing to the Drafts folder if you want to continue working on them at a later time. Messages are filtered as they come into Outlook, and messages suspected of being spam are placed in the Junk E-mail folder.

To Add Folders to Outlook

a. Click the **Folder tab**, click **New Folder** in the New group, and then type Events in the Name box. Click the **Outlook Data File** at the top of the Select where to place the folder box, and then click **OK**. The new folder appears in the Navigation Pane in a few seconds.

Troubleshooting

If necessary, click the expand arrow next to Outlook Data File to view the folders.

b. Click **New Folder** again, and then type Mid-Valley in the Name box. Click **Events** in the Select where to place the folder box, and then click **OK**. The new folder is added below the Events folder.

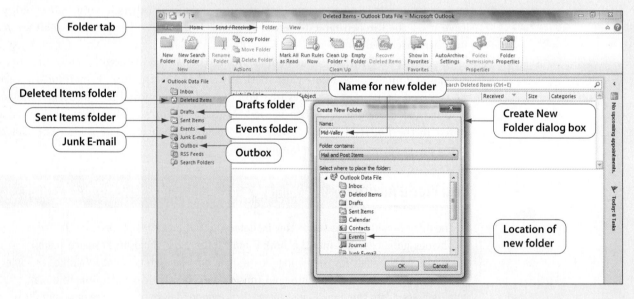

Figure 4   Add a folder

Composing an E-mail Message

It is easy to compose an e-mail message in Outlook; simply click New E-mail on the Home tab. The Message tab provides tools for composing the message, including formatting text. The Insert tab enables you to attach files, tables, graphics, links, text objects, and symbols. The Options tab contains options for themes, fields to show, and more. The Format Text tab extends the commands available on the Message tab, giving you more options for modifying the appearance of the text. The Review tab contains tools for checking spelling and grammar, and opens a Research pane or Thesaurus. The File tab can be used to save or print the message.

Just as themes are available for Microsoft Office documents, **themes** or **stationery** can be used to add interest to e-mail messages. Stationery provides preset colors, fonts, and effects. The themes extend the design choices by giving you options for vivid colors, active graphics, and background images that are not available in stationery. There are a number of themes available in Outlook. You can also select different fonts for creating messages and replying to messages. The themes and stationery are applied to all of the messages you send using the Options button on the File tab. You can also select themes, colors, fonts, and effects on the Options tab when you are creating a single e-mail message. These themes are the ones you will find in the Office 2010 software applications, such as Office, Adjacency, Essential, Flow, Solstice, and Waveform. You can also change just the background color of the page on the Options tab when you are creating an e-mail message.

Themes and stationery are applied to all of the e-mail messages you compose until you remove the theme. Keep in mind that professional e-mail should contain a professional-looking theme, with simple lines, colors, and graphics. When in doubt, it is best to create e-mail without a theme.

SIDE NOTE
Non-Outlook Applications
If the recipients of your message do not use Outlook, it is possible they will not see the message displayed with the stationery you use.

To Select a Theme or Stationery

a. Click the **File tab**, and then click **Options**. Click **Mail**, and then click **Stationery and Fonts**.

b. Click **Theme**, and then click a few of the themes in the Choose a Theme box to preview them.

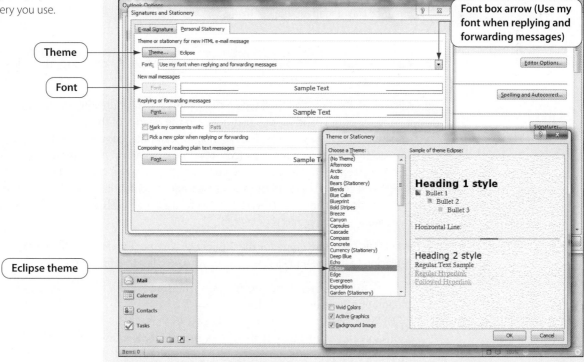

Figure 5 Applying a theme

  c. Click **Eclipse**, and then click **OK**.

  d. Click the **Font box arrow** under Theme, and then click **Use my font when replying and forwarding messages**, if necessary, to select it.

  e. Click **Font** under Replying or forwarding messages. Select **Arial** from the Font list, click the **Font color arrow**, and then select **Black**, **Text 1** from the Theme Colors palette. Click **OK**, click **OK** to accept the changes, and then click **OK** to close the Outlook Options dialog box.

Throughout this workshop you will take on different roles as you send, receive, forward, and manage e-mail. You will create a new e-mail message as if you were Patti Rochelle, the corporate events coordinator for the Painted Paradise Golf Resort and Spa. You will be responding to the inquiry message that you saw in Figure 2, which requested information. You will use your instructor's and classmates' e-mail addresses, as well as your own, to generate e-mails for this workshop.

To Create a New Message

  a. Click the **Home tab**, and then click **New E-mail** in the New group.

  b. Type your instructor's e-mail address in the **To** box. Press `Tab` to move the insertion point to the Cc box. Type your e-mail address in the **Cc** box.

Troubleshooting

Double-check the addresses you enter into the address boxes for accuracy. Mail that is incorrectly addressed is not delivered by the mail server and will "bounce" back to your Inbox as undeliverable.

  c. Click the **Options tab**, and then click **Bcc** in the Show Fields group. This adds a blind carbon copy recipient to the message.

  d. Click in the **Bcc** box, and then type a classmate's e-mail address in the Bcc box.

   The purpose of the various text boxes in the header of the e-mail message box are apparent by the names. The To text box, for example, contains the e-mail address of the recipient(s). The Cc text box (courtesy copy or carbon copy) indicates the address of other people who are to receive copies of the message. The Bcc text box is used to send blind carbon copies of the e-mail message to someone. The other recipients of the message do not know that this person received a copy because this e-mail address is not revealed when the e-mail is delivered.

  e. Press `Tab`, and then type for the Subject Lastname_Firstname_o01_ws01_Planning, replacing Lastname and Firstname with your own last and first name.

  f. Press `Tab`, and then type the following message. Press `Enter` twice between the paragraphs to create the blank lines.

   Hello Donna,

   Thanks for your interest in the Painted Paradise Golf Resort and Spa for the upcoming Mid-Valley Producers conference. As you may remember from my presentation, we have a wide variety of solutions for all of your event needs. We can provide meeting rooms, presentation/technology equipment, catering, and hotel rooms. Your guests will have access to our golf course, water park, and spa.

I am attaching a Word document that details the capacity and charges for our meeting rooms to this message. This should help you to get an idea of which room you might need based on the size of your group.

Please let me know as soon as possible about the dates you have in mind for the conference. I would like to tentatively reserve space for you so that we can continue our planning.

I look forward to working with you,

Student Name

Press Enter.

g. Click the **File tab** in the message form, and then click **Save**.

Notice that the Drafts folder now contains an item, indicated by the 1 shown next to the folder name. If the message form gets closed by mistake, the Drafts folder version can be opened and prepared so the message can be sent.

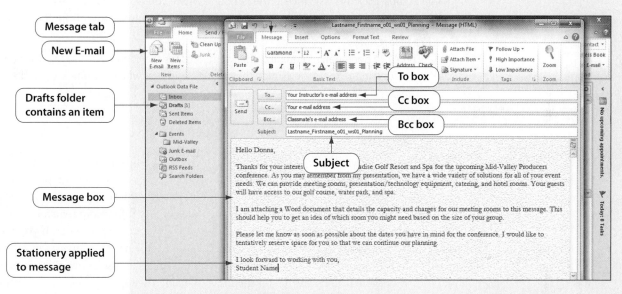

Figure 6 Composing an e-mail message

Real World Advice   Using Cc and Bcc Effectively

Think carefully before you send a carbon copy of a message to someone. Do they really need to see the message? Do they want their e-mail address revealed to the other recipients? Avoid filling the mailboxes of your friends, family, and business associates with junk mail. They will appreciate your courtesy.

In business, blind carbon copies are useful. For instance, if you send a newsletter to all of your clients, you should preserve the privacy of the recipients (and protect your e-mail list) by not listing their e-mail addresses. This also keeps them from receiving e-mail that is sent through the Reply function. Another reason for using Bcc in the business environment is to document an e-mail message by sending it to someone else, such as your supervisor. It is very effective to write a positive note to a fellow employee for a job well done, and to blind carbon copy the person's supervisor.

Attaching Documents

Attachments are often added to e-mail messages to supplement the message. You can attach files of all kinds to messages, but there are some considerations you should make. First, if you are using specialized software that the recipient may not have on their local computer, they will be unable to open the attachment. You should also consider the size of the attachment because some mail servers limit the size of the e-mail messages that can travel through the system. If the person is working with a slow Internet connection, it can take quite a while to download large attachments. Attachments can also be blocked by the e-mail recipient's mail server. Certain file types, such as .xlsm, and files with macros enabled, are quite prone to being blocked. All of these situations can cause frustration for the recipients of your message.

To Add an Attachment

a. Click the **Insert tab**, and then click **Attach File** in the Include group. In the Insert File dialog box, click the disk drive in the left pane where your student data files are located. Navigate through the folder structure and then click **o01_ws01_Planning_Rates**.

b. Click **Insert**.
   The Word document containing the room rates for the conference center is attached as described in the message. Notice that it is 16 KB in size, which is quite acceptable.

Using Signatures

Another feature you will often see in professional e-mail is a **signature**, providing additional information about the sender. The signature block contains text and often graphics. You can create more than one signature file for e-mail and select the most appropriate signature as you create your message. It is important to include contact information with e-mail messages because the message is often printed and used away from the computer. If you include your contact information, you can be assured that the recipient can contact you regardless of whether they are at their computer or not. Signatures can also contain logos or other graphics. Signatures can be created on the File tab, using the Options button, or within the message form.

To Add a Signature

a. Click the **Message tab**, click **Signature** in the Include group, and then click **Signatures**. The Signatures and Stationery dialog box opens to enable you to create an E-mail Signature.

b. Click **New**, type Professional Signature, and then click **OK**.

c. In the Edit signature box, type your name. Press [Enter], and then type Corporate Event Coordinator. Press [Enter], and then type Painted Paradise Golf Resort and Spa. Press [Enter], and then type Phone: 505-555-1489. Press [Enter], type E-mail:, and then type your e-mail address. Press [Enter], and then type Web: www.paintedparadiseresort.com. Press [Enter].

d. Select your name, and then click the **Font arrow**. Click **Brush Script MT**, click the **Font size arrow**, and then click **18**. By modifying the font you added some emphasis to the signature while maintaining the professional feel.

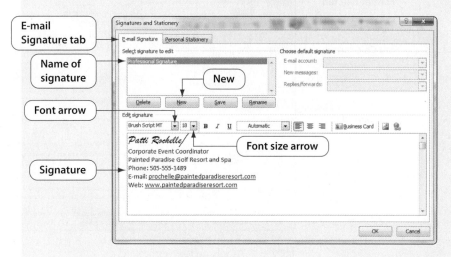

Figure 7 Creating a signature file

e. Click **Save**. Click **New** again, type Personal Class Signature for the name of the signature, and then click **OK**. With this signature selected, click in the Edit signature box, and type your name. Press ⌷Enter⌷, and then type your course name. Press ⌷Enter⌷, and then type your course number. Select **your name**, apply **Bold** and **Italic**, and then change the Font Size to **16**. Click **OK**.

f. Click **Signature** in the Include group. Notice that both signatures are listed. Click **Professional Signature**. The signature for the Painted Paradise Golf Resort and Spa appears below your message.

Emphasizing Text

Just as with other software applications, Outlook can use color to emphasize text. Keep in mind that you can easily overdo the emphasis, making your e-mail message difficult to read. If the recipients of your message do not use Outlook, it is possible they will not see the colors you have set, so make sure your message is clear without the color.

To Emphasize Text

a. Select the words **Painted Paradise Golf Resort and Spa** in the first paragraph of the e-mail message. Click the **Format Text tab**, click the **Font Size arrow**, and then click **14**. Click the **Font Color arrow**, and then click **Blue**, **Accent 1**, **Darker 25%**. Click **Bold**.

b. Repeat Step a by applying the same formatting to the words **Mid-Valley Producers**.

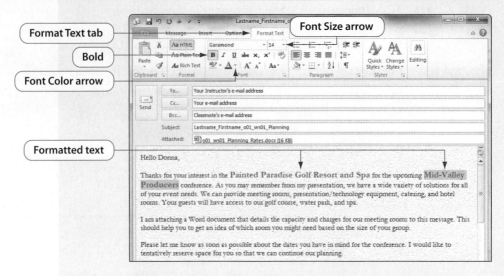

Format Text tab

Bold

Font Color arrow

Formatted text

Font Size arrow

Figure 8 Applying text formatting

c. Click the **File tab**, and then click **Save**. This creates a draft message that you can return to if a problem is encountered.

Sending and Receiving E-mail

Obviously, the reason for writing e-mail is to send it and receive replies. The e-mail must be transferred to a mail server to do this. Some computers are set up so when e-mail is placed in the Outbox, it is uploaded and new mail retrieved. Other computers rely on you to click the Send/Receive button to transfer the mail. Keep in mind that although e-mail often seems to be processed instantly, it can take time to upload, pass through the mail servers and Internet, and download. Factors such as the connection speed, size of attachments, and network traffic can all affect the speed in which e-mail is conveyed.

To Send and Retrieve E-mail

a. Click **Send**. If your Outlook system is set up to automatically send e-mail, you will briefly notice the number 1 next to the Outbox folder. If the number remains, click Send/Receive All Folders on the Quick Access Toolbar.

b. On the Home tab, click **Send/Receive All Folders** in the Send/Receive group.

A dialog box shows the progress of the process. When the process is complete, the number 1 will appear next to the Inbox to indicate there is a new unread message.

c. Click the **Inbox** folder. If necessary, click the message **Lastname_Firstname_o01_ws01_Planning** to display it in the Reading Pane. You can drag the border between the message list and the Reading Pane to see more of the message. You can use the scroll bar to view the entire message.

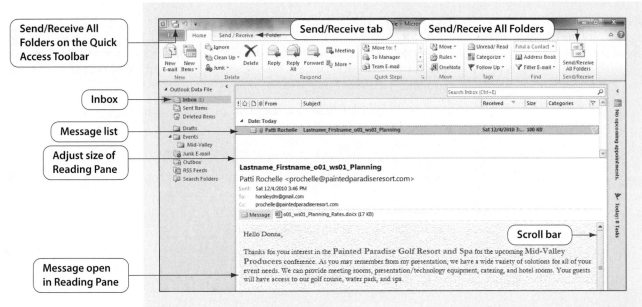

Send/Receive All Folders on the Quick Access Toolbar

Send/Receive tab

Send/Receive All Folders

Inbox

Message list

Adjust size of Reading Pane

Message open in Reading Pane

Scroll bar

Figure 9 Viewing a message

Troubleshooting

If the messages appear in your Junk E-mail folder rather than in your Inbox, you can drag them to the Inbox folder.

d. Double-click the message subject in the message list for the message you just received. The message opens in a new window, giving you more room to view the message.

e. Double-click the attachment name (**o01_ws01_Planning_Rates.docx**), and the attachment opens in Word. Review the document, and then close Word.

Replying to an E-mail Message

When you reply to an e-mail message, it is very similar to composing a new one, with the exception that Outlook automatically enters the recipient's information to the appropriate boxes. If needed, you can modify the recipient list by either adding more e-mail addresses or removing addresses you do not need. The Subject line will also be automatically adjusted with the addition of RE at the beginning of the subject. You can modify the subject as needed by typing over the text.

Whenever you view the message, you will have the options to Reply, Reply All, or Forward the message to recipients. The Reply option sends the message back to the sender. The Reply All option sends the message to everyone in the To and Cc boxes. The Forward option enables you to type a new address and mail the message to someone who did not originally receive it. Forwarded messages are designated by FW at the beginning of the Subject line. Forwarded messages will also contain any files that were attached to the original message.

In the next portion of the workshop, you will take on the role of the Mid-Valley Producers representative and respond to the first message you composed.

**Does Everyone Really
Need the Message?**
Before you use Reply All to
send a message back to
someone, pause and think
about whether all of the
people listed in the To and
Cc boxes really need to see
the e-mail. You can remove
people from the recipient list
as needed.

To Reply to a Message

a. Click **Reply** in the Respond group on the message form. Click the **Bcc** box, and then type your instructor's e-mail address. Type _Reply at the end of the Subject so it reads **RE: Lastname_Firstname_o01_ws01_Planning_Reply**.

b. Click at the top of the message box and type the following (press Enter twice between paragraphs):

Hello Your First Name,

Our planning committee has met and reviewed your room capacity and charges document. We believe that we will have 75 to 100 attendees at our conference. We would like to tentatively reserve the Eldorado Room for July 16–18.

What recommended steps should we take? We are interested in wrapping up our plans by March 15 so we can inform our members.

Thanks,

Donna Horsley

Chairman, Conference Planning

Mid-Valley Producers

c. Click the **Review tab**, and then click **Spelling & Grammar**. Make the necessary adjustments to correct mistakes. Click **OK** when the process has been completed. Proofread the message carefully.

d. Click **Send**, and then click **Send/Receive All Folders** on the Quick Access Toolbar. Wait a short period of time, and then click **Send/Receive All Folders** again to retrieve the e-mail message.

e. Close the message form that displays the original message.

Quick Reference   Using Shortcut Keys

Shortcut keys enable you to complete actions without removing your hands from the keyboard. Press F9 to Send/Receive All Folders. Press Ctrl+N to begin a New E-mail, Appointment, Contact, Task, or Note, depending on which component is currently displayed.

Forwarding a Message

When Patti received Donna's reply, she knew that she should notify other members of her staff about the tentative date for the Mid-Valley Producers conference. To do so, you will take on the role of Patti as you send the message to others.

To Forward a Message

a. Click the new message you just received, **RE: Lastname_Firstname_o01_ws01_ Planning_Reply**, on the message list. Click the **Home tab**, if necessary, and then click **Forward** in the Respond group. Notice that the e-mail addresses from the previous send were not included in the To or Cc fields.

b. Type your e-mail address in the To box. Type your instructor's e-mail address in the Cc box. Click at the end of the subject line, delete the word **Reply**, and then type Forward. The Subject line now reads **FW: Lastname_Firstname_o01_ws01_Planning_Forward**.

c. Click at the top of the message box, and type the following (press $\boxed{\text{Enter}}$ twice between paragraphs):

Hello Lesa and Thomas,

As you can see from this message, the Mid-Valley Producers are scheduling with us. Please mark your calendars.

d. Click the **Message tab**, and then click **High Importance** in the Tags group. This assigns a special character to the message that will appear in the message area when the e-mail arrives.

e. Click the **Options tab** on the message form, and then click the **Request a Read Receipt** check box in the Tracking group.

This mark causes a return message to be sent to you when the message has been opened by the recipient. It will contain the word "Read" in the Subject line. You can also request a delivery receipt that will send you a message when the message is delivered but not necessarily read.

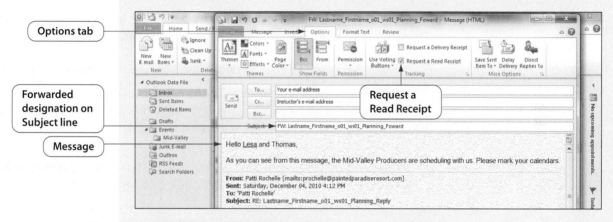

Figure 10 Forwarding a message

f. Click **Send**. If the Spelling dialog box appears, flagging Lesa's name, click **Ignore Once**. Click **Send/Receive All Folders** ⬚ on the Quick Access Toolbar. Wait a short period of time, and then click **Send/Receive All Folders** again to retrieve the e-mail message.

g. Double-click the **message** that just arrived. A Read Receipt box opens asking whether you want to send a receipt. Click **Yes**. The message then opens. Close the message form after reviewing the message.

h. Click **Send/Receive All Folders** on the Quick Access Toolbar to retrieve new e-mail. The Read Receipt appears at the top of the message list. Click the message to view the receipt in the Reading Pane.

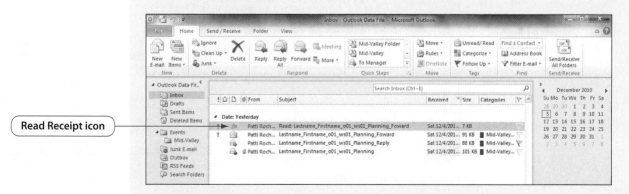

Figure 11 Receipt message

Managing E-mail

With a few messages in the Inbox, the message list and its icons can be explained. By default, Outlook arranges the messages received by date and time, with the most recent messages on the top of the list. Messages that have been read appear in regular type, while messages that are unread are shown in bold. An exclamation point ⧉ indicates the sender marked the message as High Importance. The paper clip ⧉, shown on the first message received at the bottom of the list, shows that an attachment has been added to the message. The envelope with a purple arrow ⧉ denotes a message that has been read and replied to. The envelope with a blue arrow ⧉ indicates that the message has been forwarded to another recipient. As shown in Figure 11, the circle and check mark signify that the message is a read receipt message. In the next step, you will add additional indicator elements to the message list to help organize the messages.

To Flag a Message

a. Click the **flag** ⧉ at the far right of the third message on the list, **RE: Lastname_Firstname_o01_ws01_Planning_Reply**. Click the **Expand arrow** ⧉ for the To-Do Bar to expand the pane.

   The To-Do Bar opens. By default, clicking the flag icon assigns today's date as the due date.

b. Click **Follow Up** in the Tags group on the Home tab, and then click **Next Week**.

   The flag is not as bright as the one used to flag today's date. By flagging messages, you signify that they are important and should receive further attention. The flagged items are also assigned to your Tasks list.

c. Click **Tasks** in the Navigation Pane. You see the message listed with a flag for Next Week. Click **Mail** in the Navigation Pane to return to the e-mail Inbox.

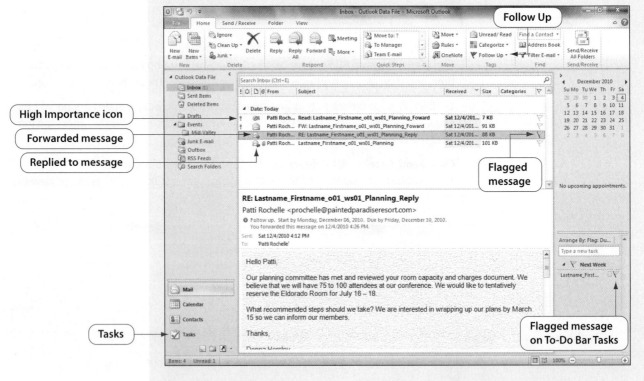

Figure 12 Follow-up icons

In addition to flagging messages for follow-up, you can add a reminder to the message. Select the message, and click the Follow Up arrow on the Home tab. Click Add Reminder, and set a start date and due date, as well as provide a date and time for the reminder to appear. For instance, you can set the start date as the current date, the due date as next Monday, and a reminder date of Friday. That way you will be reminded to follow up before the actual due date. Messages with reminders set appear on the message list with a bell icon 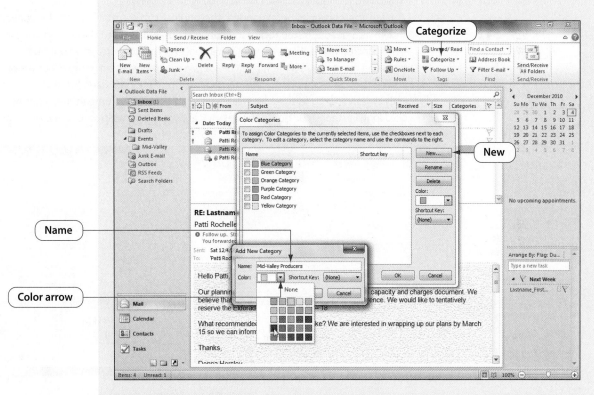 next to them.

Using Categories

Categories help you organize your work by grouping together similar items and assigning the group a name and color. You can categorize e-mail, calendar items, contacts, and tasks with color-coding. You will create a category for the Mid-Valley Producers that you will use throughout the rest of the workshop.

To Create and Assign Categories

a. On the Home tab, click **Categorize** in the Tags group, click **All Categories**, click **New**, and then type Mid-Valley Producers in the Name box.

Figure 13 Creating a color category

b. Click the **Color arrow**, click **Dark Red**, click **OK**, and then click **OK** in the Color Categories dialog box.

   Categories can reuse colors, but it is better to avoid reusing the colors if possible. It makes the category stand out if it is the only one using that color. You should now see the category next to the RE: Lastname_Firstname_o01_ws01_Planning_Reply message in the message list with the color rectangle and in the Reading Pane in the message header.

Working with Conversations

Messages can be viewed in your message list in groups called **conversations**. Conversations share the same subject line, and they can be collapsed or expanded as needed. They also include messages that were sent with the same subject line. Conversations offer an easy way to manage a number of e-mail messages from a number of people. You will experiment with the conversation you have been building in this workshop.

To View Conversations

a. Click the message with **Read** in the subject line. Click the **View tab**, click the **Show as Conversations** check box, and then click **This folder** in the dialog box. Click the first message sent, **Lastname_Firstname_o01_ws01_Planning**.

    A small triangle appears next to the message with the subject of Lastname_Firstname_o01_ws01_Planning. A white triangle indicates that the conversation can be expanded, while a black triangle shows that the conversation can be collapsed.

b. If necessary, click the **white triangle** ▷. The first message sent appears in the Reading Pane. Click the **white triangle** ▷ again to display the conversation. Notice that the messages include one that you sent to other people, the one you forwarded, and the one to which you replied.

    With the conversation expanded, the original subject that started the conversation is shown as a header at the top of the conversation group, with the related correspondence below, including replies you may have sent. As the conversation continues, the newest messages appear below the subject headers in the conversation group. When a new message arrives, the conversation group moves to the top of your message list to alert you that new activity is occurring in the conversation. The subject line of unread messages appears in a bold font. Further small dots and lines indicate the relationship among the messages.

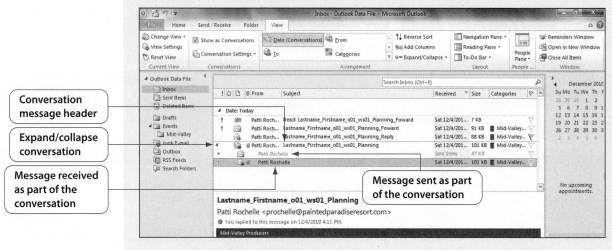

Figure 14 Viewing a conversation

c. Click the **black triangle** ◢ to collapse the conversation. Click the **View tab**, click the **Show as Conversation** check box to turn off the conversation view, and then click **This folder** in the dialog box.

Moving Messages to Folders

Earlier in this workshop you built a folder structure for managing the messages from the Mid-Valley Producers group. There are a number of ways to move messages into the folder you created.

To Move Messages to a Folder

a. Click the **Read: Lastname_Firstname_o01_ws01_Planning_Forward** message in the message list, and then drag the message into the **Mid-Valley folder** in the Navigation Pane and release it.

b. Double-click the **Mid-Valley folder** in the Navigation Pane to verify that the message has been successfully moved.

c. Click the **Inbox** folder in the Navigation Pane. Click the **Home tab**, click **More** ⯆ in the Quick Steps group, and then click **Create New**.

> **Quick Steps** enable you to set actions to occur when you select a message and then click the Quick Step. You can set multiple actions to a single Quick Step. You will create a Quick Step that moves the message to the Mid-Valley folder and assigns the Mid-Valley category to the message.

d. Type Mid-Valley Folder in the **Name** box. Click the **Choose an Action arrow**, and then click **Move to folder**. Click the **Choose folder arrow**, and then click **Mid-Valley**.

e. Click **Add Action**, click the **Choose an Action arrow**, and then click **Categorize message**. Click the **Choose category arrow**, and then click **Mid-Valley Producers**.

f. Click the **Shortcut key arrow**, and then click Ctrl + Shift + 1. Now when you select a message, you can press these keys to move the message and categorize it. Click in the **Tooltip** box, and then type Move to Mid-Valley folder and add category. Click **Finish**.

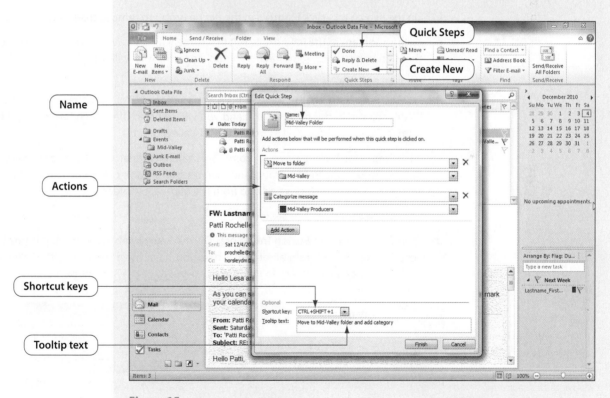

Figure 15 Creating a Quick Step

g. Point to **Mid-Valley Folder** in the Quick Steps group and observe the Tooltip. Click the **Lastname_Firstname_o01_ws01_Planning_Forward** message in the message list, and then click the **Mid-Valley Folder** Quick Step. Click the **Mid-Valley folder** in the Navigation Pane to verify that the file is in the folder and the category has been assigned. Click the **Inbox folder** in the Navigation Pane.

h. Click the message with the subject of **Lastname_Firstname_o01_ws01_Planning_Reply**, and then press Ctrl+Shift+1. Click the **Mid-Valley** folder in the Navigation Pane again to verify that the file is in the folder and the category has been assigned. Only the original message, Lastname_Firstname_o01_ws01_Planning, remains in the Inbox message list.

Filtering and Searching E-mail

When mail begins to fill your Inbox, it may be useful to filter it to find specific items. For example, you may want to check to see that you have dealt with all e-mail flagged for follow-up.

To Filter and Search E-mail

a. Click the **Inbox** folder in the Navigation Pane. Click the **Home tab**, click **Filter E-mail** in the Find group, and then click **Flagged**. A single message is displayed in the message list, and the Search tab opens.

Troubleshooting

If you do not see a single message, click Try Searching again in All Mail Items.

b. On the Search tab, click **Flagged** in the Refine group to remove the search criteria.

c. Click **Important** in the Refine group. It may appear as if nothing has been found because the High Importance items have been moved to the Mid-Valley folder.

d. Click **All Mail Items** in the Scope group and try searching again.

Now it appears that you have more e-mail than you actually have. Look at the In Folder column in the message list, and you will see that the search has included items from the Sent folder as well as from the Mid-Valley folder.

e. Click **Important** to remove it from the search criteria. On the **Search tab**, click **Categorized** in the Refine group, and then click **Mid-Valley Producers**. Three items are shown, one from the Inbox and two from the Mid-Valley folder.

f. Click **Close Search** on the Search tab.

g. Type Eldorado in the **Search Inbox** box. On the **Search tab**, click **All Mail Items** in the Scope group. E-mail from all of the folders you have been working with is displayed. Click **Close Search** to return to the Home tab and to display the Inbox folder.

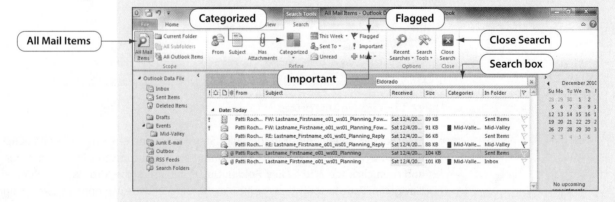

Figure 16 Performing a search

Printing an E-mail Message

In some situations you may want to print a copy of an e-mail message. You first select the message or messages that you want to print and then move to Backstage view using the File tab to access the Print command. If a message is open, the only option on the message form Backstage view that you have for printing is in Memo Style. The Memo Style provides a header to the message that lists the person the message is from, when it was sent, who the recipients were (including the people on the Cc list), the Subject, and the file name of attachments. If you set a follow-up flag or categories, these are also displayed in the header. The message follows the header, and if the message is replying to another, that message is displayed.

If a message or more than one message is selected from a folder, you have the option to print in Table Style or Memo Style. Table Style provides a list that looks like the Inbox. The name of the person who sent the message, the subject, when it was received, the size of the message, and categories or flags are shown in the Table Style. The icons indicating whether the message was opened, forwarded, or replied to also appear in the Table Style listing.

SIDE NOTE
To Print or Not to Print
Printing messages is a good way to retain documentation of a conversation. You can print the message as a Microsoft XPS file that you store on your computer, instead of printing on paper. You can also save messages using the Save As command on the File tab.

To Print an E-mail Message

a. Click the **Mid-Valley folder** in the Navigation Pane. Click the message with the subject of **Lastname_Firstname_o01_ws01_Planning_Reply**. Click the **File tab**, and then click **Print**.

b. Select the appropriate printer. Click **Memo Style**, if necessary to select it, and review the preview of the printout in the right pane. Click the **Next Page arrow** ▶ at the bottom of the preview, if necessary, to view the second page. Click **Multiple Pages** ⊞ to view the entire printout of the message.

c. Click **Print** if your instructor requests a copy of the e-mail message; otherwise, click the **Home tab** to return to Outlook.

d. Click the **Inbox folder** in the Navigation Pane, select the **Lastname_Firstname_o01_ws01_Planning** message, and click **Mid-Valley Folder** in the Quick Steps group to file this e-mail message in the correct folder.

Organizing Your Life with Contacts, Calendars, Tasks, and Notes

Outlook is so much more than just an e-mail client. It can also organize your address book, schedule, reminder lists, and notes. With these functions, Outlook becomes a desktop assistant and in the process, enables you to dynamically share information between the components by dragging items from one component to another.

Contacts, available in the Navigation Pane (as are all of the components), enable you to store a lot of information about people. While the Contact card appears very business oriented, you can add personal information and notes, even including a photograph of the person on the card.

Multiple calendars for various types of activities can be kept in Outlook and viewed separately or together. For instance, you may have one calendar for personal events and another for work. During the work day, you may focus all of your attention on the work calendar by hiding the personal calendar. Or, if you want to schedule a long weekend vacation, you may show both calendars so you can determine the best day to take off from work.

Tasks are kept on your To-Do List, making it easy to remember items as you check your e-mail. You can track your work using the Tasks component and mark tasks as complete as you finish the job.

The Notes component enables you to make quick notes to yourself. The notes can be displayed on note-shaped icons, in a list, or shown for the last seven days. You may wonder why you would need notes if you have a calendar and task list, but you will find that the notes are handy for lists and for taking quick notes such as you might do during a phone conversation.

In this section, you will use calendars, create contact cards, set tasks, and write notes.

Creating and Using Contacts

Just about everyone you know has an e-mail address. You could write each person's address in a paper address book and then type the address into an e-mail message each time you send one. However, it is much easier to use the Contacts component of Outlook to keep track of the addresses. When it is time to send a new message, you select the recipient from the Contacts folder without having to type his or her entire e-mail address. In addition to sending individual e-mail, the Contacts component enables you to create Contact Groups so you can quickly send e-mail to a predefined group of people. You will find that keeping track of people using Outlook Contacts is very efficient.

Adding Contacts

The information you have about people is entered into your Contacts folder via a contact card. You can enter as much or as little information as you want, but generally you will at least enter a name and an e-mail address. The contact card contains fields to identify the person, the company they work for, their Internet addresses, phone numbers, and physical addresses. The card is very flexible, allowing you to enter more than one e-mail address, phone number type, or different types of physical addresses. In addition, if you provide addresses and are connected to the Internet, the Map It feature can show you a Bing map of the location.

As mentioned earlier, if you have a picture of the person, it can be placed on the contact card and the photograph will show in e-mails you receive from that contact. If you click the photograph in the Reading Pane of the Mail component, the contact card will open. Extended information can also be associated with the contact card and can include personal items such as a nickname, birthday or anniversary, or business items such as department, manager's name, or assistant's name. Additional information, such as the e-mail activity with the sender, messages containing attachments, meetings you have with the person, and status updates, is available by clicking at the bottom of the contact card. You can also connect to social networks to show photos and activity updates made by others in Outlook. In this exercise you will create some real and some fictional contacts.

SIDE NOTE
Applying Your Area Code
If this is the very first time Outlook Contacts are being used, a dialog box will appear after entering a phone number. This dialog box will request input for the area code and local zone information. Type your local area code information if this dialog box appears.

To Create a Contact

a. Click **Contacts** in the Navigation Pane. Click the **Home tab**, click **New Contact** in the New group, and then **Maximize** 🔲 the contact form window, if necessary.

b. Type Patti Rochelle in the **Full Name** box. Type Painted Paradise Golf Resort and Spa as the **Company** name. Type Conference Event Coordinator for the **Job title**. Notice that the card begins to build a preview on the right side of the form as you add the fields.

c. Type prochelle@paintedparadiseresort.com in the **E-mail** box. Click in the **Web page address** box, and then type www.paintedparadiseresort.com.

d. Under the Phone numbers heading, type 505-555-1489 in the **Business** box. Click the **arrow** next to the Business phone number, and then click **Assistant**. Type 505-555-1490. Click the **Assistant** phone number arrow, and then click **Business Fax**. Type 505-555-1495.

e. Under the Addresses heading, click **Business** to open the Check Address dialog box. Type 3356 Hemmingway Circle in the Street box. Type Santa Fe for the City and New Mexico for the State/Province. Type 89566 for the ZIP/Postal code. Click **OK**.

f. Click **Add Contact Picture** (the head silhouette), navigate to the student data files, and then click **o01_ws01_Planning_Patti**. Click **OK**. Patti's photograph is shown on the preview card.

Figure 17 Adding a contact

g. Click the **Contact tab**, click **Details** in the Show group, click the **Office** box, and then type 150A Conference Center Coordination. Click in the **Assistant's name** box, and type Lesa Martin. Type 3/15/1970 in the **Birthday** box, press Enter, click **OK**, and then click **Save & Close** in the Actions group on the Contact tab. If a Microsoft Outlook dialog box displays requesting to create a birthday event in your personal Calendar, click **No**.

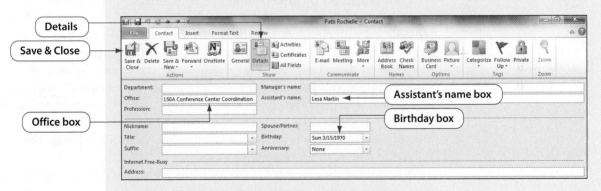

Figure 18 Adding detailed contact information

h. Using the following information, add a contact card for Lesa Martin using Steps a through g:
- **Full Name**: Lesa Martin
- **Company**: Painted Paradise Golf Resort and Spa
- **Job title**: Conference Event Assistant
- **E-mail**: lmartin@paintedparadiseresort.com
- **Web page address**: www.paintedparadiseresort.com
- **Phone number Business**: 505-555-1490
- **Address Business**: 3356 Hemmingway Circle, Santa Fe, New Mexico 89566 (Be sure to use the Check Address dialog box to enter the information.)
- Use **o01_ws01_Planning_Lesa** as the contact photograph. Click **Save & Close**.

Organizing Contacts

You have created a number of contact records, and now you will focus your attention on organizing them. Keep in mind that in a normal address book you might have hundreds of names, so having a good system for organization is important.

Contacts can be categorized with color schemes and names that can be used throughout Outlook. For instance, the Mid-Valley Producers category can be assigned to a contact in your address book. Later you could create a phone list based on just the Mid-Valley Producers records. People in your Contacts list can be in more than one category if necessary. In addition to using categories, you can also set up Contact Folders to keep contact records separated. You may maintain a folder with personal friends, another for a professional organization to which you belong, and yet another for your business.

Once you have established contact records, you can also build Contact Groups that can then be used to quickly send e-mail. You may create a Contact Group of your coworkers so you can update them all on a project or invite them all to a meeting using Outlook.

You can view Contacts in various ways in Outlook. The Business Card view shows a stylized card with the picture of the person if you provided one. The Card view focuses on the filled-in fields that you completed as you created the record. There are no pictures shown on the Card view. The Phone view shows the records, in alphabetical order by name, in a table with the available fields as columns. You can modify the columns shown in this view as needed. The List view separates the contacts into groups while displaying the records in a table. The View tab contains tools that enable you to change the arrangement of the views and to reset the views if necessary. You can also change the sorting order and add or remove columns from the views.

You will use the category for the Mid-Valley Producers, by adding Donna Horsley, your instructor, and yourself to the category. Categories are persistent throughout Outlook, meaning that you can reuse the same categories that you may have created in the Mail component in the Contacts component.

To Use Categories

d. Click the **View tab**, and then click **Categories**, if necessary, to select it. Click **Change View** in the Current View group, and then click **Business Card**.

Notice that the categories are not displayed, and in fact, the categories option is grayed out on the View tab. The Business Card view does not display the categories you have set.

e. Click **Change View** again, and then click **Phone**. Click **Categories** in the Arrangement group.

The phone list contains contact cards that have been categorized. The List view also displays categories.

Creating Contacts Folders

While Categories carry through the different components of Outlook, the Folders do not. Folders enable you to organize the contacts so you can locate or print just the ones you want. You will create a Mid-Valley Producers Contacts folder and place the contacts into the folder.

To Create Contacts Folders

a. Click the **Folder tab**, and then click **New Folder**.

b. Type Mid-Valley Producers for the Name of the folder.

c. Click **Contacts**, if necessary to select it, and then click **OK**. You placed the folder in the Contacts folder so it is displayed on the left pane.

d. Click the contact entry for **Donna Horsley**, and then drag it to the **Mid-Valley Producers** folder.

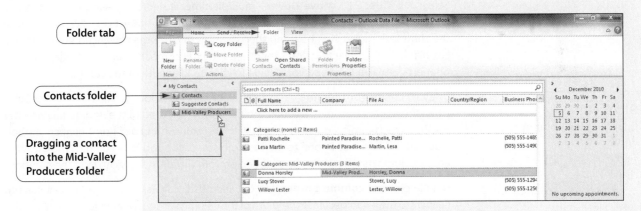

Figure 19 Organizing contacts

e. Drag the contact entries for **your instructor** and **yourself** to the Mid-Valley Producers folder.

Modifying Contacts Views

You have already seen contacts listed in Business Card, Phone, and List views. You may have noticed that you cannot see all of the information in the List view that you have entered on the contact card. Often you need to see specific fields in order to complete your work efficiently. You can alter the columns that are displayed in the Phone and

List views. You can make the columns wider and select the columns that you want to see displayed. You will remove the File As column because it is redundant to the Full Name column. You will remove other unnecessary columns. You will alter the width of the columns so all of the information is displayed.

SIDE NOTE
Different Views, Different Columns

As you change views in Contacts, the columns displayed change. You can set which columns to display in the Card, Phone, and List views. The Business Card view displays the available general information listed for each contact.

To Modify the Contacts Views

a. Click the **Mid-Valley Producers folder** in the Navigation Pane. Click the **View tab**, and then click **Change View**. Click **List**, click **View Settings** in the Current View group, and then click **Columns**.

b. Click **Icon** in the Show these columns in this order box, and then click **Remove**. This removes it from the list, but does not remove any entries you may have made on the contact cards for this column.

c. Remove the following columns from the Show these columns in this order box:
   - Attachment
   - File As
   - Country/Region
   - Department
   - Business Fax
   - Home Phone
   - Mobile Phone
   - Categories
   - Flag Status

   These columns are removed only from your current view. If you want to see the information, you can open the contact card. The remaining columns are Full Name, Job Title, Company, Business Phone, and E-mail.

d. Select **Job Title**. Click **Move Down**—multiple times if necessary—to position the Job Title under Company in the Show these columns in this order box. Click **OK** to close the Show Columns dialog box, and then click **OK** to close the Advanced View Settings: List dialog box. Notice that you cannot read the full company name, job title, business phone, or e-mail address, so you decide to change the width of the columns.

e. Drag the **column border line** between the Company and Job Title column headers, and when the pointer becomes a double-pointed arrow ⊣⊢, drag to the right to increase the width of the column. Repeat this step with the **column border line** between the Job Title and the Business Phone to increase the size of the Job Title column. The Business Phone column may be wider than needed, so you will adjust its width to fit the numbers.

f. Double-click the **column border line** between the Business Phone and E-mail column headers to the left to decrease the width of the column without removing any of the digits.

g. Drag the far-right side of the **E-mail column header** to increase the width of the column. Make adjustments to the columns so you can see all of the information in the columns. You may need to collapse the Navigation Pane and the To-Do Bar depending on your monitor resolution and screen size.

SIDE NOTE
Changing the Column Width

The column width can be changed in the Phone, List, or Card views in the Contacts component by dragging border lines. If the width of the columns exceeds the size of the window, a scroll bar appears at the bottom of the window.

Sorting Columns

If you have a lot of entries, it is helpful at times to sort the columns in different ways. Each of the columns can be sorted in ascending or descending order.

To Sort Columns

a. Click the **Company** column header.

   The contacts are now sorted by Company name. Notice the arrow next to the word Company. That indicates the sort column and the direction of sorting. An arrow that points upward means that the contacts are sorted in ascending order. An arrow pointing down indicates descending order. While sorting might not be a big deal with so few contacts, it becomes much more important when you have 100, 1,000, or 5,000 contacts.

b. Click the **Company** column header again, and then observe the change in the order of the contacts.

c. Click the **Full Name** column header. Notice that the contacts are sorted on first name because that appears first in the Full Name column.

Printing a Contacts List

There are times when you might want to have a printed copy of your contact list. You may be travelling and not have access to your computer. A printed copy can also serve as a backup copy of your information.

Each of the views of your Contacts can produce different printed documents. For instance, the Business Card view and the Card view can produce Card Style, Small Booklet Style, Medium Booklet Style, Memo Style, and Phone Directory Style printed copies. The Phone view and the List view create printed documents in the Table Style. If you open a single contact card, you can print the information in the Memo Style.

By organizing your contacts in folders, you can avoid printing all of the contact information you have stored in Outlook. You open the folder, and then print. So for instance, if you only wanted to print a copy of the employees at Painted Paradise Golf Resort and Spa, you would open the employee folder and then print the contact information. If you have arranged your contacts into categories, you can print just the entries in a category by selecting it in the List view and then printing in Table Style or Memo Style. Memo Style prints the contact card information on separate sheets.

You will print all of the contacts in the List view.

To Print a List

a. Click the **File tab**, click **Print**, and then click **Table Style** under Settings. The Preview shows the columns that were listed in the List view.

b. Click **Print Options**, and then click **Page Setup**. Click the **Paper tab**, and then click **Landscape** in the Orientation group. Click **OK**, and then click **Preview**.

c. Select the appropriate printer, and then click **Print** if your instructor requests a copy of the Contacts document. Click the **Home tab** if you did not print the document.

Real World Advice — Using Your Contacts

Another important feature of storing your Contacts in Outlook is that they dynamically interact with other applications in the Microsoft Office suite. Contacts can be used to create merged letters, envelopes, and labels in Word. You can import data from Access and Excel into the Contacts or Calendar components. A wizard for importing data files is found on the File tab, using the Open command. You can import files in the Office 97-2003 format, comma-separated values (.csv) files, and other types of data files.

To Create a Contact Group

Contact groups enable you to quickly send e-mail to a predefined group of people. You can set up a distribution list and then use the name of the list in the address box of the new e-mail message. You can also notify the entire distribution list of a meeting you are trying to arrange or assign everyone on the list to a task. Once established, your distribution list is displayed in your Contacts folder in alphabetical order with the rest of the contact names. Contacts can appear in more than one contact group, so you may reuse the contacts as you continue through this workshop.

You will create a contact group consisting of your instructor's and your own e-mail address, and then you will use the group to send an e-mail message.

To Create a Contact Group

a. On the Home tab, click **New Contact Group** in the New group.

b. Type Mid-Valley Producers in the Name box.

c. Click the **Contact Group tab**, click **Add Members** in the Members group, and then click **From Outlook Contacts**. Click the **Address Book arrow**, and then click **Mid-Valley Producers**.

d. Click **your name**, click **Members**, and then double-click **your instructor's name**. Names can be added to the Contact Group in both ways.

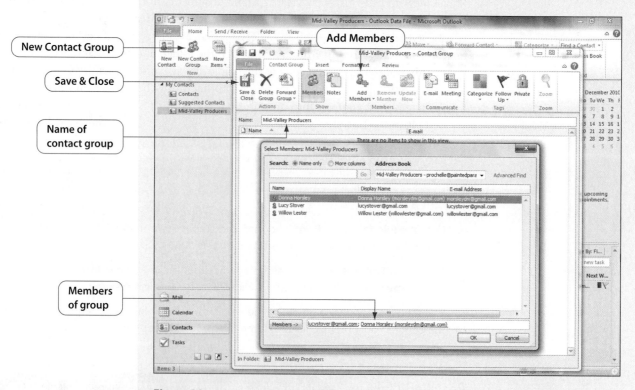

Figure 20 Contact groups

e. Click **OK**, and then click **Save & Close**. The Contact Group is displayed in the view of the contacts.

Using a Contact Group

The components of Outlook enable you to easily drag and drop items such as the contact group you just created into a component to create a new e-mail message, calendar appointment or meeting, or task. You will send your contact group an e-mail message.

To Use a Contact Group

a. Drag the **Mid-Valley Producers** contact group to the **Mail** component in the Navigation Pane. The screen will briefly flash as the new message screen opens.

b. Click the **taskbar**, and then select the **Untitled Message** form. The message already has Mid-Valley Producers in the To box.

c. Type Lastname_Firstname_o01_ws01_Planning_Group in the Subject box.

d. In the message box, type Hello, and then press Enter twice. Type As a follow-up to our meeting and tour on last Wednesday, I would like to remind you that we can offer your group more than just conference space. Attendees will be able to schedule spa treatments or tee times through our website at www.paintedparadiseresort.com. Press Enter once.

e. Click **Send**, and then click **Send/Receive All Folders** on the Quick Access Toolbar. Wait a few moments, and then click **Send/Receive All Folders** again to retrieve the message.

f. Click **Mail** in the Navigation Pane, and then select and review the message. Click **Mid-Valley Folder** in the Quick Steps group to file the message.

Managing the Calendar

Business people will tell you that the majority of their time is spent in meetings, making and returning phone calls, and managing their schedules. Using the Calendar component of Outlook, you can organize your schedule and set up reminders. You can categorize items on your calendar, just as you categorized e-mail messages and contacts. This process gives a consistent color and name to related items in Outlook to help you organize your work.

Outlook enables you to have multiple calendars and view them separately or together. For instance, you may have a personal calendar where you record appointments, and a business calendar where you schedule items related to your work world. On occasion you will want to view them both at the same time so you can make sure you don't have any conflicts.

Identifying Calendar Features

The Calendar component in Outlook contains a number of views, as shown in Figure 21, so you can select the best one for your situation. Some people like to see the calendar in a daily view, while others like to see the big picture of a weekly or monthly view. You will probably find yourself using all of the views from time to time. The Schedule View enables you to share calendars with coworkers and simultaneously view their calendars. While this is a useful view in business, it is beyond the scope of this book for workshop activities.

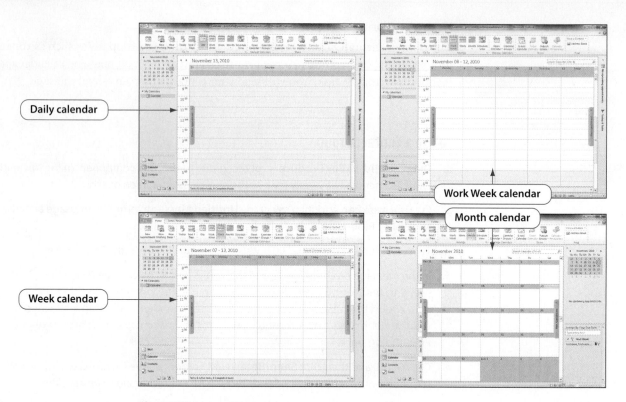

Daily calendar

Work Week calendar

Month calendar

Week calendar

Figure 21 Calendar views

The **Date Navigator** is a small month calendar that you use to select different dates quickly. It can appear in the left Navigation Pane or on the To-Do Bar on the right, depending on the setup of the calendar view. Today's date is bordered in red on the Date Navigator. The gray highlighting on the day, week, or month indicates what is displayed in the calendar view. Click a different date in the Date Navigator, and the day or days shown in the calendar view change. Click the right arrow at the top of the Date Navigator to advance the calendar by month. To return to previous months, click the left arrow on the Date Navigator. You can widen the Date Navigator to view more months by dragging the border of the calendar view as shown in Figure 22. Upcoming appointments, as well as reminders of flagged items are shown with the Date Navigator in the To-Do Bar on the right. Double-click the item to open it for review.

The **To-Do Bar** provides a quick overview of the calendar, upcoming appointments, and tasks. It can be minimized to give you more room to view other things in the window, or expanded to help keep you organized at a glance.

To Modify the Calendar Views

a. Click **Calendar** in the Navigation Pane to open the calendar.

b. Click the **Home tab**, and then click **Day** in the Arrange group. The calendar view displays the current date.

c. Click **Work Week** in the Arrange group. Note that the workweek is shown as Monday through Friday.

d. Click **Week** in the Arrange group. This calendar view shows the dates from Sunday through Saturday.

e. Click **Month** in the Arrange group to show the current month. Notice that the current day is highlighted in a gold color.

f. Click next **Wednesday** on the Date Navigator. The calendar view changes to the Day view.

g. Drag across the **weekdays for last week** on the Date Navigator. The Work Week view is shown in the calendar view.

h. Click the Expand To-Do Bar arrow, if necessary, to display the To-Do Bar. Drag the **right border** of the calendar view to increase the size of the To-Do Bar so two months are displayed in the To-Do Bar.

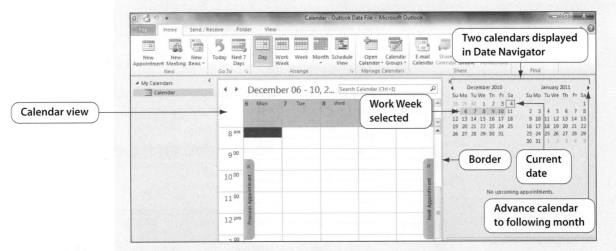

Figure 22 Date Navigator

i. Click the **right arrow** ▶ to advance the calendars in the To-Do Bar. Drag the **right border** of the calendar view to the right to decrease the To-Do Bar to a single calendar width.

Adding Calendars

The Calendar folders are shown in the left Navigation Pane of the window. You can create additional calendars as needed. For instance, you may have a calendar specifically for event planning. You will create a personal calendar and a Mid-Valley Producers calendar to help you organize events.

To Add Calendars

a. Click the **Folder tab**, and then click **New Calendar**.

b. Type Personal for the **Name**. Check to see that **Calendar** is selected in the **Select where to place the folder** box, and then click **OK**. The Personal calendar appears in the Navigation Pane, unchecked.

c. Click **New Calendar** on the Folder tab again. Type Mid-Valley Producers. Be sure **Calendar** is selected, and then click **OK**. You will use this for planning the Mid-Valley Producers event while putting some personal and professional dates on the other calendars.

d. Click the **Personal** check box in the Navigation Pane to select it and the normal Calendar. The calendars are displayed side by side in different colors. Notice that the tab at the top contains the name of the calendar.

e. Click the **Personal calendar tab**, and then click the **View in Overlay Mode arrow** ◀.
   The Personal calendar fills the calendar view. If appointments were set in both calendars, they would appear together in the Overlay Mode.

f. Click the **Calendar tab**, and then click the **View in Side-by-Side Mode arrow** ▶ to return to a view of both calendars side by side.

g. Click the **Calendar** check box in the Navigation Pane to clear the box. The Personal calendar fills the calendar view.

h. Click the **Personal** check box in the Navigation Pane to clear the box. Notice that the Calendar is automatically checked and displayed.

i. Click the **Personal** check box in the Navigation Pane, and then click the **Mid-Valley Producers** check box. All three calendars are displayed at one time, making it easy to view conflicting appointments.

j. Click the **View tab**, and then click **Month**. The monthly calendars are all displayed, but it would be hard to view any information on the dates.

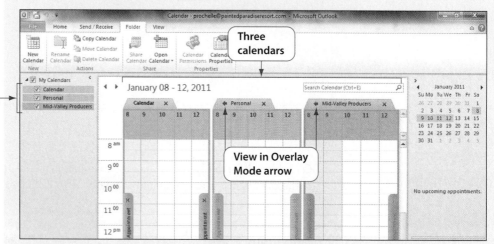

Figure 23 Three calendars viewed simultaneously in Month view

k. Click the **Personal** check box, and then click the **Calendar** check box in the Navigation Pane to show only the Mid-Valley Producers calendar.

SIDE NOTE
Change the Default Color of the Calendar
To change the color of the calendars, click the View tab, and then click Color. Select a color from the palette. Select another calendar and change the color. This can help you to quickly recognize the different calendars.

Adding Appointments

An **appointment** is defined in Outlook as an assignment of time for which you do not have to schedule other people or resources such as rooms. Examples might be doctor's appointments, conference calls in which you are a participant, and other events that you would like to attend. A **meeting** is scheduled with one or more attendees for whom Outlook will automatically create and send e-mail notifications. When you send a meeting calendar item, it appears on the other person's Outlook calendar.

Overlapping meetings or appointments are shown adjacent to one another in the same time period in which they occur. Outlook enables you to set up recurring events and to select the number of times the meeting or appointment recurs. Outlook then reserves the time for all future occurrences in the series. For instance, if you have a weekly status meeting with your staff, you can set up the calendar item once, and it will appear each week on your calendar.

Certain calendar items will be scheduled for the whole day. As an example, you may be attending a conference and want to show that you will be away from the office for three or four days of a week. As you set up a new appointment, click All day event. An alternative way to signify an all-day event is to double-click the colored bar directly below the date in the calendar view of your choice. The Event form opens so you can add the details of the event.

To Add an Appointment

a. With the Mid-Valley Producers Calendar displayed, click the **Home tab**, and then click **Today** in the Go To group. Click the date for **next Wednesday** on the Date Navigator.

b. Click **New Appointment** in the New group on the Home tab. Type Appointment with Donna Horsley in the Subject box. Type My Office in the Location box. Notice that the day is already set for next Wednesday because you selected it in the Date Navigator. Click the **Start time arrow** (the current time is displayed by default), and then click **1:00 PM**. Click the **End time arrow** (1:30 PM is now displayed by default), and then click **2:30 PM (1.5 hours)**. In the Message box, type Review time frame for Mid-Valley Producers conference, covering planning and the actual date of the event. Suggest a weekly status call. Have Lesa on standby for introductions. Tour Eldorado Room, and other appropriate facilities. Include the punctuation.

c. Click the **Appointment tab**, and then click **High Importance** in the Tags group. Click **Categorize**, and then click **Mid-Valley Producers**. Click the **Reminder arrow** in the Options group, and then click **2 hours**. This will give you time to clear your desk before the appointment and make sure you have the documents you need for the appointment.

When the Reminder option is active, each calendar entry produces a Reminder dialog box. Reminders can also be set to play a sound when they occur. You can adjust the default length of time for the reminder on the File tab, Options, Calendar. Individual appointments can also contain reminders that are for more or less time than specified by the default reminder.

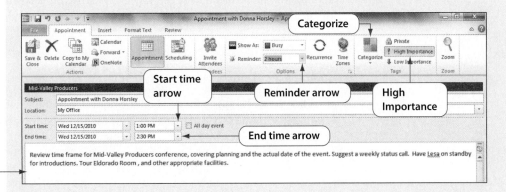

Figure 24   New appointment form

d. Click **Save & Close**. The appointment is shown in dark red on the calendar, with the time for the entire appointment blocked out.

e. Double-click the appointment to open it in the Appointment dialog box. On the **Appointment tab**, click **Copy to My Calendar** in the Actions group. Click **Calendar** in the Navigation Pane to display both calendars simultaneously. The appointment is shown on both calendars.

f. Click the **View in Overlay Mode arrow** ◄ on the **Mid-Valley Producers** calendar. Notice that you can see both instances of the appointment at 1 PM.

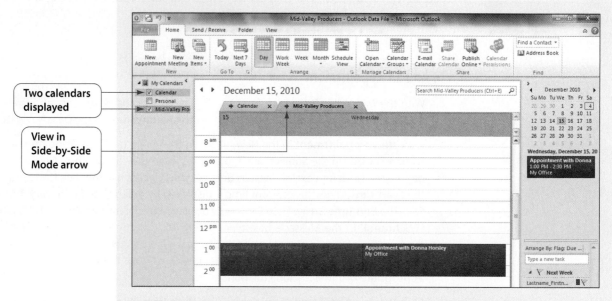

Figure 25 Two calendars viewed in Overlay Mode

g. Click the **Calendar** check box in the Navigation Pane to remove that calendar from the Calendar Pane.

Adding a Meeting

You have decided that you would like to schedule Lesa so she will definitely be available for the last half hour of the meeting with Donna so she can assist with the tour of the facilities.

To Add a Meeting

a. Click the **white space** for 2 PM on the right side of the scheduled meeting with Donna. Click the **Home tab**, and then click **New Meeting** in the New group.

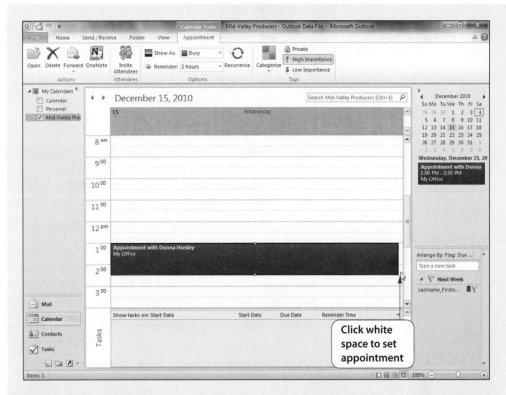

Figure 26 Adding a meeting

b. Click **To**, select **Lesa Martin**, and then click **Required**. Select **your contact information** in the Mid-Valley Producers folder, and then click **Required**. You are adding yourself to the list so Lesa knows that you will be in attendance. Click **OK**.

c. Click **High Importance** in the Tags group, click **Categorize**, and then click **Mid-Valley Producers**. Click the **Reminder arrow** in the Options group, and then click **1 hour** so Lesa will be reminded of the meeting.

d. Type Meeting with Mid-Valley Producers Representative for the Subject. Type Patti's Office for the Location. In the Message box, type Lesa, please bring layout brochures. You will join us during the tour of the facilities. Include the punctuation.

e. Click **Send**. If a message opens cautioning you that Lesa is misspelled, click Ignore All. An alert message indicates that the meeting is not in the Calendar folder and that responses will not be tallied. Because you are Lesa's supervisor, you know that she will not decline the meeting.

f. Click **Yes** to send the message. If another alert appears, asking whether you would like to update your own calendar, click **Yes**. The meeting appears next to the original appointment you set up to indicate an overlap.

g. Click **Send/Receive All Folders** on the Quick Access Toolbar.

h. Double-click the **meeting entry** on the To-Do Bar to view the appointment.

   Notice that the Respond group displays buttons that you can click to Accept the meeting, mark the meeting as Tentative, Decline the meeting, Propose a New Time for the meeting, or Respond. If you click the arrows on the buttons, you will have opportunities to edit a response, send the response, and not send a response.

i. Click **Accept**, and then click **Send the Response Now**.

j. Click **Send/Receive All Folders** on the Quick Access Toolbar. Click **Mail** in the Navigation Pane. Select the **Accepted** message, and then review the message in the Reading Pane.

Adding a Recurring Appointment

After meeting with Donna, she accepted your idea of having a weekly status call. You will set up a recurring appointment on your calendar so you can schedule 30 minutes to talk to her at 9 AM on Thursday mornings.

To Add a Recurring Appointment

a. Click **Calendar** in the Navigation Pane. If necessary, click the **Mid-Valley Producers** calendar to select it, and then click the **Calendar** check box to remove the regular calendar from the display, if necessary. Click next **Thursday** on the Date Navigator. Double-click the line for **9:00** on the Day calendar in the calendar view. The Appointment form opens.

b. Type Status Phone Call - Mid-Valley Producers in the Subject box. In the Message box, type Call Donna Horsley 505-555-8374.

c. Click the **Appointment tab**, and then click **Recurrence** in the Options group. Click **End by**, and then click the **End by arrow**. Click the **right arrow** ▶ on the calendar to advance to March. Click the first **Thursday** of the month of March, and then click **OK**.

d. Click **Categorize** in the Tags group, and then click **Mid-Valley Producers**.

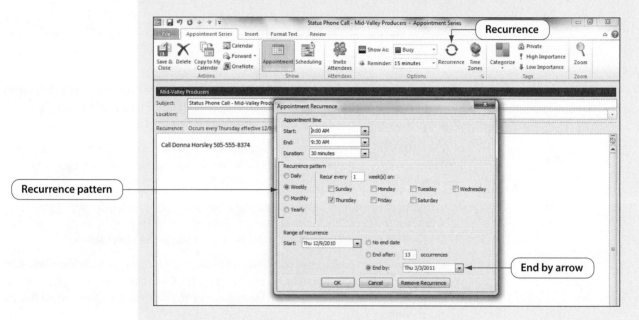

Figure 27 Recurring appointment

e. Click **Save & Close**. Click the **Home tab**, click the **Month arrow** in the Arrange group, and then click **Show High Detail**. The beginning words of the subject line are displayed on each Thursday on the monthly calendar.

Updating a Recurring Appointment

During the first phone call, Donna suggested that 9 AM did not fit well into her schedule. She requested that the status phone call be moved to 10 AM on Fridays.

To Update a Recurring Appointment

a. Double-click one of the status phone call appointments. Click **Open the series**, and then click **OK**.

b. Click the **Appointment Series tab**, and then click **Recurrence** in the Options group. Click the **Start arrow**, and then click **10:00 AM**.

c. Click **Thursday** to deselect it, click **Friday** to select it, click **OK**, and then click **Save & Close**. All occurrences of the appointment are moved to Friday in the calendar.

Setting a Private Appointment

In some situations, you would like to include a personal appointment on your calendar that will indicate to someone viewing the calendar that you have an appointment, but will not reveal the details of the appointment. You will set an appointment with the dentist on your Personal calendar and mark it as private.

To Set a Private Appointment

a. Click the **Personal calendar** check box in the Navigation Pane, and then click the **Mid-Valley Producers** check box in the Navigation Pane to deselect it. Click **New Appointment**.

b. Type Dentist Appointment in the Subject box. Type 1547 Main Street in the Location box. Click the **Start time arrow**, and select the first **Monday** of next month. Click the **Start time arrow**, and then select **9:30 AM**. Click the **End time arrow**, and then select **10:30 AM**.

c. Click the **Private** icon in the Tags group. The appointment is now marked as private.

d. Click **Save & Close**. On the Home tab, click **Week** in the Arrange group. Click the **Forward arrow** to advance to the week with the dentist appointment. The appointment is shown on your Personal calendar with a lock icon to indicate that it is private.

e. Click the **Calendar** check box in the Navigation Pane to view both the Personal and main Calendar at the same time. Drag the **Dentist Appointment** from the Personal calendar to the Calendar. Now the appointment is shown on both of your calendars.

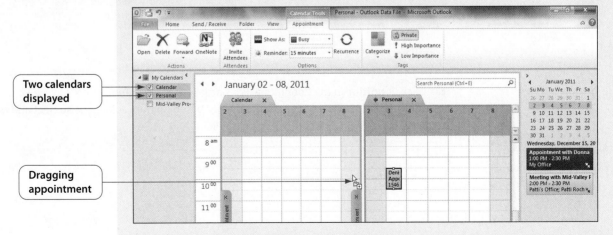

Figure 28   Dragging an appointment to another calendar

Applying Conditional Formatting

You can apply **conditional formatting**, such as blue or green shading, to appointments on your calendar to remind yourself that a meeting is important, will be away from the workplace, or requires preparation. Conditional formatting requires that you enter a rule that Outlook uses to apply the formatting. If you enter the name of the project as the rule, any other appointments or meetings that you set up later that contain the project name will be displayed with the conditional format you select.

Your dentist suggested that you return during the next month for a follow-up appointment. You will create a conditional formatting rule to highlight dental appointments in dark blue.

To Create a Conditional Formatting Rule

a. Click the **View tab**, and then click **View Settings**. Click **Conditional Formatting**.

b. Click **Add** in the Conditional Formatting dialog box. Type Dental Rule for the **Name** of the rule. Click the **Color arrow**, and then click **Dark Blue**.

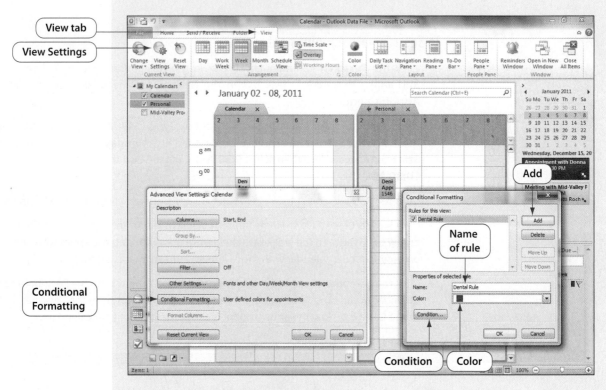

Figure 29   Conditional Formatting dialog box

c. Click **Condition** in the Conditional Formatting dialog box. Type Dentist in the Search for the word(s) box. Rules can be set to trigger based on the subject, the subject and notes fields, or on frequently used text fields. Click **OK**.

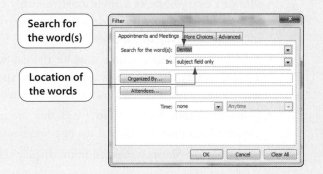

Search for the word(s)

Location of the words

Figure 30 Filter dialog box

d. Click **OK** to close the Conditional Formatting dialog box, and then click **OK** to close the Advanced View Settings dialog box. Notice that the dentist appointment is now shown with a dark blue background.

e. Click the **Home tab**, and then click **New Appointment**. Type Visit Dentist in the Subject box. Type 1547 Main Street in the Location box. Click the **Start date arrow**, and then select the first Monday of the month following the first dental appointment. Click the **Start time arrow**, and then select **10:00 AM**. Click the **Private** icon in the Tags group, and then click **Save & Close**.

f. Click **Month** in the Arrange group, and then advance the calendar to the month of the second dental appointment. The dental appointment appears on one calendar with a dark blue background. Drag the **appointment** to the other calendar, and then click the **Personal calendar** check box in the Navigation Pane so only the Calendar is displayed.

Real World Advice   Conditional Formatting or Categories?

You may wonder what the difference is between conditional formatting and categories. Categories can be assigned throughout Outlook to format e-mail messages, calendar items, contacts, and tasks. Categories are named and color-coded. You apply them by clicking them when you want to assign an item element to the category. Items can be sorted using the applied categories. Conditional formatting is based on rules, and changes to the font format or color occur automatically once the rules are set up. In the Mail, Contacts, and Tasks components changes can only be made to the font with conditional formatting. On the Calendar, conditional formatting appears as background colors in the time slots on the calendar.

Printing a Calendar View

Calendars can be printed in a variety of ways so that you can have a copy of your schedule even when you are away from the computer:

- Daily Style—Displays each hour of the work day with events listed. Calendars for the current month and the coming month are included at the top of the page. The Daily Task List and space for notes are arranged on the far right of the sheet.

- Weekly Agenda Style—Shows each day of the week following the selected date with the events listed. Calendars for the current month and the coming month are included at the top of the page.

- Weekly Calendar Style—Displays time slots for each day of the week with the events listed. Calendars for the current month and the coming month are included at the top of the page.

- Monthly Style—Shows a traditional monthly calendar with the events listed in the squares for each date. Calendars for the current month and the coming month are included at the top of the page.
- Tri-fold Style—Displays time slots for the day with the events listed for the first fold. The Daily Task List appears as the second fold and a view of the calendar for the coming week with events listed as shown on the third fold.
- Calendar Details Style—Shows days that are selected with the events for the days, giving the complete details of the appointment.
- Memo Style—Shows a selected item, displaying the details.

To Print a Calendar

a. Click the **Mid-Valley Producers** check box in the Navigation Pane, and then click the **Calendar** check box to remove the regular calendar from the display. Click **Today** in the Go To group, and then click **Month** in the Arrange group to display the full month.

b. Click the **File tab**, and then click the **Print tab**.

c. Click each of the styles under Settings to preview them. Click **Actual Size** to zoom in to see the detail and use the scroll bars to move around in the Preview Pane.

d. Click **Calendar Details Style**. Review the appointments, noting the recurring appointments. At the bottom of the page, the date the document was created, the name of the person who owns the calendar, and the page number appear in the footer.

e. Select the correct printer, and then click **Print** if your instructor directs you to make a hard copy of the document. If not, click the **Home tab**. Keep in mind that the dates shown in the figure and your Appointments may be different.

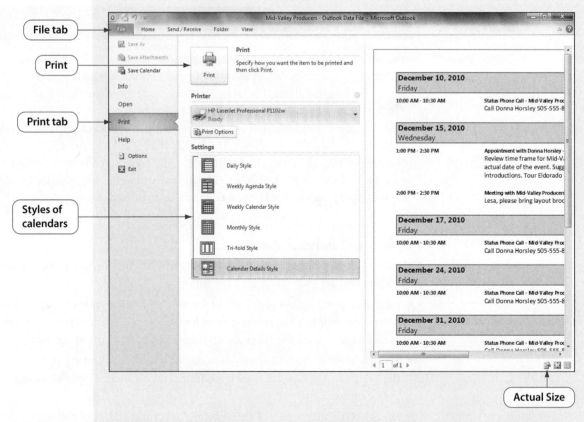

Figure 31 Printing a calendar

f. Click the **Personal calendar** check box in the Navigation Pane. Click the **right arrow** ▶ on the To-Do Bar to advance the **Date Navigator** to next month. Click the upcoming **dental appointment** in the calendar to select it. Click the **File tab**, and then click **Print**. Click **Memo Style** at the bottom of the Settings box, and then review the Preview. Print the document if requested by your instructor. If not, click the **Home tab**, and then click the **Personal calendar** check box and the **Mid-Valley Producers calendar** check box in the Navigation Pane. The Calendar is displayed by default.

g. With the Calendar displayed, click **Today** in the Go To group, and then click **Month**, if necessary. Select **Appointment with Donna**, and then press **Delete**. Select the **Meeting with Mid-Valley Producers**, and then click **Delete** in the Actions group. Click **No** to respond to the message regarding sending a response to the organizer of this meeting. Advance to the next month, delete the **Dentist Appointment**, and then delete the **Visit Dentist** appointment.

Managing Tasks and Notes

The Outlook Tasks list is an invaluable tool for planning your workday, week, or month. The tasks can be scheduled, categorized, marked as complete, and even assigned to other people. Reminders, follow-up flagged items, and tasks appear on the To-Do List shown in the main window of the Tasks component. Items with flags appear on the To-Do Bar on the right side window along with upcoming calendar appointments and meetings when viewing any of the other Outlook components. The views of the tasks can be changed from a simple list to a detailed list to filtered lists showing the completed items, active items, prioritized items, and more.

Notes, like sticky notes that you might post to remind yourself of something, are available in Outlook. Notes can be categorized and stored. They do not have dates or times associated with them, and reminders are not a feature of the Notes component. If you carry a laptop computer, you might find the Notes component to be good for taking notes during meetings.

Creating Tasks

As with the other Outlook components, tasks can be arranged in folders. Tasks placed in the folders are also shown on the main To-Do List. Tasks are displayed on the Tasks list with different characteristics based on their status. Tasks marked as completed are shown with a line drawn through them. Tasks shown in red text indicate overdue tasks as shown in Figure 32. The flag colors indicate the nearness of the deadline by turning from pink to red as the due date approaches. Just as you added and removed columns in the Contacts views, you can also modify the columns available in the Tasks component.

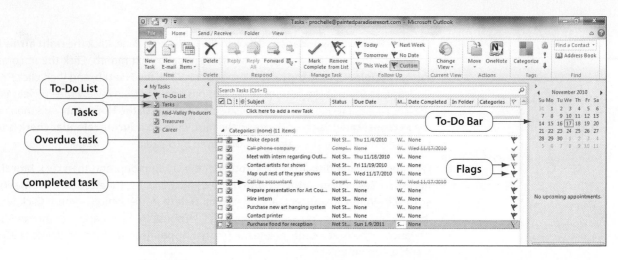

Figure 32   Tasks component

> ## Real World Advice
>
> **What Is the Difference Between the Tasks List and the To-Do List?**
>
> When the Tasks folder is selected in the Navigation Pane of the Tasks component, only the tasks in that folder are displayed. The To-Do List is a much more complete view of reminders about appointments, tasks, and flagged items.

SIDE NOTE

Alternative Methods for Adding Tasks

There are a number of ways to enter new tasks into Outlook:

- Double-click on the blank area of the Tasks component window
- Click New Task on the Home tab
- Click in the Type a new task box at the top of the Tasks list and begin typing
- Click in the Type a new task box on the To-Do Bar

To Create New Tasks

a. Click **Tasks** in the Navigation Pane. Click the **Home tab**, and then click **New Task** in the New group to open the Task form. The Task form provides extended options for tracking the task.

b. Type Prepare for Mid-Valley Producers Meeting in the Subject box. Click the **Start date arrow**, and then click **tomorrow's date**. Click the **Due date arrow**, and then click four work days from the current date. Click the **Priority arrow**, and then click **High**. Click the **Reminder** check box, and then click the **Reminder date arrow**. Click three work days from the current date.

c. Type Draft contract for Eldorado Room. Prepare idea sheet for activities after the conference day. Talk to Chef Sanchez about buffet options. in the Message box.

d. Click **Categorize** in the Tags group, and then click **Mid-Valley Producers**.

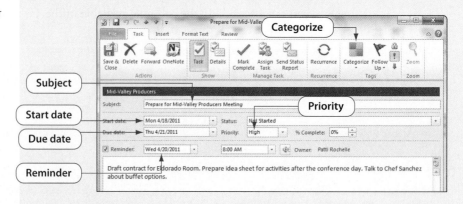

Figure 33   Task form

e. Click **Save & Close**. The task appears on the Tasks list. Also note that it is on the To-Do Bar with the reminder icon and a pink flag.

f. Click **Tasks** under My Tasks in the Navigation Pane, if necessary, to select it. Click on the **View tab**, click the **Change View** button in the Current View group, click **Simple List**. Click in the **Click here to add a new Task** box at the top of the Tasks list, and then type Plan budget for Mid-Valley Producers in the Subject box. Press Enter. This places the task on the list where some things such as priority and follow-up dates can be assigned.

g. Click the task, if necessary, to select it. On the **Home tab**, click **Categorize**, and then click **Mid-Valley Producers**.

h. Click in the **Type a new task** box on the **To-Do Bar**, and then type Discuss Mid-Valley Producers conference with Lesa. Press Enter. Select the **task** in the Tasks list, click **Categorize**, and then click **Mid-Valley Producers**.

Updating Tasks

As you work on tasks, you can use Outlook to track your progress. You can change the status of the task to Not Started, In Progress, Completed, Waiting on someone else, or Deferred. You can also provide a percentage value to quantify how close the task is to being complete.

To Update Tasks

a. Double-click the **task** you just set up in the Tasks list. The Task form opens.

b. Click the **Status arrow**, and then click **In Progress**. You have started working on the budget numbers based on your most recent conversation with Donna.

c. Click the **% Complete arrow** to change the value to **25%**. Click **Save & Close**.

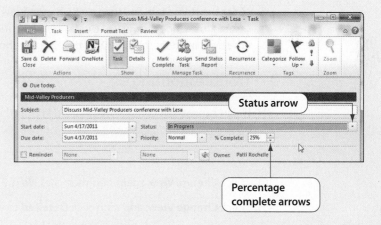

Figure 34   Updating tasks

Changing the Tasks List Views

Using different views of the Tasks list enables you to see different information for the tasks. The detailed view contains columns for status, date due, date modified or created, date completed, folder, category assigned, and flag status. Other views include Simple List, To-Do List, Prioritized, Active, and Completed, which contain different columns. You can modify the widths of the columns as needed to display the information in the column.

To Change Views of the Tasks List

a. Click **Tasks** under My Tasks in the Navigation Pane, if necessary, to select it. Click the **View tab**, and then click **Change View**. The various views show you different columns on the To-Do List.

b. Click **Detailed**. You now see the status of the task as well as the folder it is stored in, if any. One column that you probably cannot see all of is the Modified column.

c. Point to the border between the **Modified** and **Date Completed** columns at the top of the Tasks list. Drag it to the right when you see the double-pointed arrow ⊹. You can increase or decrease the width of the columns as needed.

d. Click the word **Status** at the top of the Tasks list. The items on the list are sorted in order of the status.

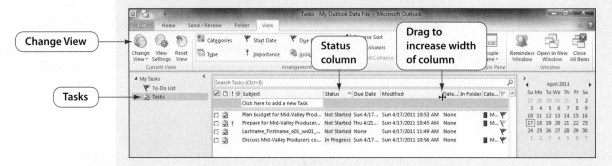

Figure 35 Detailed view of Tasks list

e. Click **Change View**, and then click **Active**. The percentage complete is shown in a column in this view.

f. Click the **Home tab**, and then click **Change View** in the Current View group. There are two places to change the view of the Task List in Outlook. Click **Today**. It appears as if some of the tasks are gone, but in reality they are not shown because they are not due today.

Troubleshooting

> If you cannot see Change View, click More in the Current View group to open the gallery to select Today.

g. Click **Change View** again, and then click **Next 7 Days**.

h. Click **Change View**, and then click **Detailed** to view all of the tasks you have set.

Managing Tasks

It is often a good idea to group tasks together to isolate them from the rest of the tasks you may have set for other projects. When you create task folders, the tasks can be moved to the folder while remaining in the normal To-Do List.

To Manage Tasks

a. Click the **Folder tab**, and then click **New Folder** in the New group.

b. Type Mid-Valley Producers in the Name box. Click **Tasks** in the Select where to place the folder box, if necessary, to select it. Click **OK**.

c. Drag all of the **tasks** to the Mid-Valley Producers folder in the Navigation Pane.

d. Click **To-Do List** in the Navigation Pane to review the list and make sure that the tasks are still on the list. Click the **Mid-Valley Producers folder** to view the tasks just for the Mid-Valley Producers conference.

e. Click the **Home tab**, click **Change View**, and then click **Prioritized**. If necessary, click **More** if no **Change View** button is available to display the gallery. You see some of the tasks have a normal priority level, while others are in the high priority group.

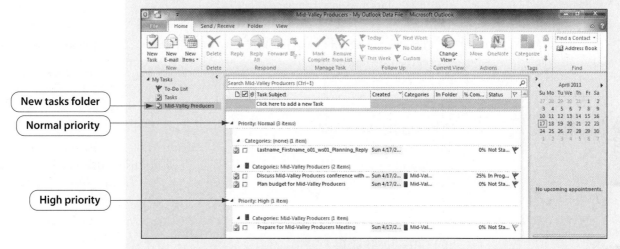

Figure 36   Prioritized tasks in Mid-Valley Producers folder

Marking Tasks as Complete

Once you have finished your work on the task, you will mark it as complete. This will make it easier for you to see at a glance what work is outstanding. It also removes the task from some of the views so that you can concentrate on just the things you have to do.

To Complete Tasks

a. Click the **flag** 🚩 for the **Plan budget for Mid-Valley Producers** task at the far right of the task. The task is now marked with a check ✔️ and is lined out as complete.

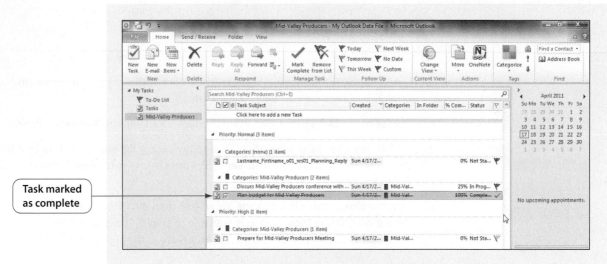

Task marked
as complete

Figure 37 Task marked as complete

b. Click the completed task in the Tasks list. On the Home tab, click **Remove from List** in the Manage Task group.

Printing a Tasks List

Often you will want a printed list of your tasks to use while away from your computer. It can document the work you have completed and help to ensure that you have all of your work scheduled.

To Print a Tasks List

a. Click the **Mid-Valley Producers folder** in the Navigation Pane, and then click the first item. You will print just one task from this folder.

b. Click the **File tab**, and then click **Print**. Two Styles are available.

c. Click **Table Style** in the Settings group. Click **Actual Size** 🖼 to view the preview.

d. Click **Memo Style** in the Settings group. All of the information is displayed for the task in this view.

e. Select the correct printer, and then click **Print**, if your instructor requests a copy of the document. If not, click the **Home tab**.

Creating Notes

Busy people often rely on sticky notes. They post them on the edges of their computer monitor, the refrigerator, and even the bathroom mirror to remind themselves of all sorts of things. Using Outlook, you can clean up your work area by using the Notes component. Notes are different than tasks, in that their purpose is to jog your memory rather than set deadlines. Notes might contain a list of things that you want to pick up at the store, whereas a task will remind you that you have to go to the store. While generally used as a quick snippet, the Notes component can be used to record meeting notes if you carry a laptop to business meetings.

The "pad" of notes is available by clicking the Notes button in the Navigation Pane and then clicking New Note on the Home tab. As you create new notes, the time and date is captured at the bottom of the note. Notes can be resized just as you would resize any other window by dragging on the bottom-right corner. You can change the default font as well as the color and size in the Options group on the File tab. You can also assign notes to categories.

To Create and Manipulate Notes

a. Click **Notes** 🔲 in the Navigation Pane.

Troubleshooting

> If you do not see the Notes icon, click the Configure buttons arrow at the bottom of the Navigation Pane, and then click Navigation Pane Options. Click Notes and then click OK to add the icon to the Navigation Pane.

b. Click the **Home tab** if necessary, and then click **Icon** in the Current View group to select it, if necessary. Click the **View tab**, and then click **Large Icons** in the Arrangement group.

c. Click the **Home tab**, and then click **New Note**. Type the following on the yellow note:
Mid-Valley Producers
Develop a menu for buffet:
Include vegetarian options for main course. Vegetables to be provided by Mid-Valley - potatoes, green beans, broccoli. Wine provided by a member of the group.

d. Click **Notes** 🗒 at the top-left corner of the note, and then click **Save & Close**.

e. Press ⌨Ctrl⌨+⌨N⌨, and then type the following on the next note:
Mid-Valley Producers
Requested audio equipment for each conference room
Computer projection only in Eldorado

f. Click **Close** ☒ in the top-right corner of the note. Notice that both notes now say Mid-Valley Producers. You will categorize them and remove the repetitive words.

g. Click **Categorize** in the Tags group, click **Mid-Valley Producers**, and then double-click the note to open it. Highlight the words **Mid-Valley Producers**, and then press ⌨Delete⌨. Be sure to delete the blank line at the top of the note.

h. **Close** ☒ the note. Repeat this step with the other note. Now the notes are color coded, and you can see the first line of the notes to jog your memory.

i. On the **Home tab**, click **Notes List** in the Current View group. The layout changes, enabling you to read the complete note.

New Note

Categorize

Notes List view

Configure
buttons arrow

Figure 38 Notes List view

j. Click the **File tab**, click **Print**, and then click **Table Style**. Both notes are shown on the Preview.

k. Click **Print Options**, and then click **Page Setup**.

 The landscape orientation is still set from earlier in the workshop. You will return to portrait orientation.

l. Click the **Paper tab**, click **Portrait** in the Orientation group, and then click **OK**. Click **Preview**. Click **Print** if directed by your instructor to submit a printout of the notes; otherwise, click the **Home tab**.

m. Click the **Folder tab**, and then click **New Folder**. Type Mid-Valley Producers for the **Name** of the folder. Check to make sure that **Notes** is selected in the Select where to place the folder box. Click **OK**. Drag both notes into the folder you just created.

 You can drag notes to a specific day on the Date Navigator on the right side of the window to schedule them into your workday. Likewise, you can drag the note to your Tasks list on the To-Do Bar. Just the first sentence of the note, rather than the contents of the note, is transferred. The components of Outlook work well together, making it easy to integrate your e-mail, calendar, contacts, and tasks.

n. Check each of the Outlook components, and then move any item you created in this workshop into the appropriate Mid-Valley Producers folder if it was not moved there previously. Click the **File tab**, and then click **Options**. Click **Mail**, click **Stationery and Fonts**, and then click the **Font arrow** under the **Theme button** and click **Use theme's font**. Click **Theme**, and then click **(No Theme)** to reset the theme to a blank. Click **OK** three times to close the dialog boxes, and then close **Outlook**.

Concept Check

1. Describe the differences between conditional formatting and categories.

2. Under what conditions would you use the Tasks component rather than the Calendar component?

3. What are the advantages of using the Notes component?

4. Lists three strengths of the Outlook application.

Key Terms

Appointment 914
Attachment 892
Category 899
Conditional formatting 920
Conversation 900
Date Navigator 912
Deleted Items folder 887
Drafts folder 888

Inbox 885
Junk E-mail folder 887
Mail client 885
Mail server 885
Meeting 914
Navigation Pane 884
Outbox folder 888
Password 885

Quick Step 901
Reading Pane 886
Sent Items folder 888
Signature 892
Stationery 889
Themes 889
To-Do Bar 912
User name 885

Visual Summary

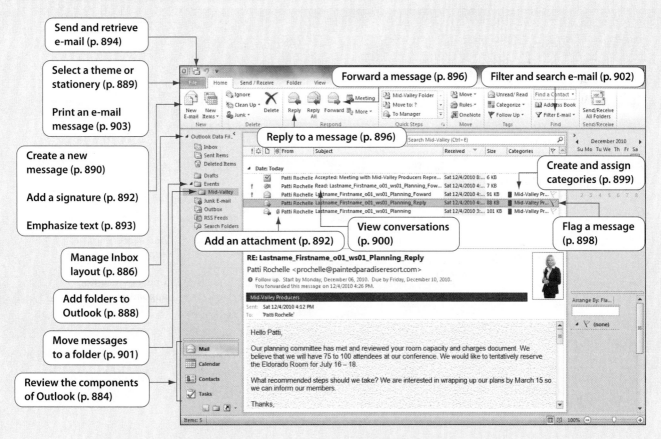

Figure 39 Managing Corporate Event Planning Using Outlook Final

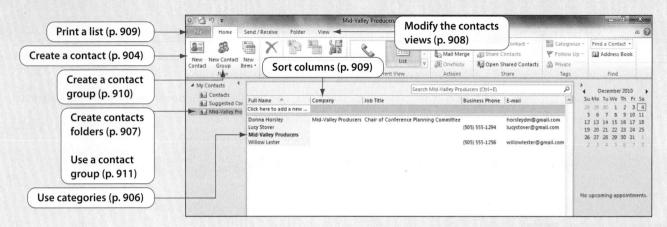

Print a list (p. 909)

Create a contact (p. 904)

Create a contact group (p. 910)

Create contacts folders (p. 907)

Use a contact group (p. 911)

Use categories (p. 906)

Modify the contacts views (p. 908)

Sort columns (p. 909)

Figure 40 Contacts

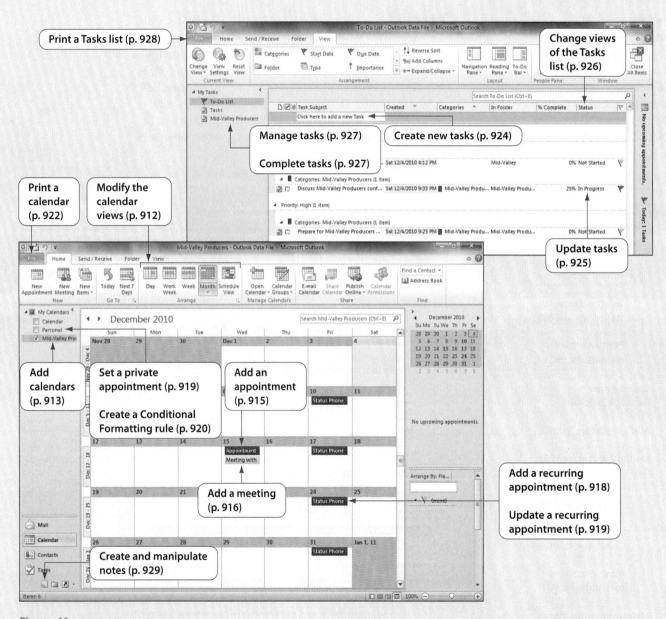

Print a Tasks list (p. 928)

Change views of the Tasks list (p. 926)

Manage tasks (p. 927)

Complete tasks (p. 927)

Create new tasks (p. 924)

Print a calendar (p. 922)

Modify the calendar views (p. 912)

Update tasks (p. 925)

Add calendars (p. 913)

Set a private appointment (p. 919)

Create a Conditional Formatting rule (p. 920)

Add an appointment (p. 915)

Add a meeting (p. 916)

Add a recurring appointment (p. 918)

Update a recurring appointment (p. 919)

Create and manipulate notes (p. 929)

Figure 41 Calendar and Tasks

Student data file needed:

o01_ws01_Gift_PO

You will save a file with the name:

Lastname_Firstname_o01_ws01_Gift_PO

You will send e-mail messages with the subject lines of:

Lastname_Firstname_o01_ws01_Gift_Request
Lastname_Firstname_o01_ws01_Gift_Forward

You will print these documents, at the direction of your instructor:

Gift Contacts Printout

Managing Contacts and E-mail for the Painted Treasures Gift Shop

Production & Operations

The gift shop, Painted Treasures, features a wide variety of products including jewelry, a house line of linens, specialty packaged foods by Chef Sanchez, and spa products. As the manager of Painted Treasures, you communicate with your suppliers via e-mail. It is handy to add new suppliers to your contact list and then send them e-mail. You will add your newest suppliers, categorize them, place them in a special folder, and send e-mail to them. You will be using your own e-mail address and that of your instructor as addresses for the new suppliers. You will make an attachment of a purchase order to an e-mail message, send the message, and forward the e-mail message to your instructor. Remember to stay organized by filing everything in folders!

a. Navigate to the student data files, and double-click **o01_ws01_Gift_PO** to open the file. Replace the words **Student Name** in the Ship To address block with your name. Save the file as Lastname_Firstname_o01_ws01_Gift_PO. Close the file, and then close Word.

b. Open **Outlook**, click **Contacts** in the Navigation Pane, click the **Folder tab**, and then click **New Folder**. Name the folder Gift Contacts. Click **OK**, and then click the **Gift Contacts** folder in the Navigation Pane to open it so you can add contacts directly to the folder.

c. Click the **Home tab**, and then click **New Contact** and add the following contact information to the Contact card:

- Full Name: Willow Lester
- Company Name: Spa Products International
- E-mail Address: willowlester@gmail.com
- Business Phone Number: 916-555-4638
- Business Address: 1564 W. Mills Street, Sacramento, CA 94203
- Notes: Customer ID PT-984

Click **Save & Close**. Continue adding contacts by adding **your instructor** and **yourself** to the Gift Contacts folder.

d. Select **Willow Lester's Contact card**, and then click **Categorize**. Click **All Categories**, and then click **New**. Name the category Gift Spa Supplier. Click **Dark Blue** for the Color, and then click **OK** twice. Click **your Contact card**, click **Categorize**, and then select the **Gift Spa Supplier** category.

e. Click **New Contact Group**, click **Add Members**, and then click **From Outlook Contacts**. Click the **Address Book arrow**, and then select **Gift Contacts**. Add **Willow Lester** and **yourself** to the group. Click **OK**. Name the Contact Group Gift Suppliers. Click **Categorize** in the Tags group, and then click **Gift Spa Supplier**. Click **Save & Close**.

f. Click **List** in the Current View group, click the **View tab**, and then click **View Settings**. Click **Columns**, and then click **Categories** in the Show these columns in this order box. Click **Remove**, click **Notes** in the Available columns box, and then click **Add**. Continue adding or removing columns until you have the ones shown here. Click **Move Up** or **Move Down** to arrange the columns in this order:

- Full Name
- Company
- E-mail
- Business Phone
- Business Address
- Notes

Click **OK** to close the Show Columns dialog box, and then click **OK** to close the Advanced View Settings: List dialog box.

g. Click the **Minimize arrows** at the top of the Navigation Pane and the To-Do Bar to collapse the panes. Double-click or drag the **border** between the headings on the Contacts List to display all of the information in the fields.

h. Click the **File tab**, and then click **Print**. Click **Print Options**, and then click **Page Setup**. Click the **Paper tab**, and then click **Landscape** in the Orientation group. Click **OK**, click **Preview**, and then carefully check the columns to ensure that all of the information will print. Click **Print** if your instructor directs you to submit a copy of the document.

i. Click the **Expand arrow** at the top of the Navigation Pane to expand the pane. Click **Mail** in the Navigation Pane, and then click the **Folder tab**. Click **New Folder**, and then type Gift E-mail as the name of the folder. Click **Inbox** if necessary to select it, and then click **OK**.

j. Click the **Home tab**, and then click **New E-mail**. Click **To**, click the **Address Book arrow**, and then click **Gift Contacts**. Click the **Gift Suppliers Contact Group** from the list of contacts, if necessary, to select it. Click **To** to select the group, and then click **OK**.

k. Click **Attach File**, and then navigate to the location where you store your project files. Double-click **Lastname_Firstname_o01_ws01_Gift_PO**. Type Lastname_Firstname_o01_ws01_Gift_ Request for the subject, and then type the following as the message:

Hello Willow, (press Enter twice)

The products you supply to the Painted Treasures Gift Shop are extremely popular. I have attached my second purchase order for some of the ones that are really selling fast. I look forward to having these in stock very soon. (press Enter twice)

Thanks,

l. Click **Signature** in the Include group on the Message tab. Click **Personal Class Signature** to add the signature you created as you completed the workshop to the message.

m. Click **Send**, and then click **Send/Receive All Folders** on the Quick Access Toolbar. Wait a few moments and click **Send/Receive All Folders** again to retrieve the message.

n. Double-click the **Lastname_Firstname_o01_ws01_Gift_Request** message that you sent (you may also see a reply from Willow Lester's e-mail account) to open it in the Reading Pane. Double-click the **attachment icon**, and then review the document. Close the Word document window.

o. Click **Forward**, and then click **To**. Click the **Address Book arrow**, and then click **Gift Contacts**. Select your instructor's contact information, and then click **To** at the bottom of the Select Names: Gift Contacts dialog box. Click **OK**.

p. Type _Forward at the end of the subject line so it reads **Lastname_Firstname_o01_ws01_Gift_Forward**. In the message box, type Hello, press Enter twice, and then continue typing The order for additional spa products has been sent. I will inform you as soon as the products are received so that you can handle payment. Press Enter twice, and then type your name.

q. Click the **Review tab**, and then click **Spelling & Grammar** in the Proofing group. Correct any misspelled words.

r. Click **Send**, and then click **Send & Receive All Folders** on the Quick Access Toolbar.

s. Drag all mail that you received into the Gift E-mail folder.

Practice 2

Student data file needed:

None needed

You will print these documents, at the direction of your instructor:

Treasures Calendar

Treasures Tasks List

Treasures Notes

Planning a Work Schedule for the Painted Treasures Gift Shop

Human Resources

As the manager of the Painted Treasures Gift Shop, you determine the schedule for the sales associates each week. At least two people are on the floor at all times, with someone taking care of stocking, cleaning duties, and covering lunch hours between noon and 4 o'clock each afternoon. The shop is open from 10 AM to 7 PM, with the associates taking a one-hour scheduled lunch between 1 and 3 PM. You will color-code the names of the associates, using conditional formatting, so they can quickly identify their work hours on the schedule. You will also create a task list to detail the closing procedures for the shop. You will make a few notes based on conversations you have had with the associates about their schedules for the coming weeks.

a. Click **Calendar** in the Navigation Pane, and then click the **Folder tab**. Click **New Calendar**, and then type Treasures as the Name. Make sure that Calendar is selected in the Select where to place the folder box, and then click **OK**. Click the **Treasures** check box in the Navigation Pane to select it, and then click the **Calendar** check box to deselect it.

b. Click the **View tab**, and then click **View Settings** in the Current View group. Click **Conditional Formatting**, and then click **Add**. Name the rule Laura Waden. Click the **Color arrow,** and then click **Yellow**. Click **Condition**, and then type Laura in the Search for the word(s) box. Click **OK** twice to close the dialog boxes. Create four more rules as follows:

Rule Name	Color	Condition Search Words
Michelle Strom	Dark Gray	Michelle
Sara Kline	Dark Peach	Sara
Jay Groth	Green	Jay
Your Name	Teal	Your First Name

c. On the **Home tab**, click **Week** in the Arrange group. Advance the calendar to display **next week**, and then click **New Appointment**. Type Laura Waden for the Subject. Click the **Start time arrow** for the date, and then click the date for **Monday** in the week displayed, if it is not already selected. Click the **Start time arrow** for the time, and then click **10 AM**. Click the **End time arrow** for the time, and then click **1 PM**. Click the **Reminder arrow** and then click **None**. Laura will not be scheduled during her lunch hour starting at 1 PM.

d. Click **Save & Close**. Repeat the previous step to schedule Laura for her afternoon work hours from **2** to **7 PM**. Continue adding new appointments to create the following schedule with a break in the schedule times for the lunch hours indicated and no reminders.

Name of Associate	Work Days/Hours	Lunch
Laura Waden	Tuesday 3–7	None
	Wednesday 10–7	2–3
	Friday 10–7	1–2
Michelle Strom	Tuesday 10–3	None
	Thursday 10–7	1–2
	Saturday 10–7	2–3
Jay Groth	Monday 10–7	2–3
	Wednesday 10–7	1–2
	Friday 10–7	2–3
	Saturday 12–4	None
Sara Kline	Tuesday 10–7	1–2
	Thursday 10–7	2–3
	Saturday 10–7	1–2
Your name	Monday–Friday 12–4	None

e. Click the **File tab**, and then click **Print**. Print the calendar in **Calendar Details Style**, if directed by your instructor to submit the document. Click the **Home tab** if you did not print.

f. Click **Tasks** in the Navigation Pane, click **Tasks** under the To-Do List and then create a new folder called Treasures in the Tasks folder. Select the **Treasures folder** to add the closing tasks for the gift shop.

g. Click the **View tab**, and then click **View Settings**. Click **Columns**, and then click **All Task fields** in the Select available columns from box. Remove all but the Subject and Categories columns. Add the Notes column between the Subject and Category by clicking **Move Up** or **Move Down** as necessary. Click **OK**, and then click **OK** again to close the Advanced View Settings dialog box.

h. Click the **Home tab**, and then click **New Task**. Type Lock front door for the Subject. Type Do not lock door before 7 PM in the Notes area. Click **Categorize**, and then click **All Categories**. Create a new category called Showroom in the color **Red**. Create another category called Register in the color **Purple**. Click **Register** to deselect the Register category check box and to assign the **Lock front door** task to the **Showroom category** only. Click **OK**, and then click **Save & Close**. Continue creating the following tasks and categorizing them.

Subject	Notes	Category
Your name	Today's date	
Tidy display shelves		Showroom
Vacuum showroom	Empty dust container afterward	Showroom
Run register tapes	Keystrokes: CTRL+REG, Click today's date	Register
Count money	Note number of each bill denomination	Register
Lock change in register	$25 in ones, $50 in fives, $50 in tens, $60 in twenties	Register
Lock excess money in safe		Register
Arm the alarm	Code: SET+6485	Showroom
Lock back door	Outside code: 3847	Showroom

i. Click the **View tab**, click **Change View**, and then click **Simple List** to select it, if necessary. Drag the **lines** between the columns so the entries can be viewed completely. Click **Categories** in the Arrangement group to sort the tasks.

j. Click the **File tab**, and then click **Print**. Print the Tasks list in **Table Style** and **Portrait** orientation if requested by your instructor.

k. Click the **Notes icon**, click **New Note**, and then type Laura Waden. Press [Enter], and then type Avoid scheduling her from 3 to 7 on Tuesdays. Press [Enter], and then type College class. Click **Close**, click **New Note**, and then type Your name. Press [Enter], and then type Wants extra afternoon hours. Click **Close**.

l. Click the **Home tab**, and click **Notes List** in the Current View group. Click the **File tab**, and then click **Print**. Print the notes in **Table Style** in Portrait orientation if your instructor requests a copy. Click the **Folder tab**, and then click **New Folder**. Type Treasures for the Name of the folder, and then click **Notes** in the Select where to place the folder box. Drag both **notes** into the Treasures folder.

Problem Solve 1

Student data file needed:

None needed

You will send e-mail messages with the subject lines of:

Lastname_Firstname_o01_ps1_Specials
Lastname_Firstname_o01_ps1_Specials_G-Grocer

You will print these documents, at the direction of your instructor:

Lastname_Firstname_o01_ps1_Specials_G-Grocer
Specials Suppliers Contacts
Specials Calendar
Specials Tasks
Specials Notes

Planning the Weekly Specials for Indigo 5

Production & Operations

Robin Sanchez, the chef at Indigo 5, uses Outlook to communicate with local farmers and other suppliers. She maintains a Contact folder, called Suppliers, with information so she can contact them quickly. As she plans the weekly specials, she lists them on the Specials calendar. She also uses the Tasks component of Outlook to organize her activities for the week. The Notes component is used to collect her ideas for new recipes. She uses categories and folders to group together all of this information. You will take on the role of Chef Sanchez as you complete Problem Solve 1.

a. Open **Contacts**, create a new folder called Specials Suppliers, and then create the following **New Contacts**. Categorize the suppliers as shown.

Name	Company	E-mail	Business Phone Number	Category/Color
Your name	The Green Grocer	Use your e-mail address	505-555-8746	Vegetables/ Green
May Andrews	Organic First	Use your instructor's e-mail address	505-555-7483	Vegetables/ Green
Edward Mitchell	Meat Unlimited	ed@unlimited-meat.com	505-555-4857	Meat/Dark Orange
Katherine Hernandez	The Catfish Farmer	khernandez@ catfishfarmer. com	505-555-6857	Meat/Dark Orange
Holly Marks	Marks Restau- rant Supply	Use a classmate's e-mail address	505-555-7513	Staples/Yellow and Vegetables/ Green

b. Display the **Specials Suppliers** contacts in **List** view with the **Categories arrangement**. Using **View Settings** on the View tab, show only the **Categories**, **Full Name**, **Company**, **Business Phone**, and **E-mail** columns, in this order.

c. Create a **New Contact Group** that includes everyone in the Vegetables category. Name the group Vegetable Suppliers. Categorize this contact group as **Vegetables/Green**.

d. Print the **Suppliers Contacts** using the **Table Style**, **Landscape** orientation, if your instructor requests a copy of the list.

e. Open **Mail**, and then create a Suppliers folder. Create the following e-mail message, sending it to the **Vegetable Suppliers Contact Group**, with the Subject of Lastname_Firstname_o01_ps1_ Specials. Mark the message as **High Importance**.

Hello,

I am setting my menus for the weekly specials. I know that corn is coming on strong now. What are your prices by the gross? I would probably need four gross next week.

Do you have any squash yet? What variety?

Thanks,

Click **Signature**, and then click **Personal Class Signature**.

f. Send the message and wait briefly to receive it from the server. Reply to the message as follows, using the Subject RE: Lastname_Firstname_o01_ps1_Specials_G-Grocer.

Hi Chef Sanchez,

We can offer you four gross of corn on Monday of next week. Our price is $62 delivered. The only squash we are currently picking is zucchini. It runs $15 a bushel.

I would be happy to drop off corn and zucchini on Monday morning.

Thanks for your business,

Your name

g. Click the **Review tab**, and then click **Spelling & Grammar**. After checking spelling, carefully proofread the message. Send the message and wait briefly to receive it from the server. Mark the message for follow-up **Tomorrow**, and then add a reminder for **12 PM**. Categorize the message as **Vegetables/Green**. Place all e-mail messages generated by this project into the Suppliers folder.

h. Print the message **Lastname_Firstname_o01_ps1_Specials_G-Grocer** in the **Memo Style**, if your instructor requests a copy.

i. Open the **Calendar**, and then create a calendar called Specials in the Calendar folder. Advance in the Specials calendar to next week. On **Monday** set an all-day event with a Subject of Summer Risotto. Type Corn Zucchini in the Notes box. Complete the specials for the rest of the week as follows:

Day	Subject	Notes
Tuesday	Spicy Barbeque Pork Loin	Grilled Corn Salsa with Lime
Wednesday	Roasted Tomato Sauce on Linguine	Caesar Salad with House Dressing
Thursday	Tuna Steak Caesar Salad	Farmer's Bread
Friday	Indigo 5 Ribs and Spuds	Corn Fritters
Saturday	Cajun Catfish	Sweet and Sour Slaw
Sunday	Your name	

j. Print the **Specials** calendar in **Calendar Details Style**, if your instructor requests a copy of the document.

k. Open **Tasks**, and then create a Specials folder. Create the following tasks in the folder:

Task	Due date	Category	Reminder
Your name			
Marinate Pork Loin	Next Monday	Meat	Monday, 4 PM
Roast 30 lbs. tomatoes	Next Tuesday	Vegetables	None
Order Catfish	Next Friday	Meat	Friday, 8 AM
Prepare Slaw	Next Friday	Vegetables	Thursday, 3 PM

l. Select the **Order Catfish** task, and then mark it as complete. You spoke with Katherine Hernandez earlier than you expected, so this task is finished.

m. Print the **Tasks** in the Specials folder in **Table Style**, **Portrait** orientation, if your instructor requests a copy of the document.

n. Open **Notes**, and then create a Specials folder. Store the notes generated in this project in this folder. Add the following notes:

Tuna Steak Caesar Salad
Marinate tuna for at least 30 minutes in lime juice, garlic, and soy sauce
Grill for 5 to 6 minutes per side, chill 2 hours
Grilled Corn Salsa
Grill the corn the night before, using garlic butter
Red onion, cilantro, salt, pepper, lime juice
Serve with lime slices
Your name
Today's date
Your course information

o. Change the Notes view to **Notes List**. Print the **Notes List** in **Table Style** if your instructor requests a copy of the document.

Student data file needed:

o01_pf1_Career_Resume

You will save your file as:

Lastname_Firstname_o01_pf1_Career_Resume

You will send e-mail messages with the subject lines of:

Lastname_Firstname_o01_pf1_Career

Lastname_Firstname_o01_pf1_Career_Response

Lastname_Firstname_o01_pf1_Career_Thanks

You will print these documents, at the direction of your instructor:

Career Calendar

Career Contacts

Career Tasks

Career Notes

Managing a Job Search with Outlook

General Business

Congratulations! You have completed your studies and are entering the job market. You have learned that the Painted Paradise Golf Resort and Spa has some openings, and you are applying for a job. Patti Rochelle has an opening for an event liaison. As people book conferences at the resort, they are assigned an event liaison, who is responsible for communication with the client and problem solving. This position requires some creative thinking and good skills in dealing with people. A successful candidate will have experience with Outlook and be able to efficiently use e-mail, calendars, and task lists to organize work. You will send an e-mail cover letter with your résumé to Patti. You will plan for a number of interviews required by the resort using the Calendar. You will create contacts for the people you will meet. You have many things to plan for and accomplish prior to the interviews, including buying clothes, getting more copies of your résumé, and sending paperwork related to the interviews such as applications, reference lists, cover letters, and thank-you notes.

a. Open the Word document **o01_pf1_Career_Resume**. Replace the words **Student Name** with your name, and **Student E-mail Address** with your e-mail address. Save the document as Lastname_Firstname_o01_pf1_Career_Resume. Start **Outlook**, and write an e-mail message that serves as a cover letter to the résumé. Create a professional signature that includes contact information. Attach the résumé file **Lastname_Firstname_ o01_pf1_Career_Resume** to the message. The Subject of the message is Lastname_ Firstname_o01_pf1_Career. Send the message to your instructor and to Patti Rochelle at prochelle@paintedparadiseresort.com. An automated reply will be returned to you from Patti's account. Mark the reply for follow-up. Forward the reply to your instructor with the Subject of Lastname_Firstname_o01_pf1_Career_Response with a **Delivery Receipt**. Include a message in the forwarded message indicating that you are sending this as confirmation of a job application. Be sure to sign your message with your full name and include your contact information signature.

b. Create a Painted Paradise category and assign the color of your choice. Create an e-mail folder called Job Search. Create a **Quick Step** that categorizes and moves e-mail into the correct folder. Apply the Quick Step to all of the e-mail generated in this exercise.

c. Create a new **Calendar** for the job search. Schedule three separate interviews on the calendar in the next month with **Patti Rochelle**, **Anthony Oskins** (Hotel Manager), and Chef **Robin Sanchez**. Set reminders for the appointments so you have some advanced notice of the appointments. Categorize the calendar entries as the **Painted Paradise category**. Print the calendar that lists each of the interviews, if your instructor requests a copy.

d. Create a **Contacts** folder named Painted Paradise for the people you will meet so you can follow up with them after the interviews, as follows:

- Use your instructor's e-mail address for Chef Robin Sanchez.
- Use your e-mail address for Anthony Oskins.
- Use Patti Rochelle's e-mail address for her contact— prochelle@paintedparadiseresort.com.

Apply the **Painted Paradise category** to the contacts. Print a copy of the **Contacts** list, showing only the columns that contain information, if your instructor requests a copy.

e. Create a **contact group** that includes Chef Sanchez, Patti Rochelle, and Anthony Oskins. Use the contact group to send a thank-you e-mail message as a follow-up to the interviews you attended. Use Lastname_Firstname_o01_pf1_Career_Thanks as the Subject. Use your **Personal Class Signature** in the e-mail.

f. Create a Career folder in **Tasks**, and add at least eight tasks that you would complete prior to the appointments that you have scheduled. Prioritize the tasks, indicate their status, set up reminders, and indicate some of the tasks with the percentage complete or as complete. Alter the columns so the information you set up for the tasks shows. Print the **Tasks list**, if your instructor requests a copy.

g. Create a Notes folder named Career. Write a series of notes, placing them in the folder for each of the people you will interview with, listing questions that you will ask them. If requested by your instructor, print your notes on individual pages so you can focus on just the questions for the person who is currently interviewing you.

h. Make sure all of the items generated by this project are stored in the Career folders.

Perform 2: How Others Perform

Student data file needed:	You will send an e-mail with the subject line of:
None needed	Lastname_Firstname_o01_pf2_Gallery_Critique

Managing an Art Gallery with Outlook

General Business

Emmy Nast, the manager of the Edwards Art Gallery has been using Outlook to schedule, plan, and communicate with artists. She has hired you to assist her in the office and has made her view of Outlook available to you. Your goal is to improve her communications and organization as you review her Outlook views.

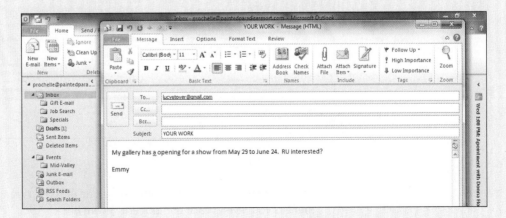

Figure 1 Art gallery e-mail

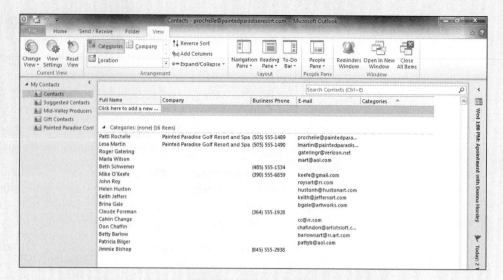

Figure 2 Art gallery contacts

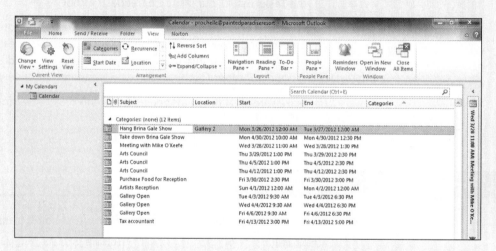

Figure 3 Art gallery calendar

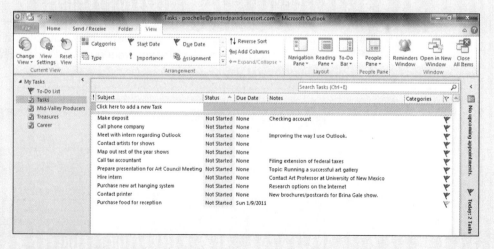

Figure 4 Art gallery tasks

a. Create a folder in the Notes component called **Art Gallery**, and compile notes for improvement as you review each component shown here.

b. Look at the e-mail message in Figure 1. What could be done to improve the content of the message? What advice would you give Emmy to improve the professional appearance of the message?

c. After reviewing the contacts, as shown in Figure 2, what recommendations would you make?

d. Review the calendar shown in Figure 3. How could you organize the calendar?

e. As you look at the tasks in Figure 4, you notice that there is a task and a calendar item (in Figure 3) that are the same. Why would this be a good or bad practice?

f. Create a new e-mail message to your instructor, summarizing how you would improve the use of each of the components based on the questions asked in Steps b through e and the notes you made. Carefully proofread the message. Add your **Personal Class Signature** to the message. Apply an appropriate **theme** or **stationery** to the message. Add your e-mail address to the Cc box. Mark the message as **High Importance**. Request a **Delivery Receipt**. Use the Subject of Lastname_Firstname_o01_pf2_Gallery_Critique. Send the message.

Objectives

1. Link an object   p. 946
2. Update a linked object   p. 950
3. Embed an object p. 954
4. Modify an embedded object   p. 955

Integrating Word and Excel

PREPARE CASE
Updated Menu

General Business

Indigo 5 is an upscale restaurant always striving to stay one step ahead of their clientele. Based on marketing and customer analysis over the past year, Alberto Dimas, the restaurant manager, has decided to add new selections to the menu. He is writing a memo in Word to his staff, and he would like to include the charts he created in Excel. Your assignment is to either link or embed the charts from Excel into the Word document.

Blend Images / Shutterstock.com

Student data files needed for this workshop:

 i01_ws01_Restaurant_Menu

 i01_ws01_Restaurant_Analysis

 i01_ws01_Restaurant_Customers

You will save your files as:

 Lastname_Firstname_i01_ws01_Restaurant_Menu

 Lastname_Firstname_i01_ws01_Restaurant_Analysis

 Lastname_Firstname_i01_ws01_Restaurant_Customers

Object Linking and Embedding

An **object** is any item that can be selected and manipulated independently of surrounding text. Examples include pictures, shapes, charts, tables, sound clips, and video. Using **OLE** (Object Linking and Embedding), a feature in Microsoft Office, an object can be inserted into a file either as a **linked object** or an **embedded object**. A linked object is an object that is inserted into a document but is still connected to the file it was created in, allowing it to be updated in both places at the same time. An embedded object is an object that is inserted into a document but is not connected to the file it was created in.

The program that creates the object is called the **source program**, and the file where the object is created is called the **source file**. The program that you insert the object into is called the **destination program**, and the file you insert the object into is called the **destination file**.

Real World Advice   To Link or Embed?

Sometimes it is easier to copy and paste an object, but when you do, you lose the advantages that come with linking and embedding objects. The choice to link or embed is determined primarily by how you want to update your object. If you want to update the object in its original source program, then you would choose to link the object to the destination file. For example, you create a chart in Excel that has data that will be changed frequently. When you link the chart to a Word document, any changes you make to the chart in Excel will be reflected in Word. On the other hand, if you want the ability to update the chart in the destination file, you would choose to embed the chart. The advantages and disadvantages are shown below in Figure 1.

	Copy & Paste	Linking	Embedding
Where copied object is located	Destination file where it is pasted	Source file where it is created	Destination file where it is inserted
How copied object is updated	In the destination file with limited options	In the source file	In the destination file
Advantages	A simple way to create a copy of an object and paste it in another location	A single chart can be displayed in multiple files and only kept up to date in the source file. Destination file size is reduced.	The destination file is a self-contained file not dependent on a source file.
Disadvantages	Objects have to be updated in both the source and destination files.	Must have access to source file to make changes	Objects have to be updated in both the source and destination files.

Figure 1   Comparing different methods of copying objects

Link an Object

Linking an object is advantageous because the data can be updated in the source file and the changes are reflected in the destination file. The data can be any object, including a chart, table, range of cells, or SmartArt.

Linking an Excel Chart to a Word Document

When you link an Excel chart to a Word document, any changes you make to the Excel data will update the chart not only in Excel, but also in the linked Word document. The chart is still part of the source document, which is the Excel file, while the Word document is the destination file that is automatically updated. For this exercise, you will link an Excel chart to an existing Word document.

To Link an Excel Chart to a Word Document

a. Start **Word**. Click the **File tab**, click **Open**, and then locate your student folder. Select **i01_ws01_Restaurant_Menu**, and then click **Open**.

b. Click the **File tab**, click **Save As**. Navigate to the disk drive and folder where you will store your project files, type Lastname_Firstname_i01_ws01_Restaurant_Menu as the file name, replacing Lastname_Firstname with your own name. Click **Save**.

c. Click the **Insert tab**, and then click **Footer** in the Header & Footer group. Select **Edit Footer** below the footer gallery. Click the **Header & Footer Tools Design tab**, click **Quick Parts** in the Insert group, select **Field**, scroll through the list of Field names, choose **FileName**, and then click **OK**.

Figure 2 Word footer

d. Click the **Header & Footer Tools Design tab**, and then click **Close Header and Footer** in the Close group.

e. Click **Save** on the Quick Access Toolbar.

f. Click **Minimize** to minimize the Word window.

g. Start **Excel**. Click the **File tab**, click **Open**, and then navigate to your student files. Select **i01_ws01_Restaurant_Analysis**, and then click **Open**.

h. Click the **File tab**, click **Save As**, and then save the workbook as Lastname_Firstname_i01_ws01_Restaurant_Analysis, replacing Lastname_Firstname with your own name. Click **Save**.

i. If necessary, click **Maximize** to maximize the Excel window. Click the **Insert tab**, and then click **Header & Footer** in the Text group. Click the **Header & Footer Tools Design tab**, click **Go to Footer** in the Navigation group, and then click in the left footer section. Click the **Header & Footer Tools Design tab**, and then click **File Name** in the Header & Footer Elements group.

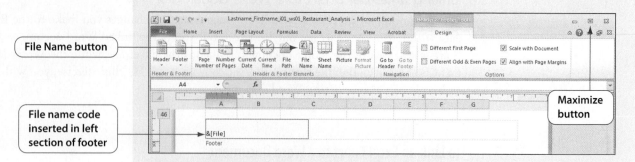

File Name button

File name code inserted in left section of footer

Maximize button

Figure 3 Excel footer

j. Click outside of the footer area, and then click **Normal** ⊞ in the bottom-right corner of the window, on the status bar, to return to the Normal view. Press Ctrl + Home to return to cell A1.

k. Select the pie chart by clicking on the **chart border** once. A grey border will appear around the edge of the object.

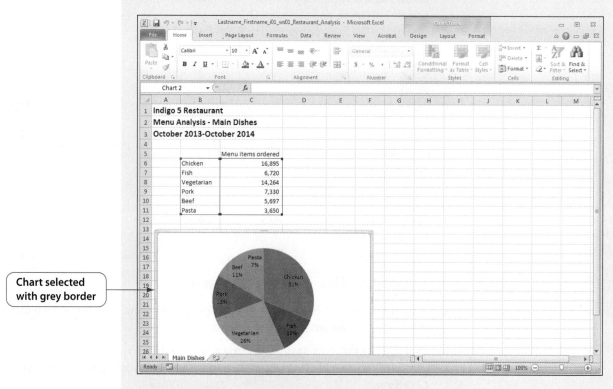

Chart selected with grey border

Figure 4 Border around selected chart

l. Click the **Home tab**, and then click **Copy** in the Clipboard group to copy the chart to the Clipboard.

m. Click **Word** W on the taskbar to display your Word document.

n. If necessary, click **Maximize** 🗖 to maximize the Word window. Click at the end of the second body paragraph. Press Enter twice to skip a line and start a new one.

SIDE NOTE
Clipboard
Once on the Clipboard, an object can be pasted into any Office program.

Troubleshooting

SIDE NOTE

The Taskbar

The buttons on a taskbar may vary from computer to computer. Any open programs will appear on your taskbar as well as any programs you have pinned there for quick access.

SIDE NOTE

Paste Button

The choices you see on the Paste button menu change depending on the object you have selected to paste.

Nonprinting Characters

To see things like spaces, paragraph marks, and other nonprinting characters, on the Home tab, click Show/Hide ¶ in the Paragraph group. With this option turned on, you will see the paragraph marks and other hidden formatting symbols. It may be easier to see the end of a paragraph with this option turned on. To hide the marks and symbols, click Show/Hide again.

o. Click the **Home tab**, click the **Paste arrow** in the Clipboard group, and then select **Paste Special**.

p. In the Paste Special dialog box, click **Paste link**, and then in the **As** box, select **Microsoft Excel Chart Object**. Click **OK**.

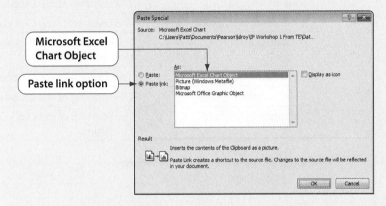

Figure 5   Paste Special dialog box

q. Click **Save** 🖫 on the Quick Access Toolbar, and then **Minimize** 🗕 Word.

Real World Advice · What Else Can Be Linked?

Any time you want to maintain continuity between data in two programs like Excel and Word, consider linking the data so when the data is updated, it is updated in two places at the same time. You can link anything between Excel and Word—objects, text, charts, or tables. You can also link from Excel to Word or from Word to Excel using the Paste link option in the Paste Special dialog box. See Figure 6 for the different Paste link options.

Continued

Continued

If the source file is in Word and you choose to Paste link As:	Depending on what has been copied, this will be pasted:
Microsoft Word Document Object	The contents of the Clipboard
Picture (Enhanced Metafile)	The contents of the Clipboard as a picture
HTML	The contents of the Clipboard as HTML format
Unicode Text	The contents of the Clipboard as Unicode Text format
Text	The contents of the Clipboard as text without any formatting
Hyperlink	The contents of the Clipboard as a Hyperlink format
Microsoft Excel Chart Object	The contents of the Clipboard as a picture so it can be edited using Microsoft Excel
Picture (Windows Metafile)	The contents of the Clipboard as an enhanced metafile
Bitmap	The contents of the Clipboard as a bitmap picture
Microsoft Office Graphic Object	The contents of the Clipboard as shapes
Formatted Text (RTF)	The contents of the Clipboard as text with font and table formatting
Unformatted Text	The contents of the Clipboard without any formatting
HTML Format	The contents of the Clipboard as HTML format
Unformatted Unicode Text	The contents of the Clipboard as text without any formatting

Figure 6 Comparing Paste link options

SIDE NOTE
A Link Is Not the Same as a Hyperlink
A link between a source and destination file is different than a hyperlink. When you click on a hyperlink, you are brought to a new location such as a website. A hyperlink is a navigation tool, a link is not.

Update a Linked Object

When both the destination file and source file are open and data is changed in the source file for a linked object, the data will be updated in the destination file only if you manually update the link for the object. This gives you control over when and how to update a link in the destination file.

When the destination file is closed and then opened, the linked object is automatically updated unless you turn off automatic updates in the Links options.

Updating a Linked Excel Chart

When data related to a chart is changed in Excel, the chart in Excel is automatically updated. However, the chart may or may not be automatically updated in the destination file depending on whether the destination file is opened or closed. For this exercise, you will make changes to a chart in Excel, and then manually update the chart in the Word document, which is open.

To Update an Excel Chart

a. Click **Excel** [icon] on the taskbar to display your Excel workbook, if necessary.

b. Click the **chart** to select it, click the **Chart Tools Design tab**, and then click **Change Chart Type** in the Type group. Select **Pie in 3-D**, and then click **OK**.

c. Click the **Chart Tools Layout tab**, click **Chart Title** in the Labels group, and then select **Above Chart**. Type Main Dishes Ordered by Type in the formula bar. Press Enter.

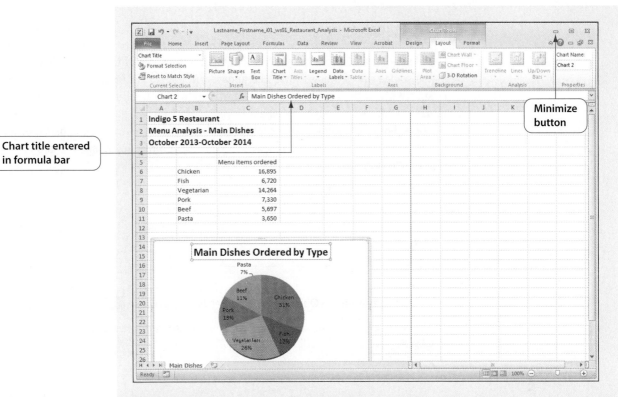

Chart title entered in formula bar

Minimize button

Figure 7 Chart Title added to Pie in 3-D chart

d. Click **Save** 🔲 on the Quick Access Toolbar, and then **Minimize** 🔲 the Excel window.

e. Click **Word** 🔲 on the taskbar to display the Word document.

f. Click the **chart** to select it, and then right-click. To update the link, select **Update Link**, and the chart is updated with the changes you made in Excel.

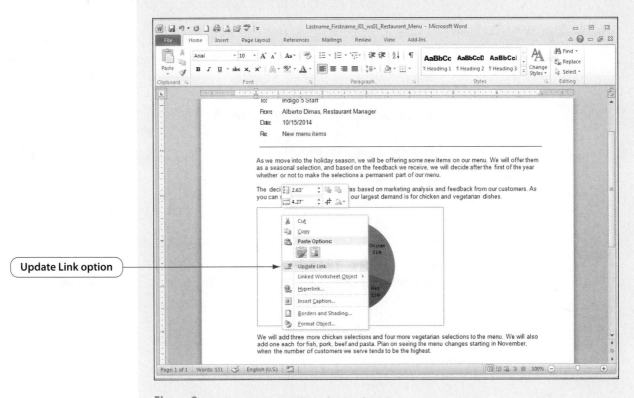

Update Link option

Figure 8 Shortcut menu with Update Link option

Troubleshooting

Did you get an error message? If you changed the name of the source file or moved the source file to a new folder, the update will not work. If Excel cannot find the source file in the same folder as the destination file, it will break the link with the destination file. To have the object linked again, you will have to open the Links dialog box and change the source file to the new location or new file name, or move the source file to the same folder as the destination file. To change the source file do the following:

1. Right-click the object in the destination file.
2. Point to Linked Worksheet Object and then click Links.
3. Click Change Source, select the new location or name of the source file, and click Open. Click OK.

g. Click **Save** 🔲 on the Quick Access Toolbar, and then **Close** ☒ Word.

h. Click **Excel** 🔣 on the taskbar, if necessary, to display your Excel workbook. **Close** ☒ Excel.

Real World Advice   Change Automatic Link Updates

There may be times when you do not want the link to be automatically updated when the destination file is opened. If you are sharing a file with people who are unfamiliar with Word, it might confuse them or frustrate them if they do not know what to do when they get the dialog box asking to update the link. Instead, you can turn off the option to update links automatically and require a manual update of the link. This option can be set for a specific object or for all objects in Word.

- To turn off the automatic update option for all linked objects in Word, on the File tab, click Options, and select Advanced. Under General (scroll down if necessary), click Update automatic links at open to clear the check box.

- To turn off the automatic update option for a specific object, right-click the object and point to Linked Worksheet Object. Click Links, and in the Links dialog box click Manual Update. Click OK.

CONSIDER THIS | To Link or Not to Link?

Teamwork is an important part of business. When sending files between team members, linking can easily cause errors because of the source file. Do you think when working in a team you should not use links? Why or why not?

Real World Advice — Teamwork and Linking Files

There are a number of options you can choose when setting up links to help preserve those links, especially when files are being shared by several people. Right-click on a linked object, point to Linked Worksheet Object (or whichever type of object is being linked), and then select Links to open the Links dialog box, where you will find the options listed in Figure 9.

Action	Effect	Advantages	Disadvantages
Convert (on shortcut menu)	The object will be changed to a non-linking object.	Another user will not have to worry about updating a link.	The destination file object will not be automatically updated to reflect changes made in the source file.
Break Link	The destination file and source file will no longer be linked by the object.	No need to worry about moving a source file or changing its name.	Changes made in the source file will no longer be reflected in the destination file.
Manual Update	When the destination file opens, the user will not get a message about there being a linked object.	If the user of the destination file is unfamiliar with Word, the manual update will not cause any confusion over what to do.	The destination file object will not be automatically updated to reflect changes made in the source file.
Locked	The object will not be updated.	When someone else is given a file you may want to have control over what data they see, so having an object that can be updated may not be beneficial.	The link will not be updated even though it has not been broken.
Change Source	Changes the source file where the object is found.	If a source file has been renamed or moved, the source file for the object can be changed to the new name or location.	If the source file has been renamed or moved but you do not know the new name or where it has been moved, then this option will not help.

Figure 9 Links options

CONSIDER THIS | Would a Hyperlink Work?

If clicking on a hyperlink can bring you to another file, do you think a hyperlink could be used more effectively than a linked object? Would using a hyperlink prevent the problem of changes to a source file name or location?

Embed an Object

When you embed an object, the object becomes a self-contained object in the destination file and can be updated independently from the object in the source file. Any changes to the object made in the source file will not be reflected in the destination file, but changes can still be made in the destination file. The difference between embedding an object and using a copy and paste command is that as an embedded object changes can still be made.

Embedding an Excel Chart in a Word Document

An Excel chart embedded in a Word document becomes part of the document and any changes made to the chart will remain in the document. Changes made to the chart in the Excel worksheet will not be reflected in the Word document. For this exercise, you will embed an Excel chart in a Word document.

To Embed an Excel Chart

a. Start **Excel**, navigate to your student files and open **i01_ws01_Restaurant_Customers**. Click the **File tab**, click **Save As**, and then save it as Lastname_Firstname_i01_ws01_ Restaurant_Customers, replacing Lastname_Firstname with your own name. **Maximize** the Excel window, if necessary.

b. Click the **Insert tab**, and then click **Header & Footer** in the Text group. Click the **Header & Footer Tools Design tab**, and then click **Go to Footer** in the Navigation group. Click in the left footer section, and then on the **Header & Footer Tools Design tab**, click **File Name** in the Header & Footer Elements group.

c. Click outside the footer area, and then click **Normal** ▦ on the status bar to return to the Normal view. Press Ctrl + Home to return to cell A1.

d. Select the line chart by clicking the **chart border** once. A grey border appears around the edge of the object.

e. Click the **Home tab**, and then click **Copy** 📋 in the Clipboard group to copy the chart to the Clipboard.

f. Click **Minimize** ⊟ to minimize the Excel window.

g. Start **Word** and open the file **Lastname_Firstname_i01_ws01_Restaurant_Menu**. Click **Yes** to the warning about updating links. Click once at the end of the last sentence of the last paragraph. Press Enter twice to skip a line and start a new one.

h. Click the **Home tab**, click the **Paste arrow** in the Clipboard group, and then select **Paste Special**.

i. In the Paste Special dialog box, click the **Paste** option, and then in the As box, select **Microsoft Excel Chart Object**. Click **OK**.

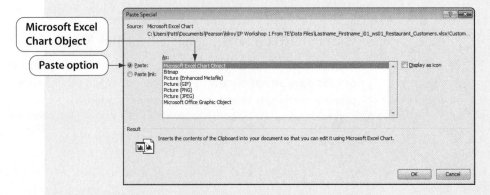

Figure 10 Paste Special dialog box

j. Click and drag the lower-right corner of each chart inward to reduce the size so they are approximately the same size and the memo fits on one page. Delete any blank pages at the end of the document.

k. Click **Save** 🖫 on the Quick Access Toolbar, and then **Minimize** 🗕 the Word window.

l. Click **Excel** 🖾 on the taskbar to display the workbook. Click **Save** 🖫 on the Quick Access Toolbar, and then **Close** ⨯ Excel.

Modify an Embedded Object

When you edit an embedded object in the destination file, the changes affect only the object in the destination file. This is what makes it different from linking or using a copy and paste command.

Modifying an Embedded Chart in a Word Document

Modifying an embedded chart in a Word document will change the chart in the document, but the chart in the Excel workbook will remain unchanged. Alternately, changing the chart in Excel will not change the chart in the Word document. However, the embedded chart can be edited using Excel tools in the Word document because it was embedded as a Microsoft Excel Chart Object. You can edit not only the chart options but also the Excel data that was used to create the chart. For this exercise, you will modify an embedded Excel chart in your Word document.

To Modify an Embedded Chart in a Word Document

a. Click **Word** 🗏 on the taskbar to display your Word document. If necessary, click **Maximize** 🗖 to maximize the Word window, and then double-click the embedded line chart. The Chart Tools tabs appear, making the various chart editing options available. The sheet tabs in the original worksheet will also be visible at the bottom of the object.

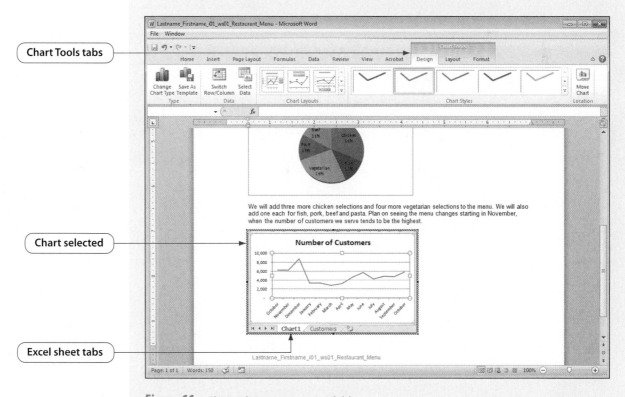

Figure 11 Chart editing options available

b. Click the **Chart Tools Design tab**, click **Change Chart Type** in the Type group, select **Line with Markers**, and then click **OK**.

c. Click the **Customers worksheet tab** in the chart window. Change October Customers in cell B6 to 8000. Click the **Chart1 worksheet tab** to see the change reflected in the chart.

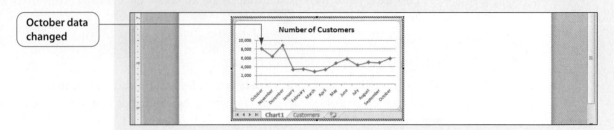

Figure 12   October data point changed

d. Click outside of the chart to deselect it.

e. Click **Save** 🖫 on the Quick Access Toolbar, and then **Close** ⊠ Word.

Concept Check

1. What is the difference between linking and embedding an object? How are these two methods different from simply copying and pasting an object?

2. Give one advantage and one disadvantage to both linking and embedding an object.

3. Why is it so important to keep source files named the same and in the same location?

4. Give two real-world examples where you might want to link data.

5. Is there any time a simple copy-and-paste operation would be sufficient instead of using Paste Special?

Key Terms

Destination file 946
Destination program 946
Embedded object 946

Linked object 946
Object 946
OLE 946

Source file 946
Source program 946

Visual Summary

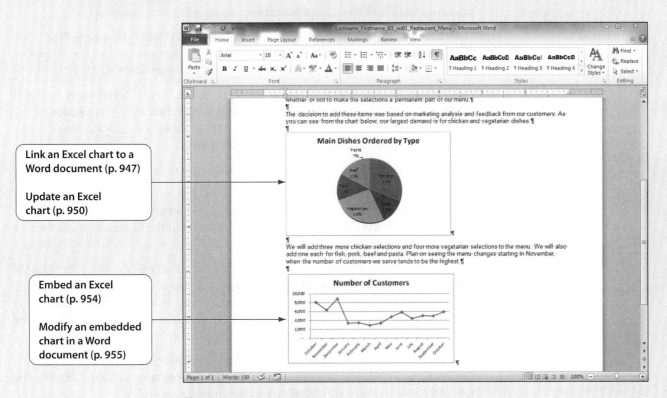

Link an Excel chart to a Word document (p. 947)

Update an Excel chart (p. 950)

Embed an Excel chart (p. 954)

Modify an embedded chart in a Word document (p. 955)

Figure 13 Updated Menu Final

Sales &
Marketing

Student data files needed:

i01_ws01_Wedding

i01_ws01_Wedding_Plan

You will save your files as:

Lastname_Firstname_i01_ws01_Wedding

Lastname_Firstname_i01_ws01_Wedding_Plan

Wedding Planning

The staff in the Event Planning department would like to promote full-service weddings at the Painted Paradise Golf Resort and Spa. A full-service wedding includes all aspects of the planning and execution of the event. One staff member wrote a short description in Word promoting the service, and another staff member put together a sample budget and time line in Excel. Your job is to link the budget and embed the time line.

a. Start **Word**. Click the **File tab**, click **Open**, and then locate your student folder. Select **i01_ws01_Wedding**, and then click **Open**.

b. Click the **File tab**, click **Save As**, and then save the document as Lastname_Firstname_ i01_ws01_Wedding, replacing Lastname_Firstname with your own name.

c. Click the **Insert tab**, click **Footer** in the Header & Footer group, and then select **Edit Footer**. Click the **Header & Footer Tools Design tab**, click **Quick Parts** in the Insert group, select **Field**, scroll through the list of field names and select **FileName**, and then click **OK**. Click the Header & Footer Tools Design tab, click **Close Header and Footer** in the Close group, and then click **Minimize** to minimize the Word window.

d. Start **Excel**, and then open the student file called **i01_ws01_Wedding_Plan**. Click the **File tab**, click **Save As**, and then save the file as Lastname_Firstname_i01_ws01_ Wedding_Plan, replacing Lastname_Firstname with your own name.

e. On the **Budget worksheet tab**, click the **Insert tab**, and then click **Header & Footer** in the Text group. Click the **Header & Footer Tools Design tab**, click **Go to Footer** in the Navigation group, and then click in the left section of the footer. Click **File Name** in the Header & Footer Elements group to enter the file name.

f. Click outside the footer area, and then click **Normal** ⊞ on the status bar to return to the Normal view. Press [Ctrl] + [Home] to return to cell A1.

g. On the **Budget worksheet tab**, select the range of cells **A4** through **C17**. Click the **Home tab**, click **Copy** in the Clipboard group to copy the data to the Clipboard, and then click **Minimize** ⊟ to minimize the Excel window.

h. Click **Word** on the taskbar to display your document. Click on the blank line after **Budget Worksheet**. Click the **Home tab**, click the **Paste arrow** in the Clipboard group, and then select **Paste Special**. Select the **Paste link** option, and then in the As box, select **Microsoft Excel Worksheet Object**. Click **OK**. Resize the object as needed so it fits on the first page. Click **Save** on the Quick Access Toolbar, and then close Word.

i. Click **Excel** on the taskbar to display your workbook. Change the **Average Cost** of the **Ceremony** to $1050, and the **Average Cost** of the **Coordinator** to $700. Click the **File tab**, click **Save**, and then click **Minimize** to minimize the Excel window.

j. Start **Word**, and then open **Lastname_Firstname_i01_ws01_Wedding**. Click **Yes** in the dialog box to accept automatic updates to the link. Because Word was closed when the changes to the table were made in Excel, when Word is reopened and you accept automatic updates, the table in Word should be updated. Click **Save** on the Quick Access Toolbar, and then click **Minimize** to minimize the Word window.

k. Click **Excel** on the taskbar to display your workbook. Click the **Timeline worksheet tab**, click the **SmartArt** to select it, and then click on the top border to ensure the whole SmartArt object is selected. A grey border appears around the edge of the object.

Click the **Home tab**, and then click **Copy** in the Clipboard group to copy the SmartArt to the Clipboard. Click **Minimize** to minimize the Excel window.

l. Click **Word** on the taskbar to display your document. Click after **Wedding Timeline**, and then press Enter to go to a new line. Click the **Home tab**, click the **Paste arrow** in the Clipboard group, and then select **Paste Special**. Make sure the **Paste option** and **Microsoft Office Graphic Object** are selected, and then click **OK**.

m. Click the embedded **SmartArt** graphic. Click the **SmartArt Tools Design tab**, select **Change Colors**, and then change the color to **Colorful - Accent Colors**. Change the heading that says **1 Month** to say 1–2 Months. Click outside of the SmartArt to deselect it. Click **Save** on the Quick Access Toolbar, and then close Word.

n. Click the **Excel** button on the taskbar to display the workbook, and then close Excel.

Practice 2

Student data files needed:

i01_ws01_Race_Flyer
i01_ws01_Race_Budget

You will save your files as:

Lastname_Firstname_i01_ws01_Race_Flyer
Lastname_Firstname_i01_ws01_Race_Budget

Running Event

Sales & Marketing

The Event Planning department is excited to organize a new competitive 5k and 10k run/walk at the resort. The event is designed to bring families to the resort for the weekend and will include a cookout, prizes, and opportunities to tour the resort. The flyer for the event was created in Word and has some charts that would be nice to include in the financial report that was created in Excel. Your assignment is to link and embed the data from Word into Excel.

a. Start **Word**. Click the **File tab**, click **Open**, locate your student folder, select **i01_ws01_Race_Flyer**, and then click **Open**.

b. Click the **File tab**, click **Save As**, and then save the document as Lastname_Firstname_i01_ws01_Race_Flyer, replacing Lastname_Firstname with your own name.

c. Click the **Insert tab**, click **Footer** in the Header & Footer group, and then select **Edit Footer**. Click the **Header & Footer Tools Design tab**, click **Quick Parts** in the Insert group, select **Field**, scroll through the list of field names, and then choose **FileName**. Click **OK**. Click the **Header & Footer Tools Design tab**, click **Close Header and Footer** in the Close group, and then click **Minimize** to minimize the Word window.

d. Start **Excel**, and then open the student file called **i01_ws01_Race_Budget**. Click the **File tab**, click **Save As**, and then save the file as Lastname_Firstname_i01_ws01_Race_Budget, replacing Lastname_Firstname with your own name.

e. Click the **Insert tab**, and then click **Header & Footer** in the Text group. Click the **Header & Footer Tools Design tab**, click **Go to Footer** in the Navigation group, and click in the left section of the footer. Click **File Name** in the Header & Footer Elements group to enter the file name.

f. Click outside the footer area, and then click **Normal** ▦ on the status bar to return to the Normal view. Press Ctrl + Home to return to cell A1. Click **Minimize** to minimize the Excel window.

g. Click **Word** on the taskbar to display your document. Select the **table** with the entry fees. Click the **Home tab**, click **Copy** in the Clipboard group to copy the table to the Clipboard, and then click **Minimize** to minimize the Word window.

h. Click **Excel** on the taskbar to display your workbook. Click in cell **E4**. Click the **Home tab**, click the **Paste arrow** in the Clipboard group, and then select **Paste Special**. Select the **Paste link** option, and then in the As box, select **Microsoft Word Document Object**. Click **OK**.

i. Click **Save** on the Quick Access Toolbar, and then close Excel.

j. Click **Word** on the taskbar to display your document. Change the **Pre-register** amount for the **10k** to $35 and the **Day of race** amount for the **10k** to $40. Click **Save** on the Quick Access Toolbar, and then click **Minimize** to minimize the Word window.

k. Start **Excel**, and then open **Lastname_Firstname_i01_ws01_Race_Budget**. Click **Enable Content** on the Security Warning bar. Update cell C4 in the workbook to 35. Click the **File tab**, click **Save**, and then click **Minimize** to minimize the Excel window.

l. Click **Word** on the taskbar to display your document. Click the **SmartArt** once to select it, and then click on the top border to ensure the whole SmartArt is selected. A grey border will appear around the edge of the object. Click the **Home tab**, and then click **Copy** in the Clipboard group to copy the SmartArt to the Clipboard. Click **Minimize** to minimize the Word window.

m. Click **Excel** on the taskbar to display your workbook. Select cell **E12**. Click the **Home tab**, click the **Paste arrow** in the Clipboard group, and then select **Paste Special**. Select the **Paste** option, in the As box select **Microsoft Office Drawing Object**, and then click **OK**.

n. Click the embedded **SmartArt** graphic. Change the order of the text to say Race Run Walk. Click off of the SmartArt to deselect it.

o. Click the **Page Layout tab**, click **Orientation** in the Page Setup group, and then select **Landscape**. In the Scale to Fit group, click the **Width arrow**, and then select **1 page** so the table and SmartArt will print on the same page as the budget. Click the **File tab**, click **Save**, and then close Excel.

p. Click **Word** on the taskbar to display your document. Click **Save** on the Quick Access Toolbar, and then close Word.

Problem Solve 1

Student data files needed:	You will save your files as:
i01_ps1_Shop_Summary	Lastname_Firstname_i01_ps1_Shop_Summary
i01_ps1_Shop_Analysis	Lastname_Firstname_i01_ps1_Shop_Analysis

First Quarter Gift Shop Update

Finance & Accounting

The gift shop, Painted Treasures, is reporting its revenue and staffing for the first quarter of the year. A short document has been created with a description of the analysis in Word, but the numbers, charts, and graphics are all in Excel. Your assignment is to link the chart created in Excel to the Word document, and embed the organization chart created in Excel in the Word document.

a. Open **i01_ps1_Shop_Summary**, and then save it as Lastname_Firstname_i01_ps1_Shop_Summary, replacing Lastname_Firstname with your own name.

b. Open **i01_ps1_Shop_Analysis**, and then save it as Lastname_Firstname_i01_ps1_Shop_Analysis, replacing Lastname_Firstname with your own name.

c. Copy the **pie chart**, and then paste it in the blank paragraph after the first body paragraph of the Word document as a linked Microsoft Excel Chart Object.

d. In the Excel source file, add a **Chart Title** above the pie chart that says Gift Shop Sales by Segment. Update the link, if necessary, in the Word document to reflect this change.

e. In the Excel source file, on the Staffing sheet, copy the **organization chart**, and then paste it in a new paragraph after the second body paragraph of the Word document as an embedded object.

f. In the Word destination file, change the SmartArt style to **3-D Polished**.

g. Resize the pie chart and the SmartArt so everything fits on one page. Delete any blank pages if necessary.

h. Insert a left-aligned footer in the Word document. Add the file name. Insert the file name footer in the left section of the workbook on the Revenue sheet. Save and close both the Excel and Word documents.

Perform 1: Perform in Your Career

Student data file needed:

None

You will save your files as:

Lastname_Firstname_i01_pf1_Photography_Letter

Lastname_Firstname_i01_pf1_Photography_Quote

Photography Quotes for Potential Customers

Sales & Marketing

You are an independent photographer who specializes in small events and small groups, including families. You are constantly sending out quotes to potential clients, and your quote form is kept in Excel, but the letters you send out are in Word. You therefore need to link your workbook data with the letter you send to potential clients. Your quote must include the date of the event, name of customer, a description of the job and its location, the approximate number of hours the job will take, any special requests, and any extra travel time required. You need the flexibility to change the data in Excel and have it change in Word at the same time.

a. Start **Word**, and then create a letter to potential clients. Include a return address, a greeting, and the date. Save the letter as Lastname_Firstname_i01_pf1_Photography_Letter, replacing Lastname_Firstname with your own name.

b. Start **Excel**, and then create a quote sheet for your services. Include a heading with your company information, headings for the date of the event, customer name, job description, number of hours required, any special requests, any extra travel time required, and the cost of the job.

c. Fill in the quote for a fictitious client. Save the file as Lastname_Firstname_i01_pf1_Photography_Quote, replacing Lastname_Firstname with your own name.

d. Copy the data for the quote, and then paste it into your Word document so it is linked to Excel. Save Lastname_Firstname_i01_pf1_Photography_Letter with the linked data.

e. Insert a left-aligned footer in the Word document and a footer in the left section of the Excel workbook with the file name.

Perform 2: How Others Perform

Student data files needed:

i01_pf2_CSS_Proposal

i01_pf2_CSS_Data

You will save your files as:

Lastname_Firstname_i01_pf2_CSS_Proposal

Lastname_Firstname_i01_pf2_CSS_Data

Computer Class Proposal

General Business

You have been asked to review a proposal for your local library to offer computer classes for adults over age 55. The written proposal contains what is supposed to be a link to a table of data in Excel and a chart for the corresponding data. The table contains the results of an informal survey done by the library.

a. Open **i01_pf2_CSS_Proposal**, and then save it as Lastname_Firstname_i01_pf2_CSS_Proposal, replacing Lastname_Firstname with your own name. Insert a left-aligned footer with the file name.

b. Based on what you know about linking and embedding objects, do you think the table was linked, embedded, copied and pasted, or added some other way? What about the chart?

c. What are the advantages to linking an object? What are the advantages to embedding an object?

d. Is there any advantage to using simple copy-and-paste commands like what was done in this example? Why or why not?

e. Fix the table and chart in the Word document so when changes are made to the table and chart in Excel, those changes will also be reflected in the Word document. Open **i01_pf2_CSS_Data**, and then save it as Lastname_Firstname_i01_pf2_CSS_Data, replacing Lastname_Firstname with your own name. Insert a footer in the left section with the file name.

f. In cell B4, change the **General Knowledge** percentage to 30%. In cell C4, change the **General Knowledge** percentage to 12%. Update the links in the Word document to make sure the data is updated in the table and the chart. Save the Excel workbook and the Word document.

Objectives

1. Prepare Excel data for import   p. 965
2. Import Excel data   p. 966
3. Prepare Access data for a mail merge   p. 969
4. Export query results from Access to Word   p. 970

Integrating Word, Excel, and Access

PREPARE CASE

Coupon Mailing

 Sales & Marketing

 Customer Service

Indigo 5 is an upscale restaurant always looking for ways to attract new customers as well as maintain relationships with current customers. Over the past year, the restaurant has been collecting comment cards from customers and recording birthdays in Excel. Each month the restaurant likes to send out birthday coupons for a free dessert to customers with birthdays in the upcoming month. Your assignment is to import the Excel data into Access, query Access for all birthdays in April, and use Word Merge with the Access list to create coupons in Word.

Andrey Armyagov / Shutterstock.com

Student data files needed for this workshop:

 i01_ws02_Birthday_List

 i01_ws02_Birthday_Flyer

You will save your files as:

 Lastname_Firstname_i01_ws02_Birthday_List

 Lastname_Firstname_i01_ws02_Birthday

 Lastname_Firstname_i01_ws02_Birthday_Merge

Use Excel Data in Access

Both Excel and Access can be used to collect, sort, and store data, but Access generally has more sophisticated tools to accomplish those tasks than Excel does. However, Excel has capabilities such as formulas, functions, and charts that are lacking in Access, so deciding where to store your data depends on what kind of data you have and what you want to do with it as summarized in Figure 1.

	Excel	Access
How data is stored	In a flat table	In a relational structure of multiple tables
What it stores best	Numbers	Text, numbers, other objects
Advantages	What-if models and analysis PivotTables Charts Conditional formatting, color bars, and other visual displays	Generates reports Multiple users Data entry forms Connecting multiple databases Data extraction

Figure 1 Storing data in Excel and Access

Data can be exchanged between Access and Excel in order to take advantage of the strengths of each program. There are multiple ways to exchange data between the two programs as shown in Figure 2.

Data from Access to Excel	Data from Excel to Access
Copy and paste	Copy and paste
Connect to Access database	Import data directly
Export data directly	Link to Excel worksheet

Figure 2 Sharing data

Import has two different meanings when referring to Excel and Access. When data is imported into Excel from Access, a permanent connection is created, so as the data in Access is updated, the data in Excel is also updated automatically. When data is imported into Access from Excel, there is no connection, so when the data is changed in Excel, the change is not reflected in Access. In this section, you will import Excel data into Access and export Access data into Word.

Real World Advice   The Fear of Access

Most people in business are either very comfortable with Excel or have some familiarity with it. Access, on the other hand, tends to be a program that not as many people are familiar with. Excel is therefore used more for data collection purposes than is necessary or appropriate, as much of the process could be done easier in Access. Having knowledge of both programs is critical so you cannot only make decisions on which to use but also move data between the two programs. For example, if your data in Access needs to be subtotaled and charted, you can import the data into Excel, apply subtotals, and then chart the data. On the other hand, if you do a lot of data entry, it would be beneficial to create a form in Access to make that data entry more user friendly.

Prepare Excel Data for Import

Data in Excel can be easily imported into an Access table. Because all data is stored in tables in Access, the data in Excel must be in a list form. Examples may be an address book, a list of inventory items, or a list of employees.

Editing an Excel List for Import

Before data is imported into Access, you need to make sure the data is compatible. The data should have column headings that will become the field names in the Access table. The rows in Excel will become the records in the Access table, so there should be no blank rows in the data you are importing. In this project, you will edit a list of data in Excel so it can be imported cleanly into Access.

To Edit Excel Data for Importing into Access

a. Start **Excel**. Click the **File tab**, click **Open**, and then locate your student folder. Select **i01_ws02_Birthday_List**, and then click **Open**.

b. Click the **File tab**, click **Save As**, and then save the workbook as Lastname_Firstname_ i01_ws02_Birthday_List, replacing Lastname_Firstname with your own name. Click **Save**.

c. Click the **Insert tab**, and then click **Header & Footer** in the Text group. Click the **Header & Footer Tools Design tab**, and then click **Go to Footer** in the Navigation group. Click in the left footer section, click the **Header & Footer Tools Design tab**, and then click **File Name** in the Header & Footer Elements group.

d. Click outside the footer area. Click **Normal** 🔳 on the status bar to return to Normal view. Press Ctrl + Home to return to cell A1.

e. In row 1, notice that only one of the two columns has a heading. Scroll through the list of names and notice the blank rows. Select **row 256** by clicking on the row number. Click the **Home tab**, click **Delete** in the Cells group, and then repeat to delete **rows 74** and **19**.

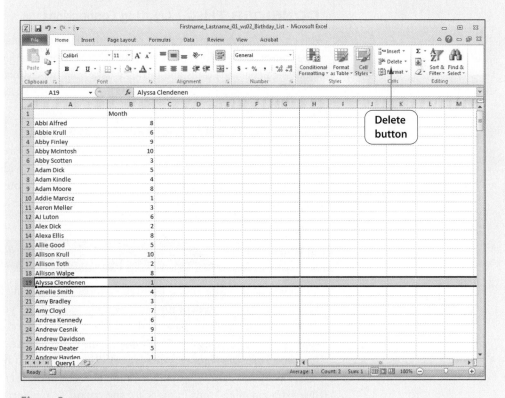

Figure 3 Blank rows deleted

Import Excel Data

When you import data from Excel into Access, Access stores the data in a new or existing table without making changes to the data in Excel. You can only import one worksheet at a time, so if you have multiple worksheets, you will have to repeat the steps for each sheet. If your data is on a worksheet with other unwanted data, you can create a **named range**, which is a specific name you give to a range of cells other than the cell references, for the data in Excel. Then, in Access you can specify that you only want the data in your named range.

Real World Advice — Data in Two Places

Once you import data from Excel to Access, the data is in two different places and is not automatically linked unless you choose to create a linked table. If a change to a record is made in Excel, it will not change the record in Access. However, imported Access data into Excel may be refreshed. Trying to maintain the same records in two different programs is not a good business practice. It is better to import or export data for a specific one-time purpose, like to query the data or create a chart from data.

CONSIDER THIS | Creating Connections

As you complete this project, you change the data in two places along the way because a permanent connection does not exist. What recommendations might you make for processing comment cards and birthday data from the customer?

Importing an Excel List into an Access Table

The Import Spreadsheet Wizard will walk you through the steps to import your Excel data into an Access table. When you import data, the Wizard provides three options: create a new table with the data, append the Excel data to an existing table, or create a linked table. For this exercise, you will import Excel data into a new Access table that will be called Birthday.

Real World Advice — Matching Fields

When you import data into a new table, Access will use the field names and data types of the imported data for the new table structure. If you import data into an existing table, the field names and data types of the imported data must match exactly the field names and data types of the existing Access table or you will get an error message. The **Import Spreadsheet Wizard** gives you the option to change the field names and data types before you import the data. Successful importing takes a few extra planning steps in order for the import to run successfully the first time.

To Import an Excel List into a New Access Table

a. Start **Access**. Click **Blank database**, and then in the **File Name** box type Lastname_Firstname_i01_ws02_Birthday, replacing Lastname_Firstname with your own name.

b. Click **Browse** 📁 and then select the folder where you have been instructed to save your files. Click **OK**, and then click **Create**.

Troubleshooting

Did you try to open an Excel workbook in Access? If you did, then Access created a link to the workbook instead of importing the data. Linking is different than importing and is not covered in this section.

c. Click the **External Data tab**, and then click **Excel** in the Import & Link group.

d. Click **Browse**, and then navigate to the folder where you save your files. Click **Lastname_Firstname_i01_ws02_Birthday_List**, and then click **Open**.

e. Select **Import the source data into a new table in the current database**, and then click **OK**.

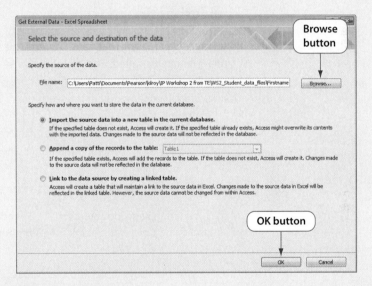

Figure 4   Import Wizard

SIDE NOTE
Primary Key
Remember that in a well-designed database, a primary key is selected for every table. If you are importing a list that does not contain a field for a primary key, Access will assign one for you.

f. In the Import Spreadsheet Wizard dialog box, verify **First Row Contains Column Headings** is checked, click **Next**, and then click **Next** again.

g. Verify **Let Access add primary key** is selected, and then click **Next**.

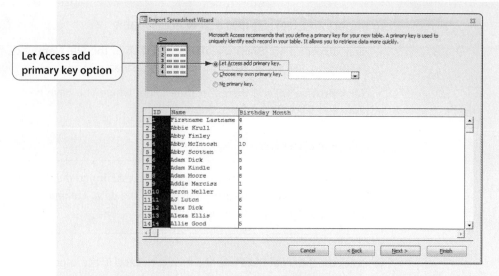

Let Access add primary key option

Figure 5   Let Access add primary key

h. Enter Birthdays for the name of the new table, and then click **Finish**.

i. Do not save the import steps. Click **Close**.

Troubleshooting

Did you receive an error that says "An error occurred trying to import file"? If so, then the import failed. If a dialog box opened up that prompts you to save the details of the operation, then the import worked, but some data may be missing. Start by opening your source file and compare it to the Access table (your destination file). If there are only a few missing pieces of information, you can add that information to the table manually. If there are large pieces, or whole columns of data missing, compare column headings and data types, revise your source data, and try to import again.

SIDE NOTE
Table1

A Table1 table is automatically created when another table is imported. Unless it is modified, it will automatically disappear once the file is closed and reopened.

j. In the Navigation Pane, double-click the **Birthdays** table to open it. Scroll to the bottom of the table and delete any blank rows without a name or birthday month. You should have a total of 298 records.

k. **Close** ☒ the Birthdays table, and then **Close** ☒ the Table1 table, which has opened by default. Leave the database and Access open if you are continuing to the next section.

Real World Advice   Save Import Steps

After you import data, you have the option to save the details of the import so you can repeat it again later without going through all the steps of the wizard. You can also create an Outlook Task if you have Outlook 2010 installed. The Outlook Task is useful if you regularly repeat an import and want Outlook to remind you when it needs to be done. The Outlook Task will even provide you with a button to run the import.

Use Access Data in Word

Access data, whether it was entered in Access directly or imported from an Excel worksheet, can be used in a Word document. One common example of using Access data in a Word document is to create a Mail Merge.

Prepare Access Data for a Mail Merge

Data for a mail merge in Word can come from either an Access table or a query. If the data is coming from a query, then the query must be created first.

Querying Data in an Access Database

To find the customers with birthdays in a particular month, you need to query the birthday table with the birthday month as the criteria. For this exercise, your will create a query to find all customers with April birthdays.

To Query Data in an Access Database

a. Click the **Create tab**, and then click **Query Design** in the Queries group. In the Show Table dialog box, click **Add** to add the Birthdays table to the query, and then click **Close**.

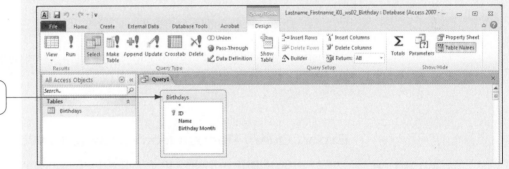

Birthdays table added to query

Figure 6   Birthdays table added to new query

b. Double-click **Name**, and then double-click **Birthday Month** to add the fields to the query design grid.

c. Click the **Show** check box under Birthday Month to hide this field. In the Criteria row for the Birthday Month field, type 4 to query for all birthdays in April. Click **Save** 🔲 and then save the query as April Birthdays. Click **OK**. Click the **Query Tools Design tab**, and then click **Run** in the Results group to run the query.

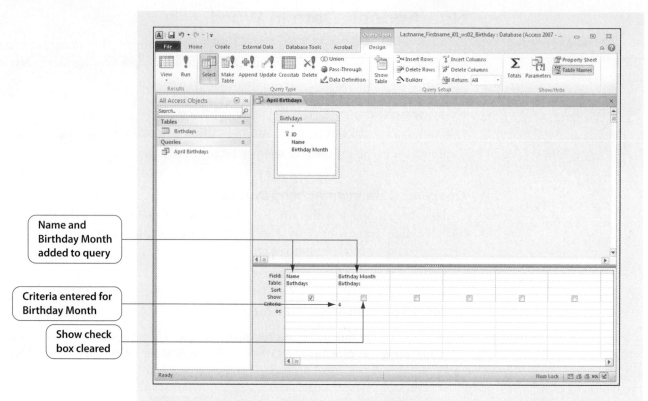

Name and Birthday Month added to query

Criteria entered for Birthday Month

Show check box cleared

Figure 7   Query design grid for April Birthdays query

d. In the Name field for the query results, double-click on the **right border** to best fit the column. Click **Save** 🖫. **Close** ✕ the query.

Export Query Results from Access to Word

Word has no import command to import data from Access, therefore the data must be exported from Access to be brought into Word. The exception to this is a mail merge, which will be discussed next. When you do use the export command in Access to export the data in a form or datasheet, or records selected in a view, that data is copied as a **Rich Text Format (.rtf)** file and put into a new Word document. From the new Word document, you can copy and paste the object into another existing Word document. Alternatively, you can copy data from an Access table, query, form, or report and paste the data into an existing document.

> **CONSIDER THIS** | **RTF Files**
>
> Importing data to an RTF file to use in another document takes two steps: creating the RTF file and copying and pasting it into another file. Are there advantages to this method versus a direct copy and paste into a document?

If the data in Access is going to be used in a merged Word document, then the Mail Merge Wizard can be used to export the data and an RTF file is not necessary. You can use the results of an Access query or any other data stored in an Access table to merge into a Word document to create customized letters or labels.

Exporting Data for a Mail Merge

To export a list of data from Access to Word, the Word Mail Merge Wizard can be used. The wizard can be started in either Access or Word. When the wizard is started in Access, it gives you the option to either create a new Word document or to use an existing one. For this exercise, you will link your data to an existing Word document to create customized birthday flyers for the customers listed in the Access query you just created.

To Mail Merge Access Query Results into Word

a. In the Navigation Pane, double-click the **April Birthdays** query to open it. Click the **External Data tab**, and then click **Word Merge** in the Export group. This opens the Microsoft Word Mail Merge Wizard.

Troubleshooting

Did you receive an error that says "The Mail Merge Wizard cannot continue because the database is in exclusive mode"? If so, then click OK and close Access. Click Yes to save changes to the layout of April Birthdays, if prompted. Start Access, and open Lastname_Firstname_i01_ws02_Birthday. If you see the Security Warning bar, click Enable Content. Then, begin again with Step a above.

b. Click **Link your data to an existing Microsoft Word document**, and then click **OK**.

c. Locate your student folder, select **i01_ws02_Birthday_Flyer**, and then click **Open**.

Troubleshooting

Did you receive an error that says "File in Use. i01_ws02_Birthday_Flyer is locked for editing." If so, the file is open on your computer and must be closed before you can use it for the mail merge. Click Cancel, close the file, and repeat, starting with Step a shown previously. If the Word document does not appear to open, check the taskbar and see whether it is minimized there.

d. In the Mail Merge pane, verify that **Use an existing list** is selected under Select recipients. Note that [April Birthdays] in "Lastname_Firstname_i01_ws02_Birthday" is selected under Use an existing list. At the bottom of the Mail Merge pane, click **Next: Write your letter**.

SIDE NOTE
Security Warning
When you open a database, you may see a **Security Warning bar** just below the Ribbon. Microsoft disables certain features to maintain security and prevent any viruses from entering your computer through a database file.

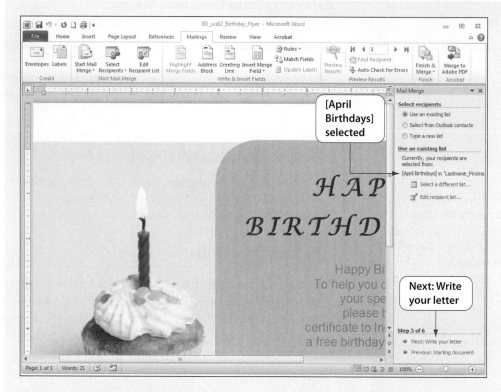

Figure 8 Mail Merge pane open in Word

e. On the birthday flyer, place the insertion point after **Happy Birthday to**, and then press Enter twice to skip a line and add a new line. In the Mail Merge pane, click **More items**.

f. In the Insert Merge Field dialog box, in the Fields box click **Name**, click **Insert**, and then click **Close**.

g. If necessary, place your insertion point after **<<Name>>**, and then press Enter so there is a blank line before and after the field. Select **<<Name>>**, click the **Home tab**, and in the Font group, change the font to **bold** and font size to **28**.

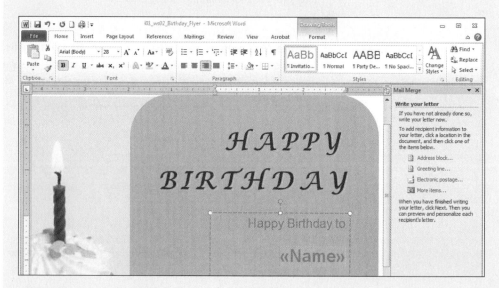

Figure 9 Name field reformatted

h. In the Mail Merge pane, click **Next: Preview your letters**. Under Preview your letters, click the **arrows** to scroll through the recipients. The first certificate should have your first and last name.

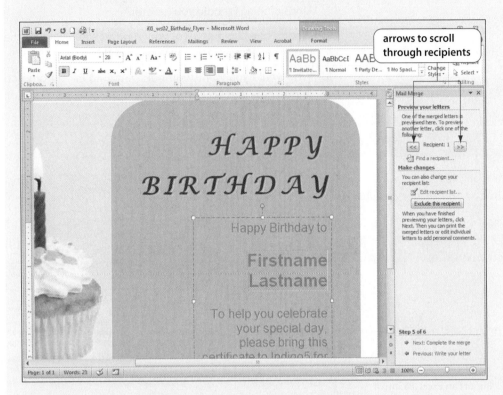

Figure 10 Certificates with merged fields formatted

i. In the Mail Merge pane, click **Next: Complete the merge**. To save the individual flyers in a new document, click **Edit Individual letters**.

j. In the Merge to New Document dialog box, select **All**, and then click **OK**. A new document opens with one page for each flyer. Save this document as Lastname_Firstname_ i01_ws02_Birthday_Merge.

k. Click the **Insert tab**, and then click **Footer** in the Header & Footer group. Select **Edit Footer**. Click the **Header & Footer Tools Design tab**, click **Quick Parts** in the Insert group, and then select **Field.** Scroll through the list of Field names, choose **FileName**, and then click **OK**.

l. Click the **Header & Footer Tools Design tab**, and then click **Close Header and Footer** in the Close group.

m. **Close** the **Lastname_Firstname_i01_ws02_Birthday_Merge** file, and then save changes if prompted. **Close** i01_ws02_Birthday_Flyer without saving changes. **Close** Access.

1. Why is it important to prepare your Excel data before importing it into Access? What kinds of things should you look for?

2. What is one common error you may get when you use the Mail Merge Wizard to export data from Access? How can you prevent this error?

3. Why would you want to import data into Excel from Access? Why would you want to import data into Access from Excel?

Key Terms

Import 964
Import Spreadsheet Wizard 966

Named range 966
Rich Text Format (.rtf) 970

Security Warning bar 971

Visual Summary

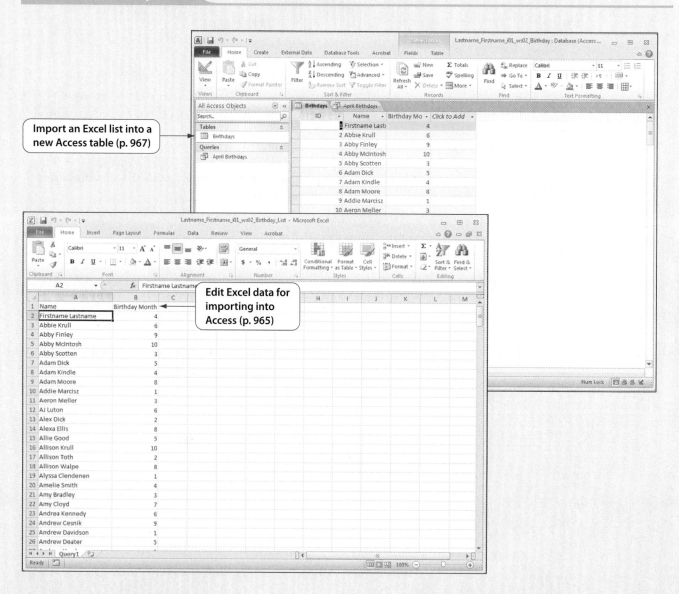

Import an Excel list into a new Access table (p. 967)

Edit Excel data for importing into Access (p. 965)

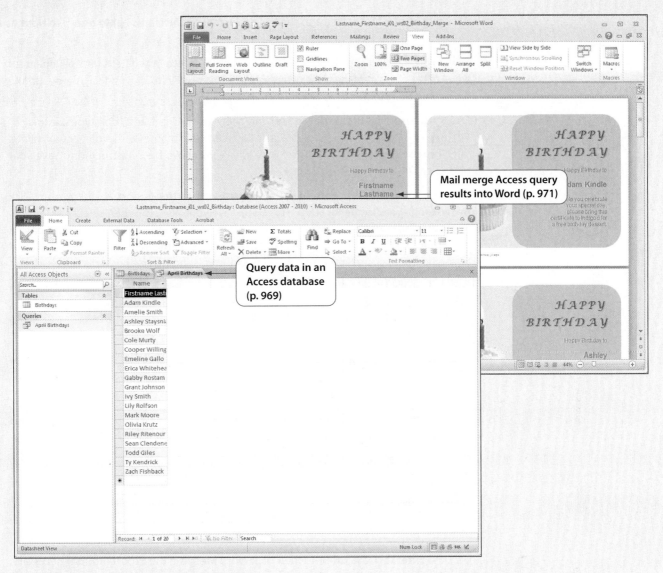

Mail merge Access query results into Word (p. 971)

Query data in an Access database (p. 969)

Figure 11 Importing and Exporting Data Final

Practice 1

Student data file needed:

i01_ws02_Library_List

You will save your files as:

Lastname_Firstname_i01_ws02_Library_List

Lastname_Firstname_i01_ws02_Library

Lastname_Firstname_i01_ws02_Library_Merge

Invitation List

Production & Operations

Painted Paradise Resort Event Planning is getting ready for an onsite library conference. You have been assigned to create name tags for only the attendees since the presenters will have special badges. You have a list of names in Excel with the library director's name, library name, and status indicating whether he or she is an attendee or a presenter. You will have to import the Excel list into Access, and then use Word Merge to create name tags using the list of data.

a. Start **Excel**, and then open the student file called **i01_ws02_Library_List**. Click the **File tab**, click **Save As**, and then save the file as Lastname_Firstname_i01_ws02_Library_List, replacing Lastname_Firstname with your own name.

b. Click the **Insert tab**, and then click **Header & Footer** in the Text group. Click the **Design tab**, click **Go to Footer** in the Navigation group, and then click in the left section of the footer. Click **File Name** in the Header & Footer Elements group to enter the file name.

Practice 1   975

c. Click outside the footer area and then click **Normal** on the status bar to return to Normal view. Press Ctrl + Home to return to cell A1.

d. Select **row 42**, click the **Home tab**, and then click **Delete** in the Cells group. Repeat for **row 18**. In cell A2, replace the existing name with your Firstname and Lastname. On the **Quick Access Toolbar**, click **Save**. Close Excel.

e. Open **Access**. Click **Blank database**, and then in the File Name box type Lastname_ Firstname_i01_ws02_Library, replacing Lastname_Firstname with your actual name. Click **Browse**, and then select the folder where you have been instructed to save your files. Click **OK**, and then click **Create**.

f. Click the **External Data tab**, and then click **Excel** in the Import & Link group. Click **Browse**, navigate to the location where you save your files, and then select **Lastname_ Firstname_i01_ws02_Library_List**. Click **Open**, select **Import the source data into a new table in the current database**, and then click **OK**. In the Import Spreadsheet Wizard dialog box, make sure **First Row Contains Column Headings** is checked, click **Next**, and then click **Next** again.

g. Make sure **Let Access add primary key** is selected, and then click **Next**. Enter Libraries for the name of the new table, and then click **Finish**. Do not save the import steps, and then click **Close**.

h. In the **Navigation Pane**, open the new table **Libraries**. Double-click the right border of the **Director** field and the **Library Name** field to best fit the column widths. Click **Save**. Close both the **Libraries** table and the **Table1** table.

i. Click the **Create tab**, and then click **Query Design** in the Queries group. Click **Add** to add the Libraries table to the query, and then click **Close**.

j. Double-click **ID**, **Director**, **Library Name**, and **Status** to add the fields to the query design grid. In the **Criteria** row for the Status field, type Attendee.

k. Click the **Query Tools Design tab**, and then click **Run** in the Results group. You should only see results for the Attendees of the conference and not the Presenters. Click **Save**, name the query Attendees, and then click **OK**.

l. Click the **External Data tab**, and then click **Word Merge** in the Export group. If necessary, close the database, reopen the database, click **Enable Content**, reopen the **Attendees** query, and then select **Word Merge** again. Select **Create a new document and then link the data to it**, and then click **OK**.

m. Switch to Word. In the Mail Merge pane, click **Labels** under Select document type. Click **Next: Starting document**, and then click **Label options** under Change document layout. In the Label Options dialog box, under Label information, make sure the Label vendor is **Avery US Letter**, and then under Product number, select **5390 Name Badges Insert Refills**. Click **OK**.

n. In the Mail Merge pane, click **Next: Select recipients**, and then click **Next: Arrange your labels**. Click **More items** under Arrange your labels. In the Insert Merge Field dialog box, double-click **Director** and **Library Name**, and then click **Close**.

o. On the nametag, click between <<Director>> and <<Library_Name>>, and then press Enter. Select both <<Director>> and <<Library_Name>> .

p. Click the **Home tab**. In the Font group, increase the font size to 18. Select only <<Director>>, and then make it bold.

q. In the Mail Merge pane, click **Update all labels** under Replicate labels. Click the **Select table button** in the top-left corner of the table to select all the records, click the **Table Tools Layout tab**, and then click **Align Center**, in the Alignment group.

r. In the Mail Merge pane, click **Next: Preview your labels**, and then click **Next: Complete the merge**.

s. In the Mail Merge pane, under Merge, click **Edit individual labels**. Under Merge records, make sure **All** is selected, and then click **OK**. Click **Save**, locate the folder in which you are storing your files, and then name the file Lastname_Firstname_i01_ws02_Library_Merge. Click **Save**, and then close the document.

t. Close the mail merge document called Document1 without saving it. Close Access.

Practice 2

Corporate Challenge

General Business

Painted Paradise Resort Event Planning is coordinating an upcoming corporate challenge event on the grounds of the resort. Each event will have a poster with the details and a list of participants. The participant information is in an Excel list. Your assignment is to import that list into Access, query for a particular event, and export the list of participants to the event flyer in Word.

a. Start **Word**. Click the **File tab**, click **Open**, and then locate your student files. Select **i01_ws02_Corporate_Flyer**, and then click **Open**.

b. Click the **File tab**, click **Save As**, and then save the document as Lastname_Firstname_i01_ws02_Corporate_Flyer, replacing Lastname_Firstname with your own name.

c. Click the **Insert tab**, click **Footer** in the Header & Footer group, and then select **Edit Footer**. Click the **Header & Footer Tools Design tab**, click **Quick Parts** in the Insert group, select **Field**, scroll through the list of field names, and then choose **FileName**. Click **OK**. Click the **Header & Footer Tools Design tab**, and then click **Close Header and Footer** in the Close group. Click **Minimize** to minimize the Word window.

d. Start **Excel**, and open the student file called **i01_ws02_Corporate_List**. Click the **File tab**, click **Save As**, and then save the file as Lastname_Firstname_i01_ws02_Corporate_List, replacing Lastname_Firstname with your own name.

e. Click the **Insert tab**, and then click **Header & Footer** in the Text group. Click the **Header & Footer Tools Design tab**, click **Go to Footer** in the Navigation group, and then click in the left section of the footer. Click **File Name** in the Header & Footer Elements group to enter the file name.

f. Click outside the footer area and click **Normal** on the status bar to return to Normal view. Press Ctrl + Home to return to cell A1.

g. Select **row 102**, click the **Home tab**, and then click **Delete** in the Cells group. Repeat for rows **58** and **35**. In cell B1, type Event for a column heading. In cell A2, replace the existing name with your Firstname and Lastname. In cell B2, change the event to 400 Meter Track Relay. Click **Save**, and then close Excel.

h. Start **Access**. Select **Blank database**, and then in the **File Name** box type Lastname_Firstname_i01_ws02_Corporate, replacing Lastname_Firstname with your own name.

i. Click **Browse**, and locate the folder where you have been instructed to save your files. Click **OK**, and then click **Create**.

j. Click the **External Data tab**, and then click **Excel** in the Import & Link group.

k. Click **Browse**, locate the folder in which you save your files, and then select **Lastname_Firstname_i01_ws02_Corporate_List**. Click **Open**, select **Import the source data into a new table in the current database**, and then click **OK**. In the Import Spreadsheet

Wizard dialog box, make sure **First Row Contains Column Headings** is selected, click **Next**, and then click **Next** again.

l. Make sure **Let Access add primary key** is selected, and then click **Next**. Enter Events for the name of the new table, and then click **Finish**. Do not save the import steps. Click **Close**.

m. In the Navigation Pane, open the new table **Events**. Double-click the right border of the **Name** field and the **Event** field to best fit the column widths.

n. Click the **Create tab**, and then click **Query Design** in the Queries group. In the Show Table dialog box, select **Events**, and then click **Add**. Click **Close** to close the dialog box. Double-click the **Name** and **Event** fields one at a time to add them to the query design grid.

o. Click **Show** under the Event field to hide this field. Click the **Criteria** row for the Event field, and then type 400 Meter Track Relay. Click **Save** and then name the query 400 Meter. Click the **Query Tools Design tab**, and then click **Run** in the Results group.

p. Double-click the right border of the **Name** field to best fit the column width. Click **Save**.

q. Select all the records in the 400 Meter query, click the **Home tab**, and then click **Copy** in the Clipboard group.

r. In the Word document **Lastname_Firstname_i01_ws02_Corporate_Flyer**, click the **Home tab**, and then click **Paste** in the Clipboard group. Move the table to the middle of the white space below the image on the flyer. Delete any extra pages as necessary. Click **Save**.

s. Close Word, close Access, and then save all changes when asked.

Problem Solve 1

Student data file needed:

i01_ps1_Inventory_List

You will save your files as:

Lastname_Firstname_i01_ps1_Inventory_List
Lastname_Firstname_i01_ps1_Inventory
Lastname_Firstname_i01_ps1_Inventory_Merge

Merchandise Labels

Production & Operations

The Gift Shop staff members would like to put merchandise labels on the different items they carry in order to quickly manage inventory and ring up sales based on the category of merchandise. The item list is in an Excel spreadsheet, and the labels are in Word. Your assignment is to import the Excel list into Access, then find the records for all items except those categorized as "Other." You will use Word Merge to create labels for the queried data.

a. Start **Excel**. Locate and open **i01_ps1_Inventory_List**, and then save it as Lastname_Firstname_i01_ps1_Inventory_List. Insert a footer in the left section with the file name. Prepare the list for importing it into Access by deleting any blank rows. Click **Save**.

b. Import the data into a new Access database called Lastname_Firstname_i01_ps1_Inventory. Save the new table as Inventory. Do not save the import steps.

c. Query the Inventory table for records in all the categories *except* **Other**. Show fields **Item** and **Category**. Save the new query as Categories.

d. Use Word Merge to create labels in a new Word document using the records in the Categories query. If necessary, save and close the database, reopen it, and then Enable Content. For Label options, choose the Avery Product number **18160 Address Labels**.

e. Add the **Item** field on the first line of the label and the **Category** field to the second line of the label. Increase the font size so the information fits well. Click on Update all labels to add fields to all the labels on the page.

f. Replicate and then preview the labels. Complete the merge, save the new document as Lastname_Firstname_i01_ps1_Inventory_Merge, and then close the document.

g. Close all documents in Word without saving. Close Access, and then close Excel, saving changes when prompted.

Perform 1: Perform in Your Career

Student data file needed:

None

You will save your files as:

Lastname_Firstname_i01_pf1_Book_Certificate

Lastname_Firstname_i01_pf1_Book_List

Lastname_Firstname_i01_pf1_Book

Lastname_Firstname_i01_pf1_Book_Merge

Award Certificates

Information Technology

You are a teacher and would like to reward your students for completing a reading program that lasted for three months. You would like to print the certificates with the students' names and the number of books they have read. You have been tracking your students in Excel for over two years, with the students' names and number of books, so you need to import the data into Access, query the data for the current year's students, and then use Word Merge to create a new Word document from the query results.

a. Start **Word**, and then create an award certificate for your students (you may use a template and modify it as necessary). Save the file as Lastname_Firstname_i01_pf1_Book_Certificate and then close Word.

b. Open **Excel**, and create a list of names, number of books read, and the year read, for at least 45 students. Approximately half of the students should have the year 2013 and the other half 2014 to represent two years of classes. The first record should have Your Name as the student name and the year 2013. Insert the filename in the left section of the footer. Save the file as Lastname_Firstname_i01_pf1_Book_List.

c. Import the Excel list into an Access database called Lastname_Firstname_i01_pf1_Book. Name the new table Books Read. Query the table for only students who completed their reading in 2013. Save the query as 2013 Students.

d. Use Word Merge to create award certificates with the results of your query. Include the student's name, number of books read, and year completed on the certificate. Save the merged document as Lastname_Firstname_i01_pf1_Book_Merge. Close Word without saving Lastname_Firstname_i01_pf1_Book_Certificate.

Perform 2: How Others Perform

Student data files needed:

i01_pf2_Pets_Newsletter

i01_pf2_Pets_Charts

i01_pf2_Pets_List

You will save your files as:

Lastname_Firstname_i01_pf2_Pets_Newsletter

Lastname_Firstname_i01_pf2_Pets_Charts

Lastname_Firstname_i01_pf2_Pets_List

Lastname_Firstname_i01_pf2_Pets_Merged

Monthly Newsletter

General Business

Your boss at Pets Plus, a national pet store chain, has written a monthly newsletter called "Pets Plus Pages" that he has been mailing each month to the six district sales managers in your company. He would like you to take over the project, which includes updating charts in Excel, importing data from Access, and summarizing all the data in the newsletter. Then you will need to personalize each newsletter with the manager's name and district name.

a. Start **Word**. Locate and open **i01_pf2_Pets_Newsletter**, and then save it as Lastname_Firstname_i01_pf2_Pets_Newsletter. Insert a left-aligned footer with the filename.

- Look at how the newsletter is laid out. How has the Year to Date Sales by District data been added?
- Is this the most efficient way to include the data, especially if the data changes each month? How else could it have been added?

b. Open **i01_pf2_Pets_Charts**, and then save it as Lastname_Firstname_i01_pf2_Pets_Charts. Insert a footer in the left section with the file name.

- Add new sales numbers for April.
- Are these changes reflected in the newsletter?
- Update the newsletter with the new chart so the chart will change in the newsletter when new data is added in Excel. You may have to rearrange how the newsletter is laid out to accommodate this change.

c. Open **i01_pf2_Pets_List**, and then save it as Lastname_Firstname_i01_pf2_Pets_List.

- Update the Access table District Rankings to show the current year-to-date rankings based on the sales in Excel.
- Change the name of the Midwest district's manager to your name.
- Run the Ranking query to sort by rank.
- For the past newsletters, your boss has exported the query table as an RTF (Rich Text Format) to a new Word document, and then has copied the data from the new Word document to the newsletter.
- Can you think of a different way to copy the query table to the newsletter in fewer steps? Copy the new query data with April rankings to the newsletter.

d. Your boss manually added the sales manager's name to each newsletter before printing. How would you do this automatically?

- Update the short letter in the top section of the newsletter. Make sure all the information fits on one page. Save the file.
- Complete a mail merge to add the manager's name and district's name to the newsletter. Save the letters individually in a file named Lastname_Firstname_i01_pf2_Pets_Merged.

Objectives

1. Work with Outlines p. 982
2. Insert Access data into a PowerPoint presentation p. 987
3. Import Access data into Excel to create a chart p. 989

Integrating Word, Excel, Access, and PowerPoint

PREPARE CASE
Restaurant Training

Human Resources

Once a year, Indigo 5 requires all staff members to undergo extensive training on customer service in its effort to remain a top-rated restaurant. The manager has written an outline in Word for the training seminar. There is a database of information with customer survey results. Your assignment is to create a PowerPoint presentation from the Word outline, then import the Access data into Excel to create a chart that can be used in the PowerPoint presentation.

Golden Pixels LLC / Shutterstock.com

Student data files needed for this workshop:

 i01_ws03_Customer_Outline

 i01_ws03_Customer_Presentation

 i01_ws03_Customer_Surveys

 i01_ws03_Customer_Chart

You will save your files as:

 Lastname_Firstname_i01_ws03_Customer_Outline

 Lastname_Firstname_i01_ws03_Customer_Presentation

 Lastname_Firstname_i01_ws03_Customer_Chart

 Lastname_Firstname_i01_ws03_Customer_Surveys

Integrate Word and PowerPoint

Text can easily be copied from Word to PowerPoint, but sometimes a copy and paste is not efficient or realistic. To copy and paste large amounts of text can be time consuming, and deciding the best way to split text up for different PowerPoint slides can often be overwhelming.

In order to efficiently use Word text in a PowerPoint presentation, a Word outline can be used. An **outline** is a hierarchical representation of paragraphs that are recognized by Word by nonprinting, end-of-paragraph marks. A paragraph can be a blank line, one or two words, or multiple sentences. When you type a paragraph into a document in **Outline view**, Word automatically assigns heading styles to the paragraph to create different levels. At the top of the hierarchy are **Level 1** paragraphs. Paragraphs at the next level are **Level** 2. These outlining levels correspond to the Heading styles available to format text located on the Home tab, in the Styles group, so paragraphs already formatted with heading styles will appear at different levels in Outline view. Paragraphs that have not been formatted with heading styles will appear as **body text** in Outline view.

Open Outline View

When Outline view is opened, a new tab on the Ribbon opens with tools available for formatting paragraphs. The Promote button and Demote button move paragraphs to different levels. When you **promote** a paragraph, you move it to a higher level in the outline. When you **demote** a paragraph, you move it to a lower level in the outline.

As your outline grows, it is often helpful to see only one level at a time. If a paragraph has levels below it, then a plus sign ⊕ appears at the beginning of the line. This plus sign is the **Collapse button** and is assigned to paragraphs with lower-level paragraphs directly beneath them. Double-clicking the Collapse button temporarily hides all the lower levels below that paragraph. The Collapse button will become the **Expand button** that allows you to show the lower levels in an outline after they have been collapsed. The minus sign ⊟ at the beginning of the line is assigned to paragraphs with no lower levels below them. Paragraphs that have a simple bullet point, that is, no plus or minus sign, are body text and cannot be collapsed or expanded. You can click Show Level to choose which levels to view at one time. When you click Show Level and select Level 2, then all Level 1 and Level 2 paragraphs will be collapsed.

Working in Outline View

You can view a normal document in Outline view at any time. When you switch to Outline view your paragraphs are listed by levels. You can make changes to the levels of the paragraphs in either Normal view or directly in Outline view. For this exercise, you will open a Word document, view it in Outline view, and make changes to the paragraph levels in Outline view.

To Work with a Document in Outline View

a. Start **Word**. Click the **File tab**, click **Open**. In the Open dialog box, click the disk drive in the left pane where your student data files are located. Navigate through the folder structure and click **i01_ws03_Customer_Outline**. Click **Open**.

b. Click the **File tab**, and then click **Save As**. In the Save As dialog box, navigate to where you are saving your files, and then type Lastname_Firstname_i01_ws03_Customer_Outline, replacing Lastname_Firstname with your own name. Click **Save**.

c. Click the **Insert tab**, click **Footer** in the Header & Footer group, and then select **Edit Footer**. Click the Header & Footer Tools Design tab, click **Quick Parts** in the Insert group, and then select **Field**. Scroll through the list of Field names, choose **FileName**, and then click **OK**.

d. Click the Header & Footer Design tab, click **Close Header and Footer** in the Close group, and then click **Save** 🔲 on the Quick Access Toolbar.

e. Click the **View tab**, and then click **Outline** in the Document Views group. Notice in the **Outline Level box** [Body Text ▾] in the Outline Tools group that all the paragraphs are considered body text.

Outlining tab ───
Outline Level box ───

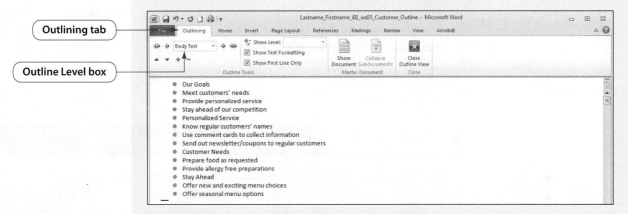

Figure 1   Outline view

f. Select all the lines of text, click the Outlining tab, and then click **Promote** 🔺 in the Outline Tools group so all the lines are promoted to Level 1. The font type and size changes, and a minus sign appears at the beginning of each line to visually show that the paragraphs are Level 1 and not body text.

Promote button ───

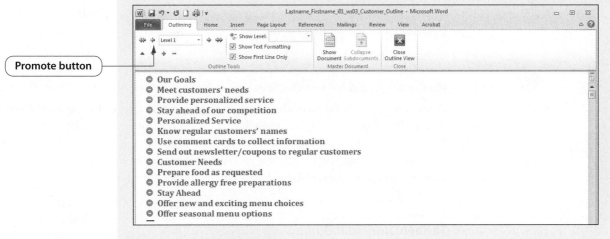

Figure 2   Level 1 paragraphs

g. Place the insertion point at the beginning of the second line, which says **Meet customers' needs**, and then click the Outlining tab, click **Demote** 🔻 in the Outline Tools group. This not only moves the paragraph to Level 2, but it changes the font type and font size as well. Note the button next to the first paragraph has changed from a minus to a plus because there is now a paragraph at a level below.

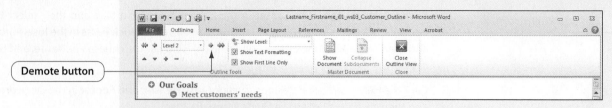

Demote button

Figure 3   Level 1 and Level 2 paragraphs

h. Select the next two lines **Provide personalized service** and **Stay ahead of our competition**. Click the Outlining tab, and click **Demote** ⬦ in the Outline Tools group.

i. Select **lines 6** through **8**, and then click **Demote** ⬦. Select **lines 10** and **11**, and then click **Demote** ⬦. Select **lines 13** and **14**, and then click **Demote** ⬦. Click the **Outlining tab**, and then click **Close Outline View** in the Close group to return to Normal view.

j. Click **Save** 🖫.

Real World Advice   Optional Outlining Method

You may want to use the Styles options on the Home tab to create your outline instead of using the Outline view. Select a paragraph and then on the Home tab, in the Styles group, select a style (Heading 1, Heading 2, and so on) to create different levels of paragraphs. By using the Style method, you will see the different formatting of the text, but you will not see the collapse button like you do in Outline view.

CONSIDER THIS | **Start at the Top**

For an existing document, you may want to promote all the paragraphs to the first level and then demote one at a time starting from there. Why would starting at the top be easier and not more time consuming?

Rearranging a Word Outline

After you have created an outline, you can move paragraphs from one part of the outline to another without changing their levels. The Outlining tab has Move Up and Move Down buttons that will move selected lines up or down one or more lines at a time. This does not change the levels, only the position of the paragraphs within the outline. For this exercise, you will reorganize your paragraphs in Outline view.

To Reorganize Your Outline

a. Press [Ctrl] + [Home].

b. Click the **View tab**, and then click **Outline** in the Document Views group.

c. Click the **Collapse** button ⊙ next to Customer Needs to select that paragraph and the two paragraphs below. Click the **Outlining tab**, then click **Move Up** ▲ in the Outline Tools group four times so all three lines are above Personalized Service.

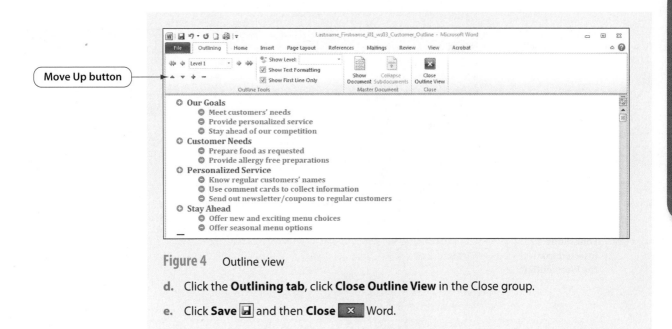

Move Up button

Figure 4   Outline view

d.   Click the **Outlining tab**, click **Close Outline View** in the Close group.

e.   Click **Save** 🔲 and then **Close** ❎ Word.

Creating PowerPoint Slides from a Word Outline

When you create PowerPoint slides from a Word outline, PowerPoint automatically uses the highest level of paragraphs in the outline as slide titles on new slides, and the next highest level of paragraphs as first-level **slide text**. Each level after the first-level slide text becomes one level lower slide text, using a bullet or number outline. Once the slides are created, you can modify them as necessary in PowerPoint by changing the formatting or the levels of text. For this exercise you will use the Word outline to create new PowerPoint slides.

SIDE NOTE
No Outlining?
If your document has no heading styles and therefore no outlining created, then PowerPoint will create slides based on paragraphs only and each paragraph will become a new slide.

To Create PowerPoint Slides from a Word Outline

a.   Start **PowerPoint**. Click the **File tab**, click **Open**, and then locate your student files. Select **i01_ws03_Customer_Presentation**, and then click **Open**.

b.   Click the **File tab**, and then click **Save As**. In the Save As dialog box, navigate to where you are saving your files, and then type Lastname_Firstname_i01_ws03_Customer_ Presentation, replacing Lastname_Firstname with your own name. Click **Save**.

c.   Click the **Home tab**, click the **New Slide arrow** in the Slides group, and then select **Slides from Outline**.

d.   In the Insert Outline dialog box, navigate through the folder structure to where your saved files are located and click **Lastname_Firstname_i01_ws03_Customer_Outline**, and then click **Insert**.

Figure 5 PowerPoint slides added

Troubleshooting

PowerPoint cannot make slides from an open Word document. If you get an error when you try to select a file, make sure the file is closed, and then try selecting the Slides from Outline option again.

e. Click the **Insert tab**, and then click **Header & Footer** in the Text group. In the Header and Footer dialog box, click the **Notes and Handouts tab**. Click **Footer** to select it, and then type Lastname_Firstname_i01_ws03_Customer_Presentation, replacing Lastname_Firstname with your own name. Click **Apply to All**.

f. Click **Save** .

g. Click **Minimize** to minimize PowerPoint to the taskbar.

Integrate Access and PowerPoint

Data can be shared between PowerPoint and Access. Access tables and queries can all be copied and pasted directly into a PowerPoint presentation. The data is therefore shared, but not linked, so any changes made to the data in Access will not be reflected in the copy and pasted selection in PowerPoint.

Insert Access Data into a PowerPoint Presentation

Unlike exporting data in Access to Word or Excel, there is no import or export command for moving Access data to a PowerPoint presentation. Instead, simple copy and paste commands are used.

Copying and Pasting Access Data

Because data must be copy and pasted from Access to PowerPoint, any data from a table or query can easily be selected, copied, and pasted using the commands on the Clipboard. For this exercise, you will copy the results of a query in Access and paste it onto a slide in PowerPoint.

SIDE NOTE
Security Warning
Microsoft disables features to prevent any malicious software from entering your computer through a database file. If you know who the database is from and are comfortable with its contents, click Enable Content.

To Copy and Paste Access Query Results to a PowerPoint Slide

a. Start **Access**. Click the **File tab**, and then click **Open**. In the Open dialog box, click the disk drive in the left pane where your student data files are located. Navigate through the folder structure and click **i01_ws03_Customer_Surveys**. Click **Open**, and then click **Enable Content** in the Security Warning bar. Click the **File tab**, click **Save Database As**, navigate to where you are saving your files, and then name the file **Lastname_ Firstname_i01_ws03_Customer_Surveys**.

b. In the Navigation Pane, double-click the query **Summarized Results** to open it in Datasheet view.

c. Click **Select All** ☐ in the top-left of the query datasheet. This selects all the records in the query datasheet.

Select All button ────→

Figure 6 Summarized Results query

d. Click the **Home tab**, click **Copy** in the Clipboard group, and then **Close** ❌ Access.

e. Click **PowerPoint** 🖥 on the taskbar to display the PowerPoint window. With **Lastname_ Firstname_i01_ws03_Customer_Presentation** open, click the **Slides tab**, and then click **Slide 2** to select it.

f. Click the **Home tab**, and then click **Paste** in the Clipboard group. Point to the edge of the table, and when your mouse pointer turns into a four-sided arrow 🔀, drag the datasheet object below the text.

SIDE NOTE
Queries and Tables
You opened and copied query results in Steps b through d. You can also open and copy a table the same way.

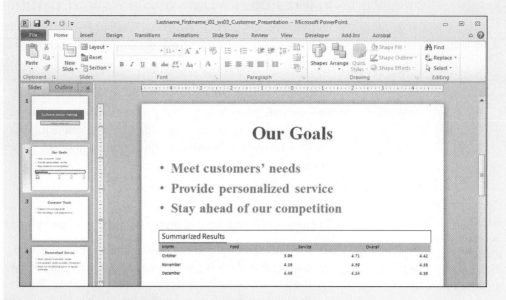

Figure 7   PowerPoint Slide 2

g. Resize the columns starting with the first column on the left. Point to the line between the Month and Food column headings, and then when your mouse pointer turns into a horizontal resize pointer ⟨↔⟩, double-click the line to best fit the data in the column so December just fits. Repeat for the other three columns.

Troubleshooting

In the Access database, the query was formatted so no decimal places were being displayed in the number. Because this is a display-only feature in Access, when the data is copied to the Clipboard, the actual data is copied, not the displayed data. Therefore, when you paste the table in PowerPoint, there will be two decimal places showing. If necessary, you can type over the numbers that are copied and replace them with a rounded number.

h. Click the **Table Tools Layout tab**, change the **Height** in the Table Size group to **2.4"** and the **Width** in the Table Size group to **3.75"**. Move the table so it is centered on the slide below the text.

i. With the table selected, click the **Table Tools Design tab**, and then select the **Themed Style 1-Accent 1** style in the Table Styles group to apply it to the table.

j. Click **Save** 🖫 and then click **Minimize** 🗕 to minimize PowerPoint on the taskbar.

CONSIDER THIS | Paste Options

You are performing a simple copy and paste with the data from Access. There are other options under Paste Special that you could have used. What are they? When would you want to use Paste Special rather than Paste?

Integrate Access, Excel, and PowerPoint

You can bring data into Excel from Access by using the copy and paste commands, by importing Access data into Excel, or by exporting Access data into the worksheet. The method you choose to use will determine whether the data is linked and can be automatically updated from one program to another. An import will create a permanent connection between Excel and Access, while a simple copy and paste will not. Figure 8 describes the various ways to share data between Access and Excel, as well as the type of connection that is made between the programs.

Sharing Data between Access and Excel	Type of Connection	Details
To bring data into Excel from Access:		
Copy and paste	None	No connection between Excel and Access after the copy and paste
Import Access data into Excel (from Excel)	Permanent	Can refresh the data in Excel when changes are made in Access
Export Access data into an Excel worksheet (from Access)	None	No connection between Excel and Access but export steps can be saved for future use
To bring data into Access from Excel:		
Copy and paste	None	No connection between Excel and Access after the copy and paste
Import an Excel worksheet into an Access datasheet (from Access)	None	No connection between Excel and Access
Link to an Excel worksheet from an Access table (from Access)	Permanent	Can refresh the data in Access when changes are made in Excel

Figure 8 Sharing data

Import Access Data into Excel

When you import data from an Access database into an Excel worksheet, a permanent connection is created and the data can be refreshed in the worksheet when data is changed in the database. If you use the copy and paste commands or export the Access data, you create a copy of the data that cannot be automatically updated.

Creating a Chart with Imported Access Data

There may be times when you have data in Access and realize that the data would be a good candidate for a chart, but Access does not have charting capabilities. If the chart is a one time project and will not need to be updated, then a copy and paste of the data will be sufficient. If, however, the data will be frequently updated in Access and therefore will require the chart to also be updated, then a link would be a better option. For this exercise you will import data from Access into Excel so when the data is changed in Access, the change is reflected in Excel.

To Import Access Data into Excel

a. Start **Excel**. Click the **File tab**, and then click **Open**. In the Open dialog box, click the disk drive in the left pane where your student data files are located. Navigate through the folder structure, click **i01_ws03_Customer_Chart**, and then click **Open**.

b. Click the **File tab**, and then click **Save As**. In the Save As dialog box, navigate to where you are saving your files, and then type Lastname_Firstname_i01_ws03_Customer_ Chart, replacing Lastname_Firstname with your own name. Click **Save**.

c. Click the **Insert tab**, and then click **Header & Footer** in the Text group. Click the Header & Footer Tools Design tab, and then click **Go to Footer** in the Navigation group. Click in the **left footer section**, and then on the Design tab, click **File Name** in the Header & Footer Elements group.

d. Click outside of the footer area, and then click **Normal** ▦ on the status bar to return to Normal view. Press Ctrl + Home to return to cell A1.

e. Select cell **A3**, click the **Data tab**, and then click **From Access** in the Get External Data group.

f. Navigate to the folder where you save your files, select **Lastname_Firstname_i01_ ws03_Customer_Surveys**, and then click **Open**.

g. If you do not see a Data Link Properties dialog box, then skip to Step i. In the Data Link Properties dialog box, under the Connection tab, verify under Step 1 that the Data Source is **Lastname_Firstname_i01_ws03_Customer_Surveys**. Under Step 2, verify that the **Use a specific user name and password** option is selected and that **Blank password** and **Allow saving password** options are selected. Click **OK**.

Troubleshooting

> The first time you get data from Access using a link on your computer, the Data Link Properties dialog box will open and require you to set a username and password. Once you have completed a successful import, this box will no longer open, and the connection will automatically be made until you close and reopen Excel again.

h. When prompted for a password, click **OK**. Because you had the Blank password option selected, no password is necessary to continue with this step.

i. In the Select Table dialog box, select **Summarized Results**. This selects the Access query to import, which has the data you need to create the desired chart. Click **OK**.

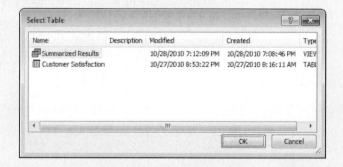

Figure 9   Select Table dialog box

j. In the Import Data dialog box, verify that **Table** is selected, and that the **Existing worksheet** text box contains **=$A$3**. This tells Excel where to put the data table in the worksheet. Click **OK**.

k. Select cells **B4:D6**. Click the **Home tab**, and then click **Decrease Decimal** in the Number group until the numbers are formatted with only two decimal places. Click **Save** and **close** Excel.

l. Start **Access**. Click the **File tab**, and click **Open**. In the Open dialog box, click the disk drive in the left pane where your student data files are located. Navigate through the folder structure and double-click **i01_ws03_Customer_Surveys**. Click the **File tab**, click **Save Database As**, navigate to the folder in which you are saving your files, and then name the file Lastname_Firstname_i01_ws03_Customer_Surveys, replacing Lastname_Firstname with your own name. Click **Save**. Click **Enable Content** in the Security Warning bar.

m. Double-click the **Customer Satisfaction** table to open it. Scroll to the last record in the table. Add a record with your Lastname, the month December, and 10 for the Food, Service, and Overall columns. **Close** the Customer Satisfaction table.

n. Double-click the **Summarized Results** query to open it and check the new query results. **Close** the Summarized Results query. **Close** Access.

o. Start **Excel**. Click the **File tab**, and click **Open**. In the Open dialog box, click the disk drive in the left pane where you are saving your files, double-click **Lastname_Firstname_ i01_ws03_Customer_Chart**, and click **Enable Content** on the Security Warning bar. Click the **Data tab**, and then click **Refresh All** in the Connections group. The linked data in the table should be updated.

Real World Advice Charting Access Data

While it may seem redundant to copy data from Access into Excel, it can be a very useful exercise. Access is best used for storing, sorting, and reporting data, while Excel is best for charting and manipulating data. Rather than recreating data in Excel, it can be easier to copy data from Access, whether from a table or a query, and then use Excel to create the chart.

Linking an Excel Chart to a PowerPoint Presentation

After you have created a chart in Excel with Access data, you can put that chart in another program like PowerPoint. If you link the chart to the presentation, then when the data is updated in Access, it can be refreshed in Excel and PowerPoint at the same time. For this exercise, you will create an Excel chart from the Access data and then link it to a slide in your PowerPoint presentation.

To Create an Excel Chart and Link it to a PowerPoint Slide

a. Select cells **A3:D6**. Click the **Insert tab**, click **Column** in the Charts group, and then select **3-D Clustered Column**.

b. Point to the top-left edge of the chart. When your mouse pointer changes to a four-sided arrow 📐, drag the **chart** so the top-left corner is in cell A8 and the bottom-right corner is in or close to cell **H22**.

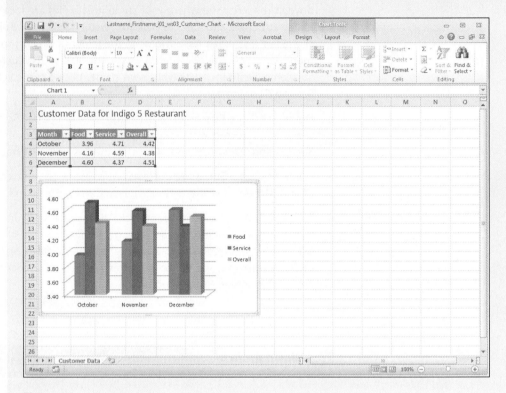

Figure 10   Excel chart

c. Click **Save** 🖫. With the chart still selected, click the **Home tab**, and then click **Copy** in the Clipboard group to copy the chart to the Clipboard.

d. Click **Minimize** ⊟ to minimize the Excel window to the taskbar.

e. Click **PowerPoint** 🗖 on the taskbar to restore the PowerPoint window. Click **Slide 3** to select it. Click the **Home tab**, click the **Paste arrow** in the Clipboard group, and then select **Paste Special**. Click **Paste link**, and then choose **Microsoft Excel Chart Object**. Click **OK**.

Troubleshooting

If you close Excel before you paste the chart in PowerPoint, then Paste Special dialog box will only give you the option to Paste and not Paste link. If you closed Excel before you pasted the chart, open Excel, copy the chart again, and keep Excel open while you paste the chart into PowerPoint.

f. Click **Minimize** ☐ to minimize PowerPoint to the taskbar, and then click **Excel** 🖾 on the taskbar to restore the Excel window. With the chart selected, click the **Chart Tools Layout tab**, click **Chart Title** in the Labels group, and then select **Above Chart**. Type the chart title Summary of Customer Surveys, and press [Enter].

g. Click **Save** 🖫. Click **Minimize** ☐ to minimize the Excel window to the taskbar, and then click **PowerPoint** 🔳 on the taskbar to restore the PowerPoint window. Note that the chart in the presentation now shows the chart title you added in Excel.

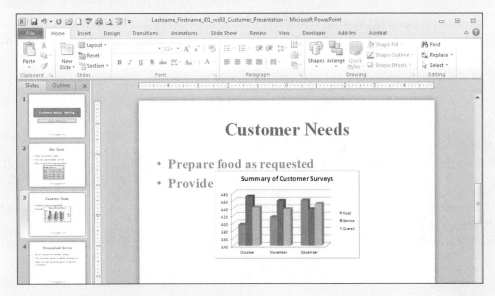

Figure 11   Chart title changed in PowerPoint

h. Move the chart so it is centered on the slide below the text. Click **Save** 🖫. **Close** ✖ PowerPoint and **Close** ✖ Excel, saving changes if prompted.

Real World Advice   Link, Embed, or Copy and Paste?

As you recall, the source file is the file that the original data comes from and the destination file is where the data is copied to. When a chart is linked to an Excel worksheet, any changes in the worksheet are made to the linked chart as well. This is helpful if you are planning to change the data on a regular basis, such as a monthly or quarterly report. If you do not plan on changing the original data but would like the option to make changes to the chart in the destination file, then you can embed the chart. This allows you to change layout, design, and formatting options of the chart in either the destination or source file, but not both. If you do not need that kind of flexibility, then copying and pasting is the simplest method for copying the chart from one file to another.

1. How is working with a Word outline different than working in Normal view with a document?

2. If an outline has three Level 1 paragraphs and each Level 1 paragraph has two Level 2 paragraphs, describe what the PowerPoint slides would look like if you used the outline to create them.

3. What is the advantage to being able to expand and collapse the different level paragraphs in an outline?

4. What is the difference between copying and pasting data from Access to Excel and exporting data from Access to Excel? Why would you copy and paste? When would you use an export?

5. Why would you want to export Access data to Excel?

Body text 982
Collapse button 982
Demote 982
Expand button 982

Level 1 982
Level 2 982
Outline 982
Outline view 982

Promote 982
Slide text 985

Work with a document in Outline view (p. 982)

Reorganize your outline (p. 984)

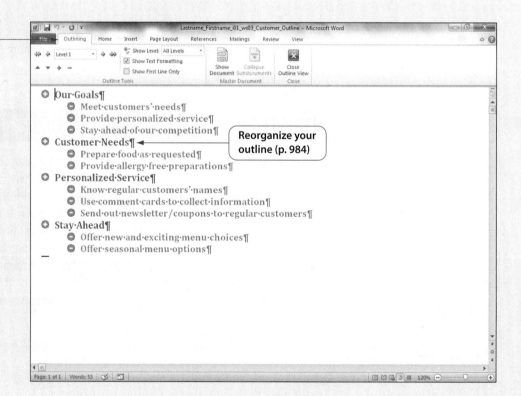

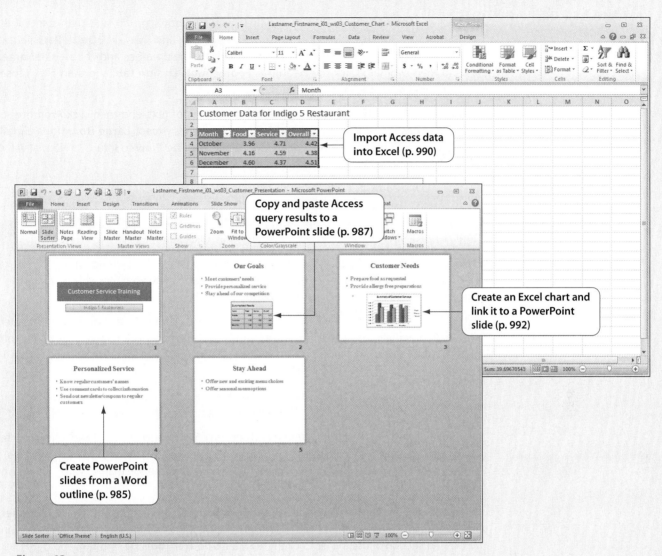

Figure 12   Restaurant Training Final

Practice 1

Student data files needed:

i01_ws03_Fundraiser_Outline

i01_ws03_Fundraiser_Presentation

i01_ws03_Fundraiser_Chart

i01_ws03_Fundraiser_Results

You will save your files as:

Lastname_Firstname_i01_ws03_Fundraiser_Outline

Lastname_Firstname_i01_ws03_Fundraiser_Presentation

Lastname_Firstname_i01_ws03_Fundraiser_Chart

Auction Fundraiser Summary

**General
Business**

Patti Rochelle, corporate event planner, has been asked to put together a presentation to summarize the recent Auction Fundraiser her group has coordinated. She has put together an outline in Word, and an Access database with donor information. Your assignment is to use the Word outline to create PowerPoint slides, and then import Access data into Excel to create charts to include in the presentation.

a.   Start **Word**. Click the **File tab**, click **Open** to locate your student folder, select **i01_ws03_Fundraiser_Outline**, and then click **Open**.

b.   Click the **File tab**, click **Save As**, and then navigate to where you are saving your files. Save the document as Lastname_Firstname_i01_ws03_Fundraiser_Outline, replacing Lastname_Firstname with your own name. Click **Save**.

c. Click the **Insert tab**, click **Footer** in the Header & Footer group, and then select **Edit Footer**. Click the **Header & Footer Tools Design tab**, and then click **Quick Parts** in the Insert group. Select **Field**, scroll through the list of field names and choose **FileName**, and then click **OK**. Click the **Header & Footer Tools Design tab**, and then click **Close Header and Footer** in the Close group.

d. Click the **View tab**, click **Outline**, select all the lines of text, and then click **Promote** so all the lines are promoted to Level 1. Demote all lines except **Large Donations**, **Small Donations Summary**, and **Donors**. Click **Close Outline View** to return to Normal view. Click **Save**. Close Word.

e. Start **PowerPoint**. Click the **File tab**, click **Open**, and then locate your student files. Select **i01_ws03_Fundraiser_Presentation**, and then click **Open**. Click the **File tab**, click **Save As**, navigate to where you are saving your files, and name the presentation Lastname_Firstname_i01_ws03_Fundraiser_Presentation. Click **Save**.

f. Click the **Home tab**, click the **New Slide arrow** in the Slides group, and then select **Slides from Outline**. Locate the folder where you are saving your files, select **Lastname_Firstname_i01_ws03_Fundraiser_Outline**, and then click **Insert**.

g. Click the **Insert tab**, and then click **Header & Footer** in the Text group. In the Header and Footer dialog box, click the **Notes and Handouts tab**. Click **Footer** to select it, and then type Lastname_Firstname_i01_ws03_Fundraiser_Presentation. Click **Apply to All**. Click **Save**.

h. Click **Minimize** to minimize the PowerPoint window to the taskbar. You need to keep PowerPoint open to complete the remainder of this workshop.

i. Start **Excel**, locate your student folder, and open **i01_ws03_Fundraiser_Chart**. Click the **File tab**, click **Save As**, navigate to where you are saving your files, and save the file as Lastname_Firstname_i01_ws03_Fundraiser_Chart, replacing Lastname_Firstname with your own name. Click **Save**.

j. Click the **Insert tab**, and then click **Header & Footer** in the Text group. Click the **Header & Footer Tools Design tab**, click **Go to Footer** in the Navigation group, and then click in the left section of the footer. Click the **Header & Footer Tools Design tab**, and then click **File Name** in the Header & Footer Elements group to enter the file name.

k. Click outside the footer area, and then click **Normal** on the status bar to return to the Normal view. Press Ctrl + Home to return to cell A1.

l. Select cell **A4**. Click the **Data tab**, and then click **From Access** in the Get External Data group. Locate your student folder, select **i01_ws03_Fundraiser_Results**, and then click **Open**.

m. If you do not see a Data Link Properties dialog box, then skip to Step o. In the Data Link Properties dialog box under the Connection tab, verify under Step 1 that the Data Source is **i01_ws03_Fundraiser_Results**. Under Step 2, verify that **Use a specific user name and password** is selected and that **Blank password** and **Allow saving password** options are selected. Click **OK**.

n. When prompted for a password, click **OK**. Because you had the Blank password option selected, no password is necessary to continue with this step.

o. In the Select Table dialog box, click **Summary of Amounts**, and then click **OK**. In the Import Data dialog box, verify that **Table** is selected, and that the Existing worksheet text box contains **=$A$4**. Click **OK**.

p. Select cells **B5:E7**. Click the **Home tab**, and then click **Accounting Number Format** in the Number group to format the numbers with a dollar sign and two decimal places.

q. Select cells **A4:B7** of the table. Click the **Insert tab**, click **Pie** in the Charts group, and then select **Pie in 3-D** under the 3-D Pie category. Move the chart so the top-left corner is in cell A9 and the bottom-right corner is in or close to cell E24.

r. Select the chart, and then edit the chart title to say Summary of Donor Values. Click the **Home tab**, and then click **Copy** in the Clipboard group. Click **Save**, and then click **Minimize** to minimize the Excel window to the taskbar.

s. Click the **PowerPoint button** on the taskbar to restore the PowerPoint window. Click **Slide 4** to select it. Click the **Home tab**, click the **Paste arrow** in the Clipboard group, and then select **Paste Special**. Click **Paste link**, choose **Microsoft Excel Chart Object**, and then click **OK**. Move the chart so it is to the right of the bullet points.

t. Click **Save**. Close PowerPoint and close Excel, saving changes if prompted.

Practice 2

Student data files needed:

i01_ws03_Wedding_Outline

i01_ws03_Wedding_Presentation

i01_ws03_Wedding_List

You will save your files as:

Lastname_Firstname_i01_ws03_Wedding_Outline

Lastname_Firstname_i01_ws03_Wedding_Presentation

Wedding Presentation

Customer
Service

The staff in the event planning group has been asked to create a PowerPoint presentation for an upcoming wedding. The bride and groom, who both work for the airline industry and love geography, have a Word outline listing the topics they want in the presentation. They also have an Access database with the guest list. Your assignment is to create a PowerPoint presentation from the Word outline and insert a query table into the presentation to show how many guests, by state, will be at the wedding.

a. Start **Word**. Click the **File tab**, click **Open**, and then locate your student folder. Select **i01_ws03_Wedding_Outline**, and then click **Open**.

b. Click the **File tab**, click **Save As**, navigate to where you are saving your files, and then save the document as Lastname_Firstname_i01_ws03_Wedding_Outline, replacing Lastname_Firstname with your own name. Click **Save**.

c. Click the **Insert tab**, click **Footer** in the Header & Footer group, and then select **Edit Footer**. Click the **Header & Footer Tools Design tab**, click **Quick Parts** in the Insert group, select **Field**, scroll through the list of field names, and then select **FileName**. Click **OK**. Click the **Header & Footer Tools Design tab**, and then click **Close Header and Footer** in the Close group.

d. Select the first line **The Bride**, click the **Home tab**, and then click **Heading 1** in the Styles group. Repeat for the following lines: **The Groom, The Bridal Party**, and **Our Guests**. Select the remaining lines, and then apply the style **Heading 2**. Click **Save**. Close Word.

e. Start **PowerPoint**. Click the **File tab**, click **Open**, and then locate your student files. Select **i01_ws03_Wedding_Presentation**, and then click **Open**. Click the **File tab**, click **Save As**, navigate to where you are saving your files, name the presentation Lastname_Firstname_i01_ws03_Wedding_Presentation, and then click **Save**.

f. Click the **Home tab**, click the **New Slide arrow** in the Slides group, and then select **Slides from Outline**. Locate the folder where you are saving your files, select **Lastname_Firstname_i01_ws03_Wedding_Outline**, and then click **Insert**.

g. Click the **Insert tab**, click **Header & Footer** in the Text group, and then in the Header and Footer dialog box, click the **Notes and Handouts tab**. Click **Footer** to select it, and then type Lastname_Firstname_i01_ws03_Wedding_Presentation. Click **Apply to All**. Click **Save**.

h. Click **Minimize** to minimize the PowerPoint window to the taskbar. You will need to keep PowerPoint open to complete this workshop.

i. Start **Access**. Click the **File tab**, click **Open**, locate your student folder, and then select **i01_ws03_Wedding_List**. Click **Open**, and then click **Enable Content** in the Security Warning bar.

j. In the Navigation Pane, double-click the query **States Represented** to open it in Datasheet view.

k. Click **Select All** at the top left of the query datasheet to select all the records in the query datasheet.

l. Click the **Home tab**, and then click **Copy** in the Clipboard group. Close Access.

m. Click the **PowerPoint button** on the taskbar to restore the PowerPoint window. Click **Slide 5** to select it. Click the **Home tab**, and then click **Paste** in the Clipboard group. Resize the columns starting with the first column on the left. Move the table so it is to the right of the text. Resize the text box with the bullet point to fit the text to the left of the table.

n. Select the table, click the **Table Tools Design tab**, and then select the **Themed Style 2-Accent 1** style in the Table Styles group to apply to the table.

o. Click **Save**. Close PowerPoint.

Problem Solve 1

Student data files needed:	You will save your files as:
i01_ps1_Shop_Outline	Lastname_Firstname_i01_ps1_Shop_Outline
i01_ps1_Shop_Presentation	Lastname_Firstname_i01_ps1_Shop_Presentation
i01_ps1_Shop_List	Lastname_Firstname_i01_ps1_Shop_Chart

Vendor Presentation

Sales & Marketing

The manager for Painted Treasures Gift Shop has to give a sales presentation to the resort board of directors for the month of January. There is an existing Access database with information on items sold as well as a Word outline with the basic information for the presentation. Your assignment is to create a PowerPoint presentation from the Word outline, copy Access query results into the presentation, and finally import the Access data into Excel to create a chart for the presentation.

a. Start **Word**, and then open the file **i01_ps1_Shop_Outline**. Save the file as Lastname_Firstname_i01_ps1_Shop_Outline. Insert a left-aligned footer with the file name.

b. Promote and demote the paragraphs so **January Trends, January Sales by Category**, and **February Strategy** are all Level 1 paragraphs. The other paragraphs should all be Level 2. Close Outline view, save, and close the file.

c. Start **PowerPoint**, and open **i01_ps1_Shop_Presentation**. Save the presentation as Lastname_Firstname_i01_ps1_Shop_Presentation. Insert a **Notes and Handouts footer** with the file name, and then apply to all pages. Insert new slides using the file **Lastname_Firstname_i01_ps1_Shop_Outline**.

d. Start **Excel**, open a new workbook, and save it as Lastname_Firstname_i01_ps1_Shop_Chart. Insert a footer in the left section with the file name. Save the workbook.

e. Get external data from the query **January Sales** in the Access database **i01_ps1_Shop_List**. Insert the table in cell **A1**. Format cells **B2:B9** with the **Accounting Number Format**. Create a **3-D Clustered Column Chart** from the data table. Change the chart title to January Sales. Move the chart below the data table. Copy the chart to the Clipboard. Save the workbook, and then minimize Excel.

f. Click **PowerPoint** on the taskbar, select **Slide 3**, and then paste the Excel chart as a link. Move the chart so it fits well on the slide and all the text is visible. Save the presentation, and then minimize PowerPoint.

g. Start **Access**, open **i01_ps1_Shop_List**, and then **Enable Content**. Copy the **January Sales** query results to the Clipboard. Close Access. Paste the table onto Slide 2 in the PowerPoint presentation. Resize the columns, and then apply a style to the table. Move the chart so it fits well on the slide and all the text is visible. Save the presentation. Close PowerPoint.

h. Close Excel.

Perform 1: Perform in Your Career

Student data file needed:

None

You will save your files as:

Lastname_Firstname_i01_pf1_Grant_Outline
Lastname_Firstname_i01_pf1_Grant_Presentation
Lastname_Firstname_i01_pf1_Grant_Schools
Lastname_Firstname_i01_pf1_Grant_Chart

Grant Presentation

General Business

You are the director of a new and innovative high school and are looking for ways to increase the technology available to your students. You come across a grant that would pay for netbooks for each of your students to use throughout the school year. Your goal is to become a leading school in technology, and you have Access data that shows how most schools are lacking in this area. Along with writing the grant, you need to create a presentation for the school board with the grant proposal information. The project name is Student Technology Grant Proposal. The grant presentation must include the following information:

- An Introduction to your school with background information and a mission statement
- A Project Summary of what your project is and its most important benefit
- A Problem Statement that identifies the problems the project will address, including statistics
- A list of Key Benefits the project will add to your school
- A Statement of Work explaining the items and resources required
- A Budget for the project

a. Start **Word**, and then create a Word outline that will eventually become your PowerPoint slides. You must have all the preceding bulleted information in your presentation. There should be Level 1 and Level 2 paragraphs for each slide. Insert a left-aligned footer that includes the file name. Save the document as Lastname_Firstname_i01_pf1_Grant_Outline.

b. Start **PowerPoint**, and then create slides from the Word outline created in Step a. Add a title and subtitle to the presentation. Insert a footer into Notes and Handout view with the file name. Apply a theme to the presentation. Save the presentation as Lastname_Firstname_i01_pf1_Grant_Presentation.

c. Start **Access**, and then create a new database called Lastname_Firstname_i01_pf1_Grant_Schools. Add the following fields after the ID field: **School Name**, **School Enrollment**, and **Computer Ratio**. Add at least 12 records to fill in this table. The first record should have your Firstname and Lastname as the School Name. The records should show that the minimum Computer Ratio is 4:1. That is, all records should be 4:1, 5:1, or higher. Copy all the records in the Access table, and then paste it into the appropriate slide in your PowerPoint presentation. Resize the columns and apply a style to the table. Save the presentation.

d. Start **Excel**, and then create a budget for the project. Assume there are 426 students. Include the cost of the actual computer, the cost of any additional hardware or software, and the estimated cost of maintenance per student and for the total project. Create a chart for the data. Insert a footer in the left section that includes the file name. Save the worksheet as Lastname_Firstname_i01_pf1_Grant_Chart.

e. Link the Excel data and the chart to a slide in your PowerPoint presentation.

f. Save the PowerPoint presentation. Close all the applications.

Perform 2: How Others Perform

Student data files needed:

i01_pf2_Class_Presentation
i01_pf2_Class_Outline
i01_pf2_Class_Enrollment

You will save your files as:

Lastname_Firstname_i01_pf2_Class_Outline
Lastname_Firstname_i01_pf2_Class_Presentation
Lastname_Firstname_i01_pf2_Class_Charts

Presentation Gone Wrong

General
Business

Your coworker at Classes For You, a computer training company, needed to put together a presentation to show how many students have signed up for classes in May. He created an outline in Word and tried to make PowerPoint slides from it, but he ended up with a slide for each class, instead of a slide for each series. The series are *Office Series*, *Basic Computer Series*, and *Special Series*. When students enroll in a class, their data is entered in an Access database. Queries have been created to track the number of students in each class and in each series of classes. Your coworker would like to import this data into Excel to create charts, but he cannot do that until his slides are correct.

a. Start **PowerPoint**, and then open **i01_pf2_Class_Presentation**.
   • Look at how the slides were created from the Word outline.
   • Open **i01_pf2_Class_Outline**.
   • Why did the outline create the slides in the presentation the way it did?

b. Fix the Word outline so the three series names will be the titles on three different slides and the class names will be the details on each slide.
   • Save the file as Lastname_Firstname_i01_pf2_Class_Outline.
   • Insert a left-aligned footer with the file name, and then save the document.

c. Create a new PowerPoint presentation, and save it as Lastname_Firstname_i01_pf2_Class_Presentation. Use the outline **Lastname_Firstname_i01_pf2_Class_Outline** to create the slides. There should be three slides from the Word outline and a title slide.
   • Add an appropriate title and subtitle to slide 1.
   • Insert a Notes and Handout footer with the file name. Save the presentation.

d. Open a new Excel workbook, and save it as Lastname_Firstname_i01_pf2_Class_Charts.
   • Change the orientation to Landscape and the width to 1 page.
   • Insert a footer in the left section with the file name.
   • Import data from the file **i01_pf2_Class_Enrollment**. Import from the three tables: Basic Computer Series classes, Office Series classes, and Special Series classes.
   • Create a column chart for each table. Change the chart titles to match the name of the tables. Save the workbook.

e. Open the presentation from Step c. Link the charts to the appropriate slide in the PowerPoint presentation. What is the advantage to importing the data rather than just copying and pasting? Save the presentation.

Integrated Projects

Objectives

1. Collect Access data using e-mail data collection forms   p. 1002

2. Manage e-mail replies   p. 1006

3. E-mail collected Access data   p. 1008

4. Other e-mail options using PowerPoint and Word   p. 1010

5. Use mail merge to send an e-mail in Outlook   p. 1012

Integrating Word, PowerPoint, Access, Excel, and Outlook

PREPARE CASE
Restaurant Survey Data Collection

Customer Service

Krishna Vargas, a server manager at Indigo 5 Restaurant, has to put together a new program to collect customer surveys about the restaurant's service and food. He sends an e-mail to customers who have provided their e-mail addresses to the restaurant. The e-mail consists of a short form the customer fills out, rating service on a scale of 1–5. When the customer replies to the e-mail, the data is automatically added to an existing Access database table.

Paul Vinten / Shutterstock.com

Once the most recent data has been collected, Krishna e-mails the results to Alberto Dimas, the restaurant manager. He always sends the Access data as an Excel workbook with a chart added for a visual display of the data.

Finally, Krishna sends all the customers who have responded to the survey a personalized e-mail with a coupon to use in the restaurant as a thank-you for completing the survey.

Krishna needs your help to send out the customer e-mail collection form, send the data that has been collected in the Access table as an Excel workbook to Alberto Dimas, and then send the coupon by e-mail using mail merge.

Student data files needed:

 i01_ws04_Survey

 i01_ws04_Survey_Responses

 i01_ws04_Survey_Presentation

 i01_ws04_Survey_Email

You will save your files as:

 Lastname_Firstname_i01_ws04_Survey

 Lastname_Firstname_i01_ws04_Survey_Responses

 Lastname_Firstname_i01_ws04_Survey_Chart

 Lastname_Firstname_i01_ws04_Survey_Presentation

 Lastname_Firstname_i01_ws04_Survey_Theme

 Lastname_Firstname_i01_ws04_Survey_Template

 Lastname_Firstname_i01_ws04_Survey_Email

 Personal e-mails (2) for the data collection forms sent

Create Data Collection Forms

Using Microsoft Outlook, you can easily collect or update information by e-mail and have that data automatically stored in Access. For example, you can send out a survey form through e-mail for your recipients to fill out. When the e-mail is returned with the form filled in, the results are saved in a new folder created in Outlook, and the data can be automatically added to an Access table that you have created. An exception to this is if the recipient replies through Hotmail, Yahoo!, or Google, in which case the data cannot be added to the table. E-mail addresses for the recipients can come from your Outlook address book or a field in an Access table from the same database used for data collection. In this section, you will create a data collection form to add data to an existing Access table.

> **CONSIDER THIS** | **Different E-mail Providers**
>
> Data can be collected only if the sender and the recipient are using Outlook and the recipient replies from their Outlook program. What options do you have if you are not sure what e-mail program the recipient is using?

Collect Access Data Using E-mail Data Collection Forms

Before you can collect data through an e-mail message, both Access 2007 or later and Outlook 2007 or later must be installed on the sender's computer. Outlook must be configured to send and receive e-mail, so if you have never used Outlook before, you must start Outlook and follow the Startup Wizard's instructions.

Data is collected using either an **HTML form** or an **InfoPath form**. If you plan on using an InfoPath form, then you must also have InfoPath 2007 or later installed on both the sender's and recipient's computers. If you do not have InfoPath installed on your computer, you will not have the option to use an InfoPath form.

Data is collected and saved in an existing database. If you do not have an existing database you must create one before you can proceed with the data collection. The tables in the database must meet the requirements for accepting form data. Attachment, AutoNumber, OLE, and Lookup field types cannot be used for data collection. Collected data can only be placed in one table, so if you need data to fill multiple tables in the same database, you would have to do a select query and use that to collect the data.

When setting up the data collection process, you can choose whether to add new records to a table or update existing records. If your table has existing records, then you will specify for Outlook to add new records to the table. If your table is empty, then Outlook will assume you want to add new records.

Using the Data Collection Wizard

To begin the data collection process, you will open the **Data Collection Wizard** in Access. The wizard will walk you through the steps necessary to create a data collection form.

Before you start the wizard, you should consider the steps involved in setting up the data collection form and be prepared to tell the wizard how you want to handle each step and the various options offered.

Step 1: Choose the Type of Data Entry Form to Use

An Access form cannot be used to collect data. You must choose between an HTML form and an InfoPath form. An InfoPath form offers better data entry options and is easier to edit. Unfortunately, it can only be used if both the sender and recipient have InfoPath installed on their computers. An HTML form can be created and used by any user whose e-mail supports HTML; however, data collected from Hotmail or Yahoo! cannot be automatically added to the

Access database table. From this point forward, this textbook assumes you will be using an HTML data entry form and that both sender and recipient are using Outlook for their e-mail.

Step 2: Choose Whether to Collect New Data or Update Existing Data

A **data collection form** is used to collect new data from the recipient or to update existing data. If the form is for collecting new data, then the user will complete the form, and the results will be input for an Access table. If the form is for updating existing data, then the recipient will be provided data that is currently in the database and will be asked to make changes to the data using the form. The existing data in the table will be updated with the new data the recipient provides.

You can usually choose whether to collect new data or update existing data, but there will be some cases where you will only be able to collect new data:

- When you are collecting data to populate two or more tables
- When the table you are using does not have a primary key field
- When the table you are using does not have any existing records
- When the e-mail addresses of the recipients are not stored as a field in one of the database tables

Step 3: Specify the Data You Want to Collect

You can usually select the fields you want to include in the form. There are two exceptions: fields that have the Required property set to Yes will automatically be included, and unsupported fields (AutoNumber, Attachment, OLE Object, or multivalued Lookup fields) cannot be included.

Deciding whether to include a primary key field in the data collection form depends on whether or not the field is an AutoNumber field type. The only time you will include a primary key field in a data collection form is when you are collecting new data. If the recipient enters a value in a primary key field that is already included in the table, then their reply will not be processed.

Step 4: Specify Whether You Want to Automatically or Manually Process the Data

To process data, either manually or automatically, from the e-mails you receive, the following criteria must be met:

- Outlook must already be open and running on your computer
- Access must be installed on your computer (but does not have to be running)
- The database you are adding records to must not be password protected or be open in Exclusive mode. The database must also be named the same and be located in the same place as when you sent the original data collection e-mail.
- The names of the tables and queries as well as the field properties of the fields included in the form must not have changed since the original data collection e-mail was sent.

If you choose to process the replies manually, then you will be required to start the export operation to transfer the data to the Access table. Manually updating the database requires you to select each reply in Outlook and select the Export option.

If you choose to process the replies automatically, then Access and Outlook will work together as the e-mails are received, and the data will be exported without any additional steps by you. When you choose to automatically process the replies you can also choose how many replies to process at once, and when to start and stop the automatic processing to avoid e-mails being processed when you are not expecting them.

Step 5: Select Where the Recipients' E-mail Addresses Are Located

The e-mail addresses you use for collecting data can be stored in the database or in your address book. You have the option of using a field in the database, typing each e-mail individually in the e-mail message, or selecting e-mails from your address book. The only time e-mail addresses must be stored in the database is if you are updating records.

Krishna needs you to create a data collection form to send to these customers so they can fill out a short survey rating the restaurant. When the customers reply to the e-mail the data is automatically added to the table. As a test, you will add your own personal data into the table, and send a collection form to yourself to make sure the form looks the way you expect.

To Send a Collection Form

a. Start **Access**. Click the **File tab**, and click **Open**. Locate your student folder and select **i01_ws04_Survey**. Click **Open**. Click the **File tab**, and click **Save Database As**. In the Save As dialog box, navigate to where you are saving your files. In the File name box, type Lastname_Firstname_i01_ws04_Survey, replacing Lastname_Firstname with your own name. Click **Save**. If necessary, click **Enable Content** in the Security Warning bar.

b. Double-click the **Customer List** table in the Navigation Pane to open it in Datasheet view.

c. Add a record at the end of the table with your Firstname and Lastname, your e-mail address, and the month December. Press ⎡Tab⎤ four times until the record selector is on the next line and your record has been added to the table.

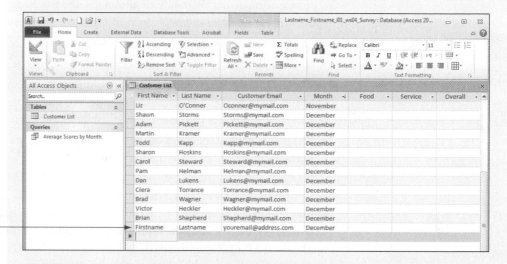

Your record added to the table

Figure 1 Customer List table with your name added

d. Click the **External Data tab**, and then click **Create E-Mail** in the Collect Data group. Read the steps involved in creating a data collection e-mail, and then click **Next**.

e. Select **HTML form**, and then click **Next**.

f. Click **All Fields** [>>], and then click **Next**.

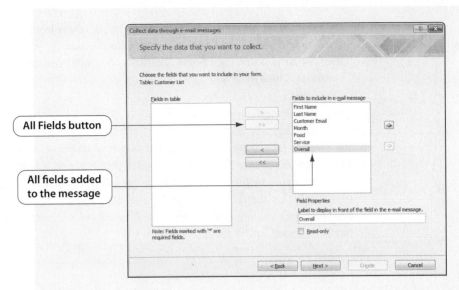

All Fields button

All fields added to the message

Figure 2 Data Collection Wizard—Specify the data you want to collect

g. Click **Automatically process replies and add data to Customer List** to select it, and then click **Next**.

h. Select **Use the e-mail addresses stored in a field in the database**, and then click **Next**.

i. Make sure **The current table or query** is selected and **Customer Email** is listed in the field box, and then click **Next**.

j. In the Subject box, type Customer Feedback Requested. In the Introduction box, type Thank you for visiting Indigo 5. If you would take a moment to fill out the following short survey we would appreciate your feedback. Please rate the food, service, and your overall visit on a scale of 1 to 5, with 5 being Outstanding, 4 being Great, 3 being Just OK, 2 being Not Very Good, and 1 being Unacceptable. For your time, if you make sure your name and e-mail address are up to date, we will send you a thank-you coupon by e-mail once your response is processed. Click **Next**, read the messages in the wizard dialog box, and then click **Next** again.

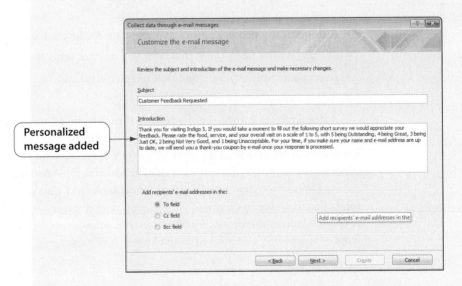

Personalized message added

Figure 3 Review subject and introduction to e-mail message

k. Click the **Select All** check box to clear the check marks from the contact list, and then scroll to find your e-mail address listed. Click the **box** for your e-mail address to send the form to yourself. Click **Send**. The dialog box will close once the sending process is complete. **Close** Access.

Troubleshooting

Did you see your name listed in the list of e-mail addresses when you went through the wizard? Make sure that when you enter your name as a new record, you actually enter the record by pressing Tab or Enter. If the pencil 🖉 is still visible in the row selector for the record with your name, then the record has not been added to the table, and you are still in edit mode. The wizard will not find your record until it has been added to the table.

Managing E-mail Replies

To respond to your e-mail, the recipient will click Reply, fill out the form, and then click Send. The replies will come to a new folder created in your Outlook account called **Access Data Collection Replies** so you can see all the replies in one place. In Access, if the reply is successful, the status of the reply in the Manage Data Collection Messages dialog box will be *Collecting data using e-mail was successful*.

You can open a reply in the Access Data Collection Replies folder in Outlook to see how the reply looks from the recipient. The replies cannot be replied to, re-sent, or forwarded. To ask for more information, a new data collection form must be sent or the original must be re-sent to the recipients.

By default, Outlook will process 25 messages automatically. If you need more messages processed, you must change this under Message Options. You can also set a date and time to stop automatic message processing. This option is helpful when you want to prevent a recipient from replying when you are not expecting it. Other import settings you can turn on or off include the following:

- Automatically process replies and add data to the database
- Discard replies from those to whom you did not send the message
- Accept multiple replies from each recipient
- Allow multiple rows per reply

A data collection form can be re-sent through the Manage Data Collection Messages dialog box. You can also delete a message, send the message to new users, or choose a different e-mail address field for your recipients. If the Resend this E-Mail Message button is not available, then you will have to **synchronize** your message settings with Outlook. Access checks to make sure the destination table and query still exist and includes the forms you included in the message. If Access does not find any problems with the table(s), it resynchronizes the message and allows you to re-send it, but if Access does find problems, you will be prompted to resynchronize the message.

Real World Advice   Maintaining a Database

When data collection is done in Access, it is important not to make changes to the field names, sizes, or data types in the table you are using for data collection. If Access cannot find a field to put the collected data in, or if the table cannot be found, then you will not be able to re-send the message or the data will not be able to be added to the table. It is important to have one person maintain a database that is being used for data collection so these problems do not arise.

In this case, you will change the number of messages to automatically process at one time, and then re-send the e-mail. You will choose yourself as the only recipient to make sure it works the way you want it to.

To Manage E-mail Replies

a. **Start** Access. Click the **File tab**, and click **Open**. Navigate to where you are saving your files and click **Lastname_Firstname_i01_ws04_Survey**. Click **Open**. If necessary, click **Enable Content** in the Security Warning bar. Double-click the **Customer List** table in the Navigation Pane to open it in Datasheet view.

b. Click the **External Data tab**, and then click **Manage Replies** in the Collect Data group. If necessary, click on the Message details **The settings of this e-mail message must be synchronized with Microsoft Outlook. Click to synchronize now**. to synchronize the settings.

c. In the Select a Data Collection message box, select **Customer Feedback Requested**.

Select message here ⟶

Message Options button ⟶

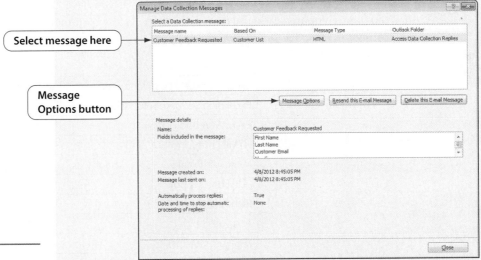

Figure 4 Manage Data Collection Messages dialog box

d. Click **Message Options**. Change the **Number of replies to be processed** to **30** and then click **OK**.

e. Click **Resend this E-mail Message**. Verify that **Automatically process replies and add data to Customer List** is selected, and then click **Next**.

SIDE NOTE

Number of Replies

When processing replies, the higher the number, the longer it will take for Outlook to actually complete the send. Would there be an advantage to sending out smaller groups rather than all at once? Why?

f. Click **Use the e-mail addresses stored in a field in the database**, and then click **Next**.

g. Verify that **The current table or query** is selected and **Customer Email** is selected in the box, and then click **Next**.

h. In the Introduction box, type If you have already replied to our previous e-mail, please disregard this. We apologize if you received duplicate e-mails. Click **Next**, and then click **Next** again.

i. Click the **Select All** check box to clear the check marks from the contact list, and then scroll to find your e-mail address listed. Click **your e-mail address** to send the form to yourself, and then click **Send**. The dialog box will close once the sending process is complete. Click **Close**, and then **Close** [×] Access.

Real World Advice — Send a Test E-mail

When you are sending out a mass e-mail with a data collection form, you should test it on yourself first by sending it and then replying to it. This is the simplest way to find out if it really works before you send it to everyone on your list. You can always delete any records that are added from your test reply before you send out the real data collection form.

E-mail Collected Access Data

Once data is collected and is in a new or existing table, the data can be managed like any other data in Access. One option is to e-mail the data to someone. The data can be sent directly from Access through Outlook as long as you have Outlook and Access installed on your computer. When data is sent from Access by e-mail, it is sent as an **attached object** in one of the formats listed in Figure 5.

Excel 97–Excel 2003 Workbook (.xls)
Excel Binary Workbook (.xlsb)
Excel Workbook (.xlsx)
HTML (.htm, .html)
Microsoft Excel 5.0/95 Workbook (.xls)
PDF Format (.pdf)
Rich Text Format (.rtf)
Text Files (.txt)
XPS Format (.xps)

Figure 5 Formats available for sending output from Access through e-mail

Sending Data as an Excel Workbook

In this exercise, all the replies have been received and added to the Customer List table. The database you will start with is identical to i01_ws04_Survey except that it has the results from the data collection form. You need to send an e-mail to the restaurant manager, Alberto Dimas, with the summarized data in an Excel workbook. Note for this case you will send the e-mail to yourself as a test so you can view and print the message.

To E-mail Data as an Excel Workbook

a. Start **Access**. Click the **File tab**, and click **Open**. Click the disk drive in the left pane where your student data files are located. Navigate through the folder structure and click **i01_ws04_Survey_Responses**. Click **Open**. Click the **File tab**, and click **Save Database As**. In the Save As dialog box, navigate to where you are saving your files. In the File name box, type Lastname_Firstname_i01_ws04_Survey_Responses, replacing Lastname_Firstname with your own name, and then click **Save**. Click **Enable Content** in the Security Warning bar.

b. Double-click the **Customer List** table in the Navigation Pane to open it. Add a record at the end with your Firstname and Lastname, your e-mail address, the month December, and a 5 for each of the three columns Food, Service, and Overall. Press Tab to move to a new row and add the record to the table.

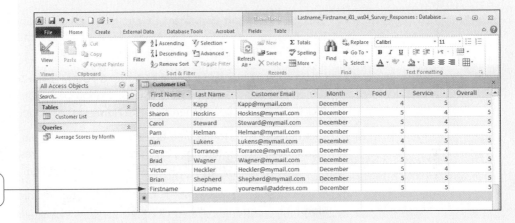

New record added with your data

Figure 6 Customer List table with your name and data added

c. Double-click the **Average Scores by Month** query in the Navigation Pane to open it in Datasheet view. Click the **External Data tab**, and then click **E-mail** in the Export group.

d. Select **Excel Workbook (*.xlsx)** as the output format. This will send the Access query results as an Excel workbook attachment. Click **OK**.

e. An Outlook Message window opens with the Excel workbook attached. In the To box, type your e-mail address. In the Subject box, type Summary of Customer Surveys. In the message area, type Alberto, and press Enter twice. Type I've attached the last quarter survey summary for your review. Please let me know if you have any questions. Press Enter twice. Type your Firstname and Lastname.

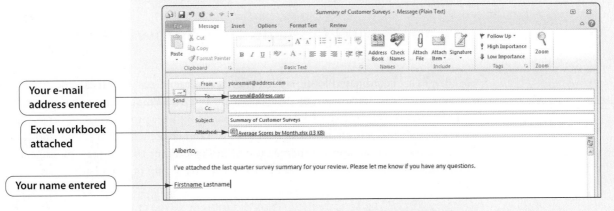

Your e-mail address entered

Excel workbook attached

Your name entered

Figure 7 Outlook Message window with Excel attachment

f. Right-click the **Average Scores by Month** attachment in the Attachment line, and then click **Open**. Click **Enable Editing** in the Protected view message bar.

g. Select cells **A1** through **D4**. Click the **Insert tab**, click **Column** in the Charts group, and then select **3-D Clustered Column**. Click the **Design tab**, and then click **Switch Row/Column** in the Data group so the columns represent the areas being reviewed.

Figure 8 Creating an Excel chart from Access query data

h. Click the **Layout tab**, click **Chart Title** in the Labels group, and then select **Above Chart**. Type Average Survey Scores by Month and press Enter. Move the chart so the top-left corner is in cell A6. Click outside the chart.

i. Click the **Insert tab**, and then click **Header & Footer** in the Text group. Click the **Design tab**, and then click **Go to Footer** in the Navigation group. Click in the **left footer section**, click the **Design tab**, and then click **File Name** in the Header & Footer Elements group.

j. Click outside of the footer area, and then click **Normal** 🖼 in the bottom-right corner of the window, on the status bar, to return to Normal view. Press Ctrl+Home to return to cell A1. Click **Save** 🖫 on the Quick Access Toolbar, and then **Close** ✖ Excel.

k. In the Outlook message window, right-click the attached file name **Average Scores by Month.xlsx**, and then click **Save As**. Save the file as Lastname_Firstname_i01_ws04_Survey_Chart, replacing Lastname_Firstname with your own name. Click **Save**. In the Message window, click **Send**, and then **Close** ✖ Access.

Real World Advice 　　Access Data as an E-mail Attachment

Sending an e-mail attachment with Access data formatted as some other object can be extremely helpful because not everyone has Access installed on their computers. It is also helpful because you can modify the data with formatting or charts before you send it. It is almost like a shortcut to importing data from Access to Excel.

Other E-mail Options Using PowerPoint and Word

Themes are coordinated fonts, colors, effects, and backgrounds you can add to a presentation, workbook, document, or even an e-mail. In PowerPoint there are a number of built-in themes you can use to make your correspondence look professional and coordinated. If you cannot find a built-in theme you like, you can create a custom theme and save it for future use. You can apply a theme created in PowerPoint to an e-mail message and then use Mail Merge in Word to send a mass e-mail to a group of e-mail addresses.

Use a Custom Theme in E-mail

Because themes are saved independent from the program they are created in, themes can be created in one program and easily used in another. This means a theme created in PowerPoint can easily be saved and then applied to an e-mail message in Outlook. This can be helpful if you are giving a presentation and want to carry the theme of your presentation to an e-mail invitation sent to those who are attending your event. Or maybe you have a color theme for your business that you use for letterhead and other correspondence and you want to apply this to a mass e-mail you are sending to your customers.

Creating a Custom Theme in PowerPoint

In Office 2010, themes and templates are managed in a similar way. Because a template is a saved collection of fonts, colors, effects, and backgrounds, you can use a template or a theme to apply to your e-mail message. In this exercise, Krishna, the restaurant manager, likes to have his correspondence look professional and follow a coordinated theme. He has created a PowerPoint presentation with a theme he would like you to use for the e-mail coupon that will be sent to the customers. You will save this theme as a custom theme to be used in other documents. You will also save the presentation as a template, so Krishna will have the option to use either the theme or template in other documents.

To Create a Custom Theme in PowerPoint

a. Start **PowerPoint**. Click the **File tab**, click **Open**, then locate your student folder and select **i01_ws04_Survey_Presentation**. Click **Open**. Click the **File tab**, and click **Save As**. In the Save As dialog box, navigate to the location where you are saving your files. In the File name box, type Lastname_Firstname_i01_ws04_Survey_Presentation, replacing Lastname_Firstname with your own name. Click **Save**.

b. Click the **Insert tab**, and then click **Header & Footer** in the Text group. Add a footer with the file name in the Notes and Handouts tab. Click **Apply to All**.

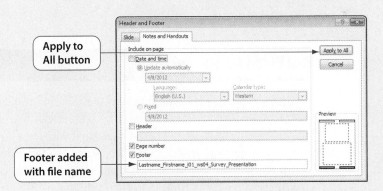

Figure 9 Header and Footer dialog box

c. Click the **Design tab**, click **More** ▾ for the Themes Gallery in the Themes group, and then select **Save Current Theme**.

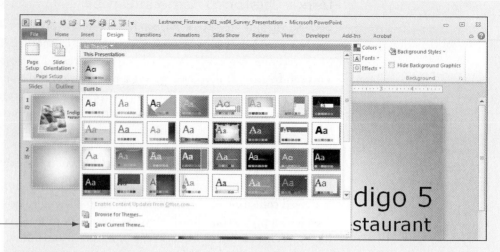

Figure 10 Themes Gallery

d. In the Save Current Theme dialog box, navigate to where you are saving your files. In the File name box, type Lastname_Firstname_i01_ws04_Survey_Theme, replacing Lastname_Firstname with your own name, and then click **Save**.

e. Click the **File tab**, and then click **Save As**. In the Save as type list, select **PowerPoint Template**, and navigate to the location where you are saving your files. In the File name box, type Lastname_Firstname_i01_ws04_Survey_Template, replacing Lastname_Firstname with your own name, and then click **Save**.

f. Click the **Insert tab**, and then click **Header & Footer** in the Text group. Click the **Notes and Handouts tab**, and then change the **Footer** to Lastname_Firstname_i01_ws04_Survey_Template, replacing Lastname_Firstname with your own name. Click **Apply to All**, and then click **Save** 🖫.

g. Click the **File tab**, and then click **Close** ❌. **Close** ❌ PowerPoint.

Real World Advice ▶ Saving Templates

When you save a theme or template, they are saved in special folders so Microsoft Windows can find them and show them automatically when you are searching for themes or templates. This is the folder that will come up as the default folder. For this case, you will save both the theme and the template to the folder where you are saving your files so you can find them easily. Normally, you would want to save each of them in the default folder so Microsoft Windows can find them.

Use Mail Merge to Send an E-mail

You can use Mail Merge to send a personalized mass e-mail message to a list of e-mails in your address book or in another location such as an Access table. Each e-mail is sent individually, so the recipient only sees their e-mail address in the To line. If you are using an Access database for the mail merge, then any fields in the tables and/or queries may be used to personalize the message.

Using Access Data to Create an E-mail Mail Merge in Outlook

To mail merge a letter in Outlook, certain conditions must be met:

- You must have an e-mail program that is **MAPI (Messaging Application Program Interface)** compatible. This is what makes it possible for Outlook and Word to share information about the merged e-mail.

- You must have the same versions of Outlook and Word.

- You cannot add recipients to the Cc line of the e-mail message. Only addresses listed in the To line are recognized.

In this exercise, you will create an e-mail message in mail merge and apply a PowerPoint custom theme so it will look consistent with other restaurant correspondence.

To Create an E-mail Using Mail Merge with Access Data

a. Start **Word**. Click the **File tab**, click **Open**, and then click the disk drive in the left pane where your student data files are located. Navigate through the folder structure and click **i01_ws04_Survey_Email**. Click **Open**.

b. Click the **Page Layout tab**, click **Themes** in the Themes group, and then select **Browse for Themes**. Click the disk drive in the left pane where your files are located. Navigate through the folder structure and click **Lastname_Firstname_i01_ws04_Survey_ Theme**. Click **Open**. Notice that the font changes in the e-mail message to match the theme's font.

c. Click the **Mailings tab**, and then click **Start Mail Merge** in the Start Mail Merge group. Select **E-mail Messages**. This switches the document to Web Layout view.

d. Click the **Mailings tab**, click **Select Recipients** in the Start Mail Merge group, and then select **Use Existing List**. Locate the folder where you are saving your files and select **Lastname_Firstname_i01_ws04_Survey_Responses**, and then click **Open**. If necessary, in the Confirm Data Source dialog box, select **OLE DB Database Files** in the Open data source list box and click **OK**. Select the **Customer List** table, and then click **OK**.

SIDE NOTE
Changing Themes
When you change the theme, the difference may be subtle depending on the theme settings. In this case, the only change you see is a different font. The original font was Calibri (Body), and the new font should be TW Cen MT (Body).

Customer List table selected

Figure 11 Select Customer List table

e. Place the insertion point in the blank line after **This coupon entitles**. Click the **Mailings tab**, and then click the **Insert Merge Field arrow** in the Write & Insert Fields group. Select **First_Name** to insert the field in the document, and then press [Spacebar]. Repeat to insert **Last_Name**.

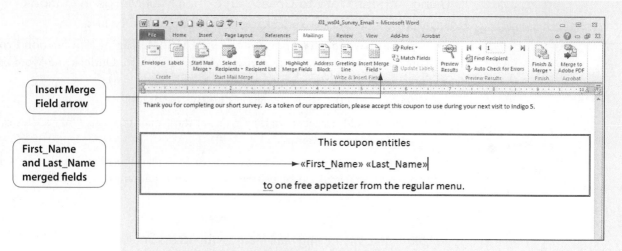

Insert Merge Field arrow

First_Name and Last_Name merged fields

Thank you for completing our short survey. As a token of our appreciation, please accept this coupon to use during your next visit to Indigo 5.

This coupon entitles

«First_Name» «Last_Name»

to one free appetizer from the regular menu.

Figure 12 Insert Merge Field button

f. Click the **Mailings tab**, and then click **Edit Recipient List** in the Start Mail Merge group. Click the **Data Source check box** to clear all recipients listed. Scroll through the list of names to find your name and e-mail address. Click the check box next to your name and e-mail address so the e-mail will be sent to only you. Click **OK**.

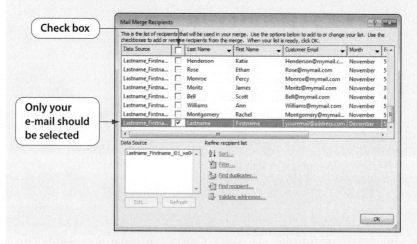

Check box

Only your e-mail should be selected

Figure 13 Mail Merge Recipients with only your name selected

g. Click the **Mailings tab**, and then click **Finish & Merge** in the Finish group. Select **Send E-mail Messages**.

h. In the Merge to E-mail dialog box, click the **To** arrow, and then select **Customer_Email**. In the Subject line box type Thank you from Indigo 5, and then click **OK**.

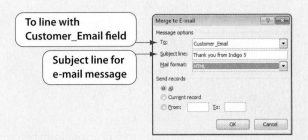

To line with
Customer_Email field

Subject line for
e-mail message

Figure 14 Merge to E-mail dialog box

i. Click the **Mailings tab**, and then click **Finish & Merge** in the Finish group. Select **Edit Individual Documents**, click **Current record** in the Merge to New Document dialog box, and then click **OK**. You should have a document with your name in the coupon. If necessary, select and delete the additional blank box added below the one with your name.

j. Click the **File tab**, click **Save**, navigate to the folder where you are saving your files, and then name the document Lastname_Firstname_i01_ws04_Survey_Email, replacing Lastname_Firstname with your own name. Click **Save**. Click the **File tab**, and then click **Close** to close Lastname_Firstname_i01_ws04_Survey_Email. Click the **File tab**, and then click **Close** to close **i01_ws04_Survey_Email**. Do not save the changes. **Close** ❌ Word.

1. What are the two types of forms you can use to collect data? What are the requirements of each of the two types? How would you choose which type to use?

2. What are the conditions under which you can only collect new data versus update existing data?

3. What does it mean to have to synch your form before you can re-send it? Are you required to synch every time you want to re-send a form? Why or why not?

4. You can create themes and apply them to two different documents. What are the two formats of themes you can apply to another document? Are there advantages to using one format over the other?

5. Have you ever received an e-mail that looks like it is a mass e-mail but only comes to your e-mail address? How is the sender able to customize a mass e-mail like this and have it look like it was sent to only you?

Key Terms

Access Data Collection Replies 1006
Attached object 1008
Data collection form 1003

Data Collection Wizard 1002
HTML form 1002
InfoPath form 1002

MAPI (Messaging Application
Program Interface) 1013
Synchronize 1006

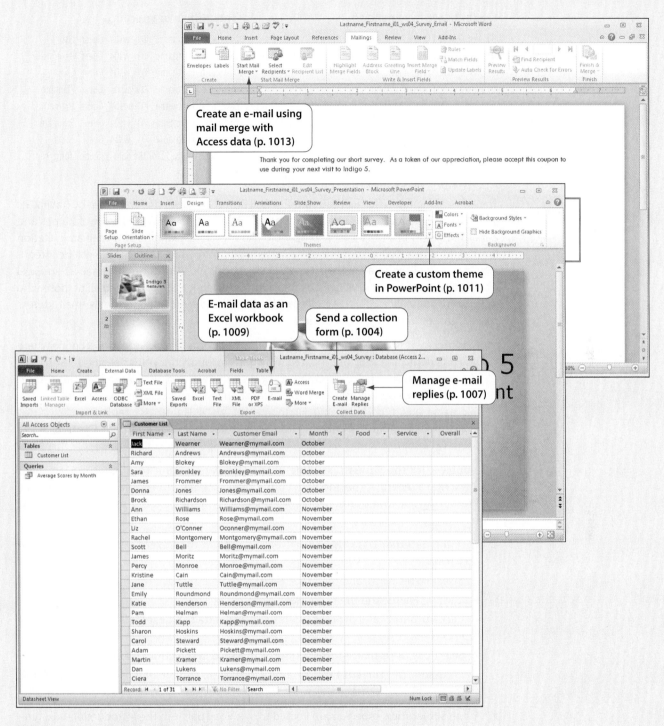

Figure 15 Restaurant Survey Data Collection Final

Holiday Party

Production & Operations

The event planning staff at Painted Paradise Golf Resort and Spa has been asked by Travel2Go, a local travel agency, to host its holiday party. Travel2Go has provided a list of names and e-mail addresses of the guests, and it would like the event planners to e-mail an invitation form to the guests to find out if they can attend and if so, how many people will be attending. The staff will send a summary of the replies to Travel2Go through e-mail as an Excel workbook. Finally, e-mails will be sent to confirm attendance at the party to all of those who responded. Note that for this case, all e-mails sent will be sent to your personal e-mail address so you can view and print the messages.

a. Start **Access**. Click the **File tab**, and click **Open**. Click the disk drive in the left pane where your student data files are located. Navigate through the folder structure and click **i01_ws04_Guest_List**. Click **Open**. Click the **File tab**, and click **Save Database As**. In the Save As dialog box, navigate to the location where you are saving your files. In the File name box, type Lastname_Firstname_i01_ws04_Guest_List, replacing Lastname_ Firstname with your own name. Click **Save**. If necessary, click **Enable Content** in the Security Warning bar.

b. Double-click the **Guest List** table in the Navigation Pane to open it in Datasheet view. Add a record at the end with your e-mail address and Firstname and Lastname. Press Tab five times until the record selector is on the next line and your record has been added to the table.

c. Click the **External Data tab**, click **Create E-mail** in the Collect Data group, and then click **Next**.

   • Select **HTML form**, and then click **Next**.

   • Click **All Fields**, and then click **Next**.

   • Click **Automatically process replies and add data to Guest List** to select it, and then click **Next**.

   • Select **Use the e-mail addresses stored in a field in the database**, and then click **Next**.

   • Make sure **The current table or query** is selected and **Email** is listed in the field box. Click **Next**.

d. In the Subject box, type You are invited to a holiday party. In the Introduction box, type Please complete the following RSVP form. Click **Next**, and then click **Next** again. Click the **Select All** check box to clear the check marks from the contact list. Click the check box for your e-mail address to send the form to yourself, and then click **Send**.

e. Click the **External Data tab**, click **Manage Replies** in the Collect Data group, and then in the Select a Data Collection message box, select **You are invited to a holiday party**.

f. Click **Message Options**. Change the **Number of replies to be processed** to 15 and then click **OK**.

   • Click **Resend this E-mail Message**. Verify that **Automatically process replies and add data to Guest List** is selected, and then click **Next**.

- Select **Use the e-mail addresses stored in a field in the database**, and then click **Next**.
- Verify that **The current table or query** is selected and **E-mail** is selected in the box, and then click **Next**.
- In the Introduction box, type Please RSVP immediately if you have not already. Click **Next**, and then click **Next** again.

g. Click the **Select All** check box to remove the check marks from the contact list. Click the check box for your e-mail address to only send the form to yourself. Click **Send**, click **Close**, and then on the File tab, click **Close Database** to close the database but not Access.

h. Click the **File tab**, click **Open**, and then locate your student folder. Select **i01_ws04_ Guest_Responses**, and then click **Open**. Click the **File tab**, click **Save Database As**, navigate to where you are saving your files, and then in the File name box, type Lastname_Firstname_i01_ws04_Guest_Responses, replacing Lastname_Firstname with your own name. Click **Save**, and then click **Enable Content** in the Security Warning bar.

i. In the Navigation Pane, double-click the **Guest List** table to open it in Datasheet view. Edit the last record replacing **youremail@address.com** with your own **e-mail address** and **Firstname** and **Lastname** with your own name. Click outside the record to save the record changes.

j. In the Navigation Pane, double-click the **Adults and Children Attending** query to open it. On the External Data tab, click **E-mail** in the Export group. Select **Excel Workbook (*.xlsx)** as the output format, and then click **OK.**

k. Click in the **To** line, and then type your e-mail address. In the Subject, type Summary of Guest Responses. In the message area, type Susan, and press Enter twice. Type Here are the RSVPs for the party. I will get in touch with you in a few days to discuss the party. Press Enter twice. Type Firstname Lastname, replacing Firstname Lastname with your own name.

l. Right-click the **Adults and Children Attending.xlsx** attachment in the Attached line, and select **Open**. Click **Enable Editing** in the Protected View message bar. Select cells **A1** through **B2**. Click the **Insert tab**, click **Pie** in the Charts group, and then select **Pie in 3-D**. Click the **Layout tab**, click **Chart Title** in the Labels group, and then select **Above Chart**. Type Attendance by Age Group and then press Enter. Move the chart so the top corner is in **A4**. Click outside the chart.

m. Click the **Insert tab**, and then click **Header & Footer** in the Text group. Click the **Design tab**, and then click **Go to Footer** in the Navigation group. Click in the **left footer section**, click the **Design tab**, and then click **File Name** in the Header & Footer Elements group.

n. Click outside of the footer area, and then click **Normal** on the status bar to return to the Normal view. Press Ctrl+Home to return to cell A1. Click **Save**. Close Excel.

o. In the Outlook message window, right-click the attached file named **Adults and Children Attending.xlsx**, and then select **Save As**. Navigate to where you are saving your files, and in the **File name** box type Lastname_Firstname_i01_ws04_Guest_Chart, replacing Lastname_Firstname with your own name. Click **Save**. In the Message window, click **Send** and then close Access.

p. Start **PowerPoint**. Click the **File tab**, click **Open**, locate your student folder and select **i01_ws04_Guest_Planning**, and then click **Open**. Click the **File tab**, click **Save As**, navigate to where you are saving your files, and then in the File name box, type Lastname_Firstname_i01_ws04_Guest_Planning, replacing Lastname_Firstname with your own name. Click **Save**. Click the **Insert tab**, click **Header & Footer** in the Text group, and then add a footer with the file name in the **Notes and Handouts tab**. Click **Apply to All**.

q. Click the **Design tab**, click **More** in the Themes Gallery in the Themes group, and then select **Save Current Theme**. In the Save Current Theme dialog box, navigate to where you are saving your files. In the File name box, type Lastname_Firstname_i01_ws04_Guest_Theme, replacing Lastname_Firstname with your actual name, and then click **Save**.

r. Click the **File tab**, and then click **Save As**. In the Save as type list, select **PowerPoint Template**. Navigate to the folder where you are saving your files. In the File name box, type Lastname_Firstname_i01_ws04_Guest_Template, replacing Lastname_Firstname with your own name. Click **Save**. Click the **Insert tab**, click **Header & Footer** in the Text group, click the **Notes and Handouts tab**, and then change the **Footer** to the new file name. Click **Apply to All**. Click **Save** and then close PowerPoint.

s. Start **Word**, and then open **i01_ws04_Guest_Email**. Click the **Mailings tab**, click **Start Mail Merge** in the Start Mail Merge group, and then select **E-mail Messages**.

t. Click the **Page Layout tab**, click **Themes** in the Themes group, and then select **Browse for Themes**. Locate the folder where you are saving your files, and then select **Lastname_Firstname_i01_ws04_Guest_Theme**. Click **Open**. Note the background will only change when you are in Web Layout view.

u. Click the **Mailings tab**, click **Select Recipients** in the Start Mail Merge group, and then select **Use Existing List**. Locate the folder where you are saving your files and then open **Lastname_Firstname_i01_ws04_Guest_Responses**. Click **Open**. If necessary, in the Confirm Data Source dialog box, select **OLE DB Database Files** in the Open data source list box and click **OK**. Select the **Guest List** table, and then click **OK**.

v. Place the insertion point in the second column, first row of the table. Click the **Mailings tab**, and then click the **Insert Merge Field** arrow in the Write & Insert Fields group. Select **First_Name**. Move to the second row in the second column. Insert the **Last_Name** field. Repeat for **Adults** and the **Children**.

w. Click the **Mailings tab**, and then click **Edit Recipient List** in the Start Mail Merge group. Click the **Data Source** check box. Click the check box next to **your name** and **e-mail address** so the e-mail will be sent only to you, and then click **OK**.

x. Click the **Mailings tab**, click **Finish & Merge** in the Finish group, and then select **Send E-mail Messages**. In the Merge to E-mail dialog box, in the To list, select **Email**. In the Subject line box, type Thank you for your response, and then click **OK.**

y. Click the **Mailings tab**, and then click **Finish & Merge** in the Finish group. Select **Edit Individual Documents**, click **Current record** in the Merge to New Document dialog box, and then click **OK.** Click the **File tab**, click **Save As**, navigate to where you are saving your files, and then in the File name box, type Lastname_Firstname_i01_ws04_Guest_Email, replacing Lastname_Firstname with your own name. Click **Save**, and then close the document. Close **i01_ws04_Guest_Email** without saving it. Close Word.

Student data files needed:

i01_ps1_PNO
i01_ps1_PNO_Responses
i01_ps1_PNO_Presentation
i01_ps1_PNO_Email

You will save your files as:

Lastname_Firstname_i01_ps1_PNO
Lastname_Firstname_i01_ps1_PNO_Responses
Lastname_Firstname_i01_ps1_PNO_Chart
Lastname_Firstname_i01_ps1_PNO_Presentation
Lastname_Firstname_i01_ps1_PNO_Theme
Lastname_Firstname_i01_ps1_PNO_Template
Lastname_Firstname_i01_ps1_PNO_Email
Personal e-mails (2) for the data collection forms sent

Parent Night Out

Production &
Operations

The Painted Paradise Golf Resort and Spa is planning a Parent Night Out (PNO) for its guests. The resort will have a "kids only" event one night where parents can drop their kids off for a few hours and know they will be safe. The event planning staff is sending e-mail invitations to all current and past guests, asking them to fill out an e-mail form for registration. The results will be sent to Matt Williams, the children's event director. An e-mail confirmation will be sent to all those who sign up for the event.

a. Start **Access**. Click **Open**, locate your student folder, and then select **i01_ps1_PNO**. Click **Open**, click the **File tab**, click **Save Database As**, navigate to where you are saving your files, and in the File name box type Lastname_Firstname_i01_ps1_PNO, replacing Lastname_Firstname with your own name. Click **Save**. If necessary, click **Enable Content** in the Security Warning bar.

b. Double-click the **Registrations** table in the Navigation Pane to open it in Datasheet view. Add a record at the end with your Firstname, Lastname, and e-mail address. Press Tab two times until the record selector is on the next line, and your record has been added to the table.

c. Click the **External Data tab**, click **Create E-mail** in the Collect Data group, and then click **Next**.

- Select **HTML form**, and then click **Next**.
- Click **All Fields**, and then click **Next**.
- Select **Automatically process replies and add data to Registrations**, and then click **Next**.
- Select **Use the e-mail addresses stored in a field in the database**, and then click **Next**.
- Make sure **The current table or query** is selected and **Parent Email** is listed in the field box, and then click **Next**.

d. In the Subject box, type Parent Night Out. In the Introduction box, type If you would like your child to participate in the upcoming Parent Night Out, please complete the following registration form. Click **Next**, and then click **Next** again. Click the **Select All** box to clear the check marks from the contact list, and then scroll to find your e-mail address listed. Click the check box for your **e-mail address** to send the form to yourself. Click **Send**.

e. Click the **External Data tab**, and then click **Manage Replies** in the Collect Data group. In the Select a Data Collection message box, select **Parent Night Out**.

f. Click **Message Options**. Change the **Number of replies to be processed** to 75 and then click **OK**.

- Click **Resend this E-Mail Message**.
- Verify that **Automatically process replies and add data to Registrations** is selected, and then click **Next**.

- Select **Use the e-mail addresses stored in a field in the database**, and then click **Next**.
- Verify that **The current table or query** is selected and **Parent Email** is selected in the box, and then click **Next**.
- In the Introduction box, type Last chance to sign your child up for Parent Night Out. Click **Next**, and then click **Next** again.

g. Click the **Select All** box to clear the check marks from the contact list, and then scroll to find your e-mail address listed. Click the box next to your **e-mail address** to only send the form to yourself. Click **Send**, click **Close** to close the Manage Data Collection Messages dialog box, click the **File tab**, and then click **Close Database** to close the database but not Access.

h. Click the **File tab**, click **Open**, locate your student folder, select **i01_ws04_PNO_Responses**, and then click **Open**. Click the **File tab**, click **Save Database As**, navigate to where you are saving your files, and then in the File name box type Lastname_Firstname_i01_ps1_PNO_Responses, replacing Lastname_Firstname with your own name. Click **Save**, and then click **Enable Content** in the Security Warning bar.

i. In the Navigation Pane, double-click the **Registrations table** to open it in Datasheet view. Edit the last record for **Firstname Lastname** with your actual first name, last name, and e-mail address. Click outside the record to save the record changes.

j. Double-click the **Age Breakdown** query listed in the Navigation Pane to open it. Click the **External Data tab**, click **E-mail** in the Export group, and then select **Excel Workbook (*.xlsx)** as the output format. Click **OK**.

k. In the To line, type your e-mail address. In the Subject, type Summary of Ages. In the message area, type Matt, and press ⎵Enter twice. Type The breakdown of ages for PNO is attached. Press ⎵Enter twice. Type Firstname Lastname, replacing Firstname and Lastname with your own name.

l. Right-click the **Age Breakdown.xlsx** attachment in the Attached line, and then select **Open**. Click **Enable Editing** on the Protected view message bar. Select cells **A1** through **B8**. Click the **Insert tab**, click **Pie** in the Charts group, and then select **Pie in 3-D**. Move the chart so the top corner is in **A10**. Click outside the chart.

m. Click the **Insert tab**, and then click **Header & Footer** in the Text group. Click the **Design tab**, and then click **Go to Footer** in the Navigation group. Click in the left footer section, click the **Design tab**, and then click **File Name** in the Header & Footer Elements group.

n. Click outside of the footer area, and then click **Normal** on the status bar to return to Normal view. Press ⎵Ctrl+⎵Home to return to cell A1. Change the cell **B2** heading to Count. Click **Save** and then close Excel.

o. In the Outlook message window, right-click on the Attached file name **Age Breakdown**, and then select **Save As**. In the Save As dialog box, navigate to the location where you are saving your files. In the File name box, type Lastname_Firstname_i01_ps1_PNO_Chart, replacing Lastname_Firstname with your own name. Click **Save**. In the Message window, click **Send**. Close Access.

p. Start **PowerPoint**, Click the **File tab**, and click **Open**. Locate your student folder and open **i01_ws04_PNO_Presentation**. Click the **File tab**, and click **Save As**. In the Save As dialog box, navigate to where you are saving your files. In the File name box, type Lastname_Firstname_i01_ps1_PNO_Presentation, replacing Lastname_Firstname with your own name. Click **Save**. On the **Insert tab**, click **Header & Footer** in the Text group, and then add a footer with the file name in the **Notes and Handouts** tab. Click **Apply to All**.

q. Click the **Design tab**, click **More** for the Themes Gallery in the Themes group, and then select **Save Current Theme**. In the Save Current Theme dialog box, locate the folder where you save your student files. In the File name box, type Lastname_Firstname_ i01_ps1_PNO_Theme, replacing Lastname_Firstname with your own name, and then click **Save**.

r. Click the **File tab**, and then click **Save As**. In the Save as type list, select **PowerPoint Template**. Navigate to the folder where you are saving your files. In the File name box, type Lastname_Firstname_i01_ps1_PNO_Template, replacing Lastname_Firstname with your own name. Click **Save**, click the **Insert tab**, and then click **Header & Footer** in the Text group. Click the **Notes and Handouts tab**, and then change the **Footer** to the new file name. Click **Apply to All**. Click **Save** and then close PowerPoint.

s. Start **Word**, and then open **i01_ps1_PNO_Email**. Click the **Mailings tab**, click **Start Mail Merge** in the Start Mail Merge group, and then select **E-mail Messages**.

t. Click the **Page Layout tab**, click **Themes** in the Themes group, and then select **Browse for Themes**. Navigate to the folder where you are saving your files, and select **Lastname_ Firstname_i01_ps1_PNO_Template**. Click **Open**.

u. Click the **Mailings tab**, click **Select Recipients** in the Start Mail Merge group, and then select **Use Existing List**. Locate the folder where you are saving your files, and then open **Lastname_Firstname_i01_ps1_PNO_Responses**. If necessary, in the Confirm Data Source dialog box, select **OLE DB Database Files** in the Open data source list box and click **OK**. Select the Registrations table, and then click **OK**.

v. Place the insertion point in the first column, second row of the table. Click the **Mailings tab**, and then click the **Insert Merge Field arrow** in the Write & Insert Fields group. Select **First_Name**, and then press [Spacebar]. Click the **Insert Merge Field arrow**, and then select **Last_Name**. Press [Tab] to move to the next cell under **Child's Age**, and then insert the field for **Age_of_Child**.

w. Click the **Mailings tab**, and then click **Edit Recipient List** in the Start Mail Merge group. Click the **Data Source** check box. Scroll through the list of names and find your name and e-mail address. Click the box next to **your name and e-mail address** so the e-mail will be sent to only you. Click **OK**.

x. Click the **Mailings tab**, click **Finish & Merge** in the Finish group, and then select **Send E-mail Messages**. In the Merge to E-mail dialog box, click the **To** arrow, and then select **Parent_Email**. In the Subject line box, type Parent Night Out Confirmation. Click **OK**.

y. Click the **Mailings tab**, and then click **Finish & Merge** in the Finish group. Select **Edit Individual Documents**, click **Current record** in the Merge to New Document dialog box, and then click **OK**. Click **Save**. In the Save As dialog box, navigate to where you are saving your files. In the File name box, type Lastname_Firstname_i01_ps1_PNO_Email, replacing Lastname_Firstname with your own name. Click **Save**. Close the document, and then close **i01_ws04_PNO_Email** without saving it. Close Word.

Student data files needed:

i01_ps2_Preorder
i01_ps2_Preorder_Responses
i01_ps2_Preorder_Email

You will save your files as:

Lastname_Firstname_i01_ps2_Preorder
Lastname_Firstname_i01_ps2_Preorder_Responses
Lastname_Firstname_i01_ps2_Preorder_Chart
Lastname_Firstname_i01_ps2_Preorder_Email
Personal e-mails (2) for the data collection forms sent

Gift Shop Jewelry Preorder

Sales & Marketing

The gift shop, Painted Treasures, is having a special promotion for Anna Kachina's newest jewelry. Because Anna creates unique jewelry on an "as ordered" basis, she would like the gift shop to send out an e-mail to take preorders. The gift shop has an e-mail list in Access that can be used. Once the data is collected, the gift shop will send Anna a list of the preorders in an Excel workbook. Finally, an e-mail receipt will be sent to each customer who preordered confirming that it was received.

a. Start **Access**. Open **i01_ps2_Preorder**, and then save the database file as Lastname_Firstname_i01_ps2_Preorder. Click **Enable Content**, and then add your name and e-mail to the Customer List table.

b. Set up a data collection form to automatically update all the fields in the **Customer List** table with the replies. The e-mail addresses to use are in the **Email** field in the **Customer List** table. Write a short message to go with the collection form explaining that customers can order either a custom necklace or bracelet and that they should specify which they would prefer. Send the e-mail to yourself only as a test.

c. Re-send the message (again, only to yourself) with a message that says this is the last chance to order a bracelet or necklace. Change the number of replies to be processed to 100.

d. Open **i01_ps2_Preorder_Responses**. Edit the last record and replace **youremail@address.com** with your e-mail address. Replace **Firstname** and **Lastname** with your first and last name. Save the database as Lastname_Firstname_i01_ps2_Preorder_Responses.

e. Open the **Items ordered** query listed in the Navigation Pane. Attach the query to an e-mail message as an Excel workbook. Modify the workbook so it shows a column chart with the different products and quantities ordered. Add a footer to the workbook in the left section with the file name. Save the workbook in the e-mail with the original name and close Excel. Save the attachment to the folder where you are saving your files as Lastname_Firstname_i01_ps2_Preorder_Chart. Send the e-mail message to yourself. Close Access.

f. Start **Word**, and then open **i01_ps2_Preorder_Email**. Create a mail merge document using the e-mail addresses and data from the **Customer List** table in **Lastname_Firstname_i01_ps2_Preorder_Responses**.

g. Edit the recipients so you are the only one receiving the merged e-mail. Insert the appropriate merge fields into the second row cells and be sure to include a space between the **First_Name** and **Last_Name** merge fields for the first column of the second row. Send the merged e-mail. Save the current record in a new document, and then save the file as Lastname_Firstname_i01_ps2_Preorder_Email. Close the file, and then close **i01_ps2_Preorder_Email** without saving it. Close Word.

Student data file needed:

None

You will save your files as:

Lastname_Firstname_i01_pf1_Employees

Lastname_Firstname_i01_pf1_Employees_Responses

Lastname_Firstname_i01_pf1_Employees_Table

Lastname_Firstname_i01_pf1_Employees_Theme

Lastname_Firstname_i01_pf1_Employees_Presentation

Lastname_Firstname_i01_pf1_Employees_Email

Personal e-mails (2) for the data collection forms sent

Update Information

Production & Operations

You have taken over a regional sales office for Custom Ride, Inc., a company that sells customized car products such as seat covers and steering wheel covers. The manager before you did not keep updated records, and you are trying to get organized as you settle in to your new position. You need to collect updated information from your local sales offices. You will need to create a database with a table that includes the contact information for your local sales managers. You need to find out how many people they have working for them so you can see if the offices need to hire more sales people. Once you have collected the data, you will send a summary of what you have collected to your manager. Finally, you will send out a merged e-mail to all your sales managers with the data you have collected, asking them to check it over and get back to you if necessary.

a. Start **Access**. Create a table in a new, blank database named Sales Managers with the following fields and data types:

Field Name	Data Type
First Name	Text
Last Name	Text
E-mail Address	Text
Sales Office Name	Text
Full Time Employees	Number
Part Time Employees	Number

b. Add data for the **First Name**, **Last Name**, **E-mail Address**, and **Sales Office Name** fields only. The sales offices should include **Northside**, **Downtown**, **Eastside**, **Westside**, **Southside**, and **Main**. Your name and actual e-mail address should be listed as one of the managers. Save the database as Lastname_Firstname_i01_pf1_Employees.

c. Set up a data collection form to send to the managers for each sales office. Include all the fields. Change the option so Access will automatically process replies and add the data to the **Sales Managers** table and use the e-mail addresses stored in the Sales Managers table. Include a message to please fill out the information and reply back to you. Change the recipients so you are the only one to actually receive the e-mail collection form.

d. Copy **Lastname_Firstname_i01_pf1_Employees**, and then name it Lastname_Firstname_i01_pf1_Employees_Responses. **Enable Content** if necessary. Because you only sent the e-mail collection form to yourself, you need to add data to this table as if you received responses. You should only have to enter the number of Full Time and Part Time Employees for the managers listed.

e. Send the **Sales Managers** table as an Excel workbook e-mail attachment. Insert a footer in the left section with the file name. Change the orientation to **Landscape** and the width to **1 page**. Save the file, close Excel, and then from the e-mail message window, save the attachment as Lastname_Firstname_i01_pf1_Employees_Table.

f. Send the e-mail to yourself, and then close Access.

g. Start **PowerPoint**, and then create a 2 slide presentation with a built-in theme. Change the colors of the theme, and then save the theme as Lastname_Firstname_i01_pf1_Employees_Theme. Save the presentation as Lastname_Firstname_i01_pf1_Employees_Presentation. Close PowerPoint.

h. Start **Word**. Use mail merge to create an e-mail to send to the managers who sent you their data. Use the file **Lastname_Firstname_i01_pf1_Employees_Responses** for the merged fields. Add all the fields in the message. Select the recipients so you are the only one receiving the e-mail.

i. Apply the PowerPoint theme **Lastname_Firstname_i01_pf1_Employees_Theme** to the message. Send the e-mail. Save the current record in a new document called Lastname_Firstname_i01_pf1_Employees_Email. Close Word without saving the merged document.

Perform 2: How Others Perform

Student data file needed:

i01_pf2_Running_Today

You will save your file as:

Lastname_Firstname_i01_pf2_Running_Today

Running Today

Production & Operations

Adam James, event coordinator for *Running Today*, has sent out multiple e-mail collection forms to past race participants asking them to update their information and register for an upcoming half-marathon, which means updating an existing table in Access. None of the data collection forms worked—either the replies were not added to the table or he did not receive any replies. Look carefully at each screen shot that follows and read the scenario that explains how each data collection form was sent. Answer the questions to help Adam understand what went wrong each time.

Start **Word**. Open **i01_pf2_Running_Today**. Insert a footer with the file name. Save the file to your student folder as Lastname_Firstname_i01_pf2_Running_Today, replacing Lastname_Firstname with your own name. After each question, insert your answer as thoroughly as possible and on as many pages as necessary.

a. Adam chose to send his e-mail messages as an HTML form because he did not have InfoPath installed on his computer. He does not know what kind of e-mail programs his recipients have, but most of the e-mail addresses in his list were either Yahoo!, Hotmail, or Google. Refer to Figure 1. The option he chose says any recipient who uses an e-mail application that supports HTML can read and reply to this message. Why did the replies not update the Access table? How can Adam get the new data into his Access table?

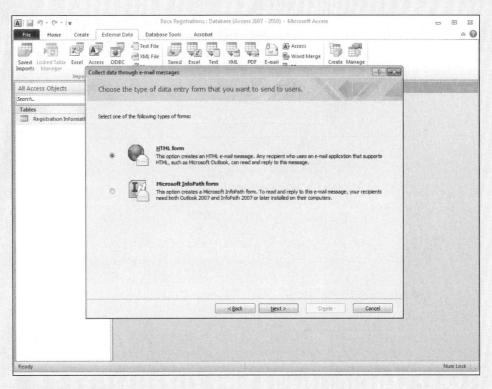

Figure 1 Scenario 1

b. Adam sent the e-mail message to a list of past participants who have always been able to reply and update a table. For this e-mail he has received replies, but his table is not updating automatically as it always has in the past. Looking at Figure 2, why isn't the table updating? What will Adam have to do to process (update) the table?

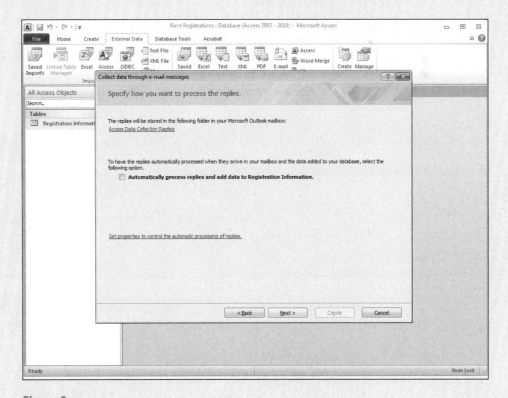

Figure 2 Scenario 2

c. Adam would like the past participants to update their existing data in a table if necessary. The design of his table records is as shown in Figure 3. Whenever he sends an e-mail collection form, the fields are all blank and do not show existing information so the recipient can update it. What is the issue with the table that will not allow him to update existing information, and what does he need to do to fix it?

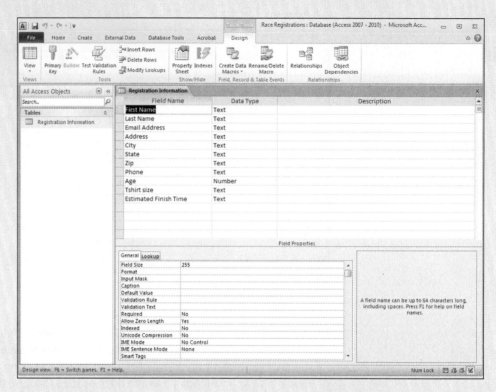

Figure 3 Scenario 3

d. Adam sent out 55 e-mail data collection forms, but only 25 had their data added to the Access table. He knows for certain that some individuals who replied did not have their data added to the table. The options set for Adam's data collection form are shown in Figure 4. Why were only 25 out of 55 replies actually processed? What does Adam have to do to automatically process all 55 replies?

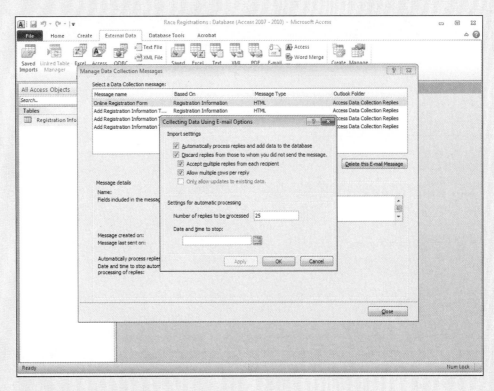

Figure 4 Scenario 4

e. Adam opened the Manage Data Collection Messages dialog box to re-send his message, but he is not able to click the Resend this E-mail Message button. Refer to Figure 5. Why can't Adam re-send the message? What does Adam need to do to re-send the message?

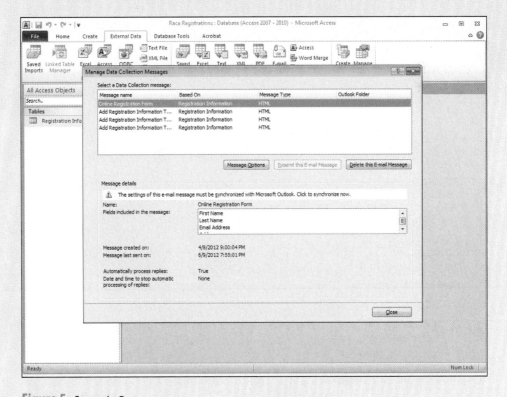

Figure 5 Scenario 5

WORD PROCESSING

Perform 1

Student data file needed:

None

You will save your file as:

Team_Number_RequestFunding

Request for Funding

Sales & Marketing

The Painted Paradise Resort and Spa would like to begin offering their own house brand of bath salts in an attempt to diversify their revenue streams. Outside funding will need to be secured in order to make this a reality. In this exercise, you will collaborate with a team of three to five students to create a request for funding.

a. Select one team member to set up the document by completing Steps b–d.

b. Point your browser to either **https://skydrive.live.com** or **https://drive.google.com**, depending on which cloud collaboration tool you choose. To ensure that changes made to this document are tracked, be sure that all members of the team have either a Microsoft or Google account.

c. Create a new document used for word processing, and then name it Team_Number_ RequestFunding. Replace *Number* with the number assigned to your team by your instructor. Insert a page footer in the document. Indicate which cloud collaboration tool your team used, your team number, and page number.

d. Share the document with the other members of your team. Make sure that each team member has the appropriate permission to edit the document.

e. The request for funding must include opening and closing paragraphs in addition to two to three paragraphs outlining the business plan. Use the information below to write the letter.

f. Add today's date to the document in the upper-right corner.

g. Address the request for funding to:

Ms. Veronica Smithers
99902 Poplars Blvd.
Santa Monica, CA 90401

h. Use the information below to assist your team in writing your request for funding.

- Ms. Smithers was recommended by Mr. Ronald Smith, of Smith & Sons Capital.
- Ms. Smithers believes that when businesses are responsible for the production of their own brand of products, the quality is improved at a lower cost, benefiting everyone.
- The Finance department expects an additional $250,000.00 needs to be secured.
- The Finance department recommends Ms. Smithers receive 7% of all profits from bath salts sales in return for the initial investment.
- Business plan summary:
  - Replace current line of bath salts with a line of house brand products for all spa services in addition to selling gift baskets in the local gift shop.
  - Market the house brand of products in local grocery stores and beauty shops.

i. Be sure that every member of the team contributes to the letter and that it is formatted appropriately and reads as if one person wrote it. After the closing, have the team member who completed Steps b–d add their first and last name as the signature.

j. Once the document is complete, share it with your instructor. Make sure that your instructor has permission to edit the document.

WORD PROCESSING

Student data file needed:
None

You will save your file as:
Team_Number_LessonsLearned

Lessons Learned

In this exercise, you will collaborate with a team of three to five students to create a document that summarizes what you have learned from the topics and skills discussed in this volume. Each member of the team will select a different module from one of the Microsoft Office Units about which to write. Each member of the team will contribute one to two paragraphs about the module chosen. Your team may choose to use Microsoft's SkyDrive or Google's Google Drives to collaborate on this document.

a.   Select one team member to set up the document by completing Steps b–d.

b.   Point your browser to either **https://skydrive.live.com** or **https://drive.google.com**, depending on which cloud collaboration tool you choose. To ensure that changes made to this document are tracked, be sure that all members of the team have either a Microsoft or Google account.

c.   Create a new document used for word processing, and then name it Team_Number_ LessonsLearned. Replace *Number* with the number assigned to your team by your instructor. Insert a page footer in the document. Indicate which cloud collaboration tool your team used, your team number, and page number.

d.   Share the document with the other members of your team. Make sure that each team member has the appropriate permission to edit the document.

e.   Begin by creating a title page, listing the names of the team members and any other information required by your instructor.

f.   Add a section heading for each of the modules that will be discussed, such as Microsoft Word 2010 - Module 2 for one section and Microsoft PowerPoint 2010 - Module 1 for another.

g.   Once the document is complete, share it with your instructor. Make sure that your instructor has permission to edit the document.

Perform 1

Student data file needed:

None

You will save your file as:

Team_Number_ProShopExpenses

Red Bluff Golf Course Financials

Finance & Accounting

You and your team have been selected by the management team at the Red Bluff Golf Course to demonstrate your online collaboration and spreadsheet skills. In this exercise, you will collaborate with a team of three to five students to create a spreadsheet that can be used to help track the daily finances of the Red Bluff Golf Club.

a. Select one team member to set up the document by completing Steps b–e.

b. Point your browser to either **https://skydrive.live.com** or **https://drive.google.com**, depending on which cloud collaboration tool you choose. To ensure that changes made to this document are tracked, be sure that all members of the team have either a Microsoft or Google account.

c. Create a new spreadsheet document, and then name it Team_Number_ProShopExpenses. Replace *Number* with the number assigned to your team by your instructor.

d. Rename Sheet1 as Contributors. List the names of each of the team members on the worksheet, and then add a heading above the name to read Team Members. Include any additional information on this worksheet required by your instructor.

e. Share the spreadsheet with the other members of your team. Make sure that each team member has the appropriate permissions to edit the document.

f. Create a new worksheet, and then name it Expenses. Enter the information from the table below into the Expenses worksheet.

Date	Item	Amount
05/01/2013	Starting Balance	$35,000.00
05/01/2013	Operational Expenses	-$8,000.00
05/02/2013	Marketing Expenses	-$7,350.00
05/03/2013	Operational Expenses	-$10,125.50
05/05/2013	Sales Revenue	$9,049.10
05/10/2013	Operational Expenses	$-12,500.00
05/12/2013	Sales Revenue	$8,210.95

g. Merge and center a title of Red Bluff Golf Club Finances - May 2013 above the table of data you entered. Make the font 18pt in size, bold, and green.

h. Add a column entitled Running Balance to keep track of available funds after each time money is withdrawn or deposited into the account.

i. Apply conditional formatting to the data in the Running Balance column to place emphasis on values that fall below $10,000.00. Make those values appear with a red fill and white font color. Note: If using SkyDrive you will need to open the document in Excel to apply conditional formatting.

j. Insert a line chart into the Expenses worksheet that illustrates the trend of the Running Balance for each date. The running total values should run along the y-axis, and the dates should run along the x-axis. Give the chart a title of Daily Running Balance - Trend.

k. Once the document is complete, share it with your instructor. Make sure that your instructor has permission to edit the document.

SPREADSHEET

Student data file needed:

None

You will save your file as:

Team_Number_LoanAnalysis

Loan Analysis

Finance &
Accounting

You and your teammates are looking to invest in a new startup company. In addition to the monies you already have, you need to finance an additional $75,000.00. In this exercise you will collaborate with a team of three to five students to conduct analysis on two loan options. Your team may choose to use Microsoft's SkyDrive or Google's Google Drive to collaborate on this spreadsheet.

a. Select one team member to set up the document by completing Steps b–e.

b. Point your browser to either **https://skydrive.live.com** or **https://drive.google.com**, depending on which cloud collaboration tool you choose. To ensure that changes made to this document are tracked, be sure that all members of the team have either a Microsoft or Google account.

c. Create a new spreadsheet document, and then name it Team_Number_LoanAnalysis. Replace *Number* with the number assigned to your team by your instructor.

d. Rename Sheet1 as Contributors. List the names of each of the team members on the worksheet, and then add a heading above the name to read Team Members. Include any additional information on this worksheet required by your instructor.

e. Share the spreadsheet with the other members of your team. Make sure that each team member has the appropriate permission to edit the document.

f. Create a new worksheet entitled Option1. The details of Option1 are as follows:
Annual Interest Rate: 4.75%
Loan Amount: $75,000.00
Term: 5 years

g. Calculate the monthly payment amount needed to pay off the loan in 60 monthly payments.

h. Create an amortization schedule that will track the beginning balance, principal payment, interest payment, and ending balance for each of the monthly payments. Be sure that all monetary values are formatted as Currency with 2 decimal places.

i. Create another worksheet entitled Option2. The details of Option2 are as follows:
Annual Interest Rate: 3.69%
Loan Amount: $75,000.00
Term: 7 years

j. Calculate the quarterly payment amount needed to pay off the loan in 28 quarterly payments.

k. Create an amortization schedule that will track the beginning balance, principal payment, interest payment, and ending balance for each of the quarterly payments. Be sure that all monetary values are formatted as Currency with 2 decimal places.

l. Create another worksheet entitled Summary. This worksheet will be used to summarize some of the data from the loan worksheets and create a chart to help determine which option best fits your needs.

m. Create a table, and then calculate the total interest payments for each of the two loan options. Also calculate the total amount paid for each of the two loan options. Be sure to write your formulas so that they can be automatically updated if the loan amount changes.

n. Create a column chart that compares the total interest paid amounts for option 1 and option 2. Give the chart a title of Total Interest Paid on Loan. Modify the y-axis values to have a minimum value of 7,000 and a maximum value of 11,000 in increments of 1,000.

o. Once the document is complete, share it with your instructor. Make sure that your instructor has permission to edit the document.

DATABASE

Perform 1

Student data file needed:

None

You will save your files as:

Team_Number_Events

Team_Number_EventsDB_Plan

Red Bluff Golf Events

Production & Operations

The Red Bluff Golf Club has started hosting events for people in the community who may want to learn the basics of golf without the commitment of joining the club. In this exercise, you will work with a team of three to five students to build an Access database to help them manage these events. The database must include:

- Tables to store information about customers, event staff, event locations, and events
  - Relationships between tables with referential integrity enforced
- Forms for entering data into each of the tables
- Three queries, of which one must be an unmatched query
- One report, which must contain a subtotal calculation
- Each of the team member's names must be included in the table storing the customer data.
- Enough data in the tables so that each query contains at least two records
- Be sure to incorporate database concepts you have learned to ensure a well-built, user-friendly database.

a. Select one team member to set up the database by completing Steps b–e.

b. Start **Access**, create a blank database, and then name it Team_Number_Events. Replace *Number* with the number assigned to your team by your instructor.

c. Point your browser to **https://skydrive.live.com**, create a new folder, and then name it Team_Number_Assignment. Replace *Number* with the number assigned to your team by your instructor.

d. Upload the **Team_Number_Events** database to the **Team_Number_Assignment** folder, and then share the folder with the other members of your team. Make sure that the other team members have permission to edit the contents of the shared folder and that they are required to log in to SkyDrive to access it.

e. Because databases can only be opened and edited by one person at a time, it is a good idea to plan ahead by determining what each team member will be responsible for contributing. Create a new Word document in the Team_Number_Assignment folder in SkyDrive, and then name it Team_Number_EventsDB_Plan. Replace *Number* with the number assigned to your team by your instructor.

f. In the Word document, each team member must list his or her first and last name as well as a summary of their planned contributions. As work is completed on the database, this document should be updated with the specifics of each team member's contributions.

g. Insert a page footer in the document and include your team number and page number.

h. Once the assignment is complete, share the *Team_Number_Assignment* folder with your instructor. Make sure that your instructor has permission to edit the contents of the folder.

Perform 2

Student data file needed:

None

You will save your files as:

Team_Number_MusicPromo
Team_Number_MusicPromoDB_Plan

Concert Event Management

Production & Operations

You have been hired by a local music promotion company that is responsible for booking local bands into various clubs and music venues in the area. In this exercise, you will work with a team of three to five students to build an Access database to help them manage their business. The database must include:

- Tables to store information about bands/performers, music venues, and events
  - Relationships between tables with referential integrity enforced
- Forms for entering data into each of the tables
- Three queries, of which one must be an unmatched query
- One report
- Each of the team member's names must be included in the table storing the band/performer data.
- Enough data in the tables so that each query contains at least two records
- Be sure to incorporate database concepts you have learned to ensure a well-built, user-friendly database.

a. Select one team member to set up the assignment by completing Steps b–e.

b. Start **Access**, create a blank database and name it Team_Number_MusicPromo. Replace *Number* with the number assigned to your team by your instructor.

c. Point your browser to **https://skydrive.live.com**, if you haven't already in the previous case, create a new folder, and name it Team_Number_Assignment. Replace *Number* with the number assigned to your team by your instructor.

d. Upload the **Team_Number_MusicPromo** database to the **Team_Number_Assignment** folder, and then share the folder with the other members of your team. Make sure that the other team members have permission to edit the contents of the shared folder and that they are required to log in to SkyDrive to access it.

e. Because databases can only be opened and edited by one person at a time, it is a good idea to plan ahead by determining what each team member will be responsible for contributing. Create a new Word document in the Team_Number_Assignment folder in SkyDrive and name it Team_Number_MusicPromoDB_Plan. Replace *Number* with the number assigned to your team by your instructor.

f. In the Word document, each team member must list his or her first and last name as well as a summary of their planned contributions. As work is completed on the database, this document should be updated with the specifics of each team member's contributions.

g. Insert a page footer in the document and include your team number and page number.

h. Once the assignment is complete, share the TeamNumber_Number_Assignment folder with your instructor. Make sure that your instructor has permission to edit the contents of the folder.

PRESENTATION

Perform 1

Student data file needed:
None

You will save your file as:
Team_Number_CollaborationTools

Cloud Collaboration Tools

Management at the Painted Paradise Resort and Spa have come to realize the value of online cloud collaboration. Microsoft and Google offer their own set of collaboration tools, each with its own strengths and weaknesses. In this exercise, you will collaborate with a team of three to five students to create a presentation outlining the strengths and weaknesses of each and to recommend one over the other. You will focus on just the presentation online collaboration tool for this exercise.

a. Select one team member to set up the presentation by completing Steps b–e.

b. Point your browser to either **https://skydrive.live.com** or **https://drive.google.com**, depending on which cloud collaboration tool you choose. To ensure that changes made to this document are tracked, be sure that all members of the team have either a Microsoft or Google account.

c. Create a new presentation, and then name it Team_Number_CollaborationTools. Replace *Number* with the number assigned to your team by your instructor.

d. Select a theme for your presentation from the available options.

e. Share the document with the other members of your team. Make sure that each team member has the appropriate permissions to edit the document.

f. Create a title slide for your presentation, type Cloud Collaboration for the title, and then type Google vs. Microsoft for the subtitle.

g. Create an agenda slide that outlines the topics that will be addressed as well as the names of all contributors to the presentation.

h. At a minimum, the presentation must include one slide listing three strengths and one slide listing three weaknesses for both SkyDrive and Google Drive as well as a conclusion slide outlining the reasons you chose the tool you used to create the presentation.

i. The presentation must include transitions between each slide as well as at least two different animations.

j. Once the presentation is complete, share it with your instructor using the share feature. Make sure that your instructor has permission to edit the document.

PRESENTATION

Perform 2

Student data file needed:	You will save your file as:
None	Team_Number_Interests

Your Interests

In this exercise, you will collaborate with a team of three to five students to create a presentation that demonstrates a personal interest of each of the team members. You may choose a favorite musician, sports team, actor/actress, hobby, and so on. Your team may choose to use Microsoft's SkyDrive or Google's Google Drives to collaborate on this presentation.

a. Select one team member to set up the presentation by completing Steps b–e.

b. Point your browser to either **https://skydrive.live.com** or **https://drive.google.com**, depending on which cloud collaboration tool you choose. To ensure that changes made to this document are tracked, be sure that all members of the team have either a Microsoft or Google account.

c. Create a new presentation, and then name it Team_Number_Interests. Replace *Number* with the number assigned to your team by your instructor.

d. Select a theme for your presentation from the available options.

e. Share the document with the other members of your team. Make sure that each team member has the appropriate permissions to edit the document.

f. Create a title slide, type Our Interests with a subtitle of Contributions by:, and then list the first and last names of all team members.

g. Create an agenda slide that outlines the interests that are a part of the presentation.

h. At a minimum, the presentation must include two slides for every team member in addition to the title and agenda slides. Include additional information about each interest, such as awards, favorite movie/album, and so on.

i. The presentation must include transitions between each slide as well as animations.

j. The presentation must include images and/or embedded multimedia objects such as audio or video.

k. Once the presentation is complete, share it with your instructor using the share feature. Make sure that your instructor has permission to edit the document.

Microsoft Windows 8

Objectives

1. Understand Windows 8 p. 1042
2. Start and shut down Windows 8 p. 1043
3. Explore the Windows 8 interface p. 1045
4. Use Charms and Windows search for files p. 1060
5. Use Gestures p. 1064

Understanding the Windows 8 Interface

PREPARE CASE

Painted Paradise Golf Resort and Spa — Employee Introduction to Microsoft Windows 8

Aidan Matthews, chief technology officer of the Painted Paradise Golf Resort and Spa, has decided to upgrade computers from Windows 7 to the brand new Windows 8 operating system. The vendor who supplies the hotel's software has a new version optimized for Windows 8. This software will fix some of the problems the company has had with the software.

Robert Kneschke/Shutterstock

There is a considerable difference between Windows 7 and Windows 8, and Painted Paradise employees have asked for help in making the transition. You have been asked to plan a workshop to train personnel in all departments to use their new operating system efficiently. Aidan has asked that you start by learning the Windows 8 interface. He wants you to focus on fundamental skills but would also like you to introduce new features that will enhance productivity, such as the enhanced search functionality. Making the transition to Windows 8 will not only require employees to learn the new version of the hotel's software, it will also require them to be comfortable using the operating system on a daily basis. In this workshop, you will focus on demonstrating new features in Windows 8.

Student data file needed for this workshop:

 01_windows_8_appendix folder

You will save your files as:

 Lastname_Firstname_w801_app_wordpad

 Lastname_Firstname_w801_app_start_snip

 Lastname_Firstname_w801_app_experience

 Lastname_Firstname_w801_app_search

Understanding Windows 8

Microsoft Windows 8 is the latest version of the Windows **operating system**. The operating system is **system software**, which controls and coordinates computer hardware operations so other programs can run efficiently. The operating system acts as an intermediary between **application software**—programs that help the user perform specific tasks, such as word processing—and the computer hardware. It also helps you perform essential tasks such as displaying information on the computer screen, saving data on a storage device, and sending documents to a printer. You can have multiple programs open at the same time and switch between programs easily using several different methods. A good operating system is like a good thief. You can tell a thief is good at their job by how little you notice them. The same idea applies to an operating system. Most people notice Windows only when problems arise.

Microsoft releases a new version of Windows every few years to take advantage of improvements made to hardware and to add new features. Windows 8 replaces Windows 7, which was released in late 2009. Like previous versions of Windows, Windows 8 uses a **graphical user interface (GUI)**, an interface that uses **icons**, which are small pictures representing commands, programs, and documents. This type of interface helps you interact with the hardware and software in a simpler fashion. However, Windows 8 introduces a number of new features that will leave even an experienced user in need of some retraining. Since the release of Windows 95, the center of the Windows experience has been the Start button. Windows 8 has moved away from the Start button and moved towards a touch screen type of interface, similar to what many users have become accustomed to with smartphones. Windows 8 also supports **gesture recognition**, which allows users with touch screens to control the computer with gestures instead of mouse clicks. **Gestures** allow users to perform actions like zooming and switching programs by performing certain actions. If you have an eBook reader or iPad, this may already be second nature. Windows 8 is introducing other new features to this version of the operating system, including support for **ARM devices**. An ARM device uses a different processor than personal computers. Devices with ARM chips use less power than a traditional PC processor. By supporting ARM processors for the first time, Windows 8 allows for new innovations in computing. Smaller, more power-efficient laptops may now be feasible in a way never before available. Some vendors anticipate battery lives of 10 hours or more for devices running an ARM processor. ARM processors are also less susceptible to viruses, at the moment. Most computer viruses affect the traditional PC CPU, and do not affect ARM chips. This is why there are fewer viruses found on mobile devices. They are not impossible to create, but virus writers currently focus on Windows PCs.

Windows RT is Microsoft's alternative to the Android and Apple devices. What sets this apart may be the integration of standard desktop applications, such as Microsoft Office. This new version of Microsoft Office includes not only keyboard and mouse support, but touch screen support as well. By combining work functions with the functions casual users like, Microsoft presents some stiff competition for competitors.

The fundamental changes to the Windows operating system will lead to exciting changes in the way we use computers. Most home users do not have touch-screen monitors on their desktop or laptop computers, primarily because the operating system and applications were not designed to take advantage of touch-screen features. Because the demand has been low, prices have remained high for touch-screen devices on personal computers. If this version of Windows is well received, touch-screen monitors will become the standard for home users. As demand goes up, supply goes up, and prices fall.

Starting and Shutting Down Windows 8

Windows 8 starts automatically when your computer is switched on unless you are more technical and have configured your computer to dual-boot. Several different things might occur, depending on where you are using your computer. You may be brought directly to the Windows **Start screen**—the working area of the Windows 8 screen (see Figure 1). If user accounts are set up, you may be required to log in before you see the Start screen. You may be required to **click**—press the left mouse button one time—your user icon, and then you may be asked to enter a password. This prevents other users from accessing your documents or other personal data. Your school or business may have a different logon procedure because many people may be sharing a network.

Windows 8's significantly faster startup time is due to a new form of technology called **hybrid boot**. In previous versions of the operating system, users tended to shut down completely rather than use the sleep and hibernate options. This served the dual purpose of having the computers start up faster, as well as conserve power when not in use. As the hibernate option often had to save gigabytes of information to the hard drive before shutting down, it led to long shut downs. Hybrid boot allows users to decrease the time it takes to shut down, while making start up times quicker. It is now the default shutdown option and has been seamlessly integrated in to the system.

Figure 1   Windows 8 Start screen

After starting the machine, you may be confused when it is time to shut down. Shutting down is now done using **Charms**, buttons appearing on the right side of the screen. Charms were introduced in Windows 8. Charms are hidden from view, so you will need to point the mouse to the bottom-right corner of the screen. This will bring up a menu with a link labeled Settings. From Settings, there is a power icon which allows you to select either Shut down or Restart. You may occasionally see an option labeled Update and restart, which will appear if your computer has downloaded updates to Windows 8.

You will begin your workshop by showing the participants how to start and shut down the machine.

To Start and Shut Down Windows

a. Switch on your computer, and then wait a few moments. If necessary, follow any logon instructions required for the computer you are using. The Windows Start screen is displayed.

b. Bring your mouse to the bottom-right corner of the screen to display the Charms and click **Settings**.

Figure 2 Windows 8 Charms

c. Click the **Power** icon, and then select **Shut down**.

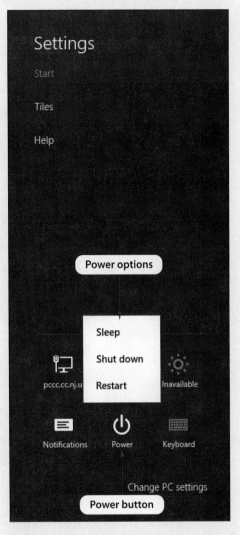

Figure 3   Power button options

Exploring the Windows 8 Interface

The Windows 8 operating system has replaced the standard desktop interface with a new interface. The idea behind this redesign was to make the operating system simpler to use, relying on simple, easy-to-read commands instead of small icons.

In addition to this, Microsoft is attempting to minimize the clutter around the screen—such as the taskbar. Instead of active tasks using screen space, users will be able to access these by pointing to the edge of the screen or performing certain gestures on a touch-screen device, such as swiping. If this sounds familiar, it is similar to the way many touch-screen devices such as the iPad and some mobile phones interact with users. Though the idea is similar to the iPad, the implementation is a bit different. Users with iPad experience will still need to do some retraining due to the differences.

The default screen for the operating system is now the Start screen. The Start screen can be identified by the word "Start" in the upper-left area of the screen, and a number of colored **tiles** on the rest of the screen. The tiles represent programs that can be opened. These are similar to shortcut icons found on the desktop or taskbar in previous versions of Windows. Much like icons in previous versions of Windows, they can be manipulated. You can change the placement and size of the tiles, as well as add and delete tiles.

Tiles designed for Windows 8 may be **Live Tiles** (see Figure 4). These tiles give users a constant stream of information. For example, the Weather tile shows the current weather for your location, updated frequently. Some Internet connections, including some cell phone networks and satellite, do not include unlimited data. In such a case, a user may wish to switch the option off.

Figure 4   Windows 8 Start screen tiles

To find installed applications not shown on the Start screen, users can right-click in any blank area of the Start screen. This will bring up a menu at the bottom of the screen allowing users to click "All apps."

The original Windows desktop is still available. By default, the Start screen will have a tile labeled Desktop. The **desktop** is the interface that users are familiar with from previous versions of Windows. The **taskbar** is the bar at the bottom of the desktop showing all open programs. All programs not specifically written for Windows 8 will use the desktop interface (see Figure 5). However, the Start button has been removed, and users will need to get comfortable with the Windows 8 interface for greater efficiency. The Start button is no longer the center of the Windows experience.

Figure 5 Windows 8 desktop

Existing applications will run under the Windows 8 interface. However, the touch screen functionality may not work as well with older applications as they will on applications designed for Windows 8. Expect many companies to release new versions of their software as Windows 8 gains acceptance.

Real World Advice — Reluctant to Retrain?

Users are often reluctant to retrain, and converting to Windows 8 will likely be met with resistance. A company named Stardock has already released a program to bring back the Start menu in Windows 8, called Start8. This is not a new phenomenon. When Microsoft released Office 2007, users were accustomed to the Office 2003 style menus, and did not want to move to the Office 2007 Ribbon interface. A company named Addintools released a tool called Classic Menu that restored the older interface for users uninterested in retraining. However, business users will likely find their employers uninterested in purchasing and deploying these tools. A user who has retrained is more valuable to a company than a user who has not. In any career involving technology, retraining is going to be a fact of life.

The next part of your workshop will focus on showing Painted Paradise Resort employees how to use the Start screen. You will also show users how to launch, interact with, switch between, and close programs. You will demonstrate the Snipping Tool and WordPad. As the Painted Paradise Resort computers do not yet have touch screens, you will focus on showing the employees how to interact with the operating system using a mouse.

Exploring the Windows 8 Start Screen

You will ask Painted Paradise Resort employees to explore the Windows 8 Start screen. They will examine various elements on the Start screen and learn correct terminology. Additionally, they should learn how to interact with elements of the Start screen and manipulate icons. Because the Painted Paradise Resort computers do not yet have touch screens, you will focus on showing the employees how to interact with the operating system using a mouse.

To Explore the Windows 8 Start Screen

a. If your computer is not already started, switch the computer on and log in if necessary.

b. Notice the new Windows Start screen. Somewhere on the screen you will see a **mouse pointer**—an arrow that shows the position of the mouse. A mouse or other pointing device is used to interact with objects on the screen, to open programs, or select commands. **Right-clicking**—pressing the right mouse button—opens a **shortcut menu**—a group or list of commands—containing commands related to the right-clicked item; these menus may also be referred to as contextual menus.

c. If the entire Start screen does not fit on your screen, you will see a **scroll bar** at the bottom of the page. The scroll bar allows users to access parts of the screen that are otherwise hidden from view due to screen size issues. Users can also zoom out to see more of the screen. They do this by clicking the Zoom button in the bottom-right corner of the screen. If the screen has already been zoomed out, users can click this button to zoom in.

Figure 6 Windows 8 Zoom button

d. Locate the **Weather** tile. If the Weather tile does not display your current weather conditions, click on the tile, and click **Allow** to display current weather, and then return to the Start screen. Right-click the **Weather** tile, which displays the current weather conditions. Four options are displayed at the bottom of the screen. Unpin from Start allows users to remove the Weather tile from the Start screen. Uninstall removes the Weather application from your computer completely. Smaller allows a user to make an icon smaller. If this icon is already small, you may instead be able to click on Larger. As the Weather tile also includes live content—updated weather—it is considered a Live Tile. On this specific right-click menu, you can also click Turn live tile off. Please note other tiles may have different options available. Select the option **Smaller** from the right-click menu to make the Weather appear in a smaller tile.

Figure 7 Right-click menu for Weather

e. Tiles can be moved. To do so, users need to **drag** the icon to a new location. To drag, users click and hold the left mouse button down on an icon. They then move the pointer where they would like the item to appear, and release the mouse button. Drag **Weather** to a different location—any location will do.

f. Users can also add new tiles to the Start screen. To add a new tile, right-click in a blank area of the Start screen. You are presented with the option to click All apps. If you do not see this, ensure you are pointing to a blank area on the Start screen. Click **All apps**.

Figure 8 All apps location

Figure 9 All apps menu

g. Locate the icon for the Snipping Tool. Right-click **Snipping Tool**, and select **Pin to Start**. This will make this tool available on the Start screen.

h. Point to the bottom-left corner of the screen, and select **Start** to go back to the main Start screen. Note when you are switching to the Start screen in this fashion, you need to move the pointer on to the Start screen thumbnail and click. This can be tricky. Verify a link to the Snipping Tool now appears on your Start screen. Note that you may need to scroll if your screen resolution does not show the entirety of the Start screen.

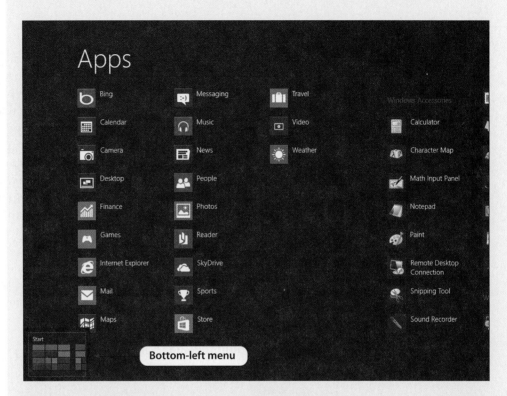

Figure 10   Bottom-left menu

Figure 11   Snipping Tool added to Start screen

i. If the icon for the Reader app is not on your Start screen, right-click a blank area of your screen, and locate the icon for Reader. Right-click **Reader**, and select **Pin to Start**.

j. If the icon for the Photos app is not on your Start screen, right-click a blank area of your screen, and locate the icon for Photos. Right-click **Photos**, and select **Pin to Start**.

Using the Snipping Tool

To have your workshop attendees take before-and-after images of their screen, you will use the **Snipping Tool**. The Snipping Tool allows users to take a picture of their current screen, called a **snip**. For many years, people could take pictures of what was on their screen using the Print Screen key on their keyboard, but that would require users pasting the image into a photo-editing tool to save it. The Snipping Tool was introduced to personal computers in Windows Vista to streamline this process.

This tool can be used in any area that requires taking snips of what is on a screen. Authors can use the Snipping Tool to take pictures of their screens to add to a textbook. People creating manuals for software can take snips to help users understand how to use their product. The tool can be used to show a technical support person what an error on the screen looks like. Any time a user needs an image of screen contents, they can do so using this program, which comes with Windows 8.

One drawback to the Snipping Tool is that it does not allow you to take snips of the Start screen. In order to do so, you will need to press the Print Screen key on your keyboard, open the Paint program, and then paste. You can then save your image.

To Use the Snipping Tool and Print Screen Tool

a. Locate the program **WordPad** using the All apps method discussed earlier. Start **WordPad**.

b. Return to the Start screen and click **Snipping Tool**. The Snipping Tool window opens.

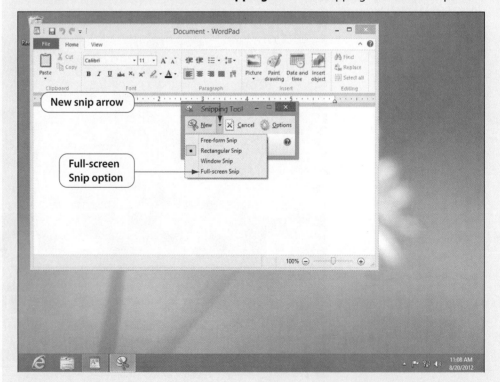

Figure 12 Snipping Tool options

c. Click the **New Snip arrow**, and then click **Full-screen Snip**. The Snipping Tool window opens and then the image is displayed.

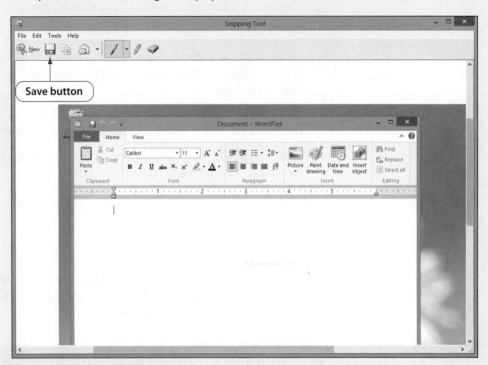

Figure 13   Snip of WordPad

d. Click the **Save** button, and browse to the location of your data files. Click the New folder button to create a new subfolder. Name this subfolder Windows 8 Workshop 1. Press **Enter**. Double-click the Windows 8 Appendix folder.

e. Click the **Save as type arrow**, and then click **JPEG file**. In the File name box, type Lastname_Firstname_w801_app_wordpad, and click the **Save** button.

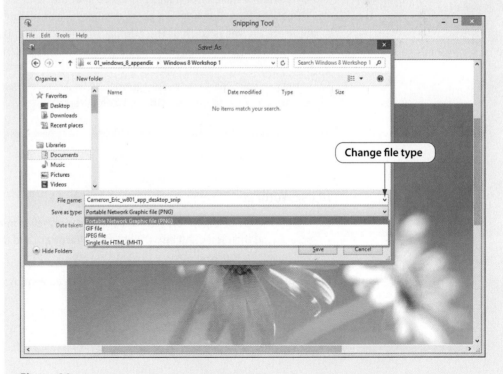

Figure 14   Save options for Snipping Tool

f. Click **Close** ⬛ in the top-right corner of the Snipping Tool window to close it.

g. Point to the Start screen thumbnail, and click the Start screen.

h. Press the Print Screen key on your keyboard.

i. Return to the Start screen. Right-click on a blank area of the Start screen, and select All apps. Click **Paint** to launch the Paint program. Click **Paste**. The image of your Start screen shows up in Paint.

j. Click the **File** menu and select **Save**. Browse to the Windows 8 Appendix folder you created earlier. Save the file as Lastname_Firstname_w801_app_start_snip.

k. Click Close ⬛ in the top-right corner of Paint to close the program. If prompted to save the file, click **Don't Save**. Do the same to close WordPad.

Using WordPad

You want to have your workshop attendees use the computer to take notes. All versions of Windows include a text-editing program named **WordPad**. Though not as powerful as full-feature word-processing programs—such as Microsoft Word or OpenOffice Writer—WordPad is free and preinstalled.

Real World Advice — Note-Taking Software

Certain versions of Microsoft Office include the OneNote tool. OneNote is designed to allow you to keep track of notes in electronic notebook files. OneNote features the option to type anywhere on a page, can organize related pages into sections, and you can keep many sections within a notebook. You may have a notebook for your computer class, with sections for each chapter of the main textbook. Each section may contain a number of pages related to that section.

OneNote also allows you to paste documents and pictures from the Internet, and automatically keeps track of the original website address. Users with tablets can use a digitizer pen and handwrite notes as well. Windows 8 handwriting recognition has greatly improved over previous versions.

You can save the files to the Internet as well, so you can open and modify the document from a number of different computers.

To Use WordPad

a. If WordPad is not shown on your Start screen, right-click in any blank area of the Start screen, and then select **All apps**. Right-click **WordPad**, and then select **Pin to Start**. This will make this tool available on the Start screen.

b. From the Start screen, click **WordPad**. The WordPad window opens.

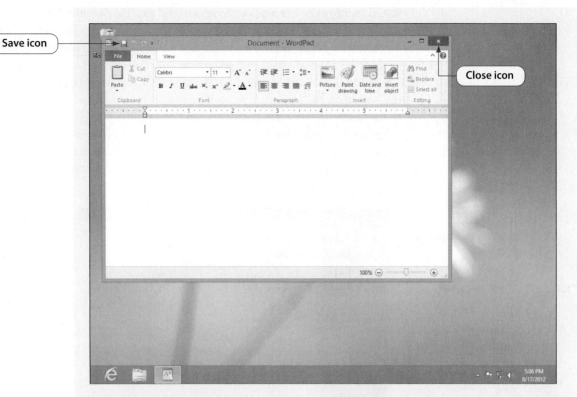

Save icon

Close icon

Figure 15 WordPad interface

c. Type a paragraph describing your experience so far with Windows 8. Click the **Save** icon near the top-left corner of the screen.

d. Navigate to your 01_windows_8_appendix folder. In the **File name** box, type Lastname_Firstname_w801_app_experience. Click **Save**.

e. Click Close ![close icon] in the top-right corner of the WordPad window to close the program.

f. Point to the Start screen thumbnail and click the Start screen.

Switching Between Programs

The Windows operating system supports **multitasking**, or the ability to run more than one program at once. Many users take full advantage of this feature. Users may be running Internet Explorer to log on to Facebook while they type a document in Microsoft Word, listen to music in iTunes, and play World of Warcraft. Users may not realize that while they are running these programs, other applications like their antivirus are also open. The ability to multitask presents great advantages over older operating systems like Microsoft's DOS, but it can also slow down the computer. Just because a computer can run 10 applications at once does not mean it should necessarily. If users find their computer is running slow, a quick fix might be to do less multitasking. Windows 8 will also attempt to manage some of this for the user with better management of open programs.

Windows 8 has changed the way users switch between programs. You can access open programs through the **task switcher** by pointing to the top-left corner of the screen. When the mouse is pointed there, an icon for the most recent application used aside from the current one is displayed (see Figure 16). So, for example, if you open Internet Explorer and then open the Snipping Tool, when you bring the mouse to the top-left of the screen, the Internet Explorer icon is displayed. If you want to see all open applications, you would point to the top-left of the screen and wait for the thumbnail to be displayed. You would then move the mouse along the left side of the screen to bring up a complete list of running software. If you have experience using the [Alt]+[Tab] key combination in older versions of Windows, you will recognize this type of interface.

Applications not designed for Windows 8 allow users to switch using the taskbar at the bottom of the screen. All non-Windows 8 programs will be shown on the taskbar of the desktop. So, if a user opens WordPad and the Snipping Tool, as well as the Windows 8 Reader app, the only two options at the top-left of the screen would be to switch to the Reader app or the desktop containing the taskbar with links to WordPad and the Snipping Tool.

Figure 16 Switching program comparison

To Switch Between Open Applications

a. From the Start screen, click **Snipping Tool**. The Snipping Tool window opens.

b. Bring the mouse to the bottom-left of the screen, and then click the **Start screen** icon.

c. From the Start screen, right-click a blank area of the screen, and then click **All apps** at the bottom of the screen. Locate and click **WordPad** to open the program.

d. Notice the taskbar at the bottom of the screen shows two programs open. One is WordPad and the other is the Snipping Tool. Click on the **icons** at the bottom of the screen to switch between the open programs.

e. Click the Start screen thumbnail to return to the Start screen. Click the **Photos** tile on the Start screen. The Photos tool opens.

f. Click the Start screen thumbnail to return to the Start screen. Click the **Reader** tile on the Start screen. The Reader tool opens. You now have three programs open: Photos, Reader, and the desktop. The desktop contains WordPad and the Snipping Tool.

g. Point to the top-left of the screen and notice a preview of Photos appears, as Photos was the most recently used application aside from the current Reader application.

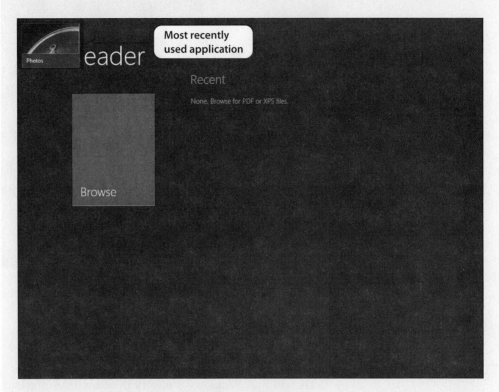

Figure 17 Switching to most recently used application

h. Move the mouse along the left edge of the screen. Notice all other open programs appear on the left side of the screen. Click **Photos** to switch to it.

i. Display the task switcher, and then bring the mouse pointer along the left edge of the screen. All open programs are displayed. Click **Reader** to switch back to that application.

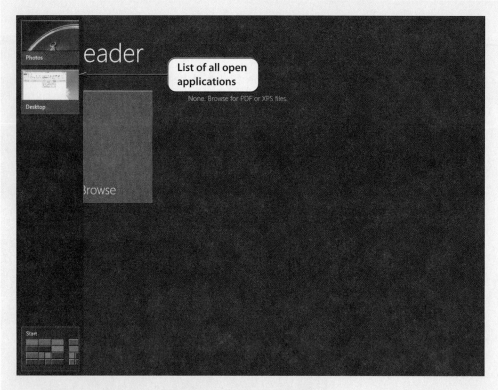

Figure 18 All open applications

Opening and Closing Programs

Users will find Windows 8 is very different than previous versions of Windows when dealing with programs. Users are accustomed to a taskbar at the bottom of the screen that shows all running programs, and a set of icons in the top-right corner of each window to close programs. Applications designed for earlier versions of Windows will open in the Windows desktop view. These applications will include the standard Close button in the top-right corner of the window to allow users to close them. All applications not designed for Windows 8 will open in the desktop view.

Applications designed for Windows 8 will not include the Close buttons users have become accustomed to. Instead, you are expected to trust the operating system to manage the computer's resources. If you do not wish to trust Windows you can also close an application manually by pointing to the task switcher and moving the mouse pointer down the left side of the screen. Any application shown there can be right-clicked and closed. You can also use gestures to close an application on a touch-screen device. A list of gestures is shown in the Using Gestures section of this appendix.

One of the reasons the Close option was removed from Windows 8 is because the operating system **suspends** programs when they are not being used. A suspended application will not use any processing power, and thus leads to Windows 8 devices being more energy-efficient than previous versions of Windows. Instead of expecting users to manage applications, the operating system is attempting to handle application management. This is similar to how cell phones work.

Users will find applications designed for Windows 8 have a different interface than applications not designed for this operating system. You will demonstrate both of these to your workshop.

To Open and Close a Program

a. Most programs can be started either from the Start screen or from All apps. If it is not already started from the previous section, click the **Photos** tile on the Start screen. The Photos application opens.

b. If it is not already started from the previous section, return to the Start screen and click the **Reader** tile. The Reader application opens.

c. As Reader is designed for Windows 8, it does not have the options users may be used to in earlier versions of Windows. Bring the mouse to the top-left corner of the screen, and bring the mouse down the left side of the screen. A list of open programs appears.

Right-click menu for Windows 8 application

Figure 19   Closing an application designed for Windows 8

d. Right-click the **Photos** application, and then click **Close**. The program has been closed.

e. Return to the Start screen, and click the **Snipping Tool**, if it is not already started from the previous section. Notice this program opens in the Windows 7 style desktop.

f. Return to the Start screen, and click **WordPad**, if it is not already open from the previous section. This program also opens in the Windows 7 style desktop.

g. Click **Close** in the top-right corner of the Snipping Tool. The program has been closed.

h. Click **Close** in the top-right corner of WordPad. The program has been closed.

Close button for older Windows apps

Figure 20 Closing a non-Windows 8 application

Using Charms and Windows Search

Charms are buttons which provide quick access to a number of useful functions. Charms bring together some functions that were found in different places in previous versions of Windows. From this menu, users have five options to choose from. Users can access the new and improved Search charm, which has greatly improved Windows search functionality. Users can access the Share charm to send information to social networking sites, such as Facebook or Twitter; blogging sites; and email. The Start charm will bring users back to the main Start screen. The Devices charm allows users to access devices such as display devices. The Settings charm gives users the chance to shut down the machine, access the Control Panel, use Personalization options, find information about the computer, get help, and change options related to wireless connections, audio, display brightness, display of notifications, and language.

Microsoft Windows has always included a search tool. However, in earlier versions of Windows, users did not always use this functionality due to a confusing interface. Windows 7 improved search functionality, but users still had to go to two different places to search effectively. The search on the Start menu was easy to use, but did not offer advanced options. The search in Windows Explorer was more powerful to use, but was not as obvious. Windows 8 has added a search charm, which will allow users to search applications, settings, and files by default. If users log in to a Microsoft account, they will also have the option to search many other areas, including Mail, Maps, People, and Photos. Search will find results not only for file names, but also for contents of files. The only requirement for the advanced find is that the file be on an **indexed** folder. Indexed folders are locations the Windows search tool has already searched and produced a keyword list for. Common indexed locations include the My Documents folder on the hard drive. Removable media, such as USB flash drives and CDs, cannot be indexed by the Windows search tool. Users can also search by simply typing from the Start screen. This is a quick way to find applications not shown on the Start screen.

You will demonstrate the Charms and the Windows search function to your workshop (see Figure 21). As your users will need to search files, you will have them copy files to the hard drive for your demonstration.

Figure 21 Charms

To Use Charms and Search for Files

a. If you have not already done so, copy the **01_windows_8_appendix** folder to your computer's My Documents folder.

b. From the Start screen, bring the mouse pointer to the bottom-right corner of the screen. The Charms are displayed on the right side of the screen.

c. After displaying the Charms, you can display the labels for them by moving the mouse along. Click the **Search** charm.

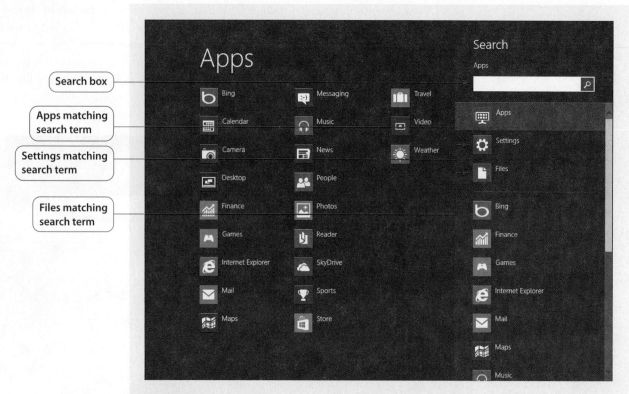

Search box

Apps matching search term

Settings matching search term

Files matching search term

Figure 22 Search charm

d. Click inside the search box at the top of the page. Your data files contain a list of workshop attendees. You will search for a name in the files. Type in the word **Abdelfattah**, and then click the **Search** icon.

No results for Apps

One result for Files

Figure 23 Search results for Abdelfattah

e. Notice you are given three sets of results by default. Apps will show you all applications matching the phrase. Settings will match settings on the computer matching the phrase. Files will show you a list of all files matching the phrase. As you wish to see results from files, click **Files**. If your data files are set up correctly, the number 2 will follow the Files icon.

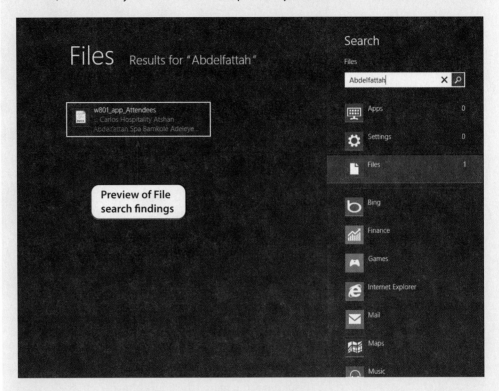

Figure 24 Search results for Abdelfattah in Files

f. The search results will show a list of files matching the search criteria. Your results should have a minimum of one result. Make a note of how many files match the search criteria.

g. Click the Start screen thumbnail.

h. Locate and click **WordPad** to open a new document.

i. Type Search Results for Abdelfattah:, and then follow this with the number of files found. Save the document as Lastname_Firstname_w801_app_search in your Windows 8 Appendix folder.

j. Display the Charms and select the Search charm. If necessary, click Close ![icon] next to the Search button to clear the search box. Enter the phrase Internet Explorer in the search box, and then click the **Search** icon.

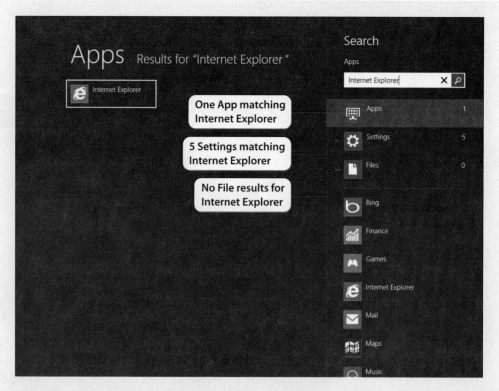

Figure 25 Search results for Internet Explorer

k. Notice your results include **Apps**, **Settings**, and **Files** matching this criteria. Make a note of how many files match the search criteria for each of these three categories. Your results may not match the figure above.

l. Display the task switcher and select the desktop icon to switch back to WordPad.

m. Press **Enter**. Type Search Results for Internet Explorer in Apps:, and then follow this with the number of files found for Apps. Press **Enter**. Type Search Results for Internet Explorer in Settings:, and then follow this with the number of files found for Settings. Press **Enter**. Type Search Results for Internet Explorer in Files:, and then follow this with the number of files found for Files. Press **Enter**. Save the document, and then close WordPad.

n. Click the Start screen thumbnail.

Using Gestures

As mentioned earlier, one of the key features that sets Windows 8 apart from previous versions is the built-in touch-screen recognition. At first, this functionality will likely be for mobile devices, but it would be a surprise if this technology is not embraced by home users to replace some mouse clicking. Many gestures are available from the bezel, or the edge of the screen. Users can swipe from off-screen on to the screen to make certain actions happen, as you will see in the table below.

You will provide your workshop attendees with a list of Windows 8 gestures, so when the touch-screen devices become available, they have a reference.

Desired Action	Gesture	Gesture
Bring up additional menu options	Swipe down from the top bezel, or swipe up from the bottom bezel	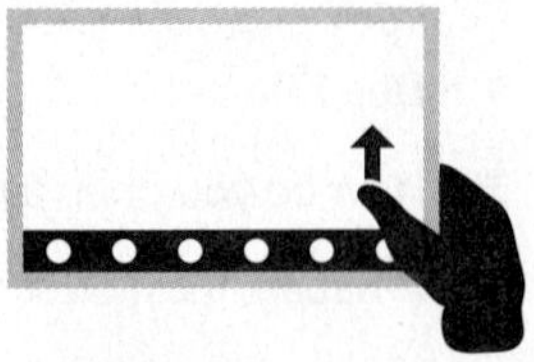
Bring up tile options on the Start screen	Swipe down on the tile	
Close the current application	Swipe down from the top bezel to the bottom	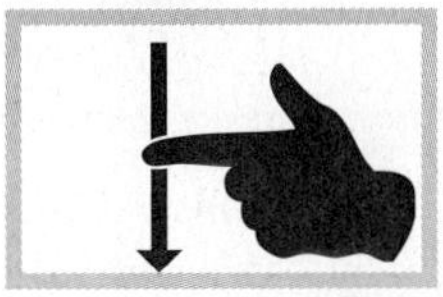
Displays Charms	Swipe from the right bezel towards the left	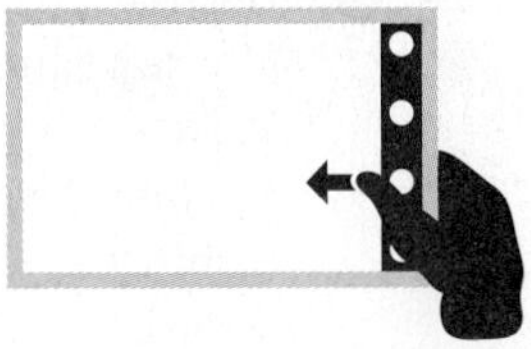
Show all open applications	Swipe out from the left bezel a little, and then swipe back to the left bezel quickly	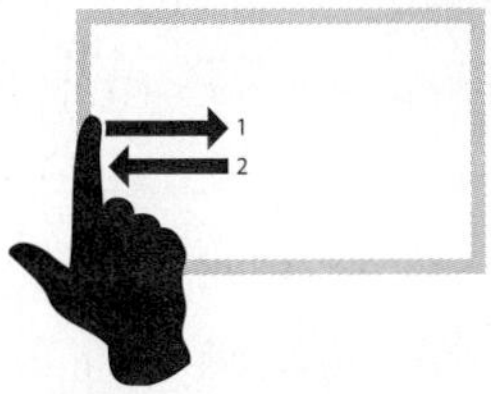
Switch between applications	Swipe from the left bezel towards the right	
Zoom in	Pinch	
Zoom out	Stretch—start two fingers pinched and spread fingers apart	

Figure 26 Windows 8 gestures

1. Describe two differences between earlier versions of Windows and Windows 8.

2. How do you open a program when no shortcuts are available?

3. What are tiles? Describe the difference between a tile and a Live Tile.

4. How do you add a tile to the Start screen?

5. What is the purpose of the Snipping Tool?

6. What are Charms?

7. What is gesture recognition? List three examples of gestures and what they do.

Key Terms

Application software   1042
ARM device   1042
Charm   1043, 1060
Click   1043
Desktop   1046
Drag   1049
Gesture   1042
Gesture recognition   1042
Graphical user interface (GUI)   1042
Hybrid boot   1043

Icons   1042
Indexed   1060
Live Tile   1046
Mouse pointer   1048
Multitasking   1055
Operating system   1042
Right-click   1048
Scroll bar   1048
Shortcut menu   1048
Snip   1052

Snipping Tool   1052
Start screen   1043
Suspend   1058
System software   1042
Taskbar   1046
Task switcher   1055
Tile   1045
Windows RT   1042
WordPad   1054

Visual Summary

Start and shut down Windows (p. 1044)

Explore the Windows 8 Start screen (p. 1048)

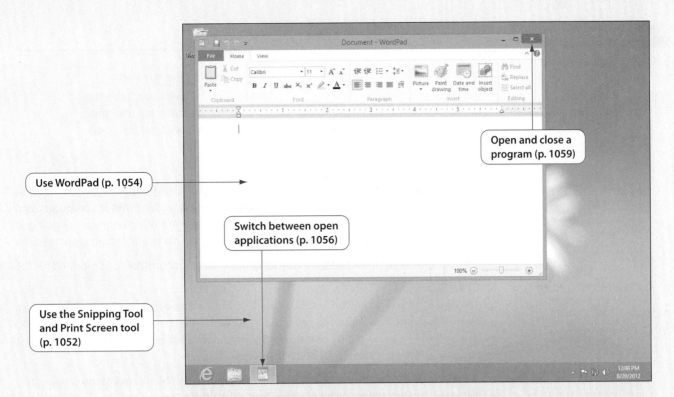

Open and close a program (p. 1059)

Use WordPad (p. 1054)

Switch between open applications (p. 1056)

Use the Snipping Tool and Print Screen tool (p. 1052)

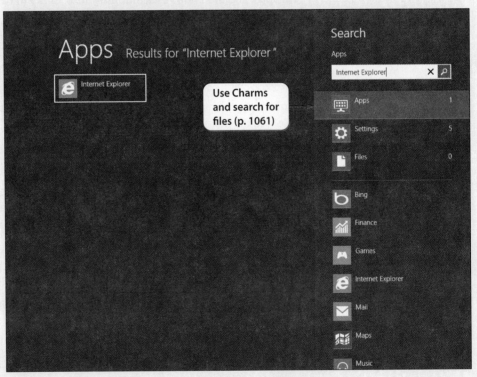

Use Charms and search for files (p. 1061)

Figure 27   Painted Paradise Golf Resort and Spa — Employee Introduction to Microsoft Windows 8 Final

Student data file needed:

01_windows_8_appendix folder

You will save your files as:

Lastname_Firstname_w801_app_before_snip

Lastname_Firstname_w801_app_after_snip

Lastname_Firstname_w801_practice1_search

Using New Features in Windows 8

Patti Rochelle, corporate event planner at Painted Paradise Golf Resort and Spa, would like you to work with her staff to help them customize their new Windows 8 computers and become comfortable with the new Search feature. To assess your workshop, you are going to have users take before and after snips of their screens, and perform and record search results.

a. Switch on your computer and, if necessary, follow any logon instructions required for the computer you are using.

b. Use the Print Screen key on your keyboard to create a screenshot of your Start screen. Paste this image into Paint, and save it as a JPG file named Lastname_Firstname_w801_app_before_snip in your **01_windows_8_appendix** folder, replacing last name and first name with your last name and first name. Close Paint.

c. If the Snipping Tool is not on your Start screen, right-click a blank area of the screen, click **All apps**, and then right-click **Snipping Tool**. Click **Pin to Start**.

d. Right-click **People** or any other large tile. Select **Smaller** to make the icon appear as a smaller tile.

e. Locate the Snipping Tool tile. Move the tile near the tile you made smaller in the previous step.

f. Right-click a blank area on the Start screen, click **All apps**, and then select any other tool to pin to the Start screen.

g. Locate the tile for the program you added to your Start screen. Move the tile near the tile you made smaller in step d.

h. Use the Print Screen key on your keyboard to create a screenshot of your Start screen. Paste this image into Paint, and save the snip as a JPG file named Lastname_Firstname_w801_app_after_snip in your **01_windows_8_appendix** folder. Close Paint.

i. Right-click a blank area on the Start screen, and then select **All apps**. Locate and click **WordPad** to open a new document. Save the created file as Lastname_Firstname_w801_practice1_search in your 01_windows_8_appendix folder.

j. Click the bottom-right area of the screen to make the Charms visible. Select the **Search** icon.

k. Use the Search charm to locate the name **Ishaaya** in your data files. Switch to WordPad, and then add the text Number of files containing Ishaaya:, and follow that text with the number of files your search found.

l. Use the Search charm to locate the text series of sensors in your data files. Switch to **WordPad**, add the text Number of files containing series of sensors:, and then follow that text with the number of files your search found.

m. Save your WordPad document, and exit the program.

n. Submit the three files as instructed.

Student data file needed:

01_windows_8_appendix folder

You will save your files as:

Lastname_Firstname_w801_app_proposal1
Lastname_Firstname_w801_app_proposal2
Lastname_Firstname_w801_app_proposal3
Lastname_Firstname_w801_app_sample_search

Presenting Windows 8 to Management

Kathleen Lordelo, manager of Painted Paradise Golf Resort and Spa's Information Technology services, is hoping to enlist your assistance in creating model Start screens. She has asked you to move some icons around and add tools you think most users need, and remove any you think they would not. She would like you to create three different snips of your ideas, from which she would allow management to choose the best one. She has also asked for your assistance in demonstrating the Search charm. Members of the management team saw a demonstration of Windows 8 and noticed the ability to search for programs is gone. She has asked you to take screen shots of a few searches that demonstrate that the Search feature still works.

a. As you cannot find information within files through the Search charm unless they are in an indexed location such as your My Documents folder, ensure your 01_windows_8_ appendix folder has been downloaded and copied to your computer's Documents folder.

b. Think about applications and tools you think would fit well on a Start screen. Add and remove tiles as necessary. Using Print Screen, take a picture of your Start screen, paste it into Paint, and save it as a JPG file named Lastname_Firstname_w801_app_proposal1. jpg in your 01_windows_8_appendix folder.

c. Create a second arrangement by adding and removing tiles as necessary. Using Print Screen, take a picture of your Start screen, paste it into Paint, and save it as a JPG file named Lastname_Firstname_w801_app_proposal2.jpg in your 01_windows_8_appendix folder.

d. Create a third arrangement by adding and removing tiles as necessary. Using Print Screen, take a picture of your Start screen, paste it into Paint, and save it as a JPG file named Lastname_Firstname_w801_app_proposal3.jpg in your 01_windows_8_appendix folder.

e. Perform a search for any Windows application you know is installed on the system. Make a note of how many apps, settings, and files match the results for this search. Create a WordPad document named Lastname_Firstname_w801_app_sample_search in your 01_windows_8_appendix folder, and summarize how many results match each criteria.

f. Browse the contents of w801_app_attendees.docx, found in your 01_windows_8_appendix folder. Find a distinctive name, and then perform a search for the name. If you get no results, ensure your data files are stored in the computer's Documents folder. Summarize how many apps, settings, and files match the criteria inside the file you created in the previous step, Lastname_Firstname_w801_app_sample_search. Save the file, and then exit WordPad.

g. Submit the files as directed.

Glossary

A

Absolute cell reference The exact address of a cell, when both the column and row need to remain a constant regardless of the position of the cell when the formula is copied to other cells.

Access Data Collection Replies folder A new folder that is automatically created in Outlook to collect replies from a data collection form.

Action button A special shape that is predefined to include actions that navigate through slides.

Active cell Identifiable as the cell with the thick black border. Only the active cell can have data entered into it.

Active window The window in which you can move the mouse pointer, type text, or perform other tasks.

Active worksheet The worksheet that is visible in the Excel application window. The active worksheet tab has a white background.

Address bar A toolbar that displays the path to the active file, folder, or window.

Adobe PDF file A file format that is easy to send through e-mail and preserves the original document look and feel so it opens the same way every time for the recipient.

Aggregate function Calculations that perform arithmetic operations, such as averages and totals, on records displayed in a table or query.

Alignment The positioning of content in a cell, either horizontally left, centered, or horizontally right; vertically bottom, middle, or top.

All Programs Provides access to programs and utilities installed on your computer.

Animation The movement of elements on a slide.

Annotate Make notations or marks on slides as you give a presentation.

Annotated bibliography A special type of bibliography that compiles references along with a short paragraph summarizing or reviewing the value of the source to the research project.

APA A writing style guide preferred by the social sciences.

Append row The first blank row at the end of the table.

Application software Programs that help the user perform specific tasks, such as word processing.

Appointment An assignment of time for which you do not have to schedule other people or resources.

Area chart Emphasize magnitude of change over time and depict trends.

Argument Inputs used in functions for calculating a solution. A value passed to a function, either as a constant or a variable.

ARM device A device using a different processor than personal computers. Uses less power than a traditional PC processor, and is less susceptible to viruses.

Attached object Data that is sent directly from Access via an e-mail message.

Attachment A file created in a variety of software applications that is appended to an e-mail message for transmission to the recipient. When received, the file can be opened using the appropriate software or saved to the local computer.

Attribute Information about the entity.

AutoCorrect A feature that corrects common typographical errors and misspellings as they are typed.

AutoFill Copies information from one cell, or a series in adjacent cells, into adjacent cells in the direction the fill handle is dragged.

AutoFit A method to change the column width of a field to match the widest data entered in that field.

AutoSum function Shortcuts to using the SUM functions.

AVERAGE function A function that returns a weighted average from a specified range of cells.

B

Backstage view Provides access to the file-level features, such as saving a file, creating a new file, opening an existing file, printing a file, and closing a file, as well as program options.

Backup database An extra copy of a database created in case the database is lost. Access appends the current date to the file name.

Banding Alternating the background color of rows and/or columns to assist in tracking information.

Bar chart Displays data horizontally and is used for comparisons among individual items.

Bibliography A list of references used in the development of a paper.

Bit-mapped graphics Images created with pixels or bits in a grid, most often used for photographs.

Block A common business letter style in which all text is left aligned and single spaced.

Body text The lowest level text in an outline.

Bound control A control on a report or form whose data source is a field in the table.

Built-in cell style Predefined and named combination of cell and content formatting properties.

Built-in function A function included in the Excel application that can be categorized as financial, statistical, mathematical, date and time, text, etc.

Bullet Symbol or graphic that identifies a summary point.

Business communication Communication between members of an organization for the purpose of carrying out business activities.

C

Calculated control A control on a report or form whose data source is a calculated expression.

Caption Text box linked to photographs within a photo album.

Cardinality The number of instances of one entity that relates to one instance of another entity. Cardinality is expressed as one-to-many, many-to-many, or one-to-one.

Category An organizational feature that enables you to color-code and name groups of e-mail, appointments, contacts, or tasks. This groups similar items together for easy retrieval.

Cell The intersection of a row and a column in a worksheet.

Cell reference Refers to a particular cell or range of cells within a formula or function instead of a value.

Center tab Tab stop at which text aligns from the center.

Centered Text aligned horizontally at the center of the page.

Charm Buttons appearing on the right side of the screen.

Chart A graphical representation of numeric data.

Chart sheet A tabbed sheet that only holds a chart.

Chicago A writing style guide that is primarily concerned with the preparation and editing of papers and books for publication.

Citation A reference to a published or unpublished source used in the development of a paper.

Click The act of pressing the left mouse button one time.

Clip Art A graphic illustration that can be inserted in a document as an object.

Clipboard An area of memory that is reserved to temporarily contain items that you have cut or copied.

Clipboard task pane Boxed area that shows up to 24 cut or copied items that you can paste or delete.

Collapse button To hide all lower levels in an outline.

Color tone The color temperature of a photograph, measured in Kelvin.

Column Part of a spreadsheet that is lettered in ascending sequence from left to right.

Column chart Used to compare across categories, show change, sometimes over time.

Command bar A toolbar that displays commands related to the open window.

Comments Short notes, stored on slides, explaining your thoughts.

Compacting An Access function that rearranges objects in your database to use space more efficiently.

Comparison operator An operator used in a query to compare the value in a database to the criteria value entered in the query.

Composite key A primary key composed of two or more fields.

Compress To reduce the size of folders and files.

Conditional formatting Allows the specification of rules that apply formatting to cells, appointments, contacts, or tasks as determined by the rule outcome.

Constant A value that does not change.

Content Elements appearing on the slide, including text and graphics.

Content pane Area in the center of Windows Explorer that displays the content of whatever is selected in the Navigation Pane.

Context sensitive Commands related to a right-clicked item.

Contextual tab A Ribbon tab that contains commands related to selected objects so you can manipulate, edit, and format the objects.

Control A part of a form or report that is used to enter, edit, or display data.

Conversation A group of e-mail messages that share the same subject line and appear together with graphics indicating the relationship between the messages. Replies to messages are shown as well as the messages received.

Copy Duplicate a selection to the Clipboard, while leaving the original in the same location.

Copyrights The legal rights afforded to the creator of written and/or artistic works.

Corporate identity The visual elements, such as a logo, that make a company and their products recognizable.

COUNT function A function that returns the number of cells in a range of cells that contain numbers.

Cropping handles Lines around selected graphic objects that enable you to cut away unneeded portions.

CSE A writing style guide preferred by the sciences.

Custom slide show A subset of a PowerPoint presentation containing only part of the slides in the presentation.

Cut Remove a selection from its original location to the Clipboard.

D

Data Facts about people, events, things, or ideas.

Data bars Graphical display of data that is overlaid on the data in the cells of the worksheet.

Data collection form A form in an e-mail message that is used to collect new data or to update existing data in an Access table.

Data Collection Wizard A step-by-step guide to walk you through setting up a data collection form.

Data point An individual piece of data being graphed.

Data series A set or subset of data that is graphed.

Data source A document that contains variable information that is used in a mail merge process.

Data type The characteristic that defines the kind of data that can be entered into a field, such as numbers, text, or dates.

Database management system (DBMS) Database management software that can be used to organize, store, manipulate, and report on your data.

Datasheet view A view of an Access object that shows data.

Date Navigator A monthly calendar, shown in the Navigation Pane, that can be used to select a date for display on the calendar.

Decimal tab Tab stop at which text aligns from the decimal point.

Default A setting that is automatically in place unless you specify otherwise.

Delay The length of time in seconds before an animation or transition plays.

Deleted Items folder A recycle bin that contains e-mail that has been deleted. Messages stay in the Deleted Items folder until the folder is emptied or the individual item is deleted within the folder.

Delimiter A character used in a text file to separate the fields; it can be a paragraph mark, a tab, a comma, or another character.

Demote To move a paragraph to a lower level in the outline.

Design themes A set of elements, such as a color palette, font group, and slide backgrounds that enable you to create consistent slides.

Design view A view of an Access object that shows the detailed structure of a table, query, form, or report.

Desktop The working area of the Windows screen. The taskbar is found at the bottom of the screen.

Desktop background The picture or pattern that is displayed on the desktop.

Destination file The file that a linked or embedded object is inserted into.

Destination program The program that a linked or embedded object is inserted into.

Details pane Pane at the bottom of Windows Explorer that displays the properties of the file or folder selected.

Dialog box A window that provides more options or settings beyond those provided on the Ribbon and requires a response from the user.

Dialog Box Launcher An icon on the Ribbon that opens a corresponding dialog box or task pane.

Document Depending on the application a document can be a letter, memo, report, brochure, resume, or flyer.

Double-click Pressing the left mouse button two times in rapid succession.

Draft view A document view that provides the most space possible for typing, without displaying margins.

Drafts folder A folder that stores e-mail that has been saved but not sent. Click the Save icon as you compose a long message to save it to this folder. Most often draft messages are saved as you navigate away from the message window.

Drag To click and hold the left mouse button down, move the pointer where you would like the item to appear, and release the mouse button.

Drop cap A design element in which the first letter of a paragraph is shown as a large graphic representation of the character.

Duration The length of time in seconds that it takes an animation or transition to play.

E

Edit mode A mode that allows you to edit or change the contents of a field or change the name of a file or folder.

Effect option Alternative transition or animation choice, often determining the way the effect enters the window.

Embedded object An object that is inserted into a document but is not connected to the file it was created in. Any updates must be done in the new document.

Emphasis Adds any group of features to characters in a font that includes bold, italics, and underline.

Emphasis action The effect that occurs after an object is displayed on a slide.

Endnote A reference that appears in a numerical list at the end of a paper, providing a information on the source.

Entity Person, place, item, or event that you want to keep data about.

Entrance animation The effect that occurs as objects enter the slide.

Exit animation The effect that occurs as objects leave the slide.

Expand To show lower levels in an outline.

Expression Builder A tool that helps you format your calculated fields correctly by providing a list of expressive elements, operators, and built-in functions.

F

Field An item of information associated with something of interest. A collection of fields about an item of interest from a record.

Field size The maximum length of a data field.

File extension A suffix that helps Windows understand what kind of information is in a file and what program should open it.

File list Displays the contents of a selected folder.

Fill color The background color of a cell.

Filter A condition applied temporarily to a table or query to show a subset of the records.

Filter by selection Selecting a value in a record and filtering the records that contain only the values that match what has been selected.

Find and Replace The process of finding a specified item, formatting, or punctuation, and replacing it with another.

Find command A command used to find records in a database with a specific value.

First-line indent An indent style where the first line of a paragraph is indented a specified distance from the right margin—by default, at 1/2".

Font A style of displaying characters, numbers, punctuation, and special characters.

Font groups Font combinations, for the headings and body content, that become part of the theme.

Footer Text or graphics that are printed in the bottom margin of a document.

Footnote A reference to a source that is placed numerically at the foot of the page in which the reference is made.

Foreign key The field that is included in the related table so the field can be joined with the primary key in another table for the purpose of creating a relationship.

Form Object that allows you to enter or view your data.

Form view Data view of a form.

Format How Access displays data.

Format Painter A tool that enables you to copy the format of objects, such as text or pictures, to paste on other objects.

Formatting marks Special characters that are displayed in a document to indicate where nonprinting characters, such as Enter, Tab, or Space, are located.

Formula Performs a mathematical calculation (or calculations) using information in the worksheets to calculate new values and can contain cell references, constants, functions, and mathematical operators.

Full Screen Reading view A document view that shows pages side by side, without a Ribbon at the top of the screen.

Function A built-in program that performs operations against data and returns a value such as SUM or AVERAGE. Some functions, null functions, do not require arguments.

G

Gadget A miniprogram that can be added to your desktop.

Gesture Allows users to perform actions like zoom and switching programs by performing certain movements.

Gesture recognition Allows users with touch screens to control the computer with gestures instead of mouse clicks.

Google Drive An extension of Google Docs, offering online file storage and collaboration tools.

Graphic Pictures, clip art, SmartArt, shapes, and charts that can enhance the look of your documents.

Graphical format The presentation of information in charts, graphs, and pictures.

Graphical user interface (GUI) Interface that uses icons and pictures to represent commands, programs, and documents.

Group A collection of records along with some introductory and summary information about the records.

Group footer The area of a report where summary information about a group is included.

Group header The area of a report where introductory information about a group is included.

Gutter A margin that adds extra space to the side or top of a document that is to be bound.

H

Handout master The layout of elements, such as the header and footer, on the handout pages.

Hanging Indent An indent style where the first line begins at the left margin, with all other lines in the paragraph indented.

Hard drive A disk drive inside your computer, also called the local drive.

Hard return What is inserted into a document when you press Enter.

Hard-coding Including actual data in formulas, making it necessary to edit the formula whenever the number needs to be changed.

Header Text or graphics that are printed in the top margin of a document.

HTML form A form created for and used by any user whose e-mail supports HTML.

Hybrid boot Allows users to decrease the time it takes to shut down, while making start up times quicker. Introduced in Windows 8.

Hyperlink An object, such as text or a graphic, that provides a path to nonlinear slides or to Internet resources, such as e-mail or websites.

I

Icon A small picture that represents a command, program, or document.

Import To bring data into one program from another.

Import Spreadsheet Wizard Step-by-step instructions in Access to help successfully import data from another source.

Importing The process of copying data from another file, such as a Word file or Excel workbook, into a separate file, such as an Access database.

Inbox A default folder that receives incoming e-mail.

Indexed Folders that the Windows search tool has already searched and produced a keyword list for. Speeds up searches.

InfoPath form A form created for and used by any user who has InfoPath installed on his or her computer.

Information Data that has been manipulated and processed to make it meaningful.

Information management program Provides the ability to track and print schedules, task lists, phone directories, and other documents.

Input mask A field property that determines the data that can be entered and how the data is displayed.

Insertion point The blinking black bar that indicates the location where text that you next type will be placed.

J

Join Create a relationship between two tables based upon a common field.

Jump List A list displaying commands or files related to an option on the Start menu.

Junction table A table that breaks down the many-to-many relationship into two one-to-many relationships.

Junk E-mail folder A folder that contains messages identified as possible spam by the Junk E-mail Filter. This folder should be regularly viewed and unneeded messages deleted.

Justified Text aligned so that it extends evenly between the left and right margins.

K

Key tip A form of keyboard shortcuts. Pressing (Alt) will display Key Tips (or keyboard shortcuts) for items on the Ribbon and Quick Access Toolbar.

Keyboard shortcut Keyboard equivalents for software commands that allow you to keep your hands on the keyboard instead of reaching for the mouse to make Ribbon selections.

Kiosk A stand-alone computer system that provides information to people in nontraditional places, such as museums, grocery stores, banks, sporting events, and more.

KISS principle An acronym for Keep It Short and Simple.

L

Label An unbound control. It may be the name of a field or other text you manually enter.

Landscape orientation For page layout and printing purposes, landscape indicates the longer dimension of the page is on the horizontal axis.

Layout selector A tool that allows you to move a whole table at one time.

Layout view Shows data and allows limited changes to a form or report design.

Leader A row of dots or dashes that are displayed before a tab stop.

Left indent Indenting an entire paragraph from the left margin.

Left tab Tab stop at which text aligns from the left.

Left-aligned Text aligned flush with the left margin, with a ragged right edge.

Level 1 The highest level in a Word outline.

Level 2 The second highest level in a Word outline.

Library Virtual folders that display the contents of multiple folders as though the files were stored together in one location.

Library pane Pane at the top of Windows Explorer that is displayed only when a library is selected.

Line chart Used to show continuous data over time, great for showing trends.

Line spacing Spacing between lines in a paragraph.

Linked object An object that is inserted into a document but is still connected to the file it was created in, allowing it to be updated in both places at the same time.

Live Preview A feature that shows the effect of a proposed change to selected text before the change is made.

Live Tile Give users a constant stream of information. For example, the Weather tile shows the current weather for your location, updated frequently.

Logical operator An operator used in a query to combine two or more criteria.

M

Mail client A program such as a Microsoft Outlook 2010 on your computer that enables you to compose, send, and receive e-mail messages.

Mail merge A process that simplifies the task of preparing documents that contain identical formatting, layout, and text but where only certain portions of each document vary.

Mail server A special-purpose computer with an Internet connection that functions as a central post office and provides private mailboxes to people authorized to use its services.

Main document A document that consists primarily of text that will not change during a mail merge process.

Main form The primary, or first table, selected when creating a form.

Many-to-many relationship A relationship between tables where one record in one table has many matching records in a second table, and a single record in the related table has many matching records in the first table.

Margin Empty space at the top, bottom, left, and right of a document.

Mathematical operators Parentheses (), exponentiation ^, division /, multiplication *, addition +, subtraction −.

MAX function A function that examines all numeric values in a specified range and returns the maximum value.

Maximize The button is located in the top-right corner of the title bar; it offers the largest workspace.

Meeting An event scheduled with one or more attendees for whom Outlook will automatically create and send e-mail notifications.

Menu bar A toolbar from which you can access menus of commands.

Merge field Reference to a field in the data source of a mail merge process.

Messaging Application Program Interface (MAPI) A program that makes it possible for Outlook and Word to share information about a merged e-mail.

Microsoft Word 2010 The word-processing package included in the Microsoft Office 2010 software suite.

MIN function A function that examines all numeric values in a specified range and returns the minimum value.

Mini toolbar Appears after text is selected and contains buttons for the most commonly used formatting commands, such as font, font size, font color, center alignment, indents, bold, italic, and underline.

Minimize To reduce a window to a taskbar button.

Mixed cell reference Using a combination of absolute cell referencing and relative cell referencing for a cell address within a formula by preceding either the column letter or the row value with a dollar sign to "lock" as absolute while leaving the other portion of the cell address as a relative reference.

MLA A writing style guide preferred by the humanities.

Modified block A business letter style in which the body is left-aligned and single-spaced, with the date and closing centered.

Mouse pointer An arrow that shows the position of the mouse on the screen.

Multitasking The ability to run more than one program at once.

N

Named range A set of cells that have been given a name, other than the default column and row cell address name, that can then be used within a formula or function.

Natural primary key A primary key that is a natural part of your data.

Navigation bar Provides a way to move through records in table, query, report, and form objects.

Navigation mode Allows you to move from record to record or field to field using keystrokes and the Navigation bar.

Navigation Pane A pane on the Outlook window that contains folders, calendars, and buttons for organizing information for each of the components of Outlook.

Newsletter A printed or electronic news report for a group.

Nonprinting characters Characters that are included in a document, but do not print, such as Enter, Tab, and Space.

Normal view The default view of PowerPoint that displays the Ribbon and tools for creating and modifying slides.

Normalization The process of minimizing the duplication of information in a relational database through effective table design.

Notes master The layout of elements, such as the slide thumbnail and note placeholder, on the speaker notes pages.

Notification area Area of the taskbar that displays information about the status of programs running in the background; it also includes a clock and the Show desktop button.

Nper The number of periods or total number of payments that will be made for a loan.

Number data type A data type that can store only numerical data. The data field will be used in calculations.

Numeric key A primary key with a number data type. AutoNumber is often used for numeric keys.

O

Object (Access) An Access table, query, form, or report.

Object (Word) An item, such as a picture or text box, that can be worked with independently of surrounding text.

OLE The abbreviation for Object Linking and Embedding, which is a feature in Microsoft Office that allows you to insert an object into a file either as a linked object or an embedded object.

One-to-many relationship A relationship between two tables where one record in the first table corresponds to many records in the second table—the most common type of relationship in Access.

One-to-one relationship A relationship between tables where a record in one table has only one matching record in the second table.

Operating system Software that controls and coordinates the computer hardware to make other programs run efficiently. Windows 8 is an example of an operating system.

Order of operations The order in which Excel processes calculations in a formula that contains more than one operator.

Orphan A line that is alone at the bottom of a page or a foreign key in one table that does not have a matching value in the primary key field of a related table.

Outbox folder A folder that contains all of the written messages that have not yet been uploaded to the server. When connected to the server, these messages are automatically transferred to the server.

Outline A hierarchical representation of paragraphs, which are recognized by a nonprinting end-of-paragraph mark.

Outline tab Tab in the Normal view used to place content on the slide in a hierarchy relationship.

Outline view A document view that shows levels of detail and organization, as identified by headings and subheadings.

P

Paragraph spacing Space between paragraphs.

Parameter A special form of variable included in a worksheet for the sole purpose of inclusion in formulas and functions.

Password A secret word or series of characters that protects your account, and with your user name, gives you access to your mailbox on the server.

Paste Placing a cut or copied selection in a new location.

Paste Preview A feature that shows the effect of a paste operation before the paste occurs.

PDF (Portable Document Format) A file type that preserves most formatting attributes of a source document regardless of the software the document was created in.

Pecha Kucha A type of presentation that displays 20 slides for 20 second each, during which the presenter speaks.

Peek Turn open windows transparent to reveal the desktop.

Photo album An efficient way to place a large number of photographs into a presentation.

Picture A photo or graphic that is saved on a disk.

Picture Styles Formatting, applied to graphics, to create borders, shapes, or effects such as shadowing or beveling.

Pie chart Displays a comparison of each value to a total.

Pinned programs area Area on the top of the left pane of the Start menu.

Placeholder A container for text or graphics, used on the layout to position the objects on the slide.

Plagiarism The act of falsely attributing ideas, or phrasing, as original to a writer, when in fact they originated with another person.

Portable Document Format (PDF) A file format developed by Adobe Systems in 1993 that has become a standard for storing files.

Portrait Orientation For page layout and printing purposes, portrait indicates the longer dimension of the page is on the vertical axis.

PowerPoint PDF A conversion of a slide show into Portable Document Format, so it can be opened by the Adobe Reader application.

PowerPoint Show A slide show that opens full screen without opening PowerPoint first.

Presenter view A two monitor setup enabling you to see the speaker notes on one monitor while the audience sees the presentation full screen on the other monitor.

Preview pane Pane on the right of Windows Explorer that displays the contents of a selected file.

Primary key The field that uniquely identifies a record in a table.

Primary sort field The first field chosen in a multiple field sort.

Print Layout view A document view that shows top, bottom, left, and right margins.

Print Preview View that allows you to preview how your document will print on the monitor before actually printing to paper or to a file.

Printer-friendly fonts Fonts that are easy to read on a printed page.

Promote To move a paragraph to a higher level in the outline.

Proofing tools PowerPoint tools to assist you with spelling, research, and finding synonyms using the Thesaurus.

Protected view The file contents can be seen and read, but you are not able to edit, save, or print the contents until you enable editing.

Pseudo-code The rough draft of a formula or code. It is intended to help you understand the logic and determine the structure of a problem before you develop the actual formula.

PV The present value of an investment or loan.

Q

Query Object that retrieves specific data from one or more database objects—either tables or other queries—and then, in a single datasheet, displays only the data you specify.

Query by example A type of query where a sample of the data is set up as criteria.

Query design grid Selected fields in a query. Shown at the bottom of a query's Design view.

Query results A recordset that provides an answer to a question posed in a query.

Query workspace Source for data in the query. Shown at the top of a query's Design view.

Quick Access Toolbar Located at the top left of the Office window, it can be customized to offer commonly used buttons.

Quick Step Multiple commands compressed into a single click accessed from the Ribbon e-mail component of Outlook.

Quick Styles Styles shown in the Styles gallery.

R

Range A group of cells in a worksheet that have been selected or highlighted, performed commands will affect the entire range.

Rate The periodic interest rate used for calculating interest accrued.

Reading Pane The portion of the Outlook window that displays the text of a selected message, appointment, contract, or task. The Reading Pane can appear on the right or bottom of the window. It can also be turned off.

Reading view A PowerPoint view where the slide is displayed full screen, with buttons on the status bar to move to the next or previous slide, or to a menu of slides.

Recolor Alter the colors of a photograph or other graphic to create a monochromatic effect.

Record All of the categories of data pertaining to one person, place, thing, event, or idea, and that is formatted as a row in a database table.

Record selector The small box at the left of a record in Datasheet view that is used to select an entire record.

Recordset A run time table.

Recycle Bin A storage area for files that have been deleted.

Redundancy Data that is repeated in a manner that indicates poor database design.

Relational database A 3-dimensional database able to connect data in separate tables to form a relationship when common fields exist—to offer reassembled information from multiple tables.

Relationship An association that you establish between two tables based on common fields.

Relative cell reference Default cell reference in a formula to a cell reference position that will automatically adjust when the formula is copied or extended to other cells, the cell being referenced changes relative to the placement of the formula.

Replace command A command used to automatically replace values in a table or query.

Report Object that summarizes the fields and records from a table or query in an easy-to-read format suitable for printing.

Report view A view that allows you to see what the printed report will look like in a continuous page layout.

Restore Returns a maximized window to its previous size and location.

Restore Down Allows you to arrange and view several windows at a time when multiple applications are open.

Reuse slides Import slides from another presentation for use in the current presentation.

Ribbon Where you will find most of the commands for the application. The Ribbon differs from program to program, but each program has two tabs in common: the File tab and the Home tab.

Ribbon button Located just below the Minimize and Close buttons in the top-right corner of the window (and directly next to the Help button, which looks like a question mark), it can hide or show the Ribbon.

Rich Text Format (RTF) A file format that retains the formatting of the original document when you import it into another program.

Right indent Indenting an entire paragraph from the right margin.

Right tab Tab stop at which text aligns from the right.

Right-aligned Text aligned flush with the right margin, with a ragged left edge.

Right-click To press the right mouse button one time.

Row Part of a spreadsheet that is numbered in ascending sequence from top to bottom.

Rule of 6's A rule that advises no more than six words per line, and no more than six lines per slide.

Ruler A horizontal and vertical bar at the top and side of a document showing measurements.

Run time An object that is created at the time of request.

S

Sans serif fonts Font styles that do not have end strokes (serifs) on the letters.

Scatter chart Shows the relationship between numeric variables.

Screen saver A moving graphic that starts when a computer sits idle for a specified amount of time.

Screen-friendly fonts Fonts that can be read easily from a distance while projected on a screen.

Screenshot An image of a window or screen display that is manipulated as an object.

ScreenTip Provides a name or other information about the object to which you are pointing.

Scroll bar A bar that appears when all items are not visible on the screen.

Scroll box The box in the scroll bar used to reposition items.

Search box A box within which you type a word or phrase to search.

Secondary sort field The second and subsequent fields chosen in a multiple field sort.

Section A document area that can be formatted differently from other sections.

Security Warning bar A yellow warning bar that appears just below the ribbon when you open an Access database.

Semiblock A business letter style in which the body is left-aligned and single-spaced, the date and closing are centered, and each paragraph is indented 1.2".

Sent Items folder A folder that contains copies of messages that have been uploaded to the mail server.

Serif font A font that includes decorative strokes and provides a visual connection between letters and words.

Shake To shake the title bar to minimize all other windows.

Shortcut menu A group or list of context-sensitive commands related to a selection that appears when you right-click.

Show Formulas view Displays toggle feature that allows for viewing the formula(s) in the spreadsheet cells instead of the output, or value, of the formula(s).

Signature A block of text and graphics that is added to the end of e-mail messages to provide additional information about the sender.

Sizing handle Small boxes, or circles, in the center and corners of the border surrounding an object that can be used to resize the object.

SkyDrive An online workspace provided by Microsoft. SkyDrive's online filing cabinet is a free Windows Live Service.

Slide footer Information at the bottom of the slide that can include the slide number, date, and other information.

Slide layout The placement of objects, such as the title and body content, on the slide.

Slide master Special slide used to create a template, which details fonts, placement of footers, background colors, and other characteristics for the presentation.

Slide sections Organizational tool used on the Slides tab, which can expand or collapse a group of slide thumbnails.

Slide Show view The full-screen display of a slide presentation, as it would be shown to an audience.

Slide Sorter view A PowerPoint view where the slides are displayed as thumbnails, enabling you to apply transitions and animations to the slides, and to reorder the slides in the presentation.

Slide text Text on a PowerPoint slide that appears in the content section of the slide.

Slides tab Thumbnails of the slides used to navigate between the slides in Normal view.

SmartArt A graphic object that presents information visually.

Snip A screen or part of a screen captured using the Snipping Tool.

Snipping Tool A feature that allows you to capture screen shots, or snips of any object on your screen.

Soft return The action whereby Word automatically wraps text from one line to the next when a line reaches the right margin.

Sort field A field used to determine the order of the records in a table.

Sorting The process of rearranging records into a specific order.

Source file The file a linked or embedded object is stored in.

Source program The program used to create a linked or embedded object.

Sparkline Small charts embedded into cells on a spreadsheet.

Speaker notes Notes that are stored with the presentation in the Notes pane.

Special operator An operator used to compare text values in a query.

Split form A form created from one table with a Form view and a Datasheet view in the same window.

Spreadsheet A software application that organizes data in a row and column format and supports manipulation of data to support decision making.

Start button On the far left of the taskbar; opens the Start menu.

Start menu The major link to your computer's programs, management tools, and file storage structure.

Start screen The working area of the Windows 8 screen.

Stationery Preset colors, fonts, and effects used to add interest to e-mail messages.

Status bar Is displayed at the bottom of windows and provides information about the selected window or object.

Storyboard A hand-drawn plan depicting the content, layout, and visual elements of a slide show.

Style A set of formatting characteristics that you can apply to selected text.

Style guide A set of standards for designing documents.

Subfolder A folder within a folder.

Subform The form created for the secondary table records when creating a form from two or more tables.

Subreport The report section created for the secondary table records when creating a report from two or more tables.

Subtotals Controls added to a report to perform calculations on a group of records.

Suspend Allows applications to not use processing power. Saves energy.

Symbol A character not available on a standard keyboard, such as the copyright symbol or foreign language accent marks.

Synchronize A process in managing a data collection form that verifies the destination table and query still exist and still include the forms you created in the original message.

Syntax The structure and order of the function and the arguments needed to run the function.

System software Controls and coordinates computer hardware operations so other programs can run efficiently. See operating system.

T

Tab A location where the insertion point will stop when the Tab key is pressed.

Table An organized grid of information, arranged in rows and columns.

Table style A predefined set of formatting properties that determine the appearance of a table.

Tabular format The presentation of information such as text and numbers in tables.

Tag A custom file property that is added to a file to help search for and locate files more quickly.

Target audience The general characteristics of the group of people you are planning to present to.

Task pane A smaller window pane that often appears to the side of the program window and offers options or helps you to navigate through completing a task or feature.

Task switcher Displays a thumbnail for most recent application. Displayed by pointing to the top-left corner of the screen.

Taskbar In Windows 7, displays the Start button, pinned taskbar buttons, notification area, and Show desktop button. In Windows 8, the bar at the bottom of the desktop screen showing all open programs.

Template A file with layouts, theme colors and fonts, and sample content to enable you to quickly produce a professional, consistent slide show.

Template folder The default storage location for any presentation being saved as a template.

Text box A bound control that represents the actual value of a field or a drawing object that can contain text.

Text data type A data type that can store either text or numerical characters.

Text filter Filters that allow you to create a custom filter to match all or part of the text in a field that you specify.

Text hierarchy The relationship of text elements on the slide, usually depicted with groups and subgroups.

Text wrap The way that text wraps around an object.

Theme A set of design elements that enables you to create professional, color-coordinated documents.

Thesaurus A research tool that enables you to select synonyms for words in the presentation.

Thumbnail A small picture of the open program file displayed.

Tile Colored icons that represent programs that can be opened from the Windows 8 Start screen.

Title bar Bar at top of window that displays the Minimize, Maximize/Restore Down, and Close buttons on the right side. May also display a program icon, and the name of the program and the active document.

To-Do Bar A pane on the right side of the Outlook window that provides a quick overview of the calendar, upcoming appointments and tasks. It can be minimized to give you more room to view other things in the window, or it can be expanded to help keep you organized at a glance.

Toggle A command that reverses itself when it is clicked or enacted a second time.

Total row A temporary row that can be added to the end of a datasheet that displays the results of statistical calculations of field values.

Transition The visual and audio elements that occur as the slides change.

Trendline Graphing the trend in the data with the intent of helping predict the future.

Trigger Text or graphic that enables animation to occur.

U

Unbound control A control on a form or report that does not have a source of data.

USB Flash drive A small storage device that plugs into your computer's USB port, also just called a USB drive.

User name A unique identifier for your account on the mail server that corresponds to your mailbox on the server. You type your user name and password to provide identification to the server.

V

Variable A value stored in a cell and used in a formula or function.

Vector graphics Object-oriented graphics based on geometric formulas, most often used for line art graphics.

View One of several perspectives of an object.

W

Wait time The time before the screen saver starts.

Watermark Text or a picture that appears behind document text.

Web Layout view A document view that displays pages as they would appear in a Web browser.

What-if analysis Changes values in spreadsheet cells to investigate the effects on calculated values of interest, and allows you to examine the outcome of the changes to values in an worksheet.

White space Space in a document that does not contain data of any kind.

Widow A paragraph's last line that is alone at the top of a page.

Wildcard A special character that represents none or many other characters (depending upon the wildcard).

Wildcard character Special symbols used as placeholders for unknown parts of a value or to match a certain pattern in a value.

Window A rectangular frame that displays a program, folder, or file.

Windows Aero Incorporates subtle animations and translucent glass windows on your desktop.

Windows Explorer A program used to create and manage folders and files.

Windows RT Microsoft's alternative to Apple and Android devices.

Wizard Step-by-step guide to complete a task.

WordPad A free text editing program that comes preinstalled with Windows.

Word processing Software that enables you to create, edit, and print documents.

Word wrap The feature whereby Word automatically wraps text from one line to the next.

WordArt A Word feature that modifies text to include shadows, outlines, colors, gradients, and 3D effects.

Workbook A file that contains at least one worksheet.

Workbook theme A collection of built-in cell styles all associated with a theme name.

Works cited A complete list of sources referenced in the preparation of a paper.

Worksheet Traditionally referred to as a spreadsheet.

Index